BEHAVIOR IN ORGANIZATIONS

BEHAVIOR IN ORGANIZATIONS

Ninth Edition

Jerald Greenberg

The Ohio State University

Robert A. Baron

Rensselaer Polytechnic Institute

PEARSON

Prentice
Hall

Upper Saddle River, New Jersey 07458

Library of Congress Cataloging in Publication Data

Greenberg, Jerald.
    Behavior in organizations / Jerald Greenberg, Robert A. Baron. — 9th ed.
    p. cm.
    Includes bibliographical references and index.
    ISBN 0-13-154284-2 (casebound)
    1. Organizational behavior. I. Baron, Robert A. II. Title.
    HD58.7.G7176 2008
    658.3—dc21

                                        2006027249

Editor-in-Chief: David Parker
VP/Editorial Director: Jeff Shelstad
Product Development Manager: Ashley Santora
Project Manager: Claudia Fernandes
Editorial Assistant: Kristen Varina
Media Project Manager: Ashley Lulling
Marketing Manager: Anne Howard
Marketing Assistant: Susan Osterlitz
Associate Director, Production Editorial: Judy Leale
Managing Editor: Renata Butera
Production Editor: Kelly Warsak
Permissions Coordinator: Charles Morris
Associate Director, Manufacturing: Vinnie Scelta
Manufacturing Buyer: Diane Peirano
Design/Composition Manager: Christy Mahon
Composition Liaison: Suzanne Duda
Designer: Steve Frim

Interior Design: Jill Little
Cover Design: Steve Frim
Cover Illustration: Stephen Cimini
Illustration (Interior): Laserwords
Director, Image Resource Center: Melinda Patelli
Manager, Rights and Permissions: Zina Arabia
Manager, Visual Research: Beth Brenzel
Manager, Cover Visual Research & Permissions: Karen
    Sanatar
Image Permission Coordinator: Angelique Sharps
Photo Researcher: Diane Austin
Composition: Laserwords
Full-Service Project Management: Thistle Hill Publishing
    Services, LLC
Printer/Binder: Quebecor World – Versailles
Cover Printer: Phoenix Color Corp.
Typeface: 10/12 Times

Credits and acknowledgments borrowed from other sources and reproduced, with permission, in this textbook appear on appropriate page within text.

Pearson Education LTD.
Pearson Education Singapore Pte. Ltd
Pearson Education Canada, Ltd
Pearson Education–Japan

Pearson Education Australia PTY, Limited
Pearson Education North Asia Ltd
Pearson Educación de Mexico, S.A. de C.V.
Pearson Education Malaysia, Pte. Ltd.

10 9 8 7 6 5 4 3 2
ISBN-13: 978-0-13-154284-6
ISBN-10: 0-13-154284-2

To my old professors, who taught me the practical value of scientific knowledge and to my students, who remind me—like it or not—that I am their old professor. For helping me realize my position in the ongoing cycle of science and practice, I dedicate this book to them.

Jerald Greenberg

To Rebecca who, as I once told the owner and patrons of a cozy restaurant in France, is *truly* "La femme qui jete des rayons de soleil sur mon ame!"

Robert A. Baron

Brief Contents

Appendixes

Contents

Appendixes

Preface—Welcome to the World of Organizational Behavior

Over the years, we've taught untold thousands of college students not only facts and figures but, more importantly, how to be critical thinkers and impartial analysts of behavior in organizations. In so doing, we've also learned a great deal from them. By listening carefully to their insights, drawing on their experiences, and discussing the world of work with them, we've come away with a strong sense of what they want to know about human dynamics in the workplace. After all, most of today's students already have held jobs, or are working while completing their studies, and chances are that they have given more than passing thought to jobs they will be performing in the future. As it becomes apparent to students that knowing about the field of organizational behavior (OB) can provide valuable insight into behavior on the job, we have been there to guide them.

Fortunately, we've been able to draw on our experiences as active scholarly researchers, journal editors, involved members of professional groups, and consultants to and trainers of people in a large number of organizations to offer students the guidance they require. From our vantage points as educators and working professionals, we've been able to give students both what they *want* to know and what they *need* to know. Indeed, our efforts to accomplish this are reflected in the pages of this book. Critical insight into individual processes (i.e., what "makes people tick"), social dynamics (i.e., how groups and teams operate), and organizational practices (i.e., the activities of companies as whole entities) combined with knowledge of real world sensitivities, demands, and practices—that's the focus of the field of OB. Not coincidentally, this is also what this book is all about.

Our Major Objective: To Spotlight Organizational Behavior

People enjoy learning about behavior in organizations. It gives us unique insight into everyday processes and phenomena we often take for granted. After all, such knowledge helps us understand a key part of the world in which we live. For a book such as ours, the implications of this assumption are threefold: (1) It must be accessible to readers, (2) it must provide added value by focusing on unique insight, information that goes beyond what common sense would suggest, and, of course, (3) it must be relevant to readers. We have gone out of our way to incorporate these qualities into this book.

Accessibility to Readers

- We use a friendly and approachable writing style, speaking directly to readers in straightforward prose. Hopefully, we have refrained from the condescension of speaking down to readers and the elitism of going over their heads.
- By carefully selecting material to which students can relate—such as accounts of organizational practices in companies with which they may be familiar—they are likely to find the material engaging.
- Key points are easy to find because of the way the book is designed and by features such as **key terms** appearing in margins and a **"Summary and Review of Learning Objectives"** appearing at the end of each chapter.

- Graphics are used to enhance explanations of material for visually oriented learners. For example, our **"talking graphics"** help readers take away the key findings of research.

These are among the several key features of this book that help bring the material to life for students by making a fascinating topic readily understandable.

Unique—Beyond Common Sense—Insight

As authors, we are highly sensitive to the need to help students understand "what's under the hood?" of behavior in the workplace. In this book, we provide that information in the form of a feature entitled, **"OB: Making Sense Out of Common Sense."** These are special sections in each chapter that explain OB phenomena that shed new light on seemingly commonsensical beliefs about behavior in organizations, offering deeper-than-usual insight into that behavior. Here are just a few such examples.

- Good Ethics Is Good Business (Chapter 2)
- Autonomy in the Orchestra Strikes a Sour Note (Chapter 7)
- Organizational Development Is Inherently Unethical—Or, Is It? (Chapter 16)

When reading these and similar sections in this book, we hope students will think to themselves, "Hmmm, that's interesting; I didn't know that." After all, inside knowledge into behavior in organizations is likely to be fascinating.

Focusing on Relevance

The field of OB is *not* about curiosity for its own sake. Rather, it's about finding real, scientifically based answers to practical questions. Thus, relevance is vital. "Theories and research are important," many students believe, so long as they offer insight into appropriate action, what to do. In preparing this book, our mission was to spotlight this relevance in a form that could enlighten our target audience—college students who desire to learn about the complexities of human behavior in organizations. We do this in three ways.

First, we provide concrete information on putting OB to practical use in special sections in each chapter entitled, **"How to Do It."** These features present several concrete tips for readers to follow when attempting to carry out some practice related to the field of OB. Examples include:

- Telecommunicating as a Business Communication Strategy (Chapter 1)
- Managing Anger in the Workplace (Chapter 5)
- How to Inspire Innovation (Chapter 14)

A second way in which we promote relevance is by identifying practices in real organizations that demonstrate how OB principles are put to use. Such examples are incorporated everywhere throughout this book. By weaving such examples throughout this book we are attempting to bring OB to life for readers by illustrating how what might be seen as arcane and irrelevant academic concepts are, in reality, quite the opposite—namely, the basis for real, organizational practices in today's organizations. Examples include:

- Using feedback to promote self-efficacy at CHP (Chapter 3)
- Unisys employees learn good listening skills (Chapter 9)
- Practices used to "make organizational changes stick" at Sears, Royal Dutch Shell, and the United States Army (Chapter 16)

A third way in which we emphasize relevance is by highlighting diversity as a feature of today's workplace. Our most ostensible effort in this regard comes in the form of a special feature entitled, **"OB in a Diverse World."** These are sections within each chapter that highlight ways in which differences between individuals with respect to their race, gender, sexual preference, or nationality impact various OB phenomena. Examples include:

■ Starbucks and Dell Actively Advance the Interests of Women (Chapter 2)
■ Inequity in Housework: Comparing Married Women and Men (Chapter 7)
■ Joint Ventures in China: Beware of Obstacles (Chapter 15)

Balancing Basic Science and Practical Application

Because the field of OB is a blend of research, theory, and practical application, so too, quite deliberately, is this book. Indeed, we have taken extensive steps to ensure that it is the best of these seemingly disparate worlds. Consider just a few examples.

■ In Chapter 3, we cover both theories of learning and how these theories are involved in such organizational practices as training, organizational behavior management, and discipline.
■ In Chapter 6, we identify specific ways in which the various theories of motivation can be put into practice.
■ In Chapter 10, it is not only various scientific studies of decision making that are identified, but also various practices that can be, and are being, followed to enhance the effectiveness of group decisions.

More than simply indicating how various theories *may be* applied, we identify precisely how they *are being* applied in today's organizations. In addition to the many in-text examples noted in conjunction with our earlier discussion of relevance, we also should note our widespread use of tables listing organizational examples.

Another place in which we highlight organizational practices is in extended figure captions. Many of these may be considered to be micro-cases illustrating key points made in the text.

Balancing Knowledge and Skills

Educators tell us that there is a fundamental distinction between teaching people about something—providing *knowledge*—and showing them how to do something—developing their *skills*. In the field of OB, this distinction becomes blurred. After all, to fully appreciate how to do something, you have to have the requisite knowledge. For this reason, we pay attention in this book to both knowledge and skills. Consider the following illustrations:

■ In Chapter 5, we describe the ways in which stress operates as well as techniques that can be used to alleviate the adverse effects of stress. We also include an exercise designed to help in this regard.
■ In Chapter 9, we describe not only the process of listening, but also ways of enhancing listening skills. Then, to help readers become effective listeners, we present an exercise designed to promote active listening skills.
■ Chapter 16 explains not only the reasons underlying people's resistance to organizational change but also various ways in which this resistance may be overcome. We then give students an opportunity to practice doing this in an exercise.

By doing these things—not only in these examples, but throughout the book—we intend not only to enable readers to understand OB, but also to help them practice it in their own lives.

New Chapters and Coverage

In the course of revising this book we made many changes. Some of these came in the process of seeking that balance to which we just referred, and others were necessitated by our ongoing commitment to highlighting the latest advances in the field. Many of the changes we made are subtle, referring only to how a topic was framed relative to others. A good many other changes are more noticeable and involve the shifting of major topics into new places and the addition of brand new topics. Doing this required the creation of a new chapter and the addition of several new features. Highlights of new coverage include the following.

- Engagement (Chapter 1)
- Entirely new chapter on Organizational Justice, Ethics, and Corporate Social Responsibility (Chapter 2)
- Stereotype threats (Chapter 3)
- Core self-evaluations (Chapter 4)
- Emotional contagion (part of expanded coverage of emotions in Chapter 5)
- Religious intolerance (Chapter 6)
- Horizontal and vertical stretch goals (Chapter 7)
- Faultlines (Chapter 8)
- Pipedreams (Chapter 9)
- Defensive avoidance (Chapter 10)
- OCB-I and OCB-O (Chapter 11)
- Quid pro quo harassment and hostile environment harassment (part of expanded coverage of sexual harassment in Chapter 12)
- Authentic leadership (Chapter 13)
- Hierarchy, market, clan, and adhocracy cultures (part of expanded coverage of organizational culture in Chapter 14)
- Vertically integrated organizations (Chapter 15)
- Offshoring (Chapter 16)

End-of-Chapter Pedagogical Features

At the end of each chapter, two groups of pedagogical features may be found. The first, named **"Points to Ponder,"** includes three types of questions:

- **Questions for Review**. These are questions designed to help students determine the extent to which they picked up the major points contained in each chapter.
- **Experiential Questions.** These are questions that get students to understand various OB phenomena by thinking about various experiences in their work lives.
- **Questions to Analyze.** The questions in this category are designed to help readers think about the interconnections between various OB phenomena and/or how they may be applied.

The second category of pedagogical features found at the end of each chapter is referred to as **"Experiencing OB."** This includes the following three types of experiential exercises.

- **Individual Exercise.** Students can complete these exercises on their own to gain personal insight into various OB phenomena.
- **Group Exercise.** By working in small groups, students completing these exercises will be able to experience an important OB phenomenon or concept. The experience itself also will help them develop team-building skills.

■ **Practicing OB.** This exercise is applications-based. It describes a hypothetical problem situation and challenges the reader to explain how various OB practices can be applied to solving it.

Case Features

Each chapter contains two cases. Positioned at the beginning of each chapter, a **Preview Case** is designed to set up the material that follows by putting it in the context of a real organizational event. These are either completely new to this edition or updated. Just a few examples of new Preview Cases include the following:

■ Southwest Airlines: Employee Relations Back on Time (Chapter 11)
■ "An Indiscriminate Jerk" (Chapter 12)
■ Commercial Metals Company "Steels" the Show (Chapter 15)

The end-of-chapter case, **Case in Point,** is designed to review the material already covered and to bring that material to life. Specific tie-ins are made by use of discussion questions appearing after each Case in Point feature. These also are new or updated for this edition. Several examples of new cases include the following.

■ The Scoop on Communications at Cold Stone Creamery (Chapter 9)
■ Amazon.com: Innovation via the "Two-Pizza Team" (Chapter 14)
■ Royal Bank of Canada: Changes You Can Bank On (Chapter 16)

Updated Supplements Package for Instructors

Instructors adopting this book have available a wide array of ancillary materials at the **Instructor Resource Center**: www.prenhall.com/irc. Among the most popular features found at this site are the following.

■ Instructors can access a variety of print, media, and presentation resources available with this text in downloadable, digital format.
■ Register only once. Access new titles and/or editions with the same username and password.
■ Our dedicated Technical Support team is ready to assist instructors with questions about the media supplements that accompany this text. Visit: http://247.prenhall.com/ (for answers to frequently asked questions and toll-free user support phone numbers)

A full complement of hard copy supplements is also available to instructors. For detailed descriptions of all of the supplements listed below, please visit: www.prenhall.com/irc

■ **Instructor Resource Center (IRC) on CD-ROM**—ISBN: 0-13-154289-3
■ **Printed Instructor's Manual**—ISBN: 0-13-154290-7
■ **Printed Test Item File**—ISBN: 0-13-154288-5
■ **TestGen test generating software**—Visit the IRC (both online and on CD-Rom) for this text.
■ **PowerPoints**—Visit the IRC (both online and on CD-Rom) for this text.
■ **Videos on DVD**—ISBN: 0-13-154286-9

Updated Supplements Package for Students

To help students, we also have available a wide variety of materials that supplement the material in the text. These include the following.

- **Companion Website: www.prenhall.com/greenberg** contains free access to a student version of the PowerPoint package and chapter quizzes.
- **SafariX Textbooks Online**—Developed for students looking to save up to 50% on textbooks, SafariX eTextbooks Online also allows students to search for specific keywords or page numbers, make notes online, print out reading assignments that incorporate lecture notes, and bookmark important passages for later review. For more information, see: www.safarix.com.

Finally—and Most Importantly—Acknowledgments

Writing is a solitary task. However, turning millions of bytes of information stored on a handful of plastic disks into a book is a magical process that requires an army of talented folks. In preparing this text, we have been fortunate enough to be assisted by many dedicated and talented people. Although we cannot possibly thank all of them here, we wish to express our appreciation to those whose help has been most valuable.

First, our sincere thanks to our colleagues who read and commented on various portions of the manuscript for this and earlier editions of this book. Their suggestions were invaluable and helped us in many ways. These include:

Royce L. Abrahamson, Southwest Texas State University

Rabi S. Bhagat, Memphis State University

Ralph R. Braithwaite, University of Hartford

Stephen C. Buschardt, University of Southern Mississippi

Dawn Carlson, University of Utah

M. Suzzanne Clinton, Cameron University

Roy A. Cook, Fort Lewis College

Cynthis Cordes, State University of New York at Binghamton

Julie Dziekan, University of Michigan–Dearborn

Janice Feldbauer, Austin Community College

Patricia Feltes, Southwest Missouri State University

Olene L. Fuller, San Jacinto College North

Richard Grover, University of Southern Maine

Courtney Hunt, University of Delaware

Ralph Katerberg, University of Cincinnati

Paul N. Keaton, University of Wisconsin at LaCrosse

Mary Kernan, University of Delaware

Daniel Levi, California Polytechnic State University

Jeffrey Lewis, Pitzer College

Rodney Lim, Tulane University

Charles W. Mattox, Jr., St. Mary's University

Daniel W. McAllister, University of Nevada–Las Vegas

James McElroy, Iowa State University

Richard McKinney, Southern Illinois University

Linda Morable, Richland College

Paula Morrow, Iowa State University

Audry Murrell, University of Pittsburgh

David Olsen, California State University–Bakersfield

William D. Patzig, James Madison University

Shirley Rickert, Indiana University–Purdue University at Fort Wayne

David W. Roach, Arkansas Tech University

Dr. Meshack M. Sagini, Langston University

Terri A. Scandura, University of Miami, Coral Gables

Holly Schroth, University of California Berkeley

Marc Siegall, California State University, Chico

Taggart Smith, Purdue University

Patrick C. Stubbleine, Indiana University—Purdue University at Fort Wayne

Paul Sweeney, Marquette University

Craig A. Tunwall, SUNY Empire State College

Carol Watson, Rider University

Philip A. Weatherford, Embry-Riddle Aeronautical University

Richard M. Weiss, University of Delaware

Stan Williamson, University of Louisiana-Monroe

Second, we wish to express our appreciation to our editor, Jennifer Simon, who saw us through this project. Her enthusiasm was contagious, and her constant support and good humor helped us bring this book to completion. Jennifer's assistant, Richard Gomes, was always there to help, as was the project manager, Claudia Fernandes. And, of course, we would be remiss in not thanking Jeff Shelstad and members of the PH team, for their steadfast support of this book.

Third, our sincere thanks go out to Prentice Hall's top-notch production team for making this book so beautiful—Kelly Warsak, Production Editor; Ashley Santora, Product Development Manager; Steve Frim, Designer; Jane Scelta, Permissions Coordinator; and Diane Austin, Photo Researcher; as well as Angela Urquhart at Thistle Hill Publishing Services and the staff at Laserwords Private Limited. Their diligence and skill with the many behind-the-scenes tasks required in a book such as this one—not to mention their constant refinements—helped us immeasurably throughout the process of preparing this work. It was a pleasure to work with such kind and understanding professionals, and we are greatly indebted to them for their contributions.

Finally, Jerald Greenberg wishes to acknowledge the special support of three key sources. First, he once again thanks the family of the late Irving Abramowitz for their generous endowment to the Ohio State University, which provided invaluable support during the writing of this book. Second, he cannot strongly enough express his appreciation for his colleagues and students whose support has helped bring this book to fruition. In particular, the intellectual nurturance and assistance of his research partners throughout the world, including Chad Brinsfield, Joseph Cooper, and Dustin Sleesman at the Ohio State University, Marissa Edwards at the University of Queensland, and Aino Salimäki at the Helsinki University of Technology have proven invaluable. Last, but not least, he is indebted to his long-devoted and loving spouse, Carolyn, whose steadfast support makes not only this book possible, but life worth living.

To all these truly outstanding individuals, and to many others too, our warm personal regards.

In Conclusion: An Invitation for Feedback

We would appreciate hearing from you! Let us know what you think about this textbook either by writing directly to Jerald Greenberg or to the publisher's Web site at college_marketing@prenhall.com. Please include "Feedback about Greenberg 9e" in the subject line. If you have questions related to this book, please contact our customer service department online at www.247.prenhall.com

Jerald Greenberg
greenberg.1@osu.edu

Robert A. Baron
baronr@rpi.edu

BEHAVIOR IN ORGANIZATIONS

THE FIELD OF ORGANIZATIONAL BEHAVIOR

Chapter Outline

Organizational Behavior: Its Basic Nature

What Are the Field's Fundamental Assumptions?

OB Then and Now: A Capsule History

OB Responds to the Rise of Globalization and Diversity

OB Responds to Advances in Technology

OB Is Responsive to People's Changing Expectations

Special Sections

OB **Making Sense Out of Common Sense**

Check Your Assumptions at the Door

OB **In a Diverse World**

What in the World Is That Name?

How to Do It

Telecommuting as a Business Continuity Strategy

After reading this chapter, you should be able to:

1. Define the concepts of organization and organizational behavior.
2. Describe the field of organizational behavior's commitment to the scientific method and the three levels of analysis it uses.
3. Trace the historical developments and schools of thought leading up to the field of organizational behavior today.
4. Identify the fundamental characteristics of the field of organizational behavior.
5. Describe how the field of OB today is being shaped by the global economy, increasing racial and ethnic diversity in the workforce, and advances in technology.
6. Explain how people's changing expectations about the desire to be engaged in their work, the need for flexibility in work, and the pressure to promote quality have influenced the field of OB.

PREVIEW CASE

Yvon Chouinard: The Head Patagoniac

An executive who claims, "We prefer the human scale to the corporate," is likely to raise the eyebrows of skeptics. To those who know Yvon Chouinard, however, founder and owner of the outdoor clothing company Patagonia, there can be no doubt about the statement's veracity. Chouinard launched the company in 1972 to manufacture clothing for mountain-climbing enthusiasts like himself. Patagonia now offers a full line of rugged, good-looking products for everything from Alpine climbing to yoga. Nearing 70, Chouinard remains an avid outdoorsman who is more likely to be found wearing the latest high-tech, seamless waterproof coat while racing down a ski mogul than donning a sport coat at a cozy country club with another business mogul.

To many, Yvon Chouinard is best known for his commitment to the environment. For over a decade, for example, Patagonia has been using only high-quality organic cotton grown using sustainable resources and ecologically sound pesticides. Chouinard hasn't been alone in his quest to preserve the environment. He founded "1% for the Planet," an alliance of businesses—now pushing 250-strong—whose members donate 1 percent of their total sales to carefully selected programs designed to preserve the natural environment. To date, Patagonia's own contributions have totaled over $22 million. And, since the company is privately held, this comes right out of Chouinard's own pocket.

As he explains in his recent book, *Let My People Go Surfing,* Chouinard's personal commitment to his employees runs as deep as the chasms he is likely to span in his outings. Take something as basic as child care, for example. To many executives, it's an obligation left up to parents to figure out themselves. At Patagonia's Ventura, California, headquarters, however, the approach couldn't be more different. Instead of the typical "drop 'em off and we'll keep 'em out of trouble" babysitting services found in many firms, Patagonia offers highly specialized learning environments for children aged 2–10 at its fully accredited Great Pacific Child Development Center. The idea is simple: To give parents peace of mind that allows them to focus on their work instead of worrying about their children.

This is not all. Many of the so-called "Patagoniacs," employees who work at headquarters or at one of four dozen retail outlets throughout the world, also are active product testers, even if usually desk-bound at work. Call the company's Service Center in Reno, Nevada, for example, and you might find yourself talking to an 11-time world champion freestyle Frisbee player. And, when she's not managing direct mail and Internet sales operations, Morelee Griswold may be found kayaking at the World Championship Kayak Surf

Competition off Ireland's rugged west coast. Most company execs would cringe at the thought of granting such an individual a five-week leave for this occasion, but Morlee's bosses at Patagonia did so with their blessings. "Patagonia has provided me a wonderful marriage of job and life," she said. "The company has reinforced that you don't have to do things like everyone else does them—that you can be different and still be successful." Indeed, Patagonia is both.

I t's clear that Yvon Chouinard has a passion for outdoor sports that has driven him to manufacture and sell the best clothing. But the success at Patagonia goes beyond the company's products. Chouinard also has a passion for people that enables them to be their best and to give their all to the company. Not just an avid sportsman, Chouinard has an avid appreciation for life in general, be it the living things in the environment (Patagonia even has a program to teach children about insects!), or the human beings in his facilities. In fact, it is safe to say that he has a profound appreciation for the importance of the human side of work, which happens to be the topic of this book.

Mr. Chouinard appears to be aware of a key fact: No matter how good a company's products may be, there can be no company without people—particularly a successful one (see Figure 1.1). From the founder to the loyal employees, it's all about people. If you've ever run or managed a business, you know that "people problems" can bring an organization down very rapidly. Hence, it makes sense to realize that people are a critical element in the effective functioning—indeed, the basic existence—of organizations. It is this people-centered orientation that is taken in the field of *organizational behavior* (*OB* for short)—the field specializing in the study of human behavior in organizations.

FIGURE 1.1

Wegman's Puts People First

These employees at Wegman's Food Markets, the 70-store grocery chain based in Rochester, New York, have good reason to be smiling. They and 32,000 fellow employees are among the best-treated employees in the U.S. according to Fortune magazine. New full-time employees are flown by chartered jet to the company headquarters where they are welcomed by Danny Wegman, CEO of this family-owned business. At Wegman's, the work atmosphere is friendly and wages are higher than the industry average. Given such positive treatment, it's little wonder that there are an average of 3 applicants for every new job and that the rate of voluntary turnover is an industry low at 8 percent. Says Chairman Robert Wegman, "No matter what we have invested in our people, we've gotten more in return. I have always believed that our path to great customer service began with that investment. That philosophy has proven itself many times over."

OB scientists and practitioners study and attempt to solve problems by using knowledge derived from research in the *behavioral sciences,* such as psychology and sociology. In other words, the field of OB is firmly rooted in science. It relies on research to derive valuable information about organizations and the complex processes operating within them. Such knowledge is used as the basis for helping to solve a wide range of organizational problems. For example, what can be done to make people more productive and more satisfied on the job? When and how should people be organized into teams? How should jobs and organizations be designed so that people best adapt to changes in the environment? These are just a few of the many important questions that are addressed by the field of organizational behavior.

As you read this text it will become very clear that OB specialists have attempted to learn about a large variety of issues involving people in organizations. In fact, over the past few decades, OB has developed into a field so diverse that its scientists have examined just about every conceivable aspect of behavior in organizations.[1] The fruits of this labor already have been enjoyed by people interested in making organizations not only more productive, but also more pleasant for those working in them.

In the remainder of this chapter we will give you the background information you will need to understand the scope of OB and its importance. With this in mind, this first chapter is designed to introduce you to the field of OB by focusing on its history and its fundamental characteristics. We will begin by formally defining OB, describing exactly what it is and what it seeks to accomplish. Following this, we will summarize the history of the field, tracing its roots from its origins to its emergence as a modern science. Then, in the final sections of the chapter, we will discuss the wide variety of factors that make the field of OB the vibrant, ever-changing field it is today. At this point, we will be ready to face the primary goal of this book: to enhance your understanding of the human side of work by giving you a comprehensive overview of the field of organizational behavior.

Organizational Behavior: Its Basic Nature

As the phrase implies, OB deals with organizations. Although you already know from experience what an organization is, a formal definition helps to avoid ambiguity. An **organization** is a structured social system consisting of groups and individuals working together to meet some agreed-upon objectives. In other words, organizations consist of people, who alone and together in work groups strive to attain common goals. Although this definition is rather abstract, it is sure to take on more meaning as you continue reading this book. We say this with confidence because the field of OB is concerned with organizations of all types, whether large or small in size, public or private in ownership (i.e., whether or not shares of stock are sold), and whether they exist to earn a profit or to enhance the public good (i.e., *nonprofit organizations,* such as charities and civic groups). Regardless of the specific goals sought, the structured social units working together toward them may be considered organizations.

To launch our journey through the world of OB, we will answer two key questions that you are likely to have on your mind: (1) What is the field of organizational behavior all about? (2) Why is it important to know about OB?

What Is the Field of Organizational Behavior All About?

The field of **organizational behavior** deals with human behavior in organizations. Formally defined, organizational behavior is the multidisciplinary field that seeks knowledge of behavior in organizational settings by systematically studying individual, group, and organizational processes. This knowledge is used both by scientists interested in understanding human behavior and by practitioners interested in enhancing organizational effectiveness and individual well-being. In this book we will highlight both these purposes, focusing on how scientific knowledge has been—or may be—used for these practical purposes.

Our definition of OB highlights four central characteristics of the field. First, OB is firmly grounded in the scientific method. Second, OB studies individuals, groups, and organizations. Third, OB is interdisciplinary in nature. And fourth, OB is used as the basis

organization
A structured social system consisting of groups and individuals working together to meet some agreed-upon objectives.

organizational behavior
The field that seeks increased knowledge of all aspects of behavior in organizational settings through the use of the scientific method.

for enhancing organizational effectiveness and individual well-being. We will now take a closer look at these three characteristics of the field.

OB Applies the Scientific Method to Practical Managerial Problems. In our definition of OB, we refer to seeking knowledge and to studying behavioral processes. This should not be surprising since, as we noted earlier, OB knowledge is based on the **behavioral sciences.** These are fields such as psychology and sociology that seek knowledge of human behavior and society through the use of the scientific method. Although not as sophisticated as many scientific fields, such as physics or chemistry—nor as mature as them—OB's orientation is still scientific in nature. Thus, like other scientific fields, OB seeks to develop a base of knowledge by using an empirical, research-based approach. That is, it is based on systematic observation and measurement of the behavior or phenomenon of interest. As we will describe in Appendix 1, organizational research is neither easy nor foolproof. Yet it is widely agreed that the scientific method is the best way to learn about behavior in organizations. For this reason, the scientific orientation should be acknowledged as a hallmark of the field of OB.

As they seek to improve organizational functioning and the quality of life of people working in organizations, managers rely heavily on knowledge derived from OB research. For example, researchers have shed light on such practical questions as:

- How can goals be set to enhance people's job performance?
- How may jobs be designed so as to enhance employees' feelings of satisfaction?
- Under what conditions do individuals make better decisions than groups?
- What can be done to improve the quality of organizational communication?
- What steps can be taken to alleviate work-related stress?
- What do leaders do to enhance the effectiveness of their teams?
- How can organizations be designed to make people highly productive?

Throughout this book we will describe scientific research and theory bearing on the answers to these and dozens of other practical questions. It is safe to say that the scientific and applied facets of OB not only coexist, but complement each other. Indeed, just as knowledge about the properties of physics may be put to use by engineers, and engineering data can be used to test theories of basic physics, so too are knowledge and practical applications closely intertwined in the field of OB.

OB Focuses on Three Levels of Analysis—Individuals, Groups, and Organizations. To best appreciate behavior in organizations, OB specialists cannot focus exclusively on individuals acting alone. After all, in organizational settings people frequently work together in groups and teams. Furthermore, people—alone and in groups—both influence and are influenced by their work environments. Considering this, it should not be surprising to learn that the field of OB focuses on three distinct levels of analysis—*individuals, groups,* and *organizations* (see Figure 1.2).

The field of OB recognizes that all three levels of analysis must be considered to fully comprehend the complex dynamics of behavior in organizations. Careful attention to all three levels of analysis is a central theme in modern OB and will be fully reflected throughout this text. For example, we will be describing how OB specialists are concerned with individual perceptions, attitudes, and motives. We also will be describing how people communicate with each other and coordinate their activities among themselves in work groups. Finally, we will examine organizations as a whole—the way they are structured and operate in their environments, and the effects of their operations on the individuals and groups within them.

OB is Multidisciplinary in Nature. When you consider the broad range of issues and approaches taken by the field of OB, it is easy to appreciate the fact that the field is multidisciplinary in nature. By this, we mean that it draws on a wide variety of social science disciplines. Rather than studying a topic from only one particular perspective, the field of OB is likely to consider a wide variety of approaches. These range from the highly

---

behavioral sciences
Fields such as psychology and sociology that seek knowledge of human behavior and society through the use of the scientific method.

FIGURE 1.2

The Three Levels of Analysis Used in Organizational Behavior

To fully understand behavior in organizations, we must consider three levels of analysis: processes occurring within individuals, groups, and organizations.

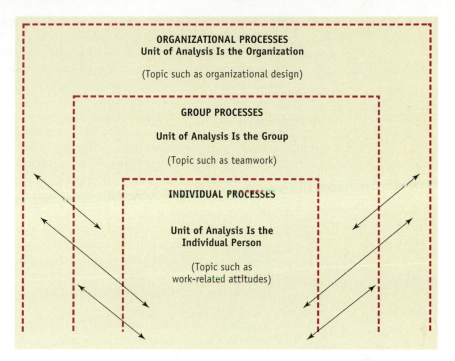

individual-oriented approach of psychology, through the more group-oriented approach of sociology, to issues in organizational quality studied by management scientists.

For a summary of some of the key fields from which the field of OB draws, see Table 1.1. If, as you read this book, you recognize some particular theory or approach as familiar, chances are good that you already learned something about it in another class. What makes OB so special is that it combines these various orientations together into a single—very broad and very exciting—field.

OB Seeks to Improve Organizational Effectiveness and the Quality of Life At Work. In the early part of the twentieth century, as railroads opened up the western portion of the United States and the nation's population rapidly grew (it doubled from 1880 to 1920!), the demand for manufactured products was great. New manufacturing plants were built, attracting waves of new immigrants in search of a living wage and laborers lured

TABLE 1.1 The Multidisciplinary Roots of OB

Specialists in OB derive knowledge from a wide variety of social science disciplines to create a unique, multidisciplinary field. Some of the most important parent disciplines are listed here, along with some of the OB topics to which they are related (and the chapters in this book in which they are discussed).

Discipline	Relevant OB Topics
Psychology	Perception and learning (Chapter 3); personality (Chapter 4); emotion and stress (Chapter 5); attitudes (Chapter 6); motivation (Chapter 7); decision making (Chapter 10); creativity (Chapter 14)
Sociology	Group dynamics (Chapter 8); socialization (Chapter 8); communication (Chapter 9)
Anthropology	Organizational culture (Chapter 14); Leadership (Chapter 13)
Political science	Interpersonal conflict (Chapter 11); organizational power (Chapter 12)
Economics	Decision making (Chapter 10); negotiation (Chapter 11); organizational power (Chapter 12)
Management science	Technology (Chapter 16); organizational quality and change (Chapter 16)

off farms by the employment prospects factory work offered. These men and women found that factories were gigantic, noisy, hot, and highly regimented—in short, brutal places in which to work. Bosses demanded more and more of their employees and treated them like disposable machines, replacing those who died from accidents or who quit with others who waited outside the factory gates.

Clearly, the managers of a century ago held very negative views of employees. They assumed that people were basically lazy and irresponsible, and treated them with disrespect. This very negativistic approach, which has been with us for many years, reflects the traditional view of management, called a **Theory X** orientation. This philosophy of management assumes that people are basically lazy, dislike work, need direction, and will only work hard when they are pushed into performing.

Today, however, if you asked corporate officials to describe their views of human nature, you'd probably find some more optimistic beliefs. Although some of today's managers still think that people are basically lazy, most would argue that the vast majority of people are capable of working hard under the right conditions. If employees are recognized for their efforts (such as by being fairly paid) and are given an opportunity to succeed (such as by being well trained), they may be expected to put forth considerable effort without being pushed. Management's job, then, is to create those conditions that make people want to perform as desired.

The approach that assumes that people are not intrinsically lazy, but that they are willing to work hard when the right conditions prevail, is known as the **Theory Y** orientation. This philosophy assumes that people have a psychological need to work and seek achievement and responsibility. In contrast to the Theory X philosophy of management, which essentially demonstrates distrust for people on the job, the Theory Y approach is strongly associated with improving the quality of people's work lives (for a summary of the differences, see Figure 1.3).

The Theory Y perspective prevails within the field of organizational behavior today. It assumes that people are highly responsive to their work environments, and that the ways they are treated will influence the ways they will act. In fact, OB scientists are very interested in learning exactly what conditions will lead people to behave most positively—that is, what makes work both productive for organizations and enjoyable for the people working in them.

Why Is It Important to Know About OB?

Have you ever had a job where people don't get along, nobody knows what to do, everyone is goofing off, and your boss is—well, putting it politely—unpleasant? We can't imagine

Theory X
A traditional philosophy of management suggesting that most people are lazy and irresponsible, and will work hard only when forced to do so.

Theory Y
A philosophy of management suggesting that under the right circumstances, people are fully capable of working productively and accepting responsibility for their work.

FIGURE 1.3

Theory X vs. Theory Y: A Summary

The traditional, Theory X orientation toward people is far more negativistic than the more contemporary, Theory Y approach, which is widely accepted today. Some of the key differences between these management philosophies are summarized here.

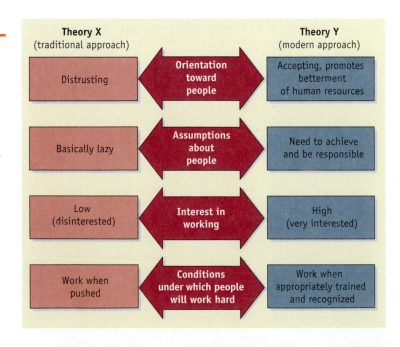

that you liked working in that company at all. Now, think of another position in which everyone is friendly, knowledgeable, hard working, and very pleasant. Obviously, that's more to your liking. Such a situation is one in which you are likely to be interested in going to work, doing your best, and taking pride in what you do. What lies at the heart of these differences are all issues that are of great concern to OB scientists and practitioners—and ones we will cover in this book.

The key reason to know about OB is simple—it matters. Indeed, OB makes a very big difference in the world of work. Not only does OB explain how people feel about their work, but importantly, how well they perform. In a recent survey of a wide range of professional workers, it was found that three factors were related to job performance: (1) management and organization, (2) information technology, and (3) workplace design.[2] Although the topics of information technology and workplace design are the primary focus of other fields, they also are related to OB. As a result, we discuss them both in this chapter and elsewhere in this book (e.g, Chapter 8). The first factor, however, management and organization, is precisely what OB is all about. Thus, studying OB provides important insight into work performance. And in today's competitive business world, not having this knowledge is a luxury no one can be without.

"Okay," you may be asking yourself, "in some companies things are nice and smooth, but in others, relationships are rocky—does it really matter?" As you will see throughout this book, the answer is a resounding *yes*! For now, here are just a few highlights of specific ways in which OB matters to people and the organizations in which they work.

- Companies whose managers accurately appraise the work of their subordinates enjoy lower costs and higher productivity than those that handle their appraisals less accurately.[3]
- People who are satisfied with the way they are treated on their jobs generally are more pleasant to their co-workers and bosses, and are less likely to quit than those who are dissatisfied with the way others treat them.[4]
- People who are carefully trained to work together in teams tend to be happier and more productive than those who are simply thrown together without any definite organizational support.[5]
- Employees who believe they have been treated unfairly on the job are more likely to steal from their employers and to reject the policies of their organizations than those who believe they have been treated fairly.[6]
- People who are mistreated by their supervisors on the job have more mental and physical illnesses than those who are treated with kindness, dignity, and respect.[7]
- Organizations that treat employees well with respect to pay/benefits, opportunities, job security, friendliness, fairness, and pride in company are, on average, twice as profitable as the Standard & Poor's 500 companies.[8]
- Companies that offer good employee benefits and that have friendly conditions are more profitable than those that are less people-oriented.[9]

By now, you might be asking yourself: Why, if OB is so important, is there no one person in charge of it in an organization? After all, companies tend to have officials who are responsible for other basic areas, such as finance, accounting, marketing, and production. Why not OB? If you've never heard of a vice president of OB or a manager of organizational behavior, it's because organizations do not have any such formal posts. So who is responsible for organizational behavior? In a sense, the answer is everyone! Although OB is a separate area of study, it cuts across all areas of organizational functioning. Managers in all departments have to know such things as how to motivate their employees, how to keep people satisfied with their jobs, how to communicate fairly, how to make teams function effectively, and how to design jobs most effectively. In short, dealing with people at work is everybody's responsibility on the job. So, no matter what job you do in a company, knowing something about OB is sure to help you do it better. This is precisely why it's so vitally important for you to know the material in this book. However, many of the things people think about behavior in organizations are untrue. That is, they are inconsistent with the findings of careful research on which the field is based. For a look at some such beliefs, see the *OB: Making Sense Out of Common Sense* section, below).

What Are the Field's Fundamental Assumptions?

The field of OB is guided by two straightforward assumptions—fundamental ideas that are widely accepted by everyone who does scientific research on OB or who puts these findings into practice in organizations. First, OB recognizes that organizations are dynamic and always changing. Second, the field of OB assumes there is no one single best way to behave in organizations, and that different approaches are called for in different situations.

OB Making Sense Out of Common Sense

Check Your Assumptions at the Door

Because we've all done some kind of work and know other people also work, it's not surprising that we assume various things about how people behave on the job. After all, it's something we experience all the time. However—and this is important—whatever we may believe to be the case about behavior in organizations cannot be trusted. Even if you already have a good intuitive sense about how people behave on the job, at least some of what you think may be questionable. Not only might anyone's casual observations be inconsistent with established research findings (many of which are noted in this book), but also, some of the things we believe to be the case might not reflect all the complexities and subtle nuances of human behavior that only scientists are prepared to determine. That's why we title this section, "Check Your Assumptions at the Door."

To get a feel for this, answer each of the following questions true or false. The results may be enlightening.

1. People who are satisfied with one job tend to be satisfied with other jobs too.
2. "Two heads are better than one," so groups make better decisions than individuals.
3. The best leaders always act the same, regardless of the situations they face.
4. Specific goals make people nervous; people work better when asked to do their best.
5. People get bored easily, leading them to welcome organizational change.
6. Money is the best motivator.
7. Today's organizations are more rigidly structured than ever before.
8. People generally shy away from challenges on the job.
9. Multiple channels of communication (e.g., written and spoken) tend to add confusion.
10. Conflict in organizations is always highly disruptive.

Now, the moment of truth: The first statement is true; all the others are false. When we say that something is true, we mean that it has been supported by research. This may be the case even if it's inconsistent with what our common sense tells us.

How did you do on this quiz? If you answered honestly, you probably didn't get them all correct. If so, don't be surprised. We're not. After all, many of the things people routinely believe about behavior in organizations are only partially true—that is, true under some conditions, but not always. In other words, this topic tends to be far more complex and nuanced than meets the eye. This is precisely why when it comes to studying OB, we cannot rely on our common sense as a guide. Instead, we rely on scientific research (see Appendix 1 for a summary of how such research is conducted).

Although it's certainly not always perfect, the fact that research is carefully designed to describe and explain behavior in an unbiased fashion enhances our confidence in what it reveals. Indeed, OB is a science, and as such, the things we know about it are based not on what we think or hope or believe to be the case, but rather, on what research reveals. So, as you read this book you can be assured that the things we say are based on the results of careful scientific investigation, some of which we will describe in the course of our discussions.

Before moving on, you probably have some questions about our ten statements. Information bearing on them will be discussed in this book, but if you want to peek ahead to see why the answers are as we say, here's where the relevant points are discussed. Question 1, Chapter 5. Question 2, Chapter 9. Question 3, Chapter 12. Question 4, Chapter 4. Question 5, Chapter 16. Question 6, Chapter 4. Question 7, Chapter 14. Question 8, Chapter 4. Question 9, Chapter 8. Question 10, Chapter 10.

OB Recognizes the Dynamic Nature of Organizations

Although OB scientists and practitioners are interested in the behavior of people, they also are concerned about the nature of organizations themselves. Under what conditions will organizations change? How are organizations structured? How do organizations interact with their environments? These and related questions are of major interest to specialists in OB.

OB scientists recognize that organizations are not static, but dynamic and ever-changing entities. In other words, they recognize that organizations are **open systems**—that is, self-sustaining systems that use energy to transform resources from the environment (such as raw materials) into some form of output (for example, a finished product).[10] Figure 1.4 summarizes some of the key properties of open systems and provides an interesting example.

This diagram illustrates the open systems nature of symphony orchestras, but it applies to all types of organizations. They receive input from their environments and continuously transform it into output. This output gets transformed back to input, and the cyclical operation continues. Consider, for example, how organizations may tap the human resources of the community by hiring and training people to do jobs. These individuals may work to provide a product in exchange for wages. They then spend these wages, putting money back into the community, allowing more people to afford the company's products. This, in turn, creates the need for still more employees, and so on. If you think about it this way, it's easy to realize that organizations are dynamic and constantly changing.

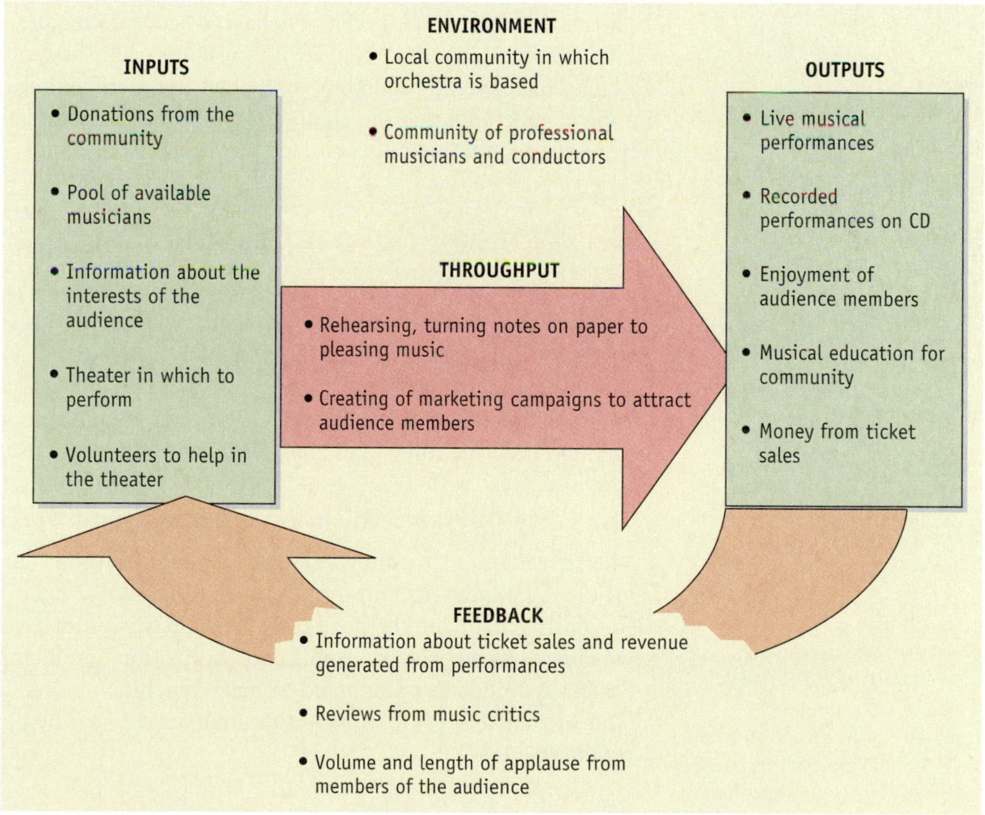

open systems
Self-sustaining systems that transform input from the external environment into output, which the system then returns to the environment.

ENVIRONMENT
- Local community in which orchestra is based
- Community of professional musicians and conductors

INPUTS
- Donations from the community
- Pool of available musicians
- Information about the interests of the audience
- Theater in which to perform
- Volunteers to help in the theater

THROUGHPUT
- Rehearsing, turning notes on paper to pleasing music
- Creating of marketing campaigns to attract audience members

OUTPUTS
- Live musical performances
- Recorded performances on CD
- Enjoyment of audience members
- Musical education for community
- Money from ticket sales

FEEDBACK
- Information about ticket sales and revenue generated from performances
- Reviews from music critics
- Volume and length of applause from members of the audience

FIGURE 1.4

Organizations as Open Systems: Overview and Example

The open systems approach is characteristic of modern-day thinking in the field of OB. It assumes that organizations are self-sustaining—that is, within the environments in which they operate they transform inputs to outputs in a continuous fashion. This example illustrates the symphony orchestra as an open system, but the same concepts apply to all organizations.

The dynamic nature of organizations can be likened to the operations of the human body. As people breathe, they take in oxygen and transform it into carbon dioxide. This, in turn, sustains the life of green plants, which emit oxygen for people to breathe. The continuous nature of the open system characterizes not only human life, but the existence of organizations as well.

OB Assumes There Is No "One Best" Approach

What's the most effective way to motivate people? What style of leadership works best? Should groups of individuals be used to make important organizational decisions? Although these questions are quite reasonable, there is a basic problem with all of them. Namely, they all assume that there is a simple, unitary answer—that is, one best way to motivate, to lead, and to make decisions.

Specialists in the field of OB today agree that there is no one best approach when it comes to such complex phenomena. To assume otherwise is not only overly simplistic and naive, but, as you will see, grossly inaccurate. When it comes to studying human behavior in organizations, there are no simple answers. For this reason, OB scholars embrace a **contingency approach**—an orientation that recognizes that behavior in work settings is the complex result of many interacting forces. This orientation is a hallmark of modern OB. Consider, for example, how an individual's personal characteristics (e.g., personal attitudes and beliefs) in conjunction with situational factors (e.g., an organization's climate, relations between coworkers) may all work together when it comes to influencing how a particular individual is likely to behave on the job.

With this in mind, explaining OB phenomena often requires saying, "it depends." As our knowledge of work-related behavior becomes increasingly complex, it is difficult to give "straight answers." Rather, it is usually necessary to say that people will do certain things "under some conditions" or "when all other factors are equal." Such phrases provide a clear indication that the contingency approach is being used. In other words, a certain behavior occurs "contingent upon" the existence of certain conditions—hence, the name.

OB Then and Now: A Capsule History

Although today we take for granted the importance of understanding the functioning of organizations and the behavior of people at work, this was not always the case. In fact, it was only 100 years ago that people first became interested in studying behavior in organizations, and only during the last 50 years that it gained widespread acceptance.[11] To enable you to appreciate how the field of OB got to where it is today, we now will outline its history and describe some of the most influential forces in its development.

The Early Days: Scientific Management and the Hawthorne Studies

The first attempts to study behavior in organizations came out of a desire by industrial efficiency experts to improve worker productivity. Their central question was straightforward: What could be done to get people to do more work in less time? This question was posed in a period of rapid industrialization and technological change in the United States. As engineers attempted to make machines more efficient, it was a natural extension of their efforts to work on the human side of the equation—making people more productive too.

Scientific Management and Its Detractors.   Among the earliest pioneers in this area was Frederick Winslow Taylor, an engineer who noticed the inefficient practices of the employees in the steel mill in which he worked and attempted to change them (see Figure 1.5).[12] This led Taylor to study the individual movements of laborers performing different jobs, searching for ways to perform them that resulted in the least wasted movements. Research of this type was referred to as **time-and-motion studies**. In 1911, Taylor advanced the concept of **scientific management,** which not only identified ways to design manual labor jobs more efficiently, but also emphasized carefully selecting and training

contingency approach
A perspective suggesting that organizational behavior is affected by a large number of interacting factors. How someone will behave is said to be contingent upon many different variables at once.

time-and-motion study
A type of applied research designed to classify and streamline the individual movements needed to perform jobs with the intent of finding "the one best way" to perform them.

scientific management
An early approach to management and organizational behavior emphasizing the importance of designing jobs as efficiently as possible.

FIGURE 1.5

Frederick Winslow Taylor (1856–1915)

Frederick Winslow Taylor was an industrial engineer who developed techniques for boosting people's efficiency on the job. He is considered to be the first person to study the behavior of people at work.

human relations movement
A perspective on organizational behavior that rejects the primarily economic orientation of scientific management and recognizes, instead, the importance of social processes in work settings.

Hawthorne studies
The earliest systematic research in the field of OB, this work was performed to determine how the design of work environments affected performance.

people to perform them. Although we take these ideas for granted today, Taylor is acknowledged to be the first person to carefully study human behavior at work.[13]

Despite his successes, Taylor's approach was credited with destroying the soul of work, of dehumanizing factories, making men into automatons. Getting people to work more efficiently was like designing a machine more efficiently, but people are not machines. So, inspired by the prospects of scientific management, but taking a more humanistic approach, other work experts advanced the idea that social factors operating in the workplace are an important determinant of how effectively people work. At the forefront of this effort was Elton W. Mayo, an organizational scientist and consultant widely regarded as the founder of what is called the **human relations movement.**[14] This approach emphasized that the social conditions existing in organizations—the way employees are treated by management and the relationships they have with each other—influence job performance.[15]

The Hawthorne Studies. Mayo's orientation was developed in the first investigations of organizational behavior, known as the **Hawthorne studies,** begun in 1927 at Western Electric's Hawthorne Works near Chicago. Mayo and his associates were interested in determining, among other things, how to design work environments in ways that increased performance. With this objective in mind, they systematically altered key aspects of the work environment (e.g., illumination, the length of rest pauses, the duration of the work day and work week) to see their effects on work performance. What they found was baffling: Productivity improved following almost every change in working conditions.[16] In fact, performance remained extremely high even when conditions were returned to normal, the way they were before the study began. However, workers didn't always improve their performance. In another set of studies, workers sometimes restricted their output deliberately. Not only did they stop working long before quitting time, but in interviews, they admitted that they easily could have done more if they desired.

What accounts for these fascinating findings? Mayo recognized that the answer resided in the fact that how effectively people work depends not only on the physical characteristics of the working conditions, but also the social conditions encountered. In the first set of studies, where productivity rose in all conditions, people simply were responding favorably to the special attention they received. Knowing they were being studied made them feel special and motivated them to do their best. Hence, it was these social factors more than the physical factors that had such profound effects on job performance. The same explanation applies to the case in which people restricted their performance. Here, the employees feared that because they were being studied, the company was eventually going to raise the amount of work they were expected to do each day. So as to guard against the imposition of unreasonable standards (and, hopefully, to keep their jobs!), the workers agreed among themselves to keep output low. In other words, informal rules were established about what constituted acceptable levels of job performance. These social forces at work in this setting proved to be much more potent determinants of job performance than the physical factors studied.

This conclusion, based on the surprising findings of the Hawthorne studies, is important because it ushered in a whole new way of thinking about behavior at work. It suggests that to understand behavior on the job, we must fully appreciate people's attitudes and the processes by which they communicate with each other. This way of thinking, so fundamental to modern OB, may be traced back to Elton Mayo's pioneering Hawthorne studies.

Classical Organizational Theory

classical organizational theory
An early approach to the study of management that focused on the most efficient way of structuring organizations.

During the same time that proponents of scientific management got people to begin thinking about the interrelationships between people and their jobs, another approach to managing people emerged. This perspective, known as **classical organizational theory,** focused on the efficient structuring of overall organizations. The idea was that there is an ideal way to efficiently organize work in all organizations—much as proponents of scientific management searched for the ideal way to perform particular jobs.

division of labor
The practiced of dividing work into specialized tasks that enable people to specialize in what they do best.

One of the most influential classical organizational theorists was Henri Fayol, a French industrialist who pioneered various ideas about how organizations should be structured. For example, Fayol advocated that there should be a **division of labor,** the practice of dividing work into specialized tasks that enable people to specialize in what they do best. He also argued that in any organization it always should be clear to whom each worker is responsible— that is, which managers have authority over them. Although many of these ideas are regarded as simplistic today, they were considered quite pioneering some 80 years ago.

bureaucracy
An organizational design developed by Max Weber that attempts to make organizations operate efficiently by having a clear hierarchy of authority in which people are required to perform well-defined jobs.

Another well known classical organizational theorist is the German sociologist Max Weber.[17] Among other things, Weber is well known for proposing a form of organizational structure known as the **bureaucracy**—a form of organization in which a set of rules are applied that keep higher-ranking organizational officials in charge of lower-ranking workers, who fulfill the duties assigned to them. As the description suggests, bureaucracies are organizations that carefully differentiate between those who give the orders and those who carry them out. A fan of bureaucracies, Henry Ford openly endorsed "the reduction of the necessity for thought on the part of the worker."[18] Making this possible are a set of rules such as those summarized in Table 1.2.

TABLE 1.2 Characteristics of an Ideal Bureaucracy

According to Max Weber, bureaucracies are the ideal organizational form. To function effectively, bureaucracies must possess the characteristics identified here.

Characteristic	Description
Formal rules and regulations	Written guidelines are used to control all employees' behaviors.
Impersonal treatment	Favoritism is to be avoided, and all work relationships are to be based on objective standards.
Division of Labor	All duties are divided into specialized tasks and are performed by individuals with the appropriate skills.
Hierarchical structure	Positions are ranked by authority level in clear fashion from lower-level to upper-level ones.
Authority structure	The making of decisions is determined by one's position in the hierarchy; higher-ranking people have authority over those in lower-ranking positions.
Lifelong career commitment	Employment is viewed as a permanent, lifelong obligation on the part of the organization and its employees.
Rationality	The organization is committed to achieving its ends (e.g., profitability) in the most efficient manner possible.

Given your own experiences with bureaucracies, you're probably not surprised to hear that this particular organizational form has not proven to be the perfect way to organize all work. Weber's universal view of bureaucratic structure contrasts with the more modern approaches to organizational design (see Chapter 15), which claim that different forms of organizational structure may be more or less appropriate under different situations. (This is the contingency approach we described earlier.) Also, because bureaucracies draw sharp lines between the people who make decisions (managers) and those who carry them out (workers), they are not particularly popular today. After all, contemporary employees prefer to have more equal opportunities to make decisions than bureaucracies permit. Still, contemporary OB owes a great deal to Weber for his many pioneering ideas.

Late Twentieth Century: Organizational Behavior as a Social Science

Based on contributions noted thus far, the realization that behavior in work settings is shaped by a wide range of individual, group, and organizational factors set the stage for the emergence of the science of organizational behavior. By the 1940s, doctoral degrees were awarded in OB and the first textbooks were published.[19] By the late 1950s and early 1960s, OB was clearly a going concern. By the 1970s, active programs of research were going on—investigations into such key processes as motivation and leadership, and the impact of organizational structure.[20]

Unfortunately—but not unexpectedly for a new field—the development of scientific investigations into managerial and organizational issues was uneven and unsystematic in the middle part of the twentieth century. In response to this state of affairs, the Ford Foundation sponsored a project in which economists carefully analyzed the nature of business education in the United States. They published their findings in 1959 in what became a very influential work known as the *Gordon and Howell report*.[21] In this work, it was recommended that the study of management pay greater attention to basic academic disciplines, especially the social sciences. This advice had an enormous influence on business school curricula during the 1960s and promoted the development of the field of organizational behavior. After all, it is a field that draws heavily on the basic social science disciplines recommended for incorporation into business curricula in this report.

Stimulated by this work, the field of OB rapidly grew into one that borrowed heavily from other disciplines. In fact, the field of OB as we know it today may be characterized as a hybrid science that draws from many social science fields. For example, studies of personality, learning, and perception draw on psychology. Similarly, the study of group dynamics and leadership relies heavily on sociology. The topic of organizational communication networks, obviously, draws on research in the field of communication. Power and politics is studied by political scientists. Anthropologists study cross-cultural themes. And OB scientists look to the field of management science to understand ways to manage quality in organizations. By the time the twentieth century drew to a close, OB clearly was a multidisciplinary field that was making important contributions to both science and practice.

OB in Today's Infotech Age

A century ago, when scientists first became aware of the importance of managing people, their primary challenge involved getting people to work efficiently, and they did so by treating people like the machines with which they worked—pushing them as hard as possible, sometimes until they broke down. Then, as we became more aware of the importance of the human element in the workplace, it became fashionable to treat people in more humane fashion. Today, in what has been called *the infotech age,* computer technology has made it possible to eliminate vast amounts of grunt-work that laborers used to have to perform. Much boring, monotonous, and dangerous physical labor has been eliminated by computer technology, and this has changed the way people work (see Figure 1.6).

Work in Today's Infotech Age

Technology has changed—and continues to change—the way many jobs are performed. We doubt that this will be one of them, but you never can tell.

"It appears to be some kind of wireless technology."

Modern technology also has changed the way managers operate. Traditionally, low-level workers gathered information and fed it to higher-level workers, who carefully analyzed it all and made decisions for lower-level workers to carry out. Today, however, easy access to information in computer databases has made it possible for almost any worker to gather the facts needed to make his or her own decisions. And, although some managers still make decisions on behalf of their workers, today we are likely to see employees making many of their own decisions with the aid of information stored on computers. Because managers no longer have to be highly involved in their subordinates' work, they are freed to concentrate on the big picture, to come up with innovative ways to improve the whole organization.

At the same time, the best managers have learned that they could use this opportunity, as one observer said, "to tap employees' most essential humanity, their ability to create, judge, imagine, and build relationships."[22] It is this focus that characterizes today's organizations—hence, the field of OB. Today, people are likely to care at least as much about the work they do as the money they make. They are likely to be deeply concerned about what their organization stands for and the extent to which they can make meaningful contributions to it. In short, contemporary OB recognizes that people care more than ever about the interpersonal side of work—recognition, relationships, and social interaction.

Despite the fact that technology has advanced, changing the way employees work, people themselves have not changed. All of us are human, and just because we work differently than before, we should not discard the things about the behavior of people we have learned over the years.[23] Twenty-first-century OB scientists are busily at work cultivating that humanity by doing things that make it possible for people to do work that is more challenging, meaningful, and interesting to them than ever before. Although this focus is not entirely unique to the twenty-first century, it's safe to say that its keen emphasis is indeed a key characteristic of modern OB.

To fully appreciate the nature of OB as a contemporary field, it is important to recognize its connection to the various economic, social, and cultural trends and forces that shape today's society. Specifically, these include three prominent trends: (1) the rise of global businesses with culturally diverse workforces, (2) rapid advances in technology, and (3) the rising expectations of people in general. We will discuss these forces in the three remaining sections of this chapter.

OB Responds to the Rise of Globalization and Diversity

When your grandfather went to work, chances are good that he faced a world of work that is quite different from the kind that exists today. For one, the company he worked for was likely to be headquartered in the U.S. and faced competition from other U.S-based organizations. He also was unlikely to find many women on the job—at least, not in high-ranking positions—nor were there as many African Americans, Hispanics, and Asian Americans working along with him. And, when he reached 65, in all likelihood, he would retire. As we will describe here, this picture has all but disappeared. Today's organizations are global in nature and are populated by women and people of color, not to mention individuals who are working well into what would have been considered "retirement years." All of this, as we will note, has important implications for OB.

International Business and the Global Economy

To fully understand behavior in organizations we must appreciate the fact that today's organizations operate within an economic system that is truly international in scope.[24] The nations of the world are not isolated from one another economically; what happens in one country has effects on other countries. For example, when Hurricane Katrina struck the U.S. Gulf Coast in late August of 2005, it sent ripples throughout the economic markets of the world for many months (e.g., because of disruptions in shipping and petroleum processing).[25] This tendency for the world's countries to be influenced by one another is known as **globalization**—the process of interconnecting the world's people with respect to the cultural, economic, political, technological, and environmental aspects of their lives.[26]

The trend toward globalization, which has been widespread in recent years, has been fueled by three major forces. First, technology has been involved in several ways. It has drastically lowered the cost of transportation and communication, thereby enhancing opportunities for international commerce. Technology also has helped companies bridge some of the inevitable cultural gaps (for an interesting example, see the *OB in a Diverse World* section on p. 18). Second, laws restricting trade generally have become liberalized throughout the world (e.g., in the United States and other heavily industrialized countries, free trade policies have been advocated). Third, developing nations have sought to expand their economies by promoting exports and opening their doors to foreign companies seeking investments.

If international trade is the major driver of globalization, then the primary vehicles are **multinational enterprises (MNEs)**—organizations that have significant operations (typically 25 percent or more of their output capacity) spread throughout various nations but are headquartered in a single nation. Currently, the four largest MNEs in the world are Exxon Mobil, Wal-Mart Stores, General Motors, and Ford Motor Company.

General Electric (GE) is a particularly good example of an MNE. It employs 313,000 people in companies located in more than 100 different countries. Yet they all draw resources from company headquarters in Fairfield, Connecticut. They also adhere to the same strategy—to insist on excellence for customers in all endeavors. As you might imagine, the rise of MNEs has resulted in large numbers of people, known as **expatriates,** who are citizens of one country living and working in another country (see Figure 1.7).

While working abroad, people are exposed to different **cultures**—the set of values, customs, and beliefs that people have in common with other members of a social unit (e.g., a nation).[27] And, when people are faced with new cultures, it is not unusual for them to become confused and disoriented—a phenomenon known as **culture shock.**[28] People also experience culture shock when they return to their native cultures after spending time away from it—a process of readjustment known as **repatriation.** In general, the phenomenon of culture shock results from people's recognition of the fact that others may be different from them in ways that they never imagined, and this takes some getting used to.

Scientists have observed that the process of adjusting to a foreign culture generally follows a U-shape curve (see Figure 1.8).[29] That is, at first, people are optimistic and

globalization
The process of interconnecting the world's people with respect to the cultural, economic, political, technological, and environmental aspects of their lives.

multinational enterprises (MNEs)
Organizations that have significant operations spread throughout various nations but are headquartered in a single nation.

expatriates
People who are citizens of one country, but who are living and working in another country.

culture
The set of values, customs, and beliefs that people have in common with other members of a social unit (e.g., a nation).

culture shock
The tendency for people to become confused and disoriented as they attempt to adjust to a new culture.

repatriation
The process of readjusting to one's own culture after spending time away from it.

OB In a Diverse World

What in the World Is That Name?

 In the United States and most English-speaking countries, we know that people named "Margaret" often go by "Peggy," that "Jack" may be "John," "James" may be "Jim," and that "Robert" may be called "Bob." If you know the culture, these alternative names are not surprising. But, if you're doing business on a global scale, such name variations are likely to be as foreign to you as the native language itself.

Besides being polite and avoiding embarrassment in business meetings, why might anyone care about this? To IBM, which in March of 2006 purchased Language Analysis Systems (LAS), a company that developed multicultural name recognition technology, there are several reasons.[30] For example, banks and insurance companies attempting to combat money laundering and fraud may need to be aware of criminals attempting to disguise their identities by using variations of their names. The service is also useful to companies whose clients don't have nefarious motives, but who forget what nickname they used on a given occasion. Airlines, for example, find it useful to be able to search for reservations and other information provided using different names. Similarly, hospitals use the technology to avoid duplicating medical procedures.

Although the exact way the LAS technology works is highly technical, what it does is straightforward. Drawing upon a database of nearly a billion names from around the world, the software verifies the origin, cultural variations, and meaning of names. It focuses on nicknames, titles, format changes, and typographical errors. (Since the name of the first author of this book is "Jerald," you might imagine he has found his name listed as "Gerald" or "Gerold" on more than one occasion.)

IBM's acquisition of LAS was not an isolated move. Rather, it was the seventeenth company acquired in five years (2001 to 2006) to help customers use technology to manage and deliver information in today's global business world. In its announcement of this acquisition, IBM's official statement underscores its commitment to such technology:

Names are often times overlooked as miniature databases of knowledge, but that's precisely what they are. In our global society, the ability to accurately recognize and manage the building blocks of an individual's name can provide the key to recognizing identities across cultures, genders, and meanings. This is where IBM's global name recognition technology can help.[31]

To companies around the world, this represents a useful service. To readers of this book, however, the existence of this service reflects a key point: namely, that technology plays a central role in helping today's organizations address the challenges of globalization. Name recognition may seem minor to most of us, but on a global scale it's quite important—and as IBM officials surely hope, big business.

---

excited about learning a new culture. This usually lasts about a month or so. Then, for the next several months, they become frustrated and confused as they struggle to learn the new culture (i.e., culture shock occurs). Finally, after about six months, people adjust to their new culture and become more accepting of it and satisfied with it. These observations imply that feelings of culture shock are inevitable. Although some degree of frustration may be expected when you first enter a new country, the more time you spend learning its ways, the better you will come to understand and accept it.[32]

In general, culture shock results from the tendency for people to be highly *parochial* in their assumptions about others, taking a narrow view of the world by believing that there is one best way of doing things. They also tend to be highly *ethnocentric*, believing that their way of doing things is the best way. For example, Americans tend to be highly parochial by speaking only English (whereas most Europeans speak several languages), and ethnocentric by believing that everyone else in the world should learn their language. As we just explained, over time, exposure to other cultures teaches people that there may be many different ways of doing the same thing (making them less parochial), and that these ways may be equally good, if not better (making them less ethnocentric). Although these biases may have been reasonable for Americans 50 years ago when the United States was the world's dominant economic power (producing three-quarters of its wealth), they would be extremely costly today. Indeed, because the world's economy is global in nature, highly parochial and ethnocentric views cannot be tolerated.

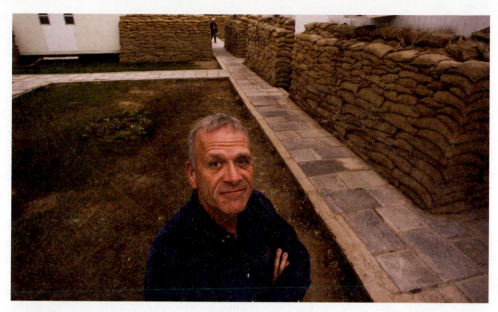

FIGURE 1.7

An Expatriate's Home Away from Home

As a project manager for Bechtel, one of the world's premier engineering, construction, and project management companies, it's not unusual for Clifford Mumm to find himself working for long periods of time in other countries. In his latest assignment in Baghdad, Mr. Mumm oversees the rebuilding of war-torn Iraq. This requires him and his associates to live in a camp composed of sandbag-reinforced prefab trailers in the Coalition Provisional Authority's "Green Zone," where safety cannot be ensured. Although there are many expatriates working today, fortunately only some undertake assignments that require them to endure such uncomfortable and unsafe conditions.

FIGURE 1.8

Adjusting to Foreign Culture: The General Stages

People's adjustment to new cultures generally follows the U-shaped curve illustrated here. After an initial period of excitement, culture shock often sets in. Then, after this period of adjustment (about 6 months), the more time spent in the new culture, the better it is accepted.

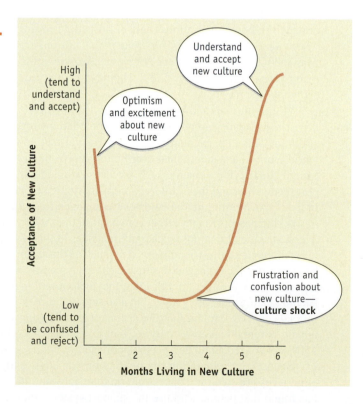

Analogously, highly narrow and biased views about the management of people in organizations may severely limit our understanding about behavior in organizations. During the 1950s and 1960s management scholars tended to overlook the importance of cultural differences in organizations. They made two key assumptions: (1) that principles of good management are universal, and (2) that the best management practices are ones that work well in the United States.[33] This highly inflexible approach is known as the **convergence hypothesis.** Such a biased orientation reflects the fact that the study of behavior in organizations first emerged at a time in which the United States was the world's predominant economic power.

With the ever-growing global economy, it has become clear that an American-oriented approach may be highly misleading when it comes to understanding the practices that work best in various countries. In fact, there may be many possible ways to manage effectively, and these will depend greatly on the individual culture in which people live. This alternative approach, which is widely accepted today, is known as the **divergence hypothesis.** Following this orientation, understanding the behavior of people at work requires carefully appreciating the cultural context within which they operate. For example, whereas American cultural norms suggest that it would not be inappropriate for an employee to question his or her superior, it would be taboo for a worker in Japan to do the same thing. Thus, today's organizational scholars are becoming increasingly sensitive to the ways in which culture influences organizational behavior.

The Shifting Demographics of the Workforce: Trends Toward Diversity

Thus far, we have been discussing cultural differences between people from companies in different nations. However, widespread cultural differences also may be found *within* organizations. Several such trends are notable: the prevalence of women in the workforce, the reality of racial and ethnic diversity, and the fact that people are living and working longer than ever before. We now consider these.

More Women Are in the Workforce Than Ever Before. In the 1950s, the "typical American family" was characterized by a man who went to work and his wife, who stayed at home and watched the children. Although this profile still may be found, it is quite uncommon. In fact, about three-quarters of women between ages 25 and 54 are employed outside the home, and almost half of all people in the workplace are women, many of whom also are mothers.[34] This trend stems not only from economic necessity, but also from the widespread acceptance of women working outside the home. As women, who for many years worked only inside the home, have moved to working outside the home, the economy has grown.

With both men and women working, companies have found it beneficial—or, even necessary, in some cases—to make accommodations for individuals who take care of their children. This is particularly necessary insofar as people in today's hectic professional world work longer hours than ever before (up from 47 weekly hours to 49 for men, and from 39 to 43.5 for women).[35] Also, because single mothers typically have to work to support themselves and their children, more are doing so than ever before—about two-thirds, in fact.[36] As a result, organizations have engaged in several efforts to help meet the needs of working parents as they struggle to balance their work and nonwork responsibilities. For a look at some of the most successful practices in this regard, see Table 1.3.[37]

Although family-friendly practices such as those summarized in Table 1.3 are likely to be expensive, the organizations that use them generally are convinced that they are in several respects wise investments. First, they help retain highly valued employees—not only keeping them from competitors, but also saving the costs of having to replace them. In fact, officials at AT&T found that the average cost of letting new parents take up to a year of unpaid parental leave was only 32% of an employee's annual salary, compared with the 150% cost of replacing that person permanently.[38]

Second, by alleviating the distractions of having to worry about nonwork issues, employees are freed to concentrate on their jobs and to be their most creative. Research has found that people who use the support systems their employers provide are not only

---

convergence hypothesis
A biased approach to the study of management, which assumes that principles of good management are universal, and that ones that work well in the U.S. will apply equally well in other nations.

divergence hypothesis
The approach to the study of management which recognizes that knowing how to manage most effectively requires clear understanding of the culture in which people work.

TABLE 1.3 Employee Support Policies: Some Exemplary Practices

With increasing frequency, companies are taking proactive steps to help employees meet their personal needs and family obligations. In so doing, they make it possible for employees to satisfy the demands imposed by their nonwork lives. This allows companies to draw on the talents of a diverse group of prospective employees who otherwise might not be able to lend their talents to the organization. Three practices have proven especially useful in this regard.

Practice	General Description	Exemplary Practice
Child-care facilities	Sites at or near company locations at which parents can leave their children while they are working.	America West believes so strongly in the importance of providing child care that it offers these services 24 hours a day. The company even maintained these benefits while it was going through bankruptcy proceedings.
Elder-care facilities	Sites at or near company locations at which employees can leave elderly relatives (e.g., parents, grandparents) for whom they serve as caretakers while the employees are working.	Lancaster Laboratories (in Lancaster, Pennsylvania) provides a facility where employees can bring adult family members who are in need of care during working hours. This enables employees to enter the workforce while meeting their caretaking responsibilities.
Personal support policies	Widely varied practices that help employees meet the demands of their family lives, freeing them to concentrate on their work.	Wilton Connor Packaging (Charlotte, North Carolina) provides even more unusual forms of support, such as an on-site laundry, high school equivalency classes, door-to-door transportation, and a children's clothing swap center.

Sources: Family Support America, 2006 and other sources; see Note 36.

child-care facilities
Sites at or near company locations where parents can leave their children while they are working.

elder-care facilities
Facilities at which employees at work can leave elderly relatives for whom they are responsible (such as parents and grandparents).

personal support policies
Widely varied practices that help employees meet the demands of their family lives, freeing them to concentrate on their work.

more active in team problem-solving activities, but also almost twice as likely to submit useful suggestions for improvement. Commenting on such findings, Ellen Galinsky, co-president of the Families & Work Institute, said, "There's a cost to *not* providing work and family assistance."[39]

A third benefit—and an important one, at that—is that such policies help attract the most qualified human resources, giving companies that use them a competitive edge over those that do not.[40] And, of course, in today's competitive work environment, companies need all the advantages they can get.

Racial and Ethnic Diversity Is Reality. Just as yesterday's workers were primarily males, they also were primarily white. However, just as growing numbers of women have made men less of a majority, so too have an influx of people from different racial and ethnic groups made white people a smaller majority. Specifically, although white non-Hispanic workers are currently the dominant group, their proportion dropped from 79.8 percent in 1986 to 75.3 percent in 1996, and to 72.7 percent by 2006.[41] At the same time, increases in the numbers of African Americans, Hispanics, and Asian Americans in the workforce are projected—in large part due to liberal immigration policies and differential birth rates in various groups (see Figure 1.9).[42] Figure 1.9 tells a clear story about the changing face of the American workforce. Today, about 1 in 4 Americans is a member of a minority group, but by 2050, that is expected to be almost 1 in 2. That certainly

FIGURE 1.9

Minorities in the Workplace: Their Numbers Are Rising

It is projected that the relative percentage of whites in the U.S. workforce, although currently the largest group, will be declining whereas the figures are rising for other racial and ethnic groups. Eventually, what it means to be a member of a "minority group" will have to be reconsidered.

Source: Based on data reported by the U.S. Department of Labor, 2006; see Note 42.

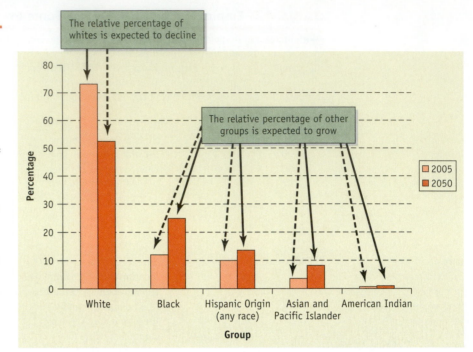

baby boom generation
The generation of children born in the economic boom period following World War II.

would be a good reason to rethink what it means to be a member of a "minority group."[43] Also, Hispanics are about to overtake blacks as the largest minority group. In some states, such as California, this already has occurred.

People Are Living—and Working—Longer Than Ever Before. In the years after World War II the peacetime economy flourished in the United States. With it came a large increase in population as soldiers returned from war and started families. The generation of children born during this period is widely referred to as the **baby boom generation**. Today, the first of these baby boomers have turned 55 and are considered "older workers" by labor economists. And, only a few years from now, the number of older people in the workplace will swell dramatically. Living in a period in which retirement is no longer automatic at age 65, aged baby boomers will comprise a growing part of the population in the years to come. In fact, people over 85 years old are already the fastest-growing segment of the U.S. population.[44] Clearly, this trend has profound implications for the traditional patterns of work and retirement that have developed over the years.

Implications for OB. In commenting on the growing diversity in the American workplace, the office of the Secretary of the Department of Labor said:

> To set the stage for understanding what work, workers, and workplaces will be like in twenty-first-century America, we need first to appreciate the demographic, educational, and employment changes that have shaped the American workforce of today.[45]

We could not agree more. That more women, people of color, and older workers are in the workforce than ever before is not merely an idle sociological curiosity. It also has important implications for OB—and ones that we will examine more closely in this book. After all, the more people differ from each other, the more challenges they are likely to face when interacting with one another.

How these challenges play out is likely to be seen on the job in important ways. For example, as we will describe, differences in age, gender, and ethnic group membership are likely to bring with them differences in communication style that must be addressed for organizations to function effectively (see Chapter 10). It also is the case that people at different stages of their lives are likely to be motivated by different things (see Chapter 6) and to be satisfied with different aspects of their jobs (see Chapter 5). And, as workers adjust to a wider variety of people in the workplace, issues about their norms and values (see Chapter 8) are likely to come up, as well as their willingness to accept others who are different from themselves (see Chapter 5). This can have important implications for potential conflict in the workplace (see Chapter 12) and their career choices (see Chapter 7), which may be expected to influence their capacity to work effectively as members of the same work teams (see Chapter 9).

OB Responds to Advances in Technology

Since the Industrial Revolution, people have performed carefully prescribed sets of tasks— known as *jobs*—within large networks of workers who answered to those above them— hierarchical arrangements known as *organizations*. This picture, although highly simplistic, does a good job of characterizing the working arrangements that most people had during much of the twentieth century. However, today, in the twenty-first century, the essential nature of jobs and organizations as we have known them is changing. Although many factors are responsible for such change, experts agree that the major catalyst is rapidly advancing computer technology, especially the use of the Internet and wireless technology.[46]

As you might imagine, this state of affairs has important implications for organizations— and, hence, the field of OB. After all, as more work is shifted to digital brains, some work that was once performed by human brains becomes obsolete. At the same time, new opportunities arise as people scurry to find their footing amidst the shifting terrain of the high-tech revolution. The implications of this for OB are considerable. We will now consider some of the most prominent trends in the world of work that have been identified in recent years. These involve how work is organized and performed, as well as the need for flexibility.

Leaner Organizations: Downsizing and Outsourcing

Technology has made it possible for fewer people to do more work than ever before. Automation, the process of replacing people with machines, is not new, of course; it has gone on, slowly and steadily, for centuries. Today, however, because it is not large mechanical devices but digital data that are manipulated, scientists refer instead to the "informating" of the workplace.

informate
The process by which workers manipulate objects by "inserting data" between themselves and those objects.

The term **informate** describes the process by which workers use computer information technology to transform a once-physical task into one that involves manipulating a sequence of digital commands.[47] Thanks to this process, for example, today's auto workers can move around large hoods and trunk lids by pressing a few buttons on a keypad instead of physically manipulating them by hand. Likewise, the process of placing sales orders often is informated. Thanks to computer systems analysts, an order entered into a salesperson's laptop computer can trigger a chain of events involving everything associated with the job: placing a sales order, manufacturing the product to exact specifications, delivering the final product, sending out the bill, and even crediting the proper commission to the salesperson's payroll check.

Unlike the gradual process of automation, today's technology—and the process of informating—is occurring so rapidly that the very nature of work is changing as fast as we can keep up. With this, many jobs are disappearing, leaving organizations (at least the most successful ones!) smaller than before.[48] Product manufacturing also has been informated. At GE's Fanuc Automation plant in Charlottesville, Virginia, for example, circuit boards are manufactured by half as many employees as required before informating the facility.[49] But it is not only blue-collar, manual labor jobs that are eliminated, but white-collar, mental labor jobs as well. In many places, middle managers are no longer needed to make decisions that can now be made by computers. It's little wonder that middle managers, while only 10 percent of the workforce, comprise 20 percent of recent layoffs.

downsizing
The process of adjusting the number of employees needed to work in newly-designed organizations (also known as *rightsizing*).

Indeed, organizations have been rapidly reducing the number of employees needed to operate effectively—a process known as **downsizing**.[50] Typically, this involves more than just laying off people in a move to save money. It is directed at adjusting the number of

rightsizing
See *downsizing*.

employees needed to work in newly designed organizations, and is therefore also known as **rightsizing**.[51] Whatever you call it, the bottom line is clear: Many organizations need fewer people to operate today than in the past—sometimes, far fewer. The statistics tell a sobering tale. From January 1997 through December 1999, 3.3 million American workers found their jobs eliminated.[52] Since 2000, most job losses have occurred in Internet-based ("dot-com") companies, retail stores, the auto industry, and media (e.g., publishing and advertising). Downsizings are not a unique manifestation of current economic trends. During the past decade some degree of downsizing has occurred in about half of all companies—especially in the middle management and supervisory ranks (to see who's most likely and least likely to get laid off, see Table 1.4).[53] Experts agree that rapid changes in technology have been largely responsible for much of this.

Another way organizations are restructuring is by completely eliminating those parts of themselves that focus on noncore sectors of the business (i.e., tasks that are peripheral to the organization) and hiring outside firms to perform these functions instead—a practice known as **outsourcing**.[54] By outsourcing secondary activities an organization can focus on what it does best, its key capability—what is known as its **core competency**. Companies like ServiceMaster, which provides janitorial services, and ADP, which provides payroll processing services, make it possible for their client organizations to concentrate on the business functions most central to their missions. So for example, by outsourcing its maintenance work or its payroll processing, a manufacturing company may grow smaller and focus its resources on what it does best, manufacturing.

outsourcing
The process of eliminating those parts of organizations that focus on noncore sectors of the business (i.e., tasks that are peripheral to the organization), and hiring outside firms to perform these functions instead.

core competency
An organization's key capability, what it does best.

Some critics fear that outsourcing represents a "hollowing out" of companies—a reduction of functions that weakens organizations by making them more dependent on others.[55] Others counter that outsourcing makes sense when the work that is outsourced is not highly critical to competitive success (e.g., janitorial services), or when it is so highly critical that it only can succeed by seeking outside assistance.[56] For example, it is a widespread practice for companies selling personal computers today to outsource the manufacturing of various components (e.g., hard drives, CD-ROMs, and chips) to other companies.[57] Although this practice may sound atypical compared to what occurs in most manufacturing companies, it isn't. In fact, one industry analyst has estimated that 30 percent of the largest American industrial firms outsource over half their manufacturing.[58]

The Virtual Organization

As more and more companies are outsourcing various organizational functions and are paring down to their core competencies, they might not be able to perform all the tasks required to complete a project. However, they can certainly perform their own highly specialized part of it very well. Now, if you put together several organizations whose

TABLE 1.4 Are You Likely to Become a Victim of Downsizing?

Based on prevailing patterns of downsizing, some people are more vulnerable to getting laid off, whereas others are generally safer. Here are some rough guidelines for assessing your own vulnerability to downsizing.

You Are Vulnerable to Getting Laid Off If . . .	You Are More Immune from Layoffs If . . .
You are paid over $150,000.	You have a good relationship with your boss.
You are inflexible and unwilling to transfer to a new job or to another city.	You have a midrange salary.
You work in retail, automotive, or manufacturing businesses.	You generate revenue for the company
You are a top executive of a division that is not performing up to expectations.	You have expertise in a technical field
You lack computer skills.	You have demonstrated willingness to work long hours whenever necessary
You do not have good leadership skills.	You are willing to relocate to another city or to transfer to another position in the company

Source: Based on suggestions by McGinn & Naughton, 2001; see Note 53.

virtual organization

A highly flexible, temporary organization formed by a group of companies that join forces to exploit a specific opportunity.

competencies complement each other and have them work together on a special project, you'd have a very strong group of collaborators. This is the idea behind an organizational arrangement that is growing in popularity—the **virtual organization**. A virtual organization is a highly flexible, temporary organization formed by a group of companies that join forces to exploit a specific opportunity.[59]

For example, various companies often come together to work on special projects in the entertainment industry (e.g., to produce a motion picture—see Figure 1.10) and in the field of construction (e.g., to build a shopping center). After all, technologies are changing so rapidly and skills are becoming so specialized these days that no one company can do everything by itself. And so, they join forces temporarily to form virtual organizations—not permanent organizations, but temporary ones without their own offices or organization charts. Although virtual organizations are not yet common, experts expect them to grow in popularity in the years ahead.[60] As one consultant put it, "It's not just a good idea; it's inevitable."[61]

Telecommuting: Going to Work Without Leaving Home

telecommuting (telework)

The practice of using communications technology so as to enable work to be performed from remote locations, such as the home.

In recent years, the practice of **telecommuting** (also known as **teleworking**) has grown in popularity from an interesting, out-of-the ordinary possibility for some people to a mainstream reality for many. This is the practice of using communications technology so as to enable work to be performed from remote locations, such as the home, a ship, a hotel room, or anywhere an Internet connection can be made. Years ago, telecommuting was used mostly by sales reps and consultants, but today it is used regularly by many employees, such as researchers, attorneys, accountants, and people in a variety of creative positions (e.g., artists, photographers, and writers). Indeed, telecommuting has gone mainstream and is used in one way or another in the vast majority of companies, big and small, public and private.

Telecommuting is in full swing today. A 2005 survey found that some 45.1 million Americans use broadband connections from various places to do work that they otherwise

FIGURE 1.10

Virtual Organizations in the Movie Business

Next time you exit the movie theater, take a close look at the credits. Not only are various actors and actresses listed along with technicians of all types, but also a number of different companies. The making of a modern motion picture, such as Walt Disney Pictures Pirates of the Caribbean (starring Orlando Bloom), is a good example of a so-called virtual organization. Various organizations with different areas of expertise (e.g., casting, sound recording, special effects, etc.) join forces long enough to bring a final product to fruition.

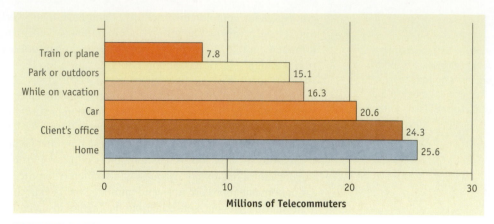

FIGURE 1.11

From Where Do People Telecommute?

Technology makes it possible for many of today's employees to do their work from locations other than their offices. As summarized here, several locations are particularly popular.

Source: IATC, 2005; see Note 62.

would have done in an office.[62] As shown in Figure 1.11, there are a wide variety of locations in popular use. Many people rely on more than just one, an average of 3.4 locations, in fact. For many, their local Starbucks represents "the third space" beyond office and home, wherever a notebook computer, a wireless network, and a latte may be found. But, with a 60 percent increase in the availability of broadband connections in people's homes, the home is the fastest-growing location.

Both employees and employers enjoy the benefits of telecommuting. For example, telecommuting makes it possible for employees to avoid the hassle and expenses of daily commuting, which, in an era of congested roads and expensive fuel costs, can be dramatic. Employees working at home also enjoy saving money that they would have spent purchasing work clothing (unless you happen to wear ties or pantyhose around the house) and buying meals in restaurants and from vending machines. In fact, it has been estimated that in 2005 each teleworker was able to save approximately $20,000 per year, taking into account all expenses.[63] Saving money is not the only reason why most telecommuters like the arrangement. They also enjoy the flexibility it gives them to balance work and family matters.[64] In fact, over 83 percent of the 4,000 employees at IBM's Midwest Division indicate that they are not interested in returning to the traditional office environment.

Telecommuting also makes it possible for companies to save millions of dollars in expenses for office facilities.[65] At Hewlett-Packard, for example, about $230 million is being saved in annual office expenses. This occurs because companies are able to get more work done in the same space. Cisco Systems, for example, has so many teleworkers that it now takes only the physical space of 88 workers to do the work of 140 employees.[66] IBM also has been able to slash its office space by as much as 55 percent in some locations. As you might imagine, the savings are particularly important to small, start-up companies, which can hire workforces without having to make large investments in office space.

Importantly, telecommuting allows companies to comply with governmental regulations (e.g., the Federal Clean Air Act of 1990) requiring them to reduce the number of trips made by their employees. In fact, the federal government is a major proponent of telecommuting. The Securities and Exchange Commission (SEC), the State Department, the Department of Justice, and four other large federal agencies now are required by law to offer all eligible workers the opportunity to telecommute.

A particularly interesting and all-too-real reason to use telecommuting is to help organizations get up and running after a disaster strikes. After all, if an organization's assets are spread out—as is the case if they are in the hands of employees who are geographically dispersed—they are less vulnerable to attacks by human threats (e.g., terrorist strikes, arsonists) and natural disasters (e.g., floods, hurricanes, and tornadoes). Preparing accordingly, of course, requires some effort. For some useful guidelines in this regard, see the *How to Do It* section on page 28.

Despite these benefits, as you might imagine, telecommuting is not for everyone; it also has its limitations.[67] It works best on jobs that require concentration, have well-defined beginning and end points, are easily portable, call for minimal amounts of special equipment, and can be done with little supervision.[68] Fortunately, at least some aspects of most sales and professional jobs meet these standards. Even so, making telecommuting work requires careful adjustments in the way work is done. Also, many people just don't have the kind of self-discipline needed to get work done without direct supervision. To see if you and your associates have what it takes to succeed at telecommuting, see the *Group Exercise* at the end of this chapter.

OB Is Responsive to People's Changing Expectations

OB scientists do not work in a vacuum. Instead, they are highly responsive to people's changing expectations with respect to various aspects of work. This is the case with respect to three particular areas of concern to the field of OB: (1) employees' and employers' desire for engagement, (2) the flexibility employees expect from employers, and (3) the pressure to produce high-quality goods and services. We now discuss each of these forces and their impact on modern OB.

Employees and Employers Desire Engagement

When referring to people who are preparing to wed, we say that they are "engaged." Typically, such individuals believe in each other, they want to share a bright future together, they are respectful to each other, and they are willing to do what it takes to ensure the other's happiness and success. We also use the term *engagement* to refer to employers and employees who share similar commitments to one another.

engagement

A mutual commitment between employers and employees to do things to help one another achieve each other's goals and aspirations.

In the field of OB the term **engagement** refers to a mutual commitment between employers and employees to do things to help one another achieve goals and aspirations.[69] Thus, engagement is a two-way process. Typically, it works like this: Organizations take steps to engage their employees, and employees, in turn, respond by engaging their organizations. This takes several forms, such as the following:

- High levels of pride in the organization
- Pride in the organizations' products and services
- Belief that the organization helps employees do their best
- Willingness to help others on the job
- Understanding "the big picture" and being willing to go beyond formal job requirements when necessary

Because engagement begins with employers, it's important to note what organizations can do to get the ball rolling. Organizations can do several specific things to promote feelings of engagement in their employees. Not surprisingly, these are practices that we will be describing (and recommending) in various places throughout this book. The four key drivers of engagement are as follows:

- Involving employees in making decisions (see Chapter 10)
- Giving employees opportunities to express their ideas and opinions (see Chapter 2)
- Providing opportunities for employees to develop their jobs (see Chapter 5)
- Showing concern for employees' well-being as individuals (see Chapter 7)

Considering this, we may ask, are today's employees are engaged in their jobs? An extensive survey by the Gallup Organization revealed three groups of employees.[70] Only 31 percent truly were *engaged*. These individuals worked with passion and felt deep connections to their companies, helping move their companies forward. The majority, however, some 52 percent, were classified as *not engaged*. These people "checked out" of their jobs and went through the

How to Do It

Telecommuting as a Business Continuity Strategy

For the average person, poignant memories of the 9/11 terrorist attacks and Hurricane Katrina tragically linger on, but their toll on business adds another dimension of suffering among the untold thousands whose businesses and livelihoods either were disrupted or vanished in their wake. As extreme as these acts were, they are but a few of the many disasters of one form or another that disrupt the operations of about 1 in 5 American businesses in an average year.[71] Even less dramatic events—such as toxic spills, earthquakes, water main breaks, or communication cables severed by careless construction workers—can disrupt business operations, underscoring the need for businesses to have sets of procedures in place to get up and running in the event of such disruptions.

Such preparations, known as **business continuity plans,** are in place in about only 2 in 5 small organizations, leaving the others vulnerable in times of crisis. Specifically, these refer to systematic sets of plans designed to help organizations get up and running again in the event of a disruption of some sort. Indeed, although small businesses are the least prepared they have the most to lose because their limited resources make it difficult, if not impossible, to sustain any disruption. Large organizations are somewhat better prepared, with plans in place in 4 out of 5 businesses. But, given that the average loss per hour of downtime in *Fortune* 1000 firms runs about $78,000, and that disruptions may last for days, weeks, or even months, no organization can afford to ignore to prepare for the inevitable.

Telecommuting is a key part of any business continuity plan. The reasons are not hard to understand. Emergencies result in loss of workspace, loss of technology, and loss of staff. In each instance, telework helps reduce the risk because it allows organizations to disperse employees quickly and to set up offices elsewhere. Besides allowing for the speedy resumption of business, teleworking helps in emergencies because it allows employees to remain in the presence of their families, where they desire to be at such times.

Organizations should take the following steps to ensure that telecommuting provides the help needed in emergencies.

1. Keep company records, especially vital ones, on several backup servers. These should be geographically disbursed in the event that a disaster strikes a particular local area.
2. Ensure that workers have a list of locations where they can go to find access to electricity and the Internet. These should be both local and regional in nature.
3. Maintain databases of addresses, phone numbers, e-mail addresses, and emergency addresses (e.g., relatives living elsewhere) where everyone can be contacted.
4. Train all workers to be able to perform at least part of their jobs from distant locations, including how to use computers.
5. Keep training current and thorough. Just because someone once may have been computer-savvy does not ensure that he or she will continue to be so. Thorough training in distance collaboration and peer communication technology is key.
6. Emphasize the business necessity of such a plan so that everyone will take it seriously without being seen as alarmist.

Following these measures, of course, will not ward off disasters. They remain a real and unforeseen risk for all organizations. However, by using telecommuting, businesses will be better prepared to cope with their inevitable aftermath.

---

business continuity plans
Systematic sets of plans designed to help organizations get up and running again in the event of a disruption of some sort.

motions. They put in time, but displayed very little energy or passion. Finally, 17 percent of the respondents were classified as being *actively disengaged.* Such individuals weren't only unhappy, but acted out their unhappiness on the job. Far too often, they undermined the accomplishments of their highly engaged counterparts (e.g., by sabotaging their work).

Generally, and this comes as no big surprise, people who are not engaged or who are actively disengaged do not enjoy their work experiences. At the same time, such individuals are not helping—and actively are hurting—their organizations. This comes at considerable cost to organizations, not only by making life miserable for everyone, but also financially. Specifically, the Gallup Organization's extensive, representative survey of U.S. workers age 18 and older revealed two disturbing findings (see summary in Figure 1.12): (1) The percentage of employees who are actively disengaged has not been dropping over

FIGURE 1.12

The High Cost of Active Disengagement

Employees who are actively disengaged at work comprise about 17% of the American workforce. These 23.3 million employees cost their organizations between $323 billion and $417 billion annually due to lost productivity.

Source: Copyright © 2006 The Gallup Organization, Princeton, NJ. All rights reserved. Reprinted with permission. Visit the *Gallup Management Journal* at http://gmj.gallup.com.

the years, and (2) the cost of employing such individuals is dramatic—about $370 billion in the third quarter of 2005.

As alarming as these figures may be, there is good news: They can be lowered! And, although it's not always easy, the path to doing so is hardly a mystery. In fact, you hold the answer in your hands right now. Following the good management practices revealed by the field of organizational behavior is the key to promoting not only engagement, but a wealth of other beneficial outcomes both for organizations and the people who work in them.

In Search of Flexibility: Responding to Needs of Employees

Earlier, we mentioned that organizations are doing many different things to accommodate workers from two-income families, single-parent households, and people taking care of elderly relatives. Often, what's most needed is not a formal program, but greater flexibility. The diversity of lifestyles demands a diversity of working arrangements. Some organizations have proven to be so flexible that they even accommodate employees taking care of their dogs (see Figure 1.13). Although Fido might not be a common sight in today's offices (even if, as some say, business has "gone to the dogs"), several practices have gained in popularity in recent years that provide the flexibility today's workers need.

Idiosyncratic Work Arrangements. Traditionally, when new employees were hired they were offered a standard set of benefits and working arrangements. People in various positions were paid salaries and had work conditions that were predetermined based on their position. Of course, this still occurs most of the time. But, with increasing frequency, however, the arrangements between today's employers and employees are being negotiated to satisfy the unique interests of each. Such arrangements are known as **idiosyncratic work arrangements**, or more simply, **i-deals**. These are uniquely customized agreements negotiated between individual employees and their employers with respect to employment terms benefiting each party. Such arrangements are called i-deals because the deals are not only idiosyncratic in nature, but also to reflect the fact that these arrangements are intended to be ideal for both employers and employees alike.[72]

I-deals are *not* a form of favoritism, which, of course, benefits one employee while disadvantaging another. Rather, they are designed to help everyone. Consider, for example, a law firm that hires a very highly regarded new attorney who, for personal reasons (e.g., having to take children to school), cannot come to the office until 10:00 A.M. Might this make the

idiosyncratic work arrangements (i-deals)
Uniquely customized agreements negotiated between individual employees and their employers with respect to employment terms benefiting each party.

FIGURE 1.13

Autodesk Offers Fido-Friendly Flexibility

Although dogs are not a common sight in offices, some companies, such as the software firm Autodesk, are allowing their employees to share workspaces with their pets. Cindy Brogan, who works at the company's San Rafael, California, headquarters, not only enjoys the companionship of her Weimaraner, Chelsea, while at work, but she is also relieved of the responsibility of having to arrange for "dogsitting" while away from home. This policy is in keeping with the company's interest in helping employees promote a balance between their work and home lives.

workload harder for everyone while this individual is out of the office? Yes, but the firm's partners might agree to the deal anyway on the basis of the fact that everyone would benefit. Specifically, the newly hired person would benefit by being given hours that accommodate his or her personal needs. The firm benefits, of course, by having the services of this individual. And, because this individual is so highly regarded, everyone else benefits because of the new business he or she brings in as well as the gain in prestige that comes from having this person on board. So, the arrangement, although out of the ordinary, stands to be beneficial all around.

Flexible Hours. If you take a look around your workplace, you'll find people at different stages of their lives. Some are single and just getting started in their careers, others may be raising families, and still others may have tried retirement but have chosen to return to work. These different individuals are likely to require different working hours. This has led contemporary organizations to put programs into place that allow for flexibility. One popular way of doing this is by implementing what are known as **flextime programs**—policies that give employees some discretion over when they can arrive and leave work, thereby making it easier to adapt their work schedules to the demands of their personal lives.

Typically, flextime programs require employees to work a common core of hours, such as 9:00 A.M. to 12 noon and 1:00 P.M. to 3:00 P.M. Scheduling of the remaining hours, within certain spans (such as 6:00 to 9:00 A.M. and 3:00 to 6:00 P.M.), is then left up to the employees themselves. Generally, such programs have been well received and have been linked to improvements in performance and job satisfaction, as well as drops in employee turnover and absenteeism.[73] In recent years, many companies, both large and small, have found that flexible work scheduling has helped their employees meet the demands of juggling their work and family lives.[74]

The Contingent Workforce: "Permanent Temporary" Employees. Recognizing that not all jobs are required to be performed all the time, many organizations are eliminating permanent jobs and hiring people to perform them whenever required. Such individuals comprise what has been referred to as the **contingent workforce**—people hired by organizations temporarily, to work as needed for finite periods of time.[75] This practice serves not only the needs of companies that cannot afford to have full-time employees in part-time positions, but also individuals who are interested in working only occasionally. The contingent workforce includes not only the traditional part-time employees, such as department store Santas, but also freelancers (i.e., independent

flextime programs
Policies that give employees some discretion over when they can arrive and leave work, thereby making it easier to adapt their work schedules to the demands of their personal lives.

contingent workforce
People hired by organizations temporarily, to work as needed for finite periods of time.

contractors who are self-employed), on-call workers (i.e., people who are called into work only when needed), and workers provided by temporary help agencies. According to the Bureau of Labor Statistics, contingent workers comprise only about 4 percent of the total workforce, most of whom are young (under 25) and poorly educated (high school dropouts). As shown in Figure 1.14, the specific jobs contingent workers do are most frequently in clerical fields.[76] Such highly flexible arrangements make it possible for organizations to grow or shrink as needed, and to have access to experts with specialized knowledge when these are required.

The trend toward corporate restructuring has caused many companies to keep their staff sizes so small that they must frequently draw on the services of Manpower, or any other of the nation's 7,000 temporary-employment firms for help.[77] As a result, many professionals are working on a part-time or freelance basis. For example, about 43 percent of new attorneys leave their first job within three years because they are being asked to work long hours that interfere with the time spent with their families. Growing numbers of lawyers choose to work permanently on a part-time basis.[78] This comes at a cost, however. As you might imagine, people who work half time earn less than those who work full time—but considerably less than half as much. For example, according to the Institute for Women's Policy Research, managers who earn $3,200 per month working full time can expect to earn as little as $800 to $1,200 per month working half time.[79]

compressed workweeks
The practice of working fewer days each week, but longer hours each day (e.g., four 10-hour days).

Compressed Workweeks. Instead of working five days of eight hours each, growing numbers of people are enjoying working **compressed workweeks**—the practice of

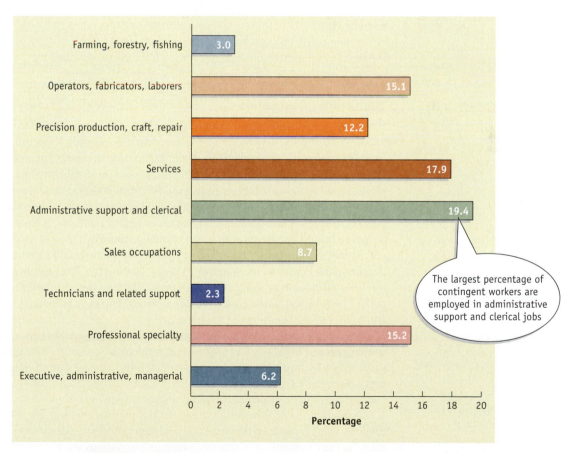

FIGURE 1.14

Contingent Workers: What Kinds of Jobs Do They Do?

As summarized here, contingent workers perform a wide variety of jobs. Most of these are in service businesses and in administrative support and clerical positions.

Source: Based on data from the Bureau of Labor Statistics, 2005; see Note 76.

working fewer days each week, but longer hours each day (e.g., four 10-hour days). The popular practice among firefighters of being on duty for 24 hours, and then off duty for 48 hours is a good example of the compressed workweek. Shell Canada has found that compressed workweek schedules have helped it make more efficient use of its manufacturing plant in Sarnia, Ontario. The Royal Bank of Canada, headquartered in Montreal, has found that compressed workweek options greatly help its recruitment efforts by offering prospective employees the choice of schedules based on either compressed workweeks (four 9.5-hour days) or standard five-day workweeks.[80]

job sharing

A form of regular part-time work in which pairs of employees assume the duties of a single job, splitting its responsibilities, salary and benefits in proportion to the time worked.

Job Sharing. **Job sharing** is a form of regular part-time work in which pairs of employees assume the duties of a single job, splitting its responsibilities, salary, and benefits in proportion to the time worked. Job sharing is rapidly growing in popularity as people enjoy the kind of work that full-time jobs allow, but require the flexibility of part-time work. Often, job sharing arrangements are temporary.

At Xerox, for example, several sets of employees share jobs, including two female employees who once were sales rivals, but who joined forces to share one job when they each faced the need to reduce their working hours so they could devote time to their new families.[81] Pella (the Iowa-based manufacturer of windows) has found that job sharing has been successful in reducing absenteeism among its production and clerical employees.[82]

voluntary reduced work time (V-time) programs

Programs that allow employees to reduce the amount of time they work by a certain amount (typically 10 or 20 percent), with a proportional reduction in pay.

Voluntary Reduced Work Time (V-time) Programs. Programs known as **voluntary reduced work time (V-time) programs** allow employees to reduce the amount of time they work by a certain amount (typically 10 or 20 percent), with a proportional reduction in pay. Over the past few years, these programs have become popular in various state agencies in the United States. For example, various employees of the New York State government have enjoyed having professional careers, but with hours that make it possible for them to also meet their family obligations. Not only does the state benefit from the money saved, but the employees also enjoy the extra time they gain for nonwork pursuits.

The Quality Revolution

For many years, people complained, but could do little when the goods they purchased fell apart, or the service they received was second-rate. After all, if everything in the market is shoddy, there are few alternatives. Then, Japanese companies such as Toyota and Nissan entered the American auto market. Their cars were more reliable, less expensive, and better designed than the offerings from Ford, General Motors, and Chrysler, companies that became complacent about offering value to their customers. When Japanese automakers began capturing the American auto market in record numbers, American companies were forced to rethink their strategies—and to change their ways.

Today's companies operate quite differently than the American auto companies of decades past. For them, the watchword is not "getting by," but "making things better," what has been referred to as *the quality revolution*. The best organizations are ones that strive to deliver better goods and services at lower prices than ever before. Those that do so flourish, and those that do not tend to fade away.

total quality management (TQM)

An organizational strategy of commitment to improving customer satisfaction by developing techniques to carefully manage output quality.

One of the most popular approaches to establishing quality is known as **total quality management (TQM)**—an organizational strategy of commitment to improving customer satisfaction by developing techniques to carefully manage output quality. TQM is not so much a special technique as a well-ingrained set of corporate values—a way of life demonstrating a strong commitment to improving quality in everything that is done.

According to W. Edwards Deming, the best-known advocate of TQM, successful TQM requires that everyone in the organization—from the lowest-level employee to the CEO—must be fully committed to making whatever innovations are necessary to improve quality. This involves both carefully measuring quality (through elaborate statistical procedures) and taking whatever steps are necessary to improve it. Typically, this requires continuously improving the manufacturing process in ways that make it possible for higher quality to result.

For example, when Toyota engineers developed the highly regarded luxury sedan from its Lexus division, the LS 400, it purchased competing cars from Mercedes and BMW, disassembled them, examined the parts, and developed ways of building an even

benchmarking

The process of comparing one's own products or services with the best from others.

quality control audits

Careful examinations of how well a company is meeting its standards.

Malcolm Baldrige Quality Award

An award given annually to American companies that practice effective quality management and make significant improvements in the quality of their goods and services.

better car. This process of comparing one's own products or services with the best from others is known as **benchmarking.** Spending some $500 million in this process, Toyota was clearly dedicated to creating a superior product. And, given the recognition that Lexus continues to receive for its high quality, it appears as if Toyota's TQM efforts have paid off.

Another key ingredient of TQM is incorporating concern for quality into all aspects of organizational culture (a concept we will discuss more fully in Chapter 13).[83] At Rubbermaid, for example, concern for quality is not only emphasized in the company's manufacturing process, but also its concern for cost, service, speed, and innovation. To assure that it is meeting quality standards, many companies conduct **quality control audits**—careful examinations of how well it is meeting its standards. For example, companies such as Pepsi Cola and FedEx regularly interview their clients to find out what problems they may be having. These responses are then taken very seriously in making whatever improvements are necessary to avoid such problems in the future.

Some companies have been so very successful at achieving high quality in all respects that they have been honored for their accomplishments by being given the **Malcolm Baldrige Quality Award.** This annual award recognizes American companies—both large and small, and in both service and manufacturing—that practice effective quality management and make significant improvements in the quality of their goods and services.[84] The major goal of the award is to promote quality achievement by recognizing those companies that deliver continually improving value to customers while maximizing their overall productivity and effectiveness. To ensure that all companies can benefit from the winner's experiences, winning companies are expected to share their successful quality strategies with other American firms. This has been done in the form of personal presentations, books, and cases presented on videotape.[85] Indeed, companies that have won over the years, such as various divisions of IBM and TRW, have set high quality standards to which other companies aspire (see Figure 1.15).[86]

FIGURE 1.15

The First Auto Dealer to Win the Malcolm Baldrige Quality Award

Diagnostic specialist Joe Lake (left) and mechanic Shawn Harris, shown here performing a brake job, take considerable pride in their work in the shop at Park Place Lexus in Grapevine, Texas (between Dallas and Fort Worth)—and with good reason. They are part of a team of professionals whose commitment to providing exceptional service has helped earn this dealership a 2005 Malcolm Baldrige Quality Award in the small business category, the only auto dealer to date to have received this honor. Upon accepting the award from President George W. Bush in December, 2005, Ken Schnitzer, chairman of Park Place Dealerships, noted that it reflects "the commitment we have for our clients, members, and vendors to provide exceptional service in every area of our dealerships." Not surprisingly, Park Place was the highest rated Lexus dealership in the nation, with an unprecedented new car client satisfaction index of 99.8 percent.

Summary and Review of Learning Objectives

1. **Define the concepts of organization and organizational behavior.**
   An organization is a structured social system consisting of groups and individuals working together to meet some agreed-upon objectives. Organizational behavior is the field that seeks knowledge of behavior in organizational settings by systematically studying individual, group, and organizational processes.

2. **Describe the field of organizational behavior's commitment to the scientific method and the three levels of analysis it uses.**
   The field of OB seeks to develop a base of knowledge about behavior in organizations by using an empirical, research-based approach. As such, it is based on systematic observation and measurement of the behavior or phenomenon of interest. The field of OB uses three levels of analysis—individuals, work groups, and entire organizations—all relying on the scientific method.

3. **Trace the historical developments and schools of thought leading up to the field of organizational behavior today.**
   The earliest approaches to organizational behavior relied on scientific management, an approach that essentially treated people like machines, emphasizing what it took to get the most out of them. For example, this approach relied on time-and-motion study, a type of applied research designed to find the most efficient way for people to perform their jobs. As this approach grew unpopular, it was supplanted by the human relations movement, which emphasized the importance of noneconomic, social forces in the workplace—an approach that remains popular to this day. Such factors were demonstrated in the Hawthorne studies, the first large-scale research project conducted in a work organization that demonstrated the importance of social forces in determining productivity. In contrast with scientific management's orientation toward organizing the work of individuals, proponents of classical organizational theory developed ways of efficiently structuring the way work is done. Weber's concept of bureaucracy is a prime example of this approach. Contemporary OB is characterized not by one best approach to management, but by systematic scientific research inspired from several social science disciplines. It takes a contingency approach to OB, recognizing that behavior may be influenced by a variety of different forces at once, thereby rejecting the idea that there is any single most effective approach to managing behavior in organizations.

4. **Identify the fundamental assumptions of the field of organizational behavior.**
   The field of OB assumes: (1) that organizations can be made more productive while also improving the quality of people's work life, (2) that there is no one best approach to studying behavior in organizations, and (3) that organizations are dynamic and ever-changing.

5. **Describe how the field of OB today is being shaped by the global economy, increasing racial and ethnic diversity in the workforce, and advances in technology.**
   The world's economy is becoming increasingly global, a trend that is affecting the field of OB in several distinct ways. For example, organizations are expanding overseas, requiring people to live and work in different countries, requiring considerable adjustment. As this occurs, much of what we thought we knew about managing people is proven to be limited by the culture in which that knowledge was developed (U.S. culture, in most cases). Racial and ethnic diversity in the workplace is in large part the result of shifting patterns of immigration that have brought more foreign nationals into the workforce. It also is the result of changes in social values and the economy that have made the presence of women common in today's workplace. Also, thanks to modern medicine, people are living longer, hence retiring from work later than ever before. Because technology has it possible for fewer people to do more work, many organizations have been growing smaller, downsizing. Furthermore, as technology becomes increasingly specialized, organizations have found it useful to hire other companies to do nonessential aspects of their operations that they once performed themselves—a process known as outsourcing.

6. **Explain how people's changing expectations about the desire to be engaged in their work, the need for flexibility in work, and the pressure to promote quality have influenced the field of OB.**

   Both employers and employees benefit when they are highly engaged with one another—that is, when they are highly committed to satisfying one another's interests. This drives organizations to follow various OB practices so as to avoid the extremely high costs of having actively disengaged workers. Today's employees also desire to have a high degree of flexibility in their work arrangements. This takes several forms: using idiosyncratic work arrangements, offering flexible hours, relying on contingent workers, using compressed workweeks, job sharing, and voluntary reduced work time programs. Because today's consumers are demanding high-quality products and services, companies are working hard to meet these demands—thereby remaining in existence and possibly staying ahead of competitors. The popular policy of continuously improving products and services, referred to as total quality management (TQM), is a response to this trend.

Points to Ponder

Questions for Review

1. How can the field of organizational behavior contribute to both the effective functioning of organizations *and* to the well-being of individuals? Are these goals inconsistent? Why or why not?
2. What is the "contingency approach" and why is it so popular in the field of OB today?
3. Explain how the field of organizational behavior stands to benefit by taking a global perspective. What would you say are the major challenges associated with such a perspective?
4. How has the growing quest for quality products and services affected your own work?

Experiential Questions

1. Think about a person with whom you may have worked who happens to be very different from you, such as someone of the opposite sex who also is a member of a different racial group and/or from a different country. In what ways was this experience challenging for you? In what ways did these differences prove to be beneficial? What insight do you believe the field of OB can give you with respect to this experience?
2. How have your own life and the lives of your family members changed because of flexible new working arrangements that have become popular in recent years?
3. Describe some ways in which you may have been treated by your boss that helped you become an engaged employee, a not-engaged employee, or an actively disengaged employee. How did you respond as a result?

Questions to Analyze

1. Although only some people in an organization need to know about marketing or accounting or production, almost everyone benefits by knowing about organizational behavior. Do you agree with this statement? If not, why not? If so, exactly how can knowing OB help you in your own work?
2. The practice of engineering is constantly evolving, but the basic rules of physics on which it rests remain relatively unchanged. Do you think the same relationship exists between technology and OB? In other words, do the things that have made organizations and individuals successful in yesterday's low-tech era remain relevant today, or are they changing along with technology?
3. Although many employees enjoy the flexibility of working lots of part-time jobs or working for a series of employees on a temporary basis, it comes at a cost: Such employees often make low wages, have little security, and cannot count on having fringe benefits. How do you think this trend affects organizations? How are companies helped and how are they harmed by this trend? Do you think this trend has any adverse effects on a company's products?

Experiencing OB

Individual Exercise

Are You an Engaged Employee?

Employees who feel engaged tend to put forth the extra effort required to do their best on their jobs. Although engagement is not the only key to job performance, research has established a link between engagement and the bottom line. Are you such an engaged employee? This questionnaire will help you find out.

Directions

Using the following scale, answer each of these 10 questions by indicating the extent to which the statement describes your situation on your current job:

- 1 = not at all
- 2 = slightly
- 3 = moderately
- 4 = somewhat
- 5 = greatly

Scale

To what extent . . .

1. Do you have a have a clear idea of what you are expected to do on the job?
2. Do you have access to the resources (e.g., materials, supplies, equipment, etc.) needed to perform your job correctly?
3. Does your job give you an opportunity to do the things that you are able to do best?
4. Are you regularly praised or acknowledged for doing a good job?
5. Does your boss or any superior seem to care about you as an individual?
6. Does someone on the job help you grow and develop professionally?
7. Do you believe that your opinions about things on the job are given serious consideration by others?
8. Do you believe that your job is important because it is in keeping with the company's mission or objectives?
9. Are the people with whom you work devoted to doing the best possible job?
10. Do you receive information from others that helps you improve your job performance?

Source: Adapted from the Q12 questionnaire from the Gallup Organization.

Scoring and Interpretation

1. Add together your responses to the 10 questions. You will get a number between 10 and 50.
2. Higher scores reflect higher degrees of engagement with your job. Scores of 15 or lower reflect low degrees of engagement. Scores of 35 or higher reflect high degrees of engagement.

Questions for Discussion

1. What do your responses suggest about your degree of engagement? Was it high or low? Was this a surprise to you, or did you pretty much find what you expected?
2. In your opinion, what factors contribute most to the degree to which you are engaged on the job? What, if anything, do you think might be able to help increase the degree to which you are engaged on the job?
3. Why do you think research has shown that engagement promotes bottom-line success? Do you think this occurs for all people performing all kinds of jobs?

Group Exercise

Is Your Team Ready for Telecommuting?

What happens when people who might ordinarily come into contact with one another on their jobs no longer have that social contact? Several things may happen. For example, when employees do not see each other on a regular basis, it is difficult to build the team spirit that is needed to establish quality goods and services in some organizations. As a result, telecommuting does not lend itself to all jobs and to all individuals. This exercise will help you determine if you and members of your work team are ready for telecommuting.

Directions

Working independently, each member of a work team should complete the following questionnaire by indicating the extent to which each statement describes his or her own characteristics or current job situation.

1 = not at all

2 = slightly

3 = moderately

4 = somewhat

5 = greatly

Scale

To what extent. . .

1. Does your job allow you to work independently of others?
2. Is it important for you to see the people with whom you work face-to-face?
3. Are you able to complete jobs without being watched closely?
4. Are you comfortable using computers and high-tech equipment?
5. Is your company able to train you to use technology to do your job?
6. Are you able to manage your own time effectively?
7. Are you capable of finding a safe, secure, and nondistracting place to work?
8. Does your job performance depend on measurable aspects of your individual performance?
9. Would you miss the socializing that goes on in the office if you were away from it?
10. Is it possible for you to have access to the equipment and supplies needed to do your job while away from the office?

Scoring and Interpretation

1. Add together your scores for items 1, 3, 4, 5, 6, 7, 8, and 10.
2. Add together your scores for items 2 and 9. Subtract this sum from 12.
3. Add together the number from step 1 and the number from step 2. You will get a number from 10 to 50. This is your individual score.
4. Higher scores reflect higher degrees of individual readiness for telecommuting. Scores of 15 or lower reflect low degrees of readiness. Scores of 35 or higher reflect high degrees of readiness.
5. Add together the individual scores from all the members of your team. Then divide this number by the number of people in your team. This is your team's average readiness for telecommuting score.
6. Higher scores in step 5 reflect higher degrees of team readiness for telecommuting. Scores of 15 or lower reflect low degrees of team readiness. Scores of 35 or higher reflect high degrees of team readiness.

Questions for Discussion

1. In scoring the scale responses, why do you think questions 2 and 9 were treated differently from the others? How are they different?

2. Does your individual score (step 4) suggest that you are ready for telecommuting? Do you do so already? Might it be possible to telecommute some of the time if you are not doing so already?
3. Does your team score (step 6) suggest that your team is ready for telecommuting? Do some members of the team engage in telecommuting already? If so, how are the other members of the work team affected by this? If not, why do you think this is not already going on?

Practicing OB

When in Rome

You are the regional director of a large U.S.-based import-export company that is expanding international operations. This requires three of your top managers to move to Rome, Italy, for no less than two years, maybe longer. Given their lengthy stay, they will be moving their families along with them and setting up new households.

1. What problems would you anticipate these executives will have as they adjust to their new surroundings?
2. What specific measures could be taken to help these individuals avoid the symptoms of culture shock that are likely to arise?
3. What difficulties might these individuals have when they return to their own country at the end of their assignments? What could be done to minimize these problems?

CASE IN POINT   Good-Bye to the Cubicle? Don't Count On It

The name Robert Probst probably doesn't show up on any "Most Wanted" list, but if people knew who he is, he probably would be a marked man. At least, this might be the case among the 40 million American workers who toil daily in cubicles—the open-plan office system Probst designed in 1968. Originally known as the "action office system," and still referred to as such today by Herman Miller, the large furniture company behind the concept, the cubicle by any name is reviled by workers.

Cartoonist Scott Adams satirized the cubicle in his popular cartoon strip, *Dilbert,* but most find working in such "soulless boxes" anything but funny as they endure excessive noise and a lack of privacy that makes concentrating on the task at hand extremely challenging for most. After working in cubicles for a while, their originator, Mr. Probst, eventually disavowed his own creation, referring to it as "monolithic insanity." Yet cubicles have the staying power of crabgrass and outsell all other forms of office furniture to the tune of some $3 billion a year.

Believe it or not, cubicles were not intended to be a cruel hoax. Rather, they were born of a noble purpose—to introduce some privacy into the world of people who worked in open "bullpens" of desks. And, by allowing people to spread out all their work on the walls and desktops that surrounded them, they could—at least in theory—be more productive than would be possible by stacking up all their work in an "in box." Furthermore, the flexible nature of the partitions was designed to promote communication by making it possible for spaces to be opened up or closed, providing ready access to others or denying it, as dictated by the task at hand.

As this flexible design was being touted, Uncle Sam entered the picture. Changes to the corporate income tax code made it possible for companies to recover their costs more quickly if they bought cubicles than if they built permanent offices. Realizing the financial benefits, more and more companies began cramming more and more people into tighter spaces. Open and flexible designs soon gave way to small cubicles that never moved. Today, we still find "cube farms," sprawling tracts of cubicles arranged in vast matrices that fill spaces as large as the facilities that house them.

In addition to the financial benefits of cubicles, many executives like them because of their inherently egalitarian nature. In fact, they prove it with their office chairs. Because nobody has a large corner office into which he or she may retreat, everyone is considered the same—at least insofar as the absence of any "trappings of success may suggest." This is particularly likely to be the case in today's high-tech firms. For example, eBay's CEO, Meg Whitman, works in a cubicle as did Intel's former CEO, Andy Grove (his was only 8 feet by 9 feet), giving their employees ready access to them.

Attempts to change or even unseat the reign of the cubicle have occurred for almost as long as cubicles have been around. Improvements in personally controlled lighting and ventilation are being introduced by the office furniture manufacturer, Steelcase. But these are merely efforts to tweak an existing design instead of a radical new design. Such efforts have been made over the years, though. One advertising executive even went so far as to do away with individual desks entirely, allowing people to work in lounge-like settings. The absence of a place (besides a gym locker) in which to place one's personal belongings proved so unpopular that cubicles began looking good by comparison. So active have been efforts to improve upon the cubicle that over 100 variations (e.g., more cockpit-like or capsule-like workstations) have been introduced over the past three decades.

If there is any one trend that is chipping away at the popularity of cubicles, it's the use of telecommuting, which we described in this chapter. Instead of driving to an office and sitting behind a computer in a cubicle, the ready availability of broadband Internet connections is making it possible for many of today's workers to do the same work from home. Despite this trend, the sale of cubicles rose 11 percent in 2005, suggesting that they aren't going away anytime soon. But, as one expert predicts, "as the office occupies a smaller part of companies' budgets, cubes will claim a smaller share of employees' lives."

Questions for Discussion

1. If you ever have worked in a cubicle, what did you like or dislike about it? If not, what do you think you would like or dislike about it?
2. What does the use of cubicles and people's reactions to them suggest about the nature of people in organizations? Also, what are the implications of housing people in cubicles for managing them? (Hint: Think about Theory X.)
3. Although telecommuting may keep people from working in cubicles, it may have its own limitations. What do you believe these may be? How would you compare the problems of telecommuting compared to the problems of working in cubicles?

Chapter 2

Organizational Justice, Ethics, and Corporate Social Responsibility

Chapter Outline

Organizational Justice: Fairness Matters

Strategies for Promoting Organizational Justice

Ethical Behavior in Organizations: Its Fundamental Nature

Why Does Ethical Behavior Matter in Organizations?

Ethics in the International Arena

Why Do Some People Behave Unethically—At Least, Sometimes?

Using Corporate Ethics Programs to Promote Ethical Behavior

Beyond Ethics: Corporate Social Responsibility

Special Sections

OB **Making Sense Out of Common Sense**

Good Ethics Is Good Business

How to Do It

Conducting an Ethics Audit: In Search of the "Triple Bottom-Line"

OB **In a Diverse World**

Starbucks and Dell Actively Advance the Interests of Women

After reading this chapter, you should be able to:

1. Identify four different forms of organizational justice and the organizational impact of each.

2. Describe strategies that can be used to promote organizational justice.

3. Explain what is meant by ethical behavior and why organizations should be concerned about ethics.

4. Explain ways of behaving ethically when conducting business internationally.

5. Describe the individual and situational factors responsible for unethical behavior in organizations and methods for minimizing such behavior.

6. Explain what is meant by corporate social responsibility, the forms it takes, and the nature of the relationship between responsible behavior and financial profitability.

PREVIEW CASE

The NFL: The National "Fairness" League?

Parents always admonish children to "play fairly," and doing so is expected of them even more emphatically if they grow up to be athletes. Indeed, the sanctity of athletic events is predicated on fairness. For an athlete to gain an unfair advantage by taking performance-enhancing drugs or by breaking a rule (e.g., using a "corked bat" in baseball) is not tolerated because it gives him or her an unfair advantage. Likewise, in recent years, many fans and analysts of college football have taken issue with the Bowl Championship Series (BCS) formula used to determine the national championship team on the grounds that it does not always identify the absolute best team. So outraged was Utah's Senator Orin Hatch about the BCS formula that in the fall of 2003 he criticized the BCS method "for calling into question the notion of basic fairness."

One organization that has gone out of its way to ensure "a level playing field" for athletics is the National Football League (NFL), professional football's official governing body. Within the NFL, a Competition Committee (composed of officials such as team owners and managers) is always tweaking the rules so as to make the game as fair as possible. As an example, consider the simple coin toss used to determine which team will kick or receive the ball when a game begins. For 22 years, this was accomplished by having the captain of the visiting team call "heads or tails" as a coin was tossed into the air by a referee before the game. Then something happened. On Thanksgiving 1998, referee Phil Luckett misunderstood the call made by the Pittsburgh Steelers' Jerome Bettis, allowing the Detroit Lions to get possession of the ball at the beginning of a critical overtime period. To avoid such an "unfortunate incident" in the future, as then-NFL Commissioner Paul Tagliabue called it, the procedure was changed. Starting with the following weeks' games, the heads-or-tails calls were made *before* the coin was tossed, thereby allowing any uncertainties to be addressed before the outcome was determined.

Although this is a seemingly small thing, it can make a big difference because of the "sudden death" method used to determine winners of NFL games that are tied after the regulation 60 minutes have been played. This procedure has the teams play until one team breaks the tie by scoring. At this point, although the other team might not get the ball, the game is over (unlike baseball, in which both the top and bottom halves of extra innings are played if necessary to determine a winner). For this reason, it follows that teams entering an overtime period will desire to possess the ball first. As you might imagine, however, this practice has been called into question by some critics who believe it puts too much weight on a simple coin toss. Although, statistically, winners of tie games are no more likely to be those possessing the ball first than those possessing the ball second, many analysts still find the present procedure inherently unfair.

To put to rest any further claims of unfairness, the NFL uses an "instant replay rule." This allows coaches an opportunity to challenge (within certain limits) rulings made by officials on the field they believe are erroneous. Once a decision is challenged, a game official reviews videotaped playback of the play in question and decides whether or not to reverse the call made on the field. Following a seven-year hiatus, this procedure was reinstated by the NFL in 1999 in the wake of public outcries about blatantly erroneous calls by referees in several critical games during the previous season. Although the procedure is considered far from perfect, it is recognized as a useful way to enhance the fairness of the game. Accordingly, the rule was reinstated in slightly revised form just prior to the 2004 season. It has remained in place since, with minor revisions.

The NFL's efforts to make the game of football as fair as possible go beyond the field itself to the financial books of the teams. Since 1994 the NFL has had a "salary cap" in effect, a rule that equalizes the total yearly amount that each team can pay its players (currently about $68 million). The underlying idea was that the game would be made fairer by preventing the wealthier teams from dominating the sport by "buying" the best athletes at prices the poorer teams could not afford (as has happened in the case of the New York Yankees baseball team). Notwithstanding the successes of the New England Patriots in the early 2000s, this practice has resulted in having a wider variety of teams win championships in recent years than ever before, eliminating the winning "dynasties" of past years. Many take this as evidence that today, athletic talent plays a greater role than organizational wealth in creating winning football teams. Although this practice is not without controversy, NFL officials are convinced that it's in the best interest in keeping the game as fair as possible.

Football fans surely will argue whether the NFL's actions really promote the fairness of the game. Then again, controversy is natural in such situations; fans revel in analyzing and debating decisions about the sports they love. And besides, few topics are as controversial as what should be done in the name of justice—particularly in the workplace, where well-intentioned parties often disagree about what's fair. Although this may be unclear, it is quite clear that people care dearly about matters of justice on the job. Just ask any worker who feels that the small pay raise he received does not adequately reflect his important contributions, or who suspects that the boss is playing favorites by giving one of her coworkers more desirable work assignments. Workers in these cases are bound to cry foul, claiming that they have been treated unfairly. Indeed, people are very sensitive to matters of justice and injustice in the workplace and are inclined to express their feelings in significant ways. Not surprisingly, OB specialists have studied these dynamics in the growing field of *organizational justice,* one of the major topics covered in this chapter.[1]

The quest to maintain justice in the workplace is part of a broader concern that people have for *ethics*—doing the right thing—the second major topic we will discuss in this chapter. Given that great philosophers over the years have not reached consensus about what constitutes "the right thing" to do, we shouldn't be surprised that distinguishing between right and wrong in the workplace is rarely a straightforward matter.[2] Yet, it's clear from cases that have been in the news in recent years—Enron being the most visible—of executives who have been accused of various improprieties that we often know what's wrong when we see it.[3] And, as we will describe in this chapter, the field of OB provides a great deal of insight into why such unethical behavior occurs—and can offer suggestions on how to curtail it.

As a natural outgrowth of the quest to behave ethically, many organizational leaders are going beyond merely doing what's right by proactively attempting to make things better in the communities in which they operate.[4] Indeed, many of today's organizations are demonstrating what is known as *corporate social responsibility*—not only attempting to meet prevailing legal and ethical standards, but exceeding them by embracing values that promote the greater welfare of society at large. Whether it involves donating money to charities, staffing community welfare projects, or taking steps to make our air and water clean, engaging in socially responsible behavior has been a great concern to leaders of today's organizations. Here again, OB specialists have sought to explain this behavior, and their efforts will be outlined in this chapter.

Organizational Justice: Fairness Matters

Suppose you received a failing grade in a course. You don't like it, of course, but can you say that the grade is unfair? To answer this question, you would likely take several things into consideration. For example, does the grade accurately reflect how well you performed in the course? Were your scores added accurately and were they computed in an unbiased fashion? Has the professor treated you in a polite and professional fashion? Finally, has the professor communicated the grading process to you adequately? In judging how fairly you have been treated, questions such as these are likely to be raised—and your answers are likely to have a considerable impact on how you feel about your grade, the professor, and even the school as a whole. Moreover, they are likely to have a profound effect on how you respond, such as whether you quietly accept the grade, complain about it to someone, or even quit school entirely.

Although this example involves you as a student, the same considerations are likely to arise in the workplace. In that context, instead of talking about grades from professors, concerns about justice may take analogous forms. Does your salary reflect your work accomplishments? How was your performance evaluation determined? Were you treated with dignity and respect by your boss? Were you given important job information in a thorough and timely manner? Matters such as these are relevant to **organizational justice**—the study of people's perceptions of fairness in organizations. Our discussion of organizational justice focuses on three key areas—the major forms of organizational justice, the relationships between these forms, and suggestions for promoting justice in organizations.

organizational justice
The study of people's perceptions of fairness in organizations.

Forms of Organizational Justice and Their Effects

The idea that justice is a multifaceted concept follows from the variety of questions just raised, everything from how much you get paid to how well you are treated by your boss. Not surprisingly, OB scientists have recognized that organizational justice takes several

FIGURE 2.1

Forms of Organizational Justice and Their Effects

Organizational justice takes the four different forms identified here. Each of these forms of justice has been found to have different effects in organizations.

Source: Based on suggestions by Colquitt, Greenberg, & Zapata-Phelan, 2005; see Note 8.

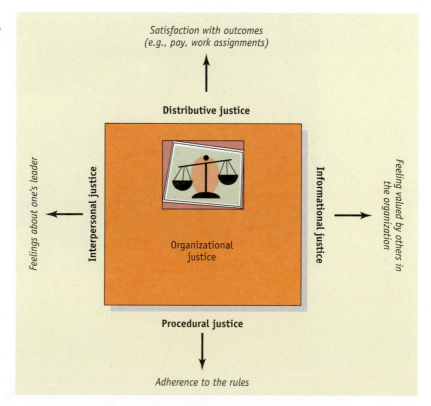

different forms. These are known as *distributive justice, procedural justice, interpersonal justice,* and *informational justice* (see Figure 2.1).[5]

Distributive justice. On the job, people are concerned with getting their "fair share" of resources. We all want to be paid fairly for the work we do and we want to be adequately recognized for our efforts and any special contributions we bring to the job. **Distributive justice** is the form of organizational justice that focuses on people's beliefs that they have received fair amounts of valued work-related outcomes (e.g., pay, recognition, etc.). For example, workers consider the formal appraisals of their performance to be fair to the extent that these ratings are based on their actual level of performance (for an example, see Figure 2.2).[6]

People who believe that they have been dealt a distributive injustice on the job tend to experience high levels of stress (see Chapter 5) and also feel dissatisfied with their jobs and the companies in which they work. (Related to this, as you will see in the discussion of *equity theory* in Chapter 7, feelings of distributive justice can have a great impact on people's motivation to perform their jobs.) A recent study provides good insight into this process.[7] Researchers conducting this investigation compared two groups of workers with respect to their feelings about distributive justice: a group of local workers from Singapore and a group of foreign workers, Chinese people who worked in Singapore. In this setting, foreign workers tend not to be paid commensurate with their skills. Not surprisingly, the foreign workers expressed higher levels of distributive injustice and were less productive on their jobs. Because they received less, they did less, as distributive justice dictates.

These findings are illustrative of many that demonstrate people's keen sensitivity to their perceptions of the fairness by which resources are distributed on the job.[8] In general, the more people believe that their rewards (e.g., pay, work assignments) are distributed in a fair manner, the more satisfied they are with them.

Procedural Justice. Recall our earlier example regarding receipt of a failing grade. In assessing the fairness of this situation you would want to know precisely *how* your grade was determined. After all, if the professor made an error in calculating your grade, it would be unfair for you to be penalized. In other words, fairness involves consideration of not

distributive justice
The form of organizational justice that focuses on people's beliefs that they have received fair amounts of valued work-related outcomes (e.g., pay, recognition, etc.).

FIGURE 2.2

Extra Fair Performance Appraisals at KFC

Among diners, KFC makes people think of delicious chicken. In the business world, the company also is known for the particularly fair performance appraisals it gives its employees. Among other things, company officials are careful to adhere to distributive justice by rewarding good performance. One Chicago-area Assistant Restaurant Manager received a paid day off and a watch with a symbolic gold emblem featuring the KFC logo recognizing his outstanding work.

only *how much* of various outcomes you receive (i.e., distributive justice) but also the process by which those outcomes are determined—that is, *procedural justice.* Specifically, **procedural justice** refers to people's perceptions of the fairness of the procedures used to determine the outcomes they receive.

procedural justice
People's perceptions of the fairness of the procedures used to determine the outcomes they receive.

Again, let's consider as an example the formal appraisals of an individual's job performance. Workers consider such ratings to be fair to the extent that certain procedures were followed, such as when raters were believed to be familiar with their work and when they believed that the standards used to judge them were applied to everyone equally.[9] As you might imagine, matters of procedural justice take a variety of different forms and are involved in many different situations.

Let's consider an illustration. A few years ago, New York City cab drivers went on strike to protest then-Mayor Giuliani's imposition of new safety rules.[10] As it worked out, the drivers had few gripes with the rules themselves. However, they felt it was unfair for the mayor to impose the rules without consulting them. In their eyes, fairness demanded having a voice in the decision-making process. This too is a major consideration when it comes to judging procedural justice. For a more complete list of some of the principal factors that people take into account when forming judgments about procedural justice, see Table 2.1.

Maintaining procedural justice is a key concern of people in all types of institutions. In legal proceedings, for example, cases may be dismissed if unfair procedures are used to gather evidence. And, in organizations, people also reject decisions based on unfair practices. In fact, following unfair procedures not only makes people dissatisfied with their

TABLE 2.1 Procedural Justice Criteria

In forming judgments of procedural justice, people take different factors into consideration. Some of the major ones are identified here, along with descriptions and examples of each.

Criterion	Description	Example
• Voice in the making of decisions	Perceptions of procedural justice are enhanced to the extent that people are given a say in the decisions affecting them.	Workers are given an opportunity to explain their feelings about their own work to a supervisor who is evaluating their performance.
• Consistency in applying rules	To be fair, the rules used as the basis for making a decision about one person must be applied equally to making a decision about someone else.	A professor must use the same exact standards in evaluating the term papers of each student in the class.
• Accuracy in use of information	Fair decisions must be based on information that is accurate.	A manager calculating the amount of overtime pay a worker is to receive must add the numbers accurately.
• Opportunity to be heard	Fair procedures are ones in which people have a readily available opportunity to correct any mistakes that have been made.	Litigants have an opportunity to have a judge's decision reconsidered in the event that an error was made in legal proceedings. (See also the instant replay rule used by the NFL as described in the *Preview Case.*)
• Safeguards against bias	A person making a decision must not have any opportunity to bias the results.	Lottery drawings are held in such a manner that each number is selected in a completely random, unbiased fashion.

Source: Based on information in Greenberg & Colquitt, 2005; see Note 1.

outcomes (as in the case of distributive justice), but leads them to reject the entire system as unfair.[11] Not surprisingly, as shown in Figure 2.1, procedural justice affects people's tendencies to follow organizational rules: Workers are not inclined to follow an organization's rules when they have reason to believe that its procedures are inherently unfair. And, of course, when this occurs, serious problems are likely to arise. Accordingly, everyone in an organization—especially top officials—would be well advised to adhere to the criteria for promoting procedural justice summarized in Table 2.1.

Interpersonal Justice. Imagine that you were just laid off from your job. You're not happy about it, of course, but suppose that your boss explains this situation to you in a manner that takes some of the sting out of it. Although your boss cannot do anything about this high-level corporate decision, he or she is very sensitive to the harm this causes you and expresses concern for you in a highly sensitive and caring manner. Research has shown that people experiencing situations such as this tend to accept their layoffs as being fair and hold positive feelings about their supervisors (see Figure 2.1). Importantly, such individuals are less inclined to sue their former companies on the grounds of wrongful termination than those who believe they were treated in an opposite manner—that is, an insensitive and disrespectful fashion.[12] The type of justice demonstrated in this example is known as **interpersonal justice**. This refers to people's perceptions of the fairness of the manner in which they are treated by others (typically, authority figures).

Informational Justice. Imagine that you are a heavy smoker of cigarettes and learn that your company has just imposed a smoking ban. Although you may recognize that it's the right thing to do, you are unhappy about it because the ruling forces you to change your behavior and break an addictive habit. Will you accept the smoking ban as fair and do your best to go along with it? Research suggests that you will do so only under certain circumstances—if you are given clear and thorough information about the need for the smoking ban (e.g., the savings to the company and improvements to the health of employees).[13] The form of justice illustrated in this example is known as **informational justice**. This refers to people's perceptions of the fairness of the information used as the basis for making a decision. Because detailed information was provided about the basis for implementing the smoking ban, informational justice was high, leading people to accept the fairness of the smoking ban.

A key explanation for this phenomenon is that informational justice prompts feelings of being valued by others in an organization. This is known as the **group-value explanation** of organizational justice.[14] The basic idea is that people believe they are considered an important part of the organization when an organizational official takes the time to explain thoroughly to them the rationale behind a decision. And people experiencing such feelings may be expected to believe that they are being treated in a fair manner. In Figure 2.2 we referred to KFC as adhering to distributive justice. This company also is very sensitive to interpersonal justice among its employees. According to Adonis Chapel, a KFC manager, the trick is not only in "doing chicken right," as its advertising slogan goes, but also "treating people right."[15]

Relationships Between Various Forms of Justice

Although we have been describing the various forms of organizational justice separately, it would be misleading to assume that they are completely independent of one another. In fact, researchers have found some well-established relationships between the various forms of justice.

The Interactive Relationship Between Distributive Justice and Procedural Justice. Imagine once again that you have received either an excellent grade or a poor grade in a class. Given that most of us tend to perceive ourselves more positively than others see us (we will discuss such perceptual biases in Chapter 3), you are likely to believe that a high grade is more fairly deserved than a low grade. In other words, the positive outcome is likely to be perceived as being more distributively just than the negative outcome. (The

---

interpersonal justice
People's perceptions of the fairness of the manner in which they are treated by others (typically, authority figures).

informational justice
People's perceptions of the fairness of the information used as the basis for making a decision.

group-value explanation (of organizational justice)
The idea that people believe they are an important part of the organization when an organizational official takes the time to explain thoroughly to them the rationale behind a decision.

FIGURE 2.3

The Relationship Between Outcome Favorability and Procedural Justice

Many different studies have reported that the relationship between outcome favorability and procedural justice takes the form summarized here. Specifically, people's reactions to favorable outcomes are affected little by the fairness of the procedure, whereas people's reactions to unfavorable outcomes are enhanced by the use of fair procedures.

Source: Based on suggestions by Brockner & Weisenfeld, 2005; see Note 16.

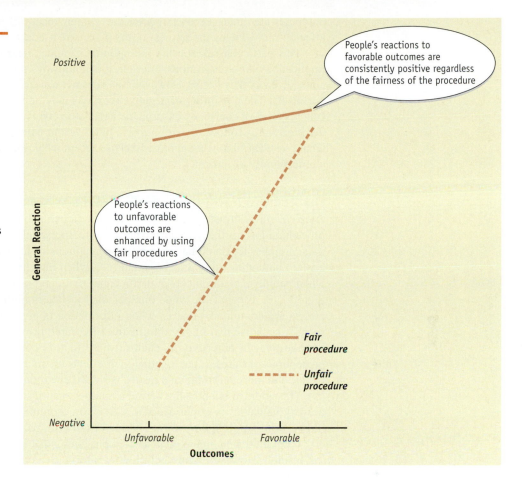

same would apply to other outcomes as well, such as pay or recognition on the job.) Now, imagine that your grade either was the result of a simple arithmetic error (i.e., procedural justice was low) or that it was computed in an accurate, unbiased fashion (i.e., procedural justice was high). Generally speaking, you will respond more positively to the fair procedure than the unfair procedure, thinking more favorably of the professor and the school as a whole. (Of course, the analogous effect also would apply in organizations.) So far, this is nothing new.

Consider, however, what happens when you combine these effects, looking at the overall relationship between the favorability of outcomes together with the fairness of procedures to arrive at those outcomes. This relationship, which takes the interactive form shown in Figure 2.3, has been very well established among scientists studying organizational justice.[16] Let's illustrate this relationship using the course grade example. The right side of the diagram describes what happens when the outcome is favorable—in other words, when you get a high grade. In this instance, you would be inclined to have a positive reaction because you are so very pleased with your high grade. Although you don't like the fact that it was not computed fairly, you are willing to overlook this given that you got what you wanted.

Now, however, look at the left side of the diagram, the part representing unfavorable outcomes. In this case, where you received a low grade, your feelings about the professor and even the school as a whole are likely to be influenced greatly by the fairness of the procedure. Specifically, you will be highly dissatisfied with the low grade when it results from an unfair procedure. After all, the grade doesn't reflect your true performance. However, your reactions are inclined to be far more positive when the low grade was based on a fair procedure. Again, although you don't particularly like the grade, believing that it was computed in an accurate and unbiased fashion (i.e., that it is procedurally fair) will get you to respond in a positive fashion. Put differently, although people's reactions to unfavorable outcomes are enhanced by fair procedures, their reactions to unfavorable outcomes are affected very little by the fairness of the procedure used.

This particular relationship is important to understand because it has very practical implications. In organizations, after all, it is not always possible to give people the favorable outcomes they desire. However, this does not necessarily mean that they will respond negatively. The possibility of negative reactions may be minimized by following fair procedures (and, of course, by ensuring that everyone involved is well aware of the fairness of the procedures followed). To borrow a phrase from Mick Jagger, "you can't always get what you want," but you are more likely to accept what you get when it was determined in a procedurally just manner.

The Additive Relationship Between Interpersonal Justice and Informational Justice. In contrast to the interactive relationship between distributive justice and procedural justice, the relationship between interpersonal justice and informational justice is far simpler. Research has shown that perceptions of justice are enhanced when people explain outcomes using a lot of detail (i.e., when informational justice is high) and also when people explain outcomes in a manner that demonstrates a considerable amount of dignity and respect (i.e., when interpersonal justice is high). What happens when these effects are combined—that is, when information is presented in a manner that is both socially sensitive *and* highly informative? Research provides a clear answer: The effects are additive. In other words, each of these factors contributes somewhat to people's perceptions of fairness, but together their effects are magnified.[17] The more interpersonal justice and more informational justice is shown, the more people believe things are fair.

This additive relationship between interpersonal justice and informational justice can be very valuable for supervisors to take into account when managing employees. The implications are straightforward: Sharing lots of information about outcomes makes workers accept those outcomes better, as does presenting that information in a sensitive and caring fashion. However, being both highly informative *and* highly sensitive and caring in one's presentation style at the same time enhances feelings of justice and promotes positive behavior most effectively of all.

A good illustration of this is provided in a study conducted recently by one of the authors.[18] In this investigation, nurses at two hospitals suffered a distributive injustice resulting from a new compensation system that reduced their pay by about 10 percent. At two other hospitals, the nurses were paid similarly to begin with, but did not have their pay cut. In one hospital in each group the supervisors of the nurses studied were given extensive managerial training that emphasized interpersonal and informational justice. Assuming that being treated in informationally and interpersonally fair ways would make nurses feel better about their pay cuts, it was reasoned that the nurses whose supervisors were trained in ways of promoting both these forms of justice (and who presumably followed what they learned in their treatment of the nurses they supervised) would suffer less stressful reactions to the pay cut than those whose supervisors were less attuned to promoting these important forms of justice. Specifically, in this study, stress was measured in terms of the nurses' insomnia, which was assessed using their responses to a questionnaire measuring problems getting to sleep and maintaining sleep throughout the night. Although we will discuss stress in considerable detail in Chapter 5, from your personal experiences, you probably are not surprised to learn that losing sleep is a common, and widespread, response to stress. These measures were collected at various points over 39 consecutive weeks.

The results, summarized in Figure 2.4, tell an interesting story. Nurses whose pay was unchanged over the study period experienced no significant changes in insomnia, whether or not their supervisors were trained. However, insomnia jumped from relatively low levels to relatively high levels immediately after the distributively unfair pay was introduced. This suggests that nurses found the distributive injustice to be stressful. Importantly, these effects were reduced dramatically among the nurses whose supervisors were trained in ways to promote informational and interactional justice. The combined effects of being treated with high degrees of informational and interpersonal justice effectively combated the negative impact of distributive injustice.

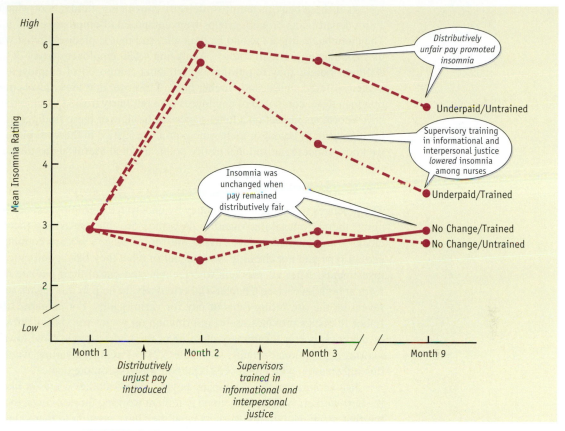

FIGURE 2.4

Losing Sleep over Injustice Can be Overcome

A recent study by one of the authors found that nurses suffered insomnia after their pay was changed in a manner that left them paid less than before (i.e., a distributive injustice). However, these insomnia reactions were reduced among nurses whose managers were trained in ways to promote interpersonal justice and informational justice.

Source: Adapted from Greenberg, 2005; see Note 18.

This is important to know because it has profound implications for managers. Although managers generally can do very little about distributive injustices because pay and fringe benefits are determined by organizational policies, they can do a great deal to promote informational justice (e.g., by explaining things) and interpersonal justice (e.g., by showing dignity and respect). Thus, there are specific things managers can do to promote organizational justice. Extending this idea, we now will consider several ways of promoting organizational justice.

Strategies for Promoting Organizational Justice

Treating people fairly on the job surely is a noble objective. Although many people are concerned about being fair for its own sake, of course, there's also a good practical reason for treating employees fairly. Specifically, individuals who believe they have been unfairly treated in any or all of the ways described respond quite negatively. We know, for example, that people who feel unfairly treated are likely to do such things as work less hard, steal from their employers, do poor-quality work, or even quit their jobs altogether—and then sue their former employers.[19] Naturally, managers are likely to seek organizational justice to avoid these problems. In addition to minimizing such negative reactions managers also are likely to seek the positive reactions associated with being perceived as fair. For example, fairness has been associated with such desirable behaviors as helping one's fellow workers and going along with organizational policies.[20]

As if these benefits aren't sufficiently convincing, think about what it would be like if entire departments or work groups were composed of employees who felt unfairly treated. The cumulative impact would be dramatic, and that is precisely what was found by scientists conducting a recent study.[21] Analyzing 4,539 employees from 783 departments in 97 different hotels, they found that departments composed of employees who felt unfairly treated suffered significantly higher rates of turnover and lower levels of customer satisfaction than those composed of employees who felt fairly treated. And, of course, these factors have enormous impact on a hotel's success. In view of these findings, there is good reason for managers to go out of their way to promote justice in the workplace. Fortunately, what we know about organizational justice points to some useful suggestions for doing so.

Pay Workers What They Deserve

The practices of saving a little money by underpaying employees—or informally discouraging them from taking vacation days they are due, or asking them to work "off the clock"—are doomed to fail. Paying the "going wage" in your community for work of a certain type and not cheating workers out of what they have coming to them are far wiser investments. After all, workers who feel cheated out of their pay are unmotivated to perform at high levels (see Chapter 7). Fortunately, to help in this regard surveys are available revealing the prevailing rates of pay for various jobs. For example, the U.S. Bureau of Labor Statistics provides useful information on wages for various jobs in various regions of the country (for a summary of some of the highest-paying and lowest-paying jobs for various occupational groups, see Table 2.2).[22] Paying prevailing wage rates and sharing this information with employees is a good way to promote justice.

Just as importantly, a company paying below-market wages is likely to lose because the best workers will be disinclined to remain working there, or even to accept jobs there in the first place. Not giving workers what they have coming to them clearly is "penny wise and pound foolish," as the saying goes.

Offer Workers a Voice

One of the best established principles of procedural justice is that people will better accept outcomes when they have had some input into determining them than when they are not involved.[23] This is known as the **fair process effect**. Often, promoting fairness in this manner is accomplished simply by conducting regular meetings with employees to hear what they have to say. The benefits of doing so result not only from making better-quality decisions (because it taps workers' expertise), but also from merely involving workers in the process. After all, workers whose input is solicited are inclined to feel better accepted as valued members of their organization than those who are ignored (this is the *group-value explanation* noted earlier). As shown in Figure 2.5, this leads them to perceive both that the resulting outcome is fair and that the procedure used to determine it is fair. And, as noted earlier, perceptions of distributive justice and procedural justice are quite beneficial to organizations.

What can be done to promote voice in organizations? Although there are many good possibilities, here are some of the most widely used methods.

- *Meet regularly and invite input.* Discussing how to do things—especially things that affect the individuals involved—is one of the most effective ways to promote voice. This gives people input into the making of decisions, promoting the perceived fairness—and acceptance—of those decisions. With this in mind, many managers hold regular meetings in which they solicit input from everyone.
- *Conduct employee surveys.* Companies conduct surveys among employees for many reasons. Among the most straightforward is to collect and systematically share employees' ideas about how to do things better. FedEx is one company that has made widespread use of this technique.
- *Keep an "open door policy."* Probably the easiest and most straightforward way to give employees voice is by letting them know that you are always available to talk. Managers who use such an "open door policy" send a strong message that they are

---

fair process effect
The tendency for people to better accept outcomes into which they have had some input in determining than when they have no such involvement.

TABLE 2.2 Highest and Lowest Paying Occupations

One of the most important ways of promoting justice in organizations is by paying people prevailing wages. The U.S. Bureau of Labor Statistics keeps records of the average rates of pay for people performing different jobs. Here are some of the highest-paying and lowest-paying jobs within various occupational categories for the year 2000.

Major Occupational Group	Highest-Paying Occupation			Lowest-Paying Occupation		
	Occupation	Mean Hourly Earnings (in $)	Rank	Occupation	Mean Hourly Earnings (in $)	Rank
Professional and technical	Airplane pilots and navigators	95.80	1	Health record technologists	11.18	347
Executive	Managers, marketing, advertising, and public relations	37.24	25	Legislators	10.74	360
Sales occupations	Sales engineers	33.59	35	Sales counter clerks	7.88	417
Administrative support	Supervisors, computer equipment operators	23.18	105	Hotel clerks	8.81	407
Precision production	Elevator installers and repairers	26.88	73	Brickmason and stonemason apprentices	9.73	387
Machine operators	Separating, filtering, and clarifying machine operators	16.77	206	Laundering and dry cleaning machine operators	7.72	421
Transportation	Longshore equipment operators	28.91	58	Parking lot attendants	8.58	408
Handlers	Stevedores	21.43	124	Nursery workers	8.03	415
Service occupations	Public transportation attendants	30.13	51	Waiters and waitresses	3.99	427

Source: Reproduced from Buckley, 2002; see Note 22.

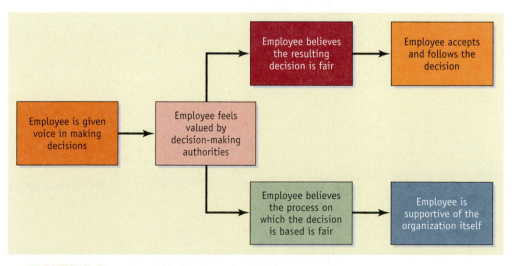

FIGURE 2.5

The Fair Process Effect: A Summary

According to the fair process effect, employees who are given voice in the making of decisions affecting them will feel valued by the decision-making authorities (e.g., top company leaders). In turn, this leads employees to believe that both the decision-making procedure and the outcomes resulting from it are fair. As a result, employees will accept and follow the decision and be supportive of the organization itself.

interested in what their employees have to say. This not only results in good ideas but also makes it clear to employees that they are valued members of the workplace.

■ *Use suggestion systems.* To encourage employees to share ideas, many companies have online sites at which employees can share ideas (see Figure 2.6). Frequently, an employee whose idea is implemented is given a reward that reflects the degree to which the suggestion led to savings for the company. Even paper-and-pencil "suggestion boxes" still are used for this purpose in more low-tech-oriented companies.

Openly Follow Fair Procedures

In Table 2.1 we identified several standards to be followed in being procedurally fair. Specifically, it is important for managers to be consistent, unbiased, and accurate in their treatment of employees in all ways. It also is important for them to make it clear that they are willing to be corrected or overturned if they are wrong.

Although these considerations come into play in many organizational activities, some of the clearest examples may be seen with respect to performance appraisal. For example, in assessing a worker's job performance procedural fairness requires that a manager apply the same standards to everyone doing the same job. Of course, these judgments also must be made in a manner that is devoid of bias and based on accurate information about the individual's work. Just as the NFL uses an "instant replay rule," as noted in our Preview Case, and courts allow verdicts to be appealed, so too does fairness demand that managers allow their judgments of workers' performance to be corrected so as to make them as accurate as possible. This would be the case, for example, if a worker brings to the manager's attention information about his or her performance that was ignored or misrepresented in his or her appraisal.

Before moving on, we must note an important qualification of this advice. Namely, although it is important to be procedurally fair, merely doing these things is insufficient. To reap the maximum benefits of your fair actions, it helps to ensure that others in the organization are keenly aware that you are doing so. Blatantly touting the fairness of one's actions

FIGURE 2.6

Suggestion Systems: An Example

Although we tend to think of suggestion systems as popular in large companies, they also are used widely in the non-profit sector. Here, for example, is a screenshot of the Web page at which employees of the State of Nebraska can share their suggestions. As shown here, the "Ideas Pay Off!" program not only invites a wide variety of suggestions, but it also can be profitable for those who use it.

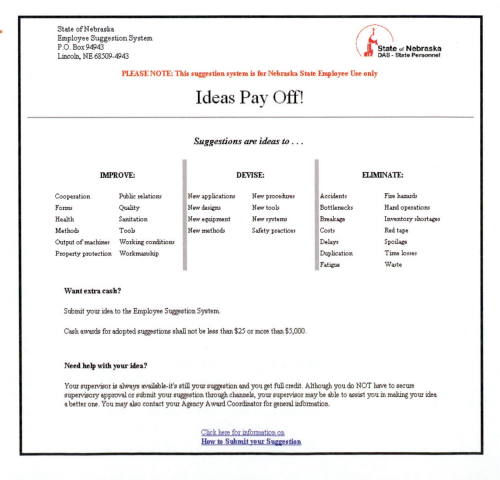

State of Nebraska
Employee Suggestion System
P.O. Box 94943
Lincoln, NE 68509-4943

State of **Nebraska**
DAS - State Personnel

PLEASE NOTE: This suggestion system is for Nebraska State Employee Use only

Ideas Pay Off!

Suggestions are ideas to . . .

IMPROVE:		DEVISE:		ELIMINATE:	
Cooperation	Public relations	New applications	New procedures	Accidents	Fire hazards
Forms	Quality	New designs	New tools	Bottlenecks	Hand operations
Health	Sanitation	New equipment	New systems	Breakage	Inventory shortages
Methods	Tools	New methods	Safety practices	Costs	Red tape
Output of machines	Working conditions			Delays	Spoilage
Property protection	Workmanship			Duplication	Time losses
				Fatigue	Waste

Want extra cash?

Submit your idea to the Employee Suggestion System.

Cash awards for adopted suggestions shall not be less than $25 or more than $5,000.

Need help with your idea?

Your supervisor is always available-it's still your suggestion and you get full credit. Although you do NOT have to secure supervisory approval or submit your suggestion through channels, your supervisor may be able to assist you in making your idea a better one. You may also contact your Agency Award Coordinator for general information.

Click here for information on
How to Submit your Suggestion

not only may be inappropriately immodest, of course, but also may arouse suspicion about one's true motives ("Why is she making such a big deal about how fair she is?"). At the same time, however, it is very useful to let people know that you are following fair procedures and to assure them of this by announcing all decisions publicly within the company and graciously explaining how they were made to anyone who wants to know. Making decisions in such an open fashion not only promotes perceptions of fairness, but demonstrates to workers precisely what they have to do to be recognized (see Chapter 3).

Explain Decisions Thoroughly in a Manner Demonstrating Dignity and Respect

To be fair, both interpersonally and informationally, it is essential for managers to take great care in presenting decisions to their employees. Specifically, fairness demands giving employees lots of information about how decisions were made and explaining those decisions in a manner that demonstrates dignity and respect for them. This is especially important when the decisions made have a negative impact on workers. After all, it's bad enough to learn something negative (e.g., a poor performance appraisal, a pay cut, or a layoff) without having a supervisor add insult to injury by not bothering to explain that decision thoroughly or by demonstrating a lack of concern for your feelings.

Illustrating this point, consider what it's like to have to live through a long pay freeze. Although it's bound to be painful, people may be more accepting of a pay freeze, accepting it as fair, if the procedure used to determine the need for the pay freeze is believed to be thorough and careful—that is, if "a fair explanation" for it can be provided. This was precisely what was found in an interesting study of manufacturing workers' reactions to a pay freeze.[24] Specifically, the researchers made comparisons between two groups of workers: those who received a thorough explanation of the procedures necessitating the pay freeze (e.g., information about the organization's economic problems), and those who received no such information. Although all workers were adversely affected by the freeze, those receiving the explanation better accepted it. In particular, the explanation reduced their interest in looking for a new job. (For a recent example of this practice in action see Figure 2.7.[25])

The practical lesson to be learned from this is important: Even if managers cannot do anything to eliminate distributive injustice (e.g., their "hands may be tied" by company policies), they may be able to reduce some of the sting by providing explanations as to *why* these unfortunate conditions are necessary and doing so in a sensitive and caring fashion. In fact, behaving in this manner can be one of the most effective cost-free things a manager can do.

Train Workers to Be Fair

Most people perceive themselves as fair individuals. However, as is clear from this section of the chapter, being fair involves several very specific forms of behavior. And, when facing the everyday pressure to get the job done, managers may not be taking into account as many of the principles of organizational justice as they should. With this in mind, it makes sense to train managers in ways of treating employees in a manner they will perceive to be fair. (In Chapter 3, we discuss the essential elements of training in general terms.)

Although training employees in ways of enhancing organizational justice is a relatively new practice, the results have been very promising. Several studies have been conducted in which managers have been thoroughly trained in techniques for promoting justice in the workplace using much the same information described in this chapter.[26] The training has consisted of sharing this information along with a series of case studies and exercises designed to increase managers' sensitivity to justice in the workplace. Managers who have been so trained reap several benefits compared to their untrained counterparts. Not only are the employees of the trained managers less inclined to respond in a negative fashion (e.g., by stealing from the company), but they also are more inclined to pitch in and help others in the organization (a phenomenon known as *organizational citizenship behavior,* which we describe in Chapter 6). Recall as well the study on insomnia whose results are summarized in Figure 2.4. This is the experiment showing that managers trained in ways of promoting informational justice and interpersonal justice behave in ways that help their subordinates cope successfully with the stresses of a new pay system they believed to be unfair.

FIGURE 2.7

Explaining Pay Cuts at Delta
Following the September 11, 2001, terrorist attacks on the United States, airlines faced major financial troubles. To help keep his company afloat in difficult times, Delta Airlines' Chairman and CEO Leo Mullin found it necessary to seek financial concessions from employees. This required thoroughly explaining the nature and extent of the problem (i.e., demonstrating informational justice) along with extreme sensitivity and caring for the employees (i.e., interpersonal justice). To help the cause, Mr. Mullins took a $9.1 million pay cut, which he explained to Delta employees in a three-page memo.

Our discussion of strategies for combating workplace injustice identifies two key issues worth highlighting. First, some sources of injustice stem from organization-wide policies involving key practices, such as the determination of pay or the appraisal of performance, that are believed to be unfair. Changing such practices requires a commitment from top executives. However, by understanding the importance of organizational justice, all managers have at their disposal a set of tools for promoting fairness in the workplace. After all, there is generally nothing to stop anyone from sharing more information or from treating others with dignity and respect. And, as we have shown, such actions from individual managers go a long way toward reducing the harmful effects that may be caused by system-wide sources of injustice.

Ethical Behavior in Organizations: Its Fundamental Nature

When philosophers talk about justice, they usually conceive of it as part of a larger interest in the topic of ethics. Of course, people in organizations also are concerned about ethics, but focus on the special ethical considerations involved in organizational settings, using the term **business ethics** to refer to the study of people's tendencies to behave in morally appropriate ways in organizations. This, of course, raises a key question: What do we mean by *morals* and *ethics?* Before proceeding further, we define and distinguish these terms.

business ethics
The study of people's tendencies to behave in morally appropriate ways in organizations.

Morals and Ethics: What's the Difference?

In addressing a group about making key military decisions, U.S. General H. Norman Schwarzkopf once said, "The truth of the matter is that you always know the right thing to do. The hard part is doing it."[27] This notion is central to the distinction between two key terms—*moral values* and *ethics*—that are essential to understanding the nature of ethical behavior in organizations.

When social scientists speak of **moral values** (usually more simply referred to as **morals**), they are referring to people's fundamental beliefs regarding what is right or

moral values (morals)
People's fundamental beliefs regarding what is right or wrong, good or bad.

wrong, good or bad. One of the most important sources of moral values is the religious background, beliefs, and training we receive. Although people's moral values may differ, several are widely accepted. For example, most people believe that being charitable to someone in need is right whereas killing an innocent person is wrong. Based on these beliefs, people are guided in ways that influence the decisions they make and the actions in which they engage. These standards are referred to as *ethics*. Thus, **ethics** refers to standards of conduct that guide people's decisions and behavior (e.g., not stealing from others).[28] For a summary of the distinction between moral values and ethics, see Figure 2.8.

When looking at Figure 2.8 please note the row of rounded boxes at the bottom. These identify some of the factors affecting moral values, ethics, decisions, and behavior. The ones corresponding to ethics and values are described in this section of the chapter. However, as indicated in the box in the lower right corner, the decisions people make and the behavior in which they engage are determined by a wide variety of considerations beyond ethics. Accordingly, these are discussed elsewhere throughout this book (note the references to other chapters throughout this book).

Most organizational scientists acknowledge that it is *not* a company's place to teach employees moral values. After all, these come with people as they enter the workplace. However, it *is* a company's responsibility to set clear standards of behavior and to train employees in recognizing and following them.[29] Just as organizations prescribe other kinds of behavior that are expected in the workplace (e.g., when to arrive and leave), so too should they prescribe appropriate ethical behavior (e.g., how to complete expense reports and what precisely is considered a bribe). Not surprisingly, most top business leaders recognize that clearly prescribing ethical behavior is a fundamental part of good management. After all, says Kent Druyversteyn, former vice president of ethics at General Dynamics, "Ethics is about conduct."[30]

The Epidemic of Ethical Scandals

Pick up any newspaper today and you're bound to find a story or two about some sort of ethically questionable act alleged to have occurred in the world of business. Consider just the following now-classic examples from recent years.[31]

ethics
Standards of conduct that guide people's decisions and behavior (e.g., not stealing from others).

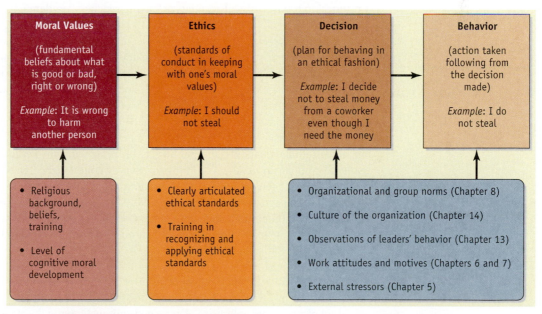

FIGURE 2.8

Moral Values Versus Ethics

As summarized here, moral values (which reside within an individual) provide the basis for ethics (which are standards of behavior that can be regulated by organizations). Ethical standards influence both decisions and behavior in the workplace, which also are affected by a host of other variables identified throughout this book.

- *Adelphia Communications.* The nation's sixth-largest cable television service provider filed for bankruptcy and is under federal investigation. The company's founder, John Rigas, and his two sons were arrested and charged with using company funds as personal income.
- *Arthur Andersen.* This accounting firm was found guilty of obstructing justice by destroying documents related to the investigation of Enron, its client over which it had auditing responsibility.
- *Enron.* The bankruptcy of this former giant energy company has been a catalyst for many of today's ethics probes. Company officials were charged with creating bogus partnerships that allowed managers to shift debt off the books. This enabled officials to become enormously wealthy as Enron's stock soared.
- *Global Crossing.* Officials from this telecommunications company were alleged to have entered into deals with other firms that were designed solely to artificially inflate its revenue. This allowed the company's chairman to sell $750 million in stock before the company collapsed.
- *Tyco International.* The chief executive officer of this company was indicted on charges of tax evasion and evidence tampering in the wake of investigations in which he and others were accused of receiving improper bonuses and company loans.
- *WorldCom.* Former top executives of this large long-distance provider were accused of misrepresenting the company's financial picture, making some $3.8 billion in accounting errors to artificially inflate the company's bottom line.
- *Halliburton.* This Houston-based provider of services to the oil and gas industry is alleged to have wasted the $18 billion it was awarded by the Pentagon to help rebuild war-torn Iraq.
- *Martha Stewart Omnimedia.* Ms. Stewart was imprisoned after being convicted of conspiring with her stockbroker to obstruct a federal investigation into her sale of personal ImClone Systems stock (see Figure 2.9).
- *Parmalat.* This large Italian dairy-foods company was forced to declare bankruptcy after an accounting fraud resulted in $8.5 to $12 billion in missing assets.

Considering these incidents, it comes as no surprise that one newspaper reporter referred to today's ethical scandals as having reached "epidemic levels."[32] Although all of these examples are from the past few years, it would be misleading to suggest that ethical misconduct is a recent phenomenon. Indeed, the history of American business is riddled with sordid tales of magnates who did whatever it took to become successful, even if in the process it involved devastating the country's natural resources, abusing people, upsetting the public's trust in the business world, and wiping out the hopes and dreams of millions of honest, hard-working people. For some historically relevant examples, see Table 2.3.[33]

Although the tendency for people to be greedy has been a longstanding and prominent feature of the business scene, things have been changing in recent years. In response to the spate of ethical scandals, the public has been growing intolerant of unethical behavior among company officials. According to a survey conducted between 1994 and 2005, workers report that top managers have become more inclined to keep their promises, less inclined to engage in misconduct, less likely to feel pressure to be unethical, and perceive greater attention paid to practicing honesty and respect for others. At the same time, 55 percent of employees who observe ethical misdeeds report them to organizational authorities.[34] In the words of one expert,

> Ethical standards, whether formal or informal . . . are considerably higher. Business-people themselves, as well as the public, expect more sensitive behavior in the conduct of economic enterprise. The issue is not just having the standards, however. It is living up to them.[35]

To the extent that people are increasingly intolerant of unethical business activity, it should not be surprising to learn that OB scientists are interested in combating unethical practices. Before reviewing strategies for doing this, we focus on the fundamental issue—namely, why we should care about ethics in the first place.

FIGURE 2.9

Martha Stewart: Target of One of Several Recent Ethical Scandals

For several months spanning parts of 2004 and 2005, Martha Stewart served time in a federal penitentiary after being indicted on charges of obstructing justice. Far from the luxurious life she lived as a media mogul, the so-called "domestic diva" and former Chair of the company she founded and to which she lent her name, was punished for failing to disclose evidence bearing on the sale of personal stock following an illegal inside tip. Her personal reputation as well as her company suffered greatly as a result. Ms. Stewart is one of several highly visible high-ranking company officials who have been embroiled in ethical and legal scandals in the past few years.

Why Does Ethical Behavior Matter in Organizations?

It may seem obvious that we should care about ethics simply because behaving ethically is the right thing to do. Indeed, many famous people agree that ethical behavior is of paramount importance. For example, President George W. Bush said, "At this moment, America's highest economic need is higher ethical standards—standards enforced by strict laws and upheld by responsible business leaders."[36] In the same vein, Robert D. Hass, former chairman of Levi Strauss & Co., observed that "A company's values—what it stands for, what its people believe in—are crucial to its competitive success."[37]

Despite these lofty and well-meaning statements from leaders, we already noted that people do not always do the right thing. Under the right circumstances, even seemingly ethical people behave unethically. Pressure to meet sales quotas, for example, have led some stockbrokers to boost their commissions by convincing unknowing clients to make bad investments.[38] Clearly, this is wrong on moral grounds. Although managers may be uncomfortable changing their morals, they must be concerned about promoting ethical behavior for two sound business reasons. First, over the long run, being ethical is profitable. Second, being ethical satisfies many of today's legal regulations.

Ethics and the Bottom Line

Imagine that you have a small neighborhood grocery store. Competing with the big chains has been very challenging, and margins are razor thin. One day, out of desperation, you decide that you can make a few extra pennies at the butcher counter by rigging your scales

TABLE 2.3 Famous Ethical Scandals from Decades Past

Despite all the attention they have been receiving lately, ethical scandals are nothing new. Described here are a few of the most prominent ethical scandals from throughout the twentieth century.

When?	Who?	What?
1920s	Charles Ponzi	Created a fraudulent investment scheme promising a 50 percent profit to investors in 90 days. Initial backers were paid with money from later investors. Eventually, the so-called "Ponzi scheme" failed, defrauding 40,000 people out of $15 million ("real money" back then).
1930s	Ivar Krueger	This "Swedish Match King" ran companies making two-thirds of the world's matches. During the Great Depression, he made hundreds of "off-the-books" schemes that defrauded investors and banks.
1960s	Billy Sol Estes	Ran a vast scam getting federal agricultural subsidies. Until eventually being imprisoned, he received $21 million a year for "growing" and "storing" nonexistent crops of cotton.
1960s	Bernie Cornfeld and Robert Vesco	Cornfeld invented Investors Overseas Services (IOS), a collection of fraudulent mutual funds, eventually raising $2.5 billion before defaulting. Brought in to save the company by investing $5 million, Vesco looted the company of some $250 million and fled to Cuba.
1980s	Charles Keating	The founder of Lincoln Savings & Loan sold fraudulent "junk bonds" and manipulated financial statements to make the institution appear profitable before failing.
1990s	Officials of the International Olympic Committee	Bribes allegedly were accepted as inducements to select Sydney, Australia and Salt Lake City, Utah as cities for the 2000 and 2002 Olympic Games.

Sources: Fordyce, 2004; Zagorian, 2005; see Note 33.

so that a sale of 0.95 pound appears as 1.00 pound on the meter. No one would be the wiser, you think, and the odds of getting caught by the local agency that regulates weights and measures are small. When "weighed" against the added profit that you stand to make over time, the temptation is too great to dismiss. Besides, you rationalize that nobody will get hurt by your actions, although the benefit to you and your employees will be great because it will help you stay profitable—or even, remain in business at all (see Figure 2.10).

FIGURE 2.10

Ethics and Profitability: You Can Have Them Both!

Too many people believe that being profitable requires being unethical, at least sometimes. This proves to be untrue in the long run. In fact, the evidence is clear that "good ethics is good business" and that "bad ethics is bad business."

Source: Reprinted by permission of Carol*Simpson.

"A 34% cut in our corporate ethics should return us to profitability."

Although you might not have your own grocery store, chances are good that you can relate to this situation because in one way or another we all are tempted to do something unethical in our business practices. "Just a little thing," we readily rationalize, "won't matter," and the odds of getting caught are small. Surely this is what was going through the minds of the individuals responsible for the ethical scandals we noted earlier. The truth, however, as we have learned, is that many people do, in fact, get caught for their misdeeds, paying consequences that far outstrip any benefits they hoped to gain. Besides the fear of getting caught, there is another good reason why ethical behavior is in a company's best interests—namely, it pays off on the bottom line. For a look at several ways in which this occurs, see the *OB: Making Sense Out of Common Sense* section, below.

Even if you are not convinced that "good ethics is good business," then look at the other side of the coin—that "bad ethics is bad business." In this connection, consider the findings of a recent survey in which consumers were asked how they would respond if they learned that a company with whom they were doing business engaged in some unethical behavior.[39] The results, summarized in Figure 2.11 (p. 60), indicate some highly damaging responses, which companies clearly cannot afford to ignore.

Admittedly, it is one thing for people to say that they would respond in certain ways, as in the case of these survey findings, and quite another for them actually to do them.

OB **Making Sense Out of Common Sense**

Good Ethics Is Good Business

For many years, people have quoted philosophers to argue that it is "best in the long run" to behave ethically and that "good ethics is good business."[40] To some, the idea of being pointed by a strong moral compass became a commonsense guide to their business practices. Today, we know that there are several sound empirical bases for the claim that "good ethics is good business." In fact, the evidence bearing on this is quite convincing.[41] This evidence takes several impressive forms.

First, scientists have established *a link between ethical behavior and financial performance*. If you have any doubt that ethics pays off on the bottom line, consider this. A few years ago, researchers compared companies with respect to the extent to which their top executives made explicit statements expressing a commitment to ethics in the messages contained in their annual reports. Whereas some CEOs said such things as, "We are committed to ethics in everything we do," others simply made no mention of ethics. The scientists then used standard measures of financial success (e.g., return on investment) to compare those companies whose executives made explicit commitments to ethics to those that did not. The findings were dramatic: Companies whose leaders explicitly expressed a strong commitment to ethical behavior financially outperformed those whose leaders were more casual about ethical issues, returning about twice the value to shareholders.[42] Although these findings do not reveal that ethical behavior causes successful financial performance, these results are difficult to ignore.

Second, it has been established that *companies with reputations for treating people well and being good citizens of the world are highly sought as employers*.[43] As it is often said, "we are known by the company we keep," and this appears to apply to the companies for which we work as well as the company we keep socially. After all, nobody wants to be associated with a company that has a questionable moral reputation because this cannot help but reflect negatively on us as individuals. And, given that it often is difficult to attract and retain the best employees, having a reputation as an ethical citizen of the world is bound to give a company a strong competitive advantage.[44]

As an extension of this idea, it also is known that not only prospective employees, but *prospective customers are drawn to businesses that deliver products and services in an ethically responsible manner*.[45] Because of this, several apparel manufacturers have gone out of their way to publicize that their products are not being made in sweatshops or by using child labor. Given that some companies have lost business as a result of such claims, it's easy to understand how emphasizing an ethical stand can help companies attract and retain customers.[46]

In view of these findings, it's clear that companies whose officials are tempted to cheat or behave unethically in one way or another are merely taking a short-term perspective. In the long run, it is clear that in several important ways, "good ethics" is indeed "good business."

FIGURE 2.11

Consumers' Adverse Responses to Unethical Business Practices

A survey asked American consumers how they would respond to companies alleged to be involved in unethical business practices. As shown here, high percentages of people indicate that they would respond in a variety of negative ways.

Source: Based on data reported by the Cone Corporate Citizenship Study, 2002; see Note 39.

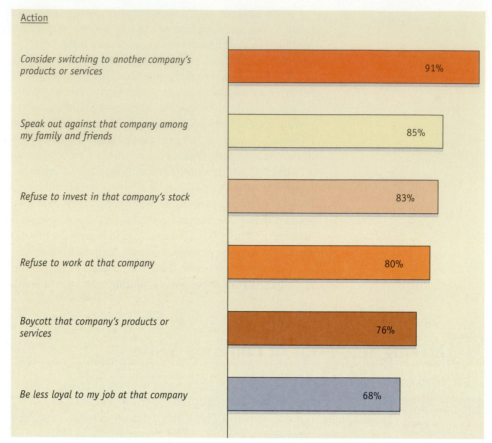

Percentage indicating that they would do this

However, case studies provide abundant evidence that companies whose reputations are sullied by ethical scandals are both scorned by consumers and deserted by stockholders.[47] As a case in point, see Figure 2.12 (p. 61).[48]

Ethics and the Law

> It is not enough to simply say that our conduct is lawful. The law is the floor. Compliance with it will be the absolute minimum with respect to the PPG associate, no matter where he or she works. Our ethics go beyond the legal code.[49]

This quotation from a former CEO of the big glass company, PPG, underscores two important points—namely, (1) that following ethical standards is *not* merely the same as obeying the law, and (2) that the law may be considered the minimum acceptable standard to which companies must adhere. Over the years, as people have become appalled by breaches of ethics in the government and corporate worlds, it is not surprising that they have looked to their political leaders for long-term solutions. For some examples of U.S. laws from the past two decades designed to discourage unethical business practices, see Table 2.4 (p. 61).[50]

Of all the laws listed in Table 2.4, the ones with the greatest influence on the practice of ethics have been the Federal Sentencing Guidelines and the Sarbanes-Oxley Act. In the case of the Federal Sentencing Guidelines, its influence may be seen in the form of the many practices it has encouraged so that companies can promote ethical behavior.[51] Specifically, because of this law, companies now take the following steps to promote ethics.

- Create and widely disseminate clear standards for following the law.
- Have a high-ranking official, usually an *ethics officer,* oversee adherence to legal and ethical practices (we describe this role further on p. 71).

FIGURE 2.12

One Individual's Ethical Misdeeds Leads Many to Suffer: An Example

In the 1990s, the president of one local chapter of a United Way agency was accused of misusing agency funds. Although only one person was involved, other chapters were adversely affected as donations slowed to a trickle and 20 percent of previous donors stopped giving altogether. It took 5 full years before donations to this venerable charity recovered fully. The real losers, of course, were the millions of people who would have been helped by the agency's efforts.

TABLE 2.4 U.S. Laws Bearing on Ethical Behavior in Organizations

Several federal laws have been enacted that reflect people's disdain for unethical behavior in government and business organizations. Summarized here are some of the most important U.S. laws bearing on ethical behavior in organizations from the last quarter century.

Law	Year Enacted or Revised	Description
False Claims Act	1986	Provides mechanisms for reporting fraudulent behavior against U.S. government agencies and protects individuals who do so.
Foreign Corrupt Practices Act	1988	Prohibits company officers from soliciting business by paying bribes to foreign officials
Federal Sentencing Guidelines for Organizations	1991	Specifies guidelines for federal judges to follow when imposing fines on organizations whose employees engage in criminal acts. Its underlying rationale is that the more steps companies take to discourage criminal behavior by its employees, the less they will be penalized should such acts occur. This law specifies several actions which, if taken, will be recognized as efforts to discourage illegal behavior. As a result, companies are actively engaged in following these courses of action
Sarbanes-Oxley Act	2002	Enacted to guard against future accounting scandals, such as occurred at Enron, this law raises the standards that public companies must use to report accounting data. Specifically, this law has kept companies actively involved in monitoring the ethical behavior of their officers.
Federal Prosecution of Business Organizations	2003	A revision to the Federal Sentencing Guidelines for Organizations that is designed to protect investors against unscrupulous acts by top executives (also in response to the Enron scandal). The focus on boards of directors is intended to discourage unethical behavior, given that such individuals often are the only parties with sufficient clout to prevent wrongdoing by top company officials.

Sources: See Note 50.

- Closely monitor and audit behavior to be able to detect unethical acts.
- Follow a clear policy for disciplining rule violators.

In recent years, companies have gone out of their way to comply with the ethical requirements specified by the Sarbanes-Oxley Act. Although there are many specific requirements, some of the most prominent ones can be illustrated by examining the response of one particular company—the large pharmaceutical firm, GlaxoSmithKline (GSK). Although this company is considered well run and has not been accused of any questionable accounting practices, its officials—like those of other publicly held companies (i.e., those in which people can purchase stock)—had to revise various policies to ensure compliance. Specifically, policies were introduced that did the following.

- ***Limited acceptance of entertainment and gifts by employees.*** Because accepting gifts and entertainment from suppliers may unduly influence an employee's business judgment, all 100,000 GSK employees worldwide are limited to accepting offers only if they are customary in nature and occur infrequently. Although the written policy provides no specific numbers as guidelines, it asks employees to consider how it would look to others if they accepted an offer. If they feel they would be embarrassed if others found out about a gift they took, then they are asked to refrain from doing so.
- ***Raised standards for accurate documentation of company performance.*** The policy specifies that "no false, artificial, intentionally misleading or incomplete entry shall be made or data established for any reason, and no employee shall engage in any arrangement that results in the creation of such entry or data." Further clarifying expectations to avoid financial misrepresentations, that policy also stipulates that "The books and records of GSK . . . are accurate and sufficiently, clear, detailed, and timely, to record the true nature of GSK's business, its transactions and liabilities."[52]

We shared GSK's responses because they are typical of those enacted in many companies. The company's policy changes fell more into the category of small adjustments than major overhauls. In most cases they merely formalized several practices that already were in effect informally.

Ethics in the International Arena

Our discussion thus far suggests that figuring out how to behave ethically isn't always easy. If that's the case when conducting business at home, then imagine how much more complex things become when conducting business in other countries. After all, people in different cultures often have different ethical standards. Consider the examples:

- In China, using pirated software is considered acceptable.
- In Indonesia, bribing an official is considered an acceptable cost of doing business.
- In Japan, you cannot conduct business unless you give the other party a small gift.

In North America, of course, all such acts would be frowned upon and considered illegal and/or unethical. Clearly, the implications for conducting business globally are confusing. Given that most business conducted today is international in nature, it's important to consider the special ethical challenges this creates. Specifically, how does one behave ethically when conducting business abroad? The answer, as we now discuss, is complex and highly nuanced, but can be mastered by adhering to several guiding principles that we will identify.

Ethical Relativism and Ethical Imperialism: Two Extreme Positions

Over the years, philosophers have approached the matter of international business ethics by distinguishing between two extreme approaches—*ethical relativism* and *ethical imperialism* (see Figure 2.13). As you will see, each of these viewpoints is problematic. However, understanding them is important because it helps you understand the most effective approach, which lies in between these two extremes.

ethical relativism

The belief that no culture's ethics are better than any other's and that there are no internationally acceptable standards of right and wrong (the opposite of *ethical imperialism*).

Ethical Relativism: Nothing Is Sacred. To some, the matter of how to conduct oneself when doing business abroad is as easy as, "when in Rome, do what the Romans do." This calls for adopting the ethics of whatever country in which one does business—an approach, known as **ethical relativism**. The rationale is that no culture's ethics are better than any other's, and that there are no internationally acceptable standards of right and wrong.

The problem with this approach is that it may lead to condoning acts that violates one's own sense of morality.[53] Consider this example. Some time ago, several European pharmaceutical companies and tanneries were looking for places where they could dispose of toxic chemical waste. Government officials from most countries they approached said no, fearing the health risks to their people. Nigeria, however, agreed to the business even though local workers, who didn't have any protective clothing, had a good chance of coming into contact with deadly substances as they moved the barrels that contained them. Despite the fact that the practice was permitted in Nigeria, it's easy to see how the risks to the workers make the practice ethically questionable.

Ethical Imperialism: What Is Different May Be Wrong. Given that following ethical relativism may lead to moral transgressions, then how about the opposite approach? That is, what if, wherever they are, people use their own country's ethical standards? In other words, they do everywhere whatever they consider to be right while at home. This approach, which is the opposite of ethical relativism, is known as **ethical imperialism**.

ethical imperialism

The belief that the ethical standards of one's own country should be imposed when doing business in other countries (the opposite of *ethical relativism*).

It too has limitations. Highly absolute in its approach, ethical imperialism asserts that there is only a single set of rules regarding right and wrong—one's own. Thus, whatever is different is wrong. Obviously, this is very limiting because it fails to recognize cultural and situational differences that may influence ethical behavior. For example, North American–type training in avoiding sexual harassment (see Chapter 5) likely would be questioned in Middle Eastern countries, where the treatment of women is highly regulated by social and religious customs. Likewise, in parts of the world where people are dying from

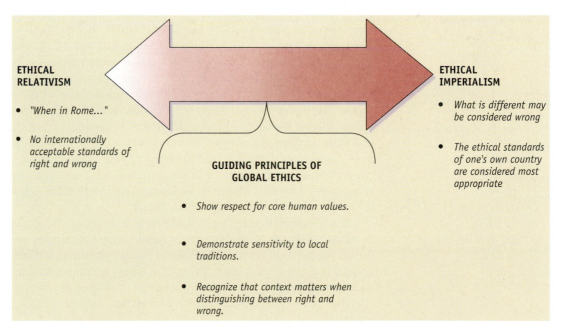

FIGURE 2.13

Approaches to Global Ethics: Two Extremes and a Middle Ground

Too often, people attempting to make ethical decisions in international settings follow one of the two ill-advised, extreme approaches identified here—*ethical relativism* and *ethical imperialism*. By adopting qualities of both approaches, a middle ground can be found in which people can be guided by three principles of global ethics.

Source: Based on suggestions by Donaldson, 1996; see Note 53.

malnutrition, it may be ill-advised to impose standards for the use of agricultural chemicals that make sense in more developed countries, where lower crop yields are not problematic.

Given that the two extreme approaches to global business ethics are problematic, you may be thinking that the best approach lies somewhere in between. So too do most of today's experts in business ethics.

Three Guiding Principles of Global Ethics

It has been recommended that company officials doing business abroad should adopt a stance between the extremes of ethical relativism and ethical imperialism. In this connection, they may be guided by three key principles: (1) show respect for core human values, (2) demonstrate sensitivity to local traditions, and (3) recognize that context matters when distinguishing between right and wrong.[54]

Show Respect for Core Human Values.
Certain practices, considered core human values, constitute the minimum ethical standards for organizations to follow. Although everyone might not agree with all values that might be included in this list, few would argue against the idea that the right to safe working conditions, the right to be free, and the right to be treated with dignity and respect are moral values that should guide all behavior in the business world (and elsewhere too, of course).

To be ethical, company officials must use their "moral compasses" to guide people toward acceptable practices and away from intolerable ones. For example, taking steps to promote a healthy workplace, one that is free from physical danger and psychological abuse, is ethically appropriate. At the same time, companies should refuse to do business with suppliers, such as those in the garment industry, who use *sweatshops*. These are factories, often located in developing countries, in which people are required to work long hours under dangerous conditions for extremely little pay and often live in squalid company-owned housing. After all, most would consider it highly unethical to condone such practices by hiring the companies that follow them (see Figure 2.14).[55]

Demonstrate Sensitivity to Local Traditions.
Being ethical requires following local traditions, so long as these don't violate core human values, of course. As a case in point, consider the practice of gift-giving among business partners in Japan. Although many American companies frown on such acts because they fear that the giving of gifts might be a way of unfairly influencing someone by cultivating his or her favor, this is not the case in Japan. This is not to say that bribery is condoned there. Such acts are not meant to be bribes. Rather, the act of giving small gifts is a customary ritual that connotes politeness and trust between the parties. To not accept a gift from a business partner would be considered highly impolite and insulting. These days, because American companies conduct so much business in Japan, officials are coming to accept this practice as acceptable. After all, when you understand precisely what the act means in Japanese culture, it hardly can be considered unethical.

It is important to note that demonstrating sensitivity to local traditions does *not* equate to moral relativism. A moral relativist would accept all actions as ethical in a country if they are deemed ethical there. The case of dumping hazardous waste in Nigeria, mentioned earlier, is a good illustration. Doing that surely violates core human values because it endangers people. Merely showing awareness of another country's cultural norms and adapting one's behavior accordingly, by contrast, may be a highly effective way of promoting ethical behavior.

Recognize that Context Matters when Distinguishing Between Right and Wrong.
Ethical rules are not hard and fast. Sometimes what's right in one context may be considered wrong in another. Being ethical requires taking into account the nature of the setting in which acts occur.

In the United States, for example, it would be considered unethical (and potentially illegal) to hire one's own relatives instead of a more qualified non–family member. Such blatant nepotism is frowned upon. By contrast, conditions in India are such that such a practice

FIGURE 2.14

Closing the Gap on Sweatshops

People who work in sweatshops, often children, are subjected to long hours of labor for extremely low wages in oppressive and dangerous conditions. Cracking down on such violations of core human values, the Gap employs over 90 full-time employees who inspect thousands of clothing manufacturing factories worldwide to ensure that working conditions are safe and humane. As one of the approved facilities, the Qualytel de Puebla plant in Puebla, Mexico, produces garments for the Gap and other concerned companies as well.

makes sense. There, jobs are difficult to find, and some of the most successful companies offer as a perk to their employees the opportunity to hire their children once they graduate from school. This eases unemployment, thereby strengthening the economy. Additionally, Indians believe that keeping the family together is more important than pursuing economic opportunities. For these reasons, the practice of hiring relatives may be considered ethical—but only in India, where conditions are unique. That's our point: Different contexts may require different ethical guidelines.

If, upon reading this, you realize the complexities of attempting to behave ethically in international settings, you have reached the same conclusion as many a seasoned businessperson. As one business expert put it, "Managers living and working abroad who are not prepared to grapple with moral ambiguity and tension should pack their bags and come home."[56]

Why Do Some People Behave Unethically—At Least, Sometimes?

Management experts long have considered the matter of why some people, at least, behave unethically on at least some occasions. Put differently, is it a matter of good people who are led to behave unethically because of external forces acting on them (i.e., "good apples in bad barrels") or is it that bad people behave inappropriately in whatever settings they are in (i.e., "bad apples in good barrels")? Acknowledging the key role of leaders in determining the ethical climate of an organization, some scientists have considered the possibility that because of their profound influence, some unethical leaders (so-called "bad apples") have made their companies unethical as well (turning "good barrels into bad"), or poisoning the whole barrel, so to speak.[57] Although the relative importance of "apples" and "barrels" has yet to be firmly decided, it is clear that ethical and unethical behavior is determined by *both* of these classes of factors—that is, individual factors (the person), and situational factors (the external forces people confront in the workplace). In this section of the chapter, we consider both sets of factors.

Individual Differences in Cognitive Moral Development

As you know from experience, people appear to differ with respect to their adherence to moral considerations. Some individuals, for example, refrain from padding their expense accounts even if they believe they will not get caught, solely because they believe that doing so is wrong. They strongly consider ethical factors when making decisions. However, this is not true of everyone. Still others, as you know, would not think twice about padding their expense accounts, often rationalizing that the amounts of money in question are small and that "the company expects me to do it." A key factor responsible for this difference is what psychologists refer to as **cognitive moral development**—that is, differences between people in the capacity to engage in the kind of reasoning that enables them to make moral judgments.

The most well-known theory of cognitive moral development was introduced over three decades ago by the psychologist Lawrence Kohlberg.[58] According to **Kohlberg's theory of cognitive moral development**, people develop over the years in their capacity to understand what is right. Specifically the theory distinguishes between three levels of moral development (for a summary, see Figure 2.15).

Preconventional Level of Moral Reasoning. The first level is referred to as the **preconventional level of moral reasoning**. People at this level (children and about one-third of all adults) haven't developed the capacity to assume the perspective of others. Accordingly, they interpret what is right solely with respect to themselves: It is wrong to do something if it leads one to be punished. Because their cognitive skills are not sufficiently advanced, such individuals generally cannot comprehend any argument you may make about something being wrong because it violates their social obligations to others.

Conventional Level of Moral Reasoning As people interact with others over the years, most come to use higher-level cognitive processes to judge morality. In a more sophisticated fashion, they judge right and wrong in terms of what is good for the others around them and society as a whole. This second level is referred to as the **conventional level of moral reasoning**. Approximately two-thirds of adults fall into this category. What they do is governed strongly by what's expected of them by others, and they carefully scour the social environment for cues as to "what's right." People who engage in conventional moral reasoning obey the law not only because they fear the repercussions of not doing so, but also because they recognize that doing so is the right thing to do insofar as it promotes the safety and welfare of society as a whole.

Postconventional Level of Moral Reasoning. Finally, Kohlberg's theory also identifies a third level of cognitive moral development, the **postconventional level of moral reasoning**. At this level, people judge what is right and wrong not solely in terms of their interpersonal and societal obligations, but in terms of complex philosophical principles of duty, justice, and rights. Very few people ever attain this level. Those who do, however, follow their own "moral compass," doing what they are convinced is truly right, even if others don't agree.

Research has found that people behave in very different ways as a function of their levels of cognitive moral development. For example, as you might expect, people who are at higher levels of cognitive moral development (typically, conventional as opposed to pre-conventional) manifest their greater ethical behavior in several ways. Specifically, they are less inclined to harm others, less likely to misreport information even if it makes them look bad, and steal less from their employers.[59] Although efforts to raise people's level of moral reasoning through training have been successful, few such efforts have been used in organizations.[60] This is in large part because most workers already function at the conventional level, making them sensitive to efforts to promote ethical behavior predicated on changing the social norms that exist within organizations.

Situational Determinants of Unethical Behavior

Although it's likely that many situational factors play a role in the tendency for people in organizations to behave unethically, three particular forces feature prominently: organizational norms that encourage unethical behavior, managerial values that discourage integrity, and the impact of unethical behavior by leaders.

cognitive moral development

Differences between people in the capacity to engage in the kind of reasoning that enables them to make moral judgments.

Kohlberg's theory of cognitive moral development

The theory based on the idea that people develop over the years in their capacity to understand what is right and wrong.

preconventional level of moral reasoning

In Kohlberg's theory of cognitive moral development, the level at which people (e.g., young children and some adults) haven't yet developed the capacity to assume the perspective of others, leading them to interpret what is right solely with respect to themselves:

conventional level of moral reasoning

In Kohlberg's theory of cognitive moral development, the level attained by most people, in which they judge right and wrong in terms of what is good for others and society as a whole.

postconventional level of moral reasoning

In Kohlberg's theory of cognitive moral development, the level at which people judge what is right and wrong not solely in terms of their interpersonal and societal obligations, but in terms of complex philosophical principles of duty, justice, and rights.

FIGURE 2.15

Kohlberg's Theory of Cognitive Moral Development

This theory distinguishes among the three major levels of cognitive moral development summarized here. According to the theory, people at different levels define what is wrong in different ways limited by their capacity for moral reasoning.

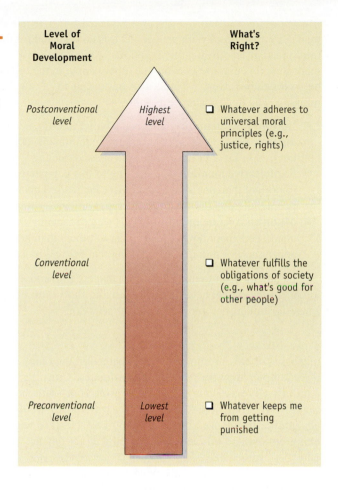

Level of Moral Development | What's Right?

Postconventional level — *Highest level* — ☐ Whatever adheres to universal moral principles (e.g., justice, rights)

Conventional level — ☐ Whatever fulfills the obligations of society (e.g., what's good for other people)

Preconventional level — *Lowest level* — ☐ Whatever keeps me from getting punished

Some Organizational Norms Discourage Ethical Behavior. In organizations, people tend to follow practices that are accepted and recognized by others as appropriate—even if these are questionable. Sometimes, for example, people are expected to remain silent about ethically inappropriate behavior they may have witnessed. This practice of willingly hiding relevant information by being secretive and deceitful, known as **stonewalling**, occurs when organizations punish individuals who are open and honest and reward those who go along with unethical behavior. A classic example may be seen in the case of B.F. Goodrich. In 1968, employees of this company were alleged to have helped secure government safety certification for its aircraft brakes by falsifying and withholding data.[61]

In this case, the *counternorms* of secrecy and deceitfulness were accepted and supported by the organization. **Counternorms** refer to practices that are accepted within an organization although they are contrary to the prevailing ethical standards of society at large. For a summary of some of the most common counternorms found in organizations, see Figure 2.16 (p. 69).[62]

It is interesting to note that sometimes, unethical counternorms are institutionalized, usually quite unintentionally, in the pay systems or formal rules of organizations. Consider, for example, the widespread practice in the long-haul trucking industry of paying drivers by the mile, but for safety reasons, limiting them to working only a certain number of hours per week. To maximize their pay, it is not unusual for drivers to fail to count the time spent while their rigs are being loaded or unloaded. By keeping these hours "off the clock," drivers are working well in excess of the maximum number of hours permitted, leading them to be fatigued, sometimes causing accidents. In this case, the unethical behavior (inaccurately logging working hours)—and the tragic results—although the result of individual decisions, are encouraged by incentives built into the companies' standard practices.

stonewalling

The practice of willingly hiding relevant information by being secretive and deceitful, which occurs when organizations punish individuals who are open and honest and reward those who go along with unethical behavior.

counternorms

Practices that are accepted within an organization despite the fact that they are contrary to the prevailing ethical standards of society at large.

bottom line mentality
The belief that an organization's financial success is the only thing that matters.

exploitative mentality
The belief that one's own immediate interests are more important than concern for others.

Madison Avenue mentality
A way of viewing the world according to which people are more concerned about how things appear to others than how they really are—that is, the appearance of doing the right thing matters more than the actual behavior.

corporate ethics programs
Formal, systematic efforts designed to promote ethics by making people sensitive to potentially unethical behavior and discouraging them from engaging in unethical acts.

code of ethics
A document describing what an organization stands for and the general rules of conduct expected of employees (e.g., to avoid conflicts of interest, to be honest, and so on).

Managerial Values Sometimes Discourage Ethical Behavior. Although most managers are basically ethical people, it is not unusual for them to have developed ways of thinking that lead to unethical actions. And, considering the considerable influence of managers, this may well encourage other people in the organization to engage in unethical behavior themselves.[63] Thus, it is important to be aware of these forms of unethical thinking. The major ones are as follows.[64]

- **Bottom line mentality**. This is the belief that financial success is the only thing that matters. When this line of thinking predominates, ethical considerations tend to be ignored in favor of more financially based ones.
- **Exploitative mentality**. According to this perspective, concern for others is less important than one's own immediate interests. This results in taking advantage of people, thereby promoting stereotypes and undermining empathy and compassion.
- **Madison Avenue mentality**. This way of viewing the world leads people to be more concerned about how things appear to others than how they really are. It is the appearance of doing the right thing that matters more than the actual behavior.

It's not difficult to imagine how managers who endorse these various perspectives tend to undermine ethical behavior. Emphasizing short-term benefits at the expense of people is a sure formula for promoting unethical behavior.

Subordinates Emulate their Managers' Unethical Behavior. Although very few managers openly promote unethical behavior, they may do so unwittingly with respect to the examples they set for their subordinates. Consider, for example, that you ask your administrative assistant to type and print your son's homework assignment during her regular working hours. This sends a clear, albeit unintentional, message that it's acceptable to misuse company resources. Despite what you may say publicly about being ethical and efficient, your unethical actions are likely to speak louder than your ethical words.

Indeed, this is precisely what happens. According to a recent survey, almost four times as many employees observe unethical behavior in workplaces in which managers behave unethically than in workplaces in which managers behave ethically.[65] With this in mind, managers should be advised, as they say, to "walk the talk" with respect to behaving ethically. Managers who fail to behave ethically themselves run the risk of poisoning the ethical climate of their entire work group. In the words of Robert Noyce, the inventor of the silicon chip, "If ethics are poor at the top, that behavior is copied down through the organization."[66]

Using Corporate Ethics Programs to Promote Ethical Behavior

Most companies today, particularly large ones, have in place some sort of formal, systematic mechanisms designed to promote ethics. These efforts, known as **corporate ethics programs**, are designed to create organizational cultures (see Chapter 14) that both make people sensitive to potentially unethical behavior and discourage them from engaging in them.

Components of Corporate Ethics Programs

Typically, corporate ethics programs consist of some combination of the following components: a code of ethics, ethics training, bodies formally responsible for ethics, a mechanism for communicating ethical standards, and the use of ethics audits.[67]

Code of Ethics. A **code of ethics** is a document describing what an organization stands for and the general rules of conduct expected of employees (e.g., to avoid conflicts of interest, to be honest, and so on). Some codes are highly specific, stating, for example, the maximum size of gifts that can be accepted, whereas others are far more general. The vast majority of codes cover all employees, from the lowest-ranking employee to the people at

FIGURE 2.16

Ethical Norms Versus Organizational Counternorms

Although societal standards of ethics dictate the appropriateness of certain actions, counternorms that encourage and support opposite practices sometimes develop within organizations.

Source: Based on suggestions by Jansen & Von Glinow, 1985; see Note 62.

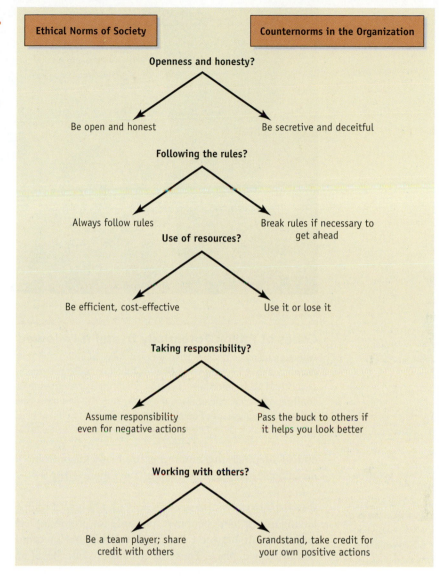

the very top. Although codes differ, there are several things that are commonly addressed by most codes of ethics.[68] These are as follows:

- Responsibilities of employees (e.g., to produce high-quality goods and service, to adhere to the law, and to protect the environment)
- Relationships with people (e.g., to be open, honest, and fair)
- Prohibitions against inappropriate behavior (e.g., conflicts of interest, corruption, and fraud)

Today, about 83 percent of all large U.S.-based companies have codes of ethics in place.[69] One-quarter of these companies, however, don't do anything to ensure that their employees comply with them, leading to the possibility that they are merely "window dressing" (see Figure 2.17).

Ethics Training. Codes of ethics are especially effective when they are used in conjunction with training programs that reinforce the company's ethical values.[70] About 68 percent of companies that have codes of ethics provide any training on the requirements and responsibilities they specify. When conducted, ethics training efforts consist of everything ranging from lectures, videotapes, and case studies to more elaborate simulations. Citicorp, for example, has trained more than 40,000 employees in over 60 countries using an elaborate corporate ethics game, "The Work Ethic," that simulates

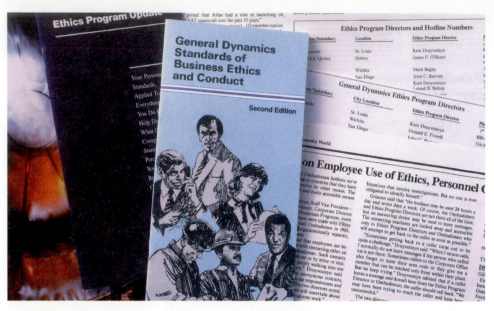

FIGURE 2.17

Codes of Ethics: Potentially Useful if Followed

Although many companies have adopted codes of ethics, too frequently they are ignored—either distributed to employees when hired but then ignored, or hung on the wall for show and not taken seriously. This is unfortunate because ethics codes can provide important guidance to people confronting ethical dilemmas in the workplace. This requires carefully training people in the code and incorporating it as part of an ongoing commitment to ethical behavior in an ethics program.

ethical dilemmas that employees are likely to confront.[71] (For an example of a particularly novel approach to ethics training, see Figure 2.18.[72]

ethics committee

A group composed of senior-level managers from various areas of an organization who assist an organization's CEO in making ethical decisions by developing and evaluating company-wide ethics policies.

Bodies Formally Responsible for Ethics.   Although ethics is everyone's business, having one or more people responsible for promoting ethical behavior helps ensure that it does not fall between the cracks. With this in mind, some companies have **ethics committees** in place. These are groups of senior-level managers from various areas of the organization who assist an organization's CEO in making ethical decisions. Members of the committee develop and evaluate company-wide ethics policies.

FIGURE 2.18

Lights, Camera, Ethics!

As an aid to helping employees become more sensitive to ethical issues, the large defense contractor Lockheed Martin, has adopted a highly creative approach. The company has launched a film festival in which employees create and submit brief films (in any format) demonstrating ways of handling the ethical dilemmas they confront on the job. The best entries are awarded a prize and are used in the company's ongoing ethics training programs.

ethics officer
A high-ranking organizational official (e.g., the general counsel or vice president of ethics) who is expected to provide strategies for ensuring ethical conduct throughout an organization.

As today's companies scramble to comply with the Federal Sentencing Guidelines for Organizations and the Sarbanes-Oxley Act, they are putting people in place who are responsible for managing ethical behavior in the company. Such an individual, known as an **ethics officer**, is a high-ranking organizational official (e.g., the general counsel or vice president of ethics) who is expected to provide strategies for ensuring ethical conduct throughout an organization. Although only 55 percent of companies have an ethics officer in place, this number is growing.[73]

A Mechanism for Communicating Ethical Standards. To be effective, ethics programs must clearly articulate—and reinforce—a company's ethical expectations to employees. Many companies fail to do this, however. In fact, fewer than half of companies with codes of ethics in place communicate with their employees about it as many as three times per year.[74] When this is done, it often takes the form of face-to-face meetings and/or articles in the company newsletter.

ethics hotlines (or helplines)
Special telephone lines that employees can call to ask questions about ethical behavior and to report any ethical misdeeds they may have observed.

To promote communications, growing numbers of companies are putting into place **ethics hotlines** (or **helplines**), special phone lines that employees can call to ask questions about ethical behavior and to report any ethical misdeeds they may have observed. To promote easy access, some companies are even printing the phone number of their company's ethics hotline on the back of each employee's identification card. (For a particularly effective example of this and other practices designed to encourage ethical behavior, see the *Case in Point* section on p. 84.)

ethics audit
The practice of assessing an organization's ethical practices by actively investigating and documenting incidents of dubious ethical value, discussing them in an open and honest fashion, and developing a concrete plan to avoid such actions in the future.

Ethics Audits. Just as companies regularly audit their books to check on irregularities in their finances, they regularly should assess the morality of their employees' behavior so as to identify irregularities in this realm as well. Such assessments are known as **ethics audits**. These require actively investigating and documenting incidents of dubious ethical value, discussing them in an open and honest fashion, and developing a concrete plan to avoid such actions in the future. Conducting an ethics audit can be quite revealing. For some useful guidelines on how to do so, see the *How to Do It* section on page 72.[75]

How Effective Are Corporate Ethics Programs?

By themselves, codes of ethics have only limited effectiveness in regulating ethical behavior in organizations.[76] However, an integrated ethics program that combines a code of ethics with additional components (e.g., an ethics officer, ethics training, etc.) can be quite effective. Specifically, it has been found that compared to companies that don't have ethics programs in place, within those that do, employees: (a) are more likely to report ethical misconduct to company authorities, (b) are considered more accountable for ethics violations, and (c) face less pressure to compromise standards of business conduct.[77] Clearly, the effects of the ethics programs are being felt.

Additional evidence from a recent study shows that an ethics program also may effectively reduce employee theft, a particularly costly form of unethical behavior.[78] This investigation compared the rate of petty theft between two groups of employees who worked for the same financial services company—one whose office had a corporate ethics program in place for the past six months, and one in a distant city that had no ethics program in place. The ethics program consisted of a code of ethics, an ethics committee, and 10 hours of training. Prior to the study, employees were tested to identify their level of cognitive moral development. Some employees were found to be at the preconventional level whereas others were at the conventional level. The workers volunteered to complete a questionnaire sponsored by the company for one hour after work. They were told to expect "fair pay" for this task, but were actually paid considerably less than their standard hourly wage ($2, as opposed to about $10). This motivated the workers to steal from the company in order to get even. In addition, workers were given an opportunity to steal by being allowed to take their own pay from a bowl of pennies in front of them while nobody watched. Because the researcher knew exactly how many pennies were in the bowl beforehand, it could be determined precisely how much money was taken. Amounts in excess of $2 were considered by the researcher to constitute theft.

HOW TO DO IT

Conducting an Ethics Audit: In Search of the "Triple Bottom-Line"

Historically, accountants have been called upon to audit a company's financial records to ensure that its financial picture is accurate. These days, it's becoming increasingly common for companies to assess their officers' and employees' ethical behavior as well. That is, in addition to focusing exclusively on the financial picture, officials also are interested in assuring that their companies are doing well with respect to promoting environmental quality and social justice. With these three foci in mind, companies are said to be looking at not one, but three separate measures of success that also take into account the company's ethical performance. This is known as the **triple bottom-line**.

With an eye toward assessing the environmental and social aspects of corporate performance, growing numbers of companies are taking steps to regularly assess the morality of their employees' behavior so as to identify inappropriate behavior by conducting regular *ethics audits.* These consist of investigating and documenting ethically inappropriate behavior, analyzing them thoroughly to find out why they occurred, and developing a plan to promote more ethical behavior in the future. Specifically, here are six guidelines that you can follow to conduct an ethics audit of your own work group.[79]

1. ***Step 1: Obtain approval.*** Instead of jumping right in, make sure that your own superiors and your company's top executives buy into your plan. It's important to gain assurance that they are not only committed to conducting the audit, but importantly, that they are prepared to deal with whatever it reveals. This step should not be overlooked, no matter how certain you are that the audit should be performed. Simply "nosing around" without permission is sure to land you in trouble, so be sure to get clear approval from the highest levels before proceeding.

2. ***Step 2: Plan and conduct a survey.*** Putting together a team of employees at all levels and from various departments, draft a questionnaire assessing the company's ethical climate and the ethical behavior of its associates. The questions should look at what the company is doing (e.g., feelings about its treatment of employees) as well as current ethical problems (e.g., pressure to cheat customers). Using open-ended questions, the questionnaire also should examine people's ideas about why various unethical acts have occurred and what the company should be doing in the future. Administer this questionnaire broadly throughout the company in a manner that ensures complete anonymity (i.e., no identifying information should be provided).

3. ***Step 3: Investigate company records.*** In addition to what your colleagues tell you, it's also important to look at objective measures. As such, your audit should involve careful analyses of official documents, such as ethical mission statements and codes of ethics. You want to see how clear and thorough they are and what purpose they serve. Are people regularly trained in these standards or do they merely serve as "window dressing"?

4. ***Step 4: Benchmark your results.*** To interpret what your company is doing, it's useful to compare your company's ethical practices to those of other organizations in the same industry. Such information may be obtained from various sources such as the Internet, industry reports, trade publications, and informal information based on your past experiences.

5. ***Step 5: Develop an action plan.*** Now that you have a good sense of what the company is doing and how it may be improved, you should identify concrete steps that can be taken to improve the situation. Be as clear as possible, specifying precisely who will do what and how things will improve as a result. To be effective, your plan must be practical and not overly grandiose. So, don't attempt too much. If you can address the major issues, that's a great beginning.

6. ***Step 6: Prepare a written report.*** You now are ready to draft a thorough report documenting your main findings along with your plans for addressing them. Before presenting this document to all concerned parties, it's a good idea to circulate it among all those who were involved in conducting the ethics audit. After all, you want to ensure that this important report is accurate and thorough before moving forward.

It's important to acknowledge that conducting an ethics audit is a major commitment and that its findings must be taken seriously. Because this process involves "stirring the pot," so to speak, it's not surprising that some companies are reluctant to initiate the process. Those that do, however, stand to benefit from following the steps outlined here.

triple bottom-line
The contemporary notion that in addition to focusing on an organization's financial performance, officials also are interested in assuring that their companies are performing well with respect to promoting environmental quality and social justice.

Did those workers who had a code of ethics in place at their office steal less from the company than those who did not? As shown in Figure 2.19, the answer depended on the workers' level of cognitive moral development. Workers whose office did not have an ethics program in place stole an average of just under 20 cents regardless of their level of cognitive moral development. Likewise, people from offices that had an ethics program stole about the same amount when they were at the preconventional level of moral development. However, hardly any theft occurred at all among workers at the conventional level who worked at an office that had an ethics program in place. In other words, the ethics program was effective in combating employee theft, but only among employees who had attained a sufficiently high level of moral development for the program to have an effect on them. By contrast, among workers at the preconventional level of moral development, the ethics program apparently had little, if any, impact. Given that such individuals are unlikely to fully comprehend and accept their ethics training, this makes perfect sense.

Although the amount of theft examined in this study was small, the underlying conclusion to be drawn is straightforward. A corporate ethics program may have only limited effectiveness because it will influence only some workers—those who have reached a sufficiently high level of moral development. Fortunately, this constitutes about two-thirds of the population as a whole. Reaching the other one-third, those at the preconventional level, may well require other methods, such as emphasizing clear penalties for breaking the rules.

Beyond Ethics: Corporate Social Responsibility

Usually, when we think of business organizations, we focus on their financial responsibilities to stockholders and investors—that is, to make money. Of course, this is not their only responsibility. To quote Henry Ford, "A business that makes nothing but money is a poor kind of business."[80] As we have been discussing all along, organizations also are responsible for obeying the law and answering to yet a higher standard, behaving ethically. In addition to these considerations, many of today's organizations are going beyond their ethical responsibilities by taking proactive steps to help society at large by virtue of their philanthropic (i.e., charitable) contributions.

Together, these four types of responsibilities—economic responsibilities, legal responsibilities, ethical responsibilities, and philanthropic responsibilities—reflect an organization's most fundamental forms of responsibility. Collectively, this is referred to as the **pyramid of corporate social responsibility** (see Figure 2.20).[81] The pyramid metaphor is used to reflect the fact that the most basic form of responsibility—economic responsibility—is at the base of the pyramid. After all, unless a company makes money, it will go out of business, making it impossible to attend to its other responsibilities.

pyramid of corporate social responsibility
The term used to describe an organization's four most basic forms of responsibility, in order from economic responsibility, to legal responsibility, to ethical responsibility, to philanthropic (i.e., charitable) responsibility.

corporate social responsibility
Business practices that adhere to ethical values that comply with legal requirements, that demonstrate respect for individuals, and that promote the betterment of the community at large and the environment.

What Is Corporate Social Responsibility?

The term **corporate social responsibility** typically focuses at the top of the pyramid. It describes business practices that adhere to ethical values that comply with legal requirements, that demonstrate respect for individuals, and that promote the betterment of the community at large and the environment. It involves operating a business in a manner that meets or exceeds the ethical, legal, and public expectations that society has of business. Some examples of highly socially responsible actions from companies around the world are as follows:

- *Alcoa.* Through its charitable foundation, this large aluminum products company has been helping the community by funding programs in violence and injury prevention, providing health care for those who cannot afford it, and improving opportunities for people with disabilities.[82]
- *Chiquita Brands International.* The world's top producer of bananas also is considered a leader in corporate social responsibility. The company has a Corporate Responsibility Officer at the vice president level, avoids using toxic chemicals, and unlike some competitors, refrains from mistreating and underpaying its laborers (see Figure 2.21, p. 76).[83]
- *McDonald's.* So extensive is this restaurant chain's commitment to social responsibility that it publishes a worldwide *Corporate Responsibility Report,* which in 2004 was 88 pages long.[84] Among its many activities, the Ronald McDonald House

FIGURE 2.19

The Effectiveness of an Ethics Program Depends on Cognitive Moral Development: Summary of Research Findings

An experiment compared the amount that employees stole from their company as a function of whether or not their office had an ethics program in place and their level of cognitive moral development. It was found that an ethics program had no appreciable effect on employee theft among workers at the preconventional level but that an ethics program successfully reduced employee theft among workers at the conventional level.

Source: Based on data reported by Greenberg, 2002; see Note 79.

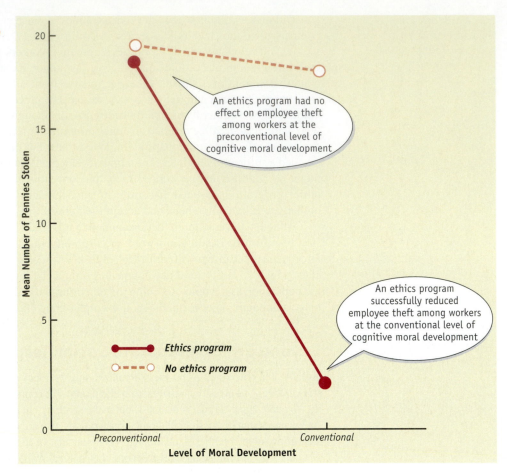

FIGURE 2.20

The Pyramid of Corporate Social Responsibility

To be socially responsible, companies must meet the four different types of responsibilities identified here. The most basic responsibilities, financial, are shown at the bottom because organizations would go out of business if they failed to meet their financial responsibilities.

Source: Based on suggestions by Carroll, 1991; see Note 81.

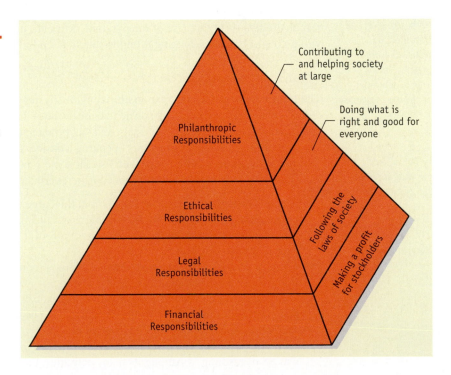

Charities works to improve the health and well-being of children and families around the world. The company also is actively engaged in protecting the environment by recycling and using innovative ways to conserve resources.

- *UPS.* For over 50 years, this large package delivery firm has set up a separate nonprofit company, the UPS Foundation, to help the community. Recently, it has contributed generously to Keep America Beautiful, a volunteer organization dedicated to improving the quality of the physical environment.[85]

It is important to note that corporate social responsibility is not merely a collection of isolated practices or occasional gestures, nor does it involve initiatives motivated by marketing or public relations benefits. Instead, corporate social responsibility is a comprehensive set of policies, practices, and programs that are integrated throughout business operations, and decision-making processes that are supported and rewarded by top management. Importantly, social responsibility involves more than simply making a few charitable donations. It must be a commitment to doing what's best for people and the community—as is the case with the companies spotlighted in these examples. For a particularly good example of this, see Figure 2.21.

In recent years, many of the largest companies in the United States have been going out of their way to behave in a variety of socially responsible ways. For a summary of some of the most socially responsible companies in a recent year, along with just a single noteworthy example of their commitment to social responsibility, see Table 2.5.[86]

Forms of Socially Responsible Behavior

Our examples make it clear that corporate social responsibility takes many different forms.[87] The major ones are as follows.

- *Helping the community by making charitable contributions.* One of the most popular ways for companies to be socially responsible is by making donations back to the communities in which they operate. Such acts are not only helpful and generous, of course, but also stand to be good business practices insofar as helping the community promotes business and helps develop future employees. Cisco Systems, the large computer networking firm, is a good example. Its various grant programs donate money and computer equipment to schools that train underprivileged children. In addition, many organizations provide assistance in various forms when disasters strike, such as the tsunami that devastated parts of southeast Asia and east Africa on December 26, 2004 (for various examples, see Table 2.6, p. 78).[88]
- *Preserving the environment.* Many companies, particularly those that derive products from natural resources, are involved actively in efforts to preserve the natural environment. As one example, the large paper and building products company Boise Cascade has ceased harvesting timber from old-growth forests and endangered forests. Likewise, the large oil company Royal Dutch Shell preserves the environment by refraining from mining or drilling for oil in regions with special biological or cultural significance.
- *Socially responsible investing.* Another popular form of being socially responsible involves being highly selective in making investments. Typically, this involves making investments in companies that promote the well-being of society and refraining from investing in companies that may do harm. A good example is the Co-operative Bank located in the United Kingdom. This firm has gone out of its way to keep from investing its money in companies that engage in such socially irresponsible practices as financing weapons, the fur trade, and companies involved in animal testing. Although some individuals might not share these values, the bank has chosen to act in ways that reflect the values of its leaders.
- *Promoting the welfare of employees.* One of the most fundamental ways of being socially responsible is by promoting the welfare of a company's own employees. Several companies have gone out of their way to avoid abusive labor practices even if they prevail in the industry. As an illustration, the Brazilian cosmetics firm Natura Cosmeticos shows its support for human rights by not using child labor. It also gives generously to educational programs and encourages its employees to do volunteer work for nonprofit organizations.

FIGURE 2.21

A "Top Banana" in Social Responsibility

Chiquita Brands International is not only the world's top producer of bananas, but it is also considered a leader in corporate social responsibility. The company's commitment to social responsibility has been institutionalized into its management structure, such as by having a Corporate Responsibility Officer at the vice-president level. Chiquita also is committed to preserving the environment by avoiding the use of toxic chemicals and by carefully controlling soil and water pollution. And, in an industry in which many employees are mistreated and underpaid, Chiquita treats its employees well. It is not surprising that the company has won several awards in recognition of its commitment to social responsibility.

Do not be misled by these examples. Being socially responsible involves more than just a few isolated generous practices or occasional kind gestures. Moreover, it is not motivated by an interest in promoting a company's marketing or public relations efforts. It is far more integrative in nature and genuine in intent. Instead, corporate social responsibility is a comprehensive set of policies, practices, and programs that are integrated throughout business operations, and decision-making processes that are supported and rewarded by top management. (For an example of such an approach, see the *Case in Point* section on page 84.)

Profitability and Social Responsibility: The Virtuous Circle

Do socially responsible companies perform better financially than those that are less socially responsible? The answer is—generally, yes. Recently, a group of researchers examined this question by systematically examining 52 different studies conducted over 30 years that compared corporate social responsibility with corporate financial performance.[89] Despite the fact that different researchers measure social responsibility and financial performance in different ways, it was found that these variables were positively correlated with one another (see Appendix 1). This finding is consistent with other observations. For example, in the four decades from 1950 to 1990, such highly socially responsible companies as Johnson & Johnson, Coca-Cola, Gerber, IBM, Deere, Xerox, J.C. Penney, and Pitney Bowes grew at an annual rate of 11.3 percent compared to only 6.2 percent for other companies on the Dow Jones Industrials list over the same period.[90] Likewise, there is considerable evidence showing that companies that are more actively involved in preserving the environment also tend to be more profitable.[91]

Although there are surely many different reasons for this, a key one, which we also mentioned in connection with ethics, is that people often support the socially responsible activities of organizations with their patronage and investments. With this in mind, there exist mutual funds that invest only in socially responsible companies (such as Calvert, identified in the *OB*

TABLE 2.5 Top 10 Most Socially Responsible Companies in the U.S.: 2000–2005

A research firm recently analyzed the level of corporate social responsibility among the largest companies in the United States for the first half of the 2000s. Basing their analysis on such key considerations as the companies' contributions to the community, attention to employees' needs, preservation of the environment, and advancement of minorities and women, the top 10 performers are listed here. As indicated, these companies excelled in different ways.

Rank	Company	Notable Socially Responsible Action
1	Fannie Mae	Created a Native American Conventional Lending Initiative to help finance $75 million in loans on trust land for the Navajo Nation of Arizona, Oneida Nation of New York, and Menominee of Wisconsin.
2	Procter & Gamble	Helped UNICEF fund tuberculosis vaccinations for 8 million children in developing countries.
3	Intel	On-the-job safety is emphasized so strongly that the accident rate among employees is 96% lower than the industry average.
4	St. Paul Companies	An active volunteer program gets employees involved in tutoring in schools, helping the cleanup after natural disasters, and helping the homeless.
5	Deere & Co.	Decided to forgo selling prime real estate to a developer; instead donated $1.5 million in land and facilities to Western Illinois University, allowing it to better serve the community, including Deere's employees.
6	Avon Products	Raised $250 million in support of breast cancer research, education, and screening for medically underserved women.
7	Hewlett-Packard	Built a worldwide network of employee volunteers to develop ways to help the company to sustain the environment.
8	Ecolab	Quick to develop creative new products for unexpected modern hazards, such as a fungicide to clean up anthrax spores and another new product to combat SARS at the Toronto Airport.
9	IBM	Donated $71 million in grants to help schools and $127 million in programs to help needy people around the world.
10	Herman Miller	Funded the start-up of the United States Green Building Council, a nonprofit organization dedicated to understanding and promoting sound environmental building practices.

Sources: Based on information reported by *Business Ethics Magazine,* 2006, see Note 86; and the Web sites of the companies listed.

in a Diverse World section, p. 79), and books that provide detailed information on the socially responsible (and irresponsible) behavior of companies that consumers and investors can use to guide their decisions.[92] Today, individuals who desire to support socially responsible companies by "voting with their dollars" can find it easy to get the information they need. That this may contribute to the financial well-being of a company is important, of course, since financial considerations are an organization's most basic responsibility (which is why they are at the base of the corporate social responsibility pyramid shown in Figure 2.20, p. 74). That said, it is important to keep in mind that most companies that engage in socially responsible behavior do so for its own sake, and not as a path to profitability.

Although profit may not be the primary objective for engaging in socially responsible behavior, it is clear that there is a strong link between the two. Moreover, this connection appears to be bidirectional in nature. The idea is straightforward: Companies that

TABLE 2.6 A Flood of Corporate Aid to Tsunami Victims

Many different companies demonstrated their commitment to corporate social responsibility by making generous donations of money, materials, and services to aid the relief of victims. A small sampling of examples is shown here.

Form of Assistance	Company	Description of Assistance
Online solicitations	Amazon.com	Links on its Web site took visitors to the site of the International Federation of the Red Cross, where over $4 million in relief aid was donated in the first few days after the disaster.
	eBay	Sellers participating in the "Giving Works" program are able to donate from 10% to 100% of their proceeds to one of eight charities that aid victims.
Matching funds	TimeWarner	In addition to its own donations, the company matched its employees' donations up to $1,000 each (up to $500,000) to relief groups.
	Starbucks	For each pound of Sumatra coffee sold in January 2004, the company donated $2 to various charities providing relief to victims' families.
Products and services	Coca-Cola; PepsiCo	Each of these soft drink giants provided generous amounts of drinking water and soft drinks to people in devastated areas.
	Johnson & Johnson; Pfizer	These firms donated millions of dollars worth of medicine and medical supplies to agencies helping thousands of injured people.
	Northwest Airlines	Cargo transportation services were provided to enable supplies to reach people in need of them.
	FedEx	Shipped 200,000 pounds of medical supplies to hospitals.
Cash	Wal-Mart Stores	Donated $2 million to the Red Cross earmarked to aid tsunami relief efforts.
	Exxon Mobil	Gave $5 million to relief efforts and also has a matching program for employees.

Sources: CNNMoney; see Note 88.

virtuous circle
The tendency for companies that are successful financially to invest in social causes because they can afford to do so (i.e., they "do good by doing well") and for socially responsible companies to perform well financially (i.e., they "do well by doing good").

are successful financially invest in social causes because they can afford to do so (i.e., they "do good by doing well") and socially responsible companies tend to perform well financially (i.e., they "do well by doing good"). This relationship, which has been referred to as the **virtuous circle**, is summarized in Figure 2.22.[93]

With the virtuous circle in mind, it is not surprising to find that some of the world's most profitable organizations are also among the most philanthropic. Two particular examples are noteworthy. In 2006 Exxon Mobil headed the Fortune 500 list of most profitable companies. This enormous company also was among the most actively involved in corporate giving. In 2003 alone, it donated over $100 million to worldwide causes, half of which went to higher education and to community and civic groups.[94] By donating $26.5 million to higher education, it's clear that the company is promoting good will. That this results in increased profits is a distinct possibility. As this occurs, it becomes possible for Exxon Mobil to make still more generous charitable contributions. In this manner, the virtuous cycle continues.

As another example, the highly profitable Microsoft Corporation regularly makes multimillion-dollar charitable contributions to worthwhile causes in the form of cash and software. In addition, a generous $24 million donation from its co-founder Bill Gates has made it possible for more good work to be accomplished around the world through the Bill and Melinda Gates Foundation. Although many big companies have been accused of exploiting people and harming society, examples like these make it clear that there is also another side to the story—and a very munificent and socially responsible one, at that.[95]

FIGURE 2.22

The Virtuous Circle

It has been suggested that socially responsible companies perform well financially because they are supported by customers and investors. As a result, they become wealthier, making it easier for them to become even more philanthropic. This is known as the virtuous circle.

Source: Based on suggestions by Trevino & Nelson, 1999; see Note 92.

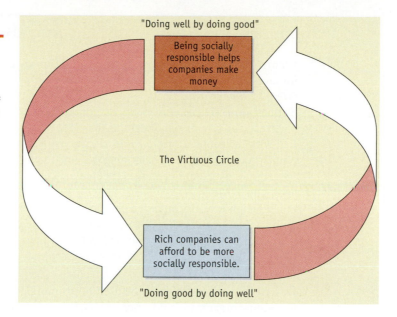

"Doing well by doing good"

Being socially responsible helps companies make money

The Virtuous Circle

Rich companies can afford to be more socially responsible.

"Doing good by doing well"

OB In a Diverse World

Starbucks and Dell Actively Advance the Interests of Women

Although there's nothing particularly special about seeing a woman use a Dell notebook computer while sipping coffee at Starbucks, these two companies recently have done something very special to help that woman. They were the first global corporations to endorse the Calvert Women's Principles, the first global code of conduct designed to empower and advance the interests of women throughout the world.[96] Developed in 2004 by Calvert, the large family of mutual funds investing in socially responsible companies, the Principles are the first code of conduct to focus exclusively on women's rights. As described by Noeleen Heyzer, executive director of the United Nations Development Fund for Women, the Principles are "a concrete set of indicators for tracking the progress of gender justice in the corporate community."[97]

By endorsing the Women's Principles, Dell and Starbucks are committing themselves to promoting proactively the interests of women in all their business practices. Specifically, these guidelines promote the interests of women in seven major ways.

1. Publicly disclosing the things they do to promote gender equality among employees.
2. Paying the legal wage to all women, giving men and women equal pay for equal work. This also includes failing to consider a woman's reproductive status as a basis for personnel decisions.

3. Protecting women against dangers of violence in the workplace, both physical and psychological.
4. Forbidding business activities or community practices that may exploit women in any way.
5. Being proactive in recruiting and appointing women to high-level company positions.
6. Promoting access to educational opportunities for women, such as those involving literacy, professional development, and the enhancement of vocational skills.
7. Publicly respecting the rights of women in advertising and promotion and ensuring that vendors and suppliers adhere to these principles as well.

While Dell and Starbucks go about their business, Calvert will be carefully monitoring their compliance with these Principles. The investment firm also hopes to pick up more major adopters of its Principles in the years ahead.

Getting companies to endorse these Principles goes beyond being socially responsible. It also makes good business sense. Calvert's CEO Barbara Krumsiek put it well when she said, "No nation can achieve its full economic and human potential if half of its population remains marginalized and disempowered, and no corporation can meet the demands of sustainable development while ignoring the untapped potential of women."[98] We suspect that officials from Dell and Starbucks are thinking much the same.

Summary and Review of Learning Objectives

1. **Identify four different forms of organizational justice and the organizational impact of each.**

   Organizational justice, people's perceptions of fairness in organizations, takes four distinct forms. *Distributive justice* refers to the perceived fairness of rewards (e.g., pay) received. People who feel they have received fair amounts of reward feel satisfied with their jobs. *Procedural justice* refers to people's perceptions of the fairness of the procedures used to determine the outcomes they receive. When high levels of procedural justice are perceived, people are inclined to follow organizational rules and policies. *Interpersonal justice* refers to the fairness of interpersonal treatment by others. High levels of interpersonal justice are related to high levels of satisfaction with one's supervisor. Finally, *informational justice* refers to people's perceptions of the fairness of the information used as the basis for making a decision. People tend to be highly valued by organizations in which they perceive high levels of informational justice.

2. **Describe strategies that can be used to promote organizational justice.**

   Promoting organizational justice can be done in several ways. First, it is important to pay workers what they deserve—the "going rate" for the work done wherever they work. Underpaying workers promotes dissatisfaction, leading to turnover. Second, workers should be given a voice—that is, some input into decisions. This may involve such strategies as holding regular meetings, conducting employee surveys, keeping an "open door policy," and using suggestion systems. Third, follow openly fair procedures. Specifically, promote procedural fairness, such as by using unbiased, accurate information and applying decision rules consistently. Managers also should openly describe the fair procedures they are using. Fourth, managers should explain decisions thoroughly in a manner demonstrating dignity and respect. Fifth, workers should be trained to be fair, such as by adhering to the principles described in this chapter.

3. **Explain what is meant by ethical behavior and why organizations should be concerned about ethics.**

   Whereas *moral values* are people's fundamental beliefs regarding what is right and wrong, *ethics* refers to standards of conduct that guide people's decisions and behavior. Organizations are concerned about promoting ethical behavior in organizations. Behaving ethically is highly desirable for two important reasons. First, good ethics is good business. In various ways, organizations in which ethical behavior prevails tend to be more successful than those marked by low levels of ethics. Second, behaving ethically is consistent with many legal requirements—most notably, the Federal Sentencing Guidelines for Organizations and the Sarbanes-Oxley Act.

4. **Explain ways of behaving ethically when conducting business internationally.**

   Behaving ethically when conducting international business is challenging because different norms of ethics apply in different cultures. Managers should resist the temptation to engage in *ethical relativism* by blindly adopting whatever ethical norms prevail in a certain country, and *ethical imperialism* by insisting on applying their own country's ethical standards wherever they do business. Instead, it is preferable to adopt a stance between these two extremes. This involves following the following guiding principles of global ethics: (1) show respect for core human values, (2) demonstrate sensitivity to local traditions, and (3) recognize that context matters when distinguishing between right and wrong.

5. **Describe the individual and situational factors responsible for unethical behavior in organizations and methods for minimizing such behavior.**

   People behave ethically or unethically due to a combination of individual and situational factors. A key individual factor is the individual's level of *cognitive moral development.* According to Kohlberg's theory of cognitive level of moral development, over time people develop the capacity to make moral judgments. The more highly developed this capacity, the more likely people are to engage in ethical behavior. However, situational factors also dictate behavior. For example, some organizational norms (e.g., stonewalling) discourage ethical behavior, managerial values sometimes discourage ethical behavior, and subordinates emulate their manager's unethical acts. Unethical behavior may be minimized by corporate ethics programs that use codes of ethics, ethics training, have bodies formally responsible for ethics, have a mechanism for communicating ethical standards, and use ethics audits.

6. **Explain what is meant by corporate social responsibility, the forms it takes, and the nature of the relationship between responsible behavior and financial profitability.**

   Corporate social responsibility refers to business practices that adhere to ethical values, that comply with legal requirements, and that promote the betterment of individuals and the community at large. Its most popular forms include making charitable contributions to the community, preserving the environment, investing in a socially responsible manner, and promoting the welfare of employees. Generally, research shows that socially responsible companies tend to be more profitable than companies that are less socially responsible. This reflects the *virtuous circle,* the tendency for successful companies to be socially responsible because they can afford to do so, which in turn, helps their chances of being even more financially successful.

Points to Ponder

Questions for Review

1. What is organizational justice, and how are its four different types different from one another?
2. What specific things can managers do to help promote perceptions of fairness in their organizations?
3. What is the difference between ethics and moral values, and why should managers be concerned about promoting ethical behavior?
4. What special ethical challenges are created by doing business internationally?
5. What are the components of an ethics program, and how effective are such programs at promoting ethical behavior?
6. What is meant by corporate social responsibility, and why should organizations be concerned about being socially responsible?

Experiential Questions

1. Think about a time in which you were a victim of organizational injustice. What specific types of justice were violated? How did you feel, and how did you react? What could have been done to avoid these injustices?
2. What do you believe are the major ethical challenges faced by the employees of the company in which you work? What might be done to make people in your company behave more ethically?
3. How socially responsible is the company in which you work? What particular things does it do to enhance the community, the lives of its employees, and/or the environment? What else might it do to be more socially responsible?

Questions to Analyze

1. The people in a company believe that they are being unfairly treated. What forms might this take? Why is this problematic? What can be done to overcome this situation?
2. The people in your company are behaving unethically, making you feel uncomfortable. What might be responsible for this situation, and what might be done to overcome it?
3. A company desires to become more socially responsible. What particular things might it do to achieve this objective, and what benefits might be expected to result from these actions?

Experiencing OB

Individual Exercise

Assessing Organizational Justice Where You Work

To learn about how workers respond to various types of injustices they may experience in the workplace, scientists have found it useful to use rating scales like the one shown. By completing this scale, you will gain some useful insight into your own feelings about the fairness experienced in the organization in which you work.

Directions

1. Using the following scale, respond to each of the questionnaire items by selecting a number from 1 to 5 to indicate the extent to which it applies to you.
   1 = almost never
   2 = slightly
   3 = moderately
   4 = greatly
   5 = almost always
2. In responding to each item, think about a particular organization in which you work—or, if you are a student, think about a particular class.
3. Where you see the word "(outcome)," substitute a specific outcome that is relevant to you (e.g., for a worker, pay; for a student, a grade).
4. Where you see the word "(superior)," substitute a specific authority figure that is relevant to you (e.g., for a worker, one's supervisor; for a student, one's teacher).

Scale

To what extent . . .

1. _____ Is it possible for you to express your views about your (outcome)?
2. _____ Are your (outcomes) generally based on accurate information?
3. _____ Do you have an opportunity to correct decisions made about your (outcome)?
4. _____ Are you rewarded appropriately for the effort you put into your work?
5. _____ Do the (outcomes) you receive reflect the quality of your work?
6. _____ Is your (outcome) in keeping with your performance?
7. _____ Are you treated politely by your (superior)?
8. _____ Does your (superior) treat you with dignity and respect?
9. _____ Does your (superior) refrain from making inappropriate comments?
10. _____ Does your (superior) communicate openly with you?
11. _____ Does your (superior) tell you things in a timely fashion?
12. _____ Does your (superior) explain decisions to you in a thorough fashion?

Source: Adapted from Colquitt, 2001; see Note 5.

Scoring Procedure and Interpretation

1. Add your responses to questions 1, 2, and 3. This is your *distributive justice* score.
2. Add your responses to questions 4, 5, and 6. This is your *procedural justice* score.
3. Add your responses to questions 7, 8, and 9. This is your *interpersonal justice* score.
4. Add your responses to questions 10, 11, and 12. This is your *informational justice* score.
5. For each score, higher numbers (e.g., 12–15) reflect higher perceived amounts of the type of fairness in question, whereas lower scores (e.g., 3–6) reflect lower perceived amounts of that type of fairness.

Discussion Questions

1. With respect to what particular type of fairness did you score highest? What specific experiences contributed to this assessment?
2. With respect to what particular type of fairness did you score lowest? What specific experiences contributed to this assessment?
3. What kinds of problems resulted from any violations of any type of organizational justice you may have experienced? What could have been done to avoid these violations?

Group Exercise

Taking Credit for Another Person's Ideas: Analyzing an Ethical Dilemma

More often than you might imagine, managers confront situations in which they have to decide the right thing to do. Such "ethical dilemmas," as they are known, are usually quite challenging. Discussing ethical dilemmas with others is often a useful way of shedding light on the ethical path by identifying ethical considerations that you may have overlooked on your own. This exercise will give you an opportunity to analyze an ethical dilemma.

Directions

1. Divide the class into multiple groups of three or four students.
2. Read the following ethical dilemma.
3. Working together with the others in your group, analyze the dilemma by answering the following questions:
   a. As the person in this situation, what do you think you would do? What factors enter into your decision?
   b. What do you think would be the *right thing* to do? Explain the basis for your answer.

Ethical Dilemma

You are a mechanical engineer working on developing new products for a large company. Your product-development team is composed of specialists in different fields from throughout the organization. Everyone shares ideas freely with one another, and the team as a whole shares credit for its accomplishments. At, least, you think so. One day you learn that the team leader, an older gentleman who resents having to work with others, has been bad-mouthing several members of the team. Worse yet, he's also been taking credit for their ideas. Once, you even overheard him say, "Those guys can't do anything without me. I'm really the brains behind the operation. That idea for the new packaging design was all mine, but I let them take credit for it." Although you are not the direct victim of this assault—at least on this occasion—you are concerned about the effects on your team's morale and performance. You also fear that one day, it might be your ideas for which he is taking credit. You know this is wrong, but you don't know how best to handle the situation.

Discussion Questions

1. Did the members of your group generally agree or disagree about what they would do in the situation described? What new viewpoints, if any, did you learn from others in your group?
2. Did the members of your group generally agree or disagree about what they thought was the right thing to do? What were the major points of agreement and disagreement?
3. Have you or members of your group ever been in similar situations? If so, how were they handled? From your own experiences and the experiences of others, what did you learn about handling an ethical dilemma of this nature?

Practicing OB

Employee Theft in Convenience Stores

The district manager of a chain of 24-hour convenience stores is very concerned about her stores' rate of employee theft, which is currently about twice the industry average and rising rapidly. Because this problem has arisen suddenly, you and she suspect that it is a response to some recently introduced changes in the company's overtime policy. Managers who used to be paid time-and-a-half for each hour they worked over 40 are now paid a flat salary that typically results in lower total wages for the same amount of work. Answer the following questions based on the information in this chapter.

1. What form of justice appears to have been violated by the new pay policy? Explain your answer.
2. In this case, the new pay policy was implemented without first discussing it with store managers. Do you think that the theft rate might have been lower had this been done? What else could be done to reduce the growing theft rate?
3. The company's code of ethics expressly prohibits theft, but other than being handed a copy along with other company documents and forms upon being hired, hardly anyone pays attention to it. What do you think could be done, if anything, to enhance the effectiveness of the code of ethics as a weapon for combating the theft problem?

CASE IN POINT

Exelon Excels at Managing Ethics

In 2000, Exelon was formed by the merger of two electric utility companies, Unicom and PECO Energy. The creation of a new company provided an opportunity for an emphasis on ethics to be built into the company's structure from the ground floor. It was with this in mind that Eliecer Palacios, who was ethics and compliance director at Unicom at the time of the merger and who is now director of ethics and compliance at Exelon, got actively involved in the process of integrating the two companies. Palacios believed that this was important insofar as large utilities face ethical challenges along several fronts, such as stock trading practices (e.g., avoiding insider trading), protection of the environment (e.g., avoiding air and water pollution), procurement (e.g., avoiding bribes and kickbacks), and following fair labor practices (e.g., avoiding harassment and discrimination). And, given that the energy industry is deregulated, customers have the opportunity to express their dissatisfaction with any ethical missteps by taking their business elsewhere. To avoid any ethical scandals, Palacios built in several safeguards to ensure that Exelon would remain "squeaky clean."

At the heart of the company's ethics initiatives is a 16-person Ethics and Compliance Committee. One of the key things this body does is review Exelon's code of ethics on a quarterly basis. Members, consisting of vice presidents and lower level employees from throughout the company as well as several attorneys, carefully review the extent to which the company is meeting its legal and ethical obligations. Is it obeying the law? Is it meeting its obligations to shareholders, employees, and the environment? Among the specific things on which the committee focuses are the company's efforts at training its tens of thousands of employees on proper ethical behavior. Like other big companies, Exelon has a code of ethics, but unlike many, it is actively involved in ensuring that its employees both understand and follow it. With this in mind, Exelon employees are required to complete an intensive ethics training program using the company's intranet. On an annual basis, employees are required to be certified as having completed the training. Also unlike many companies, ethics training at Exelon involves more than only the lowest level employees. Instead, everyone from entry-level employees to the CEO is required to be trained and recertified annually.

In addition to its training efforts, Exelon maintains an active "helpline" that employees can call to lodge complaints about seemingly unethical behavior or to make inquiries about how to avoid unethical behavior. The helpline, staffed by Palacios and an assistant, receives about 300 calls per year. Most of these involve inquiries about behavior that is considered ethically appropriate (e.g., accepting gifts from a contractor valued at over $25 is considered inappropriate).

Calls about allegations of waste, fraud, and abuse, although only about 10% to 15% of all received, also occur. All allegations are carefully investigated, and to ensure that these efforts are effective, the company strictly enforces a nonretaliation policy.

At its Web site, Exelon lists among its core values, "commitment in operating facilities safely, protecting the environment, and developing our businesses responsibly." From the ethics initiatives reported here, it's clear that the company is going out of its way to translate these values into everyday practice.

Questions for Discussion

1. What are the key things Exelon does to promote ethics?
2. What do you believe are the limitations of these tactics?
3. Which of the things Exelon does do you believe would work and would not work in the company in which you work? Why?

VIDEO CASES

No Smoking Employees

Howard Weyers, a health nut in his personal life, runs a health-care benefits company. One day, he decided that his employees at Weyco also should be healthy. With this in mind, he gave all the smokers at the company 15 months to quit smoking. He offered to pay for all the smoking cessation treatments, but anyone who still was smoking at the end of the 15 months would be terminated. Some employees claim that he violated their rights.

Discussion Questions

1. What are some of the organizational/situational variables that led Mr. Weyers to make this decision?
2. In your opinion, are Mr. Weyers's actions ethical? Was it acceptable for him to get involved in the personal behavior of his employees?
3. What could Mr. Weyers have done to ensure the privacy rights of his employees while also maintaining the best interests of the company?

Nepotism

For most people, the word *nepotism* has negative connotations. Mobsters like television's Tony Soprano practice nepotism. Adam Bellow, author of *In Praise of Nepotism,* discusses how nepotism often is a good thing.

Discussion Questions

1. Based on the information presented in the video, do you agree with Mr. Bellow that nepotism is a good thing? Explain your answer.
2. Is nepotism a form of unethical behavior? Why or why not?
3. Discuss the extent to which the practice of nepotism constitutes a violation of each of the following forms of justice: (a) distributive justice, (b) procedural justice, and (c) interactional justice. Explain your answers.

Micro "Soft" on Gay Rights?

Historically, Microsoft has been very supportive of employees of varied sexual orientations. The company had to answer to many different stakeholders, however, when faced with the decision about whether or not to support a bill in the Washington State Senate outlawing discrimination against gays. Forced to choose between succumbing to pressure from conservative groups and supporting its gay employees and customers, the software giant was in a difficult position.

Discussion Questions

1. Who are the different stakeholders involved in Microsoft's policy with respect to this issue? How, in particular, is each likely to be affected by the company's decision?
2. What social obligations does Microsoft have in this case? Does the firm have an obligation to consider the sexual preferences of all its employees? What benefits, if any, are likely to result from being sensitive to this issue?
3. How do distributive justice, procedural justice, and interactional justice enter into this situation? According to each perspective, what would be the fair thing to do?

PERCEPTION AND LEARNING: UNDERSTANDING AND ADAPTING TO THE WORK ENVIRONMENT

Chapter Outline

Social Perception and Social Identity: Understanding Others and Ourselves

The Attribution Process: Judging the Causes of Others' Behavior

Perceptual Biases: Systematic Errors in Perceiving Others

Stereotyping: Fitting People into Categories

Perceiving Others: Organizational Applications

Learning: Adapting to the World Around Us

Training: Learning and Developing Job Skills

Organizational Practices Involving the Use of Reward and Punishment

Special Sections

OB **Making Sense Out of Common Sense**

A Creative Approach to Avoiding Stereotyping

OB **In a Diverse World**

Performance Evaluations: Comparing the United States and Japan

How to Do It

Using 360-Degree Feedback: Three Success Stories

After reading this chapter, you should be able to:

1. Distinguish between the concepts of social perception and social identity.
2. Explain how the attribution process works and describe the various sources of bias in social perception.
3. Understand how the process of social perception operates in the context of performance appraisals, employment interviews, and the cultivation of corporate images.
4. Define learning and describe the two types most applicable to OB: operant conditioning and observational learning.
5. Describe how principles of learning are involved in organizational training and innovative reward systems.
6. Compare the way organizations use reward in organizational behavior management programs and how they can use punishment most effectively when administering discipline.

■ PREVIEW CASE

Keeping the Enterprise Growing

In 1957, Jack Taylor, the sales manager of a Cadillac dealership in St. Louis, had an intriguing idea: Instead of selling cars outright, it might be more profitable to rent them repeatedly on a short-term basis. Enterprise Rent-A-Car was born. Rather than competing with industry giants Hertz and Avis, who targeted business travelers by offering rentals at airports, Taylor aimed Enterprise toward a different market—individuals seeking temporary replacements for their damaged or stolen cars. From this modest start, Enterprise Rent-A-Car has grown into a company with more than 57,000 employees in 6,800 offices (within 15 minutes of 90 percent of the U.S. population). And, with over 800,000 vehicles in operation it is the largest car rental company in North America.

As the business was growing, Taylor's son, Andy, helped his father by working in rental branches, assisting customers, washing cars, doing whatever was needed. Picking up all he could about the business, Andy Taylor worked his way up the ladder and now is chairman and CEO. Under his leadership, Enterprise quickly became a multibillion-dollar company (revenue of about $9 billion in 2006) that expanded into Europe (the United Kingdom, Germany, and Ireland) and developed spin-off businesses (e.g., corporate fleet services and truck rental).

To help ensure success, Taylor works tirelessly, acknowledging that "It doesn't matter how smart or talented you are if you are not willing to put in the work for future success." To ensure that employees do, he put a plan into place that rewards them for their performance. From the assistant manager level upward, Enterprise employees are paid a salary plus a percentage of their branch's profits. As a result, they benefit directly from their hard work and those of their teammates with whom they work closely.

Taylor acknowledges that the business experience he got on the job was invaluable, saying, "Through my early experiences at Enterprise I was able to see firsthand the importance of customer service and employee development." So that today's employees can benefit from the same types of experiences, Enterprise promotes people from within the company. In fact almost all of the company's senior managers started out staffing rental offices and worked their way up the corporate ladder as management trainees. In fact, Taylor believes that advancing in Enterprise's training program is like picking up your MBA on the job—"an MBA without the IOU," as he puts it.

Andy Taylor emphasizes that Enterprise's success comes not from an overarching focus on profit, but the fundamental belief that he and his father share—that profit follows naturally when you put people first. Indeed, making Enterprise a pleasant place for people to do business is the company's objective. One way Taylor does this is by visiting local offices to keep his finger on the pulse of the business—and to not pass up any opportunities to share his beliefs about the importance of keeping customers satisfied. He also puts people first by giving back to the community by making generous donations (both personal and corporate) to local charity groups, such as the United Way. As Taylor put it, "It will be very satisfying if people say that, no matter how big our company got, we always stayed true to our goals of putting people first and always doing the right thing."

Based on recent indications, this is being recognized by others: In 2006, Enterprise was named as the best rental car company (by Market Mettix) and the rental car company ranked highest in customer satisfaction (by J. D. Power and Associates), and in 2007 it was featured as offering the best entry-level jobs (in *Princeton Review*). If there is any merit to these accolades, it's safe to say that Mr. Taylor's approach to business appears to be paying off.

Clearly, Enterprise Rent-A-Car represents a major business success. We believe that OB plays a big part in this for two reasons. First, it's clear that Andy Taylor learned a great deal about what it took to succeed by observing his father. And *learning,* as you might imagine, is a vital process when it comes to performing effectively on the job, whether it's at the very top, as in this case, or learning lower-level skills. Second, Mr. Taylor demonstrated a keen sensitivity to his employees, recognizing how they felt and how they wished to be treated. At the same time, he also was concerned about the way other people perceived him and the company, a key element of the process known as *social perception.*

Because social perception and learning are so fundamental to the way people behave in organizations, we devote this chapter to describing these topics in detail. Specifically, we begin by discussing the various processes that are responsible for social perception, and discuss the specific ways they operate in organizations. Then, we move on to the topic of learning. Here too, we cover both the basic principles that are responsible for successful learning, followed by specific applications of these principles on the job. After reading this chapter, you will come away with a good understanding of some of the basic psychological processes that occur not only at Enterprise, but in all organizations on an ongoing basis.

Social Perception and Social Identity: Understanding Others and Ourselves

Obviously, when it comes to forming opinions about people, there is a subtle, yet powerful, process going on—a process by which people come to judge and understand the people and things with which they come into contact. This process, known as *social perception,* will be described here. Then, after focusing on how we come to make judgments of others, we will examine the other side of the coin—namely, how we come to develop identities of ourselves. As you read about these phenomena, you will learn about processes that are so basic that you probably never thought about them before. As you will see, a great deal of insight can be derived by making explicit these important processes that we generally take for granted.

Social Perception: What Are Others Like?

Suppose you meet your new boss. You know her general reputation as a manager, you see the way she looks, hear the words she says, and read the memos she writes. In no time at all, you're trying to figure her out. Will she be easy to work with? Will she like you? Will she do a good job for the company? On the basis of whatever information you have available to you, even if it's very little, you will try to understand her and how you will be affected by her (see Figure 3.1). Put differently, you will attempt to combine the various things you learn about her into a meaningful picture. This process is known as **social perception**—the process of combining, integrating, and interpreting information about others to gain an accurate understanding of them.

social perception
The process of combining, integrating, and interpreting information about others to gain an accurate understanding of them.

FIGURE 3.1

Meeting New People: An Opportunity for Social Perception

Meeting new people presents many opportunities to combine, integrate, and interpret a great deal of information about them—the process of social perception.

The social perception process is so automatic that we are almost never aware that it's happening. Yet it goes on all the time in organizations. Indeed, other people—whether they're bosses, coworkers, subordinates, family, or friends—can have profound effects on us. To understand the people around us—to figure out who they are and why they do what they do—may be very helpful. After all, you wouldn't want to ask your boss for a raise when you believe he or she is in a bad mood! Clearly, social perception is very important in organizations, which is why we examine it so carefully in this chapter.[1]

Specifically, we explore various aspects of the social perception process in the sections that follow. To begin, we describe the **attribution** process—that is, the way people come to judge the underlying causes of others' behavior. Then we will note various imperfections of this process, errors and sources of bias that contribute to inaccurate judgments of others—as well as ways of overcoming them. Finally, we will highlight specific ways in which the attribution process is used in organizations. Before getting to this, however, we first turn attention to an even more basic matter—coming to understand who we are, ourselves.

Social Identity: Who Are You?

How would you answer if someone asked, "Who are you?" There are many things you could say. For example, you could focus on individual characteristics, such as your appearance, your personality, and your special skills and interests—that is, your **personal identity**. You also could answer in terms of the various groups to which you belong, saying, for example, that you are a student in a particular organizational behavior class, an employee of a certain company, or a citizen of a certain country—that is, your **social identity**. The conceptualization known as **social identity theory** recognizes that the way we perceive others and ourselves is based on both our unique characteristics (i.e., personal identity) and our membership in various groups (i.e., social identity).[2] For an overview of this approach, see Figure 3.2.

Social identity theory claims that the way we identify ourselves is likely to be based on our uniqueness in a group. Say, for example, that you are the only business major in an English class. In this situation, you will be likely to identify yourself as "the business major," and so too will others come to recognize you as such. In other words, that will become your identity in this particular situation. Because we belong to many groups, we are likely to have several unique aspects of ourselves to use as the basis for establishing our identities (e.g., you may be the only left-handed person, the only one to have graduated

attribution
The process through which individuals attempt to determine the causes behind others' behavior.

personal identity
The characteristics that define a particular individual.

social identity
Who a person is, as defined in terms of his or her membership in various social groups.

social identity theory
A conceptualization recognizing that the way we perceive others and ourselves is based on both our unique characteristics (see *personal identity*) and our membership in various groups (see *social identity*).

FIGURE 3.2

Social Identity Theory: An Overview

According to *social identity theory,* people identify themselves in terms of their individual characteristics and their own group memberships. They then compare themselves to other individuals and groups to help define who they are, both to themselves and others.

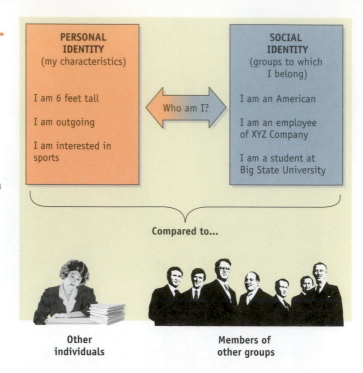

college, or even the only one to have sung in a rock band). How do we know which particular bases for defining our personal identities people will choose?

Given the natural desire to perceive ourselves positively and to get others to see us positively as well, we are likely to identify ourselves with groups we believe to be perceived positively by others. We know, for example, that people in highly regarded professions, such as doctors, are more inclined to identify themselves with their professions than those who have lower-status jobs.[3] Likewise, people tend to identify themselves with winning sports teams by wearing the colors and logos of those teams. In fact, the tendency to wear clothing that identifies oneself as a fan of a certain team depends on how successful that team has been: The better a team has performed, the more likely its fans are to sport apparel that publicly identifies them with that team.[4]

In addition to explaining how we perceive ourselves, social identity theory also explains how we come to perceive others. Specifically, the theory explains that we focus on the differences between ourselves and other individuals as well as members of other groups (see the lower portion of Figure 3.2). In so doing, we tend to simplify things by assuming that people in different groups share certain qualities that make them different from us—even if they really are not so different after all.

Not only do we perceive others as different from ourselves, but different in negative ways. This is particularly so when we are competing against them (see Chapter 11). Take athletic competitions, for example. If you ever have heard the negative things that students from one college or university say about those from other schools that they are competing against in various sports, then you know this phenomenon quite well. Although such perceptions tend to be exaggerations—and inaccurate, as a result—most of us stick with these perceptions, nevertheless. The reason why is simple. Making such categorizations helps bring order to the world. After all, distinguishing between "the good guys" and "the bad guys" makes otherwise complex judgments quite simple. And, after all, bringing simplicity to a complex world is what social perception is all about.

The Attribution Process: Judging the Causes of Others' Behavior

A question we often ask about others is "why?" Why did Tonya not return my call? Why did John goof up the order? Why did the company president make the policy she did? When we ask such questions, we are attempting to get at two different types of information: (1) What is someone really like? (that is, what traits and characteristics does he or she possess?) and (2) what made the person behave as he or she did? (that is, what accounted for his or her actions?). As we will see, people attempt to answer these questions in different ways.[5]

Making Correspondent Inferences: Using Acts to Judge Dispositions

Situations frequently arise in organizations in which we want to know what someone is like. Is your opponent a tough negotiator? Are your coworkers prone to be punctual? The more you know about what people are like, the better equipped you are to know what to expect and how to deal with them. How, precisely, do we go about identifying another's traits?

Generally speaking, the answer is that we learn about others by observing their behavior and then inferring their traits from this information. The judgments we make about what someone is like based on what we have observed about him or her are known as **correspondent inferences**.[6] Simply put, correspondent inferences are judgments about people's dispositions, their traits and characteristics that correspond to what we have observed of their actions (see Figure 3.3).

correspondent inferences
Judgments about people's dispositions, their traits and characteristics, that correspond to what we have observed of their actions.

Challenges In Judging Others Accurately. At first blush, it would appear to be a simple matter to infer what people are like based on their behavior. A person with a disorganized desk may be perceived as being sloppy. Someone who slips on the shop floor may be considered clumsy. Such judgments might be accurate, but not necessarily! After all, the messy desk actually may be the result of a coworker rummaging through it to find an important report. Similarly, the person who slipped could have encountered oily conditions under which anyone, even the least clumsy individual, would have fallen. In other words, it is important to recognize that the judgments we make about someone may be inaccurate because there are many possible causes of his or her behavior. Someone's underlying characteristics certainly may play a large role in determining what they do, but as we will explain in the next section, it also is possible for behavior to be shaped by external forces. (In our examples, these external factors would be the coworker's actions and the slippery floor.) For this reason, correspondent inferences may not always be accurate.

Correspondent inferences also might not be accurate because people on the job tend to conceal some of their traits—especially those likely to be viewed as negative. So, for example, a sloppy individual may work hard in public to appear to be organized. Likewise, the unprincipled person may talk a good show about the importance of being ethical. In other words, people often do their best to disguise some of their basic traits. In summary, because behavior is complex and has many different causes, and because people sometimes purposely disguise their true characteristics, forming correspondent inferences is a risky business.

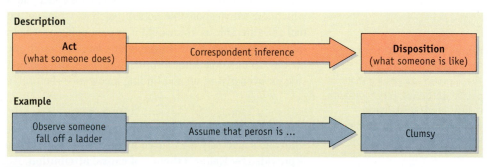

FIGURE 3.3

Correspondent Inferences: Judging Dispositions Based on Behavior

One of the ways in which we come to judge what others are like is by making inferences about them that follow from what we have observed of their behavior. Such judgments, known as *correspondent inferences,* are frequently misleading. How might the inference summarized here be inaccurate?

Making Accurate Inferences About Others. Despite such difficulties, we can use several techniques to help make more accurate correspondent inferences.

First, we can focus on others' behavior in situations in which they do not *have to* behave in a pleasant or socially acceptable manner. For example, anyone would behave in a courteous manner toward the president of the company, so when people do so, we don't learn too much about them. However, only those who are *really* courteous would be expected to behave politely toward someone of much lower rank—that is, someone toward whom they don't have to behave politely. In other words, someone who is polite toward the company president, but condescending toward a secretary is probably really arrogant. The way people behave in situations in which a certain behavior is not clearly expected of them may reveal a great deal about their basic traits and motives.

Similarly, we can learn a great deal about someone by focusing on behavior for which there appears to be only a single logical explanation. For example, imagine finding out that your friend accepts a new job. Upon questioning him, you learn that the position is very high paying, involves interesting work, and is in a desirable location. What have you learned about what's important to your friend? Not too much. After all, any of these are good reasons to consider taking a position. Now, imagine finding out that the work is very demanding and that the job is in an undesirable location, but that it pays very well. In this case, you're more prone to learn something about your friend—namely, that he highly values money. Clearly, the opportunity to make accurate correspondent inferences about people is far greater in situations in which there is only one plausible explanation for their behavior.

Causal Attribution of Responsibility: Answering the Question "Why?"

Imagine finding out that your boss just fired one of your fellow employees. Naturally, you'd ask yourself, "Why did he do that?" Was it because your coworker violated the company's code of conduct? Or was it because the boss is a cruel and heartless person? These two answers to the question "why?" represent two major classes of explanations for the causes of someone's behavior:

internal causes of behavior
Explanations based on actions for which the individual is responsible.

external causes of behavior
Explanations based on situations over which the individual has no control.

- **Internal causes of behavior**—explanations based on actions for which the individual is responsible
- **External causes of behavior**—explanations based on situations over which the individual has no control

In our example, the internal cause would be the person's violation of the rules, and the external cause would be the boss's cruel and arbitrary behavior.

Generally speaking, it is very important to be able to determine whether an internal or an external cause was responsible for someone's behavior. Knowing why something happened to someone else might better help you prepare for what might happen to you. For example, in this case, if you believe that your colleague was fired because of something for which she was responsible herself, such as violating a company rule, then you might not feel as vulnerable as you would if you thought she was fired because of the arbitrary, spiteful nature of your boss. In the later case, you might decide to take some precautionary actions, to do something to protect yourself from your boss, such as staying on his good side, or even giving up and finding a new job—before you are forced to do so.

Kelley's theory of causal attribution
The approach suggesting that people will believe others' actions to be caused by internal or external factors based on three types of information: *consensus, consistency,* and *distinctiveness.*

Kelley's Theory of Causal Attribution. When it comes to social perception, the question of interest to social scientists is: How do people go about judging whether someone's actions were caused by internal or external causes? An answer to this question is provided by **Kelley's theory of causal attribution**. According to this conceptualization, we base our judgments of internal and external causality on observations we make with respect to three types of information.[7] These are as follows:

consensus
In *Kelley's theory of causal attribution,* information regarding the extent to which other people behave in the same manner as the person we're judging.

- **Consensus**—the extent to which other people behave in the same manner as the person we're judging. If others do behave similarly, consensus is considered high; if they do not, consensus is considered low.

consistency
In *Kelley's theory of causal attribution,* information regarding the extent to which the person we're judging acts the same way at other times.

distinctiveness
In *Kelley's theory of causal attribution,* information regarding the extent to which a person behaves in the same manner in other contexts.

- **Consistency**—the extent to which the person we're judging acts the same way at other times. If the person does act the same at other times, consistency is high; if he or she does not, then consistency is low.
- **Distinctiveness**—the extent to which a person behaves in the same manner in other contexts. If he or she behaves the same way in other situations, distinctiveness is low; if he or she behaves differently, distinctiveness is high.

According to the theory, after collecting this information, we combine what we have learned to make our attributions of causality. Here's how. If we learn that other people act like this one (consensus is high), this person behaves in the same manner at other times (consistency is high), and that this person does not act in the same manner in other situations (distinctiveness is high), we are likely to conclude that this person's behavior stemmed from *external* causes. In contrast, imagine learning that other people do not act like this one (consensus is low), this person behaves in the same manner at other times (consistency is high), and that this person acts in the same manner in other situations (distinctiveness is low). In this case, we would conclude that this person's behavior stemmed from *internal* causes.

An Example. Because this explanation is highly abstract, let's consider an example that helps illustrate how the process works. Imagine that you're at a business lunch with several of your company's sales representatives when the sales manager makes some critical remarks about the restaurant's food and service. Further imagine that no one else in your party acts this way (consensus is low), you have heard her say the same things during other visits to the restaurant (consistency is high), and that you have seen her acting critically in other settings, such as the regional sales meeting (distinctiveness is low). What would you conclude in this situation? Probably that she is a "picky" person, someone who is difficult to please. In other words, her behavior stems from internal causes.

Now, imagine the same setting, but with different observations. Suppose that several other members of your group also complain about the restaurant (consensus is high), that you have seen this person complain in the same restaurant at other times (consistency is high), but that you have never seen her complain about anything else before (distinctiveness is high). By contrast, in this case, you probably would conclude that the restaurant really *is* inferior. In this case, the sales manager's behavior stems from external causes. For a summary of these contrasting conclusions, and an example, see Figure 3.4.

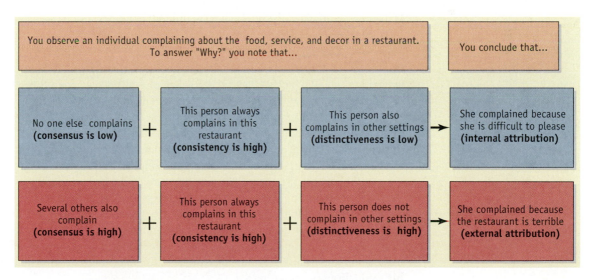

FIGURE 3.4

Kelley's Theory of Causal Attribution: A Summary
In determining whether others' behavior stems mainly from internal or external causes, we focus on the three types of information illustrated here.

Perceptual Biases: Systematic Errors in Perceiving Others

Computers may analyze information in an accurate, unbiased, tireless fashion, but the same cannot be said about human beings. We are far from perfect when it comes to gathering information about others and then making judgments about them. In fact, it is more likely to be the rule than the exception that our judgments of others will be imperfect. After all, we are not exactly unbiased in the judgments we make. As you might imagine, this can lead to serious problems for individuals and the organizations in which they work. In this section, we explore this state of affairs in some detail.

Researchers have noted that there are several systematic biases that interfere with making completely accurate judgments of others. These reflect systematic biases in the ways we think about others in general. Collectively, these biases are referred to as **perceptual biases**. We consider several such biases in this section of the chapter.

The Fundamental Attribution Error

Despite what Kelley's theory may imply, people are *not* equally predisposed to reach judgments regarding internal and external causality. Rather, they are more likely to explain others' actions in terms of internal causes rather than external causes. In other words, we are prone to assume that others' behavior is due to the way they are, their traits and dispositions (e.g., "she's just that kind of person"). So, for example, we are more likely to assume that someone who shows up for work late does so because she is lazy rather than because she got caught in traffic. This perceptual bias is so strong that it has been referred to as the **fundamental attribution error**.[8]

This particular bias stems from the fact that it is far simpler to explain someone's actions in terms of his or her traits than to recognize the complex pattern of situational factors that may have affected their actions. As you might imagine, this tendency can be quite damaging in organizations. Specifically, it leads us to prematurely assume that people are responsible for the negative things that happen to them (e.g., "he wrecked the company car because he is careless"), without considering external alternatives, ones that may be less damning (e.g., "another driver hit the car"). And this can lead to inaccurate judgments about people.

The Halo Effect: Keeping Perceptions Consistent

Have you ever heard someone say something like, "She's very smart, so she also must be hard-working"? Or, "He's not too bright, so I guess he's lazy"? If so, then you are already aware of a common perceptual bias known as the **halo effect**.[9] Once we form a positive impression of someone, we tend to view the things that person does in favorable terms—even things about which we have no knowledge. Similarly, a generally negative impression of someone is likely to be associated with negative evaluations of that person's behavior. Both of these tendencies are referred to as halo effects (even the negative case, despite the fact that the word "halo" has positive connotations).

In organizations, the halo effect often occurs when superiors rate subordinates using a formal performance appraisal form. In this context (which we will describe more fully later in this chapter), a manager evaluating one of his or her employees highly on some dimensions may assume that an individual who is so good at this particular thing also must be good at other things. The manager would then be likely to evaluate that person highly on other dimensions (see Figure 3.5). Put differently, the halo effect may be responsible for finding high correlations between the ratings given to people on various dimensions. When this occurs, the resulting evaluations are lacking in accuracy, and the quality of the resulting evaluations is compromised.

The halo effect applies not only to individuals, but to work teams as well (a topic we will discuss in Chapter 8). Consider, for example, the way we tend to bias our perceptions of the teams for which we root as sports fans. Because we desire to see our team in a favorable light, we attribute positive characteristics to it when it wins ("This is the greatest team

perceptual biases

Predispositions that people have to misperceive others in various ways. Types include the *fundamental attribution error,* the *halo effect,* the *similar-to-me-effect, first-impression error,* and *selective perception.*

fundamental attribution error

The tendency to attribute others' actions to internal causes (e.g., their traits) while largely ignoring external factors that also may have influenced behavior.

halo effect

The tendency for our overall impressions of others to affect objective evaluations of their specific traits; perceiving high correlations between characteristics that may be unrelated.

FIGURE 3.5

The Halo Effect: A Demonstration

One manifestation of the halo effect is the tendency for people rating others to give either consistently high ratings (if the individual is generally perceived in a positive manner), or low ratings (if the individual is generally perceived in a negative manner). Because each rating dimension is not considered independently, inaccurate evaluations may result.

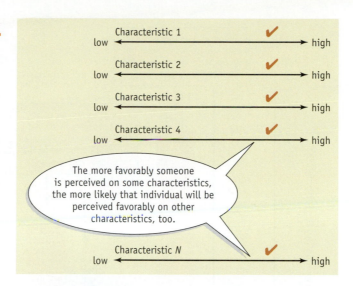

team halo effect

The tendency for people to credit teams for their successes but not to hold them accountable for their failures.

similar-to-me effect

The tendency for people to perceive in a positive light others who are believed to be similar to themselves in any of several different ways.

selective perception

The tendency to focus on some aspects of the environment while ignoring others.

ever"). However, if our team loses, we tend to blame the loss on the mistakes or poor performance of one particular player ("The team is still good, but that one player ruined it for us"). This is known as the **team halo effect**—the tendency for people to credit teams for their successes but not to hold them accountable for their failures.

The team halo effect has been demonstrated clearly in a recent study.[10] In this investigation researchers asked college students to recall either a successful team experience or an unsuccessful team experience in which they had participated. They were then asked to complete a questionnaire indicating the extent to which they attributed that outcome to either the team as a whole or to the performance of a particular individual. The results, summarized in Figure 3.6, support the existence of the team halo effect. Specifically, whereas the team as a whole was believed to be much more responsible for good performance than for poor performance, specific team members were believed to be only slightly more responsible for good performance than for poor performance. In fact, participants attributed poor team performance more to certain individuals on the team than to the teams as a whole.

The Similar-to-Me Effect: "If You're Like Me, You Must Be Pretty Good"

Another common type of perceptual bias involves the tendency for people to perceive more favorably others who are like themselves than those who are dissimilar. This tendency, known as the **similar-to-me effect**, constitutes a potential source of bias when it comes to judging other people. In fact, research has shown that when superiors rate their subordinates, the more similar the parties are, the higher the rating the superior tends to give.[11] This tendency applies with respect to several different dimensions of similarity, such as similarity of work values and habits, similarity of beliefs about the way things should be at work, and similarity with respect to demographic variables (such as age, race, gender, and work experience).

This effect appears to be partly the result of the tendency for people to be able to empathize and relate better to similar others and to be more lenient toward them. However, it also appears that subordinates tend to be more trusting and confident in supervisors whom they perceive as similar to themselves than those perceived as dissimilar.[12] As a result, they may have a more positive relationship with such individuals, and this may lead superiors to judge similar subordinates more favorably.

Selective Perception: Focusing on Some Things While Ignoring Others

Another perceptual bias, known as **selective perception**, refers to the tendency for individuals to focus on certain aspects of the environment while ignoring others.[13] Insofar as we operate in complex environments in which there are many stimuli that demand our attention, it makes sense that we tend to be selective, narrowing our perceptual fields.

FIGURE 3.6

Evidence for the Team Halo Effect

According to the team halo effect, people tend to recognize teams more for their successes than for their failures. This effect was demonstrated in an experiment showing that people held teams much more responsible for good performance than for poor performance whereas individual team members were considered only slightly more responsible for good performance than for poor performance.

Source: Based on data reported by Naquin & Tynan, 2003; see Note 10.

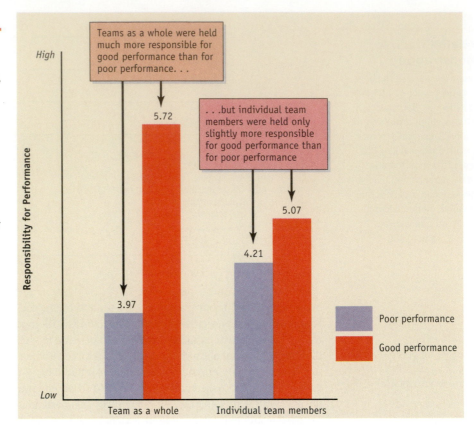

This constitutes a bias insofar as it limits our attention to some stimuli while heightening our attention to other stimuli.

As you might imagine, this process occurs in organizations. In fact, research has shown that top executives asked to indicate the functions of their organizations that contribute most strongly to its effectiveness tend to cite functional areas that matched their backgrounds.[14] For example, executives whose backgrounds were in sales and marketing perceived changes in a company's line of products and services as being most important. Similarly, those who worked previously in research and development focused more on product designs than on other issues in their perceptions of the business environment. In other words, executives tend to be affected by selective perception. That is, they give greatest attention to those aspects of the business environment that match their background experiences. Keeping this tendency in mind, it is easy to understand why different people may perceive the same situations very differently.

First-Impression Error: Confirming One's Expectations

Often, the way we judge someone is not based solely on how well that person performs now, but rather, our initial judgments of that individual—that is, our *first impressions.* To the extent that our initial impressions guide our subsequent impressions, we have been victimized by **first-impression error**.

first-impression error
The tendency to base our judgments of others on our earlier impressions of them.

As you might imagine, this error can be especially problematic in organizations, where accurately judging others' performance is a crucial managerial task. When a subordinate's performance has improved, that needs to be recognized, but to the extent that current evaluations are based on poor first impressions, recognizing such improvement is impossible. Likewise, inaccurate assessments of performance will result when initially good performers leave positive impressions that linger on even when confronted with evidence suggesting that one's performance has dropped (for a summary, see Figure 3.7).

Research suggests that the first-impression error may take very subtle forms.[15] For example, in one study, corporate interviewers evaluated prospective job applicants by viewing the application blanks and test scores of prospective employees. The more highly

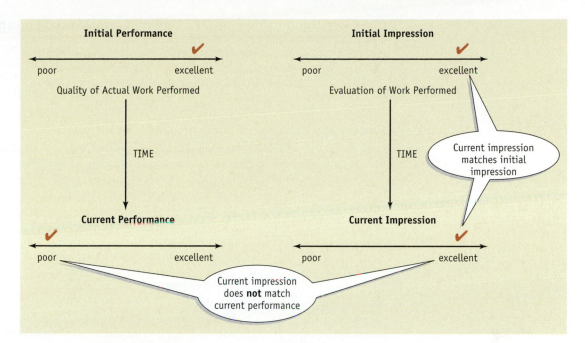

FIGURE 3.7

First-Impression Error: A Summary

When a first-impression error is made the way we evaluate someone is more highly influenced by our initial impressions of that person than by his or her current performance. In this example, someone who was initially perceived as performing well continues to be rated highly despite a downturn in performance.

interviewers judged the applicants based on these two criteria alone, the more positively the applicants were treated during the interview process. In fact, candidates who made initially positive impressions were treated more positively during the interview (e.g., they were spoken to in a more pleasant interpersonal style). Thus, instead of using the interviews to gather additional unbiased information, as you would expect (and hope!), the recruiters studied appeared to use the interviews simply to confirm the first impressions they had already developed on the basis of the test scores and application blanks. This study provides clear evidence of the first-impression error in action.

Because the perceptual errors we've discussed thus far can lead to poor judgment on the job, it's important to consider some ways of overcoming them. For some suggestions in this regard, see the suggestions summarized in Table 3.1. Although some of these guidelines may be difficult to follow, they can help the many forms of perceptual errors we've discussed thus far. As such, the effort required to put them into practice promises to be well worthwhile.

Self-Fulfilling Prophecies: The Pygmalion Effect and the Golem Effect

self-fulfilling prophecy
The tendency for someone's expectations about another to cause that person to behave in a manner consistent with those expectations. This can be either positive (see the *Pygmalion effect*) or negative (see the *Golem effect*) in nature.

Pygmalion effect
A positive instance of the *self-fulfilling prophecy*, in which people holding high expectations of another tend to improve that individual's performance.

In case it already isn't apparent just how important perceptions are in the workplace, consider the fact that the way we perceive others actually can dictate how effectively people will work. Put differently, perceptions can influence reality! This is the idea behind what is known as the **self-fulfilling prophecy**—the tendency for someone's expectations about another to cause that individual to behave in a manner consistent with those expectations.

Self-fulfilling prophecies can take both positive and negative forms. In the positive case, holding high expectations of another tends to improve that individual's performance. This is known as the **Pygmalion effect**. This effect was demonstrated in a study of Israeli soldiers who were taking a combat command course.[16] The four instructors who taught the course were told that certain trainees had high potential for success, whereas the others had either normal potential or an unknown amount of potential. In reality, the trainees identified as belonging to each of these categories were assigned to that condition at random.

TABLE 3.1 Suggestions for Overcoming Bias in Social Perception

Biases in social perception are inevitable. Fortunately, however, there are things we can do to reduce their impact. Here are several guidelines to follow to help you perceive others more accurately in the workplace. We realize that many of these tactics are far easier to say than to do. However, to the extent that we conscientiously try to apply these suggestions to our everyday interactions with others in the workplace, we stand a good chance of perceiving people more accurately.

Suggestion	Explanation
Do not overlook the external causes of others' behavior.	The fundamental attribution error leads us to discount the possibility that people's poor performance may be due to conditions beyond their control. To combat this, ask yourself if anyone else might have performed just as poorly under the same conditions. If the answer is yes, then you should not automatically assume that the poor performer is to blame.
Evaluate people based on objective factors.	The more objective the information you use to judge others, the less your judgments will be subjected to perceptual distortion. So, whenever possible, judge work performance more on quantifiable measures of quantity (e.g., sales volume) and quality (e.g., error rate) than on personal judgments.
Avoid making rash judgments.	It is human nature to jump to conclusions about people, but when you can, take the time to get to know people better before judging them. What you learn may make a big difference in your opinion.

Golem effect

A negative instance of the *self-fulfilling prophecy,* in which people holding low expectations of another tend to lower that individual's performance.

Despite this, trainees who were believed to have high potential were found at the end of the training session to be more successful (e.g., they had higher test scores). This demonstrates the Pygmalion effect: Instructors who expected their trainees to do well found that the trainees actually did so.

Researchers also have found that the self-fulfilling prophecy works in the negative direction—that is, low expectations of success lead to poor performance. This is known as the **Golem effect.** Illustrating the Golem effect, researchers have found that paratroopers whose instructors expected them to perform poorly in their training class did, in fact, perform worse than those about whom instructors had no advance expectations.[17] Clearly, this effect can be quite devastating, but fortunately, it can be overcome.

A recent study compared the performance of female military recruits enrolled in a special training program for Israeli soldiers whose limited schooling and mental test scores put them at risk for success in the military.[18] Platoon leaders in the experimental group were told, "You will be training recruits whose average ability is significantly higher than usual for special recruits" and that "you can expect better than average achievement from the recruits in your platoon." Leaders of the control group were not given any such information, and their recruits showed the Golem effect. However, no such effect was found in the experimental group, suggesting that even those who are expected to perform poorly can be kept from doing so by being led to believe that success is possible.

Why do self-fulfilling prophecies occur, both the Pygmalion effect and the Golem effect? Research into the underlying processes responsible for self-fulfilling prophecies suggest that both types of self-fulfilling prophecies operate according to the four steps summarized in Figure 3.8.[19]

The lesson to be learned from research on self-fulfilling prophecies is very clear: Managers should take concrete steps to promote the Pygmalion effect and to discourage the Golem effect. When leaders display enthusiasm toward people and express optimism about each person's potential, such positive expectations become contagious and spread throughout the organization. As a case in point, consider the great enthusiasm and support that Gordon Bethune showed toward employees of Continental Airlines in 1995 when he took over as that bankrupt company's CEO.[20] It would have been easy for him to be unsupportive and to show his disappointment with the workforce, but he did just the opposite.

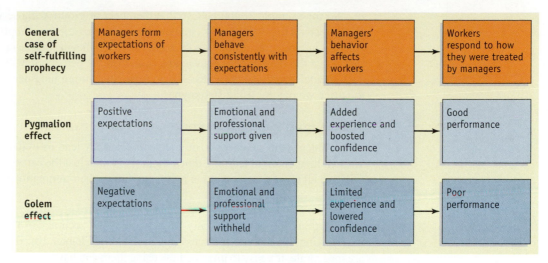

FIGURE 3.8

The Self-Fulfilling Prophecy: A Summary

The processes underlying the self-fulfilling prophecy are summarized here. As indicated, it may produce positive effects (known as the *Pygmalion effect*) or negative effects (known as the *Golem effect*).

Only a few years after Bethune was at the helm, the airline turned around to become one of the most successful carriers in the sky today. Although the changes he made to the airline's systems and equipment helped, these things alone would not have been enough if the employees felt like failures. Indeed, Bethune's acceptance and enthusiasm toward members of Continental's workforce contributed greatly to giving the encouragement needed to bring the airline "from worst to first."

Stereotyping: Fitting People into Categories

What comes to mind when you think about people who wear glasses? Are they studious? Eggheads? Although there is no evidence of such a connection, it is interesting to note that for many people, such an image lingers in their minds. Of course, this is only one example. You can probably think of many other commonly held beliefs about the characteristics of people belonging to specific groups. Such statements usually take the form: "People from group *X* possess characteristic *Y*." In most cases, the characteristics described tend to be negative. Assumptions of this type are referred to as **stereotypes**—beliefs that members of specific groups tend to share similar traits and behaviors.

Deep down inside many of us know, of course, that not all people belonging to a specific group possess the negative characteristics with which we associate them. In other words, most of us accept that the stereotypes we use are at least partially inaccurate. After all, not *all X*'s are *Y;* there are exceptions (maybe even quite a few!). If so, then why are stereotypes so prevalent? Why do we use them?

Why Do We Rely on Stereotypes?

To a great extent the answer resides in the fact that people tend to do as little cognitive work as possible when it comes to thinking about others.[21] That is, we tend to rely on mental shortcuts. If assigning people to groups allows us to assume that we know what they are like and how they may act, then we can save the tedious work of learning about them as individuals. After all, we come into contact with so many people that it's impractical, if not impossible, to learn everything about them we need to know. So, we rely on readily available information—such as someone's age, race, gender, or job type—as the basis for organizing our perceptions in a coherent way. It's simply efficient to do so.

stereotype
A belief that all members of specific groups share similar traits and are prone to behave the same way.

So for example, if you believe that members of group *X* (those who wear glasses, for example) tend to possess trait *Y* (studiousness, in this case), then simply observing that someone falls into category *X* becomes the basis for your believing that he or she possesses *Y*. To the extent that the stereotype applies in this case, then the perception will be accurate. However, such mental shorthand often leads us to make inaccurate judgments about people. This is the price we pay for using stereotypes.

The Dangers of Using Stereotypes in Organizations

The problem with stereotypes, of course, is that they lead us to judge people prematurely, without the benefit of learning more about them than just the categories into which they fit. Still, we all rely on stereotypes at least sometimes; their temptation is far too great to resist.

Negative Organizational Impact: Inaccurate Information.

As you might imagine, organizational decisions can only be as good as the accuracy of the information that goes into making them (we will discuss this in detail in Chapter 10). Because stereotypes often are inaccurate, it's easy to imagine how using them can have detrimental effects on the kinds of judgments people make in organizations. For example, if a human resources officer believes that members of certain groups are lazy, then she purposely may avoid hiring or promoting individuals who belong to those groups. That officer may firmly believe that she is using good judgment—gathering all the necessary information and listening to the candidate carefully. Still, without being aware of it, the stereotypes she holds may influence the way she judges certain individuals. If the individual in question would have been a good hire, the company loses out—and of course, so too does the individual.

The result, of course, is that the fate of the individual in question is sealed in advance—not necessarily because of anything he or she may have done or said, but by the mere fact that he or she belongs to a certain group. In other words, even people who might not intend to act in a bigoted fashion still may be influenced by the stereotypes they hold.

Negative Individual Impact: Stereotype Threats.

It is important to note that stereotypes don't influence only how people are perceived and treated by those who hold stereotypes, but also how members of stereotyped groups act as a result. Consider, for example, how people tend to live up to—or more properly, "down to"—the negative stereotypes that people hold about them. In an important study, African Americans and whites took a verbal ability test.[22] Consistent with the stereotype that they are intellectually inferior (although actually false), the African Americans performed more poorly than the whites. But, this occurred *only* when the test was described as a measure of intelligence. In other words, the African Americans conformed to the stereotype. Importantly, however, when the same test was given to a comparable group of African Americans and whites, but was described in ways that suggested nothing about intelligence, both groups performed equally well.

This idea—that stereotypes constrain behavior when a member of a stereotyped group is placed in a situation in which poor performance can be taken as an indication of the group's deficiency—is the basis of what is known as a *stereotype threat*.[23] Specifically, a **stereotype threat** is the uncomfortable feeling that people have when they run the risk of fulfilling a negative stereotype associated with a group to which they belong. Apparently, individuals facing situations in which they run the risk of substantiating a negative stereotype become so fearful of performing poorly in that situation that their performance actually suffers, making it possible for them to be taken as evidence of the very stereotype that they hoped to disprove (for a summary, see Figure 3.9).

Stereotype threats apply not only to African Americans, but to any group whose members are subjected to stereotypes—which, potentially, is anyone.[24] In one study, for example, a stereotype threat was created in a group of white male students by telling them that the research in which they were participating was designed to determine why Asian students perform better than Caucasians on tests of mathematical ability.[25] It was found that these participants performed significantly more poorly than a comparable group of white men who were not told anything about the reason for the test (i.e., a control group in which

stereotype threat
The uncomfortable feeling that people have when they run the risk of fulfilling a negative stereotype associated with a group to which they belong.

FIGURE 3.9

Stereotype Threat: An Overview

When members of a negatively stereotyped group are in a situation in which poor performance can be taken as an indication of their group's deficiency, they tend to substantiate the stereotype by performing poorly. The uncomfortable feeling experienced in this situation is known as a *stereotype threat*. Everyone is subject to experiencing stereotype threats.

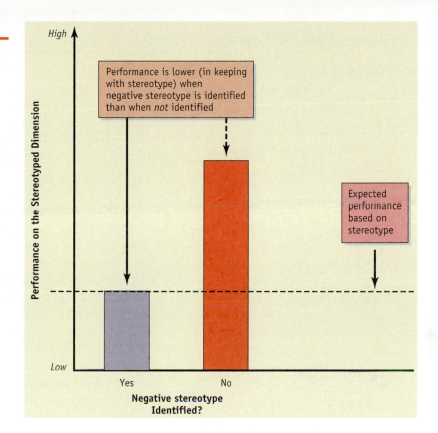

no stereotype threat was triggered). Here again, concern about substantiating the negative stereotype lowered task performance. Stereotype threats represent a key process by which stereotypes can exact stiff tolls on their victims.

In some cases, the negative effects of stereotyping go beyond hurt feelings, lowered performance and lost opportunities. Stereotyping also can be very costly to its victims financially. A study by the National Bureau of Economic Research conducted over a 10-year period found that white women who were overweight by an average of 65 pounds earned hourly wages that were, on average, 7 percent lower than wages of their nonoverweight counterparts.[26] As the scientists noted, that's like losing the pay boost that would have been earned by a year of education or three years of work experience. Interestingly, both overweight and nonoverweight women held the same kinds of jobs and had the same levels of experience, suggesting that the lower pay of obese women reflects society's negative stereotypes toward them. It's fascinating to note that the same effects of weight on pay were *not* found among African American women. Although there may be several possible explanations for this racial difference, greater acceptance of different body types and fewer negative stereotypes about obese women among African Americans appears to be a key factor.

It's important to acknowledge that the effects of stereotyping others are not always as profound. Referring to accountants as "bean counters" and professors as "absent minded" are observations that also reflect stereotypes—ones that appear to be only mildly negative. Still, it must be cautioned that holding stereotypes of people in various groups run the risks of promoting unfair discrimination (Chapter 6), causing miscommunication (Chapter 9), and generating interpersonal conflict (Chapter 11). Given the problems associated with stereotyping, it is important to consider ways of combating it. For a look into this issue, see the *OB: Making Sense Out of Common Sense* section on page 104.

Perceiving Others: Organizational Applications

Thus far, we have identified some of the basic processes of social perception and have alluded to ways in which they are involved in organizational behavior. Now, in this section,

OB Making Sense Out of Common Sense

A Creative Approach to Avoiding Stereotyping

As you know from experience, it's hard to refrain from stereotyping. It comes to us automatically and we do it unintentionally. If you have an image of a particular group in mind, you will be inclined to conjure it up whenever you encounter a member of that group. Accordingly, it would appear that stereotyping others is something about which we really cannot do too much.

Research has shown, however, that stereotyping might not be as inevitable as you think.[27] What, then, can be done to put the brakes on the stereotyping process? For one, this can occur when people are motivated to keep from stereotyping (e.g., because doing so threatens their images of themselves). In other words, those who really don't want to engage in stereotyping can keep themselves from doing so. More precisely, they can keep themselves from acting on whatever stereotypes they may have.

However, it's also possible to ensure that stereotypical images never enter your mind in the first place. In other words, if your thinking takes different routes, it's possible to avoid activating stereotypes. The trick is to adopt a mindset to "think differently." After all, if you avoid your typical associations between groups and their stereotypical characteristics, they are unlikely to come to mind.

You might think that you can do this simply by suppressing those thoughts from consciousness. This doesn't work, however. If you intentionally try to keep a thought out of your head, you actually are making yourself even *more* aware of it—what scientists refer to as making it "hyper-accessible." To do this you would have to think about the very thing you want to avoid, which makes you think of it even more. This is known as the **rebound effect.** So, forcing stereotypes out of your mind isn't going to help.

There's another approach, however. Instead of intentionally trying to avoid stereotypes, actually thinking differently by attempting to be creative (see Chapter 14)—or even thinking about times you were creative—can eliminate triggers of the well-established connections on which stereotypical thoughts are based. Research has found that people who were asked to think of various creative things they did over the years were significantly less inclined to describe members of various groups in stereotypical ways than were others who were not asked to think about their own creativity.[28] Scientists take this as an indication that focusing on "thinking differently" helps people overcome the automatic activation of stereotypes. In other words, adopting the mindset to "think differently" interferes with the kind of thinking required to trigger stereotypes (which, of course, tend to be well engrained).

This raises an important and provocative question: What can be done to discourage stereotyping in the workplace? The answer isn't easy, of course. In keeping with the rebound effect, simply telling yourself *not* to engage in stereotyping isn't going to work. However, keeping yourself thinking creatively, taking different approaches to things in the work you do, *is* likely to keep your mind from letting those stereotypes come to awareness. This is a fragile process, as you might imagine, because—again, as per the rebound effect—as soon as you catch yourself thinking that you are fighting stereotypes, you are likely to become more aware of them.

Although this notion hasn't yet been tested in the workplace, it would seem that adopting the "think differently" mindset on a regular basis might be not such a bad idea. For those whose jobs permit creative thinking, and for individuals who are capable of pulling it off, it just may keep stereotypes from entering into your mind. If your focus on thinking differently doesn't make you any more stereotype-resistant than those around you, then at least your efforts stand to make you more creative, and that can't hurt (again, see Chapter 14).

---

rebound effect
The tendency to think about something when you try intentionally not to think about it.

impression management
Efforts by individuals to improve how they appear to others.

we will make these connections more explicit. Specifically, we will describe the role of perception in three organizational activities: the *employment interview, employee performance appraisal,* and the organization's *corporate image.*

Employment Interviews: Managing Impressions to Prospective Employers

The desire to make a favorable impression on others is universal. In one way or another, we all do things to attempt to control how other people see us, often attempting to get them to think of us in the best light possible. This process is known as **impression management.**[29] Generally, individuals devote considerable attention to the impressions they create in the eyes of others—especially when these others are important, such as prospective employers.

The impressions prospective employers form of us may be based on subtle behaviors, such as how we dress and speak, or more elaborate acts, such as announcing our accomplishments (see Figure 3.10).[30] They may be the result of calculated efforts to get others to think of us in a certain way, or be the passive, unintended effects of our actions.

When it comes to the employment interview, for example, there are several things job candidates commonly do to enhance the impressions they make. In an interesting study researchers audiotaped the interviews between college students looking for jobs and representatives of companies that posted openings at the campus job placement center.[31] The various statements made by the candidates were categorized with respect to the impression management techniques they used. Several tactics were commonly observed. Table 3.2 lists these specific tactics, gives an example of each, and shows the percentage of candidates who used these techniques. Interestingly, the most common technique was *self-promotion*, flatly asserting that one has certain desirable characteristics. In this case, candidates commonly described themselves as being hardworking, interpersonally skilled, goal-oriented, and effective leaders.

Importantly, the study also found that candidates used these impression management techniques with great success. The more they relied on these tactics, the more positively they were viewed by the interviewer along several important dimensions (e.g., fit with the organization). This study not only confirms that job candidates do indeed rely on impression management techniques during job interviews, but also that these cultivate the positive impressions desired. With this in mind, the job interview may be seen as an ongoing effort on behalf of candidates to present themselves favorably, and for interviewers to try to

FIGURE 3.10

Dressing for Success Requires Dressing for the Job

It's important for employees to make favorable impressions on their coworkers by wearing the clothing expected of them on the job. For many today, this consists of "business casual" attire. At most small, high-tech companies, for example, where casual dress (sometimes, very casual) is standard, an employee would look out of place showing up in a formal business suit. Likewise, a T-shirt and jeans would make an unfavorable impression in the executive suite, where the classic business suit remains standard attire. The most positive impressions may be made by dressing in the manner considered appropriate for the job.

TABLE 3.2 How Do Job Applicants Go About Presenting Themselves Favorably?

Researchers have systematically recorded and categorized what job applicants say to present themselves favorably to recruiters interviewing them. Here is a list of techniques found during one study along with the percentages of participants using them. Descriptions and examples of each technique are given as well.

Impression Management Technique	Description	Percentage Using Technique
Self-promotion	Directly describing oneself in a positive manner for the situation at hand (e.g., "I am a hard worker").	100
Personal stories	Describing past events that make oneself look good (e.g., "In my old job, I worked late anytime it was needed").	96
Opinion conformity	Expressing beliefs that are assumed to be held by the target (e.g., agreeing with something the interviewer says).	54
Entitlements	Claiming responsibility for successful past events (e.g., "I was responsible for the 90 percent sales increase that resulted").	50
Other enhancement	Making statements that flatter, praise, or compliment the target (e.g., "I am very impressed with your company's growth in recent years").	46
Enhancements	Claiming that a positive event was more positive than it really was (e.g., "Not only did our department improve, it was the best in the entire company").	42
Overcoming obstacles	Describing how one succeeded despite obstacles that should have lowered performance (e.g., "I managed to get a 3.8 grade point average although I worked two part-time jobs").	33
Justifications	Accepting responsibility for one's poor performance but denying the negative implications of it (e.g., "Our team didn't win a lot, but it's just how you play the game that really matters").	17
Excuses	Denying responsibility for one's actions (e.g., "I didn't complete the application form because the placement center ran out of them").	13

Source: Based on information in Stevens & Kristof, 1995; see Note 31.

see through those attempts, trying to judge candidates accurately. As the evidence suggests, this task may not be as simple as it seems.

Performance Appraisal: Formal Judgments about Job Performance

performance appraisal
The process of evaluating employees on various work-related dimensions.

One of the most obvious instances in which social perception occurs is when someone formally evaluates the job performance of another. This process, known as **performance appraisal**, may be defined as the process by which people (typically superiors) evaluate the performance of others (typically subordinates), often on an annual or semi-annual basis, usually for purposes of determining raises, promotions, and training needs.[32]

An Inherently Biased Process. Ideally, this process should be completely rational, leading to unbiased and objective judgments about exactly how well each employee performed and how he or she should be treated. However, based on what we have said about perception thus far, you're probably not surprised to learn that the performance evaluation process is far from objective. Indeed, people have a limited capacity to process, store, and retrieve information, making them prone to bias when it comes to evaluating others.[33]

Several such biases have been observed by researchers. For example, it has been found that people's ratings of others' performance depends on the extent to which that performance is consistent with their initial expectations. Researchers in one study, for example, asked bank managers to indicate how well they expected their newest tellers to perform their jobs.[34] Then, four months later, they were asked to rate the tellers' actual job performance. It was found that managers gave higher ratings to those tellers whose performance matched their earlier expectations than to those who did either better or worse than predicted. These effects are unsettling insofar as they suggest that the improved performance of some employees may go unrecognized—or, worse yet, be downgraded! Of course, to the extent that human resource management decisions are made on the basis of several sources of information, besides judgments by a single superior, it is unlikely that such biased judgments will go uncorrected. Nevertheless, these findings clearly underscore a key point: Perceptions are based not only on the characteristics of the person being perceived, but the perceiver as well.

This conclusion is supported by research showing several different attribution biases in evaluations of job performance. Consider, for example, research illustrating how the similar-to-me effect operates in a performance appraisal situation. A study conducted at a bank, for example, has shown that the more tellers do things to cultivate positive impressions on their superiors (e.g., do favors for them, agree with their opinions), the more the superiors view those tellers as being similar to themselves. And, the more similar they are believed to be, the more highly the superiors evaluated their work.[35]

As you might imagine, employees often attempt to make themselves look good to superiors by offering explanations of their work that focus on the internal reasons underlying their good performance and the external reasons underlying their poor performance. Indeed, two equally good performers are unlikely to receive the same performance ratings when different attributions are made about the underlying causes of their performance. Managers tend to give higher ratings to individuals whose poor performance is attributed to factors outside those individuals' control (e.g., someone who is trying hard, but is too inexperienced to succeed) than to those whose poor performance they attribute to internal factors (e.g., those who are believed to be capable, but who are just lazy and holding back). In other words, our evaluations of others' performance are qualified by the nature of the attributions we make about that performance.

Findings such as these illustrate our point that organizational performance evaluations are far from the unbiased, rational procedures one would hope to find. Instead, they represent a complex mix of perceptual biases—effects that must be appreciated and well understood if we are to have any chance of ultimately improving the accuracy of the performance evaluation process. As you will see in the *OB in a Diverse World* section (p. 108), cultural differences in the performance appraisal process complicate things further.

Corporate Image: Impression Management by Organizations

corporate image
The impressions that people have of an organization.

It is not only individuals who desire to cultivate positive impressions of themselves, but entire organizations too—what has been termed **corporate image**.[36] Just as people can think positive things about you as an individual with respect to many aspects of yourself, so too can corporate images be based on many aspects of an organization's activities.

Positive Corporate Images: Who Has Them And Why Do They Matter? Each
year, *Fortune* magazine asks thousands of executives to rate the images of companies throughout the world. The survey asks respondents to focus on eight particular aspects of company performance: innovation, employee talent, use of corporate assets, social responsibility, quality of management, financial soundness, long-term investment, and quality of products/services. Recent survey results, *Fortune's* top 10 "most admired companies" for 2006, are identified in Table 3.3.[37] As you might expect, this list contains lots of familiar names. It also identifies a wide variety of things that companies do that contribute to these positive images.

As you might imagine, the impression an organization makes on people can have a considerable effect on the way they relate to it. Indeed, a positive image pays off handsomely: Companies that present positive images of themselves to the public are favored by consumers. In fact, many individuals go out of their way to support companies that have good images.[38] For example, companies adopting sound environmental practices (e.g., by following appropriate laws and guidelines and avoiding unnecessary pollution or other negative environmental practices) enjoy positive corporate images and tend to perform well financially.[39]

At the other extreme, people sometimes go so far as to boycott organizations that engage in practices they find undesirable. Over the years, for example, some people credit boycotts aimed at Nestlé for getting that company to stop allegedly dangerous practices

OB In a Diverse World

Performance Evaluations: Comparing the United States and Japan

Beyond individual biases that make the process of evaluating work performance inherently imprecise, widespread cultural differences also are likely to make a big difference when it comes to performance appraisal. In other words, the way people tend to evaluate others' work is likely to be influenced by the nations from which they come.[40] This shouldn't be too surprising if you consider that people from various countries differ with respect to several key variables involved in the performance appraisal process, such as how willing people are to be direct with others and how sensitive they are to differences in status. This point is illustrated clearly by comparing U.S. and Japanese companies with respect to the performance appraisal practices they use.

Although direct supervisors are likely to conduct appraisals in both countries, the ways they go about doing so are very different in several key respects. For example, the American worker's job performance typically is appraised annually. However, in Japan, judgments of how effectively a worker is developing on the job usually occur monthly. Then, an overall evaluation of performance effectiveness is given only after a long time has passed—usually 12 years—making it possible for a highly meaningful assessment to occur. Although this may make little sense in the United States, where long-term commitments to companies are atypical, this approach is possible in Japan, where employees and companies tend to be highly loyal to each other, and where loyalty is rewarded by lifetime employment and regular promotion.[41]

The United States and Japan differ as well in terms of precisely how performance appraisals are conducted. In the United States, companies almost always rely on an official form to provide a precise written record of a supervisor's evaluation. In Japan, however, such directness would be considered inappropriate, and comments about performance are handled orally in a very subtle manner. In keeping with their bluntness, Americans generally are not reluctant to rebut (or, at least, to ask questions about) the judgments made about them. However, very few Japanese employees would consider challenging their supervisors so overtly, politely accepting their supervisors' judgments.

Finally, in the United States, it is almost always the individual worker who is evaluated. In Japan, however, the group or work team tends to be judged as a whole. This reflects the fact that Japanese society generally values collective efforts; people pitching in to work together is what matters most. Americans, by contrast, tend to be far more concerned about their individual performance and their individual rewards.[42]

Although you may find these differences to be interesting curiosities, Americans doing business in Japan and Japanese people doing business in the United States widely recognize the importance of such differences. Indeed, the willingness of American managers from General Motors and Japanese managers from Toyota to understand what it takes to appraise one another's work is considered a key determinant of the long-term success of the joint venture between these two automotive giants.[43]

---

regarding sales of its infant formula, and at General Electric (now, the world's most admired company) for getting it out of the nuclear power plant business.[44] Bottom line: Corporate images matter greatly to consumers.

But consumer support is not the only benefit. Extending our discussion of the job recruitment setting, not only do individual candidates want to make good impressions on prospective employers, but employers want their job offers to be accepted by the best candidates. Research has shown that a company's image is strongly related to people's interest in seeking employment with it.[45] Specifically, the more favorably a company's reputation is considered to be (based on the *Fortune* magazine survey), the more interested prospective employees are in working there. This is important because to function effectively, organizations must do a good job of recruiting the best prospective employees.

How Are Corporate Images Communicated? In light of the importance of having a positive corporate image, it is important to consider the means through which organizations communicate those images to others. In other words, how do we come to make judgments about what various organizations are like? Obviously, we learn a great deal from stories in the news and from what other people tell us. However, as you might imagine, organizations also take proactive steps to communicate positive images of themselves.

TABLE 3.3 Which Companies Have the Best Reputations?

Based on a systematic survey of 10,000 executives and experts in various industries, *Fortune* magazine determined the most admired companies for 2006. As indicated, these companies were admired in many different ways.

Rank	Company	Admirable Qualities
1	General Electric	Breeds the best management talent and has engaged in some of the most successful management practices. GE also has been very quick to adopt changes when necessary.
2	FedEx	Besides offering top delivery service, FedEx also has several programs in place to help sustain the environment. It also offers great perks to employees, such as free rides on its airplanes anywhere in the United States.
3	Southwest Airlines	The longtime leader in low fares and reliable service, Southwest is one of the very few consistently profitable air carriers.
4	Procter & Gamble	Never staying still, P&G has made enormous investments in scientific research to help make its everyday household products highly innovative. The company also has many initiatives in place to promote diversity in the workplace.
5	Starbucks	This profitable company is regarded highly for its generous treatment of its employees (e.g., profit is shared), its socially responsible behavior (e.g., "fair trade" coffee policy), and its high-quality products (around the world, Starbucks' products are consistently good).
6	Johnson & Johnson	As the world's most comprehensive manufacturer of health-care products, J&J is involved actively in research designed to improve the health and well-being of people everywhere. A talented management team has kept the company growing in size and profitable.
7	Berkshire Hathaway	This financial management company regularly has outperformed various stock market indexes. The company is so well managed that despite losses due to Hurricane Katrina, its insurance division, GEICO, has enjoyed unprecedented gains in market share and profitability.
8	Dell	In the computer industry, in which many companies (e.g., IBM, Gateway, Compaq) either have shrunk greatly in size or have been forced to consolidate with others, Dell is firmly entrenched as the top manufacturer of personal computers.
9	Toyota	Despite technical problems and resistance from dealers, Toyota's Prius has proven to be a successful gas-electric hybrid—the first serious alternative to the internal combustion engine in automotive history. The company is highly innovative, although incredibly conservative and methodological in its approach to business and engineering.
10	Microsoft	Ongoing innovations in operating systems and the continuous development of new products have been making Microsoft even more of a leader in the market for computer software than ever. The company also has been extremely generous in giving back to the communities in which it operates.

Sources: Based on information reported by *Fortune,* 2006, see Note 41; and the Web sites of the companies listed.

One thing that influences a company's image is the amount of information people have about it from *recruitment ads.* In general, longer ads are associated with more positive images. This may not only be because of what is said in the ad, but the mere length of the ad itself. Specifically, because recruitment ads emphasize the benefits of employment with a firm, longer ads describe more benefits than shorter ones, thereby creating even stronger positive images. Moreover, to the extent that people believe that longer ads reflect a company's commitment to obtaining good employees (by their willingness to invest in a large ad), they may be more impressed with a company as a prospective place to work (see Figure 3.11).

Another mechanism that organizations use to promote their corporate images is their *annual reports*—a company's official statement to its stockholders on its activities and financial state. These booklets contain such things as letters from CEOs and descriptions of projects and future plans—in short, information that helps shape the image of the company both in the minds of employees and stockholders.

Traditionally, annual reports have been strikingly beautiful glossy booklets with elaborate photography and glitzy images, trappings of success designed to instill confidence in the minds of investors. In recent years, however, many companies—St. Paul Companies and Avery Dennison among them—have spared such expenses, issuing bare-bones annual reports.[46] The reason: To promote an image of austerity. Because today's

FIGURE 3.11

Employee Recruitment Advertising: An Important Way of Promoting a Corporate Image

As you look at this ad, what image comes to mind of the Jersey City Fire Department? Chances are, you think of it as a place in which you can do exciting, challenging work that really makes a difference in the community. This is precisely the image that the Jersey City Fire Department has in mind as it endeavors to attract dedicated firefighters to its force. The fact that you may be getting this impression illustrates just how powerful recruitment ads can be when it comes to promoting corporate images.

Source: Reprinted by permission of the Jersey City Fire Department.

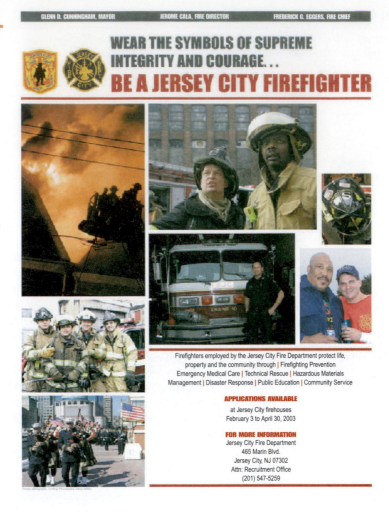

investors are looking for value, companies are going out of their way to cultivate the impression that they're not wasting money. Looking *too* successful by squandering money on elaborate annual reports may raise questions about where the profits are going.

So, whether these publications are elaborate or just plain vanilla, annual reports are designed to cultivate "the right" corporate image—whatever that may be. Clearly, just like individuals, organizations also stand to benefit by making positive impressions on others and work hard at doing so.

Learning: Adapting to the World Around Us

Thus far in this chapter we have focused on perception, one of the basic human psychological processes most actively involved in explaining behavior in organizations. However, another process is equally important—*learning*. After all, learning is involved in a broad range of organizational behaviors, ranging from developing new vocational skills, through changing the way people do their jobs, to managing them in ways that foster the greatest productivity. Not surprisingly, the more a company fosters an environment in which employees are able to learn, the more productive and profitable that organization is likely to be.[47] Naturally, scientists in the field of OB are extremely interested in understanding the process of learning—both how it occurs, and how it may be applied to the effective functioning of organizations.

learning
A relatively permanent change in behavior occurring as a result of experience.

Before we turn our attention to these matters, we should first explain exactly what we mean by learning. Specifically, we define **learning** as a relatively permanent change in behavior occurring as a result of experience.[48] Despite its simplicity, several aspects of this definition bear pointing out. First, it's clear that learning requires that some kind of change occur. Second, this change must be more than just temporary. Finally, it must be the result of experience—that is, continued contact with the world around us. Given this definition, we cannot say that short-lived performance changes on the job, such as those due to illness or fatigue, are the result of learning. Like so many concepts in the social sciences, learning is a difficult concept for scientists to understand because it cannot be observed directly. Instead, it must be inferred on the basis of relatively permanent changes in behavior.

Although there are several different kinds of learning, we will examine two that are most inclined to occur in organizations. These are *operant conditioning* and *observational learning*.

Operant Conditioning: Learning through Rewards and Punishments

operant conditioning
The form of learning in which people associate the consequences of their actions with the actions themselves. Behaviors with positive consequences are acquired; behaviors with negative consequences tend to be eliminated.

Imagine you are a chef working at a catering company where you are planning a special menu for a fussy client. If your dinner menu is accepted and the meal is a hit, the company stands a good chance of picking up a huge new account. You work hard at doing the best job possible and present your culinary creation to the skeptical client. Now, how does the story end? If the client loves your meal, your grateful boss gives you a huge raise and a promotion. However, if the client hates it, your boss asks you to turn in your chef's hat. Regardless of which of these outcomes occur, one thing is certain: Whatever you did in this situation, you will be sure to do it again if it was successful, and to avoid doing again if it failed.

instrumental conditioning
See *operant conditioning*.

This situation nicely illustrates an important principle of **operant conditioning** (also known as **instrumental conditioning**)—namely, that our behavior produces consequences and that how we behave in the future will depend on what those consequences are. If our actions have had pleasant effects, then we will be likely to repeat them in the future. If, however, our actions have unpleasant effects, we are less likely to repeat them in the future. This phenomenon, known as the **Law of Effect**, is fundamental to operant conditioning. Our knowledge of this phenomenon comes from the work of the famous social scientist B. F. Skinner.[49] Skinner's pioneering research has shown us that it is through the connections between our actions and their consequences that we learn to behave in certain ways. We summarize this process in Figure 3.12.

Law of Effect
The tendency for behaviors leading to desirable consequences to be strengthened and those leading to undesirable consequences to be weakened.

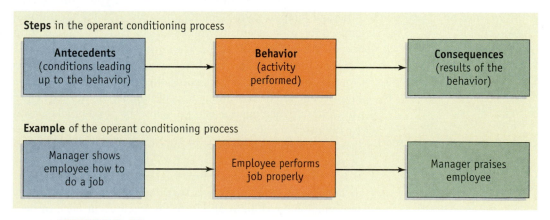

FIGURE 3.12

The Operant Conditioning Process: An Overview
The basic premise of operant conditioning is that people learn by connecting the consequences of their behavior with the behavior itself. In this example, the manager's praise increases the subordinate's tendency to perform the job properly in the future. Learning occurs by providing the appropriate antecedents and consequences.

positive reinforcement
The process by which people learn to perform behaviors that lead to the presentation of desired outcomes.

negative reinforcement
The process by which people learn to perform acts that lead to the removal of undesired events.

avoidance
See *negative reinforcement.*

punishment
Decreasing undesirable behavior by following it with undesirable consequences.

extinction
The process through which responses that are no longer reinforced tend to gradually diminish in strength.

contingencies of reinforcement
The various relationships between one's behavior and the consequences of that behavior—positive reinforcement, negative reinforcement, punishment, and extinction.

continuous reinforcement
A schedule of reinforcement in which all desired behaviors are reinforced.

partial reinforcement
A schedule of reinforcement in which only some desired behaviors are reinforced. Types include: fixed interval, variable interval, fixed ratio, and variable ratio.

intermittent reinforcement
See *partial reinforcement.*

Reinforcement Contingencies.   Operant conditioning is based on the idea that behavior is learned because of the pleasurable outcomes that we associate with it. In organizations, for example, people usually find it pleasant and desirable to receive monetary bonuses, paid vacations, and various forms of recognition. The process by which people learn to perform acts leading to such desirable outcomes is known as **positive reinforcement**. Whatever behavior led to the positive outcome is likely to occur again, thereby strengthening that behavior. For a reward to serve as a positive reinforcer, it must be made contingent on the specific behavior sought. So, for example, if a sales representative is given a bonus after landing a huge account, that bonus will only reinforce the person's actions *if* he or she associates it with the landing of the account. When this occurs, the individual will be more inclined in the future to do whatever helped get the account.

Sometimes we also learn to perform acts because they permit us to avoid undesirable consequences. Unpleasant events, such as reprimands, rejection, probation, and termination are some of the consequences faced for certain negative actions in the workplace. The process by which people learn to perform acts leading to the avoidance of such undesirable consequences is known as **negative reinforcement**, or **avoidance**. Whatever response led to the termination of these undesirable events is likely to occur again, thereby strengthening that response. For example, you may stay late at the office one evening to revise a sales presentation because you believe that the boss will "chew you out" if it's not ready in the morning. You learned how to avoid this type of aversive situation, and you behave accordingly.

Thus far, we have identified responses that are strengthened—either because they lead to positive consequences, or the termination of negative consequences. However, the connection between a behavior and its consequences is not always strengthened; such links also may be weakened. This is what happens in the case of **punishment**. Punishment involves presenting an undesirable or aversive consequence in response to an unwanted behavior. A behavior accompanied by an undesirable outcome is less likely to reoccur if the person associates the negative consequences with the behavior. For example, if you are chastised by your boss for taking excessively long coffee breaks, you may be considered punished for this action. As a result, you will be less likely to take long breaks again in the future.

The link between a behavior and its consequences also may be weakened by withholding reward—a process known as **extinction**. When a response that was once rewarded is no longer rewarded, it tends to weaken and eventually die out—or be *extinguished*. Let's consider an example. Suppose for many months you brought boxes of donuts to your weekly staff meetings. Your colleagues always thanked you as they gobbled them down. You were positively reinforced by their approval, so you continued bringing the donuts. Now, after several months of eating donuts, your colleagues have begun dieting. So, although tempting, your donuts go uneaten. After several months of no longer being praised for your generosity, you will be unlikely to continue bringing donuts. Your once-rewarded behavior will die out; it will be extinguished.

The various relationships between a person's behavior and the consequences resulting from it—*positive reinforcement, negative reinforcement, punishment,* and *extinction*—are known collectively as **contingencies of reinforcement**. They represent the conditions under which rewards and punishments will either be given or taken away. The four contingencies we discussed are summarized in Table 3.4. As we will see later in this chapter, administering these contingencies can be an effective tool for managing behavior in organizations.

Schedules Of Reinforcement: Patterns Of Administering Rewards.   Thus far, our discussion of whether a reward will be presented or withdrawn has assumed that the presentation or withdrawal will follow each occurrence of behavior. However, it is not always practical (or, as we will see, advisable) to do this. Rewarding *every* desired response made is called **continuous reinforcement**. Unlike animals performing tricks in a circus, people on the job are rarely reinforced continuously. Instead, organizational rewards tend to be administered following **partial reinforcement** (also known as **intermittent reinforcement**) schedules. That is, rewards are administered intermittently, with some desired responses reinforced and others not. Four varieties of partial reinforcement schedules have direct application to organizations.[50]

TABLE 3.4 Contingencies of Reinforcement: A Summary

The four contingencies of reinforcement may be distinguished by the presentation or withdrawal of a pleasant or an unpleasant stimulus. Positively or negatively reinforced behaviors are strengthened, whereas punished or extinguished behaviors are weakened.

Stimulus Presented or Withdrawn	Desirability of Stimulus	Name of Contingency	Strength of Response	Example
Presented	Pleasant	Positive reinforcement	Increases	Praise from a supervisor encourages continuing the praised behavior.
	Unpleasant	Punishment	Decreases	Criticism from a supervisor discourages enacting the punished behavior.
Withdrawn	Pleasant	Extinction	Decreases	Failing to praise a helpful act reduces the odds of helping in the future.
	Unpleasant	Negative reinforcement	Increases	Future criticism is avoided by doing whatever the supervisor wants.

fixed interval schedules
Schedules of reinforcement in which a fixed period of time must elapse between the administration of reinforcements.

- **Fixed interval schedules** are those in which reinforcement is administered the first time the desired behavior occurs after a specific amount of time has passed. For example, the practice of issuing paychecks each Friday at 3:00 P.M. is an example of a fixed interval schedule insofar as the rewards are administered at regular times. Fixed interval schedules are not especially effective in maintaining desired behavior. For example, employees who know that their boss will pass by their desks every day at 11:30 A.M. will make sure they are working hard at that time. However, without the boss around to praise them, they may take an early lunch or otherwise work less hard because they know that they will not be positively reinforced for their efforts or punished for not working.

variable interval schedules
Schedules of reinforcement in which a variable period of time (based on some average) must elapse between the administration of reinforcements.

- **Variable interval schedules** are those in which a variable amount of time (based on some average amount) must elapse between administering reinforcements. For example, a bank auditor may make surprise visits to branch offices an average of every six weeks (e.g., visits may be four weeks apart one time, and eight weeks apart another time). The auditor may be said to be using a variable interval schedule. Because the bank managers cannot tell exactly when their branch may be audited, they cannot afford to slack off. Another inspection may just be closer than they think! Not surprisingly, variable interval schedules generally are more effective than fixed interval schedules.

fixed ratio schedules
Schedules of reinforcement in which a fixed number of responses must occur between the administration of reinforcements.

- **Fixed ratio schedules** are those in which reinforcement is administered the first time the desired behavior occurs after a specified number of such actions have been performed. For example, suppose members of a sales staff know that they will receive a bonus for each $1,000 worth of goods they sell. Immediately after receiving the first reward, performance may slack off. But as their sales begin to approach $2,000, the next level at which reward is expected, performance will once again improve.

variable ratio schedules
Schedules of reinforcement in which a variable number of responses (based on some average) must occur between the administration of reinforcements.

- **Variable ratio schedules** are those in which a variable number of desired responses (based on some average amount) must elapse between the administration of reinforcements. People playing slot machines provide a good example. Most of the time when people put a coin into the slot they lose. But, after some unknown number of plays, the machine will pay off. Because gamblers can never tell which pull of the handle will win the jackpot, they are likely to keep on playing for a long time. As you might imagine, variable ratio schedules tend to be more effective than fixed ratio schedules.

schedules of reinforcement
Rules governing the timing and frequency of the administration of reinforcement.

The various **schedules of reinforcement** we described here have a number of important similarities and differences. We have summarized these in Figure 3.13. As you review this diagram, it is important to keep in mind that these schedules represent "pure" forms. Used in practice, several different reinforcement schedules may be combined, making complex new schedules. Still, whether they operate separately or in conjunction with one another, it is important to recognize the strong influences that schedules of reinforcement can have on people's behavior in organizations.

FIGURE 3.13

Schedules of Reinforcement: A Summary

The four schedules of reinforcement summarized here represent different ways of administering reward intermittently.

Observational Learning: Learning by Imitating Others

Although operant conditioning is based on the idea that we engage in behaviors for which we are directly reinforced, many of the things we learn on the job are *not* directly reinforced. Suppose, for example, on your new job you see one of your fellow sales representatives developing a potentially valuable sales lead by joining a local civic organization. Soon thereafter, talking to people around the office, you find out that yet another one of your colleagues has picked up a lucrative lead from a civic group to which he belongs. Chances are, after observing this several times, you too will eventually make the connection between joining such groups and getting sales leads. Although you may not have made useful contacts from such groups yourself, you would come to expect these leads to pan out on the basis of what you have observed from others. This is an example of a kind of learning known as **observational learning**, or **modeling**.[51] It occurs when someone acquires new knowledge *vicariously*—that is, by observing what happens to others. The person whose behavior is imitated is referred to as the *model*.

observational learning (or modeling)
The form of learning in which people acquire new behaviors by systematically observing the rewards and punishments given to others.

Steps In The Observational Learning Process. For people to learn by observing models, several processes must occur (for a summary of these, see Figure 3.14).

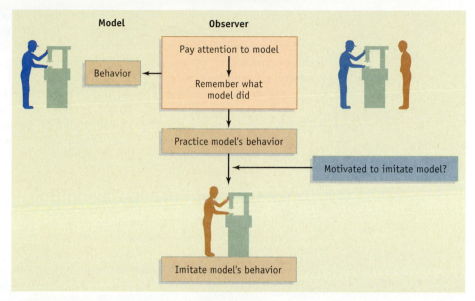

FIGURE 3.14

Observational Learning: An Overview

The process of observational learning requires that an observer pay attention to and remember a model's behavior. By observing what the model did and rehearsing those actions, the observer may learn to imitate the model, but only if the observer is motivated to do so (i.e., if the model was rewarded for behaving as observed).

1. The learner must pay careful *attention* to the model; the greater the attention, the more effective the learning will be. To facilitate learning, models sometimes call attention to themselves. This is what happens when supervisors admonish their subordinates to "pay close attention" to what they're doing.
2. People must have good *retention* of the model's behavior. It helps to be able to develop a verbal description or a mental image of someone's actions in order to remember them. After all, we cannot learn from observing behavior we cannot remember.
3. There must be some *behavioral reproduction* of the model's behavior. Unless people are capable of doing exactly what the models do, they will not be able to learn from observing them. Naturally, this ability may be limited at first, but improve with practice.
4. Finally, people must have some *motivation* to learn from the model. Of course, we don't emulate every behavior we see, but focus on those we have some reason or incentive to match—such as actions for which others are rewarded.

Examples Of Observational Learning In Organizations. A great deal of what is learned about how to behave in organizations can be explained as the result of the process of observational learning.[52] For example, observational learning is a key part of many formal job instruction training programs.[53] As we will explain in the next section, trainees given a chance to observe experts doing their jobs, followed by an opportunity to practice the desired skills, and given feedback on their work, tend to learn new job skills quite effectively.

Observational learning also occurs in a very informal, uncalculated manner. For example, people who experience the norms and traditions of their organizations and who subsequently incorporate these into their own behavior may be recognized as having learned through observation. Indeed, people tend to learn the culture of their organizations (a topic that we will discuss in Chapter 14) through observational learning.

It is important to note that people learn not only what to do by observing others, but also what *not* to do. Specifically, research has shown that people observing their coworkers getting punished for behaving inappropriately on the job tend to refrain from engaging in those same actions themselves.[54] As you might imagine, this is a very effective way for people to learn how to behave—and without ever experiencing any displeasure themselves.

The principles of learning we have discussed thus far are used in organizations in many different ways. In the remaining part of this chapter, we discuss formal approaches to incorporating the various principles of learning in organizations: *training,* and practices involving the systematic use of rewards and punishments: *organizational behavior management* and *discipline.*

Training: Learning and Developing Job Skills

training
The process of systematically teaching employees to acquire and improve job-related skills and knowledge.

Probably the most obvious use to which principles of learning may be applied in organizations is **training**—the process through which people systematically acquire and improve the skills and knowledge needed to better their job performance. Just as students learn basic educational skills in the classroom, employees must learn job skills. Training is used not only to prepare new employees to meet the challenges of the jobs they will face, but also to upgrade and refine the skills of existing employees. In fact, it has been estimated that American companies spend about $365 billion on training annually (a billion dollars per day!).[55] What's more, the amount of time and money spent training employees has been increasing steadily over the years.[56]

Varieties of Training

Training takes many forms. Some training is quite informal in nature, consisting of having experienced employees take new employees under their wings to show them how to do the job in question. Most of the time, however, training involves highly systematic, formal efforts to teach employees how to do specific things that are required for job success. We now review these methods.

classroom training
The process of teaching people how to do their jobs by explaining various job requirements and how to meet them.

Classroom Training. As a student, you already are familiar with **classroom training.** In this method, instructors describe various requirements of the job and provide tips on how to meet them. Typically, people learning new skills in the classroom are given an opportunity to practice these skills, either in a simulated work setting or on the job itself.

Consider, for example, how people are trained as account representatives at the collection agency, OSI. The account reps are the individuals who call consumers to arrange payment on seriously delinquent accounts. The reps receive four days of intensive classroom training, covering things such as approaches to take in getting people to pay, procedures to follow for sending payment, payment programs available to the consumer, and the laws that bill collectors are required to follow. This classroom training is supplemented by making simulated practice calls in which the budding reps get to practice their new skills. Following this training, they are allowed to make actual calls, but these are closely monitored by experienced personnel who stand ready to guide the trainee as needed.

apprenticeship programs
Formal training programs involving both on-the-job and classroom training usually over a long period, often used for training people in the skilled trades.

Apprenticeship Programs. Growing in popularity today are formal **apprenticeship programs**, in which classroom training is systematically combined with on-the-job instruction over a long period (often several years in the case of skilled tradespeople such as carpenters, electricians, and masons). Recognizing the importance of such programs in developing human resources, the federal government has invested hundreds of millions of dollars in apprenticeship programs, encouraging training partnerships between government and private industry.[57] To ensure that people going into various trades are trained to appropriately high standards, many apprenticeship programs often are designed and regulated by professional trade associations (for an example, see Figure 3.15)

FIGURE 3.15

Training Today's Apprentices To Become Tomorrow's Chefs

Demonstrating a pan-searing technique for his students at York Community College in Maine, this chef-instructor is training culinary arts students to become professionals chefs. These students are among thousands trained in apprenticeship programs overseen by the American Culinary Federation throughout the United States. This trade group certifies programs to ensure that graduates are proficient in key skills (e.g., how to prepare various dishes) and have knowledge of core material (e.g., food safety and kitchen sanitation procedures), enabling them to meet professional standards. The three-year program includes both classroom study and hands-on experience in restaurant kitchens.

Cross-Cultural Training. Today, given the increasing globalization of the workplace, it is not surprising that companies are sending their employees to work abroad. A growing number of companies are discovering that employees are more likely to succeed in their overseas assignments when they have been thoroughly trained in the culture of the country in which they will be living. Sure, it helps to know the language of the host country, but that's just the beginning. If you've ever lived in another country, or even visited one, for

TABLE 3.5 Summary of Techniques Used in Cross-Cultural Training (CCT)

People working overseas often are trained for their assignments using one or more of the techniques described here.

Cultural briefings	Explain the major aspects of the host country culture, including customs, traditions, everyday behaviors
Area briefings	Explain the history, geography, economy, politics, and other general information about the host country and region
Cases	Portray a real-life situation in business or personal life to illustrate some aspect of living or working in the host culture
Role playing	Allows the trainee to act out a situation that he or she might face in living or working in the host country
Culture assimilator	Provides a written set of situations that the trainee might encounter in living or working in the host country. Trainee selects from a set of responses to the situation and is given feedback as to whether it is appropriate and why.
Field experiences	Provide an opportunity for the trainee to go to the host country or another unfamiliar culture to experience living and working for a short time

Source: International Organizational Behavior: Text Readings Cases, by Francesco & Gold, © 1998. Electronically reproduced by Pearson Education, Inc., Upper Saddle River, NJ. See Note 58.

cross-cultural training (CCT)
A systematic way of preparing employees to live and work in another country.

that matter, then you can appreciate how vital it would be to understand fully the culture of the people in any country in which you are doing business. With this in mind, many companies have been investing in **cross-cultural training (CCT),** a systematic way of preparing employees to live and work in another country.[58] Actually, CCT is not a single method, but a variety of specific training techniques that have proven effective. For a summary of some of the most effective CCT methods, see Table 3.5.

Corporate Universities. Many companies (e.g., Apple Computer, the Tennessee Valley Authority, and Sprint, to name only a few), are so serious about training that they have developed their own **corporate universities**—facilities devoted to handling a company's training needs on a full-time basis.[59] Established in 1927 and still going strong, the first corporate university is the "General Motors Institute," which trains employees on almost every skill required by GM's tens of thousands of worldwide employees. Among the best known facilities is McDonald's "Hamburger University," in which McDonald's franchisees learn and/or polish the skills needed to successfully operate a McDonald's restaurant. Like several other companies, such as Saturn and Motorola, McDonald's has its own campus with full-time instructors (see Figure 3.16).

corporate universities
Centers devoted to handling a company's training needs on a full-time basis.

Most corporate universities, however, are less elaborate programs run by either the human resources department or a few top executives. Even very small Internet start-ups can have their own corporate universities by using any of a growing number of firms that provide this service. Although the curricula vary widely, most corporate universities emphasize leadership development (which we address in Chapter 13).

executive training programs
Sessions in which companies systematically attempt to develop their top leaders, either in specific skills or general managerial skills.

Executive Training Programs. Another popular form of training is **executive training programs**—sessions in which companies systematically attempt to develop the skills of their top leaders, such as how to use computer software, or more general skills, such as how to get along with others.[60] This is accomplished either by bringing in outside experts to train personnel in-house, or by sending them to specialized programs conducted by

FIGURE 3.16

Corporate Training at McDonald's Hamburger University

Headquartered in a beautiful park-like campus in Oak Brook, Illinois, and with branches in seven different countries, Hamburger University (HU) is the center for formal managerial training at McDonald's. Executives and mid-level managers are offered various courses in leadership skills and financial management. Even lower-level managers are trained in ways of maintaining and troubleshooting restaurant equipment. Training at HU is considered a stepping-stone along the path to career advancement: Among HU's 75,000 graduates are some of McDonald's top executives.

private consulting firms, or by colleges and universities.[61] Taking advantage of today's high-tech opportunities, many companies are finding that it's both convenient and effective to offer executive training online, using *e-training*.

E-Training. These days, because the investment in computer technology required to reach people in remote locations is so small, the vast majority of companies conducting training do at least some of it online. The term **e-training** is used to describe training based on disseminating information online (e.g., through the Internet or a company's internal intranet network). Online training is so popular, in fact, that savvy investment companies (e.g., Chase Capital and Merrill Lynch) have been funneling tens of millions of dollars into companies such as Ninth House and GlobalLearningSystems, which provide multimedia employee training.[62]

In recent years, many companies have found it useful to use e-training. For example, the Buffalo, New York–based Delaware North, a contract foodservice company, has used e-training as an efficient way to bring employees up to speed on new operations. According to Sherri Steinback, the company's manager of technical training and special projects, "We were rolling out a new financial application to over 125 units, and we needed an efficient way to train a diverse group scattered across the country."[63] E-training also has been used in a wide variety of different industries (see Figure 3.17).[64]

Compared to traditional, classroom-based corporate training programs, the primary benefits of online training are: (1) the flexibility it offers trainees, (2) the speed and efficiency it offers, and (3) reduced cost. Despite these benefits, e-training is far from perfect. One problem that many companies are facing is that it is very costly for them to produce self-paced, online training materials (about six to eight times more, in many cases), which drastically cuts into any short-term savings that may result.

e-training
Training based on disseminating information online, such as through the Internet or a company's internal intranet network.

FIGURE 3.17

E-Training in the Restaurant Business

These employees of the Bahama Breeze restaurant chain are discussing modifications in service policies communicated as part of the Web-based training system used by the parent company, Darden. Such e-training efforts are central to efforts to ensure high quality, uniform training at Darden's restaurants throughout the country.

Probably the most serious limitation is that many workers are uncomfortable with it. Even the most computer-savvy employees may find it deceptively easy to click ahead, thinking they know material that they really don't know that well. Others simply miss the social aspect of learning, the one-on-one experience they have in the classroom with their peers and the trainer (which, for some, may be a distraction). Indeed, some experts agree that one advantage of the traditional classroom experience is that it brought people together out of the office, a benefit that the more impersonal experience of sitting in front of a computer screen just cannot offer. In view of this, online technology may best be considered an adjunct to the total training package, a single tool rather than a replacement for the traditional, in-person training experience.

Principles of Learning: Keys to Effective Training

principles of learning

The set of practices that make training effective: participation, repetition, transfer of training, and feedback. (See *transfer of training*.)

As you might imagine, no one approach to training is ideal. Some techniques are better suited to learning certain skills than are others. The reason for this is that various techniques incorporate different **principles of learning**, that is, the set of practices that make training effective. Not surprisingly, the best training programs often use many different approaches, thereby assuring that several different learning principles may be incorporated into training.[65]

To appreciate what these particular principles are, just think about some of the ways you learned skills such as how to study, drive, or use a computer. Four major principles are most relevant.

participation

Active involvement in the process of learning; more active participation leads to more effective learning.

Participation. People not only learn more quickly, but also retain the skills longer when they have been involved actively in the learning process. This is the practice of **participation**. The benefits of **participation** apply to the learning of both motor tasks as well as cognitive skills. For example, when learning to swim, there's no substitute for actually getting in the water and moving your arms and legs. In the classroom, students who listen attentively to lectures, think about the material, and get involved in discussions tend to learn more effectively than those who just sit passively.

repetition

The process of repeatedly performing a task so that it may be learned.

Repetition. If you know the old adage "Practice makes perfect," you are already aware of the benefits of **repetition** on learning. Perhaps you learned the multiplication table, or a poem, or a foreign language phrase by going over it repeatedly. Indeed, mentally "rehearsing" such cognitive tasks has been shown to increase our effectiveness at performing them.[66] Scientists have established not only the benefits of repetition on learning, but have shown that these effects are even greater when practice is spread out over time than when it is lumped together. After all, when practice periods are too long, learning can suffer from fatigue, whereas learning a little bit at a time allows the material to sink in.

transfer of training

The degree to which the skills learned during training sessions may be applied to performance of one's job.

Transfer of Training. As you might imagine, for training to be most effective, what is learned during training sessions must be applied to the job. This is the idea of **transfer of training**, the degree to which training generalizes to actual work experiences. In general, the more closely a training program matches the demands and conditions faced on a job, the more effective that training will be. A good example is the elaborate simulation devices used to train pilots and astronauts. By closely simulating actual job conditions and equipment, the skills trained are expected to transfer to the job.[67]

feedback

Knowledge of the results of one's behavior.

Feedback. It is extremely difficult for learning to occur in the absence of **feedback**—that is, knowledge of the results of one's actions. Feedback provides information about the effectiveness of one's training, indicating improvements that need to be made.[68] For example, it is critical for people being trained as word processing operators to know exactly how many words they correctly entered per minute if they are to be able to gauge their improvement (see Figure 3.18).

360-degree feedback

The practice of collecting performance feedback from multiple sources at a variety of organizational levels.

One type of feedback that has become popular in recent years is known as **360-degree feedback**—the process of using multiple sources from around the organization to evaluate the work of a single individual. This goes beyond simply collecting feedback from superiors, as is customary, but extends the gathering of feedback from other sources, such as one's peers, direct reports (i.e., immediate subordinates), customers, and even oneself (see Figure 3.19).[69] Many companies—including General Electric, AT&T, Monsanto, Florida Power and Light, DuPont, Westinghouse, Motorola, Fidelity Bank, FedEx, Nabisco, and Warner-Lambert—have used 360-degree feedback to give more complete performance information to their employees, greatly improving not only their own work, but overall corporate productivity as well.[70] To get a feel for how some companies are using this technique, see the *How to Do It* section on page 123.

In sum, these four principles—*participation, repetition, transfer of training,* and *feedback*—are key to the effectiveness of any training program. The most effective training programs are those that incorporate as many of these principles as possible.

Organizational Practices Involving the Use of Reward and Punishment

Earlier, in describing operant conditioning, we noted that the consequences of our behavior determines whether we repeat it or abandon it. Behaviors that are rewarded tend to be strengthened, repeated in the future. With this in mind, it is possible to administer rewards selectively to help reinforce behaviors that we wish repeated in the future. This is the basic

FIGURE 3.18

Feedback: A Critical Principle of Learning

For learning to be effective, people must have *feedback* about how well they are performing. Specific information of this type helps learners make adjustments in their performance so as to bring it up to standards. Although feedback comes from many sources, this is unlikely to be one of them.

Source: www.CartoonStock.com

FIGURE 3.19

360-Degree Feedback: An Overview

Many companies rely on 360-degree feedback to provide valuable insight into how performance may be improved. As summarized here, this technique involves collecting performance feedback from multiple sources.

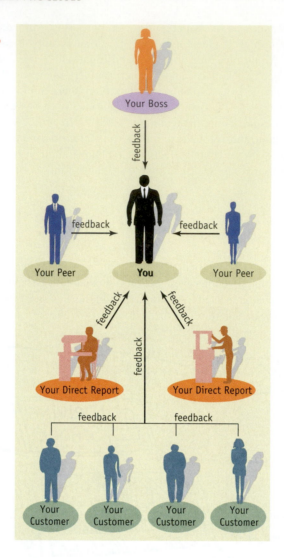

principle behind *organizational behavior management*. It's also possible to influence workers' behavior by using discipline. This, of course, involves the use of *punishment,* a contingency of reinforcement we described earlier. We now describe both organizational behavior management and discipline in organizations.

Organizational Behavior Management

organizational behavior management

The practice of altering behavior in organizations by systematically administering rewards.

When management experts refer to **organizational behavior management** (or **OB Mod**, for short), they are describing the systematic application of positive reinforcement principles in organizational settings for the purpose of raising the incidence of desirable organizational behaviors.[71]

OB Mod programs have been used successfully to stimulate a variety of behaviors in many different organizations.[72] For example, a particularly interesting and effective program has been used in recent years at Diamond International, the Palmer, Massachusetts company of 325 employees that manufactures Styrofoam egg cartons. In response to sluggish productivity, a simple but elegant reinforcement was put into place. Any employee working for a full year without an industrial accident is given 20 points. Perfect attendance is given 25 points. Once a year, the points are totaled. When employees reach 100 points, they get a blue nylon jacket with the company's logo on it and a patch identifying their membership in the "100 Club." Those earning still more points receive extra awards. For example, at 500 points, employees can select any of a number of small household appliances. These inexpensive prizes go a long way toward symbolizing to employees the company's appreciation for their good work.

HOW TO DO IT

Using 360-Degree Feedback: Three Success Stories

If you think about it, the practice of giving questionnaires to various people in an organization to assess how large groups of them feel about each other can serve a lot of purposes. Not only might the survey findings be used to help assess job performance, but it also can be used for many other purposes as well. For example, 360-degree feedback can be used to systematically assess training needs, to determine new products and services desired by customers, to gauge team members' reactions to each other, and to learn about a variety of potential human resource problems.[73] To better understand these and other uses of this popular tool, we will now consider three specific examples of 360-degree feedback in action.[74]

- *Promoting change at the Landmark Stock Exchange.* The Landmark Stock Exchange is one of several smaller stock exchanges that operate in the United States. Eclipsed by the giant exchanges, such as the New York Stock Exchange and NASDAQ, Landmark has been striving to become the best marketplace in the world by providing faster and more accurate movement of stock than its well-known competitors. Meeting this objective requires a willingness to go along with rapid change and innovation. To see how it was doing in this regard, Landmark implemented a 360-degree feedback program that provided employees with feedback in such key areas as consulting others, inspiring others, team building, and networking. This feedback was then used as the basis for providing systematic training in ways to change any behaviors found lacking.

- *Developing leaders at Leher McGovern Bovis.* Leher McGovern Bovis (LMB) was responsible for the renovation and restoration of such New York City landmarks as the Statue of Liberty and Grand Central Terminal. LMB is unique in the construction industry in the attention it pays to developing its employees' leadership skills, preparing them for senior positions in the company. Company officials implemented a 360-degree feedback program that helped identify people's readiness for advancement to leadership positions within the company and the best candidates for management training. The 360-degree feedback program helped reduce turnover among project managers from 12 percent down to only 2 percent.

- *Identifying training and selection requirements at Northwestern Mutual Life Insurance Company.* To meet growing competition, Northwestern Mutual Life (NML) restructured its offices, which required them to identify many new managers. The company used a 360-degree feedback program to assess the potential of individual agents to be promoted to these new managerial positions. Also, by systematically noting shortcomings, they use this information to identify the most-needed forms of management training. NML's 360-degree feedback program has made the task of selecting and training managers more effective than ever.

As these examples illustrate, 360-degree feedback can be a very successful tool to help meet a wide variety of organizational objectives. For this reason, it continues to be very popular and may be expected to remain in widespread use in the future.

This program has helped improve productivity dramatically at Diamond International. Compared to before the OB Mod program began, output improved 16.5 percent, quality-related errors dropped 40 percent, grievances decreased 72 percent, and time lost due to accidents was lowered by 43.7 percent. The result of all of this has been over $1 million in gross financial benefits from the company—and a much happier workforce. Needless to say, this has been a very simple and effective organizational behavior management program. Although not all such programs are equally successful, evidence suggests that they are generally quite beneficial. For example, highly successful OB Mod programs have been used at such companies as General Electric, Weyerhauser, and General Mills.

Discipline: Eliminating Undesirable Organizational Behaviors

discipline
The process of systematically administering punishments.

Just as organizations systematically use rewards to encourage desirable behavior, they also use punishment to discourage undesirable behavior. Problems such as absenteeism, lateness, theft, and substance abuse cost companies vast sums of money, situations many companies attempt to manage by using **discipline**—the systematic administration of punishment.

By administering an unpleasant outcome (e.g., suspension without pay) in response to an undesirable behavior (e.g., excessive tardiness), companies seek to minimize that behavior. In one form or another, using discipline is a relatively common practice. Survey research has shown, in fact, that 83 percent of companies use some form of discipline, or at least the threat of discipline, in response to undesirable behaviors.[75] But, as you might imagine, disciplinary actions taken in organizations vary greatly. At one extreme, they may be very formal, such as written warnings that become part of the employee's permanent record. At the other extreme, they may be informal and low-key, such as friendly reminders and off-the-record discussions between supervisors and their problem subordinates.

In a survey, nursing supervisors were asked to list the disciplinary actions they most used and to rank them with respect to their severity.[76] The results, summarized in Figure 3.20, reveals that a broad range of disciplinary measures are used, ranging from very lenient to very harsh. Although this represents the responses of a limited sample, we suspect that these results are fairly typical of what would be found across a wide variety of jobs.

Disciplinary Practices In Organizations.   One very common practice involves using punishment *progressively*—that is, starting mildly, and then increasing in severity with each successive infraction. This is the idea behind **progressive discipline**—the practice of basing punishment on the frequency and severity of the infraction.[77]

Let's consider an example of how progressive discipline might work for a common problem such as chronic absenteeism or tardiness. First, the supervisor may give the employee an informal oral warning. Then, if the problem persists, there would be an official meeting with the supervisor, during which time a formal warning would be issued. The next offense would result in a formal written warning that becomes part of the employee's personnel record. Subsequent offenses would lead to suspension without pay. And finally, if all this failed, the employee would be terminated. In the case of more serious offenses—such as gambling, for example—some of the preliminary steps would be dropped, and a formal written warning would be given. For the most serious offenses, such as stealing or intentionally damaging company property, officials would move immediately to the most severe step, immediate dismissal.

Companies with the most effective disciplinary programs tend to *make the contingencies clear,* such as by publicizing punishment rules in the company handbook. When this is done, employees know exactly what kind of behaviors the company will not tolerate, often minimizing the need to actually use discipline at all.

progressive discipline
The practice of gradually increasing the severity of punishments for employees who exhibit unacceptable job behavior.

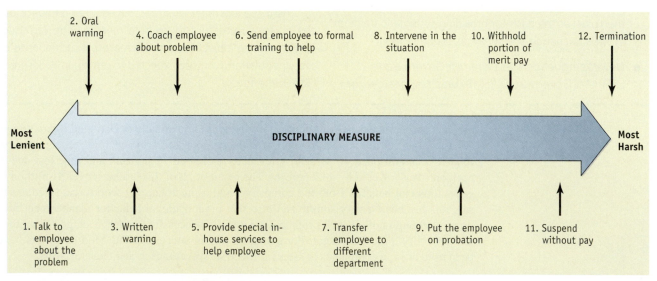

FIGURE 3.20

A Continuum of Disciplinary Measures

Ranked from mildest to most severe, these are the most commonly used disciplinary tactics used by nursing supervisors.

Source: Based on findings reported by Trahan & Steiner, 1994; see Note 76.

It probably comes as no surprise to you that supervisors do not always punish all inappropriate behaviors they encounter.[78] A key reason for this is that supervisors may feel constrained by limitations imposed by labor unions or by their own lack of formal authority. Also, in the absence of a clear company policy about how to use discipline, individuals may fear strong negative emotional reactions from the punished individual, if not also revenge and retaliation. As a result, many supervisors may turn the other way and simply do nothing when employees behave inappropriately. Although doing nothing may be easy in the long run, ignoring chronic problems is a way of informally approving of them, leading to increasingly serious problems in the future.

With this in mind, companies with the best disciplinary programs make it a practice to *take immediate action.* At Honda of America, for example, human resource specialist Tim Garrett notes that the company pays very close attention to all infractions of the rules, including ones "that other companies wouldn't think of paying attention to," adding, "If there's a problem, we'll pay attention to it right away."[79]

Keys To Using Punishment Effectively. Obviously, it isn't easy to know exactly when and how to administer punishment, and how it can be done in a way that is considered fair and reasonable. Fortunately, research and theory have pointed to some effective principles that may be followed to maximize the effectiveness of discipline in organizations.[80] We summarize these in Table 3.6. If, after going through this list, you are thinking that it is truly difficult to properly administer rewards and punishments in organizations, you have reached the same conclusion as experts in the field of organizational behavior and many practicing managers. Indeed, one of the key skills that make some managers so effective is their ability to influence others by properly administering rewards and punishments.

TABLE 3.6 Tips for Using Discipline Effectively

Disciplining employees is not as easy as it looks. It can be full of pitfalls, and most people don't know how to do it appropriately. The suggestions on this list represent some useful guidelines to follow in making your own disciplinary efforts as effective as possible. When reviewing these suggestions, be sure to think about the explanations for each one and how the suggestion is illustrated by the example.

Suggestion	Explanation	Example: *Bob is Often Late to Work, so the Manager Should . . .*
Deliver punishment immediately after the undesirable response occurs.	The less time that passes between the occurrence of an undesirable behavior and the administration of a negative consequence, the more strongly people will make the connection between them.	Talk to him about it immediately after he arrives.
Give moderate levels of punishment— nothing too high or too low.	If the consequences for performing an undesirable action are not very severe, then it is unlikely to operate as a punishment. If they are too severe, people are likely to protest.	Avoid being too lenient (e.g., by rolling his or her eyes) or too harsh (e.g., firing Bob if he is only a minute or two late).
Punish the undesirable behavior, not the person.	Punishment should be impersonal in nature and focus on an individual's actions rather than his or her personality.	Refrain from calling Bob "lazy" but explain the problems that result (e.g., customers cannot reach him) when he is not at his desk on time.
Use punishment consistently across occasions.	If you sometimes fail to punish a wrongdoing, you may send the message that you sometimes can get away with breaking the rules.	"Write up" Bob each and every time he is late.
Punish everyone equally for the same infraction.	If some people are punished while others are not, you will be accused of favoritism and will be considered unfair.	"Write up" all employees whenever they are late, just as is done with Bob.
Clearly communicate the reasons for the punishment given.	Making clear exactly what behaviors lead to what disciplinary actions makes punishment more effective.	Explain to Bob that his punishment is "nothing personal" but is based on his lateness.
Do not follow punishment with noncontingent rewards.	Sometimes people attempt to minimize the pain of punishment by doing something nice to make up for it. This may make everyone feel better, but it reinforces the undesirable behavior.	Resist the temptation to let Bob go home early (with pay) to "think about the problem."

Summary and Review of Learning Objectives

1. **Distinguish between the concepts of social perception and social identity.**

   Social perception is the process through which people select, organize, and interpret the information around them as it pertains to other people. According to social identity theory, the way we perceive others and ourselves is based on both our own unique characteristics (known as personal identity) and our membership in various groups (known as social identity).

2. **Explain how the attribution process works and describe the various sources of bias in social perception.**

   The process of attribution involves judging the underlying reasons for people's behavior. Some of our judgments are based on inferences made on the basis of observing others' behavior. These judgments, known as correspondent inferences, are often inaccurate. Our search for explanations about the causes of others' behavior leads us to make either judgments of internal causality (the individual is responsible for his own actions) or external causality (someone or something else is responsible). Kelley's theory of causal attribution explains that such judgments will be based on three types of information: consensus (whether others act in a similar manner), consistency (whether the individual previously acted this way in the same situation), and distinctiveness (whether this person acted similarly in different situations).

   Several types of systematic errors, known as perceptual biases, limit the accuracy of social perception. These include: the fundamental attribution error (the tendency to attribute others' actions to internal causes), the halo effect (the tendency to perceive others in either consistently positive or negative terms), the similar-to-me effect (the tendency to perceive similar others in a favorable light), first-impression error (the tendency for initial impressions to guide subsequent ones), and selective perception (the tendency for people to focus on only certain aspects of the environment). Perceptual inaccuracies also result from the tendency for people to rely on the use of stereotypes (the judgments of others based on the categories to which they belong).

   Perceptual biases can result in self-fulfilling prophecies (the tendency for someone's expectations about another to cause that individual to behave in a manner consistent with those expectations). These can be positive in nature, such as when expecting someone's performance to be good actually makes it so (known as the Pygmalion effect). They also can be negative, such as when someone's performance is bad because it was expected to be bad (known as the Golem effect).

3. **Understand how the process of social perception operates in the context of performance appraisals, employment interviews, and the cultivation of corporate images.**

   Biased judgments about others sometimes occur during the process of performance appraisal. In this context, people judge as superior those individuals whose performance matches their expectations, and those whose good performance is attributed to internal sources and whose poor performance is attributed to external sources. People are generally interested in getting others to perceive them favorably, and their efforts in this regard are referred to as impression management. This process is particularly important in employment interviews, although it sometimes interferes with the accuracy of information presented about individuals or companies. An organization's overall impression on people, its corporate image, is a determinant of its ability to attract qualified job applicants.

4. **Define learning and describe the two types most applicable to OB: operant conditioning and observational learning.**

   Learning refers to relative permanent changes in behavior occurring as a result of experience. In organizations, learning generally takes the form of *operant conditioning* and *observational learning*. In operant conditioning, individuals learn to behave certain ways based on the consequences of those actions. Stimuli that increase the probability of the behaviors preceding it are known as reinforcers.

Reinforcement may be either *positive,* if it is based on the presentation of a desirable outcome, or *negative,* if it is based on the withdrawal of an unwanted outcome. The probability of certain responses can be decreased if an unpleasant outcome results (punishment), or if a pleasant outcome is withdrawn (extinction). Observational learning involves learning by modeling the behavior of others. By paying attention to and rehearsing the behavior of others, we can learn vicariously, that is, through the model's experiences.

5. **Describe how principles of learning are involved in organizational training and innovative reward systems.**
   Learning is directly involved in efforts to teach people to acquire new job skills, the process known as training. Training is most effective when people can actively participate in the learning process, repeat the desired behaviors, receive feedback on their performance, and learn under conditions closely resembling those found on the job. Today, companies are experimenting with innovative reward systems that include skill-based pay (i.e., paying people for the various skills they have demonstrated on the job) and team-based rewards (i.e., paying people for their contributions to team performance).

6. **Compare the way organizations use reward in organizational behavior management programs and how they can use punishment most effectively when administering discipline.**
   Organizational behavior management is a systematic attempt to apply principles of reinforcement to the workplace so as to improve organizational functioning. Reinforcing desired behaviors can improve organizational functioning greatly. In contrast to applications of reinforcement, discipline is the systematic application of punishments to minimize undesirable organizational behaviors. The effects of discipline are most effective when punishment is applied immediately after the undesirable activity, moderately severe, focused on the activity rather than the individual, applied consistently over time, and for all employees, clearly explained and communicated, and not weakened by the use of inadvertent rewards.

Points to Ponder

Questions for Review

1. What is social perception and how is it applicable to the field of OB?
2. How do people come to make judgments about what others are like (known as the attribution process)?
3. In what ways is the attribution process biased, and what can be done about it?
4. How do operant conditioning and observational learning operate in the workplace?
5. What are the fundamental principles of learning and how are they involved in organizations?
6. What should be done to ensure that efforts to punish employees are as effective as possible?

Experiential Questions

1. Think of a time when you made judgments about a new workmate as you got to know him or her. In what ways were these judgments biased? As you got to know this person better, did you change your mind? What lesson can you learn about reaching judgments about people prematurely?
2. As a manager, it's important not to judge employees based on your expectations. If you do, the Pygmalion effect or the Golem effect may occur. Think back at a situation on the job or at school in which either you or your supervisor/teacher had expectations that led to one of these self-fulfilling prophecies. Exactly what happened? How was everyone involved affected, both positively and negatively? What could have been done to avoid this problem?
3. Think about any work-related training programs in which you may have been involved. In what ways were these efforts successful? What might have been done to make them even more effective?

Questions to Analyze

1. The attribution process is inherently inaccurate and subject to bias. In view of this, what chance do you think managers have of making accurate assessments of their subordinates' job performance? What could be done to combat these limitations, thereby making these important assessments more accurate?

2. E-learning is very popular today. What specific advice would you give anyone launching a corporate e-learning program who wants to make it as effective as possible? Do you think e-learning can ever be as effective as in-person training? In what ways might it be even more effective than in-person training?

3. Overall, do you think that managers will be able to more effectively change their subordinates' performance by using reward or by using punishment? However you answer, what specific steps would you take to make these efforts most effective? Explain your recommendations.

Experiencing OB

Individual Exercise

Identifying Occupational Stereotypes

Although we usually reserve our concern over stereotypes to those about women and members of racial and ethnic minorities, the simple truth is that people can hold stereotypes toward members of just about *any* group. And, in organizations, people are likely to hold stereotypes based on a variable whose importance cannot be downplayed—the occupational groups to which they belong. What we expect of people, and the way we treat them, is likely to be affected by stereotypes about their professions. This exercise will help you better understand this phenomenon.

Directions

Using the following scale, rate each of the following occupational groups with respect to how much of each characteristic people in these groups tend to show.

1 = not at all

2 = a slight amount

3 = a moderate amount

4 = a great amount

5 = an extreme amount

ACCOUNTANTS	PROFESSORS	LAWYERS
_____ interesting	_____ interesting	_____ interesting
_____ generous	_____ generous	_____ generous
_____ intelligent	_____ intelligent	_____ intelligent
_____ conservative	_____ conservative	_____ conservative
_____ shy	_____ shy	_____ shy
_____ ambitious	_____ ambitious	_____ ambitious

CLERGY	PHYSICIANS	PLUMBERS
_____ interesting	_____ interesting	_____ interesting
_____ generous	_____ generous	_____ generous
_____ intelligent	_____ intelligent	_____ intelligent
_____ conservative	_____ conservative	_____ conservative
_____ shy	_____ shy	_____ shy
_____ ambitious	_____ ambitious	_____ ambitious

Questions for Discussion

1. Did your ratings of the various groups differ? If so, which were perceived most positively and which were perceived most negatively?

2. On what characteristics, if any, did you find no differences with respect to the various groups? What do you think this means?
3. To what extent did your ratings agree with those of others? In other words, was there general agreement about the stereotypical nature of people in various occupational groups?
4. To what extent were your responses based on specific people you know? How did knowledge, or lack of knowledge, of members of the various occupational groups influence your ratings?
5. Do you believe that by becoming aware of these stereotypes you will perpetuate them in the future, or refrain from behaving in accord with them? Explain.

Group Exercise

Role Play: Conducting a Disciplinary Interview

Knowing how to discipline employees who behave inappropriately is an important managerial skill. The trick is to change the bad behavior into good behavior permanently, getting people to accept their mistakes and understand how to correct them. As you might imagine, this is often far more difficult than it sounds. After all, people are generally reluctant to admit their errors, and may have developed bad work habits that must be overcome. In addition, they tend to resist being chastised and don't like listening to criticism. With this in mind, disciplining others represents quite a challenge for managers, making it a skill worth developing.

Directions

1. Select four students from the class and divide them into two pairs. One person from each pair should read only the role sheet for Andy F., machine operator, and the other person from each pair should read only the role sheet for Barry B., his supervisor. Send both pairs outside the room until called upon.
2. Members of the class will serve as observers and should read both role sheets.
3. Call in the first pair of role players and ask them to spend about 10–15 minutes playing their roles—that is, acting as they would if they were the characters about whom they just read in the role sheets. They should feel free to assume any additional facts not described in these sheets.
4. Members of the class should observe the role play, taking careful notes. The class should *not* get involved in what the actors are saying, but pay close attention to it.
5. Repeat steps 3 and 4 with the second pair of role players.

Role Sheets

Andy F., Machine Operator

You have worked at Acme Manufacturing for six years now and have had a good record. Because you do your job so well, you sometimes take liberties and horse around with your buddies. For example, one Friday afternoon you were caught dancing around the shop floor when a good song came on the radio. Barry B., your supervisor, called you on the carpet for leaving your station. You think he has it in for you and is trying to run you off the job. Although you were acting silly, you are convinced that it doesn't matter since you were getting your job done. Now, he has called you in to see him to discuss the situation.

Barry B., Supervisor

After several years of experience in other shops, you were hired by Acme Manufacturing to be its new shop supervisor, a job you've had for only four months. Things have gone well during that time, but you've been having trouble with one machine operator, Andy F.

Andy seems to do an acceptable job, but is not giving it his all. Part of the problem is that he goofs around a lot. You have spoken to him about this informally a few times on the floor, but to no avail. One Friday afternoon you caught him away from his station, dancing around the shop floor. Not only wasn't he doing his own job, but he was distracting the others. You have just called Andy in to see you to discuss the situation.

Questions for Discussion

1. Did the supervisor, Barry B., define the problem in a nonthreatening way ?
2. Did each party listen to the other, or did they shut them out, merely explaining their own sides of the story?
3. Did Barry B. suggest specific things that Andy F. could do to improve? Were the specific punishments associated with future bad acts spelled out explicitly?
4. Were the discussions impersonal in nature, or did the parties focus on each other's personalities?
5. Considering all these questions, which supervisor would you say did a better job of administering discipline? What could be done to improve the way each supervisor conducted the disciplinary meeting?

Practicing OB

Managing People Who Are Goofing Off

Employees at a corporate call center have not been spending enough time at their cubicles answering phones, as required. Instead, they've been walking throughout the facility, talking to each other about personal matters. In other words, they're socializing and goofing off instead of working. Important calls have gone unanswered and customer service problems have arisen as a result.

1. What types of attributions would you be prone to make about these employees, and how would these be related to the performance evaluations you give them?
2. What types of errors would you be prone to make while making these judgments, and what might you do to overcome them so that you can make more accurate judgments?
3. How might you use training, innovative reward systems, organizational behavior management programs, and discipline to address the problem?

CASE IN POINT

Smiling Might Not Be Such a Safe Way to Treat Safeway Customers

Any training course on the essentials of customer service will advise you always to smile at customers and to make eye contact with them. In fact, it seems so commonsensical as to not need repeating. Little would you imagine, therefore, that doing precisely this actually would cause problems for some supermarket clerks! Nonetheless, this is precisely what happened to a dozen female employees at a Safeway supermarket in Martinez, California. The women claimed that their eye contact and smiles elicited unwanted attention from some male shoppers who mistook these friendly gestures as acts of flirting. Some clerks even had to resort to hiding in the store to escape customers who were hungry for services that weren't for sale. A produce clerk at one northern California store was even followed to her car and propositioned by a supermarket shopper who got the wrong idea.

The root of the problem, argue the twelve clerks who filed grievances with the United Food and Commercial Workers Union, is Safeway's "Superior Service" policy, which explicitly requires them to smile at customers and to maintain three seconds of eye contact with each one. It also expects clerks to anticipate customer's needs, to help them find items for which they're looking, and to call them by name if paying by check or credit card.

This policy was in place for five years before Safeway officials started enforcing it by using undercover shoppers to spot violators, who were sent letters warning them of the negative evaluations and disciplinary measures (even firing!) that could result from failing to comply. Soon thereafter, the incidents of customer harassment began. The union is seeking a modified policy that gives workers some discretion in the matter, allowing them to choose whether or not to maintain eye contact or to refuse to carry a customer's bags to his car at night.

From its headquarters in Pleasanton, California, Safeway officials acknowledged that although some customers get out of hand, this is not the result of their policy. They add that not one of the store's employees, currently about 200,000, ever has been fired for failing to be friendly. However, 100 have been sent to a daylong remedial training class on friendliness, what they call "Smile School." This, says Safeway spokesperson Debra Lambert, "is not about discipline. It's about treating customers well and training employees to do that." Think about this when you complain about that surly clerk who doesn't even look up to acknowledge you the next time you're in your local supermarket looking for laundry detergent.

Questions for Discussion

1. How, specifically, is the process of attribution illustrated in this case?
2. What do you suppose is being done to help train people to be friendlier toward customers? In other words, what would you imagine goes on in Safeway's "Smile School"?
3. Describe what you believe might be the progressive discipline steps outlined in the warning letter sent to unfriendly Safeway clerks.

Chapter 4

INDIVIDUAL DIFFERENCES: PERSONALITY, SKILLS, AND ABILITIES

Chapter Outline

Personality: Its Basic Nature

Major Work-Related Aspects of Personality: The "Big Five," Positive versus Negative Affectivity, and Core Self-Evaluations

Additional Work-Related Aspects of Personality

Abilities and Skills: Having What It Takes to Succeed

Special Sections

How to Do It

Increasing Self-Efficacy Among Employees

 In a Diverse World

Achievement Motivation and Economic Growth Around the World

 Making Sense Out of Common Sense

Is Job Performance Linked to Cognitive Intelligence?

After reading this chapter, you should be able to:

1. Define personality and describe its role in the study of organizational behavior.

2. Identify the Big Five dimensions of personality and elements of core self-evaluations and describe how they are related to key aspects of organizational behavior.

3. Distinguish between positive and negative affectivity and describe its effects on organizational behavior.

4. Describe achievement motivation and distinguish among learning, performance, and avoidance goal orientations.

5. Describe Machiavellianism and the difference between morning and evening persons and their role in work-related behavior.

6. Differentiate among cognitive intelligence, emotional intelligence, and practical intelligence and explain their influences on behavior in organizations.

PREVIEW CASE

Charles Schwab Brings Back Charles Schwab

In the early 2000s, even the savviest of Wall Street investors was in for a rough ride. The easy-to-come-by gains of the previous decade were only a memory, and the brokerage firm Charles Schwab was feeling the pinch. Between 2000 and 2002 assets plummeted from almost $700 million to only $100 million. Something had to give, and what would give way, the firm's board of directors decided, was the job of CEO David Pottruck. After five years in office, he was asked to step down, paving the way for the return of the company's founder and namesake. Charles Schwab, everyone believed, was special and the company that bore his name once again begged for his special touch.

Schwab founded the firm with a single office in Seattle back in 1977. Unlike his competitors at the time (including giants like the venerable Merrill Lynch), which charged sizable fees on stock trades to customers—primarily companies and wealthy individuals—Schwab had a maverick idea: Charge much lower commissions so that the average person could invest in the stock market with modest amounts of cash, bringing Wall Street to Main Street. Lower commissions, though, required higher sales volume. To make this viable, Schwab made another bold, bet-the-company move: He invested in a mainframe computer system designed to streamline transactions. This was in 1979, when computers were major expenses (often requiring huge, temperature-controlled rooms) and were not in widespread use.

The investment really began to pay off in 1984, when the first personal computers were introduced. That's when Schwab debuted The Equalizer, a now-prehistoric (DOS-based) computer program for everyday investors, which eventually pointed the way toward an online future. Shortly thereafter, long before the Internet trading frenzy of the late 1990s—before the Internet was developed, in fact—Schwab made online investing available to CompuServe subscribers, reaching out to his new market: individual investors who knew what financial products they wanted to purchase and who didn't require much advice. Soon, the novelty wore off, competition for discount brokerage services set in, and when times got tough, navigating the stock market successfully required professional know-how. This is when everyday people became disenchanted (and much poorer), causing the company to lose customers.

This was in 2004, when the visionary Schwab was handed back the reins of the now-stumbling company and asked to rework his magic on it. What he found was not the same prestigious firm he left earlier. Throughout the company, morale was low. "We lost the emotional connection with our clients," he observed. The firm had antagonized clients by raising some fees and marketing products in an impersonal manner. The firm lost momentum, Schwab believed, because it became disconnected with its customers. Realizing this almost immediately, he lowered commissions and changed operations and policies so as to regain those precious connections. Only 18 months into his second term as CEO, not only has Charles Schwab, the man, gotten the company to regain its dominance in the field, but he grew Charles Schwab, the firm, to $1.2 trillion in assets through the first half of 2006.

Today, it's no longer advances in technology that Schwab is using to strengthen its business. Everybody has the latest computers. Rather, Schwab's secret weapon through 2010 is much more old-fashioned: people. "I'd like to have every client of Schwab have the sense that they have a relationship with Schwab," he says, "which includes that they have somebody that they can trust, that they can talk to." And this, he emphasizes in egalitarian fashion, "goes from the largest clients we have to even some of the smallest."

If you were to describe Mr. Schwab, what terms would you use? Would you say he's dedicated? Innovative? A visionary? A risk-taker? Surely, he's all these things and more. He's also highly sensitive to people—both his employees (whose low morale he observed) and his customers (whose dissatisfaction he noted). No matter how you put it, Charles Schwab is quite special and a highly successful businessperson, to say the least. Many of us surely find it difficult to relate to such a unique individual. That makes sense. However, in our own ways—even if we aren't the founders or CEOs of giant brokerage firms—we are each unique. After all, each of us has a one-of-a-kind mix of traits, characteristic, skills, and abilities—a combination that makes us different, in various ways, from every other human being on the planet.

individual differences

The many ways in which individuals can differ from each other.

Scientists refer to the ways in which people differ from one another as **individual differences**, and such unique qualities can have major influences on our thinking and behavior as well as our lives and careers. Because such factors play a role in many aspects of behavior in work settings, they have long been of interest to experts in the field of organizational behavior. As such, in this chapter we provide a broad overview of this knowledge.

Our plan is as follows. First, we focus on *personality,* one very important aspect of individual differences. Here, we first consider the matter of how various facets of personality combine with elements of the work environment to influence behavior. This is important, of course, because according to the popular *interactionist perspective* to organizational behavior, how we behave is based on both who we are (i.e., individual influences) and the contexts in which we operate (i.e., situational influences).[1] Following this, we turn to the question of how personality can be measured. Since traits and abilities are not physical quantities that can be observed readily, this is not the easiest thing to do, but, as you'll see, something scientists are able to do quite effectively. Then, after describing these measurement methods, we describe a wide variety of personality variables that have been found to have important effects in the workplace. Finally, in another major section, we'll examine several *abilities* (mental and physical capacities to perform various tasks) and *skills* (proficiency at performing specific tasks acquired through training or experience) and their effects on various aspects of organizational behavior.

Personality: Its Basic Nature

Deep down, I'm pretty superficial. (Ava Gardner, American actress, 1983)

That's a fairly devastating self-description by a famous movie star of the 1940s and 1950s. How would *you* describe your own personality in a single sentence? Admittedly, that's a very difficult task, because what makes each of us unique is complex and hard to put into words. But personality involves more than just uniqueness—it has other important features, too. Since understanding the nature of personality is crucial to appreciating its potential role in organizational behavior, we begin by taking a closer look at this important concept.

What Is Personality?

personality
The unique and relatively stable patterns of behavior, thoughts, and emotions shown by individuals.

As we noted earlier, we are all, in some ways, *unique*—that is, we all possess a distinct pattern of traits and characteristics not fully duplicated in any other person. Further, this pattern of traits tends to be stable over time. Thus, if you know someone who is optimistic, confident, and friendly today, then chances are good that he or she also showed these same traits in the past and that this person will continue to show them in the future. Together, these two features form the basis for a useful working definition of **personality**—the unique and relatively stable pattern of behavior, thoughts, and emotions shown by individuals (see Figure 4.1).[2] Just how stable are various aspects of personality—or individual differences in general? Evidence suggests that they are quite stable.[3] For instance, consider job satisfaction, a topic we'll examine in Chapter 6. Interestingly, scientists have found that although some people are satisfied under almost any working conditions, others tend to be dissatisfied under almost any conditions (even when these are truly excellent).[4] Such individuals are difficult to satisfy. This doesn't imply that job satisfaction cannot be changed or that it is not affected by working conditions; as you will see in Chapter 6, this is not the case. However, this scientific observation does illustrate a key point: Stable individual differences play an important role in job satisfaction—and, as we will see, in many other aspects of organizational behavior.

Personality and Situations: The Interactionist Approach

interactionist perspective
The view that behavior is a result of a complex interplay between personality and situational factors.

Earlier, we noted that personality often combines with situational factors to influence behavior. This is a key point, so we'll clarify it now. What it means is that although people possess stable traits and characteristics that predispose them to behave in certain ways, these qualities by themselves do not completely determine how someone will behave in any given situation. Situations also introduce forces that affect how one is likely to behave. Together, both the personal factors and the situational factors influence behavior. In other words, behavior usually is the result of both characteristics possessed by an individual (his or her knowledge, abilities, skills, and personality) and the nature of the situation in which that person operates. This approach, known as the **interactionist perspective**, is very popular in the field of OB today.[5]

FIGURE 4.1

Personality: Defining Characteristics

When we speak of personality, we are referring to each individual's unique blend of traits that is relatively stable over time.

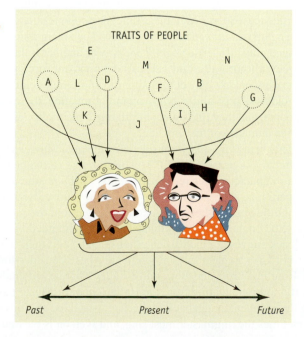

Let's consider an example. Someone with a quick temper may be predisposed to act aggressively, but he or she may refrain from expressing anger (e.g., by screaming at a coworker) because of the negative consequences of doing so in that setting (e.g., losing a job, getting into legal trouble). In this case, the situation imposes demands to hold aggression in check. It's also possible, of course, that someone's aggressive tendencies are so strong that they override the demands of the situation, leading to tragic consequences. It's useful to think of the interactionst perspective as illustrated in Figure 4.2, as a combined set of forces—individual and situational—that can tip the balance so as to influence behavior in a certain way at any given time.

With respect to organizational behavior, for instance, the question of whether various aspects of personality affect job performance has long been of interest.[6] As we will note later in this chapter, certain aspects of personality are indeed related to job performance. Although this is important, it doesn't tell the whole story, however. The strength of the effects of personality depends on many situational factors. These may include such factors as *job demands* (i.e., the set of tasks and duties associated with a specific job that motivate people to behave in certain ways; see Chapter 7) and *social norms* (i.e., pressures to go along with others in one's group; see Chapter 8). Overall, both personality and situational factors can serve as *facilitators*—factors encourage certain behaviors, or *constraints*—factors that discourage certain behaviors.[7]

We present these in generic form in Figure 4.2, but let's now consider some specific scenarios. First, as depicted in *situation 1,* suppose you are a very quiet person, someone who is inclined to keep quiet most of the time. This would discourage you from saying anything, but you would be even more strongly disinclined from saying anything if you perceive the organization as discouraging people from speaking their minds (e.g., by punishing those who speak up at meetings). Now, consider *situation 2,* in which things are opposite. Here, suppose you are a very expressive person, someone who is inclined to speak up when things occur. This would facilitate speaking up, but you would be especially likely to speak up (and to do so strongly) when organizational norms and culture (see Chapter 14) also send strong signals that this is acceptable. As you might suspect, it's easy for people when they encounter *situation 1* or *situation 2* because all forces lead them in the same direction. Both who they are as individuals and the demands of the situations they face lead them in the same directions.

However, things are more difficult in *situations 3 and 4,* in which one's personality encourages one to behave one way whereas the demands of the situation encourage one to behave another. In these cases (illustrated in the two diagrams in the lower half of Figure 4.2), people are likely to be conflicted. Here, the balance can be tipped slightly in either direction, depending on which force is stronger, the inhibiting influences or the constraining influences. So, for example, a quiet person in a situation that places a high premium on speaking up (*situation 3*) and an expressive person in a situation in which expression is discouraged may go ever so slightly one way or another if the balance is tipped. Of course, the balance will not go too far because the opposite force will keep it from doing so. As a result, we wouldn't expect to find particularly high degrees of expressiveness or of quietness under such conditions. As you might imagine, these are highly conflicting situations for people, and they find it uncomfortable to be in settings in which who they are is at odds with the demands of the situation.

person-job fit
The extent to which the traits and abilities of individuals match the requirements of the jobs they must perform.

This brings up a key consideration involved in selecting certain career options (see Appendix 2)—**person-job fit**. This term refers to the degree to which a person's unique blend of characteristics (e.g., personality, skills) is suited to the requirements for success on a particular job.[8] As you may suspect, the more closely individuals' personalities, traits, and abilities match those required by a given job, the more productive and satisfied they tend to be on those jobs.[9] Fortunately, through interacting with others, people often receive feedback suggesting the particular jobs that best fit their personalities (see Figure 4.3).

For an example of person-job fit at its best, consider Jonathan Lee Iverson, ringmaster for Ringling Bros. and Barnum & Bailey Circus. He landed this unusual job at age 22, shortly after graduating from the Hartt School of Music in Hartford, Connecticut, reflecting the excellent match between his talents and the abilities needed for this demanding job. Sometimes the ringmaster must sing, and Iverson is blessed with a wonderful voice with a

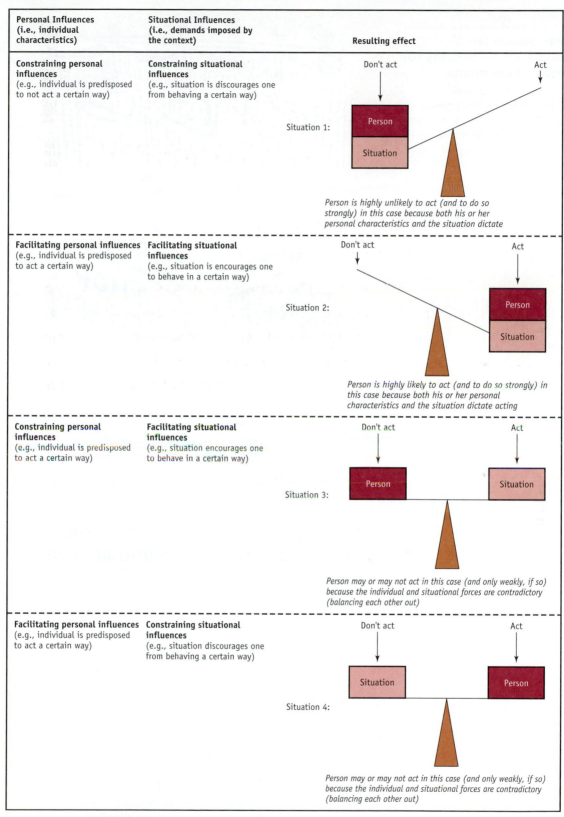

FIGURE 4.2

The Interactionist Perspective

This popular approach to the study of personality suggests that behavior in almost any context is a joint function of both characteristics of the individuals being considered and aspects of the specific context in which they are behaving. Various ways in which personalities and situations may either constrain or facilitate behavior are summarized here.

FIGURE 4.3

Person-Job Fit: Matching Personality to Job Requirements

By virtue of the qualities they bring to the jobs they perform, people's personalities predispose them in varying degrees *toward* success on particular jobs—a concept known as *person-job fit*. Hopefully, this is not one such example of good person-job fit.

Source: www.CartoonStock.com

"I've watched you, Bastable. You are domineering, foulmouth and agressive - how would you like to be foreman?"

great range, which suits him for the job. Also, he is friendly and outgoing. And of course, he is simply not afraid to control the entire show—three rings with 180 performers and 80 animals. Clearly, not everyone could do this job, but Iverson, who has now been with Ringling Bros. for several years, has precisely what the job takes—and as a result, loves it and is highly successful at it.

How Is Personality Measured?

Physical traits such as height and weight can be measured readily by means of simple tools. Various aspects of personality, however, cannot be assessed quite so simply. There are no rulers that we can put to the task. How, then, can we quantify differences between individuals with respect to their various personality characteristics? Several methods exist for accomplishing this task. In this section, we'll describe two of the most important and will then consider some of the essential requirements that all procedures for measuring individual differences must meet.

Objective Tests: Paper-And-Pencil Measures of Who We Are. Have you ever completed a questionnaire in which you were asked to indicate whether each of a set of statements is true or false about yourself, the extent to which you agree or disagree with various sentences, or which of several pairs of activities you prefer (e.g., attending a football game versus reading a book)? If so, chances are good that you have completed what is known as an **objective test**—a paper-and-pencil inventory in which people are asked to respond to a series of questions designed to measure one or more aspects of their personality. Objective tests are the most widely used method of measuring both personality and mental abilities (such as intelligence).

objective tests
Questionnaires and inventories designed to measure various aspects of personality.

People's answers to the questions on objective tests are scored by means of special answer keys. The score obtained by a specific person is then compared with those obtained by hundreds or even thousands of other people who have taken the test previously. In this way, an individual's relative standing on the trait or ability being measured can be determined. This can then be used to predict various aspects of behavior, such as success in specific kinds of job or training. Such tests are considered "objective" because they are scored by comparing individuals' answers to special scoring keys; subjective judgments by the test-givers do not play a role.

Projective Tests. A very different approach to measuring personality is adopted in what are known as *projective tests*. These tests present individuals with ambiguous stimuli—for instance, a drawing of a scene in which it is not clear what the persons shown are doing. Individuals taking such tests then report what they perceive, and their answers are used as a basis for reaching conclusions about their personalities. Presumably, one reason why different people report "seeing" different things in the ambiguous stimuli they examine is that they differ with respect to personality; and such differences then, supposedly, become visible in their responses.

Do such tests really work—do they really provide insights into personality? There is considerable controversy over this issue so except for a few widely used tests (e.g., one that measures the need for achievement), projective tests are not very popular among researchers in the field of OB. Instead, most prefer to use the objective tests described earlier. Now, let's turn to questions that relate to all measures of personality—questions about whether these measures really allow us to accurately assess the variables we want to measure.

Reliability and Validity: Essential Requirements of Personality Tests. Imagine that you weigh yourself on your bathroom scale every morning. One day, the weight reads "150 pounds." The next day, it reads "140 pounds." Although you may be happy with the result, you would probably suspect that something is wrong because you could not possibly have lost 10 pounds overnight. Instead, it is much more likely that there is something wrong with the scale. It is not recording your weight accurately. More formally, we would say that it is not measuring your weight in a *reliable* manner.

reliability
The extent to which a test yields consistent scores on various occasions, and the extent to which all of its items measure the same underlying construct.

Clearly, if we are to have confidence in something we measure—weight, various aspects of personality, or anything else—we must be able to do so reliably. The **reliability** of a measure refers to the extent to which it is stable and consistent over time. As you might imagine, a measure of personality must have a high degree of reliability in order to be useful. Only those tests that show high degrees of reliability are used in research in the field of OB. After all, tests that do not yield reliable results may tell us little—or, even worse, they may be misleading.

In addition to being reliable, a test must also be *valid*—that is, it must really measure what it claims to measure. To understand, think about those "tests" that often appear in popular magazines, such as ones with the provocative title, "Are You Compatible with Your Mate?" Considering that this is an interesting question, you go through the questions, check a few boxes, and then go to the scoring key to see if you'll be enjoying a life of bliss or if you'll end up in divorce court. Although you might find this exercise interesting and fun, and it might cause you to think about important things in your relationship, chances are good that this so-called test is not valid. In other words, such an exercise probably hasn't been tested by scientists to see if people's scores really do predict how their relationship ends up. In this case, we would say that the measure is low in *validity*. The term **validity** refers to the extent to which a test really measures what it claims to measure. Naturally, we seek tests that have

validity
The extent to which a test actually measures what it claims to measure.

high degrees of validity because we can be confident of what their scores mean. Tests that are low in validity, however, are essentially useless.

How do we assess a test's validity? In actual practice, the process is complex, requiring many steps and sophisticated statistical procedures. In essence, though, a test's validity is established by demonstrating that scores on it are related to other aspects of behavior that already are known to reflect the trait being measured. In other words, a test of a personality trait is valid to the extent that what it measures is closely related to the "true" measure of that trait, as assessed by other established tests. For instance, a test of sales ability would be valid to the extent that successful salespersons score high on it whereas those who are unsuccessful score low. Only to the extent that its validity has been so established would it be useful for selecting potential employees—ones likely to succeed at selling. Scientists refer to this type of validity as **predictive validity**. This term refers to the extent to which scores on a test administered at one time are correlated with scores on some performance measure assessed at a later time (see Figure 4.4).

Another example of predictive validity can be seen in the test you might have taken for admission into college, graduate school, or professional school. Such tests are considered highly valid because the individuals who score high on them tend to perform better in school. This positive correlation between the test score and a measure of success is an indication of its predictive validity. And this, of course, is precisely why colleges and universities rely on such tests. After all, if they didn't help predict success in their programs, there'd be no reason to use them.

At this point, we should note that all of the traits and abilities considered in this chapter are measured by tests known to be both reliable and valid. Thus, you can have confidence in the findings we report concerning their effects on important aspects of organizational behavior.

Do Organizations Have Personalities Too?

If you ask people what qualities come to mind when they think of Microsoft, chances are good that they'd say things like "arrogant" and "dominant." However, if you asked them about the Walt Disney Company, they'd likely say "family-oriented" and "friendly." Such responses seem to suggest that people think of organizations, much like people, as having certain traits—unique, stable characteristics that set them apart from other organizations—that is, distinct *personalities*. Can this be true? In one sense, it cannot. After all, organizations are not living entities and do not possess emotions, thoughts, or memories. In another sense, though, there is no doubt that we often *think about* organizations as though they do have distinct personalities (see Figure 4.5).

---

predictive validity

The extent to which the score achieved on a test administered to a person at one time predicts (i.e., is correlated with) some measure of his or her performance at some later time.

FIGURE 4.4

Predictive Validity

When a test has a high degree of predictive validity it is able to predict performance assessed at some later point in time. The positive correlation between the test score and the measure of job performance shown here provides evidence of a high degree of predictive validity. This is desirable because it makes it possible to predict how someone will behave in the future based on tests administered in the present.

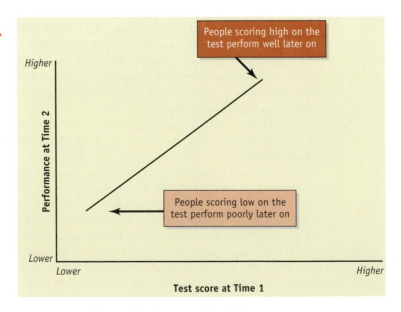

People scoring high on the test perform well later on

People scoring low on the test perform poorly later on

Performance at Time 2 — Higher / Lower

Test score at Time 1 — Lower / Higher

What Are These Organizations Like?

When asked to describe organizations, people tend to use qualities akin to human personality traits. For example, research has shown that although both Nike and Disney are considered to be highly innovative, Disney also is considered a friendly, Boy Scout-type company, whereas Nike also is considered a highly dominant and stylish company.

Source: Based on findings by Slaughter, Zickar, Highhouse, & Mohr, 2004; see Note 10.

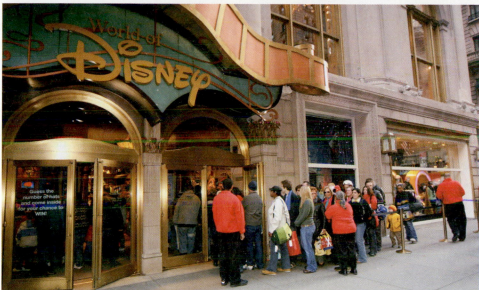

If organizations have personalities, then what particular traits describe them? A recent study examined this question.[10] In this research, hundreds of business school students were asked to rate several familiar companies (e.g., AT&T, Ford, McDonald's, Kroger, Wal-Mart, Subway, Bob Evans, JC Penney, Disney, Microsoft, Reebok, and Nike) on various traits. Interestingly, several distinct clusters emerged, with various companies rated highly on each. These clusters, traits describing them, and some of the companies rating highly on them are as follows:

- *Boy Scout:* friendly, attentive to people—Disney, Bob Evans
- *Innovative:* interesting, unique—Nike, Disney
- *Dominant:* successful, popular—Nike, Microsoft
- *Thrifty:* poor, sloppy—Bob Evans, JC Penney
- *Stylish:* modern, contemporary—Nike, Reebok

It's interesting that some companies rated highly on more than one cluster of characteristics. This shouldn't be too surprising because, just as individuals may posses high amounts of more than one personality characteristic, so too may organizations. For example, that Nike was perceived to be innovative, dominant, and stylish may square well with your own perception of this company.

Clearly, different companies are viewed as possessing different clusters of traits, but are these related to anything important? Do they really matter? The researchers who conducted this study predicted that organizational personalities would be linked to *organizational attractiveness*—the extent to which individuals perceive organizations as attractive places in which to work. To test this prediction, they prepared descriptions of a fictitious company (Stage Clothing Downtown) that depicted it possessing high amounts of the characteristics associated with each cluster (e.g., to make the company appear stylish, it was described as a place in which people concerned about fashion would shop). Participants were shown one of these descriptions and were asked to rate the company's personality and their attraction to it as a place in which to work. Results were clear: Ratings of the company's personality corresponded to the descriptions provided. Also, companies depicted as high on the Boy Scout, innovative, and stylish dimensions were rated as the best places in which to work.

In sum, it appears that we do tend to think about organizations as having personalities, and that our perceptions in this regard influence our interest in working in such companies. Clearly, then, even if organizational personality does not exist in the same sense as individual personality, it can have important effects—ones savvy organizations should consider carefully when planning their advertising and recruitment campaigns.

Major Work-Related Aspects of Personality: The "Big Five," Positive versus Negative Affectivity, and Core Self-Evaluations

Now that we have defined personality and described how it is measured, we will consider several aspects of it that have been found to be closely linked to important aspects of organizational behavior. In this first section, we'll consider aspects of personality widely considered to be especially important because they influence many aspects of behavior in work settings. After that, we'll consider several additional aspects of personality that also have important implications for behavior in work settings, but whose effects may be somewhat less general in scope.

The Big Five Dimensions of Personality: Our Most Fundamental Traits

Big Five dimensions of personality
Five basic dimensions of personality that are assumed to underlie many specific traits.

extraversion
A tendency to seek stimulation and to enjoy the company of other people; one of the Big Five personality dimensions.

agreeableness
A tendency to be compassionate toward others; one of the Big Five personality dimensions.

conscientiousness
A tendency to show self-discipline, to strive for competence and achievement; one of the Big Five personality dimensions.

neuroticism
A tendency to experience unpleasant emotions easily; one of the Big Five personality dimensions.

How many different personality traits can you list? Would you believe 17,953? That's the number of personality-related words found in a search of an English language dictionary in a study conducted over sixty years ago.[11] Even after combining words with similar meanings, the list still contained 171 distinct traits. Does this mean that we must consider a huge number of traits to fully understand the role of personality in organizational behavior?

Fortunately, the answer is no. A growing body of evidence suggests that there are five key dimensions to consider. Because these same five dimensions have emerged in so many different studies conducted in so many different ways, they are often referred to as the **Big Five dimensions of personality**.[12] These are as follows:

- **Extraversion:** A tendency to seek stimulation and to enjoy the company of other people. This reflects a dimension ranging from energetic, enthusiastic, sociable, and talkative at one end, to retiring, sober, reserved, silent, and cautious on the other.
- **Agreeableness:** A tendency to be compassionate toward others. This dimension ranges from good-natured, cooperative, trusting, and helpful at one end, to irritable, suspicious, and uncooperative at the other.
- **Conscientiousness:** A tendency to show self-discipline, to strive for competence and achievement. This dimension ranges from well organized, careful, self-disciplined, responsible, and precise at one end, to disorganized, impulsive, careless, and undependable at the other.
- **Neuroticism:** A tendency to experience unpleasant emotions easily. This dimension ranges from poised, calm, composed, and not hypochondriacal at one end, to nervous, anxious, high-strung, and hypochondriacal at the other.

openness to experience
A tendency to enjoy new experiences and new ideas; one of the Big Five personality dimensions.

■ **Openness to experience:** A tendency to enjoy new experiences and new ideas. This dimension ranges from imaginative, witty, and having broad interests at one end, to down-to-earth, simple, and having narrow interests at the other.

These five basic dimensions of personality are measured by means of questionnaires in which the people whose personalities are being assessed answer various questions about themselves. Some sample items similar to those on popular measures of the Big Five dimensions are shown in Table 4.1. By completing them, you gain a rough idea of where *you* stand on each of these dimensions.

The Big Five dimensions of personality are very important and they are related strongly to work performance.[13] This is the case across many different occupational groups (e.g., professionals, police, managers, salespersons, skilled laborers), and several kinds of performance measures (e.g., ratings of individuals' performance by managers or others, performance during training programs, personnel records). In general, *conscientiousness* shows the strongest association with task performance: The higher individuals are on this dimension, the higher their performance.[14] Many companies are aware of this relationship. For instance, a major university offers the following guidelines to managers regarding information to be imparted to incoming employees.

Establish attendance and punctuality expectations at hiring interviews and during orientation. Make sure applicants and employees understand that maintenance of good attendance is a condition of employment. Explain that sick leave should only be used for legitimate illness or injury and should be stockpiled for potential serious conditions. . . . Explain that excessive unscheduled absences disrupt the department workflow, cause a burden on co-workers and may limit the department's ability to meet customer service demands. Note that sick leave taken on a repeated basis may be viewed as abuse of the system, and may affect consideration for promotions, transfers and pay raises.

TABLE 4.1 The Big Five Dimensions of Personality

The items listed here are similar to ones used to measure each of the *big five dimensions of personality.* Answering them may give you some insight into these key aspects of your personality.

Directions: Indicate the extent to which you agree or disagree with each item by entering a number in the space beside it. Enter 5 if you agree strongly with the item, 4 if you agree, 3 if you neither agree nor disagree, 2 if you disagree, and 1 if you disagree strongly.

Conscientiousness:

    ____ I keep my room neat and clean.

    ____ People generally find me to be extremely reliable.

Extraversion:

    ____ I like lots of excitement in my life.

    ____ I usually am very cheerful.

Agreeableness:

    ____ I generally am quite courteous to other people.

    ____ People never think I am cold and sly.

Emotional Stability:

    ____ I often worry about things that are out of my control.

    ____ I usually feel sad or "down."

Openness to Experience:

    ____ I have a lot of curiosity.

    ____ I enjoy the challenge of change.

Scoring: Add your scores for each item. Higher scores reflect greater degrees of the personality characteristic being measured.

Similar recognition of the importance of this basic aspect of personality is present in many other organizations. Another Big Five dimension, *emotional stability,* also is related to task performance (although not as strongly or consistently): The more emotionally stable individuals are, the better their task performance.[15]

Other dimensions of the Big Five also are linked to task performance, but in more specific ways. For instance, *agreeableness* is related positively to various interpersonal aspects of work (e.g., getting along well with others). And for some occupations—ones requiring individuals to interact with many other people during the course of the day (e.g., managers, police officers, salespeople)—extraversion is related positively to performance. The Big Five dimensions also are related to team performance. Specifically, the higher the average scores of team members on conscientiousness, agreeableness, extraversion, and emotional stability, the higher their teams perform.[16] Overall, then, it appears that the Big Five dimensions are indeed one determinant of job performance for teams as well as individuals.

In addition, the Big Five traits also are linked to other important organizational processes.[17] For example, several of the Big Five dimensions play an important role in determining who becomes a leader (for a thorough discussion of leadership, see Chapter 13).[18] People scoring high in extraversion, in openness to experience, and in agreeableness (e.g., the tendency to trust others, at least initially) are more likely to become leaders than others who score low on these dimensions.[19]

It's also interesting that the Big Five dimensions influence business success among entrepreneurs. Specifically, the higher entrepreneurs are in conscientiousness, the longer their new ventures tend to survive—and, of course, the longevity of new ventures is linked closely to their financial success.[20]

Positive and Negative Affectivity: Tendencies toward Feeling Good or Bad

It is a basic fact of life that our moods fluctuate rapidly—and sometimes greatly—throughout the day. An e-mail message containing good news may leave us smiling, while an unpleasant conversation with a coworker may leave us feeling gloomy. Such temporary feelings are known as *mood states* and can strongly affect anyone at almost any time. However, mood states are only part of the total picture when considering the effects of how our feelings and emotions can affect our behavior at work.

As you probably know from your own experience, people differ not just in terms of their current moods—which can be affected by many different events—but also with respect to more stable tendencies to experience positive or negative feelings.[21] Some people tend to be "up" most of the time whereas others tend to be more subdued or even depressed; and these tendencies are apparent in a wide range of contexts. In other words, at any given moment people's *affective states* (their current feelings) are based both on temporary conditions (i.e., ever-changing moods) *and* relatively stable differences in lasting dispositions to experience positive or negative feelings (i.e., stable traits) (see Figure 4.6).

These differences in predispositions toward positive and negative moods are an important aspect of personality. In fact, such differences are related to the ways in which individuals approach many events and experiences on their jobs and in their lives in general. Some people, as you know, are generally energetic, exhilarated, and have a real zest for life. You know them to be "up" all the time. Such individuals may be said to be high in **positive affectivity**. They may be characterized as having an overall sense of well-being, seeing people and events in a positive light, and usually experiencing positive emotional states. By contrast, people who are low in positive affectivity are generally apathetic and listless. Another dimension of mood is known as **negative affectivity**. It is characterized at the high end by people who are generally angry, nervous, and anxious, and at the low end by those who feel calm and relaxed most of the time.[22] As indicated in Figure 4.7, positive affectivity and negative affectivity are not the opposite of each other, but rather, two separate dimensions.

As you might suspect, people who are high in positive affectivity behave differently from those who are high in negative affectivity with respect to several key aspects of organizational behavior—and in undesirable ways. In fact, 42 percent of office workers responding to a recent survey indicated that they worked with people who could be

positive affectivity
The tendency to experience positive moods and feelings in a wide range of settings and under many different conditions.

negative affectivity
The tendency to experience negative moods in a wide range of settings and under many different conditions.

FIGURE 4.6

Positive and Negative Affectivity: An Important Aspect of Personality

Everyone experiences changes in mood throughout the day. But individual differences in stable tendencies to experience either positive affect or negative affect also exist. These stable differences in affective state have been found to be related to important aspects of organizational behavior.

described as "negative"—perpetual pessimists who think everything will turn out badly, criticizers who find fault with everything, and people who are just plain negative—they are simply "down" all the time.[23] Not only do such individuals perform poorly themselves, but their negativity also interferes with the performance of others. In other words, they create an atmosphere that reduces productivity and that, of course, can be costly. Among the forms this takes are the following.

- *Decision making*—People with high levels of positive affectivity make superior decisions than those with high levels of negative affectivity.[24]
- *Team performance*—Work groups that have a positive affective tone (those in which the average level of positive affectivity is high) function more effectively than groups that have a negative affective tone (those in which the average level of negative affectivity is high).[25]
- *Aggressive behavior*—Because they tend to be very passive in nature, people who are high in negative affectivity are likely to be targets of aggression from others in their organizations.[26]

FIGURE 4.7

Positive and Negative Affectivity

Positive affectivity and negative affectivity are two independent dimensions. The mood state associated with high levels and low levels of each are shown here.

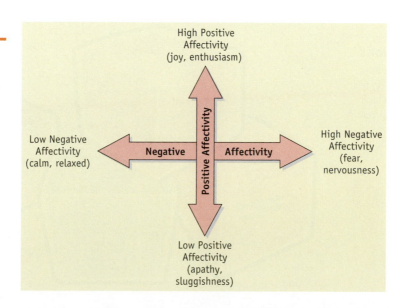

In view of these findings, it's little wonder that positive and negative affectivity are considered important personality traits when it comes to understanding organizational behavior.

Core Self-Evaluations: How Do We Think of Ourselves?

What is your image of yourself? To what extent is your self-concept positive or negative? Although most of us tend to view ourselves in positive terms, not everybody does so to the same degree. Moreover, the particular way in which we view ourselves is not indicative of a single personality variable, but rather, four distinct elements of personality known as **core self-evaluations**. These refer to people's fundamental evaluations of themselves, their bottom-line conclusions about themselves.[27]

People's core self-evaluations are based on four particular personality traits (see Figure 4.8). These are as follows:

- **Self-esteem**—The overall value one places on oneself as a person
- **Generalized self-efficacy**—A person's beliefs about his or her capacity to perform specific tasks successfully
- **Locus of control**—The extent to which individuals feel that they are able to control things in a manner that affects them
- **Emotional stability**—The tendency to see oneself as confident, secure, and steady (the opposite of *neuroticism,* one of the Big Five personality variables)

Individually, each of the four dimensions of core-self evaluations has been researched extensively, and each is associated with beneficial organizational outcomes. For example, take self-esteem. Individuals with high levels of self-esteem tend to view opportunities to perform challenging jobs as valued opportunities and enjoy rising to the occasion. Not surprisingly, they also put forth a great deal of effort and perform at high levels. By comparison, people who have low self-esteem perceive difficult work situations as threats and dislike them. As a result, they either try to avoid such tasks or don't give it their full effort because they expect to fail, and as a result, they tend to perform poorly.[28] In view of this, it's important to consider how to raise self-esteem on the job. For some suggestions in this regard, see the *How to Do It* section on page 147.

Now, let's consider generalized self-efficacy. Individuals who have high amounts of this trait are confident that they can do well at whatever they do. This, in turn, encourages them to take on such challenges and because they believe they will succeed they are unlikely to give up when things get rough. As a result, they tend to be successful at these jobs. Then, because they associate the work with success, they are inclined to be satisfied with the jobs themselves.

core self-evaluation
People's fundamental evaluations of themselves, their bottom-line conclusions about themselves.

self-esteem
The overall value one places on oneself as a person.

generalized self-efficacy
A person's beliefs about his or her capacity to perform specific tasks successfully.

locus of control
The extent to which individuals feel that they are able to control things in a manner that affects them.

emotional stability
The tendency to see oneself as confident, secure, and steady (the opposite of *neuroticism,* one of the Big Five personality variables).

FIGURE 4.8

Core Self-Evaluations

In assessing who we are as individuals, people rely on four aspects of personality, which together are known as *core self-evaluations*. These various components are shown here.

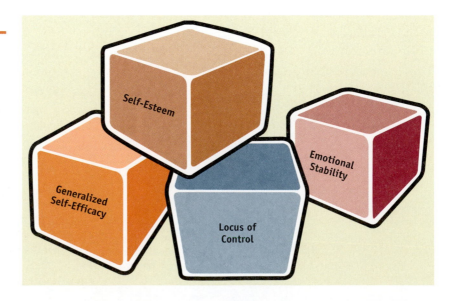

HOW TO DO IT

Increasing Self-Efficacy Among Employees

When people believe that they can do a job and do it well, the chances that they really *can* succeed often increase. Why? Because heightened feelings of self-efficacy (belief in one's ability to accomplish a specific task) have important benefits. They increase both motivation and persistence ("Why give up? I know I can make it!") and encourage individuals to set challenging goals ("I know I can do much better than before"). So encouraging high levels of self-efficacy among employees is well worthwhile. How can companies reach this objective? Here are some concrete tips.

1. ***Give Constructive—Not Destructive— Feedback:*** If you think about it, there is only one rational reason to give people feedback on their work: to help them improve. Other motives certainly exist (e.g., some managers give employees negative feedback to "put them in their place" or "even the score"), but these reasons are *not* rational and in fact are counterproductive from the point of view of increasing self-efficacy. On the other hand, constructive feedback that focuses on how an employee can improve his or her performance can add to self-efficacy because it helps reassure the recipients that they *can* get there—that they have or can soon acquire the skills or strategies necessary for success.

   One company that focuses on delivering *only* constructive feedback to employees is CHP, an HMO located in the Northeast. At CHP, managers are trained specifically to recognize that "feedback" is synonymous with "helping." They attend workshops in which they practice giving their subordinates feedback *only* when it can help them improve and *only* to reach this goal. The result? After this program was instituted, turnover dropped more than 30 percent and employee satisfaction rose significantly.

2. ***Expose Employees to Models of Good Performance—and Success:*** How do people learn to do their jobs effectively? From direct practice, of course; but in addition, they acquire many skills and strategies from others. And the more of these they possess, the

more likely they are to perform well—and so to experience increased self-efficacy. This suggests that companies that adopt carefully planned mentoring programs—programs in which inexperienced employees work closely with successful, experienced ones—can help build self-efficacy among their employees.

   The university where one of us works has adopted such a program for junior faculty. Each new faculty member is assigned a more senior faculty member—and, importantly, a successful one—by her or his department chair or dean. These faculty mentors are not there to look over the shoulders of new faculty; rather, their role is to give their junior colleagues advice on their careers and on how the system works. The program has been very successful: Junior faculty members report that it has helped them "get up to speed" very quickly, and saved them countless disappointments. There is no direct evidence that the program builds self-efficacy, but informal discussions with the faculty members involved suggest that this is indeed one of the benefits.

4. ***Seek Continuous Improvement:*** Another technique for enhancing self-efficacy involves the quest for continuous improvement. GE's "Six Sigma" program, for instance, rests on the basic idea that "we can do it better—always!" The term "six sigma" refers to outstanding performance far above average (sigma is a statistical term relating to the normal distribution, and six sigma units above the mean is far above it indeed!). Although some employees find this approach daunting at first, meetings and workshops soon convince them that they are part of a truly superb organization that will simply not settle for "average." The result? Employees come to view themselves as superior, and both self-efficacy and performance benefit.

   Through these and related steps companies can boost the self-efficacy of their employees—and hence, their performance. In the words of the famous author, Aldous Huxley: *"Those who believe that they are competent are generally those who achieve."*

Locus of control also is related positively to job satisfaction and performance. Specifically, someone with a highly internal locus of control is likely to believe that he or she can do what it takes to influence any situation. He or she feels confident in being able to bring about change. As a result, individuals with a high internal locus of control tend to be satisfied with their jobs because they either make them better or seek new ones (not remaining in bad jobs because they believe their fates are sealed). And as a result of making situations better, they tend to perform at high levels as well.

Finally, emotional stability also makes a difference. As we noted earlier, in conjunction with the Big Five dimensions of personality, emotional stability is the opposite of neuroticism (i.e., they are opposite ends of the same personality dimension). Somebody who is high on emotional stability is predisposed to have low levels of negative affect, which takes its toll on their general well-being. As we noted earlier, people with high levels of negative affect tend to experience low levels of job satisfaction and also tend to perform poorly on those jobs.

It's important to note that these individual effects tend to be particularly strong when taken together. In the aggregate, core self-evaluations are "among the best dispositional predictors of job satisfaction and performance."[29] As a result, it's not surprising that OB scientists have paid a great deal of attention to core self-evaluations in recent years.[30]

Additional Work-Related Aspects of Personality

Although many experts on personality consider the dimensions we have considered so far to be the most important, these are not the only ones with implications for organizational behavior. We'll now examine several others that have also been found to affect important forms of behavior in work settings.

Machiavellianism: Using Others to Get Ahead

In 1513, the Italian philosopher Niccolò Machiavelli published a book entitled *The Prince*. In it, he outlined a ruthless strategy for seizing and holding political power. The essence of his approach was *expediency:* Do whatever is required to defeat others or gain an advantage over them. Among the guiding principles he recommended were the following:

■ Never show humility; arrogance is far more effective when dealing with others.
■ Morality and ethics are for the weak; powerful people feel free to lie, cheat, and deceive whenever it suits their purpose.
■ It is much better to be feared than loved.

In short, Machiavelli urged those who desired power to adopt an approach based totally on expedience or usefulness. Let others be swayed by friendship, loyalty, or beliefs about decency and fair play; a truly successful leader, he suggested, should always be above those factors. He or she should be willing to do whatever it takes to win.

Clearly (and fortunately!), the vast majority of people with whom we interact don't adopt Machiavelli's philosophy. But some do seem to embrace many of these principles. This fact has led some researchers to propose that acceptance of this ruthless creed involves yet another dimension of personality—one known, appropriately, as **Machiavellianism**. Persons high on this dimension (high Machs) accept Machiavelli's suggestions and seek to manipulate others in a ruthless manner.[31] In contrast, persons low on this dimension (low Machs) reject this approach and *do* care about fair play, loyalty, and other principles Machiavelli rejected. Machiavellianism is measured by means of a relatively brief questionnaire known as the *Mach Scale*. Items similar to the ones in this scale are shown in Table 4.2.

Machiavellianism
A personality trait involving willingness to manipulate others for one's own purposes.

The Characteristics of High Machs. What are persons who score high on the Machiavelliansm scale like? Research suggests that in general, they are smooth and charming, lie easily, have no qualms about manipulating or conning others, have little remorse or guilt over harming others, and are callous and show little empathy toward others. In addition, they also tend to be impulsive, irresponsible, and prone to feeling bored. If this description sounds to you like the "con artists" we often read about in the news, you are correct: People scoring high in Machiavellianism show precisely these characteristics.[32]

For example, consider Eric Stein, who bilked more than 1,800 investors out of more than $34 million in the late 1990s. From his jail cell, he confessed several things about his activities during an interview with the *Wall Street Journal*.[33] Apparently, his scheme for becoming rich was simple: He arranged with telemarketers to phone thousands of prospective victims

TABLE 4.2 Measuring Machiavellianism

The items listed here are similar to those included in one of the most widely used measures of Machiavellianism. One's score on this scale reflects the willingness to manipulate others in order to get ahead

Directions: In the space next to each item, enter a number that characterizes your own feelings about that statement. If you disagree strongly, enter 1; if you disagree, enter 2; if you neither agree nor disagree, enter 3; if you agree, enter 4; if you strongly agree, enter 5.

____1. The best way to handle people is telling them what they want to hear.

____2. When you ask someone to do something for you, it is best to give the real reasons for wanting it rather than giving reasons that might carry more weight.

____3. Anyone who completely trusts anyone else is asking for trouble.

____4. It is hard to get ahead without cutting corners and bending the rules.

____5. It is safest to assume that all people have a vicious streak—and that it will come out when given a chance.

____6. It is never right to lie to someone else.

____7. Most people are basically good and kind.

____8. Most people work hard only when they are forced to do so.

Scoring: Add your responses to items 1, 3, 4, 5, and 8. To this number add the sum of 2, 6, and 7 after scoring them in reverse (so, if you responded with a 5, add 1 point; if you responded with a 4, add 2 points; if you responded with a 3, add 3 points; if you responded with a 2, add 4 points; and if you responded with a 1, add 5 points). Then, add your scores. The higher your score, the more Machiavellian you tend to be.

and tell them about a wonderful new investment—buying shares in a company that was developing commercials for television. Investors were told that they were being called because the company needed investors to expand its operations; they were promised a 25 percent return in 90 days. How were the prospective targets chosen? Their names were purchased from companies that specialize in identifying people nearing retirement—a prime group for telemarketing investment scams. These people know that they are running out of time and want to build their retirement funds as quickly as possible, so they tend to accept the claims they hear even though their common sense tells them they are too good to be true. Mr. Stein's scam, like many others, was a so-called Ponzi system: Early investors were indeed paid, using money from later ones. All such systems come crashing down eventually, though, and this is precisely what happened to Mr. Stein. Did he feel pangs of guilt over bilking retirement-age people out of their life savings? As he describes it, "Not at the time. But now, I regret it every day . . . I'm taking those energies and creativity that was used to create that scam and putting it toward something more positive and trying to repay these people."

Clearly, Mr. Stein, like many other confidence artists, shows all the characteristics of high Machiavellianism. Is he sincere about wanting to make amends for his previous betrayal of people who trusted him and his team of telemarketers? Only time will tell; but as a general rule, confidence artists don't usually reform—they claim that they have "seen the light" but often go back to their old patterns of bilking others as soon as they can.

Machiavellianism and Success. If high Machs (and we assume that Mr. Stein is one) are willing to do whatever it takes to succeed, you might expect that they would tend to be successful. However, this is not always so. How well they do depends on two important factors—the kind of jobs they have, and the nature of the organizations in which they work.

First, research has shown that Machiavellianism is *not* closely related to success in the kinds of jobs in which people operate with a great deal of autonomy. These are jobs—such as salesperson, marketing executive, and university professor—in which employees have the freedom to act as they wish. This gives them good opportunities to free themselves from the clutches of high Machs or to avoid interacting with them altogether![34] On the other hand, high Machs tend to be quite successful in organizations that are *loosely structured* (i.e., ones in which there are few established rules) rather than those that are *tightly structured* (i.e., ones in which rules regarding expected behavior are clear and explicit).[35] Why? Because when rules are vague and unclear, it is easy for high Machs to "do their thing." When rules are clear and strict, in contrast, high Machs are far more limited in what they can do. So while high Machs are always a danger, they are more likely to do harm to their coworkers in some environments than others.

Achievement Motivation: The Quest for Excellence

Can you recall the person in your high school class who was named "most likely to succeed"? If so, you probably are thinking of someone who was truly competitive, an individual who wanted to win in every situation—or, at least, in all the important ones. Now, in contrast, can you think of someone you have known who was not at all competitive—who could not care less about winning? As you bring these people to mind, you are actually focusing on another important aspect of personality—one known as **achievement motivation** (also known as **need for achievement**). It refers to the strength of an individual's desire to excel at various tasks—to succeed and to do better than others. Individual differences on this dimension are measured in several ways, but some of these involve the kind of *projective tests* described earlier in this chapter—tests in which individuals are shown ambiguous scenes and asked to describe what is happening in them. Their answers can then be used to measure their need for achievement, and several other aspects of personality as well.

achievement motivation (or need for achievement)
The strength of an individual's desire to excel—to succeed at difficult tasks and to do them better than other persons.

Need Achievement and Attraction to Difficult Tasks. One of the most interesting differences between persons who are high and low in the need for achievement involves their pattern of preferences for tasks of varying difficulty. As we will note, these differences may have important effects on managerial success.

Because high need achievers so strongly desire success, they tend to steer away from performing certain kinds of tasks—those that are very easy and those that are very difficult. Very simple tasks are not challenging enough to attract high need achievers, and especially difficult ones are certain to result in failure, an unacceptable outcome. Not surprisingly, high need achievers are most strongly attracted to tasks that are moderately challenging, and thereby prefer tasks of intermediate difficulty.[36]

In contrast, the opposite pattern occurs among people who are low in achievement motivation. That is, they much prefer very easy and very difficult tasks to ones that are moderately difficult. Why is this so? The explanation goes something like this. Persons low in achievement motivation like to perform easy tasks because success is virtually certain. At the same time, they also prefer tasks that are very difficult because if they fail, this can be attributed to external causes and does not threaten their self-esteem. In contrast, failure on a moderately difficult task may be the basis for making unflattering attributions about oneself (see Chapter 3), so low need achievers prefer to avoid such tasks (see Figure 4.9). Although these differences between persons high and low in need achievement are interesting by themselves, their real value becomes apparent when considering the role they play in managers' success.

Are High Need-Achievers Successful Managers? We have described people high in achievement motivation as having a highly task-oriented outlook. They are strongly concerned with getting things done, which encourages them to work hard and to strive for success. But do they always succeed, especially in managerial positions? As in the case of so many other questions in the field of OB, the answer is far from simple.

Given their intense desire to excel, it seems reasonable to expect that people high in achievement motivation will attain greater success in their careers than others. This is true to a limited extent. Research has shown that people high in achievement motivation tend to gain promotions more rapidly than those who are low in achievement motivation, at least early in their careers.[37] Their focus on attaining success "jump starts" their careers. However, as their careers progress, their unwillingness to tackle difficult challenges becomes a problem that interferes with their success. Further, they tend to be so highly

FIGURE 4.9

Achievement Motivation and Attraction to Tasks

People who are high in achievement motivation are attracted to tasks of moderate difficulty, whereas people who are low in achievement motivation are attracted to tasks that are extremely easy or extremely difficult.

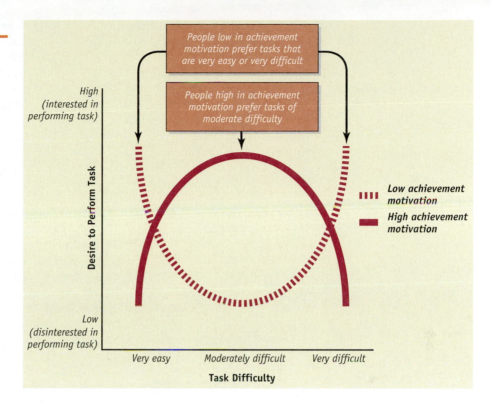

focused on their own success that they sometimes are reluctant to delegate authority to others, thereby failing to get the help they often need from subordinates. Research has shown that CEOs who are high in achievement motivation tend to keep organizational power in the hands of just a few people, failing to empower their team members as needed (see Chapter 12). This can prove disastrous from the point of view of being an effective manager.[38]

At the same time, people who are high in achievement motivation have an important "plus" going for them—the fact that they have a strong desire for feedback regarding their performance. In other words, because they want to succeed so badly, they have a strong interest in knowing just how well they are doing at any given point in time. As a result, people who are high in need achievement have a strong preference for *merit-based pay systems*—ones in which pay and other rewards are based on performance. This is so because such systems recognize people's individual achievements. Conversely, persons high in need for achievement tend to dislike seniority-based pay systems (i.e., those in which pay is based on how long one has worked in the company) because these fail to focus on differences in employees' job-based achievements.[39]

learning goal orientation
The desire to perform well because it satisfies an interest in meeting a challenge and learning new skills.

performance goal orientation
The desire to perform well to demonstrate one's competence to others.

avoidance goal orientation
The desire to achieve success to avoid appearing incompetent and to avoid receiving negative evaluation from others.

Achievement Motivation and Goal Orientation: Do People Differ in the Kind of Success They Seek? So far, our discussion has implied that the desire to excel or achieve is an important dimension along which people differ. But individuals also differ with respect to the *kind* of success they seek. In fact, individuals can have any one of three contrasting *goal orientations* when performing various tasks.[40] These are as follows.[41]

- **Learning goal orientation**—The desire to perform well because it satisfies an interest in meeting a challenge and learning new skills
- **Performance goal orientation**—The desire to perform well to demonstrate one's competence to others
- **Avoidance goal orientation**—The desire to achieve success to avoid appearing incompetent and to avoid receiving negative evaluations from others

The existence of these three different goal orientations (contrasting reasons for wanting to do well in various tasks) has important implications for performance in work settings. For instance, a learning goal orientation is related strongly to general self-efficacy, which we described earlier as a particular element of core self-evaluations.[42] The higher one's learning goal orientation, the greater is his or her general self-efficacy. Since self-efficacy exerts strong effects on performance, it is clear that a learning orientation can be very helpful when it comes to performing many jobs.

Similarly, a learning goal orientation also may be helpful with respect to benefiting from on-the-job feedback. Specifically, people high in this orientation want to receive feedback and pay careful attention to it since it will help them to learn. In contrast, neither a performance goal orientation nor an avoidance goal orientation seems to offer similar benefits.[43] So overall, organizations should strive to select people who have a learning goal orientation or to encourage such an orientation among their employees.

This raises a key question: How can a learning goal orientation be attained? The answer lies in part by giving employees an opportunity to acquire new skills on their jobs and by rewarding them for doing so—not just for being competent at what they already know. For instance, United Technologies promotes a learning goal orientation by encouraging employees to take advanced courses in their specialty, or in management. Indeed, United Technologies, as well as many other companies, actually cover the entire cost of an MBA for individuals they consider to be on the "fast track" in their careers.

That achievement motivation influences the success of individuals is far from surprising. But can it also contribute to the economic growth and well-being of entire societies? For information suggesting that it can, see the *OB in a Diverse World* section on page 153.

Morning Persons and Evening Persons

According to the U.S. Department of Labor, about 15 percent of people in the U.S. labor force work at night or on rotating shifts.[44] Unfortunately, this can be costly given that the health and well-being of many individuals suffer when they work at night.[45] Yet, as you probably know from experience, there are some people who seem to thrive on "the graveyard shift" and actually prefer it. (In fact, if you are up late at night reading this, you may be one of them!)

The suggestion that there may be individual differences in the times of day at which people feel most alert and energetic is supported by evidence showing that such differences do, in fact, exist and that they are stable over time. Specifically, it appears that most people fall into one of two categories—either they are **morning persons**, who feel most energetic early in the day, or they are **evening persons**, who feel most energetic late in the day or at night.

morning persons
Individuals who feel most energetic and alert early in the day.

evening persons
Individuals who feel most energetic and alert late in the day or at night.

Presumably, evening persons would find the task of adapting to night work less stressful than morning persons and, consequently, would do better work when exposed to such conditions. Evidence indicates that this is indeed the case. For example, consider a study involving college students asked to keep diaries in which they reported the times each day when they slept and when they studied.[46] In addition, information was obtained from university records concerning the students' class schedules and their academic performance. All participants also completed a brief questionnaire measuring the extent to which they were morning or evening persons.

Results revealed intriguing differences between participants who were classified as morning persons or evening persons. As might be expected, morning persons reported sleeping primarily at night and studying in the morning, whereas evening persons reported the opposite pattern. Similarly, class schedules for the two groups also indicated interesting differences: Students classified as morning persons tended to schedule their classes earlier in the day than those classified as evening students. Perhaps most interesting of all, morning students did better in their early classes than in their later ones, while the opposite was true for students classified as evening persons (see Figure 4.10, p. 154).

These findings and those of many other studies suggest that individual differences in preferences for various times of day are not only real, but also that they are very important when it comes to job performance.[47] Ideally, only individuals who are at their best late in the day should be assigned to night work; this would constitute a good application of the

OB In a Diverse World

Achievement Motivation and Economic Growth Around the World

 Economists have demonstrated that a wide variety of factors—including the price and availability of natural resources, labor costs, and government policies that encourage or discourage growth—contribute to national differences in economic expansion. However, these factors do not tell the whole story. Indeed, it appears that an aspect of personality, too, may play a role: national differences in achievement motivation. Although achievement motivation, strictly speaking, relates to individuals, considerable evidence suggests that it also varies across different cultures. What's more, these differences are related to important economic variables.

This point is illustrated dramatically in a classic study in which researchers analyzed children's stories from 22 different cultures with respect to the degree to which they contained themes of achievement motivation (e.g., the story "The Little Engine That Could," which was read by millions of children in the United States, reflects a great deal of achievement motivation).[48] The investigators then related the levels of achievement motivation indicated by these stories to key measures of economic development (e.g., per capita income and per capita electrical production). Their findings were impressive: The greater the emphasis placed on achievement in the children's stories in various nations, the more rapid was the economic growth in these nations as the children grew up!

Interestingly, these findings are not just a fluke; similar results have been reported in other research.[49] For example, a massive study involving more than 12,000 participants in 41 different countries has confirmed the idea that national differences in achievement motivation can be quite real and that they are related to differences in economic growth.[50] Specifically, it was found that various attitudes toward work, such as competitiveness, were different across countries, and that those countries whose citizens were most competitive tended to be those that had higher rates of economic growth.

But how, you may be wondering, can this be so? How can achievement motivation, which is a characteristic of individuals, influence economic activity? One possibility is as follows. First, economic trends are, ultimately, the reflection of actions by large numbers of individuals. Second, in societies where the average level of achievement motivation is high, and an *individualistic cultural orientation* exists (that is, much emphasis is placed on individual performance), entrepreneurship may be encouraged. In other words, a high average level of achievement motivation, coupled with the view that individual accomplishment is appropriate, may encourage large numbers of persons to start their own companies. And there is growing evidence that the level of entrepreneurial activity in a given society is a good predictor of its economic growth.[51] So the fact that achievement motivation is related to the economic growth of entire societies may not be as mysterious as it at first seems.

At present, this reasoning is mainly conjecture: Direct evidence for it does not exist. But it fits well both with findings concerning achievement motivation and a growing body of evidence concerning the economic benefits of entrepreneurial activity. In any case, existing evidence *does* demonstrate clearly that achievement motivation is one predictor of economic success not only for individuals, but for entire societies, too, and we view that, in itself, as a very thought-provoking fact.

---

principle of *person-job fit*, which we described earlier in this chapter. According to this principle, the closer the alignment between individuals' skills, abilities, and preferences and the requirements of their jobs, the more successful at these jobs they will be. The results of following such a policy might well be better performance, better health, and fewer accidents for employees—outcomes beneficial both to them and to their organizations.

Abilities and Skills: Having What It Takes to Succeed

abilities
Mental and physical capacities to perform various tasks.

skills
Dexterity at performing specific tasks, which has been acquired through training or experience.

To do easily what is difficult for others is the mark of talent. To do what is impossible for talent is the mark of genius. (Henri-Frédéric Amiel, Swiss philosopher, poet, and critic, 1856)

As this quotation suggests, people differ greatly with respect to their **abilities**—the capacity to perform various tasks—and also differ greatly with respect to specific **skills**—dexterity at performing specific tasks, which has been acquired through training

FIGURE 4.10

Academic Performance by Morning and Evening Persons

Students who felt most alert and energetic early in the day (i.e., *morning persons*) did better in classes that met in the morning than in ones that met in the afternoon or evening. The opposite was true for students who felt most alert and energetic late in the day (i.e., *evening persons*)—they did better in classes that met in the afternoon or evening.

Source: Based on data from Guthrie, Ash, & Bendapudi, 1995; see Note 50.

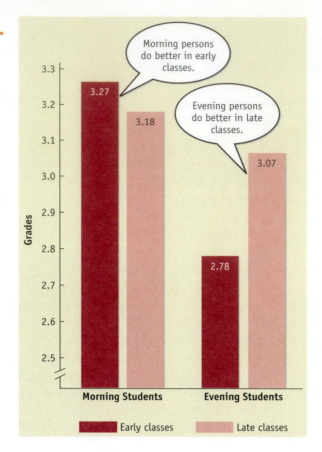

or experience.[52] For example, no matter how hard we might have tried, neither of the authors of this book could ever have made it as a professional basketball player. We are neither sufficiently tall nor athletic to succeed. In other words, we lack the basic physical abilities required by this sport. However, we have other abilities—at least, we like to think that we do!—that have allowed us to have happy lives outside the arena of professional sports.

Both abilities and skills are important, of course, but since abilities are more general in nature and have implications for a broader range of organizational behavior, we'll pay a bit more attention to them in this section of the chapter. Our discussion of abilities will focus on two major types: *intellectual abilities* (or simply, *intelligence*), which involve the capacity to perform various cognitive tasks, and *physical abilities,* which refer to the capacity to perform various physical actions.

Intelligence: Three Major Types

When most people speak about intelligence or intellectual abilities, they generally are referring to one's capacity to understand complex ideas. Of course, this is certainly very important.[53] To succeed on a job, one must have the mental capacity to undertake the intellectual challenges associated with it. However, this kind of mental prowess is not the only kind of intelligence there is.[54] In fact, on the job, several distinct types of intelligence have proven to be very important. We now consider these.

cognitive intelligence
The ability to understand complex ideas, to adapt effectively to the environment, to learn from experience, to engage in various forms of reasoning, and to overcome obstacles with careful thought.

Cognitive Intelligence. "Oh yes, Jessica is very smart," someone might tell you in reference to the new person hired in your department. But what exactly is meant by "smart"? Traditionally, the term is used to refer to a specific kind of intellectual ability that psychologists term **cognitive intelligence**. This involves the ability to understand complex ideas, to adapt effectively to the environment, to learn from experience, to engage in various forms of reasoning, and to overcome obstacles by careful thought.[55]

As you know from discussions about intelligence (or IQ) tests in the media, people possess this type of intelligence to varying degrees. You also probably realize that different jobs require contrasting levels of cognitive intelligence for success. As you might suspect, the concept of cognitive intelligence is rather broad; it consists of a wide variety of different cognitive skills and abilities. Among these are abilities involving words, numbers, and visual images, including the following.

- *Verbal comprehension*—The ability to understand written material quickly and accurately
- *Verbal reasoning*—The ability to analyze verbal information so as to make valid judgments on the basis of logical implications of material
- *Word fluency*—The ability to express oneself rapidly, easily, and with flexibility
- *Numerical ability*—The ability to perform basic mathematical operations quickly and accurately
- *Numerical reasoning*—The ability to analyze logical relationships and to recognize the underlying principles underlying them
- *Space visualization*—The ability to visualize three-dimensional forms in space and to be able to manipulate them mentally.
- *Symbolic reasoning*—The ability to think and reason abstractly using symbols rather than words or numbers, to manipulate abstract symbols mentally, and to make logically valid judgments based on them

It probably comes at no surprise that different jobs require different blends of these abilities. As some obvious examples, writers have to be adept at word fluency, statisticians have to be good at numerical ability and numerical reasoning, and architects have to be skilled at spatial visualization. As you read Appendix 2, you'll come to appreciate how various aspects of cognitive intelligence (and other types of intelligence too, as we will see), are involved in people's selections of various career alternatives. Interestingly, it is assumed widely that people who have high amounts of cognitive intelligence have an edge over those who don't when it comes to job performance. As you will see from the *OB: Making Sense Out of Common Sense* section on page 156, there is more to this than meets the eye.

Practical Intelligence: Solving the Problems of Everyday Life. Consider the following hypothetical incident.

> Two people—a business executive and a scientist—are walking in the woods, when they spot a large grizzly bear. The bear starts running toward them, growling angrily, obviously intending to attack. Both the executive and the scientist start running, but after a few yards, the scientist stops, and calls to the executive: "There's no point in running. I have done the calculations, and there is no way we can outrun that bear." The executive shouts back over his shoulder: "I don't have to outrun the bear . . . I only have to outrun you!"

Although you may find this story a bit unsettling, it provides a clear illustration of individual differences in **practical intelligence**—the ability to devise effective ways of getting things done.[56] Growing evidence suggests that practical intelligence is indeed different from the kind of intelligence measured by IQ tests, and that it is especially important in business settings.[57] In particular, people with high amounts of practical intelligence are very proficient at solving a wide range of business problems. The secret to their success resides in what is known as **tacit knowledge**—knowledge about *how* to get things done. In contrast to *formal academic knowledge,* which, as you know, often involves memorizing definitions, formulas, and other information, tacit knowledge is far more practical in nature. Specifically, tacit knowledge includes the following major characteristics.

- *Action-oriented.* It involves "knowing how" to do something as opposed to "knowing that" something is the case. For example, skilled athletes can perform amazing

practical intelligence
Adeptness at solving the practical problems of everyday life.

tacit knowledge
Knowledge about how to get things done.

OB Making Sense Out of Common Sense

Is Job Performance Linked to Cognitive Intelligence?

 For over a hundred years, psychologists have measured the general cognitive ability of millions of people of all ages and in all walks of life throughout the world. In the U.S. military alone, the general intelligence of more than 1 million people is assessed each year, and along with it, measures of people's success on just about every imaginable job. As you might imagine, quite an extensive database has been amassed. Careful analysis of this information confirms something that many people already believe: General intelligence predicts job performance. Put differently, people with higher levels of cognitive intelligence are more successful on their jobs than those with lower levels of cognitive intelligence.

"Not surprising" you say? We agree—but, when you consider this not-so-startling finding a bit more closely, some interesting points emerge. For example, is it really the case that people become successful because of their higher intelligence, as you might suspect? Possibly, but not necessarily. In fact, it may not be their innate intelligence that is responsible for the success of people who score highly on tests, but rather the subsequent treatment they receive. Specifically, people who score highly on intelligence tests often are given special opportunities that their counterparts with more modest scores are denied. For example, students and soldiers whose aptitude test scores suggest that they are gifted are put into special classes and are given other unique training opportunities. This special treatment itself may account for their success. Maybe others with more modest scores would succeed as well if they were given these opportunities. But, because they tend to be denied, it's hard to say.

It's also important to note that the relationship between job success and general intelligence differs for people in different types of jobs. Because some jobs require more of what cognitive intelligence tests measure than others, it's not surprising that it's a better predictor of success on those jobs. For example, a study of more than 1,000 enlistees in the U.S. Air Force found that although general intelligence was related to job success overall, this relationship was considerably higher among individuals performing jobs that required more cognitive skills (e.g., precision measurement equipment laboratory specialist) than those whose work was less intellectually demanding (e.g., radio operator).

Perhaps the most important thing of all to note is a message that many psychologists have been sending in recent years: Cognitive intelligence as measured by standard intelligence tests assesses only one kind of intelligence. Consider, for example, that the study of Air Force enlistees found a very low correlation between intelligence test scores and job performance among air traffic controllers. This may seem surprising because such individuals have to be "pretty sharp" to perform their jobs (in fact, you surely wouldn't want to trust your life to a not-so-smart controller when you're on a plane).

The low correlation suggests something that's both fundamental and extremely important: There's more than one kind of intelligence, and the particular form of intelligence measured by the test does not get at what it takes to succeed at that particular job. This surely makes a great deal of sense if you think about it. What it takes to be "intelligent" as a carpenter (e.g., knowledge of how to use woodworking tools with great precision), for example, is not measured on the test, whereas what it takes to be "intelligent" on a more academic job—physicist, say—is, in fact, tapped by the test. (In this chapter, the sections on *practical intelligence* and *emotional intelligence* make this point clearly.) It's important to keep this in mind when you consider what it really means when statements are made about the relationship between general intelligence and job success.

feats on the playing field but may not be able to put into words just *how* they perform these actions.

- ■ *Allows individuals to achieve goals they personally value.* As such, it is practically useful, focusing on knowledge that is relevant to them.
- ■ *Acquired without direct help from others.* Such knowledge often is acquired on one's own, largely because it goes unspoken. As such, people must recognize it, and its value, for themselves. For instance, although no one may ever tell an employee that getting help from a more senior person will aid his or her career, this person may recognize this fact and act on it.

People with high amounts of practical intelligence are adept at solving the problems of everyday life, including how they relate to their jobs. Of importance, there is more to intelligence than the verbal, mathematical, and reasoning abilities that often are associated with academic success. Practical intelligence, too, is important and contributes to success in many areas of life—including something that may be of interest to you, success as a manager. Don't be misled by the term "practical" into thinking that this form of intelligence applies only to people who work with their hands, such as mechanics and plumbers. Clearly, such individuals do have to know how to perform certain physical actions, but they also have to have cognitive skills as well so they can assess problems they confront on the job. At the same time, as suggested in Figure 4.11, people who perform jobs involving high degrees of cognitive intelligence also must have practical intelligence so they can succeed.

Emotional Intelligence: Managing the Feeling Side of Life. A third important kind of intelligence that can often play an important role in behavior in organizations is known as **emotional intelligence (EI)**.[58] Originally, emotional intelligence was defined as a cluster of abilities relating to the emotional or "feeling" side of life, and was viewed as involving four basic components: (1) the ability to recognize and regulate our own emotions (e.g., to hold our temper in check), (2) the ability to recognize and influence others' emotions (e.g., the ability to make them enthusiastic about our ideas), (3) self-motivation (the ability to motivate oneself to work long hours and resist the temptation to give up), and (4) the ability to form effective long-term relationships with others. However, extensive research on EI suggests that a more appropriate model of this kind of intelligence includes the following factors instead:[59]

- *Appraisal and expression of emotions in oneself*—An individual's ability to understand his or her own emotions and to express these naturally
- *Appraisal and recognition of emotions in others*—The ability to perceive and understand others' emotions

emotional intelligence (EI)
A cluster of skills relating to the emotional side life (e.g., the ability to recognize and regulate our own emotions, to influence those of others, to self-motivate).

FIGURE 4.11

Practical Intelligence in Action—Even Where You Least Expect It

When you think of university professors, you are inclined to think of them as having vast amounts of academic knowledge. However, they also must have practical knowledge, such as awareness of what behaviors are most highly valued on their jobs. Should they work on increasing enrollment in their classes? Should they publish a systematic series of scientific articles in prestigious scholarly journals? Should they make presentations to civic and community groups about the latest advances in their fields? Although all surely are important, the way they decide to spend their time is likely to depend on the values of the institutions in which they work. Sensitivity to this is a key aspect of practical intelligence.

- *Regulation of emotions in oneself*—The ability to regulate one's own emotions
- *Use of emotions to facilitate performance*—The ability to use emotions by directing them toward constructive activities and improved performance (e.g., by encouraging oneself to do better)

Is emotional intelligence real? Growing evidence suggests that it is predictive of important aspects of organizational behavior. In one study, for example, employees at a large factory in China were asked to rate the EI of their coworkers.[60] Then, these ratings were correlated with the performance ratings by the coworkers' supervisors. The results were clear: Individuals who had the highest levels of EI (as rated by their coworkers) had the highest levels of job performance (as assessed by supervisors). This suggests that EI is indeed related to on-the-job performance.

Evidence also suggests that EI is related to other aspects of organizational behavior. For instance, entrepreneurs who have considerable ability to "read others" accurately (a basic aspect of EI) earn more money from their businesses than others who are relatively low on this ability.[61] Likewise, scientists who are adept at accurately "reading others," and who, partly because of this ability, tend to be liked by their colleagues, are more productive than scientists who are lower in this aspect of emotional intelligence.[62] So overall, being high in various aspects of emotional intelligence can be an important determinant of career success.

Obviously, the ability to be keenly aware of others and sensitive to them can be an important contributor to success on many jobs. However, a recent study suggests that there may be more to it than this.[63] Participants in this research were a diverse group of employees at a large university who completed standard measures of cognitive intelligence and of emotional intelligence, and whose job performance was rated along several key dimensions by their supervisors. The relationship between these variables, summarized in Figure 4.12, is very interesting. Employees who scored highly on the intelligence test outperformed those who scored more poorly, but only among those who were low in emotional intelligence. In contrast, people who possessed high degrees of emotional intelligence performed at high levels regardless of their cognitive intelligence. In other words, when it comes to job performance, having high levels of emotional intelligence appears to compensate for having lower levels of cognitive intelligence. In view of these findings, it's little wonder why emotional intelligence is so very important—and a factor that begs to be given far more attention in organizations than traditionally has been the case.

Physical Abilities: Capacity to Do the Job

physical abilities
People's capacities to engage in the physical tasks required to perform a job.

When we speak of **physical abilities** we are referring to people's capacities to engage in the physical tasks required to perform a job. Although different jobs require different physical abilities, there are several types of physical ability that are relevant to a wide variety of jobs. These include the following.

- *Strength:* The capacity to exert physical force against various objects
- *Flexibility:* The capacity to move one's body in an agile manner
- *Stamina:* The capacity to endure physical activity over prolonged periods
- *Speed:* The ability to move quickly

If we were to consider all jobs that people perform, it might be possible to identify those that require primarily intellectual abilities and those that require primarily physical abilities. For example, being a chemist in a research laboratory of a large company involves mainly intellectual abilities, whereas being a construction worker involves mainly physical abilities. However, such oversimplification can be misleading. Almost all jobs require *both* cognitive and physical abilities for success. For example, consider a firefighter. Obviously, such individuals must have high degrees of strength, flexibility, stamina, and speed to be able to perform their jobs well. At the same time, however, such individuals also must possess appropriate cognitive abilities so they can assess the complex demands of the scene (e.g., wind velocity, structure of the building on fire, likely presence of victims, sources of oxygen, and so on). In sum, when it comes to assessing

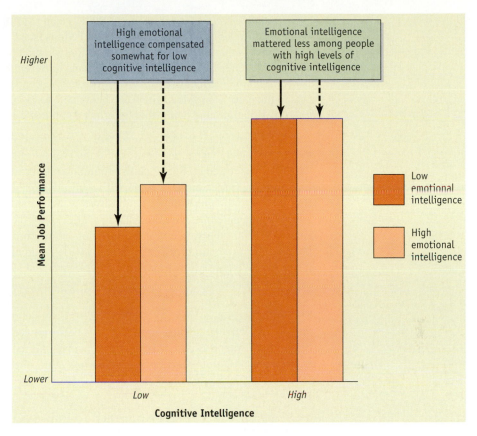

FIGURE 4.12

Emotional Intelligence Compensates for Cognitive Intelligence

Overall, people with higher degrees of cognitive intelligence out-perform those with lower degrees of cognitive intelligence. However, even people with lower cognitive intelligence perform at higher levels on a variety of jobs if they also have high levels of emotional intelligence. In other words, emotional intelligence compensates for cognitive intelligence when it comes to job performance.

Source: Based on data reported by Côté & Miners, 2006; see Note 63.

the physical demands of a job relative to the more cognitive demands, it's safest to consider this a matter not of "which?" but of "how much of each at any given time?"

Social Skills: Interacting Effectively with Others

In Chapter 3, we discussed various kinds of *employee training* and noted that many companies spend large sums of money training their employees. A major goal of such training is that of equipping employees with new *skills*—proficiencies in performing various tasks. Because skills are often linked closely to particular jobs or tasks, we cannot possibly examine even a tiny sample of them here. Instead, we'll focus on one particular cluster of skills that plays a key role in success in many different contexts: **social skills**—the capacity to interact effectively with others.[64]

social skills
The capacity to interact effectively with others.

Types of Social Skills. What do social skills involve? Although there is far from total agreement on their precise nature, most researchers who have studied social skills and their role in organizational behavior would include the following:

■ *Social perception*—Accuracy in perceiving others, including accurate perceptions of their traits, motives, and intentions (see Chapter 3)
■ *Impression management*—Proficiency in the use of a wide range of techniques for inducing positive reactions in others (see Chapter 3)

- *Persuasion and social influence*—Skill at using various techniques for changing others' attitudes or behavior in desired directions (see Chapter 12)
- *Social adaptability*—The ability to adapt to a wide range of social situations and to interact effectively with people from many different backgrounds
- *Emotional awareness/control*—Proficiency with respect to a cluster of skills relating to the emotional side of life (e.g., being able to regulate one's own emotions in various situations and being able to influence others' emotional reactions; see Chapter 5)

If these particular skills remind you of emotional intelligence, that's not surprising; there is considerable overlap between EI and social skills. However, social skills are somewhat broader in scope. Social skills are important because they have considerable effects on behavior. For example, people with well-developed social skills tend to make good impressions on job interviews, get positive evaluations of their performance, and perform well when negotiating with others.[65] In fact, a study of over 1,400 employees found that social skills are the single best predictor of job performance ratings and assessments of potential for promotion for employees in a wide range of jobs.[66] In view of these benefits, it's reasonable to ask how to improve your own social skills. For some suggestions in this regard, see Table 4.3.

The Importance of Social Skills: A Demonstration. Social skills have very broad and general effects, helping individuals to perform well in a wide range of contexts and on many different jobs. For instance, consider one recent, revealing study designed to investigate the joint effects of *conscientiousness,* one of the Big Five dimensions we

---

TABLE 4.3 The SOFTEN Approach to Improving Your Social Skills

Considering the benefits of having well-developed social skills, it's important to identify things you can do to improve your own ability to interact effectively with others. The following guidelines, following the acronym SOFTEN, generally prove helpful.

Suggestion	Explanation
*S*mile	Smiling at someone sends a very pleasant message. This is important because few of us want to interact with anyone having a sour disposition.
*O*pen posture	By keeping your arms open (maintaining an open posture) when interacting with others, you send the message that you are welcoming the conversation. In contrast, covering yourself with your arms (maintaining a closed posture) sends the message that you are "closed for business," so to speak—uninterested in interacting with others.
*F*orward lean	Leaning forward while talking to others brings you closer to them. It speaks clearly of your engagement in the conversation. Leaning away, however, sends the message that you wish to escape them.
*T*ouch	In some situations, and for some people, touching someone else is a sign that you are interested in what they have to say. You have to be careful about this, however, because some people may find it inappropriate or offensive, particularly in certain cultures. So, follow this suggestion with caution.
*E*ye contact	Looking someone in the eye when you speak to them or listen to them is an essential way to show that you are interested in the conversation. Looking away, however, makes it clear that you really don't want to be there.
*N*od	As we note in Chapter 9, nodding is very helpful feedback for speakers because it shows that you are listening and understanding them. This keeps the conversation moving along, which, of course, is essential to ensuring a positive relationship.

discussed earlier, and social skills.[67] The researchers hypothesized that people with high levels of conscientiousness will perform well, but only when they have the requisite social skills to succeed.[68] The idea is that highly conscientiousness people who lack social skills may be seen as unreasonably demanding and inflexible by their coworkers. In other words, without social skills to soften the impact of their highly methodical and task-oriented behavior, they may be perceived negatively, as "driven drudges" rather than as valuable coworkers. And since cooperation and good relations with one's coworkers is often required for success on many tasks, such individuals may work at below average levels.

To test these predictions, the scientists measured the conscientiousness, social skills, and job performance of a wide variety of workers. As expected, the benefits of conscientiousness were greatest for people high in social skills, smaller for those with average social skills, and weakest for those who were low in social skills (see Figure 4.13). In other words, high levels of conscientiousness translated into excellent performance only for persons who were also socially skilled. For individuals who were low in social skills, in fact, high levels of conscientiousness actually reduced performance slightly. The conclusion is clear: The importance of social skills on the job cannot be overstated.

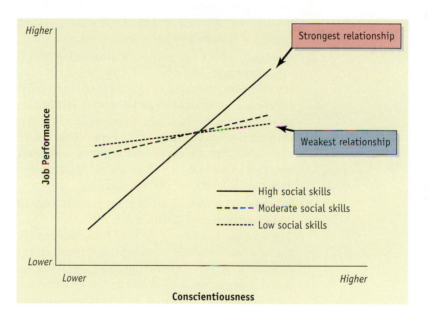

FIGURE 4.13

Social Skills, Conscientiousness, and Task Performance

As shown here, people who are highly conscientious show higher task performance than those who are low in conscientiousness, but only when they are also high in social skills. Individuals who are high in conscientiousness but low in social skills may come across as unreasonably demanding and inflexible, and this may lead other employees to avoid working with—or helping—them.

Source: Based on data from Witt & Ferris, 2003; see Note 68.

Summary and Review of Learning Objectives

1. **Define personality and describe its role in the study of organizational behavior.**
   Personality is the unique and relatively stable pattern of behavior, thoughts, and emotions shown by individuals. It, along with abilities (the capacity to perform various tasks) and various situational factors combine to determine behavior in organizations. This idea is reflected by the interactionist perspective, which is widely accepted in the field of organizational behavior today.

2. **Identify the Big Five dimensions of personality and elements of core self-evaluations and describe how they are related to key aspects of organizational behavior.**
   The Big Five dimensions of personality—so named because they seem to be very basic aspects of personality—appear to play a role in the successful performance of many jobs. These are: *conscientiousness, extraversion-introversion, agreeableness, neuroticism,* and *openness to experience.* Two of these dimensions, conscientiousness and emotional stability, have been found to be good predictors of success in many different jobs. This is especially true under conditions where job autonomy is high. Core self-evaluations are elements of personality reflecting people's fundamental evaluations of themselves, their bottom-line conclusions about themselves. These are: self-esteem, generalized self-efficacy, locus of control, and emotional stability (opposite of the Big Five trait, neuroticism). Each of the four dimensions of core self-evaluations is associated with beneficial organizational outcomes.

3. **Distinguish between positive and negative affectivity and describe its effects on organizational behavior.**
   Positive affectivity and negative affectivity refer to stable tendencies for people to experience positive or negative moods at work, respectively. Compared to people scoring high in negative affectivity, those who are predisposed toward positive affectivity tend to make higher quality individual decisions and are more willing to help others. Negative affectivity on the part of customers can generate negative emotional reactions in service providers, and so reduce customers' satisfaction with the treatment they receive.

4. **Describe achievement motivation and distinguish among learning, performance, and avoidance goal orientations.**
   Achievement motivation (or need for achievement) refers to the strength of an individual's desire to excel, to succeed at difficult tasks and to do them better than others. A learning goal orientation involves the desire to succeed in order to master new skills. A performance goal orientation involves the desire to succeed to demonstrate one's competence to others. An avoidance goal orientation involves the desire to succeed to avoid criticism from others or appearing to be incompetent.

5. **Describe Machiavellianism and the difference between morning and evening persons, and their role in work-related behavior.**
   People who adopt a manipulative approach to their relations with others are described as being high in Machiavellianism (known as high Machs). They are not influenced by considerations of loyalty, friendship, or ethics. Instead, they simply do whatever is needed to get their way. High Machs tend to be most successful in situations in which people cannot avoid them and in organizations in which there are few established rules. *Morning persons* are individuals who feel most energetic early in the day. *Evening persons* are those who feel most energetic at night. People tend to do their best work during that portion of the day that they prefer and during which they are most energetic.

6. **Differentiate among cognitive intelligence, emotional intelligence, and practical intelligence, noting their influences on behavior in organizations, and explain the importance of social skills in the workplace.**
   Cognitive intelligence is the ability to understand complex ideas, to adapt effectively to the environment, to learn from experience, to engage in various forms of reasoning,

to overcome obstacles by careful thought. Traditionally, this is what we have in mind when we refer to intelligence. However, other forms of intelligence play important roles in organizational functioning. These are practical intelligence, the ability to come up with effective ways of getting things done, and emotional intelligence, a cluster of abilities relating to the emotional or "feeling" side of life. Social skills play an important role in success in many business contexts because getting along well with others is essential for obtaining positive outcomes, and may even influence the effects of key aspects of personality (e.g., conscientiousness) on performance.

Points to Ponder

Questions for Review

1. Why might two individuals whose personalities are very similar behave differently in a given situation?
2. What is the difference between being in a good mood and having the characteristic of *positive affectivity*?
3. Suppose you are considering jobs with two different companies. Would your perceptions of the "personalities" of those companies affect your decision? Should it?
4. How does having low *self-efficacy* interfere with task performance?
5. Would you prefer to hire employees who are high in learning goal orientation or performance goal orientation? Why?
6. Why are social skills so beneficial to many different kinds of careers?

Experiential Questions

1. Have you ever worked for an organization that selected future employees by means of psychological tests? If so, do you think the test made sense—for instance, did it really measure what it was supposed to measure?
2. Have you ever known someone who was high in conscientiousness but low in social skills? If so, was this individual successful in his or her career? Why? Why not?
3. Where do you think *you* stand with respect to generalized self-efficacy? Are you fairly confident that you can accomplish most tasks you set out to do? Or do you have doubts about your ability to succeed in many situations?
4. Have you ever encountered someone who was very high in cognitive intelligence (the kind IQ tests measure), but low in practical intelligence? How could you tell?

Questions to Analyze

1. Suppose you had to choose an assistant. Would you prefer someone who is high in conscientiousness but low in agreeableness, or someone who is high in agreeableness but low in conscientiousness? Why?
2. Are you a morning or an evening person? When did you first decide that you were one or the other? Has the fact that you are a morning or an evening person affected your career decisions in any way?
3. Many persons who attain very high levels of business success were only below-average students in school. Why this might be so?

Experiencing OB

Individual Exercise

How Good Are Your Social Skills?

As we've noted at several points in this chapter, having good social skills—being adept at getting along well with others—can be very valuable to your career. Where do *you* stand in this respect? Are you high, average, or low in social skills? To find out, complete this brief questionnaire and complete the steps that follow.

Step 1:   Complete the questionnaire by answering each of the following questions as honestly as possible using the following scale.

> 1 = totally untrue
> 2 = slightly untrue
> 3 = neither true nor untrue
> 4 = slightly true
> 5 = totally true

1. _____ I'm a good judge of other people.
2. _____ I can usually recognize others' traits accurately by observing their behavior.
3. _____ I can usually read others well—tell how they are feeling in a given situation.
4. _____ I can easily adjust to being in just about any social situation.
5. _____ I can talk to anybody about almost anything.
6. _____ People tell me that I'm sensitive and understanding.
7. _____ People can always read my emotions even if I try to cover them up.
8. _____ Whatever emotion I feel on the inside tends to show on the outside.
9. _____ Other people can usually tell pretty much how I feel at a given time.
10. _____ I'm good at flattery and can use it to my own advantage when I wish.
11. _____ I can readily seem to like another person even if this is not so.

Step 2:   Score the questionnaire as follows:

- Add your answers for items 1–3 and divide by 3. This is your social perception score, your ability to "read" others accurately.
- Add your answers for items 4–6 and divide by 3. This is your social adaptability score, your ability to fit into almost any social situation.
- Add your answers for items 7–9 and divide by 3. This is your expressiveness score, the extent to which you express your own feelings and emotions clearly.
- Add your answers for items 10–11 and divide by 2. This is your impression management score, your ability to control others' impressions of you.

Step 3:   Compare your results to those of others.

- Ask two or three of your friends to rate you on the same questions.
- Compare their answers with yours.

Questions for Discussion

1. On what social skills did you score highest? Lowest?
2. Were your own scores similar to the scores when your friends rated you? If they are, you are perceiving your own social skills accurately. If not, you are not as aware of your own social skills as you might prefer.
3. Imagine that you gave this questionnaire to people in different fields or occupations. Do you think you would find differences between these various fields? For instance, among the following persons, who would score highest? Lowest? Engineers; attorneys; university professors; salespersons; actors; physicians. Why do you think this is?

Group Exercise

Machiavellianism in Action: The $10 Game

People who are high in Machiavellianism (high Machs) often come out ahead in deal-ing with others because they are true pragmatists. That is, they tend to be willing to do or say whatever it takes to win or to get their way. Several questionnaires exist for measuring Machiavellianism as a personality trait. However, tendencies in this direc-tion also can be observed in many face-to-face situations. The following exercise offers one useful means for observing individual differences with respect to Machiavellianism.

Directions

1. Divide the class into groups of three.
2. Hand the three people in each group a sheet with the following instructions.
3. Imagine that I have placed a stack of ten $1 bills on the table in front of you. This money will belong to *any two of you* who can decide how to divide it.
4. Allow groups up to 10 minutes to reach a decision on this task.
5. Ask each group whether they reached a decision, and what it was. In each group, you probably will find that two people agreed on how to divide the money, leav-ing the third "out in the cold."

Questions for Discussion

1. How did the two-person groups form? Was there a particular person in each group who was largely responsible for the formation of the winning coalition?
2. Why did the third person get left out of the agreement? What did this person say or do—or fail to say or do—that led to his or her being omitted from the two-person coalition that divided the money?
3. Do you think that actions in this situation are related to Machiavellianism? How? In other words, what particular things did anyone do that you took as an indicator of being a high Mach?

Practicing OB

Predicting Sales Success

A life insurance company has developed a test believed to measure success at per-sonal face-to-face sales. It has used this test to choose new life insurance agents, believing that persons selected in this way will generate high levels of sales. Yet this has not happened. People who score very high on the test are not outselling the com-pany's existing agents, who never took the test before they were hired. What's going on here?

1. Do you think the test of "selling ability" might be at fault? For instance, could it be that this test is not really valid? How would you find out if it is or is not?
2. What other factors might be involved? Assuming the test *is* valid, could the fact that the new agents lack experience be contributing to their relatively poor perfor-mance? If so, would you expect this will improve as they gain experience?
3. If you conclude that the test of selling ability is not really valid, how could you help the company develop a better test—one that really does measure this impor-tant ability?

Generous to a Fault?

In May 2006, Malden Mills signed a large contract resulting in the sale of $10 million worth of one of its most important products, Polartec synthetic fleece, to a company that was using it in jackets worn by U.S. soldiers in Afghanistan and northern Iraq. Ordinarily, this would be just another deal in the textile business, but an incident occurring a decade earlier makes it appear to be much more—a sign of resurrection for an embattled national hero.

Tragically, in 1996, the company's facility in Lawrence, Massachusetts, burned to the ground. Like most textile firms in the United States, Malden Mills had suffered through hard times for years, so many observers expected aging owner Aaron Feuerstein to pocket the $300 million insurance settlement, walk away from the business, and retire. But he did not. Instead, he kept all of his employees on the payroll while he sought to gain enough funds, both from the insurance companies and new investors, to continue operations. This almost unheard-of generosity won him public acclaim.

In fact, Feuerstein was featured on the television program *Sixty Minutes,* where he explained his philosophy of management and the obligations he felt to employees who had worked in his company—founded by his father, Henry, 90 years earlier. As Feuerstein described it, he felt that his employees were "like his family" because, after all, they gave many years of their lives to the company. How, after all this commitment on their part, could he turn his back on them and walk away? He could not; he was more willing to risk his own financial ruin by struggling to keep the company afloat than to sacrifice the welfare of the people who worked so diligently in his factory.

For a while, stimulated by new products and a renewed sense of commitment from grateful employees, Malden Mills prospered. Soon, however, as cheaper textiles from overseas flooded the U.S. market, the company struggled once again to stay afloat. Late in 2001, after another dismal year, lenders forced the company into Chapter 11 bankruptcy. This time, the company was $180,000,000 in debt, partly because of Mr. Feuerstein's generosity to employees and partly because of losses from operations. Again, almost everyone expected Mr. Feuerstein, who then was 77 years old, to give up. But once more, he surprised the world: Instead of surrendering, he hired a consultant skilled at rescuing sinking companies and redoubled his efforts to save Malden Mills. This time, he faced the daunting task of raising $92 million to prevent creditors from seizing the company and, in all probability, selling off its assets.

In the face of these enormous difficulties, Feuerstein stood his ground, and his employees pitched in to help. They agreed to work for lower wages and they gave up overtime pay. This was a big concession, which when taken along with Feuerstein's efforts helped to save the company. Every day he got on the phone, seeking to raise the needed money. As he put it: "I've got vultures on every side . . . but I'm getting close . . . . I can't imagine that I won't succeed with this last $10 million . . . . Every day I think tomorrow will be the day I get it done." And succeed he did. In October 2003, Malden Mills emerged from bankruptcy, and continues operations today—still providing jobs for many of the same employees Feuerstein vowed to protect.

In recognition of his humanitarian efforts, in 2005 Aaron Feuerstein received the Pace Award from the Ethics Resource Center. In an era in which corporate greed dominated the headlines, this top executive represented a refreshing departure from selfishness. Indeed, Feuerstein's generosity was the ultimate in selflessness. Today, Malden Mills continues to build business in many ways. In fact it is one of the leaders in the manufacturing of so-called "healthy textiles," fabrics that are not treated with chemicals.

Questions for Discussion

1. What particular Big Five personality traits and what elements of core self-evaluation appear to characterize Mr. Feuerstein?
2. How do you think Mr. Feuerstein's social skills may have contributed to his capacity to raise money for his ailing company?
3. What evidence, if any, do you believe points to the possibility that Mr. Feuerstein has a high level of achievement motivation?

Chapter 5

COPING WITH ORGANIZATIONAL LIFE: EMOTIONS AND STRESS

Chapter Outline

Understanding Emotions and Mood

The Role of Emotions and Mood in Organizations

Managing Emotions in Organizations

Organizational Stress and Its Causes

Adverse Effects of Organizational Stress and How to Combat Them

Special Sections

How to Do It

Managing Anger in the Workplace

OB **Making Sense Out of Common Sense**

Who Faces More Stress: Police Officers, Firefighters, or Librarians?

OB **In a Diverse World**

Do Women and Men Respond Differently to Stress?

After reading this chapter, you should be able to:

1. Distinguish between emotions and moods.
2. Explain how emotions and mood influence behavior in organizations.
3. Describe ways in which people manage their emotions in organizations.
4. Identify the major causes of organizational stress.
5. Describe the adverse effects of organizational stress.
6. Identify various ways of reducing stress in the workplace.

PREVIEW CASE

Stressing Stress-Free Jobs at Kaiser Permanente

The expression "physician, heal thyself" suggests that doctors should take doses of their own medicine, so to speak, following their own advice to keep healthy. Kris Ludwigsen, a psychologist at a Kaiser Permanente medical facility in the San Francisco Bay Area is one health-care professional who not only gets this point, but who acts on it.

In the course of counseling patients, Dr. Ludwigsen observed that many suffered physical maladies stemming from the stresses in their lives. But it was not only her patients who needed treatment, she noted; so too did the doctors and nurses with whom she worked. Since medical professionals often have to make life-and-death decisions and face considerable pressures to lower costs while raising service quality, Dr. Ludwigsen wasn't at all surprised that her colleagues showed signs of stress-related illness. Many were forgetful, irritable, quick to cry, easily distracted, and had difficulty concentrating. Unlike her patients, though, most of her colleagues didn't bother to seek treatment.

If they wouldn't come to her, she figured, she would reach out to them. With this in mind, Dr. Ludwigsen launched a comprehensive multistep work stress program for both Kaiser Permanente members and employees. Since many people—even medical professionals—don't recognize their stress-related symptoms, she began by building awareness. Group sessions were held (strictly confidential, of course) in which people were made aware of some of the signs of stress they were exhibiting. Fatigue, migraines, hypertension, stomach problems, and even panic attacks are indications that it's time to take action.

Since some of the most effective things to do involve getting the stress "out of your system," Dr. Ludwigsen got Kaiser Permanente to help. For example, the company sponsors programs to improve employees' experiences outside of work. These include fitness and health classes, seminars to enrich personal relationships, and even training to show expectant mothers how to manage pregnancy in the workplace. On the more active side, they also have extensive new exercise facilities, and to help people relax, they offer massages and teach yoga classes. In the words of one employee who has taken advantage of these opportunities, "It's really been helpful. My stomach's been fine and I'm sleeping better at night."

Interestingly, one of Dr. Ludwigsen's most important bits of advice was to get people to avoid working long hours so they could rest and spend more time with their families. Although hospital officials might have been concerned that this would cut into the productivity of doctors and nurses, who routinely work long shifts, it wasn't a problem. The resulting gains in productivity resulting from good health more than offset any increased costs linked to shorter shifts, creating benefits for everyone.

These various efforts suggest that Dr. Ludwigsen's message came across loud and clear: Efforts at preventive health care are, in the long run, less expensive and more effective than treating disease. Although Kaiser Permanente may be said to be in the "pound of cure" business, it's also clear that it is committed strongly to offering at least "an ounce of prevention."

There's no mistaking the wisdom of Kaiser Permanente's efforts to preserve the health and well-being of their employees and of Dr. Ludwigsen in sparking efforts at doing so. If you have any doubt, consider this: The workplace is the single greatest source of *stress* in people's lives. And its cost to American organizations is $200 to $300 billion annually.[1] Stress makes differences in how well people perform, the number of errors they make, and even whether or not they show up for work or remain on their jobs at all. Given that stress plays such an important role in the behavior of people in organizations, it clearly warrants the attention we devote to it in this chapter.

To understand stress fully, it helps to look more broadly at the wide range of emotions that people have in everyday work situations and their reactions to them. Whether your experiences are positive (e.g., getting a raise), negative (e.g., receiving a poor performance appraisal), or neutral (e.g., doing your job as usual), these everyday feelings—*emotions* and *moods*—play an important role in how we think and act. If emotions and moods seem to be trivial, it's simply because their effects are so widespread that we take them for granted. However, their impact on the way we work can be considerable.[2] Accordingly, we will examine them in this chapter as well.

We begin this chapter with an overview of emotions and mood in organizations, describing their basic nature and the important role they play in organizations. Following this, we examine the nature of stress on the job, focusing closely on specific steps that can be taken to minimize its often harmful effects.

Understanding Emotions and Mood

Consider, for a moment, the following situations. To help, imagine how you would feel if you were the character described in each.

- After a gloomy winter, a beautiful, sunny day finally arrived, making Mark happy. He was inspired to come up with lots of new ideas for his clients.
- Janet was so upset about not making any progress on her sales report that she couldn't take it any more. She left the work piled up on her desk and went to the gym to work out.
- It was a special day for Kimberly. She was so excited that Michael had asked her to marry him that she made her way through her delivery route in half the usual time—and with a lively spring in her step.

There's nothing special, here, right? Mark is happy, Janet is upset, and Kimberly is excited. These are everyday situations to which people have typical reactions. You have them all the time yourself. But don't let these rather ordinary feelings mislead you into thinking that they are unimportant, especially on the job. Indeed, scientists acknowledge that people's feelings at any given time are important. They also recognize that two different kinds of feelings are involved—*emotions* and *mood*. These states, as you will see, are far more important than you might imagine, and in highly complex ways.

Properties of Emotions

emotions
Overt reactions that express feelings about events.

By definition, **emotions** are overt reactions that express feelings about events. You get angry when a colleague takes advantage of you. You become sad when your best friend leaves to take a new job. And you become afraid of what the future holds when a larger firm merges with the company in which you've worked for the last 15 years. These are all examples of emotional reactions. To understand them, we now consider the various properties of emotions and the different forms they take.

Emotions Always Have an Object. Something or someone triggers emotions. For example, you may recognize that your boss made you angry when he falsely accused you of making a mistake or that your boyfriend surprised you with an engagement ring. In each case, there is someone who caused your emotional reaction.

emotional contagion
The tendency to mimic the emotional expressions of others, converging with them emotionally.

The Spread of Emotions Is Contagious. A key trigger of emotions in people is the emotions of others with whom they interact. This is described using the term **emotional contagion**, defined as the tendency to mimic the emotional expressions of others,

FIGURE 5.1

Emotional Contagion in the Workplace

The emotions we display tend to be picked up by others, resulting in a convergence of emotions. This occurs regularly in the workplace, where emotions are regularly spread from person to person. Can you think of situations on the job in which you "caught" the emotions of others with whom you came into contact? How about occasions in which you "spread" your emotions to others?

converging with them emotionally.[3] This phenomenon is prevalent on the job, where workers frequently display the same emotional responses of the higher-ranking others with whom they interact (see Figure 5.1).[4]

Expression of Emotions Is Universal. People throughout the world generally portray particular emotions by using the same facial expressions. In fact, even people living in remote parts of the world tend to express the same emotions in the same manner.[5] As a result, we can do a pretty good (but not perfect) job of recognizing the emotional states of others if we pay attention to their facial expressions. We have to be careful, however, because as we will point out later, people do not always express the emotions they really feel. When they do, however, we are fairly good at recognizing them.

Culture Determines How and When People Express Emotions. Although people throughout the world generally express their emotions in the same manner, informal standards govern the degree to which it is acceptable for them to do so.[6] These expectations are known as **display rules**. For example, Italian cultural norms accept public displays of emotion (e.g., hugging good-bye at the airport, or yelling at one another in public), whereas cultural norms frown upon such public displays in Great Britain, encouraging people there to "tone down" their emotional displays.

display rules
Cultural norms about the appropriate ways to express emotions.

Types of Emotions

Despite what you might think, people do not have an infinite (or even a very large) number of unrelated emotions. Rather, people's emotions may be categorized in different ways. Depending on how you categorize them, different features of emotion are highlighted. We now describe three such ways of categorizing emotions.

Major Emotions and Their Subcategories. Some scientists have noted that there are six major categories of emotions into which various subcategories may be classified. As shown in Figure 5.2, these major categories are anger, fear, joy, love, sadness, and surprise.[7] With one exception, each of these has associated with it various specific emotions that constitute subcategories of these major emotions. The underlying idea is that the six major groups of emotions are different from one another, but within each group, the various subcategories of emotions share similar characteristics (and, as a result, are difficult to distinguish from one another).

Self-Conscious Emotions vs. Social Emotions. Another useful way of distinguishing between emotions is by comparing those that come from internal sources and those that

FIGURE 5.2

Major Categories of Emotion and Associated Subcategories

Scientists have found it useful to categorize people's emotions into the six major categories (and associated subcategories) identified here.

Source: Based on information reported by Weiss & Cropanzano, 1996; see Note 7.

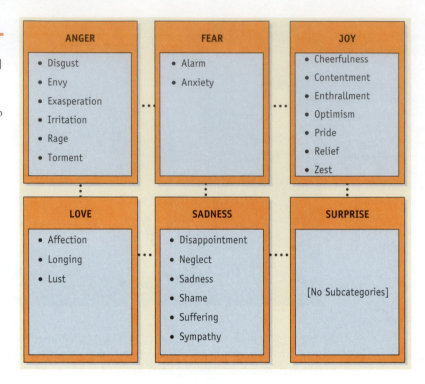

self-conscious emotions
Feelings that stem from within, such as shame, guilt, embarrassment, and pride.

come from external sources. This is the essence of the distinction between so-called *self-conscious emotions* and *social emotions.*

Self-conscious emotions refer to feelings that stem from within. Examples include *shame, guilt, embarrassment,* and *pride.*[8] Scientists believe that self-conscious emotions developed within people to help them stay aware of and regulate their relationships with others. For example, we feel shame when we believe we have failed to meet expectations, and in such cases we are likely to humble ourselves to others, allowing them to have the upper hand. So, if we have done something to harm a coworker, we are likely to demonstrate—and express—feelings of embarrassment and shame, which help appease the relationship with that individual.[9] Interestingly, research has shown that our brains are involved closely in this process: People who have suffered damage to the orbitofrontal portions of their brains tend to be less effective at experiencing self-conscious emotions and at regulating the behaviors they guide than those whose brains are intact.[10]

social emotions
People's feelings based on information external to themselves, such as pity, envy, jealousy, and scorn.

Social emotions refer to people's feelings based on information external to themselves. Examples include *pity, envy, jealousy,* and *scorn.* For example, a worker may experience envy if she covets something that another has (e.g., a better work assignment) or pity if she feels sorry for someone else (e.g., someone who was hurt in an accident). These are all emotions likely to be experienced in the workplace.[11]

The Circumplex Model of Affect. A popular way for scientists to differentiate between emotions has been by combining two different dimensions—the degree to which emotions are pleasant or unpleasant, and the degree to which they make one feel alert and engaged (a variable known as *activation*). This two-dimensional perspective is known as the **circumplex model of affect** (see Figure 5.3).[12] This diagram illustrates how various emotions are interrelated with respect to these two dimensions. Four major categories result.

circumplex model of affect
A theory of emotional behavior based on the degree to which emotions are pleasant or unpleasant and the degree to which they make one feel activated (i.e., feeling alert and engaged).

To understand how to read this diagram (hence, to understand the circumplex model of affect), look, for example, at the upper right part of Figure 5.3. It shows that being elated is a pleasant emotion (because it makes us feel good) and that it also is a highly activated emotion (because it encourages us to take action). They fall into the activated positive affect category. The same applies to the two other emotions in that part of the diagram

FIGURE 5.3

The Circumplex Model of Affect

This conceptualization summarizes emotions in terms of two key dimensions: activated-unactivated and pleasant-unpleasant. The emotions within each grouping are similar to one another. Those across from one another in this diagram are considered opposite emotions.

Source: Based on Huelsman et al., 2003; see Note 12.

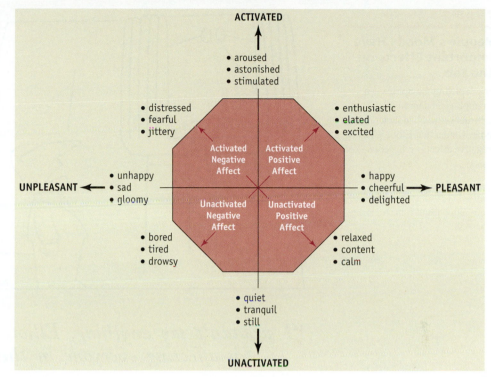

The Basic Nature of Mood

(enthusiastic and excited). Within the diagram, any emotions that lie directly opposite each other are characterized in the opposite manner. So, following through on our example, being bored, tired, and drowsy are emotions considered opposite to enthusiastic, elated, and excited. They are at the opposite ends of the two main dimensions—that is, they generate unactivated negative affect.

mood
An unfocused, relatively mild feeling that exists as background to our daily experiences.

In contrast to emotions, which are highly specific and intense, we also have feelings that are more diffuse in scope, known as *moods*. Scientists define **mood** as an unfocused, relatively mild feeling that exists as background to our daily experiences. Whereas we are inclined to recognize the emotions we are feeling, moods are more subtle and difficult to detect. For example, you may say that you are in a good mood or a bad mood, but this isn't as focused as saying that you are experiencing a certain emotion, such as anger or sadness.

Moods, as we all know, fluctuate rapidly, sometimes widely, during the course of a day. Whereas favorable feedback from the boss may make us feel good, harsh criticism may put us in a bad mood. Such temporary shifts in feeling *states*—short-term differences in the way we feel—are only partly responsible for the moods that people demonstrate. Superimposed over these passing conditions are also more stable personality *traits*—consistent differences between people's predispositions toward experiencing positive or negative affect, as we discussed in Chapter 3. Mood, in other words, is a combination of both who we are, personality-wise, and the conditions we face (see Figure 5.4).[13]

Not surprisingly, then, the moods we experience can be based on our individual experiences (e.g., receiving a raise), as well as the general characteristics of our work groups or organizations (e.g., the extent to which they are upbeat, energetic, and enthusiastic). For example, the importance of having fun at work is emphasized at several companies, with Southwest Airlines and Ben and Jerry's Homemade Ice Cream being notable examples.[14] It's not surprising, then, that people working for these companies are generally in a good mood. Because promoting positive moods in employees can be so useful, specialized companies have been created to help other organizations create fun in their workplaces (see Figure 5.5).

People's Moods Have Important Effects on the Job

By depicting the Sphinx—a mythological demon of destruction and bad luck—it's little wonder that Elliot is having a negative effects on his coworkers' moods.

Source: © The New Yorker Collection 1992, Charles Barsotti from cartoonbank.com. All rights reserved.

"I wouldn't say anything, Elliot, but your mood is affecting everyone in the office."

FIGURE 5.5

Playfair Helps Companies Promote Positive Moods

Since 1975, Playfair, based in Berkeley, California, has helped a wide variety of companies—even traditionally staid and conservative ones, such as the Federal Reserve Bank and the Internal Revenue Service—promote fun in their workplaces. To help create lighthearted workplaces, they have gotten clients to do such things as have employees dress up in funny costumes, bring in baby pictures of themselves, and take "joy breaks" in which they play marbles.

The Role of Emotions and Mood in Organizations

A keen observer of the human condition, William Shakespeare expressed the benefits of happiness poetically in *The Winter's Tale,* in which he said, "A merry heart goes all the day. Your sad tires in a mile-a." Do the famous playwright's remarks apply to work performance? We now consider this question.

Are Happier People More Successful on Their Jobs?

Before answering this question, let's clarify what we mean by "happy." To social scientists, happy individuals are those who frequently experience positive emotions in their lives. Based on this definition, do people do better on their jobs when they are happy? Research shows that the answer is "yes"; happy workers enjoy multiple advantages over their less happy peers.[15] This takes two major forms.

Job Performance. Happier people tend to outperform less happy people in several different ways. To begin with, they tend to get better jobs—that is, ones that give them high levels of autonomy, meaning, and variety.[16] Then, once on their jobs, they perform their jobs more successfully.[17] This occurs among people in jobs ranging from dormitory resident advisors to cricket players.[18] Interestingly, this same effect also occurs at the highest echelons of organizations. Happier CEOs of companies tend to have happier employees working for them. And, of course, happy employees are less inclined to resign (see Chapter 6).[19] In part because of this, their organizations tend to be more profitable.[20] Obviously, the importance of happiness cannot be overstated when it comes to job performance.

Income. Do happier people earn higher incomes? Yes, they do. Research has found this to be the case in countries throughout the world. For example, high correlations between happiness and income were found among people in Germany and Russia.[21] Fascinatingly, this same relationship was found even among indigenous Malaysian farmers, whose only income was the value of their property and belongings.[22] In these cases, because the relationships are correlational in nature, it's unclear whether people make more money because they're happy or people become happy because they make more money. In either case, this connection is quite strong.

Why Are Happier Workers More Successful?

What is behind these strong connections between happiness and work success? As in most OB phenomena, there are several answers.

Distraction. Suppose an employee is upset because he received an unsatisfactory performance rating. This individual may be expected to be so distraught that he will lose the capacity to pay attention and become distracted from his work. Not only is this likely to impede task performance, but it also is likely to interfere with the potentially useful feedback that he might receive from the supervisor giving the evaluation.

It is for this reason that experts advise managers to refrain from even trying to get messages across to people who are upset. In the case of the poorly performing employee, it may be best to wait for another time when the employee can be better focused to help him learn ways of improving. After all, if someone is too distracted to take in the message, it is wasted.

Memory. It has been shown that mood is related to memory in an interesting fashion. Being in a positive mood helps people recall positive things, whereas being in a negative mood helps people recall negative things.[23] This idea is known as **mood congruence**. For example, if you go to work while you're in a good mood, chances are that this will help you remember those things on the job that also put you in a good mood, such as the friendly relationships you have with your coworkers. Likewise, someone who is in a bad mood is likely to recall negative things associated with work, such as a recent fight with the boss. Focusing on positive things (the result of being in a positive mood) is likely to

mood congruence
The tendency to recall positive things when you are in a good mood and to recall negative things when you are in a bad mood.

promote successful job performance because it encourages people to put forth extra effort (a form of motivation discussed in Chapter 7), which they would be unlikely to do when focusing primarily on how bad things are (see Figure 5.6).

Decision Quality.   Research has found that people showing high positive affectivity do a better job of making decisions than those showing high negative affectivity.[24] Specifically, people make decisions that are more accurate and more important to the group's effectiveness, and they have greater managerial potential. This ability to make better decisions is a particularly good reason why happy people tend to be successful.

Evaluation.   Mood also biases the way we evaluate people and things. For example, people report greater satisfaction with their jobs while they are in a good mood than while they are in a bad mood.[25] Being in a good mood also leads people to perceive (and admit to perceiving) the positive side of another's work. Because being in a good mood keeps managers from perceiving even the good behavior of their subordinates as bad, it helps them offer the kind of encouraging feedback that is likely to help their subordinates to improve their performance (see Chapter 7). By contrast, managers whose bad moods keep them making negative evaluations are unlikely to be able to help their subordinates improve their work. This, of course, makes those managers less than effective themselves.

Cooperation.   Mood strongly affects the extent to which people help each other, cooperate with each other, and refrain from behaving aggressively (forms of behavior we will discuss in more detail in Chapter 11). People who are in good moods also tend to be highly generous and are inclined to help their fellow workers who may need their assistance. People who are in good moods also are inclined to work carefully with others to resolve conflicts with them, whereas people in bad moods are likely to keep those conflicts brewing. This is yet another reason why being in a good mood enhances job performance.

Clearly, people's moods and emotions have profound effects on their performance in organizations, and for a variety of reasons. Given this importance, it's not surprising that today's organizational scientists have been devoting a great deal of attention to this topic.[26]

affective events theory (AET)

The theory that identifies various factors that lead to people's emotional reactions on the job and how these reactions affect those individuals.

Affective Events Theory

In recent years, one of the guiding forces in the study of emotions in organizations has been **affective events theory (AET)**.[27] This theory identifies various factors that lead to people's emotional reactions on the job and how these reactions affect those individuals (see Figure 5.7).[28]

FIGURE 5.6

The Effects of Mood Congruence

The concept of mood congruence suggests that people's memories match their emotions. For example, people experiencing positive moods are inclined to have positive memories, things that put them in a good mood. This, in turn, encourages people to put forth extra effort, thereby improving their job performance. Just the opposite occurs in the case of negative moods.

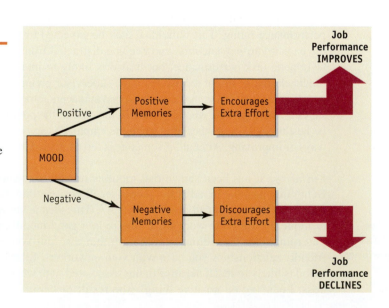

FIGURE 5.7

Affective Events Theory

According to affective events theory, people's job performance and job satisfaction are influenced by their positive and negative emotional reactions to events on the job. These events, in turn, are influenced by aspects of the work environment. People's emotional reactions to these events depend on such individual characteristics as their moods and aspects of their personalities.

Source: Based on suggestions by Ashkanasy and Daus, 2002; see Note 28.

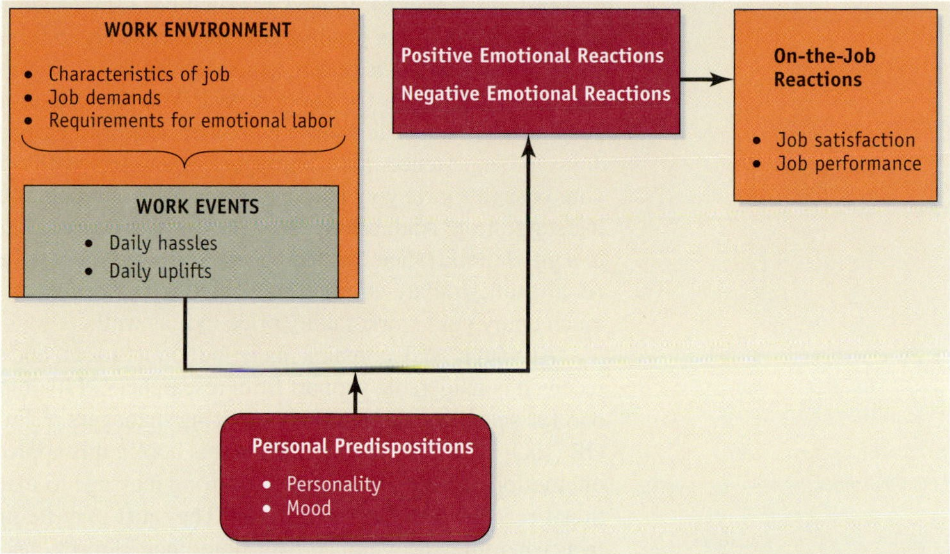

WORK ENVIRONMENT
- Characteristics of job
- Job demands
- Requirements for emotional labor

WORK EVENTS
- Daily hassles
- Daily uplifts

Positive Emotional Reactions
Negative Emotional Reactions

On-the-Job Reactions
- Job satisfaction
- Job performance

Personal Predispositions
- Personality
- Mood

emotional labor
The psychological effort involved in holding back one's true emotions.

daily hassles
Unpleasant or undesirable events that put people in bad moods.

daily uplifts
Pleasant or desirable events that put people in good moods.

Beginning on the left side of Figure 5.7, AET recognizes that people's emotions are determined, in part, by various features of the work environment. For example, the way we feel is likely to be determined by various characteristics of the jobs we do (e.g., we are likely to feel good about jobs that are interesting and exciting), the demands we face (e.g., how pressured we are to meet deadlines), and by requirements for *emotional labor*.

The concept of **emotional labor** refers to the degree to which people have to work hard to display what they believe are appropriate emotions on their jobs. People in service professions (e.g., waitresses and flight attendants), for example, often have to come across as being more pleasant than they really feel. As you might imagine, having to do this repeatedly can be very taxing. (And, as described in this chapter's Case in Point (see p. 199), this can take its toll.)

These various features of the work environment are likely to lead to the occurrence of various events. These include confronting **daily hassles**, unpleasant or undesirable events that put people in bad moods (e.g., having to deal with difficult bosses or coworkers). They also include experiencing more positive events known as **daily uplifts**. These are the opposite—namely, pleasant or desirable events that put people in good moods (e.g., enjoying feelings of recognition for the work you do).

As Figure 5.7 shows, people react to these various work events by showing emotional reactions, both positive and negative. However, as the diagram also shows, the extent to which this occurs depends upon (or, as scientists say, is "moderated by") each of two types of personal predispositions: personality and mood. As we noted in Chapter 4, personality predisposes us to respond in varying degrees of intensity to the events that occur. In keeping with our discussion, for example, a person who has a high degree of positive affectivity is likely to perceive events in a positive manner, whereas one who has a high degree of negative affectivity is likely to perceive those same events more negatively.

Mood also is a moderator of the relationship between work events and emotional reactions, as Figure 5.7 suggests. This is in keeping with the point we made earlier, that the mood we are in at any given time can exaggerate the nature of the emotions we experience in response to an event. So, for example, an event that leads a person to experience a negative emotional reaction (e.g., having a fight with a coworker) is likely to make that individual feel even worse if he or she is in a bad mood at the time.

And finally, as the theory notes, these affective reactions have two important effects. First, they promote high levels of job performance. This should not be surprising, given that we already noted that happy people perform their jobs at high levels. Second, AET also notes that affective reactions are responsible for people's job performance and *job satisfaction*—that is, the extent to which they hold positive attitudes toward their jobs (we will discuss this in detail in Chapter 6). Indeed, research has established very strongly that people who are inclined to experience positive emotions are likely to be satisfied with their jobs.[29]

Putting this all together, consider the following example. You have been happily employed at Google for about a year. You find the work pleasantly challenging and in keeping with your talents as a computer network engineer. Over the course of your workdays you experience many enjoyable encounters with others. On this particular occasion, your boss just gave you a big pat on the back in recognition of your latest revenue-generating suggestion. And, because you have a high degree of positive affect and you are already in a good mood when this happened, you experience a very positive reaction to this event. As a result, you are strongly motivated to perform your job at a high level and you very much enjoy your work, taking pride in it as well.

Although AET contains many individual ideas, and it is relatively new, it already has received considerable support from researchers.[30] Its importance rests on two key ideas—one for scientists and one for practicing managers.[31] First, unlike many other theories of OB (such as the others described in this book), this approach recognizes the important role of emotions. Second, AET sends a strong message to managers: Do not overlook the emotional reactions of your employees. They just may be more important than you think. In fact, when they accumulate over time, their impact can be considerable. Thus, it is clear that anyone in a supervisory capacity has to pay attention to managing emotions in the workplace. In view of this, we now turn to this topic.

Managing Emotions in Organizations

As we discussed in Chapter 4 when describing *emotional intelligence,* emotions are important on the job insofar as people who are good at "reading" and understanding emotions in others, and who are able to regulate their own emotions, tend to have an edge when it comes to dealing with others.[32] As we will now describe, this is only one possible way in which people manage their emotions in organizations.

Emotional Dissonance

Imagine that you are a flight attendant for a major airline. After a long flight with rude passengers, you finally reach your destination. You feel tired and annoyed, but you do not have the option of expressing how you really feel. You don't even have the luxury of acting neutrally and expressing nothing at all. Instead, you are expected to act peppy and cheerful, smiling and thanking the passengers for choosing your airline and cheerfully saying goodbye (more like "b'bye") to them as they exit the plane. The conflict between the emotion you feel (anger) and the emotion you are required to express (happiness) may take its toll on your well-being. This example illustrates a kind of situation that is all too typical—one in which you are required to display emotions on the job that are inconsistent with how you actually feel.

emotional dissonance
Inconsistencies between the emotions we feel and the emotions we express.

This phenomenon, known as **emotional dissonance**, can be a significant source of work-related stress (the major topic that we will discuss later in this chapter).[33] Emotional dissonance is likely to occur in situations in which there are strong expectations regarding the emotions one is expected to display by virtue of one's job requirements. Our flight attendant example illustrates this point. The same applies to sales clerks, bank tellers, entertainers—just about anyone who provides services to the public at large.

When emotional dissonance occurs, people often have to try very hard to ensure that they display the appropriate emotions. As we noted earlier, the psychological effort involved in doing this is referred to as *emotional labor.* If you ever find yourself "biting your tongue"—that is, holding back from saying what you want to say—you are expending a great deal of emotional labor. Actually, not saying what you really think is only part of the situation. Emotional labor also is invested in saying things you don't really feel. For example, one would have to invest a great deal of emotional labor when confronting a coworker who comes to you asking you how you feel about her new hairdo. You don't like it at all, but you struggle to keep your feelings to yourself (and not even to "leak" them nonverbally; see Chapter 3). When pressed to say something, you engage in "a little white lie," by telling her how very flattering it is. Although this is a form of dishonesty, it

felt emotions
The emotions people actually feel (which may differ from *displayed emotions*).

displayed emotions
Emotions that people show others, which may or may not be in line with their *felt emotions*.

is considered widely appropriate to keep from hurting people's feelings by saying the right thing (see Figure 5.8).

This discussion underscores an important idea: The emotions people actually experience, known as **felt emotions**, may be discrepant from the emotions they show others, known as **displayed emotions**. This is not at all surprising. After all, our jobs do not always give us the luxury of expressing how we really feel. To do so, such as by expressing the anger you really feel toward your boss, is likely to lead to problems. As sociologists tell us, social pressure compels people to conform to expectations about which particular emotions are appropriate to show in public and which are not. As we noted earlier, such *display rules* vary among cultures. But they also appear to differ as a function of people's occupational positions.

It is an unspoken rule, for example, that an athletic coach is not supposed to be openly hostile and negative when speaking about an opponent (at least, when doing so in public). It also is expected that people considered "professionals," such as doctors and lawyers, demonstrate appropriate decorum and seriousness when interacting with their patients and clients. Should your own doctor or lawyer respond to your difficult situation by saying, "Wow, I sure wouldn't want to be in your shoes," you may find yourself looking for someone else to help you.

Controlling Anger (Before It Controls You)

Quite often, behaving appropriately in business situations requires controlling negative emotions, particularly anger. After all, to be successful we cannot let the situations we face get the better of us. It's perfectly natural for anyone to get angry, particularly on the job, where there may be a great deal to anger us. We can be made angry, for example, by feeling unfairly treated (see Chapter 2), by believing that we are disrespected by others, by feeling that we are being attacked or threatened in some way, and the like.

Although we all know what *anger* is, and we have experienced it many times (perhaps too many), a precise definition is in order. By **anger**, scientists are referring to a heightened state of emotional arousal (e.g., increased heart rate, rapid breathing, flushed face, sweaty palms, etc.) fueled by cognitive interpretations of situations. Anger reactions can run the gamut from irritation to outrage and fury.

Importantly, there are situations in which displaying anger can be purposeful and constructive. For example, to get a subordinate to take immediate action in a dangerous situation, a supervisor may express anger by raising her voice and looking that subordinate straight in the eye. This would be the case should a military officer display her anger purposely to express urgency when ordering a soldier under her command to move immediately out of

anger
A heightened state of emotional arousal (e.g., increased heart rate, rapid breathing, flushed face, sweaty palms, etc.) fueled by cognitive interpretations of situations.

FIGURE 5.8

Emotional Labor: Not Uncommon When Interacting with Others

So as to maintain positive relationships with others on the job, it is necessary to be sensitive to their feelings. This sometimes leads people to say things they don't really feel or to exaggerate their true feelings. Such efforts are said to require emotional labor.

a combat zone. Because of its constructive and highly controlled nature, anger of this type is not problematic. In fact, it can be quite valuable. Where anger can be dangerous, however, is when it erupts violently and is out of control. We need to be concerned about this because aggression is a natural reaction to anger.

The challenge people face is to control their anger appropriately. This is the idea behind the practice of **anger management**—systematic efforts to reduce people's emotional feelings of anger and the physiological arousal it causes. Because you hardly ever can get rid of or avoid the things that anger you, nor can you alter them, it's important to learn to control your reactions. For some suggestions as to how to go about doing so, see the *How to Do It* section below.

anger management
Systematic efforts to reduce people's emotional feelings of anger and the physiological arousal it causes.

Organizational Compassion: Managing Emotion in Times of Trauma

The summer of 2005 was a highly traumatic period for many people around the world. In early July, Londoners were hit by terrorist attacks on their mass transit system and in late

HOW TO DO IT

Managing Anger in the Workplace

It is commonly believed that it's good to "let it all hang out" by expressing your anger fully. The American Psychological Association advises, however, that this belief is a dangerous myth because people sometimes use this to grant themselves license to "let it rip."[34] And this, of course, does nothing to alleviate the source of your anger. In fact, excessive displays of anger are likely to make things worse.

This raises a critical question: What, precisely, can we do to control our anger? Although it's not always easy to keep our anger in check—and indeed, there are professionals who often are hired to help people do this (although rarely in the form taken in the 2003 Adam Sandler and Jack Nicholson film, *Anger Management*)—we all can do various things to control our anger. Some of the key ones are as follows.

1. *Practice relaxation.* People who display dangerous amounts of anger often find it difficult to relax. As a result, they get frustrated easily and are inclined to "fly off the handle." By learning to relax, however, such individuals are better able to take control of their emotions. Simply taking a deep breath and counting to 10, a tried-and-true-technique, can be quite effective. There also are more sophisticated approaches. For example, later in this chapter, in discussing techniques for managing stress, we describe various relaxation techniques, including *meditation.* These techniques are very effective in getting people to keep their anger in check. In this chapter's Individual Exercise (see p. 197), we offer step-by-step guidelines for doing so.

2. *Change the way you think.* When people get angry, they tend to think irrationally, making things worse than they really are. It's important, however, to remind yourself that this will not help. Being logical about the source of your anger is what's needed, and this involves getting clear facts and thinking things through. Often, getting someone to help you do so is what's needed. So, instead of screaming your head off the next time you're angry, try to figure out what's going on. And if you cannot do so yourself, get someone to help you—a friend, for example, anyone who can help you see through any angry and illogical thoughts you may have.

3. *Use humor.* There's nothing like humor to take the edge off your fury. Being silly can diffuse anger, keeping it in check. So, the next time you find yourself thinking that someone is a "dirtbag," don't come out and say so. Instead, think about exactly what a bag of dirt looks like. Imagining that person's head atop a burlap sack of topsoil may give you pause, making you chuckle. And this momentary relief may help you regain your composure.

4. *Leave the room.* When you feel anger welling up inside, move to another room or even out of the building. Changing your surroundings may help you escape whatever or whoever is causing you to be so angry. Even such temporary avoidance may be enough to keep you from saying or doing something about which you would be sorry. Furthermore, the time spent moving elsewhere also can help by distracting you from the immediacy of the situation.

If there ever was a time to refer to something as "easier said than done," this is it. However, if there ever was something that "must be done, or else," this also is it. Because so much is riding on the proper management of anger, efforts to put this advice to work for you are sure to pay off in the long run.

August, residents of the U.S. Gulf Coast were struck by Hurricane Katrina. Only four years earlier were the September 11, 2001 terrorist strikes on the United States. Not only did thousands of people perish in these disasters, but they also took their toll on untold millions who once felt safe at home and work, but who now feel vulnerable. Indeed, the emotional toll of such events is considerable, and mental health professionals are experiencing signs of it in their practices.[35]

Events Triggering the Need for Compassion. Emotions clearly are very important whenever some sort of tragedy occurs that affects a company. This may happen for several reasons, such as the death of a leader. For example, although Mary Kay Cosmetics is a $2 billion company, the death of its beloved and charismatic founder, Mary Kay Ash, proved to be a highly personal, traumatic experience for the company's 3,600 employees.[36]

A natural disaster also might adversely affect the emotional well-being of employees, such as occurred following the closing of businesses (either temporarily or permanently) in the wake of Hurricane Katrina. And, of course, nobody can forget financial scandals, such as the collapse of Enron in 2002, and the horrific tragedies of September 11, 2001, that led to the destruction of scores of businesses and the disruption of thousands more in New York City. In these and other such disasters, be they well-known or more local in scope (e.g., the earthquake that rocked Hawaii in October, 2006), the emotions of everyone in the workplace run high as employees at all levels struggle collectively to deal with the trauma.

Although it's surely difficult (or impossible, in some cases) to avoid such disasters, fortunately, there is something that leaders and managers can do to help everyone involved return to business as usual.[37] Specifically, company officials should create an environment in which people can express their emotions and in which they can do something to alleviate their own or others' suffering. In other words, they should express **organizational compassion**.

organizational compassion
Steps taken by organizational officials to alleviate the suffering of its employees or others.

Responding to Tragedy: Two Contrasting Examples. To illustrate what we mean, let's compare the reactions of officials from two different companies to the devastation that followed when terrorist plans destroyed the World Trade Center. On September 11, 2001, Edmond English, the president of TJX, a company that lost seven employees on one of the planes that struck one of the towers, showed incredible amounts of compassion. As soon as information became available, he gathered his staff together to confirm that their colleagues were among the victims. The very day of the attacks, he brought in grief counselors to help the employees. He chartered planes to bring the victims' relatives to company headquarters near Boston and greeted each family member in person. And he also told the workers that they could take time off as needed. Most did not. Instead, they opted to come to work and help each other through the trauma. The steps that Mr. English took enabled TJX employees to express their emotions and to alleviate their own and their colleagues' suffering, and as a result, the company got back to normal relatively soon. Because people were able to bring their pain to the office, rather than being forced to ignore or suppress it, they were able to get back to work.

By contrast, consider what occurred at a publishing company close to ground zero, whose officers opted to conduct business as usual. They held regularly scheduled meetings and provided little or no support for those seeking to express their emotions. Terrified and confused employees showed up, but they couldn't concentrate on their work, as you might imagine. Even more seriously, the message that the company sent about its lack of compassion during these trying times took its toll on the loyalty of the employees. After all, who would want to work for a company that shows such callous disregard for their emotional well-being? Obviously, organizational compassion is important. With an eye toward minimizing the emotional fallout of disasters, several specific steps can be taken. For an overview of these, see Table 5.1.

Organizational Stress and Its Causes

Stress is an all-too-common part of life today, something few individuals can avoid. In fact, a nationwide survey conducted by a large life insurance company showed that nearly 46 percent of American workers believe jobs are highly stressful.[38] And growing evidence

TABLE 5.1 Coping with the Emotional Fallout of Disasters: How Can Companies Help?

Whether from terrorists or the wrath of Mother Nature, disasters leave people feeling vulnerable and unable to concentrate. This, of course, makes it difficult for them to focus on work, even if their workplaces still exist. Given the emotional fallout, companies find it necessary to cope in ways that they might never have considered earlier. Fortunately, there are several things companies can do to help.

Suggestion	Explanation
Provide accurate information.	It is not always clear what to do, but whatever is being done to promote workplace safety should be communicated clearly to all.
Encourage social interaction.	During periods of emotional stress, one of the most effective ways to cope is by interacting with others. Social networks provide comfort and support, reducing anxiety and depression. When disaster strikes, company social events should not be cancelled, but they should be held because they are useful mechanisms for fostering social support.
Promote the use of health services.	It's easy for people to become ill when their emotions are running high. As such, the company should encourage employees to take care of themselves, taking full advantage of the medical, counseling, and health club services that may be available.
Try to return to normalcy.	We all like having our routines, and these are shattered during times of trauma. To help return to normal, it is useful to try to get back to "business as usual." This is not to ignore the emotions that people feel, because these need to be acknowledged. Still, it's useful to regain the security of one's regular routine.

Source: Dutton et al., 2002; see Note 37.

suggests that high levels of stress adversely affect physical health, psychological well-being, and many aspects of task performance.[39] Such evidence makes a strong case for understanding organizational stress.

In this section of the chapter, we will review the major causes and effects of stress. Then, in the final section, we will describe various ways of effectively managing stress so as to reduce its negative impact. Before doing this, however, we will define stress more carefully and distinguish it from other concepts with which it is related.

What Is Stress?

What do each of the following situations have in common?

- You win $500,000 in the lottery.
- You find out that your company is about to eliminate your department.
- A dozen family members are coming over to your apartment for dinner.
- Your spouse is diagnosed with a serious illness.

stressor

Any demands, either physical or psychological in nature, encountered during the course of living.

The answer is that each situation, whether positive or negative in nature, creates extreme demands on us. Stimuli of this type are known as **stressors**—any demands, either physical or psychological in nature, encountered during the course of living.

When we encounter stressors, our bodies (in particular, our sympathetic nervous systems and endocrine systems) are mobilized into action, such as through elevated heart rate, blood pressure, and respiration.[40] Arousal rises quickly to high levels, and many physiological changes take place. If the stressors persist, the body's resources eventually may become depleted, at which point people's ability to cope (at least physically) decreases sharply, and severe biological damage may result. It is these patterns of responses that we have in mind when we talk about *stress*.

stress

The pattern of emotional states and physiological reactions occurring in response to demands from with or outside an organization. See *stressor*.

Specifically, scientists define **stress** as the pattern of emotional states and physiological reactions occurring in response to demands from within or outside organizations (i.e., stressors). It is important to note that although, strictly speaking, our bodies respond to both positive sources of stress (e.g., winning the lottery) and negative ones (e.g., losing a job), when we refer to stress on the job, we are referring to negative sources of stress. This

work stress
The harmful physical and emotional responses that people experience on their jobs.

cognitive appraisal
A judgment about the stressfulness of a situation based on the extent to which someone perceives a stressor as threatening and is capable of coping with its demands.

strain
Deviations from normal states of human functioning resulting from prolonged exposure to stressful events.

is not because we mean to be negative, but because people's reactions to stress on the job tend to be negative in nature, making it a concern to managers. Thus, when we speak of **work stress**, we are referring to the harmful physical and emotional responses that people experience on their jobs.[41]

As is the case in most OB phenomena, the mechanisms by which stressors lead to stress reactions are perceptual, meaning that they are not direct and mechanical in nature. Specifically, stress involves people's **cognitive appraisal** of the potential stressors they face—that is, their judgment about the stressfulness of a situation. In simple terms, for stress to occur people must perceive: (1) that the situation they face is somehow threatening to them, and (2) that they will be unable to cope with these potential dangers or demands—that the situation is beyond their control. As the Greek philosopher Epictetus put it some 2000 years ago, "People are disturbed not by things, but by their perception of things." In other words, stress does not simply shape our thoughts; it also derives from them and is affected by them strongly.

To the extent that people appraise various situations as stressors, they are likely to have stress reactions. And often, these can have damaging behavioral, psychological, and/or medical effects. Indeed, physiological and psychological stress reactions can be so great that eventually they take their toll on the body and mind, resulting in such maladies as insomnia, cardiovascular disease, and depression. Such reactions are referred to as **strain**, defined as deviations from normal states of human function resulting from prolonged exposure to stressful events. Reactions commonly take the form of physical ailments, emotional problems, and impaired job performance. For a summary of the relationship between stressors, stress, and strain, please refer to Figure 5.9. (As you probably have seen in dealing with different people in your own life, some individuals are far tougher than others. That is, they have the mental toughness to focus their minds and manage their emotions under stressful conditions.[42] To see how well you and your fellow team members fare in this regard, complete the Group Exercise on pp. 197–198.)

Causes of Stress in the Workplace

Stress is caused by many different factors. For example, stress is caused by personal factors such as problems with family members, financial problems, and illness. Stress also is caused by societal factors, such as concerns over crime, terrorism, and downturns in the economy. However, in this book, we are concerned mostly about job-related stress. What causes stress in work settings? Unfortunately, as you will see, the list is quite long; many different factors play a role in creating stress in the workplace.

Occupational Demands. By their nature, some jobs have the potential to present more uncontrollable demands on us than others. The jobs of emergency room physician and

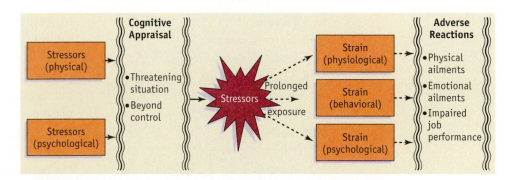

FIGURE 5.9

Stressors, Stress, and Strain: Recognizing the Distinctions

Stimuli known as stressors (which are both physical and psychological in nature) lead to stress reactions when they are cognitively appraised as being threatening and beyond one's control. The deviations from normal states resulting from stress are known as strain. Both physical and emotional ailments as well as impaired job performance result from strain.

military officer, for example, are inclined to expose the people who perform them to more stressors than do other jobs, such as college professor or janitor. This basic fact—that some jobs are potentially more stressful than others—has been confirmed by the results of a survey involving more than 130 different occupations.[43] For a listing of some of these most stressful jobs, see Table 5.2.

What, precisely, makes some jobs more stressful than others? Many such features may be identified, but five are particularly important in determining the levels of stress various jobs have the potential to generate. Specifically, people are inclined to experience higher levels of stress the more their jobs require the following activities:

- Making decisions
- Performing boring, repetitive tasks
- Repeatedly exchanging information with others
- Working in unpleasant physical conditions
- Performing unstructured rather than structured tasks

The more a job possesses these characteristics, the more stress that job has the potential to generate within the individuals who perform it. This is not to imply that people cannot experience some stress in any particular job they do. Various causes of stress can be found in just about any job; none is likely to be entirely stress-free.[44] To illustrate this point, and to give you a good sense of why the inclusion of various job characteristics suggests only the "potential" to arouse stress rather than a certainty, see the *OB: Making Sense Out of Common Sense* section on page 185.

Conflict Between Work and Nonwork. If you've ever had to face the demands of working while at the same time trying to raise a family, you are probably well aware of how difficult this can be. Not only must you confront the usual pressures to spend time at work while concentrating on what you're doing, but you also must pay attention to the demands placed on you by members of your family (e.g., to spend time with them). People

TABLE 5.2 What Jobs Are Most—and Least—Stressful?

Using a variety of standards, scientists rated 250 different jobs regarding how stressful they are. Shown here are the rankings and stress scores for selected occupations. (Higher scores reflect greater levels of stress encountered.)

Rank Score	Stress Score	Rank Score	Stress Score
1. U.S. president	176.6	47. Auto salesperson	56.3
2. Firefighter	110.9	50. College professor	54.2
3. Senior executive	108.6	60. School principal	51.7
6. Surgeon	99.5	103. Market research analyst	42.1
10. Air traffic controller	83.1	104. Personnel recruiter	41.8
12. Public relations executive	78.5	113. Hospital administrator	39.6
16. Advertising account executive	74.6	119. Economist	38.7
		122. Mechanical engineer	38.3
17. Real estate agent	73.1	124. Chiropractor	37.9
20. Stockbroker	71.7	132. Technical writer	36.5
22. Pilot	68.7	149. Retail salesperson	34.9
25. Architect	66.9	173. Accountant	31.1
31. Lawyer	64.3	193. Purchasing agent	28.9
33. General physician	64.0	229. Broadcast technician	24.2
35. Insurance agent	63.3	245. Actuary	20.2
42. Advertising salesperson	59.9		

Source: The Wall Street Journal; © 1997 Dow Jones & Company, Inc.

OB Making Sense Out of Common Sense

Who Faces More Stress: Police Officers, Firefighters, or Librarians?

If you were to compare the stressfulness of five jobs—police officer, firefighter, train operator, teacher, and librarian—which would come out on top? Before dismissing this as an "obvious question," take note of your answer and read on.

To answer this question in objective fashion, a scientist recently compared almost 300 people performing these five jobs on several indices.[45] Specifically, he gave them questionnaires assessing the degrees to which they reported experiencing various work-related stressors (e.g., workload, degree of control over work, and so on) as well as various psychological signs of stress (e.g., dissatisfaction with work that spilled over to home life). The study found that members of one group encountered the most stressors and suffered the most adverse reactions—librarians. That's right, librarians—*not* firefighters or police officers.

Why librarians, you ask? As surprising as this may be at first blush, it makes sense once you examine the study's findings more closely. For example, unlike police officers or firefighters, librarians complained about their work environments. Many reported feeling sick of being stuck between bookshelves all day. They also complained that their skills were not used much. Stamping due dates onto the backs of books and issuing 10-cent fines is, after all, rather dull and uninspiring work for individuals who are highly trained in research skills. By contrast, although police officers and firefighters regularly put their lives on the line, they found their work environments interesting and they almost always got to use the skills for which they were trained. Unlike librarians, they faced challenges and enjoyed them, thereby making their jobs less stress-arousing in these key ways.

Still, you may be thinking that catching criminals and carrying children out of burning buildings puts far greater demands on people than does re-shelving books and asking patrons to be quiet (although we know, of course, that

librarians do much more). Although this is true if you take into account only the characteristics of a job, we also have to take into consideration preparedness for stressors. Specifically, whereas police officers and firefighters are highly trained in ways to deal with the stressors they face, librarians are less likely to receive such training (although perhaps they should!). As a result, librarians are less well equipped to deal with whatever stressors they face—even if these do not involve life-and-death situations. In fact, the training of police officers and firefighters allows them to perceive as quite unremarkable situations that would be stressful to most anyone else (e.g., confronting an irate motorist).

Finally, one more factor accounts for these surprising findings. People respond differently to stressors in their lives; some hardier individuals like—and can take—more stress than others. As you might suspect, individuals who pursue dangerous lines of work enjoy the thrills these jobs provide and are predisposed to respond well to such conditions. (We will have more to say about this in our discussion of careers later in this chapter.) Such so-called "adrenaline junkies," in fact, are likely to experience higher levels of stress when performing tamer jobs (e.g., librarian). With this in mind, it makes sense that police officers and firefighters might not perceive their jobs as being especially stressful, allowing them to respond in perfectly normal fashion to conditions that the rest of us would find very stressful.

Before closing, we offer some consolation: If you answered this section's opening question incorrectly, don't be disheartened. At first, even the researcher himself was quite surprised at what he found. However, that's precisely why we do research—to establish if the things we suspect to be the case are indeed correct. In this case, the seemingly surprising findings shed light on a major complexity that's important to know. If nothing else, this might make you more empathic toward a librarian the next time he or she tells you to "shhhh."

---

role conflict

Incompatibilities between the various sets of obligations people face.

confronting such incompatibilities in the various sets of obligations they have are said to experience **role conflict** (see Chapters 9 and 11). As you might expect, when we experience conflicts between our work and nonwork lives, something has to give. Not surprisingly, the more time people devote to their jobs, the more events in their nonwork lives (e.g., personal errands) adversely affect their jobs (e.g., not being able to get the job done on time).

role juggling

The need to switch back and forth between the demands of work and family.

The stressful nature of role conflicts is particularly apparent among one group whose members are often expected to rapidly switch back and forth between the demands of work and family—a source of stress known as **role juggling**. This is an especially potent source of stress among one very large segment of the population—parents (see Figure 5.10).

Indeed, the more people, such as working mothers and fathers, are forced to juggle the various roles in their lives, the less fulfilling they find those roles to be, and the more stress they suffer in their lives.[46]

Role Ambiguity: Stress from Uncertainty.   Even if individuals are able to avoid the stress associated with role conflict, they still may encounter an even more common source of job-related stress: **role ambiguity.** This occurs when people are uncertain about several aspects of their jobs (e.g., the scope of their responsibilities, what's expected of them, how to divide their time between various duties). Most people dislike such uncertainty and find it quite stressful, but it is difficult to avoid. In fact, role ambiguity is quite common: 35 to 60 percent of employees surveyed report experiencing it to some degree.[47] Clearly, managers who are interested in promoting a stress-free workplace should go out of their way to help employees understand precisely what they are expected to do. As obvious as this may sound, such advice is all too frequently ignored in actual practice.

Sexual Harassment: A Pervasive Problem in Work Settings.   There can be no doubt that a particularly troublesome source of stress in today's workplace is **sexual harassment**—unwanted contact or communication of a sexual nature, usually against women. The stressful effects of sexual harassment stem from both the direct affront to the victim's personal dignity and the harasser's interference with the victim's capacity to do the job. After all, it's certainly difficult to pay attention to what you're doing on your job when you have to concentrate on ways to ward off someone's unwanted attentions! Not surprisingly, sexual harassment has caused some people to experience many severe symptoms of illness, including various forms of physical illness, and voluntary turnover.[48]

Unfortunately, this particular source of work-related stress is shockingly common. Indeed, when asked in a *New York Times*/CBS News poll whether they had ever been the object of sexual advances, propositions, or unwanted sexual discussions from men who supervise them, fully 30 percent of the women surveyed answered "yes." And this is not a one-sided perception: When asked if they had ever said or done something at work that could be construed by a female colleague as harassment, fully 50 percent of the men polled indicated that they had done so.[49]

role ambiguity
Uncertainty about what one is expected to do on a job.

sexual harassment
Unwanted contact or communication of a sexual nature, usually against women.

FIGURE 5.10

Working At Home: One Solution to Stress Caused by Work-Family Conflict

A few years ago, Shannon Entin founded FitnessLink, a health and fitness Web site, as a part-time business from her home in Lambertville, New Jersey. Shortly thereafter, around the time her son Logan was born, the company began to take off. To maintain a balance between her work and family life, Shannon and husband Paul quit their full-time jobs and run the company out of their home office.

There's good news, however. These days, many companies are training employees in ways to avoid sexual harassment. In fact, by California law (AB 1825), as of January 1, 2006, all employers must provide two hours of sexual harassment training and education to all supervisory employees. Efforts of this type (whether or not mandated by law) are helping people become aware of ways they are behaving that may be considered inappropriate. What's more, this seems to be having a beneficial effect on the numbers of sexual harassment cases. As shown in Figure 5.11, U.S. government figures have shown a steady decline in the number of sexual harassment cases reported since 2000.[50] Although it surely is an encouraging sign that this important source of stress may be on the decline as today's employees become more enlightened, it's important to note that sexual harassment is far from gone. It remains a far too prevalent source of stress in today's workplace.

Overload and Underload. When the phrase "work-related stress" is mentioned, most people envision scenes in which employees are asked to do more work than they possibly can handle. Such an image is indeed quite legitimate, for such *overload* is an important cause of stress in many work settings. Findings of a recent study bear this out.[51] Half of the 1,300 Americans completing a survey about their work lives indicated that they routinely skip lunch to complete the day's work. And 52 percent reported that they often had to work more than 12 hours a day to get their jobs done.

If you think about it, this isn't particularly surprising. In today's business environment, where many companies are trimming staff size (the phenomenon known as *downsizing,* which we will discuss in Chapter 16), fewer employees are required to do more work than ever before. Not only does this cause overload, but so too does the proliferation of information with which people are bombarded today as life involves communication via more sources than ever before. Scientists use the term **information anxiety** to refer to pressure to store and process great deals of information in our heads and to keep up constantly with gathering it. This constitutes an all-too real source of overload today.

information anxiety
Pressure to store and process a great deal of information in our head and to keep up constantly with gathering it.

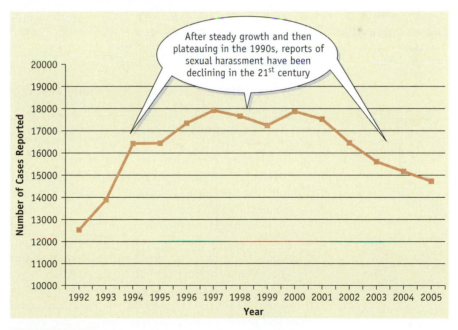

FIGURE 5.11

Sexual Harassment: Is It on the Decline?

Sexual harassment has been one of the most prevalent sources of stress for women in the workplace. These statistics from the U.S. Equal Employment Opportunity Commission reveal that its prevalence rose in the early 1990s, plateaued in the mid-late 1990s, and has been on the decline ever since. Although it appears that things are improving—perhaps as growing numbers of workers are becoming more sensitive to the problem through training—there is still a long way to go.

Source: Based on data reported by the Office of Research, Information and Planning, 2006; see Note 51.

Overload is only part of the total picture when it comes to stress. Although being asked to do too much can be stressful, so too can being asked to do too little. In fact, there seems to be considerable truth in the following statement: "The hardest job in the world is doing nothing—you can't take a break." *Underload* leads to boredom and monotony. Since these reactions are quite unpleasant, underload, too, can be stressful.

Responsibility for Others: A Heavy Burden. By virtue of differences in their jobs, some people (such as managers and supervisors) tend to deal more with people than others. And people, as you probably suspect, can be major sources of stress. As a result, managers tend to experience high levels of stress, often showing more outward signs (e.g., tension, anxiety, ulcers, hypertension) than their counterparts in nonsupervisory positions. In fact, stress has become so widely associated with managerial work that many managers think of stress as a normal, everyday part of their jobs.

Not only might subordinates be sources of stress among their managers, but it's also the case that managers may be sources of stress among their subordinates. Managers who deal with people ineffectively, for example—such as those who communicate poorly and who treat people unfairly—add stress to the lives of the individuals they supervise. As you surely know from your own experiences, a poor manager can be quite a significant source of stress. That said, it is clear that knowing and effectively practicing what you have learned about OB in this book can help alleviate stress among others in the workplace.

Adverse Effects of Organizational Stress and How to Combat Them

By now, we're sure you are probably convinced that stress stems from many sources, and that it exerts important effects on the people who experience it. What may not yet be apparent, though, is just how powerful and far-reaching such effects can be. In fact, so widespread are the detrimental effects of stress (i.e., strain) that it has been estimated that its annual costs exceed 10 percent of the U.S. gross national product![52] For some other alarming statistics about stress, see Table 5.3.[53]

Negative Effects of Stress: Their Many Forms

To get a good sense of our concern about stress, let's consider the various ways in which its negative effects manifest themselves in the workplace.

Stress and Task Performance. The most current evidence available suggests that stress exerts mainly negative effects on task performance. In other words, performance can be disrupted even by relatively low levels of stress: The greater the stress people encounter on the job, the more adversely affected their job performance tends to be.[54]

As tempting as it may be to accept this idea, it is a bit more complex than it appears on the surface. In particular, you probably know some individuals who seem to "rise to the occasion" when situations appear to be stressful and turn in exceptional performances on such occasions. This may result from the fact that they are truly expert in the tasks being performed, making them so confident in what they are doing that they appraise a potentially stressful situation as a challenge rather than a threat. Thus, it's important to keep in mind that people's various skills and abilities may contribute to the degree to which potentially stressful situations, are in fact, perceived—and responded to—as such.

Stress and Health: The Silent Killer. How strong is the link between stress and personal health? The answer, say medical experts, is "very strong, indeed." Problems at work are more strongly related to people's health complaints than are any other stressor they face in their lives (even financial or family problems).[55]

Consider the evidence. A team of medical researchers followed 10,308 British civil servants (aged 35–55) over a 14-year period.[56] They compared those who suffered chronic levels of work stress with those who were relatively stress-free on several health-related

TABLE 5.3 Some Alarming Statistics About Stress Today

Recent statistics tell a sobering story about the effects of stress today. In general, people are aware of the effects of stress in their lives but are still doing things that promote stress, creating dramatic costs in the workplace.

People feel the effects of stress:

- 40 percent feel their jobs are very stressful or extremely stressful.
- 36 percent feel used up at the end of the workday.
- 28 percent work so hard they do not have time or energy to spend with their families.
- 26 percent feel emotionally drained by their work.

People are aware that they may be contributing to their own stress levels:

- 83 percent of people would prefer to have a $10,000 per year raise than an extra hour per day at home.
- 71 percent of people are unwilling to make trade-offs between home and work.
- 49 percent of people indicate that they are not in control of how many hours they work.

Stress is costly:

- 40 percent of job turnover is due to stress.
- 60–80 percent of accidents on the job are stress related.
- On average, companies spend a quarter of their after-tax profits on medical bills.
- In the United States, stress-related problems are linked to half of all premature deaths.
- In Norway, sickness at work costs 10 percent of the gross national product.
- 65 percent of workers report that workplace stress caused difficulties for them.

Sources: Based on data reported by various sources in Note 53.

metabolic syndrome
A combination of factors (e.g., obesity around the abdomen, high triglyceride levels, glucose intolerance, etc.) that together are linked to such serious maladies as diabetes and hypertension.

measures. Chronic work stress was defined as experiencing various sources of stress (e.g., high job demands, lack of social support) at least 75 percent of the time over the 14-year study period. The findings were dramatic: Chronically stressed workers were over twice as likely as their nonstressed counterparts to suffer **metabolic syndrome**—a combination of factors (e.g., obesity around the abdomen, high triglyceride levels, glucose intolerance, etc.) that together are linked to such serious maladies as diabetes and hypertension.

Clearly, physiological strain reactions can be quite severe. In fact, some authorities estimate that stress plays a role in anywhere from 50 to 70 percent of all forms of physical illness.[57] Moreover, included in these figures are some of the most serious and life-threatening ailments known to medical science. A list of some of the more common ones, as shown in Table 5.4, makes it clear that the health-related effects of stress are not only quite widespread, but also extremely serious.[58]

Recently, research has found that the health-related impact of stress extends to the children of workers experiencing stressful conditions over long periods of time. The study involved 28,794 men who worked in any of 14 sawmills in the Canadian province of British Columbia for at least one year (between 1950 and 1998), and the 19,883 children of these men who lived with their fathers at least one of the years they worked there.[59] Based on the judgments of experts, researchers examined the degree of stressors to which the workers were exposed (e.g., amount of control over the job, demands placed on them, exposure to noise, and availability of social support).

The results were striking. The more stressful the conditions under which the men worked, the more likely their children were to attempt suicide (226 did so) or actually to commit suicide (26 did so). These results suggest that children's prolonged exposure to fathers suffering adverse stress reactions is a source of stress in those children. One of the study's authors speculates that men experiencing stress on their jobs take it out on their families when they come home, thereby victimizing their children.[60] And children having difficulty coping with stressful conditions (e.g., because they see no escape from poor conditions) may come to believe that they are in desperate situations, making them inclined to

TABLE 5.4 Health-Related Consequences of Stress

Stress causes a variety of different health problems, including medical, behavioral, and psychological problems. Listed here are some of the major consequences within each category.

Medical Consequences	Behavioral Consequences	Psychological Consequences
Heart disease and stroke	Smoking	Family conflict
Backache and arthritis	Drug and alcohol abuse	Sleep disturbances
Ulcers	Accident proneness	Sexual dysfunction
Headaches	Violence	Depression
Cancer	Appetite disorders	
Diabetes		
Cirrhosis of the liver		
Lung disease		

Source: Based on material reported by Quick et al., 1992; see Note 39.

take their own lives (or at least, to attempt to do so). Although the correlational nature of this study does not permit us to make such causal statements, of course (see Appendix 1), these findings tell a compelling story about intergenerational dangers of work stress that we cannot afford to ignore.

Stress as a Source of Desk Rage. A particularly unsettling manifestation of stress on the job that has become all too prevalent in recent years is known as **desk rage**—lashing out at others in response to stressful encounters on the job.[61] Just as angered drivers have been known to express their negative reactions to others in dangerous ways (commonly referred to as *road rage*), so too have office workers been known to behave violently toward others when stressed out by long hours and difficult working conditions.

One thing that makes desk rage so frightening is how extremely widespread it is. Indeed, 42 percent of American workers surveyed reported that yelling and verbal abuse took place where they worked, and 29 percent admitted that they themselves had yelled at their coworkers.[62] Fortunately, experts have identified several tactics that managers can use to neutralize the effects of desk rage where you work (see Table 5.5).[63]

Burnout: Stress and Psychological Adjustment. Most jobs involve some degree of stress. Yet, somehow, the people performing them manage to cope. That is, they continue to function despite their daily encounters with various stressors. Others, however, are not so fortunate, and over time, find themselves worn down by chronic levels of stress.[64] Such people are often described as suffering from **burnout**—a syndrome of emotional, physical, and mental exhaustion coupled with feelings of low self-esteem or low self-efficacy, resulting from prolonged exposure to intense stress and the strain reactions following from them. Burnout is a problem because it has an adverse impact on job performance: People who are burned out tend to "go through the motions" instead of engaging actively in their work. Also, as you might imagine, it is linked to the same adverse health effects as stress.

Fortunately, some of the signs of burnout are clear, if you know what to look for. The distinct characteristics of burnout are as follows (for a summary, see Figure 5.12, p. 192).

1. *Physical exhaustion.* Victims of burnout have low energy and feel tired much of the time. In addition, they report many symptoms of physical strain such as frequent headaches, nausea, poor sleep, and changes in eating habits (e.g., loss of appetite).
2. *Emotional exhaustion.* Depression, feelings of helplessness, and feelings of being trapped in one's job are all part of burnout.
3. *Depersonalization.* People suffering from burnout often demonstrate a pattern of attitudinal exhaustion known as **depersonalization**. Specifically, they become cynical about others, tend to treat them as objects rather than as people, and hold negative attitudes toward them. In addition, they tend to derogate themselves, their jobs, their

desk rage
Lashing out at others in response to stressful encounters on the job.

burnout
A syndrome of emotional, physical, and mental exhaustion coupled with feelings of low self-esteem or low self-efficacy, resulting from prolonged exposure to intense stress, and the strain reactions following from them.

depersonalization
A pattern of behavior occurring in burnout marked by becoming cynical toward others, treating others as objects, and holding negative attitudes toward others.

TABLE 5.5 Dealing with Desk Rage: Useful Tips for Managers

Because desk rage is all too prevalent, it's important for managers to recognize how to address it. Experts have offered the following tips.

Tip	Comment
Take control of your emotions whenever an employee seems to lose control.	Don't do anything that might keep the argument going or make it worse.
Carefully consider what led the person to be so angry.	By identifying the trigger, you are in a good position to straighten things out, such as by offering an explanation about something.
Immediately encourage everyone involved to take a deep breath.	Breathing deeply helps people calm down, and this will help you to discuss the situation calmly.
Take the feud outside the workplace.	Discussing heated personal issues in the workplace may involve others, but going outside—to lunch, say—moves the discussion to neutral territory where calm heads may prevail.
If someone seems to be having a particularly bad day, ask if there's anything you can do to help.	By intervening, you may be able to help with problems (e.g., overload), thereby eliminating conditions that promote anger.
Stay physically clear of someone who may be losing control.	By keeping an angry individual at arm's length, you may avoid a physical confrontation.
If you witness someone yelling at a coworker, intervene directly only if you are a supervisor. If you are a colleague, report this to your supervisor.	Direct intervention by a colleague would only make things worse by getting him or her involved as well. However, anyone witnessing acts of desk rage should report them at once to their supervisor.

Source: Lorenz, 2004; see Note 63.

organizations, and even life in general. To put it simply, they come to view the world around them through dark gray rather than rose-colored glasses.

4. *Feelings of low personal accomplishment.* People suffering from burnout conclude that they haven't been able to accomplish much in the past and assume that they probably won't succeed in the future, either.

Might you find differences between women and men with respect to their responses to stress, such as their likelihoods of showing signs of burnout? For a look at this question, see the *OB in a Diverse World* section on page 193.

Managing Stress: What Organizations Are Doing

Stress stems from so many different factors and conditions that to eliminate it entirely from our lives is impossible. However, there still are many things companies can do reduce the intensity of stress on employees and to minimize its harmful effects when it occurs.[65] It is quite popular for them to introduce different types of systematic programs to help employees reduce and/or prevent stress. The underlying assumption of these programs is that by minimizing employees' adverse reactions to stress, they will be healthier, less likely to be absent, and consequently, more productive on the job—which, in turn, has beneficial effects on the bottom line. We now describe some of these programs.

Employee Assistance Programs. About two-thirds of today's companies have some kind of formal program in place to help employees with various problems they may face in their personal lives (e.g., substance abuse, career planning, financial and legal problems).[66] Such efforts are known as **employee assistance programs (EAPs)**. Sometimes, such programs supplement or take the place of similar programs sponsored by trade unions. In such cases, they are known as **member assistance programs (MAPs)**.

employee assistance programs (EAPs)
Plans offered by employers that provide their employees with assistance for various personal problems (e.g., substance abuse, career planning, financial and legal problems).

member assistance programs (MAPs)
Plans offered by trade unions that provide their members with assistance for various personal problems (e.g., substance abuse, career planning, financial and legal problems).

FIGURE 5.12

Burnout: Its Four Major Components

Burnout results in adverse impact on job performance and personal health. As summarized here, it results from exposure to intense and prolonged work-related stress. It consists of four major components: physical exhaustion, emotional exhaustion, depersonalization, and feelings of low personal accomplishment.

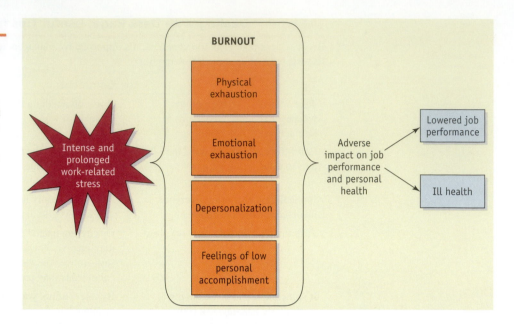

Interest in offering systematic ways of promoting the welfare of employees has grown so great that many companies today are seeking the assistance of specialized organizations with whom they can contract to offer assistance programs for their employees. By outsourcing these services to firms that are expert in this area, companies are free to focus on their usual business while ensuring that they are taking care of their employees as needed. Such efforts are paying off. According to the Employee Assistance Professionals Association, a trade group for companies offering professional EAP services to organizations, employee work loss is avoided in 60 percent of the cases in which EAP services are provided.[67]

stress management programs

Systematic efforts to train employees in a variety of techniques that they can use to become less adversely affected by stress.

Stress Management Programs. Systematic efforts known as **stress management programs** involve training employees in a variety of techniques (e.g., meditation and relaxation) that they can use to become less adversely affected by stress. (We describe many of these techniques in the following paragraphs.) These are used by about a quarter of all large companies.

Among them is the Equitable Life Insurance Company. Its "Emotional Health Program" offers training in a variety of ways that employees can learn to relax, including napping. Although some managers might not like the idea of seeing their employees asleep on the job, others recognize that brief naps can, in fact, help their employees recharge and combat the negative effects of stress.

wellness programs

Company-wide programs in which employees receive training regarding things they can do to promote healthy lifestyles.

Wellness Programs. About 56 percent of today's larger companies have **wellness programs** in place. These are systematic efforts to train employees in a variety of things they can do to promote healthy lifestyles. Very broad-based, wellness programs usually consist of workshops in which employees can learn many things to reduce stress and maintain their health. Exercise, nutrition, and weight-management counseling are among the most popular areas covered.

As an interesting example, Blue Cross Blue Shield of Oklahoma built a financial incentive into the wellness program it uses for its 1,300 employees.[68] The company offers "Weight Watchers at Work" meetings. Employees have to pay to participate in the 16-week program—but as an incentive, if they attend at least 14 weekly sessions, they are reimbursed. In the five-year period between 1999 and 2004, Blue Cross Blue Shield employees collectively have lost nearly 10 tons of excess weight.

As you might imagine, companies that have used such programs have found that they pay off handsomely. For example, at its industrial sites that offer wellness programs, DuPont has found that absenteeism is less than half of what it is at sites that do not offer

OB In a Diverse World

Do Women and Men Respond Differently to Stress?

Although anyone's life can be stressful, it seems that women generally face more stressors than men. If nothing else, women are more likely than men to carry the primary responsibility for raising children at home while also facing responsibilities on the job. Women also are more likely than men to be victims of sexual harassment on the job. And women are more likely than men to confront discriminatory practices that keep them from advancing as rapidly on the job. Considering these things, it is not surprising that surveys have found that women face more stressors and are affected more adversely by them than men.[69]

Women and men differ not only with respect to the overall amounts of stress they face, but also with respect to its various forms. In fact, compared to men, women confront stress from a wider variety of sources. Women encounter more changes and greater pressure to perform well on the job. For them, signs of stress are most likely to be found whenever their jobs are chaotic or demanding. For men, however, work is most likely to be stressful when facing ambiguous demands about what to do or when working in a highly competitive atmosphere.

Interestingly, both men and women seek relief from stress by engaging in some of the same leisure-time activities. For example, both groups do things that made them laugh and also seek to reduce stress by attending religious services. However, research shows that men and women also differ in their particular choices of leisure activities to help cope with stress.[70] For example, whereas men are inclined to play hard by engaging in strenuous sports, women are more likely to engage in artistic and cultural activities and to relax. Women also are more likely than men to respond to stress by maintaining healthy habits (e.g., eating properly and exercising regularly) and by seeking social support (e.g., talking to their friends about their problems).

Although both women and men take steps to cope with stress, women generally have a harder time of it. Overall, women cope less effectively with the stress they face. They suffer more physical symptoms (e.g., elevated blood pressure), behavioral symptoms (e.g., sleeplessness), and emotional symptoms (e.g., anxiety and depression).

Why is this? There are several possibilities.

1. **Volume of stressors.** One possibility is that women cope less effectively because the overall levels of stress they face are so much higher than those faced by men.
2. **Coping.** Another possibility is that what women are doing to cope with the stressors they face is less effective than what men do to cope with their stressors.
3. **Physiological predisposition.** Another possibility is that the generally greater physical strength and stamina of men predisposes them to respond less adversely to whatever stressors they encounter.

Of course, various combinations of these explanations may be involved, as well as numerous other factors. Regardless of the reason, one thing is sure: When attempting to get employees to be affected less adversely to work stress, managers need to focus especially carefully on women. Going out of the way to include women in stress management programs appears to be a wise investment.

---

such programs. Companies such as The Travelers Corporation and Union Pacific Railroad have enjoyed consistently high returns for each $1.00 they invest in employee wellness. And when it comes to saving money by promoting employee health, there is a lot at stake. Consider, for example, that the annual cost of health insurance in the United States due to obesity alone is $7.7 billion.[71]

As you might imagine, such programs help not only by reducing insurance costs, but also by reducing absenteeism due to illness. There's yet another way in which stress management efforts promise to help companies' bottom lines, and one of which most people are unaware. We are referring to the problem of **presentism**—the practice of showing up for work but being too sick to be able to work effectively. Paying workers who are not performing well is not only costly on its own, but also indirectly given that it may lower morale, and depending on the particular illness people have, it may spread disease throughout a workplace, compounding the problem. We tend to see this on an annual basis, for example, in places such as schools, where flu epidemics are so severe that it's sometimes necessary to close facilities for a while.

presentism
The practice of showing up for work but being too sick to be able to work effectively.

Managing Your Own Stress

Even if your own company does not have a formal program in place to manage stress, there still are several things you can do by yourself to help control the stress in your life. We now describe several such tactics.

Manage Your Time Wisely. People who don't use their time effectively find themselves easily overwhelmed, falling behind, not getting important things done, and having to work longer hours as a result. Not surprisingly, **time management**, the practice of taking control over how we spend time, is a valuable skill for reducing one possible stressor. Some of the most effective time management practices are summarized in Table 5.6.

time management
The practice of taking control over how we spend time.

Seek Social Support. According to an old saying, "misery loves company." With respect to stress, this statement implies that if we have to face stressful conditions, it's better to do so along with others (and with their support) rather than alone. Does this strategy actually work? In general, the answer is yes. When people believe they have the friendship and support of others at work—that is, when they have **social support**—their ability to resist the adverse effects of stress increases. For example, research has found that police officers who felt they could talk to their colleagues about their reactions to a traumatic event (such as a shooting) experienced less stressful reactions than those who lacked such support.[72] Clearly, social support can be an important buffer against the effects of stress.[73]

social support
The friendship and support of others, which helps minimize reactions to stress.

Eat a Healthy Diet and Be Physically Fit. Growing evidence indicates that reduced intake of salt and saturated fats, and increased consumption of fiber- and vitamin-rich fruits and vegetables are steps that can greatly increase the body's ability to cope with the physiological effects of stress.[74] Regular exercise also helps. People who exercise regularly obtain many benefits closely related to resistance of the adverse effects of stress. For example, fitness reduces both the incidence of cardiovascular illness and the death rate from such diseases. Similarly, physical fitness lowers blood pressure, an important factor in many aspects of personal health.

With this in mind, it is not surprising that growing numbers of companies are taking steps to ensure that their employees maintain proper weight by eating properly and exercising regularly. Some even are offering monetary incentives for doing so.[75]

Relax and Meditate. Many people find that it helps to relieve stress by engaging in **meditation**, the process of learning to clear one's mind of external thoughts, often by repeating a single syllable (known as a *mantra*) over and over again. Those who follow this systematic way of relaxing claim that it helps greatly to relieve the many sources of stress in their lives. (For some guidelines in how to meditate, see the Individual Exercise on page 197, at the end of this chapter.)

meditation
The process of learning to clear one's mind of external thoughts, often by repeating a single syllable (known as a *mantra*) over and over again.

Get a Good Night's Sleep. One of the most effective ways to alleviate stress-related problems is one of the simplest—if you can do it—sleeping. We all need a certain amount of sleep to allow our bodies to recharge and function effectively. Eight hours per day is average, although some need more and others can function just fine on less. Although a restful night's sleep can help people ward off the harmful effects of stress, the problem for many is that they are so stressed that they cannot get to sleep.

Avoid Inappropriate Self-Talk. This involves telling ourselves over and over how horrible and unbearable it will be if we fail, if we are not perfect, or if everyone we meet does not like us. Such thoughts seem ludicrous when spelled out in the pages of a book, but the fact is that most people entertain them at least occasionally. Unfortunately, such thoughts can add to personal levels of stress, as individuals *awfulize* or *catastrophize* in their own minds the horrors of not being successful, perfect, or loved. Fortunately, such thinking can be readily modified. For many people, merely recognizing that they have

TABLE 5.6 Three Key Suggestions for Managing Your Time

Managing time well can be an effective means of reducing stress because it allows people to avoid last-minute crises, and because it permits work to flow in a regular manner. Although these three suggestions may be easier said than done, following them can be very helpful.

Tip	Explanation
Prioritize your activities.	Distinguish between tasks that are urgent (ones that must be performed right away) and important (ones that must be done, but can wait). When determining how to spend your time, assign the greatest priority to tasks that are both important and urgent, a lower priority to tasks that are important but less urgent, and the lowest priority of all to tasks that are neither important nor urgent.
Allocate your time realistically—do not overcommit.	When planning, accurately assess how much time needs to be spent on each of the various tasks you perform. Budgeting too much time can lead to underload and too little time can lead to overload. It also helps to build in buffers, some extra time to handle unexpected issues that might arise.
Take control of your time.	Make a "to do" list and carefully keep track of what you have to accomplish. Unless an urgent situation comes up, stay focused and don't allow others to derail you. The more you allow other people to interfere with your time, the less you will have accomplished at the end of the day.

implicitly accepted such irrational and self-defeating beliefs is sufficient to produce beneficial change and increased resistance to stress.

Take a Time-Out. When confronted with rising tension, people may find it useful to consciously choose to insert a brief period of delay known as a **time-out**. This can involve taking a short break, going to the nearest restroom to splash cold water on one's face, or any other action that yields a few moments of breathing space. Such actions interrupt the cycle of ever-rising tension that accompanies stress and can help to restore equilibrium and the feeling of being at least partly in control of ongoing events.

time-out
A brief delay in activities designed to reduce mounting tension.

Summary and Review of Learning Objectives

1. **Distinguish between emotions and moods.**
    Whereas *emotions* are overt reactions that express people's feelings about a specific event, moods are more general. Specifically, *moods* are unfocused, relatively mild feelings that exist as background to our daily experiences.

2. **Explain how emotions and mood influence behavior in organizations.**
    Emotions and mood affect behavior in organizations in various ways. Generally, happier people are more successful on their jobs; they perform at higher levels and they make higher incomes. One reason for this is that people who are very upset tend to neither listen to nor understand the performance feedback they receive. Furthermore, happier people tend to make better decisions, remember positive events, give positive evaluations when appropriate, and cooperate with others.

3. **Describe ways in which people manage their emotions in organizations.**
    One way people manage their emotions is by keeping their negative feelings to themselves. Rather than offending another with our actual negative feelings we may engage in the *emotional labor* of disguising our true feelings. The inconsistency between the emotions we express and the emotions we feel is known as *emotional dissonance*. People in organizations also manage their emotions by managing their anger and by

displaying *compassion* for others when needed. This is especially important during major crises and emergencies.

4. **Identify the major causes of organizational stress.**

   Stress is caused by many different factors, including occupational demands, conflicts between the work and nonwork aspects of one's life (i.e., *role conflict*), not knowing what one is expected to do on the job (i.e., *role ambiguity*), overload and underload, having responsibility for other people, and experiencing sexual harassment.

5. **Describe the adverse effects of organizational stress.**

   Experiencing high levels of organizational stress has negative effects on task performance. It also adversely affects people's physical and mental health in a wide variety of ways. Stress also is a major cause of such serious problems as desk rage and burnout.

6. **Identify various ways of reducing stress in the workplace.**

   To help reduce employees' stress, companies are doing such things as using *employee assistance programs, wellness programs, absence control programs,* and *stress management programs.* As individuals, we can control the stress we face in our lives by following good *time management* techniques, eating a healthy diet and being physically fit, relaxing and meditating, seeking social support, avoiding inappropriate self-talk, and taking control over our reactions.

Points to Ponder

Questions for Review

1. What are *emotions* and *moods,* and how do they influence people's behavior in organizations?
2. What does affective events theory say about the effects of people's emotions on their behavior in organizations?
3. What advice would you give to leaders of a company who are interested in managing their employees' emotions?
4. What are the differences among *stressors, stress,* and *strain?*
5. What are the primary causes and consequences of stress on the job?
6. What steps can be taken to minimize the potentially harmful effects of stress on the job?

Experiential Questions

1. Think of a time when it was necessary for you to express compassion on the job in response to a traumatic situation. What were the circumstances? What did you do that was effective? What steps might you take to become even more effective the next time it is necessary to express compassion on the job?
2. What was the most stressful situation you ever encountered on the job? What were the stressors, and how did you react, both physically and psychologically? What role did social support play in helping you manage this stress?
3. What experiences have you had using stress-management techniques—either formally or informally? For example, do you meditate? Do you find that physical exercise helps you relieve stress? Does talking to others help at all? Of the various techniques described in this chapter, which one do you think you would find most beneficial?

Questions to Analyze

1. We all experience emotions, but some people disguise their true feelings better than others. Do you think this is a helpful or harmful thing to do? Under what conditions do you think it would be most useful to express your true feelings? Likewise, when do you think it would be best to keep your feelings to yourself?
2. Social support can be a very helpful means of reducing stress. However, do you think it's wise to seek social support on the job, where you stand to make yourself vulnerable by talking about your work-related stressors (e.g., by showing your weaknesses or by speaking negatively about your bosses)? Or do you think that only your coworkers are in a good

position to understand your work-related stressors, suggesting that you should talk to them about the work-related stress you are experiencing?

3. Stress management programs generally work well, but they are not always as effective as hoped. What problems and limitations do you believe may interfere with the effectiveness of stress management programs? How can these problems and limitations be overcome?

Experiencing OB

Individual Exercise

Meditation Through Relaxation

As we have explained in this chapter meditation can help people gain better control of negative emotions, such as anger, and it also can help lessen negative reactions to stress. For these reasons, learning to meditate can be very useful. Although there are several different types of meditation, the relaxation approach is both easiest to learn and among the most effective.[76] Give it a try.

Directions

1. Go to a quiet, dark place where you will not be disturbed. Sit in a comfortable position. Let your mind go blank and slowly relax your muscles.
2. Focus into space, slowly letting everything out of your mind. Do not let thoughts intrude. If they do, work at pushing them away.
3. Breathe slowly and in a regular rhythm. As you breathe in, slowly make the sound "haaah" as you would when slipping into a hot bath. Then, as you exhale, slowly produce the sound "saaah," sounding and feeling like a sigh.
4. Repeat this process, breathing slowly and naturally. When you do, inhale through your nose and pause for a few seconds. Then exhale through your mouth, again pausing for a few seconds.
5. Should thoughts enter your mind while attempting this process, don't feel badly about it. Instead, realize that this is natural and pick up the process once again. This will take time to master, so be patient. With practice, you will be able to do this more quickly.
6. Continue this process for what feels like about 20 minutes. Don't look at the clock, though. As the time draws to a close, maintain awareness of your breathing and sit quietly. Then, slowly becoming aware of where you are, open your eyes and get up gradually.

Questions for Discussion

1. How successful were you at being able to relax and meditate your first time? Did it come easily?
2. What were the major challenges you faced in following this procedure? How do you think you can overcome them?
3. After trying this for a while, does it work? Do you feel more relaxed and stress-free? Does this help you get through your workday more effectively?

Group Exercise

Are You Tough Enough to Endure Stress?

A test known as the Attentional and Interpersonal Style (TAIS) inventory has been used in recent years to identify the extent to which a person can stay focused and keep his or her emotions under control—the core elements of performing well under high-pressure conditions (see Note 42). Completing this exercise (which is based on questions similar to those actually used by such groups as Olympic athletes and U.S. Navy Seals) will help you understand your own strengths and limitations in this regard. And, by discussing these scores with your teammates, you will come away with a good feel for the extent to which those with whom you work differ along this dimension as well.

Directions

1. Gather in groups of three or four people whom you know fairly well. If you are part of an intact group, such as a work team or a team of students working on a class project, meet with your fellow group members.
2. Individually, complete the following questionnaire by responding to each question as follows: "never," "rarely," "sometimes," "frequently," or "always."

   1. _____ When time is running out on an important project, I am the person who should be called upon to take control of things.
   2. _____ When listening to a piece of music, I can pick out a specific voice or instrument.
   3. _____ The people who know me think of me as being "serious."
   4. _____ It is important to me to get a job completely right in every detail, even if it means being late.
   5. _____ When approaching a busy intersection, I easily get confused.
   6. _____ Just by looking at someone, I can figure out what he or she is like.
   7. _____ I am comfortable arguing with people.
   8. _____ At a cocktail party, I have no difficulty keeping track of several different conversations at once.

3. Discuss your answers with everyone else in your group. Item by item, consider what each person's response to each question indicates about his or her ability to focus.

Questions for Discussion

1. What questions were easiest to interpret? Which were most difficult?
2. How did each individual's responses compare with the way you would assess his or her ability to focus under stress?
3. For what jobs is the ability to concentrate under stress particularly important? For what jobs is it not especially important? How important is this ability for the work you do?

Practicing OB

Stressed-Out Employees Are Resigning

As the managing director of a large e-tail sales company, you are becoming alarmed about the growing levels of turnover your company has been experiencing lately. It already has passed the industry average, and you are growing concerned about the company's capacity to staff the call center and the warehouse during the busy holiday period. In conducting exit interviews, you learned that the employees who are leaving generally like their work and the pay they are receiving. However, they are displeased with the way their managers are treating them, and this is creating stress in their lives. They are quitting so they can take less stressful positions in other companies. Answer the following questions based on material in this chapter.

1. Assuming that the employees' emotions and moods are negative, what problems would you expect to find in the way they are working?
2. How should the company's supervisors behave differently so as to get their subordinates to experience less stress on the job (or, at least, get them to react less negatively)?
3. What could the individual employees do to help manage their own stress more effectively?

The Emotional Labor of Wanderlust's Adventure Guides

David and Aleta Nissen live and work in central Oregon, where scenic beauty abounds. Since 1993, their small company, Wanderlust Tours, has helped thousands of tourists discover the joy of these beautiful surroundings by taking them on various adventure trips. Wanderlust's guides lead small groups on full-day or half-day excursions by canoeing, snowshoeing, and/or hiking across this natural and remote area.

The company's slogan, "Discover what's around this bend!" is brought to life by several young local guides who know the area well and who delight in sharing its stories. These individuals play a vital role in cultivating guests' emotional experiences, making them exciting and fun. Their gestures and smiles, their eye contact, and of course, their words and the tone of their speech say a lot about the excursion's excitement. Even a humdrum encounter can be made exciting by raising one's voice, telling a good story, and opening one's eyes in wonder. And Wanderlust guides know it. If the guides express the routine nature of their own experiences, guests are likely to pick up on their boredom, making their own experiences far less than the exciting ones for which they paid. However, Wanderlust has been successful in large part because of their guides' capacity to communicate excitement even if they don't really feel it. In other words, part of their job involves high levels of emotional labor.

Although people in lots of jobs have to invest high levels of emotional labor, these often are brief. For example, waitresses may have to act friendly toward guests on a few visits to a table during the course of a meal. But conditions are more extreme for Wanderlust's guides. They spend as much as a full day with their guests, and in close physical encounters. As a result, sustained high levels of emotional labor are required. Even a brief out-of-character reference to their personal concerns about picking up dry cleaning might be enough to quell the experience for some guests.

As you might imagine, staying in character, not truly being yourself, for long periods of time can be quite challenging. How, then, do Wanderlust's guides stay in character as long as they do? Three factors have been the key to their success.

1. *Backstage breaks.* Many guides found it useful to escape from their groups for brief periods of time during which they could be by themselves. Whether they claimed to be going to the bathroom, leaving to check a weather radio, or to organize equipment, these breaks helped the guides by giving them relief from their roles as leaders of the excitement.

2. *Deep acting.* In addition to escaping from guests for brief periods, guides also worked hard to stay in character by "buying in" to the experience, engaging in "deep acting"—that is, giving convincing performances to make the trip as exciting as possible for guests. The resulting sense of authenticity was in keeping with the company's high-quality culture and was reinforced by others.

3. *Separating image from person.* At Wanderlust, guides were expected to be not only courageous and calm at all times, cultivating an image of safety, but also caring, giving, friendly, and of course, fun-loving. They knew that this was an image that their guests got to know, but that it wasn't really them. Keeping in mind that they were really just putting on a show helped them through the challenges. Interestingly, though, although they know deep inside that they're really acting, it helps them through the situation as they come to believe that what they are portraying are, in fact, their real emotional reactions.

Questions for Discussion

1. How successful do you think you would be if, like these adventure guides, you had to portray certain emotions to strangers for long periods of time?
2. Do you believe that sustaining high levels of emotional labor might have long-term effects on people? Is it a source of stress, for example?
3. Do you believe certain types of people are attracted to jobs requiring particularly high or low levels of emotional labor? How does this compare with your own work experiences?

VIDEO CASES

Surfer Girl Makes Comeback

Bethany Hamilton was well on her way to becoming a professional surfer when tragedy struck. While she was waiting to catch a wave one Halloween morning, a shark attacked Bethany and bit off her entire left arm. After this traumatic event, Bethany's attitude helped her heal both emotionally and physically, and it propelled her back into the water, where to this day she still competes as a surfer.

Discussion Questions

1. Besides the obvious (watch out for sharks!), what do you think Bethany learned from her ordeal? In particular, what did she learn about herself, and how would this help her on the job?
2. Which of the personality characteristics described in Chapter 4 best characterizes Bethany? Explain.
3. Based on the depiction of stress and emotions in Chapter 5, describe what you think Bethany has been experiencing.

Recipe for Success

College isn't for everyone; some young people just want to get trained for a profession in which they'll be able to get a decent-paying job after high school. The Careers Through Culinary Arts program takes kids from some of the toughest high schools in America and places them in some of the top restaurant kitchens. Students, who often start out directionless, come out of the program interested in becoming some of the best chefs in the United States.

Discussion Questions

1. Which one of the learning theories presented in the text would best explain student learning in the culinary arts program?
2. What attributions are the chef-instructors likely to make about their students before the training begins? How is this likely to influence the nature of the training received?
3. What particular stressors are likely to be encountered by the students as they undergo their training? How does the training help them address these stressors?

Dilley Six Pack

In the nurture vs. nature controversy, the notion of personality is often aligned with the nurture side of the debate. Meet the sextuplets of Becki and Keith Dilley, and it becomes apparent that personality also has a genetic component and that it is a force all its own. Each of the six children has a distinct personality and each needs to be treated differently.

Discussion Questions

1. How does this experiment in personality apply to the rest of the world?
2. In what other ways could this debate be tested?
3. What are the implications of this case for organizations?

Colorism

Usually, racism is understood in terms of discrimination by white people against African Americans and other people of color. Racism doesn't stop there, however. Based on the shade of their skin, some African Americans also discriminate against other African Americans,

Discussion Questions

1. How does the process of perception influence the responses of the people surveyed in the video?
2. What particular perceptual processes and perceptual errors described in Chapter 3 affect how skin color can distort people's judgments of others? Explain.
3. What other groups are likely to be subject to perceptual distortions based solely on their appearance?

Age Discrimination (SPC Ruling)

The U.S. Supreme Court ruled that employees can sue their employers for discrimination based on age, even if the company's discrimination was not intentional. The ruling gives workers age 40 and older protection from being squeezed out by younger workers (who also are likely to be lower paid). Typically, this form of age discrimination is embedded within company policies.

Discussion Questions

1. What role does perception play in this legislation?
2. According to this ruling, will it matter if there is a discrepancy between the employee's perception of discrimination and the reality of discrimination?
3. What sources of stress are likely to result from this legislation, and for whom?

Building Confidence

Although social interaction skills are necessary to succeed in a wide variety of jobs, many people suffer from debilitating social anxiety, which leads their work performance to suffer. Ann Demarais, author of *First Impressions,* helps a woman overcome her fear of talking to strangers. Dr. Demarais gives the woman the confidence to approach potential clients and hand out her business cards.

Discussion Questions

1. What is confidence? Is it a personality trait, an emotion, or a mood?
2. If Rita "makes" herself do things, like get business cards, is that a felt or displayed emotion? In your opinion, if you display an emotion you don't feel, will that eventually lead you actually to feel that emotion?
3. How is the concept of emotional labor involved in the approach taken by Dr. Demarais?

Stress Test: Ways Men and Women Handle Stress

Stress, stress, stress; who isn't stressed? It's an epidemic. Some may fall prey to stereotypes and say that men handle stress better than women. Think again. Researchers at UCLA tell us there's evidence women actually handle stress more effectively than men.

Discussion Questions

1. Which of the two approaches to stress are you more likely to take—"fight and flight" or "friend and befriend"? Has it been your own experience that men and women differ in these responses?
2. How do these gender differences in stress responses relate to gender differences in emotions?
3. On the job, who do you think is more successful in dealing with stress, men or women? To what extent do you believe that any such differences are related to differences in the kind of stressors members of each gender are likely to encounter?

Stress Test: What Stress Does to Your Body

An article in the *New England Journal of Medicine* reveals some disturbing findings about the serious damage that chronic stress does to our bodies. After a stressful episode, the body releases a hormone called cortisol to calm down the nervous system. This chemical initially helps the body, but ultimately, it turns into a substance that promotes illness.

Discussion Questions

1. What are some of the possible sources of stress discussed in the video clip? Add to the list from your own experiences. Which of these are environmental, organizational, or personal?
2. What are some of the possible outcomes associated with each of the possible stressors you listed for Question 1?
3. The video clip mentioned several ways in which individuals attempt to relieve their stress. What are some ways in which you attempt to reduce your stress level? To what extent are these effective?

WORK-RELATED ATTITUDES: PREJUDICE, JOB SATISFACTION, AND ORGANIZATIONAL COMMITMENT

Chapter Outline

Attitudes: What Are They?

Prejudice: Negative Attitudes Toward Others

Strategies for Overcoming Workplace Prejudice: Managing a Diverse Workforce

Theories and Measures of Job Satisfaction

Consequences of Job Dissatisfaction—and Ways to Avoid Them

Organizational Commitment: Attitudes Toward Companies

Special Sections

How to Do It

Promoting Diversity as a Competitive Weapon: Taking a Tip from Allstate

OB **Making Sense Out of Common Sense**

Is Job Satisfaction Related to Financial Performance?

OB **In a Diverse World**

Absenteeism: Does It Mean the Same Thing in Different Cultures?

After reading this chapter, you should be able to:

1. Define attitudes and work-related attitudes and describe the basic components of attitudes.

2. Distinguish between prejudice and discrimination and identify various victims of prejudice in organizations.

3. Describe some of the steps being taken by organizations today to manage diversity in the workforce and their effectiveness.

4. Describe the concept of job satisfaction and summarize four major theories of job satisfaction.

5. Describe the consequences of job dissatisfaction and ways to promote job satisfaction.

6. Describe the concept of organizational commitment, its major forms, the consequences of low levels of organizational commitment, and how to overcome them.

PREVIEW CASE

Amidst Tragedy, Some Good Emerges

The September 11, 2001 terrorist strikes on the U.S. and America's war with Iraq and its subsequent occupation had unsettling effects on not only the business economy, but also the personal lives of people in many organizations. If you have any doubt, just ask Mona Abdalall, a veteran employee of the Ford Motor Company who's worked at its Dearborn, Michigan headquarters for over 20 years. This situation was particularly hard on Abdalall, an American of Muslim faith and of Middle Eastern descent. Like so many people, she grieved following the attacks and contributed to fundraising efforts to aid the families of victims. But as things slowly returned to normal for others, they were far from normal for her. Abdalall encountered rejection and hostility from many of Ford's non-Islamic employees, making life stressful for her and creating a tense environment on the job.

Fortunately, Abdalall did not have to face this situation alone. Because Dearborn is home to one of the United States' largest Arab-American communities and many Muslim immigrants from Middle Eastern countries, she helped form a grassroots group of Middle Eastern workers. With the help of this community and Ford's Interfaith Network (FIN; a group representing seven different religious groups within the company), it became clear that something had to be done—and could be done—to turn things around.

The crux of the problem, Abdalall realized, was that many people were ignorant about her culture, which they mistakenly perceived as militant and anti-American. An educational campaign was needed, and to help, Abdalall organized "Islam 101" meetings, sessions designed to help people understand what Islam is all about. A high-ranking Muslim spiritual leader was brought in for the occasion, who reassured those gathered that the Koran (the Muslim bible) forbids killing in all forms. The terrorists, he explained, were radicals, who misinterpreted their religion and were not at all like the millions of other peace-loving Muslims around the world.

To everyone's surprise, more than 500 people showed up at the first meeting. Given this interest, Ford followed up by scheduling smaller, more intimate meetings of 60. Although a few non-Muslims remained skeptical, the vast majority left the sessions with a better understanding of Islamic culture and the Muslim religion—an understanding which, slowly but surely, has bred tolerance and acceptance during a particularly difficult period.

When the 2003 U.S. war with Iraq began, anti-Muslim feelings reemerged, so holding Islam 101 meetings once again helped promote interpersonal acceptance within the company. According to Samia Barnat, a manufacturing engineer who is Muslim, the results of these sessions are immediately noticeable. The year before the meetings, for example, coworkers used to offer her food during Ramadan, the month-long holiday, not realizing that Muslims fast during the days. Now, however, as more people have learned about her religious beliefs and customs, she feels better accepted.

Of course, things are far from perfect, and eventually interest in training sessions began to wane. To its credit, though, Ford has maintained its commitment to religious tolerance through the Ford Interfaith Network. With the company's help, FIN has been working on ways to promote tolerance for people of all religious faiths, allowing them to come together to express their faiths in appropriate and meaningful ways. For example, through the efforts of this group, Ford maintains on-site prayer and meditation rooms for employees, and it allows flexible scheduling of work hours so as to accommodate religious practices. Although hostile feelings and suspicions toward others die slowly, it's clear that through the efforts of its employees, Ford is doing its part to foster a tolerant and accepting work environment.

Although regrettable that it took an unspeakable tragedy to kindle a spirit of personal inquisitiveness and acceptance among its employees, Ford is surely fortunate that such feelings now exist. Instead of being ignorant about Islamic people—or, worse yet, harboring suspicions about them—Ford employees now have a greater understanding of this culture than ever before. This, in turn, has eased tensions and makes it easier for people of various races and religions to work together in harmony. As a result, Ford now can draw on its valuable human capital to improve business. And this, in turn, keeps employees feeling good about working for the giant automaker, thereby helping to keep them on the job.

Obviously, such feelings about people and things—*attitudes,* as they are called—represent an important part of people's lives, particularly on the job. Indeed, people tend to have definite feelings about everything related to their jobs, whether it's the work itself, superiors, coworkers, subordinates, or even such mundane things as the food in the company cafeteria. Feelings such as these are referred to as *work-related attitudes,* the topic of this chapter. As you might imagine, not only may our attitudes toward our jobs or organizations have profound effects on the way we perform, but also on the quality of life we experience while at work.

We will carefully examine these effects in this chapter. Specifically, our discussion of work-related attitudes focuses on three major targets—attitudes toward others (including a special kind of negative attitude known as *prejudice*), attitudes toward the job (known as *job satisfaction*), and attitudes toward the organization (known as *organizational commitment*). Before getting to these specific work-related attitudes, however, we begin by examining the nature of attitudes in general.

Attitudes: What Are They?

If we asked you how you feel about your job, we'd probably find you to be very opinionated. You might say, for example, that you really like it and think it's very interesting. Or perhaps you may complain about it bitterly, noting that it makes you bored out of your mind. Maybe you'd hold views that are more complex, liking some things (e.g., "my boss is great") and disliking others (e.g., "the pay is terrible"). These feelings reflect the attitudes we hold. With this in mind, we now take a closer look at the nature of attitudes.

Three Essential Components of Attitudes

Regardless of exactly how you might feel, the attitudes you express may be recognized as consisting of three major components: an *evaluative component,* a *cognitive component,* and a *behavioral component.*[1] Because these represent the basic building blocks of our definition of attitudes, it will be useful for us to take a closer look at them (see Figure 6.1).

So far, we've been suggesting that attitudes have a great deal to do with how we feel about something. Indeed, this aspect of an attitude, its **evaluative component**, refers to our liking or disliking of any particular person, item, or event (what might be called the

evaluative component (of attitudes)
Our liking or disliking of any particular person, item, or event.

FIGURE 6.1

Three Basic Components of Attitudes

Attitudes are composed of the three fundamental components shown here: the evaluative component, the cognitive component, and the behavioral component.

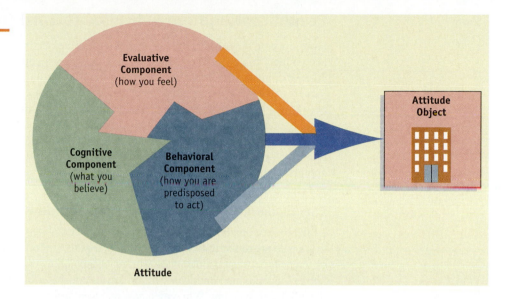

cognitive component (of attitudes)

The things we believe about an attitude object, whether they are true or false.

behavioral component (of attitudes)

Our predisposition to behave in a way consistent with our beliefs and feelings about an attitude object.

attitudes

Relatively stable clusters of feelings, beliefs, and behavioral intentions toward specific objects, people, or institutions.

work-related attitudes

Attitudes relating to any aspect of work or work settings.

attitude object, the focus of our attitude). You may, for example, feel positively or negatively toward your boss, the sculpture in the lobby, or the fact that your company just landed a large contract.

Attitudes involve more than feelings; they also involve knowledge—that is, what you believe to be the case about an attitude object. For example, you might believe that one of your coworkers is paid much more than you, or that your supervisor doesn't know too much about the job. These beliefs, whether they're accurate or even totally false, comprise the **cognitive component** of attitudes.

As you might imagine, the things you believe about something (e.g., "my boss is embezzling company funds") and the way you feel about it (e.g., "I can't stand working for him") may have some effect on the way you are predisposed to behave (e.g., "I'm going to look for a new job"). In other words, attitudes also have a **behavioral component**—a predisposition to act in a certain way. It is important to note that such a predisposition may not be perfectly predictive of one's behavior. For example, although you may be interested in taking a new job, you might not actually take one if a better position isn't available, or if there are other aspects of the job you like enough to compensate for the negative feelings. In other words, your intention to behave a certain way may or may not dictate how you will actually behave.

Basic Definitions

Combining these various components we can define **attitudes** as relatively stable clusters of feelings, beliefs, and behavioral predispositions (i.e., intentions toward some specific object). By including the phrase "relatively stable" in the definition, we are referring to something that is not fleeting and that, once formed, tends to persist. Indeed, as we will explain throughout this chapter (and again in Chapter 16), changing attitudes may require considerable effort.

When we speak about **work-related attitudes**, we are talking about those lasting feelings, beliefs, and behavioral tendencies toward various aspects of the job itself, the setting in which the work is conducted, and/or the people involved. As you will discover as you read this chapter, work-related attitudes are associated with many important aspects of organizational behavior, including job performance, absence from work, and voluntary turnover.

Now that we have identified the basic nature of attitudes, we are prepared to turn our attention to specific work-related attitudes. We begin by describing a very fundamental work-related attitude—*prejudice,* attitudes toward other people.

Prejudice: Negative Attitudes Toward Others

How do you feel about your associate in the next cubicle? How about your boss, or accountants in general? Our attitudes toward other people are obviously very important when it comes to understanding behavior in organizations. Such attitudes are highly problematic—when they are negative—especially when these feelings are based on misguided beliefs that prompt harmful behavior. *Prejudice* is the term used to refer to attitudes of this type. Specifically, **prejudice** may be defined as negative feelings about people belonging to certain groups. Members of racial or ethnic groups, for example, are victims of prejudice when they are believed to be lazy, disinterested in working, or inferior in one way or another. Prejudicial attitudes often hold people back, creating barriers to their success.

prejudice

Negative attitudes toward the members of specific groups, based solely on the fact that they are members of those groups (e.g., age, race, sexual orientation).

The Challenge of Organizational Demography

At the root of prejudicial feelings is the basic fact that people tend to be uncomfortable with those who are different from themselves. Today, as we chronicled in Chapter 1, demographic differences between people in the workplace are not the exception, but the rule. For example, not so long ago the American workforce was composed predominantly of white males. But that has been changing. White men now represent less than half of the current American work force, and most new entrants to the workforce are expected to be women and people of color.[2]

This is due to three key trends. First, there have been unequal shifts in the birth rate. Presently, three-quarters of the growth in the U.S. population is coming from African Americans, Hispanic Americans, and Asian Americans.[3] Second, growing numbers of foreign nationals are entering the American workforce, making it more ethnically diverse than ever before. Finally, we now see gender parity in the workforce.[4] About half of today's workforce is composed of women, and well over half of all adult American women work outside the home.

Regardless of the reasons behind these demographic shifts, it's important to note their implications. Clearly, they bring with them several important personal challenges. White males, for example, must recognize that their era of dominance in the workplace is over. In fact, many white men, so used to being in the majority, are highly threatened by the prospect of losing this status.[5] For females and members of ethnic minority groups, old barriers to success must be broken, and acceptance by others must be gained as old stereotypes and prejudicial attitudes fade away only slowly. As you probably already know, this is not an easy thing to do.

Increased organizational diversity also brings challenges—as well as opportunities—for organizations. Overall, the nature of the composition of a workforce with respect to various characteristics (e.g., age, gender, ethnic makeup, etc.) is known as **organizational demography**.[6] Research on this topic has shown that people often have a difficult time working with others who are different from themselves in key ways and that this often results in turnover. For example, members of top management teams are more inclined to resign from their posts the more those teams are composed of people who are demographically different (e.g., varied in age and experience).[7] In large part, this has to do with the tendency for people who are different from others to feel uncomfortable and therefore to distance themselves from them. Ultimately, such individuals are left out of communication networks (see Chapter 9), leading organizational performance to falter as a result. In fact, some researchers have concluded that "the greater the dissimilarity (between group members), the more negative outcomes, such as conflicts, divisiveness, or turnover are likely to occur."[8]

organizational demography

The nature of the composition of a workforce with respect to various characteristics (e.g., age, gender, ethnic makeup, etc.).

This, along with the fact that today diversity is the rule rather than the exception, makes it not surprising that prejudice in the workplace is considered highly problematic. After all, if people learn to accept others and to work with them, such communication problems can be eliminated, and neither individuals nor their organizations have to suffer. In fact, under many circumstances, people enjoy the benefits of working with others who are different from themselves. And, as we will see later in this section of the chapter, beneficial outcomes *can* result from exposure to people who bring different perspectives to the organizational tasks they perform.[9] This is not surprising, given that people with different backgrounds are likely to look at the world differently, and with these varied perspectives may come good ideas that people in more homogeneous groups do not recognize.

Given the key role of prejudicial attitudes on both people and organizations, we examine them closely in this section of the chapter. To give you a feel for how serious prejudices can be, we describe specific targets of prejudice in the workplace and the special nature of the problems they confront. Then, following up on this, we discuss various strategies that have been used to overcome prejudice in the workplace. Before doing this, however, it is important to take a closer look at the concept of prejudice and distinguish it from related concepts.

Anatomy of Prejudice: Some Basic Distinctions

When people are prejudiced, they rely on beliefs about people based on the groups to which they belong. So, to the extent that we believe that individuals from certain groups possess certain characteristics, knowing that someone belongs to that group will lead us to believe certain things about them. Beliefs of this type are referred to as **stereotypes**.

stereotypes
Beliefs that individuals possess certain characteristics because of their membership in certain groups.

Stereotypes. As you surely realize, stereotypes, whether positive or negative, are generally inaccurate. If we knew more about someone than whatever we assumed based on his or her membership in various groups, we probably would make more accurate judgments. However, to the extent that we often find it difficult or inconvenient to learn everything we need to know about someone, we frequently rely on stereotypes as a kind of mental shortcut. So, for example, if you believe that individuals belonging to group X are lazy, and you meet person A, who belongs to group X, you likely would believe that person A is lazy too. Although this may be logical, engaging in such stereotyping runs the risk of misjudging person A. He or she might not be lazy at all, despite the fact that you assumed so based on the stereotype.

Nonetheless, assume you believe person A to be lazy. How do you feel about lazy people? Chances are that you don't like them—that is, your evaluation of person A would be negative. Would you want to hire a lazy individual, such as A, for your company? Probably not. Thus, you would be predisposed against hiring A. Your prejudice toward person A is clear.

discrimination
The behavior consistent with a prejudicial attitude; the act of treating someone negatively because of his or her membership in a specific group.

Discrimination. Prejudicial attitudes are particularly harmful when they translate into actual behaviors. In such instances, people become the victims of others' prejudices—that is, **discrimination** occurs. In other words, as summarized in Figure 6.2, prejudice is an attitude, whereas discrimination is a form of behavior following from that attitude.

FIGURE 6.2

Prejudice vs. Discrimination: A Key Distinction

Prejudice is an attitude, and as such, consists of the three basic components of attitudes. Discrimination refers to behavior based on that attitude. The example presented here illustrates this important distinction.

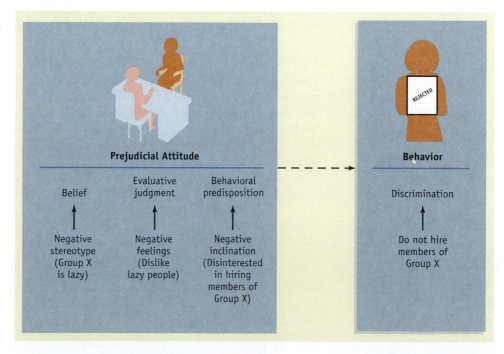

FIGURE 6.3

Anyone Can Be the Victim of Discrimination

Discrimination surely is no laughing matter when we ourselves are victims. Observing how this poor bull is being treated here helps us realize just how inappropriate it may be to discriminate against others simply by virtue of the groups to which they belong.

Source: www.CartoonStock.com

"It's because I'm a bull, isn't it".

Completing our example, you might refrain from hiring person *A,* or giving him or her a positive recommendation. By acting this way, you would be behaving consistent with your attitude. Although this might be logical, it certainly is not in the best interest of the individual involved. After all, your behavior may be based on an attitude formed on the basis of inaccurate stereotypes. For this reason, it is important to identify ways of overcoming the natural tendency to base our attitudes on stereotypes and to unfairly discriminate between people on this basis. Later in this chapter we will outline some strategies shown to be effective in this regard. Before doing so, however, it would be useful to give you a feel for the seriousness of prejudicial attitudes in organizations today.

Everybody Is a Victim of Prejudice!

Unfortunate as it may be, we are all potential victims of prejudicial attitudes. Indeed, no matter what personal characteristics we may have, there very well may be people out there who are prejudiced against us (see Figure 6.3). This is not surprising if you consider that people hold stereotypes about many different things. Whatever you look like, wherever you're from, whatever your interests, chances are good that at least some people will approach you with predisposed beliefs about what you're like. Sadly, for many groups of people, these beliefs have negative connotations, leading to discriminatory behavior. Here, we will describe some of the most prevalent targets of discrimination in American society today.

Prejudice Based on Age. As people are living longer and the birth rate is holding steady, the median age of Americans is rising all the time. Despite this trend—often referred to as the "graying of America"—prejudice against older people is all too common. Although U.S. laws (e.g., the Age Discrimination in Employment Act) have done much to counter employment discrimination against older workers, prejudices continue to exist.[10] Part of the problem resides in stereotypes that older workers are too set in their ways to train, and that they will tend to be sick or accident-prone. As in the case of many attitudes, these prejudices are not founded on accurate information. In fact, survey findings paint just the opposite picture: A Yankelovich poll of 400 companies found that older workers are considered very good or excellent, especially in such critical areas as punctuality, commitment to quality, and practical knowledge.

It is not just older workers who find themselves victims of prejudice, but younger ones as well. For them, part of the problem is that as the average age of the workforce advances (from an average of 29 in 1976 to 39 today), there develops a gap in expectations between the more experienced older workers who are in charge and the younger employees just entering the workforce.[11] Specifically, compared to older workers, who grew up in a different time, today's under-thirty employees view the world differently. They are more prone to question the way things are done, not to see the government as an ally, and not to expect loyalty. They are likely to consider self-development to be their main interest and are willing to learn whatever skills are necessary to make them marketable. These differing perspectives may lead older employees, who are likely to be their superiors, to feel uncomfortable with their younger colleagues.

Prejudice Based on Physical Condition. Counting only working-age people (21–64), there are currently some 4 million men and 3.5 million women with disabilities employed in the United States. This constitutes only 42 percent of disabled men and 34 percent of disabled women.[12] Some of the unemployed people with disabilities are unable to work at all; however, the vast majority of these individuals are ready, willing, and able to perform some type of work.

Unfortunately, however, barriers are keeping millions of potentially productive people from gainful employment. The most formidable barriers are not physical ones, but attitudinal. Most people who are not physically challenged don't know how to treat and what to expect from those who are. Experts advise that people with disabilities don't want to be pitied, but respected for the skills and commitment to work they bring to their jobs (see Figure 6.4). That is, they wish to be recognized as whole people who just happen to have a disabling condition, rather than a special class of "handicapped people."

FIGURE 6.4

Accommodating People with Physical Handicaps: Capitalizing on Human Resources

Today, companies are finding simple ways of accommodating employees who have physical handicaps. Doing so not only avoids discrimination and complies with the Americans with Disabilities Act, but also enables companies to take full advantage of their human resources. The Gap store in New York at which Freddy Laboy works has benefited from making simple accommodations for his handicap.

Legal remedies have been enacted to help break down these barriers. For example, in 1990, legislation known as the Americans with Disabilities Act (ADA) was enacted in the United States to protect the rights of people with physical and mental disabilities. Its rationale is simple: Simply because an employee is limited in some way, it does not mean that accommodations cannot be made to help the individual perform his or her job.[13] Companies that do not comply are subject to legal damages, and recent violators have paid dearly. However, probably the most important reason to refrain from discriminating against people with disabilities is not simply to avoid fines, but to tap into a pool of people who are capable of making valuable contributions if given an opportunity.

Prejudice Against Women. There can be no mistaking the widespread—and ever-growing—presence of women in today's workforce. Although 47 percent of all American workers are women, only about one large company in nine is headed by a woman.[14] Is this likely to change? Eighty-two percent of executives completing a recent *Business Week*/Harris poll indicated that it was unlikely that their company would have a female CEO in the next 10 years. Thus, it appears that "women populate corporations, but they rarely run them."[15] For some recent data on the percentage of women holding top organizational positions, see Figure 6.5.[16] It's clear that, although equality for women in the workplace is improving, it is a slow victory, to be sure.

Why is this the case? Although sufficient time may not have passed to allow more women to work their way into the top echelons of organizations, there appear to be more formidable barriers. Most notably, it is clear that powerful *sex role stereotypes* persist, narrow-minded beliefs about the kinds of tasks for which women are most appropriately suited. For example, 8 percent of the respondents to the *Business Week*/Harris poll indicated that females are not aggressive or determined enough to make it to the top. Although this number is small, it provides good evidence of the persistence of a nagging—and highly limiting—stereotype.

The existence of this problem has led growing numbers of women to venture out on their own. In fact, twice as many women than men are starting their own small businesses. As they do so, they may be expected to hire other women, potentially breaking the pattern of prejudicial behavior that has been so prevalent for so long.

Prejudice Based on Sexual Orientation. It has been estimated that between 4 percent and 17 percent of people in the workforce are gay, lesbian, or bisexual.[17] Unlike people with physical disabilities, who are protected from discrimination by federal law, no such protection exists (yet, at least!) for these individuals. (However, laws in several states and over 100 municipalities have been enacted to protect the rights of gays and lesbians in the workplace.) Unfortunately, although more people than ever are tolerant of nontraditional sexual orientations, anti-homosexual prejudice still exists in the workplace. In fact,

FIGURE 6.5

Women Still Are Not Prevalent at the Top of the Corporate Ladder

Although women and men are almost equally represented in today's workforce, very few women have worked their way up to top positions in large organizations. Today, the percentage of executives holding the most powerful titles who are women is still quite small.

Source: CATALYST, 2006; see Note 16.

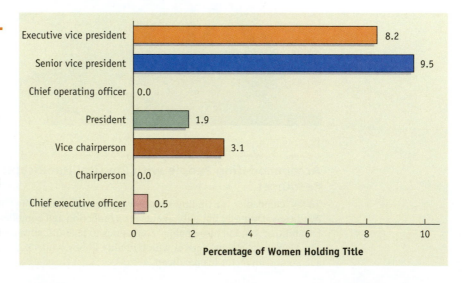

Percentage of Women Holding Title

between 25 and 66 percent of gay and lesbian employees experience discrimination in the workplace.[18] And these figures are likely to be underestimates given that many people fail to reveal their sexual identities at work. This discrimination sometimes is out in the open, as about two-thirds of CEOs from major companies admit their reluctance to put a homosexual on a top management committee. Not surprisingly, without the law to protect them and widespread prejudices against them, many gays and lesbians are reluctant to make their sexual orientations known to many others.

Fears of being "discovered," exposed as a homosexual, represent a considerable source of stress among such individuals. For example, a gay vice president of a large office-equipment manufacturer admitted in a magazine interview that he'd like to become the company's CEO, but fears that his chances would be ruined if his sexual orientation were to become known. If the pressure of going through working life with a disguised identity is disruptive, imagine the cumulative effect of such efforts on organizations in which several employees are homosexual. Such misdirection of energy can become quite a serious threat to productivity. In the words of consultant Mark Kaplan, "gay and lesbian employees use a lot of time and stress trying to conceal a big part of their identity."[19] To work in an organization with a homophobic culture, to have to endure jokes slurring gays and lesbians, can easily distract even the most highly focused employees.

To help avoid these problems—and out of respect for diverse sexual orientations— many organizations have adopted internal fair employment policies that include sexual orientation. In addition, some companies are actively working to prohibit discrimination on the basis of sexual orientation. Extending this idea, still other companies are now extending fringe benefits, which traditionally have been offered exclusively to opposite-sex partners, to same-sex domestic partners as well. For example, companies such as Ben and Jerry's Homemade, Inc. (in Waterbury, Vermont), MCA, Inc. (in Universal City, California), and Beth Israel Medical Center (in New York City) extend fringe benefits to their employees' partners regardless of whether they are of the same sex or the opposite sex. Clearly, although some companies passively discourage diversity with respect to sexual orientation, others actively encourage it, much to their own—and their employees'—advantages.

Prejudice Based on Race and National Origin. The history of the United States is marked by struggles over acceptance for people of various racial and ethnic groups. Although the American workplace is more racially diverse now than ever, it is clear that prejudice and discrimination persists. Interestingly, though, the extent to which it is considered a problem depends on whom you ask. As you might suspect, because African Americans are most likely to be victims of such discrimination, they are most aware of it (see Figure 6.6).[20]

Not only do members of various minority groups believe they are the victims of prejudice and discrimination, they are also taking action. For example, the number of complaints of discrimination based on national origin filed at the Equal Employment Opportunity Commission (EEOC) has been holding steady in the range of about 7,000–9,000 per year from 1992 to 2005, although award levels have been rising steadily.[21] Outside the courtroom, companies that discriminate pay in other ways as well— notably, in lost talent and productivity. According to EEOC Commissioner Joy Cherian, employees who feel victimized "may not take the initiative to introduce inventions and other innovations," adding, "every day, American employers are losing millions of dollars because these talents are frozen."[22] As we will see in the next section, many companies are taking concrete steps to help minimize these problems.

Prejudice Based on Religion. As illustrated by our *Preview Case* on pages 205–206, religious prejudice can be a serious problem. Although freedom of religion is the law of the land, it's sad but true that many Americans are made to feel uneasy because of their religious beliefs. In extreme cases, people have suffered through acts of **religious intolerance**, defined as actions taken against a person or group who follows a different faith. Such acts might take many forms, ranging from subtle, yet painful ridicule, to physical attacks on people and vandalism in places of worship.

A survey of a broad cross-section of Americans has shown that religious bias is a reality of the U.S. workplace.[23] It also is a serious concern for management, given that almost

religious intolerance
Actions (e.g., personal ridicule, vandalism) taken against a person or group who follows a different faith.

FIGURE 6.6

Does Racial Discrimination Exist? It Depends on Whom You Ask

A survey of American workers shows that racial discrimination is believed to be prevalent in many forms. Its main victims, African Americans, tend to be more aware of discrimination than those who are least affected by it, white Americans.

Source: Based on data reported by Fernandez & Barr, 1993; see Note 20.

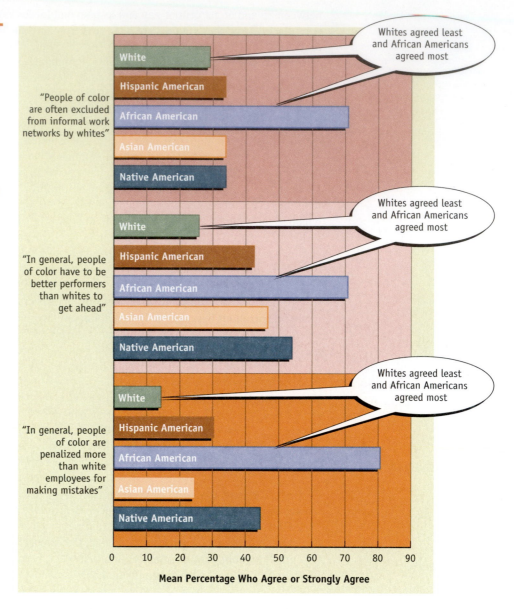

half of those who reported religious discrimination indicated that their performance was adversely affected. Equally disturbing was the finding that 45 percent of employees considered quitting because of religious discrimination. Whereas Christians and Jews were least likely to be victims of discrimination, Buddhists, Hindus, and Muslims were most likely to experience religious bias. Of these various groups, Muslims expected to receive, and actually experienced, more bias than the others.

Things are improving, however—and ironically, it appears to be a result of the September 11 terrorist attacks. A survey found that the percentage of Americans holding favorable views of Muslims rose from 45 percent several months before the attacks to 59 percent after the attacks.[24] Apparently, Americans have become better educated about the Muslim religion as the peace-loving members of this community have taken great pains to distance themselves from the horrific acts of a few extremists. And, of course, Ford (as described in our *Preview Case*) and other companies have gone out of their way to ensure that religious intolerance does not occur.

Despite such efforts, it appears that company officials don't always know how to handle religious discrimination. Less than a quarter of the people who experience religious discrimination report it to their bosses. Generally, this is because they either don't know where to go in the company to express their concerns, or because they feel that nothing would happen if they did. In fact, only 40 percent of companies provide any materials describing their policies on religious bias. In general, then, it appears that issues of religious prejudice remain largely ignored in many companies. Given the extent of the problem, coupled with the success that companies such as Ford have had in turning it around, we suspect that efforts to stem the tide of religious discrimination will become more commonplace in the years ahead.

Strategies for Overcoming Workplace Prejudice: Managing a Diverse Workforce

Having established that prejudices abound and that these may be harmful in the workplace, a question arises as to precisely what organizations are doing about this state of affairs. To begin answering this question, it is important to get a sense of the importance of diversity issues in today's organizations.

Do Companies Care About Diversity?

With this in mind, we must ask if companies care about diversity. Specifically, is it of concern to them, and if so, why? We address these issues now.

Are Matters of Diversity on Today's Corporate Agendas? A few years ago the American Society for Training and Development surveyed a sample of *Fortune* 1000 companies regarding their stance on diversity issues. The results suggest that diversity management was *not* at the top of their agenda. Only 11 percent reported that it was a high priority, but many—33 percent—indicated that they were beginning to look at it. Surprisingly, a quarter of the companies surveyed indicated that they weren't doing anything at all.[25]

However, an encouraging sign is that the trend in attention is clearly toward more activity, not less. Additional survey results found that 55 percent of employees believe that their company's management has become more strongly supportive of diversity programs over the past two years. Only 4 percent indicated a decrease in attention to diversity management efforts.[26] In fact, 91 percent indicated that their company's senior management considers the treatment of people to be the "make-or-break corporate resource" of the day.[27] So, to answer the question raised at the beginning of this section, yes, concern about diversity issues is growing—and rapidly, at that.

Why Do Companies Engage in Diversity Management Efforts? If you're a skeptic, you may believe that companies pay attention to diversity management so as to respond to government pressure. However, surveys have shown that this was identified as a contributing factor by only 29 percent of the respondents.[28] By contrast, the same survey found that the two major reasons are:

- Senior managers' awareness of the importance of diversity management programs (identified as a contributing factor by 95 percent of the respondents)
- Recognition of the need to attract and retain a skilled workforce (identified as a contributing factor by 90 percent of the respondents)

What Are Companies Doing to Foster Diversity in the Workforce? A large-scale survey by the Society for Human Resource Management and the Commerce Clearing House have found that several diversity management practices are widespread.[29] These include:

- Promoting policies that discourage sexual harassment (93 percent of organizations surveyed)
- Providing physical access for employees with physical disabilities (76 percent)
- Offering flexible work schedules (66 percent)

- Allowing days off for religious holidays that are not officially recognized (58 percent)
- Offering parental leaves (57 percent)

However, this same survey found that organizations did little by way of following up on diversity efforts. Among companies that conduct some type of diversity training only 30 percent gather any type of formal data to see if it is working. Still fewer, only 20 percent, formally reward managers for their efforts to promote diversity in the workplace.

The bottom line is clear: Although there's a lot of talk about diversity in today's organizations, there is generally more talk than action. Still, there are encouraging signs of improvement on the horizon. Given the growing awareness of the importance of diversity management activities, we suspect that more and more companies will be attempting to enhance their competitiveness in the marketplace by capitalizing on the diversity of their workforces. (For some suggestions on how to go about doing this, it's useful to consider the practices used successfully at one major company described in the *How to Do It* section on p. 217.)

What Are Today's Companies Doing to Promote Diversity?

It's one thing to identify prejudicial attitudes and quite another to eliminate them. Two major approaches have been taken toward combatting workplace discrimination—*affirmative action plans* and *diversity management programs.*

affirmative action laws

Legislation designed to give employment opportunities to groups that have been underrepresented in the workforce, such as women and members of minority groups.

Affirmative Action Plans. Traditionally, in the United States, **affirmative action laws** have been used to promote the ethical treatment of women and members of minority groups in organizations. Derived from civil rights initiatives of the 1960s, these generally involve efforts to give employment opportunities to groups of individuals who traditionally have been disadvantaged.

The rationale is quite reasonable: By encouraging the hiring of women and minority group members into positions in which they traditionally have been underrepresented, more people will be exposed to them, forcing them to see that their negative stereotypes were misguided. Then, as these stereotypes begin to crumble, prejudice will be reduced, along with the discrimination on which it is based.

After some 40 years of experience with affirmative action programs, it is clear that there have been major gains in the opportunities that have become available to women and minority groups. Yet they are not always well accepted.[30] Not surprisingly, several myths about affirmative action programs have developed over the years.[31] For a summary of these and the facts that refute them, see Table 6.1 on page 218.

Diversity Management Programs. Many of today's organizations are interested in going beyond affirmative action by not just hiring a wider variety of different people, but also creating an atmosphere in which diverse groups can flourish. They are not merely trying to obey the law or attempting to be socially responsible, but they recognize that diversity is a business issue. As one consultant put it, "A corporation's success will increasingly be determined by its managers' ability to naturally tap the full potential of a diverse workforce."[32] Or, as a top recruiter for an executive search firm put it, "There is a strong business case [for diversity]. A diverse workplace isn't a luxury, it's a necessity."[33]

diversity management programs

Programs in which employees are taught to celebrate the differences between people and in which organizations create supportive work environments for women and minorities.

It is with this goal in mind that many organizations are adapting **diversity management programs**—efforts to celebrate diversity by creating supportive, not just neutral, work environments for women and minorities.[34] Simply put, the underlying philosophy of diversity management programs is that everyone benefits when everyone, regardless of the groups to which they belong, is not just tolerated, but valued.[35] We now take a closer look at the nature of diversity management programs and their success.

Varieties of Diversity Management Programs

Diversity management programs fall into two categories: *awareness-based diversity training* and *skills-based diversity training* (see Figure 6.7, p. 219).[36]

How to Do It

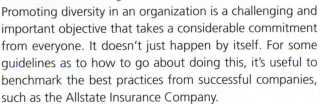

Promoting Diversity as a Competitive Weapon: Taking a Tip from Allstate

Promoting diversity in an organization is a challenging and important objective that takes a considerable commitment from everyone. It doesn't just happen by itself. For some guidelines as to how to go about doing this, it's useful to benchmark the best practices from successful companies, such as the Allstate Insurance Company.

Allstate is so committed to diversity that it uses the opportunity to promote diversity as a strategic weapon. The idea is straightforward: By reflecting the racial and ethnic diversity of its customers in its own workforce, Allstate can be sensitive to needs that otherwise may go unrecognized, and therefore, unfulfilled, by a more homogeneous group of employees. According to Ed Liddy, Allstate's chairman, president, and CEO, "Our competitive advantage is our people and our people are diverse. Nothing less than an integrated diversity strategy will allow the company to excel."[37]

Allstate's diversity management program takes a broad perspective. Not limited only to gender and ethnicity, it also pays attention to diversity with respect to age, religion, and sexual orientation. Specifically, it promotes diversity along three major fronts.

- Allstate recruiters visit historically black colleges and universities to attract members of the African American community. It also recruits from schools in Puerto Rico in an effort to expand its Hispanic customer base. From the many awards it has received for its efforts in these areas (e.g., the "Best Companies for Hispanics to Work"), such initiatives appear to be working. And the more such recognition the company receives, the easier it is for them to attract more individuals from these groups.

- Attracting recruits is half the battle, but retaining them is far trickier. With this in mind, Allstate carefully trains all its employees that they are expected to show no bias toward others. It also goes out of its way to encourage development of minority candidates by showing them the route to promotion within the company. In fact, minority candidates are considered seriously when it comes time to plan for succession up the ranks.

- Within his or her first six months on the job, each new Allstate employee receives diversity training (about three-quarters of a million person-hours have been invested thus far). This consists of classroom training that encourages people to recognize the way they see themselves and others as well as ways of sustaining a trusting environment among people who are different. Refresher courses also are given to managers from time to time.

Because it is an insurance company, it probably comes as no surprise to you that Allstate keeps careful statistical records of its diversity efforts and the company's financial success. Twice a year, the company's 53,000 employees complete a questionnaire known as the Diversity Index asking them to indicate, among other things, the extent to which they witness insensitive or inappropriate behavior at work, the amount of dignity and respect they are shown, and their beliefs about the company's commitment to delivering services to customers regardless of their ethnic background. Interestingly, the higher the overall score on the Diversity Index, the more managers are successful in promoting a diverse work environment, and the more satisfied they are. And the company's statistics show that when this happens, Allstate does a better job of satisfying and retaining its customers. Indeed, Allstate is the top insurer of lives and automobiles among African Americans and also ranks as the top insurer of homes and lives among Hispanic Americans. Clearly, at Allstate, promoting diversity is a highly successful business strategy—one that many organizations would benefit by emulating.

---

awareness-based diversity training

A type of diversity management program designed to make people more aware of diversity issues in the workplace and to get them to recognize the underlying assumptions they make about people.

Awarenesss-Based Diversity Training. The most basic approach, **awareness-based diversity training** is designed to raise people's awareness of diversity issues in the workplace and to get them to recognize the underlying assumptions they make about people. It is a very basic orientation, a starting point—one that takes a cognitive approach. Typically, it involves teaching people about the business necessity of valuing diversity and makes them sensitive to their own cultural assumptions and biases. This may involve using various experiential exercises that help people view others as individuals as opposed to stereotyped members of groups.

Skills-Based Diversity Training. Building on the awareness-based approach is **skills-based diversity training**. This orientation is designed to develop people's skills with

TABLE 6.1 Affirmative Action: Myth Versus Fact

Throughout the years, various myths about the ineffectiveness of affirmative action programs have become popular. However, as summarized here, these don't square with the facts.

Myth	Fact
Affirmative action has not led to increased representation of women and minorities in the workplace.	Gains have been substantial. Affirmative action programs have helped 5 million minority group members and 6 million white and minority women rise to higher positions.
Affirmative action programs reduce the self-esteem of women and racial minorities.	The opposite is true. By providing women and minority group members opportunities to succeed, their self-esteem actually increases.
Affirmative action plans bring unqualified people into the workplace.	Affirmative action programs specify that only qualified women and minority group members be hired.
The public no longer supports affirmative action programs.	This is overstated. Eighty percent of Americans currently believe that some sort of affirmative action is a good idea.
Although affirmative action programs may have been useful in the 1960s, they are less beneficial today.	The playing field is still far from level. For every dollar earned by white men, white women earn 75.5 cents. Among African American women and Hispanic women, this figure is even lower.

Source: Based on sources cited in Note 31.

skills-based diversity training

An approach to diversity management that goes beyond awareness-based diversity training and is designed to develop people's skills with respect to managing diversity.

respect to managing diversity.[38] As such, it goes beyond raising awareness to developing the tools needed to interact effectively with others. There are four main tools involved in this process.[39] These include:

- **Cross-cultural understanding**—Understanding the cultural differences responsible for why different coworkers behave differently on the job
- **Intercultural communication**—Learning to ensure that verbal and nonverbal barriers to communication across cultures are overcome
- **Facilitation skills**—Training in how to help others alleviate misunderstanding that may result from cultural differences
- **Flexibility and adaptability**—Cultivating the ability to patiently take new and different approaches when dealing with others who are different

Both approaches to diversity training have the same long-term goals: They strive to make interaction between diverse groups of people easier and more effective. Then, once people are paying attention to one another, the road is paved for morale to improve, for productivity to be enhanced, and for people to be able to focus their creative energies on their work.

Diversity Management Is Generally Effective

With all of these benefits in hand, organizations are positioned to attain their ultimate goal—to improve their economic position in the marketplace. Does this in fact happen? In other words, are diversity management efforts effective? Do highly diverse companies have a competitive advantage over less diverse companies? In a word, yes.

The Evidence: Diversity Is Good Business. Recent evidence paints a very positive picture of the ultimate effectiveness of diversity management efforts. Researchers reasoned that when companies use their human resources effectively they can lower their costs and thereby perform better than their competition.[40] To test this notion they compared two groups of companies from 1986 through 1992. One group was composed of organizations that received awards from the U.S. Department of Labor for their exemplary efforts at managing diversity. The other group was composed of companies that had settled large claims against them for employment discrimination.

FIGURE 6.7

Diversity Management: Two Major Approaches to Training

Skills-based diversity training builds on the approach taken by awareness-based diversity training. However, both approaches strive toward achieving the same goals.

Source: Adapted from material in Carnevale & Stone, 1995; see Note 36.

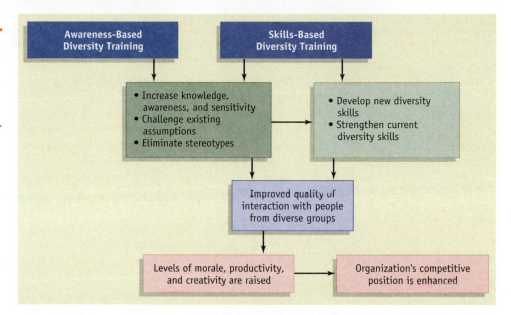

To compare the performance of these organizations, the researchers relied on a key index of economic success—stock returns. Their findings were striking: Companies that made special efforts to use their diverse human resources were considerably more profitable than those that discriminated against their employees. The researchers explain that the organizations that capitalize on the diversity of their workforces are better able to attract and retain the talented people needed for organizations to thrive. Clearly, managing diversity makes sense not only because it is the right way to treat people, but also because it is good business! With this in mind, it is not surprising to find that so many different companies have a wide variety of programs in place to celebrate diversity (see Table 6.2, p. 220).[41]

Guidelines for Ensuring Success. Given that growing numbers of companies are recognizing the benefits of having a racially and ethnically diverse workforce, it pays to consider the things that have made them so effective.[42] Based on the experiences of many companies over the years, it's clear that several steps must be taken to make diversity management work and to avoid pitfalls.[43] The key considerations are as follows:

1. *Actively pursue the best people.* Instead of waiting for talented minority candidates to come to them, the most diversity-friendly companies go out of their way to find these individuals. For example, they recruit from historically black colleges and universities, and they contact Hispanic labor organizations about good prospects.

2. *Make sure that people are accepted and fit in.* Getting a diverse group of people in the door is one thing, but developing them into good employees who feel welcome is quite another. The trick is to emphasize cooperation and teamwork between all employees, getting them to work together (we will examine these topics more closely in Chapters 11 and 8, respectively).

3. *Educate everyone.* It's not good enough for only some people in the company to value diversity. To be most effective, everyone needs to fully understand the importance of having a diverse workforce. As such, diversity management efforts should be aimed at everyone.

4. *Focus on a range of differences between people—not stereotypes.* Thinking of people in stereotypical ways can create barriers that interfere with looking at people as individuals. So, instead of looking at the *average* differences between people (which may reinforce stereotypes), experts recommend that managing diversity demands accepting a *range* of differences between people, a range that promises to become even greater in the years ahead.[44]

5. *Avoid treating someone as special because he or she is a member of a certain group.* Group membership is not as important as having unique skills or abilities. To

TABLE 6.2 Diversity Management: Some Current Practices

Many of today's companies are taking proactive steps to celebrate the diverse backgrounds of their employees. Summarized here are just a few illustrative practices.

Organization	Name of Program	Description
Pitney Bowes	Pitney Bowes Celebrates Diversity Around the World	Holds a weeklong outreach program consisting of over 100 events in which employees, customers, and community neighbors in 40 states and 11 countries recognize everyone else's ethnic backgrounds
DaimlerChrysler	Minority Dealer Program	Actively develops dealerships owned by members of the ethnic communities the company serves
Tellabs	You've Got ConneXions	Offers lavish rewards to employees for referring talented members of ethnic minorities
AT&T	Gay and Lesbian Awareness Week	Designates one week in which gay and lesbian issues are discussed and celebrated
Pace Food	Bilingual Operations	Presents all staff meetings and company publications in both English and Spanish
DuPont Corp.	Committee to Achieve Cultural Diversity	Holds focus groups that lead to career development programs for minority group members
City of Toronto	National Aboriginal Day	Showcases teaching circles, fashion shows, musicians, and traditional drummers and dancers to teach others about Aboriginal culture
NASA Glenn Research Center	Model Workplace Program	Offers multicultural training for all workers

Source: Based on information from Gingold, 2000; see Note 41.

the extent that managers are trained to seek, recognize, and develop the talents of their employees regardless of the groups to which they belong, they will help break down the barriers that made diversity training necessary in the first place.[45]

6. ***Provide total managerial support.*** Perhaps the main key to the effectiveness of diversity management is complete managerial support. Indeed, you cannot do something as complex as celebrate diversity with a one-time effort. Successful diversity management requires sustained attention to diversity in all organizational activities.[46] Without completely supporting diversity activities, organizations are bound to be disappointed with their efforts.

7. ***Assess how you're doing.*** Managing diversity, like any important goal, involves keeping careful track of progress. Only when you keep careful track of whom you're hiring and how well they're doing can you take the steps needed to improve. In other words, don't just institute a program and let it go. You also have to measure its effectiveness and revise the program as needed.

8. ***Pay attention to details.*** When managing diversity, no effort is too small. For example, you should be sensitive to cultural differences in style of dress and food preferences. After all, you don't have much of a chance of feeling wanted if the company cafeteria doesn't serve any food you'd like to eat.

9. ***Plan for the future.*** Some of the most diversity-conscious companies are not just doing things to promote diversity today, but ensuring that they will have diverse workforces tomorrow. IBM, for example, has taken steps to ensure that it will be able to hire qualified women engineers by investing in a summer science program for middle-school girls.

In conclusion, diversity management can be a highly successful way to promote equality in the workplace. This, in turn, helps attract pools of talented workers who might have been overlooked and helps companies better serve their ethnically diverse customers. However, success is not automatic. It pays to follow these nine suggestions when seeking to enhance diversity in a systematic fashion.

Now that we have described attitudes toward people in general, we turn attention to attitudes associated with various aspects of life in organizations. Next, we consider *job satisfaction,* attitudes toward one's job; following this, we turn to *organizational commitment,* attitudes toward the organizations in which we work.

Theories and Measures of Job Satisfaction

Do people generally like their jobs? In general, only about half of all working Americans claim that they do, and this number has been dropping in recent years.[47] These feelings, reflecting attitudes toward one's job, are known as **job satisfaction**. Insofar as job satisfaction plays an important role in organizations, it makes sense to ask: What factors contribute to job satisfaction?

job satisfaction
Positive or negative attitudes held by individuals toward their jobs.

As we will point out, a great deal of research, theory, and practice bears upon this question. Although there are many different approaches to understanding job satisfaction, four particular ones stand out as providing our best insight into this very important attitude—the *two-factor theory of job satisfaction,* the *dispositional model, value theory,* and the *social information processing model.*

Two-Factor Theory of Job Satisfaction

There is no more direct way to find out what causes people's satisfaction and dissatisfaction with their jobs than to ask them. Some 40 years ago, an organizational scientist assembled a group of accountants and engineers and asked them to recall incidents that made them feel especially satisfied and especially dissatisfied with their jobs.[48] His results were surprising: Different factors accounted for satisfaction and dissatisfaction. Rather than finding that the presence of certain variables made people feel satisfied and that their absence made them feel dissatisfied, as you might expect, he found that in many cases satisfaction and dissatisfaction stemmed from two different sources. For this reason, his approach is widely referred to as the **two-factor theory of job satisfaction**.

two-factor theory of job satisfaction
A theory of job satisfaction suggesting that satisfaction and dissatisfaction stem from different groups of variables (motivators and *hygiene factors,* respectively).

What are the two factors? In general, people were satisfied with aspects of their jobs that had to do with the work itself or to outcomes directly resulting from it. These included things such as chances for promotion, opportunities for personal growth, recognition, responsibility, and achievement. Because these variables are associated with high levels of satisfaction, they are referred to as *motivators.*

By contrast, dissatisfaction was associated with conditions surrounding the job, such as working conditions, pay, security, relations with others, and so on, rather than the work itself. Because these variables prevent dissatisfaction when present, they are referred to as *hygiene factors* (or *maintenance factors*). This name stems from an analogy to maintaining personal hygiene: Such practices (e.g., brushing your teeth) do not make you healthy, but they keep you from becoming unhealthy.

Rather than conceiving of job satisfaction as falling along a single continuum anchored at one end by satisfaction and at the other by dissatisfaction, this approach conceives of satisfaction and dissatisfaction as separate variables. Motivators, when present at high levels, contribute to job satisfaction, but when absent, do not lead to job dissatisfaction—just less satisfaction. Likewise, hygiene factors only contribute to dissatisfaction when absent, but not to satisfaction when present. You may find the diagram in Figure 6.8 helpful in summarizing these ideas.

Two-factor theory has important implications for managing organizations. Specifically, managers would be well advised to focus their attention on factors known to promote job satisfaction, such as opportunities for personal growth. Indeed, several of today's companies have realized that satisfaction within their workforces is enhanced when they provide opportunities for their employees to develop their repertoire of professional skills on the job. With this in mind, front-line service workers at Marriott Hotels, known as "guest services associates," are hired not to perform a single task, but a wide variety of tasks, including checking guests in and out, carrying their bags, and so on. Because they perform a variety of different tasks, Marriott employees get to call upon and develop many of their talents, thereby adding to their level of job satisfaction. (This approach, known as *job enrichment,* will be described more fully in Chapter 7 as a way to promote motivation.)

FIGURE 6.8

Two-Factor Theory of Job Satisfaction

According to *two-factor theory of job satisfaction,* job satisfaction and job dissatisfaction are not opposite ends of the same continuum, but two separate dimensions. Some examples of hygiene factors, which lead to dissatisfaction, and motivators, which lead to satisfaction, are presented here.

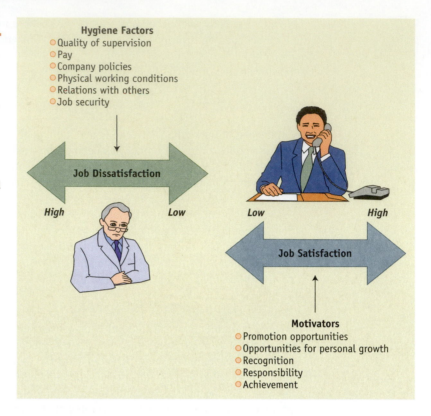

Hygiene Factors
- Quality of supervision
- Pay
- Company policies
- Physical working conditions
- Relations with others
- Job security

Job Dissatisfaction

High   Low

Low   High

Job Satisfaction

Motivators
- Promotion opportunities
- Opportunities for personal growth
- Recognition
- Responsibility
- Achievement

Two-factor theory also implies that steps should be taken to create conditions that help avoid dissatisfaction—and it specifies the kinds of variables required to do so (i.e., hygiene factors). For example, creating pleasant working conditions may be quite helpful in getting people to avoid being dissatisfied with their jobs. Specifically, research has shown that dissatisfaction is great under conditions that are highly overcrowded, dark, noisy, have extreme temperatures, and poor air quality. These factors, associated with the conditions under which work is performed, but not directly linked to the work itself, contribute much to the levels of job dissatisfaction encountered.

The Dispositional Model of Job Satisfaction

Do you know some people who always seem to like their jobs, no matter what they are doing, but others who are always grumbling about the work they do? If so, you are aware of the basic premise underlying what is known as the **dispositional model of job satisfaction**. This approach says that job satisfaction is a relatively stable characteristic that stays with people over various situations.[49] According to this conceptualization, people who like the jobs they are doing at one time also tend to like the jobs they may be doing at another time, even if the jobs are different.

Supporting this approach, researchers have found that people are consistent in liking or disliking their jobs over as long as a 10-year period, although they have had several different positions during that time. Such evidence is in keeping with the idea that job satisfaction operates much like the stable dispositions toward positive and negative affect described in Chapter 4. Indeed, research has shown that people who tend to be positive and cheerful most of the time do indeed tend to express higher job satisfaction than ones who tend to be "down" and gloomy.[50]

In keeping with this, research has shown that *genetic factors* play a role in job satisfaction. In other words, some people possess inherited tendencies to be either satisfied or unsatisfied with all aspects of their lives, including their jobs. Specifically, research has compared the levels of job satisfaction expressed by identical twins with the levels of job satisfaction expressed by unrelated persons or by fraternal twins, who share only some of their genes.[51] Results indicated that identical twins—who have the same genetic inheritance—expressed more similar levels of job satisfaction than did fraternal twins or unrelated persons. Moreover, this was true even when each member of a twin pair held very different

dispositional model of job satisfaction

The conceptualization proposing that job satisfaction is a relatively stable disposition of an individual—that is, a characteristic that stays with people across situations.

FIGURE 6.9

The Dispositional Model of Job Satisfaction

According to the dispositional model of job satisfaction, some people are consistently more satisfied with their jobs then others, even when they hold different jobs throughout their lives.

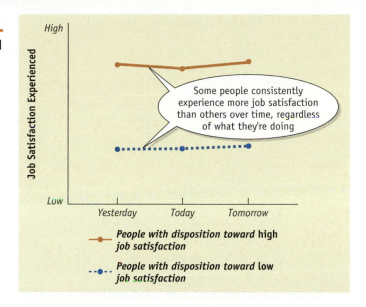

kinds of jobs. Although these findings remain somewhat controversial they have been replicated in other studies, so it does seem possible that genetic factors play a role in job satisfaction.[52]

You may be wondering how this can be so. Although genetic factors affect height, eye color, and other physical characteristics, it is much less obvious how they could influence job satisfaction. One way in which they could produce such effects involves the fact that genetic factors influence certain aspects of personality—aspects that might, in turn, be linked to job satisfaction. Such aspects of personality include the "Big Five" dimensions discussed in Chapter 4 and a general tendency to experience positive or negative moods (positive and negative affectivity).[53] Both the Big Five and positive or negative affectivity (see Chapter 4) have been found to be linked to job satisfaction, and both of these aspects of personality appear to be partly heritable (i.e., partly the result of genetic factors). So, genetic factors may influence job satisfaction indirectly through their impact on key aspects of personality (see Figure 6.10).

Direct evidence for this reasoning has been reported in a study showing that both the "Big Five" dimensions of personality and positive affectivity–negative affectivity did indeed help explain the effects of genetic factors on job satisfaction.[54] However, the effects of positive affectivity–negative affectivity appeared to be stronger. In a practical sense, these findings mean that genetic factors influence the tendency to experience positive feelings such as enthusiasm, confidence, and cheerfulness versus negative feelings such as fear, hostility, and anger, and these tendencies, in turn, influence job satisfaction. If you've ever known someone who seemed happy and cheerful in most situations or someone who was just the opposite, you get the picture. Of course, people are satisfied or dissatisfied with their jobs for lots of reasons. But some individuals, it appears, experience relatively high or low levels of job satisfaction because they possess personality traits that are determined, at least in part, by genetic factors.

Value Theory of Job Satisfaction

value theory of job satisfaction

A theory suggesting that job satisfaction depends primarily on the match between the outcomes individuals value in their jobs and their perceptions about the availability of such outcomes.

Another approach to job satisfaction, known as **value theory of job satisfaction**, takes a broader look at the question of what makes people satisfied. This theory argues that almost any factor can be a source of job satisfaction so long as it is something that people value. The less people have of some aspect of the job (e.g., pay, learning opportunities) relative to the amount they desire, the more dissatisfied they will be—especially for those facets of the job that are highly valued. Thus, value theory focuses on discrepancies between what people have and what they want: the greater those discrepancies, the more dissatisfied they will be.

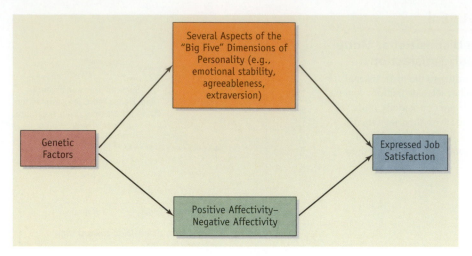

FIGURE 6.10

Genetic Factors and Job Satisfaction: The Effects Are Indirect

Genetic factors appear to influence job satisfaction, but these effects are indirect. Research suggests that genetic factors influence certain aspects of personality (e.g., positive affectivity–negative affectivity; emotional stability; extraversion) and these factors, in turn, play a role in job satisfaction.

Source: Based on findings reported by Illies & Judge, 2003; see Note 54.

This approach to job satisfaction implies that an effective way to satisfy workers is to find out what they want and, to the extent possible, give it to them. However, because it often is unknown what employees want, this is easier said than done. In fact, organizations sometimes go through great pains to find out how to satisfy their employees. With this in mind, a growing number of companies, particularly big ones, survey their employees systematically. For example, FedEx is so interested in tracking the attitudes of its employees that it has started using a fully automated on-line survey. The company relies on information gained from surveys of its 68,000 U.S.-based employees as the key to identifying sources of dissatisfaction and testing possible remedies.

Social Information Processing Model

It's your first day on a new job. You arrive at the office excited about what you will be doing, but you soon discover that your coworkers are far less enthusiastic. "This job stinks," they all say, and you hear all the details when you hang out with them during lunch. Soon, your own satisfaction with the job begins to fade. What once seemed exciting now seems boring, and your boss, who once seemed so pleasant, now looks more like an ogre. Your attitudes changed not because of any objective changes in the job or your boss, but because you changed your outlook based on the messages you received from your coworkers.

The idea that people's attitudes toward their jobs is based on information they get from other people is inherent in the **social information processing model**. This approach specifies that people adopt attitudes and behaviors in keeping with the cues provided by others with whom they come into contact.[55] The social information processing model is important insofar as it suggests that job satisfaction can be affected by such subtle things as the offhand comments others make (see Figure 6.11). With this in mind, it makes sense for managers to pay careful attention to what workers are thinking and feeling about their jobs. These things can be as important as actual characteristics of the jobs themselves when it comes to how people feel about them. This approach also suggests that managers should be very careful about what they say. A few well-chosen remarks may go a long way toward raising employees' job satisfaction. By the same token, a few offhand slips of the tongue may go a long way toward lowering morale.

social information processing model

A conceptualization specifying that people adopt attitudes and behaviors in keeping with the cues provided by others with whom they come into contact.

FIGURE 6.11

Social Information Contributes to Job Attitudes

According to the *social information processing model* of job satisfaction, the way people feel about their jobs is based on the attitudes expressed by others with whom they come into contact. For this reason, people who express negative feelings about their jobs can "poison" the job satisfaction of others.

Measuring Job Satisfaction: Assessing Reactions to Work

Although people have many different attitudes toward various aspects of their jobs, these are not particularly easy to assess. Not only can't you directly observe an attitude, but, as we noted, you cannot accurately infer its existence on the basis of people's behavior. So, for the most part, we have to rely on what people tell us to determine their attitudes. However, people may not be entirely open about their attitudes and keep much of what they feel to themselves. Moreover, sometimes our attitudes are so complex that it's difficult to express them in any coherent fashion—even if we are willing to do so.

In view of these challenges, social scientists have worked hard over the years to develop reliable and valid instruments designed to measure job satisfaction systematically.[56] Several useful techniques have been developed, including *questionnaires, critical incidents,* and *interviews.*

Questionnaires. The most common approach to measuring job satisfaction involves the use of questionnaires in which highly specialized rating scales are completed. Using this method, people answer questions allowing them to report their reactions to their jobs. Several different scales have been developed for this purpose, and these vary greatly in form and scope (see Table 6.3).

One of the most popular instruments is the **Job Descriptive Index (JDI),** a questionnaire in which people indicate whether or not each of several adjectives describes a particular aspect of their work.[57] Questions on the JDI deal with five distinct aspects of jobs: the work itself, pay, promotional opportunities, supervision, and people (coworkers). Recent research has shown that the JDI is a highly effective measure of job satisfaction insofar as it is both reliable and valid—two vital criteria for judging psychological tests that we described in Chapter 4.[58]

Another widely used measure, the **Minnesota Satisfaction Questionnaire (MSQ),** uses a different approach.[59] People completing this scale rate the extent to which they are satisfied or dissatisfied with various aspects of their jobs (e.g., their pay, chances for advancement). Higher scores reflect higher degrees of job satisfaction.

Although the JDI and the MSQ measure many different aspects of job satisfaction, other scales focus more narrowly on specific facets of satisfaction. For example, as its name suggests, the **Pay Satisfaction Questionnaire (PSQ)** is concerned with attitudes toward various aspects of pay.[60] The PSQ provides valid measures of such critical aspects as satisfaction with pay level, pay raises, fringe benefits, and the structure and administration of the pay system.[61]

Job Descriptive Index (JDI)

A rating scale for assessing job satisfaction. Individuals respond to this questionnaire by indicating whether or not various adjectives describe aspects of their work.

Minnesota Satisfaction Questionnaire (MSQ)

A rating scale for assessing job satisfaction in which people indicate the extent to which they are satisfied with various aspects of their jobs.

Pay Satisfaction Questionnaire (PSQ)

A questionnaire designed to assess employees' level of satisfaction with various aspects of their pay (e.g., its overall level, raises, benefits).

TABLE 6.3 Measures of Job Satisfaction: Some Widely Used Scales

The items shown here are similar to those used in three popular measures of job satisfaction.

Job Descriptive Index (JDI)	Minnesota Satisfaction Questionnaire (MSQ)	Pay Satisfaction Questionnaire (PSQ)
Enter "Yes," "No," or "?" for each description or word below as it applies to the particular aspect of your job identified.	Using the following scale, indicate the extent to which you are satisfied with each aspect of your present job. Enter one number next to each aspect.	Using the following scale, indicate the extent to which you are satisfied with each aspect of present pay. Enter one number next to each aspect.
Work itself: _____Routine _____Satisfactory _____Good	1 = Extremely dissatisfied 2 = Not satisfied 3 = Neither satisfied nor dissatisfied 4 = Satisfied 5 = Extremely satisfied	1 = Extremely dissatisfied 2 = Not satisfied 3 = Neither satisfied nor dissatisfied 4 = Satisfied 5 = Extremely satisfied
Promotions: _____Dead-end job _____Few promotions _____Good opportunity for promotion	_____Utilization of your abilities _____Authority _____Company policies and practices _____Independence _____Supervision-human relations	Satisfaction with pay level: _____My current pay _____Size of my salary Satisfaction with raises: _____Typical raises _____How raises are determined

Source: Based on items from the JDL, MSQ, and PSQ; see Notes 52, 54, and 55.

An important advantage of rating scales—these and others—is that they can be completed quickly and efficiently by large numbers of people. Another benefit is that when the same questionnaire already has been administered to many thousands of individuals, average scores for people in many kinds of jobs and many types of organizations are available. This makes it possible to compare the scores of people in a given company with these averages, yielding an assessment of *relative* satisfaction. Not only may this be useful information for scientists interested in studying job satisfaction, but also for companies interested in learning about trends in the attitudes of their employees.

critical incident technique
A procedure for measuring job satisfaction in which employees describe incidents relating to their work that they find especially satisfying or dissatisfying.

Critical Incidents. A second procedure for assessing job satisfaction is the **critical incident technique**. Here, individuals describe events relating to their work that they found especially satisfying or dissatisfying. Their replies are then examined to uncover underlying themes. For example, if many employees mentioned on-the-job situations in which they were treated rudely by their supervisors, or praised supervisors for sensitivity they showed in a difficult period, this would suggest that supervisory style plays an important role in their job satisfaction.

Interviews. A third procedure for assessing job satisfaction involves carefully interviewing employees in face-to-face sessions. By questioning people in person about their attitudes, it is often possible to explore these attitudes more deeply than by using highly structured questionnaires. By carefully posing questions to employees and systematically recording their answers, it is possible to learn about the causes of various work-related attitudes.

For example, a team of researchers relied on face-to-face meetings with employees to learn their feelings about their company's recent bankruptcy filing.[62] This highly personal approach to data collection was particularly effective in gathering reactions to such a complex and difficult situation.

Consequences of Job Dissatisfaction—and Ways to Avoid Them

Thus far, we have been alluding to the negative effects of job dissatisfaction, but without specifying exactly what these are. In other words, what consequences may be expected among workers who are dissatisfied with their jobs? Several effects have been well documented.

Employee Withdrawal: Voluntary Turnover and Absenteeism

As you might expect, people who are dissatisfied with their jobs want little to do with them—that is, they withdraw. An extreme form of **employee withdrawal** is quitting, formally referred to as **voluntary turnover**. Withdrawal also may take the form of *absenteeism,* staying away from the job when scheduled to work.

Organizations are highly concerned about these behaviors insofar as they are very costly. The expenses involved in selecting and training employees to replace those who have resigned can be considerable. Even unscheduled absences can be expensive—averaging between $247 and $534 per employee, by one estimate. Although voluntary turnover is permanent, whereas absenteeism is a short-term reaction, both are effective ways of withdrawing from dissatisfying jobs.

As an example, consider the reactions of the highly dissatisfied bakery workers at the Safeway market in Clackamas, Oregon, a few years ago. So upset with their jobs (particularly the treatment they received from management) were the bakery's 130 employees, that they frequently were absent, quit their jobs, and suffered on-the-job accidents. And these were no minor problems. In one year alone, accidents resulted in 1,740 lost work days—a very expensive problem. Accidents only occurred, of course, when employees showed up. At unpopular times, such as Saturday nights, it was not unusual for as many as 8 percent of the workers to call in sick. Conditions were so bad that almost no one stayed on their jobs for more than a year.

Consistent with this incident, research has shown that the more dissatisfied people are with their jobs, the more likely they are to be absent from work. This was demonstrated in a study of British health care workers whose questionnaire responses on a measure of job satisfaction were compared to records of their absenteeism over a two-year period.[63] Specifically, as summarized in Figure 6.12, workers whose levels of job satisfaction deteriorated over the study period also showed an increase in absenteeism, and those whose satisfaction increased over the study period also showed a decrease in absenteeism.

---

employee withdrawal

Actions, such as chronic absenteeism and voluntary turnover (i.e., quitting one's job), that enable employees to escape from adverse organizational situations.

voluntary turnover

A form of employee turnover in which an individual resigns freely from his or her job.

FIGURE 6.12

Relationship Between Job Satisfaction and Absence

A study tracing the levels of job satisfaction and absenteeism of health care workers over a two-year period found the relationship depicted here. Absenteeism declined among those whose satisfaction rose whereas absenteeism rose among those whose job satisfaction declined.

Source: Based on data reported by Hardy, Woods, & Wall, 2003; see Note 63.

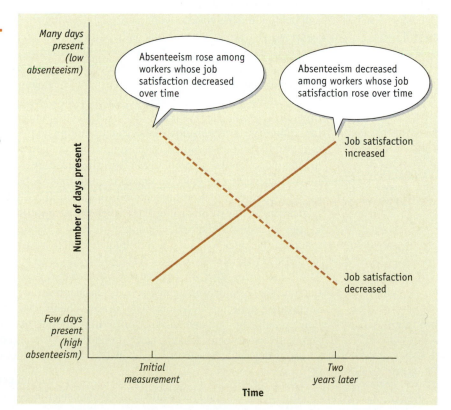

The same general relationship has been found in the case of turnover, although the relationship is more complex. Whether or not people will quit their jobs is likely to depend on several factors. Among them is the availability of other jobs. So, if conditions are such that alternative positions are available, people may be expected to resign in response to dissatisfaction. However, when such options are limited, voluntary turnover is a less viable option. Hence, knowing that one is dissatisfied with his or her job does not automatically suggest that he or she will be inclined to quit. Indeed, many people stay on jobs that they dislike.

The Honeymoon Effect and the Hangover Effect.   Thus far, we've shown that people who are dissatisfied with their jobs are inclined to resign. This isn't surprising. At that point, of course, they seek new positions. And, to their delight, they tend to be happier in those positions. This is welcome, because these individuals move to new jobs in search of higher levels of job satisfaction. That they find it, however, is not particularly surprising for several reasons. First, people in new positions need to justify their decision to leave their old jobs, which they can do by rationalizing about how wonderful their new positions are. In addition to this psychological reason, satisfaction on new jobs is likely to be high because the people associated with them are inclined to "put their best feet forward" by going out of their way to help their new colleagues feel welcome. So, for these reasons, people are likely to enjoy high levels of satisfaction on new jobs that they have taken in response to dissatisfaction with their old jobs. This is known as the **honeymoon effect**.

On the job, as in life, honeymoons only last so long, however. Eventually, reality sets in and that honeymoon glow soon fades. If one's initial satisfaction with a new job is based on limited, and often unrealistic, information, then it follows that as time goes on, people will have more realistic information about their once-new job. Reality, although not necessarily harsh, is likely to make things more negative than they appear in the honeymoon glow. In other words, people's levels of satisfaction are inclined to drop over time from when a position is brand new to when one gains more experience with it. In keeping with the idea that today's reality is harsher than yesterday's good times, this is dubbed the **hangover effect**.

Given that the honeymoon effect describes a raise in satisfaction in response to a new job and that the hangover effect describes a decline in satisfaction as that new job becomes less new, what you get when you put these together is referred to the **honeymoon-hangover effect**. That the honeymoon effect is followed by the hangover effect was demonstrated in a recent study in which scientists assessed the job satisfaction levels of several thousand high-level managers over a five-year period.[64] The changes in their satisfaction levels over this period were precisely in keeping with the honeymoon-hangover effect. We see this in Figure 6.13, which shows levels of job satisfaction among employees who took new jobs in the third year of the study. As satisfaction dropped over the first two years, participants in the study found new jobs, as you might expect. Then, reflecting the honeymoon effect, their satisfaction was particularly high during this third year, when they were new to their jobs. However, as they became more used to those jobs (i.e., when the honeymoon was over), their levels of job satisfaction dropped to about where they were when the study began. Interestingly, this pattern describes shifts in job satisfaction in lots of people, suggesting that how satisfied they are with the work they do depends on where in their job tenure you happen to assess their attitudes.

The Unfolding Model of Voluntary Turnover.   As you might imagine, the decision to quit one's job is not taken lightly; people consider a variety of different factors before making such an important decision. These have been described in a recently proposed conceptualization known as the **unfolding model of voluntary turnover**, which is summarized in Figure 6.14 on page 230.[65] According to this conceptualization, whether or not someone quits a job is said to depend on the way two key factors unfold. These are as follows:

■ *Shock to the system*—An attention-getting event that gets employees to think about their jobs (e.g., merger with another company)

---

honeymoon effect

The tendency for people to enjoy high levels of satisfaction on new jobs that they have taken in response to dissatisfaction with their old jobs.

hangover effect

The tendency for people's levels of satisfaction to drop over time from when a position is brand new to when one gains more experience with it.

honeymoon-hangover effect

The tendency for the *honeymoon effect* to occur (i.e., for job satisfaction to increase as a dissatisfied person takes a new job) followed by the *hangover effect* (i.e., for the high levels of satisfaction associated with a new job to decline over time).

unfolding model of voluntary turnover:

A conceptualization that explains the cognitive processes through which people make decisions about quitting or staying on their jobs.

FIGURE 6.13

The Honeymoon-Hangover Effect

Recent research has shown that people's levels of job satisfaction tend to shift somewhat over time. As people become dissatisfied with their jobs, they take new ones. Immediately thereafter, satisfaction increases dramatically (the *honeymoon effect*), but soon thereafter, it declines (the *hangover effect*).

Source: Based on data reported by Boswell, Boudreau, & Tichy, 2005; see Note 64.

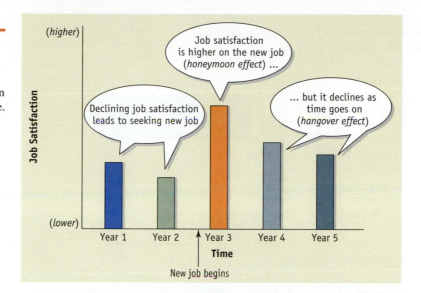

■ *Decision frames*—A set of internalized rules and images regarding how to interpret something that has occurred (e.g., "based on what I know from the past, is there an obvious response?")

As shown in Figure 6.14, the unfolding model of voluntary turnover recognizes that four possible *decision paths* can result. Trace these paths through the diagram as you read about each.

1. In *Decision Path 1*, a shock to the system occurs that matches an existing decision frame. So for example, suppose your company loses a large account. This unusual occurrence constitutes a shock to your system. Then you think about what occurred and assess what it means. If it has been your experience (directly or through others) that when accounts are lost, jobs are lost, you automatically will decide to quit. This doesn't take much consideration. Likewise, it's an easy decision for you if you reach the conclusion that lost accounts don't really mean anything, so you decide to stay.

2. In *Decision Path 2*, a shock to the system occurs, but in this case it fails to match a decision frame, and there is no specific job alternative. For example, suppose a leveraged buyout occurs (i.e., your company was taken over by another). This comes as a shock, but it's not exactly clear to you what it means. In such a case, you might assess how you feel about your organization. If upon further reflection, you decide you like it, you probably will stay, especially since there is no alternative. If, however, this gets you to think about how bad the job is, you might decide to leave anyway, even without another job to fall back upon. In either case, it's not immediately obvious to you what to do because you lack a decision frame, so you are forced to give the matter a lot of thought.

3. In *Decision Path 3*, a shock to the system occurs and it fails to match a decision frame, but here, there is a specific job alternative available. For example, suppose there's a leveraged buyout. Again, this comes as a shock, and you find it difficult to interpret because it does not match any existing decision frames. However, in this case, because there's an alternate job available, you compare your present job to this possible new one. If you think the future will be better by staying, you will be likely to do so. However, if you are so dissatisfied with your present job that you think the new one will be better, you will be inclined to leave. This, too, will be a difficult decision, although it's made easier by the presence of an alternative.

4. Finally, in *Decision Path 4*, there is no shock to the system (e.g., no lost account and no leveraged buyout). As a result, no decision frame is considered, leaving you unlikely to consider leaving in the first place. Under such circumstances, if you're

FIGURE 6.14

The Unfolding Model of Voluntary Turnover

According to the unfolding model of voluntary turnover, people make decisions about staying or leaving their current jobs based on a complex set of cognitive processes. The major considerations are whether or not there is a shock to the system (i.e., if something occurs that makes you consider leaving) and your decision frame (i.e., the things you believe). The various decision paths are summarized here.

Source: Based on suggestions by Mitchell & Lee, 2001; see Note 65.

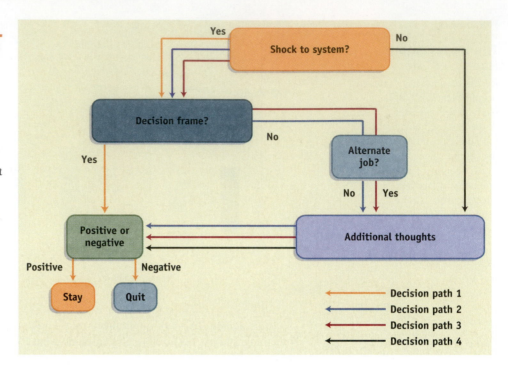

feeling dissatisfied, you may be inclined to quit if other conditions are right, but otherwise, you probably would be unwilling to bother doing so, leading you to stay. In either case, it may take a while for you to make the decision since no shock to the system has occurred.

Clearly, the unfolding model is quite complex. However, despite this complexity, and the fact that the conceptualization is new to the field of OB, it has received strong research support.[66] Accordingly, the unfolding model may be considered a valuable approach to understanding the relationship between job satisfaction and turnover.

Job Performance: Are Dissatisfied Employees Poor Performers?

How about those dissatisfied employees who remain on their jobs? Does their performance suffer? As in the case of withdrawal behaviors, the link between job performance and satisfaction also is quite modest. Indeed, several decades of research on this issue indicate that across many different jobs and organizations, the relationship between job satisfaction and work performance is relatively weak (correlations in the range of .15 to .20).[67] The strength of this relationship varies across different occupations—for instance it is stronger for scientists and engineers than for nurses—but it is not very strong for any occupation studied.[68]

Although this weak association may seem odd first, it's really not too surprising if you think about it more carefully. After all, people cannot always control all aspects of their job performance, making it impossible to do better even if they wanted to. For example, assembly-line employees are constrained by the speed at which the line moves. Similarly, people may perform poorly because they do not have access to the supplies and equipment needed to succeed. So, because people might not be able to control their job performance, they cannot adjust it (either upward or downward) in response to their attitudes. Furthermore, even someone who is inclined to lower his or her performance in response to negative job attitudes may refrain from doing so for fear of losing the job altogether (and even an undesirable job may help pay the bills).

Our discussion thus far refers only to standard forms of work performance, such as quantity and quality of work. Although people may have little control over these aspects of job performance, they tend to have considerable control over the more discretionary, voluntary forms of behavior that occurs on the job. We are referring here to such acts as helping one's coworkers or tolerating temporary inconveniences without complaint. These activities, which enhance social relationships and cooperation with the organization but go

Organizational citizenship behaviors (OCB)
Voluntary acts of cooperation that go beyond formal job requirements.

beyond the formal job requirements, are referred to as **organizational citizenship behaviors (OCB)**. Importantly, this form of behavior is highly related to job satisfaction. In fact, the more people are satisfied with their jobs, the greater the good citizenship contributions they tend to make. After all, people, people who are dissatisfied with their jobs are unlikely to go the extra mile to do anything they don't have to do. As you might imagine, these forms of behavior, although not reflected in standard performance measures (e.g., sales figures), contribute greatly to the smooth functioning of organizations. We will discuss the topic of organizational citizenship behavior more completely in Chapter 11. For now, we say only that workers who feel satisfied with their jobs may be willing to help their organizations and others who have contributed to those good feelings by engaging in acts of good organizational citizenship. (One of the most important issues about job satisfaction is whether or not it has any effects on an organization's bottom line. For a look at this issue, see the *OB: Making Sense Out of Common Sense* section below.)

OB Making Sense Out of Common Sense

Is Job Satisfaction Related to Financial Performance?

Thus far, we have been discussing the relationship between job satisfaction and various individual-level measures of performance, such as a person's productivity, his or her withdrawal behavior, and so on. Some may say that the only reason we care about this is because the better individuals perform, the more financially successful their organizations are—and this bottom-line financial performance is what matters most. After all, companies are in business to make money, so what are the financial implications of job satisfaction?

Although it may be considered short-sighted to think only of financial performance, the possibility that there may be a connection between individual job satisfaction and the financial performance of companies is intriguing. Recently, a team of researchers looked into this possibility.[69] They assessed the satisfaction of thousands of employees who worked in some of the largest and most highly esteemed companies in the United States over an eight-year period. They also computed the financial performance levels of the organizations in which these individuals worked (two key indexes that are widely used by financial analysts: return on assets and earnings per share). Because the data were collected during a period (1987–1995) in which the economy showed a variety of ups and downs, there was reason to believe that the study's findings were not the results of any fluke conditions that might have occurred. In fact, both the job satisfaction measures and the financial performance measures were highly stable over time.

By conducting sophisticated statistical analyses, the scientists arrived at two fascinating conclusions. First, job satisfaction and financial performance were, in fact, associated with each other to a considerable degree. Second, and perhaps more interestingly, this was *not* the result of

the tendency for highly satisfied workers to perform at higher levels (i.e., job satisfaction → financial performance), as you might expect. Instead, it was the other way around: The good financial performance of the companies promoted high levels of job satisfaction (i.e., financial performance → job satisfaction).

Let's consider how this appears to work. Imagine that because the company adopts policies that have been found to enhance employees' performance (e.g., involving them in key decisions, paying them for acquiring new skills), employees show high levels of performance. In turn, this good performance enhances the company's financial success. And, since it is successful, it can offer good benefits and increased pay, and enjoy a very positive reputation. The result? Employees feel well treated and are proud to work for their companies, and this leads them to experience high levels of job satisfaction. This is not just conjecture; the research found that this is precisely what occurs.

In conclusion, we return to the question that originally prompted the research and that scientists have examined for so long: Are job satisfaction and performance related? This straightforward question cannot be answered in an equally direct manner. At the moment, the best answer appears to be: Yes, to some extent, and under some conditions they are related—but the nature of the connection between them is complex and dependent on a number of variables.

Given the important financial benefits linked to job satisfaction, the investment in promoting job satisfaction in the workplace appears to be well worthwhile because it yields considerable payoffs. But, even if these financial results were not to occur, we ask you to consider another question: Isn't the satisfaction of employees a beneficial state of affairs on its own? In other words, having satisfied employees is a desirable outcome by itself.

Job Satisfaction and Injuries: Are Happy Workers Safe Workers?

Injuries at work are a serious matter—both for the employees who are hurt and their organizations. So anything that can reduce the risk of serious workplace accidents is, potentially, very valuable. Efforts to reduce workplace injuries often have focused on the design of equipment and jobs, and on restricting the number of hours employees can work so as to protect them from fatigue—all major factors in accidents. Although these practices are indeed effective, evidence suggests that enhancing job satisfaction also can have beneficial effects.

This has been demonstrated in organizations using so-called **high-performance work systems**.[70] These are organizations that offer employees opportunities to participate in decision making, provide incentives for them to do so, and emphasize opportunities to develop skills. Not only are employees highly satisfied in such organizations, but within them, they also perform their jobs very safely.[71]

A team of researchers studying this phenomenon obtained ratings of work environments from several thousand employees to assess the extent to which their work environments were high-performance systems. The researchers also obtained measures of job satisfaction from the same employees as well as records of occupational injuries from the companies in which these individuals worked. It was found that the greater the degree to which the organizations met the descriptions of high-performance organizations, the more the individuals who worked in them reported being highly satisfied with their jobs, and the lower were the levels of work-related accidents (see Figure 6.15). Further statistical analyses revealed also that to some extent the low accident rates were the direct result of the high levels of job satisfaction experienced. In view of this, the importance of promoting job satisfaction cannot be overstated.

Job Satisfaction and Life Outside Work

Here's an interesting question to ponder: Do you think that what happens to people at work "spills over" into their lives outside work? For instance, if they are satisfied with their jobs and generally feel happy at work, are they likely to take these positive reactions home with them at the end of the day? Conversely, if they are dissatisfied with their jobs and generally feel unhappy at work, will employees take these reactions home to their friends and families? A growing body of evidence indicates that in fact, there is a close link between job satisfaction and *affect*—the positive and negative feelings we experience throughout the day (see Chapter 5).[72]

In a recent study, employees at a large university were asked to rate their job satisfaction and their mood several times each day.[73] Participants did this both on work days and nonwork days, so they rated their moods and job satisfaction both at work and at home.

high performance work systems

Organizations that offer employees opportunities to participate in decision making, provide incentives for them to do so, and emphasize opportunities to develop skills.

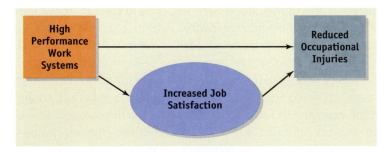

FIGURE 6.15

Job Satisfaction and Injuries at Work

Research indicates that high performance work systems (i.e., ones that provide employees with opportunities to participate in decision making, incentives that encourage them to do so, and human resource practices designed to ensure skill development) can increase performance and job satisfaction and offer the added benefit of reducing accidents. This last effect appears to stem, at least in part, from enhanced job satisfaction among employees. Apparently, positive attitudes toward their work makes employees more careful and thus helps them avoid accidents.

Source: Based on findings reported by Barling, Kelloway, & Iverson, 2003; see Note 71.

Results indicated that job satisfaction and mood were closely linked at work; in fact, each influenced the other. High job satisfaction was related to positive moods, and positive moods, in turn, were linked to experiencing high job satisfaction.

Perhaps even more interesting, job satisfaction at work also influenced the moods these employees experienced at home. High job satisfaction at work generated positive moods away from work, whereas low job satisfaction at work generates negative moods. Overall, job satisfaction did spill over into employees' moods at home. In other words, lasting as well as temporary mood states influence both job satisfaction and moods away from work.

In summary, there is no doubt that job satisfaction is very important in organizations. Under some conditions, satisfied employees are more productive than dissatisfied ones; they also are less likely to quit their jobs or to experience serious accidents and are more likely to experience positive feelings and moods at home. In view of this, we now turn to a key question: How can managers promote job satisfaction?

Guidelines for Promoting Job Satisfaction

In view of the negative consequences of dissatisfaction, it makes sense to consider ways of raising satisfaction on the job. Although an employee's dissatisfaction might not account for all aspects of his or her performance, it is important to try to promote satisfaction if for no other reason than to make people happy. After all, satisfaction is a desirable end in itself. With this in mind, what can be done to promote job satisfaction? Based on the available research, we can offer several suggestions.

Pay People Fairly. People who believe that their organizations' pay systems are inherently unfair tend to be dissatisfied with their jobs. (We discussed the importance of fairness in Chapter 2 and will revisit this topic again in Chapter 7.) This not only applies to salary and hourly pay, but also to fringe benefits. In fact, when people are given opportunities to select the fringe benefits they most desire, their job satisfaction tends to rise. This idea is consistent with value theory. After all, given the opportunity to receive the fringe benefits they most desire, employees may have little or no discrepancies between those they want and those they actually have.

Improve the Quality of Supervision. It has been shown satisfaction is highest among employees who believe that their supervisors are competent, treat them with respect, and have their best interests in mind. Similarly, job satisfaction is enhanced when employees believe that they have open lines of communication with their superiors.

For example, in response to the dissatisfaction problems that plagued the Safeway bakery employees described earlier, company officials responded by completely changing their management style. Traditionally, they were highly intimidating and controlling, leaving employees feeling powerless and discouraged. Realizing the problems caused by this iron-fisted style, they began loosening their highly autocratic ways, replacing them with a new openness and freedom. Employees were allowed to work together toward solving problems of sanitation and safety and were encouraged to make suggestions about ways to improve things. The results were dramatic: Work days lost to accidents dropped from 1,740 a year down to 2, absenteeism fell from 8 percent to 0.2 percent, and voluntary turnover was reduced from almost 100 percent annually to less than 10 percent. Clearly, improving the quality of supervision went a long way toward reversing the negative effects of satisfaction at this Safeway bakery.

Match People to Jobs that Fit Their Interests. People have many interests, and these are only sometimes satisfied on the job. However, the more people find that they are able to fulfill their interests while on the job, the more satisfied they will be with those jobs.

For example, a recent study found that college graduates were more satisfied with their jobs when these were consistent with their college majors than when these fell outside their fields of interest. It is, no doubt, with this in mind that career counselors frequently find it useful to identify people's nonvocational interests. For example, several companies, such as AT&T, IBM, Ford Motor Company, Shell Oil, and Kodak, systematically test and counsel their employees so they can effectively match their skills and interests to those positions to which they are best suited (for a further discussion of career choices, see Appendix 2). Some, including Coca Cola and Disneyland, go so far as to offer individualized counseling to employees so that their personal and professional interests can be identified and matched (Figure 6.16).

Decentralize Organizational Power. Although we will consider the concept of *decentralization* more fully later in this book (e.g., in Chapters 8 and 15), it is worth introducing here. **Decentralization** is the degree to which the capacity to make decisions resides in several people, as opposed to one or just a handful. When power is decentralized, people are allowed to participate freely in the process of decision making. This arrangement contributes to their feelings of satisfaction because it leads them to believe that they can have some important effects on their organizations. By contrast, when the power to make decisions is concentrated in the hands of just a few, employees are likely to feel powerless and ineffective, thereby contributing to their feelings of dissatisfaction.

The changes in supervision made at the Safeway bakery provides a good illustration of moving from a highly centralized style to a highly decentralized style. The power to make certain important decisions was shifted into the hands of those who were affected most by them. Because decentralizing power gives people greater opportunities to control aspects of the workplace that affect them, it makes it possible for workers to receive the outcomes they most desire, thereby enhancing their satisfaction.

This dynamic appears to be at work in many of today's organizations. For example, at the Blue Ridge, Georgia plant of Levi Strauss, the sewing machine operators run the factory themselves. In a less extreme example, a committee of employees meets monthly with the CEO of Palms West Hospital (in Palm Beach County, Florida) to make important decisions concerning the hospital's operation. High satisfaction in these facilities can be traced in large part to the decentralized nature of decision-making power. (These practices are in keeping with the use of teams, as we describe in Chapter 8).

Organizational Commitment: Attitudes Toward Companies

Thus far, our discussion has centered around people's attitudes toward one another and toward their jobs. However, to fully understand work-related attitudes we also must focus on people's attitudes toward the organizations in which they work—that is, their **organizational commitment.** The concept of organizational commitment is concerned with the degree to which people are involved with their organizations and are interested in remaining within them.

---

decentralization

The degree to which the capacity to make decisions resides in several people as opposed to one or just a handful.

organizational commitment

The extent to which an individual identifies and is involved with his or her organization and/or is unwilling to leave it (see *affective commitment, continuance commitment,* and *normative commitment*).

FIGURE 6.16

"The Real Thing": Coca Cola Helps Employees Get into the Right Jobs

One of the most successful ways of promoting job satisfaction is by ensuring that employees are working in jobs that best suit their interests and abilities. Because big companies, such as The Coca Cola Company, have many different jobs available, they are in a good position to help their employees find the jobs that are best for them. Individualized counseling is used to help identify employees' interests.

A generation or two ago, most workers remained loyal to their companies throughout their working lives. However, as a whole, today's workers are generally willing to move from job to job to advance their careers. For a look at some interesting statistics indicative of this trend, see Table 6.4.[74]

It is important to note that organizational commitment is generally independent of job satisfaction. Consider, for example, that a nurse may really like the kind of work she does, but dislike the hospital in which she works, leading her to seek a similar job elsewhere. By the same token, a waiter may have positive feelings about the restaurant in which he works, but may dislike waiting on tables. These complexities illustrate the importance of studying organizational commitment. Our presentation of this topic will begin by examining the different dimensions of organizational commitment. We will then review the impact of organizational commitment on organizational functioning, and conclude by presenting ways of enhancing commitment.

Varieties of Organizational Commitment

Being committed to an organization is not only a matter of "yes or no?" or even "how much?" Distinctions also can be made with respect to "what kind?" of commitment. Specifically, scientists have distinguished among three distinct forms of commitment, which we review here (see summary in Figure 6.17).[75]

Continuance Commitment. Have you ever stayed on a job because you just don't want to bother to find a new one? If so, you are already familiar with the concept of **continuance commitment.** This refers to the strength of a person's desire to remain working for an organization due to his or her belief that it may be costly to leave. The longer people remain in their organizations, the more they stand to lose what they have invested in the organization over the years (e.g., retirement plans, close friendships). Many people are committed to staying on their jobs simply because they are unwilling to risk losing these things. Such individuals may be said to have a high degree of continuance commitment.

Signs suggest that today, continuance commitment is not as high as it used to be. Traditionally, people sought jobs that would offer them lifetime employment. Many employees would stay on their jobs their whole working lives, starting at the bottom and working their way up to the top. But today, that scenario is atypical; the unspoken pact of job security in exchange for loyalty has all but faded from the organizational scene. In the words of a young project manager working at a New Jersey location of Prudential, "If the economy picked up, I'd consider a job elsewhere much sooner than before. I wouldn't bat

continuance commitment
The strength of a person's desire to continue working for an organization because he or she needs to do so and cannot afford to do otherwise.

TABLE 6.4 Is Loyalty Dead? Look at the Numbers

Recent statistics paint a bleak picture of the state of loyalty in the American workplace. As noted here, today's workers are not reluctant to move on to "greener pastures."

Size matters: Loyalty to small companies is greater.

- Almost 80 percent of people working in small organizations (those with fewer than 1,000 employees) feel very loyal to their companies, whereas under 50 percent of people working in large organizations (more than 10,000 employees) feel the same.

Americans are mobile: Job-hopping is not uncommon.

- In 2001, one in 10 American workers changed their employers: 6 percent took jobs at other companies, 3 percent retired, and 1 percent became self-employed.
- U.S. corporations lose about half their employees every four to five years.

Money talks: People are chasing higher salaries.

- Forty-four percent of technical workers admitted that they would be lured to a new job by a pay raise of 20 percent or less above their current salary.

Source: Based on data reported in Note 74.

FIGURE 6.17

Three Types of Organizational Commitment

Scientists have distinguished among the three different types of organizational commitment summarized here.

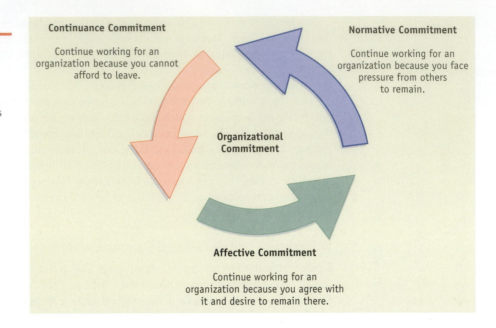

Continuance Commitment

Continue working for an organization because you cannot afford to leave.

Normative Commitment

Continue working for an organization because you face pressure from others to remain.

Organizational Commitment

Affective Commitment

Continue working for an organization because you agree with it and desire to remain there.

an eye."[76] This expression of the willingness to leave one's job reflects a low degree of continuance commitment.

affective commitment

The strength of a person's desire to work for an organization because he or she agrees with it and wants to do so.

Affective Commitment. A second type of organizational commitment is **affective commitment**—the strength of people's desires to continue working for an organization because they agree with its underlying goals and values. People feeling high degrees of affective commitment desire to remain in their organizations because they endorse what the organization stands for and are willing to help it in its mission. Sometimes, particularly when an organization is undergoing change, employees may wonder whether their personal values continue to be in line with those of the organizations in which they continue to work. When this happens, they may question whether they still belong, and if they believe not, resign.

A few years ago, Ryder Truck Company successfully avoided losing employees on this basis by publicly reaffirming its corporate values. Ryder was facing a situation in which the company was not only expanding beyond its core truck leasing business, but also facing changes due to deregulation (e.g., routes, tariffs, taxes). To help guide employees through the tumultuous time, chief executive Tony Burns went out of his way to reinforce the company's core values—support, trust, respect, and striving. He spread the message far and wide throughout the company, using videotaped interviews, articles in the company magazine, plaques, posters, and even laminated wallet-size cards carrying the message of the company's core values. Along with other Ryder officials, Mr. Burns is convinced that reiterating the company's values was responsible for the high level of affective commitment that the company enjoyed during this turbulent period.

normative commitment

The strength of a person's desire to continue working for an organization because he or she feels obligations from others to remain there.

Normative Commitment. A third type of organizational commitment is **normative commitment.** This refers to employees' feelings of obligation to stay with their organizations because of pressures from others. People who have high degrees of normative commitment are greatly concerned about what others would think of them for leaving. They would be reluctant to disappoint their employers and concerned that their fellow employees might think poorly of them for resigning. Normative commitment, like the other two forms of commitment, is typically assessed using a paper-and-pencil questionnaire. (To see what questions measuring organizational commitment look like, and to assess your own degree of organizational commitment, see the *Individual Exercise* on p. 242.)

Why Strive for a Committed Workforce?

As you might imagine, people who feel deeply committed to their organizations behave differently from those who do not. Specifically, several key aspects of work behavior have been linked to organizational commitment.[77]

Committed Employees Are Unlikely to Withdraw. The more highly committed employees are to their organizations, the less likely they are to resign and be absent (what we referred to as *withdrawal behavior* in the context of job satisfaction). Being committed leads people to stay on their jobs and to show up when they are expected to do so.[78]

This phenomenon has been demonstrated in a large-scale survey study in which dropout rates among U.S. Air Force cadets were traced over the four years required to get a degree. The more strongly committed to the service the cadets were upon entering the program, the less likely they were to drop out.[79] The finding that commitment levels could predict behavior so far into the future is a good indication of the importance of organizational commitment as a work-related attitude.

Is organizational commitment related to absenteeism and turnover all around the world? Or do cultural factors affect this relationship? For a discussion of this issue, see the *OB in a Diverse World* section below.

Committed Employees Are Willing to Make Sacrifices for Their Organizations. Beyond remaining in their organizations, those who are highly committed to them demonstrate a great willingness to share and make sacrifices required for the organization to thrive. For example, when Chrysler Corp. was in serious financial trouble in the 1970s, then-CEO Lee Iacocca demonstrated his commitment to help the company though its difficult period by reducing his annual pay to only $1. Although this move was clearly symbolic of the sacrifices the company wanted all employees to make, there is no doubt

OB In a Diverse World

Absenteeism: Does It Mean the Same Thing in Different Cultures?

 It is easy to understand why people who have low commitment to their jobs may want to stay away from them. However, the degree to which people actually express their low commitment through absence may well be influenced by cultural factors. This idea was tested in an interesting study in which large groups of employees from Canada and the People's Republic of China were surveyed about their attitudes toward being absent from work.[80]

In general, Chinese managers paid far greater attention to absenteeism than their Canadian counterparts. For the most part, absence was very strongly discouraged—so much so, that even an uncommitted Chinese employee would be unlikely to stay home from work. In keeping with this, the Chinese frowned upon absence based on illness, whereas the Canadians generally accepted illness as a valid excuse for being out of work. This is consistent with the idea that in Chinese culture, a person of good character is expected to maintain self-control, and taking time off work due to illness would be an indication of loss of such control.[81]

But there was an interesting exception to this general tendency for the Chinese to frown upon absenteeism. Specifically, compared to the Canadians, the Chinese were more likely to take time off from work to deal with personal or family issues. What's more, they believed doing this was much more appropriate than did the Canadians. There are two reasons for this. First, unlike their Canadian counterparts, the Chinese are not paid when they do not go to work. As such, they were not receiving pay for work they didn't do, avoiding the potential guilt of overpayment inequity (feeling that they were getting larger rewards than they deserved; see Chapter 7). Furthermore, during the time of the study, it first became possible in China for citizens to own private homes. Recognizing this, employers generally considered it acceptable for employees to take time off work to attend to household maintenance.

These findings underscore a key point: Whereas lack of commitment may encourage absenteeism, low commitment may not, in and of itself, lead specific employees to be absent. Several other factors, including the values of the employees' culture, will also play a role.

that Iacocca's actions cost him a great deal of real money. Had he been less committed to saving Chrysler (now, DaimlerChrysler), there would have been little incentive for him to be so generous. In fact, a less strongly committed CEO might have been expected to bail out altogether.

This example should not be taken as an indication that only highly magnanimous gestures result from commitment. In fact, small acts of good organizational citizenship are also likely to occur among people who are highly committed to their organizations.[82] This makes sense if you consider that it would take people who are highly committed to their organizations to be willing to make the investment needed to give of themselves for the good of the company.

In view of these benefits of organizational commitment, it makes sense for organizations to take the steps necessary to enhance commitment among its employees. We will now describe various ways of doing this.

Ways to Develop Organizational Commitment

Some determinants of organizational commitment fall outside of managers' spheres of control, giving them few opportunities to enhance these feelings. For example, commitment tends to be lower when the economy is such that employment opportunities are plentiful. An abundance of job options surely will lower continuance commitment, and there's not too much a company can do about it. However, although managers cannot control the external economy, they can do several things to make employees want to stay working for the company—that is, to enhance affective commitment.

Enrich Jobs. People tend to be highly committed to their organizations to the extent that they have a good chance to take control over the way they do their jobs and are recognized for making important contributions. (We will discuss *job enrichment* as an approach to motivating employees in Chapter 7.) This technique worked well for the Ford Motor Company. Years back, Ford confronted a crisis of organizational commitment in the face of budget cuts, layoffs, plant closings, lowered product quality, and other threats. In the words of Ernest J. Savoie, the director of Ford's Employee Development Office:

> The only solution for Ford, we determined, was a total transformation of our company . . . to accomplish it, we had to earn the commitment of all Ford people. And to acquire that commitment, we had to change the way we managed people.[83]

With this in mind, Ford instituted its Employee Involvement program, a systematic effort to involve employees in many aspects of corporate decision making. They not only got to perform a wide variety of tasks, but also enjoyed considerable autonomy in doing them (e.g., freedom to schedule work and to stop the assembly line if needed). A few years after the program was in place, Ford employees became more committed to their jobs—so much so, in fact, that the acrimony that usually resulted at contract renewal time had all but vanished. Although employee involvement may not be the cure for all commitment ills, it was clearly highly effective in this case.

Align the Interests of the Company with Those of the Employees. Whenever making something good for the company also makes something good for its employees, those employees are likely to be highly committed to those companies. Many companies do this quite directly by introducing **profit-sharing plans**—that is, incentive plans in which employees receive bonuses in proportion to the company's profitability. Such plans are often quite effective in enhancing organizational commitment, especially when they are perceived to be administered fairly.

For example, the Holland, Michigan auto parts manufacturer, Prince Corporation, gives its employees yearly bonuses based on several indices: the company's overall profitability,

profit-sharing plans
Incentive plans in which employees receive bonuses in proportion to the company's profitability.

the employee's unit's profitability, and each individual's performance. Similarly, workers at Allied Plywood Corporation (a wholesaler of building materials in Alexandria, Virginia) receive cash bonuses based on company profits, but these are distributed monthly as well as yearly.[84] The monthly bonuses are the same size for all, whereas the annual bonuses are given in proportion to each employee's individual contributions to total profit, days worked, and performance. These plans are good examples of some of the things companies are doing to enhance commitment (see Figure 6.18). Although the plans differ, their underlying rationale is the same: By letting employees share in the company's profitability, they are more likely to see their own interests as consistent with those of their company. And, when these interests are aligned, commitment is high.

Recruit and Select New Employees Whose Values Closely Match Those of the Organization. Recruiting new employees is important not only insofar as it provides opportunities to find people whose values match those of the organization, but also because of the dynamics of the recruitment process itself. Specifically, the more an organization invests in someone by working hard to lure him or her to the company, the more that individual is likely to return the same investment of energy by expressing commitment toward the organization. In other words, companies that show their employees they care enough to work hard to attract them are likely to find those individuals strongly committed to the company.

In conclusion, it is useful to think of organizational commitment as an attitude that may be influenced by managerial actions. Not only might people be selected who are predisposed to be committed to the organization, but also various measures can be taken to enhance commitment in the face of indications that it is suffering.

FIGURE 6.18

Profit-Sharing Plans Build Organizational Commitment

When the company does well, employees do well. That is the idea behind profit-sharing plans, which currently cover over 6 million employees. Such individuals tend to be highly committed to organizations in which such plans are in place. At Menno S. Martin Contractor, Ltd., in St. Jacobs, Ontario, Canada, a profit-sharing plan has been in place for many years, helping its workforce remain loyal.

Summary and Review of Learning Objective

1. **Define attitudes and work-related attitudes and describe the basic components of attitudes.**

   Attitudes are the stable clusters of feelings, beliefs, and behavioral tendencies directed toward some aspect of the external world. *Work-related attitudes* involve such reactions toward various aspects of work settings or the people in them. All attitudes consist of a *cognitive component* (what you believe), an *evaluative component* (how you feel), and a *behavioral component* (the tendency to behave a certain way).

2. **Distinguish between prejudice and discrimination and identify various victims of prejudice in organizations.**

   Prejudice refers to negative attitudes toward members of specific groups, and *discrimination* refers to treating people differently because of these prejudices. Today's workforce is characterized by high levels of diversity, with many groups finding themselves victims of prejudicial attitudes and discriminatory behaviors (based on many different factors, including age, sexual orientation, physical condition, racial or ethnic group membership, gender, and people from different religions than our own). Although people are becoming more tolerant of individuals from diverse groups, prejudicial attitudes persist.

3. **Describe some of the steps being taken by organizations today to manage diversity in the workforce and their effectiveness.**

   To help tap the rich pool of resources available in today's highly diverse workforce many companies are using *diversity management programs*—techniques for systematically teaching employees to celebrate the differences between people. Typically, these programs go beyond efforts to recruit and hire women and members of minority groups, to creating supportive work environments for them. The most effective programs focus on not only enhancing awareness of the benefits of a diverse workforce. (i.e., *awareness-based diversity training*) but also developing skills to help people manage diversity (i.e., *skill-based diversity training*). Although implementing diversity management programs is potentially difficult, experts acknowledge that the benefits, both organizational and personal, are considerable. For example, research has shown that companies whose employees systematically embrace diversity tend to be more profitable than those that allow discrimination to occur.

4. **Describe the concept of job satisfaction and summarize four major theories of job satisfaction.**

   Job satisfaction involves positive or negative attitudes toward one's work. According to the *two-factor theory,* job satisfaction and dissatisfaction stem from different factors. Specifically, it claims that factors leading to job satisfaction stem from factors associated with the work itself (known as *motivators*), and that factors leading to job dissatisfaction are associated with the conditions surrounding jobs (e.g., the work environment), known as *hygiene factors.* Value theory suggests that job satisfaction reflects the apparent match between the outcomes individuals desire from their jobs (what they value) and what they believe they are actually receiving. The *social information processing model* specifies that people adopt attitudes and behaviors in keeping with the cues provided by others with whom they come into contact. Finally, the *dispositional model of job satisfaction* suggests that job satisfaction is a relatively stable characteristic that stays with people over various situations.

5. **Describe the consequences of job dissatisfaction and ways to promote job satisfaction.**

   When people are dissatisfied with their jobs they tend to withdraw. That is, they are frequently absent and are likely to quit their jobs. However, evidence suggests that job performance is only very weakly associated with dissatisfaction. Levels of job satisfaction can be raised by paying people fairly, improving the quality of supervision, decentralizing control of organizational power, and assigning people to jobs that match their interests.

6. **Describe the concept of organizational commitment, its major forms, the consequences of low levels of organizational commitment, and how to overcome them.** *Organizational commitment* focuses on people's attitudes toward their organizations. There are three major types of organizational commitment. One is *continuance commitment*—the strength of a person's tendency to continue working for an organization because he or she has to and cannot afford to do otherwise. Another is *affective commitment*—the strength of a person's tendency to continue working for an organization because he or she agrees with its goals and values, and desires to stay with it. A third is *normative commitment*—commitment to remain in an organization stemming from social obligations to do so. Low levels of organizational commitment have been linked to high levels of absenteeism and voluntary turnover, the unwillingness to share and make sacrifices for the company, and negative personal consequences for employees. However, organizational commitment may be enhanced by enriching jobs, aligning the interests of employees with those of the company, and recruiting and selecting newcomers whose values closely match those of the organization.

Points to Ponder

Questions for Review

1. What are the three main components of attitudes?
2. What is job satisfaction; what are its major causes and the consequences of dissatisfaction?
3. What is organizational commitment; what are its major causes and the consequences of low levels of organizational commitment?
4. What steps can be taken to promote job satisfaction and organizational commitment?
5. What is the difference between prejudice and discrimination?
6. What steps are today's organizations taking to promote diversity, and are these efforts effective?

Experiential Questions

1. Think of a particular job you have enjoyed most. What did you like about it so much? Now, think of a particular job that you enjoyed least. What made you dislike it so much? Did the factors you liked fall into the "motivator" category of two-factor theory? Did the factors you disliked fall into the "hygiene" category of the two-factor theory?
2. Think about the particular organization at which you have worked the longest. What were the main reasons you stayed there? How do these compare to the three forms of organizational commitment described in this chapter?
3. If you have ever participated in a diversity management training program, what effects did it have on you? In what ways, if any, did your attitudes or behavior change? If you have never participated in a diversity management training program, how do you think you would react to being in one? Do you think you would find it enjoyable? Useful? What challenges to effectiveness, if any, do you suspect you might encounter?

Questions to Analyze

1. One of the strategies that has been recommended for enhancing job satisfaction is to make jobs more fun. We all like having fun, of course, but do you really think this matters when it comes to job satisfaction? In other words, is job satisfaction promoted by just having a pleasant, joking atmosphere in the workplace? Or, is what really matters making the work itself more interesting and enjoyable to perform? Explain your thoughts on this matter.
2. In today's economy, where replacing employees can be an expensive proposition, it pays to be able to maintain a highly committed workforce. Of the various things that can be done to promote commitment to an organization, which tactics do you believe may be most effective? Explain the basis for your answer.
3. Racial prejudice has been a serious problem in American society for a long time. How do you reconcile this with the fact that diversity management training generally seems to be successful? In other words, do you think diversity training actually changes people's prejudicial attitudes? Or, do you think that such programs get people to change their behavior—at least long enough to allow different kinds of people to be accepted? Explain.

Experiencing OB

Individual Exercise

Are You Committed to Your Job?

Questionnaires similar to the one presented here (which is based on established instruments) are used to assess three types of organizational commitment—continuance, affective, and normative. Completing this scale (based on Meyer & Smith, 1993; see Note 75) will give you a good feel for your own level of job commitment, and how this important construct is measured.

Directions

In the space to the left of each of the following 12 statements write the one number that reflects the extent to which you agree with it personally. Express your answers using the following scale:

> 1 = not at all
>
> 2 = slightly
>
> 3 = moderately
>
> 4 = a great deal
>
> 5 = extremely

1. _____ At this point, I stay on my job more because I have to than because I want to.
2. _____ I feel I strongly belong to my organization.
3. _____ I am reluctant to leave a company once I have been working there.
4. _____ Leaving my job would entail a great deal of personal sacrifice.
5. _____ I feel emotionally connected to the company for which I work.
6. _____ My employer would be very disappointed if I left my job.
7. _____ I don't have any other choice but to stay on my present job.
8. _____ I feel that I am part of the family at the company in which I work.
9. _____ I feel a strong obligation to stay on my job.
10. _____ My life would be greatly disrupted if I left my present job.
11. _____ I would be quite pleased to spend the rest of my life working for this organization.
12. _____ I stay on my job because people would think poorly of me for leaving.

Scoring

1. Add the scores for items 1, 4, 7, and 10. This reflects your degree of *continuance commitment*.
2. Add the scores for items 2, 5, 8, and 11. This reflects your degree of *affective commitment*.
3. Add the scores for items 3, 6, 9, and 12. This reflects your degree of *normative commitment*.

Questions for Discussion

1. Which form of commitment does the scale reveal you have most? Which do you have least? Are these differences great, or are they highly similar?
2. Did the scale tell you something you didn't already know about yourself, or did it merely reinforce your intuitive beliefs about your own organizational commitment?
3. To what extent is your organizational commitment, as reflected by this scale, related to your interest in quitting your job and taking a new position?
4. How do your answers to these questions compare to those of your classmates? Are your responses similar to theirs or different from them? Why do you think this is?

Group Exercise

Recognizing Differences in Cultural Values on the Job

One of the major barriers in understanding and appreciating people from other cultures is the fact that they may adopt widely different values—especially when it comes to basic organizational activities, such as hiring. The following exercise is designed to make you aware of such differences and to sensitize you to their impact on life in organizations.

Directions

1. Divide the class into groups of approximately 5 to 10 students.
2. Review the values differences noted in the following table.
3. As a group, identify and discuss specific examples of each of the cultural distinctions noted in the chart based on your personal experiences.
4. As a group, discuss the implications of these values differences. Note, for example, specific problems that are likely to arise as a result of such differences.
5. As a class, review the major implications identified by each group in step 4.

In mainstream American culture . . .	But, in many other cultures . . .
• People's primary obligation is toward their jobs.	• People's primary obligation is toward their family and friends.
• Employment is "at will"; an employee may be terminated at the discretion of the organization.	• Employment is for life.
• Competition is an accepted . way of life	• Cooperation is considered better because it promotes harmony between people.
• People strive for personal achievement.	• Personal ambition is frowned upon; group achievement is highly valued.

Source: Adapted from Gardenswartz & Rowe, 1994; see Note 45.

Questions for Discussion

1. Was your group, or the class as a whole, generally sensitive to the differences in values noted in this exercise?
2. What were the major organizational implications of the cultural differences in values identified by the class? What do you think could be done to help people recognize and accept these cultural differences in values?
3. Did you come away from this exercise with a better understanding of the way cultural differences between people may affect organizational activities?

Practicing OB

"I Quit!"

The president of a small manufacturing firm comes to you with a problem: The company is spending a lot of money training new employees, but 75 percent of them quit after working less than a year. Worse, they take jobs at the company's biggest competitor. Answer the following questions relevant to this situation based on the material in this chapter.

1. Drawing on research and theory on job satisfaction, what would you suspect is the cause of the turnover? What advice can you offer about how to eliminate the problem?
2. Drawing on research and theory on organizational commitment, what would you suspect is the cause of the turnover? What advice can you offer about how to eliminate the problem?
3. Suppose you find out that the greatest levels of dissatisfaction exist among employees belonging to minority groups. What would you recommend doing to eliminate the prejudice that may be responsible for the turnover?

Texaco Yesterday vs. Today: Now, Only the Oil Is Crude

Today, Texaco is a proud part of the Chevron Products Company. This large oil company proclaims proudly in its *2005 Corporate Responsibility Report* that it "is working to increase the representation of minorities in our workforce." Emphasizing further, it also states the following:

We learn from and respect the cultures in which we work. We value and demonstrate respect for the uniqueness of individuals and the varied perspectives and talents they provide. We have an inclusive work environment and actively embrace a diversity of people, ideas, talents and experiences.

Ten years earlier, however, one would have little reason to believe any of these statements. That was in 1996, a bleak year for the venerable Texaco.

One fall day while the company was in the midst of defending itself against legal charges of discrimination brought by 1,400 African American employees, a few top executives met to decide how to proceed. Secret tape recordings of that meeting revealed not only that these officials discussed destroying some incriminating documents, but worse yet, they freely used racial epithets in the course of doing so. After these tapes were shared with the plaintiffs' attorneys and the *New York Times,* Texaco found itself in the midst of a public relations nightmare. In the days that followed, the company's stock dropped so much that it lost nearly $1 billion in value.

Shortly thereafter, Texaco's chairman and CEO, Peter I. Bijur, settled the lawsuit, paying $140 million in damages and back pay to minority employees and setting aside another $35 million for a task force to monitor the company's treatment of women and minorities for the next five years. In doing so, Texaco's goal, according to Bijur, was to become "a model of workplace opportunity for all men and women." Has Texaco met this goal? Observers note that although Texaco is still not among the most hospitable companies for members of minority groups, it has made considerable strides.

Statistics tell the story. In recent years, over 40 percent of recent hires and about a quarter of all newly promoted employees have come from minority ranks. Also, over $1 billion—approximately 15 percent of the company's spending—has been directed at businesses owned by women and members of minority groups. And, although 80 percent of the company's top executives are still white men, growing numbers are coming from minority ranks. "Now," Bijur remarks, "we treat all people with the utmost respect—and that is a real achievement."

Because Texaco is under careful scrutiny—both from the courts and from the public—with respect to its treatment of women and minorities, it doesn't have much choice in the matter. Still, the company has shown that it is quite serious. Completely overhauling the way it went about hiring and treating people, Bijur took several steps to show that he would not tolerate disrespect. Rather than simply talking about promoting equality and respect for everyone, he set meaningful goals and timetables to help advance women and minorities. So serious are these goals that a portion of all top executives' and managers' annual evaluations is based on how effectively they meet them. Importantly, the company has prospered financially as it has strived toward these goals.

Clearly, changes have resulted: Corporate attorneys who used to spend time defending against discrimination lawsuits have found that virtually no such complaints have reached their desks in recent years. Even Bari-Ellen Roberts, the woman who initiated the lawsuit against Texaco, is optimistic that the company will continue its efforts to improve the treatment of women and minorities in the years ahead. "Then again," she said, "they had to—things could not remain the same."

Questions for Discussion

1. To what extent do you believe that Texaco's actions will be effective in getting its high-ranking employees to feel less prejudice toward members of minority groups?
2. How severely do you believe Texaco's public image was harmed because of this incident? Analogously, do you believe the company's image will be helped because of its new diversity management efforts?
3. What kinds of diversity management efforts do you believe would be most effective at Texaco?

MOTIVATION IN ORGANIZATIONS

Chapter 7

Chapter Outline

Motivation in Organizations: Its Basic Nature

Motivating by Meeting Basic Human Needs

Motivating by Enhancing Fit with the Organization

Motivating by Setting Goals

Motivating by Being Equitable

Motivating by Altering Expectations

Motivating by Structuring Jobs to Make Them Interesting

Special Sections

How to Do It

Recognizing Employees' Accomplishments: Easier Said Than Done

 **In a Diverse World**

Inequity in Housework: Comparing Married Women and Men

 **Making Sense Out of Common Sense**

Autonomy in the Orchestra Strikes a Sour Note

After reading this chapter, you should be able to:

1. Define motivation and explain its importance in the field of organizational behavior.
2. Describe need hierarchy theory and the motivational-fit approach, noting what each suggests about how to improve motivation in organizations.
3. Identify and explain the conditions through which goal setting can be used to improve job performance.
4. Describe equity theory and explain how it may be applied to motivating people in organizations.
5. Describe expectancy theory and how it may be applied in organizations.
6. Distinguish among job enlargement, job enrichment, and the job characteristics model as techniques for motivating employees.

PREVIEW CASE

Google: Searching for a Better Way to Work

Google, the immensely popular Web search engine, has been touted as "the closest thing the Web has to an ultimate answer machine." Although this is debatable, of course, it is far more difficult to deny that the company is, in fact, the closest thing we have to an ultimate example of business success. Founded by two computer science graduate students at Stanford University in the late 1990s, Larry Page and Sergy Brin, Google has grown astronomically. In late 1998, the search engine had 10,000 queries per day, a figure that grew to a quarter billion by 2006. Financial success likewise has been astonishing. Only four months after the initial public offering of Google stock in August 2004, its price more than doubled, making the company worth more than Ford and General Motors combined.

Although Google is in the technology business, the founders acknowledge that the company's greatest challenges lie more with people than computers. At first, Page and Brin worked with just a handful of employees out of a converted garage, but today the company has some 3,000 employees in its sprawling headquarters, known as the "Googleplex," in Mountain View, California. With such rapid growth, how can Page and Brin ensure that their many new employees share their passion for innovation and work hard to achieve it? Brin explains his strategy quite simply: "To have a good lifestyle, we have to have a good lifestyle at work."

Just about all the people who work at Google, from the most advanced computer engineers to the lowest level employees, are hand selected (or, at least, approved) by Page and Brin. They look for people who are inspired not by money, but by love of the work they do. After all, they are expected to work long hours and to achieve unparalleled levels of excellence, to come up with "the next big thing." To make this happen, they go out of their ways to make Google a great place to work. As Brin put it, "Work should be challenging, and the challenge should be fun."

With this in mind, the founders have taken strides to ensure that there's a comfortable and friendly atmosphere at Google. For example, there is no dress code; you dress however you wish to be comfortable (as stated in the company's philosophy, "You can be serious without a suit"). People even can bring their dogs to work, keeping them company throughout the day. To help everyone stay fit and to build a spirit of teamwork, there's also a very strong spirit of play at Google; at noon each day there's a volleyball game outside.

Google puts users first when it comes to online service, and it puts employees first when it comes to daily working life. Employees are treated very well. A fantastic onsite cafeteria serves gourmet meals of every kind, catering to a wide variety of dietary needs and preferences—all absolutely free of charge. According to CEO Eric E. Schmidt, this is just good business because it keeps people at their desks instead of leaving the building to eat. The company also invests in its employees in another interesting way. Every year, the company takes all its employees on an all-expenses-paid ski trip. Again, this is seen as good for the business because it promotes the spirit of friendship and closeness that's necessary in their work environment, in which the sharing of ideas is critical.

This is not to say that Google is lavish or wasteful. Although Page and Brin each made $6 billion when the company went public, and 1,000 employees also became millionaires, it is not money that keeps people going at Google. Page and Brin still share a small office and live modestly, as do most of their employees. Although they have the means to be living extremely well (and surely will do so someday), right now, the thing that keeps everyone going at Google is their zeal to use computer technology to change the world. It's all about innovation, and not getting rich quick.

To date, Google's success has been predicated on its founders' hard work and their fantastic technical abilities. Although this continues to be important, the growth of the enterprise from a converted garage to a sizeable organization now depends on another factor, the extent to which the employees, most of whom are young and new to the company, are willing to work almost as hard as the founders. So far, things are looking good. Larry Page and Sergy Brin have created a place where people want to work because it is fun and interesting, and although they are required to work hard, they are generously rewarded, both financially and personally. Why do these things stimulate people into action? In other words, what psychological mechanisms account for getting people to work hard? And from a practical perspective, what can we learn from this situation when it comes to motivating the people with whom we ourselves work every day? With an eye toward answering these questions we will examine the process of *motivation* in this chapter.

As you will see in this chapter, some of the things done at Google are very effective ways of motivating employees. We will discuss these and many other ways of motivating employees—identifying not only how to motivate people, but precisely what makes these techniques successful. In keeping with the dual orientation of the field of OB highlighted in this book, we are interested in asking both theoretical questions, such as "*What* motivates people, and *why?*" and applied questions, such as "*How* can this knowledge be put to practical use?" These dual foci will be apparent throughout this chapter.

The question of what it takes to motivate workers has received a great deal of attention by practicing managers and organizational scientists.[1] In addressing this issue, we examine six different approaches—motivating by: (1) meeting basic human needs, (2) fitting people's traits and skills with the nature of the work, (3) setting goals, (4) treating people equitably, (5) enhancing beliefs that desired rewards can be attained, and (6) designing jobs so as to make them more desirable. We will describe each of these approaches to motivation, highlighting the research bearing on it and its practical implications. This will help you develop a solid understanding of motivation as a topic of interest to organizational scientists and practitioners.

Before turning to these approaches and applications, however, we must consider a very basic matter—namely, what exactly is meant by the term *motivation*.

Motivation in Organizations: Its Basic Nature

Although motivation is a broad and complex concept, organizational scientists have agreed on its basic characteristics.[2] Drawing from various social sciences, we define **motivation** as the set of processes that arouse, direct, and maintain human behavior toward attaining some goal. The diagram in Figure 7.1 will guide our explanation as we elaborate on this definition.

Components of Motivation

The first part of our definition deals with *arousal*. This has to do with the drive or energy behind our actions. For example, people may be guided by their interest in making a good

motivation
The set of processes that arouse, direct, and maintain human behavior toward attaining some goal.

FIGURE 7.1

Basic Components of Motivation

Motivation involves the arousal, direction, and maintenance of behavior toward a goal.

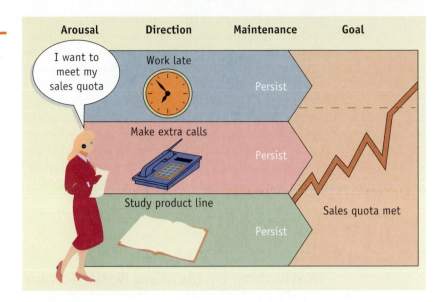

impression on others, doing interesting work, being successful at what they do, and so on. This motivates people to do what it takes to accomplish these objectives.

But how will people go about satisfying their motives? Motivation is also concerned with the choices people make, the *direction* their behavior takes. For example, employees interested in cultivating a favorable impression on their supervisors may do many different things: compliment them on their good work, do them special favors, work extra hard on an important project, and the like. Each of these options may be recognized as a path toward meeting the person's goal.

The final part of our definition deals with *maintaining* behavior. How long will people persist at attempting to meet their goal? To give up in advance of goal attainment means not satisfying the need that stimulated behavior in the first place. Obviously, people who do not persist at meeting their goals (e.g., salespeople who give up before reaching their quotas) cannot be said to be highly motivated.

To summarize, motivation requires all three components: the arousal, direction, and maintenance of goal-directed behavior. An analogy may help tie these components together. Imagine that you are driving down a road on your way home. The arousal part of motivation is like the energy created by the car's engine. The direction component is like the steering wheel, taking you along your chosen path. Finally, the maintenance aspect of the definition is the persistence that keeps you going until you arrive home, reaching your goal. In both cases, any one missing part will keep you from getting where you want to go.

Three Key Points About Motivation

Now that we have defined motivation, we should note three important points you need to keep in mind as you think further about motivation on the job.

Motivation and Job Performance Are Not Synonymous. Just because someone performs a task well does not mean that he or she is highly motivated. Motivation is just one of several possible determinants of job performance. The person who performs well may be very skillful but not put forth much effort at all. If you're a mathematical genius, for example, you may breeze through your calculus class without hardly trying. By contrast, someone who performs poorly may be putting forth a great deal of effort but is falling short of a desired goal because he or she lacks the skill needed to succeed. If you've ever tried to learn a new sport but found that you couldn't get the hang of it no matter how hard you tried, you know what we mean.

Motivation Is Multifaceted. People are likely to have several different motives operating at once. Sometimes, these conflict with one another. For example, a word processing operator might be motivated to please her boss by being as productive as possible. However, being too productive may antagonize one's coworkers, who fear that they're being made to look bad. The result is that the two motives may pull the individual in different directions, and the one that wins is the one that's strongest in that situation.

People Are Motivated by More Than Just Money. Suppose you struck it big in the lottery. Would you continue to go to work? Interestingly, most Americans say that they would, in fact, continue to work even if they didn't need the money.[3] Although money certainly is important to people, we are motivated to attain many other goals on the job as well. Specifically, the thing that most strongly motivates today's workers is not money, but the prospect of performing jobs that are interesting and challenging; getting paid was only third on the list (see Figure 7.2).[4] As you will see in the rest of this chapter, the field of OB not surprisingly considers a wide variety of factors that motivate people, including those just described.

Motivating by Meeting Basic Human Needs

As our definition suggests, people are motivated to fulfill their needs—whether it's looking good to others, as in our example, or even more fundamental needs, such as the need for food and water. Companies that help their employees in their quest to satisfy their needs are certain to reap the benefits. In fact, organizations that strive to meet the needs of their employees usually attract the best people and stimulate them to do excellent work.[5]

Some insight into how this comes about is provided by Maslow's **need hierarchy theory**.[6] The idea is simple: People will not be healthy and well adjusted in life unless their needs are met. This applies whether we're talking about becoming a functioning member of society, Maslow's original focus as a clinical psychologist, or a productive employee of an organization, a later application of his work. Specifically, Maslow identified five different types of needs, which, he claimed, are activated in a particular order. These begin at the lowest, most basic needs, and work upward to higher-level needs (which is what makes it a hierarchy) and are triggered in order from lowest to highest. Thus, each need is triggered only after the one beneath it in the hierarchy has been satisfied. The specific needs, and the hierarchical order in which they are arranged, are summarized in Figure 7.3.

need hierarchy theory
Maslow's theory specifying that there are five human needs (physiological, safety, social, esteem, and self-actualization) and that these are arranged in such a way that lower, more basic needs must be satisfied before higher-level needs become activated.

FIGURE 7.2

What Motivates People to Work?

A recent survey of people working in a wide variety of jobs in such fields as accounting, construction, insurance, and information technology were asked to indicate the job-related factors that motivated them most strongly. The top 10 things are shown here. Because people were allowed to select more than one, the figures exceed 100 percent.

Source: Based on Robson, 2004; see Note 4.

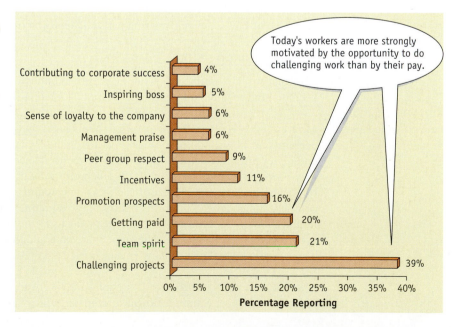

FIGURE 7.3

Maslow's Need Hierarchy Theory

Need hierarchy theory specifies that people are motivated by the five needs specified here. These are activated in order from the lowest level (shown at the bottom of the triangle) to the highest level (shown at the top of the triangle).

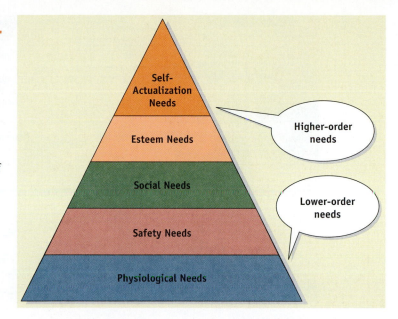

Physiological Needs

physiological needs

The lowest-order, most basic needs specified by Maslow's *need hierarchy theory,* including fundamental biological drives, such as the need for food, air, water, and shelter.

The lowest-order needs involve satisfying fundamental biological drives, such as the needs for air, food, water, and shelter. These **physiological needs**, as they are called, are the most basic needs because unless they are met people will become ill and suffer. For this reason, they are depicted at the base of the hierarchy in Figure 7.3.

There are many things that companies do to help meet their employees' basic physiological needs. Probably the simplest involves paying them a living wage, money that can be exchanged for food and shelter. But there's more to satisfying physiological needs than giving employees a paycheck. There are also coffee breaks and opportunities to rest. Presumably, even the cruelest, slave-driving bosses know the importance of giving workers time to relax and recharge their systems.

Staying physically healthy involves more than just resting; it also requires exercise, something that the sedentary nature of many of today's technologically advanced jobs does not permit. With this in mind, thousands of companies are providing exercise facilities for their employees. In fact, a survey found that the perk most desired by managers seeking new jobs is membership in a health club.[7] This makes perfectly good business sense. By keeping the workforce healthy and fit companies are paving the way for people to become productive (for an example, see Figure 7.4).[8]

Safety Needs

safety needs

In Maslow's *need hierarchy theory,* they are the need for a secure environment, to be free from threats of physical or psychological harm.

After physiological needs have been satisfied, the next level of needs is triggered—**safety needs**. These are concerned with the need to operate in an environment that is physically and psychologically safe and secure, one free from threats of harm.

Organizations help satisfy their employees' safety needs in several ways. For example, they protect shop workers from hazards in the environment by providing security and fire-prevention services and by fitting them with goggles and hard hats. Even seemingly safe work settings, such as offices, can be riddled with safety hazards. This is why efforts are made to spare office workers from eye strain, wrist injuries (such as carpal tunnel syndrome), and back pain by using ergonomically designed computer keyboards, desks, and chairs.

Psychological safety is important as well. By offering health and disability insurance, companies are promoting their employees' psychological well-being by assuring them that they will not be harmed financially in the event of illness. Although almost all companies offer health insurance benefits, a select few have taken psychological security to the extreme by having no-layoff policies.

This approach is taken by Hypertherm, the 35-year-old company specializing in high-tech metal-cutting services located in Hanover, New Hampshire. Instead of releasing

FIGURE 7.4

The Motivational and Financial Benefits of Promoting Healthy Lifestyles

LifeSteps, a comprehensive worksite wellness program sponsored by the United Auto Workers and General Motors, has helped over 800,00 employees improve their health by focusing on 13 key health risk factors (e.g., weight reduction and physical activity). Healthier employees have resulted in reduced medical costs and raises in productivity. The social aspects of the training have also promoted social bonding among employees.

employees, the company finds other ways to save money during tough times, such as by reducing corporate travel. The motivational benefits with respect to improved job security have been phenomenal, contributing greatly to the company's financial growth over the years. This is expressed nicely by Peggy Laplante, a 47-year-old machine operator at Hypertherm who does not live in fear of getting laid off. "When I see the economy sliding and hear of companies laying people off," she says, "I can remain focused on my work rather than worry about what's going on outside." Not surprisingly, this has helped boost her job performance. According to Ms. Laplante, "At Hypertherm everyone ensures that you feel special and involved. And it makes me want to do a better job, knowing that the company cares about me."[9] Given the company's success, she appears not to be alone in this regard.

Social Needs

Once people's physiological and safety needs have been satisfied, Maslow claims, **social needs** are activated. These refer to the need to be affiliative—that is, to be liked and accepted by others. As social animals we all want to be with others and to have them approve of us.

It is with this in mind that many companies help organize events that build camaraderie among their employees. Joining a company's bowling team or softball team, for example, provides good opportunities to meet social needs within an organization. In discussing physiological needs we noted that many companies provide health club facilities for their employees. Besides keeping employees physically healthy, it's easy to see how such facilities also help satisfy employees' social needs. "Playing hard" with those with whom we also "work hard" provides good opportunities to fulfill social needs on the job.

Organizations do much to satisfy social needs when they sponsor social events, such as office parties and company picnics. For example, by holding its annual "Family Day" picnic near its Armonk, New York headquarters, IBM lets employees enjoy good opportunities to

FIGURE 7.5

The Business of Fulfilling Social Needs

Because executives at many companies acknowledge the importance of satisfying their employees' social needs, companies have sprung up to provide the services needed to do so. One company, the Picnic People, in Pleasanton, California, has coordinated 5,000 picnics with over 600,000 guests for its corporate clients since 1984.

socialize with their coworkers and their families. Potentially so useful are company picnics in fulfilling social needs among employees, specialized companies have sprung up that specialize in organizing and running such events for other, usually large, organizations (see Figure 7.5).

Esteem Needs

esteem needs

In Maslow's *need hierarchy theory,* the need to develop self-respect and to gain the approval of others.

Not only do we need to be liked by others socially, but we also need to gain their respect and approval. In other words, we have **esteem needs**—that is, the need to achieve success and have others recognize our accomplishments. Consider, for example, the reserved parking spots or plaques honoring the "employee of the month" that many companies have. Both are ways of demonstrating esteem for employees. So too are awards banquets in which worthy staff members' contributions are recognized.[10] Sometimes, this is done in print by recognizing organizational contributions on the pages of a corporate newsletter. For example, employees of the large pharmaceutical company Merck enjoyed the recognition they received for developing Proscar (a highly successful drug treatment for prostate enlargement) when they saw their pictures in the company newsletter. In fact, it meant more to Merck employees to have their colleagues learn of their success internally than it did to have their accomplishments touted more widely to an anonymous audience in the pages of the *New York Times.*

The practice of awarding bonuses to people making suggestions for improvement is another highly successful way to meet employees' esteem needs. Companies such as Shell Oil, AT&T, and Campbell Soup have used a variety of small rewards in this regard, such as VCRs and computers. However, few companies have taken the practice of rewarding contributions to the same high art as Mary Kay Cosmetics. Not only are lavish banquets staged to recognize modest contributions to this company's bottom line, but top performers are awarded the most coveted prize of all—a pink Cadillac. As the company's late founder Mary Kay Ash put it, "There are two things people want more than sex and money . . . recognition and praise."[11]

Fortunately, companies that cannot afford such lavish gifts needn't be concerned about failing to satisfy their employees' self-esteem needs. After all, sometimes the best recognition is nothing more than a heartfelt "thank you." Or, as Mark Twain put it, "I can live for two months on a good compliment." (Because of the importance of recognizing employees' accomplishments, it is important to do this effectively. For some important guidelines, see the *How to Do It* section on p. 254.)

HOW TO DO IT

Recognizing Employees' Accomplishments: Easier Said Than Done

It sounds easy enough. Someone does something right and you give him or her a pat on the back. Although it seems simple, recognizing employees—effectively, at least—is fraught with so many potential problems that it often is more challenging than it seems. Avoiding these problems is an important part of any manager's job. So, to get the most out of efforts to recognize employees, here are some key things to keep in mind.

Clarify precisely what is being recognized. Remember from Chapter 3 that rewards are most successful in bringing about desired behavior when it is clear how they came about. Although managers generally don't hesitate to point out what someone did incorrectly, they often are far too vague about the reasons for the praise they give (e.g., giving someone a trophy for "best attitude"). Not only may vague praise fail to satisfy an individual's esteem needs, but it also is likely to minimize the impact of any praise that truly is deserved.

The advice to "catch someone in the act of doing something right" is very wise. Be careful, though: You should not go around the office complimenting everyone about every little thing. If you do this long enough, your messages will not be special, and after a while they won't even be heard. However, if someone did something that is particularly noteworthy, even if it's small, don't hesitate to acknowledge it.

Make time for recognition. We're all so busy these days that it often seems difficult, if not impossible, to find the time to spend with employees needed to acknowledge them. Doing so, however, is so important that it should be considered an indispensable part of any manager's job. Make it a habit to recognize people and build it into your schedule.

Before leaving for the day, for example, some managers regularly make time to write personal notes to their employees to praise them for the work they did that day. Others do the same thing via voice mail or e-mail—or, better yet, set aside time to recognize employees at regularly planned times, such as at lunch. A particularly useful practice is to schedule time at company meetings to acknowledge the noteworthy contributions of employees. By noting specifically what the individual did and how it helped the company (e.g., by saving a certain amount of money), a strong message is sent about what is valued and how one may go about receiving recognition oneself.

Be accessible; share yourself. Wandering around and observing what's going on gives managers a good chance to determine what really needs to be recognized and who is most worthy. That's always good advice, but there's more to it. Far too often, managers are away at meetings or tethered to their computers, keeping them from seeing—hence, acknowledging—their employees' work. Those things may be important, but they should not occur at the expense of sharing your presence with your subordinates. After all, one of the most powerful forms of recognition any superior can offer is simply to be present and show that he or she is interested. We're not recommending that you spy or that you "stick your nose" into other people's jobs. Rather, being accessible to employees demonstrates that you care, and this alone can be a valuable source of recognition.

By now, it's probably clear that recognizing employees effectively is more complex than you might have imagined, and that there are potential pitfalls to be avoided. Given their effectiveness, however, keeping these guidelines in mind and practicing them is well worth the effort.

Self-Actualization Needs

self-actualization

In Maslow's *need hierarchy theory,* the need to discover who we are and to develop ourselves to the fullest potential.

What happens once all an employee's lower-order needs are met? According to need hierarchy theory, people will strive for **self-actualization**—that is, they will work to become all they are capable of being. When people are self-actualized they perform at their maximum level of creativity, making them extremely valuable assets to their organizations. For this reason, companies are interested in paving the way for their employees to become self-actualized by meeting their lower-order needs.

Need hierarchy theory provides excellent guidelines with respect to ways of motivating employees, and many organizations have found its suggestions to be successful. For this reason, the theory remains popular with organizational practitioners. Scientists, however, have noted that specific elements of the theory—notably, the assertion that there are only five needs, and that they are activated in a specific order—have found limited support.[12] Despite this shortcoming, the theory's insight into the importance of meeting human needs in the workplace has made it a popular approach to motivation in organizations.

Motivating by Enhancing Fit with the Organization

Phil has a new job as a salesperson at an auto dealership. However, he doesn't have a lot of initiative and persistence, and he lacks self confidence. This makes him anxious as he approaches a prospect or tries to close a sale, impeding his capacity to succeed. In turn, this lowers his motivation to work, interfering with his performance, further lowering his motivation. The dangerous downward cycle is clear. Because Phil's particular qualities are a poor match with the requirements of the job, his motivation and performance suffer.

motivational fit approach

The framework stipulating that motivation is enhanced by a good fit between the traits and skills of individuals and the requirements of the jobs they perform in their organizations.

In Chapter 3, we noted that many different personality traits and abilities influence job performance. In the context of motivation, however, scientists have found that a few particular traits and skills have especially profound effects. This is the basic idea behind a relatively new way of looking at motivation known as the **motivational fit approach.**[13] Specifically, this framework stipulates that motivation is based on the connection between qualities of individuals and for requirements of the jobs they perform in their organizations. The better their traits and skills fit the requirements of the work environment, the more highly motivated the individual will be (for an overview, see Figure 7.6). We now will explain the motivational fit approach in more detail and describe its implications for motivating people on the job.

Motivational Traits and Skills

The motivational fit approach specifies that two particular individual characteristics, referred to as *motivational traits,* are important. These are as follows:

- *Achievement.* This refers to people's interest in excelling at what they do, accomplishing desired objectives.
- *Anxiety.* Although psychologists acknowledge that anxiety is complex and takes many forms, broadly conceived, it refers to the tendency for someone to be excessively apprehensive or nervous about things in everyday life.

Because achievement and anxiety are considered traits, they are assumed to be relatively stable individual differences between people (see Chapter 4), making some people

FIGURE 7.6

The Motivational Fit Approach: An Overview

According to the motivational fit approach, people are most highly motivated to perform when there is a good fit between certain traits and skills they possess and certain important characteristics of the work they perform. These are summarized here.

Source: Based on suggestions by Kanfer & Heggestad, 1997; see Note 13.

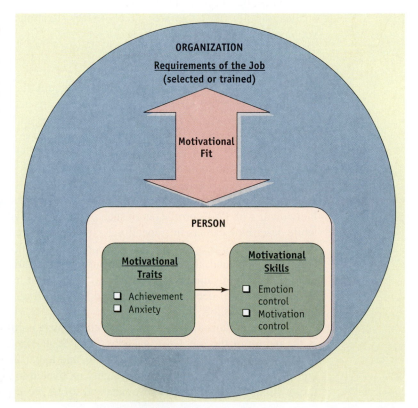

more successful than others. As it works out, the most highly motivated employees tend to be those characterized by high levels of achievement and low levels of anxiety. Such individuals not only are inclined to strive for excellence, but also lack the emotional problems associated with being excessively worried.

In addition to the traits they possess, an individual's motivation also is determined by what are known as *motivational skills*—the particular strategies used when attempting to meet objectives. Unlike traits, which are relatively stable within individuals over time, people can be trained in skills, and these also develop naturally over time as people gain experience over their careers (see Appendix 2). Two particular motivational skills are important:

■ *Emotion control.* This refers to the capacity to control one's emotions, to stay focused on the task at hand without allowing emotions to interfere.
■ *Motivation control.* The capacity to push oneself by directing attention to the job, to persist at exerting effort even when one's interest begins to wane is the idea behind motivation control.

As you might expect, employees with highly developed motivational skills are not only more strongly motivated to succeed but ultimately also more successful on their jobs than those with less well developed motivational skills. Specifically, individuals with high levels of emotional control are more successful than those with low levels of emotional control, and those with high levels of motivation control are more successful than those with low levels of motivation control. This is probably not surprising to you given that such individuals are skilled at overcoming key problems such as boredom and the frustration that inevitably occurs at work. Importantly, because these are skills rather than traits, anyone is capable of developing them.

People's motivational traits and skills do not operate independently. Rather, traits influence skills. Consider, for example, someone with high amounts of the achievement trait. Such an individual is particularly likely to seek out challenging situations. And, because such situations present considerable opportunities for failure, the person has to learn to overcome the negative emotional reactions that are likely to result (emotion control) and is likely to be driven to continue even in the face of obstacles (motivation control). By contrast, because individuals who are low in the achievement trait are inclined to avoid challenging situations, they are unlikely to face situations that allow them to develop motivational skills.

Organizational Factors: Enhancing Motivational Fit

Recognizing that people do not operate in a vacuum, the motivational fit approach specifies that it is important for people's motivational traits and skills to match the requirements of their working environments. Although this idea is admittedly abstract, we already provided a good illustration. Recall Phil, the auto salesperson lacking initiative and persistence we described at the opening of this section of the chapter. Given the nature of the work, he likely would be a bad fit with the organization.

Fortunately, however, fit can be enhanced. The motivational fit approach suggests two ways of doing so. First, the dealership can prescreen job applicants in a manner that keeps individuals with Phil's profile out of such positions (we will describe this more specifically while describing careers in Appendix 2). Indeed, research has shown that motivational fit is enhanced when people's characteristics match the unique requirements of the positions they seek.[14] Second, the company can improve motivational fit by training Phil in ways that build his motivational skills. This may take the form, for example, of training him in building self-confidence so he can avoid the self-doubts that threaten to interfere with motivation in this job.

Another organizational factor to which people's motivational traits and skills must fit is the nature of the job. On some jobs, such as research scientist, success requires the capacity to work independently, to innovate, and to persist when attempting to solve difficult problems. The individuals most highly motivated to pursue positions of this type are those with high amounts of achievement and strong motivational skills (see Figure 7.7). By contrast, among people performing more routine jobs, such as factory worker or call center operator, such characteristics are not as likely to contribute to their motivation. After all, the highly structured nature of these jobs is likely to make these traits and skills less important. Please note that "less important" does not mean "unimportant." Indeed, even among call center operators, motivational fit has been identified as a key to productivity.[15]

Because the motivational fit approach is new, it has not received as much research attention as the other frameworks described in this chapter. However, existing research has been highly supportive.[16] As a result, it already has been acknowledged as an important and especially promising way of understanding motivation on the job.[17]

Motivating by Setting Goals

goal setting
The process of determining specific levels of performance for workers to attain and then striving to attain them.

Just as people are motivated to satisfy their needs on the job and to fit with their organizations, they also are motivated by another very basic interest—to strive for, and to attain, goals—a process known as **goal setting**. The process of setting goals is one of the most important motivational forces operating on people in organizations.[18] With this in mind, we will describe the underlying psychological processes that make goal setting effective and identify some practical suggestions for setting goals on the job.

Goal-Setting Theory

goal-setting theory
A popular theory specifying that people are motivated to attain goals because doing so makes them feel successful.

self-efficacy
One's belief about having the capacity to perform a task.

Suppose that you are doing a task, such as word processing, when a performance goal is assigned. You are now expected to type 70 words per minute instead of the 60 words per minute you've been keyboarding all along. Would you work hard to meet this goal, or would you simply give up? Some insight into the question of how people respond to assigned goals is provided by a popular theory known as **goal-setting theory**.[19] This approach claims that an assigned goal influences people's beliefs about being able to perform the task in question (i.e., the personality variable of **self-efficacy**, described in Chapter 4) and their personal goals. Both of these factors, in turn, influence performance.

The basic idea behind goal-setting theory is that a goal serves as a motivator for several reasons. First, when goals are set, people direct their attention to them and gauge how well they are doing. In other words, they compare their present capacity to perform with

FIGURE 7.7

High Motivational Fit: An Example

This research scientist at 3M is working on developing and testing "cosmetic microspheres," a new type of additive that provides a luxurious feel and texture to pressed powders and other cosmetic formulations along with improved flow and smoothness. This job requires her to be highly innovative, often in the face of frustrating setbacks. Under such circumstances, she is likely to be lightly motivated to perform well when she is very interested in achieving success and has the capacity to push herself hard to attain it.

that required to succeed at the goal. To the extent that people believe they will fall short of a goal, they will feel dissatisfied and will work harder to attain it so long as they believe it is possible for them to do so. When they succeed at meeting a goal, they feel competent and successful.[20] Having a goal enhances performance in large part because the goal makes clear exactly what type and level of performance is expected (see Figure 7.8).

Goal-setting theory also claims that assigned goals will lead to the acceptance of those goals as personal goals.[21] In other words, they will be accepted as one's own. This is the idea of **goal commitment**—the extent to which people invest themselves in meeting a goal. Indeed, people become more committed to a goal to the extent that they desire to attain that goal and believe they have a reasonable chance of doing so. Likewise, the more strongly people believe they are capable of meeting a goal, the more strongly they will accept it as their own. By contrast, workers who perceive themselves as being physically incapable of meeting performance goals, for example, generally are not committed to meeting them and do not strive to do so.

Finally, goal-setting theory claims that beliefs about both self-efficacy and goal commitment influence task performance. After all, people are willing to exert greater effort when they believe they will succeed than when they believe their efforts will be in vain.[22] Moreover, goals that are not personally accepted will have little capacity to guide behavior. In fact, the more strongly people are committed to meeting goals, the better they perform.[23]

Let's illustrate this idea using an example to which college students easily can relate. Suppose you don't care about getting good grades in school (i.e., you are not committed to achieving academic success). In this case, you would not work very hard regardless of how easy or difficult the course may be. By contrast, if you are highly committed to achieving success, then a difficult (but acceptable) goal (e.g., getting a good grade in a very challenging course) will have more meaning to you than an easy goal (e.g., getting a good grade in an easy course) because it enhances your self-efficacy. As a result, you will work harder to achieve it.

Goal-setting theory has been supported by research conducted over 40 years, suggesting that it is a valuable source of insight into how the goal-setting process works.[24] In fact, goal-setting theory is so highly regarded that it has been ranked as the most influential of all OB theories by management scholars.[25] One team of scientists even referred to goal-setting theory as being "quite easily the single most dominant theory in the field [of organizational behavior]."[26]

goal commitment
The degree to which people accept and strive to attain goals.

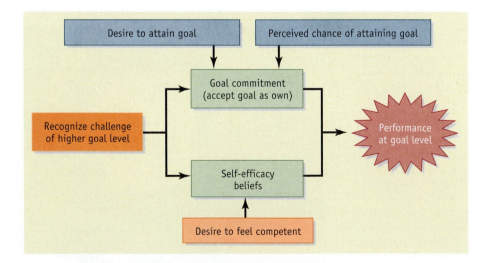

FIGURE 7.8

The Goal-Setting Process
When people are challenged to meet higher goals, several things happen. First, they assess their desire to attain the goal as well as their chances of attaining the goal. Together, these judgments affect their goal commitment. Second, they assess the extent to which meeting the goal will enhance their beliefs in their own self-efficacy. When levels of goal commitment and self-efficacy are high, people are motivated to perform at the goal level.

Guidelines for Setting Effective Performance Goals

Because researchers have been involved actively in studying the goal-setting process for many years, it is possible to summarize their findings in the form of principles. These may be taken as practical suggestions for managers to consider when attempting to enhance motivation.

1. Assign Specific Goals. Probably the best-established finding of research on goal setting is that people perform at higher levels when asked to meet a specific high-performance goal than when simply asked to "do your best," or when no goal at all is assigned. Generally, people find specific goals quite challenging and are motivated to meet them—not only to fulfill others' expectations but also to convince themselves that they have performed well.

A classic study conducted at an Oklahoma lumber camp provides a particularly dramatic demonstration of this principle.[27] The participants in this research were lumber camp crews who hauled logs from forests to their company's nearby sawmill. Over a three-month period before the study began, it was found that the crew loaded trucks to only about 60 percent of their legal capacities, wasting trips that cost the company money. Then a specific goal was set, challenging the loggers to load the trucks to 94 percent of their capacity before returning to the mill. How effective was this goal in raising performance? The results, summarized in Figure 7.9, show that the goal was extremely effective. Not only was the specific goal effective in raising performance to the goal level after just a few weeks, but these effects were long-lasting: Loggers sustained this level of performance throughout the next seven years. The resulting savings for the company was considerable.

This is just one of many studies that clearly demonstrate the effectiveness of setting specific performance goals. Research also has found that specific goals help bring about other desirable organizational objectives, such as reducing absenteeism and industrial accidents.[28] To reap such benefits, however, goals must be not only highly specific, but also challenging.

2. Assign Difficult, but Acceptable, Performance Goals. The goal set at the logging camp was successful not only because it was specific, but also because it pushed crew members to a higher standard. Obviously, a goal that is too easily attained will *not* bring about the desired increments in performance. For example, if you already type at 70 words per minute, the goal of 60 words per minute—although specific—would likely

FIGURE 7.9

Goal Setting: Some Impressive Effects

The performance of loggers loading timber onto trucks markedly improved after a specific, difficult goal was set. The percentage of the maximum possible weight loaded onto the trucks rose from approximately 60 percent before any goal was set to approximately 94 percent—the goal level—after the goal was set. Performance remained at this level as long as seven years.

Source: Adapted from Latham & Baldes, 1975; see Note 27.

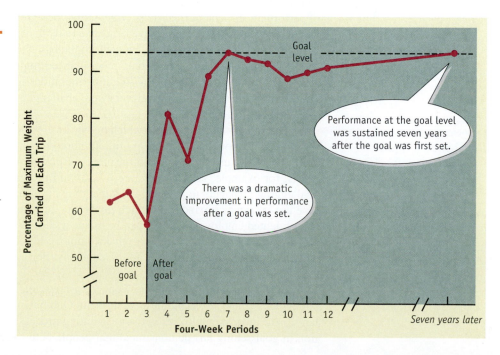

lower your performance because it is too easy. The key point is that a goal must be difficult as well as specific for it to raise performance.

It is interesting to consider *why* this occurs. The loggers were not paid any more for meeting the goal than for missing it. Still, they worked hard to meet it. Why? The answer is that the goal instilled purpose and meaning to the otherwise monotonous task of loading trucks. Loggers who met the goal took pride in doing so and found the task more interesting as a result. In fact, the challenge of meeting the goal made the job so much more fascinating that within a week after it was set, the loggers showed great improvements in attendance.[29]

Importantly, there is a limit to this effect. Although people will work hard to reach challenging goals, they only will do so when the goals fall within the limits of their capability. As goals become *too* difficult, performance suffers because people reject the goals as unrealistic and unattainable.[30] Let's consider an example to which you can relate as a student. You may work much harder in a class that challenges your ability than one that is very easy. At the same time, however, you probably would give up trying if you had to get a perfect score on all exams to pass the course—a standard you would reject as unacceptable. The underlying principle applies in most situations. Specific goals are most effective if they are set high enough to challenge people, but not so high as to be rejected.

This principle is applied in many organizations, where goals are set with respect to many important criteria. Consider these examples:

- Bell Canada's telephone operators are required to handle calls within 23 seconds, and FedEx's customer service agents are expected to answer customers' questions within 140 seconds.[31]
- At the U.S. Veteran's Administration, hospital administrators face a goal of having 68 percent of patients rate the health care they receive as good or excellent.[32]
- At Coeur d'Alene Mines, the large silver producer, the goal of reducing accidents by 10 percent each year has been in effect for some time.[33]

Despite the differences in these goals and the nature of the companies in which they were established, they have something in common. In all cases, although the goals were considered difficult when first imposed, the employees eventually met—or even exceeded—them over time. Moreover, they enjoyed the satisfaction of knowing they succeeded at doing so.

Sometimes, the difficult goals set by companies are so far beyond levels currently being achieved that employees lack a clear idea how to go about reaching them. Such goals are known as **stretch goals**. By their very nature, stretch goals are so difficult that they challenge people to rethink the way they work, thereby establishing unprecedented levels of performance. General Electric's former CEO, Jack Welch, used stretch goals at his company to help it achieve vast improvements in quality and efficiency.[34] In describing them to his colleagues, Welch likened stretch goals to the bullet trains in Japan, which run at about 200 mph. Had engineers sought only modest speed improvements, they would have limited their thinking in ways leading to minor alterations in design. However, by specifying previously unheard of speeds, engineers were challenged to think completely differently—and therefore to achieve amazing results.

Stretch goals of this type, in which higher levels of current activities are aggressively pursued (e.g., more speed, more profit, etc.) are known as **vertical stretch goals**. Some companies also use stretch goals for other purposes. At the investment firm Goldman Sachs, for example, stretch goals are used to aid professional development, such as by challenging managers to perform tasks that they never have done before.[35] Efforts of this type are known as **horizontal stretch goals**. Such initiatives help develop the company's most talented employees so they can be as successful as possible in many different ways. Not only do horizontal stretch goals make employees' jobs more interesting, but they also make them more valuable assets to the company. For a summary comparison of vertical and horizontal stretch goals, see Table 7.1.

As you read this you may be wondering how goals should be set in a manner that strengthens employees' commitment to them. One obvious way of enhancing goal acceptance is to involve employees in the goal-setting process. Research on workers' participation in goal setting has demonstrated that people better accept goals that they have been

stretch goals
Goals that are so difficult that they challenge people to rethink the way they work.

vertical stretch goals
Stretch goals that challenge people to achieve higher levels of success in current activities.

horizontal stretch goals
Stretch goals that challenge people to perform tasks that they have never done.

TABLE 7.1 Comparing the Two Types of Stretch Goals

Goals that extend performance far beyond present levels, known as *stretch goals,* take two distinct forms—*vertical stretch goals* and *horizontal stretch goals.* The differences between them are summarized here.

	Vertical Stretch Goals	Horizontal Stretch Goals
Description		
	Aggressive goals aligned with current activities	Goals that require significant new responsibilities
Purpose		
	To improve individual and/or organizational effectiveness	To improve the development of professional skills among individuals
Example		
	Instead of working to boost annual sales by 10% as usual, strive to raise sales by 50%.	An engineer is asked to lead a sales team.

Source: Based on information in Kerr & Landauer, 2004; see Note 35.

involved in setting than goals that have been assigned by their supervisors—and they work harder as a result.[36] In other words, participation in the goal-setting process tends to enhance goal commitment. Not only does participation help people better understand and appreciate goals they had a hand in setting, but it also helps ensure that the goals set are not unreasonable.

3. Provide Feedback on Goal Attainment. The final principle of goal setting appears to be glaringly obvious, although in practice it is often not followed: Feedback helps people attain their performance goals. Just as golfers interested in improving their swings need feedback about where their balls are going, so do workers need feedback about how closely they are approaching their performance goals. In both instances, the feedback helps in two important ways. First, it helps people determine how well they are doing, which potentially enhances their feelings of self-efficacy. Second, feedback also helps people determine the nature of the adjustments to their performance that are required to improve (e.g., adjusting the grip on a golf club to avoid "hooking" or "slicing" the ball down the fairway).

The importance of using feedback in conjunction with goal setting has been demonstrated in a study of pizza delivery drivers.[37] These individuals have a critical mission: to deliver their customers' pizzas quickly. But, of course, they must do so safely and in compliance with all traffic laws. All too often, however, in the interest of keeping their pizzas hot, some delivery people's driving styles are even hotter (and saucier). To speed up delivery, for example, some have been known to fail to come to complete stops at intersections.

With an eye toward curbing this behavior, officials of pizza shops in two different towns participated in a study in which their deliverers' driving behavior was observed systematically over a nine-month period. Trained observers, hidden from view, recorded various aspects of the deliverers' driving behavior during prime-time hours—in particular, the percentage of time they came to complete stops at intersections. Over a six-week period, drivers from both locations were found to come to complete stops, on average, just under half the time. Because this was unacceptable, the drivers in one location, the experimental group, were asked to come to a complete stop 75 percent of the time. And, over a four-week period, they were given regular feedback on how successfully they met this goal. Drivers in the control group were not asked to meet any goals and were not given any feedback on their driving. Following this feedback period, drivers in the experimental group were asked to maintain the 75 percent goal, but stopped getting feedback. Observations of their driving behavior, and that of control group drivers, continued during this six-month period.

How did the drivers do? The results of the study, summarized in Figure 7.10, show that goal setting in conjunction with feedback was highly successful. Specifically, it led

FIGURE 7.10

Feedback: An Essential Element of Goal Setting

Pizza delivery drivers came very close to reaching a goal—coming to a complete stop at intersections 75 percent of the time—during the period in which they were given regular feedback on goal performance. Several months later, however, after such feedback was no longer given, their performance returned to previous levels.

Source: Based on data reported by Ludwig & Geller, 1997; see Note 37.

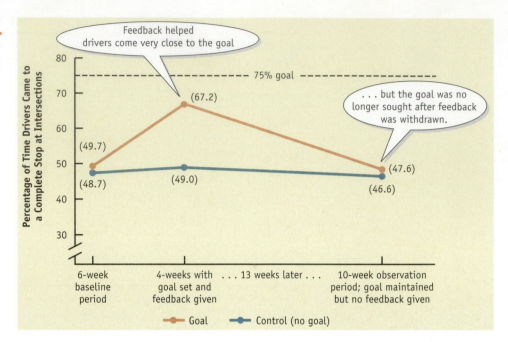

drivers to come very close to the assigned goal of coming to a complete stop at intersections three-quarters of the time. However, once that feedback was withdrawn, drivers returned to stopping only half the time—as often as they did before the study began (and as often as drivers in the control group, who received neither goals nor feedback). These findings clearly demonstrate the importance of accompanying specific, difficult goals with clear feedback about the extent to which those goals are being met. Not giving feedback on performance relative to goals forces workers to do their jobs blindly. Providing feedback, however, shines a spotlight on task performance that is essential to success.

When it comes to pizza delivery drivers, the ways of measuring performance are relatively straightforward. However, this is not usually the case among individuals who have more complex jobs with responsibilities over others, such as managers. Although it is more challenging to set, assess, and give feedback on goals for managerial performance, the same basic rules that we have been describing apply as well.

To illustrate this, let's consider how the goal-setting process is used among managers at Microsoft.[38] Although the company refers to goals as "commitments" (which makes sense, since one must commit to meeting a goal) and goal setting as "commitment setting," the process is the same. First, managers and their supervisors meet to determine specific goals to meet—ones in keeping with the company's objectives. Second, a specific plan is put in place for each of those commitments, making it clear precisely how it can be attained. Third, managers and their supervisors determine "accountabilities"—that is, specific ways of measuring each of the commitments, so that progress can be gauged. For a look at the exact form used for this purpose in the 2005 fiscal year, see Figure 7.11.

As we have shown, goal setting is a very effective tool managers can use to motivate people. Setting a specific, acceptably difficult goal and providing feedback about progress toward that goal greatly enhances job performance. Companies, both large and small, rely on the technique of goal setting, and its effectiveness has been established widely.

Motivating by Being Equitable

Our discussion this far suggests that when it comes to motivation, money isn't everything. Although money surely is important, it would be overly simplistic and misleading to say that people only want to earn as much money as possible. Even the highest-paid executives, sports figures, and celebrities sometimes complain about their pay despite their multimillion-dollar salaries.[39] Are they being greedy? Not necessarily. Often, the issue is not

Part2 FY05 Commitment Setting

Define your commitments for the next review period.
Commitments should be:
- Specific, Measurable, Achievable, Results-based, and Time-specific.
- Aligned with the commitments of your manager, organization, and *Microsoft Commitments*.
- Supported with *customer-centric actions and measures* aligned with divisional business plans.

People Managers must include at least one People Management Commitment.
For additional assistance visit: *Commitment Setting*.

Reviewer and employee, edit this section to create a prioritized list of commitments.

Commitments	Execution Plan	Accountabilities
Identify 5-7 areas of focus which are aligned with commitments of your manager, organization, and *Microsoft Commitments*.	Identify how you will achieve your commitments (key milestones and dependencies).	Define success measures and metrics to evaluate the realization of your commitments.

FIGURE 7.11

Goal Setting Among Managers at Microsoft

At Microsoft, the setting of goals is a regular part of the performance management process. Managers and their supervisors identify various goals, which they call "commitments," and for each, they jointly identify plans for attaining them along with specific ways of assessing the extent to which they are met. The form used to record this information (for the 2005 fiscal year) is shown here. In keeping with the principles of goal setting, notice the specific mention of the need for commitments to be specific and measurable.

Source: Shaw, 2004; see Note 38.

equity theory
The theory stating that people strive to maintain ratios of their own outcomes (rewards) to their own inputs (contributions) that are equal to the outcome/input ratios of others with whom they compare themselves.

outcomes
The rewards employees receive from their jobs, such as salary and recognition.

inputs
People's contributions to their jobs, such as their experience, qualifications, or the amount of time worked.

the actual amount of pay received, but rather, pay *equity*—that is, how one's pay compares to that of others doing similar work.

As an illustration, consider the National Basketball Association's Houston Rockets. In recent years, low morale on this team was linked to the fact that it had three highly paid superstars who made multimillion-dollar salaries while the majority of the team's players made the league's minimum salary (which, at the time, was $272,250).[40] Although you might not feel too sorry for someone who has to "rough it" on a quarter-million-dollar annual salary, many of these players felt underpaid because they thought that the stars who made eight or ten times more than them were not really eight or ten times better.

As we noted in Chapter 2, organizational scientists are keenly interested in explaining precisely what constitutes fairness on the job and how people respond when they believe they have been treated unfairly. One particular approach to organizational justice known as *equity theory* focuses on the motivational aspects of fairness, leading us to examine it closely here.

Equity Theory: Balancing Outcomes and Inputs

Equity theory proposes that people are motivated to maintain equitable (i.e., fair) relationships between themselves and others and to avoid those relationships that are inequitable.[41] In judging equity people compare themselves to others by focusing on two variables: **outcomes**—what we get out of our jobs (e.g., pay, fringe benefits, and prestige)—and **inputs**—the contributions made (e.g., time worked, effort exerted, units produced). It helps to think of these judgments in the form of ratios—that is, the outcomes received relative to the inputs contributed (e.g., $1,000 per week in exchange for working 40 hours). It is important to note that equity theory deals with outcomes and inputs as they are *perceived* by people, not necessarily objective standards. As you might imagine, well-intentioned people sometimes disagree about what constitutes equitable treatment.

According to equity theory people make equity judgments by comparing their own outcome/input ratios to the corresponding outcome/input ratios of others. This so-called "other" may be someone else in one's work group, another employee in the organization, an individual working in the same field, or even oneself at an earlier point in time—in short, almost anyone against whom we compare ourselves. As shown in Figure 7.12, these comparisons can result in any of three different states: *overpayment inequity, underpayment inequity,* or *equitable payment.*

Let's consider a simple example. Suppose Alice and Beth work together as paralegals in a law firm. Both women have equal amounts of experience, training, and education, and work equally long and hard at their jobs. In other words, their inputs are equivalent. But suppose Alice is paid an annual salary of $35,000 while Beth is paid only $25,000. In this case, Alice's ratio of outcomes/inputs is higher than Beth's, creating a state of **overpayment inequity** for Alice (since the ratio of her outcomes/inputs is higher), but **underpayment inequity** for Beth (since the ratio of her outcomes/inputs is lower). According to equity theory, Alice, realizing that she is paid more than an equally qualified person doing the same work, will feel *guilty* in response to her *overpayment.* By contrast, Beth, realizing that she is paid less than an equally qualified person for doing the same work, will feel *angry* in response to her *underpayment.* Guilt and anger are negative emotional states that people are motivated to change. As a result, they will seek to create a state of **equitable payment** in which their outcome/input ratios are equal, leading them to feel *satisfied.*

overpayment inequity

The condition, resulting in feelings of guilt, in which the ratio of one's outcomes-to-inputs is more than the corresponding ratio of another person with whom that person compares himself or herself.

underpayment inequity

The condition, resulting in feelings of anger, in which the ratio of one's outcomes-to-inputs is less than the corresponding ratio of another person with whom one compares himself or herself.

equitable payment

The state in which one person's outcome-input ratios is equivalent to that of another person with whom this individual compares himself or herself.

FIGURE 7.12

Equity Theory: An Overview

To judge equity or inequity, people compare the ratios of their own outcomes to inputs with the corresponding ratios of others (or of themselves at earlier points in time). The resulting states—overpayment inequity, underpayment inequity, and equitable payment—are summarized here, along with their associated emotional responses.

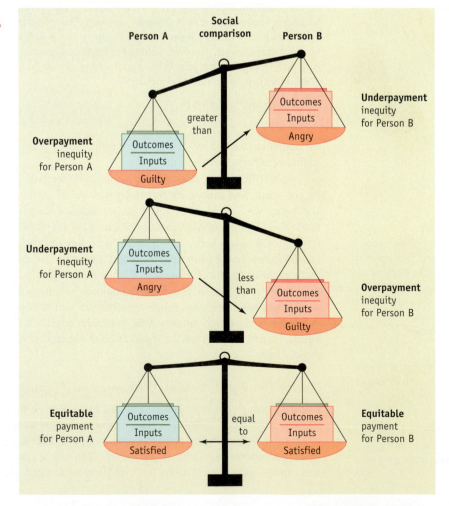

Creating Equity. How can inequitable states be turned into equitable ones? The answer lies in adjusting the balance of outcomes and/or inputs (for one logical—but highly unlikely—way to do this, see Figure 7.13). Among people who are underpaid, equity can be created by raising one's outcomes and/or lowering one's inputs. Likewise, those who are overpaid either may lower their outcomes or raise their inputs. Either action effectively would make the two outcome/input ratios equivalent. For example, the underpaid person, Beth, might lower her inputs, such as by slacking off, arriving at work late, leaving early, taking longer breaks, doing less work or lower quality work—or, in an extreme case, quit her job. She also may attempt to raise her outcomes, such as by asking for a raise, or even taking home company property, such as office supplies. By contrast, the overpaid person, Alice, may do the opposite—raise her inputs or lower her outcomes. For example, she might put forth much more effort, work longer hours, and try to make a greater contribution to the company. She also might lower her outcomes, such as by working while on a paid vacation, or not taking advantage of fringe benefits the company offers.

These are all specific *behavioral* reactions to inequitable conditions—that is, things people can *do* to turn inequitable states into equitable ones. However, people may be unwilling to do some of the things necessary to respond behaviorally to inequities. In particular, they may be reluctant to steal from their employers, or unwilling to restrict their productivity, for fear of getting caught "goofing off." In such cases, people may attempt to resolve inequity *cognitively,* by changing the way they think about the situation. As noted earlier, because equity theory deals with perceptions, inequitable states may be redressed by altering one's thinking about one's own, and others', outcomes and inputs. For example, underpaid people may rationalize that others' inputs really are higher than their own (e.g., "I suppose she really *is* more qualified than me"), thereby convincing themselves that their higher outcomes are justified. Similarly, overpaid people may convince themselves that they really *are* better and deserve their relatively higher pay. Thus, by changing the way they see things, people can come to perceive inequitable situations as equitable, effectively

FIGURE 7.13

Responding to Underpayment Inequity: An Unlikely Scenario

Nobody would be likely to ask what this speaker is asking—and no boss would be likely to comply with the request if someone actually did. According to equity theory, however, if the boss did in fact cut the other's pay, the underpaid individual may feel more fairly treated. Of course, the person whose pay is cut—Parkerson, in this case—then would feel underpaid. Not surprisingly, managers often seek to create equity in the workplace in other ways.

Source: ©The New Yorker Collection, 2001. Barbara Smaller from cartoonbank.com. All rights reserved.

B. Smaller

"O.K., if you can't see your way to giving me a pay raise, how about giving Parkerson a pay cut?"

relieving their feelings of guilt and anger, and transforming them into feelings of satisfaction. For a summary of behavioral and psychological reactions to inequity, see Table 7.2.

Responding to Inequities on the Job. From personal experience, how do you feel when you believe you have been unfairly paid? Equity theory says that you will find this highly distressing. Indeed, research has shown that the more people believe they are unfairly paid, the more negative symptoms of stress they display, such as health complaints and signs of depression and insomnia.[42]

There is a great deal of evidence to suggest that people are motivated to redress inequities at work, and that they respond much as equity theory suggests. Consider two examples from the world of sports. Research has shown that professional basketball players who are underpaid (i.e., ones who are paid less than others who perform as well or better) score fewer points than those who are equitably paid.[43] Similarly, among baseball players, those paid less than others who play comparably well tend to change teams or even leave the sport when they are unsuccessful at negotiating higher pay. Cast in terms of equity theory, the underpaid players may be said to have lowered their inputs. In 2004–2005, professional hockey players were so concerned about potential underpayment that they refused to play rather than concede to deals that would jeopardize their salaries (see Figure 7.14).[44]

We also know that underpaid workers attempt to raise their outcomes. For example, in an organization studied by one of the authors, workers at two manufacturing plants suffered an underpayment created by the introduction of a temporary pay cut of 15 percent.[45] During the 10-week period under which workers received lower pay company officials noticed that theft of company property increased dramatically, approximately 250 percent. However, in another factory in which comparable work was done by workers paid at their normal rates, the theft rate remained low. This pattern suggests that employees may have stolen property from their company in order to compensate for their reduced pay. Consistent with this possibility, it was found that when the normal rate of pay was reinstated in the two factories, the theft rate returned to its normal, low level. These findings suggest that companies that seek to save money by lowering pay may merely be encouraging their employees to find other ways of making up for what they believe is rightfully theirs.

In extreme cases, people respond to inequity by quitting their jobs.[46] This, of course, is a very costly thing to do. However, many who take this drastic step do so because they feel that their present situation is intolerable and hope that more equitable conditions can be found elsewhere. (Interestingly, many people perceive inequities in one of the most

TABLE 7.2 Possible Reactions to Inequity: A Summary

People can respond to overpayment and underpayment inequities in behavioral and/or psychological ways. A few of these are summarized here. These reactions help change the perceived inequities into a state of perceived equity.

Type of Inequity	Type of Reaction	
	Behavioral (What You Can Do Is . . .)	*Psychological* (What You Can Think Is . . .)
Overpayment inequity	Raise your inputs (e.g., work harder) or lower your outcomes (e.g., work through a paid vacation).	Convince yourself that your outcomes are deserved based on your inputs (e.g., rationalize that you work harder than others and so you deserve more pay).
Underpayment inequity	Lower your inputs (e.g., reduce effort) or raise your outcomes (e.g., get raise in pay).	Convince yourself that others inputs are really higher than your own (e.g., rationalize that the comparison worker is really more qualified and so deserves higher outcomes).

FIGURE 7.14

An Epic Struggle over Equity Eliminates the 2004–2005 National Hockey League Season

In the fall of 2004 and winter of 2005, professional hockey players and owners of National Hockey League teams failed to come to terms about fair compensation for players. Because neither side made satisfactory concessions, the entire season was delayed and eventually cancelled.

common jobs they do—housework. As chronicled in the *OB in a Diverse World* section, married men and women respond differently to perceived inequities with respect to this.)

Managerial Implications of Equity Theory

Equity theory has important implications for ways of motivating people.[47] We will highlight three key ones here.

Avoid Underpayment. Companies that attempt to save money by reducing employees' salaries may find that employees respond in many different ways so as to even the score. For example, they may steal, or they may shave a few minutes off their work days, or otherwise withhold production. In extreme cases, employees express their feelings of extreme underpayment inequity by going on strike. This has happened over many years. Consider the following examples.

- 1893: Workers who built first-class railroad sleeping cars for the Pullman Company went on strike after the company reduced the workforce by 40 percent and slashed the remaining workers' wages by 25 percent.[48]
- 1903–1904: Colorado miners went on strike, refusing to work at mines where wages were low and working hours were high.[49]
- 1997: Members of the Teamsters Union went on strike against UPS, claiming that the company was being unfair by hiring part-time workers who were paid less than full-time workers doing the same exact jobs.[50]
- 2002: Employees of the Saskatoon, Saskatchewan, Canada Public Library, who are predominantly female, went on strike, claiming that they are paid lower wages than comparably qualified city-paid workers, who are mostly men.[51]
- 2005: Employees of United Airlines agreed to go on strike should the company cut wages in an effort to save it from going out of business (see Figure 7.15, p. 269).[52]

Over the past few years, a particularly unsettling form of underpayment known as **two-tier wage structures** has been introduced in many workplaces. These are payment systems in which newer employees are paid less than those who were hired earlier to do the same work. Many of the major airlines adopted two-tier wage structures in the 1980s, much to the chagrin of those involved, particularly those in the lower tier.[53] When such a plan was instituted at the Giant Food supermarket chain, two-thirds of the lower-tier employees quit their jobs in the first three months. "It stinks," said one clerk at one Giant Food store in Los Angeles. "They're paying us lower wages for the same work."[54] Not surprisingly, proposals to introduce two-tier wage systems have met with considerable resistance among employees (often taking the form of strikes) and, when applicable, the unions representing

two-tier wage structures
Payment systems in which newer employees are paid less than employees hired at earlier times to do the same work.

OB In a Diverse World

Inequity in Housework: Comparing Married Women and Men

 Suppose you're working with a partner on an important job on which there's a recurring injustice with respect to the division of labor: That other individual does far less than his or her fair share of the work but reaps the same benefits as you. From the perspective of equity theory, this is clearly inequitable. You are underpaid and that other person is overpaid. Interestingly, this exact situation occurs regularly with respect to one of the most important jobs people perform—housework—and among the most important partners we have—our spouse. In this case, although the outcome is not money, but rather, living in a healthy and well-organized environment, the possibility that our partner's contributions to this end may be inequitable is a considerable source of conflict.

Despite the trend toward equality of the sexes, it remains the case in most households that wives do more of the housework than their husbands, even in dual-wage-earner households. Not surprisingly, this often is a source of dissatisfaction in many marriages.[55] Importantly, a recent study has found that the long-term effects of this particular source of inequity pose a serious threat to the marriage itself.[56] In this research, a large sample of married men and women from dual-wage-earner families across the United States were polled at two times eight years apart. Participants were asked to indicate the proportion of routine household tasks (e.g., house cleaning, laundry) they did and the extent to which they believed this constituted a fair division of labor as opposed to being too much or too little. The findings were dramatic. Women who perceived that they did more than their fair share of the housework were more than twice as likely to be divorced from their spouses eight years later than those who perceived the division of labor to be fair. Among men, however, no such differences were found.

That women divorce husbands with whom they have an inequitable division of labor follows from equity theory and research showing that people often resign jobs on which they feel underpaid.[57] The fact that men did not respond this way, however, reveals that husbands and wives have different thresholds as to what constitutes an equitable share of housework. Compared to men, women did a far greater proportion of the housework before believing it was too much. This is in keeping with traditional sex roles, according to which women do more housework than men. In the case of dual-earner households, however, such arrangements are impractical and generally give way to more egalitarian ones. When such expectations are violated, as often occurs because many men resent doing traditional "women's work," women experience considerable stress because they are completing most of the housework while also working outside the home. Because this puts such women in a highly stressful situation (see Chapter 5), it therefore is not surprising that they were likely to seek relief by ending their marriages.

This research is noteworthy because of the message it sends about gender equality (or lack thereof) in what is surely among the most universal of all jobs, housework. These findings provide some insight into why, even in today's allegedly enlightened era, many married women still face difficult choices between working inside and outside the home.

---

them. In recent years, however, labor unions faced with the prospect of massive job cuts by financially struggling employers reluctantly have conceded to such arrangements. As an example, although current auto workers at General Motors, Ford, and Chrysler plants average about $24/hour, under the two-tier wage system, new hires will start at $14/hour, eventually rising to only $18.50.[58]

This problem has been particularly severe among the growing legions of contingent, part-time, or permanent-temporary workers who have been staffing offices and factories in recent years (see Chapter 1). For example, at a Volkswagen manufacturing plant in Germany, new, temporary employees are paid 10 percent less than full-time employees doing the same work.[59] Because these individuals also receive fewer fringe benefits than their full-time counterparts performing the same work, they tend to feel underpaid. It is with this in mind that some organizations have taken to putting contingent workers on different shifts or having them work in different locations than full-time, permanent employees so as to keep them from talking to each other and possibly making the inequities salient.[60] This practice—which amounts to attempting to hide an inequitable pay structure—cannot be condoned on ethical grounds. Moreover, making people feel underpaid is simply an unwise and ineffective managerial practice.

FIGURE 7.15

Underpayment Inequity in "the Friendly Skies"

In recent years, pilots at major airlines, such as United Airlines, have agreed to pay cuts of 30% or more in an effort to save their companies from bankruptcy and retain their jobs. Flight attendants, mechanics, and other airline workers also have taken large concessions at several major air carriers. Hopefully, the underpayment inequity they are bound to suffer will not affect their job performance adversely.

Avoid Overpayment. You may think that because overpaid employees work hard to deserve their pay, it would be a useful motivational technique to pay people more than they merit. However, there are two key reasons why this would be problematic.[61]

- Any increases in performance in response to overpayment inequity are only temporary. As time goes on, people begin to believe that they actually deserve the higher pay they're getting and drop their work level down to normal.
- When you overpay one employee, you are underpaying all the others. When the majority of the employees feel underpaid, they will lower their performance, resulting in a net *decrease* in productivity—and widespread dissatisfaction.

With these concerns in mind, the conclusion is clear: *Managers should strive to pay all employees equitably.*

Be Open and Honest with Employees. We realize, of course, that this may be easier said than done. Part of the difficulty resides in the fact that feelings of equity and inequity are based on perceptions, and these aren't always easy to control. To help, it is useful to be open and honest about outcomes and inputs (this is in keeping with our discussion of interactional justice in Chapter 2). People tend to overestimate how much their superiors are paid and therefore tend to feel that their own pay is not as high as it should be.[62] However, if information about pay is shared, inequitable feelings are less likely to materialize. With this in mind, openness and honesty about pay is critical because it helps employees understand the basis for their pay. This, in turn, leads them to trust their company, motivating them to put forth the effort required to excel.[63]

expectancy theory
The theory that asserts that motivation is based on people's beliefs about the probability that effort will lead to performance *(expectancy),* multiplied by the probability that performance will lead to reward *(instrumentality),* multiplied by the perceived value of the reward *(valence).*

Motivating by Altering Expectations

Instead of focusing on individual needs, traits and skills, goals, or social comparisons, another popular approach to motivation, **expectancy theory**, takes a broader approach. It looks at the role of motivation in the overall work environment. The basic idea behind expectancy theory is that people are motivated to work when they expect that they will be able to achieve the things they want from their jobs. Expectancy theory characterizes people as rational beings who think about what they have to do to be rewarded and how much the reward means to them before they perform their jobs. But, as we will see, the theory doesn't only focus on what people think. It also recognizes that these thoughts combine with other aspects of the organizational environment to influence job performance.

Basic Elements of Expectancy Theory

Although several different versions of expectancy theory have been proposed, all conceive of motivation as the result of three different types of beliefs that people have.[64] These are: **expectancy**—the belief that one's effort will result in performance; **instrumentality**—the belief that one's performance will be rewarded; and **valence**—the perceived value of the rewards to the recipient (see Figure 7.16).

Expectancy. Sometimes people believe that putting forth a great deal of effort means that they will get a lot accomplished. However, in other cases, people do not expect that their efforts will have much effect on how well they do. For example, an employee operating a faulty piece of equipment may have a very low *expectancy* that his or her efforts will lead to high levels of performance. Naturally, someone working under such conditions probably would not continue to exert much effort.

Instrumentality. Even if an employee works hard and performs at a high level, motivation may falter if that performance is not suitably rewarded—that is, if the performance is not perceived as *instrumental* in bringing about rewards. So, for example, a worker who is extremely productive may be poorly motivated to perform if the pay system doesn't recognize his or her success. Often, this occurs among people who already have reached the top pay grades in their companies. Even if they have become more successful, because they cannot be paid at higher levels in recognition of this, their motivation suffers.

Valence. Finally, even if employees believe that hard work will lead to good performance *and* that they will be rewarded commensurate with their performance, they still may be poorly motivated if those so-called rewards don't mean that much to them—that is, if they have low *valence*. In other words, someone who doesn't care about the rewards offered by the organization is not motivated to attain them. For example, a reward of $100 would be

expectancy
The belief that one's efforts will positively influence one's performance.

instrumentality
An individual's beliefs regarding the likelihood of being rewarded in accord with his or her own level of performance.

valence
The value a person places on the rewards he or she expects to receive from an organization.

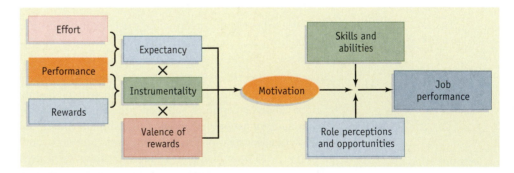

FIGURE 7.16

Expectancy Theory: An Overview

According to expectancy theory, motivation is the result of three types of beliefs. These are: expectancy (the belief that one's effort will influence performance), instrumentality (the belief that one will be rewarded for one's performance), and valence (the perceived value of the rewards expected). The theory also recognizes that motivation is only one of several factors responsible for job performance.

unlikely to motivate a multimillionaire like Donald Trump, although it may be a very desirable reward for someone of more modest means. Only those rewards that have a high positive valence to their recipients will motivate behavior.

With this in mind, many of today's companies are going out of their way to motivate employees by giving them the kinds of job perks they most desire. One particularly interesting example may be seen at Toyota. As a benefit to its U.S. employees, among whom the cost of medicine is a major concern, the company pays for the entire cost of the generic equivalent of prescription medicines, allowing employees to get them for free. Both online and onsite "Toyota Family Pharmacies" are available to employees, contributing greatly to their motivation.[65]

Combining All Three Types of Beliefs. Expectancy theory claims that motivation is a multiplicative function of all three components. This means that higher levels of motivation will result when expectancy, instrumentality, and valence are all high than when they are all low. The multiplicative assumption of the theory also implies that if any one of these three components is zero, the overall level of motivation will be zero. So, for example, even if an employee believes that her effort will result in performance, which will result in reward, motivation will be zero if the valance of the reward she expects to receive is zero.

Other Determinants of Job Performance. Figure 7.16 also highlights a point we made in our opening remarks about motivation—that motivation is not equivalent to job performance. Specifically, expectancy theory recognizes that motivation is one of several important determinants of job performance.

For example, the theory assumes that *skills and abilities* also contribute to a person's job performance. It's no secret that some people are better suited to performing their jobs than others by virtue of their unique characteristics and special skills and abilities. For example, a tall, strong, well-coordinated person is likely to make a better professional basketball player than a very short, weak, uncoordinated one—even if the shorter person is highly motivated to succeed.

Expectancy theory also recognizes that job performance will be influenced by people's *role perceptions*—in other words, what they believe is expected of them on the job. To the extent that there are disagreements about what one's job duties are, performance may suffer. For example, an assistant manager who believes her primary job duty is to train new employees may find that her performance is downgraded by a supervisor who believes she should be spending more time doing routine paperwork instead. In this case, the person's performance wouldn't suffer as a result of any deficit in motivation, but simply because of misunderstandings regarding what the job entails.

Finally, expectancy theory also recognizes the role of *opportunities to perform* one's job. Even the best employees may perform at low levels if their opportunities are limited. For example, a highly motivated salesperson may perform poorly if opportunities are restricted (such as if the territory is having a financial downturn, or if the available inventory is limited).

It is important to recognize that expectancy theory views motivation as just one of several determinants of job performance. Motivation, combined with a person's skills and abilities, role perceptions, and opportunities, influences job performance.

Expectancy theory has generated a great deal of research and has been successfully applied to understanding behavior in many different organizational settings.[66] Although the theory has received only mixed support about some of its specific aspects (e.g., the multiplicative assumption), it remains one of the dominant approaches to the study of motivation in organizations. Probably the primary reason for expectancy theory's popularity is the many useful suggestions it makes for practicing managers. We will now describe some of the most essential applications of expectancy theory, giving examples from organizations in which they have been implemented.

Putting Expectancy Theory to Work: Key Managerial Implications

Expectancy theory is a very practical approach to motivation. It identifies several important things that can be done to motivate employees.

1. Clarify People's Expectancies That Their Effort Will Lead to Performance.
Motivation may be enhanced by training employees to do their jobs more efficiently, thereby achieving higher levels of performance. It also may be possible to enhance effort-performance expectancies by following employees' suggestions about ways to change their jobs. To the extent that employees are aware of problems in their jobs that interfere with their performance, attempting to alleviate these problems may help them perform more effectively. In essence, what we are saying is: *Make the desired performance attainable.* Good supervisors don't only make it clear to people what is expected of them, but they also help them attain that level of performance.

2. Administer Rewards That Are Positively Valent to Employees. In other words, the carrot at the end of the stick must be tasty for it to have potential as a motivator. These days, with a highly diverse workforce, it would be misleading to assume that all employees care about having the same rewards. Some might recognize the incentive value of a pay raise, whereas others might prefer additional vacation days, improved insurance benefits, day care, or elder-care facilities. With this in mind, many companies have introduced **cafeteria-style benefit plans**—incentive systems allowing employees to select their fringe benefits from a menu of available alternatives.

> **cafeteria-style benefit plans**
> Incentive systems in which employee have an opportunity to select the fringe benefits they want from a menu of available alternatives.

Given that fringe benefits represent almost 40 percent of payroll costs, more and more companies are recognizing the value of administering them flexibly. In fact, a recent survey found that such cafeteria-style benefit plans are in place in as many as half of all large companies (those employing over 5,000) and 22 percent of smaller companies (those with under 1,000 employees). For example, the financial services company Primerica (a member of Citigroup) has had a flexible benefit plan in use since 1978.[67] Southwest Airlines has a modified program in place in which employees get to select their medical benefits cafeteria-style. Many of today's companies are doing highly creative things to ensure that their employees can achieve rewards that have value to them.[68] For a summary of some of these practices, see Table 7.3.

3. Clearly Link Valued Rewards and Performance. Unfortunately, not all incentive plans are as effective as they should be when it comes to rewarding desired performance. Doing so, however, is key to success. As an example, consider the pay plan IBM uses for its sales representatives. Previously, most of the pay these reps received was based on flat salary; their compensation was not linked to how well they did. Today, however, their pay is carefully tied to two factors that are essential to the company's success—profitability and customer satisfaction. So, instead of receiving commissions on the amount of the sale, as so many salespeople do, 60 percent of IBMers' commissions are tied to the company's profit on that sale. As a result, the more the company makes, the more the reps make. And, to make sure that the reps don't push only high-profit items that customers might not need, the remaining 40 percent of their commissions are based on customer satisfaction (assessed in regular surveys). Since introducing this plan in late 1993, IBM has been effective in reversing its unprofitable trend. Although there are certainly many factors responsible for this turnaround, experts are confident that this practice of clearly linking desired performance to individual rewards is a key factor.

Despite IBM's success in this arena, many organizations have a long way to go in raising their employees' instrumentality beliefs.[69] That is, managers need to do a better job of enhancing their subordinates' beliefs about instrumentality by specifying exactly what job behaviors will lead to what rewards. How can they do this? To the extent that it is possible for employees to be paid in ways directly linked to their performance—such as through piece-rate incentive systems, sales commission plans, or bonuses—expectancy theory specifies that it would be effective to do so. This is the idea behind **pay-for-performance** plans—pay plans that systematically reward employees in proportion to how well they have done their jobs.[70] Although the ideas behind such plans are very good, they too often suffer problems of implementation. In fact, 83 percent of executives polled in a recent survey reported that their company's pay-for-performance plans were generally unsuccessful.[71]

> **pay-for-performance**
> A payment system in which employees are paid differentially, based on the quantity and quality of their performance. Pay-for-performance plans strengthen *instrumentality* beliefs.

The good news is that there's no inherent reason for the rocky success of pay-for-performance plans. For them to be successful, it's exceptionally useful for them to be

TABLE 7.3 Going "Beyond the Fringe" in Benefits: Especially Creative Reward Practices

Traditionally, someone who gets a new job receives not only a salary, but a standard set of fringe benefits, such as health insurance, life insurance, a paid vacation, and a retirement plan. These days, however, these basic benefits are not enough to bring job prospects through the door. The incentives that motivate today's employees are far more varied—and, in many cases, truly lavish. Here are some particularly interesting examples.

Company	Business and Primary Location	Benefit
Staples	Office supply company; Framingham, Massachusetts	Employees can leave their children at a state-of-the-art child-care center near the office, making it possible for them to concentrate on their jobs without having to worry about their children.
Sun Microsystems	Computer products and services company; Santa Clara, California	In-house concierge service provides varied conveniences for employees, such as picking up and delivering dry cleaning, party planning, and purchasing gifts.
Quad Graphics	Printing company; Pewaukee, Wisconsin	Employees can live in modern and well-furnished rental apartments near company headquarters.
Marquardt & Roche	Marketing firm; Stamford, Connecticut	To satisfy diverse preferences, employees are permitted to take 11 of 24 different holidays throughout the year.
The Weather Channel	Cable television weather service; Atlanta, Georgia	Pet insurance is offered to employees to help defray the potentially costly expenses of caring for ill pets.
Citibank	Banking services; New York, New York	Regular financial education seminars and special auto loan programs help employees as part of the company's "Citibank at Work" program.

Source: Levering & Moskowitz, 2005; see Note 68.

carried out across many levels of the organization. An example of this may be seen in Continental Airlines, one of the few airlines today that is not experiencing serious financial problems. This was not always the case, however. In 1994, Continental was ranked dead last with respect to on-time performance—a problem that was costing the company $6 million per month.[72] To combat this, management started paying bonuses to employees to reward on-time performance: $100 per employee for a top ranking, and $65 per employee for a number two or three ranking. Since initiating this plan, Continental consistently has placed among the industry's on-time leaders, earning employees upwards of $1,000 each year.

It is very important to note that the rewards involved need not be monetary in nature; even symbolic and verbal forms of recognition for a job well done can be very effective. For example, a recent study found that companies that verbally acknowledged their employees' good attendance records experienced dramatic improvements in attendance.[73] With this in mind, many companies help recognize their employees' organizational contributions by acknowledging them on the pages of their corporate newsletter.

As a case in point, consider CalPERS, the Sacramento-based firm that manages the pension and health benefits for 1.4 million Californians. In recent years, this company has been so actively involved in acknowledging the hard work of its employees that it has won a Best Practice Award from the National Association for Employee Recognition. The employee recognition through printed and online newsletters, among other methods, has been so extensive and has generated so much goodwill that the company has been able to take on more work without having to hire additional employees.[74] Synovus, the Georgia-based bank, is so effective at acknowledging its employees that *Fortune* magazine has referred to it as having a "pat-on-the-back culture."[75] These examples illustrate the important point that recognizing employees need not be lavish or expensive. It can involve

incentive stock option (ISO) plans
Corporate programs in which a company grants an employee the opportunity to purchase its stock at some future time at a specified price.

nothing more than a heartfelt "thank you." With this in mind, some companies have used nonmonetary recognition in very creative ways. For some examples, see Table 7.4.[76]

Some companies are so serious about paying employees for their performance that they are giving their employees a small piece of the company in exchange for their contributions—a practice that is sure to link performance with rewards in their minds.[77] One popular form this has taken in many high-tech startups is known as **incentive stock option (ISO) plans.** In such plans, a company grants an employee the opportunity to purchase its stock at some future time at a specified price. So, over time, if the value of the company's stock increases, the employee can "exercise the option" by selling the stock at a profit, and with certain income tax advantages.[78] Although the exact rules to incentive stock options are complex, the underlying rationale is straightforward: They give employees a stake in the success of the company. So, what's good for the company also is good for the employee. In expectancy theory terms, ISOs may be beneficial insofar as they enhance instrumentality beliefs by rewarding employees when their company does well. And this motivates them to put forth the effort to succeed. For example, at Merck & Co., the large pharmaceutical firm, the availability of ISOs have proven to be a very successful motivational device.[79] They encourage employees to help make the company successful, and as the company becomes more successful, the more its stock value rises, making employees wealthier.

Motivating by Structuring Jobs to Make Them Interesting

job design
An approach to motivation suggesting that jobs can be created so as to enhance people's interest in doing them. See *job enlargement, job enrichment, and the job characteristics model.*

The final approach to motivation we will consider is the broadest in scope because it is directed at improving the essential nature of the work performed. The idea behind **job design** is that motivation can be enhanced by making jobs more appealing to people. As you may recall from Chapter 1, Frederick W. Taylor's principle of *scientific management* attempted to stimulate performance by designing jobs in the most efficient fashion. However, treating people like machines often meant having them engage in repetitive movements, which they found highly routine and monotonous. Not surprisingly, people became bored with such jobs and frequently quit.[80] Fortunately, today's organizational scientists have found several ways of designing jobs that can not only be performed very efficiently, but are also highly pleasant and enjoyable.

TABLE 7.4 Low-Cost Ways of Recognizing Employees

A lack of money doesn't have to be a barrier to recognizing employees effectively. Management consultant Bob Nelson, author of *1001 Ways to Reward Employees,* has compiled a list of inexpensive practices that have been very effective at various companies. Here are several that you may wish to consider using yourself.

- Whenever something positive happens, write it on a piece of paper and put it in a "smile box." On a weekly basis, draw one entry at random from the box, read it out loud, and treat the winner to a small gift card at a local store or coffee shop.

- Put a little gold star on the computer or name badge of an employee who has made a particularly important contribution. (This worked when your elementary school teacher did it!)

- Each month, have the employees give a "you da. . ." award (e.g., "you da secretary" or "you da driver") to the one person in their work group they select as having done something particularly well. The award itself can be printed on a piece of paper and prepared at the computer.

- Regularly solicit feedback from customers or suppliers. On the bulletin board, post those comments that are most glowing.

- Communicate your appreciation for employees by giving them personally written thank-you notes, sending them e-cards, or taking them to lunch at their favorite restaurant.

- On someone's birthday, instead of a cake, have everyone sign a "happy birthday" balloon and put it prominently in the person's workspace.

Source: Reprinted by permission of Bob Nelson, Ph.D., author of *1001 Ways to Reward Employees,* Second Edition. See also Note 76.

Job Enlargement and Job Enrichment

job enlargement
The practice of expanding the content of a job to include more variety and a greater number of tasks at the same level.

Imagine that you have a highly routine job, such as tightening the lugs on the left rear wheel of a car as it rolls down the assembly line. Naturally, such a highly repetitive task would be monotonous and not very pleasant. One of the first modern approaches to redesigning jobs suggested that such consequences could be minimized by having people perform an increased number of different tasks all at the same level. This approach is known as **job enlargement**. To enlarge the jobs in our example, workers could be required to tighten the lugs on all four wheels. As a result of such an action, employees have no more responsibility nor use any greater skills, but perform a wider variety of different tasks at the same level. Adding tasks in this fashion is said to increase the *horizontal job loading* of the position.

A few years ago, American Greetings Corp., Cleveland, Ohio's greeting card and licensing concern, enlarged some 400 jobs in its creative division.[81] Now, rather than always working exclusively on Christmas cards, for example, employees are able to move back and forth between different teams, such as those working on birthday ribbons, humorous mugs, and Valentine's Day gift bags. Employees at American Greetings reportedly enjoy the variety, as do those at RJR Nabisco, Corning, and Eastman Kodak, other companies that have recently allowed employees to make such lateral moves.

Although most reports of the effectiveness of job enlargement have been anecdotal, a few carefully conducted empirical studies also have examined their impact. For example, one group of researchers studied the effects of a job enlargement program instituted at a large financial services company.[82] The unenlarged jobs had different employees perform separate paperwork tasks such as preparing, sorting, coding, and keypunching various forms. By contrast, in the enlarged jobs these various functions were combined into larger jobs performed by the same individuals. Although it was more difficult and expensive to train people to perform the enlarged jobs than the separate jobs, employees expressed greater job satisfaction and less boredom. And, because one person followed the whole job all the way through from beginning to end, greater opportunities to correct errors existed. Not surprisingly, customers were satisfied with the result.

Unfortunately, in a follow-up investigation of the same company conducted two years later, it was found that not all the beneficial effects continued.[83] Notably, employee satisfaction leveled off and the rate of errors went up, suggesting that as employees got used to their enlarged jobs they found them less interesting, paying less attention to the details. Hence, although job enlargement may help improve job performance, its effects may be short-lived.

job enrichment
The practice of giving employees a high degree of control over their work, from planning and organization, through implementing the jobs and evaluating the results.

A more effective approach, **job enrichment**, gives employees not only more jobs to do, but more tasks to perform at a higher level of skill and responsibility (see Figure 7.17). Specifically, job enrichment gives employees the opportunity to take greater control over how to do their jobs. Because people performing enriched jobs have increased opportunities to work at higher levels, the job enrichment process is said to increase a job's *vertical job loading*. The idea underlying job enrichment is that by making the jobs more interesting to people, they will be more highly motivated to perform them. Generally speaking, this is the case. In fact, an interesting by-product of enriching jobs recently has been found—people performing enriched jobs tend to procrastinate (i.e., put off things they are supposed to do) less than those who perform more standard jobs.[84]

Although evidence suggests that job enrichment programs also have been successful at other organizations, several factors limit their popularity.[85] Most obvious is the *difficulty of implementation*. To redesign existing facilities so that jobs can be enriched is often prohibitively expensive. Besides, the technology needed to perform certain jobs makes it impractical for them to be redesigned. Another impediment is the *lack of employee acceptance*. Although many relish it, some people do *not* desire the additional responsibility associated with performing enriched jobs. In particular, individuals low in achievement motivation are especially frustrated with enriched jobs.[86] Similarly, people may get used to having to do their jobs in certain ways, and don't like having to change. In fact, when a group of American auto workers was sent to Sweden to work in a Saab engine assembly plant where jobs were highly enriched, five out of six indicated that they preferred their

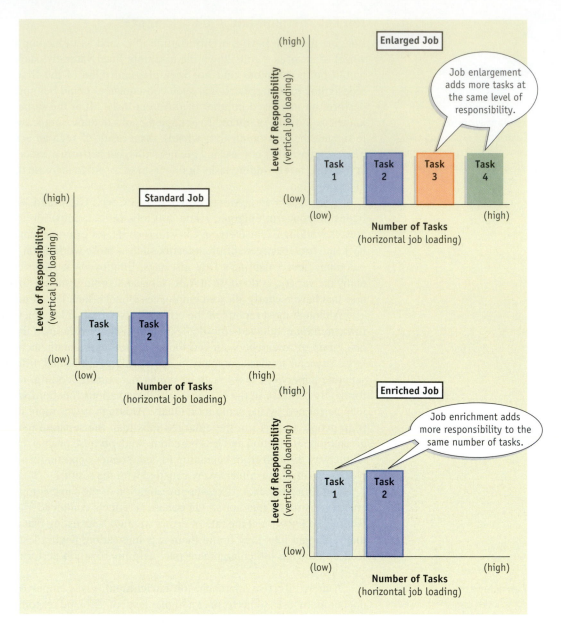

FIGURE 7.17

Job Enlargement and Job Enrichment: A Comparison

Redesigning jobs by increasing the number of tasks performed at the same level (horizontal job loading) is referred to as job enlargement. Redesigning jobs by increasing the employees' level of responsibility and control (vertical job loading) is referred to as job enrichment.

job characteristics model
An approach to job enrichment which specifies that five core job dimensions (skill variety, task identity, task significance, autonomy, and job feedback) produce critical psychological states that lead to beneficial outcomes for individuals (e.g., high job satisfaction) and the organization (e.g., reduced turnover).

traditional assembly line jobs.[87] As one union leader put it, "If you want to enrich the job, enrich the paycheck."[88] Clearly, enriched jobs are not for everyone.

The Job Characteristics Model

Thus far, we have failed to specify precisely *how* to enrich a job. *What* elements of a job need to be enriched for it to be effective? An attempt to expand the idea of job enrichment, known as the *job characteristics model*, provides an answer to this important question. The **job characteristics model** assumes that jobs can be designed so as to help people get enjoyment out of their jobs and care about the work they do. It identifies how jobs can be designed to help people feel that they are doing meaningful and valuable work. In particular, the model specifies that enriching certain elements of jobs alters people's psychological states in a manner that enhances their work effectiveness.[89] Specifically, it identifies five *core job dimensions* that help create three *critical psychological states,* leading, in turn, to several beneficial *personal and work outcomes* (see Figure 7.18).

Components of the Model. The five critical job dimensions are *skill variety, task identity, task significance, autonomy,* and *feedback.* Let's take a closer look at these.

- *Skill variety* refers to the extent to which a job requires doing different activities using several of the employee's skills and talents. For example, an office manager with high skill variety may have to perform many different tasks (e.g., do word processing, answer the telephone, greet visitors, and file records).
- *Task identity* refers to the extent to which a job requires completing a whole piece of work from beginning to end. For example, tailors will have high task identity if they do everything related to making a whole suit (e.g., measuring the client, selecting the fabric, cutting and sewing it, and altering it to fit).
- *Task significance* refers to the degree of impact the job is believed to have on others. For example, medical researchers working on a cure for a deadly disease probably recognize the importance of their work to the world at large. Even more modest contributions to the company can be recognized as being significant to the extent that employees understand the role of their jobs in the overall mission of the organization.
- *Autonomy* refers to the extent to which employees have the freedom and discretion to plan, schedule, and carry out their jobs as desired. For example, a furniture repair person may act highly autonomously by freely scheduling his or her day's work and

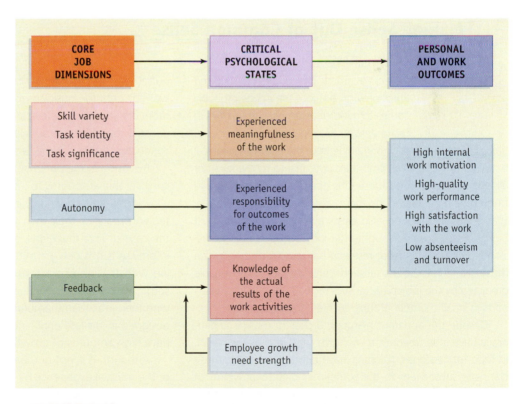

FIGURE 7.18

The Job Characteristic Model: Basic Components

The job characteristics model stipulates that certain core job dimensions lead to certain critical psychological states, which in turn, lead to several beneficial personal and work outcomes. The model also recognizes that these relationships are strongest among individuals with high levels of growth need strength.

by freely deciding how to tackle each repair job confronted. (For an example of the motivational problems created by the lack of autonomy in one particular job, see the *OB: Making Sense Out of Common Sense* section below.)

■ *Feedback* refers to the extent to which the job allows people to have information about the effectiveness of their performance. For example, telemarketing representatives regularly receive information about how many calls they make per day and the number and values of the sales made.

The model specifies that these various job dimensions have important effects on various critical psychological states. For example, skill variety, task identity, and task significance jointly contribute to a task's *experienced meaningfulness*. A task is considered to be meaningful to the extent that it is experienced as being highly important, valuable, and worthwhile. Jobs that provide a great deal of autonomy are said to make people feel *personally responsible and accountable for their work*. When they are free to decide what to do and how to do it, they feel more responsible for the results, whether good or bad. Finally, effective feedback is said to give employees *knowledge of the results of their work*. When a job is designed to provide people with information about the effects of their actions, they are better able to develop an understanding of how effectively they have performed—and such knowledge improves their effectiveness.

The job characteristics model specifies that the three critical psychological states affect various personal and work outcomes—namely: people's feelings of motivation, the quality of work performed, satisfaction with work, absenteeism, and turnover. The higher the experienced meaningfulness of work, responsibility for the work performed, and knowledge of results, the more positive the personal and work benefits will be. When they

OB Making Sense Out of Common Sense

Autonomy in the Orchestra Strikes a Sour Note

 When you think of people with limited autonomy on the job, the image probably comes to mind of assembly line workers in factories who are required to work in routinized fashion. It's easy to imagine how the highly mechanical nature of such jobs can limit their potential to motivate. After all, the people who do these jobs operate like machines and frequently are replaced by them. You probably don't realize that a similar situation also exists among one of the most highly prestigious and sought-after jobs—musicians in professional orchestras. Indeed, research has shown that orchestra musicians tend to be less satisfied with their jobs (a key variable predicted by the job characteristics model) than their counterparts in small chamber groups, such as string quartets.[90]

Despite the apparent glamour, orchestra musicians generally have little freedom to perform their jobs as they wish. In fact, for centuries, tradition has held that orchestra musicians are subservient to the sometimes dictatorial whims of the maestros who conduct them. The musicians play their instruments, but following the explicit hierarchy of the symphony orchestra, the conductor very carefully regulates precisely *how* they play them, demanding perfection down to the slightest inflection of the final note. There is no doubt who's in charge and who makes all the decisions. Believe it or

not, it was only in the past few years that orchestra unions won the right for musicians to take regularly scheduled bathroom breaks during rehearsal sessions. Until then, it was not unusual for orchestra musicians to face the wrath of angry conductors if they felt the need to heed nature's call.

By contrast, members of small musical ensembles enjoy considerable autonomy to interpret musical pieces, thereby allowing them to be highly involved in their performances, tapping more of their own talents. This is especially so in the case of jazz musicians, among whom the freedom to improvise is not only permitted, but encouraged. In keeping with the job characteristics model, it therefore is not surprising that such individuals are generally more satisfied with their jobs than members of orchestras, whose work is designed in far less enriching fashion (assuming that they have high amounts of growth need strength).

Although it is not our intention to rob you of the glory of the musical experience by explaining this to you, it is fascinating to know that the field of OB has much to say about the personal experiences of these individuals who are entertaining you. After all, as unique as their positions may be, musicians—if they are fortunate enough to be working—still hold jobs, and as such, their behavior stands to be informed by the field of OB.

perform jobs that incorporate high levels of the five core job dimensions, people should feel highly motivated, perform high-quality work, be highly satisfied with their jobs, be absent infrequently, and be unlikely to resign from their jobs.

Does the Job Characteristics Model Apply to Everyone? We should also note that the model is theorized to be especially effective in describing the behavior of individuals who are high in **growth need strength**—that is, people who have a high need for personal growth and development. People not particularly interested in improving themselves on the job are not expected to experience the theorized psychological reactions to the core job dimensions, nor consequently, to enjoy the beneficial personal and work outcomes predicted by the model.[91] By introducing this variable, the job characteristics model recognizes the important limitation of job enrichment noted earlier—not everyone wants and benefits from enriched jobs.

Putting It All Together. Based on the proposed relationship between the core job dimensions and their associated psychological reactions, the model claims that job motivation will be highest when the jobs performed rate high on the various dimensions. To assess this, a questionnaire known as the Job Diagnostic Survey (JDS) has been developed to measure the degree to which various job characteristics are present in a particular job.[92] Based on responses to the JDS, we can make predictions about the degree to which a job motivates people who perform it. This is done by using an index known as the **motivating potential score (MPS),** computed as follows:

$$MPS = \frac{Skill\ variety + Task\ identity + Task\ significance}{3} \times Autonomy \times Feedback$$

The MPS is a summary index of a job's potential for motivating people. The higher the score for a given job, the greater the likelihood of experiencing the personal and work outcomes specified by the model. Knowing a job's MPS helps one identify jobs that might benefit by being redesigned.

Evidence for the Model. The job characteristics model has been the focus of many empirical tests, most of which are supportive of many aspects of the model.[93] One study conducted among a group of South African clerical workers found particularly strong support.[94] The jobs of employees in some of the offices in this company were enriched in accordance with techniques specified by the job characteristics model. Specifically, employees performing the enriched jobs were given opportunities to choose the kinds of tasks they perform (high skill variety), do the entire job (high task identity), receive instructions regarding how their job fit into the organization as a whole (high task significance), freely set their own schedules and inspect their own work (high autonomy), and keep records of their daily productivity (high feedback). Another group of employees, equivalent in all respects except that their jobs were not enriched, served as a control group.

After employees performed the newly designed jobs for six months, comparisons were made between them and their counterparts in the control group. With respect to most of the outcomes specified by the model, individuals performing redesigned jobs showed superior results. Specifically, they reported feeling more internally motivated and more satisfied with their jobs. There were also lower rates of absenteeism and turnover among employees performing the enriched jobs. The only outcome predicted by the model that was not found to differ was actual work performance; people performed equally well in enriched and unenriched jobs. Considering the many factors that are responsible for job performance (as discussed in connection with expectancy theory), this finding should not be too surprising.

Techniques for Designing Jobs That Motivate: Some Managerial Guidelines

The job characteristics model specifies several ways in which jobs can be designed to enhance their motivating potential.[95] In Table 7.5 we present these in the form of general principles.

growth need strength
The personality variable describing the extent to which people have a high need for personal growth and development on the job. The *job characteristics model* best describes people high in growth need strength.

motivating potential score (MPS)
A mathematical index describing the degree to which a job is designed so as to motivate people, as suggested by the *job characteristics model.* It is computed on the basis of a questionnaire known as the Job Diagnostic Survey (JDS). The lower the MPS, the more the job may stand to benefit from redesign.

TABLE 7.5 Enriching Jobs: Some Suggestions from the Job Characteristics Model

The job characteristics model specifies several ways jobs can be designed to incorporate the core job dimensions responsible for enhancing motivation and performance. A few are listed here.

Principles of Job Design	Core Job Dimensions Incorporated
1. Combine tasks, enabling workers to perform the entire job.	Skill variety Task identity
2. Establish client relationships, allowing providers of a service to meet the recipients.	Skill variety Autonomy Feedback
3. Load jobs vertically, allowing greater responsibility and control over work.	Autonomy
4. Open feedback channels, giving workers knowledge of the results of their work.	Feedback

Source: Based on information in Hackman, 1976; see Note 96.

1. Combine Tasks. Instead of having several workers each perform a separate part of a whole job, it would be better to have each person perform the entire job. Doing so helps provide greater skill variety and task identity. For example, Corning Glass Works in Medford, Massachusetts redesigned jobs so that people who assembled laboratory hot plates put together entire units instead of contributing a single part to the assembly process.[96]

2. Open Feedback Channels. Jobs should be designed to give employees as much feedback as possible. The more people know how well they're doing (be it from customers, supervisors, or coworkers), the better equipped they are to take appropriate corrective action (see Figure 7.19). (You may recall that we already noted the importance of feedback in the learning process in Chapter 3, and in conjunction with goal setting earlier in this chapter.) Sometimes, cues about job performance can be clearly identified as people perform their jobs (as we noted in conjunction with goal setting). In the best cases, open lines of communication between employees and managers are so strongly incorporated into the corporate culture—as has been reported to exist at Boise Cascade's paper products group—that feedback flows without hesitation.[97]

3. Establish Client Relationships. The job characteristics model suggests that jobs should be set up so that the person performing a service (such as an auto mechanic) comes into contact with the recipient of the service (such as the car owner). Jobs designed in this manner will not only help the employee by providing feedback, but also provide skill variety (e.g., talking to customers in addition to fixing cars), and enhance autonomy (by giving people the freedom to manage their own relationships with clients).

This suggestion has been implemented at Sea-Land Service, the large containerized ocean-shipping company.[98] Once this company's mechanics, clerks, and crane operators started meeting with customers, they became much more productive. Having faces to associate with the once-abstract jobs they did clearly helped them take the jobs more seriously.

4. Load Jobs Vertically. As we described earlier, loading a job vertically involves giving people greater responsibility for their jobs. Taking responsibility and control over performance away from managers and giving it to their subordinates increases the level of autonomy the jobs offer these lower-level employees. And, according to a recent poll, autonomy is among the most important things people look for in their jobs—even more important than high pay.[99] In view of this, a growing number of companies are yielding control and giving employees increasing freedom to do their jobs as they wish (within limits, at least).

Consider, for example, Childress Buick, a Phoenix, Arizona auto dealership. This company suffered serious customer dissatisfaction and employee retention problems before the owner, Rusty Childress, began encouraging his employees to use their own judgment and

Transportation Security Administration   **Comment Card**   **Port Columbus**

The United States Department of Homeland Security, Transportation Security Administration, at Port Columbus is pleased to serve you, and we seek to provide the best service and safety possible. To achieve our goal, your feedback is vital. Will you kindly tell us how we are doing?

1. Were you treated respectfully and courteously?
   Very respectfully   1.....2.....3.....4.....5   Not at all respectfully
2. Did you experience any delay during checked-baggage screening?
   No delay   1.....2.....3.....4.....5   Unreasonable delay
3. Did you experience any delay passing through the passenger security checkpoint?
   No delay   1.....2.....3.....4.....5   Unreasonable delay
4. Do you think your personal and checked-baggage screening was thorough?
   Very thorough   1.....2.....3.....4.....5   Not at all thorough
5. Have you any suggestions or comments about our service that might help us improve?

You may give this card to any TSA employee before your departure or place a postage stamp on it and drop it in the mail. Comments may also be made directly to the Consumer Response Center by phoning (555) 555-5555. Thank you for assisting us as we aim to provide you with the safety and service you expect.

Name: _____   Phone (   ) _____

Travel Date: _____   Airline _____   Flight No. _____

Concourse Used: (circle one)   **A – B – C**   Time of Day: (circle one)   **AM** (4a-012n) – **PM** (12n-9p)

FIGURE 7.19

Gathering Feedback to Improve Service: A Serious Example

Agents of the Transportation Security Administration (TSA) perform the security screening of passengers at U.S. airports. These individuals have to balance the privacy of passengers (who sometimes have to be patted down) with the need to prevent passengers from carrying dangerous items on board. To ensure that they are handling this challenging task effectively, passengers at many airports are given the opportunity to share feedback about their experiences by completing a few questions on a card like this one and returning it to the TSA by mail. Such feedback has proven useful in identifying agents in need of further training and in helping the TSA revise its procedures as a whole.

initiative. Sometimes, previously autocratic managers are shocked when they see how hard people work when they are allowed to make their own decisions. Bob Freese, CEO of Alphatronix Inc., in Research Triangle Park, North Carolina, is among the newly converted. "We let employees tell us when they can accomplish a project and what resources they need," he says. "Virtually always they set higher goals than we would ever set for them."[100]

Summary and Review of Learning Objectives

1. **Define motivation and explain its importance in the field of organizational behavior.**
   Motivation is concerned with the set of processes that arouse, direct, and maintain behavior toward a goal. It is not equivalent to job performance, but is one of several determinants of job performance. Today's work ethic motivates people to seek interesting and challenging jobs, instead of just money.
2. **Describe need hierarchy theory and the motivational-fit approach, noting what each suggests about how to improve motivation in organizations.**
   Need hierarchy theory postulates that people have five basic needs that are activated in a specific order. The most basic, lowest-level needs, physiological needs, are activated first. After these are satisfied, people are motivated to satisfy the next need in the hierarchy, safety needs. These are followed by social needs and then esteem needs. Once all these needs have been satisfied, people can become self-actualized—reaching their full potential. Organizations do various things to help employees meet their needs to pave the way for

them to self-actualize. Instead of focusing on needs, the *motivational-fit approach* highlights the importance of motivational traits (achievement and anxiety) and motivational skills (emotion control and motivation control) in work motivation. This framework specifies that people will be most highly motivated when these traits and skills best fit the requirements of the job and the organization in which someone works.

3. **Identify and explain the conditions through which goal setting can be used to improve job performance.**
   Goal-setting theory claims that an assigned goal influences a person's beliefs about being able to perform a task (referred to as *self-efficacy*) and his or her personal goals. Both of these factors, in turn, influence performance. Research has shown that people will improve their performance when specific, acceptably difficult goals are set and feedback about task performance is provided. The task of selecting goals that are acceptable to employees is facilitated by allowing employees to participate in the goal-setting process.

4. **Describe equity theory and explain how it may be applied to motivating people in organizations.**
   Equity theory claims that people desire to attain an equitable balance between the ratios of their work rewards (outcomes) and their job contributions (inputs) and the corresponding ratios of comparison to others. Inequitable states of *overpayment inequity* and *underpayment inequity* are undesirable, motivating people to try to attain equitable conditions. Responses to inequity may be either behavioral (e.g., raising or lowering one's performance) or psychological (e.g., thinking differently about work contributions). To avoid negative reactions (e.g., strikes, reduced work, resignations), overpayment inequity and underpayment inequity should be avoided. It also is useful to explain how outcomes and inputs were determined in an open and honest fashion.

5. **Describe expectancy theory and how it may be applied in organizations.**
   Expectancy theory recognizes that motivation is the product of a person's beliefs about *expectancy* (effort will lead to performance), *instrumentality* (performance will result in reward), and *valence* (the perceived value of the rewards). In conjunction with skills, abilities, role perceptions, and opportunities, motivation contributes to job performance. Expectancy theory suggests that motivation may be enhanced by linking rewards to performance (as in *pay-for-performance plans*) and by administering rewards that are highly valued (as may be done using *cafeteria-style benefit plans*).

6. **Distinguish among job enlargement, job enrichment, and the job characteristics model as techniques for motivating employees.**
   Motivation may be enhanced at the organizational level by designing or redesigning jobs in certain ways. Popular approaches include *job enlargement* (performing more tasks at the same level) and *job enrichment* (giving people greater responsibility and control over their jobs). A more sophisticated approach, the *job characteristics model*, identifies the specific job dimensions that should be enriched (skill variety, task identity, task significance, autonomy, and feedback), and relates these to the critical psychological states influenced by including these dimensions on a job. These psychological states will, in turn, lead to certain beneficial outcomes for both individual employees (e.g., job satisfaction) and the organization (e.g., reduced absenteeism and turnover). Jobs may be designed to enhance motivation by combining tasks, opening feedback channels, establishing client relationships, and loading jobs vertically (i.e., enhancing responsibility for one's work).

Points to Ponder

Questions for Review

1. What are Maslow's five categories of needs and how might each be satisfied on the job?
2. What particular traits and skills are most important when it comes to enhancing motivation by promoting fit with one's job and organization?

3. What rules should be followed when setting goals to motivate workers?
4. What does equity theory say about the role of money as a motivator?
5. What are the basic components of expectancy theory and how are they combined to predict performance?
6. How, specifically, can jobs be designed in an effort to enhance motivation?

Experiential Questions

1. What experiences have you had in setting personal goals (e.g., for saving money, for losing weight, for getting a certain job)? Which rules of goal setting did you follow? Which rules might you have followed to be even more successful?
2. Think of a time in which you felt inequitably underpaid by your employer or manager. How did it make you feel, and how did you respond as a result?
3. Think of the job you currently do, or one that you have done recently. Describe two specific things that could be done to redesign that job so that employees will be more motivated to perform it.

Questions to Analyze

1. An employee claims to be trying very hard but is not attaining acceptable levels of job performance. According to expectancy theory, what factors would contribute to such effort? What additional factors, besides motivation, contribute to task performance?
2. Money is not the only source of work motivation, but it plays a key role. Explain the specific role of money as a motivator in each of the theories of motivation presented in this chapter.
3. Imagine that you are devising an incentive plan for your company. What particular guidelines will you follow to ensure that it is effective? What problems do you anticipate as the plan takes effect?

Experiencing OB

Individual Exercise

Are You Equitably Paid?

The desire to be paid equitably is very strong among people in the workplace. Too often, however, employees believe that they are inequitably paid—either overpaid or underpaid. The following questionnaire will help you assess how you stand in this regard.

Directions

Respond to each of the following questions by selecting the one response that most accurately describes your situation as you believe it to be.

_____1. Compared to equally experienced others doing the same job as me in my company, I am:
    a. paid less
    b. paid about the same
    c. paid more

_____2. Given my training and experience, I would say that my pay is:
    a. too low
    b. about right
    c. too high

_____3. Considering how much effort I put into my job, I would say that my pay is:
    a. too low
    b. about right
    c. too high

_____4. Over the years, my level of pay has:
    a. not kept up with my accomplishments

       b. kept up with my accomplishments

       c. exceeded my accomplishments

_____5. So far as I know, people doing the same job as me at other companies are paid:

       a. more than me

       b. about the same as me

       c. less than me

Scoring

1. Give yourself 1 point each time you answer with response "a." These responses reflect underpayment. The more points you have in this category, the more underpaid you feel.
2. Give yourself 1 point each time you answer with response "b." These responses reflect equitable payment. The more points you have in this category, the more equitably paid you feel.
3. Give yourself 1 point each time you answer with response "c." These responses reflect overpayment. The more points you have in this category, the more overpaid you feel.

Questions for Discussion

1. What do your responses to this questionnaire reveal about the perceived equitableness of your pay? Are you overpaid or underpaid? Does your score confirm what you believe about the fairness of your pay?
2. If you are equitably paid, do you feel satisfied on the job? If you are inequitably paid (either overpaid or underpaid), do you feel dissatisfied on the job?
3. On occasions in which you felt inequitably underpaid, how did you respond? Did you lower your inputs? If so, how? Did you attempt to raise your outcomes? If so, how?

Group Exercise

Does Goal Setting Really Work? Demonstrate It for Yourself

Specific, difficult goals tend to enhance task performance. The following exercise is designed to help you demonstrate this effect for yourself. All you need is a class of students willing to participate and a few simple supplies.

Directions

1. Select a page of text from a book and make several photocopies. Carefully count the words and number each word on one of the copies. This will be your score sheet.
2. Find another class of 30 or more students who do not know anything about goal setting. (We do not want their knowledge of the phenomenon to bias the results.) On a random basis, divide the students into three equal-size groups.
3. Ask the students in the first group—the "baseline" group—to copy as much of the text as they can onto another piece of paper, and give them exactly one minute to do so. Direct them to work quickly. Using the score sheet created in step 1, identify the highest number of words copied by any one of the students and then multiply this number by 2. This will be the specific, difficult goal level.
4. Ask the students in the second group—the "specific goal" group—to copy the number of words on the same printed page for exactly one minute. Tell them to try to reach the specific goal number identified in step 3.
5. Repeat this process with the third group—the "do your best" group—but instead of giving them a specific goal, direct them to "try to do your best at this task."
6. Compute the average number of words copied in the "difficult goal" group and the "do your best" group. Have your instructor compute the appropriate statistical test

(a *t*-test, in this case) to determine the statistical significance of this difference in performance levels.

Questions for Discussion

1. Was there a statistically significant difference between the performance levels of the two groups? If so, did students in the "specific goal" group outperform those in the "do your best" group, as expected? What does this reveal about the effectiveness of goal setting?
2. If the predicted findings were not supported, why do you suppose this happened? What was it about the procedure that may have led to this failure? Was the specific goal (i.e., twice the fastest speed in the "baseline" group) too high, thus making the goal unreachable? Alternatively, was it too low, thus making the specific goal too easy?
3. What do you think would happen if the goal were lowered, thus making it easier, or raised, thus making it more difficult?
4. Do you think that providing feedback about goal attainment (e.g., someone counting the number of words copied and calling this out to the performers as they worked) would have helped?
5. For what other kinds of tasks do you believe goal setting may be effective? Specifically, do you believe that goal setting can improve your own performance on something? Explain this possibility.

Practicing OB

Motivating Nurses at a Hospital

You have been hired by the director of a large suburban hospital company to help resolve problems of poor morale that have been plaguing the nursing staff. Unfortunately, the nurses don't find their jobs particularly interesting. As a result, turnover and absenteeism have been high, and patient care is at an all-time low. The problem is apparent to everyone; both doctors and patients have been complaining. Answer the following questions relevant to this situation based on the material in this chapter.

1. After interviewing the nurses, you found that they believed that no one cared how well they were doing. What theories could help explain this problem? Applying these approaches, what would you recommend the hospital should do to resolve this problem?
2. Hospital officials tell you that the nurses are well paid, adding to your surprise about the low morale. However, your interviews reveal that the nurses themselves feel otherwise. Why might this occur and why is this a problem? What could be done to help?
3. "I'm bored with my job," one highly experienced nurse tells you, and you believe she speaks for many within the hospital. What could be done to make their jobs more interesting to those who perform them? What are the limitations of your plan? Would it work equally well for other members of the hospital staff (e.g., clerical and janitorial employees)?

CASE IN POINT

Keeping the Volunteers Working Hard at Amnesty International UK

Amnesty International (AI) refers to itself as "a worldwide movement of people who campaign for internationally recognized human rights." Its primary mission is to take action that prevents and ends mental and physical abuses of people around the world. Since its inception in 1961, the organization has been putting pressure on governments and other institutions to stop human rights abuses. In just 2004 alone, for example, AI has had a hand in ceasing hundreds of unlawful killings and acts of torture, and releasing from prison hundreds more holding unpopular political ideas. It brings pressure to bear on offending political regimes by writing letters, lobbying governmental organizations, and participating in events organized by such international organizations as the United Nations. Because most of AI's support comes from donations, it relies on a network of volunteers to keep it going—some 8,000 people in 100 nations (ranging from doctors and lawyers to everyday laborers).

Keeping the legions of volunteers working hard is one of the major challenges AI faces. In the UK office of AI, located in London, where there are 100 paid staff members, Veronique Du Pont coordinates the work of 70 volunteers. Their commitment to the cause of human rights is a big motivator, she explains, but the work they do is less than glamorous. Working in the mailroom, updating the computer database, filing, and writing routine correspondence seems a far cry from getting a political dissident out of a Colombian prison.

To keep the volunteers feeling the importance of the mundane work they do, Du Pont goes out of her way to point out how even this routine work is essential to making AI's campaigns successful. One way she does this is by holding regular meetings for volunteers and having them attend the various workshops the office puts on. As Veronique points out, "Although volunteers are motivated by their involvement in the work, when they're doing quite mundane tasks, they need to feel integrated in Amnesty's projects. That means keeping volunteers informed and updated, and giving them access to information. Without a mutual respect between team members (volunteers or not) we wouldn't have happy volunteers."

If you talk to any of AI's London volunteers, it's clear that Du Pont's approach is working. Says Jamal, one of the volunteers, "I get a lot of satisfaction out of volunteering here. There are various events that help us to feel part of the organization." Among these, he cites the opportunity to attend various lectures about human rights and the work of the organization, as well as a field trip to AI's international headquarters.

Questions for Discussion

1. What specific things does Amnesty International do to motivate employees?
2. What special challenges do you believe are associated with motivating volunteers as opposed to paid employees?
3. At the company in which you work, how could you put into practice the various tactics used by Amnesty International? Would they be as effective? Why or why not?

VIDEO CASES

Fired for Being Fat

The Borgata Hotel, Casino, and Spa in Atlantic City, New Jersey, threatens to suspend or fire cocktail servers and bartenders if they put on too much weight. A former female employee describes what it was like to work in an environment in which her body size constantly was monitored.

Discussion Questions

1. What dominant values in U.S. society may have led to the Borgata's employment policy? How prevalent do you believe such policies are in organizations?
2. What does this policy communicate about this particular organization?
3. Even if you are not affected by this policy, would you suspect that the organization is discriminatory in any other way? In other words, do you believe this policy is "the tip of the iceberg" with respect to the underlying beliefs and values of the organization in question?

Gender Wage Gap

Do women really get paid less than men for equal work? Although most Americans believe this, Warren Farrell, author of *Why Men Earn More,* challenges this widely held assumption. His claim is quite simple: When women and men do comparable jobs, they receive comparable pay. Overall, however, women are paid less than men because they are inclined to do different kinds of work and to work fewer hours.

Discussion Questions

1. Based on the discussion by Warren Farrell, do you believe that men and women would be equally motivated to perform their jobs?
2. How would equity theory account for Mr. Farrell's arguments?
3. In your opinion, should women and men in the United States earn the same average salary? Explain your answer.

GROUP DYNAMICS AND WORK TEAMS

Chapter Outline

Special Sections

After reading this chapter, you should be able to:

1. Define what is meant by a group and identify different types of groups operating within organizations.

2. Describe the importance of norms, roles, status, and cohesiveness within organizations.

3. Explain how individual performance in groups is affected by the presence of others (social facilitation) and the number of others with whom one is working (social loafing).

4. Define what teams are and describe the various types of teams that exist in organizations.

5. Describe the effectiveness of teams in organizations.

6. Explain the factors responsible for the failure of some teams to operate as effectively as possible and steps that can be taken to build successful teams.

PREVIEW CASE

RAZR Gives Motorola the Edge

In the late 1990s, Rob Shaddock, a senior wireless executive at Motorola, had an idea. Calling upon the leadership of electrical engineer Roger Jellicoe, they would develop a flip-top phone that was only 0.39 inch in girth when closed. This unprecedentedly svelte phone was to be developed in the impossibly ambitious time of only one year—allowing it to be showcased in the hands of celebrities at the 2004 Academy Awards show. This association with movie stars was in keeping with the mission of creating not a phone for the masses, but rather, a high-end toy that displayed Motorola's technological prowess. Ultimately, Shaddock reasoned, this would enhance the company's reputation, luring customers to the company later on with more popular-priced items.

Going into the project knowing that he was not expected to develop a commercially popular, mass-market product freed Jellicoe to take chances with the phone's design and engineering. He sought the help of mechanical engineer Gary Weiss, and together they assembled a team of 20 engineers to create the phone, the RAZR—a cool play on the phone's razor clam shape and razor blade thinness.

Fearing that people inside the company would fight efforts to do anything radically different, Jellison kept the project top secret. To help, the team gathered after regular working hours in a separate facility in nearby Libertyville, Illinois. Details of the project were kept from most others in the company—a vast departure from Motorola's usual practices of checking with cellular carriers about features subscribers wanted and incorporating systematic feedback from consumers. For this project, though, they abandoned usual practices and moved ahead based on their own information.

While the engineers developed the phone's insides, they worked closely with the younger and hipper Chris Arnholt, who shared his vision for a phone with "rich minimalism" (of which the phone's cool backlit keypad is an example). Arnholt repeatedly sculpted mock-ups from cornstarch, revised them with masking tape, and redrew them many times before they were rendered by artists working in three-dimensional computer graphics. Throughout the late summer and early fall of 2003, team members kept on going back and forth to come up with a design and technology that worked in harmony. Aptly, Weiss refers to this process as "the dance."

Sometimes the dance wasn't elegant, but the final product benefited from the missteps. Ultimately, it boiled down to determining what features would be added at the expense of thinness. A window in which to display caller ID information was deemed necessary, which necessitated moving the phone's internal antenna to the mouthpiece. This required new technological innovations, as did other questions, such as those involving placement of the phone's battery. Ultimately, although the final product was about one-eighth of an inch thicker than planned, everyone believed this to be more than acceptable because they had created far and away the thinnest phone to date. The team also missed the deadline by margins almost as thin as the phone itself. In February 2004, movie stars didn't find the RAZR in their gift bags, but by July, the phone debuted.

Almost immediately, sales took off beyond anyone's expectations. Still priced as a high-end item, some 750,000 units sold in the first few months. Impressed with these numbers, Ron Garrique, new president of the cell phone division, saw even greater potential, and in September 2004, he gave the word for the phone to be repositioned as a mass-market item. That was all it took for the RAZR to become almost as common as Apple's iPod. In fact, the RAZR has sold close to as many RAZRs (some 50 million) in less than one-third as much time as it took the iPod to reach the same sales level. Well, so much for the initial plan to create a limited-market item!

O bviously, several aspects of Motorola's RAZR project are incredibly special and amazingly effective. Although few companies can pull off the kind of success Motorola has enjoyed with its wildly popular streamline phone, especially in such a short time, various elements of what Motorola did may be seen in factories and offices everywhere. Indeed, *work teams* are extremely popular today in all kinds of organizations—and, in view of Motorola's experiences, there's little wonder why. In the second half of the chapter we will take a close-up look at the nature of teams in the modern workplace. Acknowledging that they don't always operate as successfully as the team that developed the RAZR, we will describe the general effectiveness of teams and outline steps that can be taken to make teams as productive as possible.

To help you understand the underlying factors that contribute to team success and failure, we first must turn attention to the basic nature of *groups* in general. As you know, a great deal of the work performed in organizations is done by people working together in groups. In view of this, it makes sense to understand the types of groups that exist and the variables governing the interrelationships between them and individuals—commonly referred to as *group dynamics*. **Group dynamics** focuses on the nature of groups—the variables governing their formation and development, their structure, and their interrelationships with individuals, other groups, and the organizations within which they exist.[1] Because groups exist in all types of social settings, the study of group dynamics has a long history in the social sciences—including OB.[2]

In the first half of this chapter we will draw upon this work. Specifically, we will describe the nature of groups by defining what groups are, identifying various types of groups and why they form, explaining the various stages through which groups develop, and describing the dynamics of the way groups are structured. Following this, we shift our attention to how effectively groups operate. Specifically, we will describe how people are affected by the presence of others, how the cultural makeup of a group affects performance, and the tendency for people to withhold their individual performance under certain conditions.

group dynamics

The social science field focusing on the nature of groups—the factors governing their formation and development, the elements of their structure, and their interrelationships with individuals, other groups, and organizations.

Groups at Work: Their Basic Nature

To understand the dynamics of groups and their influence on individual and organizational functioning, we begin by raising some basic questions—namely, what is a group, what types of groups exist, why do people join groups, how do groups come into being, and how are groups structured? We will now address these questions.

What Is a Group?

Imagine three people waiting in line at the cashier's station at a supermarket. Now compare them to the board of directors of a large corporation. Which collection would you consider to be a "group"? Although in our everyday language we may refer to the people waiting in line as a group, they clearly are not a group in the same sense as the members of the board. Obviously, a group is more than simply a collection of people. But what exactly is it that makes a group a group?

Social scientists have formally defined a **group** as a collection of two or more interacting individuals with a stable pattern of relationships between them who share common goals and who perceive themselves as being a group.[3] To help us examine this definition more closely, we summarize the four key characteristics of groups in Figure 8.1.

group
A collection of two or more interacting individuals who maintain stable patterns of relationships, share common goals, and perceive themselves as being a group.

Social Interaction. One of the most obvious characteristics of groups is that they are composed of *two or more people in social interaction*. In other words, the members of a group must have some influence on one another. The interaction between the parties may be either verbal (such as sharing strategies for a corporate takeover) or nonverbal (such as exchanging smiles in the hallway), but the parties must have some impact on one another to be considered a group.

Stability. Groups also must possess a relatively *stable structure*. Although groups can change, and often do, there must be some stable relationships that keep group members together and functioning as a unit. A collection of individuals that constantly changes (e.g., the people inside an office waiting room at any given time) cannot be thought of as a group. To be a group, a greater level of stability would be required.

Common Interests or Goals. A third characteristic of groups is that their *members share common interests or goals*. For example, members of a stamp collecting club constitute a group that is sustained by the mutual interest of members. Some groups form because members with common interests help each other achieve a mutual goal. For example, the owners and employees of a sewing shop constitute a group formed around a common interest in sewing and the common goal of making money.

Recognition as Being a Group. Finally, to be a group, the individuals involved must *perceive themselves as a group*. Groups are composed of people who recognize each other as a member of their group and can distinguish these individuals from nonmembers. The members of a corporate finance committee or a chess club, for example, know who is in their group and who is not. In contrast, shoppers in a checkout line probably don't think of each other as being members of a group. Although they stand physically close to each other and may have passing conversations, they have little in common (except, perhaps, a

FIGURE 8.1

A Group: Its Defining Characteristics

To be a group, four different criteria must be met: (1) there must be two or more people in social interaction, (2) they must share common goals, (3) they must have a stable group structure, and (4) the individuals must perceive themselves as being a group.

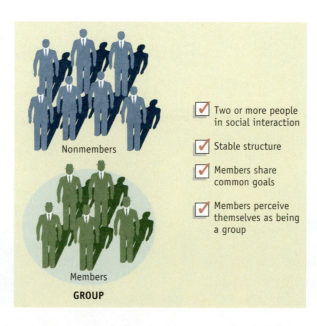

Nonmembers

Members

GROUP

- ✓ Two or more people in social interaction
- ✓ Stable structure
- ✓ Members share common goals
- ✓ Members perceive themselves as being a group

shared interest in reaching the end of the line) and fail to identify themselves with the others in the line.

By defining groups in terms of these four characteristics, we have identified a group as a very special collection of individuals (see Figure 8.2). As we shall see, these characteristics are responsible for the important effects groups have on organizational behavior. To better understand these effects, we will now review the wide variety of groups that operate within organizations.

Types of Groups

What do the following have in common: a military combat unit, three couples getting together for dinner, the board of directors of a large corporation, and the three-person cockpit crew of a commercial airliner? As you probably guessed, the answer is that they are all groups. But, of course, they are very different kinds of groups, ones people join for different reasons.

Formal Groups. The most basic way of identifying types of groups is to distinguish between *formal groups* and *informal groups* (see Figure 8.3). **Formal groups** are created by the organization and are intentionally designed to direct members toward some important organizational goal. One type of formal group is referred to as a **command group**—a group determined by the connections between individuals who are a formal part of the organization (i.e., those who legitimately can give orders to others). For example, a command group may be formed by the vice president of marketing who gathers together her regional marketing directors from around the country to hear their ideas about a new national advertising campaign. The point is that command groups are determined by the organization's rules regarding who reports to whom, and usually consist of a supervisor and his or her subordinates.

A formal organizational group also may be formed around some specific task. Such a group is referred to as a **task group**. Unlike command groups, a task group may be composed of individuals with some special interest or expertise in a specific area regardless of their positions in the organizational hierarchy. For example, a company may have a committee on equal employment opportunities whose members monitor the fair hiring practices of the organization. It may be composed of personnel specialists, corporate vice presidents, and workers from the shop floor. Whether they are permanent committees, known as **standing committees**, or temporary ones formed for special purposes (such as a committee formed to recommend solutions to a parking problem), known as **ad hoc committees** or **task forces**, task groups are common in organizations.

Margin glossary

formal groups
Groups that are created by the organization, intentionally designed to direct its members toward some organizational goal.

command group
A group determined by the connections between individuals who are a formal part of the organization (i.e., those who legitimately can give orders to others).

task group
A formal organizational group formed around some specific task.

standing committees
Committees that are permanent, existing over time.

ad hoc committee
A temporary committee formed for a special purpose.

task force
See *ad hoc committee*.

FIGURE 8.2

Is This a Group?

A collection of people waiting in line to get into a concert is not considered a group. Although the people may talk to one another and share the goal of wanting to see the performance, they are not considered a group because different people are always entering and leaving the line and because the individuals involved are unlikely to think of themselves as belonging to a group.

Varieties of Groups in Organizations

Within organizations one may find formal groups (such as command groups and task groups) and informal groups (such as interest groups and friendship groups).

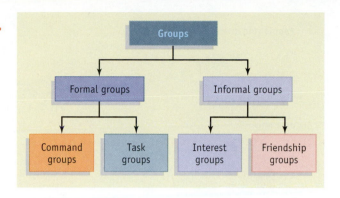

informal groups

Groups that develop naturally among people, without any direction from the organization within which they operate.

interest groups

A group of employees who come together to satisfy a common interest.

friendship groups

Informal groups that develop because their members are friends, often seeing each other outside of the organization.

Informal Groups. As you know, not all groups found in organizations are as formal as those we've identified. Many groups are informal in nature. **Informal groups** develop naturally among an organization's personnel without any direction from the management of the organization within which they operate. One key factor in the formation of informal groups is a common interest shared by its members. For example, a group of employees who band together to seek union representation, or who march together to protest their company's pollution of the environment, may be called an **interest group**. The common goal sought by members of an interest group may unite workers at many different organizational levels. The key factor is that membership in an interest group is voluntary—it is not created by the organization, but encouraged by an expression of common interests.

Of course, sometimes the interests that bind individuals together are far more diffuse. Groups may develop out of a common interest in participating in sports, or going to the movies, or just getting together to talk. These kinds of informal groups are known as **friendship groups**. A group of coworkers who hang out together during lunch may also bowl or play cards together after work. Friendship groups extend beyond the workplace because they provide opportunities for satisfying the social needs of workers that are so important to their well-being.

Informal work groups are an important part of life in organizations. Although they develop without direct encouragement from management, friendships often originate out of formal organizational contact. For example, three employees working alongside each other on an assembly line may get to talking and discover their mutual interest in basketball, and decide to get together to shoot baskets after work. As we will see, such friendships can bind people together, helping them cooperate with each other, having beneficial effects on organizational functioning.

Reasons for Joining Groups

We have already noted that people often join groups to satisfy their mutual interests and goals. To the extent that getting together with others allows us to achieve ends that would not be possible alone, forming groups makes a great deal of sense. In fact, organizations can be thought of as collections of groups that are focused toward attaining the mutual goal of achieving success for the company. But this is not the only motivation that people have for joining groups. There are also several additional reasons (see summary in Figure 8.4).

Not only do groups form for purposes of mutually achieving goals, they also frequently form for purposes of seeking protection from other groups. If you've ever heard the phrase "there's safety in numbers," you are probably already aware that people join groups because they seek the security of group membership. Historically, for example, trade unions such as the AFL/CIO, the UAW, and the Teamsters have been formed by labor for purposes of seeking protection against abuses by management. Similarly, professional associations such as the American Medical Association and the American Bar Association were created, in large part, for purposes of protecting their constituents against undesirable governmental legislation.

FIGURE 8.4

Why Do People Join Groups?

People join groups for many different reasons. Four of the most important reasons are identified and explained here.

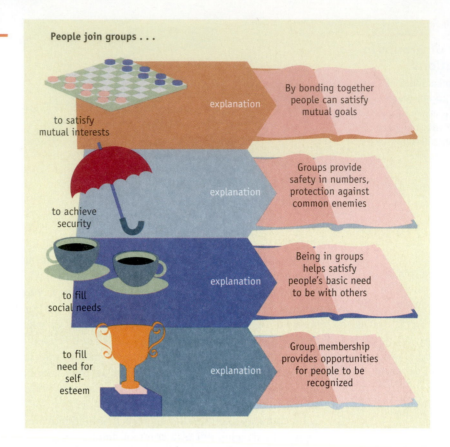

This is not to say that groups are always designed to promote some instrumental good; indeed, they also exist because they appeal to a basic psychological need to be social. As we already discussed in the context of Maslow's need hierarchy theory (in Chapter 7), people are social animals; they have a basic need to affiliate with others. Groups provide good opportunities for friendships to develop—hence, for social needs to be fulfilled.

Also as suggested by Maslow, people have a basic desire for their self-esteem to be fulfilled. Group memberships can be a very effective way of nurturing self-esteem. For example, if a group to which one belongs is successful (such as a sales group that meets its quota), the self-esteem of all members (and supporters) may be boosted. Similarly, election to membership in an exclusive group (e.g., a national honor society) will surely raise one's self-esteem.

As we have shown, people are attracted to groups for many different reasons. Despite the fact that people may have different motivations for forming groups, it is interesting to note that once formed, groups develop in remarkably similar ways. We will now turn our attention to this issue.

The Five-Stage Model of Group Formation

Social scientists long have been interested in the question of how people form groups. One popular way of answering this question is by examining the various stages through which groups develop. Just as infants develop in certain ways during their first months of life, groups also show relatively stable signs of maturation and development.[4] One popular approach, the **five-stage model**, identifies five distinct stages through which groups develop.[5] As we describe these stages, you may want to review our summary shown in Figure 8.5.

five-stage model
The conceptualization claiming that groups develop in five stages—forming, storming, norming, performing, and adjourning.

Stage 1: Forming. The first stage of group development is known as *forming*. During this stage of group development, the members get acquainted with each other. They establish the ground rules by trying to find out what behaviors are acceptable, with respect to both the job (how productive they are expected to be) and interpersonal relations (who's really in charge). During the forming stage, people tend to be a bit confused and uncertain

FIGURE 8.5

The Five Stage-Model of Group Development

In general, groups develop according to the five stages summarized here.

Source: Based on information in Tuckman & Jensen, 1977; see Note 5.

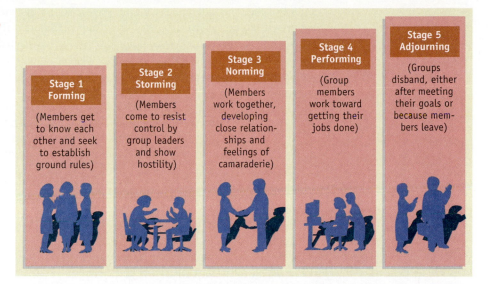

about how to act in the group and how beneficial it will be to become a member of the group. Once the individuals come to think of themselves as members of a group, the forming stage is complete.

Stage 2: Storming. The second stage of group development is referred to as *storming*. As the name implies, this stage is characterized by a high degree of conflict within the group. Members often resist the control of the group's leaders and show hostility toward each other. If these conflicts are not resolved and group members withdraw, the group may disband. However, as conflicts are resolved and the group's leadership is accepted, the storming stage is complete.

Stage 3: Norming. The third stage of group development is known as *norming*. During this stage, the group becomes more cohesive, and identification as a member of the group becomes greater. Close relationships develop, shared feelings become common, and a keen interest in finding mutually agreeable solutions develops. Feelings of camaraderie and shared responsibility for the group's activities are heightened. The norming stage is complete when the members of the group accept a common set of expectations that constitutes an acceptable way of doing things.

Stage 4: Performing. The fourth stage of group development is known as *performing*. During this stage, questions about group relationships and leadership have been resolved and the group is ready to work. Having fully developed, the group may now devote its energy to getting the job done—the group's good relations and acceptance of the leadership helps the group perform well.

Stage 5: Adjourning. Recognizing that not all groups last forever, the final stage is known as *adjourning*. Groups may cease to exist because they have met their goals and are no longer needed (such as an ad hoc group created to raise money for a charity project), in which case the end is abrupt. Other groups may adjourn gradually as the group disintegrates, either because members leave or because the norms that have developed are no longer effective for the group.

An Example. To illustrate these various stages, imagine that you have just joined several of your colleagues on your company's newly created budget committee. At first, you and your associates feel each other out: You watch to see who comes up with the best ideas, whose suggestions are most widely accepted, who seems to take charge, and the like (the forming stage). Then, as members struggle to gain influence over others, you may see a battle over control of the committee (the storming stage). Soon, this will be resolved, and an accepted leader will emerge. At this stage, the group members will become highly cooperative, working together in harmony and doing things together, such as going out to lunch as a group (the norming stage). Now, it becomes possible for committee members to work together at doing their best, giving it their all (the performing stage). Then, once the budget is created and approved, the group's task is over, and it is disbanded (the adjourning stage).

It is important to keep in mind that groups can be in any one stage of development at any given time. Moreover, the amount of time a group may spend in any given stage is highly variable. In fact, some groups may fail long before they have had a chance to work together. Research has revealed that the boundaries between the various stages may not be clearly distinct, and that several stages may be combined, especially as deadline pressures force groups to take action.[6] It is best, then, to think of this five-stage model as a general framework of group formation. Although many of the stages may be followed, the dynamic nature of groups makes it unlikely that they will progress through the various stages in a completely predictable order.

The Punctuated-Equilibrium Model

Not all scientists agree that groups develop in the order identified in the five-stage model. In fact, it has been argued that although there may not be a universal sequence of stages, there are some remarkable consistencies in the ways groups form and change. These patterns are described in the **punctuated-equilibrium model**. This approach to group formation recognizes that group members working to meet a deadline approach their task differently in the first half of their time together than in the second half.[7]

During the first half of the time, *phase 1,* groups define their task, setting a mission that is unlikely to change until the second half of the group's life. Even if group members have new ideas, these are generally not acted upon. Interestingly, as soon as groups reach the midpoints of their lives (whether this is just a few hours or several months), something curious happens. Almost as if an alarm goes off, at the midpoint of their lives groups experience a sort of "midlife crisis"—a time when they recognize that they are going to have to change the way they operate if they are going to meet their goals. This begins *phase 2* of their existence—a time when groups drop old ways of thinking and adopt new perspectives. Groups then carry out these missions until they reach the end of phase 2, when they show bursts of activity needed to complete their work. For a summary of these processes, see Figure 8.6.

The idea is straightforward: Groups develop inertia, which keeps them going (i.e., an "equilibrium") until the halfway-point, when they realize that deadlines loom large. This stimulates them to confront important issues and to initiate changes, beginning (i.e., "punctuating") a new equilibrium phase. This phase lasts until the group kicks into a final push just before the deadline.

To illustrate the punctuated-equilibrium model, consider what might happen in a group of people working to elect a political candidate. When the group first meets, one January, the members get to know each other and plan their campaign strategy. They figure out what they have to do in the 10 months that follow to get their candidate into office, and they spring into action. Then, by May or June, it becomes clear that there are problems, and the original plan needs to be changed. People working on the campaign begin taking critical looks at what they've been doing and take active steps to change things. This continues through October. Then, in the weeks or days right before the November election, the group will meet for a long time and make its final push.

Although the punctuated-equilibrium model is relatively new, studies suggest that it does a good job of describing how groups develop.[8] We think it will make great sense to you if you compare it to your own experience working with others in groups (e.g., on class projects).

The Structural Dynamics of Work Groups

As noted earlier, one of the key characteristics of a group is its stable structure. When social scientists use the term **group structure**, they are referring to the interrelationships

---

punctuated-equilibrium mode
The conceptualization of group development claiming that groups generally plan their activities during the first half of their time together, and then revise and implement their plans in the second half.

group structure
The pattern of interrelationships between the individuals constituting a group; the guidelines of group behavior that make group functioning orderly and predictable.

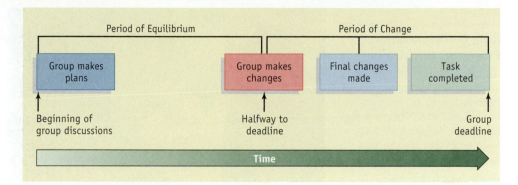

FIGURE 8.6

The Punctuated-Equilibrium Model

According to the punctuated-equilibrium model, groups go through two stages marked by the mid-point of the group's time together. The first half is a period of equilibrium, in which the group makes plans, but accomplishes little. During the second half, group members make changes that lead them to accomplish the group's task as the deadline approaches.

Source: Based on suggestions by Gersick, 1989; see Note 7.

between the individuals constituting a group, the characteristics that make group functioning orderly and predictable. In this section, we will describe four different aspects of group structure: the various parts played by group members (*roles*), the rules and expectations that develop within groups (*norms*), the prestige of group membership (*status*), and the members' sense of belonging (*cohesiveness*).

Roles: The Hats We Wear

One of the primary structural elements of groups is members' tendencies to play specific roles in group interaction, often more than one. Social scientists use the term *role* in much the same way as a director of a play would refer to the character who plays a part. Indeed, the part one plays in the overall group structure is what we mean by a role. More formally, we may define a **role** as the typical behaviors that characterize a person in a social context.[9]

In organizations, many roles are assigned by virtue of an individual's position within an organization. For example, a boss may be expected to give orders, and a teacher may be expected to lecture and to give exams. These are behaviors expected of the individual in that role. The person holding the role is known as a **role incumbent**, and the behaviors expected of that person are known as **role expectations**. The person holding the office of the president of the United States (the role incumbent) has certain role expectations simply because he or she currently has that post. When a new president takes office, that person assumes the same role and has the same formal powers as the previous president. This is the case although the new president may have very different ideas about key issues facing the nation.

The role incumbent's recognition of the expectations of his or her role helps avoid the social disorganization that surely would result if clear role expectations did not exist. Sometimes, however, workers may be confused about the things that are expected of them on the job, such as their level of authority or their responsibility. Such **role ambiguity**, as it is called, is typically experienced by new members of organizations who have not had much of a chance to "learn the ropes," and often results in job dissatisfaction, a lack of commitment to the organization, and an interest in leaving the job.[10]

As work groups and social groups develop, the various group members come to play different roles in the social structure—a process referred to as **role differentiation**. By definition, the division of people into various jobs constitutes role differentiation—different people perform different functions in an organization. In other words, role differentiation can occur on a formal basis in a work group or team (see Figure 8.7).[11]

role
The typical behavior that characterizes a person in a specific social context.

role incumbent
A person holding a particular role.

role expectations
The behaviors expected of someone in a particular role.

role ambiguity
Confusion arising from not knowing what one is expected to do as the holder of a role.

role differentiation
The tendency for various specialized roles to emerge as groups develop.

FIGURE 8.7

Role Differentiation Promotes Performance

Kurt Rambis, now an assistant coach on the Los Angeles Lakers basketball team, played with some of that team's greats in the late 1980s. Although his first love was to take shots at the basket, the team had Kareem Abdul-Jabbar and Magic Johnson to do that. Needing a defender and rebounder to help the cause, the Lakers had Rambis settle into this role. "Awareness of our roles was a huge part of our success," Rambis is quoted as saying. And, with several division championships and national championships during that period, the plan worked just fine.

task-oriented role
The activities of an individual in a group who, more than anyone else, helps the group reach its goal.

socioemotional role
The activities of an individual in a group who is supportive and nurturant of other group members and who helps them feel good.

self-oriented role
The activities of an individual in a group who focuses on his or her own good, often at the expense of others.

norms
Generally agreed on informal rules that guide group members' behavior.

prescriptive norms
Expectations within groups regarding what is supposed to be done.

proscriptive norms
Expectations within groups regarding behaviors in which members are not supposed to engage.

In addition, roles also may emerge as part of a naturally occurring process. Think of committees to which you have belonged. Was there someone who joked and made people feel better, and another member who worked hard to get the group to focus on the issue at hand? These examples of differentiated roles are typical of role behaviors that emerge in groups. Organizations, for example, often have their "office comedian" who makes everyone laugh, or the "company gossip" who shares others' secrets, or the "grand old man" who tells newcomers the stories about the company's "good old days."

Scientists have noted that roles tend to be differentiated in some standard ways. For example, in any group there tends to be one person who, more than anyone else, helps the group reach its goal.[12] Such a person is said to play the **task-oriented role**. In addition, another group member may emerge who is quite supportive and nurturant, someone who makes everyone else feel good. Such a person is said to play a **socioemotional role**. Still others may be recognized for the things they do for themselves, often at the expense of the group—individuals recognized for playing a **self-oriented role**. Many specific role behaviors can fall into one or another of these categories. For a listing of some of the most common forms that these three types of roles may take, see Table 8.1.

Norms: A Group's Unspoken Rules

One feature of groups that enhances their orderly functioning is the existence of group norms. **Norms** may be defined as generally agreed upon informal rules that guide group members' behavior.[13] They represent shared ways of viewing the world. Norms differ from organizational rules in that they are not formal and written. In fact, group members may not even be aware of the subtle group norms that exist and regulate their behavior. Yet norms have profound effects on behavior. Norms regulate the behavior of groups in important ways, such as by fostering workers' honesty and loyalty to the company, establishing appropriate ways to dress, and dictating when it is acceptable to be late for or absent from work.

If you recall the pressures placed on you by your peers as you grew up to dress or wear your hair in certain styles, you are well aware of the profound normative pressures exerted by groups. Some norms, known as **prescriptive norms**, dictate the behaviors that should be performed. Other norms, known as **proscriptive norms**, dictate specific behaviors that should be

TABLE 8.1 Roles Commonly Played by Group Members

Organizational roles may be differentiated into task-oriented, relations-oriented (or socioemotional), and self-oriented roles—each of which has several subroles. Several of these are shown here.

Task-Oriented Roles	Relations-Oriented Roles	Self-Oriented Roles
Initiator-contributors *Recommend new solutions to group problems*	Harmonizers *Mediate group conflicts*	Blockers *Act stubborn and resistant to the group*
Information seekers *Attempt to obtain the necessary facts*	Compromisers *Shift own opinions to create group harmony*	Recognition seekers *Call attention to their own achievements*
Opinion givers *Share own opinions with others*	Encouragers *Praise and encourage others*	Dominators *Assert authority by manipulating the group*
Energizers *Stimulate the group into action whenever interest drops*	Expediters *Suggest ways the group can operate more smoothly*	Avoiders *Maintain distance, isolate themselves from fellow group members*

Source: Based on Benne & Sheats, 1948; see Note 12.

avoided (see Figure 8.8, p. 300). For example, groups may develop prescriptive norms to follow their leader or to help a group member who needs assistance. They may also develop proscriptive norms to avoid absences or to refrain from telling each other's secrets to the boss.

Sometimes the pressure to conform to norms is subtle, as in the dirty looks given a manager by his peers for going to lunch with one of the assembly-line workers. (This would be the case if norms prohibit fraternizing with people at lower organizational levels.) Other times, normative pressures may be quite severe, such as when one production worker sabotages another's work because he is performing at too high a level, making his coworkers look bad. (This would be the case if norms require working within certain ranges deemed acceptable.)

Although our examples emphasize the underlying social dynamics responsible for how groups develop norms, this is only one reason. There are, in fact, several factors responsible for the formation of norms.[14] For a summary of these, see Table 8.2.

Status: The Prestige of Group Membership

Have you ever been attracted to a group because of the prestige accorded its members? You may have wanted to join a certain fraternity or sorority because it is highly regarded by the students. No doubt, members of championship-winning football teams proudly sport their Super Bowl rings to identify themselves as members of that highly regarded team. Clearly, one potential reward of group membership is the status associated with being in that group. Even within social groups, different members are accorded different levels of prestige. Fraternity and sorority officers and committee chairpersons, for example, may be recognized as more important members of their respective groups. This is the idea behind **status**—the relative social position or rank given to groups or group members by others.[15]

Within most organizations, status may be recognized as both formal and informal in nature. **Formal status** refers to attempts to differentiate between the degrees of formal authority given employees by an organization. This is typically accomplished through the use of **status symbols**—objects reflecting the position of an individual within an organization's hierarchy. Some common examples of status symbols include job titles (e.g., Director); perquisites, or perks (e.g., a reserved parking space); the opportunity to do desirable and highly regarded work (e.g., serving on important committees); and luxurious working conditions (e.g., a large, private office that is lavishly decorated).[16]

Status symbols help groups in many ways.[17] For one, such symbols remind organizational members of their relative roles, thereby reducing uncertainty and providing stability to the social order (e.g., your small desk reminds you of your lower organizational rank).

status
The relative prestige, social position, or rank given to groups or individuals by others.

formal status
The prestige one has by virtue of his or her official position in an organization.

status symbols
Objects reflecting the position of any individual within an organization's hierarchy of power.

FIGURE 8.8

Norms Dictate What to Do and Not to Do

Norms are informal rules about behaviors that are considered acceptable and unacceptable in groups. As illustrated here, it is not unusual for norms to be communicated explicitly in an effort to get others to conform to them.

Source: www.CartoonStock.com

"I don't care how young it makes you feel. You work here, you carry a briefcase."

In addition, they provide assurance of the various rewards available to those who perform at a superior level (e.g., "maybe one day I'll have a reserved parking spot"). They also provide a sense of identification by reminding members of the group's values (e.g., a gang's jacket may remind its wearer of his expected loyalty and boldness). It is, therefore, not surprising that organizations do much to reinforce formal status through the use of status symbols.

informal status

The prestige accorded individuals with certain characteristics that are not formally recognized by the organization.

Symbols of **informal status** within organizations are also widespread. These refer to the prestige accorded individuals with certain characteristics that are not formally recognized by the organization. For example, employees who are older and more experienced may be perceived as higher in status by their coworkers. Those who have certain special skills (such as the home-run hitters on a baseball team) also may be regarded as having higher status than others. In some organizations, the lower value placed on the work of

TABLE 8.2 Norms: How Do They Develop?

Group norms are likely to form according to the ways summarized here.

Basis of Norm Development	Example
Precedents set over time	Seating location of each group member around a table
Carryovers from other situations	Professional standards of conduct
Explicit statements from others	Working a certain way because you are told "that's how we do it around here"
Critical events in group history	After the organization suffers a loss due to one person's divulging company secrets, a norm develops to maintain secrecy

Source: Based on Feldman, 1984; see Note 14.

women and members of minority groups by some individuals also can be considered an example of informal status in operation.[18]

One of the best-established findings in the study of group dynamics is that higher-status people tend to be more influential than lower-status people. This phenomenon may be seen in a classic study of decision making in three-man bomber crews.[19] After the crews had difficulty solving a problem, the experimenter planted clues to the solution with either a low-status group member (the tail gunner) or a high-status group member (the pilot). It was found that the solutions offered by the pilots were far more likely to be adopted than the same solutions presented by the tail gunners. Apparently, the greater status accorded the pilots (because they tended to be more experienced and held higher military ranks) was responsible for the greater influence they wielded.

Cohesiveness: Getting the Team Spirit

cohesiveness

The strength of group members' desires to remain a part of the group.

One obvious determinant of any group's structure is its **cohesiveness**—the strength of group members' desires to remain part of their groups. Highly cohesive work groups are ones in which the members are attracted to each other, accept the group's goals, and help work toward meeting them. In very uncohesive groups, the members dislike each other and may even work at cross-purposes.[20] In essence, cohesiveness refers to a *we-feeling,* an *esprit de corps,* a sense of belonging to a group.

Several important factors influence the extent to which group members tend to "stick together." One such factor involves the severity of initiation into the group. Research has shown that the greater the difficulty people overcome to become a member of a group, the more cohesive the group will be.[21] To understand this, consider how highly cohesive certain groups may be that you have worked hard to join. Was it particularly difficult to "make the cut" on your sports team? The rigorous requirements for gaining entry into elite groups, such as the most prestigious medical schools and military training schools, may well be responsible for the high degree of camaraderie found in such groups. Having "passed the test" tends to keep individuals together and separates them from those who are unwilling or unable to "pay the price" of admission.

Group cohesion also tends to be strengthened under conditions of high external threat or competition. When groups face a "common enemy," they tend to draw together (see Figure 8.9). Such cohesion not only makes workers feel safer and better protected, but also aids them by encouraging them to work closely together and to coordinate their efforts toward the common enemy. Under such conditions, petty disagreements that may have caused dissension within groups tend to be put aside so that a coordinated attack on the enemy can be mobilized.

Research also has shown that the cohesiveness of groups is established by several additional factors.[22] For one, cohesiveness generally tends to be greater the more time group members spend together. Obviously, limited interaction cannot help but interfere with opportunities to develop bonds between group members. Similarly, cohesiveness tends to be greater in smaller groups. Generally speaking, groups that are too large make it difficult for members to interact and, therefore, for cohesiveness to reach a high level. Finally, because "nothing succeeds like success," groups with a history of success tend to be highly cohesive. It is often said that "everyone loves a winner," and the success of a group tends to help unite its members as they rally around their success. For this reason, employees tend to be loyal to successful companies.

Thus far, our discussion has implied that cohesiveness is a positive thing. Indeed, it can be. For example, people are known to enjoy belonging to highly cohesive groups. Members of closely knit work groups participate more fully in their group's activities, more readily accept their group's goals, and are absent from their jobs less often than members of less cohesive groups.[23] Not surprisingly, cohesive groups tend to work together quite well, are sometimes exceptionally productive, and have low levels of voluntary turnover.[24]

However, highly cohesive groups also can be problematic. For example, if a highly cohesive group's goals are contrary to the organization's goals, that group is in a position to inflict a great deal of harm to an organization, working against its interests.[25] Highly

Confronting Common Enemies Breeds Group Cohesiveness

Groups become highly cohesive as they work together to ward off common enemies. This applies not only to military groups, such as these American soldiers fighting in Iraq, but also to groups in business organizations whose members face less physical (but no less hostile) battles with their own enemies.

cohesive group members who conspire to sabotage their employers are a good example. With this in mind, it's important to recognize that when it comes to performance group cohesiveness is a double-edged sword: Its effects can be both helpful and harmful.

Individual Performance in Groups

Now that we have reviewed the basic nature of groups, we turn to an aspect of group dynamics most relevant to the field of organizational behavior—the effects of groups on individual performance. Specifically, we will take a look at two different issues in this connection: how people's work performance is affected by the presence of others, and how performance is affected by group size.

Social Facilitation: Working in the Presence of Others

Imagine that you have been studying drama for five years and you are now ready for your first acting audition in front of some Hollywood producers. You have been rehearsing diligently for several months, preparing for the part. Now you are no longer alone at home with your script in front of you. Your name is announced, and silence fills the auditorium as you walk to the front of the stage. How will you perform now that you are in front of an audience? Will you freeze, forgetting the lines you studied so intensely when you practiced alone? Or will the audience spur you on to your best performance yet? In other words, what impact will the presence of the audience have on your behavior?

After studying this question for a century, using a wide variety of tasks and situations, social scientists found that the answer to this question is not straightforward.[26] Sometimes people were found to perform better in the presence of others than when alone, and sometimes they were found to perform better alone than in the presence of others. This tendency for the presence of others to enhance an individual's performance at times and to impair it at other times is known as **social facilitation**. (Although the word *facilitation* implies improvements in task performance, scientists use the term *social facilitation* to refer to both performance improvements and decrements stemming from the presence of others.) What accounts for these seemingly contradictory findings?

social facilitation
The tendency for the presence of others sometimes to enhance an individual's performance and at other times to impair it.

Explaining Social Facilitation. Many scientists believe the phenomenon boils down to several basic psychological processes.[27] First, social facilitation is the result of the heightened emotional arousal (e.g., feelings of tension and excitement) people experience when in the presence of others. (Wouldn't you feel more tension playing the piano in front of an audience than alone?) Second, when people are aroused, they tend to perform the most dominant response—their most likely behavior in that setting. (Returning the smile of a smiling coworker may be considered an example of a dominant act; it is a very well learned act to smile at another who smiles at you.) If someone is performing a very well learned act, the dominant response would be a correct one (such as speaking the right lines during your fiftieth performance). However, if the behavior in question is relatively novel, newly learned, the dominant response would likely be incorrect (such as speaking incorrect lines during an audition).

Together, these ideas are known as the **drive theory of social facilitation**.[28] According to this theory, the presence of others increases arousal, which increases the tendency to perform the most dominant responses. If these responses are correct, the resulting performance will be enhanced; if they are incorrect, the performance will be impaired. Based on these processes, performance may either be helped (if the task is well learned) or hindered (if the task is not well learned). (For a summary of this process see Figure 8.10.)

Research has shown considerable support for this theory: People perform better on tasks in the presence of others if that task is very well learned, but poorer if it is not well learned. Although there are several good explanations for this effect, a key one is based on the idea of **evaluation apprehension**—the fear of being evaluated or judged by another person.[29] Indeed, people may be aroused by performing a task in the presence of others because of their concern over what those others might think of them. For example, lower level employees may suffer evaluation apprehension when they are worried about what their supervisor thinks of their work. Similarly, in the example that opened this section of the chapter, you may face evaluation apprehension in your big acting audition. After all, how well you are received by the producers will go a long way in determining the success of your career. If you know your part well, you will probably perform better in this situation than when rehearsing alone. But, if you're new to the part and can't quite get the hang of it, fear of what important others will think of you will probably lead you to blow this big opportunity.

Social Loafing in Computer-Monitored Groups. Interestingly, with the use of computers in today's workplace, it's not unusual for the presence of others to be "virtual" rather than physical in nature. That is, instead of having an individual who is physically present to observe one's work, **computerized performance monitoring** makes it possible to observe others indirectly, by computer—an "electronic presence." Imagine, for example, that you are entering data into a computer terminal. You can be monitored in a direct physical way by an individual looking over your shoulder, or indirectly by someone

---

drive theory of social facilitation

The theory according to which the presence of others increases arousal, which increases people's tendencies to perform the dominant response. If that response is well learned, performance will improve. But if it is novel, performance will be impaired.

evaluation apprehension

The fear of being evaluated or judged by another person.

computerized performance monitoring

The process of using computers to monitor job performance.

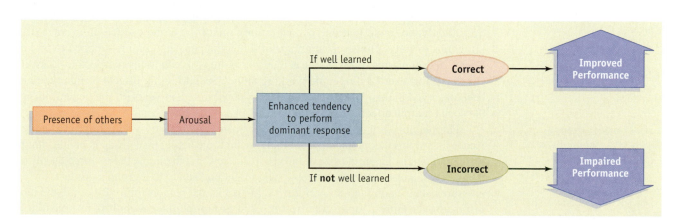

FIGURE 8.10

The Drive Theory of Social Facilitation

According to the drive theory of social facilitation, the presence of others is arousing. This, in turn, enhances the tendency to perform the most dominant (i.e., strongest) responses. If these are correct (such as if the task is well learned), then performance will be improved. However, if these are incorrect (such as if the task is novel), then performance will suffer.

checking a computerized record of the speed and accuracy of your every keystroke. If the task being performed is a complex one, the physical presence of an observer should lead to reduced performance. But does this occur when there is only an electronic presence involved? Research has shown that the answer is yes: Social facilitation occurs even when the "other" person is present only by computer.[30]

From a practical perspective this is important because it suggests that the practice of monitoring job performance so as to keep performance levels high may backfire.[31] That is, instead of causing people to improve their performance, monitoring actually might interfere with performance. Accordingly, if "Big Brother" is watching over workers to ensure that they are performing well, he just might be defeating his own purposes. This is not to say that performance monitoring always is harmful (indeed, see our discussion in Chapter 9). However, it's important to note that the "virtual presence" of others sometimes may have unintended negative effects on task performance.

Social Loafing: "Free Riding" When Working with Others

Have you ever worked with several others helping a friend move into a new apartment, each carrying part of the load from the old place to the new one? Or how about sitting around a table with others stuffing political campaign letters into envelopes and addressing them to potential donors? Although these tasks may seem quite different, they share an important common characteristic: Each requires only a single individual to perform it, but several people's work can be pooled to yield greater outcomes. Reflecting the idea that each person's contributions can be added together with another's, such tasks are known as **additive tasks**.[32]

If you've ever performed additive tasks such as the ones described here, there's a good chance that you found yourself working not quite as hard as you would have if you did them alone. Does this sound familiar to you? Indeed, a considerable amount of research has found that when several people combine their efforts on additive tasks, each individual contributes less than he or she would when performing the same task alone.[33] As suggested by the old saying "Many hands make light the work," a group of people would be expected to be more productive than any one individual. However, when several people combine their efforts on additive tasks, each individual's contribution tends to be less. Five people working together raking leaves will *not* be five times more productive than a single individual working alone; there are always some who go along for a "free ride." In fact, the more individuals who are contributing to an additive task, the less each individual's contribution tends to be—a phenomenon known as **social loafing**.[34]

This effect was first noted almost 70 years ago by a German scientist who compared the amount of force exerted by different-sized groups of people pulling on a rope.[35] Specifically, he found that one person pulling on a rope alone exerted an average of 63 kilograms of force. However, in groups of three, the per-person force dropped to 53 kilograms, and in groups of eight it was reduced to only 31 kilograms per person—less than half the effort exerted by people working alone! Social loafing effects of this type have been observed in many different studies conducted in recent years.[36] The general form of the social loafing effect is shown in Figure 8.11.

The phenomenon of social loafing has been explained by **social impact theory**.[37] According to this theory, the impact of any social force acting on a group is divided among its members. The larger the size of the group, the lower is the impact of its force on any one member. As a result, the more people who might contribute to a group's product, the less pressure each person faces to perform well—that is, the responsibility for doing the job is diffused over more people. As a result, each group member feels less responsible for behaving appropriately, and social loafing occurs.

Is Social Loafing a Universal Phenomenon? A simple way of understanding social loafing is that it occurs because people are more interested in themselves (getting the most for themselves while doing the least) than their fellow group members (who are forced to do their work for them). That this phenomenon occurs in the United States should not be particularly surprising in view of the tendency for American culture to be highly

additive tasks
Types of group tasks in which the coordinated efforts of several people are added together to form the group's product.

social loafing
The tendency for group members to exert less individual effort on an additive task as the size of the group increases.

social impact theory
The theory that explains social loafing in terms of the diffused responsibility for doing what is expected of each member of a group (see *social loafing*). The larger the size of a group, the less each member is influenced by the social forces acting on the group.

FIGURE 8.11

Social Loafing: Its General Form

According to the social loafing effect, when individuals work together on an additive task, the more people contributing to the group's task, the less effort each individual exerts.

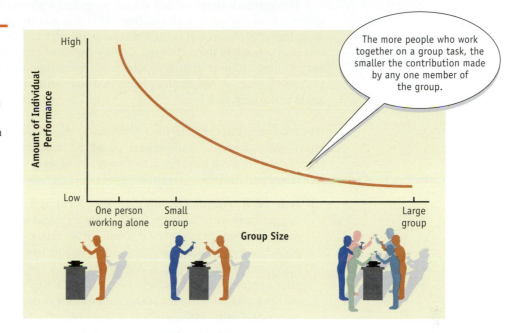

The more people who work together on a group task, the smaller the contribution made by any one member of the group.

individualistic cultures
National groups whose members place a high value on individual accomplishments and personal success.

collectivistic cultures
Cultures in which people placed high value on shared responsibility and the collective good of all.

individualistic. In **individualistic cultures** people highly value individual accomplishments and personal success.

However, in other countries, such as Israel and the People's Republic of China, people place a high value on shared responsibility and the collective good of all. Such nations are referred to as having **collectivistic cultures**. In such cultures, people working in groups would not be expected to engage in social loafing because doing so would have them fail in their social responsibility to the group (a responsibility that does not prevail in individualistic cultures). In fact, to the extent that people in collectivistic cultures are strongly motivated to help their fellow group members, they would be expected to be *more* productive in groups than alone. That is, not only wouldn't they loaf, but they would work especially hard!

These ideas were tested in an interesting experiment.[38] In this research managers from the United States, Israel, and the People's Republic of China were each asked to complete an "in-basket" exercise. This task simulated the daily activities of managers in all three countries, such as writing memos, filling out forms, and rating job applicants. They were all asked to perform this task as well as they could for a period of one hour, but under one of two different conditions: either *alone,* or as part of a *group* of 10. Research participants who worked alone were simply asked to write their names on each item they completed and to turn it in. In the group condition participants were told that their group's overall performance would be assessed at the end of the period. Fellow group members were not physically present, but were described as being highly similar to themselves with respect to their family and religious backgrounds as well as their interests. (The researchers reasoned that groups of this type would be ones whose members people would be especially reluctant to let down by loafing.) To compare the various groups, each participant's in-basket exercises were scored by converting the responses to standardized performance scores. Did social loafing occur, and in which countries? The results are summarized in Figure 8.12 (see p. 307).

These data clearly show that social loafing occurred in the United States. That is, individual performance was significantly lower among people working in groups than those working alone. However, the opposite was found in each of the two highly collectivistic cultures, the People's Republic of China and Israel. In both these countries, individuals performed at higher levels when working in groups than when working alone. In these nations, people not only failed to loaf in groups, but they worked *harder* than they did alone. Because they strongly identified with their groups and were concerned about the welfare of its members, members of collectivistic cultures placed their group's interests ahead of their own. (It is important to note that these findings only occurred when people believed that they had strong ties to the members of their groups.)

This research suggests that culture plays an important role in determining people's tendencies to engage in social loafing. Although it is tempting to think of social loafing as an inevitable aspect of human nature, it appears that the phenomenon is not as universal as you might think. Instead, loafing appears to be a manifestation of cultural values: Among cultural groups in which individualism is stressed, individual interests guide performance, but among groups in which collectivism is stressed, group interests guide performance.

Overcoming Social Loafing. Obviously, the tendency for people to reduce their effort when working with others could be a serious problem in organizations. Fortunately, research has shown that there are several ways in which social loafing can be overcome.

1. *Make each performer identifiable.* Social loafing may occur when people feel they can get away with "taking it easy"—namely, under conditions in which each individual's contributions cannot be determined. A variety of studies on the practice of *public posting* support this idea.[39] This research has found that when each individual's contribution to a task is displayed where it can be seen by others (e.g., weekly sales figures posted on a chart), people are less likely to slack off than when only overall group (or company-wide) performance is made available. In other words, the more one's individual contribution to a group effort is highlighted, the more pressure each person feels to make a group contribution. Thus, social loafing can be overcome if one's contributions to an additive task are identified: Potential loafers are not likely to loaf if they fear getting caught.

2. *Make work tasks more important and interesting.* Research has revealed that people are unlikely to go along for a free ride when the task they are performing is believed to be vital to the organization.[40] For example, research has found that the less meaningful salespeople believe their jobs are, the more they engage in social loafing—especially when they think their supervisors know little about how well they are working.[41] To help in this regard, corporate officials should deliberately attempt to make jobs more intrinsically interesting to employees. To the extent that jobs are interesting, people may be less likely to loaf.

3. *Reward individuals for contributing to their group's performance*—that is, encourage their interest in their group's performance.[42] Doing this (e.g., giving all salespeople in a territory a bonus if they jointly exceed their sales goal) may help employees focus more on collective concerns and less on individualistic concerns, increasing their obligations to their fellow group members. This is important, of course, in that the success of an organization is more likely to be influenced by the collective efforts of groups than by the individual contributions of any one member.

4. *Use punishment threats.* To the extent that performance decrements may be controlled by threatening to punish the individuals slacking off, loafing may be reduced. This effect was demonstrated in an experiment involving members of high school swim teams who swam either alone or in relay races during practice sessions.[43] In some conditions, the coach threatened the team by telling them that everyone would have to swim "penalty laps" if anyone on the team failed to meet a specified difficult time for swimming 100 yards freestyle. In a control group, no punishment threats were issued. How did the punishment threats influence task performance? The researchers found that people swam faster alone than as part of relay teams when no punishment was threatened, thereby confirming the social loafing effect. However, when punishment threats were made, group performance increased, thereby eliminating the social loafing effect.

Together, these findings suggest that social loafing is a potent force—and one that can be a serious threat to organizational performance. But, it can be controlled in several ways that counteract the desire to loaf, such as by making loafing socially embarrassing or harmful to other individual interests.

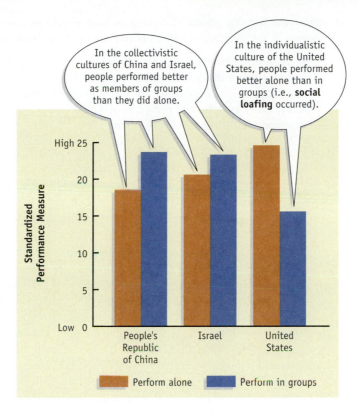

FIGURE 8.12

Social Loafing Is Not a Universal Phenomenon

Researchers compared the performance of people from the United States, Israel, and the People's Republic of China who worked alone and in groups on a managerial task. Although individual performance alone was lower than performance as part of a group in the United States (i.e., social loafing occurred), the opposite was found in China and Israel. Compared to the more individualistic nature of American culture, the highly collectivistic nature of Chinese and Israeli cultures discouraged people in these nations from letting down their fellow group members.

Source: Based on data reported by Earley, 1993; see Note 38.

Teams: Special Kinds of Groups

If you think about some of the groups we've described thus far in this chapter, such as the one in use at Motorola (described in our Preview Case, pp. 289–290) and the hypothetical budget committee (described in conjunction with the five-stage model, pp. 294–296), you'll quickly recognize that they are somehow different. Although they are each composed of several individuals working together toward common goals, the connections between the employees at Motorola appear to be much deeper in scope. The budget committee members may be interested in what they're doing, but the group members at Motorola seem more highly committed to their work and are more highly involved in the way their jobs are done. This is not to say that there is necessarily anything wrong with the corporate budget committee; in fact, it would appear to be a rather typical group. The groups at Motorola, however, are examples of special kinds of groups known as *teams*.

Defining Teams and Distinguishing Them from Groups

team
A group whose members have complementary skills and are committed to a common purpose or set of performance goals for which they hold themselves mutually accountable.

A **team** may be defined as a group whose members have complementary skills and are committed to a common purpose or set of performance goals for which they hold themselves mutually accountable.[44] At this point, it may not be entirely clear to you exactly how a team is different from an ordinary group. This confusion probably stems in part from the fact that people often refer to their groups as teams, although they are really not teams.[45] Yet there are several important distinctions between them (see Figure 8.13).

■ In groups, performance typically depends on the work of individual members. The performance of a team, however, depends on both individual contributions and *collective work products*—the joint outcome of team members working in concert.

■ Typically, members of groups pool their resources to attain a goal, although it is individual performance that is taken into consideration when it comes to issuing rewards. Members of groups usually do not take responsibility for any results other than their own. By contrast, teams focus on both individual and *mutual accountability*—that is, they work together to produce an outcome (e.g., a product, service, or decision) that represents their joint contributions, and each team member shares responsibility for that outcome. The key difference is this: In groups, the supervisor holds individual members accountable for their work, whereas in teams, members hold themselves accountable.

■ Whereas group members may share a common interest goal, team members also share a *common commitment to purpose.* Moreover, these purposes typically are concerned with winning in some way, such as being first or best at something. For example, a work team in a manufacturing plant of a financially troubled company may be highly committed to making the company the top one in its industry. Another team, one in a public high school, may be committed to preparing all its graduates for the challenges of the world better than any other school in the district. Team members focusing jointly on such lofty purposes, in conjunction with specific performance goals, become heavily invested in its activities. In fact, teams are said to establish "ownership" of their purposes and usually spend a great deal of time establishing their purposes. Like groups, teams use goals to monitor their progress. Teams, however, also have a broader purpose which supplies a source of meaning and emotional energy to the activities performed.

■ Teams differ from groups with respect to the nature of their connections to management. Work groups are typically required to be responsive to demands regularly placed on them by management. By contrast, once management establishes the mission for a team, and sets the challenge for it to achieve, it typically gives the team enough flexibility to do its job without any further interference. In other words, teams are to varying degrees *self-managing*—that is, they are to some extent free to set their own goals, timing, and the approach that they wish to take, usually without management interference. Thus, many teams are described as being *autonomous* or *semi-autonomous* in nature. This is not to say that teams are completely independent of corporate management and supervision. They still must be responsive to demands from higher levels (often, higher level teams, known as *top management teams*).

FIGURE 8.13

Groups vs. Teams: A Comparison

Groups may be distinguished from teams in terms of the various characteristics summarized here.

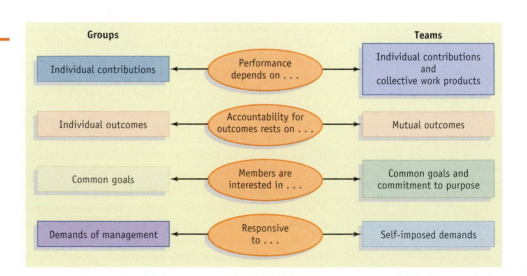

Teams are getting so much attention in the workplace these days that you'd almost think they are the latest management fad. But they are not. In fact, teams have been around for several decades—and they are here to stay. In fact, as summarized in Table 8.3, the history of business reveals many examples of highly successful teams.[46] (Obviously, attaining high levels of success is—and has been—one of the key objectives of work teams. For some suggestions on how to achieve high levels of team performance, see the *How to Do It* section on p. 310.)

Types of Teams

In view of their widespread popularity, it should not be surprising to learn that there are many different kinds of teams. To help make sense out of these, scientists have categorized teams into several different commonly found types, which vary along five major dimensions (see Figure 8.14).[47]

Purpose or Mission. The first dimension has to do with teams' major *purpose or mission*. In this regard, some teams—known as **work teams**—are primarily concerned with the work done by the organization, such as developing and manufacturing new products, providing services for customers, and so on. Their principal focus is on using the organization's resources to effectively create its results (be they goods or services). Other teams—known as **improvement teams**—are primarily oriented toward the mission of increasing the effectiveness of the processes that are used by the organization. For example, Texas Instruments has relied on teams to help improve the quality of operations at its plant in Malaysia.[48]

work teams
Teams whose members are concerned primarily with using the organization's resources to effectively create its results.

improvement teams
Teams whose members are oriented primarily toward the mission of increasing the effectiveness of the processes used by the organization.

TABLE 8.3 Some Teams That Worked Wonders

Over the years, many of the most successful business products and services have been the result of teamwork. Here are a half-dozen that *Fortune* magazine referred to as having "changed the world"—or, at least, boosted business considerably.

Date	Project	Accomplishment
1879	Electric light bulb	Four men from around the world—a British machinist, a Swiss clockmaker, a German glassblower, an American mathematician—joined famous inventor Thomas Edison in Menlo Park, New Jersey, to develop the first electric light bulb. Each contributed skills and expertise that made the invention come to fruition.
1943	Military aircraft, such as the F-104 Starfighter and the U-2 spy plane	A team of aeronautical engineers from Lockheed isolated themselves from others, devoting all their time to projects. People from various specialties, such as designers and metalworkers, worked side by side to avoid drafting anything that could not be built.
1947–1951	Housing development in Levittown, NY	In 26 precisely choreographed moves, several teams of two or three construction workers in various specialties (e.g., carpenters, electricians, plumbers, etc.) built simple, inexpensive homes for people of modest means.
1979–1982	Apple Macintosh computer	Holed up in an isolated facility, Steve Jobs (Apple's co-founder) headed a team of computer engineers who built the first Mac computers (debuting in 1983). They labored intensely, sometimes working 48 hours nonstop, to develop a user-friendly product. Team members carefully coordinated their efforts but competed intensely against other units in the company.
1980–1984	Ford Taurus	Before the Taurus, Ford developed new cars by having separate groups work in isolation, passing ideas along from one group to the next. After losing billions of dollars in this manner, Ford created a 400-person team to develop the Taurus, which debuted in 1985 (and eventually was discontinued in 2005). The jellybean-shaped car won raves and boosted sales.
1997	"Priceless" MasterCard ad campaign	A three-person creative team at the McCann Erickson advertising agency was charged with turning around business at MasterCard, which was losing ground to Visa. After brainstorming for a month, they came up with the highly successful "Priceless" ad campaign. Running in 108 countries, the campaign has helped MasterCard sign twice as many new accounts as Visa.

Source: Fortune, 2006; see Note 46.

HOW TO DO IT

Learning from High-Performance Teams

Clearly, teams are very special entities. However, some teams go far beyond the ordinary characteristics of teams and are known as **high-performance teams**. These are teams whose members are deeply committed to one another's personal growth and success.[49] The RAZR team at Motorola (described in our Preview Case, pp. 289–290) may be considered an example. Such teams are referred to as high-performance teams because they perform at much higher levels than ordinary teams (whose members lack this additional commitment to others' growth and success).[50]

Members of the best performing teams show exceptionally high levels of mutual care, trust, and respect for each other. How do they get that way? Although creating high-performance teams can be very challenging, research suggests that several characteristics must be emulated for high-performance teams to exist.[51] These are as follows.

1. *Empower people to make decisions.* In the best-performing work teams, people are free to make their own decisions without checking with others.

2. *Share responsibility.* It's not only an individual manager who is responsible for what happens, but everyone on the team.

3. *Have a common sense of purpose.* Everyone on the team must be pulling in the same direction; all members agree on what they are trying to accomplish.

4. *Focus on the task at hand.* Successful teams care about results and members coordinate their individual talents to achieving them.

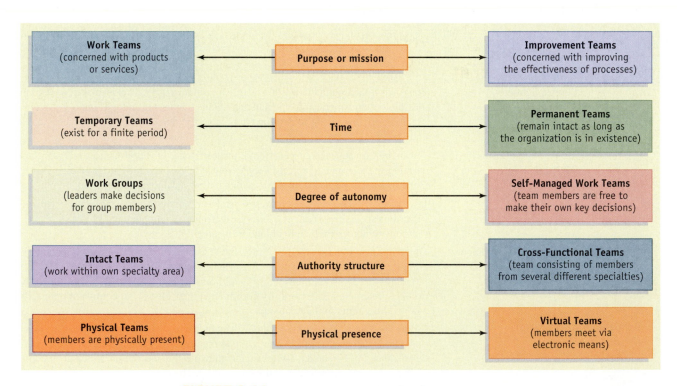

FIGURE 8.14

Types of Teams

The teams found in organizations may be distinguished from each other with respect to the five major dimensions identified here.

Source: Based on suggestions by Mohrman, 1993; see Note 47.

high-performance teams
Teams whose members are deeply committed to one another's personal growth and success.

Time. A second dimension has to do with *time*. Specifically, some teams are only *temporary* and are established for a specific project with a finite life. For example, a team set up to develop a new product would be considered temporary. As soon as its job is done, it disbands. However, other kinds of teams are *permanent* and stay intact as long as the organization is operating. For example, teams focusing on providing effective customer service tend to be permanent parts of many organizations.

Degree of Autonomy. A third distinction has to do with the degree to which teams operate autonomously.[52] This reflects the extent to which employees are responsible for making their own decisions (as opposed to having their bosses make them) and the degree to which they (as opposed to their bosses) are accountable for their own work outcomes. As shown in Figure 8.15, various points along the resulting continuum of autonomy can be conceptualized as different types of groups.

At the extreme low end of the scale (where bosses are responsible for decisions and accountable for work outcomes), we find standard *work groups*. These are groups in which leaders make decisions on behalf of group members, whose job it is to follow the leader's orders. This traditional kind of group has become less popular in recent years, as more organizations have granted employees higher degrees of responsibility for decisions and accountability for outcomes to work groups. These are known as **semi-autonomous work groups**—work groups in which employees get to share in the responsibility for decisions with their bosses and are jointly accountable for their work outcomes.

semi-autonomous work groups
Work groups in which employees get to share in the responsibility for decisions with their bosses and are jointly accountable for their work outcomes.

self-managed teams (self-directed teams)
Teams whose members are permitted to make key decisions about how their work is done.

self-directed teams
See *self-managed teams*.

At the opposite end of the scale, we find employees are free to make their own key decisions and are accountable for them. Such groups are commonly referred to as **self-managed teams** (also known as **self-directed teams**). Typically, self-managed teams consist of small numbers of employees, often around 10, who take on duties that used to be performed by their supervisors. This is likely to include making work assignments, deciding on the pace of work, determining how quality is to be assessed, and even specifying who gets to join the team.[53] A summary of the major distinctions between self-managed teams and traditional work groups is shown in Table 8.4.[54]

FIGURE 8.15

A Continuum of Autonomy

In work groups, bosses have responsibility over decisions and are accountable for work outcomes. The workers themselves have very little autonomy. By contrast, in self-managed work teams, the workers themselves have responsibility over decisions and are accountable for work outcomes. They are highly autonomous. Semi-autonomous work groups are positioned between these two extremes.

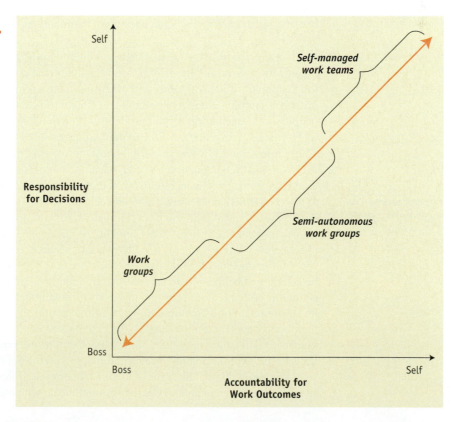

TABLE 8.4 Self-Managed Teams vs. Traditional Work Groups: A Comparison

As summarized here, self-managed teams differ from traditional work groups in many important ways.

Self-Managed Teams	Traditional Work Groups
Customer driven	Management driven
Multiskilled workforce	Workforce of isolated specialists
Few job descriptions	Many job descriptions
Information shared widely	Information limited
Few levels of management	Many levels of management
Whole-business focus	Function/department focus
Shared goals	Segregated goals
Seemingly chaotic	Seemingly organized
Purpose achievement emphasis	Problem-solving emphasis
High worker commitment	High management commitment
Continuous improvements	Incremental improvements
Self-controlled	Management controlled
Values/principle based	Policy/procedure based

Source: From K. Fisher, *Leading Self-Directed Work Teams,* © 1993. New York: McGraw-Hill. Reprinted with permission of the McGraw-Hill Companies. See Note 54.

Self-managed work teams are growing in popularity. In fact, it has been estimated that close to 50 percent of companies have at least one team in place that is self-directed to at least some extent.[55] The list of companies using teams includes many large corporations, such as Xerox, Hewlett-Packard, Honeywell, and PepsiCo. Procter & Gamble, Cummins Engine, and General Motors have used self-managed work teams for around 50 years.[56] All self-managed work teams are not alike. In fact, they differ considerably with respect to what exact aspects of the job they get to manage (for a summary, see Figure 8.16).[57] When you consider that different self-managed teams get to manage different aspects of themselves, it becomes clear why we depict the degree of autonomy in Figure 8.15 as a continuum.

Authority Structure. The fourth dimension reflects the team's connection to the organization's overall *authority structure*—that is, the connection between various formal job responsibilities. In some organizations teams remain *intact* with respect to their organizational functions. For example, at Ralston-Purina projects are structured such that people work together on certain products all the time and do not apply their specialty to a wide range of products. Within such organizations, teams can operate without the ambiguities created by straying from one's area of expertise.

With growing frequency, however, we are seeing teams that cross over various functional units (e.g., marketing, finance, human resources, and so on). Such teams are commonly referred to as **cross-functional teams**. These are teams composed of employees at identical organizational levels, but from different specialty areas, to work together on a task. Cross-functional teams represent an effective way of bringing people together from throughout the organization to cooperate with each other on the diverse tasks needed to complete large projects.

In organizations using cross-functional teams, the boundaries between all teams must be considered permeable. Indeed, people frequently are members of more than one team—a situation often required for organizations to function effectively. For example, members of an organization's manufacturing team must carefully coordinate their activities with members of its marketing team. To the extent that people are involved in several different kinds of teams, they may gain broader perspectives and make more important contributions to their various teams (for an example, see Figure 8.17).

As you might imagine, cross-functional teams are difficult to manage. It takes time for specialists in different areas to learn to communicate with each other and to coordinate their

cross-functional teams
Teams represented by people from different specialty areas within organizations.

FIGURE 8.16

Self-Managed Work Teams: What Do They Manage?

As shown here, all self-managed work teams are not alike. Whereas the vast majority are able to schedule their own work assignments and to work with outside customers, far fewer are able to do other things, such as hire and fire coworkers.

Source: Training, 1996; see Note 57.

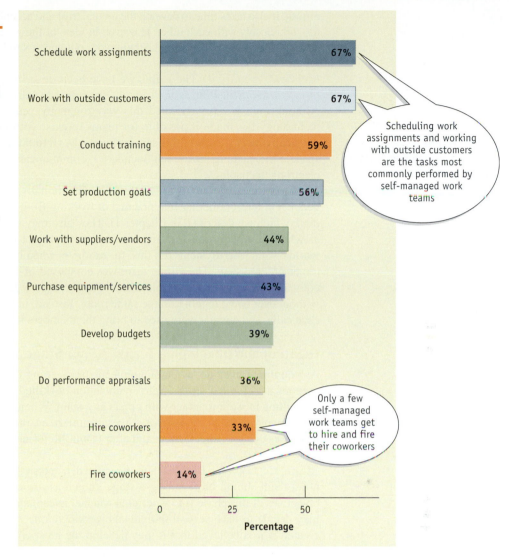

Schedule work assignments — 67%
Work with outside customers — 67%
Conduct training — 59%
Set production goals — 56%
Work with suppliers/vendors — 44%
Purchase equipment/services — 43%
Develop budgets — 39%
Do performance appraisals — 36%
Hire coworkers — 33%
Fire coworkers — 14%

Percentage

Scheduling work assignments and working with outside customers are the tasks most commonly performed by self-managed work teams

Only a few self-managed work teams get to hire and fire their coworkers

FIGURE 8.17

A Cross-Functional Team in Action

Boeing relied on cross-functional teams to design and manufacture its latest aircraft, the 777. Company officials credit the use of teams for the record speed and exceptional quality with which this enormous airplane was developed.

efforts. It also takes time to develop the mutual trust and acceptance that is required for people to work closely with each other. However, in view of the great successes of cross-functional teams, the effort required to make them work out appears to be worthwhile.

Physical Presence. The teams we have been describing this far may be considered *physical teams* insofar as they involve people who physically meet to work together. Although teams have operated this way for many years, and will continue to do so, technology has made it possible for teams to exist without ever having their members physically meet. Teams of this sort are known as **virtual teams**—teams that operate across space, time, and organizational boundaries, communicating with each other only through electronic technology.[58]

Sometimes, virtual teams form quite unintentionally, such as when valued team members begin telecommuting (the practice of working from home, but communicating via e-mail, which we described in Chapter 1). They also may be formed very deliberately, such as when it is important to bring together on a project the most talented people in the world.[59] Sun Microsystems did this, for example, when it developed a new electronic customer order system. The virtual team was composed of 15 engineers from three different companies in three different countries.[60] They worked together over a seven-month period without ever being together in the same room. Instead, intranets, teleconferencing, conference calls, and e-mails were used to bring the members together.

Creating and Developing Teams: A Four-Stage Process

As you might imagine, assembling a team and keeping it going is no easy task. Doing so requires not only having the right combination of skilled people, but also individuals who are willing to work together with others as a team. When done properly, designing a work team involves the four distinct stages summarized in Figure 8.18.[61] Note that these processes occur before, during, and after teams are formed.

Stage 1: Prework. Before teams are created, a decision has to be made about whether or not a team should be formed—a stage known as *prework*. One of the most important objectives of this phase is to determine whether a team should be created at all. A manager may decide to have several individuals working alone answer to him, or a team may be created if it is believed that it may develop the most creative and insightful ways to get things done. In considering this, it is important to note exactly what work needs to be done. The team's objectives must be established, and an inventory of the skills needed to do the job should be made. In addition, decisions should be made in advance about what authority the team should have. They may just be advisory to the manager, or they may be given full responsibility and authority for executing their task (i.e., self-regulating).

Stage 2: Create Performance Conditions. Building on the prework, organizational officials must ensure that the team has the proper resources needed to carry out its work. This involves both material resources (e.g., tools, equipment, and money), human resources (e.g., the appropriate blend of skilled professionals), and support from the organization (e.g., willingness to let the team do its own work as it sees fit). Unless managers help create the proper conditions for team success, they are contributing to its failure.

Stage 3: Form and Build the Team. Three things may be done to help a team get off to a good start. First, managers should form boundaries—clearly establish who is and who is not a member of the team. Some teams fail simply because membership in it is left unclear. Reducing such ambiguity can help avoid confusion and frustration. Second, members must accept the team's overall mission and purpose. Unless they do, failure is inevitable. Third, organizational officials should clarify the team's mission and responsibilities—make perfectly clear exactly what it is expected to do (but not necessarily *how* to do it). Will team members be responsible for monitoring and planning their own work? If so, such expectations should be spelled out explicitly.

---

virtual teams
Teams that operate across space, time, and organizational boundaries, communicating with each other only through electronic technology.

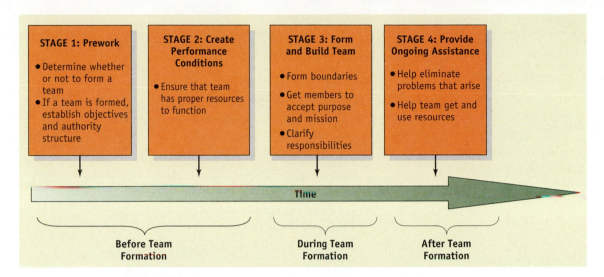

FIGURE 8.18

The Four Stages of Group Creation and Development

Successful teams are created and nurtured following the four steps summarized here.

Source: Based on suggestions by Hackman, 2002; see Note 61.

Stage 4: Provide Ongoing Assistance. Finally, once a team is functioning, supervisors may be needed to help by helping the team to eliminate problems and perform even better. For example, disruptive team members may be either counseled or replaced. Similarly, material resources may have to be replenished or upgraded. Although it may be unwise for a manager to intervene in the successful affairs of a team that has taken on its own life, it also may be unwise to neglect opportunities to help a team do even better.

As you ponder these suggestions, you doubtlessly will recognize the considerable managerial skill and hard work it takes to create and manage teams effectively. However, as managers learn these skills, and as individuals gain successful experiences as members of effective work teams, the deliberate steps outlined above may become second nature to all concerned. In the words of one expert, "When that stage is reached, the considerable investment required to learn how to use work teams well can pay substantial dividends—in work effectiveness and in the quality of the experience of both managers and [team] members."[62]

Effective Team Performance

In recent years, the popular press has been filled with impressive claims about the success of teams in improving quality, customer service, productivity, and the bottom line.[63] For a sampling of some findings cited, see Table 8.5.[64]

Clearly, we are led to believe that teams in general can produce very impressive results. However, it is important to consider whether or not such claims are valid. In this section we will examine evidence bearing on this question. Then we will focus on some of the obstacles to team success, and some of the things that can be done to help promote highly successful teams.

How Successful Are Teams?

The most direct way to learn about companies' experiences with work teams is to survey the officials of organizations that use them. One large-scale study did precisely this.[65] The sample consisted of several hundred of the 1,000 largest companies in the United States. About 47 percent used some work teams, although these were typically in place in only a few selected sites, as opposed to the entire organization. Where they were used, however, they were generally highly regarded. Moreover, teams were viewed as becoming increasingly popular over time.

TABLE 8.5 A Summary of Team Success Stories

Here are just a few of the organizational successes touted in support of teams. Despite these impressive reports, care needs to be used in generalizing. Not all teams may enjoy such success. In fact, it is far from guaranteed.

Organization	Results
P&G manufacturing	30–50% lower manufacturing cost.
FedEx	Cut service glitches (incorrect bills and lost packages) by 13% in one year.
Shenandoah Life Insurance	Case handling time went from 27 to 2 days. Service complaints "practically eliminated."
Sherwin-Williams Richmond	Costs 45% lower. Returned goods down 75%.
Tektronix Portables	Moved from least profitable to most profitable division within two years.
Rohm and Haas Knoxville	Productivity up 60%.
Tavistock coal mine	Output 25% higher with lower costs than on a comparison face. Accidents, sickness, and absenteeism cut 50%.
Westinghouse Airdrie	Reduced cycle time from 17 weeks to 1 week.
General Electrical Salisbury	Productivity improved 250%.
Aid Association for Lutherans (AAL)	Raised productivity by 20% and cut case processing time by 75%.
Cummins Engine Jamestown	Met $8,000 price of Japanese competitor for an engine expected to sell for $12,000.
Xerox	Teams at least 30% more productive than conventional operations.
Best Foods Little Rock	Highest-quality products at lowest costs of any Best Foods plant.
Volvo Kalmar	Production costs 25% less than Volvo's conventional plants.
Ford Hermosillo	In first year of operation, lower defect rate than in most Japanese automakers.
Weyerhauser Manitowoc	Output increased 33%. Profits doubled.
Northern Telecom Harrisburg	Profits doubled.
General Mills	Productivity 40% higher than traditional factories.
Honeywell Chandler	Output increased 280%. Quality stepped up from 82% to 99.5%.
American Transtech	Reduced costs and processing time by 50%.

Source: From K. Fisher, *Leading Self-Directed Work Teams,* © 1993. New York: McGraw-Hill. Reprinted with permission of the McGraw-Hill Companies. See Note 64.

These optimistic results are further supported by in-depth case studies of numerous teams in many different organizations.[66] Consider, for example, the work teams used in General Motors' battery plant in Fitzgerald, Georgia. The employees at this facility operate in various teams, including managers working together in *support teams,* middle-level employees (such as foremen and technicians) working in *coordination teams,* and *employee teams,* natural work units of three to 19 members performing specific tasks. Although the teams work closely together, coordinating their activities, they function almost as separate businesses. Because employees must perform many different tasks in their team, they are not paid based on their positions, but for their knowledge and competence. In fact, the highest-paid employees are individuals who have demonstrated their competence (usually by highly demanding tests) on all the jobs performed in at least two different teams. This is GM's way of rewarding people for broadening their perspectives, appreciating "the other guy's problems." By many measures, the Fitzgerald plant has been very effective. Its production costs are lower than comparable units in traditionally run plants. Employee satisfaction surveys also reveal that job satisfaction at this plant is among the highest found at any General Motors facility.

Although case studies report successful experiences with teams, they are not entirely objective. After all, companies may be unwilling to broadcast their failures to the world. This suggests that more objective empirical research is needed. Overall, the results of such studies have been mixed. Whereas some studies have shown that autonomous teams have significantly fewer accidents as well as lower rates of absenteeism and turnover than traditional work groups,[67] other studies have found that although many team members are satisfied with their arrangements, they are not any more productive than they were when working individually.[68]

So, what's the conclusion? Are teams effective? Taken together, research suggests that teams are well received. Most people enjoy working in teams, at least after they have adjusted to them (which can take some work). Certainly, teams help enhance commitment among employees, and as we described in Chapter 6, there are benefits to be derived from this (e.g., reduced absenteeism and turnover). From an organizational perspective, teams appear to be an effective way of eliminating layers of management, thereby allowing more work done to be done by fewer people, which also can be a valuable money-saving contribution. All of these benefits are tangible. However, it is important to keep in mind that teams are not always responsible for making individuals and organizations any more productive. Cases of companies becoming wildly successful after adopting teams, although compelling, cannot always be generalized to all teams in all situations.

Potential Obstacles to Success: Why Some Teams Fail

Although we have reported many success stories about teams, we also have hinted at several possible problems and difficulties in implementing them. After all, working in a team demands a great deal, and not everyone may be ready for them. Fortunately, we can learn from these experiences.[69] Analyses of failed attempts at introducing teams into the workplace suggest several obstacles to team success, pitfalls that can be avoided if you know them (see Figure 8.19).[70]

Unwillingness to Cooperate. First, some teams fail because their members are unwilling to cooperate with one another. This is what happened a few years ago at Dow Chemical Company's plastics group in Midland, Michigan, where a team was put into place to create a new plastic resin.[71] Some members (those in the research field) wanted to spend several months developing and testing new options, while others (those on the

FIGURE 8.19

A High-Flying Team Success

Founded by Guy Laliberté in 1984 as a troupe of 20 Montreal street performers, Cirque du Soleil now consists of 3,000 acrobats and other amazing performers (e.g., contortionists, jugglers, etc.) in 13 teams that travel the world annually. The company's success, both creatively and financially, is predicated on the mutual connections between everyone. Members are interested in cooperating with one another (especially given the consequences of falling from the trapeze), they are supported by the company (players receive 10 percent of the profits), Laliberté is willing to relinquish control to experts who know aspects of the business better than him, and core members from the various troupes cooperate with one another by sharing ideas in meetings held 10 times a year.

manufacturing end) wanted to slightly alter existing products and start up production right away. Neither side budged, and the project eventually stalled. By contrast, when team members share a common vision and are committed to attaining it, they are generally very cooperative with each other, leading to success.

Lack of Management Support.   A second reason why some teams are not effective is that they fail to receive support from management. Consider, for example, the experience at the Lenexa, Kansas plant of the Puritan-Bennett Corporation, a manufacturer of respiratory equipment.[72] After seven years of working to develop improved software for its respirators, product development teams have not gotten the job done, despite that the industry average for such tasks is only three years. According to Roger J. Dolida, the company's director of research and development, the problem is that management never made the project a priority and refused to free up another key person needed to do the job. As he put it, "If top management doesn't buy into the idea . . . teams can go nowhere."[73]

Managers' Reluctance to Relinquish Control.   A third obstacle to group success, and a relatively common one, is that some managers are unwilling to relinquish control. Good supervisors work their way up from the plant floor by giving orders and having them followed. However, team leaders have to build consensus and must allow team members to make decisions together. As you might expect, letting go of control isn't always easy for some to do. This problem emerged at Bausch & Lomb's sunglasses plant in Rochester, New York.[74] Some years ago, about 1,400 employees were put into 38 teams. After a few years, about half the supervisors had not adjusted to the change, despite receiving thorough training in how to work as part of a team. They argued bitterly with team members whenever their ideas were not accepted by the team, and eventually they were reassigned. (In addition to the difficulties associated with relinquishing power, team leaders sometimes have reason to be concerned about whether they are even needed at all. If teams are allowed to make their own decisions, it's possible that they may be able to function without any leadership. For a look at this issue, see the *OB: Making Sense Out of Common Sense* section on p. 319.)

Failure to Cooperate Between Teams.   Fourth, teams might fail not only because their members do not cooperate with each other, but also because they fail to cooperate with other teams. This problem occurred in General Electric's medical systems division when it assigned two teams of engineers, one in Waukesha, Wisconsin, and another in Hino, Japan, the task of creating software for two new ultrasound devices.[75] Teams pushed features that made their products popular only in their own countries and duplicated each other's efforts. When teams met, language and cultural barriers separated them, further distancing the teams from each other. Without close cooperation between teams (as well as within them!), organizations are unlikely to reap the benefits they hoped for when creating teams in the first place.[76]

Developing Successful Teams

Making teams work effectively is no easy task. Success is not automatic. Rather, teams need to be carefully nurtured and maintained for them to accomplish their missions.[77] As one expert expressed it, "Teams are the Ferraris of work design. They're high performance but high maintenance and expensive."[78] What, then, could be done to help make teams as effective as possible? Based on analyses of successful teams, several keys to success may be identified.[79]

Compensate Team Performance

Because the United States and Canada are highly individualistic cultures, most North American workers are used to highly individualistic compensation systems—ones that recognize individual performance. However, when it comes to teams, it is also very important

OB Making Sense Out of Common Sense

Team Leaders: When Do They Matter?

When a sports team has a poor season, the coach is likely to be ousted, often to the delight of disappointed fans hoping for a turnaround. Similarly, executives of underperforming companies and U.S. presidents serving in periods of economic downturn also are likely to be kicked out of office. Common sense suggests not only that the person at the top deserves to pay for failure by leaving his or her post, but also that things stand to improve as a result. Often, this is reasonable given that poor leaders can undermine the performance of even the most talented team members (be they athletes or employees in other industries), whereas exceptional leaders can bring out the best in team members and get them to perform at extremely high levels (see Chapter 13).

Despite their actual contributions, and the importance we accord them in society, it's important to acknowledge that leaders are only one determinant of a team's success. In fact, it's possible that some teams may succeed or fail regardless of—or even despite—their leaders' influence. This raises an interesting and important question: Under what conditions do team leaders matter most?

Scientists have identified two sets of external factors that constrain team performance in ways that limit the extent to which even the best leaders can make a difference.[80] These are: (1) team-level constraints (i.e., aspects of the technological and organizational context within which the team operates), and (2) contextual constraints (i.e., factors associated with the broad institutional context within which the team operates).

Team-level constraints. Consider the nature of work on a mechanized assembly line. Machines are paced at fixed speeds, the assembly procedures are predetermined, and the operations involved always are performed in the same highly routinized ways. In this case, the performance of the team is unlikely to be influenced by the leader. The design of the work itself largely dictates how well the team performs.

Now, consider the opposite situation, such as a product development team at a company like 3M. Scientists work at rates they determine themselves, performing highly complex work in which they have a great deal of discretion. Under such conditions, it makes sense that team leaders can make a big difference. By intervening, team leaders can contribute to their team's effectiveness by helping members gather and use resources most effectively. By contrast, of course, a leader also may disrupt task performance by interfering with what the team needs to succeed.

Contextual constraints. Just as aspects of a team's work may affect the extent to which leaders matter, so too do aspects of the organizational environments in which they operate. Consider, for example, the work done by members of an emergency rescue squad. Given the highly noble and important cause for which they labor—saving lives—it's unlikely that their leader may have much impact on members' capacity to work any harder than they already do. Similarly, constraints also are imposed by laws that dictate what must (or must not) be done. For example, members of a human resources team have to refrain from making hiring decisions on the basis of applicants' race regardless of what their leader may say or do. Finally, the labor market also constrains a team leader's impact. Consider our example of an athletic coach. Even the most talented coach can only have so much impact on a team of weak, clumsy, unmotivated players. Although the coach may help make them as good as they can be, the players' own limitations surely will make a big difference. After all, as they say, "you can't make a silk purse out of a sow's ear." In fact, it is with this in mind that leaders endeavor to select the best members of their teams.

In conclusion, we have to be careful when it comes to blaming team leaders for their team's failure or crediting them for their team's success. Leaders may make a difference, to be sure, but the degree to which they deserve the credit or blame requires taking into account the conditions under which their teams operate.

---

to recognize group performance. Teams are no places for hotshots who want to make their individual marks—rather, teams require "team players." And the more organizations reward employees for their teams' successes, the more strongly team spirit will be reinforced. Several companies in which teams are widely used—including the Hannaford Brothers retail food distribution company in New York and Westinghouse's defense and commercial electronics plant in Texas—rely on gain-sharing plans to reward teams. These plans reward team members for reaching company-wide performance goals, allowing them to share in the company's profits.

Because it is important for team members to have a variety of different skills, many companies, including Milwaukee Insurance, Colgate-Palmolive, and Sterling Winthrop, have taken to paying employees for their demonstrated skills, as opposed to their job performance. Such a system is known as skill-based pay. A highly innovative skill-based pay system has been in use at Tenessee Eastman, for example. This company's "pay-for-applied-skills-and knowledge" plan—or *PASK,* as it is known—requires employees to demonstrate their skills in several key areas, including technical skills and interpersonal skills. The pay scale is linked carefully to the number of skills acquired and the level of proficiency attained. By encouraging the development of vital skills in this manner, the company is ensuring that it has the resources for its teams to function effectively.

Communicate the Urgency of the Team's Mission

Team members are prone to rally around challenges that compel them to meet high performance standards. As a result, the urgency of meeting those standards should be expressed. For example, a few years ago, employees at Ampex Corporation (a manufacturer of videotape equipment for the broadcasting industry) worked hard to make their teams successful when they recognized the changes necessitated by the shift to digital technology. Unless the company met these challenges, the plug surely would be pulled. Realizing that the company's very existence was at stake, work teams fast-forwarded Ampex into a position of prominence in its industry by ramping up development of digital recording technology.

Train Members in Team Skills

To be effective, team members must have the right blend of skills needed for the team to contribute to the group's mission. Rather than simply putting teams together and hoping they will work, many companies are taking proactive steps to ensure that team members will get along and perform as they should. Formal efforts directed toward making teams effective are referred to as **team building**. Team building usually is used when established teams are showing signs of trouble, such as when members lose sight of their objectives and when turnover is high. Workers having high degrees of freedom and autonomy require a depth of skills and knowledge that surpasses that of people performing narrower, traditional jobs. For this reason, successful teams are those in which investments are made in developing the skills of team members and leaders. In the words of one expert, "Good team members are trained, not born."[81]

team building
Formal efforts directed toward making teams more effective.

Illustrating this maxim is Development Dimensions International, a printing and distribution facility for a human resource company, located in Pittsburgh, Pennsylvania. This small company has each of its 70 employees spend some 200 hours in training (in such areas as interaction skills, customer service skills, and various technical areas) during their first year—even more for new leaders. Then, after this initial period, all employees receive a variety of training on an ongoing basis. (Recall our detailed discussion of training in Chapter 3.)

Key Areas of Team Training. Two areas of emphasis are essential to the success of any team training effort—training in being a team member, and training in self-management.

■ *Being a team member.* Linda Godwin, a mission specialist at NASA's Johnson Space Center in Houston, likens team success to the kind of interpersonal harmony that must exist within space shuttle crews. "We have to be willing to compromise and to make decisions that benefit everyone as a whole," says Godwin, a veteran of two successful shuttle missions.[82] In this regard, there are several key interpersonal skills in which training is most useful, and these are summarized in Table 8.6.
■ *Self-management.* For teams to operate effectively, members must be able to manage themselves. However, most employees are used to being told what to do, and don't know how to manage their own behavior. Specifically, this involves the various skills summarized in Figure 8.20.[83]

Team Training Exercises. Typically, team building involves having team members participate in several different exercises designed to help employees learn how to function effectively as a team member. Among the most widely used are the following.[84]

TABLE 8.6 Interpersonal Skills Required by Team Members

Experts have advocated that team members be trained in the various interpersonal skills summarized here (many of which are described elsewhere in this book).

Skill	Description
Advocating	Ways of persuading others to accept one's point of view (see Chapter 12)
Inquiring	Listening effectively to others and drawing information out of them (see Chapter 9)
Tension management	Managing the tension that stems from conflict with others (see Chapter 11)
Sharing responsibility	Learning to align personal and team objectives (see Chapter 6)
Leadership	Understanding one's role in guiding the team to success (see Chapter 13)
Valuing diversity	Acceptance—and taking advantage—of differences between members (see Chapter 5)
Self-awareness	Willingness to criticize others constructively and to accept constructive criticism from others (see Chapters 9 and 11)

Source: Based on information Caudron, 1994; see Note 81.

■ *Role definition exercises.* Are team members doing what others expect them to be doing? Teams whose members answer "no" are destined for trouble. To avoid such problems, some team-building exercises ask members to describe their own roles and the roles of others on their team. Members then systematically discuss these perceptions and highlight areas of disagreement so these can be worked on.

■ *Goal-setting exercises.* As we described in Chapter 7, successful performance is enhanced by the setting of goals. As a team-building strategy, team members meet to clarify the various goals toward which they are working and to identify ways they can help achieve them.

■ *Problem-solving exercises.* Building successful teams requires ensuring that members are able to work together at solving important problems. To help in this regard, some team-building sessions require members to get together to systematically identify and discuss ways of solving problems more effectively.

■ *Interpersonal process exercises.* Some of the most popular team-building exercises involve activities that attempt to build trust and to open communication among members. After all, those members who harbor hostility toward each other or who have hidden agendas are unlikely to work together well. There is usually a fun aspect to interpersonal process training. Black & Decker, for example, had members of its design team participate in a Spider Web activity requiring members to crawl through a large web of woven rope suspended between two trees without touching the rope. The underlying idea is that by helping each other through these exercises, team members can develop more positive relationships with each other and come to learn how they can influence each other's potential back on the job. In doing this, companies have used such diverse activities as trekking in the wilderness, going through obstacle courses, and having paintball wars. For a particularly important example, see Figure 8.21.[85]

FIGURE 8.20

Self-Management Skills: A Key to Team Success

For teams to function successfully, it is essential for members to know how to manage themselves. Training in self-management focuses on the five skills summarized here.

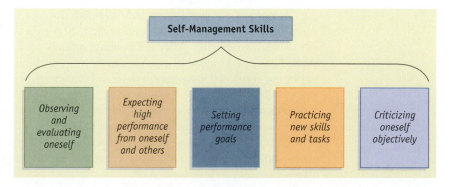

FIGURE 8.21

Teamwork Training at NASA

Although trekking in the mountain snow may be a far cry from working on a space mission, NASA officials recognize that the experience can provide a valuable learning opportunity for astronauts by simulating the interpersonal tensions crew members are likely to face while in flight. With this in mind, astronauts Clayton C. Andersen, Sunita Williams, and Edward Tsang Lu (left to right) are taking such an expedition as part of their ongoing training to work well together as a team. According to astronaut Ron Garan, "You could be the best pilot, scientist, or astronaut in the world, but if you can't work as part of a team or live with people for six months, you're no good to NASA."

As you might imagine, this list of training topics reflects only the most fundamental areas in which training in teamwork is useful. Depending on the exact nature of the work being performed and the specific working conditions involved, additional training may be required. This often is the case when team members are located in different countries throughout the world. For a look at the special challenges this creates, see, the *OB in a Diverse World* section on page 323.

Is Team Training Effective? Although these various meetings and physical exercises may be fun, we must ask if they have any value. In other words, are they worth the time and money invested in them? The answer is: *yes, but only when the training is conducted properly.* Too often, exercises are used without first thoroughly analyzing precisely what the team needs. When it comes to team building, one size does not fit all! Another problem is that team building exercises often are used as a one-time panacea. For them to be most effective, however, team-building exercises should be repeated regularly to keep the team in tip-top shape or, at least, at the very first sign of problems. And then, when on the job, everyone should be reminded of the lessons learned off-site.

A recent study shows just how effective training in teamwork skills can be.[86] The research involved over 1,000 officers in the U.S. Air Force who were trained in a wide variety of teamwork skills. After the training, officers took tests to see how effectively they picked up the relevant skills. Subsequently, various military teams consisting of these officers were compared with respect to three key measures: (1) performance in the field when doing military operations, (2) success in solving problems, and (3) performance on physical tasks. Independently of these measures, observers also rated the effectiveness of the teams overall. As summarized in Figure 8.22 (see p. 324), teams consisting of members who, as a whole, scored highly on the tests of team-relevant skills outperformed the teams whose officers performed less well. These findings highlight the potential value of administering training in teamwork skills.

OB In a Diverse World

Promoting Successful Cross-National Teams by Encouraging Ethnorelativistic Thinking

 There can be no mistaking the growth of cross-national teams in today's organizations. According to one study, 63 percent of companies plan to use teams in different locations, and 22 percent plan to locate teams across national borders.[87] This practice creates opportunities to tap a wide variety of viewpoints and talent, creating conditions that enhance team effectiveness. At the same time, however, cultural differences between people in the same team may have built-in problems.

We are referring to the natural tendency for groups consisting of culturally diverse combinations of people to break into subgroups sharing common characteristics. The extent to which this occurs, however, depends on the way characteristics are distributed across people in those subgroups. Consider, for example, a group composed of engineers and designers, some of whom are men and some of whom are women. If all the engineers happen to be of one gender while all the designers are of the opposite gender, then a so-called **faultline** is created. This refers to a condition in which the key attributes of group members are correlated across group membership instead of cutting across group membership.[88] This precisely describes our example. Managers need to be concerned about faultlines in groups because they weaken the overall cohesion of groups by promoting conflict (see Chapter 11). Analogously, geologists are concerned about faultlines in the earth because of the unstable geological conditions they create.

When groups are geographically distributed, particularly across national boundaries, people become keenly aware of the particular subgroups in each location. This encourages **ethnocentrism**—a bias toward one's own subgroup and against other subgroups. Thus, people who are distributed across national borders (as is likely to be the case) will favor their own groups at the expense of others. The resulting faultline makes cooperation between subgroups unlikely. And this, as you might imafine, is antithetical to the creation of successful workgroups.

If naturally occurring conditions (i.e., the use of cross-national teams) are inclined to promote ethnocentrism and the inevitable conflict it creates, then managers face a challenge.

How can they capitalize on the diverse viewpoints of people in different nations in a harmonious manner? The answer involves promoting **ethnorelativistic thinking**, taking the perspective of another group and understanding how they see the world, including one's own group.[89] Essentially, the idea is to expand people's perspectives and to show greater empathy for other groups.

Promoting ethnorelativistic learning requires getting group members to understand and to respect the differences between them and to help them relate to one another despite those differences. In all cases, this involves three key foci:

- *Perspective-taking*—Considering the way others see things
- *Empathy*—Being aware of others' feelings
- *Adaptability*—Willingness to change one's own views and behaviors

Practically, this can be accomplished using diversity training of the types described in Chapter 6.

Another way of avoiding faultlines involves using technology in ways that promote inclusive communication—that is, taking everyone's views into account. Often, this involves using teleconferences in which subgroup members share information freely about things that help others interpret their behavior correctly. This may include topics such as local customs, including holidays, work hours, use of breaks, and so on. Absent such information, misunderstandings are likely to develop.

It's also worthwhile to use such sessions to emphasize each subgroup's relative strengths and weaknesses so people in one subgroup can understand what to expect of those in another. This information, of course, is quite valuable to groups attempting to perform their tasks—and far more useful than focusing on difficulties associated with getting along with others.

In conclusion, because cross-national teams are growing in popularity, it is incumbent upon everyone to be prepared for the interpersonal challenges they create. Hopefully, this discussion will help prepare you to meet these challenges.

---

faultline

A condition in which the key attributes of group members are correlated across group membership instead of cutting across group membership.

Promote Cooperation Within and Between Teams

Team success requires not only cooperation within teams, but between them as well. As one expert put it, "Time and time again, teams fall short of their promise because companies don't know how to make them work together with other teams. If you don't get your teams into the right constellations, the whole organization can stall."[90]

FIGURE 8.22

Training in Teamwork Skills Promotes Successful Team Performance

After being trained in various teamwork skills, U.S. Air Force officers were tested on how well they learned the material. The higher the scores of officers in various military teams, the better those units performed on several important performance measures.

Source: Based on findings reported by Hirschfeld, Jordan, Felid, Giles, & Armenakis, 2006; see Note 86.

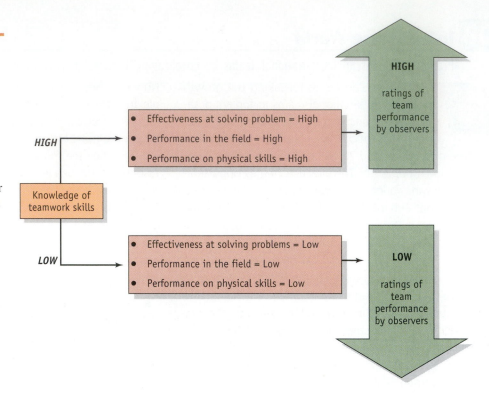

ethnocentrism

A bias toward one's own subgroup and against other subgroups.

ethnorelativistic thinking

Taking the perspective of another group and understanding how they see the world, including one's own group.

Boeing successfully avoided such problems in the course of developing its 777 passenger jet—a project involving some 200 teams (refer again to Figure 8.17, p. 313). As you might imagine, on such a large project coordination of effort between teams is essential. To help, regular meetings were held between various team leaders who disseminated information to members. And team members could go wherever needed within the organization to get the information required to succeed. As one Boeing employee, a team leader, put it, "I can go the chief engineer. Before, it was unusual just to see the chief engineer."[91] Just as importantly, if after getting the information they need, team members find problems, they are empowered to take action without getting management's approval. According to Boeing engineer Henry Shomber, "We have the no-messenger rule. Team members must make decisions on the spot. They can't run back to their functions [department heads] for permission."[92]

Select Team Members Based on Their Skills or Potential Skills

Insofar as the success of teams demands that they work together closely on a wide variety of tasks, it is essential for them to have a complementary set of skills. This includes not only job skills but also interpersonal skills (especially since getting along with one's teammates is very important). With this in mind, at Ampex, three-person subsets of teams are used to select their own new members insofar as they have the best idea about what skills are needed and who would best fit into the teams. It is also frequently important for teams to project future skills that may be needed and to train team members in these skills. Thus work teams at Colgate-Palmolive Company's liquid detergents plant in Cambridge, Ohio initially received 120 hours of training in such skills as quality management, problem solving, and team interaction, and subsequently received advanced training in all these areas.

In an effort to keep team members' skills fresh, it is important to regularly confront members with new facts. Fresh approaches are likely to be prompted by fresh information, and introducing new facts may present the kind of challenges that teams need to say innovative. For example, when information about pending cutbacks in defense spending was introduced to teams at Florida's Harris Corporation (an electronics manufacturer), new technologies were developed that positioned the company to land large contracts in nonmilitary government organizations—including a $1.7 billion contract to upgrade the FAA's air traffic control system.

A Cautionary Note: Developing Successful Teams Requires Patience

It is important to caution that although these suggestions are important, they alone do not ensure the success of work teams. Many other factors, such as the economy, the existence of competitors, and the company's financial picture also are important determinants of organizational success. Still, the fact that these practices are followed in many highly successful teams certainly makes them worthy of consideration.

However, developing effective teams is difficult, and the path to success is riddled with obstacles. It is also time-consuming. According to management expert Peter Drucker, "You can't rush teams. It takes five years just to learn to build a team and decide what kind you want."[93] And it may take most organizations over a decade to make a complete transition to teams. Clearly, teams are not an overnight route to success. But, with patience and careful attention to the suggestions outlined here, teams have ushered many companies into extraordinary gains in productivity. For this reason, they must be considered a viable option for organizing groups of work groups.[94]

Summary and Review of Learning Objectives

1. **Define what is meant by a group and identify different types of groups operating within organizations.**

   A *group* is a collection of two or more interacting individuals with a stable pattern of relationships between them who share common goals and who perceive themselves as being a group. Within organizations, there are two major classes of groups—*formal groups* (which includes *command groups* and *task groups*), and *informal groups* (which includes *interest groups* and *friendship groups*).

2. **Describe the importance of norms, roles, status, and cohesiveness within organizations.**

   Roles are the typical pattern of behavior in a social context. *Norms* are generally agreed-upon informal rules. *Status* refers to the prestige accorded group members. *Cohesiveness* is the pressures faced by group members to remain in their groups. Together, these factors determine the dynamics of people working in groups.

3. **Explain how individual performance in groups is affected by the presence of others (social facilitation), the cultural diversity of group membership, and the number of others with whom one is working (social loafing).**

   Individual productivity is influenced by the presence of other group members. Sometimes, a person's performance improves in the presence of others (when the job they are doing is well learned), and sometimes performance declines in the presence of others (when the job is novel). This phenomenon is known as *social facilitation*. Not only is performance influenced by the presence of others, but by the group's racial/ethnic diversity. Performance in diverse groups is initially worse than performance in homogeneous groups, although these differences disappear with repeated involvement with the group. On *additive tasks* (i.e., ones in which each member's individual contributions are combined), *social loafing* occurs. According to this phenomenon, the more people who work on a task, the less each group member contributes to it.

4. **Define what teams are and describe the various types of teams that exist in organizations.**

   Teams are special kinds of groups—ones whose members focus on collective, rather than individual, work products, are mutually accountable to each other, share a common commitment to purpose, and are usually self-managing. Teams differ with respect to several dimensions: their purpose or mission (*work teams* vs. *improvement teams*), time (*temporary teams* or *permanent teams*), degree of autonomy (*work groups, semi-autonomous work groups, self-managed teams*), authority structure (*intact teams* vs. *cross-functional teams*), and physical presence (*physical teams* vs. *virtual teams*).

5. **Understand the effectiveness of teams in organizations.**

   In general, teams are well received. Most people enjoy working in teams, at least after they have adjusted to them (which can take some work). Teams help enhance commitment among employees and are effective in promoting organizational efficiency by eliminating layers of management. However, teams are not always responsible for making individuals and organizations any more productive. Cases of companies becoming wildly successful after adopting teams, although compelling, cannot always be generalized to all teams in all situations.

6. **Explain the factors responsible for the failure of some teams to operate as effectively as possible and identify things that can be done to build successful teams.**

   Despite some evidence of the team successes, some teams fail. This is often because: team members are unwilling to cooperate with each other, they fail to receive support from management, some managers are unwilling to relinquish control, and some teams fail to coordinate their efforts effectively with other teams. With some effort, teams can yield exceptionally high levels of performance. To build successful teams, it helps to do the following: provide training in team skills, compensate team performance, provide managerial support, promote employee support, promote cooperation within and between teams, and select team members based on their skills or potential skills.

Points to Ponder

Questions for Review

1. What is a group and how do groups form?
2. How do norms, roles, status, and cohesiveness influence the operation of groups?
3. How do the phenomena of social facilitation and social loafing influence the performance of individuals in group settings?
4. What are teams and how do they differ from groups?
5. What does the evidence reveal about the effectiveness of work teams?
6. What are the major obstacles to team success and how can they be overcome?

Experiential Questions

1. Think of a group in which you have been working. How do the *five-stage model* and the *punctuated-equilibrium model* apply to this experience?
2. Describe an incident of *social loafing* in which you may have been involved (e.g., a class project). What might be done to overcome this effect?
3. How have your own experiences in work teams compared to those described in this chapter? Based on what you read, what could be done to make your own team experiences more successful?

Questions to Analyze

1. Imagine that you are about to go on stage to give a solo piano recital. How would the phenomenon of social facilitation account for your performance?
2. Based on the evidence regarding the effectiveness of teams, would you say that the popularity of teams today is well-founded?
3. Think of any professional sports team, such as a professional baseball, football, or basketball team. In what ways do they fit the description of definition of teams used in this chapter? In what ways do they *not* fit the description of definition of teams used in this chapter?

Experiencing OB

Individual Exercise

Are You a Team Player?

Let's face it, some people find it easier to work in teams than others. Are you already a "team player," or have you not yet developed the skills needed to work effectively with others in teams? Knowing where you stand along this dimension may come in handy when it comes to considering a new job or planning your next work assignment. The following questionnaire will give you insight into this question.

Directions

1. Read each of the following statements and carefully consider whether or not it accurately describes you on the job most of the time.
2. Then, on the line next to each statement, write "Yes" if the statement describes you most of the time, or "No" if it does not describe you most of the time. If you are uncertain, write a question mark ("?").
3. Do your best to respond to all items as honestly as possible.

Most of the time, on the job, I . . .

_____ 1. demonstrate high ethical standards.
_____ 2. deliver on promises I make.
_____ 3. take initiative, doing what's needed without being told.
_____ 4. follow the norms and standards of the groups in which I work.
_____ 5. put team goals ahead of my own.
_____ 6. accurately describe my team to others in the organization.
_____ 7. pitch in to help others learn new skills.
_____ 8. do at least my share of the work.
_____ 9. coordinate the work I do with others.
_____ 10. try to attend all meetings and arrive on time for them.
_____ 11. come to meetings prepared to participate.
_____ 12. stay focused on the agenda during team meetings.
_____ 13. share with others new knowledge I may have about the job.
_____ 14. encourage others to raise questions about the way things are.
_____ 15. affirm positive things about others' ideas before noting concerns.
_____ 16. listen to others without interrupting them.
_____ 17. ask questions to others to make certain I understand them.
_____ 18. make sure I attend to a speaker's nonverbal messages.
_____ 19. praise others who have performed well.
_____ 20. give constructive, nonjudgmental feedback to others.
_____ 21. receive constructive feedback without acting defensively.
_____ 22. communicate ideas without threats or ridicule.
_____ 23. explain the reasoning behind my opinions.
_____ 24. demonstrate my willingness to change my opinions.
_____ 25. speak up when I disagree with others.
_____ 26. show disagreement in a tactful, polite manner.
_____ 27. discuss possible areas of agreement with others with whom I am in conflict.

(*Source:* Based on material appearing in McDermott et al., 1998; see Note 94.)

Scoring

1. Count the number of times you responded by saying "yes."
2. Then, count the number of times you responded by saying "no."
3. Add these two numbers together.
4. To compute your *team player score,* divide the number of times you say yes (step 1) by the total (step 3). Then, multiply by 100. Your score will be between 0 and 100. Higher scores reflect greater readiness for working in teams.

Questions for Discussion

1. What was your score, and how did it compare to those of others in your class?
2. What underlying criteria of team success are assessed by this questionnaire?
3. What does this questionnaire reveal about the ways in which you are best equipped to work in teams?

4. What does this questionnaire reveal about the ways in which you are most deficient when it comes to working in teams? What do you think you could do to improve your readiness for working in teams?

Group Exercise

Demonstrating the Social Loafing Effect

The social loafing effect is quite strong and is likely to occur in many different situations in which people make individual contributions to an additive group task. This exercise is designed to demonstrate the effect first-hand in your own class.

Directions

1. Divide the class into groups of different sizes. Between five and 10 people should work alone. In addition, there should be a group of two, a group of three, a group of four, and so on, until all members of the class have been assigned to a group. (If the class is small, assign students to groups of vastly different sizes, such as two, 7, and 15.) Form the groups by putting together at tables people from the same group.
2. Each person should be given a page or two from a telephone directory and a stack of index cards. Then, have the individuals and the members of each group perform the same additive task—copying entries from the telephone directory onto index cards. Allow exactly 10 minutes for the task to be performed, and encourage everyone to work as hard as they can.
3. After the time is up, count the number of entries copied.
4. For each group, and for all the individuals, compute the average per-person performance by dividing the total number of entries copied by the number of people in the group.
5. At the board, the instructor should graph the results. Along the vertical axis show the average number of entries copied per person. Along the horizontal axis show the size of the work groups—one, two, three, four, and so on. The graph should look like the one in Figure 8.11 (see p. 305).

Questions for Discussion

1. Was the social loafing effect demonstrated? What is the basis for this conclusion?
2. If the social loafing effect was not found, why do you think this occurred? Do you think it might have been due to the possibility that your familiarity with the effect led you to avoid it? Test this possibility by replicating the exercise using people who do not know about the phenomenon (e.g., another class), then compare the results.
3. Did members of smaller groups feel more responsible for their group's performance than members of larger groups?
4. What could have been done to counteract any "free riding" that may have occurred in this demonstration?

Practicing OB

Gearing Up for Self-Managed Teams

Officials of a large manufacturing company are concerned about the stagnant productivity they've seen in the past year. Although sales have been good, employees in the company's manufacturing plant are having a hard time keeping up with demand. Right now, they are working on an assembly line, requiring each individual to perform only one or two highly specific tasks. To remedy the situation, they are considering moving to self-managed teams. You have been asked to give your advice on this matter.

1. Do you think teams would be effective in this situation? Why or why not?
2. What potential problems do you think would be associated with the move to teams, and how might these be overcome?
3. What advice would you give to help the teams work as effectively as possible?

CASE IN POINT

Inside the Peloton: Social Dynamics of the Tour de France

Each July, bicyclists race across the French countryside in the Tour de France. The race, first run in 1903, now consists of about 180 of the world's best cyclists, who meander their ways through tiny villages, up and down steep mountain grades, and after a grueling 3,407 kilometers (slightly over 2,117 miles), complete their 23-day-long journey along Paris's famed Champs-Elysées. To the winner goes 400,000 euros (currently about 517,840 U.S. dollars). For seven consecutive years (as of now, at least), American Lance Armstrong crossed the finish line first, but despite how it may look from the outside, the Tour, as it is called for short, is very much a team sport.

To appreciate the team dynamics, it's necessary to understand what goes on inside the *peloton,* a cycling term for pack—a picturesque mob of competing teams seen gliding along the route. The complex social arrangements that occur within them belie the bucolic surroundings in which they peddle. As one observer put it, "What appears to be a random mass of bicycles is really an ordered, complex web of shifting alliances, crossed with brutal competition, designed to keep or acquire the market's most valued currency: energy."

Pelotons consist of about 20 teams of 9 riders, each of whom has a specialty. For example, there are *roulers,* two or three particularly fast riders who help create drafts for their team's leader in flat terrain; *hill specialists,* who have the strength and stamina to support the leader in gaining ground by creating a slipstream (a field of low wind resistance) as they go up mountains; and *domestiques,* usually new riders who wear shoulder bags to help carry supplies between the team car and various team members. Together, these individuals have a common objective: to position leaders for a win.

It's not only members of one's own teams who work together, but sometimes, tiny groupings of enemies from different teams who form momentary alliances when race decisions dictate—sometimes hundreds per day. For example, members of two opposing teams riding knuckle-to-knuckle at 60 mph may help one another by cutting temporary deals, each taking turns blocking others through upcoming twists and turns. As longtime Tour commentator Phil Liggett observed, "You have to make friends of enemies. And just as quickly, enemies of friends."

Within the peloton, unspoken rules develop. For example, riders may be given a chance to lead the pack, such as when they enter their home towns (allowing them to enjoy the glory and admiration) and when they go to areas with lots of television coverage (allowing them to please their sponsors). Cooperation between teams also is important when nature calls. Usually, bathroom breaks (more actually, trips to the woods) occur when everyone agrees they will.

During one race, however, French rider Dante Coccolo took it upon himself to defy the rules. When everyone stopped for a break, he charged ahead. Later, when he took his own bathroom break, some other cyclists grabbed his bike and threw it into a ditch. Slowed down and ostracized, Coccolo's team had to get him another bike. He finished in next-to-last place that year and never again rode in the Tour. Lesson learned.

Questions for Discussion

1. What examples of role differentiation are found in this case? To what extent do they help achieve the desired goals?
2. What social norms are illustrated? How do they help each team's mission, and how are they enforced?
3. Teams of nine are used in this case. Do you think they would be more effective if they were smaller in size or does the situation dictate the team size used? To what extent would larger sizes help or hinder effectiveness?

COMMUNICATION IN ORGANIZATIONS

Chapter 9

Chapter Outline

Special Sections

After reading this chapter, you should be able to:

1. Describe the process of communication and its fundamental purposes in organizations.

2. Identify various forms of verbal media used in organizations, and explain which ones are most appropriate for communicating messages of different types.

3. Describe how technology has influenced organizational communication.

4. Describe how people's communication patterns differ as a function of their sex and culture.

5. Distinguish between the various forms of formal and informal communication that occur in organizations and how they operate.

6. Explain how you can improve your effectiveness as a communicator in organizations.

PREVIEW CASE

The Home Depot's Extreme Communication Makeover

With over 1,800 "orange box" stores throughout North America and more than 350,000 employees, The Home Depot has become the world's largest home improvement retailer. Although it's a landmark today, the company is relatively new—founded in 1978. To say that its growth has been staggering is an understatement: The Home Depot is the fastest growing retailer in history and the youngest retailer in the Fortune 50. Its sales volume is so enormous that in 2005 alone, it sold enough carpet to pave a two-lane road from company headquarters in Atlanta to Los Angeles, then up to New York and back again to Atlanta. The company enjoys annual sales of over $67 billion, it has 22 million customers per week, and it opens a new store every 50 hours.

As impressive as these figures are, The Home Depot's vast size, rapid growth, and geographic diversity have created a number of challenges—not the least important of which are the complexities of communication. After all, employees speak not only English, but Spanish (in parts of the United States and in Mexico) as well as French (in Québec)—not to mention the various mother tongues spoken by suppliers and immigrant employees. And of course, the company faces the Herculean task of getting the word out to store employees about such vital issues as price changes, promotional campaigns, and product recalls. To make all this happen, The Home Depot has developed a two-pronged plan that capitalizes on technology.

The challenge of communicating in multiple languages is so extensive that The Home Depot has a translation supervisor, Juan Morales, who oversees the translation of everything from the labeling of boxes and the creation of training manuals to in-store promotional campaigns. To receive perfect translations very quickly, the company has partnered with a firm specializing in international translation services, Bowne Global Solutions (BGS). They installed a Web-based system through which Home Depot managers can submit translation projects, ranging from simple in-store notices to lengthy operational manuals, for rapid translations that sound completely natural to native speakers. To date, BGS has completed over 800 translation projects not only for Home Depot departments in the United States, Canada, and Mexico, but also its numerous suppliers throughout the world. Mr. Morales has noted that the quick turnaround and high-quality translations it gets from BGS have been instrumental to The Home Depot's success.

Another communication challenge at The Home Depot is the need to coordinate all the information sent to sales associates and managers in a way that ensures that nothing is missed—but without overwhelming them. Over the years, these have been problems for the giant retailer, as messages in various forms would pour into stores daily, creating a deluge of phone calls, faxes, snail mails, and e-mails. According to Shannon Roh, the director of store operations, there was a need to coordinate this ongoing stream of information. To streamline and prioritize the information, The Home Depot again sought the expertise of an outside firm, Reflexis Systems, which developed a Web-based system in which all messages are organized in a single place. Now, not only can managers access all the information required to plan and track their assignments, but they also can track their progress and report their results on a real-time basis.

The biggest challenge in implementing the system, which was rolled out in September 2002, involved training more than 13,000 employees in every store. Ms. Roh has been pleased with the more streamlined and consistent flow of information that has resulted in the past few years. Says she, "We've achieved a single pipeline for all managers to receive all action-required communication and we've eliminated duplication in our communication," adding that store managers "no longer have to read the same e-mail three times because it was sent to them by so many different people." Also important, the clarity and greater visibility of important messages has made it possible for stores to be in perfect compliance with requirements for handling product recalls and safety alerts, which benefits customers. And this, of course, contributes to The Home Depot's efforts to provide outstanding customer service.

There can be no mistaking the major role of *communication* in the success enjoyed by The Home Depot in recent years. The company has experienced not only steady increases in profitability, but also considerable recognition among its employees as a desirable place to work.[1] Without the company's success at coordinating massive amounts of information in understandable forms, these benefits would be unlikely. The resulting confusion surely would lead to frustration among employees and customers.

As you might imagine, although The Home Depot surely is special, it is far from alone when it comes to emphasizing communication in its business plans. Indeed, communication is considered a key ingredient in the recipe for business success by executives throughout the world. Consider, for example, Ben Verwaayen, chief executive of British Telecom Group (BT), who in 2005 won the World Communication Award for being the "Most Influential Person."[2] Given his extraordinary efforts to stay connected to his staff and customers, this is not at all surprising. Mr. Verwaayen regularly maintains close relations with the company's 100,000 employees by traveling to its offices throughout the United Kingdom.[3] And, as if this is not enough, he has set up his own Web site from which he fields an average of 200 e-mails a day from BT's employees. Although many factors contribute to business success—indeed, BT has enjoyed steady profit for many years—industry analysts are convinced that the company's chief executive's efforts to stay in touch with his employees is a key factor. After all, unless the person at the helm and those who answer to this individual are all pulling in the same direction, there is little reason to be optimistic about the success of business activities.

Both Home Depot and BT illustrate the central role of *communication* as a factor enabling the coordination of individuals within organizations. With this important function in mind, in this chapter we will explain how the communication process works and how to foster communication in organizations. This is important considering that managers spend as much as 80 percent of their time engaging in some form of communication, such as speaking or listening to others, or writing to and reading material from them.[4]

Communication is an especially important contributor to the effective functioning of today's organizations.[5] There are several key reasons for this.

- ■ *Technology has sped up the pace of work.* As work gets done faster, communication must be more effective because there is less time to correct errors or misunderstandings.
- ■ *Work is more complex than ever before.* People interact with lots of others, requiring the careful coordination of information.

FIGURE 9.1

Technology has Transformed Communication, Opening Up Work Options

Advances in communication technology have made it possible for countless men and women to work full-time from their homes. Using the Internet and telephone, they are able to transmit work and maintain regular contact with their colleagues. The practice of *telecommuting*, popular today, not only allows people to spend time with their children, but also to save time and money by not having to commute to a distant office.

- ■ *Employees are likely to be distributed geographically.* It's not unusual for people to work from home and to keep in close contact with their home office while traveling on business. And, when people are out of sight, the normal opportunities to communicate when seeing someone in person are eliminated.
- ■ *Knowledge and information are key to success.* For today's organizations to be successful, they not only must produce goods, but they also must stay abreast of rapidly changing markets. This requires information to be accessed and shared in a coordinated fashion.
- ■ *Technology has transformed the way people do their jobs.* In today's electronically sophisticated world, we count on a wide variety of communication media that have transformed the way people do their jobs (see Figure 9.1).

Given the vital role of communication in organizations, we will examine this process closely in this chapter. To begin, we will define the process of communication and characterize its role in organizations. Following this, we will describe the two basic forms of communication: verbal and nonverbal. Because much of today's communication is high tech in nature, we will highlight computer-mediated communication techniques. Next, we will distinguish between two major types of communication in which we all engage—formal communication and informal communication. Then, recognizing that people don't always communicate in the same fashion, we will examine two key individual differences with respect to communication—sex differences and cross-cultural differences. Finally, we will conclude this chapter by offering a series of concrete suggestions regarding how you can become a better communicator.

Communication: Its Basic Nature

For you to appreciate fully the process of organizational communication, we need to address some fundamental issues. To begin, we will formally define what we mean by communication and then elaborate on the process by which it occurs. Following this, we will describe the various purposes and levels of communication in organizations.

Defining Communication and Describing the Process

What do the following situations have in common? The district manager posts a notice stating that smoking is prohibited on company property. An executive prepares a report about the financial status of a potential corporate takeover prospect. A taxi dispatcher directs Cab 54 to pick up a fare at 1177 Regency Drive. A foreman smiles at one of his subordinates and pats him on the back in recognition of a job well done. The answer, if you haven't already guessed it, is that each of these incidents involves some form of *communication.* Although you probably already have a good idea of what communication entails, we can better understand communication in organizations by defining it precisely and describing the nature of the communication process.

With this in mind, we define **communication** as the process by which a person, group, or organization (the *sender*) transmits some type of information (the *message*) to another person, group, or organization (the *receiver*). To clarify this definition and to further elaborate on how the process works, we have summarized it in Figure 9.2. You may find it helpful to follow along with this diagram as we review the various steps.

Encoding. The communication process begins when one party has an idea that it wishes to transmit to another (either party may be an individual, a group, or an entire organization). It is the sender's mission to transform the idea into a form that can be sent to and understood by the receiver. This is what happens in the process of **encoding**— translating an idea into a form, such as written or spoken language, that can be recognized by a receiver. We encode information when we select the words we use to write a letter or speak to someone in person. This process is critical if we are to clearly communicate our ideas. If you've ever had difficulty finding the right words to express your ideas (and who hasn't!), then you know that people are far from perfect when it comes to encoding their ideas. Fortunately, as we will note later, this skill can be improved.

Channels of Communication. After a message is encoded, it is ready to be transmitted over one or more **channels of communication** to reach the desired receiver—that is, the pathways along which information travels. Telephone lines, radio and television signals, fiber-optic cables, mail routes, and even the air waves that carry the vibrations of our voices all represent potential channels of communication. Of course, the form of encoding largely determines the way information may be transmitted. Visual information—such as pictures and written words—may be mailed, delivered in person by a courier, shipped by an express delivery service, or sent electronically, such as via e-mail, uploaded onto a Web

communication

The process by which a person, group, or organization (the sender) transmits some type of information (the message) to another person, group, or organization (the receiver).

encoding

The process by which an idea is transformed so that it can be transmitted to, and recognized by, a receiver (e.g., a written or spoken message).

channels of communication

The pathways over which messages are transmitted (e.g., telephone lines, mail, etc.).

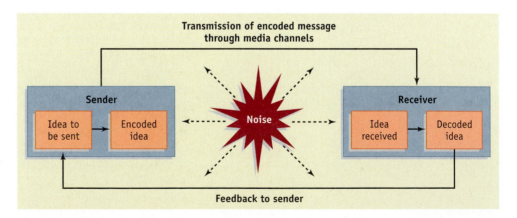

FIGURE 9.2

The Communication Process

Communication generally follows the steps outlined here. Senders *encode* messages and transmit them via one or more communication channels to receivers, who then *decode* them. The process continues as the original receiver sends feedback to the original sender. Factors distorting or limiting the flow of information, known as *noise,* may enter into the process at any point.

site, or faxed. Oral information may be transmitted over the telephone, via radio and television signals—and, of course, the old-fashioned way, in person. Whatever channel is used, the goal is the same: to send the encoded message accurately to a desired receiver.

decoding

The process by which a receiver of messages transforms them back into the sender's ideas.

Decoding.   Once a message is received, the recipient must begin the process of **decoding**—converting the message back into the sender's original ideas. This involves many different subprocesses, such as comprehending spoken and written words, interpreting facial expressions, and the like. To the extent that the sender's message is decoded accurately by the receiver, the ideas understood will be the ones intended. Of course, our ability to comprehend and interpret information received from others may be imperfect. For example, this may be restricted by unclear messages, by our own language skills, or by one's existing knowledge (see Figure 9.3). Thus, as in the case of encoding, limitations in our ability to decode information represent another potential weakness in the communication process—but, as we will describe later in this chapter, one that can be developed.

feedback

Knowledge about the impact of messages on receivers.

Feedback.   Finally, once a message has been decoded, the process can continue, with the receiver transmitting a new message back to the original sender. This part of the process is known as **feedback**—knowledge about the impact of messages on receivers. Receiving feedback allows senders to determine whether their messages have been understood properly. At the same time, giving feedback can help convince receivers that the sender really cares about what he or she has to say. Once received, feedback can trigger another idea from the sender, and another cycle of transferring information may begin. For this reason, we have characterized the process of communication summarized in Figure 9.2 as continuous.

FIGURE 9.3

Decoding: A Challenging Process

Although the police officer appears to be encoding the directions very clearly, the man to whom he is speaking does not appear to be getting the message. In other words, he is not *decoding* the message well. This might occur because the man is so unfamiliar with the neighborhood that he cannot accurately figure out exactly what the police officer means. Such problems occur widely in organizations, leading to obvious problems.

Source: © The New Yorker Collection, 1976, James Stevenson from cartoonbank.com. All rights reserved.

noise

Factors capable of distorting the clarity of messages at any point during the communication process.

spam

Uncolicited commercial e-mail messages.

Noise. Despite the apparent simplicity of the communication process, it rarely operates as flawlessly as we have described it here. As we will see, there are many potential barriers to effective communication. The name given to factors that distort the clarity of a message is **noise**. As we have shown in Figure 9.2, noise can occur at any point along the communication process. For example, messages that are poorly encoded (e.g., written in an unclear way) or poorly decoded (e.g., not comprehended), or channels of communication that are too full of static (e.g., receivers' attentions are diverted from the message) may reduce communication's effectiveness.

One particularly annoying source of noise in e-mail communication these days is **spam**, unsolicited commercial bulk e-mail messages (see Figure 9.4). The statistics are shocking:

- Approximately 206 billion junk e-mailings were estimated to have been sent in 2006 (1,400 per consumer), doubling from 2005.[6]
- The annual cost of spam to U.S. corporations is $8.9 billion, $2.5 billion for European businesses.[7]
- Approximately 80 percent of e-mail messages received are considered spam, and despite efforts to stop it, the figure is rising rapidly.[8]

Given these figures, it's not surprising that spam, a modern form of noise, contributes greatly to the inefficiency of e-mail systems—bogging them down with unwanted information, making it difficult to search for desired messages, and often exposing people to distasteful material.

Not only spam, but a variety of factors (e.g., time pressure, organizational politics) contribute to the distortion of information transmitted from one party to another and to the resulting complexity of the communication process. As you continue reading this chapter you will come to appreciate many of the factors that make the process of organizational communication so very complex and important.

Purposes and Levels of Organizational Communication

In a sense, discussing the purpose of communication in organizations seems unnecessary since it's so obvious: You have to communicate with others to share information with them, which is necessary to get things done. This is true, of course, but communication

FIGURE 9.4

Spam as Noise

Unsolicited commercial bulk e-mail, known as *spam,* has become so widespread that it has been interfering with the efficient use of e-mail, making people less productive. Spam activity is growing rapidly—doubling from year to year, recently—due to its low cost and the ease with which it is transmitted. If you've ever been slowed down in searching for your e-mail messages because of such spam, you know how much noise they can add to a communication system.

actually serves a much broader range of purposes. In fact, communication serves at least eight critical functions in organizations.[9] These are as follows:

- *Directing action.* Communication between people is necessary to get others to behave in a desired fashion. Managers must communicate with subordinates to tell them what to do, to give them feedback on their performance, to discuss problems with them, to encourage them, and so on.

- *Linking and coordination.* For organizations to function effectively, individuals and groups must carefully coordinate their efforts and activities, and communication makes this possible. In a restaurant, for example, a waiter must take customers' orders and pass them along to the chef.

- *Building relationships.* Communication is essential to the development of interpersonal relationships. Building friendships and promoting trust (see Chapter 11) requires careful communication. Doing so can help create a pleasant atmosphere in the workplace.

- *Explaining organizational culture.* By communicating with others, employees come to understand how their companies operate, what is valued, and what matters most to people. In other words, they learn about the *culture* of their organizations (we will discuss organizational culture in detail in Chapter 14).

- *Interorganizational linking.* People communicate not only with others in their own organizations but also with representatives of other organizations. This makes it possible for companies to work together to coordinate their efforts toward achieving mutual goals, such as occurs in *joint ventures* (see Chapter 15).

- *Presenting an organization's image.* Organizations send messages about themselves to broad groups of others. For example, companies publish information about goods and services to attract prospective customers. These forms of communication are designed to present certain images of the organization to the world.

- *Generating ideas.* Communication is used to generate ideas and to share them as necessary. When people brainstorm with one another, for example, the communication process helps create new ideas (see Chapter 10 for a discussion of the brainstorming process).

- *Promoting ideals and values.* Many organizations "stand for something" and have purposes that must be communicated clearly. For example, a stated purpose of the National Organization for Women (NOW) is to help women participate fully in society. Communication is required for this mission to be understood—and accomplished.

As these descriptions suggest, communication not only plays a vital role in organizations, but it also occurs at various levels. Specifically, organizational communication occurs at the five distinct levels summarized in Table 9.1. These range from interpersonal communication at one end, involving people on an individual basis, all the way to mass communication, in which information is shared with large numbers of people. This broad range of approaches lends itself to study by different professional groups. Indeed, specialists in the field of OB are not the only professionals interested in organizational communication. This topic also is of interest to many social scientists, such as psychologists and sociologists, as well as people in other fields, notably advertising and journalism. Among OB specialists, the focus primarily is on the three lowest levels, interpersonal communication, group-level communication, and organizational-level communication. You will see these various emphases in this chapter.

Now that we have established the nature of communication in organizations, we will continue by examining the two major forms it takes—*verbal communication* (communicating by using words) and *nonverbal communication* (communicating without words).

Verbal and Nonverbal Communication: Messages with and Without Words

verbal communication

The transmission of messages using words, either written or spoken.

Because you are reading this book, we know you are familiar with **verbal communication**—the process of using words to transmit and receive ideas. Whether it's a face-to-face chat with a coworker, a phone call from a supplier, an e-mail message from the boss, or a faxed memo from company headquarters, people in today's organizations use a variety of different

TABLE 9.1 Levels of Organizational Communication

As summarized here, communication occurs at many different levels. These range from the "micro-level" communication between individuals through broader, "macro-level" forms, involving communication within and between organizations as a whole.

Level of Communication	Description	Example
Interpersonal communication	Individuals sharing information, formally or informally	A supervisor meets with her direct report to discuss ways of improving this person's work.
Group-level communication	Sharing of information within groups or teams	The member of a sales team coordinate their efforts at developing a new sales campaign.
Organizational-level communication	Sharing of information between subunits of the same organization	Representatives of various company departments assemble to create a strategic plan.
Interorganizational communication	Sharing of information between organizations	Firms working together on a joint venture make plans for sharing resources required to create a new product.
Mass communication	A company sending messages to large numbers of people	An automobile manufacturer notifies its dealers and owners of a safety recall.

communications media. When we speak of verbal media, we are referring to communication involving the use of words. These may be transmitted either orally or in written form, and both play an important role in organizations.

Also, as you know, much of what people communicate occurs without using words, which is known as **nonverbal communication**. Whether we're talking about people's facial expressions or body language (to which we referred in Chapter 3), or other subtle cues that we will describe here, nonverbal communication carries a great deal of weight when it comes to sending messages in organizations. In this section of the chapter we discuss both verbal and nonverbal communication.

Verbal Media

When most of us think about communication, we think of **verbal media**—forms of communication involving the use of words. Face-to-face conversations, letters, and telephone conversations are clear examples. The various forms of verbal media can be distinguished with respect to their capacity to convey information.[10]

Some verbal media, such as *face-to-face conversations,* are considered especially *rich.* Not only do they provide vast amounts of information, but they also are highly personal in nature and provide opportunities for immediate feedback. A bit less rich are non-face-to-face interactive media, such as the *telephone.* However, not all business communication requires a two-way flow of information. For example, further toward the *lean* end of the continuum are personal, but static media, such as *memos* (written messages used for communication within an organization) and *letters* (written messages used for external communication).[11] This includes one-way communications sent either physically (e.g., letter), or electronically (e.g., fax or e-mail). (Given their growing importance in today's organizations, we will describe high-tech forms of communication in more detail in the next section.) Finally, at the leanest end of the continuum are highly impersonal, static media, such as *flyers* and *bulletins,* written information that is targeted broadly and not aimed at any one specific individual. For an overview of this continuum of verbal media, see the horizontal arrow at the top of Figure 9.5.

Two types of written media deserve special mention because of the important role they play in organizations—*newsletters* and *employee handbooks.* Although they are impersonal and aimed at a general audience, **newsletters** serve important functions in organizations.

nonverbal communication
The transmission of messages without the use of words (e.g., by gestures, the use of space).

verbal media
Forms of communication involving the use of words (e.g., telephone messages, faxes, books, etc.).

newsletters
Regularly published internal documents, either hard copy or electronic in nature, describing information of interest to employees regarding an array of business and nonbusiness issues affecting them.

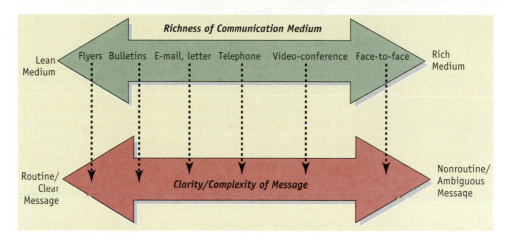

FIGURE 9.5

Media Richness Theory

Verbal communication media may be characterized along a continuum ranging from highly rich, interactive media, such as face-to-face discussions, to lean, static media, such as bulletins. According to *media richness theory,* lean media are most effectively used to communicate routine/clear messages, whereas rich media are most effectively used to communicate nonroutine/ambiguous messages.

Source: Based on material in Lengel & Daft, 1988; see Note 10.

Newsletters are regularly published internal documents describing information of interest to employees regarding an array of business and nonbusiness issues affecting them.[12] Approximately one-third of companies rely on newsletters, typically as a means of supplementing other means of communicating important information, such as group meetings.[13] Traditionally, newsletters were printed and distributed to employees, but these days many are distributed electronically. Not only are online newsletters far less expensive to create, but they also allow information to be updated far more rapidly, making them current and useful to everyone.

employee handbook
A document describing to employees basic information about a company; a general reference regarding a company's background, the nature of its business, and its rules.

Another important internal publication used in organizations is the **employee handbook**—a document describing to employees basic information about the company. It is a general reference regarding the company's background, the nature of its business, and its rules.[14] Specifically, the major purposes of employee handbooks are: (1) to explain key aspects of the company's policies, (2) to clarify the expectations of the company and employees toward each other, and (3) to express the company's philosophy.[15] Handbooks are more popular today than ever before. This is not only because clarifying company policies may help prevent lawsuits, but also because corporate officials are recognizing that explicit statements about what their company stands for are a useful means of effectively socializing new employees and promoting the company's values.

Matching the Medium to the Message

What types of communication are most effective under various circumstances? In general, communication is most effective when it uses multiple channels, such as both oral and written messages.[16] Apparently, oral messages are useful in getting people's immediate attention, and the follow-up written portion helps make the message more permanent, something that can be referred to in the future. Oral messages also have the benefit of allowing for immediate two-way communication between parties, whereas written communiqués frequently are only one-way, or require too long for a response.

Not surprisingly, two-way communications (e.g., face-to-face discussions, telephone conversations) are more commonly used in organizations than one-way communications (e.g., memos). For example, in a study of civilian employees of a U.S. Navy agency, approximately 83 percent of the communications taking place used two-way media.[17] In fact, 55 percent of all communications were individual face-to-face interactions. One-way, written communications tended to be reserved for more formal, official messages that needed to be referred to in the future at the receiver's convenience (e.g., official announcements about position openings). Clearly, both written and spoken communications have their place in organizational communication. The trick to any communication medium is not only *when* to use it but how to use it wisely.[18] For some valuable suggestions in this regard, see Table 9.2.

In essence, a medium's effectiveness depends on how appropriate it is for the kind of message being sent. Specifically, according to a conceptualization known as **media richness theory**, the effectiveness of any verbal medium depends on the extent to which it is appropriate in view of the ambiguity of the message being sent. In particular, oral media (e.g., telephone conversations, face-to-face meetings) are more effective than written media (e.g., notes, memos) when messages are nonroutine or ambiguous.[19] This is because the information contained in such messages is likely to be unclear to recipients, requiring the additional assistance in interpretation that oral media provide. If you've ever found yourself giving up on e-mail and calling someone to discuss something that is too complex, then you know what we mean.

media richness theory
A conceptualization specifying that the effectiveness of any verbal medium depends on the extent to which it is appropriate in view of the ambiguity of the message being sent.

TABLE 9.2 Guidelines for Properly Using Popular Communication Media

The most widely used communication media are e-mail, fax, postal mail, telephone, and of course, face-to-face discussions. Each of these can be very useful if a few simple rules are followed, such as those summarized here.

Medium	Best Use	Rules for Use
E-mail	Sending key information, confirming and documenting facts and appointments	■ Keep messages brief. ■ Words stay forever, so don't be sarcastic or insulting. ■ Don't ignore conventional rules of grammar.
Fax	Sending complete documents requiring a signature, drafts for approval, or notes to someone who doesn't have e-mail	■ Phone ahead to announce that your fax is forthcoming. ■ Follow up faxes with a quick phone call or e-mail to confirm receipt. ■ Avoid sending personal or confidential information that might be seen by others.
Postal mail	Sending long and complicated material or short thank-you notes	■ Verify spelling and grammar. ■ Summarize key points at the beginning. ■ Avoid long sections; break up with bullet points.
Telephone	Communicating information in which emotion must be conveyed (if face-to-face discussions are not possible)	■ Stay focused; avoid multitasking while on the phone. ■ Make appointments to have important phone calls ("phone dates"). ■ Let the other person finish speaking before talking.
Face-to-face	Communicating highly sensitive and delicate information	■ Keep discussions brief and focused on the issues. ■ Make sure personal discussions cannot be overheard. ■ Plan for meetings and arrive prepared to discuss the topic.

Source: Based on information in Gantenbein, 2002; see Note 18.

By contrast, written media are more effective when messages are clear. For example, using e-mail to send someone a billing address or a phone number or directions to a company location—all very clear and highly specific information—is more effective because it avoids errors. Problems of mishearing a number, for example, are eliminated, and people easily can refer to the written message when the information it contains is called for. In view of this, the quest for effective communication should be seen not simply as a question of what communication medium is best, but rather, what medium is best suited to the particular message being sent (recall the summary in Figure 9.5).

Importantly, managers who follow these practices by matching the type of communications media they use to the kind of message they are sending, considered *media-sensitive,* generally perform their jobs more effectively than those who do not do so, considered *media-insensitive.*[20] Fortunately, many of us are likely to have a good intuitive sense for selecting the appropriate medium for the messages we wish to send. If you've ever found yourself thinking that it's best to discuss some "sensitive" or "delicate" matters in person instead of via e-mail or phone, then you know what we mean. Matters that are "difficult" because they are emotionally charged—those pertaining to serious illness or job termination, for example—are best handled in person instead of in writing because of the added opportunities they offer to demonstrate sensitivity and concern. Also, in terms of media richness theory, they are nonroutine and sufficiently ambiguous in nature to require face-to-face explanations. However, not all managers demonstrate this sensitivity. As an extreme example, administrators in one California school district not only informed teachers that they were being laid off by giving them curt written notices, but delivered them to the teachers while standing in front of their classes![21] The resulting embarrassment for all is easy to envision. Clearly, these individuals would have been well served to learn a bit about media richness theory (not to mention everyday politeness).

Nonverbal Communication

It has been estimated that people communicate at least as much *nonverbally* (i.e., without words) as they do verbally.[22] Indeed, there can be no doubt that many of the messages we send others are transmitted without words. Here are just a few examples of how we communicate nonverbally in organizations.

- *Mode of dress.* Much of what we say about ourselves to others comes from the way we dress. For example, despite the general trend toward casual clothing in the workplace, higher-status people tend to dress more formally than lower-ranking employees.[23]
- *Waiting time.* Higher-status people, such as managers and executives at all ranks, tend to communicate their organizational positions nonverbally by keeping lower-ranking people waiting to see them—a gesture that sends the message that one's time is more important.[24]
- *Seating position.* Higher-ranking people also assert their higher status by sitting at the heads of rectangular tables, a position that not only has become associated with importance over the years, but that also enables important people to maintain eye contact with those over whom they are responsible.[25]
- *Body language.* When communicating in other countries, it's useful to learn not only the verbal language spoken, but also the nonverbal, body language used. People from various cultures interpret various nonverbal signs very differently than people do in the United States.[26] Avoiding serious miscommunications requires familiarizing oneself with such information (see Figure 9.6)

As you read this, you may be asking yourself, "What can I do to present myself more favorably to those around me on the job?" Specifically, what can you do nonverbally to cultivate the impression that you have the qualities of a good leader, and that you are worthy of promotion? Just as you can say certain things to enhance your image as a strong, effective employee, there also are several things you can do nonverbally that will enhance your image. For a summary of these, see Table 9.3.

FIGURE 9.6

Beware of Nonverbal Miscommunication in Different Countries

Successfully conducting business in another country involves learning not only that country's spoken language, but its nonverbal mannerisms as well. As suggested here, even the best intentioned communicators run the risk of sending the wrong message—some of which can be quite serious.

Source: Based on information in Barnum & Wolniansky, 1989; see Note 26.

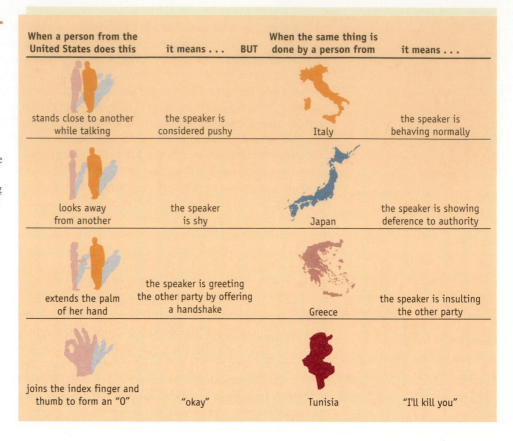

When a person from the United States does this	it means ...	BUT	When the same thing is done by a person from	it means ...
stands close to another while talking	the speaker is considered pushy		Italy	the speaker is behaving normally
looks away from another	the speaker is shy		Japan	the speaker is showing deference to authority
extends the palm of her hand	the speaker is greeting the other party by offering a handshake		Greece	the speaker is insulting the other party
joins the index finger and thumb to form an "O"	"okay"		Tunisia	"I'll kill you"

The Role of Technology: Computer-Mediated Communication

To this point, we have discussed mostly traditional, low-tech forms of verbal communication. However, these days a great deal of communication that takes place in organizations occurs online, such as through e-mail, chat rooms, instant messaging, and video conferences. These are considered forms of **computer-mediated communication** because the messages are transmitted using computers.[27]

Recently, General Motors has been making a concerted effort to use computer-mediated communication to get messages out to key employees—and, importantly, to hear back from them. Since 2005, for example, Michael Wiley, GM's director of new media communications, has been using bi-weekly *podcasts* (named "For Immediate

computer-mediated communication

Forms of communication that are aided by the use of computer technology (e.g., e-mail, instant messaging).

TABLE 9.3 How to Communicate Your Leadership Potential Nonverbally

People who are self-confident not only speak and write with assurance, but they also project their capacity to lead others in the various nonverbal ways summarized here.

- Stand and sit using an erect posture. Avoid slouching.
- When confronted, stand up straight. Do not cower.
- Nod your head to show that you are listening to someone talk.
- Maintain eye contact and smile at those with whom you are talking.
- Use hand gestures in a relaxed, nonmechanical way.
- Always be neat, well groomed, and wear clean, well-pressed clothes.

Source: Based on suggestions by DuBrin, 2001; see Note 27.

podcast

A prerecorded message distributed for playback on Apple's iPod MP3 player (i.e., an iPod broadcast).

RSS feed

Information, usually news, delivered to Web sites on a real-time basis, as events occur.

blogs (Web logs)

Web pages in which people express their personal experiences and feelings; an Internet-based diary.

synchronous communication techniques

Forms of communication in which the parties can send and receive messages at the same time.

asynchronous communication techniques

Forms of communication in which senders and receivers must take turns sending and receiving messages.

video-mediated communication (VMC)

Conferences in which people can hear and see each other using computers.

Release") and *RSS feeds* on various topics (e.g., high-tech advances) to get the latest developments to engineers in the company's small-block engine development group. A **podcast** (an iPod broadcast) is a message distributed for playback on Apple's iPod MP3 player; and an **RSS feed** is information, usually news, delivered to Web sites as events occur. And, as a means of hearing back from these engineers, the company has been relying on **blogs** (short for Web logs)—Web pages in which an individual expresses personal feelings and experiences, an Internet-based diary. The particular blog that Wiley created is called "GM FastLane Blog." Given the success of these efforts, in 2006 Wiley began introducing these high-tech media to communicate with dealers and customers. The benefit, says Wiley, is that "instead of going to message boards to talk *about* us, they have an opportunity to come and talk directly *to* us."[28] This, Wiley emphasizes, is key to becoming a better company and to developing better products. And, in today's highly competitive automotive market, this is a luxury no company can afford to ignore.

A useful way of distinguishing between various forms of computer-mediated communication is by noting differences between those in which communication occurs in *synchronous* fashion and those in which communication occurs in *asynchronous* fashion. **Synchronous communication techniques** are ones in which the parties can send and receive messages at once. Telephone conversations fall into this category, for example. However, some other communication technologies, such as walkie-talkies, are considered **asynchronous communication techniques** because people must take turns sending and receiving messages (in other words, the sender's message and the receiver's messages are not synchronized). Some widely used forms of computer-mediation communication may be found in each category.

Synchronous Communication: Video-Mediated Communication

These days, it's not unusual for people to work together although they physically may be in different locations. This is because technology can be used to bring them together, allowing people to communicate by sharing information in real time whether they are across the street or across the planet. Just as the telephone revolutionized business communications a century ago, today, advances in technology have driven down the costs of more advanced techniques, such as *videoconferences* or *Webcasts* (short for Web broadcasts), making them extremely popular communication tools. These are known more generally as forms of **video-mediated communication (VMC)**. Simply put, these are ways of simultaneously transmitting audio and video between two or more computers. The inexpensive "Webcams" with which you are likely to be familiar on your personal computer are, in fact, rudimentary forms of this technology.

Companies use VMC as inexpensive ways of linking employees in distant locations—allowing them to have *cybermeetings* (see Figure 9.7). Not only are these much less expensive than air travel—with respect to both money and time—but because they require limited preparation, they also allow for meetings to be scheduled at the last minute. Boeing, for example, regularly uses VMC to connect the employees in the company's Chicago headquarters with others in satellite locations.[29]

Although meeting others via computer makes it impossible to experience the human touch associated with actually being there, VMC is considered much more effective than other, more traditional forms of linking people in distant locations—such as phone, e-mail, and fax. In fact, there are several situations in which VMC is preferable to these other communications media.[30] This is the case, for example, when visual information needs to be shared with several people at once, especially when the information involved is stored on computers.

Asynchronous Communication: E-Mail and Instant Messaging

Some of the most widely used forms of communication technology fall into the asynchronous category. Because they rely on less sophisticated technologies, asynchronous forms of communication—such as fax machines and voice mail—are older (around since the 1980s and 1990s), making them very well established. In these techniques, one party must

FIGURE 9.7

Video-Mediated Communication: Linking People Through Technology

Brian Bodge (standing at the podium), 787 program senior specialist engineer at Boeing, leads a technical discussion between three team members in the Global Collaboration Center in Everett, Washington, and Jeff Swada (left screen, far right), senior lead engineer in Wichita, Kansas. The collaborative technology enables a virtual workspace that allows engineers on the 787 program, including its partners in Australia, Japan, Italy, Canada, and across the United States, to make concurrent design changes to the airplane in real time. The resulting efficiencies in engineering and cost savings help bring in the project on time and within budget.

complete a message before the other can respond to it. Also in this category are two especially popular forms of communication—*e-mail* and *instant messaging*.

e-mail (electronic mail)
A system whereby people use personal computer terminals to send and receive messages between one another using the Internet.

E-mail. Short for electronic mail, **e-mail** refers to text messages sent via the Internet. Based on your own experiences, it probably comes as no surprise to you that e-mail ranks among the most widely used communications tools in the United States. Currently, there are over 170 million corporate e-mail boxes in use, and that figure has been rising dramatically.[31] Although e-mail usage is less widespread in other countries, the growing availability of Internet access has contributed to its rapid acceptance elsewhere. E-mail has become such a popular means of communication that in 2002, it surpassed print advertising as the most widely used form of direct marketing.[32] The main reason for e-mail's popularity is the freedom it provides people to send and receive messages quickly and efficiently to people located anyplace at any time of day or night, and to organize and store messages as well.

E-mail is the preferred means of communicating facts, such as information needed to coordinate effort between individuals and work groups. Brief, factual messages (e.g., about schedule changes) and announcements (e.g., about forthcoming events) are popular uses of e-mail. E-mail also has made it easier to break down status barriers between people that often make it difficult to share ideas. For example, whereas one may find it difficult to get an in-person appointment with the head of a company, it's just as simple to send an e-mail message to that individual as it is to reach anyone else, effectively altering the flow of information within an organization.[33] Not surprisingly, many top executives rely on e-mail as an effective means of reaching out to everyone in their companies.

As popular as e-mail is today, it is far from perfect. One major problem is that e-mail contributes to *information overload*. Frequently, e-mail overwhelms people with so much information that it's tiring, frustrating, and challenging to have to sift through it all to find what's most important. Given that about 1.5 billion e-mail messages are sent each week, this is not too surprising.[34] With an eye toward reducing the number of e-mails received, and to enhance the human element in communication, several companies have instituted "e-mail-free Fridays."[35] Although first implemented among several British companies in 2002—the large confectioner, Nestlé Rowntree, among them—this practice has been slow to catch on. Clearly, although the practice reflects some people's frustrations with e-mail, the fact that many are reluctant to do without it is a good indication that many regard its benefits as outweighing its costs.

Another key problem with e-mail is that people usually find it a highly limiting medium for expressing their emotions. After all, traditional e-mail is restricted to alphanumeric characters and lacks the nonverbal information that makes face-to-face communication so rich. So, although you can change the tone of your voice or make a face to express how you feel about something in person, it's harder to do this using only the tools of the keyboard. As a result, many people overexpress their emotions by sending emotionally charged, angry messages to others—a practice known as **flaming**. This occurs because the brief response time required to respond to an e-mail that angers someone prevents that person from calming down, as would occur naturally if he or she responded using a medium whose messages required more time to prepare, such as typing a letter or talking to someone in person.[36] Research has shown that flaming is more likely to be committed by men than women and by people who are anonymous than those who are identified as the senders of messages.[37] Because it's too late to take back vitriol after clicking "send," we suspect that victims and perpetrators of flaming will have learned a sobering lesson about curbing their anger when communicating via e-mail.

Fortunately, people have found other, more benign ways of expressing their emotions via e-mail messages. In recent years, people have, rather ingeniously, developed simple graphic representations of facial expressions to express their feelings. Known as **emoticons**, short for emotional icons, these are symbols created by typing characters such as commas, hyphens, and parentheses, which when tilting one's head to the side, resemble facial expressions. Among the most common emoticons are these:

    :-)   smile, happy
    :-(frown, sad
    ;-)   wink

People generally use emoticons to qualify their emotions in important ways, such as to communicate sarcasm. For example, the presence of the smiley face in the message, "he's really smart :-)" may be used to connote that the person in question is really not so smart at all. For some more unusual, highly specialized emoticons see Table 9.4.[38] (Although using emoticons is fun, we also tend to think that they are useful in communicating our feelings. For an objective look at this issue, see the *OB: Making Sense Out of Common Sense* section on p. 346.)

Instant Messaging. Another form of distributed asynchronous communication that has become very popular in recent years is known as **instant messaging**. Services of this type (such as those offered by AOL and MSN) allow people who are online to share messages with one another instantaneously, without having to go through an e-mail program. Sending an instant message opens up a small onscreen window into which each party can type messages for the other to read. This makes it possible to exchange written notes in real time, as well as to share Web links and files of all types. Although e-mail is quite fast, sometimes even the rapid response of e-mail is not fast enough given that it requires checking for incoming messages and then having to click through a few steps to read, reply, and send the e-mail. This accounts for the popularity of instant messaging. In fact, on a typical day, over 5.7 million people use the most popular instant messaging service, AOL Instant Messenger.[39]

Although intended originally for home users, instant messaging has become a popular communications medium for business as well. In a 2004 report, it was noted that 21 percent of IM users, approximately 11 million American adults, use instant messaging at work. Not everyone is completely happy with IM, however.[40] Only 11 percent of people

---

flaming
The practice of overexpressing one's emotions by sending emotionally charged messages to another via e-mail.

emoticons (emotional icons)
Symbols typed using characters such as commas, hyphens, and parentheses for purposes of expressing emotions in online communication.

instant messaging
The practice of communicating with another online by typing messages into boxes that pop up on the screen as needed.

TABLE 9.4 Do You Know What These Emoticons Mean?

In recent years, people have created emoticons to express a wide variety of emotions. Here are some particularly interesting ones expressing a variety of different emotions.

Category of Emotion	Emotion	Meaning
Positive	:-)) *or* x-D	Laughing hard
	:'D *or* :'-D	Laughing and crying
	:-*	Kissing, pucker up
Negative	:-S	Worried, nervous
	>-[*or* >-(	Angry, upset
	T_T	Tears streaming down face
Playful	:-o~~~	Celebrating
	<):-)	Cowboy
	o-)-<]:	Skateboarder
Unhealthy	:~)	Runny nose
	:; *or* :-;	Sore tooth
	(:|	Tired, overwhelmed

Source: From information in Nancarrow, 2005; see Note 38.

OB Making Sense Out of Common Sense

Do Emoticons Really Communicate Anything?

Emoticons are used widely to communicate the sender's emotions, but do they really have the intended impact? In other words, are they effective in communicating emotions? Not necessarily. Research has revealed that emoticons do *not* always qualify the meanings of written messages as we might suspect.[41]

In one study, participants were presented with written messages that either were accompanied or unaccompanied by certain emoticons. After looking at them, they were asked to indicate what was being communicated. Generally, emoticons did not qualify the meanings of written messages as users might intend. For example, a negative message accompanied by a wink or a frown was not seen as being any more sarcastic or negative in tone than the words by themselves. Specifically, the message, "That class was awful ;-)" was perceived to be just as sarcastic as the message, "That class was awful." Likewise, saying "That class was awful :-(" was perceived just as negatively as "That class was awful."

For positive statements, the effects were interesting. Saying "That class was great :-)" suggested that the speaker was happier than saying "That class was great," but it did not send the message that the class was any better. In other words, emoticons don't always

have the effects that the communicator intended. One possible reason for this is that emoticons tend to be overused, and as a result, their impact has diminished over time.

Additional research has shown some interesting sex differences in the use of emoticons.[42] In general, women use emoticons more frequently than men. However, when men are communicating with women, they use emoticons more frequently than they do when they are communicating with other men. This is in keeping with research showing that in general men feel more comfortable expressing their emotions to women than to other men. Interestingly, men and women use emoticons differently. Whereas women use emoticons to be humorous, men use them to be teasing and sarcastic. Yeah, right ;-)

In conclusion, you should be careful using emoticons because they don't always do a good job of getting your message across. In fact, using emoticons is more likely to send a message about the gender of the communicator than it is to qualify the emotional meaning of the message itself. Most importantly, despite e-mail's incredible usefulness as a communication tool, it is just one option. When it comes to communicating emotionally charged messages, as people say, "we have to talk"—and on such occasions, e-mail just won't do.

using IM at work indicate that they cannot live without it. The vast majority, however—68 percent—see it as a mixed blessing, although mostly positive, whereas 4 percent see it as a mixed blessing, but mostly negative. Finally, 10 percent wish they could do away with it altogether. Clearly, using IM at work has both pros and cons (for a summary of the things people like and dislike about instant messaging, see Table 9.5). Despite mixed reactions to instant messaging as a tool for organizational communication, growing numbers of companies are finding it a useful way of communicating quickly and inexpensively with employees in distant locations.

The Human Impact of Computer-Mediated Communication

Despite the widespread popularity of computer-mediated communication, as we have been suggesting throughout this section of the chapter, people are not always completely receptive to it. For example, we already mentioned that people find it difficult to express their emotions when using e-mail and that e-mail contributes to information overload. These are only two of the problems that are beginning to come to the attention of social scientists. Among other concerns about computer-mediated communication are: (1) its potential for violations of privacy and (2) its capacity to dehumanize the workplace. We now discuss these.

Violations of Privacy. Before advances in technology, when the major forms of communication were speaking face-to-face, writing letters, and talking on the telephone, concerns about violating privacy were not especially great. After all, social norms discouraged people from listening in on others' conversations and peeking at their mail. Although dramatically useful, technology changed all this. Messages being communicated today, because they are heavily mediated by computers, can be—and frequently are—monitored by others. Indeed, today's companies spend an estimated $655 million monitoring their employees' actions on the Internet.[43]

Although most employees generally dislike this practice because it violates their privacy, employers counter that they have to monitor their employees because today's communication technology makes it easier than ever for employees to "goof off." Just consider these statistics:[44]

- 86.5 percent of employees use their company's e-mail systems to send personal messages.
- 30 percent of American workers watch sports online and 24 percent admit to shopping online while at work.
- 70 percent of the visits to Internet pornography sites occur during regular 9:00 A.M. to 5:00 P.M. working hours.

Given these figures, it's not surprising that nonwork-related use of the Internet has been estimated to result in a 40 percent loss in productivity for American businesses.

Besides lost productivity, there are two additional reasons why companies are monitoring their employees' communications. Both involve security. First, in recent years, terrorist attacks in New York, Madrid, and London have put the world on notice that being vigilant for terrorism in the workplace is wise. Second, many companies are losing untold

TABLE 9.5 Instant Messaging at Work: A Mixed Blessing

Among American workers who regularly use instant messaging at work, there are things about it that they both like and dislike. These likes and dislikes are summarized here, along with the percentage of people reporting them.

Likes	Percentage Reporting	Dislikes	Percentage Reporting
Saves time	50%	Encourages gossip	32%
Provides relief from daily grind	47%	Too distracting	29%
Improves teamwork	41%	Adds stress to life	11%

Source: Based on data reported by Shiu & Lenhart, 2004; see Note 39.

millions of dollars through industrial espionage and other breaches of information security.[45] These are vitally important considerations, of course. At the same time, however, employees are concerned about where to draw the line between their own personal liberties and the need for security, both national and industrial.[46]

The trick, then, is to find ways of being able to balance people's rights to privacy in the workplace with the rights of organizations to ensure that their employees are doing what they are paid to do and to protect their property as well as the obligation of government to protect its citizens. Although this surely isn't a simple matter, several suggestions for balancing these considerations should be noted.

- ■ *Establish a clear monitoring policy and follow it carefully.* All employees should be made aware of the conditions under which certain messages will be monitored. This gives them the opportunity to decide whether or not to engage in inappropriate behavior while at work, knowing all along that they might get caught.
- ■ *Apply the privacy policy equally.* Too often, policies applied to lower-level employees are ignored at the top. However, if it is wrong for low-level employees to use company e-mail for personal purposes, so too is it wrong for top executives to do the same.
- ■ *Maintain complete privacy of all company records.* Organizations never should use company records for purposes other than those to which employees have agreed when providing the information. For example, performance information may be used to make training decisions, but health records should not be used in making decisions about suitability for promotion. Clearly, information never should be shared with third parties without employees' full consent—unless, of course, a company is required to do so by court order.

Does High-Tech Communication Dehumanize the Workplace? When computers first entered the workplace, experts became concerned about the tendency for people's social needs to go unfulfilled because they come into contact with fewer others in the course of their days.[47] To a large extent, this is a valid concern.

Recently, research has revealed a particularly interesting side to this issue. Specifically, the inherently solitary nature of communication via the Internet makes it a particularly appealing communication channel for individuals lacking in interpersonal skills, those who find traditional, face-to-face communication awkward and difficult. Frequently, such individuals rely on the Internet (e.g., through e-mail, chat rooms, or instant messaging) to satisfy their basic needs for affiliation (i.e., to be connected to others) in ways that compensate for their uneasiness with in-person social interaction. However, research has shown that this appears to be a double-edged sword.[48] On the positive side, it's clear that the Internet opens up avenues of communication to individuals who otherwise might be inclined to be left out of the loop. The down side, however, is that many such individuals tend to overcompensate by being highly compulsive in their use of the Internet, finding it difficult to limit the considerable hours spent in front of the computer. The problem is so serious for some that, as a result, the time spent online causes them to miss work or social engagements (for a summary, see Figure 9.8). As such, we note that computer-mediated communication is a valuable organizational tool, but one that is not without limits or problems.

Formal Communication in Organizations

formal communication
The sharing of messages regarding the official work of the organization.

informal communication:
The sharing of unofficial messages, ones that go beyond the organization's formal activities.

Think of the broad range of messages that are communicated to you in the course of a workday. For example, your boss may ask you to complete an important sales report, another manager from across the hall may hand you a memo regarding the status of a new project, you may read an e-mail message from a co-worker regarding who won the office football pool, and the custodian may tell you a joke. From just these few examples, it's easy to distinguish between two basic types of communication that occur in organizations: **formal communication**—the sharing of messages regarding the official work of the organization, and **informal communication**—the sharing of unofficial messages that are unrelated to the organization's formal activities. Because both formal and informal communication is so widespread

FIGURE 9.8

The Negative Side of Computer-Mediated Communication

Research has shown that among individuals who are lacking in interpersonal skills, computer-mediated communication might be problematic. In contrast, people with good interpersonal skills reap benefits from computer-mediated communication. The specific connections responsible for these patterns are summarized here.

Source: Based on findings reported by Caplan, 2005; see Note 48.

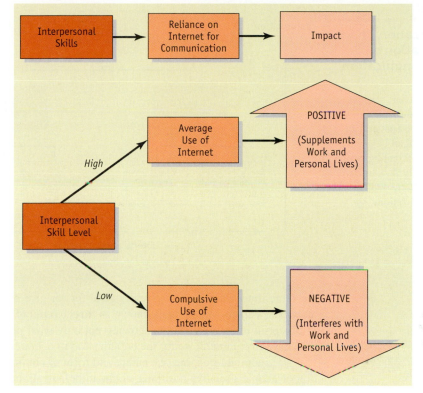

in organizations, we describe both in this chapter. First, in this section we will focus on formal communication; then in the next section we will turn to informal communication.

Organizational Structure Influences Communication

Although the basic process of communication described thus far is similar in many different contexts, a unique feature of organizations has a profound impact on the communication process—namely, their *structure*. Organizations often are set up in ways that dictate who may and may not communicate with whom. Given this, we may ask: How is the communication process affected by the structure of an organization?

The term **organizational structure** refers to the formally prescribed pattern of interrelationships existing between the various units of an organization (a topic to which we will return in Chapter 15). An organization's structure may be described using a diagram like the one shown in Figure 9.9, known as an **organization chart**. Such diagrams provide graphic representations of the formal pattern of communication in an organization (this one is fictitious). An organization chart may be likened to an X-ray showing the organization's skeleton, an outline of the planned, formal connections between individuals in various departments.[49]

Note the various boxes in the diagram and the lines connecting them. Each box represents a person performing a specific job. The diagram shows the titles of the individuals performing the various jobs and the formally prescribed pattern of communication between them. These are relatively fixed and defined. Each individual is responsible for performing a specified job. Should the people working in the organization leave their jobs, they must be replaced if their jobs are to be done. The formal structure of an organization—hence, the prescribed pattern of communication between individuals—does not change just because the personnel change. As you will see in the next section of this chapter, however, the pattern of informal communication may change dramatically under such circumstances.

The lines connecting the boxes in the organizational chart are lines of *authority* showing who must answer to whom—that is, **reporting relationships**. Each person is responsible to (or answers to) the person at the next higher level to which he or she is connected. At

organizational structure
The formally prescribed pattern of interrelationships existing between the various units of an organization.

organization chart
A diagram showing the formal structure of an organization, indicating who is to communicate with whom.

reporting relationships
Formal connections between people indicating who must answer to whom in an organization.

FIGURE 9.9

The Organization Chart: An Organization's Formal Communication Network

An organization chart, such as this simple one, shows the formally prescribed patterns of communication in an organization. Different types of messages typically flow upward, downward, and horizontally throughout organizations, as summarized here.

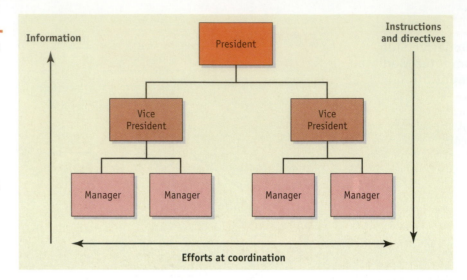

direct report

Someone in an organization, a subordinate, who must answer directly to a higher-level individual in that organization.

the same time, people are also responsible for (or give orders to) those who are immediately below them—individuals known as **direct reports**. The boxes and lines form a sort of blueprint of an organization showing not only what people have to do, but with whom they have to communicate for the organization to operate properly.

As you might imagine, the nature and form of communication vary greatly as a function of people's relative positions within an organization. Even a quick look at an organization chart reveals that information may flow up (from lower to higher levels within the same functional area), down (from higher to lower levels within the same functional area), or horizontally (between people at the same level in different functional areas). However, as summarized in Figure 9.9, and as we now describe, different types of information typically travel in different directions within a hierarchy.

Downward Communication: From Supervisor to Subordinate

downward communication

Communication from people at higher organizational levels to those at lower organizational levels.

Communication from supervisors to their subordinates is known as **downward communication** because it flows from one level to the next lowest one, slowly trickling down to the bottom of the organization chart. What types of messages do supervisors typically send their direct reports? Although many things may be communicated, official messages flowing downward generally consist of instructions, directions, and orders—messages telling subordinates what they should be doing.[50] We also would expect to find feedback on past performance flowing in a downward direction (such as when managers tell subordinates how well they have been working). A sales manager, for example, might direct members of her sales force to promote a certain product and then congratulate them for being successful.

What Do Subordinates Want to Hear? Generally, employees are only moderately satisfied with the nature of the communication they receive from their superiors. A large-scale survey found that 71 percent of employees believe their superiors keep them well informed, 65 percent believe that they are given sufficient information to do their jobs, and 51 percent believe that the downward messages they receive are candid and accurate.[51] Although the problem does not appear dire, these statistics suggest that there's clearly something missing from the information people are receiving from their superiors. This raises an interesting question: When listening to their superiors, what topics interest employees most? For what questions are they searching for answers? There appear to be six key areas of interest to employees.[52] These are as follows:

- What, exactly, does my job entail?
- How well am I doing?
- Does anyone care about me?
- How is my work unit doing?

■ Where is the organization headed?

■ How can I help the company meet its objectives?

Armed with this information, it's clear that managers should have a clear agenda when communicating downward with their subordinates. Answering these questions, whether directly in the form of one-on-one discussions, or in broader media, such as company newsletters, is a sure way of improving communication. Not only does addressing these issues stand to make workers more satisfied with the messages received from their superiors, but also with those superiors themselves. In fact, addressing these issues in messages to one's subordinates is an excellent way of managing their job performance.[53]

MUM effect

The reluctance to transmit bad news, shown either by not transmitting the message at all, or by delegating the task to someone else.

The MUM Effect. An interesting phenomenon that often occurs in the course of downward communication is known as the **MUM effect**. This refers to people's reluctance to transmit bad news to others (as in "Mum's the word," being silent about something).[54] It is only natural, for example, for doctors to be uncomfortable telling their patients that they are seriously ill and for teachers to tell their students that they are failing (yes, believe it or not, professors don't like this). Not surprisingly, the MUM effect also occurs among veterinarians who have to communicate bad news to clients about the ill health of their pets.[55] Given people's close emotional attachments to their beloved family pets, this is understandable. In general, the reluctance to transmit bad news may take several forms that threaten to impair communication. For example, people may downplay the actual serious nature of the problem, they may pass the job of sharing bad news along to someone else, or they may simply avoid saying anything whatsoever.[56] In all cases, these options keep people from information they need, leading to poor decisions (see Chapter 10).

Although the MUM effect cannot be countered completely, the task of transmitting bad news can be made less difficult for everyone concerned by following the guidelines for being a supportive communicator outlined later in this chapter (see pp. 369–370). Among the most difficult topics of downward communication involves informing someone that he or she is being terminated. Although it's never pleasant, there are several important things to take into account when it becomes necessary to do this. (For some useful guidance in this regard, see the *How to Do It* section on p. 352.)

Upward Communication: From Subordinate to Superior

upward communication

Communication from people at lower organizational levels to those at higher organizational levels.

Information flowing from lower levels to higher levels within an organization, from subordinates to supervisors, is referred to as **upward communication**. Messages flowing in this direction tend to contain the information managers need to do their jobs, such as data required for decision making and the status of various projects. In short, upward communication is designed to keep managers aware of what is going on. Among the various types of information flowing upward are suggestions for improvement, status reports, reactions to work-related issues, and new ideas.

Upward communication is not simply the reverse of downward communication. The difference in status between the communicating parties makes for some important distinctions. For example, it has been established that upward communication occurs much less frequently than downward communication. In fact, one classic study found that 70 percent of assembly line workers initiated communication with their supervisors less than once a month.[57] Further research has found that managers direct less than 15 percent of their total communication to their superiors.[58] And, when people do communicate upward, their conversations tend to be shorter than discussions with their peers.[59] Although the flattening of organizational structures (see Chapter 15) and the advent of teams in organizations (see Chapter 8) are likely to have made these figures less extreme today, it's safe to say that upward communication still remains restricted.[60]

Importantly, upward communication is often inaccurate. For example, subordinates frequently feel they must highlight their accomplishments and downplay their mistakes if they are to be looked on favorably.[61] Similarly, some individuals fear that they will be rebuked by their supervisors if they anticipate that their remarks will be perceived as threatening.[62] As a result, many people frequently avoid communicating bad news to their

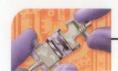

HOW TO DO IT

"You're Fired!": Doing It Better Than Donald Trump

A few years ago, millions of television viewers of the popular television show, *The Apprentice,* enjoyed watching real estate tycoon Donald Trump dismiss aspiring apprentices who failed to impress him by uttering the words, "You're fired." Despite this show's appeal, it cannot be said that Mr. Trump is serving as a role model for managers who have to "drop the ax" on an employee. Not only is communicating this devastating news unpleasant, but if done incorrectly, it's potentially costly, given that some employees who were let go may claim that they were wrongfully terminated and file lawsuits.[63] Additionally, the morale of employees who remain on the job tends to suffer if the termination of one of their colleagues is handled poorly. Fortunately, several things can be done to avoid—or, at least, minimize—these problems.[64]

1. **Document and maintain written records of performance problems.** Employers should maintain careful written logs documenting problems, goals for improvement, and a reasonable timetable for meeting these goals. Employees should be asked to sign all such documents. This will help employers defend themselves against employees who file suit against them, and it also may discourage employees from thinking about suing in the first place. Of course, this practice comes in handy for yet another reason: It guards against lapses in memory that are likely to occur over time. Having a written record to which everyone can refer will serve as a useful platform from which to launch future discussions about improvement should termination not be necessary.

2. **Give advance notice.** If an employee is doing something illegal or something that endangers others in the workplace, it is advisable to fire that person on the spot. In less extreme cases, however, firing without notice only adds insult to injury—and these injured feelings may stimulate aggrieved employees to visit their attorneys.[65] After all, failing to give advance notice demonstrates the employer's disrespect for the employee. However, giving an employee advance notice of termination helps him or her adjust to a new life outside the company and to find a new job, reducing potential gaps in employment that can lead to financial hardship.

3. **Clearly explain the termination decision.** Too often, when people are fired they claim that they had no idea why it happened.[66] Supervisors should explain the problems in clear terms. Then, after explaining the decision and emphasizing that it is final, they should move on to practical matters like severance pay and continuance of health care insurance.

4. **Be sympathetic to the fired worker's feelings.** When one loses a job, the resulting feelings of uncertainty—both personal and financial—are quite unsettling. This is bad enough, so don't make the situation worse by being insensitive and uncaring (such as by pointing a finger at someone seated across from you and saying, "You're fired"). Compassion is precisely what's needed most at such a time.

5. **Do the job in person and in private.** However tempting it may be to fire someone in writing (by e-mail or in a written letter) or by leaving a voice-mail message, don't do it. As obviously insensitive as this may be, believe it or not, this has been done! Also, although it would seem to go without saying, discussions about dismissal should occur in private. After all, they are difficult enough without the embarrassment and humiliation of having others looking on. The egregious example we noted earlier of the teachers presented layoff notices while in front of their students comes to mind as a definite example *not* to follow.

6. **Reassure surviving employees.** When someone gets fired the word tends to spread quickly, and the employees who were not fired—known as *survivors*—cannot help but wonder what the future holds for them. Will they too be let go? To the extent that uncertainty may breed distrust and spin off rumors, it is wise for supervisors to provide appropriate reassurances about the future. Such explanations can not only help layoff survivors feel better about their own futures, but the company as well.[67]

Although firing someone is never easy, following these six suggestions can make the task not only much less distasteful for all concerned. They also stand to make the termination process less expensive for the company and less emotionally draining for both layoff victims and survivors.

supervisors, or simply "pass the buck" for doing so to someone else.[68] This, of course, represents another instance of the MUM effect discussed earlier in conjunction with downward communication. Clearly, this same phenomenon occurs here as well. As you might imagine, because superiors rely on information when making decisions, keeping silent about important news, even if it's bad, may be one of the worst things a subordinate can do. As one executive put it, "All of us have our share of bonehead ideas. Having someone tell you it's a bonehead idea before you do something about it is really a great blessing."[69]

It's important to note the possibility that managers may be to blame for their subordinates' reluctance to communicate with them. Time pressure seems to be the key. Specifically, many subordinates complain that they would communicate with their superiors more frequently if they believed their superiors welcomed them, but too often they are led to believe that their superiors are unwilling to make the time for them.[70] Given the importance of accurate upward messages, it's important for managers to make time to listen to their subordinates—and importantly, to let them know that they are doing so. Also to avoid the problem of limited upward communication, many companies have incorporated large-scale programs through which employees can send messages to top company officials by completing *employee surveys*. Because of their general value in improving communication (including upward and downward communication), later in this chapter (see pp. 368–369) we will describe in detail this and other valuable tools for sending and receiving feedback.

Lateral Communication: Coordinating Messages at the Same Organizational Level

lateral communication:
Communication between individuals at the same organizational level.

Finally, we note the nature of **lateral communication** within organizations. This refers to messages that flow between different people at the same organizational level. Typically, lateral communication is characterized by efforts at coordination (attempts to work together). Consider, for example, how a vice president of marketing would coordinate her efforts to initiate an advertising campaign for a new product with information from the vice president of production about when the first products will be coming off the assembly line. Such communication is essential for organizations to operate effectively. These days, as organizations tend to be eliminating layers of hierarchy (see Chapter 15) and are having people work together in teams in which individuals are relatively equal (see Chapter 8), lateral communication is becoming increasingly common.

Because lateral communication involves people at the same organizational level, it is often friendlier in nature and less awkward than either upward or downward communication, in which the parties are at different levels. Communication between peers also tends to be more casual and occurs more quickly because fewer social barriers exist between them. Not surprisingly, people generally are satisfied with the nature of the lateral communication they experience—85 percent, according to one survey.[71] This is not to say, however, that lateral communication is free of challenges. One common problem that occurs in the case of lateral communication is that people in different departments may feel that they are competing against one another for valued organizational resources. As a result, they may show resentment toward one another, substituting an antagonistic, competitive orientation for the friendlier, cooperative one needed to get things done.[72] Fortunately, the various suggestions for improving communication that appear later in this chapter can be used to minimize this problem and to improve the quality of lateral communication.

Communicating Inside vs. Outside the Organization: Strategic Communication

All corporate communication can be distinguished with respect to whether it is aimed at other people within the organization (e.g., fellow employees) or outside the organization (e.g., the general public).[73] This prompts an interesting question: Do executives say different kinds of things when aiming their remarks inside vs. outside the company?

Research suggests that they do.[74] Illustrating this, consider a study in which scientists analyzed the comments made by CEOs of 10 forest products companies appearing in their letters to shareholders (external communications) over a 10-year period. They also examined various planning documents (internal communications) for these same companies during this period. Instead of looking at exactly what was said, they categorized these communications with respect to how they were framed. Specifically, they considered whether the statements focused on threats the company faced (e.g., the rising cost of materials) or on opportunities (e.g., growth in the housing market).

The results were quite interesting. In general, because the industry improved during the period studied, the proportion of documents framed in terms of threat dropped. However, mentions of threat were not equally likely to occur in both internal and external statements. For each year studied, a greater proportion of internal documents than external documents referred to threats. Likewise, with only few exceptions, a greater proportion of external documents than internal documents focused on opportunities.

These findings suggest that executives were attempting to present their companies in a positive light to the public (by focusing on opportunities), but were more willing to address threats internally. They may well have been thinking that whereas it is important not to frighten the investing public, it is important to keep employees appraised of any and all threats the company faces so that it can take proper steps to defend itself.

strategic communication
The practice of presenting information about the company to broad, external audiences, such as the press.

This is the idea behind what is called **strategic communication**—the practice of presenting information about the company to broad, external audiences, such as the press. The more effectively companies manage this process, the better they will be received by the general public, yielding considerable benefits, such as enhanced customer loyalty and increased sales. Given the importance of clearly and appropriately managing a corporate image through strategic communication, public relations firms are often hired to do the work.

Informal Communication Networks: Behind the Organizational Chart

Think about the people with whom you communicate during the course of an average day. Friends, family members, classmates, and colleagues at work are among those with whom you may have *informal communication,* information shared without any formally imposed obligations or restrictions. It's easy to recognize how widespread our informal connections can be. You know someone who knows someone else, who knows your best friend—and before long, your informal reach is very extensive. (Film buffs may recall that this was the premise behind the 1993 movie, *Six Degrees of Separation.*) The pattern of informal connections between people is known as an **informal communication network**.

informal communication network
The informal connections between people; the pathways through which they share informal information.

As you might imagine, informal communication networks, because they are so widespread, constitute an important avenue by which information flows in organizations.[75] In fact, middle managers ranked informal networks as better sources of organizational information than formal networks.[76] It may be said, therefore, that if an organization's formal communication network represents its skeleton, then its informal communication network constitutes its central nervous system.[77]

Organizations' Hidden Pathways

It is easy to imagine how important the flow of informal information may be within organizations. People transmit information to those with whom they come into contact, thereby providing conduits through which messages can travel.

old boys' network
A gender-segregated informal communication network composed of men with similar backgrounds.

The Old Boys' Network. We also tend to communicate most with those who are similar to ourselves on such key variables as age and time working on the job.[78] Because we are more comfortable with similar people than with dissimilar ones, we tend to spend more time with them and, of course, communicate with them more. As a result, many informal gender-segregated networks tend to form in organizations (what, among men, has been referred to as the **old boys' network**). This also occurs in the case of racial segregation, as we noted in Chapter 6.

To the extent that such restricted associations isolate people from others in power who may be different from themselves, this practice is seriously limiting.[79] At the same time, however, exposure to similar others with whom people feel comfortable provides valuable sources of information. For example, many African American business leaders have formed informal networks with others of their same race so as to help them share ways of succeeding in a business world in which they constitute an ethnic minority—alliances that have proven helpful to the careers of many.[80] This informal observation is in keeping with scientific evidence showing that the more involved people are in their organizations' communication networks, the more powerful and influential they become.[81]

The Snowball Effect. The idea that people are connected informally also has been used to explain a very important organizational phenomenon—turnover. Do people resign from their jobs in ways that are random and unrelated to each other? Research suggests that they do not, but rather, that turnover is related to the informal communication patterns between people.[82] In fact, voluntary turnover (employees freely electing to resign from their jobs) occurs in a kind of **snowball effect**. A snowball does not accumulate snowflakes randomly, but collects those that are in its path. Analogously, patterns of voluntary turnover are not independently distributed within a work group, but are the result of people's influences on each other. Thus, predicting which people will resign from their jobs may be based, in large part, on knowledge of the informal communication patterns within work groups. A person who leaves his or her job for a better one in another organization is likely to be an individual who knows someone who has already done so. For a suggestion regarding how this may operate, see Figure 9.10.

An important quality of informal communication networks is that the people in them can communicate anything to anyone else, even if they are at different organizational levels

snowball effect

The tendency for people to share informal information with others with whom they come into contact.

FIGURE 9.10

Informal Communication Networks: A Predictor of Turnover Patterns

The informal networks of communication between people (shown in dotted lines) provide channels through which messages about better job opportunities may be communicated. Patterns of voluntary turnover have been linked to the existence of such informal networks.

Source: Based on suggestions by Krackhardt & Porter, 1986; see Note 83.

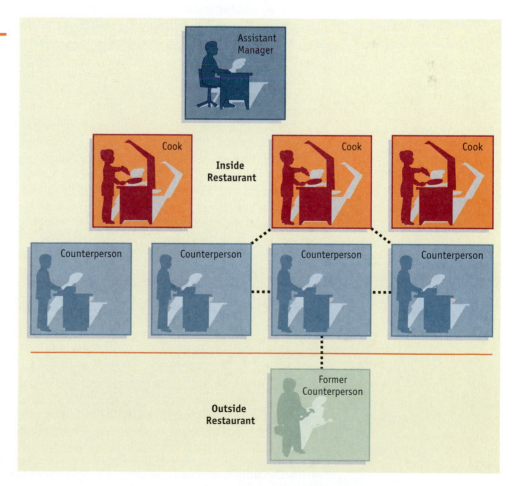

that one dare not cross in formal communications. For example, informal messages such as jokes and funny stories tend to cross levels and departments in an organizational hierarchy and are freely shared by people in both the managerial and nonmanagerial ranks of organizations.[83] This is information that's unrelated to the job. On the other hand, in many organizations it would be quite unlikely—indeed, seriously "out of line"—for a lower-level employee to communicate something to an upper-level employee about how to do the job.

The Nature of the Grapevine

grapevine

An organization's informal channels of communication, based mainly on friendship or acquaintance.

When anyone can tell something informal to anyone else, it results in a very rapid flow of information along what is commonly referred to as the **grapevine**—the pathways along which unofficial, informal information travels. In contrast to a formal organizational message, which might take several days to reach its desired audience, information traveling along the organizational grapevine tends to flow very rapidly, often within hours. This is not only because informal communication can cross formal organizational boundaries (e.g., you might be able to tell a good joke to almost anyone, not just your boss or subordinates with whom you are required to communicate), but also because informal information tends to be communicated orally.

As we noted earlier, oral messages are communicated faster than written ones, but may become increasingly inaccurate as they flow from person to person. Because of the confusion grapevines may cause, some people have sought to eliminate them, but they are not necessarily bad. Informally socializing with our coworkers can help make work groups more cohesive (see Chapter 8), and also may provide excellent opportunities for desired human contact, keeping the work environment stimulating. Grapevines must be considered an inevitable fact of life in organizations.[84]

An event occurring in early 2006 provides a cruel illustration of the potential communication problems that can result from information passed along the grapevine. On January 4 that year, an accident in the Sago Mine in Tallmansville, West Virginia left 13 miners trapped underground. Rescue workers, working under stressful conditions and wearing face masks, sent a coded message to the base that was understood to mean that all the miners were found safely. Although the message wasn't entirely clear to officials, what was believed to be good news leaked out. The joyous word spread quickly throughout the night as elated family members rejoiced and church bells rang in celebration.[85] Anxious to share in the joy, headlines of many major newspapers immediately trumpeted the news.[86] Tragically, however, the message was miscommunicated. Some 12 hours later a tearful company official came forth with the truth: Only one of the men was found alive; 12 perished in the accident. Despite heartfelt apologies from mine officials, family members of the deceased miners became enraged with the thought that the company allowed word to spread for as long as it did without setting the record straight. Not only does this incident highlight the unfortunate consequences of miscommunication, but it also draws attention to the great speed with which information—even tragically inaccurate information—can spread along the grapevine.

Today's High-tech Grapevine. These days, grapevines have gone high tech, enabling rumors to spread at lightning speed. Not only might rumors be passed along via e-mail, but also Internet bulletin boards available to people in certain industries. Although, as many argue, the Internet is one of the most important communication tools of all time, the fact that it's both easy and very inexpensive to use magnifies its potential for misuse, especially when it comes to spreading rumors.

Sometimes these rumors are spread by disgruntled employees. More often, however, they are meant to be a joke. A few years ago, for example, a seemingly innocuous hoax, targeted against clothing retailer J. Crew, reached thousands of people after a Massachusetts teenager concocted and sent an e-mail to a list of just 27 people. There have been times, however, when hoaxes and unproven assertions stem from corporate rivals. For example, there was a rumor going around the Internet alleging that a certain popular cooking product was unsafe, but a competitor deliberately spread obsolete medical data to imply that other, more popular brands were dangerous to consumers. Not surprisingly, one Internet security firm found that Internet-based rumors have been responsible for millions of dollars in lost sales and have tarnished the reputations of victims. The problem has been so extensive that a new industry has developed—companies specializing in finding and eliminating Internet rumors (see Figure 9.11).[87]

Potentially contributing to the spread of rumors because of their public nature are blogs (which, as we described earlier, are akin to Internet-based diaries). Although only 7 percent of the 120 million U.S. adults who use the Internet (over 8 million people) say they have created a blog, some 27 percent of Internet users report reading blogs.[88] This figure jumped 58 percent in 2004 over the previous year, suggesting that blogs are catching on. And, given that blogs frequently serve as places in which people can spread rumors, they represent a formidable vehicle for informal communication.[89]

It is important to note that some of the information communicated along the grapevine is accurate. In fact, one study found that 82 percent of the information communicated along a particular company's organizational grapevine on a single occasion was accurate.[90] The problem with interpreting this figure is that the inaccurate portions of some messages may alter their overall meaning. If, for example, a story is going around that someone got passed by for promotion in favor of a lower-ranking employee, it may cause quite a bit of dissension in the workplace. However, suppose everything is true except that the person turned down the promotion because it involved relocating. This important fact completely alters the situation. Only one fact needs to be inaccurate for the accuracy of communication to suffer.

Rumors and How to Combat Them

rumors
Information with little basis in fact, often transmitted through informal channels. (See *grapevine*.)

This problem of inaccuracy is clearly responsible for giving the grapevine such a bad reputation. In extreme cases, information may be transmitted that is almost totally without any basis in fact and usually is unverifiable. Such messages are known as **rumors**. Typically, rumors are based on speculation, an overactive imagination, and wishful thinking, rather

FIGURE 9.11

Tracking Internet Rumors: A High Tech Detective Job

The Colorado-based consulting firm NSI Partners provides an important service: It developed a technology that enables it to identify and track down the sources of Web-based rumors that plague its clients. The company then initiates an active "rumor management campaign" through which it attempts to set the record straight among customers (and other interested parties) by documenting and sharing the facts. Says Tom McClintock, the firm's CEO, "We really consider truth on the Internet to be a ministry of ours."

than on facts. Rumors race like wildfire through organizations because the information they present is so interesting and ambiguous. The ambiguity leaves it open to embellishment as it passes orally from one person to the next. Before you know it, almost everyone in the organization has heard the rumor, and its inaccurate message becomes taken as fact ("It must be true, everyone knows it"). Hence, even if there was, at one point, some truth to a rumor, the message quickly becomes untrue.

Types of Rumors. Scientists have noted that rumors can be classified as falling into any of four distinct categories.[91] These are as follows.

- *Pipe dreams.* Imagine a rumor going around your company that this year's bonuses will be much larger than usual. Although this may reflect the positive wishes of those who are spreading the word, if it is untrue it surely will lead to disappointment when it proves to be false. Rumors of this type, which reflect people's wishes, are known as **pipe dreams**. Although they may be positive, to the extent that they are untrue, pipe dreams have no place in organizations.

- *Bogie rumors.* A few years ago, information was posted on an Internet bulletin board stating that the Washington, DC law firm Dow, Lohnes & Albertson was laying off vast numbers of its staff attorneys. This so enraged many of the firm's staffers that they threatened to walk out. Although, in fact, a handful of attorneys were dismissed, the postings were completely overblown. According to managing partner B. Dwight Perry, the reports were "not only inaccurate" but "scurrilous . . . not to mention, potentially libelous."[92] Rumors of this, type, which are based on people's fears and anxieties, are known as **bogie rumors**. As the example suggests, such rumors are likely to arise under conditions in which people are uneasy about things, such as when budgets are exceptionally tight.

- *Wedge drivers.* Sometimes, people go out of their way to spread malicious rumors about someone with the intent of damaging that individual's reputation. Rumors of this type, known as **wedge drivers**, are the most damaging type because they are used in an intentionally aggressive fashion. Suppose, for example, someone were to come up to you and say, "Did you see that Ms. X was seen leaving the building late last night with Mr. Y, and they were holding hands?" Intending to harm Ms. X and/or Mr. Y, the person using such a wedge driver is using the rumor as a form of attack.

- *Home-stretchers.* Suppose talks have been going on in your company about an impending merger with another firm. You've been waiting for the announcement, but it hasn't come yet. Under such conditions, rumors may spread about the specifics of the merger in anticipation of something happening. Such rumors, known as **home-stretchers**, are designed to reduce the degree of ambiguity in a situation by "completing the puzzle," telling a story about something before it happens. As people become anxious about impending decisions, rumors of this type are likely to emerge.

The important thing to keep in mind about rumors, regardless of the type they may be, is that they do everyone a disservice and should not be spread. Although part of the story may be true, the fact that they are misleading makes them dangerous forms of communication that should be avoided at all costs.

How to Combat Rumors. If you've ever been the victim of a personal rumor, then you know how difficult they can be to crush, and how profound their effects can be. This is especially so when organizations are the victims of rumors. For example, rumors about the possibility of corporate takeovers may not only influence the value of a company's stock, but also are likely to threaten its employees' feelings of job security. Sometimes, rumors about company products can be very costly. To illustrate that rumors thrived long before the Internet, here are two classic examples:

- A rumor about the use of worms in McDonald's hamburgers circulated in the Chicago area in the late 1970s. Although the rumor was completely untrue, sales dropped as much as 30 percent in some restaurants.[93]

---

pipe dreams
Types of rumor that express people's wishes.

bogie rumors
Rumors that are based on people's fears and anxieties.

wedge drivers
Rumors in which people intentionally say malicious things about someone with the intent of damaging that individual's reputation.

home-stretchers
Rumors designed to reduce the degree of ambiguity in a situation by telling a story about something before it happens.

TABLE 9.6 Coca-Cola's Battle Against the Rumor Mill

Rumors involving Coca-Cola have been so extensive at times and have concerned so many issues that the company has been using its Web site to set the record straight. Here is just a small sampling of rumors that the company has denied. Remember, *these statements are false!*

Topic	Rumor
The Middle East	■ People have been warned not to buy Coca-Cola because of possible contamination by terrorists.
	■ The Coca-Cola trademark, when read backwards, reveals an anti-Muslim slogan.
Ingredients	■ The acidity of cola drinks is strong enough to dissolve teeth and bones.
	■ Phosphoric acid in Coca-Cola leads to osteoporosis.
Product and packaging	■ Soft drinks can be used by farmers as pesticides for their crops.
	■ Aluminum from soft drink cans leads to Alzheimer's disease.

Source: Coca-Cola Web site, 2005; see Note 88.

■ The consumer products giant Procter & Gamble has been subject to consistent, nagging rumors linking it to Satanism.[94] Since 1980, rumors have swirled that the company's moon-and-stars trademark was linked to witchcraft. Although the company has emphatically denied the rumor and has won court judgments against various individuals spreading such rumors, the rumor has persisted. In an effort to quash the rumor once and for all, the company changed its logo.

What can be done to counter the effects of rumors? One's immediate temptation is to refute the rumor, noting its implausibility and presenting information to the contrary. For example, Coca-Cola has been the victim of so many rumors that the company has a page on its Web site at which it identifies rumors targeted against it (see Table 9.6).[95]

Unfortunately, however, directly refuting a rumor is not completely effective. As the P&G rumor illustrates, some rumors are difficult to disprove and do not die quickly. In such cases, directly refuting the rumors only fuels the fire. When you directly refute a rumor (e.g., "I didn't do it") you actually may help spread it among those who have not already heard about it ("Oh, I didn't know people thought that") and strengthen it among those who have already heard it ("If it weren't true, they wouldn't be protesting so much"). In the case of P&G, the problem is compounded by the allegation that some parties may be making a concerted effort to keep the rumor alive. In such cases, directing the public's attention away from the rumor may help minimize its adverse impact. For example, the company can focus its advertising on other positive things the public knows about it. In research studying the McDonald's rumor, for example, it was found that reminding people of other things they thought about McDonald's (e.g., that it is a clean, family-oriented place) helped counter the negative effects of the rumor.[96]

If you should ever become the victim of a rumor, try immediately to refute it with indisputable facts if you can. But, if it lingers on, try directing people's attention to other positive things they already believe about you. Although rumors may be difficult to stop, with some effort their effects can be managed effectively.

Individual Differences in Communication

As you know from experience, people tend to communicate in different ways. Two individuals saying the same thing might do so very differently and communicate their messages in ways that may have different effects on you. Scientists have verified that such individual differences in how people communicate are indeed real. We now examine such differences with respect to two major factors—gender and nationality.

Sex Differences in Communication: Do Women and Men Communicate Differently?

Infuriated and frustrated, Kimberly stormed out of Jason's office. "I explained the problem I was having with the freelancers," she grumbled, "but he just doesn't listen!" If this situation sounds at all familiar to you, chances are good that you are already aware of the communication barriers that often exist between women and men. Deborah Tannen, a well-known sociolinguist, has explained that men and women frequently miscommunicate with one another because they have learned different ways of using language.[97] In general, what appears "natural" to women doesn't come easily to men, and vice versa (see Figure 9.12).

When it comes to communication, the basic difference between women and men, Tannen argues, is that men emphasize and reinforce their status when they speak, whereas women downplay their status. Instead, women focus on creating positive social connections between themselves and others. Thus, whereas men tend to use the word "I," women tend to say "we." Similarly, whereas men try to exude confidence and boast, thinking of questions as signs of weakness, women usually downplay their confidence (even when they are sure they are correct) and are not afraid to ask questions. (What comes to mind here is the stereotypical image of the couple that gets hopelessly lost because the man overrules the woman's pleas to ask for directions.)

This difference in style between women and men explains why they respond differently to problems. Whereas women tend to listen and lend social support, men tend to take control by offering advice. When men do this, they are asserting their power, contributing to a communication barrier between the sexes. Not surprisingly, whereas men may complain that women are "too emotional," women may complain that men "do not listen." Similarly, men tend to be much more direct and confrontative than women. Although a man might come right out and say "I think your sales figures are inaccurate," a woman might ask, "Have you verified your sales figures by comparing them to this morning's daily report?" A man may consider this approach to be sneaky, whereas a woman may believe it to be kinder and gentler than a more direct statement. Likewise, women may interpret a man's directness as being unsympathetic.

The implications of this set of differences come to the surface once we point out another of Tannen's findings: People in powerful positions tend to reward individuals whose linguistic styles match their own.[98] As a result, in most organizations, where men tend to be in charge, the contributions of women are often downplayed because the things they say tend to be misinterpreted. The woman who politely defers to a dominant male speaker at a meeting may come across (to men, at least) as being passive. As a result, her contributions may never come to the table. However, the woman who breaks from this pattern and interjects

FIGURE 9.12

Men and Women Have Different Communication Styles

Whereas men generally seek to reinforce their status when they communicate (e.g., by saying "I"), women are more interested in creating positive social connections between themselves and others (e.g., by saying we). Too often, this leads to miscommunication between the sexes.

her ideas may come across (again, to men) as being pushy and aggressive. And here too, her contributions may be discounted. In both cases, the communication barrier has caused a situation in which organizations are not only breeding conflict, they also are not taking advantage of the skills and abilities of their female employees.

The solution, although not easy, lies in appreciating and accepting the different styles that people have. As Tannen put it, "Talk is the lifeblood of managerial work, and understanding that different people have different ways of saying what they mean will make it possible to take advantage of the talents of people with a broad range of linguistic styles."[99]

Cross-Cultural Differences in Communication

In Chapter 1 we noted that the phenomenon of globalization presents many challenges. Clearly, one of the most immediate challenges has to do with communication. When people speak different languages, it follows that communication between them may be imperfect.

Part of the problem is that different words may mean different things to different people.[100] For example, as hard as it might be for people from countries with long-standing capitalist economies to realize, Russians have difficulty understanding words such as "efficiency" and "free market," which have no direct translation in their own language. People who have never known a free-market economy while they were growing up certainly may find it difficult to grasp the concept. It is therefore not surprising to find that communication barriers have been found to exist among American executives who are attempting to conduct business in Russia.[101] (Interestingly, however, because the previous edition of this book was published in Russian, we take it as a sign that things are improving.)

Another factor that makes cross-cultural communication difficult is that different cultures sometimes have very different cultural norms about using certain words. Take the simple word "no," for example. Although the term exists in the Japanese language, the Japanese people are reluctant to say no directly to someone because doing so is considered insulting. For this reason, they often rely on other ways of saying no that can be quite difficult for foreigners to understand (see Table 9.7).[102] As such, it frequently is considered wise for foreign visitors to other countries to learn not only the language of that country, but the customs about using language as well.

In addition to different vocabularies, cross-cultural communication is made difficult by the fact that in different languages even the same word can mean different things. Just imagine, for example, how confused an American executive might become when she speaks to her counterpart in Israel, where the same Hebrew word, *shalom,* means both "hello" and "good-bye" (as well as "peace"). Confusion is bound to arise. The same may be said for cultural differences in the tone of speech used in different settings. Whereas Americans might feel free to say the word "you" in both formal and informal situations,

TABLE 9.7 How to Say No in Japan

Although most Americans are not reluctant to come out directly and say "no" when necessary, doing so is frowned on by Japanese culture. The Japanese rely on the following more indirect ways of communicating "no."

Saying "no" in a highly vague and roundabout manner

Saying "yes or no" in an ambiguous fashion

Being silent and not saying anything at all

Asking questions that change the topic

Responding in a highly tangential manner

Leaving the room

Making a polite excuse

Saying, "yes, but . . ."

Delaying the answer, such as by promising a future letter

Source: Based on information in Hodgson, Sango, & Graham, 2000; see Note 94.

Spanish people have different words in each (*tu* for informal speech and *usted* for formal speech). To confuse these may be tantamount to misinterpreting the nature of the social setting, a potentially costly blunder—and all because of a failure to recognize the subtleties of cross-cultural communication. (What can be done to eliminate blunders likely to be caused by the barriers inherent in cross-cultural communication? In the *OB in a Diverse World* section, we outline several key suggestions.)

Improving Your Communication Skills

Throughout this chapter we have noted the central role of communication in organizational functioning. Given this, it is easy to understand how any efforts at improving the communication process in organizations may have highly desirable payoffs for organizations as well as for the individuals and groups working in them. Several steps can be taken to obtain the benefits of effective communication.[103] In this final section, we describe some of these techniques, including measures that can be taken by individuals, as well as tactics for improving communication that involve entire organizations.

OB In a Diverse World

Promoting Cross-Cultural Communication

 As we have noted, the potential for mis-communication between people from different cultures is considerable. However, short of becoming expert in foreign languages and cultures, there are several steps that can be taken to promote cross-cultural communication.[104]

1. **Observe, but do not evaluate.** Suppose while touring a factory in a foreign country you observe several assembly-line workers sitting down and talking instead of working. Based on your own country's culture, this would be inappropriate, a sure sign of laziness. Fearing what this means about the plant's productivity, you develop second thoughts about doing business with that company. However, as you learn more about these workers' national culture, you discover that they were engaging in a traditional work break ritual: resting while remaining on the work site. The people in question were merely doing what was expected of them culturally, and they may not be lazy after all. The point is that you evaluated the situation by applying your own cultural values and were misled by them. To avoid such problems, it is advisable in cross-cultural communications to describe what you observe (i.e., the workers are resting) rather than to use these observations as the basis for making evaluations (i.e., the workers are lazy). Doing so can help you avoid serious misinterpretation. (This relates to our discussion of the attribution process in Chapter 3.)

2. **Do not jump to conclusions.** When we perceive various situations, we tend to assume that our judgments are correct. However, when it comes to cross-national settings, we should consider our judgments more as educated guesses than as certain conclusions. If you think that something is correct (such as your interpretation of the lazy workers in the above example), it is best to compare these to the judgments of experts in the local culture than to assume you are correct. By confirming the accuracy of your judgments misinterpretation is less likely.

3. **Assume that people are different from yourself.** Most of us assume that others are similar to ourselves until we learn otherwise. However, in cross-cultural communication, such an assumption may lead us down the wrong path. Seasoned international managers know this. They take the opposite stance, assuming that others are different until proven otherwise. Because they "know that they don't know," they are less likely to be surprised by differences they don't expect—but which are inevitable.

4. **Take the other person's perspective.** Try to see situations through the eyes of your foreign colleague. Consider this individual's values and experiences, asking yourself how he or she might view things. To the extent that you can switch roles, you will be able to avoid the narrow-mindedness—referred to as *cultural myopia*—with which we tend to perceive things.

Although these measures may be easier said than done, they can be mastered with practice. Given that such steps are key to the success of international managers, the effort involved in doing so would appear to be well worthwhile.

Use Jargon Sparingly

jargon
The specialized language used by a particular group (e.g., people within a profession).

All organizations, social groups, and professions have their own **jargon**—specialized language limited to use by people in certain fields. No doubt, you've encountered a great many words and phrases in this book that may at first sound strange to you. Our point is that the use of jargon is inevitable when people within the same field or groups communicate with one another. Some degree of highly specialized language may help communication by providing an easy way for people in the same fields to share complex ideas. This is the case among football players, for example, who understand the seeming gibberish uttered by quarterbacks calling plays in the huddle.

Jargon also plays another important function. It allows professionals to identify unknown others as people in their field because they "speak the same language." For example, management professors would describe this book as dealing with the field of OB, a term that would have a very different meaning to medical doctors (for whom the acronym refers to the field of obstetrics). Obviously, within professions jargon helps communication, but it can lead to confusion when used outside the groups within which it has meaning. To illustrate that we are not beyond being confused by jargon, in Table 9.8 we have compiled a list of phrases that we have been led to believe are in use by college students when referring to the world of computers.[105] Because these phrases are more likely to reflect your jargon than ours, hopefully, they mean more to you than to us. In any case, our point should be clear: Although jargon may be useful to those who are in the know, it only confuses messages sent to the uninitiated.

TABLE 9.8 College Student Computer-Related Jargon—Or, So We Are Told

From time to time, the *Chronicle of Higher Education*, a prestigious newspaper for college professors and administrators, publishes a "Jargon Monitor" that translates some of the seemingly mysterious phrases its readers are likely to encounter on campus. We know something about computers, but we cannot personally vouch for the meaning of these computer-related phrases, although we are told that college students would understand them. Whether or not this is so, we thought you'd enjoy this peek at what professors are being told about what college students are saying.

Phrase	Definition
back-seat mouser	*noun.* An overly helpful onlooker who constantly gives directions about where to point, click, and scroll.
bar-code hairstyle	*noun.* A term used by Japanese students (who say "*baakodo haasutyru*") to describe male professors with thinning hair who comb what little they have left over their bald spots, simulating the appearance of bar codes appearing on retail products.
chalk and talk	*noun.* A derogatory term describing traditional classroom instruction, in which a professor delivers a monologue, punctuated by chalkboard scrawling, before a passive group of students.
computer snoot	*noun.* Someone on campus who knows more than you do about software or hardware and reacts to your questions by rolling his or her eyes in a haughty or pretentious manner.
cyberia	*noun.* The place to which online students feel they have been relegated when they receive no feedback from their instructor.
mouselexic	*adjective.* Someone who has difficulty using a computer mouse.
port per pillow	*noun.* Providing a high-speed Internet connection for every student living in a campus residence hall.
tick-tock tech	*noun.* A derogatory term used to describe outdated and slow machines in university computing laboratories.
netlag	*noun.* The physical condition caused by doing research on the Internet for extended periods of time.

Source: Chronicle of Higher Education, 2005; see Note 98.

Be Consistent in What You Say and Do

Managers communicating with their subordinates often send inconsistent messages by saying one thing but doing another. We're not necessarily even talking about major things such as speaking out against fraud but committing it oneself. Inconsistencies in even small things can lead to problems. Consider, for example, the case of Kristen J., the operations manager of a large consumer products company. For years, she has been telling her direct-reports to complete expense reports in a certain way that helped the accounting department—specifically, by itemizing the various expenses in a hotel bill, such as the nightly room rate, various taxes, phone charges, and so on. However, when submitting her own expense reports, Kristen hasn't been following her own directives. Rather, she simply lumps together all the expenses when submitting them for reimbursement. Although this doesn't sound like a big deal—and on its own, it surely is not—repeated instances of saying one thing but doing another have led Kristen's subordinates not to take her seriously when she issues a directive. When questioned about it one day, Kristen wasn't embarrassed, admonishing the subordinate to "Do as I say, not as I do." As you might imagine, this didn't go over very well.

To help understand such situations, one organizational analyst has developed what is known as the **say-do matrix**, a way of differentiating systematically between the consistencies and inconsistencies in communication with respect to one's actions (say) and one's words (do).[106] This conceptualization distinguishes between sending a specific message by way of one's actions (high do) or by failing to do so (low do). It also distinguishes between telling someone to do something specific (high say) or by not doing so (low say). Combining these results in a say-do matrix like the one depicted in Figure 9.13.

The various combinations of "say" and "do" create different communication situations. These are as follows.

- In the upper right corner is the *high say–high do* combination. This is the ideal—the case in which a person's words and deeds with respect to a certain message match perfectly. Making it clear that one is expected to drive safely and then following safe driving practices oneself is an example of this. There is a high degree of consistency between messages communicated verbally and behaviorally.

- In the upper left corner is the *high say–low do* case. This occurs when a manager's words and deeds do not match, such as in our example of Kristen, who fails to follow her own directives about filling out expense reports. As you might imagine, in this case communication tends to be confusing and less effective than in the high say–high do case.

- In the lower right corner is the *low say–high do* case. Here, a manager fails to articulate what to do verbally although he or she expresses it clearly by his or her actions. In such cases, the fact that the individual did not express the message verbally is likely to

say-do matrix
A way of differentiating systematically with respect to consistencies and inconsistencies in what people say and what they do.

FIGURE 9.13

The Say-Do Matrix

The say-do matrix systematically distinguishes between saying things (high say) and not saying things (low say) and doing things (high do) and not doing things (low do). The most effective communication for managers occurs when there is a high consistency between what they say and do (the high say–high do combination).

Source: Based on information in D'Aprix, 1996; see Note 52.

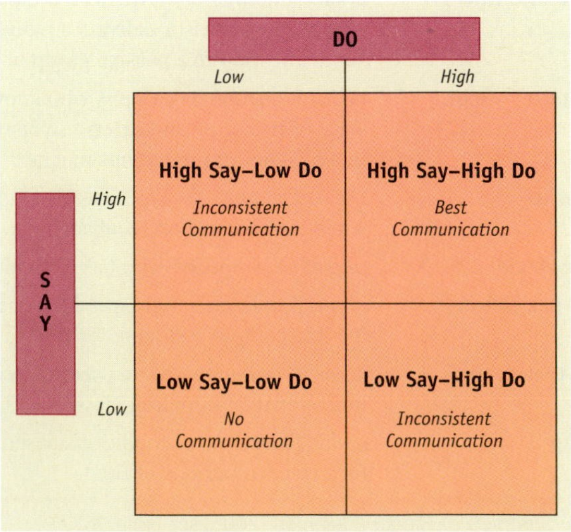

	DO	
	Low	High
SAY High	**High Say–Low Do** — *Inconsistent Communication*	**High Say–High Do** — *Best Communication*
SAY Low	**Low Say–Low Do** — *No Communication*	**Low Say–High Do** — *Inconsistent Communication*

lead to confusion insofar as it sends the message that the manager's actions are not worthy of noting. For example, our safe-driving manager is unlikely to communicate his or her concerns about road safety by not saying anything about it.

- In the lower left corner, finally, we have the *low say–low do* case. In this situation, no communication with respect to a given issue is occurring whatsoever. As odd as this may sound, such "communication voids" are not at all unusual, especially when conditions are so hectic that insufficient time is made to communicate clear expectations. In one company, for example, an office manager was hired but told almost nothing about what was expected.[107] The supervisor assumed that the manager would know what to do and how to do it. He handed her three file folders and told her to "work on these projects," and then was out of touch. A month later, the supervisor realized that the new employee had taken on responsibilities for which she was neither prepared nor able to complete. As a result, she made serious mistakes.

The practical advice is clear: Be a high say–high do manager. Communicate your intentions clearly and consistently by way of your words and your deeds. As suggested by our examples, failing to do so can have serious consequences.

Become an Active, Attentive Listener

Just as it is important to make your ideas understandable to others (i.e., sending messages), it is equally important to work at being a good listener (i.e., receiving messages). Although people do a great deal of listening, they pay attention to and comprehend only a small percentage of the information directed at them.[108]

Most of us usually think of listening as a passive process of taking in information sent by others, but when done correctly the process of listening is much more active.[109] For example, good listeners ask questions if they don't understand something, and they nod or otherwise signal when they understand. Such cues provide critical feedback to communicators about the extent to which they are coming across to you. As a listener, you can help the communication process by letting the sender know if and how his or her messages are coming across to you. *Asking questions* and *putting the speaker's ideas into your own words* are helpful ways of ensuring you are taking in all the information presented.

It is also very useful to avoid distractions in the environment and concentrate on what the other person is saying. When listening to others avoid jumping to conclusions or evaluating their remarks. It is important to completely take in what is being said before you respond. Simply dismissing someone because you don't like what is being said is much too easy. Doing so, of course, poses a formidable barrier to effective communication.

Being a good listener also involves making sure you are aware of others' main points. What is the speaker trying to say? *Make sure you understand another's ideas before you formulate your reply.* Too many of us interrupt speakers with our own ideas before we have fully heard theirs. If this sounds like something you do, rest assured that it is not only quite common, but also correctable.

Although it requires some effort, incorporating these suggestions into your own listening habits cannot help but make you a better listener. Indeed, many organizations have sought to help their employees in this way. For example, the corporate giant Unisys has for some time systematically trained thousands of its employees in effective listening skills (using seminars and self-training cassettes). Clearly, Unisys is among those companies acknowledging the importance of good listening skills in promoting effective organizational communication. Executives are so interested in training their employees in listening skills that specialized training companies have sprung up to accommodate them.

HURIER model
The conceptualization that describes effective listening as made up of the following six components: *hearing, understanding, remembering, interpreting, evaluating,* and *responding*.

The development of listening skills requires identifying the individual elements of listening, the separate skills that contribute to listening effectiveness. These may be clustered into six groups known as the **HURIER model**.[110] The term HURIER is an acronym composed of the initials of the words reflecting the component skills of effective listening: *h*earing, *u*nderstanding, *r*emembering, *i*nterpreting, *e*valuating, and *r*esponding. For a summary of these individual skills, see Figure 9.14. Although it might seem easy to do the six things needed to be a good listener, we are not all as good as we think we are in this capacity, suggesting that listening might not be as easy as it seems.

FIGURE 9.14

The HURIER Model: Components of Effective Listening

Research has shown that the six skills identified here—hearing, understanding, remembering, interpreting, evaluating, and responding—contribute greatly to the effectiveness of listening.

Source: Based on suggestions by Brownell, 1985; see Note 110.

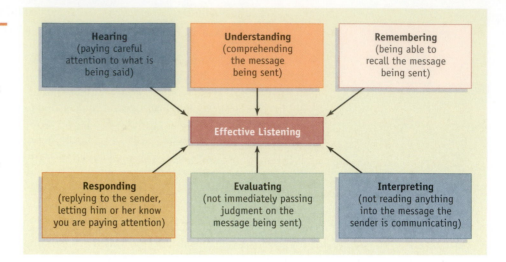

Management consultant Nancy K. Austin would agree, and she explains that when you invite people to talk to you about their problems on the job, you're implicitly making a promise to listen to them.[111] Of course, when you do, you may feel hostile and defensive toward the speaker, and become more interested in speaking up and setting the record straight if you don't like what you hear. This is the challenge of listening. Good listeners should resist this temptation and pay careful attention to the speaker. When they cannot do so, they should admit the problem and reschedule another opportunity to get together.

Austin also advises people to "be an equal opportunity listener," that is, to pay attention not only to those whose high status commands our attention, but also to anyone at any level, and to make time to hear them all in a democratic fashion. The idea is not only that people at any job level might have something to say, but also that they may feel good about you as a manager for having shown consideration to them. Austin notes that by listening to an employee, you are saying, "You are smart and have important things to say; you are worth my time."[112] Such a message is critical to establishing the kind of open, two-way communication essential for top management.

Research has confirmed the importance of listening as a management skill. In fact, it has shown that the better a person is as a listener, the more likely he or she is to rapidly rise up the organizational hierarchy and to perform well as a manager.[113] Good listening skills are an important aspect of one's ability to succeed as a manager. However, people tend to think they are much better listeners than others think they are.[114] This is unfortunate because overconfidence in one's own listening ability can be a barrier to seeking training in listening skills. After all, people who believe they are already good listeners may have little motivation to seek training in this important skill. Managers who complete formal training programs to enhance their listening skills generally benefit considerably.[115] (To get some practice in this important management skill, complete the Group Exercise at the end of this chapter, on p. 376.)

Gauge the Flow of Information: Avoiding Overload

Imagine a busy manager surrounded by a tall stack of papers, with a telephone receiver at each ear and a crowd of people gathered around, waiting to talk to her. Obviously, the many demands put on this person can slow down the system and make its operation less effective. When any part of a communication network becomes bogged down with more information than it can handle effectively, a condition of **overload** is said to exist. Consider, for example, the bottleneck in the flow of routine financial information that might result when the members of the accounting department of an organization are tied up preparing corporate tax returns. Naturally, such a state poses a serious threat to effective organizational communication. And it's only getting worse. Because today's managers face more information overload than ever before, they tend to ignore a great deal of the information they need to do their jobs. Fortunately, however, several concrete steps can be taken to manage information more effectively.

overload
The condition in which a unit of an organization becomes overburdened with too much incoming information.

gatekeepers
People responsible for controlling the flow of information to others to keep them from becoming overloaded.

queuing
Lining up incoming information so it can be managed in an orderly fashion.

For one, organizations may employ **gatekeepers**, people whose jobs require them to control the flow of information to potentially overloaded units. For example, administrative assistants are responsible for making sure that busy executives are not overloaded by the demands of other people or groups. Newspaper editors and television news directors also may be thought of as gatekeepers, since such individuals decide what news will and will not be shared with the public. It is an essential part of these individuals' jobs to avoid overloading others by gauging the flow of information to them.

Overload also can be avoided through **queuing**. This term refers to lining up incoming information so that it can be managed in an orderly fashion. The practices of "stacking" jets as they approach a busy airport and making customers take a number (i.e., defining their position in the line) at a busy deli counter are both designed to avoid the chaos that may otherwise result when too many demands are made on the system at once.

When systems are overloaded, *distortion* and *omission* are likely to result. That is, messages may be either changed or left out when they are passed from one organizational unit to the next. If you've ever played the parlor game "Telephone" (in which one person whispers a message to another, who passes it on to another, and so on until it reaches the last person), you have likely experienced—or contributed to—the ways messages get distorted and omitted. When you consider the important messages that are often communicated in organizations, these problems can be very serious. They also tend to be quite extreme. A dramatic demonstration of this was reported in a study tracing the flow of downward communication in more than 100 organizations. The researchers found that messages communicated downward over five levels lost approximately 80 percent of their original information by the time they reached their destination at the lowest level of the organizational hierarchy.[116] Obviously, something needs to be done.

One strategy that has proven effective in avoiding the problems of distortion and omission is *redundancy*. Making messages redundant involves transmitting them again, often in another form or via another channel. For example, in attempting to communicate an important message to her subordinates, a manager may tell them the message and then follow it up with a written memo. In fact, managers frequently encourage this practice.[117]

Another practice that can help avoid distortion and omission is *verification*. This refers to making sure messages have been received accurately. Pilots use verification when they repeat the messages given them by air traffic controllers (see Figure 9.15). Doing so assures both parties that the messages the pilots heard were the actual messages the controllers sent. Given how busy pilots may be during takeoffs and landings and the interference inherent in radio transmissions, coupled with the vital importance of the messages themselves, the practice of verifying messages is a wise safety measure. The practice not only is used in airline communication systems, but may be used by individual communicators as well. Active listeners may

FIGURE 9.15

Verifying Information: Critical in Some Jobs

The accuracy of communication cannot be taken for granted in some jobs. Among air traffic controllers, for example, ensuring that pilots correctly heard the information sent is a standard practice. Doing so helps avoid potentially catastrophic errors resulting from miscommunication.

wish to verify that they correctly understood a speaker. They do so by paraphrasing the speaker's remarks within a question, asking "If I understood, you were saying. . . ."

Give and Receive Feedback: Opening Channels of Communication

To operate effectively, organizations must be able to communicate accurately with those who keep them running—their employees. Unfortunately, the vast majority of employees believe that the feedback between themselves and their organizations is not as good as it should be.[118] For various reasons, people are often unwilling or unable to communicate their ideas to top management. Part of the problem is the lack of available channels for upward communication and people's reluctance to use whatever ones exist. How, then, can organizations obtain information from their employees, improving the upward flow of communication? Several approaches have been used widely.

360-degree feedback

The process of systematically giving and receiving feedback between individuals at various organizational levels.

360-Degree Feedback. A popular technique for promoting the sharing of information and ideas is known as **360-degree feedback**. In this technique, people at various organizational levels complete questionnaires in which they give feedback to and share ideas with others with whom they work in their organization. Essentially, everyone gives feedback to everyone else. At a restaurant, for example, waiters may be evaluated by restaurant managers, chefs, other service personnel, and customers. Although the process tends to be complex in operation, the basic idea is simple: By gathering information from multiple sources, information is communicated about areas of performance that need to be improved. The technique is useful because it allows such information to be collected systematically and from people who are likely to have diverse perspectives on one's work. This technique is used in many companies, including such notables as Alcoa, BellSouth, General Mills, Hewlett-Packard, Merck, Motorola, and 3M.

suggestion systems

Formal mechanisms through which employees can present ideas to their company.

Suggestion Systems. Too often, employees' good ideas about how to improve organizational functioning fail to work their way up the organizational chart because the people with the ideas do not know how to reach the people who can implement them. Even worse, they may feel they will not be listened to even if they can reach the right person. **Suggestion systems** are procedures designed to help avoid these problems by providing a formal mechanism through which employees can present their ideas to the company. Research has found that about 15 percent of employees use their companies' suggestion boxes, and that about 25 percent of the suggestions made are implemented.[119] Employees are usually rewarded for their successful suggestions, either with a flat monetary award or some percentage of the money saved by implementing the suggestion.

corporate hotlines

Telephone lines staffed by corporate personnel ready to answer employees' questions, listen to their comments, and the like.

Corporate Hotlines. Growing numbers of companies are using **corporate hotlines**— telephone lines staffed by corporate personnel ready to answer employees' questions, listen to their comments, and the like.[120] A good example of this is the hotline that Atlanta's Flag Bank set up in 2005 when it merged with First Capital Bank. As thousands of customers and employees sought information about what the merger would mean for them, the hotline proved to be a useful means of sharing needed information. In general, by providing personnel with easy access to information, companies benefit in several ways. Doing so not only shows employees that the company cares about them, but it also encouraged them to address their concerns before the issues become more serious. In addition, by keeping track of the kinds of questions and concerns voiced, top management is given invaluable insight into ways of improving organizational conditions.[121]

brown bag meetings

Informal get-togethers over meals in which people discuss what's going on in their company.

Informal Meetings. Many companies have found it useful to hold informal meetings between employees at a wide variety of corporate levels as a means of facilitating communication. Sometimes called *brown bag meetings* or *skip-level meetings,* such sessions are designed to facilitate communication between people who don't usually get together because they work at different organizational levels.[122] **Brown bag meetings** are informal get-togethers over breakfast or lunch (brought in from home, hence the term "brown bag") at which people discuss what's going on in the company. The informal nature of the meetings is designed to encourage the open sharing of ideas (eating a

skip-level meetings
Gatherings of employees with corporate superiors who are more than one level higher than themselves in the organizational hierarchy.

sandwich out of a bag is an equalizer!). **Skip-level meetings** do essentially the same thing. These are gatherings of employees with corporate superiors who are more than one level higher than themselves in the organizational hierarchy. The idea is that new lines of communication can be established by bringing together people who are two or more levels apart, individuals who usually don't come into contact with one another (see Figure 9.16).

Employee Surveys. Many companies attempt to gather feedback from employees systematically by giving them questionnaires referred to as **employee surveys**. Often, these are used to collect information about employees' attitudes and opinions about key areas of organizational operations. Surveys administered at regular intervals may be useful for spotting changes in attitudes as they occur. Such surveys tend to be quite effective when their results are shared with employees, especially when the feedback is used as the basis for changing the way things are done. Some managers even go so far as to ask their employees to rate them on a "report card."[123]

employee surveys
Questionnaires designed to assess how employees feel about their organization.

Be a Supportive Communicator: Enhancing Relationships

supportive communication
Any communication that is accurate and honest, and that builds and enhances relationships instead of jeopardizing them.

To be an effective communicator, you must be supportive of others. By **supportive communication** we are referring to any communication that is accurate and honest, and that builds and enhances relationships instead of jeopardizing them.

Simply put, how you act toward another influences the nature of your relationship with that person, which in turn affects the quality of communication, which may influence various work-related attitudes (see Chapter 6) and job performance. Suppose, for example, you send someone a very abrasive, insensitive message. That person is likely to become distant and distrustful, believing that you are uncaring. This, in turn, will lead the attacked person to become defensive, spending more time and energy constructing a good defense rather than listening carefully to your message. And, of course, a message that is not carefully attended to will not be comprehended, leading to problematic job performance.

This discussion leads us to a very important question: What can you do to become a supportive communicator? Several tried-and-true tactics can be identified.[124]

Focus on the Problem, Not the Person. Referring to an individual's characteristics (e.g., saying "You are lazy") is likely to make that person defensive (e.g., thinking, "No, I'm

FIGURE 9.16

At Kellogg, Communication Is "Gr-r-reat"

As CEO of the breakfast cereal giant, Kellogg Co., Carlos M. Gutierrez recognizes that in a highly competitive market, ideas for new products are vital to the company's success. Until recently, these could come only from the head of research and development. Today, Gutierrez gladly meets with any employee of the company's Institute for Food & Nutritional Research who wants to share ideas—even Tony the Tiger.

not"). However, focusing on the problem itself (e.g., saying "We lost the account") is likely to move the conversation toward a solution (e.g., asking "What can we do about it?"). Communication tends to be far more supportive when it focuses on the problem and possible solutions than one person's beliefs about the characteristics of another that caused it. (This is in keeping with the difficulties of making accurate attributions of others noted in Chapter 3.)

Honestly Say What You Mean. Too often, people avoid difficult matters by disguising their true feelings. Instead of saying that everything's fine when it clearly isn't, for example, it helps to make it clear how you feel. Don't be afraid of saying, "I'm upset by what you did," if that's how you really feel.

Own Up to Your Decisions. Don't hesitate to make it clear exactly what you did and how you feel. It's far more supportive, for example, to explain to someone precisely why you voted to deny his or her request than to hide behind a general statement, such as "The committee saw problems in your proposal." If you were on the committee, speak for yourself.

Use Validating Language. Of course, when you do speak your mind, always avoid language that arouses negative feelings about one's self-worth, such as "What can you expect from a lawyer?" Statements of this type use what is referred to as **invalidating language**.[125] It's far more effective to state your point in a way that makes people feel recognized and accepted for who they are—that is, to use **validating language**. For example, you might say, "I'm not sure I agree, but I'm interested in hearing your side." Although you might disagree with the speaker, this is a far more supportive approach.

Strive to Keep the Conversation Going. Saying something like, "That's nice, let me tell you about my problems" is a real conversation-stopper. By deflecting the speaker's concerns to your own, you are not being at all supportive. It's far more supportive to probe for additional information (e.g., by saying "Tell me about it") or by reflecting back what you think the speaker said (e.g., "If I heard you correctly, you feel . . ."). Another trick for helping conversations move along is to use **conjunctive statements**—comments that connect what you will be saying to the speaker's remarks, instead of **disjunctive statements**—comments that are disconnected from the speaker's remarks. So, for example, it's better to say something like, "On that same topic, I think . . .," as opposed to saying something on a completely different subject. Doing so is sure to end the conversation. (To see how supportive you are as a communicator, you may enjoy completing the Individual Exercise at the end of this chapter on pp. 374–376.)

Use Inspirational Communication Tactics

The most effective leaders know how to inspire others when they communicate with them. To become an effective leader or even a more effective employee at any level, it helps to consider several key ways of inspiring others when communicating with them.[126]

Project Confidence and Power with Emotion-provoking Words. The most persuasive communicators attempt to inspire others by sprinkling their speech with words that provoke emotion. For example, it helps to use phrases such as "bonding with customers" instead of the more benign "being friendly." Effective communicators also use words in ways that highlight their power in an organization. For some linguistic tips in this regard, see Table 9.9.[127]

Be Credible. Communicators are most effective when they are perceived to be credible. Such perceptions are enhanced when one is considered trustworthy, intelligent, and knowledgeable. Bill Joy, formerly of Sun Microsystems (considered "the Thomas Edison of the Internet"), for example, has considerable credibility in the computer business because he is regarded as highly intelligent. At the very least, credibility is enhanced by backing up your claims with clear data. People might not believe you unless you support your ideas with objective information.

---

invalidating language
Language that arouses negative feelings about one's self-worth.

validating language
Language that makes people feel recognized and accepted for who they are.

conjunctive statements
Statements that keep conversations going by connecting one speaker's remarks to another's.

disjunctive statements
Statements that are disconnected from a previous statement, tending to bring conversations to a close.

TABLE 9.9 How to Project Confidence with Your Words

The most powerful and confident people tend to follow certain linguistic conventions. By emulating the way they speak, you, too, can enhance the confidence you project. Here are some guidelines.

Rule	Explanation or Example
Always know exactly what you want.	The more committed you are to achieving a certain end, the more clearly and powerfully you will be able to sell your idea.
Use the pronoun *I*, unless you are part of a team.	This allows you to take individual credit for your ideas.
Downplay uncertainty.	If you are unsure of your opinion, make a broad but positive statement, such as "I am confident this new accounting procedure will make things more efficient."
Ask very few questions.	You may come across as being weak or unknowledgeable if you have to ask what something means or what's going on. It's best to be prepared as you don't have to ask.
Don't display disappointment when your ideas are challenged.	It is better to act as though opposition is expected and to explain your viewpoint.
Make bold statements.	Be bold about ideas but avoid attacking anyone personally.

Source: Based on suggestions by Tannen, 1998; see Note 119.

Pitch Your Message to the Listener. The most effective communicators go out of their way to send messages that are of interest to listeners. Assume that people will pay greatest attention when they are interested in answering the question, "How is what you are saying important to me?" People will attend most carefully to messages that have value to them. Gillette's CEO, Jim Kilts, appeared to have this rule in mind when he explained how his company's 2005 merger with the consumer products giant Procter & Gamble would help his company's employees (who naturally felt threatened by this change in ownership) by allowing them to work for a stronger company.

Cut Through the Clutter. People are so busy these days that they easily become distracted by the many messages that come across their desks (see Figure 9.17).[128] The most effective communicators attempt to cut through the clutter, such as by making their messages interesting, important, and special. Dull and uninspiring messages are likely to get lost in the shuffle.

Avoid "Junk Words" that Dilute Your Message. Nobody likes to listen to people who constantly use phrases such as "like," "know what I mean?" and "you know." Such phrases send the message that the speaker is ill-prepared to express himself or herself clearly and precisely. Because many of us use such phrases in our everyday language, it helps to practice by tape-recording what you are going to say so you can keep track of the number of times you say these things. Make a conscious effort to stop saying these words, and use your tape-recordings to monitor your progress.

Use Front-loaded Messages. The most effective communicators come right out and say what they mean. They don't beat around the bush, and they don't embed their most important message in a long speech or letter. Instead, they begin by making the point they are attempting to communicate, and then use the remainder of the message to illustrate it and flesh out the details.

We realize that these tips for inspiring people when communicating with them might be difficult to follow. Some even may run counter to communication patterns you have established over the years (especially given that most of us are rather timid when it comes to communicating). Then again, most of us probably inspire others very little when we communicate with them. If you have aspirations for a career as a politician or a business leader, you will need to turn this around. In doing so, we're sure you'll find these suggestions to be extremely worthwhile.

FIGURE 9.17

We All Are Bombarded by Messages

The average U.S. office worker receives 189 messages per day—that's over 23 per hour. As summarized here, they come in many different forms

Source: Wurman, 2000; see Note 129.

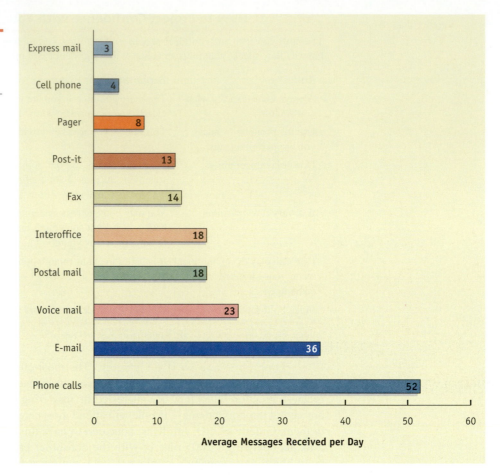

Average Messages Received per Day

Summary and Review of Learning Objectives

1. **Describe the process of communication and its fundamental purposes in organizations.**

   The process of *communication* occurs when a sender of information *encodes* a message and transmits it over communication channels to a receiver, who *decodes* it and then sends *feedback.* Factors interfering with these processes are known as *noise.* Communication serves many functions in organizations. These include: directing action, linking and coordinating, building relationships, explaining organizational culture, linking people with other organizations, presenting an organization's image, generating ideas, and promoting ideals and values.

2. **Identify various forms of verbal media used in organizations, and explain which ones are most appropriate for communicating messages of different types.**

   Communication in both oral and written forms is commonly used in organizations. Verbal media range from those that are *rich* (highly personal and provide opportunities for immediate feedback), such as face-to-face discussions, to those that are *lean* (impersonal and one-way), such as flyers. According to *media richness theory,* rich forms of communication are best for communicating ambiguous and nonroutine matters, whereas leaner forms of communication are adequate for more routine matters.

3. **Describe how technology has influenced organizational communication.**

   Technology has been a major force in facilitating organizational communication. Indeed, computer-mediated communication has been responsible for making communication faster and by making the distances between people irrelevant as a barrier to sending and receiving information. Such techniques as video-mediated communication (video conferences), e-mail, and instant messaging have revolutionized people's access to information. These media are not without problems, however. For example, people receive so many e-mails that they suffer information overload. They also find it a very limiting medium for expressing emotions. Although also very useful, many people find instant messaging too intrusive. Finally, the rapid speed of electronic communication poses another problem—it allows rumors to flow extremely rapidly, making them difficult to control, often causing damage in the process.

4. **Describe how people's communication patterns differ as a function of their sex and culture.**

   Despite similarities, women and men communicate in several different ways that may be problematic unless understood. Whereas men tend to communicate with the intent of emphasizing their status, women tend to focus on making positive social connections. Such differences frequently lead to miscommunication between men and women. Cross-cultural communication is hampered by the fact that people from different cultures frequently misunderstand each other's intentions. This may stem from different vocabularies and subtle differences in the meanings of words that may not be understood outside the culture.

5. **Distinguish between the various forms of formal and informal communication that occur in organizations and how they operate.**

   Formal communication is governed by *organizational structure,* the formally prescribed pattern of interrelationships between people in organizations. Structure dictates who must communicate with whom (as reflected in an *organization chart,* a diagram outlining these reporting relationships) and the form that communication takes. Orders flow down an organizational hierarchy, and information flows upward. However, the downward and upward flow of information is often distorted insofar as people are reluctant to share bad news with their superiors (known as the *MUM effect*). Attempts at coordination characterize *horizontal communication,* messages between organizational members at the same level. Information flows rapidly along *informal communication networks.* These informal connections between people are responsible for spreading information very rapidly because they transcend formal organizational boundaries. Informal pathways known as the *grapevine* are often responsible for the rapid transmission of partially inaccurate information known as *rumors.* Rumors may be costly to organizations as well as individuals. Fortunately, there are several ways they can be combated.

6. **Explain how you can improve your effectiveness as a communicator in organizations.**

   There are several things you can do to become a better communicator. First, keep your messages clear by avoiding *jargon* while communicating with those who may not be familiar with specialized terms. Second, you can become a better communicator by demonstrating consistency between what you say and do. Third, you can improve your *listening* skills, learning to listen actively (thinking about and questioning the speaker) and attentively (without distraction). Fourth, you can minimize the problem of *overload* by using *gatekeepers* (individuals who control the flow of information to others) or by *queuing* (the orderly lining-up of incoming information). And you can minimize the problems of *distortion* and *omission* of messages by making messages *redundant* and by encouraging their *verification.* Fifth, you can improve communication at the organizational level by using techniques that open upward channels of communication to employee feedback (e.g., *suggestion systems, corporate hotlines,* and *employee surveys*). Sixth, you should attempt to be a *supportive communicator*—someone who makes an effort to enhance his or her relationships with others, such as by focusing attention on the problem instead of the person, using *validating language.* Finally, you can enhance communication by using *inspirational communication* techniques—inspiring listeners, such as by projecting confidence, being credible, and pitching your message directly at the listener.

Points to Ponder

Questions for Review

1. What are the various steps in the communication process?
2. What types of verbal media are best suited to various situations?
3. How does technology facilitate communication in organization?
4. What can be done to improve the quality of formal and informal communication in organizations?
5. How do women and men differ in their styles of communication?
6. What steps can be taken to improve the quality of communication in organizations?

Experiential Questions

1. Think of an instance in which you had to transmit bad news to another person (e.g., firing, unwanted transfer). Were you reluctant to share this information (as per the MUM effect)? How did you respond in this situation?
2. Think of an instance in which you used a particular communication medium (e.g., e-mail) in a manner that proved to be ineffective. What occurred? In retrospect, what could you have done to avoid the problems you encountered?
3. Do you regard yourself to be a good listener? What might you do to improve your skills as a listener?

Questions to Analyze

1. What particular communication problem do you believe occurs most frequently in organizations? Why is this so? What would you recommend to combat this particular problem?
2. There's no doubt that technology has facilitated organizational communication. However, it also has brought problems. What are these limitations and how might they be overcome? Has technology been more of a help or hindrance to the communication process? Why?
3. In what ways has rapidly advancing technology helped communication in organizations and in what ways has it been a hindrance? Explain your answer.

Experiencing OB

Individual Exercise

Are You a Supportive Communicator?

As noted on pages 369–370, one key to being effective as a communicator is to be supportive of people. Supportive communication involves being accurate and honest with people in a manner that builds, rather than jeopardizes, relationships with them. This exercise will give you a good feel for how supportive you are as a communicator.

Directions

Answer each of the following questions by indicating which of the options indicated, A or B, you would be most likely to follow when interacting with someone else in the situation indicated.

_____1. You are discussing the performance of a subordinate whose work has not been up to standards. Which of the following statements comes closest to what you might say?
   A: Your sales have been lagging in the last few weeks. What do you think is wrong, and how might I be able to help?
   B: You haven't been meeting your sales quota lately. Unless you improve, you might find yourself looking for a new job pretty soon.
_____2. One of your employees has arrived at the office late many times this past week, making it difficult for his customers to reach him. Which of the following statements comes closest to what you might say?

A: You would say nothing.

B: I've noticed that you've been late this week, and I'm concerned about how this will affect your job performance.

_____3. Because of changes in your organization, it has become necessary to lay off a member of your work group. When discussing this with the individual to be laid off, which of the following statements comes closest to what you might say?

A: Because of some changes we've been making here at the company, it has become necessary to lay off some employees. I have decided that you will be released.

B: Because of some changes we've been making here at the company, it has become necessary to lay off some employees. It has been decided that you will be released.

_____4. In a meeting with the members of your work team, someone expresses an idea that seems totally ridiculous to you and, you suspect, to everyone else as well. Which of the following statements comes closest to what you might say?

A: I don't think that's a very useful idea. Please stop wasting our time so we can continue our meeting.

B: I don't quite understand that idea, but please explain it to us so we can consider it more fully.

_____5. One of your employees has been having problems with a project lately, and she has been coming up to you to complain about it. You don't understand the nature of the problem and believe she should be able to do the job. Which of the following statements comes closest to what you might say?

A: Tell me more about this so I can try to help.

B: I can't figure out why you're having this problem. You'll have to work it out yourself because I have my own work to do.

Scoring and Interpretation

1. Count the number of times you responded as follows: 1 = A; 2 = B; 3 = A; 4 = B; 5 = A.

2. The more times you responded as indicated here, the more supportive you are being as a communicator.

Let's examine each response.

Question 1: Response A is more supportive because it focuses on the problem without making negative judgments about the person. This is likely to help, whereas Response B is too threatening and may discourage the employee from trying.

Question 2: Response B is more supportive because it involves honestly saying what you mean. Merely ignoring the problem by saying nothing will not help and may make things worse because it suggest that you don't think anything is wrong.

Question 3: Response A is more supportive because you own up to your decision. This invites the person to discuss the situation with you so you can explain how the difficult decision was made. Response B is less supportive because it depersonalizes the decision, leaving the impression that nobody cares enough to stand behind it.

Question 4: Response B is more supportive because it uses validating language. It encourages the person to fully explain the idea and makes him or her feel worthwhile. Although you may not like what the person is saying, shutting the individual up, as in Response A, will discourage him or her from speaking in the future. Assuming that everyone may make a useful contribution, this is to be avoided.

Question 5: Response A is the more supportive option because it is more likely to keep the person talking to you, coming up with ways of making things better. Response B, however, makes the person feel marginalized—unimportant and not worthwhile. It gets the person off your back for now, but it also risks keeping that person from contributing anything in the future.

Questions for Discussion

1. Based on this questionnaire, how supportive are you? Did you score high, such as 4 or 5, or low, such as 1 or 2? Does this score surprise you? Did you expect to score higher or lower than you did?

2. Of the five aspects of supportive communication described in the text and assessed here, which ones are most challenging for you? How do you think you can overcome these limitations and become even more supportive in the future?

3. Based on your own past experiences, how supportive are the various people with whom you have communicated? Who are the most supportive individuals and how do they make you feel when communicating with you?

Group Exercise

Sharpening Your Listening Skills

Are you a good listener, a *really* good listener—one who understands exactly what someone else is saying to you? Most of us tend to think that we are much better than we really are when it comes to this important skill. After all, we've been listening to others our whole lives. And, with that much practice, we must certainly be okay. To gain some insight into your own listening skills, try the following group exercise.

Directions

1. Divide the class into pairs of people who do not already know each other. Arrange the chairs so that the people within each pair are facing each other, but separated from the other pairs.

2. Within each pair, select one person as the speaker and the other, as the listener. The speaker should tell the listener about a specific incident on the job in which he or she was somehow harmed (e.g., disappointed by not getting a raise, being embarrassed by another, losing a battle with a coworker, getting fired, etc.), and how he or she felt about it. The total discussion should last about 10–15 minutes.

3. Listeners should carefully attempt to follow the suggestions for good listening described on pages 365–366. To help, the instructor should discuss these with the class.

4. After the conversations are over, review the suggestions with your partner. Discuss which ones the listener followed and which ones were ignored. Try to be as open and honest as possible about assessing your own and the other's strengths and weaknesses. Speakers should consider the extent to which they felt the listeners were really paying attention to them.

5. Repeat steps 2 through 4, but change roles. Speakers now are listeners, and listeners now are speakers.

6. As a class, share your experiences as speakers and listeners.

Questions for Discussion

1. What did this exercise teach you about your own skills as a listener? Are you as good as you thought? Do you think you can improve?

2. Was there general agreement or disagreement about each listener's strengths and weaknesses? Explain.

3. After the discussion about the first listener's effectiveness, you might expect the second listener to do a better job. Was this the case in your own group or throughout the class?

4. Which particular listening skills were easiest and most difficult to put into practice? Are there certain conditions under which good listening skills may be difficult to implement?

5. Do you think you will learn something from this exercise that will help you to improve your listening skills in other situations? If so, what? If not, why not?

Practicing OB

Phone Center Chaos

The employees in a company's phone center are not paying any attention to new procedures for taking orders from clients. They are following the old procedures, which they prefer, and avoiding the changes that they dislike. What's more, they are spending so much time bickering with one another that overall productivity has been suffering. You are called in to handle this situation.

1. How might sex differences or cross-cultural differences in communication styles lie at the heart of this situation? What can be done about this?
2. How might technology be used to improve this situation?
3. What can be done to make the employees better listeners and more supportive of one another? How do you think these measures would help address the problem?

CASE IN POINT

The Scoop on Communications at Cold Stone Creamery

By 2005, CEO Doug Ducey reached his objective of having 1,000 Cold Stone Creamery ice cream shops—a goal that seemed impossible to many of his colleagues when he proposed it only four years earlier. This rapid expansion has made Cold Stone one of the top-20 fastest-growing franchises in the United States If you asked Ducey about the secret to this success he would deny—much to anyone's surprise—that it lies not in the company's butterfat-rich ice cream, served up with exotic accompaniments (such as apple pie filling and graham-cracker pie crust). Rather, he, along with many industry analysts, credit the company's success to its unusual formula for franchisee relations. This involves having a communications loop that keeps store owners happy and their businesses profitable. Specifically, his recipe for communication consists of three ingredients.

The first ingredient may be called "help them." Ducey has created a Cold Stone franchisee advisory council, a 17-member panel of store owners that serves as a clearinghouse of ideas and information. Meeting on a quarterly basis, this body makes conference calls to franchisees to see how things are going. They also take proactive steps to help, such as by launching a buying program that made it possible for owners to pay lower prices for supplies.

Ducey's second ingredient in the recipe for communication success involves "helping them help themselves." In many franchises, individual owners have difficulty reaching—and getting straight answers from—the company. Not so at Cold Stone. Jim Valentino, the company's vice president of franchisee relations, is always on-call as a representative of the company. Whether they call or e-mail him, Valentino is available to help franchisees solve their problems, guaranteeing their confidentiality in the process.

The final ingredient involves "helping them help one another." Recognizing that experience sometimes is the best teacher, Cold Stone has set up an intranet-based chat room, Creamery Talk, through which owners can communicate with other owners. In place since 2004, this tool has proven to be a little black book of tips and guidance. Topics ranging from how to repair equipment inexpensively to how to design the storefront have been lively—and highly useful—topics in this forum.

According to Cold Stone's vision statement, the company plans on becoming the top-selling ice cream in the United States by December 31, 2009. Although we will have to wait—but not long—to see if it achieves this lofty goal, given its commitment to effective communication, we wouldn't be surprised to learn that Cold Stone has indeed scooped the competition. If you have any doubt, note that Ducey wants Cold Stone to do to the ice cream business what Starbucks did to the coffee business.

Questions for Discussion

1. What specific principles or concepts of communication are illustrated in this example?
2. In addition to what is described here, what else might Cold Stone do to improve communication?
3. Do you think that the things Cold Stone is doing might be effective if they somehow were adapted for use in other industries? Why or why not?

DECISION MAKING IN ORGANIZATIONS

Chapter 10

Chapter Outline

Special Sections

After reading this chapter, you should be able to:

1. Identify the steps in the analytical model of decision making and distinguish between the various types of decisions that people make.

2. Describe different individual decision styles and the various organizational and cultural factors that influence the decision-making process.

3. Distinguish among three approaches to how decisions are made: the rational-economic model, the administrative model, and image theory.

4. Identify the various factors that lead people to make imperfect decisions.

5. Compare the conditions under which groups make superior decisions than individuals and when individuals make superior decisions than groups.

6. Describe various traditional techniques and high-tech techniques that can be used to enhance the quality of individual decisions and group decisions.

▣ PREVIEW CASE

HP to Apple: From iPod to "I Quit" in 10 Months

It could hardly lose—one of the world's largest and most successful engineering companies selling one of the all-time most successful high-tech products under its own brand name. At least, that was the logic expressed amidst much fanfare at the Consumer Electronics show in January of 2004 when Hewlett-Packard (HP) announced that it would sell Apple's wildly successful iPod digital audio player under the name "Apple iPod from HP." Carly Fiorina, HP's then CEO and chairman, had high hopes that HP and Apple would make an unbeatable pair when she announced that the first co-branded units would ship in September 2004.

Ten months later, only 5–8 percent of iPod sales came from HP—figures so negligible that the arrangement constituted "merely rounding error" for iPod sales (currently pushing 30 million total units). Preferring not to wait for a turnaround—or even foreseeing one anytime soon—in July 2004, HP's Mark Hurd announced that it would stop selling new iPods. By the middle of 2006, the last of the co-branded units in inventory was sold, leaving the product little more than history—another relic of the high-tech battlefield that took its toll on so many companies. For these large and otherwise very successful companies, the arrangement constituted what analysts considered "a nonevent" instead of a fatal failure of the type that regularly takes its toll on lesser Silicon Valley firms.

For HP, walking away from the iPod deal represents just one of several recent efforts by the company to find its identity. HP's inkjet printers revolutionized computer printing, and its industrial products (e.g., healthcare information technology solutions) have been industry leaders. Although technological development has been HP's forte and its longtime focus, its foray into making and distributing PCs, in its 2001 deal with Compaq, made the company look more like Dell, a marketer of assemble-to-order computers. Such low-margin consumer businesses hasn't served HP well, and the iPod deal is one such example. Fiorina okayed the iPod deal despite her strategy of rekindling HP's status as an inventor of world-changing products. After all, as one Wall Street analyst joked about HP, its "logo says Invent, not distribute."

Perhaps the clearest sign that the iPod deal was not HP's best strategic move was there all along. HP long has touted Microsoft's Media Center operating system as the foundation for tomorrow's digital lifestyles. Only one problem: Media Center products don't work with the iPod. Whoops. With the iPod off HP's product list, it is now selling its own non-Apple digital music players. Although these hardly represent the latest technological innovations, at least they can be integrated with the Media Center (instead of having to use Apple's iTunes service). Besides, it gives the company some neat little stocking stuffers to sell during the holiday season.

H igh-tech products, multimillion-dollar deals, and sales figures on the bottom lines of big-name companies represent only some of what this case is all about. At the heart of this episode lies a tale about a process that is extremely fundamental to all people and organizations—and thus, of considerable concern to the field of OB—the making of *decisions*. HP decided to lend its name to iPods but shortly thereafter decided otherwise and reconsidered its place in the market. Although the decisions you make as an individual may be less monumental in scope than those made by big companies such as HP, they surely are very important to you.

For example, personal decisions about what college to go to, what classes to take, and what company to work for can have a major impact on the direction your life takes. If you think about the difficulties involved in making decisions in your own life, you surely can appreciate how complicated—and important—the process of decision making can be in organizations, where the stakes are often considerable and the impact is widespread. In both cases, however, the essential nature of **decision making** is identical. It may be defined as the process of making choices from among several alternatives.

It is safe to say that decision making is one of the most important—if not *the* most important—of all managerial activities.[1] Management theorists and researchers agree that decision making represents one of the most common and most crucial work roles of executives. However true this may be, it's important to note that it's not only executives who make decisions in organizations, but in one way or another, everyone. As the late management consultant Peter F. Drucker put it,

> Most discussions of decision making assume that only senior executives make decisions or that only senior executives' decisions matter. This is a dangerous mistake. . . . Making good decisions is a crucial skill at every level.[2]

Every day, people in organizations make decisions about a wide variety of topics ranging from the mundane to the monumental.[3] Understanding how these decisions are made, and how they can be improved, is an important goal of the field of organizational behavior.

This chapter will examine theories, research, and practical managerial techniques concerned with decision making in organizations both by individuals and groups. Beginning with individuals, we will review various perspectives on how people go about making decisions. We then will identify factors that may adversely affect the quality of individual decisions and ways of combating them—that is, techniques for improving the quality of decisions. Then we will shift our focus to group decisions, focusing on the conditions under which individuals and groups are each better suited to making decisions. Finally, we will describe some of the factors that make group decisions imperfect, and various techniques that can be used to improve the quality of group decisions. But first, we begin by examining the general nature of the decision-making process and the wide variety of decisions made in organizations.

A General, Analytical Model of the Decision-Making Process

Traditionally, scientists have found it useful to conceptualize the process of decision making as a series of analytical steps that groups or individuals take to solve problems.[4] This is accomplished by the **analytical model of the decision-making process**, which can help us understand the complex nature of organizational decision making (see Figure 10.1).[5]

This approach highlights three important phases of decision-making: *formulation,* the process of understanding a problem; *consideration,* the process of determining and selecting a decision; and *implementation,* the process of carrying out the decision made.[6] As we present

decision making
The process of making choices from among several alternatives.

analytical model of the decision-making process
A conceptualization of the eight steps through which individuals and groups make decisions: identify the problem, define objectives, make a predecision, generate alternatives, evaluate alternatives, make a choice, implement choice.

FIGURE 10.1

Overview of the Decision-Making Process

The analytical model of the decision-making process describes most decisions as following the eight steps shown here. Note how each step may be applied to a hypothetical organizational problem (in this example, not having sufficient funds to meet payroll obligations).

Source: Based on information in Wedley & Field, 1984; see Note 5.

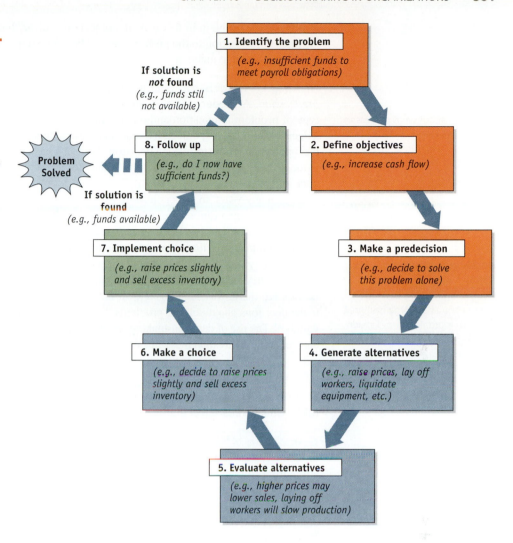

this model, keep in mind that all decisions might not fully conform to the neat, eight-step pattern described (e.g., steps may be skipped and/or combined).[7] However, for the purpose of pointing out the general way the decision-making process operates, the model is quite useful.

Decision Formulation

The first three steps in the decision-making process involve formulation. This is the process of thinking about and coming to grips with the problem at hand.

Problem Identification. The first step in the decision-making process is *problem identification.* To decide how to solve a problem, one must first recognize and identify the problem. For example, an executive may identify as a problem the fact that the company cannot meet its payroll obligations. This step isn't always as easy as it sounds. In fact, research has shown that people often distort, omit, ignore, and/or discount information around them that provides important cues regarding the existence of problems.[8] You may recall from our discussion of the social perception process (see Chapter 3) that people do not always accurately perceive social situations. It is easy to imagine that someone may fail to recognize a problem if doing so makes him or her uncomfortable. Denying a problem may be the first impediment on the road to solving it!

Defining Objectives. After a problem is identified, the next step is to *define the objectives to be met in solving the problem.* It is important to conceive of problems in such a way that possible solutions can be identified. The problem identified in our example may be defined as not having enough money, or in business terms, "inadequate cash flow." By looking at the problem in this way, the objective is clear: Increase available cash reserves. Any possible solution to the problem should be evaluated relative to this objective. A good solution is one that meets it.

Making a Predecision. The third step in the decision-making process is to *make a predecision*. A **predecision** is a decision about how to make a decision. By assessing the type of problem in question and other aspects of the situation, managers may opt to make a decision themselves, delegate the decision to another, or have a group make the decision. Decisions about how to make a decision should be based on research that tells us about the nature of the decisions made under different circumstances, many of which we will review later in this chapter.

For many years, managers have relied on their own intuition or empirically-based information about organizational behavior (contained in books like this) for the guidance needed to make predecisions. Today, however, computer programs are used that summarize much of this information in a form that gives managers ready access to a wealth of social science information that may help them decide how to make decisions.[9] Such **decision support systems (DSS)**, as they are called, can only be as good as the social science information that goes into developing them. Research has shown that DSS techniques are effective in helping people make decisions about solving problems.[10] Although they are far from perfect, they are used widely.[11] The use of decision-making technology leads to outcomes that are higher in quantity and better in quality than those made in the absence of such techniques.[12]

Decision Consideration

The decision consideration phase of the process involves three steps through which people find, evaluate, and select alternatives to solve the problem at hand.

Generating Alternatives. The fourth step in the process calls for *generating alternatives,* the stage in which possible solutions to the problem are identified. In attempting to come up with solutions, people tend to rely on previously used approaches that might provide ready-made answers for them.[13] In our example, some possible ways of solving the revenue shortage problem would be to reduce the workforce, sell unnecessary equipment and material, or increase sales.

Evaluating Alternative Solutions. Because all these possibilities may not be equally feasible, the fifth step calls for *evaluating alternative solutions.* Of the alternatives, which is best? What would be the most effective way of raising the revenue needed to meet the payroll? The various alternatives need to be identified. Some may be more effective than others, and some may be more difficult to implement than others. For example, although increasing sales would help solve the problem, that is much easier said than done. It is a solution, but not an immediately practical one.

Making a Choice. Next, in the sixth step, *a choice is made.* After several alternatives are evaluated one that is considered acceptable is chosen. As we will describe shortly, different approaches to decision making offer different views of how thoroughly people consider alternatives and how optimal their chosen alternatives are. Choosing which course of action to take is the step that most often comes to mind when we think about the decision-making process.

Decision Implementation

Once a problem has been identified and a decision has been made, the time has come to carry out the decision and to assess its impact.

Implementing the Decision. The seventh step calls for *implementing the chosen alternative.* That is, carrying out the decision that was made in step 6.

Following Up. The eighth and final step involves *following-up.* Monitoring the effectiveness of the decisions they put into action is important to the success of organizations. Does the

predecision
A decision about what process to follow in making a decision.

decision support systems (DSS)
Computer programs in which information about organizational behavior is presented to decision makers in a manner that helps them structure their responses to decisions.

problem still exist? Have any new problems been caused by implementing the solution? In other words, it is important to seek feedback about the effectiveness of any attempted solution. For this reason, the decision-making process is presented as circular in Figure 10.1. If the solution works, then the problem is solved. If not, a new solution will have to be attempted.

It is important to reiterate that this is a very general model of the decision-making process. Although it may not be followed exactly as specified in all circumstances, it paints a good picture of the general nature of a complex set of operations. Although this eight-step general, analytical model makes good sense, it is important to point out something that seems to be overlooked. Namely, decisions are not made independently from one another as our description thus far suggests. For a discussion of this important point, see the *OB: Making Sense Out of Common Sense* section below.

decision stream
An interconnected set of decisions.

OB Making Sense Out of Common Sense

No Decision Is an Island: Decision Streams

Most of the time, we consider the decisions we make as being independent of one another. Sometimes, they are. For example, in many cases your decision to wear a blue shirt may have little to do with the job you do. The blue shirt just happens to look good with your jacket. In other cases, of course, the decisions may be linked. You decide to take a job as a mechanic, and the required uniform calls for a blue shirt, so you decide to wear one. That's easy.

Other times, the connections are less apparent, but just as real. For example, in high school, you decide to take a certain seat in home room. This puts you next to Robert, whom you subsequently befriend. He decides to go to a certain university, so you apply as well. Soon, you're roommates in the same college. One Saturday afternoon you and Robert go to a football game, leading you naturally to wear your school's colors, one of which is blue. The next thing you know, you're looking through your closet for a blue sweatshirt. There you have it. One decision led to another, which led to another, and so on. As farfetched as it sounds, your decision to wear a blue sweatshirt that day was linked to your decision to select a certain seat in a classroom the previous year in a different city.

This example illustrates an important point: Despite the way we usually think of them, decisions are not made in isolation of one another. It is misleading to think of gathering information, considering alternatives, and making choices without regard to anything that has gone on before. Instead, it makes sense to think of decisions as being made in the context of other decisions that preceded them. To describe this process, the metaphor of a stream often is used, and our example illustrates why. Just as a stream meanders from one place to another, so too do our decisions flow from those that came before them to those that will follow them later. Hence, we refer to a **decision stream** as an interconnected set of decisions. For any given decision, there is a stream of decisions surrounding it: Many decisions led up to it, and many more are likely to follow from it.[14]

It's possible to look at decision streams from another perspective. Just about all decisions involve making a choice from a group of preselected alternatives resulting from all the various decisions we made earlier. The fact that you made certain decisions "activated" or "made operable" certain alternatives but "deactivated" or "made inoperable" others. Our example makes this clear. The fact that you decided to go to one particular college instead of another constrains your decisions about whom to socialize with, what sporting events to attend, what classes to take, and so on. After all, you're likely to consider alternatives based on the decision to attend that particular school. Although you don't think of it, that decision disables an entirely different set of options that might have been available had you decided differently about college.

We can summarize by noting three points. Every decision we make: (1) follows from previous decisions we made, (2) enables future decisions to be made, and (3) disables other future decisions from being made. If you think about it, then, the decisions you made in the past put limits on the decisions you can make at any given time. For example, if Heather decides to marry Michael, she cannot decide to marry anyone else. However, Heather's decision also brings with it a new set of choices and decisions. What shall she wear at the wedding? How many children should she have? And so on.

Given that every decision we make affects every other decision we ever have the opportunity to make later on, it's easy to understand what people mean when they refer to decisions as having "far-reaching consequences." From this way of looking at things, those consequences surely are more far-reaching than you probably ever imagined.

The Broad Spectrum of Organizational Decisions

As you might imagine, because decision making is so fundamental to organizations, decisions themselves tend to be of many different kinds. Understanding the wide variety of decisions that are made in organizations is an important first step toward understanding the nature of the decision-making process. With this in mind, we will distinguish among decisions in three important ways: how routine they are, how much risk is involved, and who in the organization gets to make them.

Programmed versus Nonprogrammed Decisions

Think of a decision that is made repeatedly, according to a preestablished set of alternatives. For example, a word processing operator may decide to make a backup copy of the day's work on disk, or a manager of a fast-food restaurant may decide to order hamburger buns as the supply starts to get low. Decisions such as these are known as **programmed decisions**—routine decisions, made by lower-level personnel, that rely on predetermined courses of action.

By contrast, we may identify **nonprogrammed decisions**—ones for which there are no ready-made solutions. The decision maker confronts a unique situation in which the solutions are novel. A research scientist attempting to find a cure for a rare disease faces a problem that is poorly structured. Unlike the order clerk, whose course of action is clear when the supply of paper clips runs low, the scientist in this example must rely on creativity rather than preexisting answers to solve the problem at hand.

The differences between programmed and nonprogrammed decisions can be described with respect to three important questions (see Figure 10.2). First, *what type of tasks are involved?* Programmed decisions are made on tasks that are common and routine, whereas nonprogrammed decisions are made on unique and novel tasks. Second, *how much reliance is there on organizational policies?* In making programmed decisions, the decision maker can count on guidance from statements of organizational policy and procedure. However, nonprogrammed decisions require the use of creative solutions that are implemented for the first time; past solutions may provide little guidance. Finally, *who makes the decisions?* Not surprisingly, nonprogrammed decisions typically are made by upper-level organizational personnel, whereas the more routine, well-structured decisions are usually relegated to lower-level personnel.[15]

Certain types of nonprogrammed decisions are known as **strategic decisions**.[16] These decisions are typically made by groups of high-level executives and have important long-term implications for the organization. Strategic decisions reflect a consistent pattern

programmed decisions
Highly routine decisions made according to preestablished organizational routines and procedures.

nonprogrammed decisions
Decisions made about a highly novel problem for which there is no prespecified course of action.

strategic decisions
Nonprogrammed decisions typically made by high-level executives regarding the direction their organization should take to achieve its mission.

FIGURE 10.2

Comparing Programmed and Nonprogrammed Decisions

Two major types of organizational decisions—programmed decisions and nonprogrammed decisions—differ with respect to the three dimensions summarized here.

for directing the organization in some specified fashion—that is, according to an underlying organizational philosophy or mission. For example, an organization may make a strategic decision to grow at a specified yearly rate, or to be guided by a certain code of corporate ethics. Both decisions may be considered "strategic" because they guide the future direction of the organization. Some good examples of both highly successful and unsuccessful strategic decisions made in business settings may be found in Table 10.1.[17]

Certain versus Uncertain Decisions

Just think of how easy it would be to make decisions if we knew what the future had in store. Making the best investments in the stock market simply would be a matter of looking up the changes in tomorrow's newspaper. Of course, we never know exactly what the future holds, but we can be more certain at some times than others. Certainty about the factors on which decisions are made is highly desired in organizational decision making.

Understanding Risk: Objective and Subjective Probabilities. Degrees of certainty and uncertainty are expressed as statements of *risk*. All organizational decisions involve some degree of risk—ranging from complete certainty (no risk) to complete uncertainty, "a stab in the dark" (high risk). To make the best possible decisions in organizations, people seek to "manage" the risks they take—that is, minimizing the riskiness of a decision by gaining access to information relevant to the decision.[18]

What makes an outcome risky or not is the *probability* of obtaining the desired outcome. Decision makers attempt to obtain information about the probabilities, or odds, of certain events occurring given that other events have occurred. For example, a financial analyst may report that a certain stock has risen 80 percent of the time that the prime rate has dropped, or a meteorologist may report that the precipitation probability is 50 percent (i.e., in the past it rained or snowed half the time certain atmospheric conditions existed). These may be considered reports of *objective probabilities* because they are based on concrete, verifiable data (for another example, see Figure 10.3).

It is not only in organizations, of course, that risk is involved. There is a certain degree of risk associated with every decision we make in life.[19] Given that roughly half of all marriages end in divorce, having a successful marriage is a fairly risky proposition. However, the odds of becoming president of the United States are far less, only 1 in 10 million,

TABLE 10.1 **Successful and Unsuccessful Strategic Decisions: Some Examples**

The history of business is full of examples of major successes and equally serious failures in strategic decision making. Here are a few of the most visible examples.

Unsuccessful Strategic Decisions	Successful Strategic Decisions
■ 1927: Warner Brothers rejected the idea of producing motion pictures with soundtracks.	■ 1905: Sears widened its audience by presenting its products in the form of a catalog.
■ 1938: IBM, GM, and DuPont turned down photocopying technology	■ 1914: Ford created a market for its cars by paying auto workers enough money to buy one ($5/day).
■ 1962: Decca records refused to sign the Beatles to a recording contract.	■ 1944: Coca-Cola developed brand loyalty by selling soft drinks to soldiers for 5 cents per bottle.
■ 1975: Sony decided not to license its Betamax technology, allowing Matsushita to dominate the home videotape market with VHS.	■ 1981: Microsoft decided to license its computer operating system (DOS) to IBM.
■ 1984: Coca-Cola changed its long-successful formula (at least until public outcry forced them to change it back).	■ 1994: Amazon.com launched the Web commerce market by selling books over the Internet.

FIGURE 10.3

Relying on Objective Probabilities

This manager and employee of a Boston Chicken restaurant in Bethesda, Maryland, are discussing how many chickens to cook. Such decisions, and many others made by restaurant managers during the course of a day (e.g., how many employees to schedule), are based on *objective probabilities* computed from previous sales records over similar periods. This makes it possible to boost the quality of routine decisions, improving service and reducing waste as a result.

which gives you about the same chance of getting killed by parts falling off an airplane.[20] Of course, knowing such odds helps people make decisions about certain precautions to take (e.g., getting counseling to improve the odds of having a successful marriage), or even whether they want to engage in certain behavior at all (e.g., running for president is desirable to many, but the low chances of success keep even more from trying).

In addition to making decisions on objective probabilities, people also make decisions based on *subjective probabilities*—personal beliefs or hunches about what will happen. For example, a gambler who bets on a horse because it has a name similar to one of his children's, or a person who suspects it's going to rain because he just washed his car, is basing these judgments on subjective probabilities. Despite the considerable effort that's put into making rational, objective decisions, we cannot deny the fact that people, on at least some occasions, base their decisions on subjective probabilities, or "gut feelings."

Reducing Uncertainty in Decision Making. Obviously, uncertainty is an undesirable characteristic in decision-making situations. We may view much of what decision makers do in organizations as attempting to reduce uncertainty (i.e., putting the odds in their favor) so they can make better decisions. How do organizations respond when faced with highly uncertain conditions, when they don't know what the future holds for them? Studies have shown that decision uncertainty can be reduced by *establishing linkages with other organizations*. The more an organization knows about what another organization will do, the greater certainty it will have in making decisions.[21] This is part of a general tendency for organizational decision makers to respond to uncertainty by reducing the unpredictability of other organizations in their business environments. Those outside organizations with which managers have the greatest contact are most likely to be the ones whose actions are copied.[22]

In general, what reduces uncertainty in decision-making situations? The answer is *information*. Knowledge about the past and the present can be used to help make projections about the future. A modern executive's access to data needed to make important decisions may be as close as the nearest computer terminal. Indeed, computer technology has aided greatly managers' ability to make decisions quickly, using the most accurate and thorough information available.[23] A variety of online information services are designed to provide organizational decision makers with the latest information relevant to the decisions they are making.

Of course, not all information needed to make decisions comes from computers. Many managerial decisions are also based on the decision maker's past experiences and intuition.[24] This is not to say that managers rely on subjective information in making decisions (although they might), but that their history of past decisions—both successes and failures—is often given great weight in the decision-making process. In other words, when it comes to making decisions, people often rely on what has worked for them in the past. Part of the reason this strategy is often successful is because experienced decision makers tend to make better use of information relevant to the decisions they are making.[25] Individuals who have expertise in certain subjects know what information is best to use and how to interpret it once collected, when making decisions. It is therefore not surprising that people seek experienced professionals, such as doctors and lawyers who are seasoned veterans in their fields, when it comes to making important decisions. With high levels of expertise comes information relevant to assessing the riskiness of decision alternatives and how to reduce it.

Top-Down Versus Empowered Decisions

Traditionally, in organizations the job of making all but the most menial decisions belonged to managers. In fact, organizational scientist Herbert Simon, who won a Nobel prize for his work on the economics of decision making, has gone so far as to describe decision making as synonymous with managing.[26] Subordinates collected information and gave it to superiors, who used it to make decisions. This approach, known as **top-down decision making**, puts decision-making power in the hands of managers and leaves lower-level workers little or no opportunities to make decisions. If this sounds familiar to you, it's probably because this has been the way most organizations have operated.

Today, however, a new approach has come into vogue, which is in many ways exactly the opposite. The idea of **empowered decision making** allows employees to make the decisions required to do their jobs without first seeking supervisory approval. As the name implies, it gives them the power to decide what they need to do so as to perform their jobs effectively. (For a comparison between top-down decision making and empowered decision making, see Figure 10.4.) The rationale for this philosophy of decision making is that the people who do the jobs know what's best, so having someone else make the decision may not make the most sense. In addition, when people are empowered to make their own decisions they are more likely to accept the consequences of those decisions. If the decision was a good one, they can feel good about it. If not, then they have learned a valuable lesson for the next time. In either case, people are more committed to courses of action based on decisions they have made themselves than ones based on decisions that others have made. And such commitment can be important to keeping the organization functioning effectively.

It is important to note that managers who empower their subordinates to make their own decisions are not abdicating their responsibility. Rather, they are delegating some power they have to others who are capable of making decisions. When empowering workers, managers provide general guidance about how to make decisions, but they do not set up specific rules to be followed in each possible circumstance. This gives workers discretion about what to do. For example, a manager at a car rental agency may empower agents at rental counters to offer free upgrades or discounts as appeasement to customers who have reasonable complaints. In this case, the worker is making the decision as deemed necessary but within guidelines set by the manager (who, of course, ultimately is responsible). Not only does empowerment motivate many workers (as noted in Chapter 7) and serve as a source of job satisfaction (as noted in Chapter 6), but it also frees up the time of higher-level personnel. Instead of "micro-managing" by making small decisions, empowering lower-level workers enables higher-level managers to concentrate on making the higher-level decisions that only they, themselves, can make.

top-down decision making
The practice of vesting decision-making power in the hands of superiors as opposed to lower-level employees.

empowered decision making
The practice of vesting power for making decisions in the hands of employees themselves.

Top-Down vs. Empowered Decisions: A Comparison

Traditionally, decision making in organizations was a top-down practice. Upper-level workers made decisions, which they then imposed on lower-level workers, who carried them out. Although this still goes on of course, many decisions today are made by lower-level workers who are empowered to make certain decisions for themselves.

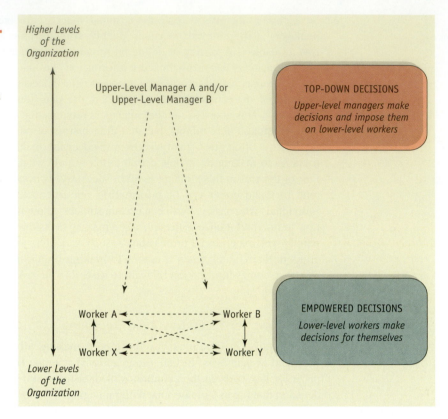

We find illustrations of empowerment in many different organizations. Consider these examples.

■ Individual employees at the Ritz-Carlton Hotel chain are empowered to spend up to $2,000 of the company's money per day to resolve any customer problem they find.[27] Instead of getting approval, they can make arrangements directly with the appropriate individuals in the company to fix the problem.

■ Teams at the Chesapeake Packaging Company's box plant in Baltimore, Maryland are organized into eight separate internal companies.[28] Each such unit is empowered to make its own decisions about key issues, such as ordering, purchasing new equipment, or measuring their own work (see the discussion of self-management in Chapter 8).

■ At Disney World, empowering employees to deal with customers is the rule rather than the exception.[29] Employees are given the authority to do whatever it takes (within reason, of course) make customers happy on the spot. Management interference is discouraged.

These examples not only illustrate some of the great lengths to which companies are going to empower their employees to make decisions, but also highlight a key trend. Empowering workers is not a fad, but a practice that is here to stay.[30]

Factors Affecting Decisions in Organizations

Given how fundamental the decision-making process is in organizations, it makes sense that it is influenced by a wide variety of factors. In fact, as we will see, organizational decisions are affected by all factors associated with three levels of analysis in the field of OB—individuals, groups, and organizations (see Chapter 1). We now consider each of these factors.

Individual Decision Style

Do all individuals go about making decisions the same way, or are there differences in the general approaches people take? In general, research has shown that there are meaningful

decision style
Differences between people with respect to their orientations toward decisions.

decision style model
The conceptualization according to which people use one of four predominant decision styles: *directive, analytical, conceptual,* or *behavioral.*

differences between people with respect to their orientation toward decisions—that is, their **decision style**.

Whereas some people are primarily concerned with achieving success at any cost, others are more concerned about the effects of their decisions on others. Furthermore, some individuals tend to be more logical and analytical in their approach to problems, whereas others are more intuitive and creative. Clearly, important differences exist in the approaches decision makers take to problems. The **decision style model** classifies four major decision styles (see summary in Figure 10.5).[31]

■ *Directive style*—Characterized by people who prefer simple, clear solutions to problems. Individuals with this style tend to make decisions rapidly because they use little information and do not consider many alternatives. They tend to rely on existing rules to make their decisions and aggressively use their status to achieve results.

■ *Analytical style*—Individuals who are willing to consider complex solutions based on ambiguous information. People with this style carefully analyze their decisions using as much data as possible. Such individuals tend to enjoy solving problems. They want the best possible answers and are willing to use innovative methods to achieve them.

■ *Conceptual style*—People who are socially oriented in their approach to problems. Their approach is humanistic and artistic. Such individuals tend to consider many broad alternatives when dealing with problems and to solve them creatively. They have a strong future orientation and enjoy initiating new ideas.

■ *Behavioral style*—People who have a deep concern for the organizations in which they work and the personal development of their coworkers. They are highly supportive of others and very concerned about others' achievements, frequently helping them meet their goals. Such individuals tend to be open to suggestions from others, and therefore tend to rely on meetings for making decisions.

It is important to point out that although most managers may have one dominant style, they use many different styles. In fact, those who can shift between styles—that is, those who are most flexible in their approach to decision making—have highly complex, individualistic

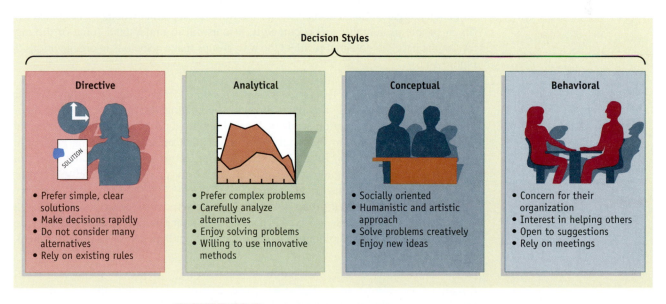

FIGURE 10.5

Decision-Style Model: A Summary

According to the *decision-style model,* people may be characterized as adhering to one of the four decision styles summarized here.

Source: Based on information in Rowe, Boulgaides, & McGrath, 1984; see Note 31.

styles of their own. Despite this, people's dominant style reveals a great deal about the way they tend to make decisions. Not surprisingly, conflicts often occur between individuals with different styles. For example, a manager with a highly directive style may have a hard time accepting the slow, deliberate actions of a subordinate with an analytical style.

Researchers have argued that being aware of people's decision styles is a potentially useful way of understanding social interactions in organizations. With this in mind, Rowe and his associates have developed an instrument known as the *decision-style inventory,* a questionnaire designed to reveal the relative strength of people's decision styles.[32] The higher an individual scores with respect to a given decision style, the more likely that style is to predominate in his or her decision making. (To give you a feel for how the various decision styles are measured, and your own decision style, see the Individual Exercise on pp. 419–420.)

Research using the decision style inventory has revealed some interesting findings. For example, when it was given to a sample of corporate presidents, their scores on each of the four categories were found to be approximately equal. Apparently, they had no one dominant style, but were able to switch back and forth between categories with ease. Further research has shown that different groups tend to have, on average, different styles that dominate their decision making. For example, military leaders were found to have high conceptual style scores. They were not the highly domineering individuals that stereotypes suggest. Rather, they were highly conceptual and people-oriented in their approach. Such findings paint a far more humanistic and less authoritarian picture of military officers than stereotypes suggest.

In conclusion, research on decision styles reveals that people tend to take very different approaches to the decisions they make. Their personalities, coupled with their interpersonal skills, lead them to approach decisions in consistently different ways—that is, using different decision styles. Although research on decision styles is relatively new, it is already clear that understanding such stylistic differences is a key factor in appreciating potential conflicts likely to arise between decision makers.

Group Influences: A Matter of Trade-Offs

As you might imagine, groups influence organizational decisions in a vast array of ways, potentially positive and negative. We say "potentially" because the wide variety of factors influencing organizational decisions makes it difficult to predict whether anticipated benefits or problems actually will occur. Still, it is useful to understand some of the major forces that have the potential to affect the way groups make decisions in organizations (see Figure 10.6).

Potential Benefits of Decision-Making Groups.   Much can be gained by using decision-making groups. For example, bringing people together may increase the amount of knowledge and information available for making good decisions. In other words, there may be a *pooling of resources.* A related benefit is that in decision-making groups there can be a *specialization of labor.* With enough people around to share the work load, individuals can perform only those tasks at which they are best, thereby potentially improving the quality of the group's efforts.

Another benefit is that group decisions are likely to enjoy *greater acceptance* than individual decisions. People involved in making decisions generally understand those decisions better and are more committed to carrying them out than decisions made for them by someone else.[33]

Potential Problems of Decision-Making Groups.   Of course, there are also some problems associated with using decision-making groups. One obvious drawback is that groups are likely to *waste time.* The time spent socializing before getting down to business, for example, may be a drain on the group and be very costly to organizations.

Another possible problem is that potential disagreement over important matters may breed ill will and *group conflict.* Although constructive disagreement may lead to better group outcomes, highly disruptive conflict may interfere with group decisions. Indeed,

FIGURE 10.6

Group Decision Making: An Important Process with Mixed Results

Groups, such as members of the "Bring New Orleans Back Commission" shown here, are charged with the responsibility for making decisions—in this case, how to rebuild this city devastated by Hurricane Katrina. Although groups sometimes make better decisions than individuals (which, hopefully is the case here), this is not always so.

with corporate power and personal pride at stake, it is not at all surprising to find that lack of agreement can cause bad feelings to develop between group members.

Finally, we may expect groups to be ineffective sometimes because of members' *intimidation by group leaders.* A group composed of several "yes men" or women trying to please a dominant leader tends to discourage open and honest discussion of solutions. In view of these problems, it is easy to understand the old adage, "A camel is a horse put together by a committee."

Groupthink: Too Much Cohesiveness Can Be a Dangerous Thing. As we described in Chapter 8, sometimes members of groups become so concerned about not "rocking the boat" that they are reluctant to challenge the group's decisions. When this happens, group members tend to isolate themselves from outside information, and the process of critical thinking deteriorates. This phenomenon is referred to as **groupthink.**[34]

To illustrate the phenomenon of groupthink, consider the tragic decision to launch the space shuttle *Challenger* in January, 1986. Analyses of conversations between key personnel suggested that NASA officials made the decision to launch the shuttle under freezing conditions while ignoring admonitions from engineers.[35] Given that NASA had such a successful history, the decision makers operated with a sense of invulnerability. They also worked so closely together and were under such intense pressure to launch the shuttle without further delay that they all collectively went along with the launch decision, creating the illusion of unanimous agreement. For a more precise description of groupthink and a practical guide to recognizing its symptoms, see Figure 10.7.

Groupthink doesn't occur only in governmental decision making, as you might imagine, but in the private sector as well (although in such cases, the failures may be less well publicized). For example, analyses of the business policies of large corporations such as British Airlines, Lockheed, and Chrysler have suggested that it was the failure of top management teams to respond to changing market conditions that at one time led these firms to the brink of disaster.[36] The problem is that members of very cohesive groups may have considerable confidence in their group's decisions, making them unlikely to raise doubts about these actions (i.e., "the group seems to know what it's doing"). As a result, they may suspend their own critical thinking in favor of conforming to the group. When group members become fiercely loyal to each other, they may ignore potentially useful information from other sources that challenges the group's decisions. The result of this process is that the group's decisions may be completely uninformed, irrational, or even immoral.[37] (Fortunately, several concrete steps can be taken to avoid groupthink. For some suggestions, see the *How to Do It* section.)

groupthink
The tendency for members of highly cohesive groups to so strongly conform to group pressures regarding a certain decision that they fail to think critically, rejecting the potentially correcting influences of outsiders.

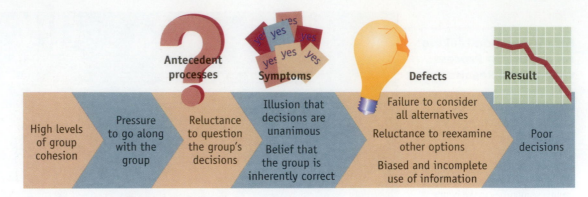

FIGURE 10.7

Groupthink: An Overview

Groupthink occurs when highly cohesive conditions in groups discourage members from challenging their group's overall decision. Poor quality decisions result.

HOW TO DO IT

Strategies for Avoiding Groupthink

Because scientists have such a good feel for why groupthink occurs, it is possible to identify several tactics aimed at weakening the dynamics that trigger it in the first place. With this in mind, here are several tried-and-true recommendations.

1. *Promote open inquiry.* Remember, groupthink arises in response to group members' reluctance to "rock the boat." Thus, group leaders should encourage members to be skeptical of all solutions and to avoid reaching premature agreements. It sometimes helps to play the role of *devil's advocate* by intentionally finding fault with a proposed solution.[38] Research has shown that when this is done, groups make higher-quality decisions.[39] In fact, some corporate executives use exercises in which conflict is intentionally generated just so the negative aspects of a decision can be identified before it's too late.[40] This is not to say that leaders should be argumentative. Rather, raising a nonthreatening question to force both sides of an issue can be very helpful in improving the quality of decisions.

2. *Use subgroups.* Because the decisions made by any one group may be the result of groupthink, basing decisions on the recommendations of two groups is a useful check. If the two groups disagree, a discussion of their differences is likely to raise important issues. However, if the two groups agree, you can be relatively confident that their conclusions are not *both* the result of groupthink.

3. *Admit shortcomings.* When groupthink occurs, group members feel very confident that they are doing the right thing. Such feelings of perfection discourage people from considering opposing information. However, if group members acknowledge some of the flaws and limitations of their decisions, they may open themselves to corrective influences. No decision is perfect, of course, so asking others to point out misgivings about a group's decisions may help avoid the illusion of perfection that contributes to groupthink.

4. *Hold second-chance meetings.* Before implementing a decision, it is a good idea to hold a *second-chance meeting* during which group members are asked to express any doubts and propose any new ideas they may have. Alfred P. Sloan, former head of General Motors, is known to have postponed acting on important matters until any group disagreement was resolved.[41] As people get tired of working on problems, they may hastily reach agreement on a solution. Second-chance meetings can be useful devices for seeing if a solution still seems good even after "sleeping on it."

Given the extremely adverse effects groupthink can have on organizations, managers would be wise to put these suggestions into action. The alternative—facing the consequences of groupthink—clearly suggests that they should be taken seriously.

Organizational Influences on Decision Making

In addition to individual and group forces that affect decision making, we also have to be aware of forces stemming from within organizations themselves. Two key ones in this regard are political pressures and time pressures.

Political Pressures. Sometimes, the quality of decisions people make in organizations is limited by the pressures they face to look good to others (i.e., to "save face") even though the resulting decisions might not be in the best interest of their organizations. Imagine, for example, how an employee might distort the available information needed to make a decision if the correct decision would jeopardize his job. This would be the case if a sales rep inflated his quarterly sales figures to make himself look good although that might lead to an overly optimistic picture of a product's popularity. Unfortunately, such misuses of information to support desired decisions are all too common.

A study on the topic of political face-saving found that a group of businesspeople working on a group decision-making problem opted for an adequate—although less than optimal—decision rather than risk generating serious conflicts with their fellow group members.[42] In an actual case, a proponent of medical inoculation for the flu was so interested in advancing his pro-inoculation position that he proceeded with the inoculation program although there was only a 2 percent chance of an epidemic.[43] Apparently, people often make the decisions they need to make to cultivate the best impressions although these may not be the best ones for their organizations.

Time Pressure: Making Decisions in Emergencies. An unavoidable fact of life in contemporary organizations is that people often have only limited amounts of time to make important decisions. The rapid pace with which businesses operate these days results in severe pressures to make decisions almost immediately. Among firefighters, emergency room doctors, and fighter pilots, it's clear that time is of the essence. But, even those of us who toil in less dramatic settings also face the need to make good decisions quickly. The practice of thoroughly collecting information, carefully analyzing it, and then leisurely reviewing the alternatives is a luxury few modern decision makers can afford. In one survey, 77 percent of a broad cross-section of managers polled felt that the number of decisions they were required to make each day has increased, and 43 percent reported that the time they can devote to making decisions has decreased.[44] Often, the result is that bad—and inevitably, costly—decisions are made.

Highly experienced experts, psychologists tell us, are able to make good decisions quickly because they draw on a wealth of experiences collected over the years.[45] Whereas novices are very deliberate in their decision-making, considering one option at a time, experts are able to make decisions quickly because they are able to assess the situations they face and compare them to experiences they have had earlier in their careers. They know what matters, what to look for, and what pitfalls to avoid. What is so often considered "gut instinct" is really nothing more than the wealth of accumulated experiences. The more experiences a person has from which to draw, the more effectively he or she can "size up" a situation and take appropriate action.

"Fine, but I'm not yet an expert," you may be thinking, "so what can I do to make good decisions under pressure?" The answer lies in emulating some of the things that experts do.[46] For some of these, see Table 10.2.

Thus far, our discussion has focused on individual, group, and organizational influences on decision making. We must not forget, however, that all such decisions occur in contexts in which the effects of national culture also may be at play. To appreciate the role of such factors, we invite you to read the *OB in a Diverse World* section on page 395.

How Are Individual Decisions Made?

Now that we have identified the types of decisions people make in organizations, we are prepared to consider the matter of *how* people go about making them. Perhaps you are thinking, "What do you mean, you just think things over and do what you think is best?" Although this may be true, you will see that there's a lot more to decision making than

TABLE 10.2 Making Decisions Under Pressure: Some Guidelines

No matter what you do, you're likely to have to make a split-second decision at one time or another. Because these cannot be made in deliberate fashion, the quality of such decisions may suffer. However, following the suggestions outlined here will help prepare you for whatever quick decisions you have to make.

Suggestion	Description	Example
Recognize your prime objectives.	Many organizations have cardinal rules by which they must live. Relying on these can help you make decisions quickly.	For newspaper editors, the news has to get out quickly, but it also has to be right. With this in mind, editors at the *Washington Post* follow a "when in doubt, leave it out" policy. According to Mary Hadar, an assistant managing editor, this makes it easy to decide whether or not to run a particular story.
Rely on experts.	Although you might not be an expert, chances are good that there is someone in your organization on whose expertise you can draw for help in making decisions.	Tina Carlstrom, an institutional sales trader for Merrill Lynch, often has to make quick decisions that can mean the difference between making and losing millions of dollars. When a buying opportunity comes along for a company she doesn't know well, she turns to experts on staff for quick answers.
Anticipate crises.	Anticipate crises in advance so that if they ever should occur, you already have an idea of how to respond.	Some managers prepare for handling hostile employees by practicing what to do in training sessions. By doing so, it becomes easier for them to jump into action should they ever confront such an individual.
Learn from mistakes.	Although mistakes are inevitable, they should not be dismissed. Rather, it's essential to learn from them. Think of each poor decision you make as preparation for the next time.	One criticism leveled against NASA is that the 2003 explosion of its space shuttle *Columbia* resulted from lessons it failed to learn from the 1986 explosion of the space shuttle *Challenger.*

meets the eye. In fact, scientists have considered several different approaches to how individuals make decisions. Here, we review three of the most important ones.

The Rational-Economic Model: In Search of the Ideal Decision

We all like to think that we are "rational" people who make the best possible decisions. But what exactly does it mean to make a *rational* decision? Organizational scientists view **rational decisions** as ones that maximize the attainment of goals, whether they are the goals of a person, a group, or an entire organization.[47] What is the most rational way for an individual to go about making a decision? Economists interested in predicting market conditions and prices have relied on a **rational-economic model** of decision making, which assumes that decisions are optimal in every way. An economically rational decision maker will attempt to maximize his or her profits by searching systematically for the *optimum* solution to a problem. For this to occur, the decision maker must have complete and perfect information and be able to process all this information in an accurate and unbiased fashion.[48]

In many respects, rational-economic decisions follow the same steps outlined in our analytical model of decision making (recall Figure 10.1, p. 381). However, what makes the rational-economic approach special is that it calls for the decision maker to recognize *all* alternative courses of action (step 4), and to accurately and completely evaluate each one (step 5). In other words, it views decision makers as attempting to make *optimal* decisions.

rational decisions
Decisions that maximize the chance of attaining an individual's, group's, or organization's goals.

rational-economic model
The model of decision making according to which decision makers consider all possible alternatives to problems before selecting the optimal solution.

OB In a Diverse World

The Impact of National Culture on Organizational Decisions

 People are people, and the process of decision making is essentially the same all over the world—right? Not exactly. Even if people were to follow the same basic steps when making decisions, there exist widespread differences in the *way* people from various cultures go about doing so.[49] Because we tend to take for granted the way we do things in our own countries, especially such basic tasks as making decisions, some of these differences may seem quite surprising.

What's the problem? The role of fate. Suppose you are managing a large construction project when you discover that one of your most important suppliers will be several months late in delivering the necessary materials. What would you do? You're probably thinking, "This is a silly question; I'd simply try to get another supplier." If you're from the United States, this is probably just what you'd do. But, if you're from Thailand, Indonesia, or Malaysia, chances are good that you'd simply accept the situation as fate and allow the project to be delayed. In other words, to the American, Canadian, or Western European manager, the situation may be perceived as a problem in need of a decision, whereas no such problem would be recognized by Thai, Indonesian, or Malaysian managers. Thus, as basic as it seems that decision making begins with recognizing that a problem exists, it is important to note that not all people are likely to perceive the same situations as problems.

Who makes the decision? Cultures also differ with respect to the nature of the decision-making unit they typically employ. In the United States, for example, where people tend to be highly individualistic, individual decisions are made routinely. However, in more collectivist cultures, such as Japan, it would be considered inconceivable for someone to make a decision without first gaining the acceptance of his or her immediate colleagues.

Consider also that culture dictates the extent to which people expect to be involved in the decision-making process. In Sweden, for example, it is traditional for employees at all levels to be involved in the decisions affecting them. This is so much the case, in fact, that Swedes may totally ignore an organizational hierarchy and contact whomever is needed to make a decision however high-ranking that decision maker may be. However, in India, where autocratic decision making is expected, it would be considered a sign of weakness for a manager to consult a subordinate about a decision.

Time urgency. Another cultural difference in decision making has to do with the amount of time taken to make a decision. For example, in the United States, one mark of a good decision maker is that he or she is "decisive," willing to take on an important decision and make it without delay. However, in some other cultures, time urgency is downplayed. In Egypt, for example, the more important the matter, the more time the decision maker is expected to take in reaching a decision. Throughout the Middle East reaching a decision quickly would be perceived as overly hasty.

As these examples illustrate, there exist some interesting differences in the ways people from various countries go about formulating and implementing decisions. Understanding such differences is an important first step toward developing appropriate strategies for conducting business at a global level.[50]

Of course, the rational-economic approach to decision making does not fully appreciate the fallibility of the human decision maker. Based on the assumption that people have access to complete and perfect information and use it to make perfect decisions, the model can be considered a *normative* (also called *prescriptive*) approach—one that describes how decision makers ideally ought to behave so as to make the best possible decisions. It does not describe how decision makers actually behave in most circumstances. This task is undertaken by the next major approach to individual decision making, the *administrative model*.

The Administrative Model: The Limits of Human Rationality

As you know from your own experience, people generally do not act in a completely rational-economic manner. To illustrate this point, consider how a personnel department might select a new receptionist. After several applicants are interviewed, the personnel manager might choose the best candidate seen so far and stop interviewing. Had the manager been following a rational-economic model, he or she would have had to interview all possible candidates before deciding on the best one. However, by ending the search after finding someone considered good enough to do the job, the manager is using a much simpler approach.

administrative model

A model of decision making that recognizes that people have imperfect views of problems, which limits the making of optimally rational-economic decisions.

satisficing decisions

Decisions made by selecting the first minimally acceptable alternative as it becomes available.

bounded rationality

The major assumption of the administrative model—that organizational, social, and human limitations lead to the making of *satisficing* rather than optimal decisions.

bounded discretion

The tendency to restrict decision alternatives to those that fall within prevailing ethical standards.

The process used in this example characterizes an approach to decision making known as the **administrative model**.[51] This conceptualization recognizes that decision makers may have a limited and imperfect view of the problems confronting them. The number of solutions that can be recognized or implemented is limited by the capabilities of the decision maker and the available resources of the organization. Also, decision makers do not have perfect information about the consequences of their decisions, so they cannot tell which one is best.

How are decisions made according to the administrative model? Instead of considering all possible solutions, decision makers consider solutions as they become available. Then they decide on the first alternative that meets their criteria for acceptability. Thus, the decision maker selects a solution that may be just good enough, although not optimal. Such decisions are referred to as **satisficing decisions**. Of course, a satisficing decision is much easier to make than an optimal decision. In most decision-making situations, satisficing decisions are acceptable and are more likely to be made than optimal ones.[52] The following analogy is used to compare the two types of decisions: Making an optimal decision is like searching a haystack for the sharpest needle, but making a satisficing decision is like searching a haystack for a needle just sharp enough with which to sew.

As we have noted, it is often impractical for people to make completely optimal, rational decisions. The administrative model recognizes the **bounded rationality** under which most organizational decision makers must operate. The idea is that people lack the cognitive skills required to formulate and solve highly complex business problems in a completely objective, rational way.[53]

In addition, decision makers limit their actions to those that fall within the bounds of current moral and ethical standards—that is, they use **bounded discretion**.[54] So, although engaging in illegal activities such as stealing may optimize an organization's profits (at least in the short run), ethical considerations strongly discourage such actions (see Figure 10.8).

It should not be surprising that the administrative model does a better job than the rational-economic model of describing how decision makers actually behave. The administrative approach is said to be *descriptive* (also called *proscriptive*) in nature because it describes what actually occurs. This interest in examining the actual, imperfect behavior of decision makers, rather than specifying the ideal, economically rational behaviors that

FIGURE 10.8

Bounded Discretion: A Constraint on Decision Making

People making decisions in business situations often confront opportunities to engage in illegal and/or unethical behavior. In most situations (but certainly not all), people considering various decision alternatives limit themselves to only the acceptable options.

Source: www.CartoonStock.com

"Our scientists say it would be a public health hazard, but market research shows it would sell like hot cakes - what do you think?"

decision makers ought to engage in, lies at the heart of the distinction between the administrative and rational-economic models. Our point is not that decision makers do not want to behave rationally, but that restrictions posed by the innate capabilities of the decision makers preclude "perfect" decisions.

Image Theory: An Intuitive Approach to Decision Making

If you think about it, you'll probably realize that some, but certainly not all, decisions are made following the logical steps of our general model of decision making. Consider Elizabeth Barrett Browning's poetic question "How do I love thee? Let me count the ways."[55] It's unlikely that anyone would ultimately answer the question by carefully counting what one loves about another (although many such characteristics can be enumerated). Instead, a more intuitive-based decision making is likely, not only for matters of the heart, but for a variety of important organizational decisions as well.[56]

The point is that selecting the best alternative by weighing all the options is not always a major concern when making a decision. People also consider how various decision alternatives fit with their personal standards as well as their personal goals and plans. The best decision for someone might not be the best for someone else. In other words, people may make decisions in a more automatic, *intuitive* fashion than is traditionally recognized. Representative of this approach is **image theory**.[57] This approach to decision making is summarized in Figure 10.9.

Image theory deals primarily with decisions about adopting a certain course of action (e.g., should the company develop a new product line?) or changing a current course of action (e.g., should the company drop a present product line?). According to the theory, people make decisions on the basis of a simple two-step process. The first step is the *compatibility test*, a comparison of the degree to which a particular course of action is consistent with various images—particularly individual principles, current goals, and plans for the future. If any lack of compatibility exists with respect to these considerations, a rejection decision is made. If the compatibility test is passed, then the *profitability test* is carried out. That is, people consider the extent to which using various alternatives best fits their values, goals, and plans. The decision is then made to accept the best candidate. These tests are used within a certain *decision frame*—that is, with consideration of meaningful information about the decision context (such as past experiences). The basic idea is that we learn from the past and are guided by it when making decisions. The example shown in Figure 10.9 highlights this contemporary approach to decision making.

image theory

A theory of decision making that recognizes that decisions are made in an automatic, intuitive fashion. According to the theory, people will adopt a course of action that best fits their individual principles, current goals, and plans for the future.

FIGURE 10.9

Image Theory: An Overview and Example

According to *image theory*, decisions are made in a relatively automatic, intuitive fashion following the two steps outlined here.

Source: Adapted from Beach & Mitchell, 1990; see Note 57.

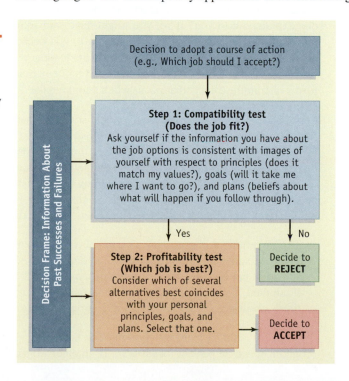

According to image theory, the decision-making process is very rapid and simple. The theory suggests that people do not ponder and reflect over decisions, but make them using a smooth, intuitive process with minimal cognitive processing. If you've ever found yourself saying that something "seemed like the right thing to do," or "something doesn't feel right," you're probably well aware of the kind of intuitive thinking that goes on in a great deal of decision making. Recent research suggests that when it comes to making relatively simple decisions, people tend to behave as suggested by image theory.[58] For example, it has been found that people decide against various options when past evidence suggests that these decisions may be incompatible with their images of the future.[59]

To summarize, we have described three major approach to decision making. The rational-economic approach represents the ideal way optimal decisions may be made. However, the administrative model and image theory represent ways that people actually go about making decisions. Both approaches have received support, and neither should be seen as a replacement for the other. Instead, several different processes may be involved in decision making. Not all decision making is carried out the same way: Sometimes decision making might be analytical, and sometimes it might be more intuitive. Modern organizational behavior scholars recognize the value of both approaches, each of which recognizes the fallibility of the human decision maker. With this in mind, we now turn attention to the imperfect nature of individual decisions.

The Imperfect Nature of Individual Decisions

Let's face it, as a whole, people are less than perfect when it comes to making decisions. Mistakes are made all the time. Obviously, people have limited capacities to process information accurately and thoroughly, like a computer. For example, we often focus on irrelevant information in making decisions.[60] We also fail to use all the information that's available to us, in part because we may forget some of it.[61] Beyond these general limitations in human information-processing capacity, we may note several systematic determinants of imperfect decisions, factors that contribute to the imperfect nature of people's decisions. These variables reside not only within individuals themselves (e.g., biases in the way people make decisions) but also the organizations within which we operate. We now examine several major factors contributing to the imperfect nature of individual decisions.

Framing Effects

framing
The tendency for people to make different decisions based on how the problem is presented to them.

Have you ever found yourself changing your mind about something because of *how* someone explained it to you? If so, you might have said something like, "Now that you put it that way, I agree." This may sound familiar to you because it describes a well-established decision-making bias known as **framing**—the tendency for people to make different decisions based on how the problem is presented to them. Scientists have identified three major forms of framing effects that occur when people make decisions.[62]

risky choice framing effect
The tendency for people to avoid risks when situations are presented in a way that emphasizes positive gains, and to take risks when situations are presented in a way that emphasizes potential losses that may be suffered.

Risky Choice Frames. For many years, scientists have noted that when problems are framed in a manner that emphasizes the positive gains to be received, people tend to shy away from taking risks and go for the sure thing (i.e., decision makers are said to be *risk-averse*). However, when problems are framed in a manner that emphasizes the potential losses to be suffered, people are more willing to take risks so as to avoid those losses (i.e., decision makers are said to make *risk-seeking* decisions).[63] This is known as the **risky choice framing effect**. To illustrate this phenomenon consider the following example:

> The government is preparing to combat a rare disease expected to take 600 lives. Two alternative programs to combat the disease have been proposed, each of which, scientists believe, will have certain consequences. *Program A* will save 200 people, if adopted. *Program B* has .a one-third chance of saving all 600 people, but a two-thirds chance of saving no one. Which program do you prefer?

When such a problem was presented to people, 72 percent expressed a preference for Program A, and 28 percent for Program B. In other words, they preferred the "sure thing" of saving 200 people over the one-third possibility of saving them all. However, this did not occur when the description of the programs was framed in negative terms such as the following:

> *Program C* was described as allowing 400 people to die, if adopted. *Program D* was described as allowing a one-third probability that no one would die, and a two-thirds probability that all 600 would die. Now which program would you prefer?

Compare these four programs. Program C is just another way of stating the outcomes of Program A, and Program D is just another way of stating the outcomes of Program B. However, Programs C and D are framed in negative terms, which led to opposite preferences: 22 percent favored Program C and 78 percent favored Program D. In other words, people tended to avoid risk when the problem was framed in terms of "lives saved" (i.e., in positive terms), but to seek risk when the problem was framed in terms of "lives lost" (i.e., in negative terms). This classic effect has been replicated in several studies.[64]

Attribute Framing. Risky choice frames involve making decisions about which course of action is preferred. However, the same basic idea applies to situations not involving risk, but involving evaluations. Suppose, for example, you're walking down the meat aisle of your local supermarket when you spot a package of ground beef labeled "75% lean." Of course, if the same package were to say "25% fat," you would know exactly the same thing. However, you probably wouldn't perceive that to be the case. In fact, consumer marketing research has shown that people rated the same sample of ground beef as being better tasting and less greasy when it was framed with respect to a positive attribute (i.e., 75% lean) than when it was framed with respect to a negative attribute (i.e., 25% fat).[65]

attribute framing effect
The tendency for people to evaluate a characteristic more positively when it is presented in positive terms than when it is presented in negative terms.

Although this example is easy to relate to, its generalizability goes way beyond product evaluation situations. In fact, the **attribute framing effect**, as it is known, occurs in a wide variety of organizational settings. In other words, people evaluate the same characteristic more positively when it is described in positive terms than when it is described in negative terms. Take performance evaluation, for example. In this context, people whose performance is framed in positive terms (e.g., percentage of shots made by a basketball player) tend to be evaluated more positively than those whose identical performance is framed in negative terms (e.g., percentage of shots missed by that same basketball player).[66]

Goal Framing. A third type of framing, *goal framing,* focuses on an important question: When attempting to persuade someone to do something, is it more effective to focus on the positive consequences of doing it or the negative consequences of not doing it? For example, suppose you are attempting to get women to engage in self-examination of their breasts to check for signs of cancer. You may frame the desired behavior in positive terms:

> "Research shows that women who *do* breast self-examinations have an *increased* chance of finding a tumor in the early, more treatable stages of the disease."

Or you may frame it in negative terms:

> "Research shows that women who *do not* do breast self-examinations have a *decreased* chance of finding a tumor in the early, more treatable stages of the disease."

Which approach is more effective? Research has shown that women were significantly more likely to engage in breast self-examination when they were presented with the consequences of not doing it rather than the benefits of doing it.[67] This is an example of the **goal framing effect** in action. According to this phenomenon, people are more strongly persuaded by the negatively framed information than by the positively framed information.

goal framing effect
The tendency for people to be more strongly persuaded by information that is framed in negative terms than information that is framed in positive terms.

A General Note About Framing. The three kinds of framing we have described here, although similar in several key ways, are also quite different. Spceifically they focus on different types of behavior: preferences for risk in the case of *risky choice framing*; evaluations of characteristics in the case of *attribute framing*; and taking behavioral action in the case of *goal framing*. For a summary of some these three effects, see Figure 10.10.

Scientists believe that framing effects are due to the tendency for people to perceive equivalent situations framed differently as not really equivalent.[68] In other words, focusing on the glass as "half full" leads people to think about it differently than when it is presented as being "half empty," although they might recognize intellectually that the two are really the same. Such findings illustrate our point that people are not completely rational decision makers, but are systematically biased by the cognitive distortions created by simple differences in the way situations are framed.

Reliance on Heuristics

Framing effects are not the only cognitive biases to which decision makers are subjected. It also has been established that people often attempt to simplify the complex decisions they face by using **heuristics**—simple rules of thumb that guide them through a complex array of decision alternatives.[69] Although heuristics are potentially useful to decision makers, they represent potential impediments to decision making. Two very common types of heuristics may be identified—the availability heuristic and the representativeness heuristic (see Figure 10.11).

The Availability Heuristic. The **availability heuristic** refers to the tendency for people to base their judgments on information that is readily available to them—even though it might not be accurate. Suppose, for example, that a real estate executive needs to know the percentage of available houses in a particular neighborhood. There is not enough time to gather the appropriate statistics, so she bases her judgments on her knowledge of available property nationwide. If the neighborhood in question is atypical, her estimate will be off accordingly (see the top portion of Figure 10.11). In other words, basing judgments solely on information that just happens to be available increases the possibility of making inaccurate decisions. Yet people often use the availability heuristic when making decisions.[70]

The Representativeness Heuristic. The **representativeness heuristic** refers to the tendency to perceive others in stereotypical ways if they appear to be typical representatives of the category to which they belong.

heuristics

Simple decision rules (rules of thumb) used to make quick decisions about complex problems. (See *availability heuristic* and *representativeness heuristic*.)

availability heuristic

The tendency for people to base their judgments on information that is readily available to them although it may be potentially inaccurate, thereby adversely affecting decision quality.

representativeness heuristic

The tendency to perceive others in stereotypical ways if they appear to be typical representatives of the category to which they belong.

Type of Framing	Negative Frame		Positive Frame
Risky choice framing	Avoid losses (lives lost)	Likelihood of taking risks	Experience gains (lives saved)
	more likely	←———————→	less likely
Attribute framing	Negative qualities (25% fat)		Positive qualities (75% lean)
	negative	←——— Evaluation ———→	positive
Goal framing	Suffer loss (no breast exam → decreased chance of finding early tumor)		Experience gain (breast exam → increased chance of finding early tumor)
	more likely	Likelihood of performing exam ←———————→	less likely

FIGURE 10.10

Framing Effects: A Summary of Three Types

Information presented (i.e., framed) negatively is perceived differently than the same information presented positively. This takes the three different forms summarized here—*risky choice framing, attribute framing,* and *goal framing.*

Source: Based on suggestions by Levin et al., 1998; see Note 59.

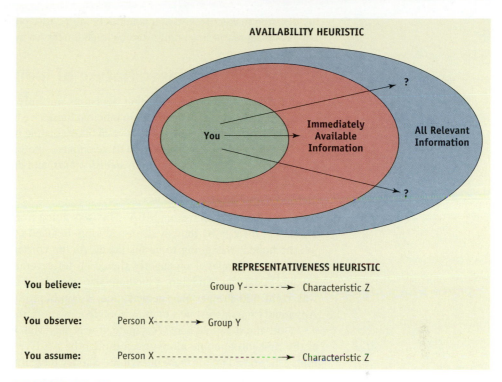

AVAILABILITY HEURISTIC

You → Immediately Available Information → ?

All Relevant Information

REPRESENTATIVENESS HEURISTIC

You believe: Group Y -------→ Characteristic Z

You observe: Person X -------→ Group Y

You assume: Person X --------------------→ Characteristic Z

FIGURE 10.11

The Availability Heuristic and the Representativeness Heuristic

People making decisions often rely on simple rules of thumb, known as heuristics, to help them. Sometimes, however, these actually hinder decision-making quality. This occurs in the case of the *availability heuristic,* in which people are inclined to consider immediately available information (e.g., what they already know) instead of all relevant information. The *representativeness heuristic* is another example. Here, people are likely to assume that people possess the characteristics they associate with others in those individuals' groups—that is, that people we meet are representative of the groups to which they belong.

For example, suppose you believe that accountants are bright, mild-mannered individuals, whereas salespeople are less intelligent, but much more extroverted. Further, imagine that there are twice as many salespeople as accountants at a party. You meet someone at the party who is bright and mild-mannered. Although mathematically the odds are two-to-one that this person is a salesperson rather than an accountant, chances are you will guess that the individual is an accountant because she possesses the traits you associate with accountants (see the bottom portion of Figure 10.11). In other words, you believe this person to be representative of accountants in general—so much so that you would knowingly go against the mathematical odds in making your judgment. Research has found that people tend to make this type of error in judgment, thereby providing good support for the existence of the representativeness heuristic.[71]

The Helpful Side of Heuristics. It is important to note that heuristics do not *always* deteriorate the quality of decisions made. In fact, they can be quite helpful. People often use rules of thumb to help simplify the complex decisions they face. For example, management scientists employ many useful heuristics to aid decisions regarding such matters as where to locate warehouses or how to compose an investment portfolio.[72] We also use heuristics in our everyday lives, such as when we play chess ("control the center of the board") or blackjack ("hit on 16, stick on 17").

However, the representativeness heuristic and the availability heuristic may be recognized as impediments to superior decisions because they discourage people from collecting and processing as much information as they should. Making judgments on the basis of only readily available information, or on stereotypical beliefs, although making things simple for the decision maker, does so at a potentially high cost—poor decisions. Thus, these systematic biases represent potentially serious impediments to individual decision making.

The Inherently Biased Nature of Individual Decisions

As individuals, we make imperfect decisions not only because of our overreliance on heuristics, but also because of certain inherent biases we bring to the various decision making situations we face. Among the several biases people have when making decisions, four have received special attention by OB scientists—the bias toward *implicit favorites,* the *hindsight bias,* the *person sensitivity decision bias,* and the *escalation of commitment* bias.

Bias Toward Implicit Favorites

Don was about to receive his MBA. This was going to be his big chance to move to San Francisco, the city by the bay. Don had long dreamed of living there, and his first "real" job, he hoped, was going to be his ticket. As the corporate recruiters made their annual migration to campus, Don eagerly signed up for several interviews. One of the first was Baxter, Marsh, and Hidalgo, a medium-size consulting firm in San Francisco. The salary was right and the people seemed nice, a combination that pleased Don very much. Apparently the interest was mutual; soon Don was offered a position.

Does the story end here? Not quite. It was only March, and Don felt he shouldn't jump at the first job to come along, even though he really wanted it. So, to do "the sensible thing," he signed up for more interviews. Shortly thereafter, Sparling and Fox, a local firm, made Don a more attractive offer. Not only was the salary higher, but, there was every indication that the job promised a much brighter future than the one in San Francisco.

What would he do? Would he accept the better local job or go to the merely acceptable one in San Francisco? Actually, Don didn't consider it much of a dilemma. After thinking it over, he reached the conclusion that the work at Sparling and Fox was much too low-level—not enough exciting clients to challenge him. And the starting salary wasn't really all *that* much better than it was at Baxter, Marsh, and Hidalgo. The day after graduation Don was packing for his new office overlooking the Golden Gate Bridge.

Do you think the way Don made his decision was atypical? He seemed to have his mind made up in advance about the job in San Francisco, and didn't really give the other one a chance. Research suggests that people make decisions in this way all the time. That is, people tend to pick an **implicit favorite** option (i.e., a preferred alternative) very early in the decision-making process.[73] Then, the other options they consider subsequently are not given serious consideration. Rather, they are merely used to convince oneself that the implicit favorite is indeed the best choice. An alternative considered for this purpose is known as a **confirmation candidate**. It is not unusual to find that people psychologically distort their beliefs about confirmation candidates so as to justify selecting their implicit favorites. Don did this when he convinced himself that the job offered by the local firm really wasn't as good as it seemed (see Figure 10.12).

Research has shown that people make decisions very early in the decision process. For example, in one study of the job recruitment process investigators found that they could predict 87 percent of the jobs that students would take as early as two months before the students acknowledged that they actually had made a decision.[74] Apparently, people's decisions are biased by the tendency for them to not consider all the relevant information available to them. In fact, they tend to bias their judgments of the strengths and weaknesses of various alternatives so as to make them fit their already-made decision—that is, to select their implicit favorite.[75] This phenomenon clearly suggests that people not only fail to consider all possible alternatives when making decisions, but that they even fail to consider all readily available alternatives. Instead, they tend to make up their minds very early and convince themselves that they are right. As you might imagine, this bias toward implicit favorites is likely to limit severely the quality of decisions that are made.

Hindsight Bias

"Hindsight is 20-20," is a phrase commonly heard. It means that when we look back on decisions that already were made, we know better what we should have done. Indeed,

implicit favorite
One's preferred decision alternative, selected even before all options have been considered.

confirmation candidate
A decision alternative considered only for purposes of convincing onself of the wisdom of selecting the *implicit favorite.*

FIGURE 10.12

Biasing Decisions toward Implicit Favorites

People often develop implicit favorites (i.e., preferred alternatives) early in the process of making decisions. They then use the remainder of the decision making process to convince themselves that their implicit favorite is, in fact, the best course of action. This often occurs when making decisions about job opportunities, for example.

hindsight bias
The tendency for people to perceive outcomes as more inevitable after they have occurred (i.e., in hindsight) than they did before they occurred (i.e. , in foresight).

research has revealed that this phenomenon is quite pervasive. For example, studies have shown that people tend to distort the way they see things so as to conform to what they already know about the past. This effect, known as the **hindsight bias**, refers to the tendency for people to perceive outcomes as more inevitable after they occurred (i.e., in hindsight) than they did before they occurred (i.e., in foresight). Hindsight bias occurs when people believe that they could have predicted past events better than they actually did—that is, when they say, "I knew it all along."

The hindsight bias occurs because people feel good about being able to judge things accurately. As such, we may expect that people will be more willing to say that they expected events from the past to have occurred whenever these are positive about themselves or their work team, but not when these events are negative. After all, we look good when we can take credit for predicting successes, but we look bad when we anticipated negative outcomes without doing anything to stop them. Indeed, recent research has shown precisely this.[76] This qualification of the hindsight bias may have important effects on the way people make decisions (for example, see Figure 10.13).

Let's consider a classic example. During the 1970s, a group of public utilities known as the Washington Public Power Supply System (WPPSS) made plans to build seven nuclear power plants in an effort to meet the need for energy, estimated as growing by 7 percent each year. Through the early 1980s, 27,000 investors bought bonds to support this project. As things worked out, however, consumers found ways to conserve energy as energy prices rose, resulting in far smaller increases in energy demands than anticipated. As a result, only one of the seven planned power plants was ever completed, and in 1983, the WPPSS defaulted on bonds valued at $2.25 billion. When investors sued, they claimed that the WPPSS "should have known" that the demand for energy was going to change, thereby precluding the need for the power plants. In other words, they were biased such that they saw the decision to invest in ways that made themselves look good and the WPPSS look bad. Likewise, officials from the WPPSS claimed that they had no way of anticipating the changes the future was going to bring, therefore justifying their decision to raise money and build power plants as a wise one.

Person Sensitivity Bias

President George W. Bush first took office in January 2001, following a highly controversial election that some don't believe he won fairly and squarely. Many disapproved of his foreign policy, claiming that he was ill-suited to the position. Then, only eight months later, following the September 11 terrorist attacks, President Bush unified the country with impassioned speeches that sent his approval ratings into the stratosphere. His stance with

FIGURE 10.13

Hindsight Bias: An Example

These doctors from the Family Medical Center in Bakersfield, California, are meeting to make important decisions about medical procedures to be followed at their facility. In keeping with the *hindsight bias,* when reviewing cases that had positive outcomes, they are likely to claim that they "knew it all along." However, they are unlikely to acknowledge that they were able to predict the outcomes of cases having negative results.

person sensitivity bias
The tendency for people to give too little credit to others when things are going poorly and too much credit when things are going well.

respect to foreign policy was now widely praised. Then, years later when the war in Iraq faltered, his approval rating plummeted. This mini history lesson nicely illustrates an interesting aspect of human nature (beyond the fickle nature of politics, that is): When things are going poorly, nobody likes you, but when things are going well, everyone's your friend. Scientists refer to this as **person sensitivity bias**. Formally, this refers to the tendency for people to blame people too much when things are going poorly and to give them too much credit when things are going well.

Evidence for the person sensitivity bias has been reported in an interesting experiment.[77] Participants in the study were people asked to judge the performance of either individuals who staffed an assembly line or machines that performed the same assembly task. The people or the machines also were described either as exceeding the company standards or not meeting them. When people were said to be responsible for exceeding the standards, they were perceived more positively than machines that also exceeded the standard. However, when the standards were not met, participants judged other people more harshly than the machines (see Figure 10.14). These findings are in keeping with both the positive and negative aspects of the person sensitivity bias.

The person sensitivity bias is important insofar as it suggests that the decisions we make about others are not likely to be completely objective. As people, we need to understand others (as we emphasized in Chapter 3), and it makes things easier for us if we keep our perceptions consistent: what's good is very good; what's bad is very bad. With such a bias underlying our judgments of others, it's little wonder that the decisions we make about them may be highly imperfect. After all, to the extent that effective decisions rely on accurate information, biases such as the person sensitivity bias predispose us to perceive others in less than objective ways.

Escalation of Commitment Bias

Because decisions are made all the time in organizations, some of these inevitably will be unsuccessful. What would you say is the rational thing to do when a poor decision has been made? Obviously, the ineffective action should be stopped or reversed. In other words, it would make sense to "cut your losses and run." However, people don't always respond in this manner. In fact, it is not unusual to find that ineffective decisions are sometimes followed up with still further ineffective decisions.

Imagine, for example, that you have invested money in a company that now appears to be failing. Rather than lose your initial investment, you may invest still more money in the hope of salvaging your first investment. The more you invest, the more you may be tempted to save those earlier investments by making later investments. That is to say, people sometimes

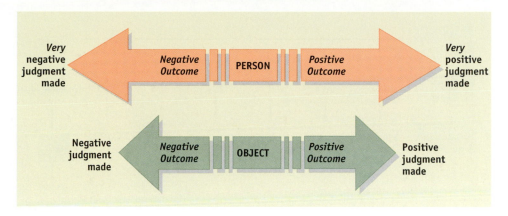

FIGURE 10.14

Person Sensitivity Bias: An Overview

According to the *person sensitivity bias,* we are likely to blame people too much when things are going poorly and to give them too much credit when things are going well. The same positive decision outcomes are perceived as being more positive when caused by people than by inanimate objects, such as computers. Likewise, equally negative decision outcomes are perceived as being more negative when caused by people than by objects.

Source: Based on suggestions by Moon & Conlon, 2002; see Note 77.

escalation of commitment phenomenon
The tendency for individuals to continue to support previously unsuccessful courses of action.

may be found "throwing good money after bad" because they have "too much invested to quit." This is known as the **escalation of commitment phenomenon**—the tendency for people to continue to support previously unsuccessful courses of action because they have sunk costs invested in them.[78]

Although this might not seem like a rational thing to do, this strategy is frequently followed. For example, Motorola has invested over $1.3 billion dollars in its Iridium Satellite System, a network of 66 low-orbiting communication satellites that make it possible to make wireless telephone calls from anywhere on earth. In recent years, however, it has become clear that the system has serious technical limitations. Moreover, the service has failed to attract anywhere near as many subscribers as expected. And now, Motorola is beginning to face competition from other major companies. Instead of accepting its losses and walking away from the project, Motorola officials are investing still more in the Iridium project, hoping that each successive dollar invested will be the one needed to turn the project around to make it profitable.[79]

Why do people do this? If you think about it, you may realize that the failure to back your own previous courses of action in an organization would be taken as an admission of failure—a politically difficult act to face in an organization. In other words, people may be very concerned about "saving face"—looking good in the eyes of others and oneself.[80] Researchers have recognized that this tendency for *self-justification* is primarily responsible for people's inclination to protect their beliefs about themselves as rational, competent decision makers by convincing themselves and others that they made the right decision all along and are willing to back it up.[81] Although there are other possible reasons for the escalation of commitment phenomenon, research supports the self-justification explanation.[82] For a summary of the escalation of commitment phenomenon, see Figure 10.15.

Researchers have noted several conditions under which people will refrain from escalating their commitment to a failing course of action.[83] Notably, it has been found that people will stop making failing investments under conditions in which the available funds for making further investments are limited, and the threat of failure is overwhelmingly obvious.[84] For example, when the Long Island Lighting Company decided in 1989 to abandon plans to operate a nuclear power plant in Shoreham, New York, it was in the face of 23 years' worth of intense political and financial pressure (a strong antinuclear movement and billions of dollars of cost overruns).[85]

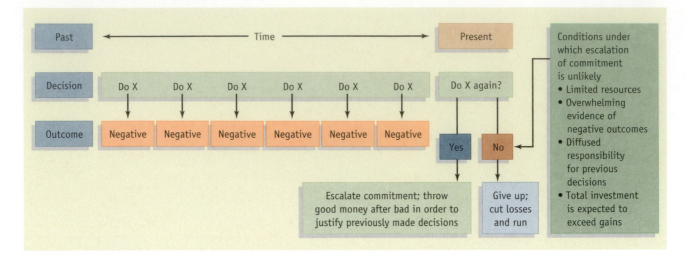

FIGURE 10.15

Escalation of Commitment: An Overview

According to the escalation of commitment phenomenon, people who have repeatedly made poor decisions continue to support those failing courses of action to justify their earlier decisions. Under some conditions, however, as summarized here, this effect will not occur.

It also has been found that people will refrain from escalating commitment when they can diffuse their responsibility for the earlier failing actions. That is, the more people feel they are just one of several people responsible for a failing course of action, the less likely they are to commit to further failing actions.[86] In other words, the less one is responsible for an earlier failure, the less one may be motivated to justify those earlier failures by making further investments in them.

Third, escalation of commitment toward a losing course of action will be low in organizations in which the people who have made ineffective decisions have left and are replaced by others who are not linked to those decisions. In other words, turnover lessens an organization's commitment to a losing course of action. Illustrating this, recent research has shown that although some banks continue to make bad (i.e., uncollectable) loans to customers to whom they have loaned money in the past, this is less likely to occur in banks whose top executives (individuals who are considered responsible for those loans) have left their posts.[87]

Finally, it has been found that people are unwilling to escalate commitment to a course of action when it is made clear that the total amount invested exceeds the amount expected to be gained.[88] Although people may wish to invest in projects that enable them to recoup their initial investments, there is little reason for them to do so when it is obvious that doing so will be a losing proposition. Under such conditions, it is difficult to justify doing so, even if one "hopes against hope" that it will work out. Indeed, research has shown that decision makers do indeed refrain from escalating commitment to decisions when it is made clear that the overall benefit to be gained is less than the overall costs to be borne.[89] This finding was more apparent among students with accounting backgrounds than those without such backgrounds, presumably because their training predisposed them to be more sensitive to these issues.

To conclude, the escalation of commitment phenomenon represents a type of irrational decision making that has the potential to occur. However, whether or not it does occur will depend on the various circumstances that decision makers confront.

Group Decisions: Do Too Many Cooks Spoil the Broth?

Decision-making groups are a well-established fact of modern organizational life. Groups such as committees, study teams, task forces, or review panels are often charged with the responsibility for making important business decisions.[90] They are so common, in fact, that it has been said that some administrators spend as much as 80 percent of their time in committee meetings.[91]

In view of this, it is important to ask how well groups do at making decisions compared to individuals. Given the several advantages and disadvantages of having groups make decisions we described earlier, this question is particularly important. Specifically, we may ask: Under what conditions might individuals or groups be expected to make superior decisions? Fortunately, research provides some good answers.[92]

When Are Groups Superior to Individuals?

Whether groups will do better than individuals or worse than individuals depends on the nature of the task. Specifically, any advantages that groups may have over individuals will depend on how complex or simple the task is.

Complex Decision Tasks. Imagine a situation in which an important decision has to be made about a complex problem—such as whether one company should merge with another. This is not the kind of problem about which any one individual working alone would be able to make a good decision. After all, its highly complex nature may overwhelm even an expert, thereby setting the stage for a group to do a better job.

However, this doesn't happen automatically. In fact, for groups to outperform individuals, several conditions must exist. First, we must consider who is in the group. Successful groups tend to be composed of *heterogeneous group members with complementary skills.* So, for example, a group composed of lawyers, accountants, real estate agents, and other experts may make much better decisions on the merger problem than would a group composed of specialists in only one field. Indeed, research has shown that the diversity of opinions offered by group members is one of the major advantages of using groups to make decisions.[93]

As you might imagine, it is not enough simply to have skills. For a group to be successful, its members must also be able to freely communicate their ideas to each other in an open, nonhostile manner. Conditions under which one individual (or group) intimidates another from contributing his or her expertise can easily negate any potential gain associated with composing groups of heterogeneous experts. After all, *having* expertise and being able to make a contribution by *using* that expertise are two different things. Indeed, research has shown that only when the contributions of the most qualified group members are given the greatest weight does the group derive any benefit from that member's presence.[94] Thus, for groups to be superior to individuals, they must be composed of a heterogeneous collection of experts with complementary skills who can freely and openly contribute to their group's product.

Simple Decision Tasks. In contrast to complex decision tasks, imagine a situation in which a judgment is required on a simple problem with a readily verifiable answer. For example, make believe that you are asked to translate a phrase from a relatively obscure language into English.

Groups might do better than individuals on such a task, but probably because the odds are increased that someone in the group knows the language and can perform the translation for the group. However, there is no reason to expect that even a large group will be able to perform such a task better than a single individual who has the required expertise. In fact, an expert working alone may do even better than a group. This is because an expert individual performing a simple task may be distracted by others and suffer from having to convince them of the correctness of his or her solution. For this reason, exceptional individuals tend to outperform entire committees on simple tasks.[95] In such cases, for groups to benefit from a pooling of resources, there must be some resources to pool. The pooling of ignorance does not help.

In sum, the question, "Are two heads better than one?" can be answered this way: On simple tasks, two heads may be better than one if at least one of those heads has enough of what it takes to succeed. Thus, whether groups perform better than individuals depends on the nature of the task performed and the expertise of the people involved. We have summarized some of these key considerations in Figure 10.16.

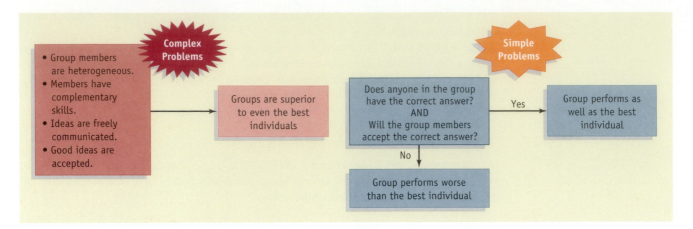

FIGURE 10.16

When Are Group Decisions Superior to Individual Decisions?

When performing complex problems, groups are superior to individuals if certain conditions prevail (e.g., when members have heterogeneous and complementary skills, when they can freely share ideas, and when their good ideas are accepted by others). However, when performing simple problems, groups perform only as well as the best individual group member—and then, only if that person has the correct answer and if that answer is accepted by others in the group.

When Are Individuals Superior to Groups?

As we have described thus far, groups may be expected to perform better than the average or even the exceptional individual under certain conditions. However, there are also conditions under which individuals are superior to groups.

Most of the problems faced by organizations require a great deal of creative thinking. For example, a company deciding how to use a newly developed adhesive in its consumer products is facing decisions on a poorly structured task. Although you would expect that the complexity of such creative problems would give groups a natural advantage, this is not the case. In fact, research has shown that on poorly structured, creative tasks, individuals perform better than groups.[96]

An approach to solving creative problems commonly used by groups is **brainstorming**. This technique was developed by advertising executive Alex Osborn as a tool for coming up with creative, new ideas.[97] The members of brainstorming groups are encouraged to present their ideas in an uncritical way and to discuss freely and openly all ideas on the floor. Specifically, members of brainstorming groups are required to follow four main rules:

brainstorming
A technique designed to foster group productivity by encouraging interacting group members to express their ideas in a noncritical fashion.

1. Avoid criticizing others' ideas.
2. Share even far-out suggestions.
3. Offer as many comments as possible.
4. Build on others' ideas to create your own.

Does brainstorming improve the quality of creative decisions? To answer this question, researchers compared the effectiveness of individuals and brainstorming groups working on creative problems.[98] Specifically, participants were given 35 minutes to consider the consequences of situations such as "What if everybody went blind?" or "What if everybody grew an extra thumb on each hand?" Clearly, the novel nature of such problems requires a great deal of creativity. Comparisons were made of the number of solutions generated by groups of four or seven people and a like number of individuals working on the same problems alone. The results were clear: Individuals were significantly more productive than groups.

In summary, groups perform worse than individuals when working on creative tasks. A great part of the problem is that some individuals feel inhibited by the presence of others even though one rule of brainstorming is that even far-out ideas may be shared. To the extent that people wish to avoid feeling foolish as a result of saying silly things, their creativity may be inhibited when in groups. Similarly, groups may inhibit creativity by slowing down the process of bringing ideas to fruition. Yet, many creative professionals strongly believe in the power of brainstorming.[99] For some suggestions on how to reap the benefits of brainstorming, see Table 10.3.

Traditional Techniques for Improving the Effectiveness of Decisions

As we have made clear in this chapter, certain advantages can be gained from sometimes using individuals and sometimes using groups to make decisions. A decision-making technique that combines the best features of groups and individuals, while minimizing the disadvantages, would be ideal. Several techniques designed to realize the "best of both worlds" have been widely used in organizations. These include techniques that involve the structuring of group discussions in special ways. An even more basic approach to improving the effectiveness of group decisions involves training decision makers in ways of avoiding some of the pitfalls of group decision making. We will begin this section of the chapter with a discussion of this training approach to improving group decisions and then go on to consider various ways of creating specially structured groups.

Training Individuals to Improve Group Performance

Earlier in this chapter we noted that how well groups solve problems depends in part on the composition of those groups. If at least one group member is capable of coming up with a solution, groups may benefit by that individual's expertise. Based on this reasoning, it follows that the more qualified individual group members are to solve problems, the better their groups as a whole will perform. What, then, might individuals do to improve the nature of the decisions they make?

TABLE 10.3 Tips for Using Brainstorming Successfully

The rules of brainstorming are simple enough, but doing it effectively requires some guidance. Many brainstorming sessions fail because people don't fully appreciate the finer points of how to conduct them. Following these guidelines stand to make your own brainstorming sessions more effective.

Suggestion	Explanation
Brainstorm frequently, at least once per month.	Practice makes perfect. The more frequently people engage in brainstorming, the more comfortable they are with it—hence, the more effective it becomes.
Keep brainstorming sessions brief, less than an hour in length.	Brainstorming effectively can be very exhausting, so limit the time dedicated to it. After about an hour, people become too inefficient to make it worthwhile to continue.
Focus on the problem at hand.	The best brainstorming sessions begin with a clear statement of the problem at hand. These shouldn't be too broad or too narrow.
Don't forget to "build" and "jump."	The best ideas to result from brainstorming sessions are those that build on other ideas. Everyone should be strongly encouraged to jump from one idea to another as they build on the earlier one.
Prepare for the session.	Brainstorming is much more effective when people prepare in advance by reading up on the topic than when they come in "cold."
Don't limit yourself to words—use props.	Some of the most effective brainstorming sessions result when people introduce objects to help model their ideas.

Source: Based on suggestions by Kelley, 2001; see Note 99.

Researchers looking into this question have found that people tend to make four types of mistakes when attempting to make creative decisions, and that they make better decisions when trained to avoid these errors.[100] Specifically, these are as follows.

hypervigilance

The state in which an individual frantically searches for quick solutions to problems, and goes from one idea to another out of a sense of desperation that one idea isn't working and that another needs to be considered before time runs out.

1. *Hypervigilance.* The state of **hypervigilance** involves frantically searching for quick solutions to problems, going from one idea to another out of a sense of desperation that one idea isn't working and that another needs to be considered before time runs out. A poor, "last chance" solution may be adopted to relieve anxiety. This problem may be avoided by keeping in mind that it is best to stick with one suggestion and work it out thoroughly, and reassuring the person solving the problem that his or her level of skill and education is adequate to perform the task at hand. In other words, a little reassurance may go a long way toward keeping individuals on the right track and avoiding the problem of hypervigilance.

unconflicted adherence

The tendency for decision makers to stick to the first idea that comes to their minds without more deeply evaluating the consequences.

2. *Unconflicted adherence.* Many decision makers make the mistake of sticking to the first idea that comes into their heads without more deeply evaluating the consequences, a mistake known as **unconflicted adherence**. As a result, such people are unlikely to become aware of any problems associated with their ideas or to consider other possibilities. To avoid unconflicted adherence, decision makers are urged (1) to think about the difficulties associated with their ideas, (2) to force themselves to consider different ideas, and (3) to consider the special and unique characteristics of the problem they are facing and avoid carrying over assumptions from previous problems.

unconflicted change

The tendency for people to quickly change their minds and to adopt the first new idea to come along.

3. *Unconflicted change.* Sometimes people are very quick to change their minds and adopt the first new idea to come along—a problem known as **unconflicted change**. To avoid unconflicted change, decision makers are encouraged to ask themselves about (1) the risks and problems of adopting that solution, (2) the good points of the first idea, and (3) the relative strengths and weaknesses of both ideas.

defensive avoidance

The tendency for decision makers to fail to solve problems because they go out of their way to avoid working on the problem at hand.

4. *Defensive avoidance.* Too often, decision makers fail to solve problems effectively because they go out of their way to avoid working on the task at hand. This is known as **defensive avoidance**. People can do three things to minimize this problem. First, they should attempt to *avoid procrastination*. Don't put off the problem indefinitely just because you cannot come up with a solution right away. Continue to budget some of your time on even the most frustrating problems. Second, *avoid disowning responsibility*. It is easy to minimize the importance of a problem by saying "It doesn't matter, so who cares?" Avoid giving up so soon. Finally, *don't ignore potentially corrective information*. It is tempting to put your nagging doubts about the quality of a solution to rest in order to be finished with it. Good decision makers would not do so. Rather, they use their doubts to test and potentially improve the quality of their ideas.

Techniques for Enhancing Group Decisions

Just as there are various things individuals can do to improve decision making, so too are there steps that groups can take to enhance the quality of their decisions. The basic idea underlying these techniques is identical: Structure the group experience so as to enable the many benefits of groups to occur without also experiencing the weaknesses.

The Delphi Technique: Decisions by Expert Consensus.

According to Greek mythology, people interested in seeing what fate the future held for them could seek the counsel of the Delphic oracle. Today's organizational decision makers sometimes consult experts to help them make the best decisions as well. A technique developed by the Rand Corporation, known as the **Delphi technique**, represents a systematic way of collecting and organizing the opinions of several experts into a single decision.[101] For a summary of the steps in this process, see Figure 10.17.

Delphi technique

A method of improving group decisions using the opinions of experts, which are solicited by mail and then compiled. The expert consensus of opinions is used to make a decision.

The Delphi process starts by enlisting the cooperation of experts and presenting the problem to them, usually in a letter or an e-mail message. Each expert then proposes what he or she believes is the most appropriate solution. The group leader compiles all of these individual responses and reproduces them so they can be shared with all the other experts in a second mailing. At this point, each expert comments on the others' ideas and proposes

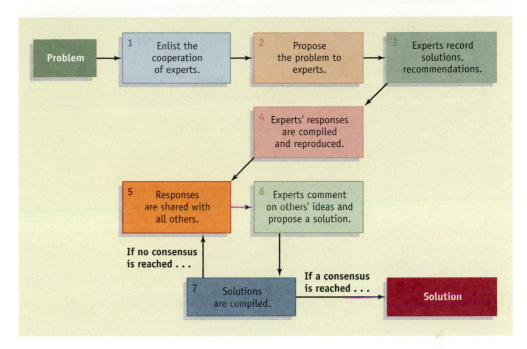

FIGURE 10.17

The Delphi Technique

The Delphi technique allows decisions to be made by several experts while avoiding many of the pitfalls of face-to-face group interaction. Its general steps are outlined here.

another solution. These individual solutions are returned to the leader, who compiles them and looks for a consensus of opinions. If a consensus is reached, the decision is made. If not, the process of sharing reactions with others is repeated until a consensus is eventually obtained.

The obvious advantage of using the Delphi technique to make decisions is that it allows expert judgments to be collected without the great costs and logistical difficulties of bringing many experts together for a face-to-face meeting. However, the technique is not without limitations. As you might imagine, the Delphi process can be very time-consuming. Sending out letters or e-mail messages, waiting for everyone to respond, transcribing and disseminating the responses, and repeating the process until a consensus is reached can take quite a long time. Experts have estimated that the minimum time required to use the Delphi technique would be more than 44 days. In one case (using regular postal mail), the process took five months to complete.[102] With the widespread use of e-mail, the Delphi approach can be sped up considerably, but it is still slow. Obviously, the Delphi approach is not appropriate for making decisions in crisis situations, or whenever else time is of the essence. However, the approach has been successfully employed to make decisions such as what items to put on a conference agenda and what the potential impact of implementing new land-use policies would be.[103]

nominal group technique (NGT)

A technique for improving group decisions in which small groups of individuals systematically present and discuss their ideas before privately voting on their preferred solution. The most preferred solution is accepted as the group's decision.

The Nominal Group Technique: A Structured Group Meeting. When there are only a few hours available to make a decision, group discussion sessions can be held in which members interact with each other in an orderly, focused fashion aimed at solving problems. The **nominal group technique (NGT)** brings together a small number of individuals (usually about 7 to 10) who systematically offer their individual solutions to a problem and share their personal reactions to others' solutions.[104] The technique is referred to as *nominal* because the individuals involved form a group in name only. The participants do not attempt to agree as a group on any solution, but rather vote on all the solutions proposed. For a summary of this process, see Figure 10.18.

FIGURE 10.18

The Nominal Group Technique

The nominal group technique structures face-to-face group meetings in such a way that the open expression and evaluation of ideas is encouraged. It follows the six steps summarized here.

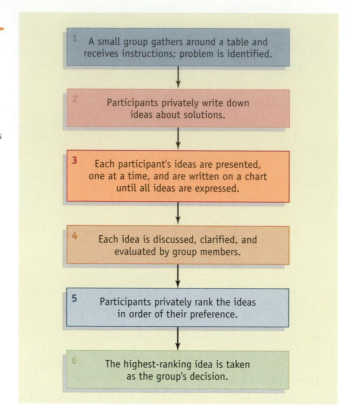

As shown in Figure 10.18, the nominal group process begins by gathering the group members together around a table and identifying the problem at hand. Then each member writes down his or her solutions. Next, one at a time, each member presents his or her solutions to the group as the leader writes these down on a chart. This process continues until all the ideas have been expressed. Following this, each solution is discussed, clarified, and evaluated by the group members. Each member is given a chance to voice his or her reactions to each idea. After all the ideas have been evaluated, the group members privately rank-order their preferred solutions. Finally, the idea that receives the highest rank is taken as the group's decision (To experience the NGT firsthand, complete the Group Exercise on p. 420.)

The NGT has several advantages and disadvantages.[105] We have already noted that it can be used to arrive at group decisions in only a few hours. This can be useful for many types of decisions—but, of course, not for urgent decisions that have to be made on the spot. The benefit of the technique is that it discourages any pressure to conform to the wishes of a high-status group member because all ideas are evaluated and the preferences are expressed in private balloting. The technique must be considered limited, however, in that it requires the use of a trained group leader. In addition, using NGT successfully requires that only one narrowly defined problem be considered at a time. So, for very complex problems, many NGT sessions would have to be run—and only *if* the problem under consideration could be broken down into smaller parts.

It is important to consider the relative effectiveness of nominal groups and Delphi groups over face-to-face interacting groups. In general, research has shown the superiority of these special approaches to decision making in many ways on a variety of decision problems.[106] Overall, members of nominal groups tend to be the most satisfied with their work and made the best-quality judgments. In addition, both nominal groups and Delphi groups are much more productive than interacting groups.

As we noted earlier, however, there is a potential benefit to be derived from face-to-face interaction that cannot be realized in nominal and Delphi groups—that is, acceptance of the decision. Groups are likely to accept their decisions and be committed to them if members have been actively involved in making them. Thus, the more detached and impersonal atmosphere of nominal and Delphi groups sometimes makes their members less likely to

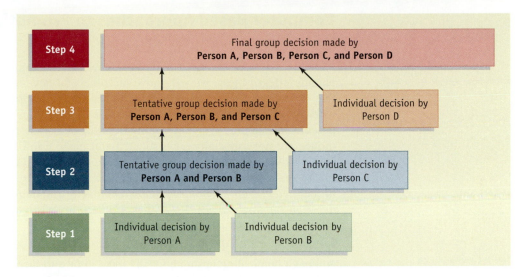

FIGURE 10.19

The Stepladder Technique

By systematically adding new individuals into decision-making groups, the stepladder technique helps to increase the quality of the decisions made.

Source: Adapted from Rogelberg & O'Connor, 1998; see Note 108.

accept their groups' decisions. We may conclude, then, that there is no one best type of group used to make decisions. Which type is most appropriate depends on the trade-offs decision makers are willing to make in terms of speed, quality, and commitment.[107]

The Stepladder Technique: Systematically Incorporating New Members. Another way of structuring group interaction is known as the **stepladder technique**.[108] This approach minimizes the tendency for group members to be unwilling to present their ideas by adding new members to a group one at a time and requiring each to present his or her ideas independently to a group that already has discussed the problem at hand. To begin, each of two people works on a problem independently, and then come together to present their ideas and discuss solutions jointly. While the two-person group is working, a third person working alone also considers the problem. Then, this individual presents his or her ideas to the group and joins in a three-person discussion of a possible solution. During this period a fourth person works on the problem alone, and then presents his or her ideas to the group and joins into a four-person group discussion. After each new person has been added to the group, the entire group works together at finding a solution. (For a summary of the steps in this technique, see Figure 10.19.)

In following this procedure, it is important for each individual to be given enough time to work on the problem before he or she joins the group. Then, each person must be given enough time to present his or her ideas to the group thoroughly. Groups then must have sufficient time to discuss the problem at hand and reach a preliminary decision before the next person is added. Next, the final decision is made only after all individuals have been added to the group.

The rationale underlying this procedure is that by forcing each person to present independent ideas without knowing how the group has decided, the new person will not be influenced by the group, and the group is required to consider a constant infusion of new ideas. If this is so, then groups solving problems using the stepladder technique would be expected to make better decisions than conventional groups meeting all at once to discuss the same problem. Research has found that this is exactly what happens. Moreover, members of stepladder groups report feeling more positive about their group experiences than their counterparts in conventional groups. Although the stepladder technique is new, this evidence suggests that it holds a great deal of promise as a way of enhancing the decision-making capacity of groups.

stepladder technique
A technique for improving the quality of group decisions that minimizes the tendency for group members to be unwilling to present their ideas by adding new members to a group one at a time and requiring each to present his or her ideas independently to a group that already has discussed the problem at hand.

Computer-Based Approaches to Promoting Effective Decisions

Now that we have reviewed traditional, low-tech techniques for improving decision-making effectiveness, we will move on to several new, technology-based approaches that have been used in recent years. Given the widespread use of computers in the workplace, it probably comes as no surprise that attempts have been made to put computers to use in improving the quality of group decisions. For the most part, these techniques are not especially sophisticated and make good use of widely available, and inexpensive, computer technology. As a result, they stand to be widely used to the extent that they are effective. With this in mind, we will examine three such techniques: *electronic meeting systems, computer-assisted communication,* and *group decision support systems.*

Electronic Meeting Systems

electronic meeting systems
The practice of bringing individuals from different locations together for a meeting via telephone or satellite transmissions, either on television monitors, or via shared space on a computer screen.

Although nominal groups traditionally meet in face-to-face settings, advances in modern technology enable them to be formed even when members are in distant locations. Specifically, **electronic meeting systems**, as they are known, involve holding teleconferences in which individuals in different locations participate in group conferences by means of telephone lines or direct satellite transmissions.[109] The messages may be sent either via characters on a computer monitor or images viewed during a teleconference. Despite their high-tech look, automated decision conferences are really just nominal groups meeting in a manner that approximates face-to-face contact. And, for the most part, they have proven to be equally effective.

Insofar as electronic meetings allow for groups to assemble more conveniently than face-to-face meetings, they are growing in popularity. Presently, such companies as GE Appliances, U.S. West, Marriott Corp., and Sun Microsystems have relied on electronic meetings, and growing numbers of companies are using them all the time (for another example, see Figure 10.20).

Computer-Assisted Communication

computer-assisted communication
The sharing of information, such as text messages and data relevant to the decision, over computer networks.

Another way of leveraging technology to facilitate group decision-making involves using **computer-assisted communication**—that is, the sharing of information, such as text messages and data relevant to the decision, over computer networks. The underlying idea of computer-assisted communication is that on-screen messages provide an effective means of sending some forms of information that can help groups make better decisions. But does

FIGURE 10.20

An Electronic Meeting in Progress

As a developer of semiconductors, firmware, and software platforms for portable multimedia products (e.g., personal media players), Portalplayer Inc. relies on the talents of technicians around the world. Engineers at the company's Santa Clara, California headquarters, (from left to right) Vallab Kulkarni, Sudhakara Ram, and Jeff Hawkey, routinely conduct teleconference meetings with project managers in India.

it really work? In other words, does being able to communicate with other team members via computer help teams make more effective decisions than they would make without computer assistance?

Research suggests that the answer is "only sometimes."[110] A study was conducted that compared the effectiveness of three-person groups whose members were allowed only to speak to each other (the talk-only condition) with other three-person groups whose members also were allowed to send text messages to one another over a computer network (the computer-assisted communication condition). Participants were asked to perform a task that simulated the kind of decisions made in a military "command and control" situation. This involved assessing the threat risk of aircraft spotted on a computer screen (based on such information as speed and size) after they were trained to perform this task. The teams' decisions were scored on the basis of accuracy and then were compared to one another. The results, summarized in Figure 10.21, revealed that the effectiveness of the teams' decisions depended on another variable.

Specifically, teams using the computer-assisted communication made better decisions than teams using verbal communication only when they were composed of individuals whose scores on a personality test indicated that they were highly open to experience. People scoring high on **openness to experience** tend to have intellectual curiosity, value learning, have an active imagination, and are intrigued by artistic endeavors. By contrast, people scoring low on this measure tend to be exactly the opposite. Apparently, because computer-assisted communication was new to many of the participants, its effectiveness was limited to those who were most accepting of the new technology and who possessed the creativity to use the technology in an efficient manner. These individuals reaped the benefits associated with the computer assistance. However, those who were less open to experience

openness to experience
A personality variable reflecting the degree to which individuals have intellectual curiosity, value learning, have an active imagination, and are intrigued by artistic endeavors.

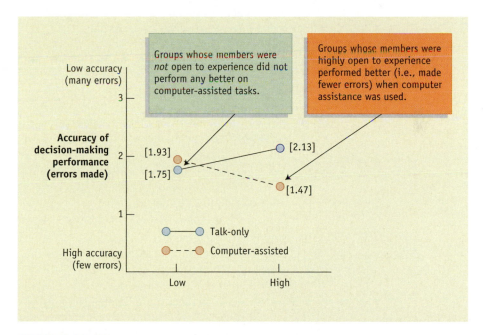

FIGURE 10.21

Computer-Assisted Communication Improves Decision Making Among People Who Are Open to Experience

Computer-assisted communication involves the sharing of information (e.g., text messages and data relevant to them) over computer networks. Research simulating a military decision-making situation has shown that the effectiveness of this technique depends on people's openness to experience. As summarized here, computer-assisted communication improved the decision-making performance of three-person teams only when they were composed of individuals who scored highly on a personality test measuring openness to experience. However, individuals who were not particularly open to experience were not helped by computer-assisted communication.

Source: Based on data reported by Colquitt et al., 2002; see Note 110.

failed to perform better when using computer-assisted communication—actually, they performed slightly worse. Apparently, the computer-assisted communication was not much "assistance" to them, after all.

Because it provides a useful means of exchanging crucial information, one might be inclined to assume that computer-assisted communication is an effective way to improve group decision quality. And, because it can be adopted readily and inexpensively, some may be tempted to put it into practice. However, given that that it appears not to be effective for everyone, implementing computer-assisted communications on a widespread basis would be unwise—at least, it may be premature. Perhaps, after such systems are in use for a while and people come to be familiar with them, even those who are not open to experiences will find them acceptable. Furthermore, training on how to integrate computer-assisted communication with more traditional forms also could compensate for any lack of openness to experience. For the moment, however, those implementing computer-assisted communication systems would be wise to proceed with caution.

Group Decision Support Systems

group decision support systems (GDSS)

Interactive computer-based systems that combine communication, computer, and decision technologies to improve the effectiveness of group problem-solving meetings.

Another approach to using technology to improve the effectiveness of decisions that has received attention in recent years is known as **group decision support systems (GDSS)**. These are interactive computer-based systems that combine communication, computer, and decision technologies to improve the effectiveness of group problem-solving meetings. They often involve having people type their ideas into a computer program and discuss these ideas anonymously with others in chat rooms. A record of these discussions is then left for all to examine as needed. Their underlying rationale is straightforward: The quality of group decisions stands to be improved insofar as this process removes some of the impediments to decision making. In this sense, just as decision support systems, described earlier (see p. 382), can be used to identify effective ways of making decisions, so too can group decision support systems.

One of the reasons why face-to-face groups sometimes make poor decisions is that group members do not always share information they have available to them that might help the group. As we discussed earlier, in connection with the phenomenon of groupthink, this may occur because people sometimes censor unpopular ideas voluntarily, even if these are good ideas that can improve the quality of group decisions. This is where GDSS can be useful. Groups using GDSS may avoid this problem insofar as the anonymous recording of ideas makes people less reluctant to share them and makes it easier than ever to have access to them. In this manner, some of the most potent impediments to group decision quality can be eliminated. Recent research has found that this is, in fact, exactly what happens in groups using GDSS. An experiment was conducted comparing the effectiveness of groups of managers asked to solve simulated management problems in face-to-face groups and using GDSS.[111] As expected, the results showed that compared to face-to-face groups, groups using GDSS not only shared considerably more information, but they also made far better decisions as a result.

For now, it seems that group decision support systems appear to be quite effective. However, because they are very new, we don't yet know all the conditions under which they will continue to be successful. As OB researchers conduct further research on this topic, we surely will learn more about this promising technique in the future.

Summary and Review of Learning Objectives

1. **Identify the steps in the analytical model of decision making and distinguish between the various types of decisions that people make.**
   According to the analytical model of decision making, the making of decisions is a multistep process through which: (1) a problem is identified, (2) solution objectives are defined, (3) a predecision is made (i.e., a decision about how to make a decision), (4) alternatives are generated, (5) these alternatives are evaluated, (6) an alternative is

chosen, (7) that alternative is implemented, and then (8) a follow-up occurs to determine if the problem still exists. Decisions made in organizations can be characterized as being either programmed, routine decisions made according to preexisting guidelines, or nonprogrammed decisions requiring novel and creative solutions. Decisions also differ with respect to the amount of risk involved, ranging from those in which the decision outcomes are relatively certain to those in which the outcomes are highly uncertain. Uncertain situations are expressed as statements of probability based on either objective or subjective information. Decisions also differ with respect to whether they are made by high-level organizational officials (top-down decisions) or by employees themselves (empowered decisions).

2. **Describe different individual decision styles and the various organizational and cultural factors that influence the decision-making process.**

There are individual differences in the way people make decisions. Generally, people demonstrate one of four dominant decision styles: *directive* (preference for simple, clear solutions), *analytical* (willingness to consider complex situations based on ambiguous information), *conceptual* (a humanistic and artistic orientation), or *behavioral* (a concern for the organization). Within organizations, decision quality made may be adversely affected by severe time constraints and by political face-saving pressures. Decisions made in organizations also are affected by the national culture in which the organization exists. For example, Americans are more likely to confront problems as decisions that need to be made, whereas people from Thailand are more likely to accept these problems as they are. Also, whereas Americans make decisions in a highly individualistic way (by looking out for themselves), Asians are more likely to make decisions in a collective manner (by taking into account the group or organization).

3. **Distinguish among three approaches to how decisions are made: the rational-economic model, the administrative model, and image theory.**

The rational-economic model characterizes decision makers as thoroughly searching through perfect information to make an optimal decision. This is a normative approach, in that it describes how decision makers ideally ought to behave to make the best possible decisions. In contrast, the administrative model is a descriptive approach, which describes how decision makers actually behave. It recognizes that limitations imposed by people's ability to process the information needed to make complex decisions (bounded rationality and bounded discretion) restrict decision makers to making satisficing decisions—solutions that are not optimal, but good enough. An alternative approach, image theory, recognizes that decisions are made in an automatic, intuitive fashion. It claims that people will adopt a course of action that best fits their individual principles, current goals, and plans for the future.

4. **Identify the various factors that lead people to make imperfect decisions**

People make imperfect decisions due to cognitive biases. One such bias, framing, refers to the tendency for people to make different decisions based on how a problem is presented. For example, when a problem is presented in a way that emphasizes positive gains to be received, people tend to make conservative, risk-averse, decisions, whereas when the same problem is presented in a way that emphasizes potential losses to be suffered, people tend to make riskier decisions. Simple rules of thumb, known as heuristics, also may bias decisions. For example, according to the availability heuristic, people base their judgments on information readily available to them, and according to the representativeness heuristic, people are perceived in stereotypical ways if they appear to be representatives of the categories to which they belong. People also are biased toward implicit favorites, alternatives they prefer in advance of considering all the options. Other alternatives, confirmation candidates, are considered for purposes of convincing oneself that one's implicit favorite is the best alternative. Decisions also are biased because of the tendency to believe that we were far better at judging past events than we actually were (known as the hindsight bias) and the tendency for people to give too little credit to others when things are going poorly and too much credit when things are going well (known as the person sensitivity bias). Finally, decisions are biased insofar as people tend to escalate commitment to unsuccessful courses of action because they have sunk costs invested in them. This occurs in large part because people need to justify their previous actions and wish to avoid having to admit that their initial decision was a mistake.

5. **Compare the conditions under which groups make superior decisions than individuals and when individuals make superior decisions than groups.**
   Groups make superior decisions than individuals when these are composed of a heterogeneous mix of experts who possess complementary skills. However, groups may not be any better than the best member of the group when performing a task that has a simple, verifiable answer. Individuals make superior decisions than face-to-face brainstorming groups on creative problems. However, when brainstorming is done electronically—that is, by using computer terminals to send messages—the quality of decisions tend to improve.

6. **Describe various traditional techniques and high-tech techniques that can be used to enhance the quality of individual decisions and group decisions.**
   Decision quality may be enhanced in several different ways. First, the quality of individual decisions has been shown to improve following individual training in problem-solving skills. Training in ethics also can help people make more ethical decisions. Group decisions may be improved in three ways. First, in the Delphi technique, the judgments of experts are systematically gathered and used to form a single joint decision. Second, in the nominal group technique group meetings are structured so as to elicit and evaluate systematically the opinions of all members. Third, in the stepladder technique new individuals are added to decision-making groups one at a time, requiring the presentation and discussion of new ideas. Contemporary techniques also employ the use of computers as aids in decision making. One of these is known as electronic meeting systems. These are computer networks that bring individuals from different locations together for a meeting via telephone or satellite transmissions, either on television monitors, or via shared space on a computer screen. Another computer-based approach is computer-assisted communication—the sharing of information, such as text messages and data relevant to the decision, over computer networks. Finally, computers have been used to facilitate decision making by way of group decision support systems. These are interactive computer-based systems that combine communication, computer, and decision technologies to improve the effectiveness of group problem-solving meetings.

Points to Ponder

Questions for Review

1. What are the general steps in the decision-making process, and how can the different types of organizational decisions be characterized?
2. How do individual decision style, group influences, and organizational influences influence decision-making in organizations?
3. What are the major differences between the rational-economic model, the administrative model, and the image theory approach to individual decision making?
4. How do each of the following factors contribute to the imperfect nature of decisions: framing effects, reliance on heuristics, decision biases, and the tendency to escalate commitment to a losing course of action?
5. When it comes to making decisions, under what conditions are individuals superior to groups and under what conditions are groups superior to individuals?
6. What traditional techniques and computer-based techniques can be used to improve the quality of decisions made by groups or individuals?

Experiential Questions

1. Think of any decision you recently made. Would you characterize it as programmed or nonprogrammed? Highly certain or highly uncertain? Top-down or empowered? Explain your answers.

2. Identify ways in which various decisions you have made were biased by framing, heuristics, the use of implicit favorites, and the escalation of commitment.
3. Think of various decision-making groups in which you may have participated over the years. Do you think that groupthink was involved in these situations? What signs were evident?

Questions to Analyze

1. Imagine that you are a manager facing the problem of not attracting enough high-quality personnel to your organization. Would you attempt to solve this problem alone or by committee? Explain your reasoning.
2. Suppose you were on a committee charged with making an important decision, and that committee was composed of people from various nations. How do you think this might make a difference in the way the group operates?
3. Argue pro or con: "All people make decisions in the same manner."

Experiencing OB

Individual Exercise

What Is Your Personal Decision Style?

As you read about the various personal decision styles, did you put yourself into any one of the categories? To get a feel for what the *Decision-Style Inventory* reveals about your personal decision style, complete this exercise. It is based on questions similar to those appearing in the actual instrument (Rowe, Boulgaides, & McGrath, 1984; see Note 31).

Directions

For each of the following questions, select the one alternative that best describes how you see yourself in your typical work situation.

1. When performing my job, I usually look for:
   a. practical results
   b. the best solutions to problems
   c. new ideas or approaches
   d. pleasant working conditions
2. When faced with a problem, I usually:
   a. use approaches that have worked in the past
   b. analyze it carefully
   c. try to find a creative approach
   d. rely on my feelings
3. When making plans, I usually emphasize:
   a. the problems I currently face
   b. attaining objectives
   c. future goals
   d. developing my career
4. The kind of information I usually prefer to use is:
   a. specific facts
   b. complete and accurate data
   c. broad information covering many options
   d. data that is limited and simple to understand
5. Whenever I am uncertain about what to do, I:
   a. rely on my intuition
   b. look for facts
   c. try to find a compromise
   d. wait, and decide later
6. The people with whom I work best are usually:
   a. ambitious and full of energy
   b. self-confident

c. open-minded

d. trusting and polite

7. The decisions I make are usually:

a. direct and realistic

b. abstract or systematic

c. broad and flexible

d. sensitive to others' needs

Scoring

1. For each *a* you select, give yourself a point in the *directive* category.
2. For each *b* you select, give yourself a point in the *analytical* category.
3. For each *c* you select, give yourself a point in the *conceptual* category.
4. For each *d* you select, give yourself a point in the *behavioral* category.

The points reflect the relative strength of your preferences for each decision style.

Questions for Discussion

1. What style did the test reveal that you have? How did this compare to the style you thought you had before you took the test?
2. Based on the descriptions of the personal decision styles in the text, were you able to guess in advance which test items were indicative of which styles?
3. What additional items may be added to the test to assess each style?

Group Exercise

Running a Nominal Group: Try It Yourself

A great deal can be learned about nominal groups by running one—or, at least, participating in one—yourself. Doing so will not only help illustrate the procedure, but demonstrate how effectively it works.

Directions

1. Select a topic suitable for discussion in a nominal group composed of students in your class. It should be a topic that is narrowly defined and on which people have many different opinions (these work best in nominal groups). Some possible examples include:

   ■ What should your school's student leaders be doing for you?
   ■ What can be done to improve the quality of instruction in your institution?
   ■ What can be done to improve the quality of jobs your school's students receive when graduating?

2. Divide the class into groups of approximately 10. Arrange each group in a circle, or around a table, if possible. In each group, select one person to serve as the group facilitator.
3. Following the steps outlined in Figure 10.18 (p. 412), facilitators should guide their groups in discussions regarding the focal question identified in step 1, above. Allow approximately 45 minutes to 1 hour to complete this process.
4. If time allows, select a different focal question and a different group leader, and repeat the procedure.

Questions for Discussion

1. Collectively, how did the group answer the question? Do you believe that this answer accurately reflected the feelings of the group?
2. How did the various groups' answers compare? Were they similar or different? Why?
3. What were the major problems, if any, associated with the nominal group experience? For example, were there any group members who were reluctant to wait their turns before speaking up?
4. How do you think your group experiences would have differed had you used a totally unstructured, traditional face-to-face group instead of a nominal group?

Practicing OB

The Intrusive Manager

A large product-distribution company is having a problem during its group meetings: One department manager is constantly disrupting the meetings while trying to get his ideas across. He has so consistently intimidated his coworkers that they are reluctant to speak up. As a result of his intrusiveness, people's good ideas are not coming across.

1. Explain what steps might be taken to avoid this problem.
2. What is your rationale for this advice?
3. What are the advantages and disadvantages of the tactic you identify?

CASE IN POINT

Helping the Broncos Buck the Odds

Each year about 1,000 incredibly strong and talented athletes vie for a handful of positions on 32 National Football League (NFL) teams. In one of these, the Denver Broncos, determining which college athletes to select as candidates for its professional team is a responsibility that falls heavily on the shoulders of Jim Goodman, that team's director of college recruiting. In this capacity, Goodman spends 363 days per year gathering information used to make vitally important selection decisions over several 15-minute chunks of time during the other two days—the NFL's annual player draft. One weekend each April, team executives and coaches look to Goodman for his input on not only which players are most likely to succeed in the pro ranks, but also which ones are best equipped to meet the Broncos' particular needs that year.

Most of Goodman's time is spent visiting colleges and universities in search of football players who are good enough to be selected for the "Big Show" (slang for the National Football League). Although being away from home is what Goodman finds the hardest part of his job, he enjoys being around college coaches (a job he had for 20 years before going into the NFL). Because of his longtime coaching experience at various Southern schools, Goodman spends most of his observation time there, leaving other regions to his assistants, who report their findings to him. Specifically, each of the eight members of the Broncos recruiting staff is responsible for schools in a particular section of the country. This specialization makes it possible for Goodman's crew to keep tabs on talented players from smaller schools, who otherwise might not get the attention of their more visible cohorts at major universities.

Whether the athlete's school is large or small, the key to Goodman's success lies in collecting all pertinent information about players in a massive database so that it can be called up when Broncos officials need to make decisions about which prospects to select as their draft choices. With this in mind, Goodman spends most of his time on the road closely watching players, both during games and in practice sessions—live from the sidelines when he can, but at least on DVD video. Goodman also talks to coaches and trainers, getting their slant on each athlete's strengths and weaknesses. Along with his own impressions, this information gets fed into the computer for use when making selection decisions on—and even before—draft weekend.

As do his counterparts at the other NFL teams, Goodman routinely gathers detailed information on players' physical qualities, such as their height, weight, speed, percentage of body fat, and height of vertical leap. This is not all, however. Goodman also pays close attention to personal qualities and intangible characteristics, such as a player's "football intelligence," his work ethic, competitiveness, and his workout habits during the off-season.

Acknowledging that such a system is only as good as the data entered into it, Goodman and his staff spend a great deal of time entering information about players into notebook computers. And, because, he can't run up and down the sidelines while typing notes into his computer, Goodman sometimes takes notes on paper or simply speaks his impressions into a microcassette recorder. Then, either while on the plane or back at the hotel, he enters all of this information into his trusty notebook computer and transmits it to the main computer on his desktop back at Denver's Invesco Field at Mile High. No matter how tired he gets and how grueling his schedule, Goodman knows that the success of his team begins with helping head coach Mike Shanahan make the best possible selection decisions—a responsibility that all begins with him.

Questions for Discussion

1. As an individual who is potentially overwhelmed by statistics and observations about individual players, how do you think Goodman's own decision processes may be biased?
2. Goodman collects lots of objective information, but decisions also are made on subjective feelings as well (e.g., assessments of "football intelligence"). In what ways do you think that the quality of the decisions about drafting players is helped or hindered by the use of such subjective information?
3. In what ways do you think that escalation of commitment may be involved in the decisions Goodman makes for the Broncos?

Chapter 11

CONFLICT, COOPERATION, TRUST, AND DEVIANCE: INTERPERSONAL BEHAVIOR AT WORK

Chapter Outline

Psychological Contracts and Trust: Building Blocks of Working Relationships

Organizational Citizenship Behavior: Going Above and Beyond Formal Job Requirements

Cooperation: Providing Mutual Assistance

Conflict: The Inevitable Result of Incompatible Interests

Deviant Organizational Behavior

Special Sections

OB **In a Diverse World**

Psychological Contracts in China and the U.S: Are They the Same?

How to Do It

Promoting the Occurrence of OCB

OB **Making Sense Out of Common Sense**

The Positive Side of Conflict

1. Describe three types of psychological contracts and the two basic kinds of trust that play a role in work relationships.

2. Describe organizational citizenship behavior and ways in which it may be encouraged.

3. Identify ways in which cooperation can be promoted in the workplace.

4. Describe the causes and effects of conflict in organizations along with techniques that can be used to manage conflict in organizations.

5. Explain why deviant organizational behavior can produce positive as well as negative effects.

6. Describe the major forms of workplace deviance, both constructive and destructive.

PREVIEW CASE

Southwest Airlines: Employee Relations Back on Time

For many years, Southwest Airlines was famous for having good relations between employees and management. The company and its employees saw eye-to-eye and agreements about working conditions and pay were met readily. Recently, though, the situation soured considerably. Negotiations regarding labor practices between the company and its employees hit the skids. In 2002 and 2003 talks between the two sides ground to a painful halt. Even worse, the tone of the negotiations became so angry and bitter that for the first time in the company's history union leaders issued strong verbal attacks against top management, including Southwest's then-CEO, James F. Parker.

Employees accused Parker of being inflexible and unreasonable, and expressed strong concerns about the quality of his leadership. Ultimately, the situation became so tense that Parker removed himself from the negotiations and asked Southwest's former CEO, Herbert D. Kelleher, to come out of retirement just to resolve the bitter dispute. Fortunately, he succeeded quickly, resolving in less than eight weeks a dispute that had lasted over two years.

For Parker, this failure on his part was the last straw, leading him to resign in mid-2004. In his resignation speech, he stated that he had never found the job to be fun and that the company deserved a leader who could take it to the next level.

Today, Kelleher remains sensitive to his company's relations with its employees. Addressing an audience at Stanford Business School in April 2006, Kelleher said, "We've never treated them [employees] as adversaries. We've always treated them as partners, because if that canoe goes down, we're all going down with it." He said Southwest makes a point of including union leaders in company functions, and "if they have an issue, we take care of it as quickly as we possibly can." During labor negotiations, "We have fights, but not vendettas. We yell, we throw things, we get a contract and then it's behind us. It's not like the Hatfields and McCoys, feuding and still killing each other after generations for reasons they don't remember." And, in today's highly competitive airline business, this surely gives Southwest an edge up on the other carriers.

Given Herb Kelleher's statement as Southwest's executive chairman of the board, it's clear that he's striving to ensure that the company's few years of bad blood with employees soon will be nothing more than a blip on the its otherwise happy radar screen of relations with employees. Today, although CEO Gary Kelly and President Colleen Barrett remain committed to Kelleher's philosophy, all recognize that making this happen will take some work. Relationships between sides that are cooperative and trusting are what they're after, and they're committed to avoiding ones that, unfortunately, are more typical in the airline business, mistrustful and even hostile relationships.[1]

This situation at Southwest illustrates the kind of complex dynamics that occur all the time among people in organizations, and that are of major importance in the field of organizational behavior. Although you may not be involved in multimillion-dollar business deals with other parties, we all have been involved in situations in which people work at cross-purposes, or even go out of their way to purposely harm one another. It is these processes of working with others and against them that is the focus of this chapter on various forms of **interpersonal behavior** at work. We will summarize a wide array of interpersonal behaviors that occur in the workplace and describe how they influence the way people work and how they feel about their jobs and organizations.

Figure 11.1 identifies the major forms of interpersonal behavior in the workplace reviewed in this chapter. This diagram organizes interpersonal behaviors along a continuum ranging from those that involve working with others, shown on the left, to those involving working against others, shown on the right. This forms a useful roadmap of how we will proceed in this chapter. Beginning on the left, we first will examine **prosocial behavior**—the tendency for people to help others on the job, sometimes even when there doesn't appear to be anything in it for them.

Following this, we will discuss situations in which people help each other and receive help from them—that is, the tendency to *cooperate.* In the world of business, as you know, people and entire companies don't always work with each other; they also *compete* against each other—that is, as one tries to win, it forces the other to lose. Under such circumstances, it is not unusual for *conflict* to emerge, breeding ill-will. And, when taken to the extreme, this results in *deviant* behavior—extreme acts such as stealing from the company or even harming another person.

Before examining these various forms of behavior, though, we consider two processes that play a role in all interpersonal relationships: developing *psychological constructs* and building *trust.* These processes are important because they often affect the extent to which people choose either to work with or against one another.

interpersonal behavior
A variety of behaviors involving the ways in which people work with and against one another.

prosocial behavior
Acts that benefit others.

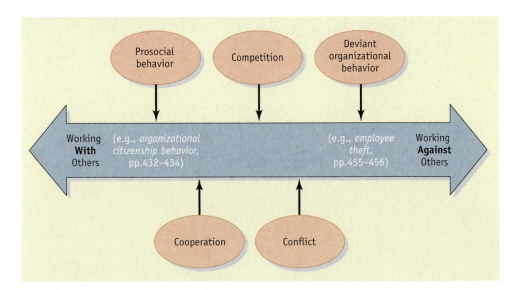

FIGURE 11.1

Varieties of Interpersonal Behavior

The five types of interpersonal behavior observed in organizations and presented in this chapter can be summarized as falling along a continuum ranging from those involving working with other people to those involving working against them.

Psychological Contracts and Trust: Building Blocks of Working Relationships

Interpersonal relationships are complex, to say the least. They range in nature from ones that are relatively short-term and have little or no emotional ties between the persons involved (e.g., interactions between temporary employees and regular employees; customers and salespersons at a used car lot), to ones that are long-term and involve powerful emotional bonds (e.g., co-founders of a new venture; employees who have worked closely together for many years). In a sense, then, all interpersonal relationships are unique. Yet, despite this fact, there are basic themes or building-blocks that play a role in most, if not all of them. Among these, two that are especially important are *psychological contracts* and *trust.*

Psychological Contracts: Our Expectations of Others

Whenever people enter into relationships with each other, they quickly develop expectations about what these relationships will be like—what each side is expected to do and provide. For instance, if you leave a phone message for a friend, you expect her to return your call. If you report for work on a regular basis and do a good job, you certainly expect to be paid at the end of the pay period. These examples illustrate what is known as the **psychological contract**—a person's perceptions and expectations about the mutual obligations in an employment relationship (or, for that matter, any other relationship).[2]

psychological contract
A person's beliefs about what is expected of another in a relationship.

Although psychological contracts generally are not written down on paper, they guide what we expect of others in much the same way. However, unlike legal contracts, in which the terms are made explicit, psychological contracts are not written down and exist primarily in the beliefs and perceptions of the persons involved. Not surprisingly, there may well be differences of opinion regarding psychological contracts: What one person expects may not be exactly what another expects. As you know from experience, such disagreements can often lead to interpersonal friction (see Figure 11.2).

Types of Psychological Contracts. Although psychological contracts can vary in many ways and are, in a sense, unique to each working relationship, most can be described in terms of three basic dimensions.[3] First, psychological contracts vary with respect to *time frame*—how long they are expected to last. Temporary employees anticipate only a short-term relationship with their employers, while employees in large Japanese and European companies have, until recently, expected that once they are hired, they are there for life or at least the long term.

Second, psychological contracts vary in terms of *performance requirements*—how close the relationship is between performance demands (what employees are expected to do) and the rewards they receive.[4] For some jobs, pay is related directly to output, while for others, this relationship is less clear-cut, and much more than pay is involved: The relationship is *not* defined purely in economic terms (e.g., employees expect emotional and social support from their companies as well as pay). Together, these two dimensions point to the existence of three basic kinds of psychological contracts: *transactional, relational,* and *balanced.*[5]

Transactional contracts are informal expectations between individuals whose relationships are exclusively economic in nature and of relatively brief duration. Suppose, for example, that you are a student working at a summer job. You have been hired to take over for regular employees while they are on vacation. You know that your relationship with your employer is short-term and that it is based on a clearly defined set of economic terms. You go to work each day as scheduled, you do your job, you get your paycheck, and at the end of the season, it's over—and you go back to school.[6]

By contrast, **relational contracts** are informal expectations between individuals whose relationships are close and personal in nature. They are not tied to specific pay or other rewards and generally are longer-term in nature. For example, if you have worked in the same company for the same boss for more than 20 years, chances are good that your relationship is based not simply on an exchange of specific benefits and contributions that are largely economic in nature; rather, other factors, such as friendship, loyalty, and years of shared experiences matter, too. You expect that relationship to last well into the future, and you feel a sense of commitment to your boss, your job, and your company that no temporary employees, working under transactional psychological contracts, can share.

A third type of psychological contract combines the open-ended, long-term features of relational psychological contracts with the well-specified reward-performance contingencies of transactional contracts. Such **balanced contracts**, as they are known, are informal expectations between people that result in each side receiving some benefit from the other.[7] As an example, consider an individual who wants to start her own company. She may spend several years working in a large organization because this helps her develop the needed skills and contacts for founding a new venture. She is committed to staying in this company until she acquires these skills and contacts (perhaps for several years), and forms close relationships with the people who are helping her toward her goal. Clearly, then, she is exchanging her time, effort, and talent for pay and these other, less tangible benefits. The term "balanced contracts" reflects the fact that each side receives benefits from the arrangement between them. For an overview of the three types of psychological contracts, see Figure 11.3.

Relations between employees and management in many companies fit under the heading of balanced relationships. For instance, in response to growing pressure from competitors, DaimlerChrysler has sought concessions from its German employees with respect to wages and working hours.[8] Although these may sound like straightforward economic issues, the situation is complicated by the fact that representatives of labor sit on the company's board of directors and long have been involved in shaping DaimlerChrysler's policies. Further, German employees expect long-term employment even in changing economic times, and long have believed that their health and well-being should be just as important to the company as profits. As a result, when employees accepted wage cuts and an increase in working hours for at least some employees, Daimler Chrysler reciprocated by cutting the salaries of top executive by 10% and agreed to trim the pay of 3,000 lower-level managers, too. In this way, the company acknowledged the fact that more was stake than purely economic issues: It was also important to demonstrate that the employees, too, are "part of the team." Clearly, the psychological contract between DaimlerChrysler and its employees goes well beyond ones that are merely transactional in nature.

Effects of Psychological Contracts. As you might expect, the three different kinds of psychological contracts have contrasting effects both for individuals and organizations. For instance, relational and balanced contracts tend to encourage individuals to go beyond the basic requirements of their jobs, helping others or their companies on a voluntary basis (we will describe this kind of behavior, known as *organizational citizenship behavior,* in the next major section of this chapter).[9]

---

transactional contract
A variety of psychological contract in which the parties have a brief and narrowly defined relationship that is primarily economic in focus.

relational contract
A variety of psychological contract in which the parties have a long-term and widely defined relationship with a vast focus.

balanced contracts
Psychological contracts that combine the open-ended, long-term features of relational psychological contracts with the well-specified reward-performance contingencies of transactional contracts.

FIGURE 11.3

Three Kinds of Psychological Contracts: A Summary

Psychological contracts may be considered either transactional, relational, or balanced. The key characteristics of transactional and relational contracts are shown at opposite ends of each continuum. Balanced contracts, however, combine various aspects of each, typically at the point indicated by "X" on each dimension.

Source: Based on suggestions by Rousseau, 2004; see Note 2.

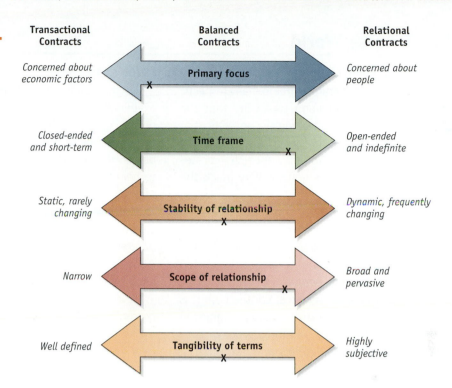

Similarly, individuals with certain personal characteristics are more likely to form relational contracts, while others are more likely to form transactional ones. Specifically, people who are low in emotional stability (see Chapters 4 and 5) and who also are highly sensitive to being treated fairly (see Chapter 2) are inclined to form transactional contracts, whereas those who are high in conscientiousness and self-esteem are inclined to form longer-term relational contracts.[10] Can you see why? Persons low in emotional stability do not like long-term commitments—ones that demand high levels of social skills and trust.[11] On the other hand, persons high in conscientiousness and in self-esteem are often more concerned with doing a good job and with opportunities for growth and achievement than with purely economic benefits, especially short-term ones. So they tend to prefer—and to develop—relational contracts.

In sum, although psychological contracts aren't written on paper, they play an important role in many aspects of organizational behavior, including the extent to which individuals work with or against each other—the main theme of this chapter. (Do these three kinds of psychological contracts exist around the world? For a discussion of this issue, please see the *OB in a Diverse World* section on p. 430.)

Trust in Working Relationships

One thing that makes relationships based on transactional contracts so different from those based on relational contracts is the degree to which the parties *trust* each other. By **trust,** we are referring to a person's degree of confidence in the words and actions of another.[12] Suppose, for example, that your supervisor, the local sales manager, will be talking to his boss, the district sales manager, about getting you transferred to a desirable new territory. You are counting on your boss to come through for you because he says he will. To the extent you believe that he will do what he promises—make a strong case on your behalf— you trust him. However, if you believe that his recommendation will not be too enthusiastic, or that he will not recommend you at all, you will trust him less; you do not believe that he will do what he says he will do.

trust
A person's degree of confidence in the words and actions of another.

calculus-based trust
A form of trust based on deterrence; whenever people believe that another will behave as promised out of fear of getting punished for doing otherwise.

Calculus-Based Trust. The concept of trust is a bit more complex than you might expect. In fact, there appear to be two distinct kinds of trust (see Figure 11.4). The first is known as **calculus-based trust,** a kind of trust based on deterrence.[13] Calculus-based trust

OB In a Diverse World

Psychological Contracts in China and the U.S: Are They the Same?

Because cultures differ in many respects, it's an interesting possibility that the types of psychological contracts that people use in various nations reflect these differences. Interestingly, though, research indicates that psychological contracts are actually very much the same across various cultures.[14]

This has been shown in a study of psychological contracts in China.[15] The researchers asked Chinese employees to complete a scale designed to measure the types of psychological contracts they use. In the United States, it has been clear that people use transactional, relational, and balanced psychological contracts, but is this also the case in China? The study's results suggested that in China, just as in the U.S., all three types of contracts are used. Just like their American counterparts, Chinese employees are aware of the nature of their relationships with their employers and understand that these can vary in terms of time frame (length of duration) and performance requirements (strictly pay-for-specific performance or a much broader array of mutual obligations).

In the same research project, the researchers also examined the extent to which people were interested in helping others in their organizations and the types of relationships they had with them. Employees in relational or balanced relationships with their employers were inclined to help their colleagues and the organization itself in an effort to strengthen their relationships with their supervisors. However, employees whose relationships with their employers were transactional in nature also helped, but for different reasons—as a means of demonstrating respect. Again, these findings matched those found among employees in the United States.

Overall, this research suggests that the basic nature of psychological contracts is indeed the same in the U.S. and China, despite their very different cultures. However, it was clear from the research that the specific nature of these contracts and the forms they took were influenced by cultural factors to some degree. As is often the case, then, basic processes of organizational behavior are much the same around the world, but they should be viewed through the lens of specific cultures to obtain an accurate understanding of the specific forms they take in different countries.

---

exists whenever people believe that another person will behave as they promise out of fear of getting punished for doing otherwise. We trust our employers to contribute their share to our Social Security accounts because they risk fines and penalties if they fail to do so. Similarly, if your company hires a catering firm to provide the food for an important social function, you trust this business to show up with the items you have ordered; if they fail to do this, you won't pay them the balance due and may warn others not to hire them.

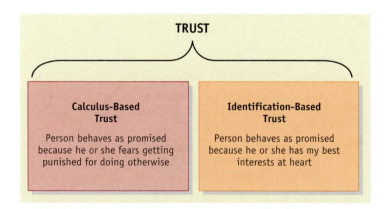

FIGURE 11.4

Two Major Forms of Trust: A Comparison

When we are confident in another's words and actions, we trust that individual. That trust can be based on the two major considerations summarized here. *Calculus-based trust* is based on deterrence, whereas *identification-based trust* is based on accepting and understanding the other party.

Calculus-based trust is characteristic of many business relationships—ones based on transactional contracts, in which each side knows what it is expected to deliver. Although calculus-based trust may not sound like the kind you would like others to have in you, it is essential for most businesses: It is the basis for a good reputation, and that, as everyone knows, often is the foundation for success.

identification-based trust
A form of trust based on accepting the wants and desires of another person.

Indentification-Based Trust. A second kind of trust, known as **identification-based trust**, is based on accepting and understanding another person's wants and desires. Identification-based trust occurs when people know and understand each other so well that they are willing to allow that individual to act on their behalf. The example we described earlier in which you allow your boss to discuss your transfer with a higher-ranking official illustrates identification-based trust.

Another example is provided by Myomatrix, Inc. a start-up biotech company in New York. The company was founded by two partners from very different backgrounds—one is an M.D. practicing in the area of cardiology, and the other holds a Ph.D. and an MBA, and is a university professor in the field of bioengineering. After meeting socially, they developed a close personal relationship and they grew to know and respect each other. The result? When they founded Myomatrix, both got the right to sign checks on the company's account; they trusted each other to do what was good for their company and to spend wisely and well. The two partners continue to work together very closely (e.g., they both participate in all negotiations), and this working relationship definitely rests on identification-based trust.

Now, look at the cartoon in Figure 11.5. If the people shown actually *do* hand blank checks to Dogbert, what kind of trust will they be showing? We think it is more an illustration of identification-based than calculus-based trust. After all, once Dogbert has the checks, he can cash them with little fear of punishment because the people involved gave them to him voluntarily. On the other hand, the fact they are willing to give him blank checks indicates that they believe he will not do anything harmful to them. This involves identification-based trust. In this case, though it may *not* be well-founded! Ordinarily, identification-based trust occurs in close, long-term relationships—ones based on relational contracts instead of the kind of short-term relationship shown here.

How Does Trust Develop? What factors influence the development of trust? Although many play a role, two are especially important. First, as you may already know from experience, some people tend to be more trusting than others—there are consistent individual differences in this respect (see Chapter 4). You probably have met people at both ends of this continuum—ones who are cynical and mistrusting, and others who seem to trust everyone they meet, as least initially. As we saw in Chapter 4, trust is closely related to one of the Big Five dimensions of personality, *agreeableness*.[16]

FIGURE 11.5

Trust: How Not to Use It!

Dogbert is clearly trying to use trust for his own benefit. This is not the way trust operates in organizations, and we definitely do not recommend this approach!

Source: DILBERT © Scott Adams/Dist. by United Features Syndicate, Inc.

Second, some people develop reputations for being trustworthy or not trustworthy. Just as reputations are important for businesses, they are very important for individuals, too. If someone warns you about another person, saying something like "Don't trust him," you are likely to take it seriously and to treat this person with caution. You will be on the lookout for violations of any agreement you make with this person, or for ulterior motives they may have for being nice to you. Who knows . . . perhaps they are high in Machiavellianism, an unsavory aspect of personality we discussed in Chapter 4. On the other hand, if several people tell you that another person is one you can trust, you may approach her or him in a very different way, assuming that this person will honor commitments—legal or psychological.

How to Promote Trust in Working Relationships. Our comments so far suggest that you should do everything in your power to develop a reputation for being trustworthy. The success of your working relationships, and your career, may depend on it. But how, specifically, can we demonstrate to others that we are to be trusted? Clearly, the key is to not let them down—to keep our word and honor our commitments. Beyond this, there are specific things you can do to strengthen others' perceptions that you are trustworthy. Here are some of the most useful.

- *Always meet deadlines.* If you promise to get something done on time, it is essential to meet that deadline. Although one or two incidents of lateness may be overlooked, people who are chronically late in meeting deadlines rapidly gain a reputation for being untrustworthy. And, when others believe that you will not meet important deadlines, they are likely to skip you when it comes to getting any important, career-building assignments.
- *Follow through as promised.* It is not only important to do things on time, but to perform those tasks in the manner in which others expect them to be done. If you do not—for instance, if you provide only part of what others expect you to provide— you may acquire a reputation for being untrustworthy, and that can be very damaging to your career.
- *Spend time sharing personal values and goals.* Identification-based trust requires a keen understanding and appreciation of another person. Gaining this understanding requires spending time together discussing common interests, common objectives, and so on. Perhaps this is why James F. Parker (former CEO of Southwest Airlines) was not able to negotiate an agreement with the company's unions, while Herbert Kelleher was, in fact, able to do so: Employees *trusted* Kelleher and believed he had their best interests at heart, but they did not feel the same way about Parker. To the extent this was true—and observers close to this situation report that it was—it is not at all surprising that Parker decided to resign. He understood clearly that trust, once gone, is hard to restore, and so he did the best thing he could do—leave!

Organizational Citizenship Behavior: Going Above and Beyond Formal Job Requirements

Imagine the following scene. It's coming up on 5:00 P.M. and you're wrapping up your work for the day. You're anxiously looking forward to getting home and relaxing. While this is going on, the scene is quite different at the next cubicle. One of your colleagues has been working feverishly to complete an important report, but appears to have hit a snag. She now has little hope of getting the report on the boss's desk before he leaves for the day—that is, without your help. Pitching in to help your colleague is something you don't have to do. After all, there's nothing in your formal job description that makes it necessary for you to do so. What's more, you're quite weary after your own long day's work. However, when you see the bind your colleague is in, you put aside your own feelings and offer to stay and help her out.

In this case, although you're probably not going to win any medals for your generosity, you are being helpful, and you have gone "above and beyond the call of duty." Actions

organizational citizenship behavior (OCB)

An informal form of behavior in which people go beyond what is formally expected of them to contribute to the well-being of their organization and those in it.

OCB-I

Acts of organizational citizenship directed at other individuals in the workplace (i.e., helping coworkers in ways that go beyond what is expected).

OCB-O

Acts of organizational citizenship directed at the organization itself (i.e., helping the company in ways that go beyond what is expected).

such as these, which exceed the formal requirements of one's job, are known as **organizational citizenship behavior** (or **OCB,** for short).[17] It is easy to imagine how such behaviors, although informal and sometimes minor in nature, play a very important role when it comes to the smooth functioning of organizations.

Forms of OCB

The example we just gave of volunteering to help one of your coworkers is just one of five different forms that OCB can take. For a summary of all five, including examples of each, see Table 11.1.

If you look at the examples in Table 11.1, it becomes apparent that organizational citizenship behavior can be directed both at an *individual* (in which case it is referred to as **OCB-I**) and at the *organization* itself (in which case it is referred to as **OCB-O**).[18] Some examples of OCB-O include the following:

- Speaking favorably about the organization to outsiders
- Being receptive to new ideas
- Being tolerant to temporary inconveniences without complaining
- Offering ideas to improve the functioning of the organization
- Expressing loyalty toward the organization

Some examples of OCB-I include the following:

- Doing a favor for someone
- Assisting a coworker with a personal problem
- Bringing in food to share with others
- Collecting money for flowers for sick coworkers or for funerals
- Sending birthday greetings to others in the office

Why Does OCB Occur?

As you know, people sometimes are selfish and do not engage in OCB. What, then, lies behind the tendency to be a good organizational citizen? Although there are several factors involved, evidence strongly suggests that people's beliefs that they are being treated fairly by their organization (especially their immediate supervisors) is a critical factor. The more people believe they are treated fairly by the organization, the more they trust its management, and the more willing they are to go the extra mile to help out when needed.[19] By contrast,

TABLE 11.1 Organizational Citizenship Behavior: Specific Forms and Examples

Organizational citizenship behavior (OCB) can take many different forms, most of which fall into the five major categories shown here.

Form of OCB	Examples
Altrusim	■ Helping a coworker with a project
	■ Switching vacation dates with another person
	■ Volunteering
Conscientiousness	■ Never missing a day of work
	■ Coming to work early if needed
	■ Not spending time on personal calls
Civic virtue	■ Attending voluntary meetings and functions
	■ Reading memos; keeping up with new information
Sportsmanship	■ Making do without complaint ("Grin and bear it!")
	■ Not finding fault with the organization
Courtesy	■ "Turning the other cheek" to avoid problems
	■ Not "blowing up" when provoked

those who feel that their organizations are taking advantage of them are untrusting and not at all likely to engage in OCB.

OCB also occurs for other reasons. For example, OCB tends to occur at a high level when employees hold positive attitudes toward their organizations.[20] OCB also is likely to occur when people hold good relationships with their supervisors.[21] It's interesting to note that not everyone is equally predisposed to engage in OCB. Personality characteristics also are linked to OCB. Specifically, individuals who are highly conscientious (see Chapter 4) and who are highly empathic (i.e., those who are inclined to take others' perspective and to share their feelings and reactions) are inclined to engage in OCB.[22] This isn't too surprising, of course, since such individuals probably would be highly interested in "going the extra mile" to make others feel good.

Does OCB Really Matter?

As you might imagine, the effects of OCB are difficult to assess because OCB is generally not included as part of any standard performance measures that a company gathers about its employees. However, OCB does have important effects on organizational functioning. Specifically, people's willingness to engage in various types of OCB is related to such work-related measures as job satisfaction and organizational commitment, which, as described in Chapter 6, are related to organizational functioning in a number of complex ways.[23]

In addition, being a good organizational citizen can have important effects on recruiting efforts. After all, the more positive statements current employees make about the companies where they are employed, the more effectively those companies will be able to recruit the best new employees.[24] In conclusion, although the effects of OCB may be indirect and difficult to measure, they can be very profound. In view of this, it's important to consider promoting OCB in the workplace. For some useful guidelines in this regard, see the *How to Do It* section on page 435.

Cooperation: Providing Mutual Assistance

That individuals often help others at work is clear; but in fact, another pattern—one in which helping is mutual and both sides benefit—is even more common. This pattern is known as **cooperation** and involves situations in which individuals, groups, or even entire organizations work together to attain shared goals.

Cooperation can be highly beneficial; through it, groups or organizations can often attain goals they could never reach by themselves. Surprisingly, though, cooperation does *not* always develop. Frequently, individuals belonging to a group try to coordinate their efforts, but somehow fail to do so. Even worse, they may perceive their personal interests as incompatible, with the result that instead of working together and coordinating their efforts, they work *against* each other, with each individual, group, or organization attempting to maximize its own outcomes and defeat the others.

Although this is often the required pattern for organizations—each seeks to maximize its own market share and profitability—*competition* also frequently occurs within organizations, in ways that may interfere with their overall performance. A key goal for managers, then, is often that of maximizing cooperation to the extent that this is feasible. In this section, we'll examine the factors that influence the occurrence of cooperation between individuals, and also between entire organizations, in what are known as *interorganizational alliances.*[25]

Cooperation Between Individuals

Given the obvious benefits of cooperation, an interesting question arises: If it is so useful, then why does it sometimes fail to occur? In other words, why do people with similar goals sometimes keep from joining forces? Although there may be many different possibilities, the answer in many situations is simply that cooperation cannot occur because the goals sought by the individuals or groups involved are incompatible—that is, they cannot be shared. For example, two people going after the same job cannot both get it. Likewise, when two companies court the same merger candidate, only one can be victorious. This

cooperation
A pattern of behavior in which assistance is mutual and two or more individuals, groups, or organizations work together toward shared goals for their mutual benefit.

How to Do It

Promoting the Occurrence of OCB

Although many people view OCB as something that comes from within individuals—either they want to help or they do not—in fact, it can be encouraged or discouraged by conditions existing in an organization. Here are some steps managers can take to increase the frequency of OCB in their work groups.

1. *Be a model of helpful behavior.* Helping, it appears, is contagious. This means that once it begins, it tends to increase. Managers can get the ball rolling by being helpful to their subordinates and to their peers. In this way, they become models of helpful behavior and may encourage its occurrence.

2. *Make voluntary functions worth attending.* Why should employees attend voluntary meetings if these are dull and boring? Making meetings interesting and fun, on the other hand, may encourage employees to attend and to show the civic virtue aspect of OCB. For instance, if you are having a voluntary meeting in the morning, be sure to provide coffee and something to eat. There's nothing like food to bring in a crowd!

3. *Demonstrate courtesy.* Courtesy, too, is contagious, so managers always should be sure to demonstrate it in their own behavior. Show respect for employees, treat them with politeness—and the result will be that these aspects of OCB, too, become the norm.

4. *Don't complain!* If managers complain a lot, this sets the tone for similar behavior by employees—and OCB will go right out the window. So even if conditions are not ideal, be a "good sport" and refrain

from complaining. This, too, will increase OCB in your work group.

5. *Demonstrate conscientiousness.* If *you,* as manager, aren't willing to come in early, stay late, and go beyond the requirements of your position, how can you expect your subordinates to do so? So be sure to demonstrate these aspects of OCB clearly and openly. It will encourage your subordinates to do the same.

6. *Treat employees fairly.* Perhaps the single factor that exerts the strongest effects on OCB is perceived fairness: When employees perceive that they are being treated fairly, their willingness to engage in OCB increases. So it is *essential* to ensure that all actions and procedures in an organization lead to this conclusion (see Chapter 2). This may require considerable effort (e.g., to ensure that performance appraisals are conducted fairly), but it is well worthwhile in terms of the significant increases in OCB it will generate.

Although these suggestions may all seem like common sense, they certainly are *not* common practice. Often, managers do not set a very good example for their subordinates where OCB is concerned. They don't show courtesy, complain frequently, "pull rank" on subordinates, and take advantage of their positions through such actions as disappearing for two-hour lunches. Needless to say, these actions have a "chilling" effect on helpfulness by employees: Why should they go beyond the requirements of their jobs if their boss doesn't? So although it may seem very simple, being a model of OCB can also be highly effective. Try it; we're confident the results will be positive.

---

competition
A pattern of behavior in which each person, group, or organization seeks to maximize its own gains, often at the expense of others.

describes a type of behavior known as **competition**—the pattern of behavior in which each person, group, or organization seeks to maximize its own gains, often at the expense of others. (For a comparison between cooperation and competition, see Figure 11.6.) With this background, we now consider some of the factors associated with people's tendencies to cooperate with one another.

Social Dilemmas: Situations in Which Cooperation Could Occur, But Often Doesn't. Another way to think about situations in which cooperation potentially could develop but does not is to view them as ones involving what are known as **social**

social dilemmas
Situations in which each person can increase his or her individual gains by acting in a purely selfish manner, but if others also act selfishly, the outcomes experienced by all are reduced.

dilemmas—situations in which each person can increase his or her individual gains by acting in a purely selfish manner, but if others also act selfishly, the outcomes experienced by all are reduced.[26] As a result, the persons in such situations must deal with **mixed motives**: There are reasons to cooperate (avoid negative outcomes for all), but also reasons to *compete*—to do what is best for oneself, since if only one or a few persons engage in such behavior, they will benefit while the others will not.

FIGURE 11.6

Cooperation Versus Competition: A Comparison

When cooperating with each other, people work together to attain the same goal, which they share. However, when competing against one another, each person works to attain the same goal to the exclusion of the other.

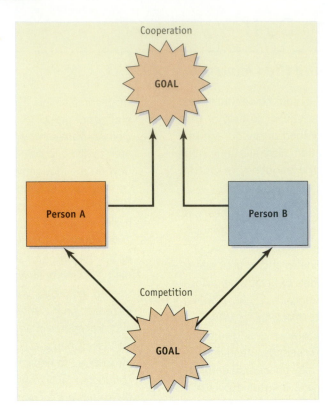

Cooperation

GOAL

Person A

Person B

Competition

GOAL

mixed-motive situations
Contexts in which people are interested in both competition and cooperation, to varying degrees.

A good example of such a situation is provided by players on a professional basketball team. Here, each one has much to gain from cooperating with team members: They will increase their chances of beating their opponents. But they also have much to gain from "showboating"—from increasing their individual records by shooting instead of passing the ball to teammates; this may help them get higher salaries and bonuses (for another example, see Figure 11.7). So again, there is a strong basis for cooperating—*and* strong temptations for each player to maximize his own outcomes.

The Reciprocity Principle. The "Golden Rule" tells us to "do unto others as we would have them do unto us." However, this doesn't describe exactly the way people behave. Instead of treating others as we would like to be treated, most people tend to treat others

FIGURE 11.7

Mixed Motives on the Playing Field

When Chicago White Sox hitter Tadahito Iguchi makes a sacrifice bunt—here, against the Los Angeles Angels in the 2005 American League Championship Series—he is doing something for the good of his team even though it lowers his individual statistics. Although Iguchi was called out, by advancing the base runner from first to second he contributed greatly to the team's success. (The White Sox went on to win the World Series.)

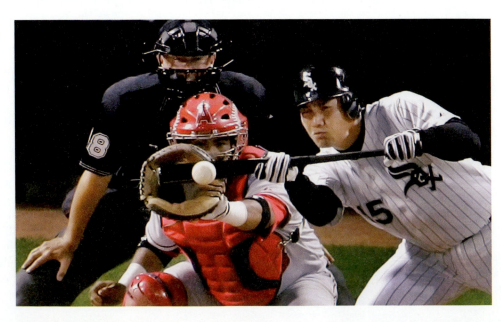

reciprocity
The tendency to treat others as they have treated us, popularly referred to as "the golden rule."

the way those others have treated them in the past. In short, we are more inclined to follow a different principle: "an eye for an eye and a tooth for a tooth." Social scientists refer to this as the principle of **reciprocity**—the tendency to treat others as they have treated us, popularly referred to as "the golden rule."

To a great extent, the principle of reciprocity describes the way people behave when cooperating with others.[27] Because this is so, the key task in establishing cooperation in organizations is straightforward: getting it started. Once individuals or teams have begun to cooperate, the process may be largely self-sustaining. That is, one unit's cooperation encourages cooperation among the others. To encourage cooperation, therefore, managers should attempt to get the process under way.

Personal Orientation. As you know from experience, some people tend to be more cooperative, by nature, than others. In contrast, others tend to be far more competitive—interested in doing better than others in one way or another. Not surprisingly, scientists have found that people can be reliably classified into four different categories in terms of their natural predispositions toward working with or against others.[28] These are as follows.

competitors
People whose primary motive is doing better than others, besting them in open competition.

individualists
People who care almost exclusively about maximizing their own gain and don't care whether others do better or worse than themselves.

cooperators
People who are concerned with maximizing joint outcomes, getting as much as possible for their team.

equalizers
People who are primarily interested in minimizing the differences between themselves and others.

- **Competitors**—People whose primary motive is doing better than others, beating them in open competition
- **Individualists**—People who care almost exclusively about maximizing their own gain, and don't care whether others do better or worse than they do
- **Cooperators**—People who are concerned with maximizing joint outcomes, getting as much as possible for their team
- **Equalizers**—People who are primarily interested in minimizing the differences between themselves and others

Because these differences exist and are the result of a lifetime's experience, they tend to be difficult to change. In view of this fact, it is often useful for managers to take the time to get to know their subordinates' personal orientations, so that they can match these to the kinds of tasks they ask them to perform. For example, competitors may be effective in negotiation situations whereas cooperators may be most effective in teamwork situations. In other words, managers should attempt to put these existing individual preferences to work rather than trying to change them.

Organizational Reward Systems. It is not only differences between people that lead them to behave cooperatively; differences in the nature of organizational reward systems matter, too. Despite good intentions, companies often create reward systems that encourage their employees to compete against each other. This would be the case, for example, in an organization in which various divisions sell competing products. For instance, Lennox International Inc. has purchased many previously independent heating contractors throughout the United States. Because they have established reputations, these companies continue to operate as if they are independent, and they compete vigorously against each other for business. In fact, however, they all belong to the same parent company, so this may well generate extra costs. The basic idea is that the local reputations of these companies are so good that this offsets these costs, but this is a new business model, so no one knows for certain whether it will work.

Just as individuals differ in their overall preference for competition or cooperation, they also differ greatly in their reactions to cooperative and competitive reward structures. As an illustration of this, let's consider the findings of a particularly interesting study.[29] The researchers arranged for teams of business students to play a game that simulated complex military situations. Their task was to keep unfriendly forces from moving into certain restricted areas while allowing friendly forces to move freely in these areas. The game was structured either as cooperative or competitive in nature. In the cooperative condition, the teams were told that the *team* with the best overall performance would receive a cash award. In the competitive condition, teams were told that the top-performing *individuals* would receive cash awards.

Additionally, the researchers measured the students' extraversion and agreeableness to determine whether these aspects of personality were related to performance under the two reward structures. It was predicted that persons high in both agreeableness and extraversion would do better in the cooperative reward structure condition, while those low on these dimensions would do better in the competitive reward structure condition. Why? Because people high in agreeableness and extraversion trust others and like to interact with them, so they prefer cooperation to competition. People low on these dimensions show the opposite pattern. Results offered clear support for these predictions. In addition, and perhaps even more interestingly, two aspects of task performance—*speed* and *accuracy*—were affected in different ways by the reward structures of the game. Accuracy was higher under a cooperative reward structure, whereas speed was higher under a competitive reward structure (see Figure 11.8). This appeared to be the case because in the cooperative reward structure, teams worked closely together, taking time for discussion and information sharing. Under the competitive reward structure, in contrast, individuals more or less "did their own thing" as much as possible, and this speeded up the performance of the entire team.

Whatever the precise basis for these findings, they suggest that the task of choosing between these two different ways of structuring tasks is trickier than most people would guess. Managers wanting to do a good job in this respect should take into account the personal characteristics of team members (the degree to which they are high or low in agreeableness and extraversion) and also whether speed or accuracy is more important. Truly, such decisions will be complex; but given the strong effects of these factors on team and individual performance, they are well worth considering carefully.

Cooperation Between Organizations: Interorganizational Alliances

In business, competition is the natural order of things; company competing against company is the standard state of affairs. This does not mean, however, that it must always be the case. Sometimes, in fact, companies find it beneficial to work together to maximize their joint profits—to cooperate. This occurs in several different ways, including *partnering with suppliers, research and development partnerships,* and joining forces against *external threats.*

Partnering with Suppliers. Years ago, companies used to think of suppliers (other companies from whom they purchase goods and services) as more or less interchangeable. They'd select the best one and ignore the others, and if the situation changed, they switched suppliers quickly. Today, however, companies are far more likely to work closely with their suppliers to ensure that they can provide high-quality products.

FIGURE 11.8

Effects of Competitive and Cooperative Reward Structures on Performance

As shown here, speed is increased by a competitive reward structure, whereas accuracy is enhanced by a cooperative reward structure. This suggests that the choice between these two possible reward structures is complex and depends on whether speed or accuracy is of primary importance.

Source: Based on data from Beersma et al., 2003; see Note 29.

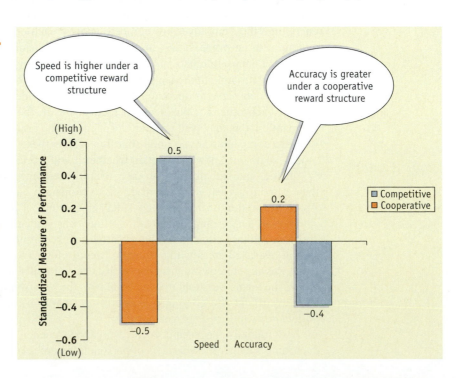

Consider Kontron, a German company that provides data to Microsoft about the effectiveness of its new operating systems. Rather than being forced to guess what Microsoft wants, Kontron officials work closely with Microsoft engineers to provide the kind of information that is most useful to them. Many auto companies also have developed close, cooperative relationships with their suppliers (e.g., various manufacturing companies) to ensure a constant flow of high-quality components required to stay competitive.

Research and Development (R&D) Partnerships. In certain industries, the costs of research and development can present a staggering burden to individual companies, especially ones that are relatively small in size. Under these conditions, it often makes sense for two or more organizations to pool their resources and share in the potential rewards.[30]

This occurs in many different industries, but perhaps the biotech industry is the best single example. In this industry, hundreds of small start-up firms struggle to advance the drugs they are developing through the rigorous testing procedures required by the U.S. government. Only drugs that pass each of many different hurdles can be brought to market. Modern science is expensive, and to deal with these costs, these small companies often form research and development partnerships. In these partnerships, each company often brings something unique to the table—special facilities, specific kinds of knowledge, useful ties with larger companies. The hope, of course, is that by cooperating in this manner, all participants in the partnership will benefit greatly when—and if—their drugs pass the required tests.

Interorganizational Alliances and Social Dilemmas. Recall our discussion of social dilemmas—situations in which there are strong reasons to cooperate with others *and* strong reasons to defect (to compete while one's opponent is still acting cooperatively). If you think about it for a moment, you will see that this basic model fits many instances of interorganizational cooperation. Yes, the participating companies have much to gain by working together; but the temptation to take advantage of the situation and seek selfish, individual gain can be strong.

Recently, research has called attention to this possibility.[31] Specifically, it was noted that in a multiparty alliance (i.e., one in which many companies participate), noncooperative behavior by one is relatively easy to conceal—much easier than in a situation involving just two companies. Similarly, any harm produced by selfish actions on the part of one company is diffused across the many partners, and this may make it easier to conclude, "I'll gain, and no one will be hurt very much." Finally, since there are many partners in the alliance, it is difficult for each to influence the decisions of the others through its own actions, and therefore, more difficult to insist on cooperation by the threat of withdrawal. The result is that multiparty alliances between organizations are especially subject to the risks inherent in all social dilemma situations: One or more participants will stop cooperating while the others continue to cooperate, and so reap large, individual gains—at their cost!

How can these risks be reduced? Several procedures may be effective, including taking steps to ensure that the payoffs for universal cooperation are much greater than those for universal defection, increasing the level of communication between members, focusing the alliance on long-term rather than short-term goals, and establishing a high level of identification with the alliance. Through these and other steps—which are all designed to strengthen incentives for cooperation and weaken temptations to compete (i.e., defect from the alliance)—the likelihood that interorganizational alliances will succeed is increased. And as we noted earlier in this discussion, this is the essential nature of cooperation. When it works, it provides larger rewards for the persons or groups who participate in it than they could obtain alone.

Conflict: The Inevitable Result of Incompatible Interests

Recall the Preview Case at the start of this chapter, in which James F. Parker, the CEO of Southwest Airlines, resigned after a prolonged labor dispute that he seemed unable to resolve. This is almost a "textbook" example of *conflict*—and the high costs it often exacts

conflict

A process in which one party perceives that another party has taken or will take actions that are incompatible with one's own interests.

from the parties to it. Because of this continuing clash between labor and management, morale at the company suffered and the company's long-standing "culture of cooperation" came under stress. If we conceive of prosocial behavior and cooperation as being at one end of a continuum (as in Figure 11.1), then it makes sense to conceive of *conflict* as approaching the opposite end.

In the context of organizations, **conflict** may be defined as a process in which one party perceives that another party has taken or will take actions that are incompatible with one's own interests. As you might imagine, conflict occurs quite commonly in organizations. In fact, it has been estimated that about 20 percent of managers' time is spent dealing with conflict and its effects.[32] Considering this, it makes sense to examine the types of conflict that exist, the causes and consequences of conflict, and ways to effectively manage conflict that occurs in the workplace.

Types of Conflict

As you might imagine, all conflict is not alike. In fact, scientists have distinguished among three major types of conflict that commonly occur.[33] These are as follows:

substantive conflict

A form of conflict that occurs when people have different viewpoints and opinions with respect to a decision they are making with others.

affective conflict

A form of conflict resulting when people experience clashes of personality or interpersonal tension, resulting in frustration and anger.

- *Substantive conflict*—It is not unusual for people to have different viewpoints and opinions with respect to a decision they are making with others. This variety of conflict is known as **substantive conflict**. In most cases, substantive conflict can be very beneficial to helping groups make effective decisions because it forces the various sides to clearly articulate their ideas. (We discussed group decision making more fully in Chapter 10.)
- *Affective conflict*—When people experience clashes of personalities or interpersonal tension of some sort, the frustration and anger that result are signs of **affective conflict**. It is not unusual for affective conflict to result whenever people from different backgrounds are put together to perform tasks. Until they learn to accept one another, affective conflict is likely, resulting in disruption to group performance. After all, people who do not see the world in the same manner are likely to clash, and when they do, their joint performance tends to suffer.
- *Process conflict*—In many work groups controversies arise about how they are going to operate—that is, how various duties and resources will be allocated and with whom various responsibilities will reside. This is known as **process conflict**. Generally, the more process conflict exists, the more group performance will suffer.[34]

process conflict

A form of conflict resulting from differences of opinion regarding how work groups are going to operate, such as how various duties and resources will be allocated and with whom various responsibilities will reside.

As this discussion suggests, conflict takes several different forms and can have different effects—both positive and negative in nature. With this in mind, let's now turn to a discussion of the underlying causes of conflict.

Causes of Conflict

The conflicts we face in organizations may be viewed as stemming from a variety of causes, including both our interactions with other people and the organization itself. Here are just a few of the most important sources of organizational conflict.

Grudges.   All too often, conflict is caused when people who have lost face in dealing with someone attempt to "get even" with that person by planning some form of revenge (see Figure 11.9). Employees involved in this kind of activity are not only going out of their way to harm one of their coworkers, but by holding a grudge, they are wasting energy that could be devoted to more productive organizational endeavors.

Malevolent Attributions.   Why did someone do something that hurt us? To the extent that we believe that the harm we suffer is due to an individual's malevolent motives (e.g., the desire to hurt us), conflict is inevitable. However, whenever we believe that we suffered harm because of factors outside someone's control (e.g., an accident), conflict is less likely to occur. (This is an example of the attribution process addressed in Chapter 3.) This causes problems in cases in which we falsely attribute the harm we suffer to another's negative intent when, in reality, the cause was externally based.

FIGURE 11.9

FIGURE 11.9

Holding Grudges: An All-Too-Common Source of Conflict

When people find it shameful to look bad in the eyes of others, they may hold grudges against them. Sometimes, this takes the form of seeking revenge by sabotaging another's work (e.g., this woman is unplugging a colleague's computer). This, of course, only escalates the conflict between the parties.

destructive criticism

Negative feedback that angers the recipient instead of helping him or her do a better job.

Destructive Criticism. Communicating negative feedback in organizations is inevitable. All too often, however, this process arouses unnecessary conflict. The problem is that some people make the mistake of using **destructive criticism**—that is, negative feedback that angers the recipient rather than helps this person do a better job. The most effective managers attempt to avoid conflict by using constructive criticism instead. For some important comparisons between these two forms of criticism, see Table 11.2.

Distrust. The more strongly people suspect that some other individual or group is out to get them, the more likely they are to have a relationship with that person or group that is riddled with conflict. In general, companies that are considered great places in which to work are characterized by high levels of trust between people at all levels.

Competition Over Scarce Resources. Because organizations never have unlimited resources (such as space, money, equipment, or personnel), it is inevitable that conflicts will arise over the distribution of those resources. This occurs in large part because of a self-serving tendency in people's perceptions (see Chapter 3)—that is, people tend to overestimate their own contributions to their organizations. Believing that we made greater contributions leads us to feel more deserving of resources than others. Inevitably, conflict results when others do not see it this way.

Consequences of Conflict

The major problem with conflict, as you know from experience, is that it yields strong negative emotions (see Chapter 5). However, these emotional reactions mark only the beginning of a chain of reactions that can have harmful effects in organizations.

The negative reactions, besides being quite stressful, are problematic in that they trigger negative emotions that divert people's attention from the task at hand. For example, people who are focused on getting even with a coworker and making him look bad in front of others are unlikely to be attending to the most important aspect of their jobs. In particular, communication between individuals or teams may be so adversely affected that any coordination of effort between them is compromised (see Chapter 9). Not surprisingly, such lowered coordination tends to lead to decrements in organizational functioning. In short, organizational conflict has costly effects on organizational performance.

Consider this example. In July 2004, the Graves Museum in Dania Beach, Florida, closed its doors indefinitely.[35] Museum closings are rare, so it's interesting to ask, "What happened to produce this dismal outcome?" The answer seems to involve bitter disputes

TABLE 11.2 Constructive Versus Destructive Criticism: A Comparison

The factors listed here distinguish *constructive criticism* (negative feedback that may be accepted by the recipient to improve his or her performance) from *destructive criticism* (negative feedback likely to be rejected by the recipient and unlikely to improve his or her performance).

Constructive Criticism	Destructive Criticism
Considerate—protects the recipient's self-esteem	Inconsiderate—harsh, sarcastic, biting
Does not contain threats	Contains threats
Timely—occurs as soon as possible after the substandard performance	Not timely—occurs after an inappropriate delay
Does not attribute poor performance to internal causes	Attributes poor performance to internal causes (e.g., lack of effort, motivation, ability)
Specific—focuses on aspects of performance that were inadequate	General—a sweeping condemnation of performance
Focuses on performance, not on the recipient	Focuses on the recipient—his or her personal characteristics
Motivated by desire to help the recipient improve	Motivated by anger, desire to assert dominance over the recipient, desire for revenge
Offers concrete suggestions for improvement	Offers no concrete suggestions for improvement

among board members. Several members of the museum's board wanted to sell the property and relocate. The founder, Gypsy Graves, opposed this action. The dispute between them over this issue intensified when, in 1996, the board brought in an outside group to provide corporate structure for the museum. This resulted in a greatly reduced role for Graves, and she walked out in protest. Later, though, she launched a bitter court battle to regain her control. She succeeded in 2002, but tensions soon surfaced again and contributed to a situation in which the museum—essentially leaderless and engaged in bitter internal conflict—amassed large debts. The trustees finally acted to close it and file for bankruptcy. Sadly, this kind of devastation of a previously successful organization is all too common when conflicts get out of hand. For some helpful suggestions on how to avoid many of these problems, see Table 11.3.[36]

In short, organizational conflict has costly effects on organizational performance.[37] Conflict—especially when it gets out of hand—is stressful, unpleasant, distracting, interferes with communication, and can damage long-term relationships. That's quite a list—and it suggests that conflict is a serious issue, one that every manager and every organization should take seriously. However, it is very important to note that, despite what often is said about conflict, it also can have positive effects on behavior in organizations. For a discussion of this key point, see the *OB: Making Sense Out of Common Sense* section.

Managing Conflict Through Negotiation

When conflicts arise between individuals, groups, or even entire organizations, the most common way to resolve them is to work together to find a solution that is acceptable to all parties involved. This process is known as **bargaining** (or **negotiation**). Formally, we may define bargaining as the process in which two or more parties in dispute with each other exchange offers, counteroffers, and concessions in an attempt to find a mutually acceptable agreement.

Obviously, bargaining does not work when the parties rigidly adhere to their positions without budging—that is, when they "stick to their guns." For bargaining to be effective, the parties involved must be willing to adjust their stances on the issues at hand. And, for the people involved to be willing to make such adjustments, they must believe that they have found an acceptable outcome—one that allows them to claim victory in the negotiation process. For bargaining to be most effective in reducing conflict, this must be the case for all sides. That is, outcomes must be found for all sides that allow them to believe that

bargaining (negotiation)
The process by which two or more parties in dispute with one another exchange offers, counteroffers, and concessions in an attempt to find a mutually acceptable agreement.

TABLE 11.3 How to Manage Conflict Effectively

Although conflict is inevitable, there are concrete steps that managers can take to avoid the negative consequences that result from conflict between people in the workplace.

- Agree on a process for making decisions *before* a conflict arises. This way, when a conflict needs to be addressed, everyone knows how it is going to be handled.

- Make sure everyone knows his or her specific areas of responsibility, authority, and accountability. Clarifying these matters avoids potential conflicts when people either ignore their responsibilities or overstep their authority.

- Recognize conflicts stemming from faulty organizational systems, such as a pay system that rewards one department at the expense of another. In such cases, work to change the system rather than training employees.

- Recognize the emotional reactions to conflict. Conflicts will not go away until people's hurt feelings are addressed.

- Consider how to avoid problems rather than assign blame for them. Questions such as "Why did you do that?" only make things worse. It is more helpful to ask, "How can we make things better?"

- Conflicts will not go away by making believe they don't exist; doing so will only make them worse. Avoid the temptation not to speak to the other party and discuss your misunderstandings thoroughly.

Source: Based on suggestions by Bragg, 1999; see Note 36.

win-win solutions
Resolutions to conflicts in which both parties get what they want.

they have "won" the negotiation process—results known as **win-win solutions**. In win-win solutions, everybody wins, precisely as the name implies.

Tips for Negotiating Win-win Solutions. Several effective ways of finding such win-win solutions may be identified. (For practice in putting these techniques to use, see the Group Exercise below.)

1. *Avoid making unreasonable offers.* Imagine that a friend of yours is selling a used car with an asking price of $10,000—the car's established "book value." If you were to attempt to "lowball" the seller by offering only $1,000, your bad-faith offer might end

OB Making Sense Out of Common Sense

The Positive Side of Conflict

Have you ever worked on a team project and found that you disagreed with someone on a key matter? If so, how did you react? Chances are good that you fell short of sabotaging that person's work or acting aggressively. In fact, the conflict may have even brought the two of you to the table to have a productive discussion about the matter at hand. As a result of this discussion you may have even improved relations between the two of you and the quality of the decisions that resulted from your joint efforts. If you can relate to this scenario, then you already recognize an important fact about organizational conflict—that some of its effects are positive.

When asked recently about his management philosophy, Starbucks' CEO and founder Howard Schultz touted the importance of conflict and debate, saying, "If there's no tension, I don't think you get the best result."[38] As this

successful business leader suggests, organizational conflict can be the source of several benefits. Among these are the following.

- Conflict may improve the quality of organizational decisions (as in the above example).
- Conflict may bring out into the open problems that have been previously ignored.
- Conflict may motivate people to appreciate each other's positions more fully.
- Conflict may encourage people to consider new ideas, thereby facilitating change.

In view of these positive effects of conflict, the key is to make sure that more of these benefits occur as opposed to costs. It is with this goal in mind that managers work so diligently to effectively manage organizational conflict. We consider several ways of doing this in this chapter.

the negotiations right there. A serious buyer would offer a more reasonable price, say $9,000—one that would allow both the buyer and the seller to come out ahead in the deal. In short, extreme offers tend to anger one's opponents, sometimes ending the negotiation process on a sour note, allowing none of the parties to get what they want.

2. *Seek the common ground.* All too often people in conflict with others assume that their interests and those of the other party are completely incompatible. When this occurs, they tend to overlook the fact that they actually might have several areas of interest in common. When parties focus on the areas of agreement between them, it helps bring them together on the areas of disagreement. So, for example, in negotiating the deal for purchasing the used car, you might establish the fact that you agree to the selling price of $9,000. This verifies that the interests of the buyer and the seller are not completely incompatible, thereby encouraging them to find a solution to the area in which they disagree, such as a payment schedule. By contrast, if either party believed that they were completely far apart on all aspects of the deal, they would be less likely to negotiate a win-win solution.

3. *Broaden the scope of issues considered.* Sometimes, parties bargaining with one another have several issues on the table. When this occurs, it is often useful to consider the various issues together as a total package. Labor unions often do this in negotiating contracts with company management whenever they give in on one issue in exchange for compensation on another issue. So, for example, in return for not freezing wages, a company may agree to concede to the union's other interests, such as gaining representation on key corporate committees. In other words, compared to bargaining over single issues (e.g., the price of the used car), when the parties get to bargaining across a wide array of issues, it often is easier to find solutions that are acceptable to all sides.

4. *Uncover "the real" issues.* Frequently, people focus on the conflicts between them in only a single area although they may have multiple sources of conflict—some of which are hidden. Suppose, for example, that your friend is being extremely stubborn when it comes to negotiating the price of the used car. He's sticking firmly to his asking price, refusing to budge despite your reasonable offer, possibly adding to the conflict between you. However, it may be the case that there are other issues involved. For example, he may be trying to "get even" with you for harming him several years ago. In other words, what may appear to be a simple conflict between two people may actually have multiple sources. Finding long-lasting solutions requires identifying all the important issues—even the hidden ones—and bringing them to the table.

As you might imagine, it is almost always far easier to say these things than to do them. Indeed, when people cannot come to agreement about something, they sometimes become irrational, not seeking common ground, and not taking the other's perspective needed to find a win-win solution, but thinking only of themselves. In such circumstances, third parties can be useful to break the deadlock. One widely used way of helping out in such situations is by turning to *alternative dispute resolution techniques,* a topic to which we now turn.

Alternative Dispute Resolution

When a customer cancelled a $60,000 wedding reception, Anthony Capetola, a caterer from Long Island, New York, was able to fill that time slot with an event bringing in only half as much.[39] Although Capetola was harmed by the customer's actions, as you might imagine, that customer was unwilling to cough up the lost revenue.

Many business owners in Capetola's situation would seek restitution by taking the customer to court, resulting in a long delay and a huge bill for litigation, not to mention adverse publicity. Fortunately, in their contract, Capetola and the customer agreed to settle any future disagreements using what is known as **alternative dispute resolution (ADR)**. This refers to a set of procedures in which disputing parties work together with a neutral party who helps them settle their disagreements out of court. There are two popular forms of ADR—*mediation* and *arbitration* (see Figure 11.10).

alternative dispute resolution (ADR)

A set of procedures, such as *mediation* and *arbitration,* in which disputing parties work together with a neutral party who helps them settle their disagreements out of court.

FIGURE 11.10

Mediation Versus Arbitration: A Summary

Mediation and *arbitration* are both popular techniques for resolving conflicts. Third parties known as *arbitrators* can impose terms of agreement between the disputants, whereas *mediators* can only recommend such terms.

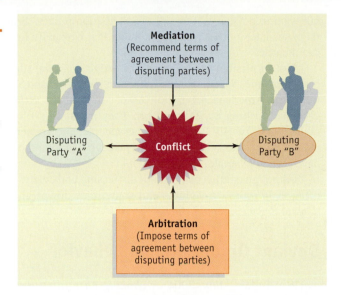

mediation

The process in which a neutral party (known as a mediator) works together with two or more parties sides to reach a settlement to their conflict.

integrative agreement

A type of solution to a conflict situation in which the parties consider joint benefits that go beyond a simple compromise.

arbitration

A process in which a third party (known as an *arbitrator*) has the power to impose, or at least to recommend, the terms of an agreement between two or more conflicting parties.

binding arbitration

A form of arbitration in which the two sides agree in advance to accept the terms set by the arbitrator, whatever he or she may be.

voluntary arbitration

A form of arbitration in which the two sides retain the freedom to reject the agreement recommended by an arbitrator.

conventional arbitration

A form of arbitration in which an arbitrator can offer any package or terms he or she wishes.

final-offer arbitration

A form of arbitration in which the arbitrator chooses between final offers made by the disputing parties themselves.

Mediation. The process of **mediation** involves having a neutral party (the *mediator*) work together with both sides to reach a settlement. Typically, mediators meet with each side together and separately, attempting to find a common ground that will satisfy everyone. Mediators do not consider who's wrong and who's right, but set the stage for finding a resolution. They have no formal power and cannot impose any agreements. Instead, they seek to clarify the issues involved and to enhance communication between the parties.

Sometimes, mediators offer specific recommendations for compromise or **integrative agreements**. These are solutions that involve taking many different factors into account. In other cases, they merely guide the parties toward developing such solutions themselves. Their role is primarily that of a facilitator—that is, someone who helps the two sides toward agreements that each will find acceptable. Because it requires voluntary compliance by the disputing parties, mediation often proves to be ineffective. Indeed, when the mediation process fails, it simply underscores the depth of the differences between the two sides.

Arbitration. As you might imagine, for mediation to work the two sides must be willing to communicate with each other. When this doesn't happen, ADR may take the form of **arbitration**. This is a process in which a third party (the *arbitrator*) has the power to impose, or at least to recommend, the terms of an agreement between two parties.[40] Four types of arbitration are most common. These are as follows:

- **Binding arbitration**—The two sides agree in advance to accept the terms set by the arbitrator, whatever they may be.
- **Voluntary arbitration**—The two sides retain the freedom to reject the recommended agreement.
- **Conventional arbitration**—The arbitrator can offer any package of terms he or she wishes.
- **Final-offer arbitration**—The arbitrator chooses between final offers made by the disputing parties themselves.

ADR Today. ADR is very popular these days because it helps disputants reach agreements rapidly (often in a matter of a day or two, compared to months or years for court trials) and inexpensively (usually for just a few thousand dollars split between the parties, compared to astronomical sums for attorney fees). Moreover, it keeps people who otherwise might end up in court out of the public eye, which could be damaging to their reputations—even the party in whose favor the judgment goes.

Because it is low-key and nonconfrontational, mediation is particularly valuable in cases in which the parties have an ongoing relationship (business or personal) that they do not want to go sour.[41] After all, the mediation process brings the parties together, helping them see each other's side—something that is usually lost for sure in the heat of a courtroom battle.

Not surprisingly, the popularity of ADR these days has led to the development of several companies specializing in rendering mediation and arbitration services. The largest of these, the American Arbitration Association, boasts offices in half the U.S. states, with a caseload pushing 80,000 per year. They maintain a file of some 18,000 arbitrators and mediators (typically lawyers, businesspeople, and former judges), enabling them to find a neutral party who is experienced in just about any kind of dispute that people are likely to have (for an example, see Figure 11.11).[42]

Although conflict can be both distressing and costly, we now turn to behaviors that are often even more damaging—and sometimes downright frightening—various forms of *deviant organizational behavior.*

Deviant Organizational Behavior

USA Today—July, 2004: *A choking haze filled the hallways, spreading like an impenetrable fog. Larry Hansel, a technician laid off by Elgar, a San Diego–based electronics company, shot out the company switchboard and set off homemade bombs. They were diversionary tactics. As fire scorched the walls and employees scrambled for cover . . . Hansel wielded a 12-gauge shotgun and searched for executives on his hit list. He found at least some of the victims he was seeking. Hansel shot and killed a vice president and a sales manager. Then he mounted his bicycle and pedaled away, the shotgun under one arm.*

FIGURE 11.11

Moving to Alternative Dispute Resolution: An Example

The U.S. Army Corps of Engineers—members of which are shown here clearing debris before rebuilding a breached levy in hurricane-ravaged New Orleans—used to assume that 80 percent of its construction projects result in some kind of litigation. Companies hired by the Corps to carry out various tasks would ultimately sued over a wide range of issues, a process that was time-consuming and expensive. In order to resolve disagreements more expediently now, the Corps has established specific milestones for each project and requires contractors to settle disputes using *alternative dispute resolution (ADR)* techniques. By so doing, the proportion of projects resulting in litigation has dropped by more than two-thirds (down to 25 percent).

In recent years, newspapers and evening news reports have been filled with such accounts of violent behavior by angry, disgruntled employees. In fact, assaults were so frequent among employees of the U.S. Postal Service that the phrase "going postal" entered our everyday language to describe this form of violence—clearly at the far negative end of the continuum of positive to negative behaviors we have been discussing.

Although acts of physical violence have been the subject of news stories, however, they represent just one very extreme form of what is often described as **deviant organizational behavior**—actions on the part of employees that intentionally violate the norms of organizations and/or the formal rules of society.[43] At first glance, you might assume that all forms of deviant organizational behavior produce negative effects. In fact, though, the issue is more complex. As we'll now see, deviant organizational behaviors—ones that violate the norms of a particular company—can produce beneficial effects if, at the same time, they are consistent with other norms, those of the broader society or culture.

Constructive and Destructive Workplace Deviance

To illustrate the fact that departures from existing organizational norms can produce a wide variety of effects, consider the following example. Imagine that an employee of a large company is ordered to find a way to dump toxic waste into a nearby river without being observed. Further, assume that the river is one used by many people for fishing, boating, and even swimming. The employee follows these orders and comes up with an effective means of dumping the chemicals. How would you describe this person's behavior? From the point of view of the organization, it is *constructive:* The employee has performed an assigned task well. From the point of view of society, though, it is highly *destructive:* Many innocent people may be harmed by the toxic chemical waste.

Now, imagine that when ordered to dump the waste, the employee refuses and, in fact, reports the company's intentions to the Environmental Protection Agency and a local newspaper. In this case, the employee's behavior is destructive from the point of view of the organization (its reputation may be harmed and it may receive a large fine), but constructive from the point of view of society.

Here's another example. Suppose that the norms in an organization support sexual discrimination: Women do not receive the raises or promotions they deserve simply because they are women. Under these conditions, managers who discriminate against women are behaving in a way consistent with organizational norms, but they are also violating societal norms against such discrimination—not to mention laws against such practices. Does this sound far-fetched? Then consider the fact that Morgan, Stanley, one of the largest brokerage companies in the United States, agreed in July 2004 to pay $54 million to settle lawsuits by former employees who claimed they had been the victims of sexual discrimination and sexual harassment. And Wal-Mart, the largest retailer in the world, is facing a huge class-action lawsuit alleging that the company routinely practices discrimination against women with respect to wages and promotions.[44] In these and related cases, many employees went along with their company's unstated norms of discrimination, thus violating fundamental societal norms and laws.

Basically, the framework we have been discussing suggests that it is useful to think about workplace deviance in terms of both constructive and destructive forms (see Figure 11.12). **Destructive organizational deviance** is a form of behavior that violates both organizational and societal norms (e.g., workplace aggression and violence). However, **constructive organizational deviance** refers to actions that deviate from organizational norms but are consistent with societal norms (e.g., the act of going public with an organizational wrongdoing, or what is called whistle-blowing). We now take a closer look at each.

Whistle-Blowing: Constructive Workplace Deviance

Sometimes employees face situations in which they recognize that their organization is behaving improperly. To right the wrong they reveal the improper or illegal practice to someone who may be able to correct it—an action known as **whistle-blowing**.[45] Formally, whistle-blowing is the disclosure by employees of illegal, immoral, or illegitimate practices by employers to people or organizations able to take action.

---

deviant organizational behavior
Actions on the part of employees that intentionally violate the norms of organizations and/or the formal rules of society, resulting in negative consequences.

destructive organizational deviance
A form of behavior that violates both organizational and societal norms.

constructive organizational deviance
Actions that deviate from organizational norms but are consistent with societal norms.

whistle-blowing
The disclosure by employees of illegal, immoral, or illegitimate practices by employers to people or organizations able to take action.

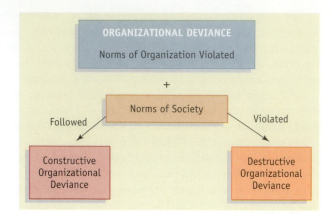

FIGURE 11.12

Constructive Versus Destructive Organizational Deviance

Behavior directed toward an organization is considered deviant if it violates its norms or rules, thereby bringing harm. If that behavior is consistent with the norms of society, it is considered *constructive organizational deviance*. However, if it is inconsistent with the norms of society and those of the organization, it is considered *destructive organizational deviance*.

Is whistle-blowing a constructive action? Although people in the organization might not think so, from the point of view of society, it usually is. In many instances, the actions of whistle-blowers can protect the health, safety, or security of the general public. For example, an employee of a large bank who reports risky or illegal practices to an appropriate regulatory agency may be protecting thousands of depositors from considerable delay in recovering their savings. Similarly, an individual who blows the whistle on illegal dumping of toxic chemicals by his or her company may save many people from serious illness. For a summary of some actual cases of whistle-blowing, see Table 11.4.[46]

TABLE 11.4 Whistle Blowing: Some Examples

As the following examples illustrate, employees blow the whistle on many different types of organizations accused of committing a wide range of questionable activities.

Whistle-Blower	Incident
Coleen Rowley	This special agent wrote a letter to the FBI director (with copies to two key members of Congress) about the bureau's failure to take action that could have prevented the terrorist attacks of September 11, 2001.
Sherron Watkins	In 2001, she notified the press about her letter to her boss at Enron identifying the company's fictitious accounting practices.
Paul van Buitenen	Went public in 1999 with claims of fraud and corruption within the European Commission.
An unnamed U.S. Customs inspector	Alerted Congress of security problems at the Miami airport in 1995 after management took no action.
Tonya Atchinson	This former internal auditor at Columbia-HCA Healthcare Corp. charged the company with illegal Medicare billing.
Daniel Shannon	An in-house attorney for Intelligent Electronics protested the company's alleged misuse of marketing funds from computer manufacturers.
Robert Young	This agent for Prudential Insurance Co.in New Jersey accused company agents of encouraging customers to needlessly sell some policies and buy more expensive ones, boosting their commissions.
Bill Bush	This manager at the National Aeronautics and Space Administration (NASA) went public with the administration's policy of discouraging the promotion of employees older than 54 years of age.

Sources: See Note 46.

Key questions about whistle-blowing include: "Why do people do it?" and "What happens as a result—what are the effects on both employees and their organizations?" Unfortunately, there is no clear-cut answer to the first question. Individual employees appear to engage in whistle-blowing for a variety of reasons, ranging from a desire to "get even" with a company they feel has treated them unfairly, through a genuine desire to stop illegal and harmful actions. A recent survey of Australian employees, though, suggests that uneasiness about being party to unlawful and dangerous or unsafe action is often a key motivator.[47]

As you might imagine, blowing the whistle on one's employer is likely to be a very costly act for employees, as they often find themselves facing a long, uphill battle attempting to prove the wrongdoing. They also frequently face ostracism and losing their jobs in response to their disloyalty. For example, five agents from State Farm Insurance were fired after they accused the company of various consumer abuses.[48]

Sometimes, when whistle-blowers have gathered sufficient evidence in support of their claims, they bear the major costs of their public disclosure. For instance, consider Jennifer P. Day, a teacher in the Boston school system (see Figure 11.13).[49] She observed her principal helping fourth-grade students to do well on a standardized systemwide exam by giving them the answers. (Principals in Boston receive bonuses for excellent performance on these exams by students in their schools.) She reported this action to the proper state authorities in June, 2004, and the result was quick in coming: She was fired!

Sadly, this can be the outcome for many whistle-blowers, and it is one reason why many persons are highly reluctant to engage in this action.[50] Although various laws prevent employers from firing people directly because they blew the whistle, organizations frequently find alternative official grounds for dismissing "troublemakers."[51] It is not surprising, therefore, that six senior employees of the company that runs the 900-mile Trans-Alaskan pipeline chose to remain anonymous when voicing their complaints about safety violations to BP Amoco.[52] Despite the risks involved, many persons do decide to blow the whistle on their companies, and although they are often discarded by their organizations, they sometimes become true heroes and heroines to their societies.

Cyberloafing: Deviant Behavior Goes High-Tech

The advent of Internet technology has brought with it increased efficiency in accessing information and communicating with others—both of which are vital objectives. However,

FIGURE 11.13

Whistle Blowers: People Who Put the Good of Society Ahead of the Good of Their Organizations

Jennifer P. Day, a teacher in the Boston school system, noticed that the principal of her school was helping students raise their scores on standardized exams by giving them the answers. When she reported this unethical behavior, she was fired. Although she did the right thing, she paid a stiff price. Such fears often prevent people from going public with wrongdoings they observe in their own organizations.

cyberloafing

The practice of using a company's e-mail and/or Internet facilities for personal use.

it also has created new ways for employees to loaf, or "goof off." Although workers have devised ways to slack off ever since people have been employed, access to the Internet and e-mail has provided tempting and more insidious opportunities than ever before. Employees who use their company's computers, such as its e-mail and/or Internet facilities, for personal use are considered to be engaged in **cyberloafing**.[53]

In the U.S., 40 million people have Internet and/or e-mail access at work and use it regularly, and are referred to as *online workers*. However, further statistics reveal that much of what online workers are doing while online is not work-related. For example:

- According to an MSNBC survey, one-fifth of all people who have visited pornographic Web sites have done so while on the job.
- One-third of workers surveyed by the Society of Financial Service Professionals reported playing computer games while at work.
- Eighty-three percent of employers surveyed by the Privacy Foundation indicated that their employees were using e-mail for personal purposes.

These and other forms of cyberloafing are costing U.S. organizations, both private and public, untold millions of dollars a year. In fact, just one $40,000/year employee can cost his or her employer as much as $5,000 annually by playing around on the Internet for one hour a day.

Executives are implicitly aware of this problem, and over three-quarters believe that some type of online monitoring and filtering efforts are needed. Recent polls found, however, that only about a third of online workers are monitored, and most of this monitoring is highly sporadic. In fact, only 38 percent acknowledge monitoring the online work of employees who already have been suspected of cyberloafing. Bottom line: Cyberloafing is a costly problem about which little is being done.

Although various software products make it possible to monitor employees (Baltimore MIMEsweeper and Websense being the most widely used), and such products are growing in popularity, this technology is not a panacea. Some problems are technical in nature, but the most notable ones are social-psychological. Specifically, employees believe that being monitored constitutes an invasion of their privacy and reject the practice as being unfair.

Decisions in federal courts are in agreement. A few years ago, for example, the 27-judge Judicial Conference of the United States repealed a proposed monitoring policy for their own employees, which they feared would violate their constitutional rights to privacy. Speaking for the group, federal appeals court judge Alex Kozinski objected to the policy's

FIGURE 11.14

Cyberloafing: Inaction in Action

Does this scene look familiar to you? If so, we're not surprised. Far too many people engage in *cyberloafing*, the practice of using the company's computer system for personal purposes. This form of workplace deviance is both widespread and extremely costly to organizations.

assertion that "court employees should have no expectation of privacy at any time while at work." The resulting policy permitted virtually no monitoring of employees' e-mail and only highly limited monitoring of their Internet use.

Where we stand now is quite interesting: Although cyberloafing is admittedly a widespread and costly problem, efforts aimed at addressing it that involve employee monitoring are not well accepted (or even legally permissible, in some cases). Clearly, the key is to find additional ways of discouraging people from cyberloafing. Admittedly, given the ancient problem of "goofing off" coupled with the vast opportunities to goof off provided by Internet access, cyberloafing looks like it's going to be a problem that stays around for years to come. Fortunately, organizational behavior specialists are now beginning to study this phenomenon, which hopefully will provide useful suggestions in the years to come.[54]

Workplace Aggression and Violence

Approximately 1.5 million Americans annually become victims of violence while on the job, resulting in direct and indirect costs to their companies of more than $4.2 billion.[55] Despite all the publicity given to incidents like the one described on page 446, though, violence is actually a rare occurrence in workplaces. Only about 800 people are murdered at work each year in the United States, and most of these crimes are committed by outsiders, such as customers or criminals during robberies, not by fellow employees.[56]

Although violence is relatively rare, other forms of **workplace aggression**—any efforts by individuals to harm others with whom they work or have worked in the past, or their organizations—are much more common.[57] What forms does workplace aggression take? Why does it occur? And who are the persons most likely to engage in it? These are the questions to which we now focus turn.

workplace aggression
Acts of verbal and physical abuse toward others in organizations, ranging from mild to severe.

Workplace Aggression: Its Many Forms. When it comes to aggression, most people would like to maximize the harm they do their intended victims while simultaneously minimizing the likelihood of retaliation. In view of this, it's not surprising that many instances of workplace aggression are largely covert (hidden, disguised) in nature. This type of aggression is especially likely in workplaces because aggressors in such settings expect to interact with their intended victims frequently in the future. Using covert forms of aggression reduces the likelihood that the victims will retaliate against them.

Of course, not all forms of workplace aggression are covert. People do indeed sometimes assault others directly, either with words or in physical assaults. Overall, it appears that most aggression occurring in workplaces can be described as falling into three major categories. (Note that most of the actions in the first two categories tend to be *covert* in nature.)

incivility
Demonstrating a lack of regard for others, denying them the respect they are due.

obstructionism
Attempts to impede another's job performance.

overt aggression
Acts that are outwardly intended to harm other people or organizations.

- *Incivility*—Behaviors demonstrating a lack of regard for others, denying them the respect they are due. Often such acts are verbal or symbolic in nature (e.g., belittling others' opinions, talking behind their backs, spreading malicious rumors about them)
- *Obstructionism*—Behaviors designed to obstruct or impede the target's performance (e.g., failure to return phone calls or respond to memos, failure to transmit needed information, interfering with activities important to the target)
- *Overt aggression*—Behaviors that have typically been included under the heading "workplace violence" (e.g., physical assault, destruction of property, threats of physical violence, direct verbal abuse)

How common are these forms of behavior? More common than you might guess. In fact, a large proportion of employees report that they have either been on the receiving end of workplace aggression or behaved aggressively toward others at some time during their working careers. So, although overt violence involving physical assaults is relatively rare, other forms of workplace aggression are much more common. In fact, in some workplaces, they are an everyday occurrence.

Workplace Aggression: Its Causes.   What are the causes of workplace aggression? As is true of aggression in any context, many factors play a role. However, one that has emerged repeatedly in research on this topic is *perceived unfairness*.[58] When individuals feel that they have been treated unfairly by others in their organization—or by their organization itself—they experience intense feelings of anger and resentment, and often seek to "even the score" by harming the people they hold responsible in some manner (see Chapter 2).

In addition, the likelihood that a specific person will engage in workplace aggression is influenced by the overall level of aggression in his or her workgroup or organization.[59] In other words, to the extent that individuals work in environments in which aggression is common, they, too, are likely to engage in such behavior. Moreover, this seems to be true for aggression outside as well as inside organizations. For instance, one recent study found that the greater the incidence of violence in communities surrounding United States Post Offices, the higher the rates of aggression within these branch offices.[60] It was as if acceptance of violence in the surrounding communities paved the way for similar behavior inside this large organization.

Additional factors play a role in workplace aggression involve changes that have occurred recently in many workplaces: downsizing, layoffs, and increased use of part-time employees, to name a few. In fact, the greater the extent to which such changes have occurred, the greater the level of stress and uncertainty experienced by employees, and the higher the level of workplace aggression that occurs. Since such changes have occurred with increasing frequency in recent years, it seems possible that the incidence of workplace aggression, too, may be increasing for this reason. In sum, workplace aggression, like aggression in other contexts, derives from many different factors rather than a single dominant cause.

Who Engages in Workplace Aggression?   What kind of person is most likely to engage in workplace aggression? Existing evidence concerning this issue paints a fairly clear picture of the characteristics that seem to equip individuals with "short fuses":[61]

- *High trait anger*—The tendency to respond to situations in a predominantly angry manner
- *Positive attitude toward revenge*—The belief that it is justifiable to get back at others who have caused one harm
- *Past experience with aggression*—A history that involves exposure to aggressive behavior
- The tendency to express anger *overtly* rather than to suppress it

Can we use these findings to create a "profile" of individuals who are likely to seek to harm others in their organization? Findings of a *USA Today* study indicate that at least in the case of the most violent offenders, perhaps we can.[62] This study examined a total of 224 fatal incidents spanning 28 years (1975–2003) to gain insight into the motives and traits of employees who kill. Results suggested that the desire for revenge was important for many of these persons, but that others—persons high in trait anger—were started down the path toward violence by an initially minor on-the-job argument or disagreement.

Others have even killed before. After being fired from his job at Bank One (now Chase Bank) in Columbus, Ohio, for example, Jerry Hessler kicked in the front door of the home where two people he blamed for this event—Brian Stevens and his wife Tracey—lived with their five-month-old daughter, Amanda. He murdered all three. Only a few minutes earlier, he murdered P. Thane Griffin, the father of a woman who rejected his advances. The bottom line: At present we don't have a clear picture of what might be termed "potentially dangerous" employees. However, continued research is coming closer to providing such a profile.

What Job Characteristics put People at Risk for Violence or Aggression?   In addition to identifying individuals whose personal characteristics predispose them to behave aggressively, scientists also have considered the possibility that aggressive behavior is triggered by the nature of the work people perform. The possibility that people performing certain kinds of jobs are more likely to become victims of aggression than those performing other kinds of jobs is important to know in advance so that appropriate precautions can be taken. With this in mind, scientists conducted a study in which they assessed the relationship between two variables in a broad sample of workers—characteristics of the work they performed (i.e., the extent to which their jobs put them in a position to do certain things, such as caring for other people, handling valuable goods, etc.), and the extent to which they experienced various forms of violence or aggression at work.[63] Their findings were quite interesting: People whose jobs led them to exercise control over others or to handle various weapons (e.g., police officers) or to have contact with people on medication or to take physical care of others (e.g., nurses) were most likely to experience violence on the job. Figure 11.15 identifies the seven job characteristics that are most strongly associated with experiencing violence on the job.

Managing Workplace Aggression. Although it often is very difficult for individual employees to deal with this problem, organizations can take steps to reduce it. Here are a few that may prove helpful:

■ *Establish clear norms against abusive treatment of employees—and clear procedures for assuring they are followed.* If it is made clear in an organization from the top down that abusiveness toward employees will not be tolerated, and employees are provided with procedures for reporting such treatment, even highly aggressive managers will be likely to get the message. After all, assuming they want to protect their own careers, they will be inclined to reduce their abusiveness, if only to avoid the negative consequences it may bring.

■ *Train managers in interpersonal skills.* Some abusive supervisors simply don't know how else to communicate with their subordinates. For them, destructive criticism is the only style they know. Training programs designed to equip such managers with better communication skills and greater understanding of others can help reduce such problems.

FIGURE 11.15

Job Characteristics That Put People at Risk for Violence

The seven job characteristics listed here were found to be most strongly related to experiencing violence on the job. Insofar as these are characteristic of the work performed by police officers and nurses, it is not surprising that individuals performing these jobs also were found to suffer the highest occurrences of violence.

Source: Based on data reported by LeBlanc & Kelloway, 2002; see Note 63.

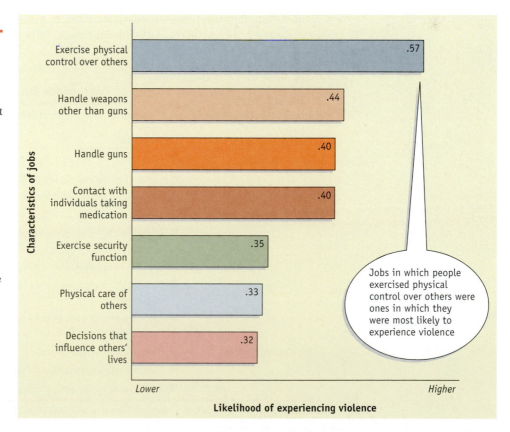

■ *Conduct periodic assessments of employee satisfaction and commitment.* If such assessments are conducted in a confidential manner that protects the identity of individual employees, managers who are acting in a hostile, abusive manner are able to be identified before their behavior becomes worse. Then, these individuals can be provided with appropriate training or counseling, and if that does not succeed, disciplinary procedures designed to change their behavior can be initiated.

Although none of these procedures is perfect, together, they can help get the message to abusive managers that their behavior is inappropriate and will not be tolerated. Not only will this create a more positive work environment, but it also can contribute to an organization's financial success. As such, they are well worth doing.

Abusive Supervision: Workplace Bullying

abusive supervision

A pattern of supervision in which a boss engages in sustained displays of hostile verbal and nonverbal behaviors.

workplace bullying

The repeated mistreatment of an individual at work in a manner that endangers his or her physical or mental health.

In recent years, OB scientists and practitioners have become interested in studying **abusive supervision**—a pattern of supervision characterized by sustained displays of hostile verbal and physical behaviors. A particularly widespread form of abusive supervision is known as **workplace bullying**.[64] This refers to the repeated mistreatment of individuals at work in a manner that endangers their physical or mental health.[65] Workplace bullying occurs by virtue of things people do intentionally to bring harm (e.g., chastising another) as well as things they don't do (e.g., withholding valuable information and training). Unlike harassment based on race or gender, bullying is not strictly illegal (unless, of course, it results in harm), and it is quite widespread.

According to a recent survey, 1 in 6 workers in the United States has been the victim of bullying in the past year.[66] Typically, bullies tend to be bosses (81 percent) who are abusing their power. Interestingly, bullies are equally likely to be women or men, but the vast majority of the targets of bullying tend to be women (especially when the bullies are themselves women).[67] For a summary of some of the most prevalent forms of workplace bullying, see Table 11.5.

An interesting thing about bullying is that it tends to repeat itself, thereby escalating its effects. For example, a bully's target is likely to complain to a higher-ranking organizational official. Typically, most higher-level managers will take some form of action (e.g., admonishing the bully), but will leave the bully in place to strike again. This time, however, the bully is likely to retaliate with vengeance. Often, this results in high levels of fear

TABLE 11.5 Prevalent Forms of Workplace Bullying

Workplace bullying takes a variety of forms. Some of the most prevalent are summarized here.

Category	Description
Constant Critic	■ Uses insulting and belittling comments, engages in name-calling
	■ Constantly harangues the victim about his or her incompetence
	■ Makes aggressive eye contact
Two-Headed Snake	■ Denies victims the resources needed to work
	■ Demands that coworkers provide damning evidence against the victim
	■ Assigns meaningless work as punishment
Gatekeeper	■ Isolates the victim; ignoring him or her with "the silent treatment"
	■ Deliberately cuts the target out of the communication loop but expects the victim to have the missing information
Screaming Mimi	■ Yells, screams, and curses
	■ Makes loud, angry outbursts and tantrums
	■ Intimidates by slamming things and throwing objects

Source: Based on information in Namie & Namie, 2000; see Note 67.

that paralyze the workplace, causing people to seek new jobs and exposing employers to litigation. Part of the difficulty in dealing with this problem is that bullies often are so highly effective that they bring other employees into their webs, getting them either to join in on the abuse or to agree to keep silent about it. Soon, what appears to be the inappropriate behavior of a lone individual becomes a serious problem for the entire organization.

Today's workplace bully is not simply a grown-up version of the same person as the schoolyard bully who threatened to beat you up after school back in second grade. Rather, workplace bullies are best understood from the same perspective as those who perpetrate domestic violence—they are individuals whose needs to control others are so extreme that they are in need of psychological counseling. As you might imagine, the workplace bully, once rooted out, should be dealt with in a swift and effective manner. This might result in a leave of absence during which professional help is provided—or, in many cases, termination. As you might imagine, of course, this is far easier said than done. After all, few among us would be willing to admit that we have a bully working in our midst, causing us to take only mild action, which, as we noted, can only make things worse. As in so many cases, the best offense here is likely to be "a good defense"—that is, to be on the lookout for bullies and to step in before they can get a foothold into the organization.

Although bullies are not commonplace in organizations, almost anyone can engage in bullying if prompted by adverse situations. For example, frequent mergers and acquisitions make working conditions insecure for lots of people, causing almost anyone to behave aggressively from time to time. This makes it more important than ever for managers to identify and respond to bullies (as they would respond to any employees who engage in aggressive behavior) by following the guidelines outlined on pages 453–454.

Employee Theft

Retail stores are very concerned with problems of shoplifting, as you know. What you might not know, however, is that companies lose more money and goods from their own employees than from customers. Although estimates of costs of employee theft are quite varied, it is clear that the figures are staggering, amounting to many billions of dollars per year (for some statistics in this regard, see Table 11.6).[68]

To understand these statistics fully, it is important to consider an important fact: Almost everyone takes home some company property—a pencil, a note pad, some paper— for personal use, but in general, we don't consider this theft. It is considered to be part of the job. Whether or not this is justified, taking company property for nonbusiness uses does

---

TABLE 11.6 Employee Theft: Some Alarming Facts and Figures

The following statistics will give you a sense of the scope and serious nature of employee theft today.

- In the restaurant business, theft by employees costs between $15 billion and $25 billion per year.

- Although fewer consumers are stealing wireless phone service than ever before, there has been a significant rise in theft of service by employees of wireless companies.

- Most employees dislike the use of video surveillance cameras at work. At a Virginia restaurant, seven cashiers resigned the day before they believed closed-circuit surveillance cameras were going to be installed.

- Fraud cost American businesses about $400 billion a year.

- The average convenience store loses $20,000 per year due to employee theft.

- In Asian retail businesses, about 3 percent of the staff steal every day and 8 percent steal every week.

- Breaches of computer security are on the rise, but most of the people who break into corporate or government computers illegally are current employees rather than outsiders.

Source: See Note 68.

indeed constitute **employee theft** in the legal sense of this term. Although taking home a few pens or pencils may seem innocent and innocuous, such *petty theft,* as it is known, is so common that cumulatively, it costs companies far more than the small number of larger thefts that often capture newspaper headlines.[69]

Why do Employees Steal? Some employees steal because they are troubled in some way (e.g., they are in serious debt or have a narcotics or gambling habit). But this appears to be the minority. Many persons engage in employee theft for another reason—*they see their coworkers doing it.* To the extent that everyone around you is taking home tools, office supplies, and even petty cash, it may quickly seem appropriate for you to do it, too. Although this doesn't make it right, of course, and it clearly costs the company money, people are quick to convince themselves that petty theft is "no big deal" and not worth worrying about.

Similarly, many employees engage in theft because in some companies, *not* stealing goes against the informal norms of the work group.[70] Unspoken rules go a long way toward determining how people behave on the job (as we discussed in Chapter 8), and in some companies, an employee has to steal to feel accepted and to belong.

For example, in some retail stores, so many clerks steal goods that those who don't go along are socially ostracized by their workmates. Finally, employees frequently also engage in theft because they want to "even the score" with employers whom they believe have mistreated them. In fact, people who believe they have been underpaid frequently steal from their employers because in so doing they are righting a wrong by taking what they believe they should have had all along. (This is in keeping with equity theory described in Chapter 7.)

Reducing Employee Theft. Although we now see security cameras just about everywhere, it's clear that they are not completely effective, and employee thefts continue.[71] Fortunately, there are several additional steps that can help to lessen the problem. Although they won't be able to stop theft by employees completely, they can make a difference:

- ■ *Involve employees in the creation of a theft policy.* It is not always clear what constitutes theft. Does your company prohibit personal phone calls or using the copy machine for personal purposes? If so, violating these policies constitutes theft of company resources, although chances are good that few will think of them as such. The trick is to develop very clear policies about employee theft and to involve employees in the process of doing so. The more involved they are, the more they will "buy into" the policies and follow them.
- ■ *Communicate the costs of stealing.* Many employees would be truly shocked to learn how much their companies are losing each year through theft; they don't realize how quickly pencils, pads, papers, and other items add up—especially when everyone takes them. To the extent that this information is shared with other employees, along with a clear indication of how it costs them (e.g. through smaller raises and bonuses), many will think twice before they take company property for personal use.
- ■ *Treat people fairly.* Many employees who steal from their employers are doing so because they are trying to strike back at companies they believe have treated them unfairly in the past. So, treating people fairly—and making sure they feel that they are being treated this way—can go a long way toward reducing such resentment and employee theft.
- ■ *Be a good role model.* One of the most effective things managers can do to discourage theft is to not engage in theft themselves. After all, to the extent that employees see their managers making personal phone calls, padding their expense accounts, or taking home office supplies, they are left with the message that doing these kind of things is perfectly acceptable. When it comes to discouraging employee theft, "walking the talk" is very important.

Again, none of these steps by themselves will be completely effective, but together they can make a difference, and even slight reductions in the rate of employee theft can go right to the bottom line and significantly increase an organization's profitability.

Summary and Review of Learning Objectives

1. **Describe three types of psychological contracts and the two basic kinds of trust that play a role in work relationships.**
   One type of psychological contract is the *transactional contract.* It is characteristic of relationships that have an exclusively economic focus, last for a brief period of time, are unchanging in nature, and have a narrow, well-defined scope. Another kind is the *relational contract.* It applies to relationships that are longer-term in scope and go beyond basic economic issues such as pay for performance. A third type is the *balanced contract;* this involves elements of both transactional and relational contracts. With respect to trust, one type is known as *calculus-based trust.* It is a form of trust based on deterrence, whenever people believe that another will behave as promised out of fear of getting punished for doing otherwise. A second type is *identification-based trust.* It is based on understanding another person plus the acceptance of this person's wants and desires.

2. **Describe organizational citizenship behavior and ways in which it may be encouraged.**
   Organizational citizenship behavior consists of acts that go above and beyond one's formal job requirements in helping one's organization or fellow employees. It is influenced by many factors, including employees' beliefs about whether they are being treated fairly, their relationships with their supervisors, their attitudes toward their company, and several personal characteristics (e.g., conscientiousness).

3. **Identify ways in which cooperation can be promoted in the workplace.**
   Although by nature some people are more cooperative than others, interpersonal cooperation may be promoted by following the reciprocity principle and by adopting reward systems that encourage cooperation with others.

4. **Describe the causes and effects of conflict in organizations along with techniques that can be used to manage conflict in organizations.**
   Conflict is caused by a wide variety of factors, including grudges, malevolent attributions, destructive criticism, distrust, and competition over scarce resources. Conflict can be not only a source of negative emotions, but it also can lead to a lack of coordination, which can make performance suffer in organizations. But conflict also can have beneficial effects. These include: bringing out into the open problems that have been previously ignored, motivating people to appreciate one anothers' positions more fully, and encouraging people to consider new ideas. Bargaining is the single most effective technique for resolving conflicts. Many factors influence the course and outcomes of bargaining, including specific tactics used by bargainers (e.g., the "big lie" technique), their overall approach to the situation (win-win versus win-lose), cognitive factors such as faulty beliefs and perceptions on the part of negotiators (e.g., the belief that keeping deadlines secret is best), and the motives and emotions of the negotiators. *Alternative dispute resolution* is another approach to resolving conflicts. It involves *mediation* (in which a neutral third party works with the conflicting parties to find a mutually satisfying solution to the conflict) and *arbitration* (in which a neutral third party proposes solutions for conflicting parties).

5. **Explain how deviant organizational behavior can produce positive as well as negative effects.**
   Deviant organizational behavior (sometimes termed *workplace deviance*) involves actions on the part of employees that intentionally violate the norms of organizations and/or the rules of society. Depending on whether such actions violate one or both of these sets of norms, they can result in beneficial or harmful effects both for the organization and society. For instance, if an employee's behavior is consistent with organizational norms but violates societal ones (e.g., dumping toxic chemical wastes into a nearby river), it produces positive effects for the organization but negative ones for society. If it violates organizational norms but is consistent with societal norms, then the opposite occurs (as occurs in the case of *whistle-blowing*).

6. **Describe the major forms of workplace deviance.**

Workplace aggression is usually covert (i.e., hidden) in nature. Direct physical or verbal assaults by one employee against another are much rarer than indirect attacks, such as spreading malicious rumors about another person or withholding important information from them. Workplace aggression stems from many different factors including employees' beliefs that they have been treated unfairly, their personal characteristics, and the general level of aggression in a work group or organization. Abusive supervision is a style of supervision involving sustained displays of hostile verbal and nonverbal behaviors by a supervisor. *Cyberloafing* is a form of deviance in which employees "goof off" by using their computers for nonwork activities. *Employee theft,* another form of deviant organizational behavior, occurs when employees take company property for personal use. It can be reduced by involving employees in the creation of a theft policy, communicating the costs of stealing, and having managers be a good role model by not stealing themselves.

Points to Ponder

Questions for Review

1. What are psychological contracts and why do different kinds develop in various working relationships?
2. What is the difference between calculus-based trust and identification-based trust?
3. What forms does organizational behavior take? Why do people engage in it?
4. What are the major determinants of cooperation between individuals and between organizations?
5. What are the major causes and consequences of organizational conflict?
6. In what ways can organizational conflict be managed effectively?
7. Why can deviant organizational behavior result in negative consequences for an organization but positive consequences for society?

Experiential Questions

1. Think of individuals whom you trust and those you don't trust. In what key ways do your relationships with these people differ?
2. What are the major sources of conflict at work within the company at which you are employed? How do you think these conflicts may be resolved?
3. Have you ever been the target of some form of workplace aggression? Why do you think this happened? What did you do to deal with it?

Questions to Analyze

1. Do you agree or disagree with the following statement? People are inherently good, but are forced into behaving in negative ways by virtue of compelling forces they encounter within their organizations.
2. What would you say are the major barriers to interpersonal cooperation within the workplace?
3. What do you think *you* would do if faced with a situation in which obeying the norms of your organization would lead you to perform actions you considered illegal or unethical? Would you resist? What would be the consequences of resisting or "going along"?

Experiencing OB

Individual Exercise

Assessing Your Personal Orientation Toward Others

On page 437, you read descriptions of four different personal orientations toward others—*competitors, individualists, cooperators,* and *equalizers.* As you read these, you probably developed some ideas as to which orientation best described you. This exercise is designed to help you find out.

Directions

Use the following scale to indicate how well each of the following statements describes you.

1 = Does not describe me at all/never

2 = Describes me somewhat/some of the time

3 = Describes me moderately/half of the time

4 = Describes me greatly/much of the time

5 = Describes me perfectly/all of the time

1. _____ I don't care how much money one of my coworkers earns, so long as I make as much as I can.
2. _____ When playing a game with a close friend, I always try to keep the score close.
3. _____ So long as I do better than the next guy, I'm happy.
4. _____ I will gladly give up something for myself if it can help my team get ahead.
5. _____ It's important to me to be the best in the class, even if I'm not doing my personal best.
6. _____ I feel badly if I do too much better than my friends on a class assignment.
7. _____ I want to get an A in this class regardless of what grade you might get.
8. _____ I enjoy it when the people in my work team all pitch in together to beat other teams.

Scoring

Insert the numbers corresponding to your answers to each of the questions in the spaces corresponding to those questions. Then, add the numbers in each column (these can range from 2 to 10). The higher your score, the more accurately the personal orientation heading that column describes you.

Competitor	Individualist	Cooperator	Equalizer
3._____	1._____	4._____	2._____
5._____	7._____	8._____	6._____
Total = _____	Total = _____	Total = _____	Total = _____

Questions for Discussion

1. What did this exercise reveal about yourself?
2. Were you surprised at what you learned, or was it something you already knew?
3. Do you tend to maintain the same orientation most of the time, or are there occasions on which you change from one orientation to another? What do you think this means?

Group Exercise

Negotiating the Price of a Used Car

This exercise is designed to help you put into practice some of the skills associated with being a good negotiator. In completing this exercise, follow the steps for negotiating a win-win solution found on pages 443–444.

Directions

1. Find a thorough description of a recent-model used car in a newspaper or online.
2. Divide the class into groups of six. Within each group, assign three students to the role of buyer and three to the role of seller.
3. Each group of buyers and sellers should meet in advance to plan their strategies. Buyers should plan on getting the lowest possible price; sellers should seek the highest possible price.

4. Buyers and sellers should meet to negotiate the price of the car within the period of time specified by the instructor. Feel free to meet within your groups at any time to evaluate your strategy.
5. Write down the final agreed-upon price and any conditions that may be attached to it.

Questions for Discussion

1. Did you reach an agreement? If so, how easy or difficult was this process?
2. Which side do you think "won" the negotiation? What might have changed the outcome?
3. How might the negotiation process or the outcome have been different had this been a real situation?

Practicing OB

Your Worst Nightmare Boss

You work for a moderate-size office-supply company. Most of the people in your work group are pleasant and easy to get along with. But your boss—that is something else entirely. She always seems to be in a bad mood, and shows it. Almost every day one or more of your coworkers (including you!) become the target of her harsh verbal abuse. She frequently storms out of her office, shouting at any subordinate unlucky enough to be in her path. And she seems to take great pleasure out of raking people over the coals publicly—humiliating them in front of others. Her management style is so obnoxious that everyone hates her, and several good people have already quit to find other jobs. Answer the following questions based on the material in this chapter.

1. Why do you think she acts this way? Is it her job? Something about her personality? Or has she merely learned that intimidation works—at least for her?
2. What effects do you think her behavior is having on the performance of your work group? Morale, clearly, has been wrecked, but what about efficiency and the quality of the work done?
3. What can members of your work group do to change her obnoxious behavior? Or are you stuck with her as long as she is the supervisor and you stay with the company?

CASE IN POINT

A Sad Sendoff for Sendo

Although Birmingham, England is better known for its steel mills than its advanced technology, this didn't deter Hugh Brogan from having high-tech dreams, and big ones at that. As CEO and co-founder of Sendo, England's only mobile phone manufacturer, Brogan envisioned making Web-enabled cellular "smart phones" that could be customized before sale to fit the needs of consumers, much like PCs. To bring his dream to realization, Brogan signed a deal with software giant Microsoft to co-develop the "Z100 Smartphone," relying on a streamlined version of the Windows operating system, code-named "Stinger."

In the months that followed, Brogan's dream rapidly turned into a nightmare. Although early prototypes of the Z100 were well received by industry analysts, a commercial version of the phone continued to be postponed because the Stinger software wasn't ready. Because it's such a small company, these delays pushed Sendo to the verge of bankruptcy, forcing Brogan to borrow $14 million from Microsoft just to stay afloat. A provision of the loan required Sendo to have a working version of the phone available by April, 2002 to avoid default, but Sendo missed the deadline. The problem, Brogan claimed, was that Microsoft failed to meet its obligation to deliver the needed software. Microsoft agreed not to call in the loan, but demanded an intense technical audit of Sendo's work on the Z100.

Only a few months later, in October 2002, Orange, a Sendo competitor and Europe's second-largest mobile carrier, released its own version of a Microsoft-powered smart phone. Suspecting foul play, Sendo severed ties with Microsoft, cancelled the Z100, and entered into a relationship with Nokia to use its software instead. On November 7, 2002, Brogan dropped this bomb on his 325 employees, noting that "We have to do this to save the company." His explanation was straightforward: "Microsoft double-crossed Sendo."

Six weeks later, Sendo filed a lawsuit against the software giant alleging that it committed "fraud, theft of intellectual property, and conspiracy to destroy the startup." Although it seems as if it would not be in Microsoft's best interest to jeopardize its relationship with Sendo, Brogan has an explanation. Under the terms of their contract, Microsoft stood to get free access to Sendo's technology if Sendo went bankrupt, so that's precisely what it was attempting to make happen. Sendo's lawsuit alleges that Microsoft had a carefully constructed plan to gain its trust and "plunder" its technology while driving it to the brink of bankruptcy.

Microsoft officials have claimed that Sendo's claims are baseless and that they are looking forward to establishing this in court. Unfortunately for tiny Sendo, however, it simply couldn't afford the protracted legal battle with the giant Microsoft. In June of 2005, the company folded, selling its assets to Motorola for almost nothing—$30,000 for intellectual property and $638,749 for its plant, machinery, and equipment.

Questions for Discussion

1. What forms of trust are involved in this case and how were they violated?
2. How are issues of cooperation and competition involved in this case?
3. To what extent do you believe that Microsoft ultimately was to blame for Sendo's demise? What could Sendo have done to avoid its fate?

VIDEO CASES

Getting Your Message Right: E-Mail Code

Text messaging, instant messaging, and e-mail have changed the way people communicate with one another. A new shorthand has evolved, and most young people are fluent in this abbreviated language. Take a crash course in instant-message speak.

Discussion Questions

1. What are some of the possible problems associated with using this form of written communication in organizations? Are any of these problems offset by strengths?
2. What are the long-term implications of this computer-aided lingo for organizational functioning?
3. Identify and define any five particular "hip" expressions you are likely to use on the job. Explain the conditions under which you would be likely to use each one (e.g., when and to whom?).

Getting Your Message Right: Innovative Gadgets

A group of inventors compete to get a chance to present their products on the Home Shopping Network (HSN). This opportunity tests their abilities to peddle their products when the stakes are high. Who will win the prize for best communication skills?

Discussion Questions

1. Brian, the inventor of the shower head, seemed to have problems communicating the worthiness of his product to the HSN buyers. What particular barriers to communication does Brian appear to be facing?
2. How do you think Brian might be able to overcome these particular problems?
3. How might Brian's communication effectiveness be affected by the use of different communication media?

Bullies on the Job

Every school has its share of bullies, but it turns out some kids grow up to be bullies at work too. In fact, about one out of every six people experiences psychological abuse in the workplace. Gary Namie, the author of *The Bully at Work,* explains the phenomenon and provides some advice on how to confront the problem.

Discussion Questions

1. Why is it necessary to eliminate office bullying? As a manager, what should you do to create a "bully-free" work environment?

2. Based on the video, what should you do if you feel you are the victim of office bullying?

3. Have you ever bullied someone else at work or been the victim of someone else's bullying? If so, describe your experiences.

POWER: ITS USES AND ABUSES IN ORGANIZATIONS

Chapter Outline

Special Sections

After reading this chapter, you should be able to:

1. Describe the nature of influence in organizations and its major forms.
2. Distinguish between various forms of individual power in organizations.
3. Define empowerment and indicate how it operates among individuals and in teams.
4. Describe how the resource-dependency model and the strategic contingencies model explain the nature of power between organizational units.
5. Describe how sexual harassment constitutes an abuse of organizational power and ways of reducing its occurrence.
6. Describe when and where organizational politics occur and the forms such behavior takes.

■ PREVIEW CASE

"An Indiscriminate Jerk"

Company policy at Holland & Knight—one of the largest and most respected law firms in the world—makes it perfectly clear: "The firm is committed to fostering a collegial work environment in which all individuals are treated with dignity and respect." To nine of the firm's female attorneys in its Tampa, Florida office, however, this sentiment is a far cry from the treatment they allegedly received from Douglas Wright, one of the firm's partners. One by one, they reported incidents in which Wright touched them in ways they believed were inappropriate and/or spoke to them in sexually explicit ways.

Among the accusations was that Wright told the women to "feel my guns," referring to his muscular arms. In the context of other things he did and said that were suggestive in nature and tone, the female associates felt highly uneasy, went out of their ways to avoid Wright at the office, and even stayed away from social functions he was attending. In 2004, they filed internal charges of sexual harassment against Wright, citing incidents dating back to 1999.

Two independent investigations followed, one by an outside law firm and another by an internal body, Holland & Wright's Fair Employment Practices Committee (FEPC). Wright denied the charges against him. However, he admitted using the phrase "feel my guns" regularly, albeit in a friendly fashion, as "an icebreaker," and not in a sexual manner. Most of the investigators didn't buy it, countering that the charges against Wright were credible. With this, the FEPC recommended reprimanding him personally and privately (although these reprimands, and the accounts themselves, subsequently were made public).

Among the recommendations were that Wright be told to refrain from asking others in the firm to "feel his muscles, guns, and/or pipes," to no longer ask people about their sex lives, to stop from monitoring adherence to the firm's dress code, and to be given professional counseling about sexual harassment. In July 2004, Howell Melton, Jr., the firm's managing partner, agreed to adhere to these guidelines for reprimanding Wright, but refused to go along with specific recommendations to bar Wright from participating in the hiring of summer associates and regular firm associates.

Furious and dissatisfied by his unwillingness to accept all the recommendations, four female accusers responded to Melton in a sharply worded memo: "The message that you have sent us . . . is that cruel behavior is tolerated so long as the perpetrator is in a position of power." This sentiment was in keeping with the FEPC's recommendation that Wright's behavior be monitored because he "has been entrusted with leadership positions" and "has made questionable use of the power inherent in those positions."

465

In a 2005 interview, the burly attorney with the frat-boy personality told the *St. Petersburg* (Florida) *Press* that he denied targeting women. "I joke and tease with everyone," he stated—adding, "I suppose some might think that makes me an indiscriminate jerk."

As you might suspect, people hold varied ideas about this incident.[1] Regardless of where you might stand, however, it's noteworthy that claims about Mr. Wright's misuse of power feature prominently in this account of *sexual harassment*. Being far more senior than his accusers, Wright was able to *influence* their careers by the things he did and said. He could play a key role in determining their fates. Moreover, this capacity to affect the young female attorneys was based on the formal *power* he held over them by virtue of his high-ranking position in the law firm. The accusers cried foul in response to the managing partner's actions, suggesting that he might have been succumbing to *organizational politics* by giving Wright "a slap on the wrist"—going too easy on a colleague, who was "one of the guys." Again, although these perspectives all are matters of opinion, to be sure, it cannot be denied that uses and abuses of power play vital roles in this episode. Indeed, they are central themes in all organizations in general, warranting their attention as the focus of this chapter.

To begin, we examine the nature of the influence process in general by describing a wide range of tactics used by individuals and groups in work settings to change others' behavior. Then, building on this, we turn to the nature of power. In this connection, we examine separately power as it is acquired and used by *individuals* and power as it is used by *groups* or units in an organization. For both discussions, the key issues will be how power is gained and used, and—especially with respect to individual power—how it sometimes is shared with others. Then, we will focus on various ways in which people abuse power in organizations. At this point, we will be more explicit about the problem we've been discussing here, sexual harassment in the workplace, including information about the extent of the problem and how to address it. Finally, in closing we will cover a fascinating form of behavior known as organizational politics, examining the tactics individuals use to attain their personal (and selfish) goals, as well as the ethical issues raised by these actions.

Influence: A Basic Organizational Process

Imagine that you are a supervisor heading a group of a dozen staff members who are working on an important project for your company. Tomorrow, you're scheduled to make a big presentation to company officials, but the report isn't quite ready. If only several staff members would work late that evening, the job could be done on time. There's a problem, however. This happens to be a night when several major events are occurring—a key basketball game, a special concert featuring a famous entertainer, and a big fund-raising benefit for a local museum. Most of the people on your team have tickets to one of these events, so if anything, they'd prefer to leave early rather than stay late. What can you do to get them to change their plans and work late in order to complete the project? In other words, how can you *influence* them to do what you want—work late that evening?

social influence

Attempts to affect another in a desired fashion, whether or not these are successful.

By definition, **social influence** involves doing something that affects someone else in one way or another. In this case, you will have influenced your subordinates successfully if you have gotten them to stay late, as intended. Your influence attempt was successful, which of course is what you wanted. In this case, it may be said that you exercised *control* over them by influencing them successfully. Strictly speaking, however, even if you were unsuccessful in your efforts to get your subordinates to help, you still will have influenced them in one way or another if they responded to you in any fashion (e.g., by making them feel bad about not going along with your request). In other words, although your efforts did not yield the desired results, you still may be said to have exerted some influence. Obviously, however, we are interested in doing things that influence people in the desired fashion—that is, successful influence attempts. As such, this will be our focus.

Every day, managers confront situations in which they attempt to influence others, much as in our example. In one way or another, managers seek to change others' behavior in a manner consistent with organizational objectives. Yet, it isn't always apparent how they can, or should, go about doing so. What specific tactics do they use, and which are most effective? These are the issues to which we now turn our attention.

Tactics for Exerting Influence

It is acknowledged widely that successful managers are adept at influencing others.[2] But precisely how do they do so? And how do *you* attempt to influence others—get them to do what you want them to do? The following techniques are used most widely to influence various target individuals.[3]

- **Rational persuasion**—Using logical arguments and facts to persuade one or more others (the target persons) that a desired result will occur
- **Inspirational appeals**—Arousing enthusiasm by appealing to a target person's values and ideals
- **Collaboration**—Somehow making it easier for a target person to agree to a request
- **Consultation**—Asking a target person to participate in decision making or planning a change
- **Ingratiation**—Getting a target person to do what you want by putting him or her in a good mood or by getting him or her to like you
- **Exchange**—Promising some benefits to a target person upon complying with a request
- **Personal appeal**—Appealing to feelings of loyalty or friendship before making a request
- **Coalition-building**—Persuading by seeking the assistance of others in a coalition, or by telling them about the support you already enjoy from others
- **Legitimating**—Calling attention to one's formal authority to make a request, or verifying that it is consistent with prevailing organizational policies and practices
- **Pressuring**—Seeking compliance by making demands or threats, or otherwise intimidating a target person.

How are these various tactics used? Not surprisingly, the answer depends on differences in status between the people involved—that is, whether one is attempting to influence another who is at a higher, lower, or equivalent organizational level as oneself.[4] For example, leaders often use inspirational appeals to influence their subordinates, or even pressure, when necessary. In contrast, subordinates are unlikely to use these techniques when attempting to influence their bosses. Instead, they generally rely on consultation or rational persuasion.

We should add that overall, people believe that techniques that involve dealing with others directly (e.g., consultation) are more appropriate than ones that involve pressuring others or "cutting the ground from under them" (e.g., pressure).[5] Accordingly, the most popular techniques used to influence people at all levels of an organization are consultation, inspirational appeals, and rational persuasion.[6] These techniques generally are viewed as being appropriate for efforts to influence others regardless of whether they are at the same level, a higher level, or lower level in the organization than the person trying to exert influence. In contrast, more coercive forms of influence, such as pressure and legitimating, are viewed as less appropriate and are used far more infrequently. In fact, pressure, when it is used, is more likely to be relied on as a follow-up technique than as a tool for one's initial influence attempt—and then, only for subordinates. Also, it is interesting that some techniques—such as ingratiation, coalition, personal appeal, and exchange—are more likely to be used in combination with other techniques than used alone.

The influence tactics we've been describing thus far are ones people working in organizations use to influence one another. But organizations often seek to influence people outside the corporate boundaries, too—customers, banks and other financial institutions, even government officials. In these contexts, all the forms listed above are used, but some others also enter the picture.

A very dramatic illustration of the range of these tactics involves the many ways in which casinos try to lure the business of the world's biggest "high rollers."[7] In this case, the stakes are incredibly high: Some of these hugely rich people can lose many millions of

---

rational persuasion
Using logical arguments and factual evidence to persuade others (targets) that an idea is acceptable.

inspirational appeals
A form of social influence in which an individual arouses enthusiasm by appealing to a target person's values and ideals.

collaboration
A form of social influence in which an individual makes it easier for a target person to agree to a request.

consultation
A form of social influence in which an individual asks a target person to participate in decision making or planning a change.

ingratiation
The process of getting someone to do what you want by putting that person in a good mood or by getting him or her to like you.

exchange
A form of social influence in which an individual promises some benefits to a target person upon complying with his or her request.

personal appeal
A form of social influence in which an individual attempts to gain a target's compliance by appealing to his or her feelings of loyalty or friendship.

coalition-building
A form of social influence in which an individual seeks the assistance of others in a coalition by telling them about the support he or she already has.

legitimating
A form of social influence in which an individual calls attention to his or her authority to make a request or verifies that the request is consistent with prevailing organizational policies and practices.

pressuring
A form of social influence in which an individual seeks a target person's compliance by making demands or threats, or otherwise intimidating him or her.

dollars on a single night, thus raising corporate earnings significantly. As Glenn Schaeffer, president and CEO of Mandalay Resort Group, put it, "It's very difficult, when you've got a $1 billion building, to make a living on slot machines." So the large casinos do things such as build special, private entrances for the "highest rollers," offer them lavish free suites, and provide sumptuous meals (see Figure 12.1). In addition—and perhaps even more surprising—the casinos offer their larges customers big discounts on their losses; in other words, they agree to refund 20–25 percent of any losses these special customers may have.

Can Managers Learn to Use Influence More Effectively?

As we noted earlier, managers' successes are determined greatly by their ability to influence others effectively. For instance, a manager who can't induce his subordinates to put forth extra effort on important projects probably will not advance very far. Similarly, a manager who can't persuade her boss to consider her views on various topics carefully probably won't be seen as a good candidate for promotion. And managers who can't get their peers to assist them in various ways will have considerable difficulty in getting ahead. So influence is certainly an important skill, and one all managers should develop. But can they learn it? Or is it something with which people simply are born and that they cannot modify?

Fortunately, the news is encouraging. We all have a chance at being influential because influence is a skill, and, like other skills (see Chapter 3), it can be improved. This was revealed in research involving employees of a regional bank who were asked to rate the extent to which their managers employed various tactics of influence, the ones discussed earlier.[8] The managers also rated themselves on their use of these tactics, so that the two ratings—those by subordinates and the self-ratings by the managers—could be compared. On the basis of these ratings, the researchers then prepared "Feedback Reports" summarizing how the managers were using four core influence tactics—*rational persuasion, inspirational appeals, consultation,* and *collaboration.* These reports were given to

FIGURE 12.1

High Rollers Leverage Their Wealth: Money Talks

Elegant suites like this one at the $1.6 billion Bellagio Hotel in Las Vegas are routinely given free of charge to wealthy gamblers; the hotels seek to attract such gamblers because of the money made from their losses. As a result, these "high rollers" have incredible influence to have their requests granted at the casinos. Besides furnishing suites with gamblers' favorite amenities (including expensive wines), some have been granted free first-class airfare to the casino, lifts on a private jet, and hundreds of thousands of dollars worth of casino chips. Because of their wealth and lavish gambling practices, such individuals have influence that most of us never will experience.

the managers, who then participated in a seven-hour workshop on their use of these skills. The workshop involved showing the managers videotapes illustrating how these tactics could be used in various situations that typically arise at banks. Examples of upward, downward, and lateral influence were included. Then, groups of managers met to discuss effective ways of using these tactics.

After the workshops were completed, subordinates of the participating managers again rated the managers' use of various influence tactics. By comparing the pre-workshop and post-workshop ratings, the effectiveness of training could be assessed. In other words, the researchers were able to determine the extent to which the workshops helped managers learn to use influence tactics more effectively. A control group of managers from the same bank received feedback, but did not participate in the workshop. (Later, after the study was completed, they, too, participated in the same workshop.)

As shown in Figure 12.2, participation in the workshop did indeed increase managers' use of these highly effective tactics of influence. Those who participated in the workshop showed a significant increase in the frequency with which they used these tactics (as rated by their subordinates). In contrast, managers in the control group, who did not participate in the workshop before the ratings were completed, showed no increase in their skill at using these tactics of influence.

In sum, effective use of influence tactics is indeed a skill that we can learn. Given the benefits of being able to influence others effectively, it seems clear that this is one skill managers should work hard to acquire. And when they do, the careers they enhance will be their own! This raises an important question: How can you increase your own use of core influence tactics? For some suggestions in this regard, see the *How to Do It* section on pages 470–471.

FIGURE 12.2

Learning to Be More Influential

Managers who participated in a workshop designed to give them feedback on how they were currently using various influence tactics, plus information on how they could use these techniques more successfully, benefited greatly from this experience. They used these effective tactics of influence more frequently after the workshop than before it. In contrast, managers who did not receive such training did not show a similar increase in use of influence tactics.

Source: Based on data from Seifert, Yukl, & McDonald, 2003, see Note 8.

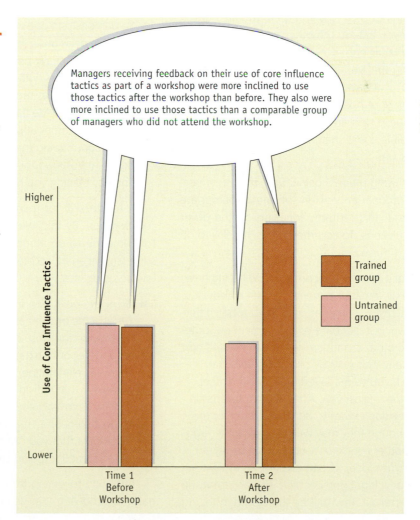

Managers receiving feedback on their use of core influence tactics as part of a workshop were more inclined to use those tactics after the workshop than before. They also were more inclined to use those tactics than a comparable group of managers who did not attend the workshop.

Trained group

Untrained group

Use of Core Influence Tactics

Higher

Lower

Time 1
Before
Workshop

Time 2
After
Workshop

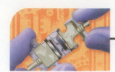

How to Do It

Cultivating Your Own Influence Skills

Clearly, we cannot review all the suggestions about improving use of influence tactics covered in the seven-hour training session that led to the research findings in Figure 12.2. However, it's possible to identify a few of the major ways of doing so for each of the four core forms of influence.

To improve your use of *rational persuasion* it's important to base your arguments on valid information and to present that information in a clear and unemotional manner. Specifically, to do this, you should consider the following suggestions.

■ *Gather the facts.* Base your arguments on clear and thorough information from objective and verifiable sources. Opinions are fine, but you will be far more influential if you can present and share the evidence on which they are based. Be prepared to share and explain all the evidence upon which your opinion was drawn.

■ *Present balanced information.* There are two sides to every story, as they say, so to enhance credibility, be sure to explain not only why you think you are right but also why you believe the other side is wrong. This double-sided tactic enhances your influence by demonstrating that you are aware of all the relevant facts and that you have taken them into account when forming your position. Even if there's some evidence that doesn't square with your position, you'll be more credible if you share it than if you ignore it or try to cover it up.

In addition to using rational persuasion, it's also important to use *inspirational* appeals in the most appropriate fashion. In general, this requires focusing on the other side's values and feelings. To accomplish this, it helps to do the following.

■ *Focus on what's best for the company.* Explaining how your position on a matter benefits yourself is likely to be of little interest to someone who has a totally different perspective. Instead, base your argument on something that the other cannot argue against—what's best for the company. This way, by taking the personal angle out of it, you've made it difficult for the other person to argue against you. After all, they can hardly claim that they don't want to do what's good for the company (although they may well have a counterargument that another course of action would be better).

■ *Point to a higher ideal.* If you present an ethical perspective or a legal perspective, it's hard to argue otherwise. After all, few will be interested in taking the side of "wrong" when what you are embracing clearly is what's "right."

As you will see later in this chapter in connection with empowering people, it's also important for managers to rely on using *consultation skills.* This involves encouraging other parties to get involved in the making of a decision. Some specific ways of doing this are as follows.

■ *Invite everyone to participate.* People like to feel that their ideas matter, making it important to ensure that everyone is invited to get involved. Someone who is not saying anything, for example, might be called upon to share his or her ideas at a meeting. The rationale is not to pick on someone, of course, but to ensure that all perspectives are heard. Doing this cannot help but make one more influential because it demonstrates one's concerns about others

■ *Encourage dissenting views.* To be influential, it helps to demonstrate one's concern for making the best possible decisions. And doing this requires making sure that you have been thorough and complete. With this in mind, it is quite useful to encourage individuals to share any ideas they might have about how a particular idea may be flawed, even if it's your favorite. When it becomes apparent to others that your concerns about doing the best thing override any personal interests, your credibility will be enhanced, thereby making you highly influential.

A fourth skill for managers to develop involves using *collaboration.* By this, we are referring to making it easier for someone to go along with your requests. Doing this successfully can be accomplished by implementing the following guidelines.

■ *Eliminate obstacles.* If someone cannot do something because he or she has other responsibilities, it helps to arrange for those other obligations to be fulfilled by another or to extend the deadlines for meeting them. By eliminating the obstacles for someone, it's easier for that individual to go along with you.

■ *Offer incentives.* People often are willing to do something if someone "makes it worthwhile" to do so. To the extent that you can provide some incentives for doing something, you can be very influential.

Although following these suggestions might not come naturally, knowing that doing so can boost your own level of influence over others surely may be an incentive to give it some effort. After all, we are not talking here about being manipulative by misusing managerial powers, but rather, ensuring that those powers are harnessed for the good of all. And that, of course, is what effective management is all about.

Individual Power: Sources and Uses

Power consists in one's capacity to link his will with the purpose of others, to lead by reason and a gift of cooperation.

Woodrow Wilson, 28th president of the United States (1856–1924),
letter to Mary A. Hulbert, September 21, 1913

power
The capacity to change the behavior or attitudes of others in a desired manner.

In this insightful comment, President Wilson made a key point about the nature of power. Putting it less articulately, **power** refers to the capacity to exert influence over others. This raises a key question: From where do people derive this capacity? In other words, what are the bases of individual power in organizations? As we now describe, there are several key answers to this important question.

Position Power: Influence That Comes with the Office

position power
Power based on one's formal position in an organization.

A great deal of the power people have in organizations comes from the specific jobs or titles they hold. In other words, they are able to influence others because of the formal power associated with their jobs. This is known as **position power**. For example, there are certain powers that the president of the U.S. has simply because of the office (e.g., signing bills into law, making treaties, etc.). These formal powers remain vested in the position and are available to anyone who holds it. When the president's term is up, these powers transfer to the new office-holder. There are four bases of position power: *legitimate power, reward power, coercive power,* and *information power.*

legitimate power
The individual power base derived from one's position in an organizational hierarchy; the accepted authority of one's position.

Legitimate Power. The power that people have because others recognize and accept their authority is known as **legitimate power**. As an example, students recognize that their instructors have the authority to make class policies and to determine grades, giving them legitimate power over the class.

It is important to note that legitimate power covers a relatively narrow range of influence, and that it may be inappropriate to overstep these bounds. For example, although a boss may require her secretary to type and fax a company document, it would be an abuse of power to ask that secretary to type her son's homework. This is not to say that the secretary might not take on the task as a favor, but doing so would *not* be the direct result of the boss's formal authority. Legitimate power applies only to the range of behaviors that are recognized and accepted as appropriate by the parties involved.

reward power
The individual power base derived from an individual's capacity to administer valued rewards to others.

Reward Power. Along with certain jobs comes the power to control the rewards others want to receive—that is, **reward power**. For example, professors have a degree of reward power over students, since they can reward them with high grades and glowing letters of recommendation. In the case of managers, the rewards available may be tangible ones such as raises and promotions, or intangible ones such as praise and recognition. In both cases, access to these desired outcomes gives power to the individuals who control them.

coercive power
The individual power base derived from the capacity to administer punishment to others.

Coercive Power. In contrast, power also results from the capacity to control punishments—that is, **coercive power**. Although most managers do not like using the threat of punishments, it is a fact of organizational life that many people rely on coercive power. If any boss has ever directly told you, "Do what I say, or else," or even implied it, you are probably all too familiar with coercive power. Often, people have power simply because others know that they have the opportunity to punish them, even if the threat of doing so is not made explicit. For example, in the military, when your commanding officer asks you to do something, you almost certainly will comply since that request can turn into an order, and there are severe consequences for failing to obey. In organizations, implied threats of demotions, suspensions without pay, and assignments to undesirable duties may enhance the coercive power of many managers.

Information Power.   The fourth source of power available to people by virtue of their positions is based on the data and other knowledge they have at their disposal—known as **information power**. Traditionally, people in top positions have available to them unique sources of information that are not available to others (e.g., knowledge of company performance, market trends, and so on), which makes them powerful. Often, it is said that "Knowledge is power," and to a large extent, this is true.

Today, however, as technology has made it possible for more information to be available to more people than ever before (which is why the field is known as *information technology*), it is an intriguing idea that information power may be losing ground as a potent source of influence in many organizations. We note, however, that although much information no longer is the unique property of a few people holding special positions, it remains the case that managers, by virtue of their positions, have access to proprietary information—that is, closely guarded information about people and processes. For example, only the owners may know for sure how profitable a privately held company truly is. Similarly, managers are expected to maintain confidentiality about a great deal of information about their employees. Thus, although far more information is available to people today than ever before, it seems safe to say that even today information remains an important source of power.

Personal Power: Influence That Comes from the Individual

So far, all the sources of influence we've discussed have been based on an individual's position in an organization. However, this is not the only way people gain power. Frequently, it also derives from an individual's own unique qualities or characteristics. This is known as **personal power**, and there are four basic types: *rational persuasion, referent power, expert power,* and *charisma.*

Rational Persuasion.   Earlier, we noted that rational persuasion is a key tactic for exerting influence—perhaps the most frequently used approach in organizations. When it is used effectively and repeatedly, however, it can also serve as a means for acquiring personal power. In other words, individuals who are truly expert at influencing others through the strength of their logical arguments and by means of an effective style for delivering those arguments, often acquire power over others. Not only can they influence them in specific situations or about specific issues, but they also gain power within their organizations by virtue of their effectiveness in doing so.

Expert Power.   Another basis of personal power lies in *expertise.* People who possess expert knowledge of a business or some facet of it often gain what is known as **expert power,** power based on expert knowledge. Consider, for example, the conductor of a symphony orchestra or band. The musicians follow this person's directions and lead not only because he or she is in charge formally (i.e., because of legitimate power), but also because this individual is a recognized expert in the field of music. When people believe that you know what you are doing, you have power over them because they are inclined to do what you say (for a fascinating example, see Figure 12.3).

Referent Power.   Imagine that you are friends with your supervisor. One day, she asks you to take on a special project that you really don't like. To anyone else, you might be inclined to say no, but because of your closeness to this individual, you may be likely to take it on as a favor. In this case, it could be said that the supervisor has power over you by virtue of your positive relationship. This illustrates another source of personal power, one

---

information power
The extent to which a supervisor provides a subordinate with the information needed to do the job.

personal power
The power that one derives because of one's individual qualities or characteristics.

expert power
The individual power base derived from an individual's recognized superior skills and abilities in a certain area.

FIGURE 12.3

Expert Power in Action

One evening, an anxious musician approached the famous conductor Arturo Toscanini minutes before a concert was about to begin. "Maestro! Maestro!" he exclaimed, "One of the keys on my instrument is broken; how will we play the concert?" Toscanini thought for a moment and then said: "All is well. That note is never played in tonight's performance." Talk about expertise! Would you follow the orders of someone with this much knowledge of their field? Probably you would, and this illustrates the basis for *expert* power.

referent power

The individual power base derived from the degree to which one is liked and admired by others.

not based on expertise, but rather, the fact that one is admired or respected by others. This type of power is known as **referent power**—that is, the power individuals have by virtue of the fact that they are liked by others. For example, senior managers who possess desirable qualities and good reputations may find that they have referent power over younger managers who identify with them and wish to emulate them. Not only might these younger individuals go along with their senior colleague because they feel they have to do so (i.e., legitimate power) or because they believe that he knows what he's doing (i.e., expert power), but simply because they like him. That represents referent power.

charisma

An attitude of enthusiasm and optimism that is contagious; an aura of leadership.

Charisma. As you know, some people seem to possess an almost magical quality: their personalities are so powerful and magnetic that they put others in a kind of trance. Such individuals are described as possessing **charisma**, and one benefit they gain from this quality is a big boost in personal power. (We'll return to this topic in Chapter 13, where we examine the nature of leadership.)

What makes them so influential—so capable of getting others to do what they want? Charismatic people have "that special something" that gets others to go along with them. Although their power seems to be magical, the "spell" cast by highly charismatic individuals, in reality, is based on several key elements. People considered to be highly charismatic have the following characteristics in common. Specifically, they

- Express clear visions of the future and how to get there
- Excite crowds by using colorful metaphors and exciting language
- Inspire trust because their integrity is beyond reproach
- Make people feel good about themselves

In your opinion, who can be described in this manner, either currently or from the past? The Rev. Dr. Martin Luther King, President John F. Kennedy, Steve Jobs, one of the founders of Apple Computer? Indeed, all these individuals have been noted for their charisma. Of course, there also are countless other individuals who are far less visible to most of us who also may be considered highly charismatic in their own worlds—and who, by virtue of this, have power over others. (We will discuss charisma more fully in Chapter 13.)

In summary, people may influence others because of the jobs or positions they hold (position power), their individual characteristics (personal power), or both. When you consider these factors, it's not difficult to understand why large differences exist in most organizations with respect to power: Some have it, and some do not. (The sources of position and personal power discussed in this section are summarized in Figure 12.4).

How Is Individual Power Used?

What bases of power do you use? Chances are good that you don't rely on just one, but several, including different types of power on different occasions. Not surprisingly, the various power bases are closely related to each other with respect to how they are used.[9]

For example, the more someone uses coercive power, the less that person is liked, and the lower his or her referent power tends to be. Similarly, managers with expert power also are likely to have legitimate power because people accept their expertise as a basis for having power over them. In addition, the higher someone's rank is in the organizational hierarchy, the more legitimate power that person has. And this, in turn, tends to be accompanied by greater opportunities to use reward and coercion.[10] Clearly, then, the various bases of power should not be thought of as completely separate and distinct from each other. They are often used together in varying combinations.

What bases of power do people prefer to use? Although the answer depends on many considerations, overall people prefer to use expert power most and coercive power least.[11] Although this is the case with respect to the specific power bases we've identified so far, an interesting picture emerges when you ask people to report exactly what sources of power they have on their jobs. Figure 12.5 presents the results of a survey in which 216 CEOs of American corporations were asked to rank-order the importance of a series of specific sources of power.[12] The numbers shown in Figure 12.5 reflect the percentage of executives who included each source of power among their top three choices. These findings indicate not only that top executives seem to derive their power from many different sources, but also that their power rests mainly on their personal characteristics (personal power) and on support from people located throughout their organizations.

Although executives use a wide variety of powers to influence their subordinates, they tend to rely most on expert power when attempting to influence peers and superiors.[13] After all, it is almost always appropriate to try to get others to go along with you if you justify your attempts on the basis of your expertise. In contrast, coercive tactics tend to be rejected in general, and are especially inappropriate when attempting to influence a higher-ranking person.[14]

Influencing superiors is tricky because of the **counterpower** they have—that is, the capacity to neutralize another's influence attempts. When attempting to influence another who is believed to have no power at his or her disposal, one doesn't have to worry about

counterpower
The capacity to neutralize another's influence attempts.

FIGURE 12.4

Sources of Individual Power: An Overview

As shown here, *individual power* can derive either from formal positions within an organization *(position power)* or from various personal characteristics *(personal power)*.

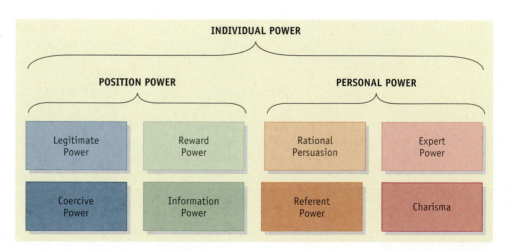

FIGURE 12.5

American CEOs: What Are Their Power Bases?

A survey of more than 200 American CEOs revealed that they obtained their power primarily by cultivating the support of others at different levels throughout the organization and by virtue of their personality and leadership skills

Source: Based on data appearing in Stewart, 1999; see Note 12.

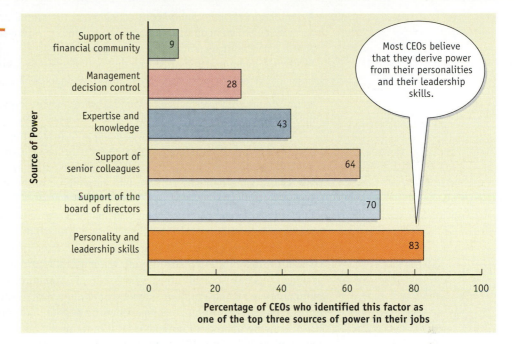

possible retaliation. When dealing with an individual with considerably greater power, however, this is a real possibility and can lead to greater compliance with the wishes of the powerful party. Flexing one's muscles in a power struggle, then, is a sure way to get the other party to flex theirs. After all, in organizations wielding power is vitally important.

The situation is complicated still further, however, by the fact that one party may have higher power on one dimension, and another party may have higher power on another dimension. Consider, for example, the case of secretaries who have acquired power because they have been with their company for many years. They know the ropes and can get things done for you if they want, or they can get you hopelessly bogged down in red tape. Their expert knowledge gives them a great sense of power over others. Although they may lack the legitimate power of their executive bosses, secretaries' expertise can be a valuable source of counterpower over those with more formal power.

Empowerment: Sharing Power with Employees

President Theodore Roosevelt was quoted as saying, "The best executive is the one who has sense enough to pick good men to do what he wants done, and self-restraint enough to keep from meddling with them while they do it."[15] Although this remark was made about 100 years ago, it's as true today as ever. In fact, an important trend has been occurring in organizations these days: Power is shifting downward. Top managers are granting more power to lower-level managers, and supervisors are putting power into the hands of employees themselves.

In other words, many of today's employees are not being "managed" in the traditional, top-down styles that have been used by managers of generations past. Instead, power is often shifted down the ladder to teams that are allowed to make decisions themselves. Survey findings tell the story clearly: When asked about how much power they currently had compared to 10 years ago, only 19 percent of CEOs surveyed reported that they now had more power. Thirty-six percent indicated that they had the same amount of power. However, the largest group, 42 percent, indicated that they had less power.[16]

These figures are in keeping with the idea of **empowerment**—the process of delegating authority to individuals at the lowest level in an organization at which competent decisions can be made.[17] Although empowerment involves many specific steps and policies, three are most central. These are:

empowerment
The passing of responsibility and authority from managers to employees.

- *Information sharing*—Providing potentially sensitive information on costs, productivity, quality, and financial performance to employees throughout the organization

■ *Autonomy through boundaries*—Using organizational designs (see Chapter 15) and practices that encourage autonomous action by employees, including work procedures, areas of responsibilities, and goals

■ *Team accountability*—Ensuring that both decision-making authority and performance accountability reside in teams (see Chapter 8)

Overall, then, empowerment is a trend toward sharing power with employees in several important ways.[18]

As you might imagine, empowerment is not just a simple yes-or-no option, but a matter of degree (see Figure 12.6).[19] At one end of the scale are companies such as the traditional assembly lines, in which workers have virtually no power to determine how to do their jobs. At the opposite end are jobs in which employees have complete control over what they do and how they do it.

We see this at companies using self-managed work teams (as described in Chapter 8). For example, at Chapparel Steel managers are free to hire, train, and use new employees however they think best.[20] At W. L. Gore, manufacturers of specialty fabrics, the empowerment philosophy is so strongly entrenched that employees work without any fixed, assigned sets of responsibilities.[21] Less extreme in nature, and found more commonly, are companies in which employees have some degree of responsibility for their work and have a voice in important decisions, but are not completely free to work however they see fit. A growing number of companies fall into this category, including the General Motors Saturn plant in Spring Hill, Tennessee.[22] Government bureaus and departments, too, have jumped on the empowerment bandwagon. For instance, in Canada, government downsizing and restructuring, undertaken to increase efficiency, has been linked with empowerment of employees. According to an account of these new policies: "In accordance with the 'New Public Management,' narrow jobs have become enriched, enlarged [see Chapter 7] and more fluid. More information and decisions are delegated to self-directed teams. Work arrangements are more flexible, with increased overtime, and more choice for employees."[23]

When employees are empowered, their supervisors cannot be thought of as "bosses" who use coercive power to "push people around." Rather, they are more likely to serve as teachers, or "facilitators" who guide their work groups by using their knowledge and experience (i.e., their expert power). Traditional managers may tell people what to do and how and when to do it, but supervisors of empowered workers are more inclined to provide assistance. They ask questions that help others solve problems and that allow them to make decisions on their own (see Figure 12.7).

If the practices we've been describing here don't fit well with your own experiences, don't be surprised. Because most managers are somewhat reluctant to surrender control, the

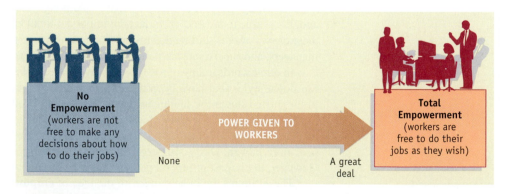

FIGURE 12.6

The Empowerment Continuum: Relinquishing Control Is a Matter of Degree

As shown here, empowering subordinate workers may take several different forms, ranging from giving workers complete power to determine how to do their jobs, to giving them no power at all.

FIGURE 12.7

Empowering People to Preserve the Environment

In her position as "Community Empowerment Leader" for the World Wildlife Fund's "Friends of the Reef" Project, Ria Fitriana is responsible for helping organize the efforts of community members to help preserve the precious coral reefs in the Asia-Pacific region. By carefully coaching and educating members of the community, she enlists their aid in contributing to the group's conservation goals.

empowered employee is still in the minority in the vast majority of today's organizations.[24] However, experts predict a change in that direction is coming, and fast.[25] Empowerment is likely to be coming to a workplace near you. If this prediction is correct, we can look forward to significant changes in the way people will use power in organizations.

Do Employees Like Being Empowered?

If empowerment is indeed a trend in today's organizations, it's important to consider how employees react to it. In general, most respond quite favorably.[26] For instance, consider Xerox. Years ago, a corporate reorganization led to having the employees take greater responsibility for their work, especially at its distribution center outside Atlanta. The head of that facility considers its 24 hourly paid, union workers as managers, and treats them as such. They are free to take responsibility for their own jobs and to solve problems as they see fit. And that's just what they've done. For example, employees have found ways to save the company money on trash removal (by recycling) and in shipping costs (by using lighter-weight pallets). They even have reorganized warehousing procedures such that 99.9 percent of orders now ship on time. Absenteeism is almost nonexistent and productivity is up dramatically.[27]

Another example of the benefits of empowerment is provided by Omni Hotels. The company recently implemented a program called the Power of One to help combat exceptionally high employee turnover and low levels of satisfaction among guests. This involved training all employees to make independent decisions that benefit guests—even if it meant bending the rules. Frontline employees also were empowered to listen to angry customers and to give them whatever they wanted (within reason, of course).[28] Within the first month, customer satisfaction surged 16 percent, and after the first year, turnover was reduced to 42 percent, from 65 percent before the plan was introduced. The hotel chain has enjoyed higher profits ever since. In fact, it placed among the top three upscale domestic hotel chains in a recent J.D. Power and Associates survey.[29]

These and many similar success stories suggest that empowerment does indeed often confer important benefits both on employees and their organizations.[30] But we don't want to paint too rosy a picture. It would be misleading to suggest that employees always react positively to empowerment. Although many like some aspects of it, they may find it challenging and stressful to take on new responsibilities. This point is in keeping with ones we made earlier in this book suggesting that not all employees are motivated to perform enriched jobs (Chapter 7) or to work in teams in which they have freedom to make decisions (see Chapter 10). There seem to be clear individual differences in the degree to which people are attracted to jobs that empower them to make decisions. To many of us, this seems like a wonderful opportunity, whereas to others, it's merely an obligation that they would rather not undertake. (In view of this, we pose an interesting question: Do employees all over the world react in the same way to empowerment? Is empowerment perceived differently in different countries? For a look at this matter, see the *OB in a Diverse World* section below.)

Empowerment in Teams

empowerment climate

A relatively enduring atmosphere in the workplace that is supportive of empowerment.

So far, we have focused on the effects of empowerment for individual employees. However, empowerment also may influence teams and work units of various types, and a recent study reveals precisely how that may occur.[31] Researchers conducting the study reasoned that organizations adopting various procedures and practices involving empowerment will create what they called an **empowerment climate**—a relatively enduring atmosphere in the workplace that is supportive of empowerment. Specifically, they hypothesized that the more strongly organizations encourage information sharing, autonomy, and holding teams accountable for their work (key aspects of empowerment), the more those organizations would have an empowerment climate. And this, in turn, would enhance the performance of teams—and also, by generating feelings of empowerment among individuals, enhance both individual performance and job satisfaction (see Figure 12.8).

To test these predictions, employees of a high-tech manufacturing company were asked to complete a questionnaire assessing their organizations' empowerment climate (e.g., "We create structures and procedures that encourage people to take initiative in improving organizational performance"). Team performance was assessed through ratings by higher-level managers who had responsibility for managing these work units, and

OB In a Diverse World

Reactions to Empowerment in Various Nations

Cultures differ greatly, and one of the ways in which they vary involves the extent to which inequalities among people in status or power are seen as appropriate. In *high-power-distance* cultures (so-called "vertical" societies, such as India and Japan), such differences are viewed as natural and acceptable and people are comfortable with hierarchical distinctions.[32] In *low-power-distance* cultures (so-called "horizontal" societies, such as the United States and Mexico), in contrast, differences in power are viewed as less acceptable and people feel uncomfortable with distinctions based on position or rank.

How do people in these two kinds of cultures react to empowerment? Presumably, people in low-power-distance cultures will react more favorably. After all, empowerment tends to reduce distinctions based on hierarchies so that managers and their subordinates are on a more equal footing, and this would be consistent with the basic values of a low-power-distance culture. In contrast, people in high-power-distance cultures might find empowerment somewhat disturbing: They are comfortable with differences based on hierarchies and might be somewhat uncomfortable with the blurring of such differences produced by empowerment.

Research has shown that this, in fact, is the case. In one intriguing project, a team of researchers asked employees

of a multinational corporation to rate the extent to which empowerment was occurring in their company and their satisfaction with their work, their supervisors, and their coworkers.[33] These measures were collected in four different countries: the United States, Poland, and Mexico (which are low in power distance) and India (which is relatively high in power distance). As you might expect, the researchers found a positive relationship between empowerment and job satisfaction in the United States, Poland, and Mexico. That is, when empowerment was high, job satisfaction was high as well. However, there was a negative relationship between these factors in India: When empowerment was high, job satisfaction was low.

These findings indicate that although empowerment is often a positive development in many organizations, its benefits may not be universal in scope. In fact, in cultures where people are used to distinctions based on hierarchies, employees may find empowerment a strange concept and—more importantly—inconsistent with traditional cultural values. Clearly, then, for management practices to succeed, they must take into account the cultures in which they are applied. Failing to do so runs the real risk of accepting a "one-practice-fits-all" mentality, and that, in turn, can undermine the very benefits that inspired their use in the first place.

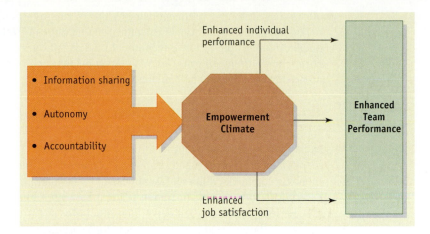

FIGURE 12.8

The Benefits of Team and Individual Empowerment

Creating an empowerment climate in an organization facilitates team performance and also encourages individual empowerment. This, in turn, enhances individual performance and job satisfaction.

Source: Based on findings reported by Seibert, Silver, & Randolph, 2004; see Note 31.

individual performance was measured by ratings from team leaders; job satisfaction was reported by individual team members.

The study's results were in keeping with Figure 12.8. Not only did empowerment climates enhance team performance, but they also contributed to feelings of psychological empowerment among employees. This, in turn, enhanced both individual performance and job satisfaction. In short, creating an organizational climate favorable to empowerment enhanced not only individual performance, but team performance as well.

Additional research has shown that team empowerment also leads to beneficial effects for teams that do not actually work together—that is, *virtual teams* (see Chapter 8).[34] One study examined empowerment in teams of employees who worked in a high-tech service organization in the travel industry, whose members met one another in person only rarely. Interestingly, the more these teams were empowered to do their work, the higher was the level of satisfaction among the customers they served.

Overall, then, evidence for the benefits of empowering employees—both as individuals and as members of teams or work-units—seems compelling. Not only does empowerment generate high motivation, enthusiasm, and satisfaction among employees, but it also enhances both individual and team performance. So while empowerment may not be a totally unmixed blessing, and its effects may vary somewhat from culture to culture (as noted in the *OB in a Diverse World* section on p. 478), evidence suggests that it is one step that modern organizations can take to bolster their own performance.

The Power of Organizational Groups

So far, we have examined the uses of power by individuals and teams. However, in organizations, it is not only people acting alone or in small teams who wield power, but also large groups and subunits, such as departments.[35] For instance, just as some individuals are considered more powerful than others, so too are some bodies of people, including branch offices, trade unions, and so on.

This is based on the tendency for power within organizations to be distributed unequally across different departments or subunits. These have responsibility for different functions such as finance, human resource management, marketing, and research and development (we will describe these arrangements more fully in Chapter 15), and some clearly have more power than others. Why? What are the sources of such power? By what means do some groups come to control the activities of other groups? Answers to these questions are offered by two theoretical models—the *resource-dependency model* and the *strategic contingencies model.* We now consider each of these, noting what they reveal about power at the group or subunit level.

The Resource-Dependency Model: Controlling Critical Resources

It is not difficult to think of an organization as a complex set of subunits that are constantly exchanging resources with each other. By this, we mean that formal organizational departments may both give to and receive from other departments such valued commodities as money, personnel, equipment, supplies, and information. These critical resources are necessary for the successful operation of organizations.

Various subunits often depend on others for such resources. To illustrate this point, imagine a large organization that develops, produces, and sells its products. The sales department provides financial resources that enable the research and development department to create new products. Of course, it cannot do so effectively without information from the marketing department about what consumers are interested in buying and how much they might be willing to pay. The production department has to do its part by manufacturing the goods on time, but only if the purchasing department can supply the needed raw materials—and at a price the finance department accepts.

It is easy to see how the various organizational subunits are involved in a complex set of interrelationships with others. To the extent that one subunit controls the resources on which another subunit depends, it may be said to have power over it. After all, controlling valued resources allows the group that has such control to successfully influence the actions of other groups. Subunits that control more resources than others may be considered more powerful in the organization. Indeed, such imbalances, or *asymmetries,* in the pattern of resource dependencies occur normally in organizations. The more one group depends on another for needed resources, the less power it has (see Figure 12.9).

resource-dependency model
The view that power resides within subunits that are able to control the greatest share of valued organizational resources.

The **resource-dependency model** proposes that a subunit's power is based on the degree to which it controls the resources required by other subunits.[36] Thus, although all subunits may contribute something to an organization, the most powerful ones are those that contribute the most important resources. Controlling the resources other departments need puts a subunit in a better position to bargain for the resources it, in turn, requires.

To illustrate this point, let's consider a classic study of differences between power wielded by departments in a large university.[37] Within a university, the various academic departments may be very unequal with respect to the power they possess. For example, some may have more students, be more prestigious in their national reputation, receive greater grant support, and have more representatives on important university committees than others. As such, they would be expected to have greater control over valued resources. This was

FIGURE 12.9

The Resource-Dependency Model: An Example

The resource-dependency model of organizational power explains that subunits acquire power when they control critical resources needed by other subunits. In this example, the accounting department would be considered more powerful than either the production department or the marketing department.

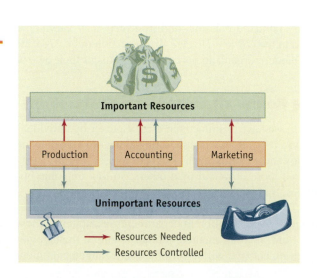

found to be the case within the large state university examined in this study. Specifically, the more powerful departments proved to be those that were most successful in gaining scarce and valued resources from the university (e.g., funds for graduate student fellowships, faculty research grants, summer faculty fellowships). As a result, they became even more powerful, suggesting that within organizations, the rich subunits tend to get richer.

A question that follows from this conclusion is: How do various organizational subunits gain such power to begin with? That is, why do certain departments come to control the most resources when an organization is newly formed? Insight into this question is provided by a study of the semiconductor industry in California.[38] Using personal interviews, market research data, and archival records, it was found that two main factors account for how much power an organizational subunit has: (1) the period within which the company was founded, and (2) the background of the entrepreneur starting the company. For example, because research and development functions were critical for the earliest semiconductor firms (founded 1958–1966), this department had the most power among the oldest firms—the ones founded in the semiconductor industry's early years. Because research and development became somewhat less important, while sales became more important in later years as the industry matured, these departments were found to be relatively more powerful in younger companies—ones founded in the 1970s and 1980s. In short, the importance of each area of corporate activity at the time the company started operations determined the relative power of that area years later (in 1985, when the study was conducted).

It also was found that the most powerful organizational subunits tended to be those that represented the founder's area of expertise. Thus, for example, the marketing and sales departments of companies founded by experts in marketing and sales tended to have the greatest amounts of power. This research provides an important missing link in our understanding of the attainment of subunit power within organizations. This tendency for the greatest corporate power to reside in areas of the founder's expertise has been found in companies all over the world. As one case in point, Mr. Ibuka, the founder of Sony (then, Tokyo Telecommunications Laboratory), was an engineer—and engineering remains very powerful in Sony to this day.

In short, the resource-dependency model suggests that a key determinant of subunit power is the control of valued resources: The greater this control, the greater the power the subunit or department can wield. However, as we will now see, control over resources is not the only factor that determines organizational power; control over the *activities* of other subunits is important, too.

The Strategic Contingencies Model: Power Through Dependence

In many companies, the accounting department has the responsibility for approving or disapproving funds requested by other departments. To the extent that it has this power, its actions greatly affect the activities of other units, which depend on its decisions. Specifically, other departments' operations are *contingent* on what the accounting department does. To the extent that a department is able to control the relative power of various organizational subunits by virtue of its actions, it is said to have control over *strategic contingencies*. For example, if the accounting department consistently approved the budget requests of the production department but rejected the budget requests of the marketing department, it would be making the production department more powerful.

Where do the strategic contingencies lie within organizations? In a classic study researchers found that power was distributed differently (i.e., across various departments) in different industries.[39] More specifically, they found that within successful firms, strategic contingencies are controlled by the departments that are most important for organizational success. For example, within a food-processing industry, where it was critical for new products to be developed and sold, successful firms had strategic contingencies controlled by the sales and research departments. In the container manufacturing field, where the timely delivery of high-quality goods is a critical determinant of organizational success, successful firms placed most of the decision-making power in the sales and production departments. Thus, successful firms focused the control over strategic contingencies within the subunits most responsible for their organization's success.

strategic contingencies model

A view explaining power in terms of a subunit's capacity to control the activities of other subunits. A subunit's power is enhanced when (1) it can reduce the level of uncertainty experienced by other subunits, (2) it occupies a central position in the organization, and (3) its activities are highly indispensable to the organization.

uncertainty

Lack of knowledge about the likelihood of certain events occurring in the future.

centrality

The degree to which an organizational unit has a key impact on others because it has to be consulted and because its activities have immediate effects on an organization.

nonsubstitutable

The degree to which an organizational unit is the only one that can perform its particular duties.

What factors give subunits control over strategic contingencies? The **strategic contingencies model** suggests that several are crucial. First, power may be enhanced by subunits that have the capacity to reduce the levels of **uncertainty** faced by others—that is, the degree to which it can provide information about the likelihood of certain events occurring in the future. For example, departments that can shed light on projections of future markets, changes in government regulations, and the availability of needed supplies, for example, can be expected to wield the most power. Accordingly, the balance of power within organizations may be expected to change as organizational conditions shift.

Consider, for example, changes that have taken place over the years in public utility companies. When public utilities first began, the engineers tended to wield the most power. But now that these companies have matured and face problems of litigation and governmental regulation (particularly over nuclear power), power has shifted to lawyers.[40] A similar shift toward greater power to the legal department has occurred in recent years in the area of human resource management, where a complex set of laws and governmental regulations have created a great deal of uncertainty for organizations. Powerful subunits are those that can help reduce such uncertainty.

Second, subunits control power to the extent that they possess a high degree of *centrality* in the organization. **Centrality** refers to the degree to which an organizational unit has a key impact on others because it has to be consulted and because its activities have immediate effects on an organization. Some organizational subunits perform functions that are more central, whereas others perform functions that are more peripheral. For example, a firm's accounting department may have to be consulted by others before expenditures can be approved. As a result, it has a very central position in its organization. A unit's centrality is also considered high to the extent that its actions have immediate effects. So, for example, in an auto company, the effects would be far more dramatic and immediate if production lines stopped than if the research and development activities ceased. Thus, the units in charge of manufacturing or production would have greater centrality—hence, wield more power—than those responsible for research and development. In other words, the central connection of some departments to immediate organizational success provides them with considerable power.

Third, a subunit controls power when its activities are **nonsubstitutable**—that is, the degree to which it is the only unit that can perform its particular duties. So, if any group can perform a certain function, then the particular subunits responsible for controlling that function are not especially powerful. In a hospital, for example, personnel on surgical teams are certainly more nonsubstitutable than personnel in the maintenance department because fewer individuals have the skills needed to perform surgical duties. Because an organization easily can replace some employees with others either within or outside it, subunits composed of individuals who are most easily replaced tend to wield very little organizational power. A summary of the three major factors included in the strategic contingencies model is provided by Figure 12.10.[41]

In sum, when combined, the resource dependency and strategic contingencies models offer important insights into the question, "Why, in a given organization, are some subunits

FIGURE 12.10

Strategic Contingencies Model: Identifying Sources of Subunit Power

The strategic contingencies model explains intraorganizational power in terms of the capacity of some subunits to control the actions of others. Subunit power may be enhanced by the factors shown here.

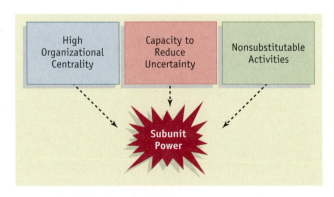

or departments more powerful than others?" This question focuses on the power of organizational units as a whole instead of individuals per se. Interestingly, the power that individuals and groups have in organizations generally is used for good—that is, to promote the objectives of the organization and the well-being of the individuals within them. Sometimes, however, as you know probably only too well, we see abuses of power, situations in which people use their power in ways that are harmful or destructive. In each of the remaining parts of this chapter, we address a particularly important form of abuse of power—*sexual harassment* and *organizational politics*. Both constitute what may be considered "the dark side" of organizational power.

Sexual Harassment: A Serious Abuse of Power

Recall this chapter's Preview Case about a prominent male attorney who was alleged to have sexually harassed as many as nine of his female colleagues over a five-year period. His actions of inappropriate behavior—or even claims about them—harmed not only the victims, but also sullied his own reputation and tarnished the image of his otherwise distinguished firm. Unfortunately, this represents only one episode of a form of behavior that is all too common in many workplaces. And because it represents an abuse of power, *sexual harassment* is a theme we address in this section of the chapter.

Before moving forward, let's underscore this point: Almost always, sexual harassment is about power. In the majority of instances, it is an abuse of power: A more powerful person (usually, but not always, a male) gives unwanted sexual attention to a less powerful person (usually, but not always, a female). And because there's a power difference between the parties, the less powerful individual is put in a difficult situation.

Nature and Scope of Sexual Harassment

To understand why there is such concern about sexual harassment, we begin by defining what is meant by this form of behavior and presenting some statistics about its prevalence and forms. This information will make it clear that sexual harassment is an issue about which we all must be highly concerned.

Definition. Although the working definitions used in various organizations may differ, the definition of **sexual harassment** from the U.S. Equal Employment Opportunity Commission is that it is:

> Unwelcome sexual advances, requests for sexual favors, and other verbal or physical conduct of a sexual nature constitute sexual harassment when this conduct explicitly or implicitly affects an individual's employment, unreasonably interferes with an individual's work performance, or creates an intimidating, hostile, or offensive work environment.[42]

sexual harassment
Unwelcome sexual advances, requests for sexual favors, and other verbal or physical conduct of a sexual nature constitute sexual harassment when this conduct explicitly or implicitly affects an individual's employment, unreasonably interferes with an individual's work performance, or creates an intimidating, hostile, or offensive work environment.

To understand this definition fully, it helps to keep in mind the following facts.

- The victim as well as the harasser may be a woman or a man. The victim does not have to be of the opposite sex.
- The harasser can be the victim's supervisor, an agent of the employer, a supervisor in another area, a coworker, or a nonemployee.
- The victim does not have to be the person harassed but could be anyone affected by the offensive conduct.
- Unlawful sexual harassment may occur without economic injury to or discharge of the victim.
- The harasser's conduct must be unwelcome.

Because sexual harassment is covered under Title VII of the Civil Rights Act of 1964, the U.S. Equal Employment Opportunity Commission (EEOC) keeps statistics on charges filed at the federal level. In 2005, for example, the EEOC received 12,679 charges of sexual harassment, 14.3 percent of which were filed by males. It recovered $47.9 million in monetary benefits for charging parties and other aggrieved individuals (not including monetary benefits obtained through litigation).

quid pro quo sexual harassment

A form of sexual harassment in which the harasser requires sexual favors in exchange for some tangible conditions, privileges, or terms of employment from a victim.

hostile environment sexual harassment

A form of sexual harassment in which individuals are subjected to negative, unwanted, or abusive conditions under which their ability to work effectively and comfortably is compromised.

Major Forms.   The law recognizes two major forms of sexual harassment. So-called **quid pro quo sexual harassment** occurs when the harasser requires sexual favors in exchange for some tangible conditions, privileges, or terms of employment from a victim. Think of this very blatant form of sexual harassment as a direct exchange of sexual favors for employment favors. At one time, this was the only recognized form of sexual harassment.

Today, however, sexual harassment also is considered to have occurred if a hostile work environment is created. This so-called **hostile environment sexual harassment** refers to the practice of subjecting individuals to negative, unwanted, or abusive conditions under which the ability to work effectively and comfortably is compromised. Hostile environments may exist not only because of the words or actions of particular individuals, but also by virtue of management's failure to prevent such actions among employees. This describes the form of sexual harassment depicted in this chapter's Preview Case. Although it was not claimed that Mr. Wright engaged in quid pro quo harassment, he was alleged to have created a hostile work environment for his accusers. This particular form of harassment is most prevalent. And, as you might imagine, by virtue of its inherent ambiguity, it also is most challenging to establish. Nonetheless, it's not difficult to imagine how its impact on victims can be quite devastating (see Figure 12.11).

Occurrence.   As you might imagine, only a small proportion of cases of sexual harassment are brought to the federal level; the vast majority are addressed as internal matters by the human resources departments within organizations. Exact figures about the prevalence of sexual harassment are difficult to come by because about 95 percent of all such incidents go unreported. However, it has been estimated that about 42 percent of women and 15 percent of men report being victims of sexual harassment.[43]

Interestingly, these figures have remained relatively flat in recent years. This appears to be the result of two countervailing forces. On the one hand, as people have become increasingly aware of sexual harassment because of accounts in the popular press, they have grown more sensitive to its inappropriate nature and the fact that they can (and should) do something about it. This leads them to report the behavior to appropriate authorities in their organizations, thereby contributing to a rising trend. However, the apparent rate of sexual harassment hasn't risen overall because at the same time, awareness of the problem has inhibited some prospective perpetrators from engaging in such behavior. Thus, there also may be less of it occurring. Overall, then, fewer incidents coupled with more widespread reporting of those incidents makes it easy to see why the occurrence of sexual harassment appears not to be a

FIGURE 12.11

Sexual Harassment: An All-Too-Common Abuse of Power

It's possible to establish that sexual harassment has occurred if a person with higher power makes unwanted sexually oriented comments to a less powerful person. Such hostile environment sexual harassment makes victims feel uncomfortable (or worse!), thereby interfering with their ability to do their jobs.

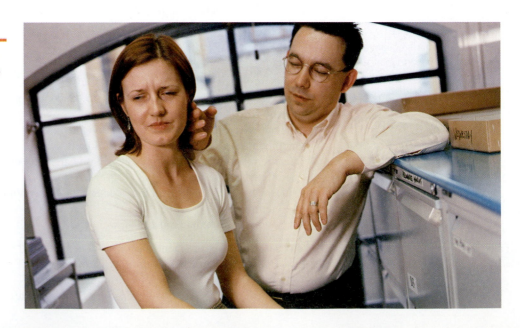

growing problem. Don't be misled, however; the problem remains quite serious and despite progress, it is nowhere close to disappearing from the scene.

Costs: Financial and Psychological. The costs of sexual harassment are considerable for all the parties involved—victims, perpetrators, and their organizations. Moreover, these costs are both financial and psychological in nature.[44]

According to *Working Woman Magazine,* a typical *Fortune* 500 corporation can expect to lose about $10 million annually due to sexual harassment, not counting the costs of litigation or legal damages. These losses take many forms, such as higher absenteeism and turnover, lower productivity, increased health-care costs, and decline in morale. This figure also does not include damage to a company's reputation, which also can be considerable. For a breakdown of some such costs for an average single case, see the figures reported in Table 12.1.[45]

For victims, of course, the costs of harassment also are great. This includes humiliation, loss of dignity, psychological (and sometimes physical) injury, and damage to professional reputation and career. Inevitably, the victims face a choice between their work and their self-esteem. Sometimes, they face a choice between their jobs and their own safety, which, of course, nobody should have to make. The health-related effects of sexual harassment are considerable in scope and severity, ranging from headaches and sleeplessness to various stress-related disorders (on the unhealthy effects of stress, see Chapter 5) and even suicide.[46]

Finally, the costs to an individual defending himself against charges of sexual harassment also can be very high. If a civil suit is brought against him, the financial costs can be substantial. Also, of course, the inevitable damage to his reputation, and loss of employment, can be devastating as well. The bottom line is clear: When sexual harassment occurs, nobody wins. At this point, you may find yourself thinking that sexual harassment is somewhat different from what you envisioned it to be. Indeed, it is the subject of several myths, ones that must be exploded before fully understanding the nature and gravity of sexual harassment, let alone ways of reducing its occurrence. For some of these myths and the problems associated with them, see the *OB: Making Sense Out of Common Sense* section on page 486.

TABLE 12.1 Sexual Harassment Claims: Their High Costs to Organizations

The costs to organizations associated with defending themselves against sexual harassment claims fall into three major categories—direct financial expenses, lost time, and bruised public image. As summarized here, the various sources of expenses falling into each category can be considerable. The figures shown are for 2002 and reflect average expenses associated with defending against a single case of sexual harassment.

Category	Source	Amount or Form
Direct financial expenses	Attorney fees	$250,000 if case goes to trial; $95 if case is settled before trial
	Settlement costs	$150,000 to $250,000 and up
Lost time	Time spent by employee preparing for the claim process and investigating the claim	120 hours (60 hours preparing and 60 hours investigating)
	Time spent by managers and employees in the claim process	80 hours (40 hours spent by each)
Bruised public image	Damage to reputation as a prospective employer	Difficulty attracting new employees
	Adverse media publicity	Potential decline in stock prices (if the company is publicly traded)

Source: Adapted from Employment Law Learning Technologies and Littler Mendelson; see Note 45.

OB Making Sense Out of Common Sense

Dispelling Myths About Sexual Harassment

To understand fully the nature of sexual harassment it is important to recognize that some of the things that often are believed about such behavior are myths. Dispelling false beliefs and acknowledging the underlying truths, however, is a necessary step toward reducing the occurrence of this highly undesirable form of behavior. With this in mind, we identify and explode several of these myths.[47]

Myth 1. If women only would say "no," harassment would stop.

Fact. This is problematic on two counts. First, it often is difficult and very embarrassing for women of lower organizational ranks to confront higher-ranking harassers by telling them to stop what they are doing. It is up to the higher-ranking men to refrain from putting women in this position by not harassing them in the first place.

Second, even if a woman says "no," some men rationalize that "no really means yes," leading them to continue harassing their victims. The fact could not be more simple: No means no. Bottom line: It's preferable to not put anyone in a situation in which they have to say "no," but if and when it is said, the offensive behavior should stop immediately.

Myth 2. Harassment will stop if the victim simply ignores it.

Fact. The opposite is true: When harassment is ignored it either continues or gets worse. This occurs because the harasser interprets the victim's silence as a sign of approval or encouragement. Remember, victims, quite understandably, may be too embarrassed to speak up, so they never should be put in a position where they have to do so. If necessary, however, any victim of sexual abuse, or witnesses to such abuse on the part of others, should report it to the proper authorities.

Myth 3: If women dressed less provocatively, there would be no sexual harassment.

Fact. Anyone can be a victim of sexual harassment no matter how that individual dresses. Often, harassment is about demonstrating power, rather than sexual interest sparked by attractiveness. Besides, dressing a certain way does not grant permission to touch or otherwise harass.

Myth 4. Most behavior considered sexual harassment is merely natural flirting and teasing between people.

Fact. This is an all-too-common rationalization. There's nothing friendly or playful about unwanted sexual innuendos, inappropriate touching, and making lewd comments. Instead of considering these innocuous expressions of friendship, recognize them for what they are—abuses of power and a need to control. If the behavior were friendly, it would not be so hurtful.

Myth 5. What some may mistake for harassment is really just a harmless compliment.

Fact. There's nothing harmless about being humiliated, or even frightened, by something that someone else says or does. Nobody should be required to endure such treatment, even if it's well intended and seemingly innocuous. If the target isn't taking it this way, then it's not so harmless after all.

Myth 6. "Nice" people, such as professionals, cannot be harassers.

Fact. Sexual harassers may not be perverts; they do not match any particular profile. Almost anyone—even a popular, highly admired professional—might be a sexual harasser. In fact, highly regarded and trusted individuals might be able to engage in harassment because potential victims are not suspicious of them.

Sexual harassment is a very serious and all too widespread form of behavior in organizations. It occurs in large part because of common misconceptions that allow people to get away with it. Hopefully, by balancing some of these myths with truths we have taken at least a small step toward reducing its occurrence.

Managing Sexual Harassment in the Workplace: What to Do

Earlier, we noted that organizations are held legally responsible for the hostile work environments created by their employees. Unless they step in to remedy the problem, they will be seen as having contributed to it by virtue of their inaction. As such, it's important to consider what managers' responsibilities are with respect to sexual harassment in the workplace. How can management help discourage sexual harassment? The success of several practices has been established.[48]

Have—and Communicate a Clear Policy. In the employee handbook or in some other statement of regulations, it's necessary for all companies to have a clearly articulated statement about sexual harassment. These generally indicate the company's intolerance of it and the actions taken against violators. Specifically, such statements make it clear that

■ The employer will not tolerate harassment based on race, sex, religion, national origin, age, or disability.

■ The employer will not tolerate retaliation against anyone who complains of harassment or who participates in an investigation.

It is imperative for all employees to familiarize themselves with these policies (some of which are likely to be quite extensive) and for managers to ensure that their subordinates are well versed in them. After all, having a policy that is neither communicated clearly nor followed consistently is worthless. This is important because the absence of a clear policy sends the message that sexual harassment is condoned (even if that is untrue). As you might imagine, because they are more formal in nature and have sophisticated human resources experts to help, larger companies are more likely to have formal sexual harassment policies in place than smaller ones (see Figure 12.12).[49]

Train Employees About What Constitutes Inappropriate Behavior. Just as employees need to be trained in how to perform their jobs, they also need to be trained regarding what constitutes appropriate and inappropriate behavior toward others in the workplace. Because the lines sometimes are gray, it's important to establish the kinds of things that can and cannot be done and said. For example, although many may consider it innocuous, others may find it sexually offensive to tell sexually oriented jokes, to say sexual things about people, to refer to people's body parts, or to refer to people in sexually related or demeaning ways. Although some individuals already may be sensitive to these things, others may not, making such training appropriate for individuals at all levels. In fact, the higher a person's rank is in an organization, the greater is that person's potential to abuse power—and hence, the more important it is for him or her to be well trained.

Make Sure There's a Clear and Effective Complaint Procedure. Any policy prohibiting sexual harassment isn't going to be particularly effective if there's no

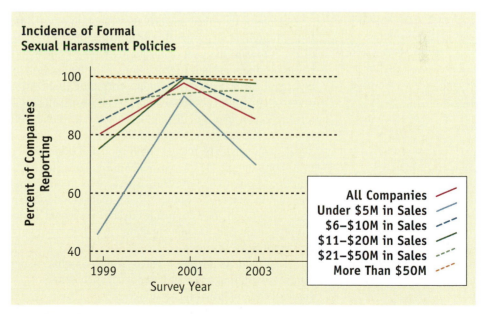

FIGURE 12.12

Formal Sexual Harassment Policies in Different Size Organizations

A survey of human resources practices in manufacturing companies revealed that a greater percentage of larger organizations have formal sexual harassment policies than smaller ones. Interestingly, although nearly every company (97 percent) reported having a formal sexual harassment policy in 2001, this figure dropped somewhat in 2003 (to 85 percent) because there was an increase in the number of smaller firms surveyed.

Source: From Ura, 2003; see Note 49.

mechanism in place to report any violations that might occur. As a result, most companies, as well as colleges and universities, have offices to which incidents of sexual harassment may be reported. The professionals in this office, usually staffed by experts in human resources management, are well equipped not only to take complaints, but also to investigate them and to make recommendations. As you may recall, such a unit, the FEPC, existed in the law firm described in this chapter's Preview Case.

Take Immediate Steps to Stop Harassment. If an employer determines that harassment occurred, it should take immediate measures to stop the harassment and to ensure that it does not recur. Perpetrators found guilty of harassment should be disciplined using measures proportional to the seriousness of the offense (for general guidelines on using discipline, see Chapter 3). In addition, the employer should correct any effects of the harassment. For example, any negative performance evaluations resulting from the harassment should be corrected.

Contribute to a Nonhostile Environment Yourself. One of the most effective things any manager can do to reduce the likelihood of sexual harassment occurring is to contribute to a positive and supportive culture himself or herself. Not only should you, as a manager, show support for the sexual harassment policy (e.g., by expressing its importance, distributing information about it, encouraging discussions about it, etc.), but it's also important to show clear conformity with it yourself. Any violations on a manager's part may be modeled by subordinates, thereby suggesting the manager's own lack of regard for it. In other words, supervisors must be good role models.

In closing, we cannot overstate the importance of managerial involvement in efforts to prevent sexual harassment. As a manager, this is one of your key responsibilities, and of course, a strong ethical obligation.

Organizational Politics: Selfish Uses of Power

When individuals working in a wide range of industries and companies are asked to list the key problems they face at work, they mention many different issues. Near the top of most lists, though, is **organizational politics**. This refers to actions by individuals that are directed toward the goal of furthering their own self-interest without regard for the well-being of others or their organizations.[50] If this sounds selfish and unprincipled—an abuse of organizational power—you are correct. Organizational politics *does* involve placing one's self-interests above the interests of the organization. Indeed, this use of power to foster one's own interests distinguishes organizational politics from uses of power that are approved and accepted by organizations.[51]

Not surprisingly, many people condemn organizational politics and those who engage in it. For example, as the outspoken billionaire and former presidential candidate H. Ross Perot once put it, "I don't want any corporate politicians . . . some guy that wants to move ahead at the expense of others."[52] Similarly, in describing why they have chosen to leave secure jobs with good companies to start their own businesses, many people note that they simply got tired of life in a big company—and especially, of having to deal with organizational politics![53]

To provide you with a broad overview of what we currently know about organizational politics, we'll first consider the roots of such behavior—why it occurs. Then we'll describe some of the important forms it takes.

Forms of Political Behavior

To give you a better sense of what, precisely, organizational politics involves, we now take a look at its various forms. In this section, then, we focus on a key question: What do people do to promote their own selfish ends by influencing others? Many strategies exist, but among the most important are the ones we describe here.[54]

Gaining Control Over and Selective Use of Information. Information is often the lifeblood of organizations. Therefore, controlling information and determining who knows

organizational politics
Unauthorized uses of power that enhance or protect one's own or one's group's personal interests

what is one of the most important ways to gain and exercise power in organizations. Although outright lying and falsifying information are relatively rare (in part because of the consequences of getting caught), there are other ways of controlling information to gain political advantage. For example, you might (1) withhold information that makes you look bad (e.g., negative sales information), (2) avoid contact with those who may ask for information you would prefer not to disclose, (3) be very selective in the information you disclose, or (4) overwhelm others with information that may not be completely relevant. These are all ways of controlling the nature and degree of information people have at their disposal. Such control often plays a key role in organizational politics.

Cultivating a Favorable Impression. People interested in enhancing their power in an organization often engage in some type of image building—attempts to enhance the favorableness of the impressions they make on others. Such efforts take many forms, such as (1) "dressing for success," (2) associating oneself with the successful accomplishments of others (or, in extreme cases, taking credit for others' successes), or (3) simply calling attention to one's own successes and positive characteristics.[55]

Building Powerful Coalitions. To successfully exert influence, it is often useful to gain the support of others within the organization. Managers may, for example, lobby for their ideas before they officially present them at meetings, ensuring that others are committed to them in advance and thereby avoiding the embarrassment of public rejection. Sometimes, of course, it's difficult even to assemble an audience of high-ranking organizational officials to whom to make your argument. This is where the "elevator pitch" often comes in: Politically active people often hang around specific elevators at particular times of day, hoping to ride next to a top executive—to whom they can "pitch" their projects or ideas.

Blaming and Attacking Others. One of the most popular tactics of organizational politics involves blaming and attacking others when bad things happen. A commonly used political tactic is finding a **scapegoat**, a person who is made to take the blame for someone else's failure or wrongdoing. A supervisor, for example, may explain that the failure of a sales plan she designed was based on the serious mistakes of one of her subordinates—even if this is not entirely true. Explaining that "it's *his* fault" can sometimes get the real culprit "off the hook" for it.

Finding a scapegoat can allow the politically astute individual to avoid (or at least minimize) association with the negative situation. For example, when corporate performance drops, powerful chief executives often resort to placing the blame on lower-ranking individuals, protecting themselves from getting fired while their subordinate gets the axe (see Figure 12.13).[56]

Associating with Powerful Others. One of the most direct ways to gain power is by connecting oneself with more powerful others. There are several means of accomplishing this goal. For example, a lower-power person may become more powerful if she has a very powerful mentor, a more powerful and better-established person who can look out for and protect her interests (for a thorough discussion of careers, see Appendix 2).

People also may align themselves with more powerful others by giving them "positive strokes" in the hope of getting these persons to like them and help them—the process of ingratiation we described in our discussion of influence.[57] Agreeing with someone more powerful may be an effective way of getting that person to consider you an ally. Such an alliance, of course, may prove valuable when you are looking for support within an organization. To summarize, having a powerful mentor, forming coalitions, and using ingratiation are all potentially effective ways of gaining power by aligning oneself with others.

Creating Obligations and Using Reciprocity. Still another way to gain power is to gather a lot of obligations—IOUs from others that will be paid back with interest. People who are adept at using this tactic do favors for others in their organization—favors that cost them relatively little. Later, they attempt to wring major benefits from such obligations. "I helped you," they suggest, "now it's your turn." They do relatively little for others, but expect a lot in return.

scapegoat
Someone who is made to take the blame for someone else's failure or wrongdoing.

FIGURE 12.13

Scapegoats: Important Players in Many Political Games

Although scapegoats are never so conveniently identified, politically astute individuals still manage to find individuals on whom they can affix blame for their own wrongdoings.

Source: www.CartoonStock.com

Why Does Political Behavior Occur?

politics
See *organizational politics.*

If you have worked in several different organizations, you probably realize that although **politics** occur almost everywhere, the amount of such activity varies greatly. In some settings, people spend large amounts of time engaging in organizational politics although in others, such actions are far less frequent. This raises an important question: What factors encourage—or discourage—such behavior? Both personal and organizational variables play a role.

Personal Determinants of Organizational Politics. Turning first to personal factors, it appears that people high in Machiavellianism, an aspect of personality we discussed in Chapter 4, are especially likely to engage in such behavior.[58] Given that high Machiavellians believe that it is acceptable to use others for their personal needs, this is hardly surprising.

social chameleons
Individuals who figure out what behaviors they believe are considered generally appropriate in their organization, and then go out of their way to make sure that others are aware that they behaved in such a manner.

We also know that some individuals, ones who are particularly adept at monitoring the effects of their behavior on others, are inclined to engage in organizational politics. After all, such **"social chameleons"** do whatever it takes to get others to like them.[59]

Finally, people who engage in organizational politics have a particular set of skills and traits that equip them for this role. In particular, they are very socially adept, highly popular, extroverted, self-confident, aggressive, ambitious, devious, intelligent, and articulate. Given this particular set of variables, it's little wonder that such individuals often succeed in their efforts to get ahead, no matter what.[60]

Organizational Determinants of Organizational Politics. Turning next to organizational factors, it appears that to the extent certain conditions exist in an organization, political behavior is likely to occur. Specifically, political behavior is likely to occur to the extent that goals and roles are ambiguous, the organization has a history or climate of political activity, and resources are scarce.[61] Further, to the degree that an organization is highly centralized (decision making and power are concentrated in the hands of a small number of individuals or units) and different individuals or units in the organization have conflicting interests or goals, political behavior is likely to occur. In other words, organizations low on empowerment are more likely to be the scene of organizational politics than ones high on empowerment.

Politics in Human Resource Management. Another important finding concerning organizational politics is that it often occurs in connection with key human resource management activities such as performance appraisal, personnel selection, and compensation decisions.[62] Given that there is often a certain amount of ambiguity associated with evaluating another's performance, this leaves lots of room for individuals to cultivate certain images as they perform this task. As a result, performance ratings are sometimes more a reflection of the rater's interest in promoting a particular image of himself or herself than an interest in accurately evaluating another's behavior.[63] Similarly, when making personnel decisions, people are at least as much concerned about the implications of their hires for their own careers (e.g., will this person support me or make me look bad?) as they are concerned about doing what's best for the organization.[64]

Finally, pay raise decisions have been shown to be politically motivated, at least in some instances. For instance, researchers conducting a management simulation exercise found that managers gave the highest raises to individuals who threatened to complain if they didn't get a substantial raise, particularly if it was known that these people had political connections within the organization.[65] Taken together, these findings suggest that the very nature of human resource management activities in organizations makes them prime candidates for various forms of organizational politics.

Politics in Large Multinational Organizations. Although organizational politics often involves actions by individuals designed to boost their own power and status, it also occurs at the corporate level between units of large multinational companies. For instance, consider Vodafone Group, the huge European-based mobile phone company. It has subsidiaries around the world, from Australia to Europe, and works hard to attain a high level of equipment and software compatibility in all its units.

Yet, because its subsidiaries retain considerable independence (often under the laws of their own countries), Vodafone lacks the power to order them to adopt a uniform array of products. How does it attempt to deal with this situation? Through the political tactic of creating accomplished fact: It strives to create the perception that systems and products it recommends are the established standard. And to some extent, this works. In some instances, however, subsidiaries carefully guard their independence and make their own choices. The result is that Vodafone, like many other companies facing the same situation, must continue to use political tactics and maneuvering to strengthen its power; under present circumstances there is, literally, no other option.

The Impact of Organizational Politics

Political behavior is selfish, by definition. So when people engage in such actions, and do so effectively, one result is that they personally benefit: They get the promotions, raises, or power that they are seeking. The effects on other persons and the organization itself, however, can be far more negative.

We know, for example, that the more frequently political behavior occurs in an organization, the less satisfied its employees are with their jobs and the less committed they are to working in those organizations.[66] Similarly, the greater the incidence of political behavior, the stronger is the intention of employees to leave (voluntary turnover).[67] As we saw in Chapter 6, job satisfaction, commitment, and turnover are all important factors in an organization's performance, so to the extent these are affected by political behavior, important consequences may result. Finally, the greater the incidence of politics in an organization, the less employees believe that they are supported by their organizations.[68] And since such feelings play a key role in work motivation (see Chapter 7), the impact of organizational politics can take its toll in a very important way.

In general, although organizational politics may benefit those who are skilled at carrying it out, at least over the short term, its occurrence tends to undermine employees' satisfaction with, and commitment to, their organizations. And in extreme cases, many persons—often the best—may choose to leave rather than put up with an environment they view as unfair, corrupt, and deceptive.

Interestingly, however, not everyone reacts to organizational politics in the same way. Some people are bothered by it more than others. In particular, people low in *conscientiousness*—one of the Big Five dimensions of personality we examined in Chapter 4— are more strongly affected. The less conscientious they are, the more adversely their job performance is affected by political behavior.[69] It's interesting to consider why this occurs. The answer lies in the fact that people who are highly conscientious are reliable, responsible, and persistent, giving them the tenacity and diligence to get things done even in a politically charged work environment. In contrast, individuals who are low in conscientiousness lack these adaptive characteristics, allowing them to become more easily distracted or discouraged by politics. In a sense, therefore, politics are most harmful to the "weakest links" in an organization's chain—those employees who are not top performers anyway.

Summary and Review of Learning Objectives

1. **Describe the nature of influence in organizations and its major forms.**
   When someone attempts to change the behavior or views of one or more others, they are engaging in attempts at exerting *influence*. Influence can take many different forms, including rational persuasion, inspirational appeal, consultation, ingratiation, exchange, personal appeal, coalition-building, legitimating, and pressure.

2. **Distinguish between various forms of individual power in organizations.**
   Overall, power refers to the capacity to influence others. One major type of power, *position power,* resides within one's formal organizational position. It includes: (1) *reward power* and (2) *coercive power,* the capacity to control valued rewards and punishments, respectively, (3) *legitimate power,* the recognized authority that an individual has by virtue of his or her organizational position, and (4) *information power,* power that stems from having special data and knowledge. A second major type of power, *personal power,* resides within an individual's own unique qualities or characteristics. It includes: (1) *rational persuasion,* using logical arguments and factual evidence to convince others that an idea is acceptable, (2) *expert power,* the power an individual has because he or she is recognized as having some superior knowledge, skill, or expertise, (3) *referent power,* influence based on the fact that an individual is admired by others, and (4) *charisma,* having an engaging and magnetic personality.

3. **Define empowerment and indicate how it operates among individuals and in teams.**
   Empowerment is a process in which authority is delegated to the lowest level in an organization at which competent decisions regarding various issues can be made. At the individual level, it has been found to enhance both performance and job satisfaction, although these beneficial effects are greater in some cultures (low power-distance cultures) than others (high power-distance cultures). To the extent organizations create an *empowerment climate,* they can empower teams as well as individuals. This can enhance the performance of both teams and individuals.

4. **Describe how the resource-dependency model and the strategic contingencies model explain the nature of power between organizational units.**
   The *resource-dependency model* asserts that power resides within the subunits that control the greatest share of valued organizational resources. The *strategic contingencies model* explains power in terms of a subunit's capacity to control the activities of other

subunits. Such power may be enhanced by the capacity to reduce the level of uncertainty experienced by another unit, having a central position within the organization, or performing functions that other units cannot perform.

5. **Describe how sexual harassment constitutes an abuse of organizational power and ways of reducing its occurrence.**

    Almost always, sexual harassment constitutes an abuse of power in which a more powerful person (usually, but not always, a male) gives unwanted sexual attention to a less powerful person (usually, but not always, a female). Because there's a power difference between the parties, the less powerful individual is put in a difficult situation. Unfortunately, this form of behavior is not uncommon, although most instances go unreported. Not only is sexual harassment patently illegal, but it also is highly costly to all involved parties, both financially and psychologically. To help reduce the occurrence of sexual harassment, it is useful for management to do the following: (1) have—and communicate—a clear policy prohibiting sexual harassment, (2) train employees about what constitutes inappropriate behavior, (3) make sure there's a clear and effective complaint procedure in place, (4) take immediate steps to stop harassment before it gets worse, and (5) as a manager, contribute to a nonhostile work environment yourself.

6. **Describe when and where organizational politics occur and the forms such behavior takes.**

    Political behavior is likely to occur in situations where goals and roles are ambiguous, the organization has a history or climate of political activity, and resources are scarce. In addition, politics is also encouraged by a high level of centralization and when different individuals or units in the organization have conflicting interests or goals. Politics often occur in connection with human resources issues and tends to increase as organizations mature and increase in size. Political tactics vary greatly and include such things as blaming and attacking others, controlling access to information, and cultivating a favorable impression.

Points to Ponder

Questions for Review

1. What is influence and how does it differ from power? From organizational politics?
2. What are the tactics of influence used most frequently in organizations?
3. What is position power? How does it differ from personal power?
4. What is empowerment? Can it work on the team as well as individual level?
5. According to the resource-dependency model of subunit power, what are the most important foundations of subunit power in an organization?
6. According to the strategic contingencies model, what is the basis of subunit power in an organization?
7. What, exactly, is sexual harassment, and what can be done to minimize its occurrence in organizations?
8. What are some of the most important antecedents of organizational politics?
9. What are the effects of organizational politics?

Experiential Questions

1. How do you attempt to influence the people with whom you work?
2. If you hold power in an organization, what is its basis? How do you prefer to exert power over others?
3. Have you ever felt empowered in an organization? If so, why? And what effects, if any, did such feelings of being empowered have on your performance?
4. Only answer the following questions if you don't mind talking about this personal issue: Have you ever engaged in sexual harassment? What, precisely, did you do that was wrong and what might have been done to prevent you from doing it?
5. Only answer the following questions if you don't mind talking about this personal issue: Have you ever been a victim of sexual harassment? How did it make you feel?
6. Have you ever engaged in organizational politics? If so, what tactics did you use?

Questions to Analyze

1. Do you think that highly influential people gain power? In other words, are influence and power related?
2. Aside from rational persuasion, what techniques of influence do you believe are used most often in organizations? Why are these particular techniques used more frequently than others?
3. Why do you think most executives prefer personal bases of power to positional bases of power?
4. Do you think that sexual harassment ever can be eliminated entirely or that some degree of harassment is inevitable in the workplace?
5. Politics often produces negative effects for organizations as a whole. What steps can an organization wishing to reduce politics take to reach this goal?

Experiencing OB

Individual Exercise

What Kinds of Influence Does Your Supervisor Use?

One of the main ways of learning about social influence in organizations is to use questionnaires in which people are asked to describe the behaviors of their supervisors. If a consistent pattern emerges with respect to the way subordinates describe supervisors, some very strong clues are provided as to the nature of that person's influence style. Questionnaires similar to this one are used for this purpose (see Schriesheim & Hinkin, 1990; see Note 3). Complete this questionnaire to get an idea of the types of social influence favored by your supervisor.

Directions

Indicate how strongly you agree or disagree with each of the following statements as it describes your immediate supervisor. Answer by using the following scale:

1 = strongly disagree

2 = disagree

3 = neither agree nor disagree

4 = agree

5 = strongly agree

For each statement select the number corresponding to the most appropriate response. Then, score your responses by following the directions below.

My supervisor can:

_____ 1. Recommend that I receive a raise.
_____ 2. Assign me to jobs I dislike.
_____ 3. See that I get the promotion I desire.
_____ 4. Make my life at work completely unbearable.
_____ 5. Make decisions about how things are done.
_____ 6. Provide useful advice on how to do my job better.
_____ 7. Comprehend the importance of doing things a certain way.
_____ 8. Make me want to look up to him or her.
_____ 9. Share with me the benefit of his or her vast job knowledge.
_____ 10. Get me to admire what he or she stands for.
_____ 11. Find out things that nobody else knows.
_____ 12. Explain things so logically that I want to do them.
_____ 13. Have access to vital data about the company.
_____ 14. Share a clear vision of what the future holds for the company.
_____ 15. Come up with the facts needed to make a convincing case about something.
_____ 16. Put me in a trance when he or she communicates to me.

Scoring

1. Add the numbers assigned to statements 1 and 3. This is the *reward power* score.
2. Add the numbers assigned to statements 2 and 4. This is the *coercive power* score.
3. Add the numbers assigned to statements 5 and 7. This is the *legitimate power* score.
4. Add the numbers assigned to statements 6 and 9. This is the *expert power* score.
5. Add the numbers assigned to statements 8 and 10. This is the *referent power* score.
6. Add the numbers assigned to statements 11 and 13. This is the *information power* score.
7. Add the numbers assigned to statements 12 and 15. This is the *rational persuasion* score.
8. Add the numbers assigned to statements 14 and 16. This is the *charisma* score.

Questions for Discussion

1. With respect to which dimensions did your supervisor score highest and lowest? Are these consistent with what you would have predicted in advance?
2. Does your supervisor behave in ways consistent with the dimension along which you gave him or her the highest score? In other words, does he or she fit the description given in the text?
3. How do you think your own subordinates would answer the various questions with respect to yourself?
4. Which of the eight forms of social influence do you think are most common and least common, and why?

Group Exercise

Recognizing Organizational Politics When You See It

A good way to make sure you understand organizational politics is to practice enacting different political tactics, and to attempt to recognize these tactics portrayed by others. This exercise is designed with these objectives in mind. The more practiced you are at recognizing political activity when you see it, the better equipped you may be to defend yourself against political adversaries.

Directions

1. Divide the class into groups of approximately four students each.
2. Each group should select at random one of the six major political tactics described on pages 488–490.
3. Meeting together for about 30 minutes, each group should prepare a brief role-play in which the four members enact the particular political tactic selected. These should be as realistic as possible, and not written simply to broadcast the answer. That is, the tactic should be presented much as you would expect to see it used in a real organization.
4. Each group should take a turn presenting its role-play to the class. Feel free to announce the setting or context in which your portrayal is supposed to occur. Don't worry about giving an award-winning performance; it's okay to keep a script or set of notes in your hand. The important thing is that you attempt to depict the political tactic in a realistic manner.
5. After each group presents its skit, members of the class should attempt to identify the specific political tactic depicted. This should lead to a discussion of the clues that suggested that answer and additional things that could have been done to depict the particular tactic portrayed.

Questions for Discussion

1. How successful was the class in identifying the various political tactics portrayed? Were some tactics more difficult to portray than others?
2. Based on these portrayals, which tactics do you believe are most likely to be used in organizations, and under what circumstances?
3. Which political tactics do you believe are most negative? Why

---

Practicing OB

Politics Is Powering the Exit Door

A rapidly growing high-tech company has recently experienced resignations by several of its best people. These individuals have left, expressing strong annoyance over the high level of politics within the company. This is a serious situation because these former employees are also spreading the word that "politics is king" in the company.

1. What steps can the top management of this company take to turn this situation around—to reduce the role of politics within the company?
2. How can the company counter the negative image it is acquiring as a result of disparaging comments by former employees concerning politics within the company?
3. Why do you think politics has become such an important issue in this company? Is it a matter of personalities—the specific persons who work there—or something about the nature of the business—how it is structured, the industry within which it works?

CASE IN POINT

The Smith Brothers: A Low-Key Approach to Gaining—and Keeping—Organizational Power

Two brothers who have both been CEOs of major companies? That's certainly a rarity in the modern world of business. But it is exactly the situation for the Smith brothers, John F. and Michael. John was president and CEO of GM until 2000 (today, he is group vice president of Global Product Planning), while his brother Mike was CEO of Hughes Electronics Corp., a leading telecommunication and satellite company that is owned by GM. So both have held powerful positions, indeed. But how, you may be wondering, did they both acquire so much power—and such a high level of success? Was it because they lusted after power and focused their lives on attaining it? People who know them well would disagree. They attribute the Smiths' rise to power more to their interests than to any powerful desire for power.

Long-time friends and acquaintances note that even as children, the Smith brothers showed tremendous interest in business. Sally Mahoney, who knew the Smith brothers and their parents, recalls that as children, they loved to play board games, especially Monopoly. "I can just remember them stacking up those hotels and houses. Money was always very interesting to them," she notes. And the Smiths themselves were aware of this interest from childhood on. "We like business. We grew up in a business-oriented family," Michael Smith says.

Although they attended different schools, the Smith brothers were both described by people who knew them as bright, hard-working, and unassuming. "Ego doesn't show," says M. Hoglund, a retired GM executive who worked with both brothers. "They are great guys to work around and as a result, generate a lot of loyalty." "Jack will wander down the halls, his head down, trying to be obscure, where the king would be looking around for recognition," says David Cole, director of the University of Michigan's Center for the Study of Automotive Transportation. So, it does not appear that the Smiths gained their power through organizational politics. Instead, they seemed to acquire it naturally because other people liked, trusted, and respected them.

In addition, the fact that they were "organization-oriented" rather than "my own career–oriented" seems to have played an important role in their rise to power. Both Smith brothers are true team players, with genuine concern for the people with whom they work as well as their companies. As we noted earlier, most top executives strongly prefer to gather power from their personal characteristics—their charisma, expertise, personality—rather than from their position. The Smith brothers seem to understand this lesson very well and have converted it into highly successful careers—and huge helpings of power. Individually and together, they suggest that the road to power in today's organizations does *not* have to follow a route dictated by self-ish self-interest. On the contrary, individuals who gain power often seem to do so because their skills and talents suit them to this role rather than because they set out, early in life, to seek it.

Questions for Discussion

1. What bases of personal power contribute to the Smith brothers' success?
2. Is their low-key, unassuming approach the best for obtaining—and keeping—power?
3. If you studied the Smith brothers' family background closely, do you think you could identify specific factors (e.g., in the way their parents raised them) that play a role in their successful rise to corporate power?

LEADERSHIP IN ORGANIZATIONS

Chapter 13

Chapter Outline

The Nature of Leadership

The Trait Approach to Leadership: Having the Right Stuff

Leadership Behavior: What Do Leaders Do?

Leaders and Followers

Change-Oriented Leadership: Future Visions

Contingency Theories of Leader Effectiveness

Leadership Development: Bringing Out the Leader within You

Special Sections

OB **Making Sense Out of Common Sense**

Boosting Cultural Intelligence

How to Do It

Coaching Tips from Some of the Best

OB **In a Diverse World**

Guanxi: Social Networking in China

After reading this chapter, you should be able to:

1. Describe the **trait approach** to leadership and identify the characteristics that distinguish successful leaders from ordinary people.

2. Distinguish between the two basic forms of leader behavior: **person-oriented behavior** and **production-oriented behavior**, explaining how **grid training** helps develop them.

3. Explain what the **leader-member exchange (LMX) model** and the **attributional approach to leadership** say about the relationships between leaders and followers.

4. Describe the nature of **charismatic leadership** and how it compares to **transformational leadership**.

5. Summarize what **LPC contingency theory** and **situational leadership theory** say about the connection between leadership style and situational variables.

6. Describe various techniques used to develop leadership in organizations.

■ PREVIEW CASE

Mary Minnick Won't Let Coke Fizzle

A "culture of politeness and consensus" long dominated at the Coca-Cola Company, where a genteel Southern style prevailed among executives. So notes Mary E. Minnick, whose own blunt and impatient style has ruffled more than a few feathers at the company's Atlanta headquarters. Yet, this was precisely why CEO E. Neville Isdell appointed Minnick executive vice president and asked her to assume the presidency of the company's Marketing, Strategy, and Innovation Group in May, 2005. Isdell was concerned that sales were flat, and he had faith that Minnick could put some fizz back into the most valuable brand in history. With archrival Pepsi nipping at Coca-Cola's heels, Minnick's challenge has been to reverse the trend.

Minnick's strategy was straightforward: Resuscitate the brand by developing new products. Indeed, she has been prolific, introducing 1,000 new products or variations around the world in her first year at the job! Among these have been the diet drink, Coca-Cola Zero, and the coffee-infused beverage, Coca-Cola Blak. However, the thing that most concerned insiders at this "sodacentric" company, where Coca-Cola Classic was the cash cow, has been Minnick's attention to new noncarbonated beverages—and lots of them. For example, instead of ceding the bottled coffee category to Pepsi, which sells Frappuccinos under the Starbucks label, Minnick has fought back by introducing Coca-Cola's own line of decadent lattes and mochas in a licensing deal with the chocolatier Godiva. And to appeal to the older, upscale crowd, Gold Peak premium iced teas were introduced to boost sales of its Nestea line. For Minnick, this is just the beginning. Currently, she is planning entirely new lines of health and beauty beverages, special drinks fortified with vitamins and minerals that have cosmetic benefits. Her plan is to create an entirely new category, in the same way that the company's Red Bull single-handedly launched energy drinks.

To accomplish all of this has been no easy feat, but Minnick has led the charge effectively. One way she has done this has been by generating excitement among Coca-Cola's 200 marketing managers around the world. At a 2006 meeting in Istanbul, Turkey, for example, she stirred the troops by getting them to share her visions of entirely new drink categories. Her images of "neutraceutical" versions of Diet Coke, beverages that could promote health and beauty, have been so compelling, for example, that the company already has been engaged in clinical trials of new products so that it could make health claims. Should this succeed, Minnick will have led the charge to redefine the company's image as a purveyor of sugar-laden "junk food."

Beyond sharing her strategic visions for the company, Minnick also has been successful in bringing them to fruition. One of the ways she has gone about this has been to win support from local bottlers by involving them in the product-development process. Traditionally, Coca-Cola delivered final products to bottlers, who then put them in containers and delivered them to restaurants and retail outlets. Instead of keeping them out of the loop, however, Minnick thought it was important to get their buy-in, which she did by involving them in the process of developing and testing new products. Now, they realize that Minnick's innovations are necessary for their own success, making them very cooperative. In the words of Ron Wilson, president of a large bottler in Philadelphia, "There are a lot of bottlers who realize now that it's innovate or die."

Although Minnick disrupted the status quo at Coca-Cola by boldly introducing new products, it looks like her efforts are going a long way toward helping the company *and* preserving its legendary status. And as one of *Fortune* magazine's "Most Powerful Women in Business," there's every reason to be confident that she'll succeed.

Despite her short time as company president, there can be little doubt that Mary Minnick has had a considerable impact on Coca-Cola's product line. Although it's too soon to tell whether or not her impatience will also pay off on the bottom line, it's clear that Minnick has a clear vision and she's bringing it to reality. Politeness and leisurely focus on carbonated beverages has given way to bluntness and urgent attention to noncarbonated beverages, and Minnick has been responsible for it. Although she's only one person, so far, she has made a huge and fundamental difference in the marketing strategy. To say that she is a strong *leader*—a very strong one, in fact—surely would be an understatement. And, as this case suggests, a strong leader can have a profound impact on an organization.

If you gathered a group of top executives and asked them to name the single most important determinant of organizational success, chances are good that most would identify "effective leadership." Indeed, it is widely believed in the world of business that *leadership* is the key ingredient in the recipe for corporate achievement. And this view is by no means restricted to business organizations. As you know from experience, leadership also is important when it comes to politics, sports, and many other activities.[1]

Is this view justified? Do leaders such as Mary Minnick and countless others really play crucial roles in shaping the fortunes of organizations? A century of research on this topic suggests that they do. Effective leadership is indeed a key determinant of organizational success.[2] Given its importance, you may not be surprised to learn that leadership has been one of the most widely studied concepts in the social sciences.[3] In view of this, we will devote this chapter to describing various approaches to the study of leadership as well as their implications for managerial practice.

To make the task of summarizing this wealth of information manageable, we will proceed as follows. First, we will consider some basic points about leadership—what it is and why being a leader is not necessarily synonymous with being a manager. Then, we will examine views of leadership focusing on the traits of leaders, followed by another view that focuses on leaders' behaviors. Next, we will examine several major theories of leadership that focus on the relationship between leaders and their followers. Following this, we will review several contrasting theories dealing with the conditions under which leaders are effective or ineffective in their important role. Finally, we conclude by describing various techniques used to enhance and develop leaders, making them highly effective.

The Nature of Leadership

In a sense, leadership resembles love: It is something most people believe they can recognize, but often find difficult to define. What, precisely, is it? And, how does being a leader differ from being a manager? We now focus on these questions.

Leadership: A Working Definition

Imagine that you have accepted a new job and entered a new work group. How would you recognize its leader? One possibility, of course, is through the formal titles and assigned roles each person in the group holds. In short, the individual designated as department head or project manager would be the one you would identify as the group's leader.

Imagine, however, that during several staff meetings, you noticed that this person was really not the most influential. Although she or he held the formal authority, these meetings were actually dominated by another person who, ostensibly, was the top person's subordinate. What would you conclude about leadership then? Probably, you would say that the real leader was the person who actually ran things—not the one with the formal title and the apparent authority.

In many cases, of course, the disparity we have just described does not exist. The individual possessing the greatest amount of formal authority is also the most influential. In some situations, however, this is not so. And in such cases, we typically identify the person who actually exercises the most influence over the group as its **leader**. These facts point to the following working definition of leadership—one accepted by many experts on this topic: **Leadership** is the process whereby one individual influences other group members toward the attainment of defined group or organizational goals.[4] We now describe the key characteristics of the leadership process (see Figure 13.1).

leader

An individual within a group or an organization who wields the most influence over others.

leadership

The process whereby one individual influences other group members toward the attainment of defined group or organizational goals.

Leadership Involves Noncoercive Influence. According to our definition, leadership is a process involving influence—one in which a leader changes the actions or attitudes of several group members or subordinates. As we saw in Chapter 12, many techniques for exerting such influence exist, ranging from relatively coercive ones—the recipient has little choice but to do what is requested; to relatively noncoercive ones—the recipient can choose to accept or reject the influence offered. In general, leadership refers to the use of noncoercive influence techniques. This characteristic distinguishes a leader from a *dictator*. Whereas dictators gets others to do what they want by using physical coercion or by threats of physical force, leaders do not.[5]

As Mao Zedong (founder of the People's Republic of China) put it, "Power grows out of the barrel of a gun." This may be true with respect to the power of dictators, but *not* the power of leaders. The point is that leadership rests, at least in part, on positive feelings between leaders and their subordinates. In other words, subordinates accept influence from leaders because they respect, like, or admire them—not simply because they hold positions of formal authority.[6]

Leadership Influence Is Goal-Directed. The definition presented above also suggests that leadership involves the exercise of influence for a purpose—to attain defined group or organizational goals. In other words, leaders focus on altering those actions or attitudes of their subordinates that are related to specific goals; they are far less concerned with altering actions or attitudes that are irrelevant to such goals.

Leadership Requires Followers. Finally, note that our definition, by emphasizing the central role of influence, implies that leadership is somewhat reciprocal. Although leaders do indeed influence subordinates in various ways, leaders are also influenced by their subordinates. In fact, it may be said that leadership exists only in relation to followers. After all, one cannot lead without followers! As former British statesman Benjamin Disraeli once put it, "I must follow the people. Am I not their leader?"[7]

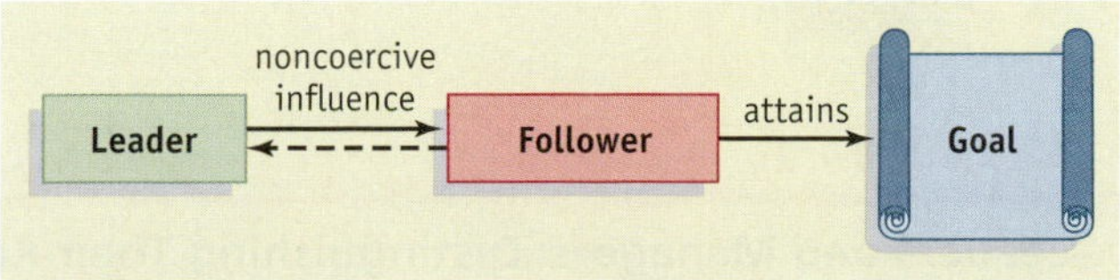

FIGURE 13.1

The Leadership Process: A Summary

Leadership is a process in which one person, a *leader*, influences a follower in a noncoercive manner to attain a goal.

Leaders Versus Managers: A Key Distinction—At Least in Theory

In everyday speech, the terms *leader* and *manager* tend to be used interchangeably. Although we understand the temptation to do so, the two terms are not identical and need to be clearly distinguished. In essence, the primary function of a *leader* is to create the essential purpose or mission of the organization and the strategy for attaining it. By contrast, the job of the *manager* is to implement that vision.

Essentially, the manager's job is to put into practice a means for achieving the vision created by the leader. Thus, whereas management is about coping with complexity, leadership is about coping with change. Specifically, managers create plans and monitor results relative to those plans. However, leaders establish direction by creating a vision of the future. Effective leaders then get people to buy into their visions and to go along with them.[8]

Although these differences are simple to articulate, the distinction between establishing a mission and implementing it is often blurred in practice (see Figure 13.2). This is so because many leaders, such as top corporate executives, frequently are called upon not only to create a vision, but also to formulate a strategy for implementing it, as well as to play a role in increasing people's commitment toward that vision and plan. By contrast, managers are charged with responsibility for implementing organizational strategy through others. At the same time, they frequently are involved also in helping to formulate strategy and increasing people's commitment and effort toward implementing that plan.

In other words, there are several overlapping roles played by leaders and managers in actual practice—a fact that makes the distinction between them difficult to make. However, some managers are considered leaders, whereas others are not. Similarly, some leaders take on more of a management role than others. Thus, although the differences are not always obvious, they are real. For this reason, we will distinguish carefully between leaders and managers throughout this chapter (for an overview, see Table 13.1).

The Trait Approach to Leadership: Having the Right Stuff

At one time or another, many people have daydreams about being a leader. They fantasize about taking charge of large groups and being viewed with great awe and respect. Despite the prevalence of such daydreams, however, relatively few individuals convert them into reality by becoming leaders. Further, among those who do make it to leadership positions, only a small proportion are considered particularly effective in this role.

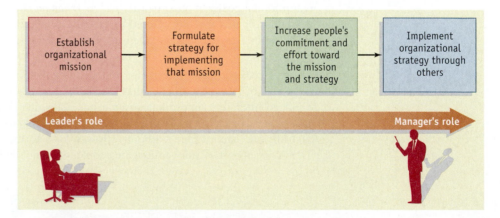

FIGURE 13.2

Leaders and Managers: Distinguishing Their Roles

Leaders are primarily responsible for establishing an organizational mission, whereas *managers* are primarily responsible for implementing that mission through others. The intermediate steps—formulating a strategy for the mission, and increasing people's commitment toward it—tend to be performed by either leaders or managers. It is these overlapping functions that often make the distinction between leaders and managers blurred in actual practice.

TABLE 13.1 Leaders Versus Managers: A Summary Comparison

According to a well-known management theorist, the distinction between managers and leaders is reflected by the 12 points of difference summarized here. Although some of these are a bit general, they provide a good flavor for the differences between managers and leaders. Also, because some managers do the things in the "leaders" column and some leaders do the things in the "managers" column, the practical distinctions between them are not always clear.

Managers . . .	Leaders . . .
■ Administer	■ Innovate
■ Ask how	■ Ask what and why
■ Focus on systems	■ Focus on people
■ Do things right	■ Do the right things
■ Maintain	■ Develop
■ Rely on control	■ Inspire trust
■ Have a short-term perspective	■ Have a longer-term perspective
■ Accept the status quo	■ Challenge the status quo
■ Have an eye on the bottom line	■ Have an eye on the horizon
■ Imitate	■ Originate
■ Emulate the classic good soldier	■ Are their own person
■ Copy	■ Show originality

Source: Bennis, 1989; see Note 3.

This fact raises an intriguing question: What sets effective leaders apart from most others? Why, in short, do some people, but not others, become effective leaders? One of the most widely studied approaches to this question suggests that effective leadership is based on the characteristics that people have. In other words, people become leaders because they are in some special ways different from others.[9]

The Great Person Theory

Are some people born to lead? Common sense suggests that this is so. Great leaders of the past such as Alexander the Great, Queen Elizabeth I, and Abraham Lincoln do seem to differ from ordinary human beings in several respects. The same applies to contemporary leaders as well, such as the president of the United States, a military general, a business tycoon such as Bill Gates. No matter what you may feel about these individuals, you'd have to agree that they all possess high levels of ambition coupled with clear visions of precisely where they want to go. To a lesser degree, even leaders lacking in such history-shaping fame seem different from their followers.

Top executives, some politicians, and even sports heroes or heroines often seem to possess an aura that sets them apart from others. One scientist expressed this idea as follows.

[I]t is unequivocally clear that *leaders are not like other people.* Leaders do not have to be great men or women by being intellectual geniuses or omniscient prophets to succeed, but they do need to have the "right stuff" and this stuff is not equally present in all people. Leadership is a demanding, unrelenting job with enormous pressures and grave responsibilities. It would be a profound disservice to leaders to suggest that they are ordinary people who happened to be in the right place at the right time. . . . In the realm of leadership (and in every other realm), the individual does matter.[10]

great person theory
The view that leaders possess special traits that set them apart from others, and that these traits are responsible for their assuming positions of power and authority.

This orientation expresses an approach to the study of leadership known as the **great person theory**. According to this orientation, great leaders possess key traits that set them apart from most other human beings. Further, the theory contends that these traits remain stable over time and across different groups.[11] Thus, it suggests that all great leaders share these characteristics regardless of when and where they lived, or the precise role in history they fulfilled.

What Characteristics Do Great Leaders Possess?

What are these characteristics? In other words, in precisely what measurable ways do successful leaders differ from people in general? Researchers have identified several such characteristics, and these are listed in Table 13.2.[12] As you review these, you will readily recognize and understand most of these characteristics (e.g., drive, honesty and integrity, self-confidence), which require no elaboration. However, we will explain several that are not quite as obvious.[13]

Leadership Motivation: The Desire to Lead. First, consider what has been termed **leadership motivation**. This refers to leaders' desires to influence others and, in essence, to lead.[14] Such motivation, however, can take two distinct forms. On the one hand, it may cause leaders to seek power as an end in itself. Leaders who demonstrate such **personalized power motivation** wish to dominate others, and their desire to do so is often reflected in an excessive concern with status. In contrast, leadership motivation can cause leaders to seek power as a means to achieve desired, shared goals. Leaders who evidence such **socialized power motivation** cooperate with others, develop networks and coalitions, and generally work with subordinates rather than trying to dominate or control them. Needless to say, this type of leadership motivation is usually far more adaptive for organizations than personalized leadership motivation.

Flexibility. Another special characteristic of effective leaders is *flexibility*. This refers to the ability of leaders to recognize what actions are required in a given situation and then to act accordingly. Evidence suggests that the most effective leaders are not prone to behave in the same ways all the time, but to be adaptive, matching their style to the needs of followers and the demands of the situations they face.[15]

Focus on Morality. In view of all the attention that has been paid to the dishonest dealings of many top business leaders in recent years (e.g., most notably the late Ken Lay and his associates at Enron), it's important to note that successful leaders do, in fact, place a considerable emphasis on ethics and morality. This emphasis is in keeping with what has been called *authentic leadership*. **Authentic leaders** are highly moral individuals who are confident, hopeful, optimistic, and resilient, and who are highly aware of the contexts in which they operate.[16] Because of their highly positive perspectives, authentic leaders play key roles in promoting the growth and development of their subordinates and, as a result, the sustained performance of their organizations.

Multiple Domains of Intelligence. Scientists have acknowledged that leaders have to "be smart" in a variety of different ways. In other words, they have to demonstrate what is known as **multiple domains of intelligence**.[17] Specifically, leaders have to be intelligent in three special ways (see Chapter 3).

TABLE 13.2 Characteristics of Successful Leaders

Research indicates that successful leaders demonstrate the traits listed here.

Trait or Characteristic	Description
Drive	Desire for achievement; ambition; high energy; tenacity; initiative
Honesty and integrity	Trustworthy; reliable; open
Leadership motivation	Desire to exercise influence over others to reach shared goals
Self-confidence	Trust in own abilities
Cognitive ability	Intelligence; ability to integrate and interpret large amounts of information
Knowledge of the business	Knowledge of industry and relevant technical matters
Creativity	Originality
Flexibility	Ability to adapt to needs of followers and requirements of situation

---

leadership motivation
The desire to influence others, especially toward the attainment of shared goals.

personalized power motivation
Leaders' desires to influence others (in essence, to lead).

socialized power motivation
Leaders' interest in cooperating with others, developing networks and coalitions, and generally working with subordinates rather than trying to control them.

authentic leaders
Highly moral individuals who are confident, hopeful, optimistic, and resilient, and who are highly aware of the contexts in which they operate.

multiple domains of intelligence
Intelligence as measured in several different ways, such as cognitive intelligence (traditional measures of the ability to integrate and interpret information), emotional intelligence (the ability to be sensitive to one's own and others' emotions) and cultural intelligence (awareness of cultural differences between people).

■ *Cognitive intelligence.* Of course, leaders must be capable of integrating and interpreting large amounts of information. However, mental genius does not seem to be necessary for leadership. Although the best leaders are surely smart, they tend not to be geniuses.[18] Moreover, research has shown that for people to become leaders, it's important for them to appear to be smart.[19] After all, people are unlikely to accept leaders whose intellectual competence is questionable.

■ *Emotional intelligence.* In Chapters 3 and 5 we described *emotional intelligence,* which refers to people's abilities to be sensitive to their own and others' emotions. As you might imagine, successful leaders must have high levels of emotional intelligence. Indeed, effective leaders are keenly aware of people's emotional states and demonstrate their ability to connect with others.[20]

■ *Cultural intelligence.* Most of the research on leadership has focused on Americans working in companies based in the United States. However, the behavior of leaders is likely to be influenced by the cultures within which they operate, requiring different approaches to leadership in different countries. Sensitivity to this fact has been referred to as **cultural intelligence**.[21] In today's global economy, cultural intelligence is more important than ever. In the words of C. R. "Dick" Shoemate, chairman and CEO of Bestfoods, "It takes a special kind of leadership to deal with the differences of a multicountry, multicultural organization such as ours."[22] Not surprisingly, most of the countries on *Fortune* magazine's list of the "Global Most Admired Companies" (such as General Electric, BASF, Berkshire Hathaway, and SBC Communications) pay considerable attention to training leaders to deal with the realities of the global economy.[23] (For a closer look at training in cultural intelligence, see the *OB: Making Sense Out of Common Sense* section below.)

cultural intelligence

A person's sensitivity to the fact that leaders operate differently in different cultures.

OB Making Sense Out of Common Sense

Boosting Cultural Intelligence

To many people, their own cultural practices are just matters of common sense that should not be challenged. The ways they think and act, because they seem perfectly normal, appear to be "correct," leading them to take them for granted.

In today's highly competitive global economy, however, no organization can afford to have employees who adopt such a narrow perspective. Culture is so well engrained into the ways we think and act, it's difficult to imagine that people really can become comfortable in other cultures, at least rapidly enough to be of use to companies seeking their help in overseas assignments. Yet, this does appear to be possible.

With this in mind, today's companies use a variety of approaches to boost the cultural intelligence of global leaders. Some of the most widely used methods are as follows.

1. In-house *leadership seminars* (focusing on many of the concepts in this chapter, and the entire book) that traditionally have been used continue to be popular. However, these are being supplemented by carefully customized programs that prepare leaders for global assignments.

2. Companies are intensely *coaching* individuals who take on overseas assignments and are carefully

planning a succession of career assignments that prepare leaders for global business. For example, the pharmaceuticals giant Pfizer systematically assigns key managers and potential leaders to project teams that will give them overseas experience. Just as the company takes a long-term perspective on developing its products, Pfizer also "takes a long-term view of developing people," says Chick Dombeck, vice president of human resources.[24]

3. Like other companies, American Express relies extensively on individual coaching, but also incorporates *international assignments* in its strategy for developing leaders. According to a company executive, American Express's goal is "to ensure our people have the required capabilities to lead the company to future success."[25]

There can be no doubt that when it comes to developing leaders, today's companies are paying careful attention to the global world in which they do business. And training them to operate effectively in this world by enhancing their cultural intelligence is an important part of the process. It appears that boosting cultural intelligence is not only possible, but necessary. As a result, thinking that this is neither necessary nor possible is not only unfounded, but dangerously narrow.

Leadership Behavior: What Do Leaders Do?

The trait approach to leadership we just reviewed focuses on the appealing idea that various traits distinguish effective leaders from others. In short, it focuses on *who leaders are*. As plausible as this approach may be, it also makes sense to consider the idea that leaders may be distinctive with respect to the way they behave. In other words, we can supplement our focus on leadership traits with attention to leadership behavior—that is, by examining *what leaders do*.

The behavioral approach is appealing because it offers an optimistic view of the leadership process. After all, although we may not all be born with "the right stuff," we certainly can at least strive to do "the right things"—that is, to do what it takes to become a leader. The general question underlying the behavior approach is quite simple: What do leaders do that make them effective as leaders? As we now describe, there are several good answers to this question.

Participative versus Autocratic Leadership Behaviors

When it comes to describing the behavior of leaders, a key variable involves how much influence they allow subordinates to have over the decisions that are made. As we will see, there are two ways of describing these behaviors.

The Autocratic-Delegation Continuum Model.
Think about the different bosses you have had in your life. Can you remember one who wanted to control virtually everything—someone who made all the decisions, told people precisely what to do, and wanted, quite literally, to run the entire show? Such a person is said to be **autocratic**. In contrast, can you recall a boss or supervisor who allowed employees to make their own decisions? This individual would be described as relying on *delegation*.

You probably also know supervisors who have acted in ways that fall between these extremes—that is, bosses who invited your input before making decisions, were open to suggestions, and who allowed you to carry out various tasks in your own way. These individuals may be said to be using a so-called **participative leadership style**.[26] More precisely, they may be *consulting* with you or involving you in a *joint decision* of some sort. In either case, you were more involved than you would be in the case of an autocratic leader but less involved than you would be in the case of a leader who delegated all responsibility to you (for a summary of this **autocratic-delegation continuum model**, see Figure 13.3).

Although the autocratic-delegation continuum model does a reasonable job of describing the role of the leader in organizational decision-making, it is regarded as overly simplistic. In fact, upon more carefully studying the way leaders make decisions, researchers have observed that describing a leader's participation in decision-making involves two separate dimensions.[27]

The Two-Dimensional Model of Subordinate Participation.
Acknowledging the need for a more sophisticated approach, scientists have proposed the **two-dimensional model of subordinate participation**. As the name implies, this conceptualization describes subordinates' participation in decisions in terms of two dimensions.

The first dimension characterizes the extent to which leaders permit subordinates to take part in decisions; this is the *autocratic-democratic* dimension. The autocratic extreme is marked by no participation whereas the democratic extreme is marked by high participation. The second dimension involves the extent to which leaders direct the activities of subordinates and tell them how to carry out their jobs; this is the *permissive-directive* dimension. The permissive extreme is marked by not telling subordinates how to do their jobs, whereas the directive extreme is marked by considerable attempts to tell subordinates how to do their jobs. Combining these two variables yields the four possible patterns described in Table 13.3. These are:

- the *directive autocrat*
- the *permissive autocrat*
- the *directive democrat*
- the *permissive democrat*

---

autocratic (leadership style)
A style of leadership in which the leader makes all decisions unilaterally.

participative leadership style
A style of leadership in which the leader permits subordinates to take part in decision making and also permits them a considerable degree of autonomy in completing routine work activities.

autocratic-delegation continuum model
An approach to leadership describing the ways in which leaders allocate influence to subordinates. This ranges from controlling everything (*autocratic*) to allowing others to make decisions for themselves (*delegating*). Between these extremes are more participative forms of leadership—*consulting* and making *joint decisions*.

two-dimensional model of subordinate participation
An approach to leadership that describes the nature of the influence leaders give followers. It distinguishes between leaders who are *directive* or *permissive* toward subordinates, and the extent to which they are *participative* or *autocratic* in their decision making. Individual leaders may be classified into four types in terms of where they fall when these two dimensions are combined.

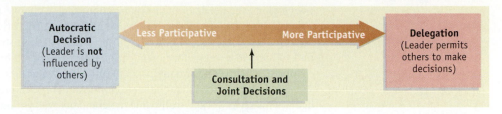

FIGURE 13.3

The Autocratic-Delegation Continuum Model

Traditionally, the amount of influence leaders give followers has been summarized as a continuum ranging from autocratic behavior (no influence) to delegation behavior (high influence). Consultation and joint decisions are intermediate forms of participation in decision-making.

Source: Based on suggestions by Yukl, 2006; see Note 1.

Although any attempt to divide human beings into discrete categories can't be perfect, these patterns do seem to make good sense. Indeed, many managers adopt a leadership style that fits, at least roughly, within one.

Given that leaders differ along these two dimensions and can, as a result, be classified as falling into one of the four patterns listed above, do any of them have a clear-cut edge? In short, is one pattern superior to the others in many, if not most, situations? Existing evidence suggests that this is doubtful. All four styles involve a mixed pattern of advantages and disadvantages. Moreover—and this is the crucial point—the relative success of each depends heavily on conditions existing within a given organization and its specific stage of development.

To illustrate this point, consider a manager who is a *directive autocrat.* Such a person makes decisions without consulting subordinates and supervises subordinates' work activities very closely. It is tempting to view such a pattern as undesirable insofar as it runs counter to the value of personal freedom. However, this approach may be highly successful in some settings—such as when employees are inexperienced or underqualified for their jobs, or when subordinates adopt an adversarial stance toward management and must be closely supervised. As you might imagine, such individuals tend to be unpopular.

In contrast, consider the case of the *permissive autocrat*—a leader who combines permissive supervision with an autocratic style of making decisions. This pattern may be useful in dealing with employees who have high levels of technical skill and want to be left alone to manage their own jobs (e.g., scientists, engineers, computer programmers), but who have little desire to participate in routine decision making.

The remaining two patterns (*directive democrat* and *permissive democrat*) are also well suited to specific organizational conditions. The key task for leaders, then, is to match their

TABLE 13.3 The Two-Dimensional Model of Subordinate Participation

Leaders can be described as having different styles based on how they involve subordinates in making decisions about how to do their jobs. Four distinct styles are summarized here.

Are Subordinates Told Exactly How to Do Their Jobs?	Are Subordinates Permitted to Participate in Making Decisions?	
	Yes (*Democratic*)	No (*Autocratic*)
Yes (*directive*)	**Directive democrat** (*makes decisions participatively; closely supervises subordinates*)	**Directive autocrat** (*makes decisions unilaterally; closely supervises subordinates*)
No (*permissive*)	**Permissive democrat** (*makes decisions participatively; gives subordinates latitude in carrying out their work*)	**Permissive autocrat** (*makes decisions unilaterally; gives subordinates latitude in carrying out their work*)

Source: Based on suggestions by Muczyk & Reimann, 1987; see Note 27.

own style to the needs of their organization, and to change as these needs shift and evolve. What happens when leaders in organizations lack such flexibility? Actual events in one now-defunct company—People Express Airlines—are instructive.[28] Don Burr, the founder and CEO, had a very clear managerial style: He was a highly permissive democrat. He involved employees in many aspects of decision making, and emphasized autonomy in work activities. Indeed, he felt that everyone at People Express should be viewed as a "manager." This style worked well while the company was young, but as it grew and increased in complexity, such practices created mounting difficulties. New employees were not necessarily as committed as older ones, so permissive supervision was ineffective with them. And, as decisions increased in both complexity and number, a participative approach became less appropriate. Unfortunately, top management was reluctant to alter its style; after all, it seemed to have been instrumental in the company's early success. This poor match between the style of top leaders and changing external conditions seems to have contributed (along with many other factors, of course) to People Express's ultimate demise.

To conclude, no single leadership style is best under all conditions and in all situations. However, recognizing the importance of differences in this respect can be a constructive first step toward assuring that the style most suited to a given set of conditions is, in fact, adopted. (Specific ideas regarding the most appropriate style for a given situation are described in our discussion of so-called *contingency theories of leader effectiveness* beginning on p. 520.)

Person-Oriented Versus Production-Oriented Leaders

Think again about all the bosses you have had in your career. Now, divide these into two categories—those who were relatively effective and those who were relatively ineffective. How do the two groups differ? If you think about this carefully, your answers are likely to take one of two forms. First, you might reply, "My most effective bosses helped me to get the job done. They gave me advice, answered my questions, and let me know exactly what was expected of me. My most ineffective bosses didn't do this." Second, you might answer, "My most effective bosses seemed to care about me as a person. They were friendly, listened to me when I had problems or questions, and seemed to help me toward my personal goals. My ineffective bosses didn't do this."

A large body of research, much of it conducted in the 1950s at the University of Michigan and at The Ohio State University, suggests that leaders do differ greatly along these dimensions.[29] Those at the high end of the first dimension, known as **initiating structure** (or **production-centered**), are concerned mainly with production and focus primarily on getting the job done. They engage in actions such as organizing work, inducing subordinates to follow rules, setting goals, and making leader and subordinate roles explicit. In contrast, other leaders are lower on this dimension and show less tendency to engage in these actions.

Leaders at the high end of the second dimension, known as **consideration** (or **person-centered**), are concerned primarily with establishing good relations with their subordinates and being liked by them. They engage in actions such as doing favors for subordinates, explaining things to them, and ensuring their welfare. Others, in contrast, are low on this dimension and don't really care much about how they get along with subordinates.

At first glance, you might assume that initiating structure and consideration are linked such that people high on one of these dimensions are automatically low on the other. In fact, this is not the case. The two dimensions are largely independent.[30] Thus, a leader may be high on both concern with production and concern for people, high on one of these dimensions and low on the other, moderate on one and high on the other, and so on (see Figure 13.4).

Is any one of these possible patterns best? Careful study indicates that this is a complex issue; production-oriented and people-oriented leadership behaviors both offer a mixed pattern of pluses and minuses. With respect to showing consideration (high concern with people and human relations), the major benefits are improved group atmosphere and morale.[31] However, since leaders high on this dimension are reluctant to act in a directive manner toward subordinates and often shy away from presenting them with negative feedback, productivity sometimes suffers. Regarding initiating structure (high concern with production), efficiency and performance are indeed sometimes enhanced by this leadership style. If leaders focus

initiating structure
Activities by a leader designed to enhance productivity or task performance. Leaders who focus primarily on these goals are described as demonstrating a task-oriented style.

production-centered
See initiating structure.

consideration
Actions by a leader that demonstrate concern with the welfare of subordinates and establish positive relations with them. Leaders who focus primarily on this task are often described as demonstrating a person-oriented style.

person-centered
See consideration.

FIGURE 13.4

Two Basic Dimensions of Leader Behavior

Leaders' behavior can vary from low to high with respect to *consideration* (person orientation) and *initiating structure* (task orientation). Patterns of leader behavior produced by variations along these two dimensions are illustrated here.

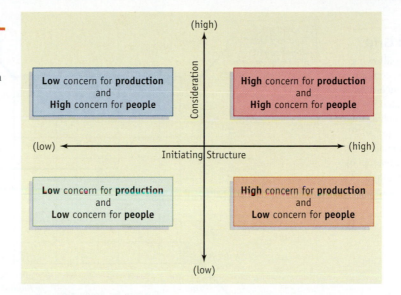

entirely on production, however, employees may soon conclude that no one cares about them or their welfare. Then work-related attitudes such as job satisfaction and organizational commitment may suffer (and, as we describe in Chapter 6, this is problematic).

Having said all this and pointed out the complexities, we add that one specific pattern appears to have an edge in many settings. This is a pattern in which leaders demonstrate high concern with both people *and* production.[32] Indeed, research has shown that high amounts of concern with people (showing consideration) and concern with productivity (initiating structure) are not incompatible. Rather, skillful leaders can combine both of these orientations into their overall styles to produce favorable results. Thus, although no one leadership style is best, leaders who combine these two concerns may often have an important edge over leaders who show only one or the other. In the words of U.S. Army Lieutenant General William G. Pagonis:

> To lead successfully, a person must demonstrate . . . expertise and empathy. In my experience, both of these traits can be deliberately and systematically cultivated; this personal development is the first important building block of leadership.[33]

Developing Successful Leader Behavior: Grid Training

grid training
A multi-step process designed to cultivate concern for people and concern for production.

How can one go about developing these two forms of leadership behavior—demonstrating concern for production and concern for people? A technique known as **grid training** proposes a multistep process designed to cultivate these two important skills.[34]

The initial step consists of a *grid seminar*—a session in which an organization's managers (who have been previously trained in the appropriate theory and skills) help organization members analyze their own management styles. This is done using a specially designed questionnaire that allows managers to determine how they stand with respect to their *concern for production* and their *concern for people*. Each participant's approach on each dimension is scored using a number ranging from 1 (low) to 9 (high).

Managers who score low on both concern for production and concern for people are scored 1,1—evidence of what is called *impoverished management*. A manager who is highly concerned about production but shows little interest in people, the *task management* style, scores 9,1. In contrast, ones who show the opposite pattern—high concern with people but little concern with production—are described as having a *country club* style of management; they are scored 1,9. Managers scoring moderately on both dimensions, the 5,5 pattern, are said to follow a *middle-of-the-road* management style. Finally, there are individuals who are highly concerned with both production and people, those scoring 9,9. This is the most desirable pattern, representing what is known as *team management*. These various patterns are represented in a diagram like that shown in Figure 13.5, known as the *managerial grid.*®

FIGURE 13.5

The Managerial Grid®

A manager's standing allowing two basic dimensions, concern for production and concern for people, can be illustrated by means of a diagram such as this, known as the *managerial grid*®. In *grid training,* people are trained to be effective leaders by demonstrating high amounts of both dimensions.

Source: Based on suggestions by Blake & Mouton, 1969; see Note 34.

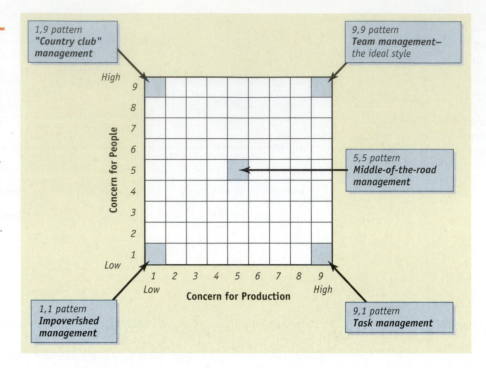

After a manager's position along the grid is determined, training begins to improve concern over production (planning skills) and concern over people (communication skills) to reach the ideal, 9,9 state. This consists of organization-wide training aimed at helping people interact more effectively with each other. Then, training is expanded to reducing conflict between groups that work with each other. Additional training includes efforts to identify the extent to which the organization is meeting its strategic goals and then comparing this performance to an ideal. Next, plans are made to meet these goals, and these plans are implemented in the organization. Finally, progress toward the goals is continuously assessed, and problem areas are identified.

Grid training is widely considered an effective way of improving the leadership behaviors of people in organizations. Indeed, the grid approach has been used to train hundreds of thousands of people in developing the two key forms of leadership behavior.

Leaders and Followers

Thus far throughout this chapter, we have focused on leaders—their traits and their behaviors. Followers, by and large, have been ignored. But, in a crucial sense, followers are the essence of leadership. Without them, there really is no such thing as leadership (see Figure 13.6). As someone once put it, "Without followers leaders cannot lead. . . . Without followers, even John Wayne becomes a solitary hero, or, given the right script, a comic figure, posturing on an empty stage."[35]

The importance of followers, and the complex, reciprocal relationship between leaders and followers, is widely recognized by organizational researchers. Indeed, major theories of leadership, such as those we consider in this section, note—either explicitly or implicitly—that leadership, is really a two-way street. We will now consider three such approaches: the *leader-member exchange model,* the practice of *team leadership,* and the *attribution approach* to leadership.

The Leader-Member Exchange (LMX) Model: The Importance of Being in the "In-Group"

Do leaders treat all their subordinates in the same manner? Informal observation suggests that, clearly, they do not. Yet many theories of leadership ignore this fact. They discuss leadership behavior in terms that suggest similar actions toward all subordinates. The

FIGURE 13.6

Leaders and Followers: An Essential Connection

Mark Hurd is president and chief executive officer of HP. As a successful leader, his effectiveness is based on his capacity to gain the support of followers. And in such large, publicly traded organizations, stockholders are among the most important followers whose favor is courted.

leader-member exchange (LMX) model

A theory suggesting that leaders form different relations with various subordinates and that the nature of such dyadic exchanges can exert strong effects on subordinates' performance and satisfaction.

importance of potential differences in this respect is brought into sharp focus by the **leader-member exchange (LMX) model**.[36]

This theory suggests that for various reasons leaders form different kinds of relationships with various groups of subordinates. One group, referred to as the *in-group*, is favored by the leader. Members of in-groups receive considerably more attention from the leader and larger shares of the resources they have to offer (such as time and recognition). By contrast, other subordinates fall into the *out-group*. These individuals are disfavored by leaders. As such, they receive fewer valued resources from their leaders.

Leaders distinguish between in-group and out-group members very early in their relationships with them—and on the basis of surprisingly little information. Sometimes, perceived similarity with respect to personal characteristics such as age, gender, or personality is sufficient to categorize followers into a leader's in-group.[37] Similarly, a particular follower may be granted in-group status if the leader believes that person to be especially competent at performing his or her job.[38]

Research has supported the idea that leaders favor members of their in-groups. For example, one study found that supervisors inflated the ratings they gave poorly performing employees when these individuals were members of the in-group, but not when they were members of the out-group.[39] Given the favoritism shown toward in-group members, it follows that such individuals would perform their jobs better and would hold more positive attitudes toward their jobs than members of out-groups.

In general, research has supported this prediction. For example, it has been found that in-group members are more satisfied with their jobs and more effective in performing them than out-group members.[40] In-group members are also less likely to resign from their jobs than out-group members.[41] And, as you might imagine, members of in-groups tend to receive more mentoring from their superiors than do members of out-groups, helping them become more successful in their careers (for a summary, see Figure 13.7).[42]

Together, these studies provide good support for the LMX model. Such findings suggest that attention to the relations between leaders and their followers can be very useful. The nature of such relationships can strongly affect the morale, commitment, and performance of employees. Helping leaders to improve such relations, therefore, can be extremely valuable in several respects.

The Challenge of Leading Work Teams

Traditionally, leaders make strategic decisions on behalf of followers, who are responsible for carrying them out. In many of today's organizations, however, where *teams* predominate (see Chapter 8), leaders are called upon to provide special resources to team members,

FIGURE 13.7

The LMX Model: A Summary

According to the *leader-member exchange (LMX) model,* leaders distinguish between groups they favor (in-groups) and those they do not favor (out-groups). Members of in-groups generally enjoy higher levels of morale, commitment, and job performance than members of out-groups.

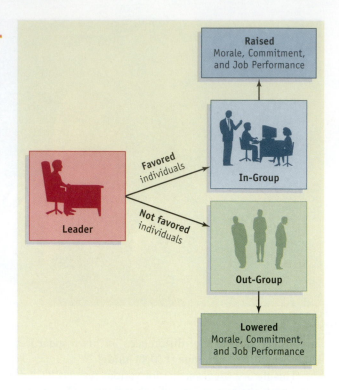

who are empowered to implement their own missions in their own ways. Instead of "calling the shots," team leaders help subordinates take responsibility for their own work. As such, they are very different from the traditional, "command and control" leadership role we have been discussing.[43] As Table 13.4 suggests, leading teams is clearly very different from leading individuals in the traditional manner.

The Role of Leaders in Self-Managed Work Teams. When most people think of leaders, they tend to think of individuals who make strategic decisions on behalf of followers and who are responsible for carrying them out. In many of today's organizations, however, where the movement toward *self-managed teams* predominates, it is less likely than ever that leaders are responsible for getting others to implement their orders to help fulfill their visions. Instead, team leaders may be called upon to provide special resources to groups empowered to implement their own missions in their own ways. They don't call all the shots, but help subordinates take responsibility for their own work.

This suggests that the role of team leader is clearly very different from the traditional approach to leadership in hierarchical organizations.[44] With this in mind, here are a few guidelines that may be followed to achieve success as a team leader.

1. Instead of directing people, *team leaders work at building trust and inspiring teamwork.* One way this can be done is by encouraging interaction between all members of the team as well as between the team and its customers and suppliers. Another key ingredient is to take initiatives to make things better. Instead of taking a reactive, "if it ain't broke, don't fix it" approach, teams may be led to success by individuals who set a good example for improving the quality of their team's efforts.

2. Rather than focusing simply on training individuals, effective *team leaders concentrate on expanding team capabilities.* In this connection, team leaders function primarily as coaches, helping the team by providing all members with the skills needed to perform the task, removing barriers that might interfere with task success, and finding the necessary resources required to get the job done. Likewise, team leaders work at building the confidence of the team, cultivating their untapped potential.

3. Instead of managing one-on-one, *team leaders attempt to create a team identity.* In other words, leaders must help teams understand their missions and recognize what they're doing to help fulfill it. In this connection, team leaders may help the group set

TABLE 13.4 Leading Groups Versus Leading Teams

The popularity of teams in today's organizations has important implications for how leaders go about fulfilling their roles. Some of the key differences between leading traditional work groups and leading teams are summarized here.

In Traditional Work Groups, Leaders . . .	But, in Teams, Leaders . . .
Tell people what to do.	Ask people what they think and share responsibility for organizing and doing the work.
Take all the credit.	Share the limelight with all their teammates.
Focus on training employees.	Concentrate on expanding their team's capabilities by functioning primarily as coaches who build confidence in team members, cultivating their untapped potential.
Relate to others individually.	Create a team identity by helping the team set goals, helping members meet them, and celebrating when they have been met.
Work at reducing conflict between individuals.	Make the most of team differences by building respect for diverse points of view and ensuring that all team members' views are expressed.
React to change.	Recognize that change is inevitable and foresee it, better preparing the organization to make appropriate adaptations.

goals—pointing out ways they may adjust their performance when they do not meet them, and planning celebrations when team goals are attained.

4. Although traditional leaders have worked at preventing conflict between individuals, *team leaders are encouraged to make the most of differences between members.* Without doubt, it is a considerable challenge to meld a diverse group of individuals into a highly committed and productive team, but doing so is important. This can be done by building respect for diverse points of view, making sure that all team members are encouraged to present their views, and respecting these ideas once they are expressed.

5. Unlike traditional leaders who simply react to change, team leaders try to *foresee and influence change.* To the extent that leaders recognize that change is inevitable (a point we will emphasize in Chapter 16), they may be better prepared to make the various adaptations required. Effective team leaders continuously scan the business environment for clues as to changes that appear to be forthcoming and help teams decide how to be responsive to them.

In conclusion, leading teams is a far cry from leading individuals in the traditional directive (or even participative) manner. The special nature of teams makes the leader's job very different. Although appreciating these differences is easy, making the appropriate adjustments may be extremely challenging—especially for individuals who are well practiced in the ways of traditional leadership. However, given the prevalence of teams in today's work environment, the importance of making the adjustments cannot be overstated. Leading new teams using old methods is a surefire formula for failure.

Grassroots Leadership. A good example of team leadership may be found in a most unlikely place—aboard a U.S. Navy warship. For 20 months D. Michael Abrashoff was commander of the USS *Benfold,* one of the U.S. Navy's most modern, most technologically advanced, most lethal warships (see Figure 13.8). Although you'd surely think that Commander Abrashoff ran this $1 billion floating computerized arsenal in the strict, top-down manner of most military companies, you couldn't be farther off.[45] In fact, he actually relied on a **grassroots leadership** approach in which the traditional management hierarchy is turned upside down. Aboard the *Benfold,* however, it's the 300 sailors who are really in charge. The commander expressed it as follows.

grassroots leadership
An approach to leadership that turns the traditional management hierarchy upside-down by empowering people to make their own decisions.

In most organizations today, ideas still come from the top. Soon after arriving at this command, I realized that the young folks on this ship are smart and talented. And I realized that my job was to listen aggressively—to pick up all of the ideas that they had for improving how we operate. The most important thing that a captain can do is to see the ship from the eyes of the crew.[46]

Abrashoff's approach to commanding the ship was highly personalized. Like all good team leaders do, he met face-to-face with each of the crew members in an attempt to understand their personal and professional goals. Moreover, he made decisions that paved the way for the sailors under his command to spend more time on mission-critical tasks and less time on unpleasant chores. No longer did they have to sand off rust and repaint the ship. Abrashoff arranged for an outside firm to replace rusting bolts with stainless steel hardware and to apply a special rust-inhibiting finish to the ship's surfaces. This not only relieved the sailors from having to perform tedious, demoralizing chores, but also freed them to spend more time on their true purpose—preparing for combat.

Grassroots leadership has been an unqualified success aboard the *Benfold*. During his command, the ship became recognized as the best in the Pacific Fleet and was recognized as the most combat-ready ship in the entire U.S. Navy. In addition, the crew became so efficient that it was able to return a third of the budget allocated for maintenance. Finally, and perhaps most impressively, literally all of the career sailors aboard the *Benfold* reenlisted for a second tour of duty, enabling the Navy to get the most from its highly trained personnel.

It is not only aboard the USS *Benfold* where one can see grassroots leadership at work. The same basic approach also has been used very successfully at Royal Dutch Shell—which, like the U.S. Navy, is an organization with a strong tradition of top-down leadership.[47] The success of grassroots leadership in such rigid and traditional organizations is a good indication that this approach may have considerable value in a wide variety of organizations.

attribution approach (to leadership)

The approach to leadership that focuses on leaders' attributions of followers' performance—that is, their perceptions of its underlying causes.

The Attribution Approach: Leaders' Explanations of Followers' Behavior

As we have just noted, leaders' relationships with individual subordinates can play an important role in determining the performance and satisfaction of these individuals. One specific aspect of such exchanges serves as focus of another contemporary perspective on leadership—the **attribution approach**.[48] This theory emphasizes the role

FIGURE 13.8

The USS *Benfold*: Grassroots Leadership at Sea

Sailors aboard the USS *Benfold*, a warship, operate as a team and are empowered to make many decisions themselves. This *grassroots leadership* approach is quite different from traditional top-down approaches to leadership found in most military and civilian organizations.

of leaders' attributions concerning the causes behind followers' behavior (see Chapter 3)—especially the causes of their job performance.

Leaders observe the performance of their followers and then attempt to understand *why* this behavior met, exceeded, or failed to meet their expectations. Since poor performance often poses greater difficulties than effective performance, leaders are more likely to engage in a careful attributional analysis when confronted with the former. When they are, they examine the three kinds of information described in Chapter 3 (consensus, consistency, and distinctiveness), and on the basis of such information, they form an initial judgment as to whether followers' performance stemmed from internal causes (e.g., low effort, commitment, or ability) or external causes (factors beyond their control, such as faulty equipment, unrealistic deadlines, or illness). Then, on the basis of such attributions, they formulate specific actions designed to change the present situation, and perhaps improve followers' performance. Attribution theory suggests that such actions are determined, at least in part, by leaders' explanations of followers' behavior. For example, if they perceive poor performance as stemming from a lack of required materials or equipment, they may focus on providing such items. If, instead, they perceive poor performance as stemming mainly from a lack of effort, they may reprimand, transfer, or terminate the person involved (for a summary example, see Figure 13.9).

Evidence for the accuracy of these predictions has been reported in several studies.[49] In one experiment, for example, researchers presented nursing supervisors with brief accounts of errors committed by nurses.[50] The incidents suggested that the errors stemmed either from internal causes (i.e., lack of effort or ability) or from external causes (i.e., overdemanding work environment). After reading about the incidents, supervisors indicated what kind of action they would be likely to take in each situation. Results showed that they were more likely to direct corrective action toward the nurses when they perceived the errors as stemming from internal causes (e.g., by showing them how to do something), but more likely to direct action toward the environment when they perceived the errors as stemming from external factors (e.g., changing schedules or improving facilities).

Thus far, we have discussed the attributions leaders make about followers' behavior. However, followers also make attributions about their leaders' behavior. In fact, recent research suggests that this takes a particularly interesting form: Followers tend to rally around their leaders in times of crisis, what is known as the **rally 'round the flag effect**. In other words, they make positive attributions about their leaders when they appear to be working to keep things together during a crisis situation. Probably the most poignant recent example of this is the dramatic boost in popularity experienced by U.S. President

rally 'round the flag effect
The tendency for followers to make positive attributions about their leaders when they appear to be working to keep things together during a crisis situation.

FIGURE 13.9

Leaders' Attributions of Followers' Poor Performance

The way leaders respond to their followers depends on the attributions leaders make regarding the causes of followers' performance. In this example, attributions made about the causes of a subordinate's poor performance direct that leader to take very different courses of action.

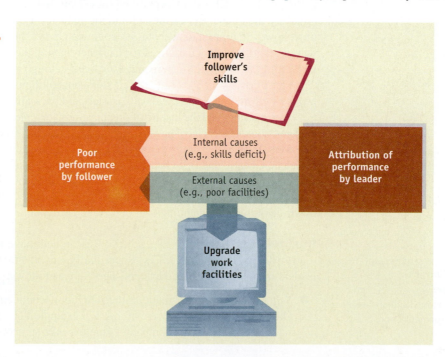

George W. Bush immediately following the terrorist attacks of September 11, 2001. The American public put aside its political differences (which were considerable given the vagaries of the 2000 presidential election) and supported the president during this crisis. As time moved on, however, this effect faded and the president's popularity waned. Interestingly, this is not the only time this has happened. A team of researchers recently organized all the militarized disputes that occurred between 1933 and 1992. They found that support for the president grew in all instances, especially during large-scale wars.[51]

Although comparable evidence has not been collected in the case of business organizations, anecdotal evidence suggests that a similar effect occurs there as well—although it takes a slightly different form. Specifically, many employees tend to stick by CEOs who are engaged in efforts to help their companies when these leaders face a crisis (such as when Microsoft had to defend itself against antitrust charges). However, when CEOs are perceived to be the cause of the problem (as in the case of Enron), or when the consequences appear to be so dire as to threaten the existence of the company, loyalty may not be found. Rather, the most qualified employees may "abandon ship," seeking employment elsewhere, before it's too late.

In summary, the attribution approach suggests that the attitudes and behaviors of leaders and followers often reflects the attributions they make about one another's behavior. From this perspective, then, leadership lies as much in the perceptions of the people who exercise such influence as in the perceptions of those who confer the right to wield it over them.

Change-Oriented Leadership: Future Visions

For organizations to thrive—let alone survive—they must be led by individuals who have a strong commitment to change. As such, leaders must have clear visions about what the future holds. The world's top leaders tend to agree. In a large-scale survey of CEOs from 20 different countries, having "a strong sense of vision" was identified by 98 percent as the most important characteristic for a CEO to have. Not surprisingly, companies with the most visionary leaders tend to outperform those with less visionary leaders in all important financial respects.

Having said this, the question arises about what precisely is involved in giving leaders the capacity to envision the most effective changes for the future. Answers are provided by two interesting approaches to leadership known as *charismatic leadership* and *transformational leadership*.

Charismatic Leadership: That "Something Special"

In the 1970s, the Chrysler Corporation (now DaimlerChrysler) was being written off as terminal by many analysts of the automobile industry. Lee Iacocca, Chrysler's CEO at the time, however, refused to accept this economic verdict. Instead, he launched a campaign to win government loan guarantees for Chrysler, paving the way for the company's survival. By setting an example of personal sacrifice—taking only $1 as salary one year during Chrysler's crisis—Iacocca rallied Chrysler's tens of thousands of employees to unheard-of levels of effort, and saved the day. Chrysler paid back all its loans ahead of schedule.

World history and the history of organizations are replete with similar examples. Through the ages, some leaders have had extraordinary success in generating profound changes in their followers. Indeed, it is not extreme to suggest that some such people (e.g., Napoleon, Nelson Mandela, Ghandi, and Bill Gates to name a few) have changed entire societies through their words and actions. Individuals who accomplish such feats have been referred to as **charismatic leaders**. These are individuals who exert especially powerful effects on followers by virtue of their commanding confidence and clearly articulated visions.

charismatic leaders
Leaders who exert especially powerful effects on followers by virtue of the attributions followers make about them. Such individuals have high amounts of self-confidence, present a clearly articulated vision, behave in extraordinary ways, are recognized as change agents, and are sensitive to the environmental constraints they face.

Qualities of Charismatic Leaders. Researchers have found that charismatic leaders tend to be special in key ways. Specifically, several factors differentiate charismatic leaders from noncharismatic leaders. These are as follows:

- *Self-confidence:* Charismatic leaders are highly confident in their ability and judgment. Others readily become aware of this. For example, John Bryan, CEO of Sara Lee, is widely regarded by his company's employees as someone who really knows his stuff.

- *A vision:* A charismatic leader is said to have vision to the extent that he or she proposes a state of affairs that improves upon the status quo. He or she also must be able to clearly articulate that vision and show willingness to make sacrifices to make it come true. This is precisely what Lee Iacocca did when he took the $1 salary during Chrysler's troubled period. For some further examples of visions stated by some well-known charismatic leaders, see Table 13.5.
- *Extraordinary behavior:* Charismatic leaders are frequently unconventional. Their quirky ways, when successful, elicit admiration. For example, much of the success of Southwest Airlines is attributed to the zany antics of its CEO, Herb Kelleher, who has been known to fall out of overhead bins to surprise passengers.
- *Recognized as change agents:* The status quo is the enemy of charismatic leaders. They make things happen. This can be said about the late Roberto Goizueta, who made Coca-Cola one of the most admired—and profitable—companies in America (a challenge being picked up today by Mary Minnick, as described in the *Preview Case* on pp. 499–500).
- *Environmental sensitivity:* Charismatic leaders are highly realistic about the constraints imposed upon them and the resources needed to change things. Consequently, they know what they can and cannot do.

Reactions to Charismatic Leaders. At first glance, it is tempting to assume that charismatic leaders are special merely because of the traits they possess. However, it also makes sense to look at charismatic leadership as involving a special relationship between leaders and their followers. That is to say, leaders are considered charismatic by virtue of their effects on followers. Such reactions include:

- Levels of performance beyond those that normally would be expected[52]
- High levels of devotion, loyalty, and reverence toward the leader[53]
- Enthusiasm for and excitement about the leader and the leader's ideas.[54]

In short, charismatic leadership involves a special kind of leader-follower relationship in which the leader can, in the words of one author, "make ordinary people do extraordinary things in the face of adversity."[55]

The Effects of Charismatic Leadership—Both Good and Bad. As you might imagine, charismatic leaders have dramatic effects on the behavior of their followers. Because these individuals are perceived as being so heroic, followers are very pleased with them—satisfaction that generalizes to perceptions of the job itself. In short, people enjoy

TABLE 13.5 Some Famous Charismatic Leaders and Their Visions

One quality that makes charismatic leaders so effective is that they share clear visions for their organizations and then help pave the way toward attaining them. The visions of a few well-known charismatic leaders are summarized here.

Charismatic Leader	Company	Vision
Steven Jobs	Apple Computer	To make computing simple and available to everyone
Charles Schwab	Charles Schwab	To provide high-quality financial services to people at reasonable prices
Herb Kelleher	Southwest Airlines	To provide excellent service and great value to the flying public
Mary Kay Ash	Mary Kay Cosmetics	To enhance the self-esteem of women by building their financial independence while providing quality cosmetics
Rupert Murdoch	News Corporation	To provide accurate access to news for people throughout the world
Walt Disney	Walt Disney Co.	To provide wholesome, high-quality entertainment to families throughout the world

working for charismatic leaders and do well under their guidance. On a larger scale, research has found that U.S. presidents believed to be highly charismatic (as suggested by biographical accounts of their personalities and their reactions to world crises) received higher ratings by historians of their effectiveness as president.[56] In short, evidence suggests that charismatic leadership can have some very beneficial effects.

It is important to caution, however, that being charismatic does not necessarily imply being virtuous. In fact, throughout history, many of the most vicious dictators (Adolf Hitler, among them) were able to rise to power because of the considerable charisma they had. Indeed, it was their clear visions of different worlds, misguided though they may have been, that led them to have such profound effects on their followers.

Are Charismatic Leaders Always Needed? It is important to note that there may not always be a place for charismatic leaders in organizations. They tend to be needed most under circumstances in which there is some crisis.[57] For example, charismatic leaders tend to emerge under wartime conditions, such as when U.S. General Norman Schwartzkopf expressed a vision of victory over Iraq and led his troops to victory in 1991's Operation Desert Storm. A crisis, such as the Great Depression, led to the election of President Franklin D. Roosevelt, the individual who would lead the United States out of its financial upheaval. And, as noted earlier, the economic crisis at Chrysler during the 1970s led to the emergence of Lee Iacocca, the man who saved the company.

By the same token, it is easy to imagine that under everyday conditions, leaders who approach others with such overwhelming levels of arrogance and self-confidence that they ignore others may be more of a liability than an asset. Such was the case, for example, at Borland International, the world's largest database software provider.[58] When the company faced financial crises in the late 1980s, charismatic president and CEO Philippe R. Kahn was most helpful in turning things around. Interestingly, however, as the company emerged from crisis, Kahn's "Barbarian" approach to leadership only interfered with the company's operations. Likewise, several of the most famous political leaders were not charismatic at all. Take Benjamin Franklin, for example. For all his accomplishments as an inventor (of bifocals, among other things) and his stature in American history (he co-wrote and signed both the Declaration of Independence and the U.S. Constitution), Franklin was not at all charismatic. Instead, he took a very functional, problem-centered approach known as **pragmatic leadership**.[59] This is a type of leadership based on methodically developing solutions to problems and working them out in a thorough manner. Clearly, although being charismatic may be useful in many situations, it is a not a necessary requirement for leadership success.

The Liabilities of Being a Charismatic Leader. In closing, we should point out a particularly interesting thing about charismatic leaders: People's reactions to them tend to be highly polarized. That is, people either love them (as is the case most of the time) or hate them. With this in mind, it is not surprising that some of the world's most charismatic leaders, such as John F. Kennedy, Martin Luther King, and Israeli leader Itzak Rabin have fallen victim to assassination. Less visionary leaders certainly would have done little to inspire would-be assassins from attempting to leave their marks on the world in such clearly inappropriate ways.

Transformational Leadership: Beyond Charisma

If you're thinking that charismatic leaders are really something special, we're inclined to agree. But being charismatic is only the beginning when it comes to doing what it takes to get followers to be their most effective. Theorists have recognized that although charisma is important, the most successful leaders also do things that revitalize and transform their organizations. Accordingly, their orientation is referred to as **transformational leadership**.

Characteristics of Transformational Leaders. Transformational leaders may be described in terms of several characteristics. First, as we said, they have *charisma*. That is, they provide a strong vision and a sense of mission for the company. As one leadership theorist put it, "If you as a leader can make an appealing dream seem like tomorrow's reality, your subordinates will freely choose to follow you."[60] Consider, for

pragmatic leadership
A type of leadership based on methodically developing solutions to problems and working them through in a thorough manner.

transformational leadership
Leadership in which leaders use their charisma to transform and revitalize their organizations.

example, the great visions expressed by the highly charismatic leaders we described in Table 13.5 on page 517.

But charisma alone is insufficient for changing the way an organization operates. For this to occur, transformational leaders also must provide the following:

- *Intellectual stimulation:* Transformational leaders help their followers recognize problems and ways of solving them.
- *Individualized consideration:* Transformational leaders give their followers the support, encouragement, and attention they need to perform their jobs well.
- *Inspirational motivation:* Transformational leaders clearly communicate the importance of the company's mission and rely on symbols (e.g., pins and slogans) to help focus their efforts.

As you might imagine, transformational leaders arouse strong emotions. They also help transform their followers by teaching them, often by serving as mentors.[61] In so doing, transformational leaders seek to elevate followers to do their own thing. By contrast, charismatic leaders may keep their followers weak and highly dependent on them. A charismatic leader may be the whole show, whereas a transformational leader does a good job of inspiring change in the whole organization. Many celebrities, be they musicians, actors, or athletes, tend to be highly charismatic, but they do not necessarily have any transformational effects on their followers. As such, although some people may idolize certain rock stars, and dress like them, these musicians' charisma is unlikely to stimulate their fans into making sacrifices that revitalize the world. When you think of it this way, it's easy to see how charisma is just a part of transformational leadership.

Profile of a Transformational Leader. Jack Welch, the past chairman and CEO of General Electric (GE), is a good example of a transformational leader. Under Welch's leadership, GE underwent a series of changes with respect to the way it does business.[62] At the individual level, GE has abandoned its previously bureaucratic ways and now does an outstanding job of listening to its employees. Not surprisingly, GE has consistently ranked among the most admired companies in its industry in *Fortune* magazine's annual survey of corporate reputations—including a number one ranking in 2002 and several previous years.[63]

In the 1980s, Welch bought and sold many businesses for GE, using as his guideline the fact that GE would only keep a company if it placed either number one or number two in market share. If this meant closing plants, selling assets, and laying off personnel, he did it, and got others to follow suit. Not surprisingly, he earned the nickname "Neutron Jack." Did Welch transform and revitalize GE? Having added $52 billion of value to the company, there can be no doubt about it.[64]

Measuring Transformational Leadership and its Effects. Scientists measure transformational leadership by using a questionnaire known as the Multifactor Leadership Questionnaire (MLQ). In completing this instrument, subordinates complete a series of questions in which they describe the behavior of their superiors. It consists of items tapping the four aspects of transformational leadership described above. So, for example, agreeing with an item such as "My leader makes me feel proud to be associated with him/her" is taken as an indication of the leader's transformational ways. The more subordinates agree with such statements as they describe the leader in question, the more highly that leader is scored as being transformational. Using this questionnaire, scientists have found that transformational leaders tend to be very effective in making their organizations highly successful.

Research has shown managers at FedEx who are rated by their subordinates as being highly transformational tend to be higher performers, and are recognized by their superiors as being highly promotable.[65] These and other studies suggest that the benefits of being a transformational leader may be considerable.

With this in mind, it certainly would be useful to consider how people might go about developing ways of transforming their organizations through their leadership. We have summarized several key guidelines in Table 13.6. Although you may find it easier to understand than to carry out some of these suggestions, the evidence regarding the effectiveness of transformational leadership suggests that the effort required to do so may be worthwhile.

TABLE 13.6 Guidelines for Becoming a Transformational Leader

Being a *transformational leader* is not easy, but following the suggestions outlined here may help leaders transform and revitalize their organizations.

Suggestion	Explanation
Develop a vision that is both clear and highly appealing to followers.	A clear vision will guide followers toward achieving organizational goals and make them feel good about doing so.
Articulate a strategy for bringing that vision to life.	Don't present an elaborate plan; rather, state the best path toward achieving the mission.
State your vision clearly and promote it to others.	Visions must not only be unambiguous but also made compelling, such as by using anecdotes.
Show confidence and optimism about your vision.	If a leader lacks confidence about success, followers will not try very hard to achieve that vision.
Express confidence in followers' capacity to carry out the strategy.	Followers must believe that they are capable of implementing a leader's vision. Leaders should build followers' self-confidence.
Build confidence by recognizing small accomplishments toward the goal.	If a group experiences early success, it will be motivated to continue working hard (see Chapter 7).
Celebrate successes and accomplishments.	Formal or informal ceremonies are useful for celebrating success, thereby building optimism and commitment.
Take dramatic action to symbolize key organizational values.	Visions are reinforced by things leaders do to symbolize them. For example, one leader demonstrated concern for quality by destroying work that was not up to standards.
Set an example; actions speak louder than words.	Leaders serve as role models. If they want followers to make sacrifices, for example, they should do so themselves.

Contingency Theories of Leader Effectiveness

That leadership is a complex process should be obvious by now. It involves intricate social relationships and is affected by a wide range of factors. Given all these complications, you may wonder why so many researchers focus so much of their time and energy on attempting to understand all of its intricacies. The answer, of course, is that effective leadership is an essential ingredient in organizational success. With effective leadership organizations can grow, prosper, and compete effectively. Without it, many simply cannot survive. Recognition of this basic point lies behind several modern theories of leadership collectively referred to as **contingency theories of leader effectiveness**.

As will soon be clear, these theories differ sharply in their content, terminology, and scope. Yet all are linked by two common themes. First, all adopt a *contingency approach*— they recognize that there is no one best style of leadership, and that the key task of organizational behavior researchers is determining which leadership styles will prove most effective under which specific conditions. Second, all are concerned with the issue of *leader effectiveness*. They seek to identify the conditions and factors that determine whether, and to what degree, leaders will enhance the performance and satisfaction of their subordinates. Several theories fall into this category.[66] Among these are five that we will describe here: *LPC contingency theory, situational leadership theory, path-goal theory, normative decision theory,* and the *substitutes for leadership* framework.

LPC Contingency Theory: Matching Leaders and Tasks

Earlier, we explained that the behaviors associated with effective leadership fall into two major categories—concern for people, and concern for production. Both types of behavior

contingency theories of leader effectiveness
Any of several theories which recognize that certain styles of leadership are more effective in some situations than others.

contribute to a leader's success. However, a more refined look at this issue leads us to ask exactly *when* each type of behavior works best. That is, under what conditions are leaders more successful when they demonstrate a concern for people compared to a concern for production?

The Basics of the Theory. This question is addressed by a widely studied approach to leadership known as **LPC contingency theory**. The contingency aspect of the theory is reflected by the assumption that a leader's contribution to successful performance by his or her group is determined both by the leader's own traits and by various features of the situation. Different levels of leader effectiveness occur under different combinations of conditions. To fully understand leader effectiveness, both types of factors must be considered.

According to the theory, *esteem (liking) for least preferred coworker* (**LPC** for short) is the most important personal characteristic. This refers to a leader's tendency to evaluate in a favorable or unfavorable manner the person with whom she or he has found it most difficult to work. Leaders who perceive this person in negative terms (low LPC leaders) are concerned primarily with attaining successful task performance. In contrast, those who perceive their least preferred coworker in a positive light (high LPC leaders) mainly are concerned with establishing good relations with subordinates. A questionnaire is used to measure one's LPC score. It is important to note that the theory views LPC as being fixed—that is, an aspect of an individual's leadership style that cannot be changed. As we will explain, this has important implications for applying the theory so as to improve leader effectiveness.

Which type of leader—one low in LPC or one high in LPC—is more effective? As suggested by the word "contingency," the answer is: "It depends." And, what it depends on is the degree to which the situation is favorable to the leader—that is, how much it allows the leaders to have control over their subordinates. This, in turn, is determined largely by three factors:

1. The nature of the *leader's relations with group members* (the extent to which he or she enjoys their support and loyalty)
2. The *degree of structure* in the task being performed (the extent to which task goals and subordinates' roles are clearly defined)
3. The leader's *position power* (as described in Chapter 11, his or her formal capacity to enforce compliance by subordinates)

Combining these three factors, the leader's situational control can range from very high (positive relations with group members, a highly structured task, and high position power) to very low (negative relations, an unstructured task, and low position power).

What types of leaders are most effective under these various conditions? According to the theory, low LPC leaders (ones who are task-oriented) are superior to high LPC leaders (ones who are relations-oriented) when situational control is either very low or very high. In contrast, high LPC leaders have an edge when situational control falls within the moderate range (refer to Figure 13.10).

The rationale for these predictions is quite reasonable. Under conditions of low situational control, groups need considerable guidance to accomplish their tasks. Without such direction, nothing would get done. For example, imagine a military combat group led by an unpopular platoon leader under battle conditions in which things are falling apart and the troops are thinking of mutinying. Any chance of effectiveness this person has would result from paying careful attention to the task at hand, rather than hoping to establish better relations with the group. (In fact, in the Army, it is often said that a leader in an emergency is better off giving wrong orders than no orders whatsoever.) Since low LPC leaders are more likely to provide structure than high LPC leaders, they usually will be superior in such cases.

Similarly, low LPC leaders are also superior under conditions that offer the leader a high degree of situational control. Indeed, when leaders are liked, their power is not challenged. When the demands of the task make it clear what a leader should be doing, it is perfectly acceptable for them to focus on the task at hand. Subordinates expect their leaders to exercise control under such conditions and accept it when they do so. And this leads to task success. For example, an airline pilot leading a cockpit crew is expected to take charge and not to seek the consensus of others as she guides the plane onto the runway for a landing. Surely, she would be less effective if she didn't take charge, but asked the co-pilot what he thought she should do.

LPC contingency theory

A theory suggesting that leader effectiveness is determined both by characteristics of leaders (their *LPC* scores) and by the level of situational control they are able to exert over subordinates.

LPC

Short for "esteem for least preferred co-worker"—a personality variable distinguishing between individuals with respect to their concern for people (high LPC) and their concern for production (low LPC).

FIGURE 13.10

LPC Contingency Theory: An Overview

LPC contingency theory predicts that low LPC leaders (ones who are primarily task-oriented) will be more effective than high LPC leaders (ones who are primarily people-oriented) when situational control is either very low or very high. However, the opposite is true when situational control is moderate.

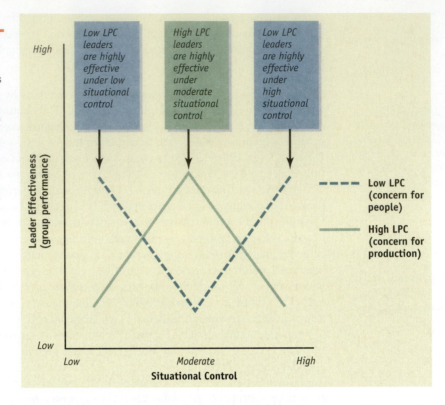

Things are different, however, when situations offer leaders moderate situational control. Consider, for example, a situation in which a leader's relations with subordinates are good, but the task is unstructured, and the leader's power is somewhat restricted. This is generally the case within a research and development team attempting to find creative new uses for a company's products. Here, it clearly would be inappropriate for a low LPC leader to impose directives. Rather, a highly nurturant leader who is considerate of the feelings of others would likely be most effective—that is, a high LPC leader (see Figure 13.11).

Applying LPC Contingency Theory. Practitioners have found LPC contingency theory to be quite useful when it comes to suggesting ways of enhancing leader effectiveness. Because the theory assumes that certain kinds of leaders are most effective under certain kinds of situations, and that leadership style is fixed, the best way to enhance effectiveness is to fit the right kind of leaders to the situations they face.

This involves completing questionnaires that can be used to assess both the LPC score of the leader and the amount of control he or she faces in the situation. Then, using these indexes, a match can be made such that leaders are put into the situations that best suit their leadership styles—a technique known as **leader match**. This approach also focuses on ways of changing the situational control variables—leader-member relations, task structure, and leader position power—when it is impractical to change leaders. For example, a high LPC leader may be moved to a job in which situational control is either extremely high or extremely low. Alternatively, we may attempt to change the situation, such as by altering relations between leaders and group members, or raising or lowering the leader's position power) so as to increase or decrease the amount of situational control encountered.

Several companies, including Sears, have used the leader match approach with some success. In fact, several studies have found that the approach is effective in improving group effectiveness on at least some occasions.

Situational Leadership Theory: Adjusting Leadership Style to the Situation

Another theory of leadership, **situational leadership theory**, is also considered a contingency theory because it focuses on the best leadership style for a given situation. Specifically, the scientists who developed this theory argue that leaders are effective when

leader match

The practice of matching leaders (based on their LPC scores) to the groups whose situations best match those in which they are expected to be most effective (according to LPC contingency theory).

situational leadership theory

A theory suggesting that the most effective style of leadership—either delegating, participating, selling, or telling—depends on the extent to which followers require guidance and direction, and emotional support.

FIGURE 13.11

Matching Leadership Style to the Situation

LPC contingency theory recognizes that the most appropriate leadership style depends on the situation leaders are confronting. The aircraft cockpit crew (pictured left) may be most effective when its leader, the pilot, uses a highly directive (low LPC) style. So too, would a military troop in a difficult battle situation (pictured center) perform best when its commanding officer adopts a low LPC style. However, a research and development team would perform poorly if its leader (pictured right) behaved this same way. In that setting, a less directive (high LPC) style would be more effective.

they select the right leadership style for the situation they face.[67] Specifically, this depends on the *maturity* of followers—that is, their readiness to take responsibility for their own behavior. This, in turn, is based on two variables with which we are already familiar: (1) *task behavior* (the degree to which followers have the appropriate job knowledge and skills—that is, their need for guidance and direction), and (2) *relationship behavior* (the degree to which followers are willing to work without taking direction from others—that is, their need for emotional support).

As shown in Figure 13.12, by combining high and low levels of these independent dimensions, four different types of situations are identified (denoted by "S" in the diagram), each of which is associated with a particular leadership style that is most effective.

- *Lower-right corner of Figure 13.12 (S1):* Situations in which followers need a great deal of direction from their leaders but don't need much emotional support from them. The practice of *telling* followers what to do is most useful in such situations. That is, giving followers specific instructions and closely supervising their work may be the best approach.
- *Upper-right corner of Figure 13.12 (S2):* Situations in which followers still lack the skill to be able to succeed, although in this case, they require more emotional support. Under these conditions, *selling* works best. Being very directive may make up for the follower's lack of ability, while being very supportive will help get them to go along with what the leader is asking of them.
- *Upper-left corner of Figure 13.12 (S3):* Conditions in which followers need very little guidance with respect to how to do their jobs, but considerable emotional hand-holding and support to motivate them. That is, low levels of task behavior, but high levels of relationship (supportive) behavior are required. A *participating* style of leadership works well in such situations because it allows followers to share their expertise while enhancing their desire to perform.
- *Lower-left corner of Figure 13.12 (S4):* Followers are both willing and able to do what is asked of them. In other words, low levels of task behavior and low levels of relationship behavior are required. Under such conditions, *delegating* is the best way to treat followers—that is, turning over to them the responsibility for making and implementing their own decisions.

According to this situational leadership theory, leaders must be able to: (1) diagnose the situations they face, (2) identify the appropriate behavioral style, and then (3) implement that response. Because the situations leaders face may change all the time, leaders

FIGURE 13.12

Situational Leadership Theory: Its Basic Dimensions

Situational leadership theory specifies that the most appropriate leadership style depends on the amount of emotional support followers require in conjunction with the amount of guidance they require to do their jobs.

Source: Hersey & Blanchard, 1988; see Note 67.

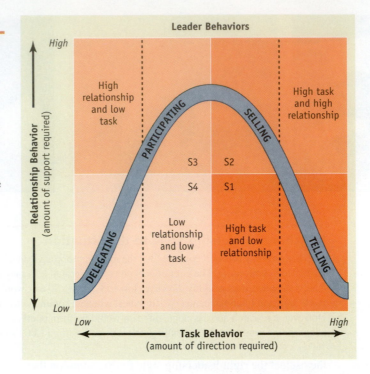

must constantly reassess them, paying special attention to their followers' needs for guidance and emotional support. To the extent that they do so, they are likely to be effective.

Specialized training in these skills has been found to be quite useful. In fact, the approach has been widely used to train leaders at such corporate giants as Xerox, Mobil Oil, and Caterpillar, as well as in the U.S. military services. (Which style of leadership are you most prone to follow in your treatment of others? To give you some insight into this question, complete the Experiencing OB section on pp. 538–539.)

Path-Goal Theory: Leaders as Guides to Valued Goals

Suppose you conducted an informal survey in which you asked 100 people to indicate what they expect from their leaders. What kind of answers would you receive? Although they would vary greatly, one common theme you might uncover would be, "I expect my leader to *help*—to assist me in reaching goals I feel are important." This basic idea plays a central role in the **path-goal theory** of leadership.[68]

path-goal theory
A theory of leadership suggesting that subordinates will be motivated by a leader only to the extent they perceive this individual as helping them to attain valued goals.

In general terms, this theory contends that subordinates will react favorably to a leader only to the extent that they perceive this person as helping them progress toward various goals by clarifying actual paths to such rewards. That is, effective leaders clarify for followers what they need to do to get from where they are to where they should be, and to help them do so. More specifically, the theory contends that actions by a leader that clarify the nature of tasks and reduce or eliminate obstacles will increase perceptions on the part of subordinates that working hard will lead to good performance and that good performance, in turn, will be recognized and rewarded. Under such conditions, the theory suggests, job satisfaction, motivation, and actual performance will all be enhanced.

How, precisely, can leaders best accomplish these tasks? The answer, as in other modern views of leadership, is: "It depends." (In fact, that's how you can tell it is a contingency theory.) And what it depends on is a complex interaction between key aspects of *leader behavior* and certain *contingency* factors. With respect to leader behavior, path-goal theory suggests that leaders can adopt four basic styles:

- *Instrumental (directive):* An approach focused on providing specific guidance, establishing work schedules and rules
- *Supportive:* A style focused on establishing good relations with subordinates and satisfying their needs

■ *Participative:* A pattern in which the leader consults with subordinates, permitting them to participate in decisions

■ *Achievement-oriented:* An approach in which the leader sets challenging goals and seeks improvements in performance

According to the theory, these styles are not mutually exclusive; in fact, the same leader can adopt them at different times and in different situations. Indeed, showing such flexibility is one important aspect of an effective leader. (Recognizing that it is important to adopt these styles, many of today's leaders have adopted an approach to leadership known as *coaching*. For a look at this orientation to leadership, see the *How To Do It* section below.)

HOW TO DO IT

Coaching Tips from Some of the Best

If you have ever played on a sports team you have experienced first-hand the important leadership function of a coach. What did your coach do? Chances are that he or she was actively involved in helping you in the following manner:

■ Analyzing ways of improving your performance and extending your capabilities

■ Creating a supportive climate, one in which barriers to development are eliminated

■ Encouraging you to improve your performance, no matter how good you already may be

Coaching has been around for a long time. However, only recently has coaching emerged as a philosophy of leadership in organizations.[69] To a large extent this appears to have been stimulated by books in which football coaches (such as the famed college coach Lou Holtz and NFL coach Bill Belichick) and executives (such as the Green Bay Packers' executive VP and general manager, Ron Wolf) have shared insight into the coaching process.[70]

These insiders to big-time sports tell us that what makes coaching a unique form of leadership is the special nature of the relationship between the coach and team members. The key to this relationship is trust. Team members acknowledge the coach's expertise and trust the coach to have his, and the team's, best interests in mind. At the same time, the coach believes in the team member's capacity to profit from his or her advice. In other words, coaching is a partnership in which both the coach and the team member play an important part in achieving success.

Additional dimensions of the coach's leadership power have been described by basketball hall of famer and former U.S. Senator Bill Bradley.[71] A key to coaching, Bradley emphasizes, is to get players to commit to something bigger than themselves. In sports this may mean winning a championship, and in other businesses it may mean landing a huge contract or surpassing a long-standing sales record. Focusing on the goal itself, and identifying how each individual may contribute to it, is key.

Bradley also advises that the best coaches don't do all the talking when someone gets out of line. Rather, they harness the power of team members to put pressure on the problem person. As a case in point, consider what happened when the Chicago Bulls' Scottie Pippin angrily took himself out of a 1994 semifinal championship game after coach Phil Jackson called for teammate Toni Kukoc to make the final, game-deciding shot. Naturally, Coach Jackson came down hard on Pippin in his postgame interview, but that was mostly for show. The real work in getting Pippin to see the error of his ways came not from the coach, but from his teammates. After the game, the coach left the locker room, announcing that the team had something to say to Pippin. Then, one by one, members of the Bulls expressed their disappointment in Pippin for letting down the team. Seeing the error of his ways, Pippin apologized on the spot and immediately went back to being the team player he had been all along. Had the coach not orchestrated this session, the effects surely would not have been as successful.

One way coaches can be supportive of their team members and earn their trust, is to refrain from bad-mouthing team members to others. Athletic coaches who use the media to send critical messages to their players live to regret it, Bradley tells us. However, behind the closed doors of the locker room, it's quite a different story. In that setting, there's no such thing as being too frank. The same applies in the office or shop as well. A manager who complains to other managers what a poor job one of her employees has been doing is not only making herself look bad, but more importantly, betraying that employee's trust. And, as we said earlier, trust is the heart of the coaching game.

Which of these styles is best for maximizing subordinates' satisfaction and motivation? The answer depends on two contingency factors. First, the style of choice is strongly affected by several *characteristics of subordinates.* For example, if followers are high in ability, an instrumental style of leadership may be unnecessary; instead, a less structured, supportive approach may be preferable. On the other hand, if subordinates are low in ability, the opposite may be true; people with poor ability need considerable guidance to help them attain their goals. Similarly, people high in need for affiliation (that is, those desiring close, friendly ties with others) may strongly prefer a supportive or participative style of leadership. Those high in the need for achievement may strongly prefer an achievement-oriented leader.

Second, the most effective leadership style also depends on several *aspects of the work environment.* For example, path-goal theory predicts that when tasks are unstructured and nonroutine, an instrumental approach by the leader may be best; much clarification and guidance are needed. However, when tasks are structured and highly routine, such leadership may actually get in the way of good performance, and may be resented by subordinates who think the leader is engaging in unnecessary meddling. (See Figure 13.13 for an overview of all these aspects of path-goal theory.)

Path-goal theory has been subjected to empirical testing in several studies.[72] In general, results have been consistent with major predictions derived from the theory, although not uniformly so. Thus, at present, path-goal theory appears to be another framework offering valuable insights into leadership and the many factors that determine the degree to which individual leaders are successful in this role.

Normative Decision Theory: The Right Time for Employee Participation

As we discussed in Chapter 10, making decisions is one of the major tasks performed by leaders. Indeed, to some, a defining characteristic of leadership positions is that they are where "the buck finally stops" and concrete actions must be taken. Since the decisions reached by leaders often have far-reaching effects on their subordinates, one major determinant of leader effectiveness clearly is the adequacy with which they perform this key task. Leaders who make good decisions will be more effective in the long run than leaders who make bad ones. But how should they go about making decisions? Specifically, how much participation should leaders invite from them? As we noted earlier, participation in decision making is an important variable in many organizational settings—one with implications for job satisfaction, stress, and productivity. Thus, the manner in which leaders handle this issue can be crucial in determining their effectiveness.

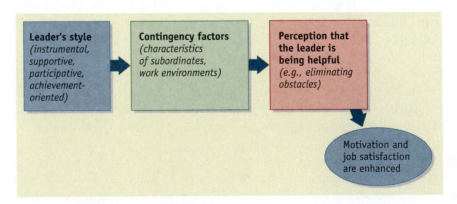

FIGURE 13.13

Path-Goal Theory: An Overview

According to *path-goal theory,* perceptions among employees that leaders are helping them reach valued goals enhance both employees' motivation and job satisfaction. Such perceptions, in turn, are encouraged when a leader's style is consistent with the needs and characteristics of subordinates (e.g., their level of experience) and aspects of the work environment (e.g., the requirements of the tasks being performed).

normative decision theory
A theory of leader effectiveness focusing primarily on strategies for choosing the most effective approach to making decisions.

But how much participation in decisions by subordinates should leaders allow? Perhaps the most useful answer to this question is provided by **normative decision theory**.[73] This is a theory of leader effectiveness that focuses primarily on strategies for choosing the most effective approach to making decisions. Specifically, research on this theory has shown that leaders often adopt one of five distinct methods for reaching decisions. These are summarized in Table 13.7, and as you can see, they cover the entire range—from decisions made solely by the leader in a totally autocratic manner through ones that are fully participative.

Are any of these approaches strongly preferable to the others? The answer is no. Just as there is no single best style of leadership, there is no single best strategy for making decisions. Each pattern offers its own mixture of benefits and costs. For example, decisions reached through participative means stand a better chance of gaining support and acceptance among subordinates. However, such decisions require a great deal of time—often, more time than a leader or organization can afford. Similarly, decisions reached autocratically (by the leader alone) can be made more rapidly and efficiently. But such an approach can generate resentment among followers and encounter difficulties with respect to actual implementation. A major task faced by leaders, then, is selecting the specific decision-making approach that will maximize potential benefits but minimize potential costs. How can this be done?

It has been proposed that leaders should attempt to select the best approach (or at least eliminate ones that are not useful) by answering several basic questions about the situation. These relate primarily to the *quality of the decision*—the extent to which it will affect important group processes such as communication or production; and to *acceptance of the decision*—the degree of commitment among subordinates needed for its implementation. For example, with respect to decision quality, a leader should ask questions such as: Is a high-quality decision required? Do I have enough information to make such a decision? Is the problem well structured? With respect to decision acceptance, he or she should ask: Is it crucial for effective implementation that subordinates accept the decision? Do subordinates share the organizational goals that will be reached through solution of this problem?

According to normative decision theory, answering such questions and applying specific rules such as those shown in Table 13.8 eliminate some of the potential approaches to reaching a given decision. Those that remain constitute a feasible set that can, potentially, be used to reach the necessary decision.

To simplify this process, theorists recommend using a decision tree such as the one shown in Figure 13.14. To apply this diagram, a manager begins on the left side and responds, in turn, to the questions listed under each letter (A, B, C, and so on). As the manager replies to each question, the set of feasible approaches narrows. For example, imagine that the manager's answers are as follows:

- Question A: Yes—a high-quality decision is needed.
- Question B: No—the leader does not have sufficient information to make a high-quality decision alone.

TABLE 13.7 Potential Strategies for Making Decisions

According to *normative decision theory*, leaders making decisions often adopt one of the five basic strategies described here.

Decision Strategy	Description
AI (autocratic)	Leader solves problem or makes decision unilaterally using available information.
AII (autocratic)	Leader obtains necessary information from subordinates but then makes decision unilaterally.
CI (consultative)	Leader shares the problem with subordinates individually but then makes decision unilaterally.
CII (consultative)	Leader shares problem with subordinates in group meeting but then makes decision unilaterally.
GII (group decision)	Leader shares problem with subordinates in a group meeting; decision is reached through discussion to consensus.

Source: Based on suggestions from Vroom & Jago, 1988; see Note 73.

TABLE 13.8 Decision Rules in Normative Decision Theory

By applying the rules shown here, leaders can eliminate decision-making strategies that are likely to prove ineffective in a given situation and select those likely to be most effective.

Rules Designed to Protect Decision Quality		Rules Designed to Protect Decision Acceptance	
■ Leader Information Rule	If the quality of the decision is important and you do not have enough information or expertise to solve the problem alone, eliminate an autocratic style.	■ Acceptance Rule	If acceptance by subordinates is crucial for effective implementation, eliminate the autocratic styles.
■ Goal Congruence Rule	If the quality of the decision is important and subordinates are not likely to make the right decision, rule out the highly participative style.	■ Conflict Rule	If acceptance by subordinates is crucial for effective implementation and they hold conflicting opinions over the means of achieving some objective, eliminate autocratic styles.
■ Unstructured Problem Rule	If the quality of the decision is important but you lack sufficient information and expertise and the problem is unstructured, eliminate the autocratic leadership styles.	■ Fairness Rule	If the quality of the decision is unimportant but acceptance is important, use the most participatory style.
		■ Acceptance Priority Rule	If acceptance is critical and not certain to result from autocratic decisions and subordinates are not motivated to achieve the organization's goals, use a highly participative style.

- ■ Question C: No—the problem is not structured.
- ■ Question D: Yes—acceptance by subordinates is crucial to implementation.
- ■ Question E: No—if the leader makes the decision alone, it may not be accepted by subordinates.
- ■ Question F: No—subordinates do not share organizational goals.
- ■ Question G: Yes—conflict among subordinates is likely to result from the decision.

As you can see, these replies lead to the conclusion that only one decision-making approach is feasible: CII, involving full participation by subordinates. (The path leading to this conclusion is shown in the broken orange line in Figure 13.14.) Of course, different answers to any of the seven key questions would have led to different conclusions.

The normative decision model is highly appealing because it takes full account of the importance of subordinate participation in decisions and offers leaders clear guidance for choosing among various methods for reaching decisions. As with any theory, though, the key question remains: Is it valid? Are its suggestions concerning the most effective style of decision making under various conditions really accurate? The results of several studies designed to test the model have been encouraging.

The latest version of the theory is more complex: Instead of seven contingency questions there are twelve, and instead of answering questions with a simple "yes" or "no," there are now five response options. This revised model is so highly complex that a computer program is used instead of a decision tree to help find the most appropriate leadership style. Preliminary evidence suggests that the resulting theory is more valid than the original, although it is far too complex to present here. Still, the basic idea is identical.

Whether we're talking about the more sophisticated version or the original version of normative decision theory, it is clear that this formulation makes an important contribution to our understanding of leadership. Insofar as there is widespread current interest in allowing subordinates to participate in decision making, normative decision theory is useful insofar as it gives leaders clear guidance as to when such a move may be expected to improve task performance.

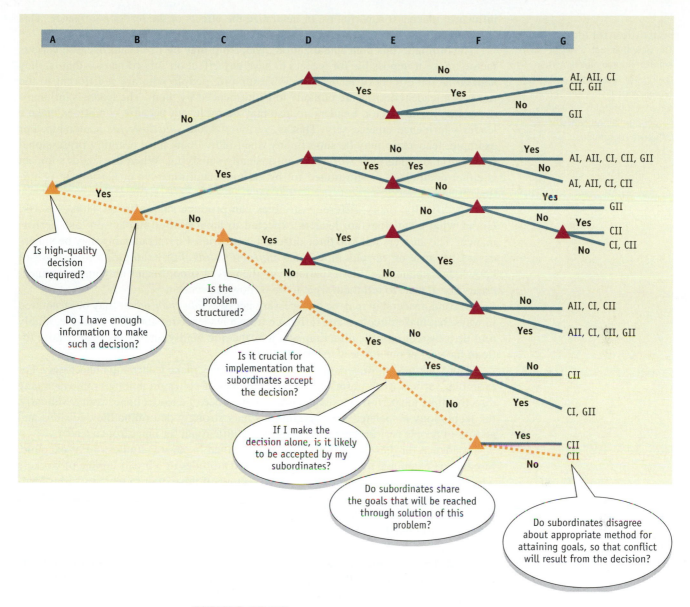

FIGURE 13.14

Normative Decision Theory: An Example

By answering the questions listed here and tracing a path through this decision tree, leaders can identify the most effective approaches to making decisions in a specific situation. Note: The path suggested by the answers to questions A through G (see pp. 527–528) is shown by the broken orange line.

Source: Based on suggestions by Vroom & Yetton, 1973; see Note 73.

Substitutes for Leadership: When Leaders Are Superfluous

Throughout this chapter, we have emphasized that leaders are important. Their style, actions, and degree of effectiveness all exert major effects on subordinates and, ultimately, on organizations. In many cases, this is certainly true. Yet, almost everyone has observed or been part of groups in which the designated leaders actually had little influence—groups in which these people were mere figureheads with little impact on subordinates. One explanation for such situations involves the characteristics of the leaders in question: They are simply weak and unsuited for their jobs. Another, and in some ways more intriguing possibility is that in some contexts, other factors may actually substitute for a leader's

substitutes for leadership
The view that high levels of skill among subordinates or certain features of technology and organizational structure sometimes serve as substitutes for leaders, rendering their guidance or influence superfluous.

influence, making it superfluous, or neutralize the effects of the leader's influence. This has been proposed in what is known as the **substitutes for leadership** framework.[74]

According to this conceptualization, leadership may be irrelevant because various factors make it impossible for leaders to have any effect on subordinates—that is, they *neutralize* the effects of leadership. For example, people who are indifferent to the rewards a leader controls are unlikely to be influenced by them. The leader's influence is negated by this factor. Leadership also may be irrelevant because conditions make a leader's influence unnecessary. That is, various factors *substitute for* leadership. For example, leadership may be superfluous when individuals have a highly professional orientation and find their work to be intrinsically satisfying. When the leader's impact is either neutralized or substituted for by various conditions, his or her impact is limited, at best.

Specifically, many different variables can produce such effects. Thus, we ask: Under what conditions are leaders expected to have limited impact on task performance? The answers fall into three different categories. First, leadership may be unnecessary because of various *individual characteristics*. For example, a high level of knowledge, commitment, or experience on the part of subordinates may make it unnecessary for anyone to tell them what to do or how to proceed.

Second, leadership may be unnecessary because *jobs themselves* may be structured in ways that make direction and influence from a leader redundant. For example, highly routine jobs require little direction, and jobs that are highly interesting also require little in the way of outside leadership stimulation.

Third, various *characteristics of organizations* may make leadership unnecessary. For example, various work norms and strong feelings of cohesion among employees may directly affect job performance and render the presence of a leader unnecessary. Similarly, the technology associated with certain jobs may strongly determine the decisions and actions of people performing them, and so leave little room for input from a leader.

Evidence for these assertions has been obtained in several studies.[75] For example, researchers examined the work performance and attitudes of a broad sample of workers who completed scales measuring their perceptions of the extent to which various leadership behaviors and substitutes for leadership were exhibited on their jobs.[76] Consistent with the theory, it was found that job performance and attitudes were more strongly associated with the various substitutes than with the leadership behaviors themselves.

If leaders are superfluous in many situations, why has this fact often been overlooked? One possibility is that people have a strong tendency to *romanticize* leadership—that is, to perceive it as more important and more closely linked to performance in many contexts than it actually is.[77] Researchers testing this possibility presented MBA students with detailed financial information about an imaginary firm, including a paragraph describing the firm's key operating strengths. The content of this paragraph was varied, so that four different groups of subjects received four different versions. These attributed the firm's performance either to its top-level management team, the quality of its employees, changing patterns of consumer needs and preferences, or federal regulatory policies, respectively.

After reading one of these paragraphs and examining other information about the firm, subjects rated two aspects of its overall performance—profitability and risk. It was reasoned that because of the tendency to overestimate the importance of leadership, subjects would rate the firm more favorably when its performance was attributed to top-level management than when it was attributed to any of the other factors. As you can see in Figure 13.15, this was precisely what occurred. The imaginary company was rated as higher in profitability and lower in risk when subjects had read the leadership-based paragraph than when they had read any of the others.

These findings, plus others, help explain why leaders are often viewed as important and necessary even when, to a large degree, they are superfluous. Note: This in no way implies that leaders are usually unimportant. On the contrary, they often do play a key role in work groups and organizations. However, because this is not always so, their necessity should never be taken for granted.

FIGURE 13.15

Overestimating the Importance of Leadership: Research Evidence

People who received information suggesting that an imaginary company's past success was attributable to its top management rated the company more favorably (higher in profitability, lower in risk) than those who received information suggesting that the identical record resulted from other causes. These findings suggest that people *romanticize leadership*, overestimating its impact in many situations.

Source: Based on data reported by Meindl & Ehrlich, 1987; see Note 77.

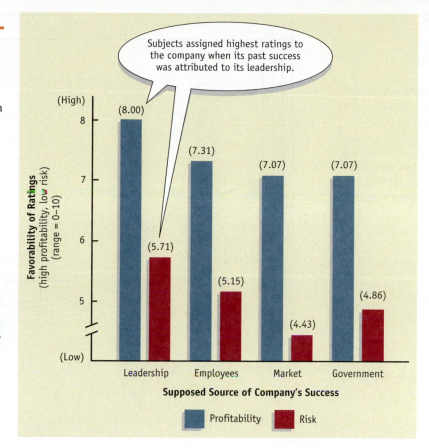

Leadership Development: Bringing Out the Leader Within You

In case it's not clear by now, being an effective leader isn't easy. If you happen to be fortunate enough to be born with "the right stuff," it helps. It also helps to find yourself in the kind of situation in which an opportunity exists to demonstrate your capacity as a leader. However, anyone can improve his or her leadership skills, honing his or her capacity to inspire others in an organization. Although we all cannot become a Jack Welch (the highly successful former CEO of General Electric described earlier), it is possible for almost anyone to develop the skills needed to become more successful as a leader.

leadership development
The practice of systematically training people to expand their capacity to function effectively in leadership roles.

The systematic process of training people to expand their capacity to function effectively in leadership roles is known as **leadership development**. In recent years, many organizations have invested heavily in leadership development efforts, recognizing that effective leadership is a source of competitive advantage for an organization (see Figure 13.16). Such efforts have focused on three major areas of emphasis. These are as follows:

- Developing networks of social interaction between people, close ties within and between organizations (see Chapter 9)
- Developing trusting relationships between oneself and others (see Chapter 11)
- Developing common values and shared visions with others

In essence, these skills focus on the development of emotional intelligence—one of the key characteristics of effective leaders we described earlier.

All leadership development programs are based on two key assumptions: (1) that leadership makes a difference in an organization's performance, and (2) that it is possible for leaders to be developed (i.e., made, if not born).[78] However, the various leadership development tools go about the mission of promoting leadership skills in different ways. We now identify some of the most widely used techniques.[79]

FIGURE 13.16

Leadership Development: An Important Organizational Activity

To avoid having people like Mr. Henderson, here, who fail to become effective leaders, today's organizations are disinclined to leave things to chance. Instead, many are involved actively in the process of *leadership development*.

Source: www.CartoonStock.com

"We're sorry, Henderson — But you never evolved into the leader the board had hoped for."

360-degree feedback
The process of using multiple sources from around an organization, and outside it, to evaluate the work of an individual—often used for leaders to learn what people think about them.

360-Degree Feedback

In Chapter 3 we described **360-degree feedback**, the process of using multiple sources from around an organization, and outside it, to evaluate the work of an individual. Here, we note that this practice has proven to be an effective way for leaders to learn what key others, such as peers, direct reports, and supervisors, think about them.[80] This is a useful means of identifying aspects of one's leadership style that are in need of change. Its basic assumption is that one's performance is likely to vary across different contexts, suggesting that different people will have different perspectives on someone's leadership.

The practice of collecting 360-degree feedback is extremely popular these days. In fact, nearly all of the *Fortune* 500 companies rely on this technique in one way or another.[81] However, collecting feedback and taking appropriate action based on it are two entirely different things. After all, many people are threatened by negative feedback and defend against it psychologically by dismissing it as invalid. Even those who agree with it might not be willing to change their behavior (a topic we will revisit in Chapter 16). Furthermore, even the most well-intentioned leaders may fail to take action on the feedback they receive if that information is too complex or inconsistent, which may well occur. To help in this regard, many companies have found that leaders who have face-to-face meetings with others in which they get to discuss the feedback they receive are particularly likely to follow up in an effective manner.[82]

Networking

networking
A leadership development tool designed to help people make connections to others to whom they can turn for information and problem solving.

Far too often, leaders find themselves isolated from things that are going on in other departments. As a result, when they need help, they don't know where to go for help within their organizations. As a leadership development tool, **networking** is designed to break down these barriers. Specifically, it is aimed at helping leaders learn to whom they should turn for information, finding out the problem-solving resources that are available to them. Networking is so important to Accenture, the worldwide consulting firm, for example, that it holds an annual five-day seminar designed to give its global partners a chance to meet one another and to exchange views. The goal is to allow partners to strengthen their personal networks, making it possible to address problems and take on projects that otherwise would have been overlooked.

Networking is beneficial to leadership development because it promotes peer relationships in work settings. These relationships are valuable insofar as they involve mutual obligations, thereby promoting cooperation. What's more, they tend to be long-lasting. In fact, it is not unusual for some peer relationships to span an entire 30-year career. Importantly, personal networks tend to be effective because they transcend organizational boundaries, thereby bringing together people from different parts of an organization who otherwise would not normally come into contact with one another. (Although networking is beneficial in organizations in all countries, it is especially important in China, where, as we describe in the *OB in a Diverse World* section below, it is an essential aspect of doing business.)

guanxi
In China, a person's network of personal and business connections.

OB In a Diverse World

Guanxi: Social Networking in China

If making connections with other people is a useful skill for American leaders, it is an absolutely essential skill for Chinese leaders, or anyone doing business in China, for that matter. In Chinese, the term **guanxi** refers to interpersonal relationships—specifically, one's network of personal and business connections.[83] For several centuries, guanxi has been a pervasive part of the Chinese business world, binding literally millions of Chinese companies into a vast social and business web. Business cannot be conducted in China without guanxi; one must have the proper network of connections to get things done. One party supports another, exchanging favors. It's not considered bribery, and it's perfectly legal. In fact, it's the glue that holds together the Chinese business enterprise. In today's fast-paced world, this is truer than ever.[84]

Behind the penchant for networking in China is the tendency for the Chinese to prefer working with people they know and trust. They are unlikely to make deals with strangers, so becoming a trusted associate is essential (and time consuming, too). Leaders who cultivate strong relationships with others become powerful because they are given opportunities that are denied to others. Doors open up for them. Suppose, for example, you want to obtain a license to market your product in a new region of China. With the right guanxi, the process can be accelerated and much less expensive. Without it, you might be hopelessly tied up in a mountain of red tape.

Guanxi is developed by cultivating a network of reciprocal obligations over time.[85] One person does a favor for another, and that original favor is subsequently reciprocated by another, and so on. Money talks when it comes to cultivating favors, but guanxi is more about interpersonal good will and personal support. For example, in China, one wouldn't think of doing business with a supplier, a bank, or even a government official without bringing a small gift, such as wine or cigarettes. Although the process might seem intrusive to the point of being blatantly pushy, it is considered completely proper in China. In fact, the giving of small gifts is absolutely necessary to cultivate, develop, and nurture the vast network of relationships needed to succeed.

Management consultant Tom Peters once wrote that a sure sign of a successful leader is one who has a Rolodex (file of business contacts) that grows larger each year. Former President Bill Clinton was considered a master of developing a vast network of business relationships. Whenever he needed a favor from someone, he would just find the Rolodex card of someone he met who might be able to help. Peters and Clinton worked their network contacts to their strategic advantage. In China, however, leaders must do the same thing just to stay in the game.

Executive Coaching

A highly effective method of developing leaders involves custom-tailored, one-on-one learning aimed at improving an individual leader's performance. This approach, known as **executive coaching**, is an extension of the practice of career counseling described in Appendix 2. Coaching can be either a one-time process aimed at addressing some specific issues, or it can be an ongoing, continuous process. In either case, executive coaching typically includes an integrative assessment of a leader's strengths and weaknesses along with a comprehensive plan for improvement. Specifically, executive coaching programs tend to follow the specific steps outlined in Figure 13.17.

In some organizations, being assigned a coach is seen as a remedial measure, a sign of weakness. In such cases, any benefits of coaching may be minimized as leaders fail to get involved in the process out of embarrassment. For this reason, organizations that use coaches are advised to provide these services to an entire executive group, thereby removing any stigma associated with coaching and putting all leaders on an equal footing. Research has found that executive coaching is particularly effective when it is used following a formal training program. In fact, the customized, one-on-one coaching provided after a standardized training program was found to increase leaders' productivity by 88 percent.[86]

Mentoring

In Chapter 6 we discussed how minority group members stand to benefit by having relationships with *mentors,* more senior associates who help show them the ropes. Again, in Appendix 2, we describe the formal process of *mentoring,* in which employees receive help, either formally or informally, from more experienced colleagues in the organization as a means of helping them develop their careers. (Mentors also may come from outside the organization, but such relationships are more likely to take the form of coaching). Although mentoring is unlikely to include a formal assessment of a leader's strengths and limitations, it is inclined to be focused on personal and professional support. Recent research shows that officials from a wide array of organizations consider mentoring one of the most effective forms of leadership development they have in place.[87]

FIGURE 13.17

Steps in the Executive Coaching Process

The process of executive coaching generally follows the four steps outlined here.

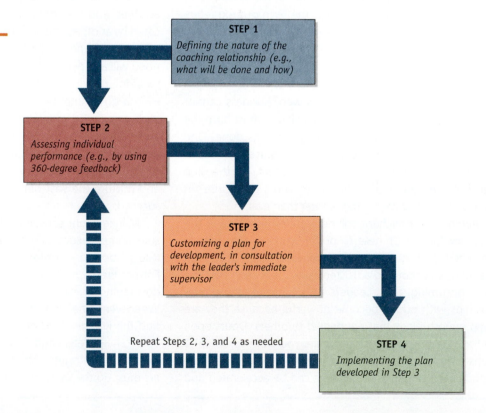

STEP 1
Defining the nature of the coaching relationship (e.g., what will be done and how)

STEP 2
Assessing individual performance (e.g., by using 360-degree feedback)

STEP 3
Customizing a plan for development, in consultation with the leader's immediate supervisor

Repeat Steps 2, 3, and 4 as needed

STEP 4
Implementing the plan developed in Step 3

A potential problem with mentoring (as we note in Appendix 2) is that protégés (i.e., the individuals helped by mentors) may become so highly connected to their mentors that they fail to think independently. Soon, what a protégé does is just what the mentor would have done. Although this can be beneficial, it is also potentially quite limiting, leading to a narrowness of thought. This problem is especially likely to occur in the case of executive coaching because protégés making important decisions may fear straying from the tried-and-true solutions of their mentors. And whenever this occurs, the organization is denied any fresh new perspective that the less seasoned executive might be able to provide.

Job Assignments

When it comes to leadership, the phrase "experience is the best teacher" seems to hold true. Indeed, one of the most effective ways of training leaders is by assigning them to positions that promise to give them needed experience.

With this in mind, several companies intentionally assign personnel to other countries so they can broaden their experiences. For example, the Coca-Cola Company recently transferred over 300 professional and managerial employees from the United States to facilities in other countries for one year in an effort to develop their skills before returning them home to assume new positions of leadership. Procter & Gamble does the same thing on a regular basis, assigning prospective leaders to positions at foreign affiliates for periods of one to three years. In many ways, this may be thought of as developing baseball players by sending them to the minor leagues. Likewise, teams from the National Football League are able to develop their players by sending them to compete on NFL Europe teams.

For job assignments to serve their developmental function, it is necessary for the newly assigned positions to provide the kind of opportunities that make learning possible. Ideally, the new positions are ones that give newly developing leaders opportunities to try out different approaches to leadership so they can see what works for them. In other words, they should have the latitude to try different approaches, even if they fail. It is important to keep in mind that the purpose of the job assignment is to facilitate learning, in which case failure is inevitable. However, should an emphasis be placed on job performance instead, it's unlikely that the new assignment will have the intended benefits, and it is destined to be looked upon unfavorably.

Action Learning

Traditionally, much of the learning that takes place when people learn to lead occurs in the classroom. The problem with this approach, however, is that shortly after the formal training sessions are over, people revert back to their old ways, resulting in little if any developmental progress. To combat this problem, many organizations have been turning to **action learning**, which is a continuous process of learning and reflection that is supported by colleagues and that emphasizes getting things done.[88] The underlying assumption of action learning is that leaders develop most effectively when they are working on real organizational problems.[89]

Citibank used action learning to help develop its leaders, who were having difficulty thinking about problems from a broad perspective.[90] Specifically, they took the following steps.

1. The issues to be worked on were selected by heads of business units. These had to be ones that affected total Citibank performance.
2. Participants were selected from throughout the world based on a through review of their talents.
3. A three-day orientation session was held off-site in which team-building skills were practiced (these are discussed in Chapter 8).
4. For two to three weeks data were collected about effective banking practices from both inside and outside Citibank.
5. These findings were systematically analyzed and recommendations were developed.
6. Findings were presented to area heads and the CEO in 90-minute meetings.

action learning
A leadership development technique involving a continuous process of learning and reflection that is supported by colleagues and that emphasizes getting things done.

7. A one-day debriefing session was held with a coach. These focused on the recommendations, team processes, and individual development opportunities.

8. One to two weeks later, senior managers followed up and made decisions regarding the various recommendations.

Although the business imperatives that drive action learning are often different, this basic process is generally quite similar. Action learning has been used not only at Citibank, but also at such organizations as General Electric (to develop new markets), ARAMARK (to promote cross-cultural opportunities), Shell Oil (to alter perceptions of the company's financial strength), and even the U.S. Army (to share lessons from battlefield experiences).[91] Because action learning is a general idea that takes different forms in different organizations, its effectiveness has been difficult to assess. However, available research generally confirms the effectiveness of training leaders by using the kind of active approaches described here instead of more passive, classroom training (see also our discussion of the factors that make training effective in Chapter 3).

Summary and Review of Learning Objectives

1. **Describe the trait approach to leadership and identify the characteristics that distinguish successful leaders from ordinary people.**

   The *trait approach to leadership,* referred to as *great person theory,* claims that successful leaders have characteristics that set them apart from other people. Such individuals tend to be higher in *leadership motivation* (i.e., the desire to be a leader), drive, honesty, self-confidence, and several other traits. Successful leaders also tend to have multiple sources of intelligence (e.g., cognitive intelligence, emotional intelligence, and cultural intelligence) and demonstrate high amounts of *flexibility*—that is, the ability to adapt their style to the followers' needs and to the requirements of specific situations.

2. **Distinguish between the two basic forms of leader behavior: person-oriented behavior and production-oriented behavior, explaining how grid training helps develop them.**

   Leaders differ with respect to the extent to which they focus on efforts to attain successful task performance—known as *initiating structure* (or being *task-oriented*)—and their concern with maintaining favorable personal relations with subordinates—known as *consideration* (or being *person-oriented*). *Grid training* is a systematic way of training managers to raise their concern for people as well as their concern for production (by training them in communication skills and planning skills).

3. **Explain what the leader-member exchange (LMX) model and the attributional approach to leadership say about the relationships between leaders and followers.**

   The *leader-member exchange (LMX) model* specifies that leaders favor members of some groups—referred to as *in-groups*—more than others—referred to as *out-groups*. As a result, in-groups tend to perform better than out-groups. The relationship between leaders and followers is also the focus of the *attributional approach to leadership.* This approach focuses on leaders' assessments of the underlying causes of followers' performance. Specifically, when leaders perceive that their subordinates poor performance is caused by internal factors, they react by helping the subordinates to improve. However, when poor performance is attributed to external sources, leaders direct their attention toward changing aspects of the work environment believed to be responsible for the poor performance.

4. **Describe the nature of charismatic leadership and how it compares to transformational leadership.**

   Some leaders—known as *charismatic leaders*—exert profound effects on the beliefs, perceptions, and actions of their followers. Such individuals have a special relationship with their followers in which they inspire exceptionally high levels of performance, loyalty, and enthusiasm. Charismatic leaders tend to have high amounts of self-confidence, present a clearly articulated vision, behave in extraordinary ways, are recognized as change agents, and are sensitive to the environmental constraints they face. In addition to being charismatic, *transformational leaders* also do things that transform and revitalize their organizations. They provide intellectual stimulation, individualized consideration, and inspirational motivation. Transformational leaders tend to be very effective.

5. **Summarize what LPC contingency theory and situational leadership theory say about the connection between leadership style and situational variables.**

   LPC contingency theory suggests that a leader's characteristics in conjunction with various situational factors determine his or her group's effectiveness. Task-oriented leaders (termed *low-LPC leaders*) are more effective than people-oriented leaders (termed *high-LPC leaders*) under conditions in which the leader has either high or low control over the group in question. In contrast, people-oriented leaders are more effective under conditions where the leader has moderate control. The *situational leadership theory* suggests that the most effective style of leadership—either delegating, participating, selling, or telling—depends on the extent to which followers require guidance and direction, and emotional support. Effective leaders are required to diagnose the situations they face and implement the appropriate behavioral style for that situation.

6. **Describe various techniques used to develop leadership in organizations.**

   One popular technique of leadership development, *360-degree feedback,* involves giving people multiple sources of feedback about their strengths and weaknesses. *Networking,* another technique, is aimed at helping leaders learn to whom they should turn for information, both inside and outside their organization. *Executive coaching* is a one-on-one experience in which a leader is given an integrative assessment of his or her strengths and weaknesses. Leadership development also involves giving people special *job assignments* that allow them to develop new skills. Finally, *action learning* is a leadership development technique in which people get to learn by experiencing real organizational problems.

Points to Ponder

Questions for Review

1. What is the difference between leadership and management? What are the characteristics that distinguish successful leaders from ordinary managers?
2. What is the difference between person-oriented leadership and production-oriented leadership?
3. How are the relationships between leaders and followers explained by the LMX model and the attribution approach to leadership? What assumptions must be made about the relationships between leaders and followers when leading work teams?
4. What makes charismatic leaders and transformational leaders so special in organizations?
5. What are the basic assumptions of contingency theories of leadership? What particular theories fall into this category?
6. What is meant by "leadership development," and what techniques are used to bring it about?

Experiential Questions

1. Do you know anyone whom you consider a charismatic leader or a transformational leader? If so, what is this person like? What has this individual done that suggests that he or she is so special?
2. Think about the leaders of teams in which you have worked and how they compare to the leaders of other groups that do not operate as teams. In what ways do these leaders behave similarly or differently?
3. Have you ever participated in a leadership development program? If so, what exactly was done? In what ways was the program effective or ineffective?

Questions to Analyze

1. As we noted, the lines between leading and managing sometimes are blurred in practice. What factors (e.g., technology, the economy, etc.) do you believe are responsible for making this distinction so vague?
2. As technology advances further in the years to come, how do you think the nature of leadership in work organizations is likely to change?

3. What techniques of leadership development do you believe would be most effective in the company in which you work? What do you see as the major impediments to the effectiveness of leadership development?

Experiencing OB

Individual Exercise

Determining Your Leadership Style

As noted on pages 522–524, *situational leadership theory* identifies four basic leadership styles. To be able to identify and enact the most appropriate style of leadership in any given situation, it is first useful to understand the style to which you are most strongly predisposed. This exercise will help you gain such insight into your own leadership style.

Directions

Following are eight hypothetical situations in which you have to make a decision affecting you and members of your work group. For each, indicate which of the following actions you are most likely to take by writing the letter corresponding to that action in the space provided.

- Action A: Let the members of the group decide themselves what to do.
- Action B: Ask the members of the group what to do, but make the final decision yourself.
- Action C: Make the decision yourself, but explain your reasons.
- Action D: Make the decision yourself, telling the group exactly what to do.

_____ 1. In the face of financial pressures, you are forced to make budget cuts for your unit. Where do you cut?

_____ 2. To meet an impending deadline, someone in your secretarial pool will have to work late one evening to finish typing an important report. Who will it be?

_____ 3. As coach of a company softball team, you are required to trim your squad to 25 players from 30 currently on the roster. Who goes?

_____ 4. Employees in your department have to schedule their summer vacations to keep the office appropriately staffed. Who decides first?

_____ 5. As chair of the social committee, you are responsible for determining the theme for the company ball. How do you do so?

_____ 6. You have an opportunity to buy or rent an important piece of equipment for your company. After gathering all the facts, how do you make the choice?

_____ 7. The office is being redecorated. How do you decide on the color scheme?

_____ 8. Along with your associates you are taking a visiting dignitary to dinner. How do you decide what restaurant to go to?

Scoring

1. Count the number of situations to which you responded by marking A. This is your *delegating* score.
2. Count the number of situations to which you responded by marking B. This is your *participating* score.
3. Count the number of situations to which you responded by marking C. This is your *selling* score.
4. Count the number of situations to which you responded by marking D. This is your *telling* score.

Questions for Discussion

1. Based on this questionnaire, what was your most predominant leadership style? Is this consistent with what you would have predicted in advance?

2. According to situational leadership theory, in what kinds of situations would this style be most appropriate? Have you ever found yourself in such a situation, and if so, how well did you do?
3. Do you think that it would be possible for you to change this style if needed?

Group Exercise

Identifying Great Leaders in All Walks of Life

A useful way to understand the great person theory is to identify those individuals who may be considered great leaders and then to consider what it is that makes them so great. This exercise is designed to guide a class in this activity.

Directions

1. Divide the class into four equal-size groups, arranging each in a semicircle.
2. In the open part of the semicircle, one group member—the recorder—should stand at a flip chart, ready to write down the group's responses.
3. The members of each group should identify the 10 most effective leaders they can think of—living or dead, real or fictional—in one of the following fields: business, sports, politics/government, humanitarian endeavors. One group should cover each of these domains. If more than 10 names come up, the group should vote on the 10 best answers. The recorder should write down the names as they are identified.
4. Examining the list, group members should identify the traits and characteristics that the people on the list have in common, but that distinguish them from others who are not on the list. In other words, what is it that makes these people so special? The recorder should write down the answers.
5. One person from each group should be selected to present his or her group's responses to members of the class. This should include both the names of the leaders identified and their special characteristics.

Questions for Discussion

1. How did the traits identified in this exercise compare to the ones identified in this chapter (see p. 504 and Table 13.2) as important determinants of leadership? Were they similar or different? Why?
2. To what extent were the traits identified in the various groups different or similar? In other words, were different characteristics associated with leadership success in different walks of life? Or were the ingredients for leadership success more universal?
3. Were some of the traits identified surprising to you, or were they all what you would have expected?

Practicing OB

"I Don't Get No Respect"

The president and founder of a small tool and die casting firm tells you, "Nobody around here has any respect for me. The only reason they listen to me is because this is my company." Company employees report that he is a highly controlling individual who does not let anyone do anything for themselves.

1. What behaviors should the president attempt to emulate to improve his leadership style? How might he go about doing so?
2. Under what conditions would you expect the president's leadership style to be most effective?
3. Do you think that these conditions might exist in his company? If not, how might they be created?

CASE IN POINT   Chan Suh Celebrates Agency.com's Tenth Anniversary

Like 'em or not, you see them all the time when you visit Web sites—those flashy ads beckoning for your attention with catchy text and animated graphics. Although you probably never think much about how they get there, that's the main thought running through Chan Suh's head, and it has been since 1995 when he co-founded Agency.com, one of today's premiere online advertising agencies.

Although interactive advertising comprises only a small portion of the $200 billion advertising market, its potential and growth has been enormous. In 1998 alone, the four-year-old Agency.com quadrupled in size as sales zoomed from $18 million to $80 million. Its client list—including 3M, DIRECTV, Gucci, Land Rover, Saab, the Olive Garden, and Visa—would be the envy of any traditional advertising agency. In 2006, it won a long list of awards for clients, including a Cannes Cyber Lions award for British Airways ("Have You Clicked Yet?").

Originally, Suh started Agency.com with a group of casually attired, body-pierced twenty-somethings in a poorly ventilated room over the loading dock in Manhattan's Time-Life building. Today, its headquarters is on New York's fashionable Madison Avenue, far plusher digs in the heart of the advertising world. With U.S. offices also in Chicago, Dallas, and San Francisco, and international offices in London, Brussels, and Amsterdam, Agency.com has come a long way in only a few years.

Suh considers himself fortunate to be where he is today. Indeed, Agency.com has come a long way since bankers laughed at his business plan in 1995. Yet Suh was determined to launch his agency. So, cashing in the goodwill he had developed with his former employer, Time-Life (for whom he earlier developed *Vibe* online before venturing out on his own), Suh struck a deal in which he got the space in exchange for completing several projects. One of these was the highly regarded Web site for the 1995 *Sports Illustrated* swimsuit edition video. On the strength of his successful experiences with Time, Suh was able to attract more blue-chip clients, for whom he struck gold. The Web site Agency.com developed for MetLife, for example, grew in popularity from 300,000 hits in 1996 to over 4 million hits in 1997. This Web site was only one of over two dozen for which the company won awards for various clients in 1998 (including a prestigious Clio for Pacific Bell). In 2001 alone, Agency.com won 15 prestigious awards for its various Web designs. Through just the first half of 2006, the firm already won over twice as many awards (for clients such as CNN, eBay, and Discovery Networks, to name just a few). Clearly, they know what they're doing.

For Agency.com to continue to grow—or even to have survived the shakeout forthcoming in the interactive advertising business—Suh had to grow the company dramatically, making it a major force in online advertising. As a result, the company's reach has broadened dramatically. Importantly, as clients grow more sophisticated, they are moving from being knocked out by the novel, whiz-bang technology to the stage where they now are demanding results—a return on their advertising investments. Suh knows that this will keep him busy hiring the most talented and creative people he can find—individuals who share his vision for taking technology to places where no advertising agency has ever been.

It's having a vision and chasing it that keeps Chan Suh navigating these uncharted waters. After all, only a true visionary and pioneer would say, "We love the fact that we get to invent the future while we live in it." If Suh's vision even comes close to being as accurate as it has been, there's every indication that he easily will reach the goal of making Agency.com a $1 billion company. Based on recent figures, he appears to be well on his way.

Questions for Discussion

1. What special qualities make Chan Suh so effective as a leader?
2. Would you say that Chan Suh is a charismatic leader or a transformational leader?
3. What challenges do you believe Agency.com is likely to face in the next few years?

VIDEO CASE

Harvard Leadership Controversy

In 2005 Harvard University president Larry Summers addressed the National Bureau of Economic Research about what proved to be a controversial topic: Why there aren't more women mathematicians and scientists in top American universities. He told the audience that he wanted to speak unofficially, off the record. That he did. His observations about women's innate abilities in math and science proved provocative and still are being discussed today.

Discussion Questions

1. In what ways do you believe that this leader's effectiveness has been threatened by his controversial stance on this topic? Explain your answer.
2. What is your own personal stance on this issue? Why do you believe women are under-represented in math and the sciences? Be prepared to defend your answer.
3. Why do you believe this particular issue proved to be as controversial as it was?

ORGANIZATIONAL CULTURE, CREATIVITY, AND INNOVATION

Chapter Outline

Special Sections

1. Define organizational culture and identify its core characteristics and the various functions it serves in organizations.

2. Describe the four major forms of organizational culture specified by the competing values framework.

3. Explain the factors responsible for creating and transmitting organizational culture and for getting it to change.

4. Define creativity and describe the basic components of individual and team creativity.

5. Describe various approaches to promoting creativity in organizations.

6. Identify the basic forms and targets of innovation and the stages of the innovation process.

PREVIEW CASE

Apple: Innovative to the Core

In the aftermath of the dot-com bust of the late 1990s, most high-tech companies slashed their research and development budgets, but not Apple Computer. Following its image of making the most elegant and easy-to-use computers, the Apple iPod has been not only the company's ticket to financial riches, but also the most influential new technology product in years (with 8.5 million sold through the middle of 2006).

The man behind this success is Apple's CEO, Steven Jobs. After founding the company in 1976, he was ousted in 1986, only to come back aboard in 1997. It was then that the company shifted into high gear with respect to innovation. A slew of new computers (e.g., various incarnations of the iMac, the Mac Mini, and others) and, of course, the iPod has made Apple one of the most highly regarded high-tech companies in the world. The secret, Jobs says, is that "We hire people who want to make the best things in the world," noting that Apple employees work very hard and care greatly about the products they make.

These products involve not only hardware, but software—where one of the greatest innovations has occurred. The company's iTunes jukebox software program morphed into the iTunes music store, which is the first online music service to sell over 1 million songs in the form of downloaded files. Innovations of this type are controlled accidents, more or less. Although the company does not legislate innovation—nor can it do so—the creative spirit is in the air throughout Apple's Cupertino, California headquarters. As Jobs put it, "Innovation comes from people meeting up in the hallways or calling each other at 10:30 at night with a new idea, or because they realized something that shoots holes in how we've been thinking about a problem. It's ad hoc meetings of six people called by someone who thinks he has figured out the coolest new thing ever and who wants to know what other people think of his idea."

Personally, Jobs contributes to the company's innovative spirit when and how he can. He spends some of his time sharing new ideas with the OS X team and some with the group doing iLife applications. "I get to spend my time on the forward-looking stuff," because, as Jobs says, "My top executives take half the other work off my plate."

One of Apple's latest ideas—and certainly its boldest—called for moving to Intel chips in its computers, allowing Macs to run Windows software as well as its own operating system. This shift, made in April 2006, was a clear effort by Apple to accommodate itself to the rest of the computer world. Although many Mac aficionados have taken pride in Apple's distinctiveness from the dominant Microsoft Windows operating system, this latest innovation was hailed by industry insiders as being in the best interest of the company and the computer industry as a whole.

There can be no doubt that Apple's software and hardware engineers bring a wealth of *creativity* and talent to their jobs. At the same time, it is not only their individual creativity that makes Apple so effective at coming up with exciting new products, but also the company's commitment to *innovation*. To be sure, there is something special about Apple that makes its engineers and developers so devoted to developing the best new products. That special something is not in the form of magic found in the company's next whiz-bang product. Rather, it is something far more human in nature—Steve Jobs's infectious enthusiasm and his willingness to make the best possible products.

If you have worked in several different organizations, it's probably been your experience that each is unique in one way or another. Even organizations concerned with the same activities or that provide similar products or services can be very different places in which to work. For example, in the world of retailing, Wal-Mart employees long have been encouraged to be agents for the customer, focusing on service and satisfaction.[1] By contrast, for many years, employees of Sears allegedly were forced to meet stringent sales quotas, which led them to pressure customers into making unnecessary purchases.[2] Both are large national chains selling a large variety of goods. Somehow, these similar businesses have taken very different approaches to customer service. Why is this so? To a great extent, the answer rests in the shared beliefs, expectations, and core values of people in the organization—what is known as *organizational culture*.[3] Once established, these beliefs, expectancies, and values tend to be relatively stable and exert strong influences on organizations and those working in them.

Among these influences lies a particularly important one—an organization's tendency toward *creativity* and *innovation*. As you know, some people regularly take novel, ingenious, and cutting-edge approaches to the problems they face. Likewise, some organizations—Microsoft and Corning among them—are far more innovative than others. It's unlikely that people in one organization, by chance alone, will just happen to be more creative than people in another. Indeed, companies such as 3M, Toyota, and Rubbermaid go out of their way to breed the kind of cultures in which creativity and innovation flourish (see Figure 14.1).[4]

What makes these companies—and others like them—the kinds of places where people routinely do the nonroutine? This question, concerning the culture of creativity and innovation, is the focus of this chapter. We will begin by describing the basic nature of organizational culture, including the role it plays in organizations. Then we will describe the processes through which organizational culture is formed and maintained. Following this, we will review the effects of organizational culture on individual and organizational functioning, examining when and how culture is subject to change. This discussion will prepare us for understanding the nature of creativity and innovation in organizations, the major topic covered in the second half of this chapter. Finally, our focus will move from consideration of what makes individuals and teams creative, to how this creativity can be harnessed to implement innovative ideas in organizations.

The Basic Nature of Organizational Culture

To fully appreciate organizational culture we have to understand its basic nature. With this in mind, we will now examine five fundamental aspects of culture: (1) its formal definition, (2) the key characteristics on which it is based, (3) the strength of organizational culture, (4) whether there is generally only one or more than one culture within organizations, and (5) the role that culture plays in organizational functioning.

organizational culture
A cognitive framework consisting of attitudes, values, behavioral norms, and expectations shared by organization members; a set of basic assumptions shared by members of an organization.

Organizational Culture: A Definition

Although we have been talking about organizational culture in general terms thus far, a specific definition is now in order. Accordingly, we define **organizational culture** as a cognitive framework consisting of attitudes, values, behavioral norms, and expectations shared by organization members.[5] Scientists often think of organizational culture as a set of basic assumptions shared by members of an organization.

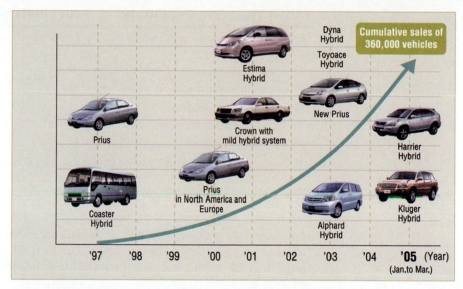

FIGURE 14.1

Hybrid Vehicles: A Major Innovation at Toyota

In 1994, Toyota began its Eco Project, designed to reduce carbon dioxide emissions from vehicles into the atmosphere and to double the fuel economy of conventional vehicles. By 1997, a new powertrain, the Toyota Hybrid System was announced (incorporating both a gasoline engine and an electric motor) and incorporated into the Prius, the first mass-produced hybrid vehicle in the world. As summarized here, sales have been rising steadily with the introduction of several models (mostly in Japan, but in North America and Europe, also with the Prius and, in 2007, the Camry). In fact, due to strong demand in 2006, sales of hybrid Toyotas have been growing by more than 20,000 vehicles monthly. Promoting this growth is in keeping with the company's *oobeya* philosophy, a system for cutting costs and boosting quality. Although hybrids make up only 3 percent of Toyota's overall world sales (though mid-2006), these vehicles contribute greatly to the company's image as an innovator.

Source: Toyota Sustainability Report 2005. Photo © 2005 Toyota. Courtesy of Toyota Motor Corporation.

Some management experts have likened the role played by organizational culture to the roots of trees. What roots do for the life of a tree, culture does for the life and performance of an organization. Just as roots provide stability and nourishment for trees, so does culture provide stability and nourishment for organizations. Culture supports and feeds everything that goes on inside an organization. As one expert put it, "the strength of a firm's 'root system' ultimately shapes and determines its ability to perform in the marketplace."[6] With this in mind, the importance of organizational culture cannot be emphasized too strongly.

Core Cultural Characteristics

At the root of any organization's culture is a set of six core characteristics that are valued collectively by members of an organization. We now describe each of these (for a summary, see Table 14.1).[7]

Sensitivity to Others. Years ago, the culture at UPS was relatively rigid and inflexible with respect to customer needs. They operated however they thought best, and forced customers to adjust to their ways. Today, however, a new culture is in place in which customer service and satisfaction are highly valued. UPS now strives to suit the needs of its customers; the culture is such that changes are driven by opportunities to better serve customers.[8] The same can be said of Amazon.com (as we describe in this chapter's Case in Point on p. 580).

Interest in New Ideas. Walt Disney Co. employees—or "cast members," as they are called—undergo lengthy orientation programs to ensure that they know exactly what to say and how to behave toward guests.[9] For the most part, their behavior is scripted. By

TABLE 14.1 Core Organizational Values Reflected in Culture

Organizations may be distinguished by their basic values, such as the fundamental ones summarized here.

- Sensitivity to the needs of customers and employees.
- Interest in having employees generate new ideas.
- Willingness to take risks.
- The value placed on people.
- Openness of available communication options.
- Friendliness and congeniality of the employees toward one another.

Source: Based on suggestions by Martin, 1996; see Note 7.

contrast, people working at Southwest Airlines are encouraged to be unique and to bring fresh ideas to their work. In fact, company founder Herb Kelleher is so adamant about this that managerial training is geared toward hiring people who bring to the job an attitude of openness and fun.[10]

Willingness to Take Risks. At some companies, such as the Bank of America, the culture is very conservative, and employees make only the safest investments. By contrast, buyers at The Limited are discouraged from making too many "safe" choices. Taking risks in the purchasing of fashion merchandise is valued.[11]

The Value Placed on People. Some companies consider their employees as valuable only insofar as they contribute to production, much as they view machinery. Such organizations, where people do not feel valued, are considered to have **toxic organizational cultures**. A recent survey found that 48 percent of people believe they work in toxic cultures.[12] Organizations with toxic cultures tend to lose good employees, and struggle to be profitable as a result. By contrast, organizations that treat people well and that inspire employees—said to have **healthy organizational cultures**—tend to have very low turnover, and generally thrive.[13] Examples of companies with healthy cultures include Enterprise Rent-A-Car, the Men's Wearhouse, and the Container Store. For an overview of the characteristics of healthy organizational cultures, see Table 14.2.[14]

Openness of Available Communication Options. In some companies, such as Yahoo!, the popular Internet media company, employees are expected to make decisions freely and to communicate with whoever is needed to get the job done—even if it means going right to CEO Timothy A. Koogle.[15] At IBM, however, the tradition has been to work within the proper communication channels and to vest power in the hands of only a few key individuals, although this has been changing in recent years.[16]

Friendliness and Congeniality. At some companies, such as Nokia Corp., the employees tend to get along well. Friendships tend to run deep, and employees see each other outside of work.[17] At the toymaker Mattel, however, the culture is far more cutthroat and competitive.[18]

Strength of Organizational Culture: Strong and Weak

As we have been suggesting, organizations differ in many key ways with respect to the nature of their cultures. However, they also differ with respect to the degree to which their organizational cultures impact the people in the organization. In some organizations, there is widespread agreement with respect to the six elements of organizational culture we just described (i.e. sensitivity to others, willingness to take risks, etc.), making it possible for these factors to exert major influences on the way people behave. An organization of this

toxic organizational cultures
Organizational cultures in which people feel that they are not valued (opposite of healthy organizational cultures).

healthy organizational cultures
Organizational cultures in which people feel that they are valued (opposite of toxic organizational cultures).

TABLE 14.2 Characteristics of Healthy Organizational Cultures

Healthy organizational cultures are ones in which value is placed on treating people well. Such organizations tend to inspire employees and have low levels of turnover. They are marked by the eight characteristics summarized here.

Characteristic	Description
■ Everyone in the organization is open and humble.	Arrogance is absent. This is good because it encourages everyone to learn from everyone else.
■ People are held accountable and accept personal responsibility for their actions.	Denial, blame, and excuses are absent. By accepting responsibility, conflict is lowered and opportunities for success are boosted.
■ Within appropriate limits, people are free to take risks.	Neither reckless risk-taking nor stiflingly high levels of control are found. Hence, freedom exists to follow new ideas.
■ The commitment to do things well is very high.	Mediocrity is not tolerated. Everyone is expected to do things appropriately, not taking shortcuts to quality.
■ Mistakes are tolerated because they are considered learning opportunities.	Healthy innovation helps the organization, but some failures are inevitable. These are accepted because they provide opportunities to learn how to improve things next time.
■ Integrity is unquestioned.	Dishonesty undermines trust, and trust is essential to success. As a result, efforts to promote integrity, such as being transparent about decisions and following up on promises, is key.
■ Collaboration and integration between units is ongoing.	Turf wars and narrow thinking are discouraged. Instead, people work together in open, friendly, collaborative environments.
■ Courage and persistence are encouraged.	Work often is challenging. In healthy cultures everyone is encouraged to persist even in the face of failure, so long as they remain realistic about what can be accomplished.

Source: Institute for Business, Technology, and Ethics, 2004; see Note 14.

strong culture
An organization in which there is widespread agreement with respect to the core elements of culture, making it possible for these factors to exert major influences on the way people behave.

weak culture
An organization in which there is limited agreement with respect to the core elements of culture, giving these factors little influence on the way people behave.

type may be said to have a **strong culture**. By contrast, other organizations may be characterized as having weaker agreement with respect to the various elements of organizational culture, thereby giving these factors limited impact on the way people behave. An organization described in this manner may be said to have a **weak culture**.

In an organization with a strong culture, the core values are held intensely and shared widely. The more members who accept the core values and the greater their commitment to those values, the stronger a culture may be said to be. Specifically, organizations with strong cultures are characterized in the following ways.

- A clear philosophy exists about how business is to be conducted.
- Considerable time is spent communicating values and beliefs.
- Explicit statements are made that describe the organization's values.
- A set of values and norms exist that are shared widely and rooted deeply.
- New employees are screened carefully to ensure fit with the culture.

Recent research has shown that organizations with strong cultures and weak cultures differ in some interesting ways.[19] For example, stronger organizational cultures are likely to be found in organizations that are newer and that have fewer employees. This suggests that perhaps as companies grow older and larger in size, the effects of culture become diffused. This would be the case, for example, as the influence of a company founder grows smaller because his or her impact is felt less in a maturing organization. Also, organizations are more successful financially when their leaders hold views that are in keeping with the organizational culture than when leaders' personal perspectives are at odds with the prevailing culture. This makes sense given that workers may find themselves responding to inconsistent and competing messages when such inconsistencies exist. Together, these findings suggest that strong cultures shape the preferences and actions of people in the organizations that have them.

Cultures within Organizations: One or Many?

Our discussion thus far has implied that each organization has only a single, uniform culture—one set of shared values, beliefs, and expectations. In fact, this is rarely the case. Instead, organizations, particularly large ones, typically have *several* cultures operating within them.

People generally have attitudes and values that are more in common with others in their own fields or work units than they do with those in other fields or other parts of the organization. These various groups may be said to have several different **subcultures**—cultures existing within parts of organizations rather than entirely through them. These typically are distinguished with respect to either functional differences (i.e., the type of work done) or geographic distances (i.e., the physical separation between people). Indeed, research suggests that several subcultures based on occupational, professional, or functional divisions usually exist within any large organization.

This is not to say, however, that there also may not be a **dominant culture**, a distinctive, overarching "personality" of an organization—the kind of culture to which we have been referring. An organization's dominant culture reflects its core values, dominant perceptions that are generally shared throughout the organization. Typically, members of subcultures who generally share additional sets of values also generally accept the core values of their organizations as a whole. Thus, subcultures should not be thought of as a bunch of totally separate cultures but, rather, as "mini" cultures operating within a larger, dominant culture.

The Role of Culture in Organizations

As you read about the various cultural values that make organizations special, it probably strikes you that culture is an intangible force—albeit one with far-reaching consequences. Indeed, culture plays several important roles in organizations (for a summary, see Figure 14.2).

Culture Provides a Sense of Identity. The more clearly an organization's shared perceptions and values are defined, the more strongly people can associate with their organization's mission and feel a vital part of it. For example, employees at Southwest Airlines feel special because of their company's emphasis on having fun and joking around on the job, a widespread practice initiated by founder Herb Kelleher.[20] Southwest's employees feel strongly associated with the company, that they belong there. As a result, they only infrequently resign to take other positions in the airline industry.

Culture Generates Commitment to the Organization's Mission. Sometimes it's difficult for people to go beyond thinking of their own interests (i.e, how will this affect me?). When there is a strong, overarching culture, however, people feel that they are part of that larger, well-defined whole and involved in the entire organization's work. Bigger than any one individual's interests, culture reminds people of what their organization is all about.

subcultures

Cultures existing within parts of organizations rather than entirely through them.

dominant culture

The distinctive, overarching "personality" of an organization.

FIGURE 14.2

The Basic Functions of Organizational Culture

Organizational culture serves the three major functions summarized here.

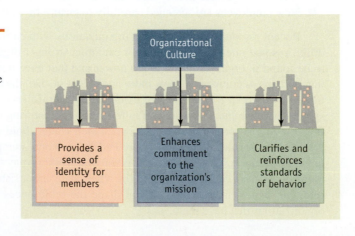

Culture Clarifies and Reinforces Standards of Behavior. Culture guides employees' words and deeds, making it clear what they should do or say in a given situation, which is especially useful to newcomers. In this sense, culture provides stability to behavior, both with respect to what an individual might do at different times, but also what different individuals may do at the same time. For example, in a company with a culture that strongly supports customer satisfaction, employees will have clear guidance as to how they are expected to behave: doing whatever it takes to please the customer.

By serving these three important roles, it is clear that culture is an important force influencing behavior in organizations.

Forms of Organizational Culture

As you might imagine, just are there are many different organizations, there also are many different organizational cultures. Although each organization may be unique in several ways, key similarities in underlying organizational cultures may be noted. Fortunately, organizational scientists have developed useful ways of organizing and identifying these cultures.

One of the most popular approaches is known as the **competing values framework.**[21] According to this approach, the cultures of organizations differ with respect to two sets of opposite values (hence, the name). These are:

- Valuing *flexibility* and *discretion* as opposed to stability, order, and control.
- Valuing *internal affairs* as opposed to what's going on in the external environment.

By combining both dimensions, as shown in Figure 14.3, scientists have been able to identify the four unique types of organizational culture we now describe.

Hierarchy Culture

Organizations described as having a **hierarchy culture** (shown in the lower left corner of Figure 14.3) have an internal focus and emphasize stability and control. Here, the most effective leaders are good coordinators of projects and emphasize a smooth-running organization, often relying on formal rules and policies to do so.

Governmental agencies and large corporations tend to fall into this category. At McDonald's, for example, key values center on maintaining efficient and reliable production, and to ensure this, both the equipment used and the procedures followed—described in a 350-page manual—are designed with this in mind. Sometimes, because organizations

---

competing values framework

A conceptualization of organizational culture that specifies that cultures of organizations differ with respect to two sets of opposite values: (1) valuing flexibility and discretion as opposed to stability, order, and control, and (2) valuing internal affairs as opposed to what's going on in the external environment.

hierarchy culture

In the competing values framework, a form of organizational culture in which organizations have an internal focus and emphasize stability and control.

FIGURE 14.3

The Competing Values Framework

According to the *competing values framework,* the cultures of organizations can be distinguished in terms of the two opposite dimensions identified here. Combining these two sets of competing values results in the four types of organizational cultures shown.

Source: Adapted from Cameron & Quinn, 1999; see Note 21.

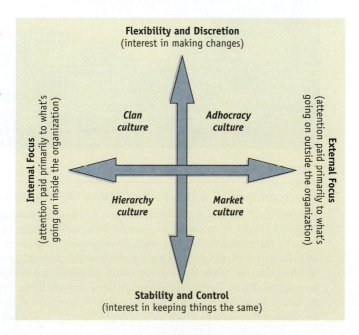

with hierarchy cultures are so attuned to internal concerns at the expense of external concerns, and so focused on stability as opposed to making necessary changes (which often are necessary; see Chapter 16), serious problems result (for a particularly tragic example, see Figure 14.4).[22]

Market Culture

market culture
In the competing values framework, a form of organizational culture in which organizations are concerned with stability and control, but are external in their orientation; core values emphasize competitiveness and productivity, focusing on bottom-line results.

The term **market culture** describes organizations that are concerned with stability and control, but are external in their orientation (see the lower right corner of Figure 14.3). In such organizations, the core values emphasize competitiveness and productivity, focusing on bottom-line results. They do this by carefully identifying the markets in which they are going to compete and then taking a very hard-driving, results-oriented approach to getting things done.

Perhaps the classic example of a market culture can be seen at General Electric. For many years, under the guidance of former CEO Jack Welch, the culture called for making each one of GE's business units either first or second in its respective markets. Otherwise, the mandate from Welch was clear—fix, sell, or close the unsuccessful business.[23] He explained this as follows:

> When you're number four or five in a market, when number one sneezes, you get pneumonia. When you're number one, you control your destiny. The number fours keep merging; they have difficult times. That's not the same if you're number four, and that's your only business. Then you have to find strategic ways to get stronger. But, GE had a lot of number ones.[24]

His approach to market success involved not making small, incremental changes slowly, but rather, making major changes quickly. In this respect, GE operates more like a small company than the enormous one it is.

FIGURE 14.4

Shortcomings of a Hierarchy Culture: A Tragic Example

Not surprisingly, as a large government agency, the National Aeronautics and Space Administration (NASA) has a *hierarchy culture*. Its sharp focus on stability created a culture that was blind to the threat posed by foam debris on its space shuttles. Furthermore, its attention to internal issues as opposed to external matters reinforced employees' convictions that that the agency was far more attuned to making decisions based on safety than it was in reality. Tragically, according to the Columbia Accident Investigation Board, flawed organizational culture was among the factors that led to the explosion of the space shuttle *Columbia* on February 1, 2003. Although not all hierarchy cultures are doomed to fail, this incident represents an extreme example of what may occur when they do.

Clan Culture

clan culture

In the competing values framework, an organization characterized by a strong internal focus along with a high degree of flexibility and discretion; with goals that are highly shared by members of the organization and high levels of cohesiveness, such organizations feel more like extended families than economic entities.

An organization is said to have a **clan culture** when it has a strong internal focus along with a high degree of flexibility and discretion (see the upper left corner of Figure 14.3). With goals that are highly shared by members of the organization and high levels of cohesiveness (see Chapter 8), such organizations feel more like extended families than economic entities. Given their highly friendly nature, it's not surprising that most people prefer clan cultures to any of the other forms of organizational culture.[25]

In the clan culture, the predominant focus is on flexibility when it comes to external needs. This is attained by concentrating on the excellence of the employees, which reflects the internal focus. An example of a company that fits the clan culture is the Finnish conglomerate, Nokia, best known for its cellular phones. At this company, the well-being of employees is a top priority. In contrast to the attention-grabbing element of most high-tech firms, Nokia's emphasis is on collegiality. As the firm's former CEO Jorna Ollila put it, "We don't snap our suspenders."[26]

Of importance, clan cultures often are characterized as enjoyable places to work, organizations in which a great deal of attention is paid to doing things to make work fun for employees. Although this makes life pleasant, of course, it's important to note that cultures in which having fun is stressed also must pay serious attention to meeting serious business objectives. For a discussion of this point, see the *OB: Making Sense Out of Common Sense* section below.

Adhocracy Culture

adhocracy culture

In the competing values framework, organizations that emphasize flexibility while also paying a great deal of attention to the external environment; characterized by recognition that to succeed an organization needs to be highly innovative and constantly assessing what the future requires for it to survive.

Organizations that have an **adhocracy culture** emphasize flexibility while also paying a great deal of attention to the external environment (see upper right corner of Figure 14.3). As defined by management consultant Robert H. Waterman, Jr., an *adhocracy* is a form of

---

OB Making Sense Out of Common Sense

Beyond the Cheerleading

The idea is straightforward, at least in theory: Create a culture in which people feel welcome and respected, and they will be willing to work hard. Organizational success then will follow. As in the case of most OB ideas, however, this formula isn't quite as simple as it seems.

For many years, executives bought into the idea that creating a winning organizational culture was mostly about cheerleading. They opened up their "cultural cupboards," as one management expert put it, throwing Friday beer bashes, putting foosball tables in the cafeterias, and even hiring "chief culture officers."[27] Not surprisingly, employees enjoyed the fun atmosphere. They felt good, but positive morale alone isn't an automatic path to business success (as we noted in Chapter 6). Sure, employees liked it. Who wouldn't? But such rah-rah isn't what business is all about.

Too often, managers who focus on morale lose sight of more traditional, financial business metrics. To be totally successful, however, organizational culture must be attuned to winning. After all, a business that doesn't make money is not likely to be around much longer, let alone having much about which to cheer. And, at the end of the day, employees of small firms in whose ownership they are likely to have

invested are likely to be more interested in business success than anything else. That's what they want to cheer about.

Having a healthy culture requires maintaining focus on the right goals, and this requires attention to specific feedback (as you will recall from Chapter 7). As such, it's important for organizations to keep careful track of financial performance in an open manner, making key information readily accessible to all. One company in the telephone software business even goes so far as to post a large football-style scoreboard in the conference room. On it are posted all the important figures, such as those regarding sales, expenses, revenues, and the like. By referring to them, employees can see how well the company is doing and make appropriate adjustments as needed. And this, it is hoped, will provide plenty of opportunities for cheering.

Such a practice of openness helps promote the belief that a company has an exciting future. As one expert put it, this makes employees "come to work with a fire inside them, a result of clearly stated leadership and business practices that everyone explicitly understands."[28] Once this occurs, there may well be plenty about which to cheer. And that's the point: Cheerleading should not be an indulgent avoidance of the development of a winning strategy. Rather, it should be part of it.

organization that cuts across normal bureaucratic lines to capture opportunities, solve problems, and get results.[29] The term *adhocracy* is a reference to the absence of hierarchy, making it the opposite of *bureaucracy* (an organizational form we discuss in Chapters 1 and 15). Typical of contemporary organizations, which often have to make rapid changes in the way they operate (see Chapter 16), the adhocracy culture is characterized by recognition that to succeed organizations need to be highly innovative (a concept we will describe later in this chapter) and constantly assessing what the future requires for survival, let alone growth.

Typical of companies with adhocracy cultures are those in the software development and filmmaking businesses, where it is widely recognized that highly innovative products and services are essential to success (for an example, see Figure 14.5). Not surprisingly, adhocracy cultures also exist in organizations in which research and development is essential. This is the case, for example, at 3M, the large American company that has been producing innovative products for over 100 years (currently, some 55,000 of them). To promote the innovative spirit at 3M, one of its earliest presidents, William McKnight, recognized the importance of a culture in which people were respected and free to take risks. Consider the three principles he articulated back in 1948, which describe an adhocracy culture (although he didn't refer to it as such):[30] (1) Delegate responsibility to encourage people to take initiative; (2) expect mistakes to be made, so be tolerant of them; and (3) criticize in a constructive, not destructive, manner (see Chapter 9).

Creating and Transmitting Organizational Culture

Now that we have described the basic nature and forms of organizational culture, we turn our attention to three additional issues of importance: how culture is created initially, how it is sustained over time (i.e., what keeps it going once it is created), and when and how it changes.

FIGURE 14.5

Adhocracy Culture in Action

Although you probably don't think of it when you're watching *Wheel of Fortune* on TV, or viewing *The Da Vinci Code* in the theater (note director Ron Howard at work here, standing in the center, wearing a hat), you're enjoying the products of Sony Pictures. Despite its enormous size (annual sales of over $7 billion), most units of Sony Pictures are considered to have a clan culture, in which individual welfare is valued. This type of organizational culture is typical of that found in most motion picture studios.

How Is Organizational Culture Created?

Why do many individuals within an organization share basic attitudes, values, and expectations? Two key factors contribute to this state of affairs and, hence, to the emergence of organizational culture—the influence of company founders and experiences with the external environment.

Company Founders. Organizational culture may be traced, at least in part, to the founders of the company.[31] These individuals often possess dynamic personalities, strong values, and clear visions of how their organizations should operate. Since they are on the scene first and play a key role in hiring initial staff, their attitudes and values are readily transmitted to new employees. As a result, their views become the accepted ones in the organization and persist as long as the founders are on the scene—and often, long afterward. For a summary of the four major steps involved in this process, see Figure 14.6.

Several good illustrations of the important role of founders may be identified. For example, the culture at Microsoft calls for working exceptionally long hours, in large part because that's what co-founder Bill Gates has always done. Sometimes, founders' values can continue to drive an organization's culture even after that individual is no longer alive. For example, the late Ray Kroc founded the McDonald's restaurant chain on the values of good food at a good value served in clean, family-oriented surroundings—key cultural values that persist today. Likewise, Walt Disney's wholesome family values are still cherished at the company that bears his name—in large part because employees ask themselves, "What would Walt think?"[32] These individuals' values continue to permeate their entire companies and are central parts of their dominant cultures.

FIGURE 14.6

How Do Founders Influence Organizational Culture?

The cultures of organizations are affected by their founders. This tends to occur over time, generally according to the four steps summarized here.

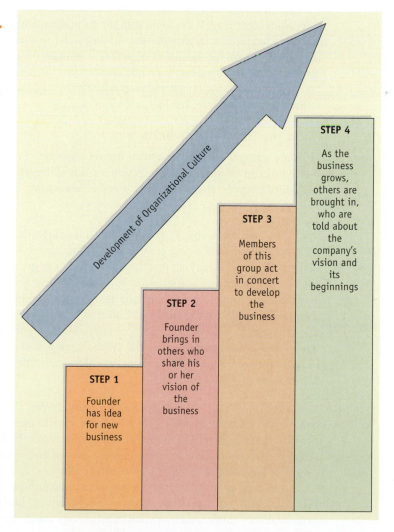

Development of Organizational Culture

STEP 1

Founder has idea for new business

STEP 2

Founder brings in others who share his or her vision of the business

STEP 3

Members of this group act in concert to develop the business

STEP 4

As the business grows, others are brought in, who are told about the company's vision and its beginnings

Experiences With the External Environment.   As critical events occur in organizations based on their experiences with the external environment, it's not surprising that their effects contribute to the development of organizational culture. It's as if organizations learn from these events and the memories are passed along from person to person, contributing to the development of organizational culture. In this connection, the term **organizational memory** is used to describe information from an organization's history that its leaders draw upon later as needed.[33] That information is stored through the recollections of these events and their shared interpretations by key individuals in the organization who pass it along to others.

As an example, consider Sony's experience with its Betamax format for home video-cassette tapes. Introduced in 1975, this format competed with the VHS format introduced by JVC the following year. If you're thinking that you've heard of VHS, but not Betamax, that's indeed the story. Sony made two critical errors with Betamax. First, unlike JVC, which permitted open sharing of its technology, Sony licensed its technology, which made it less popular among equipment manufacturers. Second, Sony failed to anticipate the demand for prerecorded movies, leading studios to release films on VHS instead. As a result, Sony's product never captured the market, and in 1988 it threw in the towel, making VHS-format VCRs.

In the aftermath of this incident, Sony executives learned an important lesson about what it takes to win the battle of formats. The organizational memory of this failure lives on at Sony, making the company more aggressive and more carefully attuned to what it takes to win a "format war." Today, an analogous battle is heating up once again, with players in the fight for dominance in the vast high-definition DVD market. Sony's Blue-Ray DVD (BD-DVD) is duking it out with Toshiba's High Definition DVD (HD-DVD) on the floors of electronics stores. Only time will tell exactly how effectively Sony learned its lesson.

The mechanism by which organizational memories help transmit organizational culture is not surprising. It has to do with the natural tendency of individuals within organizations to come into contact with one another—and to share interpretations of events when doing so. Indeed, the dynamics of people in groups (as discussed in Chapter 8) and their tendencies to communicate with one another (as discussed in Chapter 9) make it possible for incidents to be explained and interpreted to others, thereby perpetuating organizational culture (for an example, see Figure 14.7).[34]

Tools for Transmitting Culture

How are cultural values transmitted between people? In other words, how do employees come to learn about their organization's culture? Several key mechanisms are involved, including *symbols, slogans, stories, jargon, ceremonies,* and *statements of principle.*

Symbols: Objects That Say More than Meets the Eye.   Organizations often rely on **symbols**—material objects that connote meanings that extend beyond their intrinsic content. For example, some companies use impressive buildings to convey their strength and significance, signifying that the company is a large, stable place. Indeed, research has found that the way an organization is furnished provides useful insight into its culture.[35] For example, firms in which there are lots of plants and flower arrangements are believed to have friendly, person-oriented cultures, whereas those in which waiting areas are adorned with awards and trophies are believed to be highly interested in achieving success. These findings suggest that material symbols are potent tools for sending messages about organizational culture. (To demonstrate this phenomenon for yourself, try the Group Exercise on p. 579.)

Slogans: Phrases That Capture Organizational Culture.   When you think of the catchy phrases that companies use to call attention to their products and services, you may dismiss them as being merely advertising gimmicks. It should be noted, however, that slogans also communicate important aspects of an organization's culture, both to the public at large and to the company's own employees. For some examples of such slogans and what they communicate about organizational culture, see Table 14.3. As you peruse this list, you will see that slogans help convey important information about an organization's culture, such as what the company stands for and what it values.

---

organizational memory
Information from an organization's history that is stored through the recollections of events and their shared interpretations by key individuals in the organization who pass it along to others as needed.

symbols
Material objects that connote meanings that extend beyond their intrinsic content.

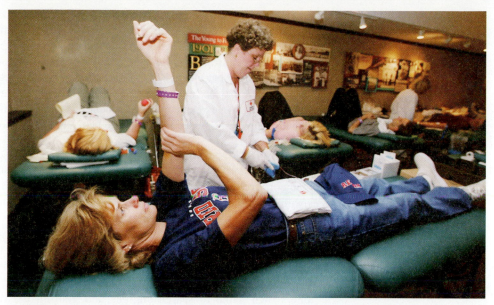

FIGURE 14.7

Sharing Interpretations of Critical Incidents Promotes Organizational Culture

Some years ago, the American Red Cross discovered that a portion of its blood supply was tainted. Immediately, a vast army of officials rallied to solve the problem by putting procedures in place that would prevent it from reoccurring. Today, as Red Cross employees and volunteers discuss this incident, they assign similar meaning to what happened, perceiving the organization in a similar manner, reinforcing its culture as one in which safety of the blood supply is valued.

TABLE 14.3 Slogans that Reflect Organizational Culture

Corporate *slogans* often send messages about the cultures of the organizations that use them. By virtue of their slogans, customers, employees, and prospective employees can learn something about the cultures of the organizations listed here. Can you think of other slogans that may reflect the culture of the organizations with which they are associated?

Company	Slogan	Message
Circuit City Stores	*We're with you.*	We offer support for the technology products we sell.
Staples	*That was easy.*	The office products we sell make your life easy, and purchasing from us is a pleasurable experience.
Wal-Mart	*Always low prices. Always.*	You can count on us for offering everyday low prices.
Home Box Office (HBO)	*It's not TV. It's HBO.*	Our service is special, not your ordinary television shows.
Hyatt Hotels	*Feel the Hyatt touch.*	We take special care of our hotel guests.
Maxwell House	*Good to the last drop.*	Our coffee keeps its flavor.
Maytag	*The dependability people.*	We are known for our trouble-free appliances.
MetLife Insurance	*Get Met. It pays.*	Purchasing our insurance is a good investment.
Pep Boys	*Cars like us. People love us.*	You will enjoy purchasing your auto parts and accessories from us.
Royal Caribbean	*Like no other vacation on earth.*	Our cruises are unique and special.
State Farm	*Like a good neighbor, State Farm is there.*	You can count on friendly and reliable service when you need it.

Stories: "In the Old Days, We Used to . . .". Organizations also transmit information about culture by virtue of the *stories* that are told in them, both formally and informally. Stories illustrate key aspects of an organization's culture, and telling them can effectively introduce or reaffirm those values to employees.[36] It is important to note that stories need not involve some great event, such as someone who saved the company with a single wise decision, but may be small tales that become legends because they communicate a message so effectively. An example may be found at Nike, where employees are told tales about how the company was founded in an effort to help athletes (for some examples, see Table 14.4).[37]

Jargon: The Special Language That Defines a Culture. Even without telling stories, the everyday language used in companies helps sustain culture. For example, the slang or *jargon* that is used in a company or in a field helps people define their identities as members of that group (see Chapter 9). Illustrating this, for many years employees at IBM referred to disk drives as "hard files" and circuit boards as "planar boards," terms that defined the insulated nature of their culture.[38] Today's jargon continues to predominate in the high-tech world. For example, within the information technology (IT) community, the term "geek keys" is used to refer to a loose deck of electronically encoded pass cards that are used to gain access to restricted areas, and "egosurfing" refers to the practice of feeding one's own name to search engines and visiting the resulting hits.[39] Over time, as departments, organizations, or professional groups develop unique language, their terms, although strange to newcomers, serve as a common factor that brings together individuals belonging to a corporate culture or subculture.

ceremonies
Celebrations of an organization's basic values and assumptions.

Ceremonies: Special Events That Commemorate Corporate Values. Organizations also do a great deal to sustain their cultures by conducting various types of **ceremonies**. These may be seen as celebrations of an organization's basic values and assumptions. Just as a wedding ceremony symbolizes a couple's mutual commitment and a presidential inauguration ceremony marks the beginning of a new presidential term, various organizational ceremonies also celebrate some important accomplishment. These events have importance that go beyond the individuals involved—in this example, the bride and groom, and the new president and vice president. They send clear messages about the institutions of marriage and the presidency to all who participate in or view the ceremony. In this manner, it's easy to see how they function as important transmitters of organizational culture.

For example, one accounting firm celebrated its move to much better facilities by throwing a party, a celebration signifying that it "has arrived," or "made it to the big time."

TABLE 14.4 The Nike Story: Just Telling It—And Keeping It Alive

New employees at Nike are told stories that transmit the company's underlying cultural values. The themes of some of the most important Nike stories are summarized here along with several of the ways the company helps keep its heritage alive.

New Employees Are Told the Following Stories . . .

- Founder Phil Knight was a middle-distance runner who started the business by selling shoes out of his car.
- Knight's running coach and company co-founder, Bill Bowerman, developed the famous "waffle sole" by pouring rubber into the family waffle iron.
- The late Steve Prefontaine, coached by Bowerman, battled to make running a professional sport and was committed to helping athletes.

To Ensure That These Tales of Nike's Heritage Are Kept Alive, the Company . . .

- Takes new hires to the track where Bowerman coached and the site of Prefontaine's fatal car crash.
- Has created a "heritage wall" in its Eugene, Oregon, store.
- Requires salespeople to tell the Nike story to employees of the retail stores that sell its products.

Source: Based on information in Ransdell, 2000; see Note 37.

Such ceremonies convey meaning to people inside and outside the organization. As one expert put it, "Ceremonies are to the culture what the movie is to the script . . . values that are difficult to express in any other way."[40]

Statements of Principle: Defining Culture in Writing. Organizational culture also may be transmitted directly using written **statements of principle**. Some organizations have explicitly written their principles for all to see. For example, Forrest Mars, the founder of the candy company M&M Mars, developed his "Five Principles of Mars," which still guide his company today.[41] These are as follows.

statements of principle
Explicitly written statements describing the principle beliefs that guide an organization. Such documents can help reinforce an organization's culture.

- *Quality.* Everyone is responsible for maintaining quality.
- *Responsibility.* All employees are responsible for their own actions and decisions.
- *Mutuality.* Creating a situation in which everyone can win.
- *Efficiency.* Most of the company's factories operate continuously.
- *Freedom.* Giving employees opportunities to shape their futures.

Not only do these principles apply, but company employees are given opportunities to share their feelings about them and their experiences with each one at the company's Web site. This technique helps reinforce the company's messages about what it stands for.

Some companies have chosen to make explicit the moral aspects of their cultures by publishing *codes of ethics,* which, as you will recall from Chapter 2, are explicit statements of a company's ethical values and expectations. According to Hershey Foods' former CEO, Richard Zimmerman, this is an effective device: "[O]ften, an individual joins a firm without recognizing the type of environment in which he will place himself and his career. The loud and clear enunciation of a company's code of conduct . . . [allows] that employee to determine whether or not he fits that particular culture."[42]

Why and How Does Organizational Culture Change?

Our comments about the relative stability of organizational culture may have left you wondering why and how culture ever changes. In other words, why isn't culture simply passed down from one generation of organizational members to the next in unchanging fashion? The answer lies in the fact that the worlds in which organizations operate are in a constant state of flux (see Chapter 16). Shifts in market conditions, new competitors, emerging technologies, altered government policies, and many other factors necessitate changing how organizations operate, and with it, their cultures. We now consider several factors that promote changes in organizational culture.

Composition of the Workforce

Over time, the people entering an organization may differ in important ways from those already in it, and these differences may impinge on the existing culture of the organization. For example, people from different ethnic or cultural backgrounds may have contrasting views about various aspects of behavior at work. They may hold dissimilar views about style of dress, the importance of being on time (or even what constitutes "on-time" behavior), the level of deference one should show to higher-status people, and even what foods should be served in the company cafeteria. When people have different views, existing cultural norms are likely to be challenged. And when this occurs, changes in organizational culture can be expected to follow suit.

Mergers and Acquisitions

culture clashes
Problems resulting from attempts to merge two or more organizational cultures that are incompatible.

Another, and even more dramatic, source of cultural change is *mergers* and *acquisitions,* events in which one organization purchases or otherwise absorbs another.[43] When this occurs, there is likely to be a careful analysis of the financial and material assets of the acquired organization. However, it is unusual for any consideration to be given to the acquired organization's culture. This is unfortunate, insofar as there have been several high-profile cases over the years in which the merger of two organizations with incompatible cultures has led to serious problems referred to as **culture clashes**. Consider these examples:[44]

■ In 2001, AOL merged with Time Warner to form AOL Time Warner. AOL officials were used to spending money freely, whereas Time Warner officials were far more conservative. Culturally, individuals from the two companies never truly merged. Reflecting this, in 2003 the AOL name was dropped, returning to Time Warner.

■ In 1998, Chrysler merged with Daimler-Benz to form DaimlerChrysler. After the new company was created, the former Chrysler officials traveled to meetings in minivans and flew economy class, whereas Daimler-Benz officials showed up in Mercedes sedans and flew first class. They tried to iron out their cultural differences for six months before realizing they were at an impasse.

■ RJ Reynolds merged with Nabisco in 1988 to form RJR Nabisco. The freewheeling lifestyles of Nabisco executives (who threw lavish parties in penthouses and used corporate jets) contrasted sharply with the modest, hard-working, community-minded orientation of the executives from RJ Reynolds. After a bitter feud erupted, the former Nabisco boss fired the RJ Reynolds executives.

cultural due diligence analysis

Before a merger or acquisition is finalized, the process of analyzing the cultures of both organizations to ensure their compatibility.

As you might imagine, life in companies with incompatible cultures tends to be conflict-ridden and highly disruptive, often resulting in arguments and considerable uncertainty about what to do. In some cases, organizations have even been known to disband because of extreme culture clashes. With this in mind, some experts have called for conducting a **cultural due diligence analysis** to ensure compatibility before a merger or acquisition is finalized.[45] This involves analyzing the cultures of both organizations in as much depth as typically is used in exploring the financials, the legal implications, and the intellectual property of the companies involved. For some useful guidelines to follow in conducting such an analysis, refer to the summary in Table 14.5. The idea is straightforward: By determining in advance the potential areas in which the companies might experience culture clashes, they may begin to focus on mutual understanding and working together on developing a totally new culture.

TABLE 14.5 Conducting a Cultural Due Diligence Analysis

Just as company officials carefully analyze the financial and legal ramifications of mergers and acquisitions before finalizing the deals, it is advised that they also carefully analyze the cultures of the individual companies to determine their cultural compatibility. This so-called *cultural due diligence* analysis involves the following activities.

Suggestion	Description
Audit the prevailing cultures.	Compare such fundamental aspects of the culture as how compensation is determined, how leaders emerge, what business practices are valued, what the tolerance is for taking risks, and so on.
Assess *intellectual capital*—that is, who knows what.	Interview people in both organizations to determine who really knows what to do and how to do it. Knowing this will help the new company put people's talents and skills to best use.
Involve different people from both companies in designing the new enterprise.	By involving diverse groups (e.g., customers, the sales force, people from different departments) in a discussion of how the new company should operate, a better understanding of each group's culture is likely to emerge.
Communicate early and often.	Throughout the process, everyone should be completely open and honest about what's going on. This should involve not only top-down communication, but discussions within and between people at all levels of both organizations.

Source: Based on suggestions by Smith, 2005; see Note 45.

Strategic Cultural Change

Sometimes, company officials deliberately decide to change organizational culture so as to help adjust to changing conditions—even positive ones, such as fantastic growth. It's probably not too surprising that the culture of a small organization has to change as the company grows in size. What once worked for a small company may no longer be successful as it becomes a much larger organization.

This describes the need for organizational culture change at Home Depot.[46] From the time it was founded in 1978, to 2000, Home Depot became an 1,100-store chain with annual revenues of over $50 billion. In the beginning, the company's culture reflected the personality of one of its co-founders, Bernie Marcus. It had a high-spirited, entrepreneurial way of doing things. Employees were willing to take risks and showed a passionate commitment to customers, colleagues, and the company as a whole. Anything bureaucratic was rejected. In fact, official directives from Atlanta headquarters often went unread as managers spent time on the sales floor with customers.

That's the culture Robert Nardelli found when he took over as CEO in 2000 (see Figure 14.8). Although this culture served Home Depot very well in the beginning, Nardelli knew that things had to change. As he put it, "What so effectively got Home Depot from zero to $50 billion in sales wasn't going to get it to go to the next $50 billion."[47] The main problem, as he saw it, was that store managers were free to do as they wished, but this had to change. Now, he believed, three key things needed to be done: (1) To get the best prices, purchasing needed to become more centralized; (2) to avoid turf wars, managers needed to collaborate with one another; and (3) sales associates needed to be trained so they could better help customers.

As logical as this all seems, Home Depot had a strong culture in which employees had a highly entrepreneurial approach to business. Now, managers had to replace their primarily intuitive approach to making decisions with data-driven decisions based on the market. And, instead of avoiding directives from the home office, store managers now were held accountable for them. As you might imagine, resistance was fierce at first (as you'll see in Chapter 16, resistance to organizational change is quite common). Many of the top managers left the company during Nardelli's first year.

Over time, though, Nardelli got others to see the wisdom of his ways and go along with his blueprint for culture change. To get company employees to embrace a new corporate culture, he took several important steps. Among them were the following.

FIGURE 14.8

Culture Change at Home Depot

Robert Nardelli has been CEO of Home Depot since 2000. His blueprint for changing organizational culture transformed the chain of over 2,000 stores from one in which an entrepreneurial spirit prevailed (which was fine when the company was smaller) to one that today is far more efficient and data-driven. Employees and customers are highly satisfied and stockholders have been enjoying profits even during difficult economic times.

- *Measure performance.* In the past, management decisions tended not to be based on objective data. Now, reflecting a new cultural priority, people were required to measure things consistently using objectively quantifiable data. Previously, for example, managers pointed to anecdotal reports of customer satisfaction to show that they were doing well. Now, however, they moved to objective questionnaires, which, by the way, showed that the stores were not quite as highly regarded as they thought.

- *Integrate the new culture.* When he became CEO, Nardelli held two-hour conference calls with his top executives (about 15 of them) every Monday morning. These helped people in various posts cooperate with one another and they provided opportunities for accountability: If you said you were going to do something, you were expected to do it by the following week's meeting.

- *Build support for culture change.* In 2002 and 2003, a series of five-day learning forums were conducted in which some 1,800 district managers and store managers participated in a series of exercises that got them to understand the need for change. Appreciating why new ways of operating were necessary, it was reasoned, would get key people to embrace the new ways of operating.

All signs suggest that the culture of Home Depot has changed, and all for the better. By 2005 it was clear that the company's focus was on process, hard data, and accountability. The fact that over 80 percent of the company's 350,000-plus employees complete regular opinion surveys suggests that they have bought into the need to collect objective information and they take it seriously. And importantly, all these changes have paid off on the bottom line: Between 2004 and 2005, sales increased 11.5 percent and earnings increased 16.7 percent.[48]

Responding to the Internet

There can be no doubt that the Internet is a major influence on organizational culture these days. Compared to traditional brick-and-mortar businesses, where things move slowly and in which people look at change skeptically, the culture of Internet businesses is agile, fast-paced, and receptive to new solutions.[49] Information-sharing is key, as such organizations not only accept, but embrace the expansion of communication networks and business relationships across organizational boundaries. When traditional businesses expand into e-commerce (in which case they sometimes are referred to as "click-and-mortar businesses"), changes in their organizational cultures follow suit. We see this, for example, at the investment firm Merrill Lynch, which launched a Web site for trading stock in an effort to compete with brokerage firms such as E*Trade, which do business only online. The organizational culture at this venerable, traditional firm has become far more fast-paced than ever since it adapted to the Internet economy.

Another interesting example of culture change in response to the Internet may be seen at Circuit City. This retail giant specializing in home electronics operates both physical stores (some 600 of them) and a virtual site from which customers can place online orders, much like at any other "e-tail" company (such as Amazon.com). Unlike its competitors, though, it has blended the two by allowing customers to place orders online but get their merchandise right away by picking it up at their nearest retail store. Reflecting their seriousness about good service, they offer a $24 gift card to customers whose purchases are not ready for them within 24 minutes of order confirmation. This policy reflects the company's growing commitment to customer service and to trying innovative new ways of delivering service to customers.[50] Circuit City's organizational culture long has been considered among those best suited to business success. But opportunities created by the Internet have enabled the company to further develop its ongoing commitment to enhancing the quality of shopping experience for customers.[51]

To conclude, it is clear that although organizational culture is generally stable, it is not immutable. In fact, culture often evolves in response to outside forces (e.g., changes in workforce composition and information technology) as well as deliberate attempts to change the design of organizations (e.g., through mergers and corporate restructuring). An important aspect of culture that organizations frequently strive to change is the degree to which it approaches problems in creative and innovative ways. With this in mind, we now turn attention to the topics of *creativity* and *innovation* in organizations.

Creativity in Individuals and Teams

creativity
The process by which individuals or teams produce novel and useful ideas.

Although you probably have no difficulty recognizing creativity when you see it, defining creativity can be a bit more challenging. Scientists define **creativity** as the process by which individuals or teams produce novel and useful ideas.[52] With this definition to guide us, we will explain how the process of creativity operates. Specifically, we begin by describing the components of individual and team creativity and then outline several steps you can take to enhance your own creativity.

Components of Individual and Team Creativity

Creativity in individuals and teams is composed of three basic components—*domain-relevant skills, creativity-relevant skills,* and *intrinsic task motivation.*

Domain-Relevant Skills. Whether it's the manual dexterity required to play the piano or to use a computer keyboard, or the sense of rhythm and knowledge of music needed to conduct an orchestra, specific skills and abilities are necessary to perform these tasks. In fact, any task you might undertake requires certain talents, knowledge, or skills. These skills and abilities that we already have constitute the raw materials needed for creativity to occur. After all, without the capacity to perform a certain task at even a basic level, one has no hope of demonstrating creativity on that task. For example, before he or she can begin to create dramatic automotive stunts, a stunt driver must have the basic skills of dexterity and eye-hand coordination required to drive a car.

Creativity-Relevant Skills. Beyond the basic skills, being creative also requires additional skills—special abilities that help people approach the things they do in novel ways. Specifically, when fostering creativity, it helps to do the following.

divergent thinking
The process of reframing familiar problems in unique ways.

- *Break mental sets and take new perspectives.* Creativity is enhanced when people do not limit themselves to old ways of doing things. Restricting oneself to the past can inhibit creativity. Take a fresh look at even the most familiar things. This involves what is known as **divergent thinking**—the process of reframing familiar problems in unique ways, producing multiple or alternative answers from available information. Divergent thinking requires creating unexpected combinations, recognizing associations between things, and transforming information into unexpected forms. Often, the result of divergent thinking is something novel and surprising, something that never before has existed.[53] For some examples of ways to promote divergent thinking, see Table 14.6.
- *Understand complexities.* Instead of making things overly simplistic, don't be afraid to consider complex ways in which ideas may be interrelated.
- *Keep options open and avoid premature judgments.* Creative people are willing to consider all options. To do so, they consider all the angles and avoid reaching conclusions prematurely. People are particularly good at this when they are new to an organization and, therefore, don't know enough to accept everything the way it is. With this in mind, some companies actually prefer hiring executives from outside their industry.

creativity heuristics
Rules that people follow to help them approach tasks in novel ways.

- *Follow creativity heuristics.* People sometimes follow certain strategies, known as **creativity heuristics**, to help them come up with creative new ideas. These are rules that people follow to help them approach tasks in novel ways. They may involve such techniques as considering the counterintuitive, and using analogies.

productive forgetting
The ability to abandon unproductive ideas and temporarily put aside stubborn problems until new approaches can be considered.

- *Use productive forgetting.* Sometimes, our creativity is inhibited by our becoming fixated on certain ideas that we just can't seem to get out of our heads. With this in mind, it helps to practice **productive forgetting**—the ability to abandon unproductive ideas and temporarily put aside stubborn problems until new approaches can be considered.

To help individuals and teams become more creative, many organizations are inviting employees to participate in training exercises designed to promote some of these skills. Although the results are not assessed scientifically, many companies have reported successes using these techniques to boost creativity in the workplace.[54]

TABLE 14.6 Ways of Triggering Divergent Thinking

To encourage divergent thinking, exercises often are conducted in which people are asked open-ended questions to which there are no correct answers. Responses are free to fall outside normal ways of thinking about things. The following are typical examples.

- Besides wearing it, list various uses for a hat.
- Make as many sentences as possible that include the following words: *melon, consider, flower, paper.*
- How could you turn a cardboard box into a temporary tent for use on a camping trip in the woods?
- Think carefully about a stone. Then indicate what you believe to be its hidden meanings.
- Consider the various resources that are available to you when writing a research paper.
- Your car is stuck in a ditch along a deserted road. Using only the things likely to be found in and around the car, how could you summon help?

intrinsic task motivation
The motivation to do work because it is interesting, engaging, or challenging in a positive way.

Intrinsic Task Motivation. The first two components of creativity, domain-relevant skills and creativity-relevant skills, focus on what people are *capable* of doing. However, the third component, intrinsic task motivation, refers to what people are *willing* to do. The idea is simple: For someone to be creative, he or she must be interested in performing the task in question. In other words, there must be a high degree of **intrinsic task motivation**—the motivation to do work because it is interesting, engaging, or challenging in a positive way. Someone who has the capacity to be creative, but who isn't motivated to do what it takes to produce creative outcomes, certainly wouldn't be considered creative. People are most likely to be highly creative when they are passionate about their work.[55]

Intrinsic task motivation tends to be high under several conditions. For example, when an individual has a *personal interest* in the task at hand, he or she will be motivated to perform it—and may go on to do so creatively. However, anyone who doesn't find a task interesting surely isn't going to perform it long enough to demonstrate any signs of creativity. Likewise, task motivation will be high whenever an individual perceives that he or she has internal reasons to be performing that task. People who come to believe that they are performing a task for some external reason—such as high pay or pressure from a boss—are unlikely to find the work inherently interesting, in and of itself, and are unlikely to show much creativity when performing it.

Putting it All Together. As you might imagine, the components of creativity are important insofar as they can be used to paint a picture of when people will be creative. In this connection, scientists claim that people will be at their most creative when they have high amounts of all three of the components shown in Figure 14.9.

Specifically, it has been claimed that there is a multiplicative relationship between these three components of creativity. Thus, people will not be creative at all if any one of these components is at zero (i.e., if it is missing completely). After all, you would be unlikely to be creative at a job if you didn't have the skills needed to do it, regardless of how motivated you were to be creative and how well-practiced you were at coming up with new ideas. Likewise, creativity is expected to be nonexistent if either creativity-relevant skills or motivation were zero. The practical implications are clear: To be as creative as possible, people must strive toward attaining high levels of all three components of creativity.

A Model of the Creative Process

Although it isn't always obvious to us how people come up with creative ideas, scientists have developed a model that outlines the various stages of the creative process.[56] Specifically, this model, summarized in Figure 14.10, specifies that the process of creativity occurs in the following four stages.

FIGURE 14.9

Components of Creativity

Scientists claim that people will be at their most creative when they exhibit high levels of the three factors shown here.

Source: Adapted from Amabile, 1988; see Note 52.

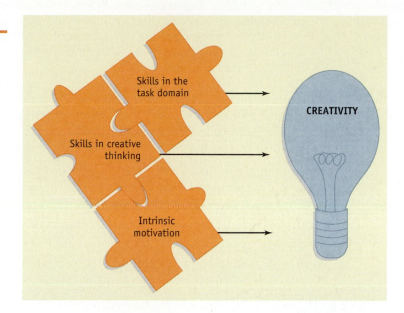

1. *Prepare to be creative.* Although we often believe that our most creative ideas come "out of thin air," people are at their most creative when they have made suitable preparations. This involves gathering the appropriate information and concentrating on the problem.
2. *Allow ideas to incubate.* Because ideas take time to develop, creativity can be enhanced by putting the problem out of our conscious minds and allowing it to incubate. If you've ever been successful at coming up with a fresh approach to a problem by putting it aside and working on something else, you know what we are describing. The phrase "sleep on it" captures this stage of the process.
3. *Document insight.* At some point during the first two stages, you are likely to come up with a unique idea. However, that idea may be lost if it is not documented. With

FIGURE 14.10

Steps in the Creative Process

Scientists have proposed that the creative process follows the four steps outlined here.

Source: Kabanoff & Rossiter, 1994; see Note 56.

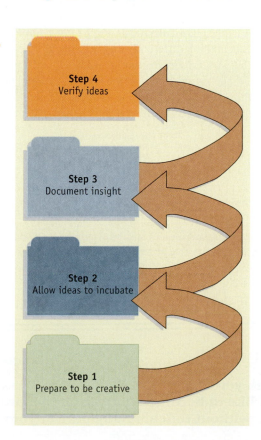

this in mind, many people carry small voice recorders that allow them to capture their ideas before they become lost in the maze of other ideas. Likewise, writers keep diaries, artists keep sketch-pads, and songwriters keep tape recorders handy to capture ideas whenever inspiration strikes.

4. *Verify ideas.* Coming up with an idea is one thing, but ensuring that it's any good is quite another. Assessing the usefulness of an idea requires consciously thinking about it and verifying it, such as by seeing what others have to say about it. In other words, you want to see if those ideas that came to you in a moment of inspiration in the middle of the night still are any good in the morning light.

Knowing about the creative process is particularly useful insofar as it can be applied to promoting individual and team productivity. We will now turn to the process of doing so.

Promoting Creativity in Organizations

Highly creative people are an asset to any organization. But what exactly do organizations do to promote creativity within their ranks? In general terms, the answer lies in things that we can do as individuals and that organizations can do as a whole. Specifically, two major approaches may be identified.

Training People to be Creative

It is true that some people, by nature, are more creative than others. Such individuals are inclined to approach various situations in new ways and tend not to be bogged down by previous ways of doing things.[57] However, there are skills that anyone can develop to become more creative, and firms have sprung up that assist organizations in doing things to promote creative employees (see Figure 14.11). Generally, training people to become more creative involves three steps.[58]

Encourage Openness to New Ideas.   Many good ideas go undeveloped because they are not in keeping with the current ways of doing things. Becoming more creative requires allowing oneself to be open to new ideas, or as it is often described, *thinking outside the box.* Some companies do this by sending their employees on *thinking expeditions*—trips specifically designed to put people in challenging situations in an effort to help them think differently and become more creative. According to the CEO of a company that specializes in running such expeditions for clients, these trips "push people out of their 'stupid zone'—a place of mental and physical normalcy—so that they can start to think differently," adding "it's an accelerated unlearning experience."[59] For an example of how this has been accomplished at one large company, see Figure 14.12.[60]

FIGURE 14.11

Creativity Training Is Big Business

Because organizations prosper when their employees are creative, they sometimes hire outside firms that specialize in helping employees bring out their creativity. This outfit apparently practices what it preaches.

Source: Used with permission of Randy Glasbergen (www.glasbergen.com).

© 1998 Randy Glasbergen.
www.glasbergen.com

GLASBERGEN

"Thank you for calling Creative Business Seminars. If you'd like to become a more creative problem solver, press 1 without touching any part of your telephone."

FIGURE 14.12

How Does This Make Betty Crocker More Efficient?

To develop creative new ideas about how to improve efficiency in their Betty Crocker factories, General Mills officials went to an unlikely place, the pit of a NASCAR auto race track, where they carefully studied how pit crews changed tires on racecars in the midst of a race. What they learned led them to creative new ways of making the changes necessary to swap factory configurations from one product to another, ultimately reducing the process from 4.5 hours to only 12 minutes. Clearly, General Mills' openness to new ideas led to some creative new ways of solving a problem.

Take the Time to Understand the Problem. Meaningful ideas rarely come to those who don't fully understand the problem at hand. Only when time is taken to examine the many different facets of the issue can people be equipped to develop creative solutions. Consider, for example, BrightHouse, the 17-employee Atlanta-based company that specializes in developing new ideas for its clients (among them have been Coca-Cola, Home Depot, and Georgia-Pacific).[61] For a fee of $500,000, the entire staff devotes a full 10 weeks to the issues their clients have in mind (e.g., how to improve billboard advertising at Turner Field, the home of baseball's Atlanta Braves).

Promote Divergent Thinking. As we noted earlier, divergent thinking involves taking new approaches to old problems. Teaching people various tactics for divergent thinking allows problems to incubate, setting the stage for creative new ideas to develop. One popular way of developing divergent thinking is known as **morphology**. A morphological analysis of a problem involves identifying its basic elements and combining them in systematically different ways. (For an example of this approach and for a chance to practice it yourself, see the Individual Exercise on pp. 577–578.)

morphology
An approach to analyzing problems in which basic elements are combined in systematically different ways.

Developing Creative Work Environments

Thus far, we have identified ways of making people more creative as individuals. In conjunction with these approaches, it also is useful for organizations to take concrete steps to change work environments in ways that bring out people's creativity.[62] Several such approaches may be identified.[63]

Provide Autonomy. It has been established that people are especially creative when they are given the freedom to control their own behavior—that is, when they have *autonomy* (see Chapter 7) and are *empowered* to make decisions (see Chapter 12). At the Japanese video game manufacturer Nintendo, creativity is so important that no one considers it odd when designers leave work to go see a movie or a play.

Provide Exposure to Other Creative People. It is widely assumed that workers are likely to be creative when they are surrounded by other creative individuals. After all, being around creative people inspires one to be creative oneself. Moreover, one can learn creativity-relevant skills from creative individuals. Although this is true under some circumstances, research suggests that the picture is not so simple. Specifically, the effect of having creative coworkers on a person's own creativity depends on the extent to which that individual is closely monitored by his or her supervisor.

A researcher conducting a recent study administered questionnaires to a group of employees to assess the extent to which they believed they were surrounded by creative coworkers as well as their beliefs about how closely they were monitored by their supervisors.[64] In addition, supervisors who were familiar with the work of each of these employees were asked to rate the degree of creativity they demonstrated in their work. The results, summarized in Figure 14.13, show that the presence of creative coworkers promoted creativity when supervisory monitoring was low, but that it actually discouraged creativity when supervisory monitoring was high.

These findings may be explained as follows. Workers who feel that they are constantly being watched, evaluated, and controlled by their bosses are reluctant to take the chances

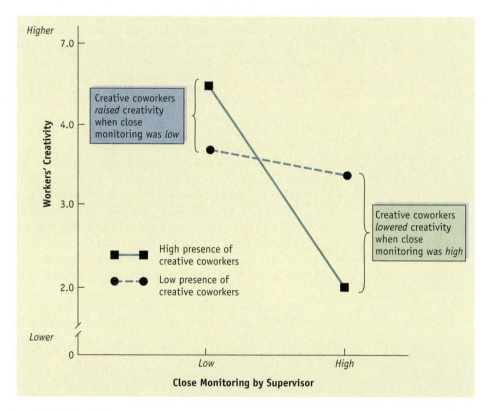

FIGURE 14.13

When Do Creative Coworkers Boost Creativity? Research Findings

The effects of having creative coworkers present on a worker's level of creativity has been found to depend on the degree to which the worker is monitored closely by his or her supervisor. According to a recent study, having creative coworkers boosted creativity when close supervisory monitoring was low (because they provided encouragement and demonstrated creativity-relevant skills). However, having creative coworkers lowered creativity when close supervisory monitoring was high (because workers were so concerned about not doing anything out of the ordinary that they merely "played it safe" by imitating the behavior of others).

Source: Based on data reported by Zhou, 2003; see Note 64.

required to behave in a creative fashion for fear of doing something that is considered inappropriate. As a result, they tend to "play it safe" by simply imitating what others are doing, thereby demonstrating less creativity than they are capable of showing. By contrast, employees who are not closely monitored by their supervisors are likely to be more willing to experiment with new ideas, thereby allowing them to reap the creative benefits of having creative coworkers around them.

Allow Ideas to Cross-Pollinate. People who work on just one project run the risk of getting stale, whereas those who work on several are likely to come into contact with different people and have a chance of applying to one project an idea they picked up on another project. This is done all the time at the design firm IDEO. For example, in coming up with an idea about how to make a more comfortable handle for a scooter, designers might use ideas they developed while working on a project involving the design of a more comfortable computer mouse. Because of the upheaval that is bound to result when companies are downsizing, ideas are unlikely to cross-pollinate. It is, therefore, not surprising that creativity tends to be considerably lower at such times.[65]

Make Jobs Intrinsically Interesting. Research has shown that people are inclined to be creative when they are intrinsically interested in the work they do. After all, nobody will want to invest the effort it takes to be creative at a task that is uninteresting. With this in mind, creativity can be promoted by enhancing the degree to which tasks are intrinsically interesting to people. The essence of the idea is to turn work into play by making it interesting.

This approach is used routinely at a marketing agency in Richmond, Virginia, appropriately named Play. Instead of coming up with ideas by sitting in boring meetings, staff members are encouraged to play. For example, to aid the process of coming up with a new marketing campaign for the Weather Channel, employees spent time in a corner office developing costumes for superheroes. According to Play's co-founder Andy Stefanovich, the idea is simple: "When you work in a place that encourages people to be themselves, have fun, and take risks, you fuel and unleash their creativity. The best ideas come from playful minds. And the way to tap into that playfulness is to play—together."[66]

Set Your Own Creative Goals. Being free to do as you wish does not necessarily imply goofing off. In fact, the freedom to make your own decisions pays off most handsomely when people set their own creative goals. For example, the famous inventor Thomas A. Edison set the goal of having a minor invention every 10 days and a major invention every six months. This kept Edison focused on being creative—and, with over 1,000 patents in his name, he clearly did an outstanding job of meeting his goals. We are not talking about strict external pressure to be creative, which rarely results in anything positive. However, creativity is aided when people strive to meet their own difficult goals for achieving creativity.[67]

Support Creativity at High Organizational Levels. Nobody in an organization is going to go out of his or her way to be creative if it is not welcomed by the bosses. Supervisors, team leaders, and top executives must encourage employees to take risks if they are to have any chance of being creative. At the same time, this involves accepting any failures that result. This idea is embraced by Livio D. DeSimone, the retired CEO of 3M, one of the most innovative companies in the world. "Failure is not fatal," he says, adding, "Innovations are simply chance breakthroughs. And when you take a chance, there is always the possibility of a failure."[68]

Have Fun! For people to be motivated to be creative, it helps to have an incentive, and one of the most potent incentives is fun. Indeed, people strive to be creative when they can have fun along the way. It is with this in mind that many companies encourage creative thinking by providing employees with opportunities to have fun on the job. This is especially so at today's high-tech jobs, where creativity is essential and where long hours at the office are typical.

With this in mind, companies have done lots of interesting things to help people have fun in the workplace (for some suggestions based on things that companies have done, see the left-hand column of Table 14.7).[69] It is important to note, however, that having fun at work must be done in ways that are appropriate and that don't harm anyone or anything. The suggestions in the right-hand column of Table 14.7 are designed to help avoid this potential problem. Remember, having fun is supposed to promote creativity and not to stifle it by coming at anyone's expense.[70]

Promote Diversity. When companies are staffed by people from diverse ethnic and cultural groups, they are bound to think differently about the situations they face. And, as we noted earlier, divergent thinking is a key element of creativity. Therefore, companies with ethnically diverse workforces are inclined to have cultures that allow creativity to flourish. In fact, some high-tech experts attribute the highly creative ideas emanating from California's Silicon Valley to the fact that over one-third of its resident engineers and scientists come from countries throughout the world.[71]

Many of today's most successful multinational corporations attribute their successes to the fact that the adjustments they have made in the course of getting different kinds of people to work together in harmony has had a beneficial, if sometimes unintended by-product—namely, boosting creativity. Although having a diverse population does not ensure creativity, to be sure, it is safe to say that *not* having one surely can limit creativity.

Today's multinational corporations are unwilling to be denied this benefit. It is not surprising, therefore, that Edgar van Ommen, chief operating officer of Arabella Sheraton Hotels, follows what he calls the "principle of the United Nations" when it comes to recruiting—hiring the best people in the world, regardless of their nationality.[72] (This discussion raises an interesting question as to whether people in some countries are more creative than those in other countries. For some insight into this matter, see the *OB in Diverse World* section on p. 569.)

The Process of Innovation

innovation
The process of making changes to something already established by introducing something new; the successful implementation of creative ideas within an organization.

Having examined the process of individual and group creativity, we now extend our analysis to situations in which people implement their creative skills for the sake of improving their organizations. This is the process of *innovation* to which we referred earlier. Specifically, **innovation** may be defined as the process of making changes to something already established by introducing something new. Put differently, innovation is the successful implementation of

TABLE 14.7 **Having Fun at Work: Doing It Right**

Creativity can be promoted by having fun at work. This can be done in many ways that are both enjoyable and productive (left column). However, to avoid having fun at anyone's expense, be sure to keep in mind the "do nots" listed here (right column).

Ways to Have Fun at Work	Ways *Not* to Have Fun at Work
Play childhood games (e.g., pitching pennies, flying paper airplanes).	Making fun of coworkers or management, (e.g., teasing or mocking them)
On an associate's birthday, hide lots of birthday cards around his or her work area.	Telling jokes that are in bad taste (ethnic jokes, off-colored jokes, etc.)
Post baby pictures of people who work in the company.	Engaging in practical jokes or pranks
Each month, sponsor a special outing (e.g., to a beach or amusement park).	Doing anything of a sexual nature
Make time to share the special hobbies that everyone has (quilting, writing poetry, etc.).	Deceiving someone
Form an all-employee band (no matter how bad everyone may be).	Gambling
Put up Nerf basketball nets around the office.	Being sarcastic
Hold fun contests, such as for paintball or spinning hula hoops.	Complaining about the company or its policies

Sources: Based on multiple sources listed in Notes 69 and 70.

OB In a Diverse World

Where in the World Is Entrepreneurial Creativity Promoted?

To be a successful entrepreneur, it helps to live someplace where the culture supports entrepreneurial activity and where people value creative thinking and innovation. Not only is entrepreneurship likely to thrive under such conditions, but the reverse is especially true: The entrepreneurial spirit is likely to be snuffed out whenever creativity and innovation are frowned upon. This applies not only to differences in organizational cultures, but national cultures as well. With this in mind, it is interesting to consider the possibility that various countries differ with respect to how strongly their cultures support creativity and innovation.[73]

In a recent study, scientists administered a questionnaire to people from Spain, Norway, Sweden, Germany, Italy, and the United States to assess citizens' perceptions of: (1) their society's admiration for people who start their own businesses, (2) the extent to which they believe that innovative and creative thinking is good, and (3) the belief that starting one's own business is a valued career option.[74]

The results were striking: People from the United States scored considerably higher than their counterparts in the European countries. That is, Americans, as a whole, believed their country was more supportive of entrepreneurial activity and the creativity and innovativeness required to make that activity successful than did people from Sweden, Norway,

Spain, Italy, or Germany. Furthermore, the Europeans all scored remarkably similar to one another.

Although these findings are interestings on their own, three important points should be taken into account when interpreting them. First, considerations in addition to the value placed on creativity are also likely to make a difference. In fact, the same study found that knowledge of how to finance, structure, and manage new businesses, and the extent to which the government provides helpful support along the way, also were important considerations. Along these dimensions, people from the two Scandinavian countries ranked highly along with the Americans.

Second, these findings do *not* mean that American entrepreneurs are destined to be more successful than their European counterparts. Clearly, many different factors are involved in determining the ultimate success of any entrepreneurial venture. Still, the findings reveal that when it comes to nurturing the creative activities that promote entrepreneurial activity, Americans appear to have the edge.

Finally, it is important to recognize that the study considered only a small number of countries. To the extent that entrepreneurs come from all over the world, it would be interesting to extend these findings to people from places such as Asia, Latin America, Africa, and the Middle East.

---

creative ideas within an organization. Thus, whereas creativity involves coming up with new ideas, innovation involves putting them into action. To understand the nature of innovation, it helps to identify the companies considered most innovative and to examine some of the especially innovative things they do. For such an overview, see Table 14.8.[75]

To understand this process we identify the major forms of innovation, the various targets of innovation and its key components. Then, we review the various stages through which innovation progresses. Before doing this, however, we address the business case for being innovative.

Innovation Pays Off on the Bottom Line

Why be innovative? The underlying assumption is that innovation pays off—that is, that highly innovative companies are more profitable than their less innovative counterparts. Is this really so? Data reveal the answer to be an unqualified "yes."

Take the top 25 most innovative companies (the first 10 of which are identified in Table 14.8). These companies enjoyed annual profit margin growths of about 3.4 percent, whereas the comparable figure for a Standard & Poors Global 1200 company was only 0.4 percent for the same period. Another financial index tells the same story. Over the past decade, the 25 most innovative companies had annual stock returns of 14.3 percent, which was 3 points higher than the comparison group.[76] Although such financial statistics surely result from many factors, it's clear that innovation is a key contributor to success. Says one consultant, "Innovation is allowing companies to grow faster [and to] have a richer product mix."[77] As you read about some of the innovative things companies are doing in the

TABLE 14.8 The Ten Most Innovative Companies in the World

The most innovative companies do not get that way by accident. As summarized here, the world's most innovative companies, as identified by *Business Week* magazine, engage in a variety of practices to help promote innovation.

Rank	Company	Innovative Practices
1	Apple	Selling songs online (now, well over 1 million downloads) coupled with a cool-looking and easy-to-use MP3 player. The iPod has been more profitable for Apple than its line of computers.
2	Google	Programmers combine powerful mapping technology with additional user information (e.g., real estate listings) to create useful "mash-ups."
3	3M	Scientists inside the company apply independently for "Genius Grants" that give them generous budgets for funding the development of new products.
4	Toyota	Working with suppliers, Toyota has streamlined the auto manufacturing process, finding new ways to cut the cost of parts and assembly.
5	Microsoft	Each year, "Hack Day" is held in which software developers are pulled from their routines, coming together for a fun event that relieves pressure and hopefully inspires creativity.
6	General Electric	Among more traditional bases for evaluation, GE's 5,000 top managers are rated on innovation-related themes such as "imagination and courage."
7	Procter & Gamble	Expanding its innovative capacity through an extensive network of connections outside the company, Procter & Gamble works with scientists, inventors, and suppliers all over the world.
8	Nokia	Nokia rewards engineers who have at least 10 patents by inducting them into its prestigious "Club 10."
9	Starbucks	Some Starbucks baristas go to trendy European coffee houses, where, like anthropologists, they observe trends that they later can put into practice at home in the United States.
10	IBM	In an "innovation Summit," some of the world's most successful innovators share their secrets with 500 IBM officials, who then consider ways of applying these ideas to their own work.

Source: McGregor, 2006; see Note 75.

remainder of this chapter, you probably will find it easy to understand the positive financial impact of innovative practices.

Major Forms of Innovation

Our definition leaves open the possibility that innovation may take several different forms. In fact, it's possible to differentiate between forms of innovation with respect to three key factors: its impact on existing business, the degree of uncertainty involved, and its sources (for a summary comparison, see Figure 14.14).

Impact on Existing Business. Over the years, wireless networking standards have changed to allow increasingly faster transmissions of data through the air. First there was 802.11a, then the faster 802.11b, followed by 802.11g, and still faster networking standards today, such as 802.11n. An improvement of this type is referred to as a **sustaining innovation** because it allows companies to approach their markets in the same manner.[78] It gives existing customers better performance. A sustaining innovation is, quite simply, the proverbial "better mousetrap."

Innovations of this type may be contrasted with others that bring significant changes to the market. For example, before it introduced its personal computer (PC), IBM was in the market of selling minicomputers, and before that, mainframe computers. The mini disrupted the market for the mainframe and the PC disrupted the market for the mini. As this description

sustaining innovation
A form of innovation that is incremental in nature; innovation that allows companies to approach their markets in the same manner as they have done in the past.

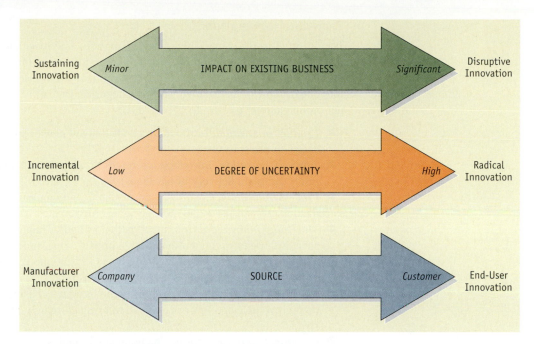

FIGURE 14.14

Forms of Innovation

Various forms of innovation may be distinguished with respect to the three dimensions summarized here.

disruptive innovation

A form of innovation that is so extreme in nature that it changes the market in which companies operate.

incremental innovation

A slow-and-steady approach to innovation, in which companies exploit existing technology and operate under conditions in which uncertainty about the future is low.

radical innovation

A form of innovation in which companies make quantum leaps; involves exploring new technology and operating under highly uncertain conditions.

manufacturer innovation

The traditional form of innovation in which an individual or organization develops an innovation for the purpose of selling it.

end-user innovation

The form of innovation in which new ideas are inspired by the individuals who use a company's products.

suggests, an innovation of this type, which completely changes the market, is known as a **disruptive innovation**. Despite what the name suggests, a disruptive innovation is desirable for the company that produces it—although, of course, it is meant to be highly disruptive to competitors.

Degree of Uncertainty. Another way to categorize innovation is with respect to the degree of uncertainty involved. On some occasions, organizations face conditions in which things have evolved slowly, making it clear what may be done. Moving ahead with innovation isn't particularly risky because the future is relatively certain. This slow-and-steady approach to innovation is known as **incremental innovation**. Companies engaging in incremental innovation exploit existing technology and operate under conditions in which uncertainty about the future is low. In other words, you can pretty much figure out what the future will be.

GE's former CEO, Jack Welch, didn't favor the incremental approach to innovation. Instead, he was inclined to do the opposite, shocking his competitors by making quantum leaps in innovation. This approach is known as **radical innovation**. In contrast to companies making incremental innovations, those making radical innovations explore new technology and operate under highly uncertain conditions.[79] Instead of making continuous, linear changes that are slow and steady, radical innovation involves a trajectory that is sporadic and discontinuous. And when it works, the payoffs of radical innovation tend to be huge. For example, radical innovations resulted in the development of Colgate Total, a new kind of toothpaste that unseated Crest as the world's leading toothpaste brand.

Source of Innovation. Traditionally, the source of innovation is the company itself. This process, known as **manufacturer innovation**, occurs when an individual or organization develops an innovation for the purpose of selling it. Intel, for example, develops faster computer chips, which it sells to customers demanding more powerful computers.

Although manufacturer innovation has been going on for some time, many of today's organizations are finding inspiration from the individuals who use their goods or services. This process, known as **end-user innovation**, is very popular today because users of products provide useful guidance with respect to what is needed.[80]

Targets of Innovation

If innovation involves introducing new changes to activities that already are established, it makes sense to ask: What business activities are the foci of innovation? In general, companies can be innovative with respect to just about anything. However, most innovation falls into one or more of the following seven categories, each of which may be considered a target of innovation.[81]

- *Product innovation.* Introducing goods that are new or substantially improved (e.g., easier-to-use software).
- *Service innovation.* Introducing services that are new or substantially improved (e.g., faster overnight delivery of packages).
- *Process innovation.* Creating a new or significantly improved production or delivery method (e.g., an easier and more accurate order-taking system for call center operators).
- *Marketing innovation.* Coming up with new and/or improved marketing methods, such as those involving product design or packaging, product promotion, or pricing.[82]
- *Supply chain innovation.* Developing quicker and more accurate ways to get products from suppliers and to deliver them to customers.
- *Business model innovation.* Revising the basic way business is done (e.g., focusing on high volume and low prices or on offering extremely high-quality goods to exclusive clients).
- *Organizational innovation.* Changing key organizational practices, such as those presented in this book (e.g., how the organization is structured; see Chapter 15).

As you might imagine, companies attempting to be innovative tend to follow more than one of these practices at a time. For example, consider a financial investment firm that is attempting to be more innovative. This may involve developing new financial products (e.g., new money market funds) and services (e.g., new interest-bearing checking accounts) for clients, combining basic financial attributes (e.g., risk-sharing, liquidity, credit) in innovative ways, and finding legal ways to minimize clients' income tax liabilities. Not only does this require creating new products and services, but also new business models, improved business processes, and so on. In other words, innovation takes many different activities that are likely to be followed in concert.

Conditions Required for Innovation to Occur

Creativity is necessary for innovation to occur, but it is not sufficient. What other factors, then, are required for innovation to occur? As it works out, the answer lies in the same basic components that are essential for creativity to occur, albeit in different ways. These are *motivation, resources,* and *skills*.

Motivation to Innovate. Just as individual creativity requires that people are motivated to do what it takes to be creative, organizational innovation requires that organizations have the kind of cultures that encourage innovation. When top executives fail to promote a vision of innovation and accept the status quo, change is unlikely. However, at companies such as Microsoft, where leaders (including co-founder Bill Gates) envision innovation as being part of the natural order of things, it is not surprising that innovative efforts are constantly underway.

Resources to Innovate. Again, a parallel to individual creativity is in order. Just as people must have certain basic skills to be creative, so too must organizations possess certain basic resources that make innovation possible. For example, to be innovative, at the very least, organizations must have what it takes in terms of human and financial resources. After all, unless the necessary skilled people and deep pockets are available to do what it takes to innovate, stagnation is likely to result.

Skills to Manage Innovation. Finally, just as individuals must hone special skills needed to be creative, so too must organizations develop special ways of managing people so as to encourage innovation—that is, *skills in innovation management*. Most notable in this regard is the matter of *balance*. Specifically, managers help promote innovation when they show balance with respect to three key matters: goals, reward systems, and time pressure.

- Organizational innovation is promoted when *goals* are linked carefully to the corporate mission. However, they should not be so specific as to tie the hands of those who put them into practice. Innovation is unlikely when such restrictions are imposed.
- *Reward systems* should recognize one's contributions generously and fairly, but they should not be so specific as to connect literally every move to a bonus or some type of monetary reward. To do so discourages people from taking the kinds of risks that make innovation possible.
- Innovation management requires carefully balancing the *time pressures* under which employees are placed. If pressures are too great, people may be unimaginative and offer routine solutions. By the same token, if pressure is too weak, employees may have no sense of time urgency and believe that the project is too unimportant to warrant any creative attention on their part.

Stages of the Organizational Innovation Process

Any CEO who snaps her fingers one day and expects her troops to be innovative on command surely will be in for disappointment. Innovation does not happen all at once. Rather, innovation occurs gradually, through a series of stages. Specifically, scientists have identified five specific stages through which the process of organizational innovation progresses.[83] We now describe each of these (see the summary in Figure 14.15).

Stage 1: Setting the Agenda. The first stage of the process of innovation begins by setting the agenda for innovation. This involves creating a **mission statement**—a document describing an organization's overall direction and general goals. The component of innovation that is most involved here is *motivation* (see Chapter 7). After all, the highest-ranking officials of the organization must be highly committed to innovation before they will initiate a push toward it.

Stage 2: Setting the Stage. Once an organization's mission has been established, it is prepared to set the stage for innovation. This may involve narrowing down certain broad goals into more specific tasks and gathering the resources to meet them. It also may involve assessing the environment, both outside and inside the organization, searching for anything that may either support or inhibit later efforts to "break the rules" by being creative. To set

mission statement

A document describing an organization's overall direction and general goals.

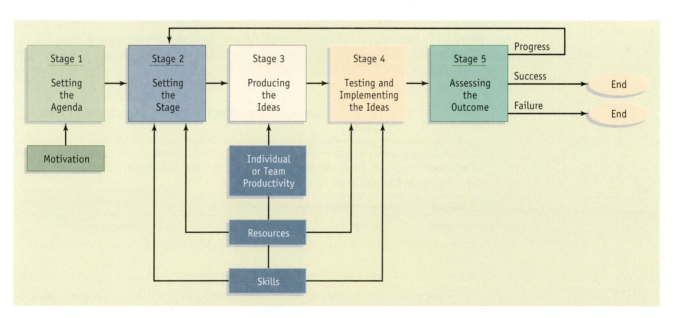

FIGURE 14.15

The Process of Innovation

The innovation process consists of the various components, and follows the steps, shown here.

Source: Adapted from Amabile, 2000; see Note 55.

the stage for innovation most effectively requires using the skills necessary for innovation management as well as full use of the organization's human and financial resources.

Stage 3: Producing the Ideas. This stage of the process involves coming up with new ideas and testing them. It is in this third stage that individual and small group creativity enters the picture. As a result, all of the components of individual creativity mentioned earlier are involved. What's more, these may combine in important ways with various organizational factors. For example, an individual who has the skills and motivation to be highly creative might find his motivation waning as he attempts to introduce novel new ideas in an organization that is not committed to innovation and that fails to make the necessary resources available. By contrast, the highly innovative nature of an organization may bring out the more creative side of an individual who may not have been especially creative.

Stage 4: Testing and Implementing the Ideas. This is the stage where implementation occurs. Now, after an initial group of individuals has developed an idea, other parts of the organization get involved. For example, a prototype product may be developed and tested, and market research may be conducted. In short, input from the many functional areas of the organization is provided. As you might imagine, resources in the task domain are important at this stage. After all, unless adequate amounts of money, personnel, material systems, and information are provided, the idea will be unlikely to survive.

Interestingly, even a good idea and resources are not enough to bring innovation to life. Skills in innovation management are critical because for good ideas to survive it is necessary for them to be "nourished" and supported throughout the organization. Even the best ideas may be "killed off" if people in some parts of the organization are not supportive. For some remarkable examples of this, see Table 14.9.[84] When you see all the great ideas that didn't quite make it at first, you realize may come to that you are in excellent company if your own ideas are rejected.

Stage 5: Assessing the Outcome. The final stage of the process involves assessing the new idea that arises. What happens to that idea depends on the results of the assessment. Three outcomes are possible. If the resulting idea (e.g., a certain product or service) has been a total success, it will be accepted and carried out in the future. This ends the process. Likewise, the process is over if the idea has been a complete failure. In this case, there is no good reason to continue. However, if the new idea shows promise and makes some progress toward the organization's objectives, but still has problems, the process starts all over again at stage 2.

Although this five-stage process does not account for all innovations you may find in organizations, this general model does a good job of identifying the major steps through

TABLE 14.9 Is Your Innovative Idea Rejected? If So, You're in Good Company

Some of the best, most innovative ideas were rejected at first because one or more powerful people failed to see their merit. When you look at these examples, you can imagine how bad these individuals must have felt about "the one that got away."

Product	Rejection Story
Star Wars	Turned down by 12 Hollywood studios before finally being accepted.
Photocopying process	Rejected as a viable technology by IBM, GM, and DuPont.
Velcro	Victor Kiam (of Remington Razor fame) turned down the patent for $25,000.
Transistor radio	In the 1950s, Sony's founder, Akio Morita, was unsuccessful in marketing this idea.
The Beatles	Turned down by Decca Records in 1962 because it was believed that "groups with guitars were on the way out."
Movies with soundtracks	In 1927, Harry Warner, president of Warner Brothers, said "nobody wanted to hear actors talk."

Source: Based on information reported by Davilla et al., 2005, and Ricchiuto, 1997; see Note 84.

which most innovations go as they travel along their path from a specific organizational need to a product or service that meets that need. (For some further suggestions on how to promote innovation in an organization, see the *How to Do It* section below.)

HOW TO DO IT

How to Inspire Innovation

The noted organizational consultant Gary Hamel believes that top management plays an important role when it comes to inspiring innovation in their companies. Radical innovation, he argues, "is no longer an option for big companies—it's the imperative," adding that top management's job is "to build an organization that can continually spawn cool new business concepts."[85] Hamel identifies several ways in which managers can go about doing this.[86] Some of these are as follows.

Set very high expectations.   In Chapter 7 we emphasized that people strive to meet performance goals. When employees are confronted with goals they find to be especially challenging—but still not impossible, of course—they are forced to consider highly novel ways of accomplishing them. At GE Capital, for example, executives are expected to grow annual earnings by at least 20 percent. This leads them to consider more creative approaches and to develop more innovative products than they would if they were required to meet a more modest goal, such as the more typical 5 percent.

Listen to new voices.   If you ask questions of the same old people, you get the same old answers. But, if you seek the opinions of outsiders free from industry prejudices, they are less likely to say "you can't do it." Indeed, Jeff Bezos was not a retailing mogul when he started Amazon.com (see the *Case in Point* on p. 580), and neither was Ted Turner a seasoned broadcast journalist when he founded CNN. With this in mind, many of today's most innovative companies are doing things like seeking out the revolutionaries in the company, those whose voices are getting muffled by the hierarchy. They also are paying special attention to newcomers to the company, especially the youngest people. Again, GE Capital provides a good example: Intentionally seeking a youthful perspective, many members of the management team at this well-established financial services firm are hired when under 30.

Create opportunities for talented employees.   It is widely believed that the best people are always interested in the best opportunities within a company. The most effective organizations capitalize on this by allowing employees to move to other jobs within the company that they find more exciting. Sometimes, this involves making the best use of a company's human resources by training employees for new positions that enable their organizations to be innova-

tive. For example, IBM has committed to spending $200 million to train 100,000 employees in high-skill jobs, such as those involving Linux systems and middleware (i.e., software that connects two otherwise separate applications, such as linking a database system and a Web server). [87]

Recognize innovation.   Many experts believe that to get people to innovate, it helps to reward them for doing so. This is practiced at South Africa's First National Bank (FNB), which in 2005 initiated the FNB Innovators competition.[88] This program identifies and rewards employees who think creatively and come up with innovations to ensure efficient and effective systems and procedures. According to Michael Jordaan, CEO of FNB, innovation can either be a new approach to an old process or a totally novel idea. In its first year, 3,000 ideas were entered. The bank's Cellphone Banking Division won first prize in 2005 for creating an entirely new way to do online banking, netting team members a whopping ZAR 1 million (approximately US$166,668).

It is important to note that the reconition for innovative activity need not always be monetary in nature. Many companies find that simply recognizing employees for their innovations contributes to efforts to keep it going. At 3M, for example, which we have acknowledged several times in this chapter for its innovative ways, a "Hall of Inventors" showcases the work of the firm's most innovative engineers. The company even has published its own book to celebrate the contributions of its innovators.[89]

Identify a cause.   Most think of Charles Schwab as a well-established, rather traditional investment firm. Although in many ways it is, that's not how president and co-CEO David Pottruck prefers to think of it. Rather, Pottruck envisions Charles Schwab's mission in far loftier terms—as guardians of its customers' financial dreams. By sharing this vision, Pottruck has gotten his employees to recognize that they are doing something important, contributing to a cause that will make a difference in people's lives. It was such thinking that inspired Schwab employees to take innovative steps, such as offering its services online, and at a sizable discount.

If you are thinking that implementing these guidelines is akin to being innovative about innovation, we are inclined to agree. Indeed, although these suggestions may be challenging to adopt, their considerable impact makes it unwise to ignore them.

Summary and Review of Learning Objectives

1. **Define organizational culture and identify its core characteristics and the various functions it serves in organizations.**
   Organizational culture is a cognitive framework consisting of attitudes, values, behavioral norms, and expectations shared by organization members. Scientists often think of organizational culture as a set of basic assumptions shared by members of an organization. Organizational culture consists of six core characteristics by which organizations may be differentiated. These are: (1) sensitivity to others, (2) interest in new ideas, (3) willingness to take risks, (4) value placed on people, (5) openness of available communication options, and (6) friendliness and congeniality. Culture plays three major roles in organizations. It provides a sense of identity for its members, it generates commitment to the organization's mission, and it also serves to clarify and reinforce standards of behavior.

2. **Describe the four major forms of organizational culture specified by the competing values framework.**
   According to the competing values framework, organizations have one of four different forms of organizational culture. Organizations that have an internal focus and that emphasize stability and control are said to have a *hierarchy culture*. In this case, effective leaders are good coordinators of projects and emphasize a smooth-running organization, often relying on formal rules and policies to do so. Organizations that are concerned with stability and control, but that are external in their orientation are said to have a *market culture*. In such organizations, the core values emphasize competitiveness and productivity, focusing on bottom-line results. They do this by carefully identifying the markets in which they are going to compete and then taking a very hard-driving, results-oriented approach to getting things done. Organizations that have a strong internal focus along with a high degree of flexibility and discretion are said to have a *clan culture*. With goals that are highly shared by members of the organization and high levels of cohesiveness, such organizations feel more like extended families than economic entities. Organizations that emphasize flexibility while also paying attention to external environments are said to have *adhocracy cultures*. Such cultures are characterized by the recognition that to succeed organizations need to be highly innovative and constantly assessing what the future requires for survival.

3. **Identify the factors responsible for creating and transmitting organizational culture and for getting it to change.**
   Organizational culture is created by two key factors—the influence of company founders and experiences with the external environment. Organizational culture is transmitted in several ways, including: symbols, slogans, stories, jargon, ceremonies, and statements of principle. Although organizational culture tends to be stable, it is subject to change. Among the factors most responsible for changing organizational culture are the composition of the workforce, mergers and acquisitions, strategic (i.e., planned) organizational changes, and changes necessitated by the Internet.

4. **Define creativity and describe the basic components of individual and team creativity.**
   Creativity is the process by which individuals or small groups produce novel and useful ideas. Creativity in organizations is based on three fundamental components: domain-relevant skills (basic knowledge needed to perform the task at hand), creativity-relevant skills (special abilities needed to generate creative new ideas), and intrinsic task motivation (people's willingness to perform creative acts).

5. **Describe various approaches to promoting creativity in organizations.**
   Creativity in organizations may be promoted by training people to be creative, by encouraging openness to new ideas (e.g., "thinking outside the box"), by taking the time to understand the problem at hand, by developing divergent thinking (e.g., using morphology). It also may be accomplished by developing creative work environments. These are ones in which autonomy is provided, people are exposed to creative

individuals, ideas are permitted to cross-pollinate, jobs are made intrinsically interesting, creative goals are set, creativity is supported within the organization, people have fun, and diversity is promoted.

6. **Identify the basic forms and targets of innovation and the stages of the innovation process.**

   Innovation refers to the implementation of creative ideas within organizations. It takes different forms depending on three factors: impact on existing business (*sustaining innovation* if impact is minor, and *disruptive innovation* if impact is major), the degree of uncertainty involved (*incremental innovation* if uncertainty is low, and *radical innovation* if uncertainty is high), and its sources (*manufacturer innovation* if ideas come from within, and *end-user innovation* if ideas come from customers). The innovation process generally proceeds in the following five stages: setting the agenda, setting the stage, producing the ideas, testing and implementing the ideas, and assessing the outcome.

Points to Ponder

Questions for Review

1. What is organizational culture, what role does it play in organizations, and how is it created?
2. How does organizational culture influence individuals and organizations, and what makes organizational culture change?
3. What are the three components of individual and team creativity, and what can be done to promote creativity in individuals, work teams, and the whole work environment?
4. What are the basic components of innovation and the stages through which the process of innovation progresses?

Experiential Questions

1. Think of an organization in which you have worked. In what ways was its culture transmitted to the people who worked in it and those who remained outside, such as the public?
2. Have you ever worked for an organization whose culture is in need of change? If so, what was the problem? What could have been done to change the culture? What obstacles would have had to be overcome for the changes to be effective?
3. Do you think of yourself as are a creative person? What could you do to become more creative when it comes to the work you do?
4. Have you ever worked for a highly innovative company? If so, what was done that made it so innovative? If not, what could have been done to make it more innovative?

Questions to Analyze

1. Organizational culture is a "mushy" concept. You can't see it, yet you know it's there. What indications are there that organizational culture really does exist?
2. Think of an organization in which you have worked. Was its culture predominantly hierarchy, market, clan, or adhocracy? Was this an effective culture given the nature of the people employed there and the type of work done?
3. Think of an instance in which you were especially creative. Did it involve a task at which you were particularly skillful and that you found interesting (e.g., composing music)? Also, did you use any of the creativity-relevant skills identified here (e.g., divergent thinking, productive forgetting)? In retrospect, what additional skills might you have used to be even more creative in that situation?

Experiencing OB

Individual Exercise

Morphology in Action: Using an Idea Box

One day, the marketing director of a company that makes laundry hampers was tinkering with ways of boosting sales in a stagnant, mature market. To trigger his imagination, he thought explicitly about something that most of us take for granted—the basic parameters of laundry hampers. Specifically, he noted that they differed in four basic ways: the materials of which they were made, their shape, their finish, and how they are positioned. For each of these dimensions, he identified five different answers, resulting in the following chart, known as an *idea box*.

Improve Design for Laundry Hamper

	Material	**Shape**	**Finish**	**Position**
1	Wicker	Square	Flat	Sits on Floor
2	Plastic	Cylindrical	Painted	On Ceiling
3	Paper	Rectangle	Clear	On Wall
4	Metal	Hexagonal	Luminous	Chute to Basement
5	Net Material	Cube	Neon	On Door

Source: Reprinted with permission from *Thinkertoys* by Michael Michalko. Berkeley, California: Ten Speed Press.

Then, by randomly combining one item from each column—net material, cylindrical shape, painted finish, and positioning on a door—he came up with a completely new idea. It was a laundry hamper made to look like a basketball net: about a yard of netting attached to a cylindrical hoop, hung from a backboard attached to the back of a door.

With some quick math, you can see that this particular idea box generates 3,125 different combinations. Given that this is a far greater number of ideas than you could probably generate without the aid of the idea box, it makes sense to practice generating idea boxes for situations you face in which creative new solutions are required. Nurture your own creativity by following the directions given here.

Directions

To generate an idea box, do the following.

1. ***Specify the challenge you are facing.*** Although you may not be interested in developing exciting new laundry baskets, you must start at the same point indicated in our example—that is, by identifying exactly what you are attempting to do.
2. ***Select the parameters of your challenge.*** Material, shape, finish, and position were the parameters of the laundry basket problem. What are yours? To help determine if the parameter you are considering is important enough to add, ask yourself if the challenge would still exist without that parameter.
3. ***List variations.*** Our example shows five variations of each parameter, but feel free to list as many key ones as you can. After all, as your idea box grows larger, it gets increasingly difficult to spot new ideas. (For example, if your idea box had 10 parameters, each of which contained 10 variations, you'd face 10 billion potential combinations to consider—hardly a practical task!)
4. ***Try different combinations.*** After your idea box is completed, work your way through the box to find some of the most promising combinations. Begin by examining the entire box, and then eventually limit yourself to the most promising combinations.

Questions for Discussion

1. Have you ever used the idea box, or something similar to it, before now? If so, how effectively has it worked?
2. For what kinds of challenges is the idea box most useful and least useful?
3. It has been said that generating an idea box is similar to writing a poem. How is this so?

Group Exercise

What Does Your Workspace Communicate About Organizational Culture?

Newcomers' impressions of an organization's culture depend greatly on the visual images of that organization they first see. Even without knowing anything about an organization, just seeing the workplace sends a message, intentional or unintentional, regarding what that organization is like. The following exercise is designed to demonstrate this phenomenon.

Directions

1. Each member of the class should take several photographs of his or her workplace and select the three that best capture, in his or her own mind, the essence of what that organization is like.
2. One member of the class should identify the company depicted in the photos, describe the type of work it does, and present the photos to the rest of the class.
3. Members of the class should then rate the organization shown in the photos using the following dimensions. Circle the number that comes closest to your feelings about the company shown.

unfamiliar	: 1 : 2 : 3 : 4 : 5 : 6 : 7 :	familiar
unsuccessful	: 1 : 2 : 3 : 4 : 5 : 6 : 7 :	successful
unfriendly	: 1 : 2 : 3 : 4 : 5 : 6 : 7 :	friendly
unproductive	: 1 : 2 : 3 : 4 : 5 : 6 : 7 :	productive
not innovative	: 1 : 2 : 3 : 4 : 5 : 6 : 7 :	innovative
uncaring	: 1 : 2 : 3 : 4 : 5 : 6 : 7 :	caring
conservative	: 1 : 2 : 3 : 4 : 5 : 6 : 7 :	risky
closed	: 1 : 2 : 3 : 4 : 5 : 6 : 7 :	open

4. Take turns sharing your individual reactions to each set of photos. Compare the responses of the student whose company pictures were examined with those of the students who were seeing the photos for the first time.
5. Repeat this process using the photos of other students' organizations.

Questions for Discussion

1. For each set of photos examined, how close did the descriptions of members of the class come to the photographers' assessments of their own companies? In other words, how well did the photos capture the culture of the organization as perceived by an "insider"?
2. As a whole, were people more accurate in assessing the culture of companies with which they were already familiar than those they didn't already know? If so, why do you think this occurred?
3. Was there more agreement regarding the cultures of organizations in some types of industries (e.g., manufacturing) than in others (e.g., service)? If so, why do you think this occurred?

Practicing OB

Stimulating a Creative Culture

The president of your organization, a small manufacturing company, has been complaining that sales are stagnant. A key problem, you discover, is that the market for the products your firm makes is fully developed—and frankly, the products themselves are not very exciting. No one seems to care about doing anything innovative. Instead, the employees seem more interested in doing things the way they have always done them.

1. What factors do you suspect are responsible for the way the culture in this organization has been over the years?
2. What do you recommend should be done to enhance the creativity of this company's employees?
3. What could be done to help make the company's products more innovative?

CASE IN POINT

Amazon.com: Innovation via the "Two-Pizza Team"

Amazon.com widely is considered the world's best online retail site, the undisputed leader of Internet commerce. Although many e-tailers pulled their plugs during the dot-com bust of the late 1990s, Amazon has become a profitable multibillion-dollar business. The man behind the company's success is its founder and CEO, Jeff Bezos. And his secret to success, he proudly proclaims, is his willingness to innovate.

His secret to being innovative is simple (to explain, at least)—being willing to take risks. As Bezos put it, "Innovation is part and parcel with going down blind alleys. You can't have one without the other." And at Amazon, being innovative is possible because it's engrained into the culture of the organization. Indeed, the very idea of starting an Internet-based bookstore in 1993 was then as unusual as it is unremarkable today.

To keep innovation going at Amazon, Bezos does several things. First, company officials go out of their way to select people who are interested in being innovative. Those who are unwilling to take risks or who demand stable working environments "flee Amazon.com in hordes," says Bezos. However, because Amazon is known for its pioneering focus, it also tends to attract individuals who buy into the company's highly innovative orientation.

Second, to keep ideas percolating, managers form teams that introduce and test ideas constantly. And, because the company's only presence is Web-based, it's easy to test ideas without making large investments. For example, it's possible to expose some customers, but not others, to some features or descriptions or prices. Then, comparisons can be made to provide instant feedback on how people behave.

Within the company's Seattle headquarters, these teams that test innovations are called "two-pizza teams." All projects involve only small numbers of people—"small enough that they can be fed on two pizzas," Bezos explains, explaining that six-person teams constitute a good size for getting things done.

At Amazon, "getting things done" is all about making the best possible experience for customers. Recently, this has taken such popular forms as "inside the book" (which allows guests to the Web site to examine and search through books before purchasing) and various deals that allow customers to have their items shipped free of charge. Both have been wildly successful.

When asked if he considers himself to be an innovator, Bezos readily acknowledges that this description fits him perfectly. "I absolutely think of myself as an innovator," he says, adding that too often "we learn that we can't improve things." However, being innovative means learning that anything can be improved upon. And if Amazon's success is any indication, this clearly is so.

Questions for Discussion

1. As Amazon.com has grown in size over the years, do you think it has become easier or more difficult for innovation to occur? Or do you think that the company's size makes no difference in this regard?
2. What role do you think Jeff Bezos has played in instilling the innovative culture at Amazon.com? How, if at all, do you think he is involved in maintaining an innovative culture?
3. Personally, would you like to work at a highly innovative company like Amazon.com, or would you be among those who leave because you prefer a more stable environment?

Chapter 15

ORGANIZATIONAL STRUCTURE AND DESIGN

Chapter Outline

Organizational Structure: The Basic Dimensions of Organizations

Departmentalization: Ways of Structuring Organizations

Organizational Design: Coordinating the Structural Elements of Organizations

Emerging Organizational Designs

Interorganizational Designs: Going Beyond the Single Organization

Special Sections

How to Do It

Designing High-Tech Organizations with Flexibility in Mind

OB Making Sense Out of Common Sense

When Should Companies Go Virtual?

OB In a Diverse World

Joint Ventures in China: Beware of Obstacles

1. Describe what is meant by organizational structure and how it is revealed by an organization chart.

2. Explain the basic characteristics of organizational structure revealed in an organization chart (hierarchy of authority, division of labor, span of control, line versus staff, and decentralization).

3. Describe different approaches to departmentalization—functional organizations, product organizations, matrix organizations, and the boundaryless organization.

4. Distinguish between classical and neoclassical approaches to organizational design and between mechanistic organizations and organic organizations, as described by the contingency approach to organizational design.

5. Describe the five organizational forms identified by Mintzberg: simple structure, machine bureaucracy, professional bureaucracy, divisional structure, and adhocracy.

6. Characterize two forms of intraorganizational design—conglomerates and strategic alliances.

PREVIEW CASE

Commercial Metals Company "Steels" the Show

Although you probably never heard of the Commercial Metals Company (CMC), chances are good that you've driven across a bridge or spent time in a building made of its steel products. And when builders repaired the Pentagon after the September 11 terrorist attack they turned to the CMC for ultra-strong structural steel girders. To industry insiders, the choice seemed obvious. Since 1915, companies building bridges, skyscrapers, vehicles, and industrial equipment have relied on CMC to provide steel and metal products of every conceivable type. The company's high-quality products coupled with its reputation for outstanding service has paid off on the bottom line. Even in an economically rocky period, the company turned in record earnings in 2006.

In a word, says company president and CEO Stanley A. Rabin, the key to the company's success can be described in a single word, "efficiency." Indeed, CMC operates a network of companies that carefully feed one another in a manner that minimizes waste. Specifically, the firm is organized into five segments: Domestic Mills; the Polish company, CMC Zawiercie (CMCZ); Domestic Fabrication; Recycling; and Marketing and Distribution. The Domestic Mills segment consists of four steel "minimills" and the Howell Metals Company, which manufactures copper tubes in Virginia. Servicing the European market, CMCZ mills 1.1 million tons of steel a year. To ensure a constant supply of raw materials for these units is CMC's Recycling Segment. Operating 34 metals-processing plants across the Sunbelt, CMC is one of the largest processors of scrap metals in the U.S., providing metal products of all types to steel mills (including the company's own facilities) and manufacturing plants.

Supporting these divisions is CMC's Marketing and Distribution segment. This portion of the business, which itself is composed of four different divisions, focuses on marketing steel, nonferrous metals, and other commodities and products through a network of offices located around the world. One of these divisions is the International Division, which knits together CMC's operations in 130 countries around the world and coordinates business ventures with companies in other nations (e.g., Australia and Germany). To help promote the manufacturing business, the marketing and distribution segment also performs vital service functions for its customers, such as providing technical information, financing, transportation and shipping, and even insurance. In short, if it's something that a metals customer may need, this segment of CMC is there to provide it. And the more seamlessly customers have their needs met, the more metal products they buy from the organization.

To say that nothing goes to waste at CMC is an understatement. Take scrap, for instance. For a quarter century CMC has been holding an annual "Scrap Can Be Beautiful" contest for art students at a high school in the Dallas area (where the company is headquartered). The company donates scrap metal to students in a metal sculpture class and awards cash prizes for the best entries. Some of the projects are displayed in the corporate office for a year, others are displayed in local galleries and museums, and still others are auctioned off to benefit Dallas-area arts organizations.

I t's safe to assume that a great part of CMC's success can be attributed to the tight interconnections between the various segments of its business. Each serves and feeds upon the others. CMS's outstanding record raises an important question: Is this approach, which works so well at CMC, a model for all companies to follow? Putting it more generally, how should companies organize themselves into separate units to be most effective? This question is a venerable one in the field of business—and, as we explain in this chapter, an extremely important one.

OB researchers and theorists have provided considerable insight into the matter by studying what is called *organizational structure*—the way individuals and groups are arranged with respect to the tasks they perform—and *organizational design*—the process of coordinating these structural elements in the most effective manner.[1]

As you may suspect, finding the best way to structure and design organizations is no simple matter. However, because understanding the structure and design of organizations is key to appreciating their functioning fully—and, ultimately, their success—organizational scientists have devoted considerable energy to this topic. We describe these efforts in this chapter. To begin, we identify the basic structural dimensions of organizations. Following this, we examine how these structural elements can be most effectively combined into productive organizational designs. In so doing, we cover some of the traditional ways of designing organizations as well as some of the rapidly developing organizational forms emerging today.

Organizational Structure: The Basic Dimensions of Organizations

Think about how a simple house is constructed. Typically, it is composed of a wooden frame positioned atop a concrete slab covered by a roof and siding materials. Within this basic structure are separate systems operating to provide electricity, water, and telephone services. Similarly, the structure of the human body is composed of a skeleton surrounded by various systems of organs, muscle, and tissue serving bodily functions such as respiration, digestion, and the like. Although you may not have thought about it much, we also can identify the structure of an organization in a similar fashion.

Consider, for example, the college or university you attend. It probably is composed of various groupings of people and departments working together to serve special functions. Individuals and groups are dedicated to tasks such as teaching, providing financial aid, maintaining the physical facilities, and so on. Of course, within each group, even more distinctions can be found between the jobs people perform. For example, it's unlikely that the instructor for your organizational behavior course also is teaching seventeenth-century French literature. Similarly, you also can distinguish between the various tasks and functions people perform in other organizations. In other words, an organization is not a haphazard collection of people, but a meaningful combination of groups and individuals working together purposefully to meet the goals of the organization.[2] The term **organizational structure** refers to the formal configuration between individuals and groups with respect to the allocation of tasks, responsibilities, and authority within organizations.[3]

organizational structure
The formal configuration between individuals and groups with respect to the allocation of tasks, responsibilities, and authorities within organizations.

organization chart
A diagram representing the connections between the various departments within an organization; a graphic representation of organizational design.

Strictly speaking, one cannot see the structure of an organization; it is an abstract concept. However, the connections between various clusters of functions of which an organization is composed can be represented in the form of a diagram known as an **organization chart**. In other words, an organization chart can be considered a representation of an organization's internal structure. As you might imagine, organization charts are useful tools for avoiding confusion within organizations regarding how various tasks or functions are interrelated (see Figure 15.1). With this in mind, we now turn our attention to the five basic dimensions of organizational structure that can be revealed by organizational charts.

Organization charts provide information about the various tasks performed within an organization and the formal lines of authority between them. For example, look at the chart depicting part of a hypothetical manufacturing organization shown in Figure 15.2. Each box represents a specific job, and the lines connecting them reflect the formally prescribed

FIGURE 15.1

Organization Charts Reveal a Great Deal

Although this man might not be flattered by his position in the organization in which he works, organization charts, like the one at which he is looking, reveal a great deal about organizations. They provide a guide to an organization's structure, indicating the formal reporting relationships between individuals at different organizational levels.

Source: www.CartoonStock.com

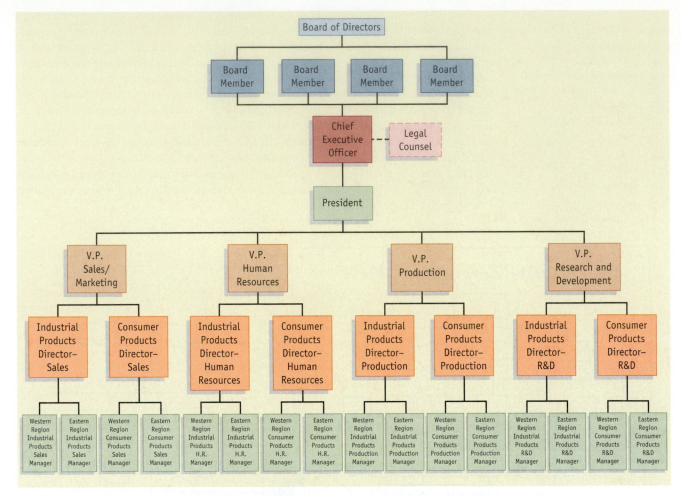

FIGURE 15.2

Organization Chart of a Hypothetical Manufacturing Firm

An organizational chart, such as this one, identifies pictorially the various functions performed within an organization and the lines of authority between the individuals performing those functions.

reporting relationships between the individuals performing those jobs. (In other words, it reveals "who answers to whom.") To specialists in organizational structure, however, such diagrams reveal a great deal more.

Hierarchy of Authority: Up and Down the Organizational Ladder

hierarchy of authority
A configuration of the reporting relationships within organizations; that is, who reports to whom.

Among the first things you see when examining an organization chart is information about who reports to whom—what is known as **hierarchy of authority**. The diagram reveals which particular lower-level employees are required to report to which particular individuals immediately above them in the organizational hierarchy. In our hypothetical example in Figure 15.2, the various regional salespeople (at the bottom of the hierarchy and the bottom of the diagram) report to their respective regional sales directors, who report to the vice president of sales, who reports to the president, who reports to the chief executive officer, who reports to the board of directors. As we trace these reporting relationships, we work our way up the organization's hierarchy. In this case, the organization has six levels. Organizations may have many levels, in which case their structure is considered *tall* (as in the top of Figure 15.3), or only a few, in which case their structure is considered *flat* (as in the bottom of Figure 15.3).

From the mid-1990s through today, many organizations have been restructuring their workforces, seeking to eliminate waste by flattening them out.[4] This is what's taking place as companies "downsize," "rightsize," "delayer," or "retrench" by eliminating entire layers

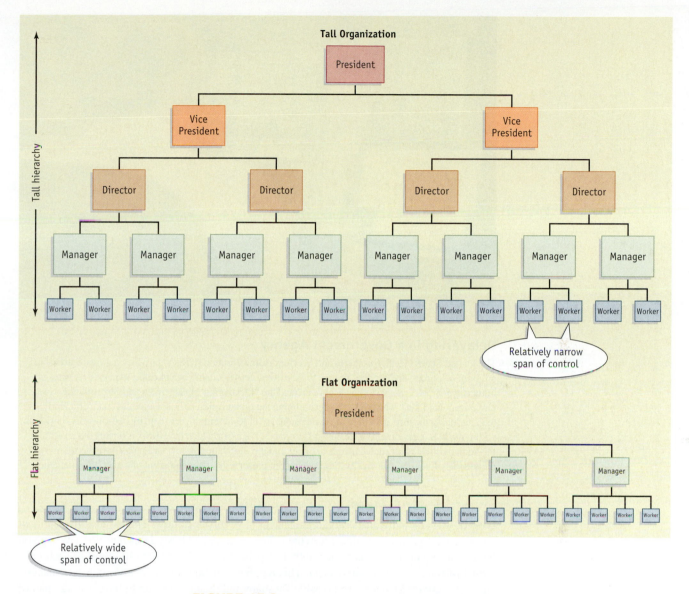

FIGURE 15.3

Tall Versus Flat Organizations: A Comparison

In tall organizations, the hierarchy has many layers and managers have a narrow span of control (i.e., they are responsible for few subordinates). However, in flat organizations, the hierarchy has few layers and managers have a wide span of control (i.e., they are responsible for many subordinates). Both of the organizations depicted here have 31 members, although each one is structured differently.

of organizational structure (we will return to this topic again in Chapter 16).[5] Job losses due to restructuring have hit particularly hard at the middle levels of many large organizations. For example, delayering has been in widespread use in health-care organizations as part of that industry's efforts to contain astronomical costs.[6] The same thing has been going on in the public sector. In fact, one of President George W. Bush's reforms has called for the delayering of government agencies to streamline them so as to make them smaller and more efficient (see Figure 15.4). In keeping with the trend toward getting work done through teams (see Chapter 8), tall organizational hierarchies become unnecessary. The underlying assumption is that fewer layers reduce waste and enable people to make better decisions (by moving them closer to the problems at hand), thereby leading to greater profitability. "Doing more with less" is the mantra of proponents of delayering.

FIGURE 15.4

Delayering in a Government Agency

The United States Health Resources and Services Administration (HRSA) provides national leadership, program resources, and services needed to improve access to quality health care. As part of its strategic initiatives for 2005, agency officials have created the "Delayering Management and Streamlining Organizational Plan," which calls for streamlining the organization so that it operates more efficiently (e.g., reducing the time it takes to make decisions) with fewer employees (e.g., by consolidating positions within the U.S. Department of Health and Human Services, of which the HRSA is a part). As a result of this initiative, the agent shown here is likely to find it easier than ever to coordinate efforts between individuals of various agencies as they endeavor to preserve health in the event of a national emergency.

Span of Control: Breadth of Responsibility

Over how many individuals should a manager have responsibility? The earliest management theorists and practitioners alike (even the Roman legions) addressed this question.[7] When you look at an organization chart, the number of people formally required to report to each individual manager is immediately clear. This number constitutes what is known as a manager's **span of control**. Managers responsible for many individuals are said to have a *wide* span of control, whereas those responsible for fewer are said to have a *narrow* span of control. In our organization chart in Figure 15.3, note how the managers in the top portion of this figure have relatively narrow spans of control (only two workers), whereas managers in the bottom have relatively broader spans of control (twice as many workers). In real organizations, some managers have spans of control so broad that they may be responsible for dozens of subordinates.

Figure 15.3 shows something important about the relationship between the tallness of its hierarchy and the span of control of its supervisory personnel. Generally speaking, when a manager's span of control is wide, the organization itself tends to have a flat hierarchy. In contrast, when a manager's span of control is narrow, the organization itself tends to have a tall hierarchy. Specifically, notice that in the "Tall Organization," there are many levels in the hierarchy and that the span of control is relatively narrow (i.e., the number of people supervised is low). By contrast, in the "Flat Organization," there are only a few levels in the hierarchy, and the span of control is relatively wide. Both organizations depicted here have 31 positions, but these are arranged differently, as you can see.

It is important to note that the organization chart may not reflect a manager's actual span of control perfectly. Other factors not immediately forthcoming from the chart itself may be involved. For example, managers may have additional responsibilities that do not appear on the chart—notably, assignments on various committees. Moreover, some subordinates (e.g., people new to the job) might require more attention than others. Also, the degree of supervisory control needed may increase (e.g., when jobs change), or decrease (e.g., when subordinates become more proficient).

span of control
The number of subordinates in an organization who are supervised by managers.

It is not readily possible to specify the "ideal" span of control that should be sought. Instead, it makes better sense to consider what form of organization is best suited to various purposes. For example, because supervisors in a military unit must have tight control over subordinates and get them to respond quickly and precisely, a narrow span of control is likely to be effective. As a result, military organizations tend to be extremely tall. In contrast, people working in a research and development lab must have an open exchange of ideas and typically require little managerial guidance to be successful. Units of this type tend to have very flat structures.

Division of Labor: Carving Up the Work to Be Done

division of labor
The process of dividing the many tasks performed within an organization into specialized jobs.

The standard organization chart makes clear that the many tasks to be performed within an organization are divided into specialized jobs, a process known as the **division of labor**. The more that tasks are divided into separate jobs, the more those jobs are *specialized* and the narrower the range of activities that job incumbents are required to perform. In theory, the fewer tasks a person performs, the better he or she may be expected to perform them, freeing others to perform the tasks that they perform best. Taken together, an entire organization is composed of people performing a collection of specialized jobs. This is probably the most obvious feature of an organization that can be observed from the organizational chart.

As you might imagine, the degree to which employees perform specialized jobs is likely to depend on the size of the organization. The larger the organization, the more opportunities for specialization are likely to exist. For example, an individual working in a large advertising agency may get to specialize in a highly narrow field, such as writing jingles for radio and TV spots for automobiles. By contrast, someone working at a much smaller agency may be required to do all writing of print and broadcast ads in addition to helping out with the artwork and meeting with clients. Obviously, the larger company might be expected to reap the benefits of using the talents of employees efficiently (a natural result of an extensive division of labor). As companies downsize, however, many managerial jobs become less specialized. For example, at General Electric, quite a few middle-management positions have been eliminated in recent years. As a consequence, the remaining managers must perform a wider variety of jobs, making their own jobs less specialized.[8] You can see this relationship in our summary in Table 15.1.

Line Versus Staff Positions: Decision Makers Versus Advisers

line positions
Positions in an organization in which people can make decisions related to doing its basic work.

staff positions
Positions in organizations in which people make recommendations to others, but are not themselves involved in making decisions concerning the organization's day-to-day operations.

The organization chart shown in Figure 15.2 reveals an additional distinction that deserves to be highlighted—that between *line positions* and *staff positions*. People occupying **line positions** (e.g., the various vice presidents and managers) have decision-making power. However, the individual shown in the dotted box set off to the right—the legal counsel—cannot make decisions, but provides advice and recommendations to be used by the line managers. Such an individual may help corporate officials decide whether a certain product name can be used without infringing on copyright restrictions.

In many of today's organizations, human resource managers may be seen as occupying **staff positions** because they provide specialized services regarding testing and interviewing procedures as well as information about the latest laws on personnel discrimination. However, the ultimate decisions on personnel selection might be made by more senior managers in specialized areas—that is, staff managers. Various assistants

TABLE 15.1 Division of Labor: A Summary

Low and high levels of division of labor can be characterized with respect to the three dimensions shown here.

Dimension	Division of Labor	
	Low	High
Degree of specialization	General tasks	Highly specialized tasks
Typical organizational size	Small	Large
Economic efficiency	Inefficient	Highly efficient

also fall into this category, holding staff positions. For an example from a large government agency, see Figure 15.5.

Differences between line and staff personnel are not unusual. Such differences may arouse conflict or even may be used to create intentional sources of conflict. For example, when Harold S. Geneen was the CEO of International Telephone and Telegraph (ITT, which now is in the hotel, insurance, and defense contracting business), staff specialists in the areas of planning and strategy were regularly brought in from headquarters to challenge the decisions made by line managers in an attempt to "keep them on their toes."[9]

Sociologists have noted that staff managers tend to be younger, better educated, and more committed to their fields than the organizations employing them.[10] Line managers might feel more committed not only because of the greater opportunities they have to exercise decisions, but also because they are more likely to perceive themselves as part of a company rather than as an independent specialist (whose identity lies primarily within his or her specialty area).

Decentralization: Delegating Power Downward

During the first half of the twentieth century, as companies grew larger and larger, they shifted power and authority into the hands of a few upper-echelon administrators—executives whose decisions influenced the many people below them in the organizational hierarchy. In fact, it was during the 1920s that Alfred P. Sloan, Jr., president of General Motors at the time, introduced the notion of a "central office"—the place where a few individuals made policy decisions for the entire company.[11] As part of Sloan's plan, decisions regarding the day-to-day operation of the company were pushed lower and lower down the organizational hierarchy, allowing those individuals who were most affected to make the decisions. This process of delegating power from higher to lower levels within organizations is known as **decentralization**. It is the opposite, of course, of *centralization*, the tendency for just a few powerful individuals or groups to hold most of the decision-making power.

decentralization
The extent to which authority and decision making are spread throughout all levels of an organization rather than being reserved for top management (centralization).

Earlier, we mentioned that flattening of organizational hierarchies has made it possible to make organizations more streamlined by eliminating many middle-management jobs. This is in keeping with the tendency toward decentralization. After all, as people are empowered to make their own decisions, they don't have to have as many supervisors to whom they must report. As a result, organization charts might show fewer positions as decision-making authority is pushed farther down the hierarchy. We see this today as many organizations are moving toward decentralization to promote managerial efficiency and to improve employee satisfaction (the result of giving people greater opportunities to take responsibility for their own actions; see Chapter 6).[12]

It is important to note that decentralization is *not* always an ideal step for organizations to take. In fact, for some types of jobs, it may be a serious hindrance to productivity. Consider production-oriented positions, like assembly-line jobs. In a classic study, researchers found that decentralization improved the performance on some jobs—notably, the work of employees in a research lab—but interfered with the performance of people performing more routine, assembly-line jobs.[13] These findings make sense once you consider that people working in research and development positions are likely to enjoy the autonomy to make decisions that decentralization allows, whereas people working on production jobs are likely to be less interested in taking responsibility for decisions and actually may welcome *not* having to take such responsibility. For a summary of the relative advantages and disadvantages of centralization, see Table 15.2 on page 592.

With this in mind, portions of many high-tech companies—including various units within Hewlett-Packard, Intel Corporation, Philips Electronics, and Lucent Technology—have introduced decentralized designs.[14] When this happens, large companies are able to operate with the agility of smaller ones, which is vital in the fast-paced world of high technology—at least, in theory. As it works out, they are not doing so perfectly. It has been reported that many of the large companies that are doing this are not setting up their Web sites so as to reflect their decentralized form. The home pages of many high-tech companies still reflect the deep complexity of their massive sizes, making it difficult to communicate with the ease of smaller firms.[15] (For some guidelines on designing highly flexble high-tech organizations, see the *How to Do It* section on p. 592.)

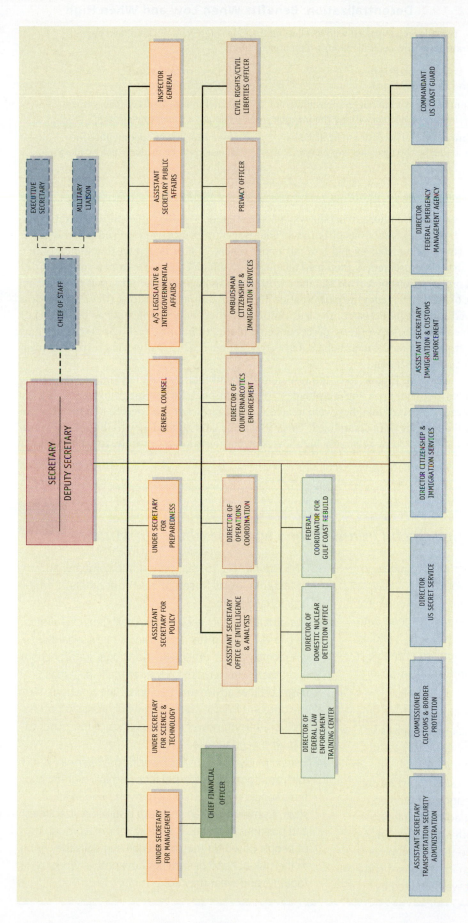

FIGURE 15.5

Line Versus Staff Positions in the U.S. Department of Homeland Security

The upper echelons of the U.S. Department of Homeland Security are organized as shown here. Note how the Chief of Staff, the Executive Secretary, and the Military Liaison have staff positions whereas all others on this organization chart have line positions.

Source: U.S. Department of Homeland Security, 2005.

TABLE 15.2 Decentralization: Benefits When Low and When High

Various benefits are associated with low decentralization (high centralization) and high decentralization (low centralization) within organizations.

Low Decentralization (High Centralization)	High Decentralization (Low Centralization)
■ Eliminates the additional responsibility not desired by people performing routine jobs	■ Can eliminate levels of management, making a leaner organization
■ Permits crucial decisions to be made by individuals who have the "big picture"	■ Promotes greater opportunities for decisions to be made by people closest to problems

Research has indicated that the way people respond to different levels of centralization is based on their perceptions of fairness: That is, centralization is perceived as being fairer under some circumstances and less fair under others.[16] This is demonstrated clearly in a study in which researchers examined the degree to which employees from a variety of different organizations perceived that their work unit was centralized.[17] This was measured in terms of their frequency of participation in organizational decisions (the more people believed to have participated, the less centralized their unit was labeled as being). They also measured these workers' perceptions of interactional justice—that is (as you may recall from Chapter 2), their beliefs that they are treated in a sensitive and respectful manner by the organization.

As shown in Figure 15.6, the researchers found that the relationship between these variables depended on the employees' organizational level. Specifically, high-level employees perceived that they were treated fairly regardless of the degree to which organizational decisions were centralized. This reflects the general tendency for high-level workers, who tend to enjoy relatively high levels of participation as a whole, to feel positively

How to Do It

Designing High-Tech Organizations with Flexibility in Mind

Most of what we have said about designing organizations is based on traditional technology. However, because today's high-tech world is so fast-paced, it is essential for today's well-designed high-tech firm to be designed with one key factor in mind: *flexibility.* In other words, it should have organizational structures and designs that enable it to "turn on a dime." This is accomplished in several ways.[18]

1. High-tech firms should be extremely flat, and have *little or no vertical hierarchy.* Because their world moves so rapidly, there is no time for the slow responses associated with seeking decisions from higher up.

2. In high-tech firms *organizational designs must be permitted to change frequently.* A design that worked when a company was small and made only a few products might be less effective after it has grown. As a case in point consider ROLM, the telecommunications company that operated as an independent company from 1969 to 1984, when it was acquired by

IBM. During this 15-year period, the company grew so fast that it was forced to have four different organizational designs.

3. *The distinction between line and staff functions should be blurred.* Thus, instead of having some specialists who merely advise others (the traditional staff function) and others who have the power to make decisions based on that advice (the traditional line function), the use of teams in many high-tech work groups is putting decision-making power into the hands of those individuals who need to take action.

4. Instead of dividing jobs into specific predetermined roles and formal hierarchical relationships, high-tech firms should *rely on informal networks and relationships.* Continuous changes make institutionalized roles and positions impractical. Instead, informal groupings of people based on the knowledge and skills they bring to the task at hand determines how people work together and what they do.

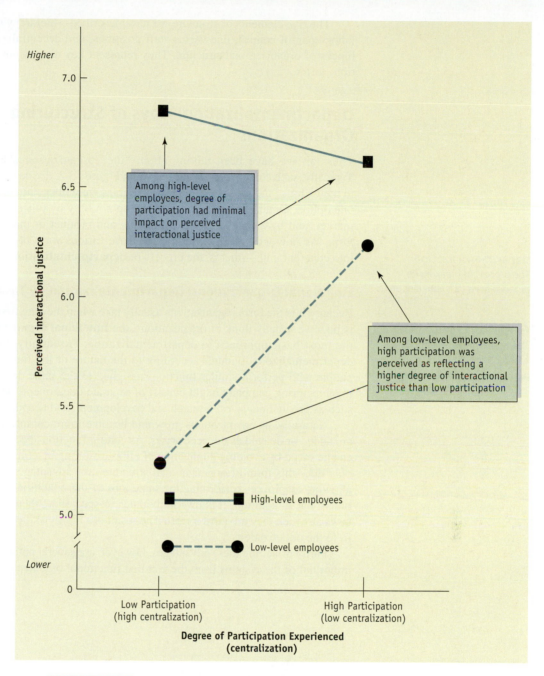

FIGURE 15.6

The Perceived Fairness of Centralization: Research Findings

A recent study found that low-level employees perceived that they were treated more fairly when their organizations were low in centralization—that is, when they believed they had good opportunities to participate in the making of decisions. However, the effects of centralization were minimal in the case of high-level employees (for whom participation tends to be high to begin with).

Source: Based on data reported by Schminke, Cropanzano, & Rupp, 2002; see Note 17.

about their work. By contrast, level of centralization made a very big difference for low-level employees. Specifically, the more low-level workers were allowed to participate in the making of decisions (i.e., the less decision making was considered centralized), the more fairly they believe they were treated. This reflects the tendency for lower-level employees to place a high value on participation because as a whole they tend to get so little out of it. As a result, the more low-level employees are given an opportunity to participate, the more positively this reflects in their eyes on the fairness of the organization.

The five elements of structure we have described—hierarchy of authority, division of labor, span of control, line versus staff positions, and decentralization—are the building blocks of organizational structure. They represent key dimensions along which organizations differ.

Departmentalization: Ways of Structuring Organizations

Thus far, we have been talking about "the" organization chart of an organization. Typically, such charts, like the one shown in Figure 15.2, divide the organization according to the various functions performed. However, as we will explain in this section, this is only one option. Organizations can be divided up not only by function, but also by product or market, and by a special blend of function and product or market known as the *matrix form*. We now will take a closer look at these various ways of breaking up organizations into coherent units—that is, the process of **departmentalization**.

departmentalization
The process of breaking up organizations into coherent units.

Functional Organizations: Departmentalization by Task

Because it is the form organizations usually take when they are first created, and because it is how we usually think of organizations, the **functional organization** can be considered the most basic approach to departmentalization. Essentially, functional organizations departmentalize individuals according to the nature of the functions they perform, with people who perform similar functions assigned to the same department. For example, a manufacturing company might consist of separate departments devoted to basic functions such as production, sales, research and development, and accounting (see Figure 15.7).

functional organization
The type of departmentalization based on the activities or functions performed (e.g., sales, finance).

Naturally, as organizations grow and become more complex, additional departments are added or deleted as the need arises. As certain functions become centralized, resources can be saved by avoiding duplication of effort, resulting in a higher level of efficiency. Not only does this form of organizational structure take advantage of economies of scale (by allowing employees performing the same jobs to share facilities and not duplicating functions), but in addition, it allows individuals to specialize, thereby performing only those tasks at which they are most expert. The result is a highly skilled workforce, a direct benefit to the organization.

Partly offsetting these advantages, however, are several potential limitations. The most important of these stems from the fact that functional organizational structures encourage

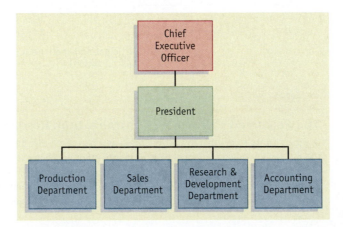

FIGURE 15.7

Functional Organization of a Typical Manufacturing Firm

Functional organizations are ones in which departments are formed on the basis of common functions performed. In the hypothetical manufacturing firm shown in this simplified organization chart, four typical functional departments are identified. In specific organizations the actual functions may differ.

separate units to develop their own narrow perspectives and to lose sight of overall organizational goals. For example, in a manufacturing company, an engineer might see the company's problems in terms of the reliability of its products and lose sight of other key considerations, such as market trends, overseas competition, and so on. Such narrow-mindedness is the inevitable result of functional specialization—the downside of people seeing the company's operations through a narrow lens.

A related problem is that functional structures discourage innovation (see Chapter 14) because they channel individual efforts toward narrow, functional areas and do not encourage coordination and cross-fertilization of ideas between areas. As a result, functional organizations are slow to respond to the challenges and opportunities they face from the environment (such as the need for new products and services). In summary, although functional organizations certainly are logical in nature and have proven useful in many contexts, they are by no means the perfect way to departmentalize people in organizations.

Product Organizations: Departmentalization by Type of Output

product organization

The type of departmentalization based on the products (or product lines) produced.

Organizations—at least successful ones—do not stand still; they change constantly in size and scope. As they develop new products and seek new customers, they might find that a functional structure doesn't work as well as it once did. Manufacturing a wide range of products using a variety of different methods, for example, might put a strain on the manufacturing division of a functional organization. Similarly, keeping track of the varied tax requirements for different types of business (e.g., restaurants, farms, real estate, manufacturing) might pose quite a challenge for a single financial division of a company. In response to such strains, a **product organization** might be created. This type of departmentalization creates self-contained divisions, each of which is responsible for everything to do with a certain product or group of products. (For a look at the structure of a product organization, see Figure 15.8.)

When organizations are departmentalized by products, separate divisions are established, each of which is devoted to a certain product or group of products. Each unit contains all the resources needed to develop, manufacture, and sell its products. The organization is composed of separate divisions operating independently, the heads of which report to top management. Although some functions might be centralized within the parent company (e.g., human resources management or legal staff), on a day-to-day basis each division operates autonomously as a separate company or, as accountants call them, *cost centers* of their own.

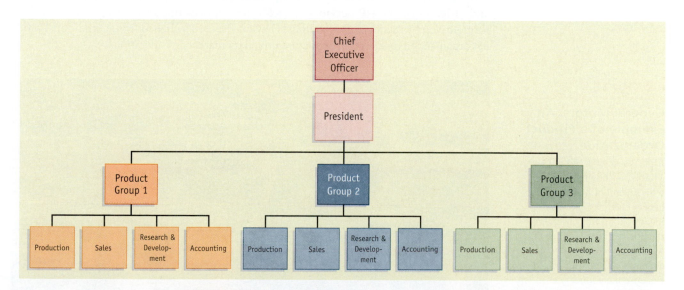

FIGURE 15.8

A Product Organization

In a *product organization,* separate units are established to handle different products or product lines. Each of these divisions contains all of the departments necessary for operating as an independent unit.

Consider, for example, how separate divisions of General Motors are devoted to manufacturing cars, trucks, locomotives, refrigerators, auto parts, and the like. The managers of each division can devote their energies to one particular business (see Figure 15.9). Organizations may benefit from a marketing perspective as well. Take Toyota, for example. In 1989 it introduced its Lexus line of luxury cars. By creating a separate division, manufactured in separate plants and sold by a separate network of dealers, the company made its higher-priced cars look special and avoided making its less expensive cars look less appealing by putting them together with superior products on the same showroom floors. Applying the same reasoning to a completely different market, Toyota launched its Scion line in 2003 to appeal to younger car buyers.

Product organizations also have several drawbacks. The most obvious of these is the loss of economies of scale stemming from the duplication of various departments within operating units. For example, if each unit carries out its own research and development functions, the need for costly equipment, facilities, and personnel is multiplied. Another problem associated with product designs involves the organization's ability to attract and retain talented employees. Since each department within operating units is necessarily smaller than a single combined one would be, opportunities for advancement and career development may suffer. This, in turn, may pose a serious problem with respect to the long-term retention of talented employees. Finally, problems of coordination across product lines may arise. In fact, in extreme cases, actions taken by one operating division may have adverse effects on the outcomes of one or more others.

A clear example of such problems is provided by Hewlett-Packard, a major manufacturer of computers, printers, and scientific test equipment.[19] For most of its history, Hewlett-Packard adopted a product design. It consisted of scores of small, largely autonomous divisions, each concerned with producing and selling certain products. As it grew—merging with Compaq in 2002—the company found itself in an increasingly untenable situation in which sales representatives from different divisions sometimes attempted to sell different lines of equipment, often to be used for the same basic purposes, to the same customers.

To deal with such problems, top management at Hewlett-Packard reorganized the company into four sectors—what they call "business groups"—based on the markets they serve: the Enterprise Systems Group (which provides information technology hardware for businesses), the Imaging and Printing Group (which focuses on printers for businesses and consumers), the Personal Systems Group (which focuses on personal computers for home and office use), and HP Services (which offers information technology services).[20] In short, driven by market considerations, Hewlett-Packard switched from a traditional product organization to an internal structure driven by market considerations.

FIGURE 15.9

General Motors: An Example of a Product Organization

Rick Wagoner, CEO of General Motors, is shown here along with several of his company's latest vehicles. Since its inception, GM has been divided into distinct divisions, each of which designs, manufactures, and sells a separate line of cars. Because the company is organized with respect to different product lines, GM is considered an example of a *product organization.*

Matrix Organizations: Departmentalization by Both Function and Product

When the aerospace industry was first developing, the U.S. government demanded that a single manager in each company be assigned to each of its projects so that it was immediately clear who was responsible for the progress of each project. In response to this requirement, TRW established a "project leader" for each project, someone who shared authority with the leaders of the existing functional departments.[21] This temporary arrangement later evolved into what is called a **matrix organization**, the type of organization in which an employee is required to report to both a functional (or division) manager and the manager of a specific project (or product). In essence, they developed a complex type of organizational structure that combines both the function and product forms of departmentalization.[22] Matrix organizational forms have been used in many organizations, such as Citibank and Liberty Mutual Insurance.[23] To better understand matrix organizations, examine the organization chart shown in Figure 15.10.

Employees in matrix organizations have two bosses (or, more technically, they are under *dual authority*). One line of authority, shown by the vertical axes on Figure 15.9, is *functional*, managed by vice presidents in charge of various functional areas. The other, shown by the horizontal axes, is *product* (or it may be a specific project or temporary business), managed by specific individuals in charge of certain products (or projects).

In matrix designs, there are three major roles. First, there is the *top leader*—the individual who has authority over both lines (the one based on function and the one based on product or project). It is this individual's task to enhance coordination between functional and product managers and to maintain an appropriate balance of power between them. Second, there are the *matrix bosses*—people who head functional departments or specific projects. Since neither functional managers nor project managers have complete authority over subordinates, they

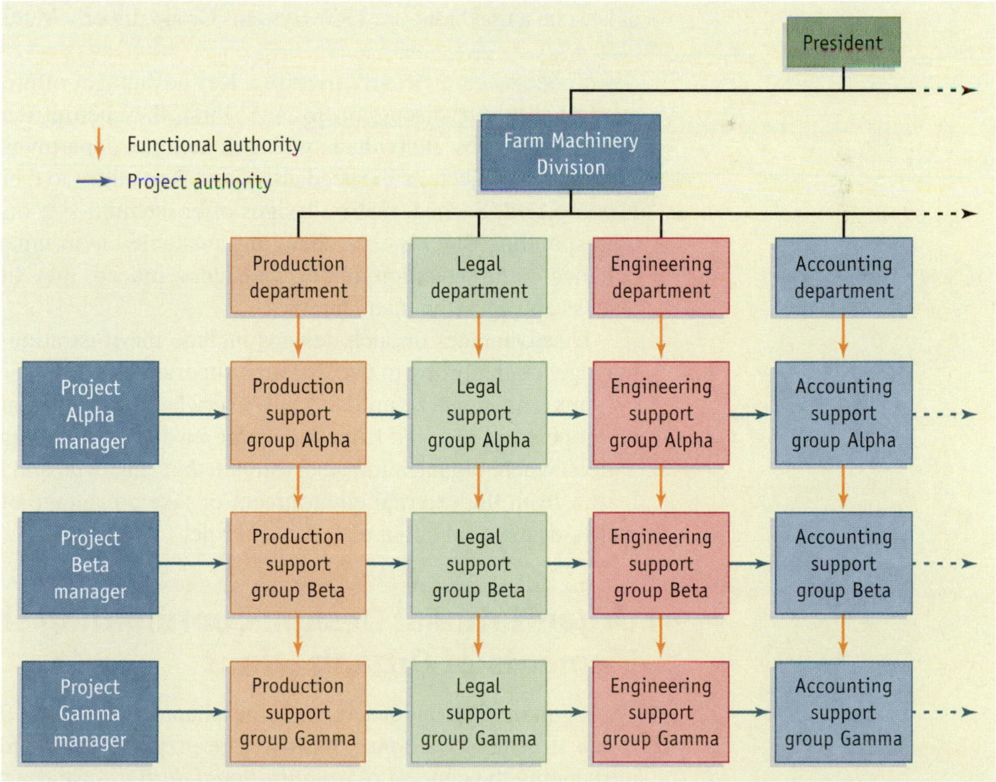

matrix organization
The type of organization in which a product or project form is superimposed on a functional form.

FIGURE 15.10

A Typical Matrix Organization

In a *matrix organization,* a portion of which is depicted here, a product structure is superimposed on a basic functional structure. This results in a dual system of authority in which some managers report to two bosses—a project (or product) manager, and a functional (departmental) manager.

must work together to ensure that their efforts mesh rather than conflict. In addition, they must agree on issues such as promotions and raises for specific people working under their joint authority. Finally, there are *two-boss managers*—people who must report to both product and functional managers and attempt to balance the demands of each.

Key Considerations. Not all organizations using the matrix structure do so on a permanent basis. Several partial, or temporary, types of matrix design have been identified.[24] First, the *temporary overlay* is a form of matrix structure in which projects are crossed with functions on a special, short-term basis. This is in contrast to a *permanent overlay,* in which project teams are kept going after each project is completed. Finally, there are *mature matrix organizations,* those in which both the functional lines and the product lines are permanent and equally strong within the organization.

With a matrix organization that has been in effect for over 25 years, Dow Corning is an example of a mature matrix organization.[25] At this company, each functional representative reports to the leaders of his or her own department, while also contributing to the design and operation of the particular product line for which he or she is responsible. Because people working in this fashion have two bosses, they must have sufficient freedom to attain their objectives. As you might imagine, a fair amount of coordination, flexibility, openness, and trust is essential for such a program to work, suggesting that not everyone adapts well to such a system.

Organizations are most likely to adopt matrix designs when they confront certain conditions. These include a complex and uncertain environment (one with frequent changes) and the need for economies of scale in the use of internal resources. Specifically, a matrix approach is often adopted by medium-size organizations with several product lines that do not possess sufficient resources to establish fully self-contained operating units. Under such conditions, a matrix design provides a useful compromise. Some companies that have adopted this structure, at least on a trial basis, are TRW Systems Group, Liberty Mutual Insurance, and Citibank.[26]

Advantages and Disadvantages. Key advantages offered by matrix designs have been suggested by our discussion so far.[27] First, they permit flexible use of an organization's human resources. Individuals within functional departments can be assigned to specific products or projects as the need arises and then return to their regular duties when this task is completed. Second, matrix designs offer medium-size organizations an efficient means of responding quickly to a changing, unstable environment. Third, such designs often enhance communication among managers; indeed, they literally force matrix bosses to discuss and agree on many matters.

Disadvantages of such designs include the frustration and stress faced by two-boss managers in reporting to two different supervisors, the danger that one of the two authority systems (functional or product) will overwhelm the other, and the consistently high levels of cooperation required from the people involved for the organization to succeed.[28] In situations where organizations must stretch their financial and human resources to meet challenges from the external environment or take advantage of new opportunities, however, matrix designs can often play a useful role.

Organizational Design: Coordinating the Structural Elements of Organizations

We began the first major section of this chapter by likening the structure of an organization to the structure of a house. Now we are prepared to extend that analogy for purposes of introducing the concept of *organizational design.* Just as a house is designed in a particular fashion by combining its structural elements in various ways, so too can an organization be designed by combining its basic elements in certain ways. Accordingly, **organizational design** refers to the process of coordinating the structural elements of organizations in the most appropriate manner.

As you might imagine, this is no easy task. Although we might describe some options that sound neat and rational on the next few pages, in reality this is hardly ever the case.

organizational design
The process of coordinating the structural elements of an organization in the most appropriate manner.

Even the most precisely designed organizations will face the need to change at one time or another, adjusting to the realities of technological changes, political pressures, accidents, and so on. Organizational designs might also be changed purposely in an attempt to improve operating efficiency, such as the promise by some recent U.S. presidents to streamline the huge federal bureaucracy.

Our point is simple: Because organizations operate within a changing world, their own designs must be capable of changing as well. Those organizations that are either poorly designed or inflexible cannot survive. If you consider the large number of banks and airlines that have gone out of business in the last few years because of their inability to deal with rapid changes brought about by deregulation and a shifting economy, you'll get a good idea of the ultimate consequences of ineffective organizational design.

Classical and Neoclassical Approaches: The Quest for the One Best Design

The earliest theorists interested in organizational design did not operate out of awareness of the point we just made regarding the need for organizations to be flexible. Instead, they approached the task of designing organizations as a search for "the one best way." Although today we are more attuned to the need to adapt organizational designs to various environmental and social conditions, theorists in the early and middle part of the twentieth century sought to establish the ideal form for all organizations under all conditions—the universal design.

In Chapter 1, we described the efforts of organizational scholars such as Max Weber, Frederick Taylor, and Henri Fayol. These theorists believed that effective organizations were ones that had a formal hierarchy, a clear set of rules, specialization of labor, highly routine tasks, and a highly impersonal working environment. You may recall that Weber referred to this organizational form as a *bureaucracy*. This **classical organizational theory** has fallen into disfavor because it is insensitive to human needs and is not suited to a changing environment. Unfortunately, the "ideal" form of an organization, according to Weber, did not take into account the realities of the world within which it operates. Apparently, what is ideal is not necessarily what is realistic.

In response to these conditions, and with inspiration from the Hawthorne studies, the classical approach to the bureaucratic model gave way to more of a human relations orientation. Organizational scholars such as McGregor, Argyris, and Likert attempted to improve upon the classical model—which is why their approach is labeled **neoclassical organizational theory**—by arguing that economic effectiveness is not the only goal of an industrial organization, but also employee satisfaction.

Specifically, Douglas McGregor was an organizational theorist who objected to the rigid hierarchy imposed by Weber's bureaucratic form because it was based on negative assumptions about people—primarily that they lacked ambition and wouldn't work unless coerced (the *Theory X* approach).[29] In contrast, McGregor argued that people desire to achieve success by working and that they seek satisfaction by behaving responsibly (the *Theory Y* approach). Another neoclassical theorist, Chris Argyris, expressed similar ideas.[30] Specifically, he argued that managerial domination of organizations blocks basic human needs to express oneself and to successfully accomplish tasks. Such dissatisfaction, he argues, would encourage turnover and lead to poor performance.

An additional neoclassical theorist, Rensis Likert, shared these perspectives, arguing that organizational performance is enhanced not by rigidly controlling people's actions, but by actively promoting their feelings of self-worth and their importance to the organization.[31] An effective organization, Likert proposed, was one in which individuals would have a great opportunity to participate in making organizational decisions—what he called a *System 4 organization*. Doing this, he claimed, would enhance employees' personal sense of worth, motivating them to succeed. Likert called the opposite type of organization *System 1*, the traditional form in which organizational power is distributed in the hands of a few top managers who tell lower-ranking people what to do. (*System 2* and *System 3* are intermediate forms between the System 1 and System 4 extremes.)

The organizational design implications of these neoclassical approaches are clear. In contrast to the classical approach, calling for organizations to be designed with a rigid, tall

classical organizational theory
Approaches assuming that there is a single best way to design organizations.

neoclassical organizational theory
An attempt to improve upon the classical organizational theory which argues that economic effectiveness is not the only goal or organizational structure, but also employee satisfaction.

hierarchy, with a narrow span of control (allowing managers to maintain close supervision over their subordinates), the neoclassical approach argues for designing organizations with flat hierarchical structures (minimizing managerial control over subordinates) and a high degree of decentralization (encouraging employees to make their own decisions). (For a summary of these differences, see Figure 15.11.) Indeed, such design features may well serve the underlying neoclassical philosophy.

Like the classical approach, the neoclassical approach also may be faulted on the grounds that it is promoted as "the one best approach" to organizational design. Although the benefits of flat, decentralized designs may be many, to claim that this represents the universal, ideal form for all organizations would be naive. In response to this criticism, more contemporary approaches to organizational design have given up on finding the one best way to design organizations in favor of finding designs that are most appropriate to various circumstances and contexts within which organizations operate. We now turn to such approaches.

The Contingency Approach: Design According to Environmental Conditions

contingency approach to organizational design

The contemporary approach that recognizes that no one approach to organizational design is best, but that the best design is the one that best fits with the existing environmental conditions.

The idea that the best design for an organization depends on the nature of the environment in which the organization is operating lies at the heart of the modern **contingency approach to organizational design.** We use the term "contingency" here in a manner similar to the way we used it in our discussion of leadership (see Chapter 13). But rather than considering the best approach to leadership for a given situation, we are considering the best way to design an organization given the environment within which the organization functions.

The External Environment: Its Connection to Organizational Design. It is widely assumed that the most appropriate type of organizational design depends on the organization's *external environment*. In general, the external environment is the sum of all the forces impinging on an organization with which it must deal effectively if it is to survive.[32] These forces include general work conditions, such as the economy, geography, and national resources, as well as the specific task environment within which the company operates—notably, its competitors, customers, workforce, and suppliers.

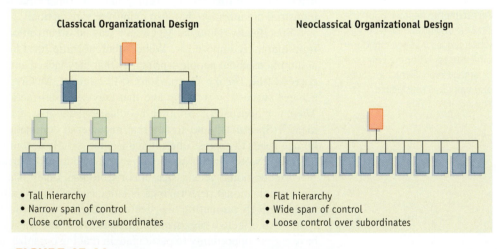

• Tall hierarchy
• Narrow span of control
• Close control over subordinates

• Flat hierarchy
• Wide span of control
• Loose control over subordinates

FIGURE 15.11

Classical Versus Neoclassical Designs: A Summary

The *classical approach* to designing organizations assumed that managers needed to have close control over their subordinates. As such, it called for designing organizations with tall hierarchies and narrow spans of control. In contrast, the *neoclassical approach* to designing organizations assumed that managers did not have to carefully monitor their subordinates. As such, it called for designing organizations with flat hierarchies and wide spans of control.

Let's consider some examples. Banks operate within an environment that is highly influenced by the general economic environment (e.g., interest rates and government regulations) as well as a task environment sensitive to other banks' products (e.g., types of accounts) and services (e.g., service hours, access to account information by computers and/or telephone), the needs of the customer base (e.g., direct deposit for customers), the availability of trained personnel (e.g., individuals suitable for entry-level positions), as well as the existence of suppliers providing goods and services (e.g., automated teller equipment, surveillance equipment, computer workstations) necessary to deliver services. Analogous examples can be found in other industries as well. For example, think about the environmental forces faced by the airlines, the computer industry, and automobile manufacturers. It's easy to recognize the features of their environments that must be taken into account when considering how organizations in these fields could be designed.

Although many features of the environment may be taken into account when considering how an organization should be designed, a classic investigation provides some useful guidance.[33] Scientists interviewed people in 20 industrial organizations in the United Kingdom to determine the relationship between managerial activities and the external environment. In so doing, they distinguished between organizations that operated in highly *stable*, unchanging environments, and those that operated in highly *unstable*, turbulent environments. For example, a rayon company in their sample operated in a highly stable environment: The environmental demands were predictable, people performed the same jobs in the same ways for a long time, and the organization had clearly defined lines of authority that helped get the job done. In contrast, a new electronics development company in their sample operated in a highly turbulent environment: Conditions changed on a daily basis, jobs were not well defined, and no clear organizational structure existed.

The researchers noted that many of the organizations studied tended to be described in ways that were appropriate for their environments. For example, when the environment is stable, people can do the same tasks repeatedly, allowing them to perform highly specialized jobs. However, in turbulent environments, many different jobs may have to be performed, and such specialization should not be designed into the jobs. Clearly, a strong link exists between the stability of the work environment and the proper organizational form. It was the researchers' conclusion that two different approaches to management existed and that these are largely based on the degree of stability within the external environment. These two approaches are known as **mechanistic organizations** and **organic organizations**.

Mechanistic Versus Organic Organizations: Designs for Stable Versus Turbulent Conditions.

mechanistic organization
An internal organizational structure in which people perform specialized jobs, many rigid rules are imposed, and authority is vested in a few top-ranking officials.

organic organization
An internal organizational structure in which jobs tend to be very general, there are few rules, and decisions can be made by lower-level employees.

If you've ever worked at a McDonald's restaurant, you probably know how highly standardized each step of the most basic operations must be.[34] Boxes of fries are to be stored 2 inches from the wall in stacks 1 inch apart. Making those fries is another matter—one that requires 19 distinct steps, each clearly laid out in a training film shown to new employees. The process is the same, whether it's done in Moscow, Idaho, or in Moscow, Russia. This is an example of a highly mechanistic task. Organizations can be highly mechanistic when conditions don't change. Although the fast-food industry has changed a great deal in recent years (with the introduction of new, healthier menu items, competitive pricing, and the like), the making of fries at McDonald's has not changed. The key to using mechanization is the lack of change. If the environment doesn't change, a highly mechanistic organizational form can be very efficient.

An environment is considered stable whenever there is little or no unexpected change in product, market demands, or technology. Have you ever seen an old-fashioned-looking bottle of E. E. Dickinson's witch hazel, which is used to cleanse the skin in the area of a wound? Since the company has been making the product following the same distillation process since 1866, it is certainly operating in a relatively stable manufacturing environment.[35] As we described earlier, stability affords the luxury of high employee specialization. Without change, people can easily specialize. When change is inevitable, however, specialization is impractical.

Mechanistic organizations can be characterized in several additional ways (for a summary, see Table 15.3). Not only do mechanistic organizations allow for a high degree of

TABLE 15.3 Mechanistic Versus Organic Designs: A Summary

Mechanistic designs and *organic designs* differ along several key dimensions identified here. These represent extremes; organizations can be relatively organic, relatively mechanistic, or somewhere in between.

	Structure	
Dimension	Mechanistic	Organic
Stability	Change unlikely	Change likely
Specialization	Many specialists	Many generalists
Formal rules	Rigid rules	Considerable flexibility
Authority	Centralized in few top people	Decentralized, diffused throughout the organization

specialization, but they also impose many rules. Authority is vested in a few people located at the top of a hierarchy who give direct orders to their subordinates. Mechanistic organizational designs tend to be most effective under conditions in which the external environment is stable and unchanging.

Now think about high-technology industries, such as those dedicated to computers, aerospace products, and biotechnology. Their environmental conditions are likely to be changing all the time. These industries are so prone to change that as soon as a new way of operating could be introduced into one of them, it would have to be altered. It isn't only technology, however, that makes an environment turbulent. Turbulence also can be high in industries in which adherence to rapidly changing regulations is essential. For example, times were turbulent in the hospital industry when new Medicaid legislation was passed, and times were turbulent in the nuclear power industry when governmental regulations dictated the introduction of many new standards that had to be followed. With the dominance of foreign automobiles in the United States, the once-stable American auto industry has faced turbulent times of late. Unfortunately, in this case, the design of the auto companies could not rapidly accommodate the changes needed for more organic forms (since the American auto industry was traditionally highly mechanistic).

The pure organic form of organization may be characterized in several different ways (see Table 15.3). The degree of job specialization possible is very low; instead, a broad knowledge of many different jobs is required. Very little authority is exercised from the top. Rather, self-control is expected, and an emphasis is placed on coordination between peers. As a result, decisions tend to be made in a highly democratic, participative manner. Be aware that the mechanistic and organic types of organizational structure described here are ideal forms. The mechanistic-organic distinction should be thought of as opposite poles along a continuum rather than as completely distinct options for organization. Certainly, organizations can be relatively organic or relatively mechanistic compared with others, but may not be located at either extreme.

Finally, organizational effectiveness is related to the degree to which an organization's structure (mechanistic or organic) is matched to its environment (stable or turbulent). In a classic study, researchers evaluated four departments in a large company—two of which manufactured containers (a relatively stable environment) and two of which dealt with communications research (a highly unstable environment).[36] One department in each pair was evaluated as being more effective than the other. It was found that for the container manufacturing departments, the more effective unit was the one structured in a highly mechanistic form (roles and duties were clearly defined). In contrast, the more effective communications research department was structured in a highly organic fashion (roles and duties were vague). Additionally, the other, less effective departments were structured in the opposite manner (i.e., the less effective manufacturing department was organically structured, and the less effective research department was mechanistically structured) (see Figure 15.12).

Taken together, the results made it clear that departments were most effective when their organizational structures fit their environments. This notion of "Which design is best

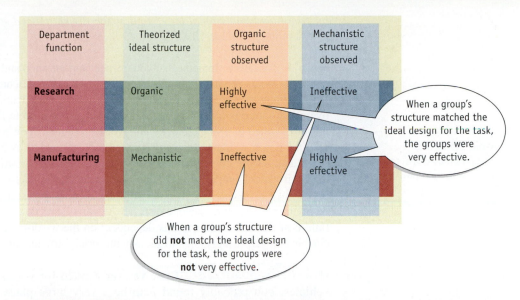

FIGURE 15.12

Matching Organizational Design and Industry: The Key to Effectiveness

In a classic study, researchers evaluated the performance of four departments in a large company. The most effective units were ones in which the way the group was structured (mechanistic or organic) matched the most appropriate form for the type of task performed (i.e., organic for research work and mechanistic for manufacturing work).

Source: Based on suggestions by Morse & Lorsch, 1970; see Note 36.

under which conditions?" lies at the heart of the modern orientation—the contingency approach—to organizational structure. Rather than specifying *which* structure is best, the contingency approach specifies *when* each type of organizational design is most effective.

Mintzberg's Framework: Five Organizational Forms

Although the distinction between mechanistic and organic designs is important, it is not terribly specific with respect to exactly how organizations should be designed. Filling this void, however, is the work of contemporary organizational theorist Henry Mintzberg.[37] Specifically, Mintzberg claims that organizations are composed of five basic elements, or groups of individuals, any of which may predominate in an organization. The one that does will determine the most effective design in that situation. The five basic elements are as follows:

- **The operating core:** Employees who perform the basic work related to the organization's product or service. Examples include teachers (in schools) and chefs and waiters (in restaurants).
- **The strategic apex:** Top-level executives responsible for running the entire organization. Examples include the entrepreneur who runs her own small business, and the general manager of an automobile dealership.
- **The middle line:** Managers who transfer information between the strategic apex and the operating core. Examples include middle managers, such as regional sales managers (who connect top executives with the sales force) and the chair of an academic department in a college or university (an intermediary between the dean and the faculty).
- **The technostructure:** Those specialists responsible for standardizing various aspects of the organization's activities. Examples include accountants, auditors, and computer systems analysts.
- **The support staff:** Individuals who provide indirect support services to the organization. Examples include consultants on technical matters and corporate attorneys.

What organizational designs best fit under conditions in which each of these five groups dominate? Mintzberg has identified five specific designs: *simple structure, machine*

operating core
Employees who perform the basic work related to an organization's product or service.

strategic apex
Top-level executives responsible for running an entire organization.

middle line
Managers who transfer information between higher and lower levels of the organizational hierarchy. (See *strategic apex* and *operating core.*)

technostructure
Organizational specialists responsible for standardizing various aspects of an organization's activities.

support staff
Individuals who provide indirect support services to an organization.

bureaucracy, professional bureaucracy, the *divisionalized structure,* and the *adhocracy* (see summary in Table 15.4).

Simple Structure. Imagine that you open an antique shop and hire a few people to help you out in the store. You have a small, informal organization in which there is a single individual with ultimate power. There is little in the way of specialization or formalization, and the overall structure is organic in nature. The hierarchy is quite flat, and all decision-making power is vested in a single individual—you. An organization so described, simple in nature, with the power residing at the strategic apex, is referred to by Mintzberg as having a **simple structure**. As you might imagine, organizations with simple structure can respond quickly to the environment and be very flexible. For example, the chef-owner of a small, independent restaurant can change the menu to suit the changing tastes of customers whenever needed, without first consulting anyone else. The down side of this, however, is that the success or failure of the entire enterprise is dependent on the wisdom and health of the individual in charge. Not surprisingly, organizations with simple structure are risky ventures.

Machine Bureaucracy. If you've ever worked for your state's department of motor vehicles, you probably found it to be a very large place, with numerous rules and procedures for employees to follow. The work is highly specialized (e.g., one person gives the vision tests, and another completes the registration forms), and decision making is concentrated at the top (e.g., you need to get permission from your supervisor to do anything other than exactly what's expected). This type of work environment is highly stable and does not have to change. An organization so characterized, where power resides with the technostructure, is referred to as a **machine bureaucracy**. Although machine bureaucracies can be highly efficient at performing standardized tasks, they tend to be dehumanizing and very boring for the employees.

Professional Bureaucracy. Suppose you are a doctor working at a large city hospital. You are a highly trained specialist with considerable expertise in your field. You don't need to check with anyone else before authorizing a certain medical test or treatment for your patient; you make the decisions as they are needed, when they are needed. At the same time, the environment is highly formal (e.g., there are lots of rules and regulations for you to follow). Of course, you do not work alone; you also require the services of other highly qualified professionals such as nurses and laboratory technicians. Organizations of this type—and these include universities, libraries, and consulting firms as well as hospitals—maintain power with the operating core, and are called **professional bureaucracies**. Such organizations can be highly effective because they allow employees to practice those skills for which they are best qualified. However, sometimes specialists become so overly

simple structure

An organization characterized as being small and informal, with a single powerful individual, often the founding entrepreneur, who is in charge of everything.

machine bureaucracy

An organizational form in which work is highly specialized, decision making is concentrated at the top, and the work environment is not prone to change (e.g., a government office).

professional bureaucracy

Organizations (e.g., hospitals and universities) in which there are lots of rules to follow, but employees are highly skilled and free to make decisions on their own.

TABLE 15.4 Mintzberg's Five Organizational Forms: A Summary

Mintzberg has identified five distinct organizational designs, each of which is likely to occur in organizations in which certain groups are in power.

Design	Description	Dominant Group	Example
Simple structure	Simple, informal, authority centralized in a single person	Strategic apex	Small, entrepreneurial business
Machine bureaucracy	Highly complex, formal environment with clear lines of authority	Technostructure	Government office
Professional bureaucracy	Complex, decision-making authority is vested in professionals	Operating core	University
Divisionalized structure	Large, formal organizations with several separate divisions	Middle line	Multidivisional business, such as General Motors
Adhocracy	Simple, informal, with decentralized authority	Support staff	Software development firm

Source: Based on suggestions by Mintzberg, 1983; see Note 37.

narrow that they fail to see the "big picture," leading to errors and potential conflict between employees.

Divisional Structure. When you think of large organizations, such as General Motors, Du Pont, Xerox, and IBM, the image that comes to mind is probably closest to what Mintzberg describes as **divisional structure**. Such organizations consist of a set of autonomous units coordinated by a central headquarters (i.e., they rely on departmental structure based on products, as described on pp. 595–596). In such organizations, because the divisions are autonomous (e.g., a General Motors employee at Buick does not have to consult with another at Chevrolet to do his or her job), division managers (the *middle line* part of Mintzberg's basic elements) have considerable control. Such designs preclude the need for top-level executives to think about the day-to-day operations of their companies and free them to concentrate on larger scale, strategic decisions. At the same time, companies organized into separate divisions frequently tend to have high duplication of effort (e.g., separate order processing units for each division). Having operated as separate divisions for the past 70 years, General Motors is considered the classic example of divisional structure.[38] Although the company has undergone many changes during this time—including the addition of the Saturn Corporation—it has maintained its divisional structure.

Adhocracy. After graduating from college, where you spent years learning how to program computers, you take a job at a small software company. Compared to your friends who found positions at large accounting firms, your professional life is much less formal. You work as a member of a team developing a new time-management software product. There are no rules, and schedules are made to be broken. You all work together, and although there is someone who is "officially" in charge, you'd never know it. Using Mintzberg's framework, you work for an **adhocracy**—an organization in which power resides with the support staff. Essentially, this is the epitome of the organic structure identified earlier. Specialists coordinate with each other not because of their shared functions (e.g., accounting, manufacturing), but as members of teams working on specific projects.

The primary benefit of the adhocracy is that it fosters innovation. Some large companies, such as Johnson & Johnson (J&J), nest within their formal divisional structure units that operate as adhocracies. In the case of J&J, it's the New Products Division, a unit that has been churning out an average of 40 products per year during recent years.[39] As in the case of all other designs there are disadvantages. In this case, the most serious limitations are their high levels of inefficiency (they are the opposite of machine bureaucracies in this regard), and the greatest potential for disruptive conflict.

The Vertically Integrated Organization

Recall our discussion of the Commercial Metals Company in this chapter's Preview Case (see pp. 583–584). One thing that makes this company so special is the fact that it relies on its own companies for supplies and raw materials (e.g., its recycling companies provide scrap metals that are recycled into sellable products). Companies of this type, which own their own suppliers and/or their own customers who purchase their products, are said to be involved in **vertical integration**. By contrast, companies that only assemble products that they buy from suppliers and sell to customers, such as Dell, are not vertically integrated.

For many years, Ford has been a good model of vertical integration because it has owned its own steel mills and its own financing arm for helping customers buy cars. This kind of efficiency associated with having built-in markets is a hallmark of vertically integrated companies, such as Ford and Commercial Metals Company. For a comparison between vertically integrated companies and non–vertically integrated companies, see Figure 15.13.

Despite the benefits of vertical integration, companies organized in this fashion often face special challenges.[40] For one, they tend to find it difficult to balance their resources in the most effective manner, providing exactly enough resources to be used in manufacturing and exactly the right number of finished products to be sold. A second drawback of vertical integration comes from the fact that because the company's suppliers are internal, they don't face competition to keep their prices down, potentially resulting in higher costs for

---

divisional structure
The form used by many large organizations, in which separate autonomous units are created to deal with entire product lines, freeing top management to focus on larger scale, strategic decisions.

adhocracy
A highly informal, organic organization in which specialists work in teams, coordinating with each other on various projects (e.g., many software development companies).

vertical integration
The practice in which companies own their own suppliers and/or their own customers who purchase their products from them.

FIGURE 15.13

The Vertically Integrated Organization

A vertically integrated organization, like the one summarized on the right, owns the suppliers and/or the customers with whom it does business (the blue boxes in this diagram). Because it is involved only in the assembly business, the organization summarized on the left is not considered vertically integrated.

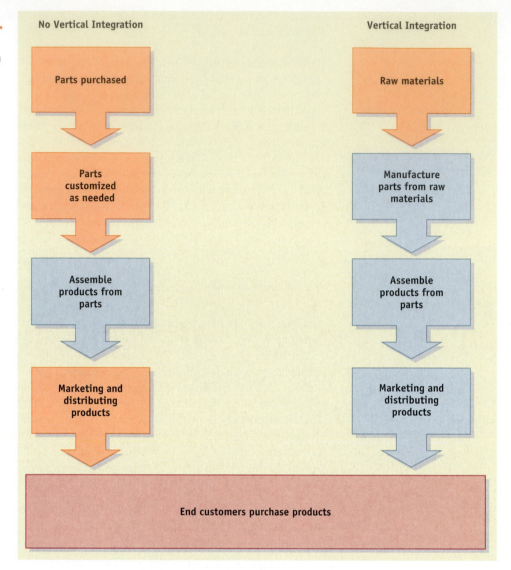

the company. Third, because the various parts of the organization are so tightly interconnected, it is very difficult for the organization to respond to changes, such as developing new products. Because this would involve changes in supplies, manufacturing, and sales, the vertically integrated company faces more challenges than its non–vertically integrated counterpart when it comes to making such changes.

Emerging Organizational Designs

Thus far, the organizational designs we have been describing have been around for a long time, and because they are so well known and often so effective, they are not likely to fade away anytime soon. However, during the past decade, several emerging forms of organizational design have come onto the scene. Given how popular and promising some of these seem to be, we will describe them here.

Team-Based Organizations

Given the growing popularity of work teams (see Chapter 8), it's not surprising that many of today's organizations rely on teams as their organizing structure. The idea is simple. Instead of organizing jobs in the traditional, hierarchical fashion by having a long chain of groups or individuals perform parts of a task (e.g., one group that sells the advertising job, another that plans the ad campaign, and yet another that produces the ads), *team-based*

team-based organizations
Organizations in which autonomous work teams are organized in parallel fashion such that each performs many different steps in the work process.

organizations have flattened hierarchies. Specifically, **team-based organizations** are organizations in which autonomous work teams are organized in parallel fashion such that each performs many different steps in the work process. Essentially, this approach calls for designing organizations around *processes* instead of tasks (see Figure 15.14).[41] For example, members of an advertising team may bring different skills and expertise to a single team responsible for all aspects of advertising.

Team-based organizations are ones in which teams focus on specific processes that need to get done instead of individual jobs. The horizontal organization is already a reality in at least parts of several of today's organizations—including AT&T (network systems division), Eastman Chemical (a division of Kodak), Hallmark Cards, and Xerox. Consider, for example, General Electric's factory in Bayamón, Puerto Rico. The 172 hourly workers, 15 salaried "advisers," plus a single manager manufacture "arresters" (surge protectors that guard power stations from lightning). That's the entire workforce; there are no support staff and no supervisors—only

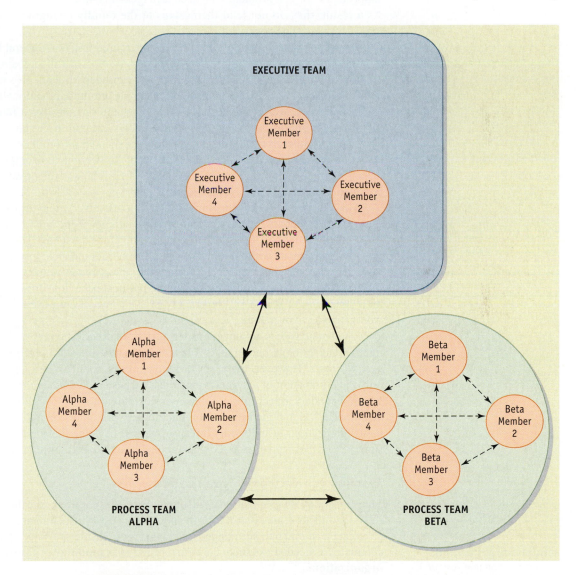

FIGURE 15.14

Team-Based Organizations

Instead of arranging individuals and tasks in hierarchical fashion, *team-based organizations* are designed with respect to the processes performed by various teams and the interconnections between them.

Source: Adapted from Mohrman et al., 1997; see Note 41.

about half as many people as you'd find in a conventional factory. Bayamón employees are formed into separate teams of approximately 10 widely skilled members who "own" such parts of the work as shipping and receiving, assembly, and so on. The teams do whatever is needed to get the job done; the advisers get involved only when necessary.

The Boundaryless Organization: Business Without Barriers

You hear it all the time: Someone is asked to do something, but responds defiantly, saying, "It's not my job." As uncooperative as this may seem, such a comment may make a great deal of sense when it comes to the traditional kind of organizational structures we've been describing—ones with layers of carefully connected boxes neatly stacked atop each other in hierarchical fashion. The advantage of these types of organizations is that they clearly define the roles of managers and employees. Everyone knows precisely what he or she is supposed to do. The problem with such arrangements, however, is that they are inflexible. As a result, they do not lend themselves to the rapidly changing conditions in which today's organizations operate.

boundaryless organization

An organization in which chains of command are eliminated, spans of control are unlimited, and rigid departments give way to empowered teams.

Sensitive to this limitation Jack Welch, the retired CEO of General Electric, proposed the **boundaryless organization**. This is an organization in which chains of command are eliminated, spans of control are unlimited, and rigid departments give way to empowered teams. Replacing rigid distinctions between people are fluid, intentionally ambiguous, and ill-defined roles. Welch's vision was that GE would operate like a family grocery store (albeit a $60 billion one)—one in which the barriers within the company that separate employees from each other and that separate the company from its customers and suppliers would be eliminated.[42] Although GE has not yet become the completely boundaryless organization Welch envisioned, it has made significant strides toward breaking down boundaries, as have other organizations.[43]

For boundaryless organizations to function effectively, they must meet many of the same requirements as successful teams. For example, there must be high levels of trust between all parties concerned. Also, everyone involved must have such high levels of skill that they can operate without much, if any, managerial guidance. Insofar as the elimination of boundaries weakens traditional managerial power bases, some executives may find it difficult to give up their authority, leading to political behavior. However, to the extent that the elimination of boundaries leverages the talents of all employees, such limitations are worth striving to overcome.

The boundaryless organizations we have been describing involve breaking down both internal and external barriers. As a result, they sometimes are referred to as *barrier-free organizations*. However, there are variations of the boundaryless organization involving only the elimination of external boundaries.[44] These include the *modular organization* (in which secondary aspects of the company's operations are outsourced) and the *virtual organization* (in which organizations combine forces with others on a temporary basis to form new organizations, usually only briefly). We will describe these below. Meanwhile, for a summary of these three related organizational designs, see Figure 15.15.

Modular (or Network) Organizations

Many of today's organizations outsource noncore functions to other companies while retaining full strategic control over their core business. Such companies may be thought of as having a central hub surrounded by networks of outside specialists that can be added or subtracted as needed. As such, they are referred to as **modular organizations** (or **network organizations**).[45]

modular organization

An organization that surrounds itself by a network of other organizations to which it regularly outsources noncore functions.

network organization

See modular organization.

As a case in point, you surely recognize Nike and Reebok as major designers and marketers of athletic shoes. However, you probably didn't realize that Nike's production facilities are limited, and that Reebok doesn't even have any plants of its own. Both organizations contract all their manufacturing to companies in countries such as Taiwan and South Korea where labor costs are low. In so doing, not only can they avoid making major investments in facilities, but they can concentrate on what they do best—tapping the changing tastes of their customers. While doing this, their suppliers can focus on rapidly retooling to make the new products.[46]

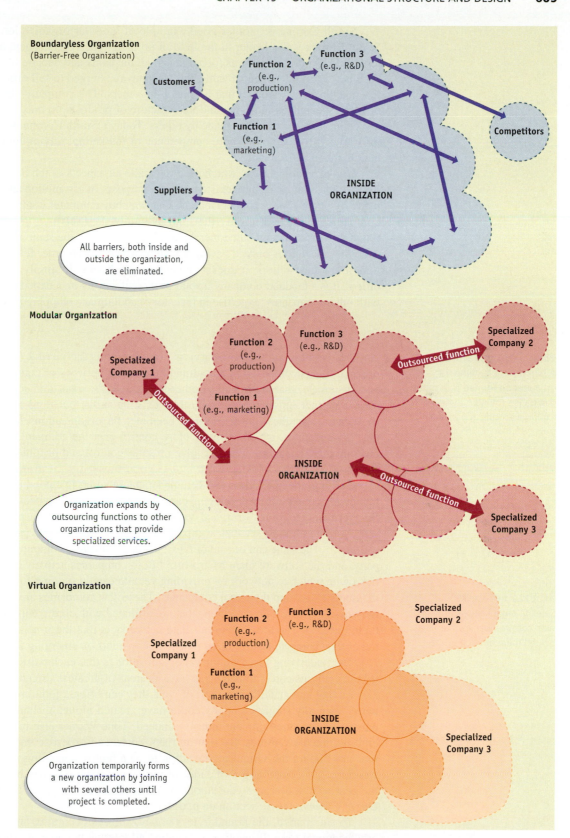

FIGURE 15.15

The Boundaryless Organization: Various Forms

The true boundaryless organization is free of both internal barriers and external barriers. Variants, such as the modular organization and the virtual organization, eliminate only external barriers. All forms of boundaryless organizations are growing in popularity.

Smith Corona is another good example of modular organization.[47] For 112 years, Smith Corona was a leader in the field of portable typewriters. Then, as word processing took hold, Smith Corona was forced to sell all its plants and declare bankruptcy. However, because the brand name had value, the company reemerged to sell office products (such as fax machines and phones) that are made by others. The company clearly switched from one that specialized in design and manufacture of products, to one that deals only in selling under its name products made by others. Today's Smith Corona is a modular company insofar as it focuses on its core competency of marketing, relying on other companies to handle the manufacturing.

Unlike Smith Corona, which used to handle all aspects of the office machine business itself, some companies have existed only for purposes of assembling and/or selling products made by others. For example, Dell and Gateway buy computer components made by other companies and perform only the final assembly themselves, putting together systems ordered by customers. Online merchants operate in much the same way. Amazon.com, for example, specializes only in having a Web presence and an order fulfillment facility. Other than a few best-sellers, it doesn't inventory any books. It simply processes and fulfills orders. It is a modular company insofar as it combines its own expertise in order fulfillment with other companies' expertise in inventory handling and shipping to serve its customers.

Virtual Organizations

virtual organization

A highly flexible, temporary organization formed by a group of companies that join forces to exploit a specific opportunity.

Another variation on the boundaryless organization is the **virtual organization**. Such an organization is composed of a continually evolving network of companies (e.g., suppliers and customers) that are linked together to share skills, costs, and access to markets. They form a partnership to capitalize on their existing skills, pursuing common objectives. In most cases, after these objectives have been met, the organizations disband.[48] Unlike modular organizations, which maintain close control over the companies with which they do outsourcing, virtual organizations give up some control and become part of a new organization, at least for a while.

Corning, the giant glass and ceramics manufacturer, is a good example of a company that builds upon itself by developing partnerships with other companies (including Siemens, the German electronics firm, and Vitro, the largest glass manufacturer from Mexico). In fact, Corning officials see their company not as a single entity, but as "a network of organizations."[49] The same can be said of NEC, the large Japanese computer and electronics company, and the software giant Microsoft.[50] Both companies actively develop new organizations with which to network by providing venture capital funding for current research staff members to develop their own companies. These new companies are referred to as **affiliate networks**—satellite organizations that are affiliated with core companies that have helped them develop. The idea behind affiliate networks is that these new firms can work with, rather than compete against, their much larger parents on emerging technology.[51]

affiliate networks

Satellite organizations affiliated with core companies that have helped them develop.

The underlying idea of a virtual organization is that each participating company contributes only its core competencies (i.e., its areas of greatest strength). By several companies mixing and matching the best of what they can offer, a joint product is created that is better than any single company could have created alone. Virtual corporations are not unusual in the entertainment industry. Indeed, Time Warner also has become part of several multimedia ventures. By sharing risks, costs, and expertise, many of today's companies are finding the virtual organization to be a highly appealing type of organizational structure. (As compelling as the idea of virtual organizations may be, they are not always the best way to design organizations. For a look at this issue, see the *OB: Making Sense Out of Common Sense* section on p. 611.)

To summarize, the boundaryless organization is becoming an increasingly popular organizational form. It involves eliminating all internal boundaries (such as those between employees) and external boundaries (such as those between the company and its suppliers). Variations on this organizational form involve only the elimination of external boundaries. These include the modular organization (in which secondary aspects of the company's operations are outsourced) and the virtual organization (in which organizations combine forces with others on a temporary basis to form new organizations, usually only briefly).

OB Making Sense Out of Common Sense

When Should Companies Go Virtual?

Form organizations as you need them by "going virtual." It just makes sense. Indeed, many of today's companies are finding it useful to downscale their hierarchies and network with other companies on an ad-hoc basis. Doing so allows them to move more quickly, standing a better chance of improving in a highly competitive environment.

As compelling as it may sound, you might want to think twice before jumping on the bandwagon because, despite what many believe, virtual organizations are far from perfect. When you think about it further you may realize that people from different companies do not share common values. As a result, interpersonal conflicts are likely to occur, and coordination is often challenging (see Chapter 11). This raises an important question: When should companies organize in a virtual manner?

The answer depends on how organizations fare with respect to two considerations: the type of capabilities the company needs, and the type of change that will be made.[52] Specifically, organizational changes may be either *autonomous* or *systemic*. **Autonomous change** is one that is made independently of other changes. For an example, an auto company that develops a new type of upholstery may do so without revising the rest of the car. **Systemic change** is such that change in one part of an organization requires changes in another part of that same organization. For example, Polaroid's development of instant photography required changes in both film and camera technologies.

A second key distinction involves the capabilities needed to complete the project. In some cases, outside capabilities are required. For example, in the early 1980s, IBM was able to develop its first personal computer in only 15 months because it went outside the company for expertise (e.g., buying chips from Intel and an operating system from Microsoft). Other times, capability can be found inside the company. For example, Ford traditionally develops many of the components used in its cars, making it less dependent on other companies (although it does far less of this than it used to).[53]

By combining these factors, it becomes clear when companies should "go virtual" and when they should work exclusively within their own walls. Virtual organizations work best for companies considering autonomous changes using technologies that exist only outside their walls. For example, Motorola has developed virtual organizations with several battery manufacturers for its cell phones and pagers. In so doing, it can focus on its core business—the delivery of wireless communication—while ensuring it has the battery power to make such devices work.

In contrast, companies should keep their focus inward when changes are systemic in nature and involve capabilities the company either already has or can create. Under such conditions, relying on outside help may be far too risky—and unnecessary. For example, these days Intel is making extensive investments to enhance its current and future capacities.

Finally, for conditions that fall between these extremes (i.e., when systemic changes are being made using capabilities that come only from outside the company, and when autonomous changes are being made using capabilities that must be created), virtual alliances should be created with extreme caution. Clearly, the virtual organization has a key place in today's organizational world. The trick, however, lies in understanding precisely what that place is. These guiding principles represent useful guidance in that respect.

---

autonomous change
A change in one part of an organization that is made independently of the need for change in another part.

systemic change
A change in one part of an organization that is related to change in another part of it.

conglomerate
A form of organizational diversification in which an organization (usually a very large, multinational one) adds an entirely unrelated business or product to its organizational design.

Interorganizational Designs: Going Beyond the Single Organization

All the organizational designs we have examined thus far have concentrated on the arrangement of units within an organization—what may be termed *intraorganizational designs*. However, sometimes at least some parts of different organizations must operate jointly. To coordinate their efforts on such projects, organizations must create *interorganizational designs*, plans by which two or more organizations come together. (For a tragic example of what occurs when such coordination fails to occur, see Figure 15.16.) Two such designs are commonly found: *conglomerates* and *strategic alliances*.

Conglomerates: Diversified "Megacorporations"

When an organization diversifies by adding an entirely unrelated business or product to its organizational design, it may be said to have formed a **conglomerate**. Some of the world's largest conglomerates may be found in Asia. For example, in Korea, companies such as

FIGURE 15.16

Interorganizational Coordination: Sometimes Tragic Results

When Hurricane Katrina struck the U.S. Gulf coast in the summer of 2005, its toll on people and property was dramatic. Given the storm's fury and the geographic vulnerability of the area it hit, destruction was inevitable. Not inevitable, however, was the human suffering that resulted from the ill-coordinated rescue efforts by public and private relief agencies. Officials from various organizations were unclear as to their jurisdiction, sometimes waiting for others to take action. The absence of a carefully organized plan in place by which the various organizations could coordinate their work made conditions frustrating and quite dangerous for victims and rescue workers alike, sometimes leading to tragic results. Learning from this episode, carefully developed plans have been drawn to facilitate coordination between the different organizations involved in responding to future disasters.

Samsung and Hyundai produce home electronics, automobiles, textiles, and chemicals in large, unified conglomerates known as *chaebols*.[54] These are all separate companies overseen by the same parent company leadership. In Japan, the same type of arrangement is known as a *keiretsu*.[55] A good example of a keiretsu is the Matsushita Group.[56] This enormous conglomerate consists of a bank (Asahi Bank), a consumer electronics company (Panasonic), and several insurance companies (e.g., Sumitomo Life, Nippon Life). These examples are not meant to suggest that conglomerates are unique to Asia. Indeed, many large U.S.-based corporations, such as IBM and Tenneco, are also conglomerates.

Companies form conglomerates for several reasons. First, as an independent business, the parent company can enjoy the benefits of diversification. Thus, as one industry languishes, another may excel, allowing for a stable economic outlook for the parent company. In addition, conglomerates may provide built-in markets and access to supplies, since companies typically support other organizations within the conglomerate. For example, General Motors cars and trucks are fitted with Delco radios, and Ford cars and trucks have engines with Autolite spark plugs, separate companies that are owned by their respective parent companies. In this manner conglomerates can benefit by providing a network of organizations that are dependent on each other for products and services, thereby creating considerable advantages.

Strategic Alliances: Joining Forces for Mutual Benefit

strategic alliance
A type of organizational design in which two or more separate companies combine forces to develop and operate a specific business. (See *mutual service consortia, joint ventures,* and *value-chain partnerships*.)

A **strategic alliance** is a type of organizational design in which two or more separate firms join their competitive capabilities to operate a specific business. The goal of a strategic alliance is to provide benefits to each individual organization that could not be attained if they operated separately. They are low-risk ways of diversifying (adding new business operations) and entering new markets. Some companies, such as GE and Ford, have strategic alliances with many others. Although some alliances last only a short time, others have remained in existence for well over 30 years and are still going strong.[57] For a good example of a strategic alliance, see Figure 15.17.

The Continuum of Alliances. A study of 37 strategic alliances from throughout the world identified three types of cooperative arrangements between organizations.[58] These may be arranged along a continuum from those alliances that are weak and distant, at one end, to those that are strong and close, at the other end. As shown in Figure 15.18, at the weak end of the continuum are strategic alliances known as **mutual service consortia**. These are arrangements between two similar companies from the same or similar industries to pool their resources to receive a benefit that would be too difficult or expensive for either to obtain alone. Often, the focus is some high-tech capacity, such as an expensive piece of diagnostic equipment that might be shared by two or more local hospitals (e.g., a magnetic resonance imaging, or MRI unit).

At the opposite end of the scale are the strongest and closest type of collaborations, referred to as **value-chain partnerships**. These are alliances between companies in different industries that have complementary capabilities. Customer-supplier relationships are a prime example. In such arrangements one company buys necessary goods and services from another so that it can do business. Because each company greatly depends on the other, each party's commitment to their mutual relationship is high. As noted earlier, Toyota has a network of 230 suppliers with whom it regularly does business. The relationship between Toyota and these various companies represent value-chain partnerships.

Between these two extremes are **joint ventures**. These are arrangements in which companies work together to fulfill opportunities that require the capabilities of the other. For example, two companies might enter into a joint venture if one has a valuable technology and the other has the marketing knowledge to help transform that technology into a viable commercial product.

mutual service consortia
A type of strategic alliance in which two similar companies from the same or similar industries pool their resources to receive a benefit that would be too difficult or expensive for either to obtain alone.

value-chain partnerships
Strategic alliances between companies in different industries that have complementary capabilities.

joint ventures
Strategic alliances in which several companies work together to fulfill opportunities that require one another's capabilities.

FIGURE 15.17

Strategic Alliances at Cisco Systems

Cisco Systems CEO, John Chambers (left), and British Prime Minister, Tony Blair (center), find their meeting with a Health Robot (right) most amusing, but at Cisco Systems, the large computer networking company headquartered in San Jose, California, forming strategic alliances is no laughing matter. The company refers to this practice as "impact partnering," and bases its choices of strategic alliances on such factors as the capacity to form new markets, to ward off potential threats, and the potential for several points of connection with the partnering company. One such alliance, with InTouch Health, led to the creation of this Health Robot used to help doctors diagnose patients in remote locations.

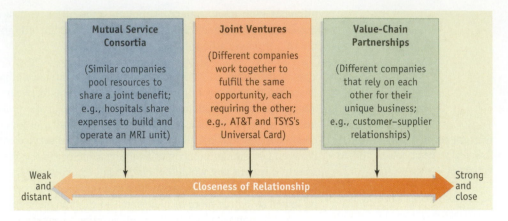

FIGURE 15.18

Strategic Alliances: A Continuum of Interorganizational Relationships

The three types of strategic alliances identified here may be distinguished with respect to their location along a continuum ranging from weak and distant to strong and close.

Source: Based on suggestions by Kanter, 1994; see Note 57.

networked incubator

Partnerships between established companies (often Internet-based firms), which provide valued resources and experience, with start-ups, which are able to develop and market products quickly.

incubator

A company that specializes in starting up new businesses.

In recent years, as information technology has flourished, many Internet-based organizations have developed joint ventures with newly forming companies (referred to as *start-ups*). Their mission: To facilitate the flow of knowledge and talent across companies in a manner that boosts their joint technical and marketing competence. This special kind of joint venture is known as a **networked incubator**.[59] These are partnerships between established companies (often Internet-based firms), which provide valued resources and experience, with start-ups, which are able to develop and market products quickly. When properly designed, networked incubators combined the best of both worlds—the scale and scope of large, established companies, and the entrepreneurial spirit of small firms.

As an example, consider Hotbank, a company known as an **incubator** because it specializes in starting up new businesses. Hotbank is managed by another company, Softbank Venture Capital (SBVC), which leases the office space, funds the projects, and provides the basic services needed to run a business (recruiting, public relations, accounting, and so on). SBVC provides the services needed to develop business ideas identified by Hotbank. For example, Hotbank's first company was Model E, a firm specializing in build-to-order vehicles and a Web-based comprehensive service packet (e.g., registration, insurance, financing). Model E was able to get off the ground because of the business ingenuity of Hotbank and the resources of SBVC. Because networked incubators are a new form of business relationship, it is too soon to tell how successful they will prove to be. However, if early reports provide any indication, it looks as if they will be quite successful.

spinoff

An entirely new company that is separate from the original parent organization, one with its own identity, a new board of directors, and a different management team.

An Alternative to the Joint Venture. Although forming joint ventures with other companies is a popular way for companies to grow in new directions, it is not the only way. An alternative that has been popular in many companies has been to create a **spinoff**—that is, an entirely new company that is separate from the original parent organization, one with its own identity, a new board of directors, and a different management team. The idea is that instead of looking around for a suitable partner, a rich and powerful company can create its own partner.

Consider, for example, the development of Expedia, Microsoft's online travel service. In 1996, Expedia was launched as just another Microsoft product.[60] As it became more successful, Expedia was set up as a separate operating unit. Then, in November 1999, Expedia was "spun off" into a separate publicly traded company (i.e., it can be purchased by anyone on the stock market). This raised $84 million for Microsoft, and because the company retains 85 percent of Expedia's stock it promises to make even more money in the future. Despite the highly competitive market within which it operates, Expedia has been flourishing, enjoying record profits in recent years. This is in large part because it was the offspring of a wealthy and successful parent (which gave Expedia a head start), but also because it was allowed to develop on its own as needed, without too much "parental supervision," so to speak. Further extending the parent-child metaphor, the spinoff company is forever associated with the parent company, provides services to it, and gets help from it. However, it also is free to develop other business relationships that stand to strengthen it further.

Strategic Alliances in the Global Economy. Strategic alliances with companies in nations with transforming economies (such as China and eastern Europe) provide good opportunities for those nations' economies to develop. Given the rapid move toward globalization of the economy, we may expect to see many companies seeking strategic alliances in the future as a means for gaining or maintaining a competitive advantage. Frequently, companies form strategic alliances with foreign firms to gain entry into that country's market.[61] Such arrangements also may allow for an exchange of technology and manufacturing services. For example, Korea's Daewoo receives technical information and is paid to manufacture automobiles for companies with which it has entered into alliances, such as General Motors, as well as Germany's Opel and Japan's Isuzu and Nissan.[62] Some companies, such as the telecommunications giant MCI, are actively involved in several strategic alliances, including one in Canada and several in New Zealand.[63]

In addition to the financial incentives (circumventing trade and tariff restrictions) and marketing benefits (access to internal markets) associated with strategic alliances, direct managerial benefits also are associated with extending one company's organizational chart into another's. These benefits come primarily from improved technology and greater economies of scale (e.g., sharing functional operations across organizations). For these benefits to be derived, a high degree of coordination and fit must exist between the parties, each delivering on its promise to the other. Finally, it is noteworthy that strategic alliances with companies in nations with transforming economies provide good opportunities for those nations' economies to develop.[64] Given the rapid move toward globalization of the economy, we may expect to see many companies seeking strategic alliances in the future as a means for gaining or maintaining a competitive advantage.[65] (For a close-up look at this process in operation in China, see the *OB in a Diverse World* section on p. 616.)

Strategic Alliances can Help Minority-Owned Businesses. Although members of minority groups represent about one-third to one-half of the U.S. population, they control a significantly lower percentage of the nation's businesses. In an effort to bring parity to this situation by boosting the number of minority-owned businesses, the U.S. government requires companies to meet specified targets for conducting business with minority-owned companies. The underlying rationale is that this practice is good for business. Jethro Joseph, DaimlerChrysler's head of special supplier relations, offers a simple explanation: "If we buy from minority suppliers, they will hire minority employees, who will have the wherewithal to buy our products. We look at it as a never-ending wheel."[66] To get this wheel moving, many large companies are finding it useful to form alliances with minority-owned companies, creating relationships from which both parties can benefit. For a sample of some of these alliances, see Table 15.5 on page 617.

Are Strategic Alliances Successful? As our descriptions of the various types of alliances illustrate, there are clear benefits to be derived from forming alliances. These result from improved technology, widened markets, and greater economies of scale (e.g., sharing functional operations across organizations). However, as you might imagine, for these benefits to be realized, a high degree of coordination and fit must exist between the parties, each delivering on its promise to the other.

As you might imagine, not all strategic alliances are successful. For example, AT&T and Olivetti once tried to work together on manufacturing personal computers. Strong differences in management styles and organizational culture (see Chapter 14) led the alliance to fail and, ultimately, to dissolve. Similarly, a planned alliance between Raytheon and Lexitron, a small word processing company, failed because of the clashes between the rigid culture of the much larger Raytheon and the more entrepreneurial style of the smaller Lexitron. Clearly, for strategic alliances to work, the companies must not only be able to offer each other something important, but they also must be able to work together to make it happen.

OB In a Diverse World

Joint Ventures in China: Beware of Obstacles

 With an enormous market that is opening its doors to Western capitalism, it's not surprising that the idea of forming joint ventures with Chinese companies is very appealing to organizations in other parts of the world. Some companies, such as Johnson & Johnson, have enjoyed considerable success in joint ventures with Chinese firms. Most others, however, are finding it difficult to make these relationships work.[67]

Consider, for example, the experiences of a U.S.-based household-products company that formed a joint venture with Shanhai Jawa Corporation, China's largest cosmetics manufacturer. The U.S. company was looking for help introducing its products into the large Chinese market by tapping into Jahwa's distribution system. It also was hoping to find what the Chinese call *guanxi,* the social and political connections required to become successful in China. Jahwa officials were looking for help in upgrading its technology and boosting its capacity to compete in the international marketplace. Unfortunately, the two companies had serious disagreements over directions and resources that paralyzed them, resulting in a failed deal. Making matters worse, joint ventures are difficult to dissolve in Chinese culture because the relationship between the two companies is based on trust. Walking away from such relationships comes at a considerable loss of face (i.e., esteem in the eyes of others).

Several factors make the prospects of forming joint ventures with Chinese firms difficult, at best. To begin with, there is the obvious matter of cultural differences. Compared to Western countries, Chinese culture and traditions are profoundly different. In particular, its social, governmental, and economic systems are far more complex. Compared to Western companies, for example, Chinese companies are more likely to become lax after achieving success, and they are less likely to consider strategies that take a long-term approach. If this were the only challenge, however, it most likely would be overcome. After all, executives interested in conducting business in various countries have been successful in learning all about the cultural ways of their hosts.[68] In China, however, there are several more unique problems.

First is the fact that the Chinese market is becoming extremely competitive as many companies are attempting to be the first to introduce their products to the vast Chinese population. Competition has become so fierce in some industries (e.g., construction, pharmaceuticals, and electronics), in fact, that companies have been aggressively pursuing market share, even if it meant lowering prices so much that they were selling at a loss. This is a game that very few companies can afford to play.

A second unique problem associated with forming joint ventures with Chinese companies is that very few have presence throughout the country. Most operate either regionally or locally. This is a vestige of the country's planned economic system, in effect until 1979, which required companies to operate in very narrow market niches. Because only the earliest companies to form joint ventures with Chinese companies (e.g., Coca-Cola Co.) managed to make contact with the few that operate nationally, it is very difficult for today's foreign companies to find a suitable partner.

A third unique problem has to do with government intervention. Although governments are involved in one way or another in businesses in all countries, their connection to Chinese businesses runs deep—so much so, in fact, that many companies are actually owned, in part, by government agencies. What makes this particularly frustrating is that different governmental rules operate in different territories. As a case in point, consider the difficulties that companies such as AT&T, NEC, and Siemens have been having in establishing telephone service through their various Chinese partners. The problem resides in the fact that Shanghai Bell has a Chinese partner, which just happens to be the Ministry of Post and Telecommunication—the government agency that controls communications. To say that Shanghai Bell has a distinct advantage, as a result, probably comes as no surprise.

In view of these considerations, experts advise companies seeking joint ventures with Chinese firms to consider all their options carefully. The benefits that stand to be gained from an enormous market may never be realized because several important obstacles stand in the way.

TABLE 15.5 Alliances Involving Minority-Owned Businesses

In recent years, many large companies have found it useful to enter into strategic alliances with small, minority-owned companies. Other companies have served as "matchmakers," bringing together firms with one or more minority group owners. Here are a few examples.

Large Company	Involvement with Small, Minority-Owned Company
Bank of America	Bank of America wanted to do business with R. J. Leeper, a black entrepreneur in the construction business. However, because he lacked experience, Bank of America helped him learn the business by getting him a job at a successful construction company and paying half his salary while he worked there. Leeper now has his own construction company, R. J. Leeper Construction, which is a supplier to Bank of America.
Procter & Gamble	Procter & Gamble purchases plastic bottles for Sunny Delight from a company that it helped create—a joint venture between Plastitec and minority-owned Madras Packaging.
DaimlerChrysler	DaimlerChrysler helped International Paper, one of its suppliers, form a joint venture with a black entrepreneur, Carlton Highsmith. His company, Specialized Packaging Group, now produces packaging for automotive parts made by DaimlerChrysler.
Ford Motor Company	Ford Motor Company officials wanted to buy conveyor systems from one of three minority-owned companies (Devon Contracting Services, Scion, and Gala & Associates), but they were too small. Ford helped these three firms merge, forming Tri-Tec, the larger and more stable company from which Ford now buys conveyor systems.
Johnson Controls	Johnson Controls purchases interior car parts from TKA Plastics. This company was the result of a partnership between two parties that Johnson Controls brought together: Del-Met, an injection molding company, and Michael Cherry, an African-American entrepreneur.

Source: Based on information in Weisul, 2001; see Note 66.

Summary and Review of Learning Objectives

1. **Describe what is meant by organizational structure and how it is revealed by an organization chart.**
   The formal configuration between individuals and groups with respect to the allocation of tasks, responsibilities, and authority within organizations is known as *organizational structure.* It is an abstract concept that can be represented by an *organizational chart,* a diagram indicating the relationships between the various units (individuals or departments) in an organization.

2. **Explain the basic characteristics of organizational structure revealed in an organization chart (hierarchy of authority, division of labor, span of control, line versus staff, and decentralization).**
   Organization charts depict five different elemental building blocks of organizational structure. These are: *hierarchy of authority* (a summary of reporting relationships), *division of labor* (the degree to which jobs are specialized), *span of control* (the number of individuals over which a manager has responsibility), *line* versus *staff positions* (jobs permitting direct decision-making power versus jobs in which advice is given), and *decentralization* (the degree to which decisions can be made by lower-ranking employees as opposed to a few higher-ranking individuals).

3. **Describe different approaches to departmentalization—functional organizations, product organizations, matrix organizations, and the boundaryless organization.**
   Within organizations, groups of people can be combined into departments in various ways. The most popular approach is the *functional organization,* an organization created by combining people in terms of the common functions they perform (e.g., sales,

manufacturing). An alternative approach is to departmentalize people by virtue of the specific products for which they are responsible, known as the *product organization.* Another form of departmentalization combines both of these approaches into a single form known as the *matrix organization.* In such organizations, people have at least two bosses; they are responsible to a superior in charge of the various functions and a superior in charge of the specific product. Employees also may have to answer to high-ranking people responsible for the entire organization, the top leader. Following the lead of General Electric, many of today's companies are moving toward *boundaryless organizations* (ones in which chains of command are eliminated, spans of control are unlimited, and rigid departments give way to empowered teams). These eliminate all internal boundaries (such as those between employees) and external boundaries (such as those between the company and its suppliers).

4. **Distinguish between classical and neoclassical approaches to organizational design and between mechanistic organizations and organic organizations, as described by the contingency approach to organizational design.**

   Organizational design is the process of coordinating the structural elements of organizations in the most appropriate way. *Classical organizational theories* (such as Weber's notion of bureaucracy) claim that a universally best way to design organizations exists, an approach based on high efficiency. *Neoclassical organizational theories* (such as those advanced by McGregor, Argyris, and Likert) also believe that there is one best way to design organizations. Their approach, however, emphasizes the need to pay attention to basic human needs to succeed and express oneself. The *contingency approach* to organizational design is predicated on the belief that the most appropriate way to design organizations depends on the external environments within which they operate. Specifically, a key factor has to do with the degree to which the organization is subject to change: A stable environment is one in which business conditions do not change, whereas a turbulent environment is one in which conditions change rapidly. When conditions are stable, a *mechanistic organization* is effective. This is one in which people perform specialized jobs, many rigid rules are imposed, and authority is vested in a few top-ranking officials. However, when conditions are turbulent, an *organic organization* is effective. This is one in which jobs tend to be very general, there are few rules, and decisions can be made by low-level employees.

5. **Describe the five organizational forms identified by Mintzberg: simple structure, machine bureaucracy, professional bureaucracy, divisional structure, and adhocracy.**

   Five specific organizational forms have been identified by Mintzberg. Organizations with *simple structure* are small and informal and have a single powerful individual, often the founding entrepreneur, who is in charge of everything (e.g., a small retail store owned by a sole proprietor). In a *machine bureaucracy* work is highly specialized, decision making is concentrated at the top, and the work environment is not prone to change (e.g., a government office). In *professional bureaucracies,* such as hospitals and universities, there are lots of rules to follow, but employees are highly skilled and free to make decisions on their own. *Divisional structure* characterizes many large organizations (such as General Motors) in which separate autonomous units are created to deal with entire product lines, freeing top management to focus on larger scale, strategic decisions. Finally, the *adhocracy* is a highly informal, organic organization in which specialists work in teams, coordinating with each other on various projects (e.g., many software development companies).

6. **Characterize two forms of intraorganizational design—conglomerates and strategic alliances.**

   Some organizational designs represent ways of combining more than one organization. Such interorganizational designs include the *conglomerate* (large corporations that diversify by getting involved in unrelated businesses) and the *strategic alliance* (organizations combining forces to operate a specific business). There are three major types of strategic alliances: *mutual service consortia, joint ventures,* and *value-chain partnerships.*

Points to Ponder

Questions for Review

1. What are the fundamental dimensions of organizations that are described by organizational structure?
2. What are the major ways that traditionally have been used to organize departments in organizations?
3. What are the major differences between classical, neoclassical, and contingency approaches to organizational design?
4. What are the five organizational forms identified by Mintzberg?
5. What is meant by "the boundaryless organization" and what forms does it take?
6. What are the major types of interorganizational design, in which two or more organizations can coordinate their efforts?

Experiential Questions

1. Think of the organization in which you currently work—specifically, the work group or department with which you are most closely affiliated. How would you characterize this unit with respect to division of labor, span of control, and centralization?
2. Based on your own experiences, do you think that traditional, hierarchical organizations are giving way to less well-structured, boundaryless forms of organization? In other words, do you see this trend in your own organizational life?
3. Have you ever worked for a company that was involved in a strategic alliance of some kind? How about a virtual organization? If so, how was the experience different from working for a traditional company?

Questions to Analyze

1. How have advances in information technology changed the way organizations are structured and designed today?
2. For what types of business endeavors do you think virtual organizations are particularly well suited, and for what type do you believe they should be avoided?
3. Much has been said about the successes of networked incubators. However, they can have problems. What do you believe are the most important limitations of this form of organizational design?

Experiencing OB

Individual Exercise

Which Do You Prefer—Mechanistic or Organic Organizations?

Because mechanistic and organic organizations are so different, it is reasonable to expect that people will tend to prefer one of these organizational forms over the other. This questionnaire is designed to help you identify your own preferences (and, in so doing, to help you learn about the different forms themselves).

Directions

Each of the following questions deals with your preferences for various conditions that may exist where you work. Answer each one by checking the one alternative that best describes your feelings.

1. When I have a job-related decision to make, I usually prefer to:

    _____ a. make the decision myself.

    _____ b. have my boss make it for me.

2. I usually find myself more interested in performing:

    _____ a. a highly narrow, specialized task.

    _____ b. many different types of tasks.

3. I prefer to work in places in which working conditions:

     _____ a. change a great deal.

     _____ b. generally remain the same.

4. When a lot of rules are imposed on me, I generally feel:

     _____ a. very comfortable.

     _____ b. very uncomfortable.

5. I believe that governmental regulation of industry is:

     _____ a. usually best for all.

     _____ b. rarely good for anyone.

Scoring

1. Give yourself 1 point each time you answered as follows: 1 = b; 2 = a; 3 = b; 4 = a; 5 = a. This score is your preference for *mechanistic organizations.*
2. Subtract this score from 5. This score is your preference for *organic organizations.*
3. Interpret your scores as follows: Higher scores (closer to 5) reflect stronger preferences, and lower scores (closer to 0) reflect weaker preferences.

Questions for Discussion

1. How did you score? That is, which organizational form did you prefer?
2. Think back over the jobs you've had. Have these been in organizations that were mechanistic or organic?
3. Do you think you performed better in organizations whose designs matched your preferences than those in which there was a mismatch?
4. Do you think you were more committed to organizations whose designs matched your preferences than those in which there was a mismatch?

Group Exercise

Comparing Span of Control in Organizational Charts

One of the easiest things to determine about a company by looking at its organizational chart is its span of control. This exercise will allow you to learn about and compare span of control within companies in your area.

Directions

1. Divide the class into four equal-size groups.
2. Assign one of the following industry types to each group: (a) manufacturing companies, (b) financial institutions, (c) public utilities, and (d) charities.
3. Within the industry assigned to each group, identify one company per student. Also, consider larger organizations inasmuch as these are more likely to have formal organizational charts. For example, if there are five students in the "financial institutions" group, name five different banks or savings and loan institutions.
4. Each student should search the Internet for a copy of the organizational chart for the company assigned to him or her in step 3.
5. Meet as a group to discuss the spans of control of the organizations in your sample.
6. Gather as a class to compare the findings of the various groups.

Questions for Discussion

1. How easy or difficult was it to find organization charts on the Internet?
2. Did you find that there were differences with respect to span of control?
3. Were spans of control different at different organizational levels? If so, how? And, were these differences the same for all industry groups?
4. In what ways did spans of control differ for the various industry groups? Were the spans broader for some industries and narrower in others? How do you explain these differences? Do these differences make sense to you?

Practicing OB

Reconsidering an Organizational Design

Fabricate-It, Inc. is a medium-size manufacturing company that uses standard assembly lines to produce its products. Its employees tend to be poorly educated and perform monotonous work. Think-It, Inc. is a software design firm that writes customized programs to solve its customers' problems. Its employees tend to be highly educated and perform highly creative work. Both are reconsidering their present organizational designs.

1. What type of organizational design would you imagine would best suit the needs of Fabricate-It? Explain your decision.
2. What type of organizational design would you imagine would best suit the needs of Think-It? Explain your decision.
3. How might each of these organizations benefit by entering into strategic alliances with other organizations?

CASE IN POINT

Biotechnology-Pharmaceutical Alliances: Unexpected Side Effects

Creating new drugs is a very long and expensive ordeal, but one with potentially phenomenal payoffs. Usually, no one company can go through the process alone. Each has a piece of the jig-saw puzzle and requires the assistance of other companies to make something happen. This is why biotechnology and pharmaceutical companies frequently are involved in partnering. In fact, between 1997 and 2002 the 20 largest pharmaceutical firms were involved in nearly 1,500 alliances. And this usually leads to success. Currently, over half of the 20 top-selling prescription drugs were developed, marketed, or licensed by more than one company.

Knoll Pharmaceuticals (a division of the German chemical company BASF) and Cambridge Antibody Technology (the UK-based biotech firm) formed an alliance in 1993. Cambridge had an extensive library of antibodies that could be tested on the various autoimmune disease targets (tumors, in particular) identified by Knoll. To everyone's delight, they were successful right away. One of Cambridge's antibodies managed to neutralize the specific tumor on which it was tested.

Recognizing the potential of this success, in 2001 Abbott Laboratories (located in suburban Chicago) bought Knoll for $7.1 billion. Under Abbott's guidance, that product was tested rigorously, meeting with continued success Then, in 2003, a product was marketed under the brand name Humira, a successful treatment for rheumatoid arthritis. By 2005, sales hit the $1.2 billion mark. Humira was hailed by a pharmaceutical executive as "a blockbuster drug," one of many that will be coming from the alliance between pharmaceutical companies and biotech companies.

Just as Humira was taking off on the market, Abbott and Cambridge became embroiled in a legal battle over the payment of royalties on shares of the profits. At issue were questions about the intellectual property that was licensed by each party. Legally, the many interconnections between the parties are fraught with potential conflicts because when two parties sign agreements regarding their intellectual property, other parties (e.g., various research institutes involved in the clinical trials, in this case) claim that their rights have been infringed.

As this case lingers on in the courts, it has implications for other similar alliances that are being made these days—one of the most recent involving GlaxoSmithKline and Theverance (a San Francisco–area biotech firm). The problem, industry observers have noted, is that alliances are based on trust. But, in the big-money world of drug development, one must wonder if expecting trust is overly optimistic. Yet, without such alliances, the next miracle drug may never be forthcoming.

Questions for Discussion

1. Based on the unhappy ending between Abbott and Cambridge, what lessons might be learned by GlaxoSmithKline and Theverance as they join forces?
2. In what ways are the images of each of the companies involved in a strategic alliance likely to change as a result of their associations with one another?
3. Besides entering into joint ventures, how else might pharmaceutical and biotech companies work together to develop new pharmaceuticals?

Chapter 16

Managing Organizational Change: Strategic Planning and Organizational Development

Chapter Outline

The Prevalence of Change in Organizations

The Nature of the Change Process

Strategic Planning: Deliberate Change

Resistance to Change: Maintaining the Status Quo

Organizational Development Interventions: Implementing Planned Change

Critical Questions About Organizational Development

Special Sections

OB **In a Diverse World**

Strategic Values: More American Than Universal

How to Do It

Making Changes Stick: Tips from Three Established Organizations

OB **Making Sense Out of Common Sense**

Organizational Development Is Inherently Unethical—Or Is It?

After reading this chapter, you should be able to:

1. Characterize the prevalence of the change process in organizations.
2. Understand what, exactly, is changed when organizational change comes about, and the forces responsible for unplanned organizational change.
3. Describe what is meant by strategic planning and the types of strategic changes that organizations make.
4. Identify the 10 steps in the strategic planning process.
5. Explain why people are resistant to organizational change and how this resistance may be overcome.
6. Identify and describe the major organizational development techniques that are used today.

PREVIEW CASE

The Eden Alternative: Graceful Aging for the Elder-Care Business

After working in the Chase Memorial nursing home in upstate New York, Dr. Bill Thomas couldn't understand why so many people in elder-care facilities were simply warehoused as if they were waiting to die. Residents suffered what he called "the three plagues" of life in a nursing home: loneliness (because they've been uprooted from their families, friends, and pets), helplessness (because they live by the institution's schedule instead of their own control), and boredom (because, short of watching television, there's little for them to do). "Why not treat the elderly with dignity and respect?" Thomas wondered. He couldn't see any reason why nursing homes couldn't be friendly and loving places where people enjoy spending their elder years.

With this in mind, Thomas spearheaded several changes at Chase Memorial. To begin, he brought in animals to live on the premises, offering loving companionship as an antidote to loneliness. Also, by caring for the animals, the elders felt important. Their importance also was recognized by allowing them to partner with staff members on such issues as how to decorate the living quarters to make them more homelike and friendly. This removed much of the hierarchical and autocratic management that traditionally exists in nursing care facilities. Although staff members at first resented the loss of power, they came to like the arrangement because a very cordial relationship developed within the home as elders and staff members worked together and grew to care about one another.

Not satisfied with transforming a single facility, Thomas toured the country in the summer of 1999 to share his experiences with nursing home administrators in 27 cities. And he hasn't stopped since. His approach—a movement known as the Eden Alternative (named after the idyllic biblical image of the Garden of Eden)—has been turning the elder-care business upside-down. Today, "the large-scale, institutional care facility is crumbling," Thomas claims, "and we now have the possibility of real transformation."

Acknowledging that the elder-care industry has little incentive to change, "you need to have people go a little nuts about what you want to do," Thomas says. Individual nursing home operators are too overwhelmed by the day-to-day pressures of caring for the elderly while meeting stringent government requirements to try anything new, he recognizes. So, to inspire them, he tries to capture their minds with his passion and conviction, inspiring others to feel the same.

This is precisely what he has done. Thomas runs the Eden Alternative foundation, which transforms elder-care facilities in ways that improve their social and physical facilities. By 2006 he has "Edenized" over 300 facilities throughout the United States, as well as several in Europe and Australia, improving the quality of life for their residents. This certification process involves adopting such principles as "surrendering the institutional point of view" and adopting the "human habitat model that makes pets, plants, and children the pivots for daily life in a nursing home." An Eden home "provides easy access to companionship," "provides opportunities to give as well as to receive care," and "imbues daily life with variety and spontaneity." Moreover, the Eden Alternative home replaces programmed activities with natural activities of daily life. You'll know one of these facilities as soon as you enter because you'll likely hear the cheerful sound of birds singing and local schoolchildren chatting with their elderly companions.

In each facility, administrators and all staff members are trained thoroughly as Eden Associates, and they receive ongoing advice from Thomas. Each step of the process—and it is a real process, not a marketing ploy—is acknowledged. In contrast to the typical "don't make waves" orientation you'll find at most other nursing homes, in Eden Alternative residences it is believed that "change is good."

To the delight of many, Dr. Thomas has been responsible for dramatic changes in the nursing home business. Of course, this isn't the only industry in which dramatic changes have been seen over the years. Just about all organizations have found it necessary to respond to changing forces. Auto companies, for example, have had to accelerate the development of hybrid cars in the wake of rising fuel prices. Identity thieves have challenged Internet service providers to guard the personal identities of their clients against predators. And many consumer electronics companies have been struggling to chip away at Apple's dominance in the portable music player market (even Pope Benedict has an iPod) by introducing new models with more features.

These and countless other examples of change in the ways businesses operate make it clear that change is the rule rather than the exception. Acknowledging just the tip of the iceberg, advances in technology have streamlined record keeping and access to medical tests by physicians, helping us all. By contrast, foreign competition and efforts to meet the growing demands of labor have forced some venerable companies to struggle. GM, for example, was forced to cut 30,000 jobs during 2005–2006 by closing assembly and components plants throughout North America, saving roughly $2.5 billion.[1] Clearly, change in the world of business—both positive and negative—is inevitable: As some companies grow, still others fail to stay afloat (see Figure 16.1).

It is an understatement to say that the impact of **organizational change** can be found everywhere. This may be defined as planned or unplanned transformations in an organization's structure, technology, and/or people. To understand this important process, we examine it from several key perspectives in this chapter. To begin, we describe the nature

organizational change
Planned or unplanned transformations in an organization's structure, technology, and/or people.

FIGURE 16.1

Change Is All Around Us

In 2005, the century-old maker of razors, toothbrushes, and batteries, Gillette, was purchased for $54.3 billion by the consumer products giant Procter & Gamble. Deals of this magnitude have not been unusual in recent years, illustrating one of the major sources of organizational change today.

of the process of change, describing forces that require organizations to change. Then we shift our focus to changes that are more deliberate, describing what is known as *strategic planning*. This involves deliberately making radical changes in the way an organization operates.

As you might imagine, most people have difficulty accepting that they may have to change the group of people they work with and the basic nature of the jobs they do. After all, if you're used to working a certain way, a sudden change can be very unsettling. In other words, as we will describe, for various reasons, people are resistant to change. Fortunately, such resistance can be overcome. With this in mind, social scientists have developed various methods, known collectively as *organizational development* techniques, which are designed to implement needed organizational change in a manner that is acceptable to employees and that enhances the effectiveness of the organizations involved.

The Prevalence of Change in Organizations

A century ago, advances in machine technology made farming so highly efficient that fewer hands were needed to plant and reap the harvest. Displaced laborers fled to nearby cities, seeking jobs in newly opened factories, opportunities created by some of the same technologies that sent them from the farm. The economy shifted from agrarian to manufacturing, and the *industrial revolution* was underway. With it came drastic shifts in where people lived, how they worked, how they spent their leisure time, how much money they made, and how they spent it.

Today, we are in the midst of *another* industrial revolution—one driven by a new wave of global economic forces and rapid technological transformation. As one observer put it, "This workplace revolution . . . may be remembered as a historic event, the Western equivalent of the collapse of communism."[2] And, as in the case of the previous industrial revolution, this one is bringing with it broad changes in the workplace to which we all must adapt.

The Message Is Clear: Change or Disappear!

Today's business landscape is not the same as it was just a few years ago. Take the auto industry, for example. Within only the past decade, Bentley was purchased by Volkswagen, Ford took a controlling stake in Jaguar, the Saab auto line (they also make jet engines) was bought by General Motors, and the Mini Cooper (formerly a British car) reemerged under ownership by the German firm, BMW. If this musical chairs ownership in the auto industry leaves your head spinning, don't even think of being able to track changes in ownership of various banks, where mergers and acquisitions leave local branch offices (and the entities they sponsor) changing signs almost every time we drive past them (see Figure 16.2). Although we shared examples from only two industries, it's clear that no industry, no organization is immune; change is everywhere.

The handwriting on the wall is clear: The world is changing, and those companies that fail to change when required find themselves out of business as a result.[3] Not surprisingly, research has shown that support for organizational change among senior managers is a characteristic that distinguishes the most successful organizations from other organizations. Specifically, managers in successful organizations support change 94 percent of the time, whereas all other managers support change only 76 percent of the time.[4] Although this alone does not mean that support for change directly causes success, of course, the sizable difference surely suggests that it may be a factor.

This is important because business failure is the rule rather than the exception: Fully 62 percent of new ventures fail to last as long as five years, and only 2 percent make it as long as 50 years.[5] In view of this, it is particularly impressive that some American companies have beaten the odds—so soundly, in fact, that they have remained in business for well over 300 years. For example, the United States' oldest company, J. E. Rhoads & Sons, now makes conveyer belts, although it originally started out in 1702 (four years before Benjamin Franklin was born) making buggy whips.[6] As you might imagine, this company has undergone many changes during its existence.

A Sign of Change in Banking and Baseball

For many years, Bank One bought out many smaller banks, making it one of the largest financial institutions in the United States. Then, in September, 2005 after Bank One merged with JP Morgan Chase, not only were thousands of banking offices renamed, but so too was the home of the Arizona Diamondbacks, from Bank One Ballpark to Chase Field.

Change Is a Global Phenomenon

Interestingly, the forces for organizational change are not isolated to the United States; they appear to be global in nature. To illustrate this point, consider the findings of a survey of 12,000 managers in 25 different countries conducted a few years ago.[7] When asked to identify the changes they've experienced in the past two years, respondents reported that major restructurings, mergers, divestitures and acquisitions, reductions in employment, and international expansion had occurred in their organizations.

Figure 16.3 shows the percentage reporting each of these activities in six selected nations. Although some forms of change were more common in some countries than others, organizations in all countries were actively involved in each of these change efforts. This evidence suggests that organizational change is occurring throughout the world. Although different forces may be shaping change at different rates in different places, the conclusion is apparent: Change is a universal fact of life in today's organizations.

The Nature of the Change Process

Given that change occurs so commonly, it is important to understand the basic nature of the change process. With this in mind, we turn attention to two key questions: (1) What, exactly, is changed when organizational change occurs? and (2) What forces are responsible for unplanned organizational change?

Targets: What, Exactly, Is Changed?

Imagine that you are an engineer responsible for overseeing the maintenance of a large office building. The property manager has noted a dramatic increase in the use of heat in the building, causing operating costs to skyrocket. In other words, a need for change exists—specifically, a reduction in the building's heat usage. You cannot get the power company to lower its rates, of course, so it's up to you to bring about changes in the use of heat. But how?

One possibility is to rearrange job responsibilities so that only maintenance personnel are permitted to adjust thermostats. Another option is to put timers on all thermostats so that the building temperature is automatically lowered during periods of nonuse. Finally, you consider the idea of putting stickers next to the thermostats, requesting that occupants do not adjust them. These three options are good examples of the three potential targets of organizational change we will consider—changes in *organizational structure, technology,* and *people* (see Figure 16.4).

FIGURE 16.3

Organizational Change: An International Phenomenon

A large cross-national survey found that various forms of organizational change are reported to occur throughout the world. Shown here are the percentages of respondents in six countries indicating that each of four different forms of change occurred in organizations within their country in the past two years. Major restructuring was found to be the most widely encountered form of change in most countries.

Source: Based on data reported by Kanter, 1991; see Note 7.

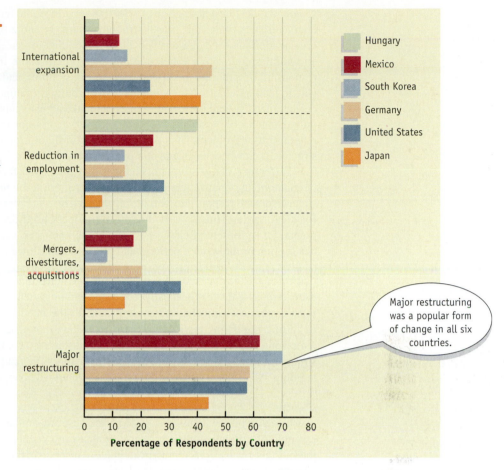

Major restructuring was a popular form of change in all six countries.

FIGURE 16.4

Organizational Change Targets: Structure, Technology, People

To create change in organizations, one can rely on altering organizational structure, technology, and/or people. Changes in any one of these areas may necessitate changes in the others.

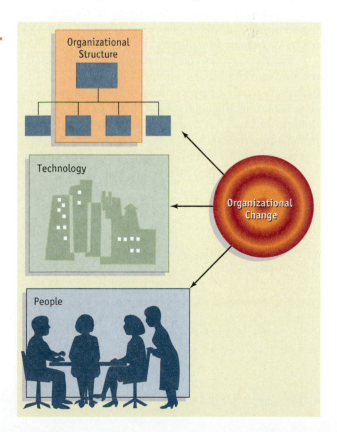

Changes in Organizational Structure. In Chapter 15 we described the key characteristics of organizational structure. Here, we note that altering the structure of an organization may be a reasonable way of responding to a need for change. In our example, a structural solution to the heat-regulation problem came in the form of reassigning job responsibilities. Indeed, modifying rules, responsibilities, and procedures may be an effective way to manage change. Changing the responsibility for temperature regulation from a highly decentralized system (whereby anyone can make adjustments) to a centralized one (in which only maintenance personnel may do so) is one way of implementing organizational change in response to a problem. This particular structural solution called for changing the power structure (i.e., who is in charge of a particular task).

Different types of structural changes may take other forms. For example, changes may be made in an organization's span of control, altering the number of employees for which supervisors are responsible. Structural changes also may take the form of revising the basis for creating departments—such as from product-based departments to functional departments. Other structural changes may be much simpler, such as clarifying someone's job description or the written policies and procedures followed.

Changes in Technology. In our example, we noted that one possible solution would be to use thermostats that automatically reduce the building's temperature while it is not in use. This is an example of a technological approach to the need to conserve heat in the building. Installing regulating devices on the thermostats that would thwart attempts to raise the temperature also would be possible. The thermostats also could be encased in a locked box, or simply removed altogether. A new, modern, energy-efficient furnace could be installed in the building. All of these suggestions represent technological approaches to change.

Changes in People. You've probably seen stickers next to light switches in hotels asking guests to turn off the lights when not in use. These are similar to the suggestion in our opening example of affixing signs near thermostats asking occupants to refrain from adjusting the thermostats. Such efforts represent attempts to respond to the needed organizational change by altering the way people behave. The basic assumption is that the effectiveness of organizations is greatly dependent on the behavior of the people working within them.

As you might imagine, the process of changing people is not easy—indeed, it lies at the core of most of the topics discussed in this book (this chapter, in particular). However, in one way or another, whatever is done involves basic steps (see Figure 16.5).

The first step is known as *unfreezing*. This refers to the process of recognizing that the current state of affairs is undesirable and in need of change. Realizing that change is needed may be the result of some serious organizational crisis or threat (e.g., a serious financial loss, a strike, or a major lawsuit), or simply becoming aware that current conditions are unacceptable (e.g., antiquated equipment, inadequately trained employees).

FIGURE 16.5

Changes Involving People: A Three-Step Process

Many organizational changes require people to do things differently. For this to occur it's necessary to follow the three general steps outlined here. As you will see later in this chapter, there are several specific ways in which these steps may be carried out.

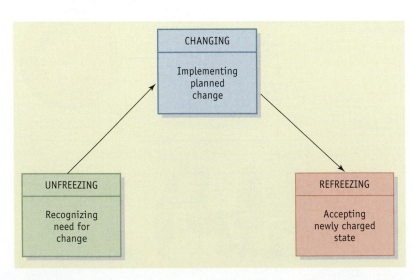

In recent years, some executives have gotten employees to accept the need to change while things are still good by creating a sense of urgency. They introduce the idea that there is an impending crisis although conditions are, in fact, currently acceptable—an approach referred to as **doomsday management**. This process effectively unfreezes people, stimulating change before it's too late to do any good.

After unfreezing, *changing* may occur. This step occurs when some planned attempt is made to create a more desirable state for the organization and its members. Change attempts may be quite ambitious (e.g., an organization-wide restructuring) or only minor (e.g., a change in a training program). (A thorough discussion of such planned change techniques will be presented in the next major part of this chapter.)

Finally, *refreezing* occurs when the changes made are incorporated into the employees' thinking and the organization's operations (e.g., mechanisms for rewarding behaviors that maintain the changes are put in place). Hence, the new attitudes and behaviors become a new, enduring aspect of the organizational system.

Magnitude: How Much Is Changed?

The changes that organizations make differ in magnitude. Whereas some changes are limited in scope and complexity (e.g., the addition of a new sales rep to an already large sales force), others are more extensive in nature (e.g., the acquisition of a new firm).

Change that is continuous in nature and involves no major shifts in the way an organization operates is known as **first-order change**. Changes of this type are apparent in the very deliberate, incremental changes that Toyota has been making in continuously improving the efficiency of its production process.[8] Similarly, a restaurant may be seen as making first-order changes as it gradually adds new items to its menu and gauges their success before completely revamping its concept.

As you might imagine, however, other types of organizational change are far more complex. **Second-order change** is the term used to refer to more radical change, major shifts involving many different levels of the organization and many different aspects of business.[9] (For a comparison between these two forms of change, see Figure 16.6.) Citing only some of the most publicized examples of second-order change from recent years, General Electric, Allied Signal, Ameritech, and Tenneco have radically altered the ways they operate, their culture, the technology they use, their structure, and the nature of their relations with employees.[10]

Forces: Why Does Unplanned Change Occur?

As organizations encounter changes in the environments in which they operate (e.g., due to changes in people, new technology, legal constraints, etc.), they face formidable challenges to adapt. Indeed, as we noted earlier, organizations must be responsive to **unplanned changes**. Such forces include changes in the demographic composition of the workforce, performance gaps, government regulation, and global competition, changing economic conditions, and advances in technology.

Shifting Employee Demographics. It is easy to see how, even within your own lifetime, the composition of the workforce has changed. As noted in Chapter 1, the American workforce is now more highly diverse than ever. To people concerned with the long-term operation of organizations, these are not simply curious sociological trends, but shifting conditions that require organizations to change.

Human resources experts need to know how the workforce is changing so they can make appropriate adjustments. For example, in recent years the growth of minority groups in the United States has been considerable (as we describe in Chapters 1 and 6). Among other things, this has made it possible to hire people from different ethnic groups in many companies and to serve members of these groups who seek service providers with whom they share common language and cultural backgrounds.[11] Besides facility in language, growing ethnic diversity has made it necessary in many companies to offer diversity management programs designed to help people from different backgrounds get along with one another (see Chapters 1 and 6). Sometimes, the changes that people have to make are

---

doomsday management
The practice of introducing change by suggesting that an impending crisis is likely.

first-order change
Change that is continuous in nature and involves no major shifts in the way an organization operates.

second-order change
Radical change; major shifts involving many different levels of the organization and many different aspects of business.

unplanned change
Shifts in organizational activities due to forces that are external in nature, those beyond the organization's control.

FIGURE 16.6

Comparing First-Order and Second-Order Change

Changes occurring in organizations differ with respect to scope and complexity. A change that is relatively minor is referred to as *first-order change*, whereas one that is more major is referred to as a *second-order change*. One example of each is shown here.

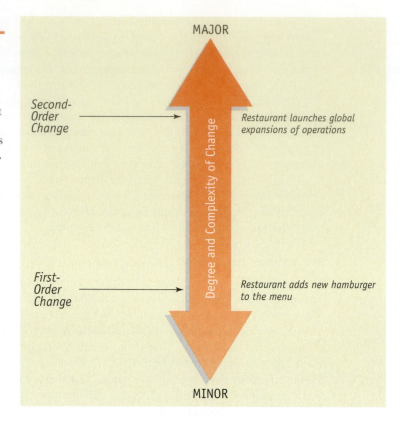

Restaurant launches global expansions of operations

Restaurant adds new hamburger to the menu

small. For example, changing the offerings in the company cafeteria to accommodate the varied tastes of people from different ethnic groups can make a big difference to employees who come to feel at home as a result.

Today's managers need to know not only about changing demographic conditions that they will be facing, but even more fundamental matters, such as the number of employees who will be available to work and the skills they will bring to their jobs. Recognizing this, a high-ranking executive at General Electric once observed that changes in workforce demographics "will turn the professional human-resources world upside down."[12]

Performance Gaps. If you've ever heard the phrase "If it's not broken, don't fix it," you already have a good feel for one of the most potent sources of unplanned internal changes in organizations—*performance gaps*. A product line that isn't moving, a vanishing profit margin, a level of sales that isn't up to corporate expectations—these are examples of gaps between real and expected levels of organizational performance.

Few things force change more than sudden and unexpected information about poor performance. Organizations usually stay with a winning course of action and change in response to failure. Indeed, a performance gap is one of the key factors providing an impetus for organizational innovation (for an example, see this chapter's *Case in Point* on p. 659). Those organizations that are best prepared to mobilize change in response to unexpected downturns are expected to be the ones that succeed.

Government Regulation. One of the most commonly witnessed unplanned organizational changes results from government regulations. For example, the federal government has been involved in both imposing and eliminating regulations in industries such as commercial airlines (e.g., mandating inspection schedules, but no longer controlling fares) and banking (e.g., restricting the amount of time checks can be held before clearing, but no longer regulating interest rates). Such activities have greatly influenced the way business is conducted in these industries (for a particularly profound example, see Figure 16.7).

FIGURE 16.7

Governmental Intervention: A Force for Change

In the wake of the financial scandals of the early 2000s that rocked corporate America (e.g., Enron, WorldCom, and Tyco), the U.S. government enacted legislation to guard against such future breaches of the public trust. In particular, the Sarbanes-Oxley Act of 2002 protects investors by improving the accuracy and reliability of corporate disclosures made by organizations (see Chapter 12). This law imposes criminal and civil penalties on executives and members of boards of directors whose firms fail to maintain adequate internal procedures for financial reporting. Broad changes in the ways public companies operate have followed.

Global Competition. It happens every day—someone builds a better mousetrap, or at least a cheaper one. As a result, companies often must fight to maintain their share of the market, advertise more effectively, and produce goods less expensively. This kind of economic competition not only forces organizations to change, but also demands that they change effectively if they are to survive.

Although competition always has been crucial to organizational success, today competition comes from all over the world. As it has become increasingly less expensive to transport materials around the world, the industrialized nations have found themselves competing with each other for shares of the marketplace in nations all over the world. This extensive globalization of the economy presents a strong need to change and to be innovative (see Chapter 14). For example, in recent years the large American automobile manufacturers have suffered by being unprepared to meet the world's growing demand for small, high-quality cars—products their Japanese competitors were only too glad to supply to an eager marketplace. With this rapidly changing growth in globalization, one thing is certain: Only the most adaptive organizations can survive.

Fluctuating Economic Conditions. The constantly changing economy has been very challenging for organizations in recent years. A recession in the early 1990s required laying off workers. The U.S. Bureau of Labor Statistics reported that from 1979 through 1995, some 43 million jobs were lost in the United States, affecting one-third of all households.[13] The number of job reductions reached a peak in 1992, and then leveled off. By the late 1990s, things had changed. Many organizations realized that they cut their workforces too deeply, and struggled to rehire many of the workers they once released. The economy was strong and unemployment was at an exceptionally low level, causing a monstrous labor crunch that led some prospective employees to be offered generous salaries and benefits.

Sometimes, cutbacks are necessary because of seasonal fluctuations in the business cycle (e.g., retail help is needed during the busy year-end holiday sales period). At other times, however, they occur as a result of unforeseen situations. For example, the terrorist attacks of September 11, 2001 forced thousands of companies to scale back in an effort to cut costs amid one of the biggest shocks to the economy in history. (For a summary of mass layoffs over the 10 years from 1996 through 2005, see Figure 16.8.)[14] Regardless of the exact form of these trends, our point is clear—namely, that economic conditions are a major source of unplanned organizational change.

From an OB perspective, these changes are important for several reasons. First, of course, they have profound implications for the individuals who lose their jobs. After all, unemployment is a major source of stress both for those who lose their jobs and those who find themselves working harder to do some of the tasks their former colleagues left behind (see Chapter 5). Second, the strength of the economy determines the degree to which organizations will expand in ways that allow new jobs to be created (e.g., companies opening new factories). Third, as the economy grows, companies are likely to invest in new technological advances that enable them to take on new and different lines of business, which has implications for the nature of the work that people will do (or even if they will have jobs at all). Fourth, as companies face more prosperous times, they are likely to be more generous toward their employees and to be more socially responsible to the communities in which they operate (see Chapter 2). For all these reasons and more, economic changes are likely to have profound effects on organizations that we can see in the field of OB.

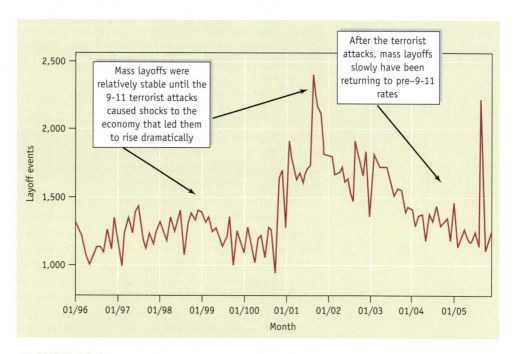

FIGURE 16.8

Mass Layoffs in the U.S. Workforce: 1995–2005

In recent years shifts in economic conditions have resulted in no less than 1,000 mass layoffs (i.e., dismissals of at least 50 employees for at least 31 days) per month—and frequently more (such as following the September 11, 2001 terrorist attacks). Such shifts are sure signs of changing workplace conditions. Declines in the size of the workplace are likely to have many effects. Among other things, to compensate for those who have departed, shifts of this nature are likely to be a major sign of—and impetus for—organizational change.

Source: Bureau of Labor Statistics, 2006; see Note 14.

Advances in Technology. As you know, advances in technology have produced changes in the way organizations operate. Senior scientists and engineers, for example, can probably tell you how their work was drastically altered in the mid-1970s, when their ubiquitous plastic slide rules gave way to powerful pocket calculators. Things changed again only a decade later, when calculators were supplanted by powerful desktop microcomputers, which have revolutionized the way documents are prepared, transmitted, and filed in an office.

Today, powerful handheld devices make portable, wireless communication a reality, further changing the way work is done. Companies that in the late 1980s and early 1990s may have considered jumping on the technology bandwagon to gain an advantage over their competitors quickly found out that doing so wasn't an option needed to get ahead—but rather, a requirement just to stay in the game. In the late 1990s, technology made it possible for people to develop new, Web-based businesses with only limited start-up capital. Businesses started by *Internet entrepreneurs* became commonplace, although vast numbers of these went bust by 2000. Today, although the Internet no longer is seen as a path to instant riches, it is clear that Internet technology has transformed the way many people work. (For a summary of ways in which computer technology has changed the way we work, see Table 16.1.)

strategic planning
The process of formulating, implementing, and evaluating decisions that enable an organization to achieve its objectives.

Strategic Planning: Deliberate Change

Thus far, we have been describing unplanned organizational change. However, not all changes that organizations make fall into this category. Organizations also make changes that are very carefully planned and deliberate. This is the idea of **strategic planning**,

TABLE 16.1 How Has Computer Technology Changed the Way We Work?

Advances in computer technology have revolutionized many of the ways we work. Some key ways in which this has been occurring are summarized here.

Area of Change	Old Way	New Technology Examples
Use of machines	Materials were moved by hand, with the aid of mechanical devices (e.g., pulleys and chains).	*Automation* is prevalent—the process of using machines to perform tasks that otherwise might be done by people. For example, computer-controlled machines manipulate materials and perform complex functions, a process known as *industrial robotics* (*IR*).
Work by employees with disabilities	People with various physical or mental disabilities either were relegated to the most simple jobs, or they didn't work at all.	*Assistive technology* is widespread—devices and other solutions that help individuals with physical or mental problems perform the various actions needed to do their jobs. For example, *telephone handset amplifiers* make it possible for people with hearing impediments to use the telephone and *voice recognition systems* read to people with visual impairments.
Monitoring employees	Supervisors used to enter the offices of employees at work and observe them from afar.	*Computerized performance monitoring* systems are in widespread use, which allow supervisors to access their subordinates' computers for purposes of assessing how well they are performing their jobs.
Customer service	Individual service providers did things to help employees, customizing goods and services as time and skill allowed.	*Personalized service* is likely to take the form of greeting visitors to one's Web page with information customized to match the goods and services in which they expressed interest in their last visit (e.g., Amazon.com does this).
Environmental friendliness	Products at the end of their lives were buried in landfills, often polluting the earth.	*Design for disassembly* (*DFD*) is the process of designing and building products so that their parts can be reused several times and then disposed of at the end of the product's life without harming the environment.

which we define as the process of formulating, implementing, and evaluating decisions that enable an organization to achieve its objectives.[15]

Basic Assumptions About Strategic Planning

To clearly understand the nature of strategic plans used in organizations today, it is important to highlight three fundamental assumptions about them.[16]

Strategic Planning Is Deliberate. When organizations make strategic plans, they make conscious decisions to change fundamental aspects of themselves. These changes tend to be radical (e.g., changing the nature of the business), as opposed to minor (e.g., changing the color of the office walls) in nature.[17] These changes may be inspired by any of several factors, such as the presence of new competitors, new technologies, and the like.

Strategic Planning Occurs When Current Objectives Can No Longer Be Met. For the most part, when a company's present strategy is bringing about the desired results, change is unlikely to occur. However, when it becomes clear that the current objectives can no longer be met, new strategies are formulated to turn things around.

New Organizational Objectives Require New Strategic Plans. Whenever a company takes steps to move in a completely new direction, it establishes new objectives—and a strategic plan is designed to meet them. Acknowledging that the various parts of an organization are all interdependent, the new strategic plan is likely to involve all functions and levels of the organization. Moreover, the plan will require adequate resources from throughout the organization to bring it to fruition.

To illustrate how these assumptions come to life, we now will describe some examples of the kinds of things about which companies tend to make strategic plans.

About What Do Companies Make Strategic Plans?

As you might imagine, organizations can make strategic plans to change just about anything. However, most of the strategic planning we see these days involves changing either (a) a company's products and services, or (b) its organizational structure.

Products and Services. Imagine that you and a friend have a small janitorial business. The two of you divide the duties, each doing some cleaning, buying supplies, and performing some administrative work. Before long, the business grows and you expand, adding new employees, and you really start "cleaning up." Many of your commercial clients express interest in window cleaning, and so you and your partner think it over and decide to expand into the window-cleaning business as well. This decision to take on a new direction to the business, to add a new, specialized service, will require a fair amount of organizational change. Not only will new equipment and supplies be needed, but also new personnel will have to be hired and trained, new insurance will have to be purchased, and new accounts will have to be secured. In short, you made a strategic decision to change the company's line of services, and this necessitates organizational change.

Organizations are required to make these kind of changes all the time. For example, Canon, Minolta, and Nikon, dominant players in the market for photography equipment, responded to the digital revolution of the 1990s by adding digital cameras to their product mix. By contrast, Polaroid, the longtime leader in instant film-based photography, was slow to jump on the digital photography bandwagon.[18] Because Polaroid executives stuck to their largely unfounded beliefs about the relative benefits of their instant film products, the company has been a minor player in the very large and popular market for digital cameras.

Organizational Structure. It is not only changes in products and services about which companies make strategic plans. They also make strategic plans to change the structures of their organizations themselves. For example, consider IBM's 2004 decision to reorganize structurally by selling its personal computer division to the China-based Lenovo Group.[19] Although IBM was the world's third largest PC maker (behind market leaders Dell and

HP), company officials made a strategic decision to strengthen its focus on the company's core business—developing information technology for corporate customers. This, of course, represents a significant departure for IBM because it was the original leader of the personal computer revolution with the release of the first IBM PC on August 12, 1981—four months before *Time* magazine named the personal computer its "man of the year."[20]

In recent years, many organizations that struggled to stay competitive responded by reducing the size and basic configurations of their organizational charts (see Chapter 15). The process of reducing the number of employees needed to operate effectively is known as **downsizing**. Earlier, we mentioned that layoffs are a common response to economic downturns. However, downsizing is likely to involve more than just laying off people in a move to save money. It is directed at adjusting the number of employees needed to work in newly designed organizations (which is why it also has been called **rightsizing**).

Another way organizations are restructuring is by completely eliminating parts of themselves that focus on noncore sectors of the business and hiring outside firms to perform these functions instead—a practice known as **outsourcing**. For example, companies like ServiceMaster, which provides janitorial services, and ADP, which provides payroll processing services, make it possible for other organizations to concentrate on the business functions most central to their mission, thereby freeing them from these peripheral support functions.

Outsourcing is particularly popular in various high-tech businesses, as when firms contract with other, specialized companies to provide such services as data storage or disaster recovery. Another widely outsourced function in computer-related businesses is customer service (see Figure 16.9). The vast majority of these services are provided by companies located in other countries, in which specialized facilities have developed to provide these services. The practice of using outsourcing services of overseas companies is known as **offshoring** (short for offshore outsourcing). Typically, this practice is followed because it allows companies to take advantage of lower labor costs. In fact, one research consulting firm has estimated that offshoring to India alone (a popular destination for outsourcing high-tech services) will free some $30 billion in new investments for American companies.[21]

Some critics have expressed concerns that outsourcing represents a "hollowing out" of companies—a reduction of functions that weakens organizations by making them more dependent on others. Others counter that outsourcing makes sense when the work that is outsourced is not highly critical to competitive success (e.g., janitorial services), or when it

downsizing
The process of systematically reducing the number of employees required to perform newly restructured jobs.

rightsizing
See *downsizing*.

outsourcing
The practice of eliminating parts of organizations that focus on noncore sectors of the business and hiring outside firms to perform these functions instead.

offshoring
Short for offshore outsourcing, the practice of using outsourcing services of overseas companies, typically because it allows companies to take advantage of lower labor costs.

FIGURE 16.9

Offshoring Technical Support Is Big Business

The ready availability of well-educated, English-speaking experts in information technology (IT), like these in the southern Indian city of Bangalore, have made their nation a haven for companies seeking the services of technical support representatives. Many businesses here, and in the Philippines as well, provide these services to American firms in 24/7 call centers, located in gigantic "IT Cyberparks." Cisco Systems is one large American company that has had considerable success with this practice.

is so highly critical that the only way to succeed requires outside assistance. If you think that outsourcing is an unusual occurrence, guess again. One industry analyst has estimated that 30 percent of the largest American industrial firms outsource over half their manufacturing—and this practice is growing rapidly.[22]

The Ten Steps of the Strategic Planning Process

The process of strategic planning typically follows 10 ordered steps, which we now describe.[23] Although these steps are not immutable and are not always followed in the exact order specified, they do a reasonably good job of describing the way companies go about planning change strategically. As we describe these, you may find it useful to follow along with the summary of steps appearing in Figure 16.10.

Define Goals. A strategic plan must begin with a stated goal. Typically, goals involve a company's market (e.g., to gain a certain position in the product market) and/or its financial standing (e.g., to achieve a certain return on equity). Organizational goals also involve society (e.g., to benefit certain groups, or the environment), or organizational culture (e.g., to make the workplace more pleasant).

It is important to note that a company's overall goals must be translated into corresponding goals to be achieved by various organizational units. For example, suppose a company wants to change its position in the market from a manufacturer of wholesale machinery to a manufacturer of consumer products. It identifies as its goal achieving 10 percent market share within the first two years. This strategic goal then must be translated into goals for the various departments. For example, the marketing department must have

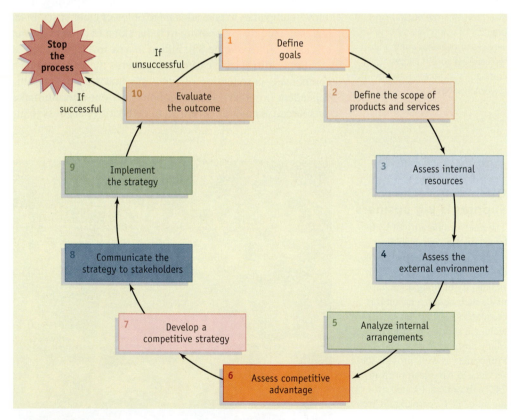

FIGURE 16.10

Strategic Planning: A Ten-Step Process

Strategic planning—the process of formulating, implementing, and evaluating decisions that enable an organization to achieve its objectives—generally follows the 10 steps summarized here.

Source: Based on suggestions by Christensen, 1994; see Note 23.

goals with respect to reaching certain consumers in its advertising. Likewise, the production department must have certain goals about being able to manufacture certain numbers of products within a specific period of time.

Define the Scope of Products or Services. For a strategic plan to be effective, company officials must clearly define their organization's *scope*—that is, the businesses in which it already operates and the new ones in which it aims to participate. If scope is defined too narrowly, the company will overlook opportunities; if scope is defined too broadly, the effectiveness of its plan will be diluted.

The matter of defining scope involves answering questions about what business a company is in, and what business it could be in. For example, Beech-Nut, long known for its infant food, faced a challenge created by lowered birthrates, thereby lowering the size of its market. That's when company officials recognized that its scope could be broadened to include the elderly—another group that has difficulty digesting hard food. Broadening its scope in this manner has been a key part of the company's strategic plan for success.[24]

Assess Internal Resources. The question with respect to internal resources is: What resources does the company have available to plan and implement its strategy? The resources in question involve funds (e.g., money to make purchases), physical assets (e.g., required space), and human assets (e.g., knowledge and skills of the workforce).

Assess the External Environment. As we have said throughout this book, organizations do not operate in a vacuum. Rather, they function within environments that influence their capacity to operate and to grow as desired. The extent to which the environment either aids or hinders a company's growth (or even its existence) depends on several key factors. Specifically, a company has a competitive advantage over others when (a) its resources cannot be easily imitated by others, (b) its resources will not depreciate anytime soon, and (c) competitors do not have resources that are any better.[25]

Analyze Internal Arrangements. By "internal arrangements," we are referring to the nature of the organization itself as identified by the characteristics described in this book. For example, are the employees paid in a way that motivates them to strive for corporate goals (Chapter 7)? Also, does the culture of the organization encourage people to be innovative and to make changes, or does it encourage them to be stagnant (see Chapter 14)? Furthermore, do people communicate with each other clearly enough (Chapter 9), and do they get along with one another sufficiently well (Chapter 11) to accomplish their goals? These and other basic questions about the organization itself must be answered to formulate an effective strategic plan. After all, unless the organization is operating properly in these key respects, even the best strategic plans may not pan out.

competitive advantage
The benefits enjoyed by an organization to the extent that its customers perceive its products or services as being superior to the products or services of another organization.

Assess Competitive Advantage. A company is said to have a **competitive advantage** over another to the extent that customers perceive its products or services as being superior to the products or services of that other company. Superiority may be assessed in terms of such factors as quality, price, breadth of product line, reliability of performance, styling, service, and company image. A company is considered to have an advantage over its competitors to the extent that customers perceived it as offering higher quality at an equal or lower price.

Develop a Competitive Strategy. A competitive strategy is the means by which an organization achieves its goal. Based on a careful assessment of the company's standing on the factors described above (e.g., the company's available resources, its competitive advantage, etc.), a decision is made about how to go about achieving its goal. Although there are many possible strategies, some of the most popular ones used in today's organizations are summarized in Table 16.2.

stakeholder
Any individual or group in whose interest an organization is run.

Communicate the Strategy to Stakeholders. The term **stakeholder** is used to describe an individual or group in whose interest an organization is run. In other words,

market-share increasing strategies
A deliberate attempt on the part of a company to develop a broader share of an existing market (such as by widening the range of products, or forming a joint venture with another company that has a presence in the market of interest).

profit strategies
Attempts to derive more profit from existing business, such as by training employees to work more effectively or salespeople to sell more effectively.

market concentration strategies
The tactic of withdrawing from markets where a company is less effective, and concentrating resources instead in markets where the company is likely to be more effective.

turnaround strategies
Attempts to reverse a decline in business by moving to a new product line, or by radically restructuring operations.

exit strategies
The tactic by which a company withdraws from a market, such as by liquidating its assets.

TABLE 16.2 Varieties of Competitive Strategies

Some of the most popular competitive strategies used by today's organizations are summarized here.

Strategy	Description
Market-share increasing strategies	Developing a broader share of an existing market, such as by widening the range of products, or by forming a joint venture (see Chapter 15) with another company that already has a presence in the market of interest
Profit strategies	Attempting to derive more profit from existing businesses, such as by training employees to work more efficiently or salespeople to sell more effectively
Market concentration strategies	Withdrawing from markets where the company is less effective and, instead, concentrating resources in markets where the company is likely to be more effective
Turnaround strategies	Attempting to reverse a decline in business by moving to a new product line or by radically restructuring operations
Exit strategies	Withdrawing from a market, such as by liquidating assets

these are individuals who have a special stake, or claim, on the company. The most important stakeholders include employees at all levels, boards of governors, and stockholders. It is essential to communicate a firm's strategy to stakeholders very clearly so they can contribute to its success, either actively (e.g., employees who pitch in to help meet goals) or passively (e.g., investors who pour money into the company to help meet goals). Without the stakeholders fully understanding and accepting a firm's strategy, it is unlikely to receive the full support it needs to meet its goals.

Implement the Strategy. Once a strategy has been formulated and communicated, the time has come for it to be implemented. When this occurs, there is likely to be some upheaval as people scramble to adjust to new ways of doing things. As we describe in the next section of this chapter, people tend to be reluctant to make changes in the way they work. However, as we also will note, several steps can be taken to ensure that the people who are responsible for making the changes come about will embrace them rather than reject them.

Evaluate the Outcome. Finally, after a strategy has been implemented, it is crucial to determine if the goals have been met. If so, then new goals may be sought. If not, then different goals may be defined, or different strategies may be followed, so as to achieve success next time. (The process of strategic planning we have been describing here may strike you as perfectly rational—so much so, in fact, that you may expect it to be universal. However, as we explain in the *OB in a Diverse World* section on p. 639, this is not the case.)

Resistance to Change: Maintaining the Status Quo

Even if people are unhappy with the current state of affairs confronting them in organizations, they may be afraid that any changes will be potentially disruptive and will only make things worse. Indeed, fear of new conditions is quite real and it creates unwillingness to accept change. For this reason people may react to organizational change quite negatively. Then again, if the process is managed effectively, people may respond to change in a very enthusiastic manner. Scientists have summarized the nature of people's reactions to organizational change as falling along a continuum ranging from acceptance, through indifference and passive resistance, to active resistance.[26] For a summary of the various forms these reactions may take, see Figure 16.11 on page 640.

OB In a Diverse World

Strategic Values: More American Than Universal

Although you may not have realized it, the process of strategic planning we have been describing has several underlying values associated with it. Specifically, the process (a) is highly deliberate, (b) is based on competition, (c) assumes that radical change is possible and desirable, and (d) assumes shareholder ownership of the company. As we will outline here, these values are not universally held, thereby casting doubt on the generalizability of the strategic planning process outside American culture.

One of the most obvious features of the strategic planning process we have been describing is its *deliberate nature*. In the United States, the companies that are most successful are the ones that carefully analyze, plan, and implement key decisions.[27] Despite this, such a deliberate process is not always used in other countries. In Southeast Asian countries, for example, intuition (gut feeling) and informal knowledge are used instead of deliberate analyses. In the words of one expert in the field, companies in these countries "don't have strategies. They do deals. They respond to opportunities."[28]

It's clear that our analysis of strategic planning is strongly based on one's position relative to the competition. However, outside the United States open expressions of *competitiveness* are not as common. Japan provides a fascinating example. In that nation, almost nothing is ever said about being competitive. Rather, the good work of the company is likely to be stressed in formal company publications. Ironically, however, Japanese companies tend to be fierce competitors in the international market. Thus, although competitive values may not be expressed in Japan (where, as a result, they are not likely to appear in any strategic plans), they certainly exist.

Our discussion of strategic planning is based on the idea that radical change is not only possible, but desirable. Again, we use Southeast Asian culture as a counterexample. In Vietnam and Thailand, for example, experts caution that radical change is doomed to fail. Instead, minor incremental adjustments to ways of operating are advised.[29]

Finally, in the United States, strategic decisions tend to be made primarily in the interest of stockholders. In fact, it is often said that the mission of a company is to raise stockholder value. Outside the United States, the interests of other stakeholders are given more weight. For example, in Germany and France, the interests of the employees tend to be accorded far greater importance in the planning process. And, in Japan, companies are considered to belong to all the stakeholders, with employees being given precedence over all others.[30]

In conclusion, it is clear that the values underlying the strategic planning process tend to prevail in the United States, but are not equally prevalent elsewhere throughout the world. As a result, it appears questionable whether the strategic planning process we've described here would work—or that it is even worth attempting—outside the United States.

---

resistance to change
The tendency for employees to be unwilling to go along with organizational changes, either because of individual fears of the unknown or organizational impediments (such as structural inertia).

As you might imagine, for organizations to make the changes needed to remain competitive—let alone to survive—they must tackle the problem of **resistance to change** head-on. With this in mind, we discuss the issue of readiness for change and examine both the individual and organizational barriers to change. Then we conclude this section of the chapter by identifying specific steps that can be taken to overcome resistance to change.

Individual Barriers to Change

People resist changes in organizations for a variety of reasons stemming from their own individual concerns, qualities, and interests.[31] Key ones are as follows.

- *Economic insecurity.* Because any changes on the job have the potential to threaten one's livelihood—by either loss of job or reduced pay—some resistance to change is inevitable.
- *Fear of the unknown.* Employees derive a sense of security from doing things the same way, knowing who their coworkers will be, and whom they're supposed to answer to from day to day. Disrupting these well-established, comfortable patterns creates unfamiliar conditions, a state of affairs that is often rejected. It is not unusual for such fears to be based on adjustments required to adapt to the use of new technology (see Figure 16.12, p. 641).
- *Threats to social relationships.* As people continue to work within organizations, they form strong bonds with their coworkers. Many organizational changes (e.g., the reassignment of job responsibilities) threaten the integrity of friendship groups that provide valuable social rewards.

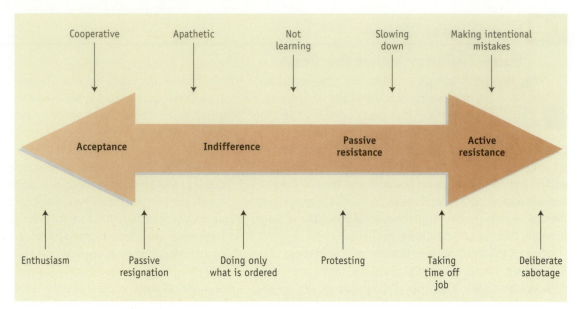

FIGURE 16.11

A Continuum of Reactions to Organizational Change

People's reactions to organizational change can range from acceptance (left) to active resistance (right). Some of the specific forms these reactions might take are indicated here.

Source: Based on suggestions by Goldstein, 2001, and Judson, 1991; see Note 26.

■ *Habit.* Jobs that are well learned and become habitual are easy to perform. The prospect of changing the way jobs are done challenges people to develop new job skills. Doing this is clearly more difficult than continuing to perform the job as it was originally learned.

■ *Failure to recognize need for change.* Unless employees can recognize and fully appreciate the need for changes in organizations, any vested interests they may have in keeping things the same may overpower their willingness to accept change.

Organizational Barriers to Change

In addition to the effects of individual factors, resistance to organizational change stems also from conditions associated with organizations themselves.[32] Several such factors are as follows.

structural inertia

The organizational forces acting on employees, encouraging them to perform their jobs in certain ways, thereby making them resistant to change.

■ *Structural inertia.* Organizations are designed to promote stability. To the extent that employees are carefully selected and trained to perform certain jobs, and rewarded for doing them well, the forces acting on individuals to perform in certain ways are very powerfully determined—that is, jobs have **structural inertia**. Thus, because jobs are designed to have stability, it is often difficult to overcome the resistance created by the forces that create stability.

work group inertia

Forces within a work group that encourage employees to perform their jobs in certain ways, thereby making them resistant to change.

■ *Work group inertia.* Inertia to continue performing jobs in a specified way comes not only from the jobs themselves but also from the social groups within which people work—**work group inertia**. Because of the development of strong social norms within groups (see Chapter 8), potent pressures exist to perform jobs in certain ways. Introducing change disrupts these established normative expectations, leading to formidable resistance.

■ *Threats to existing balance of power.* If changes are made with respect to who's in charge, a shift in the balance of power between individuals and organizational subunits is likely to occur (see Chapter 12). Those units that now control the resources, have the expertise, and wield the power may fear losing their advantageous positions as a result of any organizational change.

FIGURE 16.12

Sometimes, Change Is Not Readily Accepted

For many reasons, including fear of the unknown, people often are afraid of changing how they do their jobs. This often is the case with respect to embracing new technology—although such resistance usually isn't quite this extreme.

Source: www.CartoonStock.com

IT'S **MINE** AND YOU **CAN'T** HAVE IT

MORRIS WAS FINDING IT MORE DIFFICULT THAN MOST TO ADJUST TO THE CONCEPT OF A 'PAPERLESS' OFFICE

■ *Previously unsuccessful change efforts.* Anyone who has lived through a past disaster understandably may be reluctant to endure another attempt at the same thing. Similarly, groups or entire organizations that have been unsuccessful in introducing change in the past may be cautious about accepting further attempts at introducing change into the system.

Let's consider an example. For almost two decades, General Electric (GE) has been undergoing a series of widespread changes in its basic strategy, organizational structure, and relationship with employees. In this process, it experienced several of the barriers just identified. For example, GE managers had mastered a set of bureaucratic traditions that kept their habits strong and their inertia moving straight ahead. The prospect of doing things differently was scary for those who were so strongly entrenched in doing things the "GE way." In particular, the company's interest in globalizing triggered many fears of the unknown.

Resistance to change at GE also was strong because it threatened to strip power from those units that traditionally possessed most of it (e.g., the Power Systems and Lighting division). Changes also were highly disruptive to GE's "social architecture"; friendship groups were broken up and scattered throughout the company. In all, GE has been a living example of many different barriers to change all rolled into a single company.

Readiness for Change: When Will Organizational Change Occur?

As you might imagine, there are times when organizations are likely to change and other times during which change is less likely. In general, change is inclined to occur when the people involved believe that the benefits associated with making a change outweigh the costs.[33] The factors contributing to the benefits of making a change are:

- The amount of dissatisfaction with current conditions
- The availability of a desirable alternative
- The existence of a plan for achieving that alternative

Theorists consider that these three factors combine multiplicatively to determine the benefits of making a change (see Figure 16.13). Thus, if any one of these factors is zero, the benefits of making a change, and the likelihood of change itself, will be zero. If you think about it, this makes sense. After all, people are unlikely to initiate change if they are not at all dissatisfied, or if they don't have any desirable alternative in mind (or any way of attaining that alternative, if they do have one in mind). Of course, for change to occur, the expected benefits must outweigh the likely costs involved (e.g., disruption, uncertainties).

Factors Affecting Resistance to Change

To overcome resistance to change, it helps to discover the individual variables (e.g., personality) and aspects of the work setting to which such resistance is most closely linked. Doing this makes it possible to identify specific ways of changing people and/or changing situations so as to make them more accepting of organizational change.

This approach was taken in a study of officials who worked for a large governmental agency.[34] Using questionnaires that assessed a variety of different individual differences and situational factors, the researchers sought to identify the factors that were linked most closely to an important concept—openness to change (i.e., the extent to which someone is willing to accept changes in his or her organization). The researchers found that three variables in particular were most strongly linked to openness to change. These were as follows:

- *Resilience.* The extent to which they are capable of bouncing back from adversity (recall our discussion of this variable in Chapter 5 as it pertains to stress)
- *Information about change.* Specific facts about how things will be different
- *Change self-efficacy.* Beliefs in one's ability to function effectively despite the demands of change

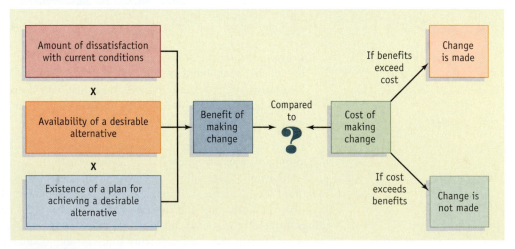

FIGURE 16.13

Organizational Change: When Will It Occur?

Whether or not an organizational change will be made depends on people's beliefs regarding the relative benefits and costs of making the change. The benefits are reflected by three considerations reviewed here.

Source: Based on suggestions by Beer, 1980; see Note 33.

As summarized at the top of Figure 16.14, the relationship between each of these variables and openness to change was positive—in other words, greater amounts of these variables was associated with greater openness to change.

Of course, it's not only what people report on a questionnaire about their openness to change that matters, but also how such openness is related to key aspects of people's work attitudes and behavior. To learn about this, the researchers also assessed a number of variables in their questionnaire. What they found was interesting. Three particular variables were strongly associated with openness to change (see bottom portion of Figure 16.14). The first was job satisfaction (see Chapter 6). The more open to change employees were, the more satisfied they were with their jobs. Furthermore, the more open the workers were to change, the less work-related irritation they showed (i.e., the less they tended to get angry or aggravated at work), and the less likely they were to quit their jobs. Thus, openness to change can make a big difference when it comes to these important aspects of the job.

In view of this, it makes sense to make an effort to make people more resilient to change, to increase the amount of information they have available about how their organizations will change, and to boost their beliefs that they will be able to respond positively to new work situations. As you will see in the next section, several of these suggestions are incorporated into specific approaches to overcoming resistance to organizational change.

How Can Resistance to Organizational Change Be Overcome?

Because organizational change is inevitable, managers should be sensitive to the barriers to change so that resistance can be overcome. This, of course, is easier said than done. However, several useful approaches have been suggested, and the key ones are summarized here.[35]

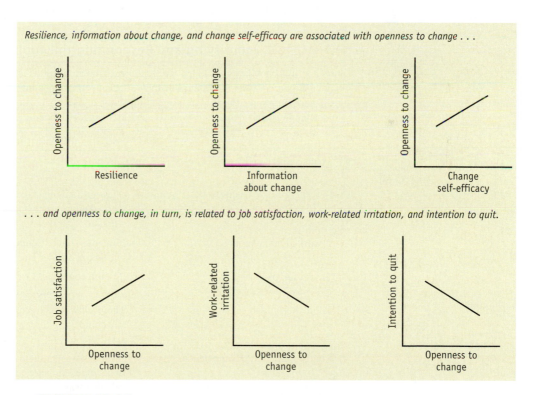

FIGURE 16.14

Variables Linked to Openness to Change: Research Findings

As summarized at the top of this diagram, three factors—resilience, information about change, and change self-efficacy—are associated positively with openness to change. And, as shown at the bottom, openness to change is in turn related to job satisfaction, work-related irritation, and intention to quit.

Source: Based on findings reported by Wanberg & Banas, 2000; see Note 34.

Shape Political Dynamics. For change to be accepted, it often is useful (if not absolutely necessary) to win the support of the most powerful and influential individuals in the company. Doing so builds a critical internal mass of support for change. Demonstrating clearly that key organizational leaders endorse the change is an effective way to get others to go along with it—either because they share the leader's vision or because they fear the leader's retaliation. Either way, their support will facilitate acceptance of change.

Identify and Neutralize Change Resisters. An important way of supporting change initiatives involves neutralizing those who resist change. Often, change is resisted because people say things publicly that express their fears of change, but organizational officials fail to respond. An offhand remark about change that expresses concerns and fears about impending change can be contagious, sending fear into the workplace. Not saying anything to counter such statements is to support that concern tacitly. As such, it is important for people promoting organizational change to identify and neutralize those who resist change. Several statements reflecting a fear of change and ways of responding to them are identified in Table 16.3.[36]

Educate the Workforce. Sometimes, people are reluctant to change because they fear what the future has in store for them. Fears about economic security, for example, may be put to rest by a few reassuring words from powerholders. As part of educating employees about what organizational changes may mean for them, top management must show a considerable amount of emotional sensitivity. Doing so makes it possible for the people affected by change to help make it work. Some companies have found that simply answering the question, "what's in it for me?" can help allay a lot of fears.

"Sell" the Need for Change. For organizational change to occur, top management must accept the idea that change is required. And quite often, it's lower-level managers,

TABLE 16.3 Identifying and Responding to People Who Resist Change

It generally is not difficult to identify employees who are most resistant to change. The things they say give them away. Unless such statements are immediately countered, they run the risk of resistance may spread further throughout the company. Here are some statements that reflect an underlying resistance to change and some guidelines for responding to them.

When They Say . . .	You Should Counter by Saying . . .
That seems risky.	Yes, but the risk is worth taking. After all, it is even riskier to do nothing.
Let's get back to basics.	The world has changed so much that what once seemed appropriate because it was "basic" no longer works today.
It worked in the past.	Maybe so, but as conditions have changed, there is reason to consider a new approach.
Things are okay as they are.	Possibly, but unless we take action, things are unlikely to be okay in the future.
I don't see any threat.	There's always a threat. Just because you don't see any compelling threat doesn't mean that one doesn't exist.
That's not our core competence.	Just because a particular area used to be an organization's core competence doesn't mean that it should stay that way.
The numbers don't work.	In the new Internet-based economy, new rules of accounting may be considered.
Once we start down that road, we can never go back.	Don't be afraid of relinquishing control. Anything that doesn't work can be stopped.
There will be unforeseen consequences.	This is always the case. In fact, that is precisely why it is necessary to consider making changes.

Source: Based on suggestions by Reich, 2000; see Note 36.

those who toil daily in the trenches, who offer the best ideas. For these ideas to be accepted and implemented, however, it's necessary for top officials to be convinced that the ideas are worthwhile. How, then, do managers "sell" their bosses on the need for change? A recent study has examined this question.[37] Scientists conducting this research interviewed managers from various departments in a large hospital, inquiring as to how they went about presenting their ideas for change to top management. Carefully analyzing the responses led them to identify three major approaches, known as "issue selling" techniques (for a summary, see Figure 16.15). These are as follows:

- **Packaging moves.** This involves combining several ideas into a coherent whole. It includes such approaches as presenting one's ideas in the form of a clear business plan, and "bundling" the idea together with other key organizational concerns, such as profitability.
- **Involvement moves.** This has to do with involving other people in the selling of the idea, such as other top-level personnel, others at the same level, or even others outside the organization.
- **Process moves.** This involves paying attention to matters of form and style, such as giving a thorough presentation with all the issues carefully thought out, and presenting ideas at the most opportune time and in a persistent fashion.

Although one cannot guarantee that top leaders always will follow the advice of their lower-level managers, for them to have any chance of doing so, they must be convinced of the merit of their ideas. And, to increase the chances that managers' good ideas will come across, it may well help to follow these moves.

Involve Employees in the Change Efforts. It is well established that people who participate in making a decision tend to be more committed to the outcomes of the decision than are those who are not involved. Accordingly, employees who are involved in

---

FIGURE 16.15

How Do Managers "Sell" Ideas About Change to Their Superiors?

Interviews with managers have revealed that to "sell" their superiors on ideas about organizational change, they rely on the three kinds of "moves" identified here.

Source: Based on suggestions by Dutton, Ashford, O'Neill, & Lawrence, 2001; see Note 37.

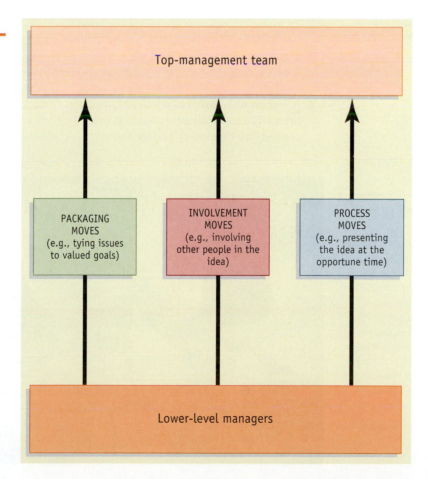

responding to unplanned change, or who are made part of the team charged with planning a needed organizational change, may be expected to have very little resistance to change. Organizational changes that are "sprung" on the workforce with little or no warning might be expected to encounter resistance simply as a knee-jerk reaction until employees have a chance to assess how the change affects them. In contrast, employees who are involved in the change process are better able to understand the need for change, and are therefore less likely to resist it. Says Duane Hartley, general manager of Hewlett-Packard's microwave instruments division, "I don't think people really enjoy change, but if they can participate in it and understand it, it can become a positive [experience] for them."[38]

Reward Constructive Behaviors. One rather obvious, and quite successful, mechanism for facilitating organizational change, as we noted in Chapter 3, is to reward people for behaving in the desired fashion. Changing organizational operations may necessitate changing the kinds of behaviors that need to be rewarded by the organization. This is especially critical when an organization is in the transition period of introducing the change. For example, employees who are required to learn to use new equipment should be praised for their successful efforts. Feedback on how well they are doing not only provides a great deal of useful assurance to uncertain employees, but also helps shape the desired behavior.

Create a "Learning Organization." Although all organizations change, whether they want to or not, some do so more effectively than others. Those organizations that have developed the capacity to adapt and change continuously are known as **learning organizations**.[39] In learning organizations, people set aside old ways of thinking, freely share ideas with others, form a vision of the organization, and work together on a plan for achieving that vision. Examples of learning organizations include Ford, General Electric, Wal-Mart, Xerox, and Motorola (see Figure 16.16).

As you might imagine, becoming a learning organization is no simple feat. In fact, it involves implementing many of the principles of organizational behavior described in this book. Specifically, for a firm to become a continuous learner, management must take the following steps.

- *Establish commitment to change.* Unless all employees clearly see that top management is committed strongly to changing and improving the organization, they will be unlikely to make the changes necessary to bring about improvements.
- *Adopt an informal organizational structure.* Change is more readily accepted when organizational structures (described in Chapter 15) are flat, cross-functional teams are created (see Chapter 8), and the formal boundaries between people are eliminated.

learning organization
An organization that is successful at acquiring, cultivating, and applying knowledge that can be used to help it adapt to changes.

FIGURE 16.16

Motorola: A Learning Organization

This woman works at a Motorola factory in Penong, Malaysia, which makes two-way radios and cell phones. Her company has been actively engaged in becoming a *learning organization*—that is, one in which people set aside old ways of thinking in an effort to make continuous changes that help the business.

■ *Develop an open organizational culture.* As we described in Chapter 14, managers play a key role in forming *organizational culture*. To adapt effectively to changes in their environments, organizations should have cultures that embrace risk taking, openness, and growth. Companies whose leaders are reluctant to confront the risk of failure are ones that will be unlikely to grow and develop.

Take the Situation into Account. Although the suggestions we have identified thus far may be very useful, they fail to take into account the nature of the situation in which change efforts are to be undertaken. Should changes be imposed on employees or should they be involved in the process of designing the change efforts? Organizational scientists have determined that precisely how one should approach the change process depends on the nature of the situation that is being faced.[40] Some strategies for ways to overcome resistance to change in various situations are summarized in Table 16.4.

Although these suggestions may be easier to state than to implement, efforts at following them will be well rewarded. Given the many forces that make employees resistant to change, managers should keep these guidelines in mind. (For some suggestions as to how some effective organizations promote change, see the *How to Do It* section on p. 648.)

Organizational Development Interventions: Implementing Planned Change

organizational development (OD)

A set of social science techniques designed to plan change in organizational work settings, for purposes of enhancing the personal development of individuals and improving the effectiveness of organizational functioning.

Now that we've shed some light on the basic issues surrounding organizational change, we are prepared to examine planned ways of implementing it—collectively known as techniques of **organizational development (OD)**. Formally, we may define organizational development as a set of social science techniques designed to plan and implement change in work settings for purposes of enhancing the personal development of individuals and improving the effectiveness of organizational functioning. By planning organization-wide changes involving people, OD seeks to enhance organizational performance by improving the quality of the work environment and the attitudes and well-being of employees.

Over the years, many different strategies for implementing planned organizational change (referred to as *OD interventions*) have been used by specialists attempting to improve organizational functioning (referred to as *OD practitioners*).[41] All the major methods of organizational development attempt to produce some kind of change in individual employees, work groups, and/or entire organizations. This is the goal of the five OD interventions we review here.

Management by Objectives: Clarifying Organizational Goals

In Chapter 7 we discussed the motivational benefits of setting specific goals. As you might imagine, not only individuals, but also entire organizations stand to benefit from setting specific

---

TABLE 16.4 Situation-Based Strategies for Overcoming Resistance to Change

An effective way to approach overcoming resistance to change is to consider the nature of the situation in which change is required and to respond accordingly. Some important ways of overcoming resistance to change in various situations are summarized here.

In Situations in Which . . .	Resistance to Change Should Be Overcome by . . .	This Is Effective Because . . .
Information is lacking or is inaccurate.	Educating employees and communicating with them	Employees can help make the changes once they appreciate their importance.
Management doesn't know what type of change is best.	Involving employees in the process of making the change	Employees' commitment to change will be enhanced.
Employees are concerned about losses resulting from change.	Negotiating an agreement about other aspects of work	It finds a way for employees to win, thereby offsetting their losses.
Changes are vital and must be made immediately.	Imposing the required changes	Time is of the essence; explanations can follow.

Source: Based on suggestions by Kotter, 1995; Kotter & Schlesinger, 1979; see Note 40.

HOW TO DO IT

Making Changes Stick: Tips from Three Established Organizations

If you want to understand change, it makes sense to look at successful organizations that have been around for a while. After all, to have made it for 100 years, an organization must be managing change quite effectively. This clearly applies to three of the world's largest organizations—Sears, Royal Dutch Shell, and the United States Army. By analyzing what they have done to manage change effectively, it's possible to identify several practices that are worth emulating.[42]

1. *Fully incorporate employees into challenges faced by the organization.* This means more than simply involving employees in the organization's operations—actively engaging employees at all levels in the problems it faces. Officials from Shell Malaysia had long been unsuccessful in getting employees to work together to beat the competition. They were far too complacent, and the competition was rapidly gaining market share. In response to this, Shell officials called together all 260 managers for a $2\frac{1}{2}$-day session in which the problem of the rapidly encroaching competition was put before them. They emerged from this marathon session with a firm plan that was put into place. Back on the job, regular follow-up meetings were held to make sure the plan was implemented. Finally, because the employees bought into the problem and met the challenge themselves, Shell was successful in changing the way it operated.

2. *Lead in a way that stresses the urgency of change.* It's not unusual for company officials to get in a rut, becoming lazy and complacent about the way they operate—even if it's necessary to take decisive action. This is *almost* what happened to Sears a few years ago. The retailing giant was losing customers rapidly as officers sat by, merely lowering sales goals. That's when CEO Arthur Martinez lit a fire under everyone by stressing the importance of turning things around—or else! He generated a sense of urgency by setting very challenging goals (e.g., quadrupling market share and increasing customer satisfaction by 15 percent). Although Martinez didn't have all the answers to Sears' problems, he provided something even more important—straightforward, honest talk about the company's problems, creating a sense of urgency that got everyone moving in the right direction.

3. *Create relentless discomfort with the status quo.* Following military maneuvers, the U.S. Army thoroughly debriefs all participants in what is called an "After Action Review." In these sessions, careful feedback is given about what soldiers did well and where they stand to improve. By focusing in a relentless, detailed manner on work that needs to be done, officers eventually get soldiers to internalize the need for excellence. Soldiers return to their home bases asking themselves how they can do something better (faster, cheaper, or more accurately), or if there is a new and better approach that could be taken. In short, the status quo is the enemy; current performance levels are never accepted. Things can always be better. Army brass liken this commitment to continuous improvement to painting a bridge: The job is never over.

Although these measures are rather extreme measures—and may not always be easy to implement—they certainly warrant careful consideration. After all, they have worked well for some of the most successful organizations in the world.

---

goals. For example, an executive may express interest in "raising productivity" and "improving the quality" of her company's goods or services. These objectives, well-intentioned though they may be, are not as useful to an organization as more specific ones, such as, "increase production of widgets by 15 percent" or "lower the failure rate of widgets by 25 percent." After all, as the old saying goes, "It's usually easier to get somewhere if you know where you're going." The late management expert Peter Drucker was well aware of this idea while consulting for General Electric during the early 1950s and is credited with promoting the benefits of specifying clear organizational goals—a technique known as **management by objectives (MBO)**.

As summarized in Figure 16.17, the MBO process consists of three basic steps. First, goals are selected that employees will try to attain to best serve the needs of the organization. The goals should be selected by managers and their subordinates working together and not simply imposed on subordinates by managers. Further, these goals should be directly measurable

management by objectives (MBO)

The technique by which managers and their subordinates work together to set, and then meet, organizational goals.

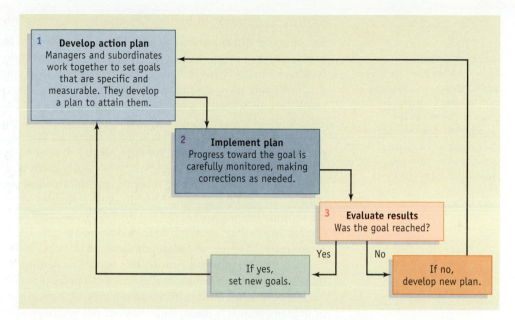

FIGURE 16.17

Management by Objectives: Developing Organizations Through Goal Setting

The organizational development technique of *management by objectives* requires managers and their subordinates to work together on setting and trying to achieve important organizational goals. The basic steps of the process are outlined here.

action plan

A carefully specified set of guidelines indicating exactly what needs to be done to attain desired results.

and have some time frame attached to them. Goals that cannot be measured (e.g., "make the company better"), or that have no time limits, are useless. It also is crucial that managers and their subordinates work together to plan ways of attaining the goals they have selected—developing what is known as an *action plan*. Specifically, an **action plan** is a carefully specified set of guidelines indicating exactly what needs to be done to attain desired results.

Once goals are set and action plans have been developed to accomplish them, the second step calls for *implementation*—carrying out the plan and regularly assessing its progress. Is the plan working? Are the goals being approximated? Are there any problems being encountered in attempting to meet the goals? Such questions need to be considered while implementing an action plan. If the plan is failing, a midcourse correction may be in order—changing the plan, the way it's carried out, or even the goal itself.

Finally, after monitoring progress toward the goal, the third step may be instituted: *evaluation*—assessing goal attainment. Were the organization's goals reached? If so, what new goals should be set to improve things still further? If not, what new plans can be initiated to help meet the goals? Because the ultimate assessment of the extent to which goals are met helps determine the selection of new goals, MBO is a continuous process.

MBO represents a potentially effective source of planning and implementing strategic change for organizations. Individual efforts designed to meet organizational goals get individual employees and their organizations working together toward common ends. When this happens, systemwide change results. Of course, for MBO to work, everyone involved has to buy into it. Because MBO programs typically require a great deal of participation by lower-level employees, top managers must be willing to accept and support the cooperation and involvement of all.

Making MBO work also requires a great deal of time—anywhere from three to five years. Hence, MBO may be inappropriate in organizations that do not have the appropriate time to commit to the process. Despite these considerations, MBO has become one of the most widely used techniques for affecting organizational change in recent years. Not only is it used on an ad hoc basis by many organizations, but it also constitutes an ingrained element of the organizational culture in some companies, such as Hewlett-Packard and Intel.

Survey Feedback: Inducing Change by Sharing Information

survey feedback

An OD technique in which questionnaires and interviews are used to collect information about issues of concern to an organization. This information is shared with employees and is used as the basis for planning organizational change.

For effective organizational change to occur, employees must understand the organization's current strengths and weaknesses. That's the underlying rationale behind the **survey feedback** method. This technique follows the three steps summarized in Figure 16.18.

First, data are collected that provide information about matters of general concern to employees, such as organizational culture (see Chapter 14), leadership style (see Chapter 13), and job satisfaction (see Chapter 6). This may take the form of intensive interviews or structured questionnaires, or both. Because it is important that this information be as unbiased as possible, employees providing feedback should be assured that their responses will be kept confidential. For this reason, this process is usually conducted by outside consultants.

The second step calls for reporting the information obtained back to the employees during small group meetings. Typically, this consists of summarizing the average scores on the information assessed in the survey. Profiles are created of feelings about the organization, its leadership, the work done, and related topics. Discussions also focus on why the scores are as they are, and what problems are revealed by the feedback.

The final step involves analyzing problems dealing with communication, decision making, and other organizational processes to make plans for dealing with them. Such discussions are usually most effective when they are carefully documented and a specific plan of implementation is made, with someone put in charge of carrying it out.

Survey feedback is used widely as an organizational development technique. This is not surprising in view of the advantages it offers. It is efficient, allowing a great deal of information to be collected relatively quickly. Also, it is very flexible and can be tailored to the needs of different organizations facing a variety of problems. However, the technique can be no better than the quality of the questionnaire used—it must measure the things that really matter to employees. Of course, to derive the maximum benefit from survey feedback, it must have the support of top management. The plans developed by the small discussion groups must be capable of being implemented with the full approval of the organization. When these conditions are met, survey feedback can be a very effective OD technique.

Appreciative Inquiry

appreciative inquiry (AI)

An OD intervention that focuses attention away from an organization's shortcoming, and toward its capabilities and its potential; based on the assumption that members of organizations already know the problems they face and that they stand to benefit more by focusing on what is possible.

Although survey feedback and MBO are highly regarded OD techniques, they focus only on deficiencies, such as negative feedback and unmet goals. By contrast, a relatively new approach to organizational development known as *appreciative inquiry* helps organizations focus on the positive and the possible.[43] Specifically, **appreciative inquiry (AI)** is an OD intervention that focuses attention away from an organization's shortcomings and toward its capabilities and its potential. It is based on the assumption that members of organizations already know the problems they face and that they stand to benefit more by focusing on what is possible.

As currently practiced, the process of appreciative inquiry involves assembling small groups of people from an organization and guiding them through four straightforward steps. These are as follows.[44]

FIGURE 16.18

Survey Feedback: An Overview

The *survey feedback* technique of organizational development follows the three steps outlined here: collecting data, giving feedback, and developing action plans.

1. *Discovery.* The discovery step involves identifying the positive aspects of the organi-zation, the best of "what is." This frequently is accomplished by documenting the positive reactions of customers or people from other organizations.
2. *Dreaming.* Through the process of discovering the organization's strengths, it is possi-ble to begin dreaming by envisioning "what might be." By discussing dreams for a the-oretically ideal organization, employees are free to reveal their ideal hopes and dreams.
3. *Designing.* The designing stage involves having a dialogue in which participants dis-cuss their ideas about "what should be." The underlying idea is that by listening to others in a highly receptive manner, it is possible to understand others' ideas and to come to a common understanding of what the future should look like.
4. *Delivering.* After having jointly discussed the ideal state of affairs, members of the organization are ready to begin instituting a plan for delivering their ideas. Specifically, this involves establishing specific objectives and directions regarding "what will be."

Because appreciative inquiry is an emerging approach to OD, it has not been used as widely as the better established OD techniques we've described thus far. However, those organizations in which it has been used have enjoyed beneficial results.[45] For a particularly interesting example of such success, see Figure 16.19.[46]

Action Labs

Usually, bringing about change in organizations is a very slow process. At a typical large company, it involves painstakingly analyzing and planning ideas and then rolling out only small changes in a deliberate sequence. However, in today's rapidly moving world, this pace is likely to be far too slow. To accelerate the change process a technique known as the *action lab* has been introduced in recent years. The action lab is meant to be a "greenhouse" in which change can be created by insulating a group of decision makers from daily operations

FIGURE 16.19

Appreciative Inquiry at Work

Change doesn't come readily in military organizations. However, high-ranking officers in the U.S. Navy have recognized that technology makes it possible for lower-ranking sailors to collect and synthesize information enabling them to make their own decisions. To develop a plan for crafting and implementing the required changes, the *appreciative inquiry* technique was used. During the course of a 4-day "Leadership Summit," 260 people ranging from seamen to admirals (all dressed in civilian clothes to equalize them) followed the 4-D steps. This session culminated in 30 projects aimed at bringing about the required changes. The Chief of Naval Operations commented, "We will not stop; we have too much invested. I say to you, let's go try it."

action lab

An OD intervention in which teams of participants work off-site to develop and implement new ways of solving organizational problems by focusing on the ineffectiveness of current methods.

and getting them to focus on a business problem. Specifically, an **action lab** is an OD intervention in which teams of participants work off-site to develop and implement new ways of solving organizational problems by focusing on the ineffectiveness of current methods.[47]

One of the unique features of action labs is that the participants are in contact with one another for such extended periods of time (e.g., every day for four weeks) that they eventually find it impossible to cling to their established ways. For example, in one particular action lab team, participants faced a frustrating few days in which bold proposals constantly were being shot down. Inevitably, an executive in the team would find some flaw and the idea was dropped in an attempt to avoid conflict. Soon, however, members of the team realized that despite the aim of treating everyone as equals, they inevitably retreated to the safety of the company's established practice of pleasing the bosses. Eventually, the lab participants figured out that the very forces that were blocking changes in the company were also present within the lab. They were more concerned with avoiding conflict than with getting new ideas out into the open. Only once this insight occurred was the way paved for the team to develop innovative new ideas.

Let's consider an example of how an action lab helped facilitate change in an organization. The Cummins Engine Company used an action lab to develop a strategy consisting of several teams that focused on ways in which the company could regain its former leadership in the diesel engine manufacturing business. An action lab was formed consisting of several teams, one of which included union stewards, manufacturing supervisors, and plant managers.[48] Carefully analyzing the situation, they discovered that customers were turning to competitors because they offered less expensive products. Cummins' long-time strategy was to attract customers by emphasizing "lifetime customer value," that is, by getting them to realize that the high quality of their engines made them less expensive over the products' lifetimes. This image served the company well, but it didn't compensate for the competitors' lower initial prices, causing sales to slip.

Analyzing the problem, the team figured out that, to remain competitive, Cummins had to reduce prices by 20 percent. The barrier was the long-standing practice of manufacturing all components in-house to ensure the highest quality standards. The lab team realized that this cherished practice had to be abandoned. Within one month's time, the team established strategic alliances (see Chapter 15) with various suppliers who could manufacture the parts less expensively. Cummins would assemble the final products and serve as the "quality watchdog" for the overall manufacturing process. Although this process has been in place for only a few years, it seems to be very successful thus far. Quality has been high and Cummins is on its way to regaining its dominance in the diesel engine business.

Quality of Work Life Programs: Humanizing the Workplace

quality of work life (QWL)

An OD technique designed to improve organizational functioning by humanizing the workplace, making it more democratic, and involving employees in decision making.

work restructuring

The process of changing the way jobs are done to make them more interesting to workers.

quality circles (QCs)

An approach to improving the quality of work life, in which small groups of volunteers meet regularly to identify and solve problems related to the work they perform and the conditions under which they work.

When you think of work, do you think of drudgery? Although many people believe these two terms go together naturally, it has grown increasingly popular to improve systematically the quality of life experienced on the job in systematic fashion. As more people demand satisfying and personally fulfilling places to work, OD practitioners have attempted to create work situations that enhance employees' motivation, satisfaction, and commitment—factors that may contribute to high levels of organizational performance. Such efforts are known collectively as **quality of work life (QWL)** programs. These programs are ways of increasing organizational output and improving quality by involving employees in the decisions that affect them on their jobs. Typically, QWL programs support highly democratic treatment of employees at all levels and encourage their participation in decision making. Although many approaches to improving the quality of work life exist, they all share a common goal: humanizing the workplace.

One popular approach to improving the quality of work life involves **work restructuring**—the process of changing the way jobs are done to make them more interesting to workers. We already discussed several such approaches to redesigning jobs—including *job enlargement, job enrichment,* and the *job characteristics model*—in our discussion of motivation in Chapter 7. These techniques are also considered effective ways of improving the quality of work life for employees.

Another approach to improving the quality of work life involves using **quality circles (QCs)**. These are small groups of volunteers (usually around 10) who meet regularly (usually weekly) to identify and solve problems related to the quality of the work they perform and the conditions under which people do their jobs. An organization may have several QCs operating at once, each of which deals with a particular work area about which it has the most expertise. To help them work effectively, the members of the circle usually receive some form of training in problem solving. Large companies such as Westinghouse, Hewlett-Packard, and Eastman Kodak, to name only a few, have included QCs as part of their QWL efforts. Groups have dealt with issues such as how to reduce vandalism, how to create safer and more comfortable working environments, and how to improve product quality. Research has shown that although quality circles are very effective at bringing about short-term improvements in quality of work life (i.e., those lasting up to 18 months), they are less effective at creating more permanent changes.

Three major benefits—even if short-term ones—may result from QWL programs. The most direct benefit usually is increased job satisfaction, organizational commitment, and reduced turnover within the workforce (see Chapter 6). A second benefit—and a major one—is increased productivity. A final benefit related to these first two is increased organizational effectiveness (e.g., profitability, goal attainment).

As you might imagine, achieving these benefits is not automatic. For success to be possible, it's crucial to incorporate the following two key provisions into any QWL program.

■ **Both management and labor must cooperate in designing the program.** Should either believe that the program is really just a method of gaining an advantage over the other, it is doomed to fail.

■ **The plans agreed to by all concerned parties must be fully implemented.** It is too easy for action plans developed in QWL groups to be forgotten. To keep this from occurring amidst the hectic pace of daily activities, it should be considered the responsibility of employees at all levels—from the highest-ranking executive to the lowest-level laborer—to follow through on their parts of the plan.

Over the years, some of the largest and best known companies, such as Ford and General Electric, have had active—and very successful—QWL programs. Their successes, in part, have been based on their careful attention to these two vitally important considerations.

Now that we've described a variety of OD techniques, you may find yourself wondering if engaging in these practices is ethical. They do, after all, encourage people to change in ways that they might find undesirable. To some, it's commonsensical that because of this, OD is unethical. However, there are several important counterarguments to this that we raise in the *OB: Making Sense Out of Common Sense* section on page 654.

Critical Questions About Organizational Development

No discussion of organizational development would be complete without addressing two fundamental questions—do the techniques work (i.e., do they bring about the desired results), and if so, where (i.e., are they culture-bound)? We now consider these two important questions.

The Effectiveness of Organizational Development: Does It Really Work?

Thus far, we have described some of the major techniques used by OD practitioners to improve organizational functioning. As is probably clear, carrying out these techniques requires a considerable amount of time, money, and effort. Accordingly, it is appropriate to ask if this investment is worthwhile. In other words, does OD really work? Given the popularity of OD in organizations, this question is very important. Most of the studies bearing on the answer show the effects of the various OD interventions to be beneficial—particularly when it comes to improving organizational functioning.[49]

We hasten to add that any conclusions about the effectiveness of OD should be qualified in several important ways.

■ **OD interventions tend to be more effective among blue-collar employees than among white-collar employees.** This likely occurs for a simple reason—namely, that most OD techniques are focused on changing the behavior of front-line people in operative roles rather than higher-level decision-makers.

■ **The beneficial effects of OD can be enhanced by using a combination of several techniques (e.g., two or more together) instead of any single technique.** Given that

OB Making Sense Out of Common Sense

Organizational Development Is Inherently Unethical—Or Is It?

By its very nature, OD applies powerful social science techniques in an attempt to change attitudes and behavior. Because of this, some people have argued over the years that its practice is inherently unethical. After all, they argued, it is only common sense that changing people in ways they might not want to be changed is manipulative and inappropriate.[50]

For example, it has been claimed that OD techniques impose the values of the organization on the individual without taking the individual's own attitudes into account. OD is a very one-sided approach, reflecting the imposition of the more powerful organization on the less powerful individual. A related issue is that the OD process does not provide for any free choice on the part of the employees. As a result, it may be seen as *coercive* and *manipulative.* When faced with a "do it, or else" situation, employees tend to have little free choice and are forced to allow themselves to be manipulated, a potentially degrading prospect.

Another argument is that the unequal power relationship between the organization and its employees makes it possible for the true intent of OD techniques to be misrepresented. As an example, imagine that an MBO technique is presented to employees as a means of allowing greater organizational participation, whereas in reality it is used as a means for holding individuals responsible for their poor performance and punishing them as a result. Although such an event might not happen, the potential for abuse of this type does exist, and the potential to misuse the technique—even if not originally intended—might later prove to be too great a temptation.

Despite these considerations, many professionals (ourselves included) do not agree that OD is inherently

unethical. Such a claim, it has been countered, is to say that the practice of management is itself unethical. After all, the very act of going to work for an organization requires one to submit to the organization's values and the overall values of society at large. One cannot help but face life situations in which others' values are imposed. This is not to say that organizations have the right to impose patently unethical values on people for the purpose of making a profit (e.g., stealing from customers). Indeed, because they have the potential to abuse their power (such as in the MBO example above), organizations have a special obligation to refrain from doing so.

Although abuses of organizational power are all too common, OD itself is not necessarily the culprit. Indeed, like any other tool (even a gun!), OD is not inherently good or evil. Instead, many proponents of OD argue that whether the tool is used for good or evil will depend on the individual using it. With this in mind, the ethical use of OD interventions will require that they be supervised by professionals in an organization that places a high value on ethics. In fact, today's OD practitioners subscribe to a Code of Ethics that holds them to clear standards with respect to ensuring the benefits to organizations and the well-being of all employees.[51]

To the extent that top management officials embrace ethical values and behave ethically themselves, norms for behaving ethically are likely to develop in organizations. When an organization has a strong ethical culture, it is unlikely that OD practitioners would even think of misusing their power to harm individuals. The need to develop such a culture has been recognized as a way for organizations to take not only moral leadership in their communities, but financial leadership as well.

---

the various techniques have strengths and weaknesses, it is not surprising that using one approach to offset the limitations of another stands to be quite helpful.

■ *The effectiveness of OD techniques depends on the degree of support they receive from top management.* The more programs are supported from the top, the more successful they tend to be. We already made this point in conjunction with QWL programs, but it is applicable to all OD interventions. If management is not fully supportive of such efforts, they are doomed to fail.

Despite the obvious importance of attempting to evaluate the effectiveness of OD interventions, a great many of them go unevaluated. There are two key reasons for this. First, we must note the difficulty of assessing change. Because many factors can cause people to behave differently in organizations, and because such behaviors may be difficult to measure, many OD practitioners avoid the problem of measuring change altogether. Second, political pressures to justify OD programs may discourage some OD professionals from honestly and accurately assessing their effectiveness. After all, in doing so, one runs the risk of scientifically demonstrating one's wasted time and money. Although these considerations are understandable, they certainly are not advisable. Assessing the effectiveness of any OD program is wise insofar as it provides valuable feedback about precisely how things can be improved in the future. Just as a medical doctor must know the effectiveness of his or her efforts to cure illness to take an appropriate course of action, so too must organizational practitioners assess the impact of their own actions.

Overall, our conclusion is positive. Despite some limitations, organizational development techniques have considerable capacity to benefit both organizations and the individuals working within them. And, as you may recall from Chapter 1, these are among the fundamental purposes of the field of OB.

Is Organizational Development Dependent on National Culture?

For organizational development to be effective, people must be willing to share their ideas candidly with others, they must be willing to accept uncertainty, and they must be willing to show concern for others, especially members of their own teams. However, not all people are willing to do these things; this pattern better characterizes the people from some countries than others. For example, this profile perfectly describes people from Scandinavian countries, suggesting that OD may be most effective in such nations. However, people from Latin American nations are much the opposite, suggesting that OD interventions will be less successful when conducted there.[52] For a summary of the extent to which the basic assumptions of OD fit with the cultural styles of people from various nations, see Figure 16.20.

Although the predominant cultural values of people from the United States places it in the middle region of the diagram in Figure 16.20, this is not to say that OD is doomed to be ineffective in American companies. Not all OD techniques are alike with respect to their underlying cultural values.[53] For example, MBO has become a very popular OD technique in the United States in large part because it promotes the American values of willingness to take risks and working aggressively at attaining high performance. However, because MBO also encourages superiors and subordinates to negotiate freely with each other, the technique has been generally unsuccessful in France, where others' higher levels of authority are well accepted.[54] Reasoning similarly, one may expect survey feedback to be unsuccessful in the southeast Asian nation of Brunei, where the prevailing cultural value is such that problems are unlikely to be confronted openly.[55]

These examples illustrate a key point: The effectiveness of OD techniques will depend, in part, on the extent to which the values of the technique match the underlying values of the national culture in which it is employed. As such, OD practitioners must appreciate fully the cultural norms of the nations in which they are operating. Failure to do so not only may make OD interventions unsuccessful, but they may even yeild unintended negative consequences.

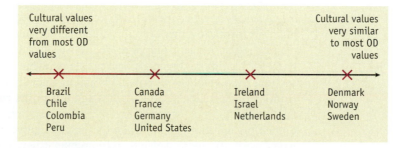

FIGURE 16.20

Organizational Development: Its Fit with National Values

Organizational development (*OD*) techniques tend to be more successful when the underlying values of the technique match the cultural values of the nations in which it is used. General OD values tend to conform more to the cultural norms of some nations, shown on the right (where OD is more likely to be accepted), than others, shown on the left (where OD is less likely to be accepted).

Source: Based on suggestions by Jaeger, 1986; see Note 52.

Summary and Review of Learning Objectives

1. **Characterize the prevalence of the change process in organizations.**
   Organizational change is very prevalent and is occurring at a rapid pace. Almost all organizations are changing in one way or another in order to survive. Inevitably, those that fail to adapt, fail. Research has shown that the tendency for organizational change to occur is not limited to organizations in North America. Change is occurring rapidly in organizations of all nations throughout the world.

2. **Understand what, exactly, is changed when organizational change comes about, and the forces responsible for unplanned organizational change.**
   The process of organizational change involves some combination of changing organizational structure, technology, and people. Unplanned change occurs in organizations due to: shifting employee demographics, performance gaps, governmental regulation, economic competition in the global arena, and advances in technology.

3. **Describe what is meant by strategic planning and the types of strategic changes that organizations make.**
   Strategic planning is the process of formulating, implementing, and evaluating decisions that enable an organization to achieve its objectives. Typically, strategic plans are made about changing either a company's products and services, or its organizational structure.

4. **Identify the 10 steps in the strategic planning process.**
   The strategic planning process follows 10 steps: (1) define goals, (2) define the scope of products or services, (3) assess internal resources, (4) assess the external environment, (5) analyze internal arrangements, (6) assess competitive advantage, (7) develop a competitive strategy, (8) communicate the strategy to stakeholders, (9) implement the strategy, and (10) evaluate the outcome.

5. **Explain why people are resistant to organizational change and how this resistance may be overcome.**
   In general, people are resistant to change because of individual factors (e.g., economic insecurity, fear of the unknown) and organizational factors (e.g., the stability of work groups, threats to the existing balance of power). However, resistance to change can be overcome in several ways, including: shaping political dynamics, educating the workforce about the effects of the changes and involving employees in the change process, involving employees in change efforts, rewarding constructive behaviors, and creating a learning organization.

6. **Identify and describe the major organizational development techniques that are used today.**
   Management by objectives (*MBO*) focuses on attempts by managers and their subordinates to work together at setting important organizational goals and developing a plan to help meet them. *Survey feedback* uses questionnaires and/or interviews as the basis for identifying organizational problems, which then are addressed in planning sessions. *Appreciative inquiry* (*AI*) is an OD intervention that focuses attention away from an organization's shortcomings and toward its capabilities and its potential. It involves having small groups of workers discover, dream, design, and deliver changes to their organizations. An *action lab* is an OD intervention in which teams of participants work off-site to develop and implement new ways of solving organizational problems by focusing on the ineffectiveness of current methods. *Quality of work life* (*QWL*) programs seek to humanize the workplace by involving employees in the decisions affecting them (e.g., through quality circle meetings) and by restructuring the jobs themselves. The rationale underlying all of these techniques is that they may enhance organizational functioning by involving employees in identifying and solving organizational problems. Overall, research suggests that they generally are effective in this regard.

Points to Ponder

Questions for Review

1. When people talk about organizational change, what precisely is being changed and what forces lead to such change?
2. Under what conditions will people be most willing to make changes in organizations? Explain your answer and give an example.
3. What is meant by strategic planning, and what are the steps in the strategic planning process?
4. What are the major techniques of organizational development?
5. Overall, how effective is organizational development in improving organizational functioning? With respect to what factors does it work or not work?
6. Argue for or against the following statement: "Organizational development doesn't work." Explain your answer.

Experiential Questions

1. Think about the one job in a company with which you are most familiar (a job you have or one that a close friend or family member has). Based on what you know about this position, how has the nature of this job changed over the years? What is done differently, and why? In what ways has technology been involved? To what extent do you believe that the company benefited from these changes?
2. Think back to one particular change that was made in the organization in which you either work or have worked. What concerns did you have about it? Were you resistant to this change? If so, what, if anything, did management do to allay your fears? What might they have done?
3. Have you ever participated in some type of organizational development effort? If so, what was done? How did you feel about the program? Do you believe the effort was effective?

Questions to Analyze

1. Suppose you are having difficulty managing a small group of subordinates who work in an office 1,000 miles away from your home base. What kinds of changes in structure, technology, and people can be implemented to more closely supervise these distant employees?
2. Suppose that you are a top executive of a large organization about to undertake an ambitious restructuring plan that involves massive changes in job responsibilities for most employees. Explain why people might be resistant to such changes and what steps could be taken to overcome this resistance.
3. Imagine that you are a manager whose unit is suffering problems due to a lack of coordination between employees. How can OD techniques be used to address this problem? Which particular technique would you use and why? What do you need to do to help ensure its success?

Experiencing OB

Individual Exercise

Developing a Strategic Plan

Developing a strategic plan is not an easy matter. In fact, doing it right requires a great deal of information and a great deal of practice. This exercise will give you a feel for some of the challenges involved in developing such a plan.

Directions

1. Suppose that you are the president of a small software development firm that has for years sold a utility that has added functionality to the operating system used in most computers. Now, you suddenly face a serious problem: Microsoft has changed its operating system such that your product no longer serves any purpose.
2. Using the 10 steps outlined in Figure 16.11, develop a strategic plan to keep your company alive. Make any assumptions you need to develop your plan, but state these in the process of describing it.

Questions for Discussion

1. How easy or difficult was it for you to develop this strategic plan? What would have made the process easier or more effective?
2. Which of the 10 steps would you imagine is easiest to implement? Which do you think would be most challenging?
3. Would you use competitive intelligence in the course of implementing your plan? If so, how?
4. What special challenges, if any, would the employees of your company face as they attempted to implement this plan? How would you attempt to overcome these challenges?

Group Exercise

Recognizing Impediments to Change—and How to Overcome Them

To confront the reality of organizational change, one of the most fundamental steps involves recognizing the barriers to change. Then, once these impediments have been identified, consideration can be given to ways of overcoming them. This exercise is designed to help you practice thinking along these lines while working in groups.

Directions

1. Divide the class into groups of approximately six and gather each group around a circle.
2. Each group should consider each of the following situations.

   ■ *Situation A.* A highly sophisticated e-mail system is being introduced at a large university. It will replace the practice of transmitting memos on paper.
   ■ *Situation B.* A very popular employee who's been with the company for many years is retiring. He will be replaced by a completely new employee from the outside.

3. For each situation, discuss three major impediments to change.
4. Identify a way of overcoming each of these impediments.
5. Have someone from the group record the answers and present them to the class for a discussion session.

Questions for Discussion

1. For each of the situations, were the impediments to change similar or different?
2. Were the ways of overcoming the impediments similar or different?
3. How might the nature of the situation confronted dictate the types of change barriers confronted and the ease with which these may be overcome?

Practicing OB

Concerns About Downsizing

You are the manager of a poorly performing research and development department. In view of the performance problems, there has been talk in the company about the possibility of downsizing your unit. This has aroused a great deal of concern in the workplace as people begin to fear for the security of their jobs. This, in turn, has been disrupting the flow of work. Productivity is slowing down as some of your top engineers have been taking new jobs.

1. Does it make sense to expect your employees to have these fears? Why or why not?
2. Describe the steps you can take to help allay these fears and to return work back to normal. How effective do you think these steps may be?
3. If large-scale downsizing were to occur, how might you use an organizational development technique to help smooth the transition?

CASE IN POINT

Royal Bank of Canada: Changes You Can Bank On

"What do you want from your bank?" This question was uppermost on Cathy Burrows's mind. As senior manager of the Royal Bank of Canada's (RBC) client relationship marketing department, the answers would lead her to changing the huge bank's products, services, and internal operations. With over 62,000 employees, 1,300 branches across Canada, and offices in over 30 countries, making changes at Canada's premier global financial services organization wasn't going to be easy. And she knew it. But, because she also realized that in today's competitive banking market staying atop customers' needs (all 10 million of them, in RBC's case) was paramount to the bank's future success, she knew the effort would be worthwhile.

Launching the initiative, RBC conducted a "gap analysis," an elaborate survey of customers designed to determine disparities between what they wanted from RBC and what they were getting. The conclusion from Toronto headquarters was striking. Clients wanted to have an integrated banking relationship, one in which their financial needs (e.g., for loans, savings, investments, ATMs, and so on) were understood and anticipated over the years.

Burrows acknowledged that these changes were not only reasonable but doable. The first step in making things happen was to empower the bank's sales force to help customers. This involved working with NCR to develop a software program—the Client Sales and Service (CSS) system—that tracked customers' use of bank products. This enabled everyone from tellers on up the line to help clients by recommending to clients ways that the bank could service their needs. The CSS, they believed, would help develop client loyalty, which was likely to be a problem as other banks offered competitive products. At the same time, RBC also found that bank personnel had too much discretion when it came to determining rates for mortgages and investment certificates. The pricing of these products was shifted to the head office, a centralization that boosted profitability.

Another important move that RBC made involved shifting its orientation from only present profitability to long-term, future profitability. This required focusing on customers' needs over the years. For example, although several banks were getting out of the relatively unprofitable (and high-risk) business of granting student loans, RBC chose to keep offering student loans so as to court long-term relationships with these customers. Today's students, they figured, might well become tomorrow's business tycoons, making the investment worthwhile.

Overall, RBC's new approach involved providing value to clients as an ongoing process, instead of an end-point in the relationship. This message comes across loud and clear at the bank's Web site, where a greeting proclaims, "At RBC, we're committed to putting you first and to finding better ways to help meet your financial needs." And its long-term orientation in this regard is suggested clearly by a letter to its clients on "The Reality of Aging" and, of course, a variety of products to help retirees.

Questions for Discussion

1. What adjustments were required at RBC as changes were made?
2. What sources of resistance to change do you suspect were encountered at RBC and how do you think they were overcome?
3. What problems, if any, are likely to be encountered at RBC as efforts are made to sustain these changes over the years?

VIDEO CASES

Boot Camp Nightmare

One glimpse into army boot camp and it's not too hard to find adjectives to describe its culture. Discipline reigns supreme. Boot camp is designed to break down the recruits slowly until they submit to the highly structured and controlled world of the military. Although it sounds torturous, high-ranking military officers assert that this rigorous orientation is essential for recruits to graduate from basic training prepared to serve.

Discussion Questions

1. Describe the culture of the boot camp experience. What elements of organizational culture are depicted in this video clip? Explain how they are illustrated.
2. In your opinion, how is the culture of a business organization similar to and different from the culture found in the military?
3. In what ways does the culture of military organizations support the mission of military organizations? Explain.

Kraft Food Gets Healthy

Obesity is a huge problem in the United States. Instead of taking responsibility for their own poor eating habits, some Americans are blaming fast-food restaurants for exposing them to unhealthy, fattening food. In the wake of the blame game, Kraft has pledged to reduce the calories, fat content, and portion size of many of the most popular products on our shelves.

Discussion Questions

1. In your opinion, do companies deserve to be blamed for childhood obesity? How do you feel about the so-called "fat lawsuits?"
2. What do you believe is Kraft's motivation to make this change? In your opinion, does the company's motivation to change matter at all if the change itself is beneficial to people?
3. This example suggests that social trends can promote organizational change. What other organizational changes appear to be the result of changing social trends?

Appendix 1

LEARNING ABOUT BEHAVIOR IN ORGANIZATIONS: THEORY AND RESEARCH

In Chapter 1, we noted that organizational behavior is a science, and as such, it relies upon the scientific method to draw conclusions about behavior in organizations. As in the case of other scientific fields, OB uses the tools of science to achieve its goals. In this case, those goals are learning about organizations and the behavior of people working in them. With this in mind, it is useful to understand the basic tools scientists use to learn about behavior in organizations. In this Appendix we will briefly describe some of these techniques. Our goal here is not to make you an expert in scientific methodology, but rather, to give you a solid understanding of the techniques you will be encountering as you venture further into this book.

Isn't It All Just Common Sense?

Although you may not be a top executive of a large business firm with decades of experience in the work world (yet, at least), you doubtlessly know *something* about the behavior of people on the job. After all, you probably learned quite a bit from whatever jobs you have had, or from talking to other people about their experiences. This isn't surprising, given that we all can observe a great deal about people's behavior in organizational settings just by paying casual attention. So, whether you're the CEO of a Fortune 500 firm or a part-time pizza delivery driver, chances are good that you already have a few ideas about how people behave on the job. Besides, there are probably some things about behavior in organizations that you take for granted.

For example, would you say that happier employees tend to be more productive? If you're like most people, you probably would say "yes, of course." It's logical, right? Well, despite what you may believe, this is generally *not* true. In fact, as we see in Chapter 5, people who are satisfied with their jobs are not necessarily more productive than those who are dissatisfied with their jobs. This contradiction of common sense is not an isolated example. This book is full of examples of phenomena studied in the field of OB that you might find surprising. To see how good you may be at predicting human behavior in organizations, answer the questions found in the section *OB: Making Sense Out of Common Sense: Check Your Assumptions at the Door* found in Chapter 1 (see p. 10). These questions are our way of demonstrating that there's more to understanding the complexities of behavior in organizations than meets the eye.

So, if we can't trust our common sense, on what can we rely? This is where the scientific method enters the picture. Although social science research is far from perfect, the techniques used to study behavior in organizations can tell us a great deal. Naturally, not everything scientific research reveals contradicts common sense. In fact, a considerable amount of research confirms things we already believe to be true. If this occurs, is the research useless? The answer is emphatically *no!* After all, scientific evidence often provides a great deal of insight into the subtle conditions under which various events occur. Such complexities would not have been apparent from only casual, unsystematic observation and common sense. In other words, the field of OB is based solidly on carefully conducted and logically analyzed research. Although common sense may provide a useful starting point for getting us to think about behavior in organizations, there's no substitute for scientific research when it comes to really understanding what happens and why.

Now that you understand the important role of the scientific method in the field of OB, you are prepared to appreciate the specific approaches used to conduct scientific research in this field. We will begin our presentation of these techniques with a discussion of one of the best-accepted sources of ideas for OB research—*theory*.

Theory: An Indispensable Guide to Organizational Research

What image comes to mind when you think of a scientist at work? Someone wearing a white lab coat surrounded by microscopes and test tubes busily at work testing theories? Although OB scientists typically don't wear lab coats or use microscopes and test tubes, it *is* true that they make use of theories. This is the case despite the fact that OB is, in part, an applied science. Simply because a field is characterized as being "theoretical" does not imply that it is impractical and out of touch with reality. To the contrary, a theory is simply a way of describing the relationship between concepts. Thus, theories help, not hinder, our understanding of practical situations.

What Is a Theory and Why Are Theories Important?

theory
A set of statements about the interrelationships between concepts that allow us to predict and explain various processes and events.

Formally, we define a **theory** as a set of statements about the interrelationships between concepts that allow us to predict and explain various processes and events. As you might imagine, such statements may be of interest to both practitioners and scientists alike. We're certain that as you read this book you will come to appreciate the valuable role that theories play when it comes to understanding behavior in organizations—and putting that knowledge to practical use.

To demonstrate the value of theory in OB, let's consider an example based on a phenomenon described in more detail in Chapter 7—the effects of task goals on performance. Imagine observing that word processing operators type faster when they are given a specific goal (e.g., 75 words per minute) than when they are told to try to do their best. Imagine also observing that salespeople make more sales when they are given quotas than when they are not given any quotas. By itself, these are useful observations insofar as they allows us to predict what will happen when goals are introduced. In addition, it suggests a way to change conditions so as to improve performance among people in these groups. These two accomplishments—*prediction* and *control*—are major goals of science.

Yet, there's something missing—namely, knowing that having specific goals improves performance fails to tell us anything about *why* this is so. What is going on here? After all, this was observed in two different settings and with two different groups of people. Why is it that people are so productive in response to specific goals? This is where theory enters the picture. In contrast to some fields, such as physics and chemistry, where theories often take the form of mathematical equations, theories in OB generally involve verbal assumptions. For example, in the present case, it might be theorized as follows:

- When people are given specific goals they know exactly what's expected of them, and
- When people know what's expected of them, they are motivated to work hard to find ways to succeed, and
- When people work hard to succeed, they perform at high levels.

This simple theory, like all others, consists of two basic elements: *concepts* (in this case goals and motives), and *assertions about how they are related*.

Developing and Testing Theories

hypotheses
Logically derived, testable statements about the relationships between variables that follow from a theory.

In science, the formation of a theory is only the beginning of a sequence of events followed to understand behavior. Once a theory is proposed, it is used to introduce **hypotheses**—logically derived statements that follow from a theory. In our example, it may be hypothesized that specific goals will only improve performance when they are not so difficult that they cannot be attained. Next, such predictions need to be tested in actual research to see if they are confirmed. If research confirms our hypotheses, we can be more confident about the accuracy of the theory. However, if it is not confirmed after several well-conducted studies are done, our confidence in the theory is weakened. When this happens, it's time to revise the theory and generate new, testable hypotheses from it. As you might imagine, given the complexities of human behavior in organizations, theories are rarely—if ever—fully confirmed. In fact, many of the field's most popular and useful theories are constantly being refined and tested. We have summarized the cyclical nature of the scientific endeavor in Figure A1.1.

It probably will come as no surprise to you to learn that the process of theory development and testing we have been describing is very laborious. In view of this, why do scientists bother to constantly fine-tune their theories? The answer lies in the very useful purposes that theories serve. Specifically, theories serve three important functions—organizing, summarizing, and guiding. First, given the complexities of human behavior, theories provide a way of *organizing* large amounts of data into meaningful propositions. In other words, they help us combine information so diverse that it might be difficult to grasp without the help of a theory. Second, theories help us to *summarize* this knowledge by making it possible to make sense out of bits and pieces of information that otherwise would be difficult—if not impossible—to understand. Third, and finally, theories provide an important *guiding* function. That is, they help scientists identify important areas of needed research that would not have been apparent without theories to guide their thinking.

As you read this text you will come across many different theories attempting to explain various aspects of behavior in organizations. When you do, we think you will appreciate the useful organizing, summarizing, and guiding roles they play—in short, how theories help provide meaningful explanations of behavior. In all cases, the usefulness of any theory is based on the extent to which it can be confirmed or disconfirmed. In other words, theories must be *testable*. A theory that cannot be tested serves no real purpose to scientists. Once it's tested, a theory—or, at least part of it—must be confirmed if it is to be considered an accurate account of human behavior. And, of course, that's what the field of OB is all about.

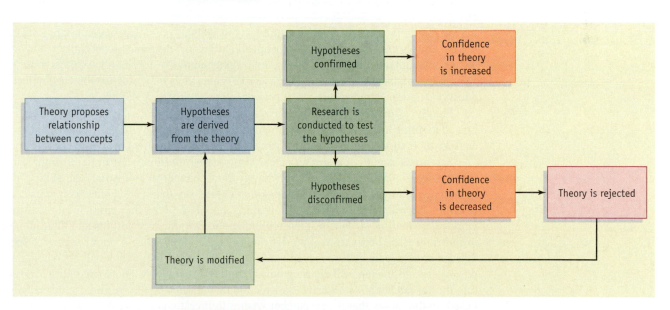

FIGURE A1.1

Theory Testing: The Research Process

Once a theory is formulated, research is conducted to test hypotheses derived from it. If these hypotheses are confirmed, confidence in the theory is increased. If these hypotheses are disconfirmed, confidence in the theory is diminished. At this point, the theory either is modified and retested, or it is rejected completely.

How are theories tested? The answer is: by conducting *research.* Unless we do research we cannot test theories, and unless we test theories, we are greatly limited in what we can learn about behavior in organizations.[1] This is why research is such a major concern of specialists in OB. So, in order for you to fully appreciate the field of OB, it's critical for you to understand something about the techniques it uses—that is, how we come to know about the behavior of people at work. As a result, throughout this book, we not only explain *what* is known about OB, but also *how* that knowledge was derived. We are confident that the better you understand OB's "tools of the trade," the more you will come to appreciate its value as a field. With this in mind, we will now describe some of the major research techniques used to learn about organizational behavior.

Survey Research: The Correlational Method

surveys
Questionnaires in which people are asked to report how they feel about various aspects of themselves, their jobs, and organizations.

The most popular approach to conducting research in OB involves giving people questionnaires in which they are asked to report how they feel about various aspects of themselves, their jobs, and their organizations. Such questionnaires, also known as **surveys**, make it possible for organizational scientists to delve into a broad range of issues. This research technique is so very popular because it is applicable to studying a wide variety of topics. After all, you can learn a great deal about how people feel by asking them a systematic series of carefully worded questions. Moreover, questionnaires are relatively easy to administer (be it by mail, phone, or in person), and—as we will note shortly—they are readily quantifiable and lend themselves to powerful statistical analyses. These features make survey research a very appealing option to OB scientists. Not surprisingly, we will be describing quite a few survey studies throughout this text.

Conducting Surveys

The survey approach consists of three major steps. First, the researcher must identify the variables in which he or she is interested. These may be various aspects of people (e.g., their attitudes toward work), organizations (e.g., the pay plans they use), or the environment in general (e.g., how competitive the industry is). They may be suggested from many different sources, such as a theory, previous research, or even hunches based on casual observations.

Second, these variables are measured as precisely as possible. As you might imagine, it isn't always easy to tap precisely people's feelings about things (especially if they are uncertain about those feelings or reluctant to share them). As a result, researchers must pay a great deal of attention to the way they word the questions they use. For some examples of questions designed to measure various work-related attitudes, see Table A1.1.

Finally, after the variables of interest have been identified and measured, scientists must determine how—if at all—they are related to each other. With this in mind, scientists analyze their survey findings using a variety of different statistical procedures.

Scientists conducting survey research typically are interested in determining how variables are interrelated—or, put differently, how changes in one variable are associated with changes in another variable. For example, let's say that a researcher is interested in learning the relationship between how fairly people believe they are paid and various work-related attitudes, such as their willingness to help their coworkers and their interest in quitting. Based on various theories and previous research, a researcher may suspect that the more people believe they are unfairly paid, the less likely they will be to help their coworkers and the more likely they will be to desire new jobs. These predictions constitute the researcher's *hypothesis*—as we explained earlier, the as-yet-untested prediction based on the theory that the researcher wishes to investigate. After devising an appropriate questionnaire measuring these variables, the researcher would have to administer it to a large number of people so that the hypothesis can be tested.

online surveys
Questionnaires presented to people either via e-mail or using a Web site, which they then complete and return to administrators using the same electronic means.

Today, the practice of conducting surveys online has become very popular.[2] **Online surveys** present questions to people either via e-mail or using a Web site, which respondents then complete and return to administrators using the same electronic means. Many employees enjoy taking surveys online because modern software programs have made

TABLE A1.1 Survey Questions Designed to Measure Work Attitude

Items such as these might be used to measure attitudes toward various aspects of work. People completing the survey are asked to circle the number that corresponds to the point along the scale that best reflects their feelings about the attitude in question.

Overall, how fairly are you paid?

Not at all fairly 1 2 3 4 5 6 7 Extremely fairly

Imagine that one of your colleagues needs to stay late to complete an important project. How likely or unlikely would you be to volunteer to help that person, even if you would not receive any special recognition for your efforts?

Not at all likely 1 2 3 4 5 6 7 Extremely likely

How interested are you in quitting your present job?

Not at all interested 1 2 3 4 5 6 7 Extremely interested

them highly user-friendly, and in some cases, fun to complete (see the samples in Figure A1.2). Many employers and researchers also prefer them to paper-and-pencil questionnaires because they are easier to administer and because they also can provide an instant summary and analysis of responses that would have taken many hours to enter into a statistical analysis program by hand.

This is not to say that online surveys are perfect, by any means. The greatest problem with them is that they cannot always be used because access to online networks is not universal. Thus, any survey results coming from people who complete questionnaires online may not be generalizable to those who either do not have access to computers or who avoid completing online questionnaires because they are uncomfortable working at computers. In short, online surveys should be considered a useful addition to the choices available to researchers interested in administering questionnaires, but not yet a replacement for more traditional, low-tech options. Until this turns around, you might want to keep that #2 pencil handy.

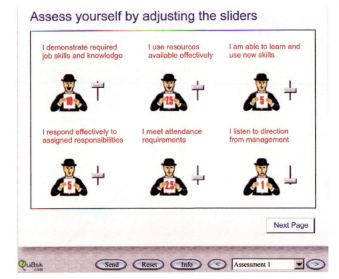

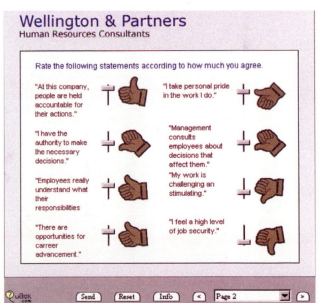

FIGURE A1.2

Online Surveys: Two Examples

Employee satisfaction questionnaires (left) and self-assessment questionnaires (right) are among the many different kinds of surveys that can be presented via e-mail or on Web pages using the "Form Caster" program by Quask. Companies such as GE Medical Systems, Lockheed Martin, and Procter & Gamble have benefited from using this technique.

Analyzing Survey Results: Using Correlations

Once the data are collected (from either paper-and-pencil surveys or online surveys), the investigator must statistically analyze them so as to compare the results to the hypothesis. Generally speaking, researchers are interested in seeing how the variables of interest are related to each other. That is, if they are "co-related"—or, that there exists a meaningful **correlation** between them. Variables are correlated to the extent that the level of one variable is associated with the level of another variable.

Suppose a researcher obtains results like those shown in the left side of Figure A1.3. In this case, the more fairly employees believe they are paid, the more willing they are to help their coworkers. In other words, the variables are related to each other such that the more one variable increases, the more the other variable also increases. Any variables described in this way are said to have a **positive correlation**.

Now, imagine what will be found when the researcher compares the sample's perceptions of pay fairness with their interest in quitting their jobs. If the experimenter's hypothesis is correct, the results will look like those shown on the right side of Figure A1.3. In other words, the more people believe their pay is fair, the less interested they are in looking for a new job. Any such case—in which the more one variable increases, the more another decreases—is said to have a **negative correlation**.

OB scientists are not only interested in the direction of the relationship between variables—that is, whether the association is positive or negative—but also, how strong that relationship is. To gauge this, researchers rely on a statistic known as the **correlation coefficient**. This is a number between -1.00 and $+1.00$ used to express the strength of the relationship between the variables studied. The closer this number is to 1.00 (either -1.00 or $+1.00$), the stronger the relationship is—that is, the more closely the variables are related to each other. However, the closer the correlation coefficient is to 0, the weaker the relationship between the variables—that is, the less strongly they are associated.

So, when interpreting a correlation coefficient, there are two things to keep in mind: its *sign* (in keeping with algebraic traditions, positive correlations are usually expressed without any sign), and its *absolute value* (that is, the size of the number without respect to its sign). For example, a correlation coefficient of $-.92$ reflects a much stronger relationship between variables than one of $.22$. The minus sign simply reveals

correlation
The extent to which two variables are related to each other.

positive correlation
A relationship between two variables such that more of one variable is associated with more of the other.

negative correlation
A relationship between two variables such that more of one variable is associated with less of the other.

correlation coefficient
A statistical index indicating the nature and extent to which two variables are related to each other.

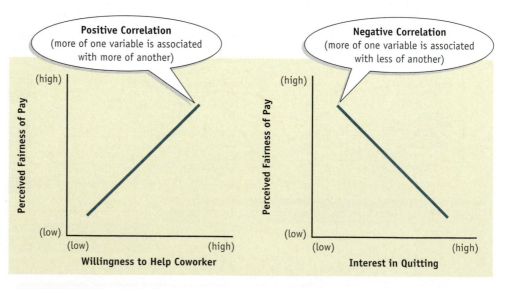

FIGURE A1.3

Positive and Negative Correlations: What They Mean

Positive correlations (left) exist when more of one variable is associated with more of another. Negative correlations (right) exist when more of one variable is associated with less of another.

that the relationship between the variables being described is negative (more of one variable is associated with less of another variable). The fact that the absolute value of this correlation coefficient is greater tells us that the relationship between the variables is stronger.

When variables are strongly correlated scientists can make more accurate predictions about how they are related to each other. So, using our example, a negative correlation between perceptions of pay fairness and intent to quit, we may expect that in general, those who believe they are unfairly paid will be more likely to quit their jobs than those who believe they are fairly paid. If the correlation coefficient were high, say over $-.80$, we would be more confident that this would occur than if the correlation were low, say under $-.20$. In fact, as correlation coefficients approach 0, it's impossible to make any accurate predictions whatsoever. In such a case, knowing one variable would not allow us to predict anything about the other. As you might imagine, organizational scientists are extremely interested in discovering the relationships between variables and rely on correlation coefficients to tell them a great deal.

Although the examples we've been using involve the relationship between only two variables at a time, organizational researchers frequently are interested in the interrelationships between many different variables at once. For example, an employee's intent to quit may be related to several variables besides the perceived fairness of one's pay—such as satisfaction with the job itself, or liking for one's immediate supervisor. Researchers may make predictions using several different variables at once using a technique known as **multiple regression**. Using this approach, researchers may be able to tell the extent to which each of several different variables contributes to predicting the behavior in question. In our example, they would be able to learn the degree to which the several variables studied, together and individually, are related to the intent to quit one's job. Given the complex nature of human behavior on the job and the wide range of variables likely to influence it, it should not be surprising to learn that OB researchers use the multiple regression technique a great deal in their work.

multiple regression
A statistical technique through which it is possible to determine the extent to which each of several different variables contributes to predicting another variable (typically, where the variable being predicted is the behavior in question).

An Important Limitation of Correlations

Despite the fact that the analysis of surveys using correlational techniques such as multiple regression can be so very valuable, conclusions drawn from correlations are limited in a very important way. Namely, *correlations do not reveal anything about causation.* In other words, although correlations tell us about how variables are related to each other, they don't provide any insight into their cause-and-effect relationships.

So, in our example, although we may learn that the less employees feel they are fairly paid the more interested they are in quitting, we cannot tell *why* this is the case. In other words, we cannot tell whether or not employees want to quit *because* they believe they are unfairly paid. Might this be the case? Yes, but it also might be the case that people who believe they are unfairly paid tend to dislike the work they do, and it is this that encourages them to find a new job. Another possibility is that people believe they are unfairly paid because their supervisors are too demanding—and it is this that raises their interest in quitting (see Figure A1.4). Our point is simple: Although all these possibilities are reasonable, knowing only that variables are correlated does *not* permit us to determine what causes what. Because it is important for researchers to establish the causal relationships between the variables they study, OB researchers frequently turn to another technique that *does* permit such conclusions to be drawn—the experiment.

Experimental Research: The Logic of Cause and Effect

experimental method
A research technique through which it is possible to determine cause-effect relationships between the variables of interest—that is, the extent to which one variable causes another.

Because both scientists and practitioners not only want to know the degree to which variables are related, but also how much one variable causes another, the **experimental method** is popularly used in OB. The more we know about the causal connections between variables, the better we can explain the underlying causes of behavior—and this, after all, is one of the major goals of OB.

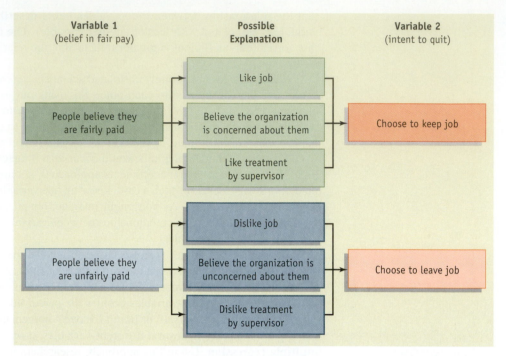

FIGURE A1.4

Correlations: What They Don't Reveal About Causation

Even if a strong negative correlation exists between pay fairness and the desire to leave one's job, we cannot tell why this relationship exists. This correlation does not show that unfairness causes people to leave. As shown here, there are many possible underlying causes that are not identified by the knowledge of the correlation alone.

A Hypothetical Experiment

To illustrate how experiments work, let's consider an example. Suppose we're interested in determining the effects of social density (the number of people per unit of space) on the job performance of clerical employees—that is, the degree to which the crowdedness of working conditions in an office influences how accurately word-processing operators do their jobs.

Although this topic might be studied in many different ways, imagine that we do the following. First, we select at random a large group of word-processing operators working in a variety of different organizations—the participants in our study. Then, we prepare a specially designed office, the setting for the experiment. Throughout the study, we would keep the design of the office and all the working conditions (e.g., temperature, light, and noise levels) alike with one exception—we would systematically vary the number of people working in the office at any given time.

For example, we could have one condition—the "high density" condition—in which 50 people are put into a 500-square-foot room at once (allowing 10 square feet per person). In another condition—the "low density" condition—we could put 5 people into a 500-square-foot room at once (allowing 100 square feet per person). Finally, we can have a "moderate density" condition in which we put 25 people into a 500-square-foot room (allowing 20 square feet per person).

Say we have several hundred people participating in the study and we assign them at random to each of these three conditions. Each word-processing operator is then given the same passage of text to type over two hours. After this period, the typists are dismissed, and the researcher counts the number of words accurately typed by each typist, noting any possible differences between performance in the various conditions. Suppose we obtain the results summarized in Figure A1.5.

Experimental Logic

Let's analyze what was done in this simple hypothetical experiment to help explain the basic elements of the experimental method and its underlying logic. First, recall that we

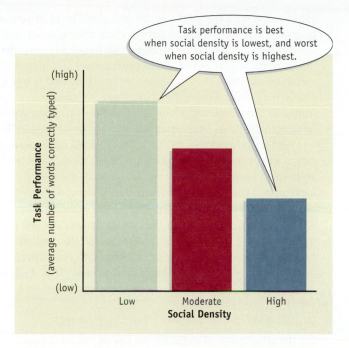

FIGURE A1.5

Example of Simple Experimental Results

In our example, word-processing operators are put into rooms that differ with respect to only one variable—social density (i.e., the number of people per unit of space). The hypothetical results summarized here show that people perform best under conditions of lowest density and worst under conditions of highest density.

selected participants from the population of interest and assigned them to conditions on a *random* basis. This means that each of the participants had an equal chance of being assigned to any one of the three conditions. This is critical because it is possible that differences between conditions could result from having many very good operators in one condition and many unproductive ones in another. So, to safeguard against this possibility, it is important to assign people to conditions at random. When this is done, we can assume that the effects of any possible differences between people would equalize over conditions.

Thus, by assigning people to conditions at random, we can be assured that there will be just as many fast operators and slow operators in each. As a result, there is no reason to believe that any differences in productivity that may be noted between conditions can be attributed to systematic differences in the skills of the participants. Given "the luck of the draw," such differences can be discounted, thereby enhancing our confidence that differences are solely the result of the social density of the rooms. This is the logic behind random assignment. Although it is not always feasible to use random assignment when conducting experiments in organizations, it is highly desirable whenever possible.

Recall that word-processing operators were assigned to conditions that differed with respect to only the variable of interest—in this case, social density. We can say that the experimenter *manipulated* this aspect of the work environment, systematically changing it from condition to condition. A variable altered in this way is called an **independent variable**. An independent variable is a variable that is systematically manipulated by the experimenter so as to determine its effects on the behavior of interest. In our example, the independent variable is social density. Specifically, it may be said to have three different *levels*—that is, degrees of the independent variable: high, moderate, and low.

The variable that is measured, the one influenced by the independent variable, is known as the **dependent variable**. A dependent variable is the behavior of interest that is being measured—the behavior that is dependent upon the independent variable. In this case, the dependent variable was word-processing performance, the quantity of words accurately typed. Besides studying this, we could have studied other dependent variables, such as

independent variable
A variable that is systematically manipulated by the experimenter so as to determine its effects on the behavior of interest (i.e., the *dependent variable*).

dependent variable
A variable that is measured by the researcher, the one influenced by the *independent variable*.

satisfaction with the work, or the perceived level of stress encountered. In fact, it would be quite likely for OB researchers to study several dependent variables in one experiment.

By the same token, researchers also frequently consider the effects of several different independent variables in a given experiment. The matter of which particular independent variables and dependent variables are being studied is one of the most important questions researchers make. Often, they base these decisions on suggestions from previous research (other experiments suggesting that certain variables are important) and existing theory (conceptualizations suggesting that certain variables may be important).

Generally speaking, the basic logic behind the experimental method is quite simple. In fact, it involves only two major steps. First, some variable of interest (the independent variable) must be systematically varied. Second, the effects, if any, of such variations must be measured. The underlying idea is that if the independent variable does indeed influence behavior, then people exposed to different amounts of it should behave differently. In our example, we can be certain that social density caused differences in processing performance because when all other factors were held constant, different amounts of density led to different levels of performance. Although our experiment is fabricated, it follows the same basic logic of all experiments—namely, it is designed to reveal the effects of the independent variables on the dependent variables.

Drawing Valid Conclusions from Experiments

For the conclusions of experimenters to be valid it is critical for them to hold constant all factors other than the independent variable. Then, if there are differences in the dependent variable, we can assume that they are the result of the effects of the independent variable. By assigning participants to conditions at random we already took an important step to ensure that one key factor—differences in the ability levels of the participants—would be equalized.

But, as you might imagine, other factors may affect the results as well. For example, it would be essential to also hold constant environmental conditions that might influence word-processing speed. In this case, more people would generate more heat, so to make sure that the results are influenced only by density—and not heat—it would be necessary to air-condition the work room so as to keep it the same temperature in all conditions at all times.

If you think about it, our simple experiment is really not that simple at all—especially if it is conducted with all the care needed to permit valid conclusions to be drawn. Thus, experiments require all experimental conditions to be kept identical with respect to all variables except the independent variable so that its effects can be determined unambiguously. As you might imagine, this is often easier said than done.

Where Are Experiments Conducted? Laboratory and Field Settings

How simple it is to control the effects of extraneous variables (i.e., factors not of interest to the experimenter) depends, in large part, on where the experiment is conducted. In the field of OB, there are generally two options available: experiments can be conducted in naturalistic organizational settings referred to as the *field,* or in settings specially created for the study itself, referred to as the *laboratory* (or *lab* for short). As summarized in Figure A1.6, there are trade-offs involved with conducting research in each setting.

The study in our example was a lab experiment. It was conducted in carefully controlled conditions specially created for the research. The great amount of control possible in such settings improves the chances of creating the conditions needed to allow valid conclusions to be drawn from experiments. At the same time, however, lab studies suffer from a lack of realism. Although the working conditions can be carefully controlled, they may be relatively unrealistic, not carefully simulating the conditions found in actual organizations. As a result, it may be difficult to generalize the findings of lab studies to settings outside the lab, such as the workplace.

However, if we conducted our study in actual organizations, there would be many unknowns, many uncontrollable factors at work. To conduct such a study we would have to distinguish between those who worked in offices differing with respect to social density and later compare people's performance. If we did this, we would be sure that the conditions studied were realistic. However, there would be so little control over the setting that many

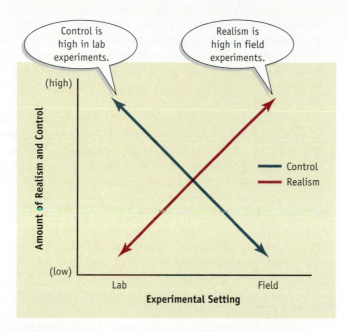

FIGURE A1.6

Trade-Offs Between Lab and Field Experiments

Researchers in OB may conduct experiments in laboratory or field settings, each of which has advantages and disadvantages. Generally, the lab offers more control but less realism, whereas the field offers less control but more realism.

different factors could be operating. For example, because people would not be assigned to conditions at random, it might be the case that people work in those settings they most desire. Furthermore, there would be no control over such factors as distractions and differences in environmental conditions (e.g., noise and temperature).

In short, field experiments, although strong in realism, are weak with respect to the level of control they provide. By contrast, lab experiments permit a great deal of control, but tend to be unrealistic. In view of these complementary strengths and weaknesses, it should be clear that experiments should be conducted in *both* types of sites. As researchers do so, our confidence can be increased that valid conclusions will be drawn about behavior in organizations.

Qualitative Research Methods

In contrast to the highly empirical approaches to research we have been describing thus far, we also should note that OB researchers sometimes use a less empirical approach. After all, probably the most obvious ways of learning about behavior in organizations are to observe it firsthand and to describe it after it occurs. Organizational scientists have a long tradition of studying behavior using these nonempirical, descriptive techniques, relying on what is known as **qualitative research**.[3] The qualitative approach to research relies on preserving the natural qualities of the situation being studied, attempting to capture the richness of the context while disturbing naturalistic conditions only minimally, if at all. The two major qualitative methods used by OB scientists are *naturalistic observation* and the *case method*.

Naturalistic Observation

There's probably no more fundamental way of learning about how people act in organizations than simply to observe them—a research technique known as **naturalistic observation**. Suppose, for example, that you wanted to learn how employees behave in response to layoffs. One thing you could do would be to visit an organization in which layoffs will be

qualitative research
A nonempirical type of research that relies on preserving the natural qualities of the situation being studied.

naturalistic observation
A research technique in which people are systematically observed in situations of interest to the researcher.

participant observation

A qualitative research technique in which people systematically make observations of what goes on in a setting by becoming an insider, part of that setting itself.

occurring and systematically observe what the employees do and say both before and after the layoffs occur. Making comparisons of this type may provide very useful insights into what's going on. As a variation of this technique, you could take a job in the organization and make your observations as an insider actually working there—giving you a perspective you might not otherwise gain. This technique, often used by anthropologists, is known as **participant observation**.

It's not too difficult to think of the advantages and disadvantages of observational research. Its major advantage is that it can be used without disrupting normal routines, allowing behavior to be studied in its natural state. Moreover, almost anyone—including people already working in the host organization—can be trained to use it.

Observational research also suffers from several important limitations. First, the potential for subjectivity among researchers is considerable. Even among the most diligent of researchers, it's inevitable that different people will make different observations of the same events. Second, being involved in the daily functioning of an organization will make it difficult for observers to be impartial. Researchers interpreting organizational events may be subject to bias due to their feelings about the people involved. Finally, because most of what goes on in an organization is fairly dull and routine, it's very easy for researchers to place a great deal of emphasis on unusual or unexpected events, possibly leading to inaccurate conclusions.

Given these limitations, most OB scientists consider observational research to be more useful as a starting point for providing basic insight into behavior than as a tool for acquiring definitive knowledge about behavior.

The Case Method

Suppose that we conducted our hypothetical study of reactions to layoffs differently. Instead of observing behavior directly, we might fully describe the company's history leading up to the event and some statistics summarizing its aftermath (e.g., how long people were unemployed, how the company was restructured after downsizing, and the like). We might even include some interviews with people affected by the event, and quote them directly. The approach we are describing here is known as the **case method**. More often than not, the rationale behind the case method is *not* to teach us about a specific organization per se, but to learn what happened in that organization as a means of providing cues as to what may be going on in other organizations.

case method

A research technique in which a particular organization is thoroughly described and analyzed for purposes of understanding what went on in that setting.

The case method is similar to naturalistic observation in that it relies on descriptive accounts of events. However, it is different in that it often involves using post hoc accounts of events from those involved as opposed to firsthand observations by scientists.

As you might imagine, a great deal can be learned by detailed accounts of events in organizations summarized in the form of written cases. Especially when these cases are supplemented by careful interviews (in which case the method would be considered quantitative rather than qualitative in nature), cases can paint a particularly detailed picture of events as they unfolded in a particular organization.

Of course, to the extent that the organization studied is unique, it may be not be possible to generalize what is learned to others. To get around this limitation, some researchers have recommended that multiple, as opposed to single, cases should be used to test theories.[4] Another problem with the case method—a limitation it shares with naturalistic observation—is that the potential for bias is relatively high. As a result, many scientists believe that while the case method may serve as a valuable source of hypotheses about behavior on the job, testing those hypotheses requires more rigorous research methods.[5]

UNDERSTANDING AND MANAGING YOUR CAREER

Throughout this book we have spoken about the work people do at any given point in time. Here, however, we turn attention to the work people do over the course of their lives. Indeed, over the course of our life we are likely to find ourselves holding a variety of different jobs in different organizations. In fact, the average American holds eight different jobs over his or her lifetime.

In most cases, these positions are interconnected in some systematic way, weaving a path, however twisted and indirect, representing a career. In this Appendix, we describe the basic nature of careers. We also elaborate on some of the key issues associated with choosing a career and the challenges encountered as our career develops over the years. To fully understand these ideas, of course, we begin with some basic definitions.

The Nature of Careers

We've all heard of, and use, the term *career,* but it begs to be defined more precisely. As you'll see, although we use the term rather loosely in everyday language, social scientists use it in far more precise fashion. With this in mind, we will define what we mean by *career,* along with various terms to which it is related. Following this, we will identify and describe various types of careers.

Basic Definitions

career
The evolving sequence of work experiences over time.

job
A predetermined set of activities one is expected to perform.

occupation
A coherent set of jobs.

Formally, a **career** can be defined as the evolving sequence of work experiences over time. In everyday language, however, people often use the terms *job, occupation,* and *career* interchangeably, so it makes sense to distinguish among these terms before going any further. Simply put, a **job** is a predetermined set of activities one is expected to perform. An **occupation,** by contrast, is a coherent set of jobs.[1] So, for example, a person working as a carpenter would be said to have an occupation in the field of construction. Eventually, he or she may shift to occupations in the field of sales, such as home sales manager. Overall, this succession of jobs represents the individual's career. For a summary, see Figure A2.1.

Careers mean a great deal to individuals—both financially and psychologically. After all, the career path you take determines a great deal about how much money you will make throughout your life. Historically, some careers are more lucrative than others. For example, in 2006 the average salary of a general practitioner physician was $149,000; for a computer operations manager it was about $80,000; for an elementary school teacher, it was $47,000, and the average retail stock clerk made only about $20,000.[2] Although money isn't everything, of course, these very large differences underscore the point that how much money you are likely to make depends greatly on your choice of career.

Careers also are important to us as individuals because they give us a sense of accomplishment and pride, and they also can give meaning to our lives (e.g., such as doctors who feel good about themselves because they save people's lives). Like it or not, your job defines your identity in the eyes of others. After all, when you meet someone at a party, the question often is asked, "What do you do?" Indeed, we define ourselves and others define us by the work we do.

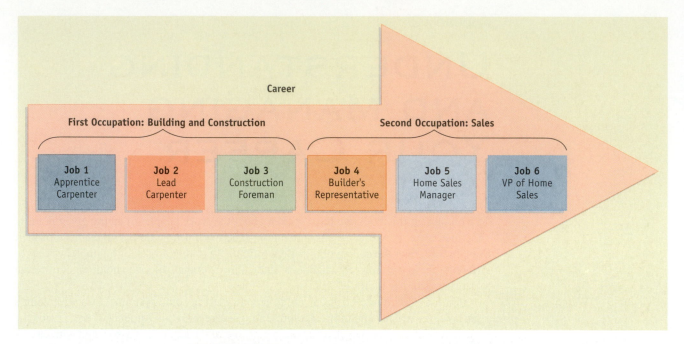

FIGURE A2.1

Distinguishing Among Career, Occupation, and Job

The typical career consists of several occupations (coherent sets of jobs), each of which is composed of a succession of individual jobs (predetermined sets of activities). A hypothetical example is presented here.

Types of Careers

Although everyone's career is unique, scientists who have studied careers have observed that there are some general patterns or categories into which the vast majority of careers fall.[3] Specifically, four different types of careers have been identified, and we now will describe each one (for a summary, see Figure A2.2).

Steady-State Careers. Bob's family owns a small bakery, Main Street Bakery. When Bob was a young boy, he used to hang out at the bakery after school, and he became interested in that line of work. After getting a degree in hospitality management from the local community college, Bob took over the family business. For all his working life, some 40 years, he ran Main Street Bakery, where he baked fine breads, cakes, and pies. Over the years, Bob had several opportunities to sell the business and do something else, but he didn't. When it came time for him to retire, he simply handed over the family business to his own son.

Bob made a career choice that led him to a lifetime commitment to a single job, what is called a **steady-state career**. People who have steady-state careers are generally very satisfied with what they are doing. Also, because they work at their jobs for so long, they tend to become highly skilled experts at what they do. After all, for Bob to have stuck it out in the bakery as long as he did, he must like what he does, and be pretty good at it, as well.

steady-state career
The type of career in which there is a lifetime of employment in a single occupation.

Linear Careers. Claire always loved tinkering with computers, even as a young girl. Nobody was surprised, therefore, when she did an internship at a software development firm before getting a bachelor's degree in computer science. After graduating, she took an entry-level position at a Silicon Valley start-up, where she did lots of different jobs and got great experience. After about four years, it became clear that the company wasn't going anywhere (except out of business, perhaps), so she moved on to a much larger company, where she took a position in which she helped develop and test new wireless products. Her assignments were small at first, but after a few years, Claire found herself taking on larger and larger projects,

FIGURE A2.2

Four Major Types of Careers

Scientists have found it useful to distinguish among four different types of careers—steady-state careers, linear careers, spiral careers, and transitory careers—each of which is depicted here.

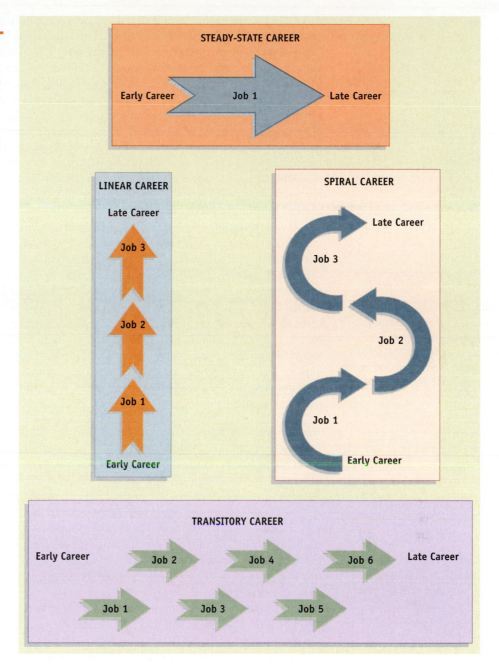

linear career

The type of career in which someone stays in a certain field and works his or her way up the occupational ladder, from low-level jobs to high-level jobs.

until eventually she became a vice president of technology for the company. It was a dream job for Claire, but she wanted more. At about the same time, the company decided to invest more of its resources in manufacturing and marketing and to outsource research and product development. So Claire sold her stock in the company and started her own firm—not a competitor, but a lab that specialized in developing new wireless technology for her old employer, and lots of other companies as well.

Claire had what's known as a **linear career**. That is, she stuck with a certain field and worked her way up the occupational ladder. Sometimes, she stayed at a single company, but at other times, she changed jobs. In all cases, however, she took on greater challenges. Linear careers are rather traditional paths. For many years, working one's way "up the corporate ladder" until "you made it" was considered the true sign of career success. Indeed, although achieving increasingly higher levels of success in a single line of work is a considerable accomplishment, it is no longer regarded as the only acceptable option for people today.

Spiral Careers. John always loved science, especially physics, so he kept going to school and getting higher degrees. Before he knew it, he had a Ph.D. and found that he enjoyed studying thermal dynamics. Fortunately, a local aeronautics lab was looking for someone in that area to conduct research, and they were impressed with John's accomplishments. Working there was satisfying for John for a few years, but research wasn't his passion. Then, one day, he was asked to give a talk about his work to a group of students at a small college nearby. John became hooked on teaching and soon took a job teaching physics courses at that same school. The pay wasn't great, and the hours were long, but John enjoyed explaining physical principles in simple ways, and he proved to be pretty good at it. The students loved him—in part, because he made complex ideas more understandable than the textbook, and far more fun, too. "If you don't like the textbook," he soon reasoned, "write one yourself." And that he did. Now, John has moved on to his third career—this time, as an author of textbooks.

Over his working life, John moved between three jobs. First, he was a laboratory scientist; second, he was a professor; and third, he was an author. These jobs are very different from one another, and each requires different skills. However, John pieced them together such that each position built upon the previous one. He did exciting, new, and different things with each career move, but they all drew upon his interest in physics. In other words, he had what's called a **spiral career**—the kind of career in which people evolve through a series of occupations, each of which requires new skills and that builds upon existing knowledge and skills. People who have spiral careers are not "job-hoppers," who move from one post to another. Rather, they are constantly growing and improving as they explore different facets of the same profession (physics, in John's case). Typically, people in spiral careers spend about 7–10 years in each position, enabling them to become pretty good at what they do.

Transitory Careers. After high school, Cheryl worked as a waitress while she tried to find a job as an actress. The tips were good, but after it became clear that Hollywood wasn't going to come calling, she took a job at an art gallery. She wasn't especially interested in art, but she had a friend who worked there, who helped her get the job. A few months later, she got bored and took a part-time job at a bookstore. To help make ends meet, she started a dog-walking and pet-sitting business for her neighbors, all while taking a few college classes at night. Although we could say more about the other jobs Cheryl had, you probably get the picture: She continuously moved from job to job, with little connection between them. In other words, Cheryl has what is known as a **transitory career**. People in transitory careers move between many different unrelated positions, spending about one to four years in each.

Although it may be tempting to dismiss Cheryl on the grounds that she is "trying to find herself," it would be unfair to assume that she is in any way inept. In fact, many people in transitory careers are those who have not been fortunate enough to discover the kind of work that allows them to derive satisfaction. In fact, many of the most successful people in the business world have been "late bloomers," who drifted between jobs until they found their calling. For example, before Ray Croc founded McDonald's at age 52, he worked such jobs as being an ambulance driver, a piano player, and a paper cup salesman.[4] Obviously, to say that he was anything other than a huge success, despite his transitory career, would be very misleading.

It also is important to acknowledge that some people simply do not find work the major source of fulfillment in their lives. Such individuals may elect to "make a career out of their hobbies," so to speak, preferring to devote their energy and talent to their avocations instead of their vocations. Perhaps you know someone who's a talented musician, but who moves from one low-level "day job" to the next, so as to have time to play local gigs at night. Although such an individual may have a transitory career during the daytime, it's quite possible that his or her career is moving along in a very linear fashion after the sun goes down. Even if the hobby brings personal satisfaction instead of occupational recognition, it clearly would be unfair to think any less of such an individual.

spiral career
The kind of career in which people evolve through a series of occupations, each of which requires new skills and that builds upon existing knowledge and skills.

transitory career
The type of career in which someone moves between many different unrelated positions, spending about one to four years in each.

Getting Started: Making Career Choices

"What do you want to be when you grow up?" This is a question you probably heard many times in your youth (if not later in life, too!). As children, we learn about different careers, based mostly on the people with whom we come into contact in real life (e.g., teachers and doctors) and on television (e.g., athletes). This continues into our adult years as well, although as adults we come into contact with a broader range of professions and we have had experiences at some. With this in mind, we now will discuss three major factors that determine people's career choices.

Person-Job Fit: Holland's Theory of Occupational Choice

person-job fit
The degree to which a particular job matches an individual's skills, abilities, and interests.

Why is it that you may decide to become a lawyer whereas your sister is interested in being a doctor, a police officer, a musician, or a chef—anything other than a lawyer? To a great extent, the answer lies in the notion of **person-job fit**. That is the degree to which a particular job matches an individual's skills, abilities, and interests. This was the basic idea of John Holland, a scientist who has specialized in studying occupational choice. Specifically, he believed that a person's occupational choice is based primarily on his or her personality (see Chapter 4).[5] His research has established two important findings:

■ People from various occupations tend to have many similar personality characteristics.

■ People whose characteristics match those of people in a given field are predisposed to succeed in that field.

So, for example, assume for argument's sake that successful lawyers tend to have certain characteristics in common: They are very inquisitive, detail-oriented, and analytical—all characteristics that help them do their jobs well. According to *Holland's theory of vocational choice,* you would be attracted to the field of law to the extent that you share many of the same characteristics. In other words, because being a lawyer "suits you," and you "have what it takes" to succeed at that field, you are likely to select that occupation. In essence, **Holland's theory of vocational choice** says that people will perform best at occupations that match their traits and personalities.

Holland's theory of vocational choice
A theory that claims that people will perform best at occupations that match their traits and personalities.

Holland's theory is quite specific with respect to the various personality types and occupational types involved. Specifically, Holland identifies six different characteristics of work environments and the personality traits and interests of the people who are most successful in those environments. These are summarized in Figure A2.3. As you look at this diagram, you probably cannot help but consider what particular type best describes you. It is important to be very cognizant of this because the more closely your personality type matches the work you do, the more successful you will be and the less stress you are likely to encounter.[6]

It's clear from Figure A2.3 that people in each type should work in certain environments, but what happens when these don't occur? Holland has noted that for people of each type there are second-best matches, third-best matches, and some jobs that constitute the worst possible match of all. These are summarized in Figure A2.4, known as **Holland's hexagon**. Interpreting this diagram is straightforward. The position of each Holland type around the hexagon indicates those occupations for which people are best suited and worst suited, based on their types. The closer a job environment comes to the associated personality type on this diagram, the more effective the person will be.

Holland's hexagon
A conceptualization specifying the occupations for which people are best suited based on which of six personality types most closely describe them.

So, for example, someone with an enterprising personality type is expected to be most successful when working in an occupation that permits enterprising qualities to come out (e.g., a sales job). However, neither people nor jobs fit perfectly into only a single category. As such, fairly good matches may occur in cases in which people in a certain category perform work in environments that favor adjacent types. So, for example, an enterprising person may perform reasonably well at jobs in social environments or in conventional environments, each of which is adjacent to the enterprising type in the hexagon. By the same token, poorer matches, such as with environments favoring artistic or realistic people, which are two steps away, are likely to be quite problematic for enterprising individuals. And finally, we

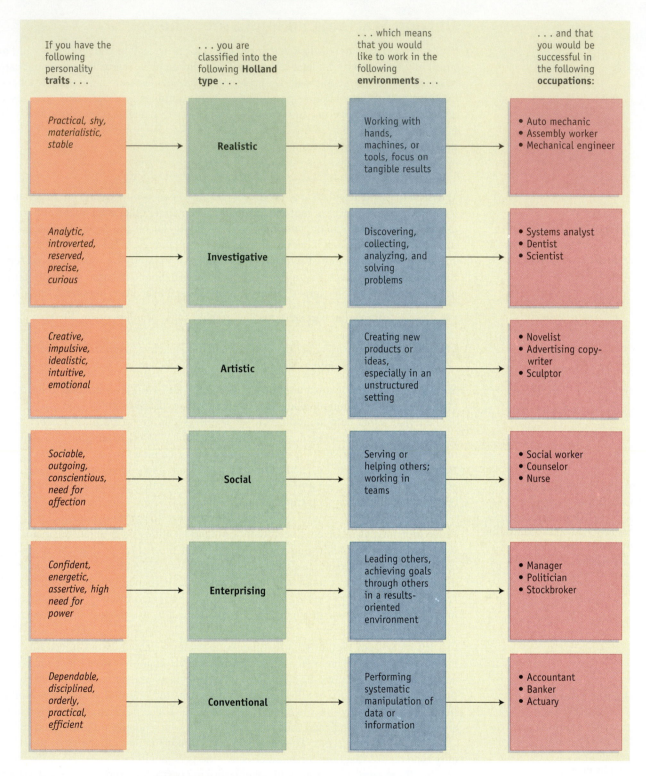

FIGURE A2.3

Holland's Theory of Vocational Choice: An Overview

Holland's theory of vocational choice specifies that people are most satisfied with occupations that match their personalities. People are classified into any of six distinct personality types, each of which is associated with a particular work environment that best suits them. These pairings and the occupations that most closely match them are summarized here.

FIGURE A2.4

Holland's Hexagon

The diagram known as Holland's hexagon summarizes the relationship between each of the six personality and work environment types. According to Holland's theory of vocational choice, the closer these are, the more satisfied one will be with one's occupational choice. Occupations with demands opposite each personality type (shown here with dashed lines) identify those for which people are most poorly suited.

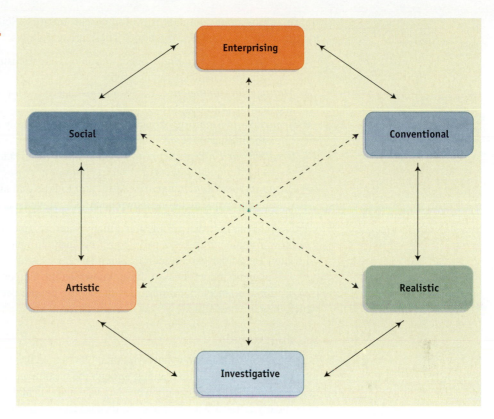

have the point along the hexagon that lies directly opposite—in the case of the enterprising type, it's the investigative environment. These represent the poorest matches. So, for example, we would expect people who do well in enterprising occupations (such as salesperson) to do poorly in occupations (such as scientist) that require the more analytical talents of the investigative type.

Holland's theory has been used widely by vocational counselors, professionals specializing in helping people find the kind of work that best suits them. The rationale is straightforward. People taking various vocational tests can determine how closely their traits and personality characteristics match those of people in various occupational groups. Then, using Holland's hexagon, people are encouraged to seek work in fields whose job incumbents tend to have those various qualities, and to avoid work in fields whose job incumbents have qualities that lie opposite their own along the hexagon. The happiest and most successful workers tend to be those for whom there is a close fit between their personality and their work environment. According to Holland, and supported by research, this is the key to successful career development.[7]

Career Anchors

Thus far, we've considered the extent to which a person's occupation matches his or her personality. However, another very important consideration when it comes to selecting careers has to do with the extent to which various jobs are in keeping with our image of ourself. For example, suppose you think of yourself as a creative kind of person, someone who likes to build or produce new things on your own. Because of this, based on your experiences and knowledge, you may find yourself moving into directions that bring out your creative side. So, instead of managing a restaurant, for example, you might come to think of yourself as a chef and be motivated to develop a new set of skills. In other words, these beliefs about yourself "anchor" your choice of careers—and, as such, they are known as *career anchors*.

Formally defined, a **career anchor** is a person's occupational self-concept based on his or her self-perceived talents, abilities, values, needs, and motives.[8] As people spend

career anchor

A person's occupational self-concept based on his or her self-perceived talents, abilities, needs, and motives.

time working, they gradually develop career anchors. Scientists studying careers have identified five major career anchors.[9] These are as follows:

- **Technical or Functional.** Concentration on jobs focusing on specific content areas (e.g., auto mechanics, graphic arts)
- **Managerial Competence.** Focus on jobs that allow for analyzing business problems and dealing with people
- **Security and Stability.** Attraction to jobs that are likely to continue into the future (e.g., the military)
- **Creativity or Entrepreneurship.** Primary interest in starting new companies from visions of unique products or services, but not necessarily running them
- **Autonomy and Independence.** Attraction to jobs that allow for freedom from constraints and working at one's own pace (e.g., novelists and creative artists)

Despite the fact that people have many interests and abilities, not all of these guide them toward careers. Instead, people are regularly attracted to careers that are in keeping with their particular career anchor. Scientists have used various questionnaires to assess people's career anchors. One of these, known as the Career Orientation Inventory, is used by vocational counselors for purposes of helping people decide the kind of occupations to which they are best suited.

Job Opportunities

Let's face it: No matter how much you think you would like to be a shepherd, and how good a job you think you might do roaming through the pasture and tending the flock, job opportunities for shepherds are not exactly what they were in biblical days. Fortunately, most people tend to be highly rational when it comes to making career choices, favoring occupations in which opportunities are most likely to exist and avoiding positions in which opportunities are declining. For a summary of recent projections of the five jobs projected to show the greatest growth by 2014 and the five jobs showing the greatest declines by this same time, see Figure A2.5.[10]

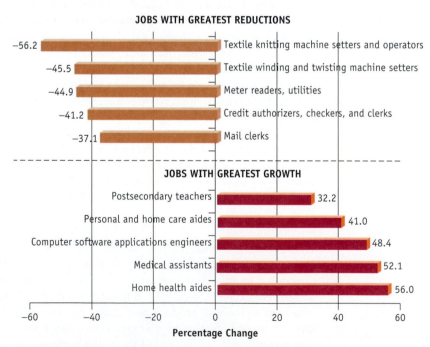

FIGURE A2.5

Job That Are Growing and Declining in Number: Outlook Through 2014

Thanks to computer technology, jobs involving the physical operation of machines are on the decline, whereas those associated with caring for the aging population are showing the greatest growth in numbers. These figures reflect projections through 2014.

Source: Based on data reported by Hecker, 2005; see Note 10.

As you look at these statistics, it's interesting to note that most of the growth is expected to come in areas related to assisting patients and doctors. Given that the baby boomers are now getting older, they are likely to require health care, accounting for the growth in this area. At the other extreme, we find that the jobs requiring fewer people are all ones that now are being replaced by computer-assisted equipment. For example, the textile-manufacturing process is now largely computerized. And that nice man who used to come around to read your electric meter is now being replaced by wireless technology that allows the same jobs to be performed more quickly and accurately.

Because openings in many high-tech jobs and medical jobs are expected to grow in the years ahead, these positions tend to capture people's attention when considering occupations they might want to enter. Not surprisingly, they also capture the attention of people administering vocational programs in high schools, technical schools, and colleges. To be popular with prospective students, these programs offer training in areas where the jobs are likely to be. The availability of such training opportunities also attracts people to the kind of jobs that require this training, creating the cycle shown in Figure A2.6.

Managing Established Careers

Although getting started in one's career can be very difficult, so too do people face considerable challenges once they've been working for a while. We now will describe three such challenges.

Confronting the Career Plateau

While people in their 20s and 30s are figuring out what they want to be, the 40-something crowd faces different challenges. This is sometimes a difficult period in which people look down the road and realize that they never may fulfill their career aspirations. As you might

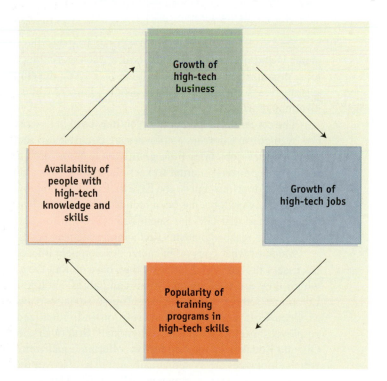

FIGURE A2.6

The Cyclical Nature of Job Growth, Training Opportunities, and Skilled Labor

As summarized here, the growth of high-tech companies leads to high-tech jobs, which leads to high-tech training, which leads to more people with high-tech skills, which further supports the growth of more high-tech jobs.

imagine, this can be problematic for both employees and their organizations. Fortunately, however, as we will describe, something can be done to help.

The Nature of the Career Plateau.   The point at which one's career has peaked and is unlikely to develop further is known as a **career plateau**. One way to identify a career plateau is by noting how long someone has been in his or her current position. Employees who have been in a particular post for five or more years would be considered immobile and to have reached a career plateau. Another popular approach for identifying a career plateau is subjective in nature. People may be considered to have plateaued whenever they no longer expect to move on to higher-status positions. Using either definition, about one employee in four is considered to have reached a career plateau.[11]

Although it is tempting to assume that employees whose careers have plateaued are no longer motivated or effective at their current jobs, this isn't always so. In fact, some people are quite satisfied to remain at their present jobs for a long time, finding it more relaxing and a source of contentment to be a "solid citizen" of the company instead of being one of its "fast trackers" or "high fliers." Of course, career plateauing can be a serious source of dissatisfaction for individuals who believe that the only path to contentment is via upward movement in the company. This is more likely to be the case among managers than for employees holding other jobs, given that people in managerial positions tend to define their success in terms of upward advancement.

Today, as companies are reducing the size of their workforces and competition for good jobs becomes intense, more people than ever are reaching career plateaus earlier than expected. Faced with poor chances for promotion and few alternatives for employment, they may feel unmotivated and simply stick out their jobs until they retire from them. If you think this picture is depressing, imagine how serious the problem becomes when companies are faced with large cohorts of mid-career employees who are unmotivated because their careers have plateaued. Surely, a workforce composed of people who are merely "going through the motions" will be neither very productive, nor satisfied.

Career Development Interventions.   To avoid the problems associated with career plateaus and other career-related issues, such as finding the right job or adjusting to new jobs, organizations have been relying on **career development interventions**. These are systematic efforts to help manage people's careers while simultaneously helping the organizations in which they work.

The career development interventions used in several companies are quite interesting. For example, at Chevron, employees are counseled to seek outside hobbies during periods in which their jobs offer little gratification. Some are encouraged to make lateral moves within the company in order to keep their work lives stimulating. Not only have Chevron employees done this, but so too have thousands of employees at General Motors, where the white collar workforce has been reduced dramatically over the last few years. In fact, it has been reported that GM has spent some $10 million per year helping employees whose careers have reached plateaus find appropriate new positions within the company.

Much of what goes on in career development interventions involves helping employees assess the skills and interests they have so that they may be placed into positions for which they are well suited. Some companies, such as Hewlett-Packard and Lawrence Livermore Laboratories, provide self-assessment exercises for this purpose. Others, such as Coca-Cola and Disneyland, rely on individualized counseling sessions in which employees meet with trained professionals. Still others, including AT&T, IBM, Ford, Shell Oil, and Kodak, take it a step further, offering organizational assessment programs through which employees are systematically tested to discover their profiles of skills and interests.

At the very least, companies such as CBS, Merck, Aetna, and General Electric all provide services such as job posting systems and career resource centers through which employees can learn about new career options within their companies. And, when companies find that they must reduce the size of their workforces, terminated employees at Exxon, Mutual of New York, General Electric, and other companies receive the services of **outplacement programs**. These generally include assistance in developing the skills needed to find new jobs (such as networking, interviewing skills, resume writing, and the

---

career plateau
The point at which one's career has peaked and is unlikely to develop further.

career development interventions
Systematic efforts to help manage people's careers while simultaneously helping the organizations in which they work.

outplacement programs
Systematic efforts to find new jobs for employees who are laid off.

like). Despite these various differences, it is safe to characterize the vast majority of career development interventions as following the six steps listed in Figure A2.7.

Making Career Changes

Changing jobs, or even entire occupations, is quite common today. In fact, most new graduates with MBA degrees expect to stay at their first jobs for no more than four years.[12] About two-thirds of all U.S. workers say that they would make major career changes if they could.[13] Each year, approximately 10 million workers do make major career changes. And, of those who made such career changes in recent years, 53 percent did so voluntarily, with the majority reporting that their incomes went up as a result.[14] People who make major career changes do so for a variety of reasons. The major ones are that they recognize that:

- They either don't like, or can't succeed, at their chosen profession.
- Prospects are poor for future employment in their present occupation.
- Their needs or interests have shifted, requiring a life change.

The traditional way of making a major career change is by starting completely anew. You may, for example, quit your present job, return to school for new training, and then begin starting over in your new career. People do this all the time. If you've done it, or if you know anyone who has, you probably know how very difficult it can be, both emotionally (because you're making a lot of changes at once) and financially (because you're likely to be without an income for a while, and then have a lower income).

FIGURE A2.7

Career Development Interventions: Step-by-Step

Although each specific career development intervention may be unique in various ways, most involve the six steps summarized here.

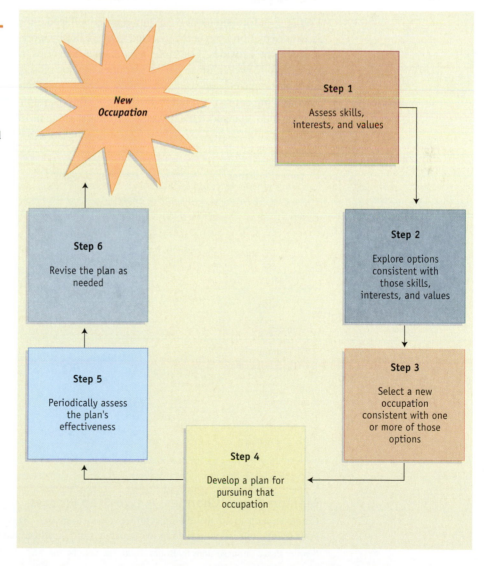

New Occupation

Step 1
Assess skills, interests, and values

Step 2
Explore options consistent with those skills, interests, and values

Step 3
Select a new occupation consistent with one or more of those options

Step 4
Develop a plan for pursuing that occupation

Step 5
Periodically assess the plan's effectiveness

Step 6
Revise the plan as needed

For example, suppose that Michelle is a lawyer who specializes in computers But, she is unhappy and looking to make a brand-new start by becoming, say, a business teacher. The hard way of doing this would be for Michelle to give up her job and go back to college, where she studies both education and business. Then, after graduating and receiving her teaching credentials, she can look for a new job. Although this would take Michelle to that new place she desires, this way of making the change would be very disruptive. So, how can Michelle go about making a major career change in a way that minimizes the disruption in her life?

Career experts advise making the changes in two steps: first changing either your occupation or your field of expertise, and then changing the other.[15] In our example Michelle has a present occupation, lawyer, and desires a new one, teacher. She also has a present field, computers, and desires a new one, business. Using the two-step method, she first may change her field, such as by expanding her practice into business law. Then, after getting established in her new field, Michelle should consider changing occupations, such as by teaching a class or two during the evenings at a local community college. After a while, she might want to take on more teaching responsibilities and limit the size of her legal practice, until eventually she is teaching business on a full-time basis. It also would be possible for Michelle to first change her occupation (e.g., by teaching law) and then her field (shifting from law to business). Either way, there you have it—from computer lawyer to business teacher in two not-so-simple steps. Again, although this transition might not be easy for Michelle, it certainly is a lot more feasible than attempting to change both occupation and field at once (see summary in Figure A2.8).

Planning for Succession and Retirement

Preparation for retirement is an important issue faced during later life. Psychologically, there is a reorientation from being directed in one's life by work activities to an increased focus on leisure time activities. For those who dislike their jobs, retirement is an anxiously awaited condition. However, those whose identities are tied closely to what they do find the decision difficult to make—and sometimes, they even change their minds and go back to work after once having retired. Probably the most visible example is basketball superstar Michael Jordan, who announced his retirement from the game in 1993 only to return in 1995. He then retired once more in 1999 before returning again as a player for the 2002–2003 season and

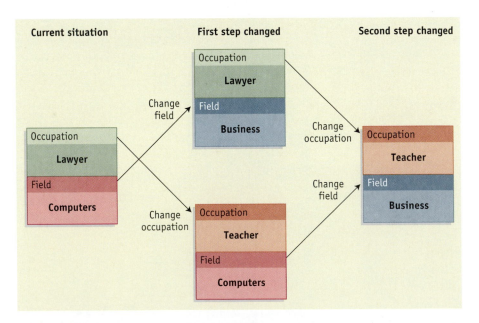

FIGURE A2.8

Making Career Changes: A Two-Step Process

Career experts advise that the most effective way to make a major career change is by changing your occupation and your field in two separate steps, as illustrated here.

Source: Based on suggestions by Bolles, 2006; see Note 14.

then retiring again at the end of the 2003 season (at age 40). Few of us have the option of changing our minds this often, but then again, we're not Michael Jordan.

Retirement. The phase of people's lives in which they reach the end of their careers and stop working for their primary income is known as **retirement**. It's important to recognize that retirement does not necessarily imply inactivity, but rather, a different kind of activity.[16] Many retired people lead very active lives, such as by working part-time, engaging in volunteer work, spending time engaged in leisure pursuits, or some combination of these activities. Generous pension plans coupled with more sophisticated investors and a generally good economy have made it possible for many people to retire earlier than ever. This, coupled with the fact that advances in health care enable people to live longer, makes it not unusual for people to spend 20 years or more in retirement.

People retire for either voluntary or involuntary reasons (see Figure A2.9). Sometimes, people retire earlier than they originally planned—that is, involuntarily—because they fear that their jobs may be eliminated or because they are in ill health. In other words, like turnover and absenteeism, sometimes retirement is a form of withdrawal.[17] Fortunately, in most cases, retirement occurs voluntarily, with employees leaving their companies on good terms and happily moving on to the next stage of their lives. Research has shown that the underlying reasons why people retire make a difference in how their retirement goes.[18] Those who retire for work-related or health-related reasons tend to be less satisfied with their retirement than those who retire as planned, by personal choice.

Today, rather than retiring from work completely, many people in their 60s are opting for brand-new careers. In fact, only about 37 percent of recent retirees expect to never return to work. The rest plan on staying active by working at least part-time.[19] Apparently, the image of retirees spending their golden years leisurely golfing and playing with their grandkids is fading fast. Speaking of golf, many professional golfers who find that aging makes it hard for them to compete against the likes of Tiger Woods no longer have to retire from the game. Instead, older golfers are discovering second careers by competing in the Senior PGA tour, where at age 50, they once again can rise to the top of their game.[20] Although precious few of us have the luxury of making a living by playing golf, many companies are finding it beneficial to hire semiretired executives as consultants. Instead of putting these talented, experienced people out to pasture, so to speak, they are taking full advantage of the expertise they can bring to the job—especially as *mentors* to young employees.[21]

Succession Planning and Mentoring. Before people retire—whether to a world of leisure or to an entirely new career—high-level executives typically assist their companies to prepare for the void created by their departure. This process is known as **succession planning**—a person's systematic attempt to identify possible holders of particular positions ahead of time as preparation for his or her departure.[22] After an individual spends years building a successful business it is unlikely that he or she would feel comfortable retiring without taking steps to preserve what has been done and to ensure that the company is left in good hands. People generally also want to pass the baton to another whose goals and values match their own. And, of course, careful planning of this nature is in the best interest of the company as well.

Formal succession-planning efforts are more likely to occur in large organizations than small ones. Large firms generally have formal plans on record, specifying exactly

---

retirement

The phase of people's lives in which they reach the end of their careers and stop working for their primary income.

succession planning

A person's systematic attempt to identify possible holders of particular positions ahead of time as preparation for his or her departure.

FIGURE A2.9

Voluntary Versus Involuntary Retirement

Retirement can occur for voluntary or involuntary reasons, some of which are identified here.

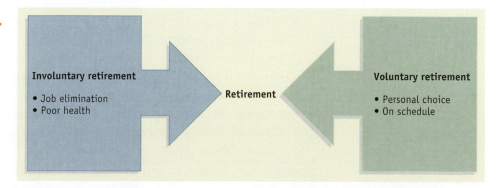

Involuntary retirement	Retirement	Voluntary retirement
• Job elimination • Poor health		• Personal choice • On schedule

short-term successors
Individuals who are considered suitable candidates, at least temporarily, to fill the position of someone who leaves his or her job unexpectedly.

mentoring
The process by which a more experienced employee (see *mentor*) advises, counsels, and otherwise enhances the professional development of a new employee (see *protégé*).

mentor
A more experienced employee who guides a newer employee (see *protégé*) in learning about the job and organization.

protégé
An inexperienced employee who receives assistance from a more experienced employee (see *mentor*).

who will move into certain positions once they are vacated. These typically include frequently updated information on the specific skills and qualifications of the individuals involved. Many succession plans identify **short-term successors**, individuals who are suitable candidates, at least temporarily, to fill a post vacated unexpectedly (e.g., through termination, resignation, or death).[23] This is not to say that leaders of small companies are unconcerned about succession. Indeed, their companies' small size makes it crucial to consider how jobs will be filled in the event of an emergency. However, leaders of small companies are more likely to discuss these things among themselves than to have a formal plan specifying succession in any systematic fashion.

One way of identifying successors, particularly for top executives, is by having the retiring individual identify and develop a successor (over a course of years, if possible).[24] This may be accomplished through the process of **mentoring**. This involves having an experienced employee, known as a **mentor**, advise and counsel the professional development of a new employee, known as a **protégé**. If you've ever had an older, more experienced employee take you under his or her wing and guide you, then you probably already know how valuable mentoring can be. Indeed, mentoring is strongly associated with career success: The more mentoring people receive, the more promotions and pay raises they subsequently receive during their careers.[25]

Mentors do many important things for their protégés.[26] For example, they provide much-needed emotional support and confidence. For those who are just starting out and are likely to be insecure about their abilities, this can be a big help. Mentors also help pave the way for their protégés' job success, such as by nominating them for promotions and by providing opportunities for them to demonstrate their competence. They also suggest useful strategies for achieving work objectives—especially ones that protégés might not generate for themselves. In doing all these things, they help bring the protégé to the attention of top management—a necessary first step for advancement. Finally, mentors often protect their protégés from the repercussions of errors and help them avoid situations that may be risky for their careers.[27]

As you might suspect, it is not only mentors and protégés who come out ahead from mentoring programs, but organizations themselves. At Scotiabank, for example, mentoring was used to reduce the time required for newly minted MBAs to become loan officers. This was necessary because these recent grads maintained traditional, not particularly service-oriented, beliefs about banking, which were holding them back. Through Scotiabank's Competency-Based Mentoring Program, however, branch managers reinforced what these new employees learned about service in their training programs. As a result, training time was reduced from a full year to nine months, allowing the bank to get these new employees fully functioning that much sooner. Clearly, mentoring can be very beneficial if it is handled properly. For a summary of some guidelines for effective mentoring, see Table A2.1.[28]

TABLE A2.1 Ten Tips for Successful Mentoring

The long-term success of mentoring can be enhanced by adhering to the suggestions identified here. Both mentors and protégés should familiarize themselves with these guidelines before entering into a relationship.

Mentors Should . . .

1. Be responsible *to* protégés, not *for* them.
2. Make the mentoring relationship fun and enjoyable.
3. Recognize that their involvement with their protégé extends beyond the workday.
4. Listen carefully to their protégés.
5. Openly acknowledge their failures as well as their successes.
6. Protect their protégés and expect their protégés to protect them.
7. Give their protégés not only directions but also options.
8. Recognize and encourage their protégés' small successes and accomplishments.
9. Encourage independent thinking among their protégés.
10. Focus not only on job skills but also on ethical values.

Source: Based on suggestions by Wickman & Sjodin, 1997; see Note 28.

Endnotes

Chapter 1

Preview Case Sources

Ellis, R. (2006, March 16). How much difference can 1% make. From: http://www.msnbc.msn.com/id/11880767/. 1% for the Planet. (2006, January). TYF takes action for the planet. Press release. From: http://onepercentfortheplanet.org/newsroom.htm. Chouinard, Y. (2005). *Let my people go surfing: Education of a reluctant businessman.* New York: Penguin. Annual Public Report. (2006). Patagonia: Labor compliance program. Fair Labor Association. From: http://www.fairlabor.org/2004report//companies/participating/complianceProgram_pat.html. About Patagonia (2006, March). From: http://www.patagonia.com/about/main_about_us.shtml.

Chapter Notes

1. Greenberg, J. (Ed.). (2003). *Organizational behavior: The state of the science* (2nd ed.). Hillsdale, NJ: Erlbaum.

2. Davenport, T. H. (2005). *Thinking for a living: How to get better performance and results from knowledge workers.* Boston, MA: Harvard Business School Press.

3. Risher, H. (1999). *Aligning pay and results.* New York: AMACOM.

4. Judge, T. A., & Church, A. H. (2000). Job satisfaction: Research and practice. In C. A. Cooper & E. A. Locke (Eds.), *Industrial and organizational psychology: Linking theory to practice* (pp. 166–198). Malden, MA: Blackwell.

5. Hackman, J. R., Wageman, R., Ruddy, T. M., & Ray, C. L. (2000). Team effectiveness in theory and in practice. In C. A. Cooper & E. A. Locke (Eds.), *Industrial and organizational psychology: Linking theory to practice* (pp. 109–129). Malden, MA: Blackwell.

6. Greenberg, J. (2001). Promote procedural justice to enhance acceptance of work outcomes. In E. A. Locke (Ed.), *A handbook of principles of organizational behavior.* Malden, MA: Blackwell.

7. Benavides, F. G., Benach, J., Diez-Roux, A. V., & Roman, C. (2000). How do types of employment relate to health indicators? Findings from the Second European Survey on working conditions. *Journal of Epidemiology & Community Health, 54,* 494–501. Roberts, S. (2000, June 26). Integrating EAPs, work/life programs holds advantages. *Business Insurance, 34*(36), pp. 3, 18–19. Vahtera, J., Kivimaeki, M., Pentti, J., & Theorell, T. (2000). Effect of change on the psychosocial work environment on sickness absence: A seven year follow up of initially healthy employees. *Journal of Epidemiology and Community Health, 54,* 484–493.

8. The Corporate Research Foundation UK. (2000). *Britain's best employers: A guide to the 100 most attractive companies to work for.* New York: McGraw-Hill.

9. Bollinger, D. (1996). *Aiming higher: 25 stories of how companies prosper by combining sound management and social vision.* New York: AMACOM.

10. Katz, D., & Kahn, R. (1978). *The social psychology of organizations.* New York: Wiley.

11. Warner, M. (1994). Organizational behavior revisited. *Human Relations, 47,* 1151–1166.

12. Kennedy, C. (1991). *Instant management.* New York: William Morrow.

13. Drucker, P. F. (1974). *Management: Tasks, responsibilities, practices.* New York: Harper & Row.

14. Mayo, E. (1933). *The human problems of an industrial civilization.* London: Macmillan.

15. Crainer, S. (2000). *The management century.* San Francisco: Jossey-Bass.

16. Roethlisberger, F. J., & Dickson, W. J. (1939). *Management and the worker.* Cambridge, MA: Harvard University Press.

17. Weber, M. (1921). *Theory of social and economic organization* (A. M. Henderson & T. Parsons, Trans.). London: Oxford University Press.

18. Colvin, G. (2000, March 6). Managing in the info era. *Fortune,* pp. F6–F9 (quote, p. F9).

19. Gardner, B., & Moore, G. (1945). *Human relations in industry.* Homewood, IL: Irwin.

20. See Note 18.

21. Gordon, R. A., & Howell, J. E. (1959). *Higher education for business.* New York: Columbia University Press.

22. See Note 21.

23. Collins, J. (2000, August 28). Don't rewrite the rules of the road. *Business Week,* pp. 206–208.

24. Cascio, W. E. (1995). Whither industrial and organizational psychology in a changing world of work? *American Psychologist, 50,* 928–939 (quote, p. 928).

25. BBC News. (2005, September 9). EU faces Katrina economic effect. From: http://news.bbc.co.uk/2/hi/business/4226712.stm.

26. Lodge, G. C. (1995). *Managing globalization in the age of interdependence.* San Francisco: Pfeifer.

27. Ogbonna, E. (1993). Managing organizational culture: Fantasy or reality? *Human Resource Management Journal, 3*(2), 42–54.

28. DeCieri, H., & Dowling, P. J. (1995). Cross-cultural issues in organizational behavior. In C. L. Cooper & D. M. Rousseau (Eds.), *Trends in organizational behavior* (Vol. 2, pp. 127–145). New York: Wiley.

29. Hesketh, B., & Bochner, S. (1994). Technological change in a multicultural context: Implications for training and career planning. In H. C. Triandis, M. D. Dunnette, & L. Hough (Eds.), *Handbook of industrial and organizational psychology* (Vol. 4, pp. 190–240). Palo Alto, CA: Consulting Psychologists Press.

30. DM Review. (2006, March 24). IBM to acquire Language Analysis Systems. From: http://www.dmreview.com/article_sub.cfm?articleId=1051183.

31. IBM. (2006, March 16). IBM to acquire Language Analysis Systems. From: http://www-306.ibm.com/software/data/globalname/.

32. Janssens, M. (1995). Intercultural interaction: A burden on international managers? *Journal of Organizational Behavior, 16,* 155–167.

33. See Note 32.

34. Porter, E. (2006, March 6) Women in the workplace—trend is reversing. *San Francisco Chronicle,* p. A. 2. Lerman, R. I., & Schmidt, S. R. (2002). *An overview of economic, social, and demographic trends affecting the labor market.* Report to the Urban Institute for U.S. Department of Labor (www.dd.gor).

35. Families and Work. (2006). A status report on workplace flexibility. From: http://familiesandwork.org/3w/research/status.html.

36. Bureau of Labor Statistics. (2006). From: www.bls.gov.

37. Family Support America. (2006). The state of family support. From: http://www.familysupportamerica.org/content/gains/index.htm. Mason, J. C. (1993, July). Working in the family way. *HRMagazine,* pp. 25–28. Shellenbarger, S. (1994, February 16). The aging of America is making "elder care" a big workplace issue. *Wall Street Journal,* p. A1. Fenn, D. (1993, July). Bottoms up. *Inc.,* pp. 57–60. Meier, L., & Meagher, L. (1993, September). Teaming up to manage. *Working Woman,* pp. 31–32, 108.

38. Mason, J. C. (1993, July). Working in the family way. *HRMagazine,* pp. 25–28.

39. See Note 38.

40. See Note 38.

41. U.S. Bureau of Labor Statistics. (2006). From: www.bls.gov.

42. Office of the Secretary. U.S. Department of Labor. (2006). The U.S. population is becoming larger and more diverse. From: http://www.dol.gov/asp/programs/history/herman/reports/futurework/report/chapter1/main.htm.

43. Carnevale, A. P., & Stone, S. C. (1995). The American mosaic: An in-depth report on the future of diversity at work. New York: McGraw-Hill.

44. See Note 43.

45. Office of the Secretary. U.S. Department of Labor. (2006). The U.S. population is becoming larger and more diverse. From: http://www.dol.gov/asp/programs/history/herman/reports/futurework/report/chapter1/main.htm.

46. It all depends where you sit. (2000, August 14). *Business Week,* Frontier Section, p. F8.

47. Zuboff, S. (1988). *In the age of the smart machine.* New York: Basic Books.

48. Bridges, W. (1994). *Job shift: How to prosper in a workplace without jobs.* Reading, MA: Addison-Wesley.

49. See Note 48.

50. Tomasko, R. M. (1990). *Downsizing: Reshaping the corporation for the future.* New York: AMACOM.

51. Hendricks, C. F. (1992). *The rightsizing remedy.* Homewood, IL: Business One Irwin.

52. Displaced workers summary. (2002, January). Bureau of Labor Statistics (www.bls.gov/news.release/disp.nr0htm.)

53. McGinn, D., & Naughton, K. (2001, February 5). How safe is your job? *Newsweek,* pp. 36–43.

54. Tomasko, R. M. (1993). *Rethinking the corporation.* New York: AMACOM.

55. Bettis, R. A., Bradley, S. P., & Hamel, G. (1992). Outsourcing and industrial decline. *Academy of Management Review, 6,* 7–22.

56. Haapaniemi, P. (1993, Winter). Taking care of business. *Solutions,* pp. 6–8, 10–13.

57. See Note 56.

58. Stewart, T. A. (1993, December 13). Welcome to the revolution. *Fortune,* pp. 66–68, 70, 72, 76, 78.

59. Byrne, J. A., Brandt, R., & Port, O. (1993, February 8). The virtual corporation: The company of the future will be the ultimate in adaptability. *Business Week,* pp. 98–102.

60. Davidow, W. H., & Malone, M. S. (1992). *The virtual corporation.* New York: Harper Business.

61. See Note 59 (quote, p. 99).

62. IATC Press Release. (2005, October 4). Annual survey shows Americans are working from many different locations outside their employer's office. Silver Spring, MD: IATC. From: http://www.workingfromanywhere.org/news/pr100405.htm.

63. Telework Statistics for 2005. (2006). The Information Society, London. From: http://www.noelhodson.com/index_files/2004_telework_statistics.htm.

64. Kugelmass, J. (1995). *Telecommuting: A manager's guide to flexible work arrangements.* New York: Lexington Books.

65. See Note 64.

66. See Note 63.

67. DuBrin, A. J. (1994). *Contemporary applied management: Skills for managers* (4th ed.). Burr Ridge, IL: Irwin.

68. Mariani, M. (2000, Fall). Telecommuters. *Occupational Outlook Quarterly,* pp. 10–17.

69. Robinson, D., Perryman, S., & Hayday, S. (2004). *The drivers of employee engagement (IES Report 408).* Brighton, England: University of Sussex, Institute for Employment Studies.

70. Krueger, J., & Killharn, E. (2006, March 9). Why Dilbert is right. *Gallup Management Journal.* From: http://gmj.gallup.com/content/default.asp?ci=21802.

71. International Telework Advisory Council. (2006). *Can your organization survive a disaster? Exploring telework as a business continuity strategy.* Scottsdale, AZ: The Telework Advisory Group for World at Work. From: http://www.workingfromanywhere.org/pdf/ITAC-ExecSummFINAL web.pdf.

72. Rousseau, D. M., Ho, V. T., & Greenberg, J. (2006). I-deals: Idiosyncratic terms in employment relationships. *Academy of Management Review.* Rousseau, D. M. (2005). *I-deals: Idiosyncratic deals employees bargain for themselves.* New York: M. E. Sharpe.

73. Cohen, A. R., & Gadon, H. (1980). *Alternative work schedules.* Reading, MA: Addison-Wesley.

74. Galen, M., Palmer, A. T., Cuneo, A., & Maremont, M. (1993, June 28). Work & family. *Business Week,* pp. 80–84, 86, 88.

75. Fierman, J. (1994, January 24). The contingency workforce. *Fortune,* pp. 30–34, 36.

76. Bureau of Labor Statistics (2005, May 24). Employed contingent and noncontingent workers by occupation and industry. From: http://www.bls.gov/news.release/conemp.t04.htm.

77. Aley, J. (1995, September 18). Where the jobs are. *Fortune,* pp. 53–54, 56.

78. Raeburn, P. (2000, March 6). The perils of part-time for professionals. *Business Week,* p. 125.

79. See Note 78.
80. Olmsted, B., & Smith, S. (1994). *Creating a flexible workplace* (2nd ed.). New York: AMACOM.
81. Meier, L., & Meagher, L. (1993, September). Teaming up to manage. *Working Woman,* pp. 31–32, 108.
82. See Note 81.
83. Walton, M. (1990). *The Deming management method at work.* New York: Perigee.
84. Hart, C. W. L., & Bogan, C. E. (1992). *The Baldrige.* New York: McGraw-Hill.
85. Hodgetts, R. M. (1993). *Blueprints for continuous improvement: Lessons from the Baldrige winners.* New York: AMACOM.
86. Boyett, J. H., Schwartz, S., Osterwise, L., & Bauer, R. (1993). *The quality journey: How winning the Baldrige sparked the remaking of IBM.* New York: Dutton.

Case in Point Sources

Schlosser, J. (2006, March 20). The great escape. *Fortune,* pp. 107–110. Tischler, L. (2005, June). Death to the cubicle! *Fast Company,* pp. 29–31. Herman Miller Co. (2006). Action office systems. From: http://www.hermanmiller.com/CDA/SSA/Product/html.

Chapter 2

Preview Case Notes

Wood, S. (2004, August 29). Overtime rule unique to NFL. *USAToday,* p. C1. Hiestand, M. (2003, October 29). Senators challenge the fairness of BCS bids. *USAToday,* p. C1. Wilson, M. (2002, January 11). Understanding the NFL salary cap. *CasinoARTICLES.com.* From: http://www.casinoarticles.com/pub/sports_nfl_football_salary_cap.html. National Football League. (1998, November 30). *NFL modifies coin toss procedure.* From: http://www.nfl.com/news/981130coin.html. National Football League. (1999, August 21). *Commissioner's news conference.* From: http://www.nfl.com/news/0123.tagliabue.html.

Chapter Notes

1. Greenberg, J., & Colquitt, J. A. (2005). *Handbook of organizational justice.* Mahwah, NJ: Lawrence Erlbaum.
2. Werhane, P., Radin, T. J., & Bowie, N. E. (2003). *Employment and employee rights.* Malden, MA: Blackwell.
3. McClean, B., & Elkind, P. (2004). *Smartest guys in the room: The amazing rise and scandalous fall of Enron.* New York: Penguin.
4. Harvard Business School Press. (2005). *Harvard Business Review on corporate responsibility.* Boston, MA: Author.
5. Colquitt, J. A. (2001). On the dimensionality of organizational justice: A construct validation of a measure. *Journal of Applied Psychology, 86,* 386–400. Greenberg, J. (1993). The social side of fairness: Interpersonal and informational classes of organizational justice. In R. Cropanzano (Ed.), *Justice in the workplace: Approaching fairness in human resource management* (pp. 79–103). Hillsdale, NJ: Lawrence Erlbaum.
6. Greenberg, J. (1996). *The quest for justice on the job: Essays and experiments.* Thousand Oaks, CA: Sage.
7. Ang, S., Van Dyne, L., & Begley, T. M. (2003). The employment relationships of foreign workers versus local employees: A field study of organizational justice, job satisfaction, performance, and OCB. *Journal of Organizational Behavior, 24,* 561–583.
8. Colquitt J. A., Greenberg, J., & Zapata-Phelan, C. (2005). What is organizational justice: An historical analysis. In Greenberg, J., & Colquitt, J. A. (2004). *Handbook of organizational justice* (pp. 3–57). Mahwah, NJ: Lawrence Erlbaum.
9. Greenberg, J. (2000). Promote procedural justice to enhance acceptance of work outcomes. In E. A. Locke (Ed.), *The Blackwell handbook of principles of organizational behavior* (pp. 181–195). Malden, MA: Blackwell.
10. Allen, M. (1998, May 15). Giuliani threatens action if cabbies fail to cancel a protest. *New York Times,* p. C1.
11. Greenberg, J., & Cropanzano, R. A. (2001). *Advances in organizational justice.* Stanford, CA: Stanford University Press.
12. Lind, E. A., Greenberg, J., Scott, K. S., & Welchans, T. D. (2000). The winding road from employee to complainant: Situational and psychological determinants of wrongful termination claims. *Administrative Science Quarterly, 45,* 557–590.
13. See Note 5.
14. Tyler, T. R., Degoey, P, & Smith, H. J. (1996). Understanding why the justice of group procedures matters: A test of the psychological dynamics of the group-value model. *Journal of Personality and Social Psychology, 70,* 913–930.
15. Gostick, (2002). *The 24-carrot manager.* Layton, UT: Gibbs Smith.
16. Brockner, J., & Weisenfeld, B. M. (2005). How, when, and why does outcome favorability interact with procedural fairness? In Greenberg, J., & Colquitt, J. A. (2004). *Handbook of organizational justice* (pp. 522–555). Mahwah, NJ: Lawrence Erlbaum.
17. See Note 5.
18. Greenberg, J. (2006). Losing sleep over injustice: Attenuating insomniac reactions to underpayment inequity with supervisory training in interactional justice. *Journal of Applied Psychology 91,* 58–69.
19. Colquitt, J. A., Greenberg, J., & Scott, B. (2005). Organizational justice: Where do we stand? In Greenberg, J., & Colquitt, J. A. (2004). *Handbook of organizational justice* (pp. 622–655). Mahwah, NJ: Lawrence Erlbaum.
20. Greenberg, J. (2006). Positive organizational justice: Moving from fair to fairer—and beyond. In J. E. Dutton & B. R. Ragins (Eds.), *Exploring positive relationships at work: Building a theoretical and research foundation* (pp. 159–178). Mahwah, NJ: Lawrence Erlbaum.
21. Simons, T., & Roberson, Q. (2003). Why managers should care about fairness: The effects of aggregate justice perceptions on organizational outcomes. *Journal of Applied Psychology, 88,* 432–443.
22. Buckley, J. E. (2002, March). Rankings of full-time occupations, by earnings, 2000. *Monthly Labor Review,* pp. 46–57.
23. Van den Bos, K. (2005). What is responsible for the fair process effect? In Greenberg, J., & Colquitt, J. A. (2004). *Handbook of organizational justice* (pp. 318–342). Mahwah, NJ: Lawrence Erlbaum.

24. Schaubroeck, J., May, D. R., & Brown, F. W. (1994). Procedural justice explanations and employee reactions to economic hardship: A field experiment. *Journal of Applied Psychology, 79,* 455–460.

25. Reed, D. (2003, April 4). Delta CEO to give up pay, bonuses up to $9.1 million. *USAToday,* p. C7.

26. Skarlicki, D. P., & Latham, G. P. (2005). Can leaders be trained to be fair? In J. Greenberg & J. A. Colquitt (Eds.), *Handbook of organizational justice.* Mahwah, NJ: Lawrence Erlbaum.

27. Tyme, J. (2005). Quotations on ethics, morals and integrity. From: www.ideasandtraining.com/Ethics-Quotations.html.

28. Ethics Resource Center. (2003). What is ethics? From: http://www.ethics.org/faq.html#eth_what.

29. Salopek, J. J. (2001, July). Do the right thing. *American Society for Training and Development.* From: http://www.astd.org/CMS/templates/index.html?template_id=1&articleid=26983.

30. Trevino, L. K., & Nelson, K. A. (1999). *Managing business ethics* (2nd ed.). New York: Wiley (quote, p. 14).

31. Business: Corporate ethics. From: www.washingtonpost.com/wp-dyn/business/ specials/corporateethics/. Myers, L. (2004, June 30). New Halliburton waste alleged. From: http://msnbc.msn.com/id/5333896/. Masters, B. A., & White, B. (2004, March 6). Stewart guilty on all charges. *Washington Post,* p. A1. Edmonson, G., & Cohen, L. (2004, January 12). How Parmalat went sour. BusinessWeek Online. From: www.businessweek.com/magazine/content/04_02/b3865053_mz054.htm.

32. McConahey, M. (2003, June 8). Ethics scandals reach epidemic level. *Press Democrat* (Santa Rosa, CA), p. A8. (Also available from: http://www.jim-carroll.com/acrobat/public-ity/pressdemocrat-1.pdf.)

33. Zagorian, A. (2005, January 24). Scambuster, Inc. *Time,* pp. 47–48. Fordyce, T. (2004, July 30). Track record on Olympic corruption. BBC Sport. From: news.bbc.co.uk/sport1/hi/other_sports/olympics_2012/3939219.stm.

34. Ethics Resources Center. (2006). *National business ethics survey: How employees view ethics in their organizations 1995–2005.* Washington, DC: Author.

35. Henderson, V. E. (1992). *What's ethical in business?* New York: McGraw-Hill.

36. George W. Bush. Corporate Responsibility Speech, July 9, 2002.

37. See Note 34 (quote, pp. 26–27).

38. Panzner, M. J. (2004). *The new laws of the stock market jungle.* New York: Financial Times Prentice Hall.

39. Cone. (2002). *2002 Cone corporate citizenship study.* Boston, MA: Author. From: www.coneinc.com/Pages/pr_13.html

40. O'Toole, J. (2005). *Creating the good life: Aristotle's guide to getting it right.* New York: Rodale.

41. MAALA Business for Social Responsibility. (2002). *Corporate social responsibility.* Tel Aviv, Israel: Author (www.maala.com.). Verschoor, C. C. (1998). A study of the link between a corporation's financial performance and its commitment to ethics. *Journal of Business Ethics, 17,*

1509–1516. Embley, L. L. (1993). *Doing well while doing good.* Englewood Cliffs, NJ: Prentice Hall.

42. See Note 41.

43. Fombrun, C. J. (1996). *Reputation: Realizing value from the corporate image.* Boston: Harvard Business School Press.

44. Alsop, R. J. (2004). *The 18 immutable laws of corporate reputation.* New York: Free Press.

45. Gaines-Ross, L. (2002). *CEO capital: A guide to building CEO reputation and company success.* New York: Wiley.

46. Bies, R. J., & Greenberg, J. (2001). Dueling images of justice in the global economy: The swoosh, the sweatshops, and the sway of public opinion. In M. Gannon & K. Newman (Eds.), *Handbook of cross-cultural management.* Oxford, England: Blackwell.

47. Fine, J. (2003, August 25). *Major advertisers drop from "Martha Stewart Living."* AdAge.Com. From: www.adage.com/news.cms?newsId=38569.

48. Johnson, D. C. (1997, November 9). United Way, faced with fewer donations, is giving away less. *New York Times,* p. A1.

49. See Note 39 (quote, pp. 30–31).

50. Ethics and Policy Integration Center (2003). *Toward an effective ethics and compliance program: The Federal Sentencing Guidelines for Organizations.* Washington, DC: Author. Also available from: http://www.ethicaledge.com/appendix1.html. Lander, G. (2003). *What is Sarbanes-Oxley?* New York: McGraw Hill. Kaplan, J. M. (2003, May/June). Justice department revises corporate prosecution standards. *Ethikos, 16*(6), pp. 1–3, 13.

51. Ethics and Policy Integration Center (2003). *Toward an effective ethics and compliance program: The Federal Sentencing Guidelines for Organizations.* Washington, DC: Author. Also available from: http://www.ethicaledge.com/appendix1.html.

52. Preventing Corrupt Practices and Maintaining Standards of Documentation. GlaxoSmithKline Corporate Policy POL-GSK-007 v04. From: www.gsk.com.about/corp-gov-sarb-oxley.htm.

53. Donaldson, T. (1996, September/October). Values in tension: Ethics away from home. *Harvard Business Review,* pp. 48–62.

54. See Note 53.

55. Gap, Inc. (2004). *Social responsibility report, 2003.* New York: Author. Also available from: http://ccbn.mobular.net/ccbn/7/645/696/index.html.

56. See Note 53 (quote, p. 55).

57. Trevino, L. K., & Youngblood, S. A. (1990). Bad apples in bad barrels: A causal analysis of ethical decision-making behavior. *Journal of Applied Psychology, 75,* 378–385.

58. Kohlberg, L. (1976). Moral stages and moralization: The cognitive-developmental approach. In T. Lickona (Ed.), *Moral development and behavior: Theory, research, and social issues* (pp. 2–52). New York: Holt, Rinehart, and Winston. Kohlberg, L. (1969). Stage and sequence: The cognitive-developmental approach to socialization. In D. A. Goslin (Ed.), *Handbook of socialization theory and research* (pp. 347–380). Chicago, IL: Rand McNally.

59. Greenberg, J. (2002). Who stole the money, and when? Individual and situational determinants of employee theft. *Organizational Behavior and Human Decision Processes, 89,* 895–1003. Blass, T. (1999). Obedience to authority: Current perspectives on the Milgram paradigm. Mahwah, NJ: Lawrence Erlbaum. Grover, S. L. (1993). Why professionals lie: The impact of professional role conflict on reporting accuracy. *Organizational Behavior and Human Decision Processes, 55,* 251–272.

60. Trevino, L. K. (1992). Moral reasoning and business ethics. *Journal of Business Ethics, 11,* 445–459.

61. Engineering.Com. (2004). *B. F. Goodrich case adapted from Texas A&M University.* From: www.engineering.com/content/ContentDisplay?contentId=41009005.

62. Jansen, E., & Von Glinow, M. A. (1985). Ethical ambivalence and organizational reward systems. *Academy of Management Review, 10,* 814–822.

63. Brass, D. J., Butterfield, K. D., & Skaggs, B. C. (1998). Relationships and unethical behavior: A social-network perspective. *Academy of Management Review, 23,* 14–31.

64. Wolfe, D. M. (1988). Is there integrity in the bottom line: Managing obstacles to executive integrity. In S. Srivastava (Ed.), *Executive integrity: The search for high human values in organizational life* (pp. 140–171). San Francisco: Jossey-Bass.

65. Ethics Resource Center. (2003). *2003 national business ethics survey.* Washington, DC: Author.

66. From: http://www.adviceonmanagement.com/advice_ethics.html.

67. Cassell, C., Johnson, P., & Smith, K. (1997). Opening the black box: Corporate codes of ethics in their organizational context. *Journal of Business Ethics, 16,* 1077–1093.

68. Gaumnitz, B. R. (2004). A classification scheme for codes of business ethics. *Journal of Business Ethics, 49,* 329–336.

69. Deloitte. (2004). *Business ethics and compliance in the Sarbanes-Oxley era: A survey by Deloitte and Corporate Board Member magazine.* From: www.deloitte.com/dtt/cda/doc/content/us_assur_ethicsCompliance(1).pdf. Weaver, G. R., Trevino, L. K., & Cochran, P. L. (1996). Corporate ethics practices in the mid-1990's: An empirical study of the Fortune 1000. *Journal of Business Ethics, 18,* 283–294.

70. Ethics Resource Center. (1994). *Ethics in American business: Policies, programs and perceptions.* Washington, DC: Author. Weaver, G. R., Trevino, L. K., & Cochran, P. L. (1996). Corporate ethics practices in the mid-1990's: An empirical study of the Fortune 1000. *Journal of Business Ethics, 18,* 283–294.

71. See Note 70.

72. Sears, B. (2004, January/February). Lights! Camera! Action! Lockheed Martin's ethics film festival. *Ethikos,* pp. 8–9.

73. See Note 72.

74. See Note 72.

75. Ferrell, O. C., Fraedrich, J., & Ferrell, L. (2002). *Business ethics* (5th ed.). Boston: Houghton Mifflin. Waddock, S., & Smith, N. (2000, Winter). Corporate responsibility audits: Doing well by doing good. *Sloan Management Review,* pp. 66–83.

76. Schwartz, M. (2001). The nature of the relationship between corporate codes of ethics and behaviour. *Journal of Business Ethics, 23,* 219–228.

77. See Note 77.

78. Greenberg, J. (2002). Who stole the money, and when? Individual and situational determinants of employee theft. *Organizational Behavior and Human Decision Processes, 89,* 985–1003.

79. Ferrell, O. C., Fraedrich, J., & Ferrell, L. (2005). *Business ethics* (6th ed.). Boston: Houghton Mifflin. Waddock, S., & Smith, N. (2000, Winter). Corporate responsibility audits: Doing well by doing good. *Sloan Management Review,* pp. 66–83.

80. From: http://www.adviceonmanagement.com/advice_ethics.html.

81. Carroll, A. B. (1991). The pyramid of corporate social responsibility: Toward the moral management of organizational stakeholders. *Business Horizons, 34*(4), 39–48.

82. From: www.alcoa.com/global/en/community/info_page/Areas_of_Excellence_Overview.asp.

83. Business for Social Responsibility (2004). *Issue brief: Overview of corporate social responsibility.* From: www.bsr.org/CSRResources.

84. McDonald's Worldwide. (2004). *Corporate responsibility report, 2004.* Oak Brook, IL: Author. Also available from: www.mcdonalds.com/corp/values/socialrespons/sr_report.RowPar.0002.ContentPar.0002.ColumnPar.0003.File.tmp/SR%20Report_output_rev_ed.pdf.

85. Corporate Social Responsibility Wire. (2005, February 1). *Press release: The UPS Foundation awards grant to Keep America Beautiful.* From: www.csrwire.com/article.cgi/3492.html.

86. Asmus, P. (2006, Spring). 100 best corporate citizens: Five years. *Business Ethics,* pp. 6–10.

87. Brady, D. (2002, February 19). The right mix of (yogurt) cultures? *BusinessWeek,* p. 57–58. Key mining and oil companies pledge to keep hands off protected sites. (2003, September 7). *Business Respect Corporate Social Responsibility Dispatches No. 62.* From: http://www.mallenbaker.net/csr/nl/62.html#anchor1058. U.S.: Boise Cascade announces zero old-growth wood policy. (2003, September 7). *Business Respect Corporate Social Responsibility Dispatches No. 62.* From: http://www.mallenbaker.net/csr/nl/62.html#anchor1058. Waddock, S. A. (2001). *Leading corporate citizens.* Burr Ridge, IL: McGraw-Hill/Irwin.

88. CNNMoney. (2005, January 5). U.S. firms helping tsunami victims. From: http://money.cnn.com/2004/12/30/news/fortune500/corporate_aid/. CNN Money. (2004, December 31). Corporations give to tsunami relief. From: http://money.cnn.com/2004/12/30/news/fortune500/corporate_aid/.

89. Orlitzky, M., Schmidt, F. L., & Rynes, S. L. (2003). Corporate social and financial performance: A meta-analysis. *Organization Studies, 24,* 403–441.

90. Margolis, J. D., & Walsh, J. P. (2001). *People and profits? The search for a link between a company's social and*

financial performance. Mahwah, NJ: Lawrence Erlbaum. Labich, K. (1992, April 20). The new crisis in business ethics. *Fortune,* pp. 167–170, 172, 174, 176.

91. Kelly, M. (2004, Winter). Holy grail found: Absolute, definitive proof CSR pays off. *Business Ethics,* pp. 4–5.

92. McIntosh, M. (2003). *Raising a ladder to the moon: The complexities of corporate social and environmental responsibility.* New York: Palgrage Macmillan. Rayner, J. (2002). *Corporate social responsibility monitor.* London: Gee. Kinder, P. D., Lydenberg, S. D., & Domini, A. L. (1994). *Investing for good: Making money while being socially responsible.* New York: HarperCollins. Domini, A. L., Lydenberg, S. D., & Kinder, P. D. (1992). *The social investment almanac: A comprehensive guide to socially responsible investing.* New York: Henry Holt.

93. See Note 92.

94. From: www.exxonmobil.com/corporate/Citizenship/ Corp_citizenship_home.asp.

95. Clark, J., & Driscoll, W. (2003). *Globalization and the poor: Exploitation or equalizer.* New York: International Debate Education Association. Steele, J. R. (2003). *"Is this my reward?" An employee's struggles for fairness in the corporate exploitation of his inventions.* New York: Pencraft Press.

96. Deane, B. (2005, January). Promoting accountability in the workplace: Starbucks and Dell first to adopt corporate code of conduct regarding women. From: www.diversityhotwire .com/business/managers_update.html.

97. See Note 96.

98 See Note 96.

Cas.e in Point Sources

Singer, A. (2003, May/June). Exelon excels at reaching out. *Ethikos, 16*(6), pp, 7–9, 13. From: www.exeloncorp.com/ corporate/about/a_overview.shtml.

Chapter 3

Preview Case Sources

Enterprise Rent-a-Car Web site. (2006). http://aboutus.enterprise.com/. Schlereth, J. (2003, July–August). Putting people first. *BizEd,* pp. 16–20. *Hoover's handbook of private companies.* (2006). Enterprise-Rent-A-Car (pp. 141–148). Austin, TX: Hoover's Online.

Chapter Notes

1. Furnham, A. (2005). *The psychology of behavior of work: The individual in the organization.* New York: Psychology Press.

2. Ashforth, B. E., & Mael, F. (1989). Social identity theory and the organization. *Academy of Management Review, 14,* 20–29.

3. LaTendresse, D. (2000). Social identity and intergroup relations within the hospital. *Journal of Social Distress and the Homeless, 9,* 51–69.

4. Cialdini, R. B., Borden, R. J., Thorne, A., Walker, M. R., Freeman, S., & Sloan, L. R. (1999). Basking in reflected glory: Three (football) field studies. In R. F. Baumeister (Ed.), *The self in social psychology* (pp. 436–445). Philadelphia: Psychology Press/Talor & Francis.

5. Weiner, B. (1995). *Judgments of responsibility.* New York: Guilford.

6. Jones, E. E., & McGillis, D. (1976). Correspondent inferences and the attribution cube: A comparative reappraisal. In J. H. Harvey, W. J. Ickes, & R. F. Kidd (Eds.), *New directions in attribution research* (Vol. 1, pp. 389–420). Hillsdale, NJ: Lawrence Erlbaum Associates.

7. Kelley, H. H. (1972). Attribution in social interaction (pp. 1–26). In E. E. Jones, D. E. Kanous, H. H. Kelley, R. E. Nisbett, S. Valins, & B. Weiner (Eds.), *Attribution: Perceiving the causes of behavior.* Morristown, NJ: General Learning Press.

8. Burger, J. M. (1991). Changes in attribution errors over time: The ephemeral fundamental attribution error. *Social Cognition, 9,* 183–193.

9. Murphy, K. R., Jako, R. A., & Anhalt, R. L. (1993). Nature and consequences of halo error: A critical analysis. *Journal of Applied Psychology, 78,* 218–225.

10. Naquin, C. E., & Tynan, R. O. (2003). The team halo effect: Why teams are not blamed for their failures. *Journal of Applied Psychology, 88,* 332–340.

11. Pulakos, E. D., & Wexley, K. N. (1983). The relationship among perceptual similarity, sex, and performance ratings in manager-subordinate dyads. *Academy of Management Journal, 26,* 129–139.

12. Turban, D. B., & Jones, A. P. (1988). Supervisor-subordinate similarity: Types, effects, and mechanisms. *Journal of Applied Psychology, 73,* 228–234.

13. Dearborn, D. C., & Simon, H. A. (1958). Selective perception: A note on the departmental identification of executives. *Sociometry, 21,* 140–144.

14. Waller, M. J., Huber, G. P., & Glick, W. H. (1995). Functional background as a determinant of executives' selective perception. *Academy of Management Journal, 38,* 943–974.

15. Dougherty, T. W., Turban, D. B., & Callender, J. C. (1994). Confirming first impressions in the employment interview: A field study of interviewer behavior. *Journal of Applied Psychology, 79,* 659–665.

16. Eden, D., & Shani, A. B. (1982). Pygmalion goes to boot camp: Expectancy, leadership, and trainee performance. *Journal of Applied Psychology, 67,* 194–199.

17. Oz, S., & Eden, D. (1994). Restraining the Golem: Boosting performance by changing the interpretation of low scores. *Journal of Applied Psychology, 79,* 744–754.

18. Davidson, O. B., & Eden, D. (2000). Remedial self-fulfilling prophecy: Two field experiments to prevent Golem effects among disadvantaged women. *Journal of Applied Psychology, 85,* 386–398.

19. Eden, D. (1997). Leadership and expectations: Pygmalion effects and other self-fulfilling prophecies in organizations. In R. Vecchio (Ed.), *Leadership: Understanding the dynamics of power and influence in organizations* (pp. 177–193). Notre Dame, IN: University of Notre Dame Press.

20. Bethune, G. (1999). *From worst to first: Behind the scenes of Continental's remarkable comeback.* New York: John Wiley & Sons.

21. Sherman, J. W. (2001). The dynamic relationship between stereotype efficiency and mental representation. In G. B. Moskowitz (Ed.), *Cognitive social psychology: The*

Princeton Symposium on the legacy and future of social cognition (pp. 177–190). Mahwah, NJ: Lawrence Erlbaum Associates.

22. Steele, C. M., & Aronson, J. (1995). Stereotype threat and the intellectual performance of African Americans. *Journal of Personality and Social Psychology, 69,* 797–811.

23. Steele, C. M., Spencer, S. J., & Aronson, J. (2002). Contending with group image: The psychology of stereotype and social identity threat. In P. P. Zanna (Ed.), *Advances in experimental social psychology* (Vol. 34, pp. 379–440). San Diego, CA: Academic Press.

24. Martens, A., Johns, M., Greenberg, J., & Schimel, J. (206). Combating stereotype threat: The effect of self-affirmation on women's intellectual performance. *Journal of Experimental Social Psychology, 42,* 236–243.

25. Aronson, J., Lustina, M. J., Good, C., & Keough, K. (1999). When white men can't do math: Necessary and sufficient factors in stereotype threat. *Journal of Experimental Social Psychology, 35,* 29–46.

26. Extra pounds, slimmer wages. (2001, January 15). *Business Week,* p. 28.

27. Blair, I. (2001). Implicit stereotypes and prejudice. In G. B. Moskowitz (Ed.), *Cognitive social psychology: The Princeton Symposium on the legacy and future of social cognition* (pp. 359–374). Mahwah, NJ: Lawrence Erlbaum Associates.

28. Sassenberg, K., & Moskowitz, G. B. (2005). Don't stereotype, think different! Overcoming automatic stereotype activation by mindset priming. *Journal of Experimental Social Psychology, 41,* 506–614.

29. Rosenfeld, P., Giacalone, R. A., & Riordan, C. A. (2002). *Impression management: Building and enhancing reputations at work.* London: Thompson Learning.

30. Giacalone, R. A. & Rosenfeld, P. (1989). *Impression management in the organization.* Hillsdale, NJ: Lawrence Erlbaum Associates.

31. Stevens, C. K., & Kristof, A. L. (1995). Making the right impression: A field study of applicant impression management during job interviews. *Journal of Applied Psychology, 80,* 587–606.

32. Mohrman, A. M., Jr., Resnick-West, S. M., & Lawler, E. E., III. (1989). *Designing performance appraisal systems.* San Francisco: Jossey-Bass.

33. Ilgen, D. R., Major, D. A., & Tower, S. L. (1994). The cognitive revolution in organizational behavior (pp. 1–22). In J. Greenberg (Ed.), *Organizational behavior: The state of the science.* Hillsdale, NJ: Lawrence Erlbaum Associates.

34. Hogan, E. A. (1987). Effects of prior expectations on performance ratings: A longitudinal study. *Academy of Management Journal, 30,* 354–368.

35. Wayne, S. J., & Liden, R. C. (1995). Effects of impression management on performance ratings: A longitudinal study. *Academy of Management Journal, 38,* 233–260.

36. Harris, P. R., & Moran, R. T. (1991). *Managing cultural differences* (3rd ed.). Houston: Gulf Publishing.

37. Lewis, R. D. (2000). *When cultures collide.* Naperville, IL: Nicholas Brealey.

38. Morrison, T., Conaway, W. A., & Douress, J. J. (2001). *Dun & Bradstreet's guide to doing business around the world.* Paramus, NJ: Prentice Hall.

39. Hodgson, J. D., Sano, Y., & Graham, J. L. (2001). *Doing business with the new Japan.* Lanham, MD: Rowman & Littlefield.

40. Garbett, T. (1988). *How to build a corporation's identity and project its image.* Lexington, MA: Lexington Books.

41. America's most admired companies. (2006, February 19). *Fortune.* From: http://money.cnn.com/magazines/fortune/mostadmired/.

42. Davies, G. (2002). *Corporate reputation and competitiveness.* Oxfordshire, UK: Taylor & Francis.

43. Bansal, P., & Clelland, I. (2004). Talking trash: Legitimacy, impression management, and unsystematic risk in the context of the natural environment. *Academy of Management Journal, 47,* 93–103.

44. Infact. (2006). *Challenging corporate abuse, building grassroots power, since 1977.* From: http://www.infact.org/aboutinf.html. Boycott Thieves. (2006). More reasons to boycott Exxon Mobil. From: http://boycott-thieves.blogspot.com/.

45. Gatewood, R. D., Gowan, M. A., & Lautenschlager, G. J. (1993). Corporate image, recruitment image, and initial job choice decisions. *Academy of Management Journal, 36,* 414–427.

46. Bongiorno, L. (1995, April 10). The duller the better: For 1994's annual reports, modesty is a virtue. *Business Week,* p. 44.

47. Wick, C. W., & Leon, L. S. (1993). *The learning edge: How smart managers and smart companies stay ahead.* New York: McGraw-Hill.

48. Atkinson, R. C., Herrnstein, R. J., Lindzey, G., & Luce, R. D. (Eds.). (1988). *Stevens' handbook of experimental psychology* (2nd ed.) (Vol. 1, pp. 218–266). New York: Wiley.

49. Skinner, B. F. (1969). *Contingencies of reinforcement.* New York: Appleton-Century-Crofts.

50. Scott, W. E., & Podsakoff, P. M. (1985). *Behavioral principles in the practice of management.* New York: Wiley.

51. Bandura, A. (1986). *Social foundations of thought and action.* Englewood Cliffs, NJ: Prentice Hall.

52. Harrison, J. K. (1992). Individual and combined effects of behavior modeling and the cultural assimilator in cross-cultural management training. *Journal of Applied Psychology, 77,* 963–963.

53. Goldstein, I. L. (1991). Training in work organizations. In M. D. Dunnette & L. M. Hough (Eds.), *Handbook of industrial and organizational psychology* (2nd ed.) (Vol. 2, pp. 507–620). Palo Alto, CA: Consulting Psychologists Press.

54. Schnake, M. E. (1986). Vicarious punishment in a work setting. *Journal of Applied Psychology, 71,* 343–345.

55. Moe, M.. & Blodgett, H. (2000). Merrill Lynch & Co., Global Securities Research and Economics Group, Global Fundamental Research Department. In *ASTD annual report.* Alexandria, VA: Author.

56. Sugrue, B. (2003). *State of the industry: ASTD's annual revue of U.S. and international trends in workplace learning*

and performance. Alexandria, VA: American Society for Training and Development.

57. Del Valle, C. (1993, April 26). From high schools to high skills. *Business Week,* pp. 110, 113.

58. Francesco, A. M., & Gold, B. A. (1998). *International organizational behavior.* Upper Saddle River, NJ: Prentice Hall.

59. Jarvis, P. (2000). *Universities, corporate universities, and the higher learning industries.* London: Kogan Page. Meister, J. C. (1998). *Corporate universities.* New York: McGraw-Hill.

60. Gist, M. E., Stevens, C. K., & Bavetta, A. G. (1991). Effects of self-efficacy and post-training intervention on the acquisition and maintenance of complex interpersonal skills. *Personnel Psychology, 44,* 837–861.

61. O'Reilly, B. (1993, April 5). How execs learn now. *Fortune,* pp. 53–54, 58.

62. Rendon, J. (2000, October). Learning potential. *Grok,* pp. 58–60.

63. Liddle, A. J. (2003, March 10). Chains upgrade to online training, downgrade teaching expenses. *Nation's Restaurant News, 37*(10), pp. 62–63 (quote, p. 62).

64. See Note 63.

65. Argyris, C. (1991, May–June). Teaching smart people how to learn. *Harvard Business Review, 69*(3), 99–109.

66. Driskell, J. E., Cooper, C., & Moran, A. (1994). Does mental practice enhance performance? *Journal of Applied Psychology, 79,* 481–493.

67. Tracey, B. J., Tannenbaum, S. I., & Kavanaugh, M. J. (1995). Applying trained skills on the job: The importance of the work environment. *Journal of Applied Psychology, 80,* 239–253.

68. Tannenbaum, S. I., & Yukl, G. A. (1992). Training and development in work organizations. *Annual Review of Psychology, 43,* 399–441.

69. Hoffman, R. (1995, April). Ten reasons you should be using 360-feedback. *HRMagazine,* pp. 83–85.

70. Edwards, M. R., & Ewen, A. J. (1996). *360° feedback: The powerful new model for employee assessment and performance improvement.* New York: AMACOM.

71. Miller, L. (1978). *Behavior management.* New York: Wiley.

72. Frederiksen, L. W. (1982). *Handbook of organizational behavior management.* New York: Wiley.

73. Tornow, W. W., & London, M. (1998). *Maximizing the value of 360-degree feedback.* San Francisco: Jossey Bass.

74. Lepsinger, R., & Lucia, A. D. (1997). *The art and science of 360-degree feedback.* San Francisco: Jossey Bass.

75. Beyer, J., & Trice, H. M. (1984). A field study of the use and perceived effects of discipline in controlling work performance. *Academy of Management Journal, 27,* 743–754.

76. Trahan, W. A., & Steiner, D. D. (1994). Factors affecting supervisors' use of disciplinary actions following poor performance. *Journal of Organizational Behavior, 15,* 129–139.

77. Oberle, R. J. (1978). Administering disciplinary actions. *Personnel Journal, 18*(3), 30–33.

78. Arvey, R. D., & Jones, A. P. (1985). The use of discipline in organizational settings: A framework for future research. In L. L. Cummings & B. M. Staw (Eds.), *Research in organizational behavior* (Vol. 7, pp. 367–408). Greenwich, CT: JAI Press.

79. Kiechell, W., III. (1990, May 7). How to discipline in the modern age. *Fortune,* pp. 179–180 (quote, p. 180).

80. Arvey, R. E., & Icancevich, J. M. (1980). Punishment in organizations: A review, propositions, and research suggestions. *Academy of Management Review, 5,* 123–133.

Case in Point Sources

Our Company. (2006). *Safeway, the start-up.* From: http://shop.safeway.com/superstore/default.asp?brandid=1& page=corphome. Safeway workers frowning upon service-with-a-smile policy (1998, September 3). *Columbus Dispatch,* p. C1. Kornheiser, T. (1998, September 13). Unsafe way? *Washington Post,* p. F1. McNichol, T. (1998, November 11). My supermarket, my friend. *SF Weekly.* From: http://www.sfweekly.com/Issues/1998-11-11/ news/feature.html.

Chapter 4

Preview Case Sources

Battelle, J. (2006, March). 1.2 trillion buck chuck. *Business 2.0,* pp. 101–103. History and evolution of the Charles Schwab Corporation. (2006). Charles Schwab Web site: http://www.aboutschwab.com/schwabcorp/history.html. Kador, J. (2002). *Charles Schwab: How one company beat Wall Street and reinvented the brokerage industry.* New York: Wiley.

Chapter Notes

1. Tett, R. P., & Burnett, D. D. (2003). A personality trait–based interactionist model of job performance. *Journal of Applied Psychology, 88,* 500–517.

2. Carver, C. S., & Scheier, M. F. (1992). *Perspectives on personality* (2nd ed.). Boston: Allyn & Bacon.

3. Steel, R. P., & Rentsch, J. R. (1997). The dispositional model of job attitudes revisited: Findings of a 10-year study. *Journal of Applied Psychology, 82,* 873–879.

4. Illies, R., & Judge, T. A. (2003). On the heritability of job satisfaction: The mediating role of personality. *Journal of Applied Psychology, 88,* 750–759.

5. George, J. M., & Zhou, J. (2001). When openness to experience and conscientiousness are related to creative behavior: An interactional approach. *Journal of Applied Psychology, 86,* 513–524.

6. Chatman, J. A., Caldwell, D. F., & O'Reilly, C.A. (1999). Managerial personality and performance: A semi-idiographic approach. *Journal of Research in Personality, 33,* 534–545.

7. See Note 1.

8. Osipow, S. H. (1990). Convergence in theories of career choice and development: Review and prospect. *Journal of Vocational Behavior, 36,* 122–131.

9. Caldwell, D. F., & O'Reilly, C. A., III (1990). Measuring person-job fit with a profile-comparison process. *Journal of Applied Psychology, 75,* 648–657.

10. Slaughter, J. E., Zickar, M. J., Highhouse, S., & Mohr, D. C. (2004). Personality trait inferences about organizations: Development of a measure and assessment of

construct validity. *Journal of Applied Psychology, 89,* 85–103.

11. Allport, G.W., & Odbert, H. S. (1936). Trait names: A psycholexical study. *Psychological Monographs, 47,* 211–214.

12. Costa, P. T., & McCrae, R. R. (1992). *The NEO-PI personality inventory.* Odessa, FL: Psychological Assessment Resources.

13. Salgado, J. F. (1997). The five-factor model of personality and job performance in the European community. *Journal of Applied Psychology, 82,* 30–43.

14. Hurtz, G. M, & Donovan, J. J. (2000). Personality and job performance: The Big Five revisited. *Journal of Applied Psychology, 85,* 869–879.

15. Mount, M. K., & Barrick, M. R. (1995). The Big Five personality dimensions: Implications for research and practice.in human resources management. In K. M. Rowland & G. Ferris (Eds.), *Research in personnel and human resources management* (Vol. 13, pp. 153–200). Greenwich, CT: JAI Press.

16. Barrick, M. R., Stewart, G. L., Neubert, M. J., & Mount, M. K. (1998). Relating member ability and personality to work-team processes and team effectiveness. *Journal of Applied Psychology, 83,* 377–391.

17. Raja, U., Johns, G. J., & Ntallanis, F. (2004). The impact of personality on psychological contracts. *Academy of Management Journal, 47,* 350–367.

18. Watson, D., & Clark, L. A. (1997). Extraversion and its positive emotional core. In R. Hogan, J. A. Johnson, & S. R. Briggs (Eds.), *Handbook of personality psychology* (pp. 767–793). San Diego, CA: Academic Press.

19. Judge, T. A., Bono, J. E., Ilies, R., & Gerhardt, M.W. (2002). Personality and leadership: A qualitative and quantitative review. *Journal of Applied Psychology, 87,* 765–780.

20. Ciaverall, M. A., Bucholtz, A. K., Riordan, C. M., Gatewood, R. D., & Stokes, G. (2004). The Big Five and ventures survival: Is there a linkage? *Journal of Business Venturing, 19,* 465–583.

21. George, J. M., & Brief, A. P. (1992). Feeling good—doing good: A conceptual analysis of the mood at work—organizational spontaneity relationships. *Psychological Bulletin, 112,* 310–329.

22. Isen, A. M., & Baron, R. A. (1992). Positive affect as a factor in organizational behavior. In B. M. Staw & L. L. Cummings (Eds.), *Research in organizational behavior* (Vol. 13, pp. 1–54). Greenwich, CT: JAI Press.

23. Magruder, J. (2004, August 5). Negative employees costing companies money. *The Arizona Republic,* p. B16.

24. Staw, B. M,, & Barsade, S. G. (1993). Affect and managerial performance: A test of the sadder-but-wiser vs. happier-and-smarter hypotheses. *Administrative Science Quarterly, 38,* 304–331.

25. George, J. M. (1990). Personality, affect, and behavior in groups. *Journal of Applied Psychology, 75,* 107–116.

26. Aquino, K., Grover, S. L., Bradfield, M., & Allen, D. G. (1999). The effects of negative affectivity, hierarchical status, and self-determination on workplace victimization. *Academy of Management Journal, 42,* 260–272.

27. Judge, T. A., Locke, E. A., & Durham, C. C. (1997). The dispositional causes of job satisfaction: A core evaluations approach. *Research in Organizational Behavior, 19,* 151–188.

28. Judge, T. A., & Bono, J. E. (2001). Relationship of core self-evaluations traits—self-esteem, generalized self-efficacy, locus of control, and emotional stability—with job satisfaction and job performance: A meta-analysis. *Journal of Applied Psychology, 86,* 80–92.

29. See Note 27.

30. Judge, T. A., Bono, J. E., Erez, A., & Locke, E. A. (2004). Core self-evaluations and job and life satisfaction: The role of self-concordance and goal attainment. *Journal of Applied Psychology, 90,* 257–268. Bono, J. E., & Judge, T. A. (2003). Core self-evaluations: A review of the trait and its role in job satisfaction and job performance. *European Journal of Personality, 17*(Suppl1), S5–S18.

31. Christie, R., & Geis, F. L. (1970). *Studies in Machiavellianism.* New York: Academic Press.

32. See Note 31.

33. Ruffenach, G. (2004, August 9). Confessions of a scam artist. *Wall Street Journal* pp. R1, R3.

34. Wilson, D. S., Near, D., & Miller, R. R. (1997). Machiavellianism: A synthesis of the evolutionary and psychological literatures. *Psychological Bulletin, 119,* 285–299.

35. Schultz, C. J., II. (1993). Situational and dispositional predictors of performance: A test of the hypothesized Machiavellianism x structure interaction among sales persons. *Journal of Applied Social Psychology, 23,* 478–498.

36. McClelland, D. C. (1985). *Human motivation.* Glenview, IL: Scott, Foresman.

37. McClelland, D. C. (1977). Entrepreneurship and management in the years ahead. In C. A. Bramletter (Ed.)., *The individual and the future of organizations* (pp. 12–29). Atlanta, GA: Georgia State University.

38. Miller, D., & Droge, C. (1986). Psychological and traditional determinants of structure. *Administrative Science Quarterly, 31,* 539–560.

39. Turban, D. B., & Keon, T. L. (1993). Organizational attractiveness: An interactionist perspective. *Journal of Applied Psychology, 78,* 184–193.

40. Dweck, C. S. (1999). *Self-theories: The role in motivation, personality, and development.* Philadelphia: Psychology Press.

41. VandeWalle, D. (1997). Development and validation of a work domain goal orientation instrument. *Educational and Psychological Measurement, 8,* 995–1015.

42. Chen, G., Gully, S. M., Whiteman, J. A., & Kilcullen, R. N. (2000). Examination of relationships among trait-like individual differences, state-like individual differences, and learning performance. *Journal of Applied Psychology, 85,* 835–847.

43. VandeWalle, D., Cron, W. K., & Slocum, J. W., Jr. (2001). The role of goal orientation following performance feedback. *Journal of Applied Psychology, 86,* 629–640.

44. U.S. Department of Labor (2005, July 1). Workers on flexible and shift schedules in 2004 summary. From: http://www.bls.gov/news.release/flex.nr0.htm.

45. Totterdell, P., Spelten, E., Smith, L., Barton, J., & Folkard, S. (1995). Recovery from work shifts: How long does it take? *Journal of Applied Psychology, 80,* 43–57.

46. Guthrie, J. P., Ash, R. A., & Bendapudi, V. (1995). Additional validity evidence for a measure of morningness. *Journal of Applied Psychology, 80,* 186–190.

47. Wallace, B. (1993). Day persons, night persons, and variability in hypnotic susceptibility. *Journal of Personality and Social Psychology, 64,* 827–833.

48. McClelland, D. C. (1961). *The achieving society.* Princeton, NJ: Van Nostrand.

49. Lynn, R. (1991). *The secret of the miracle economy.* London: SAU.

50. Furnham, A., Kirkcaldy, B. D., & Lynn, R. (1994). National attitudes to competitiveness, money, and work among young people: First, second, and third world differences. *Human Relations, 47,* 119–132.

51. Baron, R. A., & Shane, S. (2005). *Entrepreneurship: A process perspective.* Cincinnati, OH: Thomson.

52. Eysenk, M.W. (1994). *Individual differences.* Hillsdale, NJ: Erlbaum.

53. Salgado, J. F., Anderson, N., Moscoso, S., Bertua, C., de Fruyt, F., & Rolland, J. P. (2003). A meta-analytic study of general mental ability validity for different occupations in the European community. *Journal of Applied Psychology, 88,* 1068–1081.

54. Sternberg, R. J. (1986). *Intelligence applied.* New York: Harcourt Brace Jovanovich.

55. Neisser, U., Boodoo, G., Bouchard, T. J., Jr., Bykin, A.W., Brody, N., Ceci, S.J., et al. (1996). Intelligence: Knowns and unknowns. *American Psychologist, 51,* 77–101.

56. Sternberg, R. (2004). Successful intelligence. *Journal of Business Venturing, 19,* 189–202.

57. Sternberg, R. J., Wagner, R. K., Williams, W. M., & Horvath, J. A. (1995). Testing common sense. *American Psychologist, 50,* 912–927.

58. Goleman, D. (1995). *Emotional intelligence.* New York: Bantam Books.

59. See Note 58.

60. Davies, M., Stankow, L., & Roberts, R. D. 1998. Emotional intelligence: In search of an elusive construct. *Journal of Personality and Social Psychology 75,* 989–1015.

61. See note 60.

62. Baron, R. A., & Markman, G. D. (2003). Beyond social capital: The role of entrepreneurs' social competence in their financial success. *Journal of Business Venturing, 18,* 41–60.

63. Baron, R. A., & Markman, G. D. (2000). Beyond social capital: *Academy of Management Executive, 14,* 106–11.

64. Côté, S., & Miners, C. T. H. (2006). Emotional intelligence, cognitive intelligence, and job performance. *Administrative Science Quarterly, 51,* 1–28.

65. Schneider, R. J. (2002). Exploring the structure and construct validity of a self-report social competence inventory. In L. M. Hough (Chair), *Compound traits: The next frontier of I/O personality research.* Symposium presented at the 17th Annual Conference of the Society for Industrial and Organizational Psychology. Toronto, Ontario, Canada.

66. Riggio, R. E., & Throckmorton, B. (1988). The relative effects of verbal and nonverbal behavior, appearance, and social skills on valuations made in hiring interviews. *Journal of Applied Social Psychology, 18,* 331–348. Robbins, T. L., & DeNisi, A. S. (1994). A closer look at interpersonal affect as a distinct influence on cognitive processing in performance evaluations. *Journal of Applied Psychology, 79,* 341–353.

67. Wayne, S. J., Liden, R. C., Graf, I. K., & Ferris, G. R. (1997). The role of upward influence tactics in human resource decisions. *Personnel Psychology, 50,* 979–1006.

68. Witt, L. A., & Ferris, G. R. (2003). Social skill as moderator of the conscientiousness-performance relationship: Convergent results across four studies. *Journal of Applied Psychology, 88,* 809–820.

Case in Point Sources

Bushnell, D. (2006, June 15). Malden Mills increasing military sales. *Boston Globe,* p. C2. Greenbiz.com. (2006, May 26). News: Consumer demand for healthy fabrics boost green textile certification. From: www.greenbiz.com/news. Pacelle, M. (2003, May 10). Through the mill: Can Mr. Feuerstein save his business one last time? *Wall Street Journal,* pp. A1, A10.

Chapter 5

Preview Case Sources

Dealing with stress on the job and elsewhere. (2006). *Schizophrenia.Com Newsletter.* From the Web at: http://www.schizophrenia.com.newsletter/697/697stress.htm. Kaiser Permanente. (2006). Life outside of work. From: http://www.kaiserpermanentejobs.org/workinghere/lifeoutside.asp. Jacobs, L. (2003, Winter). Discovering a remedy for physician work stress. *The Permanente Journal.* From: http://xnet.kp.org/permanentejournal/winter03/group.html.

Chapter Notes

1. American Institute of Stress. (2006). *Job stress.* From the Web at: http://www.stress.org/job.htm.

2. Kanfer, R., & Klimoski, R. J. (2002). Affect and work: Looking back into the future. In R. G. Lord, R. J. Klimoski, & R. Kanfer (Eds.), *Emotions in the workplace: Understanding the structure and role of emotions in organizational behavior.* San Francisco: Jossey Bass.

3. Hatfield, E., Cacioppo, J. T., & Rhapson, R. L. (1994). *Emotional contagion.* New York: Cambridge University Press.

4. Cherulnik, P. K., Donley, K. A., Wiewel, T. S. R., & Miller, S. R. (2001). Charisma is contagious: The effects of leaders' charisma on observers' affect. *Journal of Applied Social Psychology, 31,* 2149–2159.

5. Ekman, P., Friesen, W. V., & Ancoli, S. (2001). Facial signs of emotional experience. In W. G. Parrott (Ed.), *Emotions in social psychology* (pp. 255–264). Philadelphia, PA: Psychology Press.

6. Nakamura, N. (2000). Facial expression and communication of emotion: An analysis of display rules and a model of facial expression of emotion. *Japanese Psychological Review, 43,* 307–319.

7. Weiss, H. M., & Cropanzano, R. (1996). Affective events theory: A theoretical discussion of the structure, causes, and consequences of affective experiences at work. In B. M. Staw & L. L. Cummings (Eds.), *Research in organizational behavior* (Vol. 18, pp. 1–74). Greenwich, CT: JAI Press.

8. Tangney, J. P., & Fischer, K. W. (Eds.). (1995). *Self-conscious emotions: The psychology of shame, guilt, embarrassment, and pride.* New York: Guilford Press. Tracy, J. L., & Robins, R. W. (2004). Putting the self into self-conscious emotions: A theoretical model. *Psychological Inquiry, 15,* 103–125.

9. Keltner, D., & Anderson, C. (2000). Saving face for Darwin: The functions and uses of embarrassment. *Current Directions in Psychological Science, 9,* 187–192.

10. Beer, J. S., Heery, E. A., Keltner, D., Scabini, D., & Knight, R. T. (2003). The regulatory function of self-conscious emotion: Insights from patients with orbitofrontal damage. *Journal of Personality and Social Psychology, 85,* 594–604.

11. Vecchio, R. P. (2005). Explorations of employee envy: Feeling envious and feeling envied. *Cognition and Emotion, 19,* 69–81. Poulson, C. F. II. (2000). Shame and work. In N. M. Ashkanasy, W. Zerbe, & C. E. J. Härtel (Eds.), *Emotions in the workplace: Research, theory, and practice* (pp. 490–541). Westport, CT: Quorum Books.

12. Huelsman, T. J., Furr, R. M., & Memanick, R. C., Jr. (2003). Measurement of dispositional affect: Construct validity and convergence with a circumplex model of affect. *Educational and Psychological Measurement, 63,* 655–673. Larsen, J., Diener, E., & Lucas, R. E. (2002). Emotion: Moods, measures, and differences. In R. G. Lord, R. J. Klimiski, & R. Kanfer (Eds.), *Emotions in the workplace* (pp. 64–113). San Francisco, CA: Jossey-Bass.

13. George, J. M., & Brief, A. P. (1996). Motivational agendas in the workplace: The effects of feelings on focus of attention and work motivation. In B. M. Staw & L. L. Cummings (Eds.), *Research in organizational behavior* (Vol. 18, pp. 75–109). Greenwich, CT: JAI Press.

14. Freiberg, K., Freiberg, J., & Peters, T. (1998). *Nuts!: Southwest airlines' crazy recipe for business and personal success.* New York: Bantam Doubleday. Cohen, B., Greenfield, J., & Mann, M. (1998). *Ben & Jerry's double dip: How to run a values-led business and make money, too.* New York: Fireside.

15. Lyubomirsky, S., King, L., & Diener, E. (2005). The benefits of frequent positive affect: Does happiness lead to success? *Psychological Bulletin, 131,* 803–855.

16. Staw, B. M., Sutton, R. I., & Pelled, L. H. (1994). Employee positive emotion and favorable outcomes in the workplace. *Organization Science, 5,* 51–71.

17. Cropanzano, R., & Wright, T. A. (1999). A five-year study of change in the relationship between well-being and job performance. *Consulting Psychology Journal, 51,* 252–265. Wright, T. A., & Staw, B. M. (1999). Affect and favorable work outcomes: Two longitudinal tests of the happy-productive worker thesis. *Journal of Organizational Behavior, 20,* 1–23.

18. DeLuga, R. J., & Manson, S. (2000). Relationship of resident assistant conscientiousness, extraversion, and positive affect with rated performance. *Journal of Research in Personality, 34,* 225–235. Totterdell, P. (2000). Catching moods and hitting runs: Mood linkage and subjective performance in professional sports teams. *Journal of Applied Psychology, 83,* 848–859.

19. See Note 18.

20. Foster, J. B., Hebl, M. R., West, M., & Dawson, J. (2004, April). *Setting the tone for organizational success: The impact of CEO affect on organizational climate and firm-level outcomes.* Paper presented at the annual meeting of the Society for Industrial and Organizational Psychology, Toronto, Ontario, Canada. Pritzker, M. A. (2002). The relationship among CEO dispositional attributes, transformational leadership behavior and performance effectiveness. *Dissertation Abstracts International, 62*(12-B), 6008. (UMI No. AA13035464.)

21. Lucas, R. E., Clark, A. E., Georgellis, Y., & Deiner, E. (2004). Unemployment alters the set points for live satisfaction. *Psychological Science, 15,* 8–13. Graham, C., Eggers, A., & Sukhtanar, S. (in press). Does happiness pay: An exploration based on panel data from Russia. *Journal of Economic Behaviour and Organization.*

22. Howell, C. J., Howell, R. T., & Schwabe, K. A. (in press). Does wealth enhance life satisfaction for people who are materially deprived? Exploring the association among the Orang Asli of Peninsular Malaysia. *Social Indicators Research.*

23. Clore, G. L., Schwartz, N., & Conway, M. (1994). Affective causes and consequences of social information processing. In R. S. Wyer, Jr., & T. K. Srull (Eds.), *Handbook of social cognition* (Vol. 1, pp. 323–417). Hillsdale, NJ: Lawrence Erlbaum.

24. Vohs, K. D., Baumeister, R. F., & Loewenstein, G. (in press). *Do emotions help or hurt decision making?* New York: Russell Sage Foundation Press.

25. Weiss, H. M., Nicholas, J. P., & Daus, C. S. (1999). An examination of the joint effects of affective experiences and job beliefs on job satisfaction and variations in affective experiences over time. *Organizational Behavior and Human Decision Processes, 78,* 1–24.

26. Ashkanasy, N. M. (2004). Emotion and performance. *Human Performance, 17,* 137–144.

27. Weiss, H. M., & Cropanzano, R. (1996). An affective events approach to job satisfaction. In B. M. Staw & L. L. Cummings (Eds.), *Research in organizational behavior* (Vol. 18, pp. 1–74). Greenwich, CT: JAI Press.

28. Ashkanasy, N. M., & Daus, C. S. (2002). Emotion in the workplace: New challenges for managers. *Academy of Management Executive, 16,* 76–86.

29. See Note 12.

30. Miner, A. G., & Hulin, C. L. (2000). *Affective experience at work: A test of affective events theory.* Poster presented at the 15th annual conference of the Society for Industrial and

Organizational Psychology; New Orleans, LA. Fisher, C. (1998, August). *Mood and emotions while working: Missing pieces of job satisfaction?* Paper presented at Academy of Management Conference, San Diego, CA.

31. Ashkanasy, N. M., Hartel, C. E. J., & Daus, C. S., (2002). Diversity and emotion: The new frontiers in organizational behavior research. *Journal of Management, 28,* 307–338.

32. Goleman, D. (1998). *Working with emotional intelligence.* New York: Bantam.

33. Morris, J. A., & Feldman, D. C. (1997). Managing emotions in the workplace. *Journal of Managerial Issues, 9,* 257–274.

34. American Psychological Association. (2006). Topic: Anger. Controlling anger. From the Web at: http://www.apa.org./topics/angersub1.html.

35. Boscarino, J. A., Figley, C. R., & Adams, R. E. (2003). Fear of terrorism in New York after the September 11 terrorist attacks: Implications for emergency mental health and preparedness. *International Journal of Emergency Mental Health, 5,* 199–209.

36. Wikipedia. (2006). Mary Kay. From the Web at: http://en.wikipedia.org/wiki/Mary_Kay_Cosmetics. Tribute to Mary Kay Ash. (2006). From: http://entrepreneurs.about .com/gi/dynamic/offsite.htm?zi=1/XJ&sdn=entrepreneurs &zu=http%3A%2F%2Fwww.marykaytribute.com.

37. Dutton, J. E., Frost, P. J., Workline, M. C., Lilius, J. M., & Kanov, J. M. (2002, January). Leading in times of trauma. *Harvard Business Review,* pp. 54–61.

38. Northwestern National Life Insurance Company. (1999). *Employee burnout: America's newest epidemic.* Minneapolis, MN: Author.

39. Quick, J. C., Murphy, L. R., & Hurrell, J. J., Jr. (1992). *Stress and well-being at work.* Washington, DC: American Psychological Association.

40. Selye, H. (1976). *Stress in health and disease.* Boston: Butterworths.

41. National Institute for Occupational Safety and Health. (2005). *Stress at work* (NIOSH publication no. 99–101). Cincinnati, OH: Author.

42. Kane, K. (1997, October–November). Can you perform under pressure? *Fast Company,* pp. 54, 56. Enhanced Performance Web site: www.enhanced-performance.com.

43. Stress at work (1997, April 15). *Wall Street Journal,* p. A12.

44. Heller, R., & Hindle, T. (1998). *Essential manager's manual.* New York: DK Publishing.

45. Saddiq, S. (2006, January*). Occupational stress.* Paper presented at the meeting of the British Psychological Society, Glasgow, Scotland. Reported by Hamilton, A. (2006, January 12). Stress: Shhhh . . . *Times Online.* From: http://www.timesonline.co.uk/article/0,,2-1980961,00.html. BBC News (2006, January 12). Librarians "suffer most stress." *BBC News.* From: http://news.bbc.co.uk/1/hi/uk/4605476.stm.

46. Fenn, D. (1999, November). Domestic policy. *Inc.,* pp. 38–42, 44–45. Hammonds, K. H., & Palmer, A. T. (1998, September 21). The daddy trap. *Business Week,* pp. 56–58, 60, 62, 64.

47. McGrath, J. E. (1976). Stress and behavior in organizations. In M. D. Dunnette (Ed.), *Handbook of industrial and organizational psychology* (pp. 1351–1398). Chicago: Rand McNally.

48. Fisher, A. B. (1993, August 23). Sexual harassment: What to do. *Fortune,* pp. 84–86, 88.

49. Kolbert, E. (1991, October 10). Sexual harassment at work is pervasive. *New York Times,* pp. A1, A17.

50. Office of Research, Information, and Planning. (2006). Sexual harassment charges: EEOC and FEPAs combined: FY 1992–FY 2005. From: http://www.eeoc.gov/stats/harass.html.

51. Niessen, B. (2000, November 15). Last straw survey—overworked, overwrought: "Desk rage" at work. CNN.com. From: http://archives.cnn.com/2000/CAREER/trends/11/15/rage/.

52. Sullivan, S. E., & Bhagat, R. S. (1992). Organizational stress, job satisfaction, and job performance: Where do we go from here? *Journal of Management, 18,* 353–374.

53. Job stress. (2006). From: http://www.stress.org/job.htm. Human nature at work. (2006). Stats and quotes. From: http://www.humannatureatwork.com/serious.htm. Gallup Organization. (2001). *Attitudes in the American workplace VI.* Omaha, NE: Author. Nieman, C. (1999, July–August). How much is enough? *Fast Company,* pp. 108–116. Wah, L. (2000, January). The emotional tightrope. *Management Review,* pp. 38–43.

54. Motowidlo, S. J., Packard, J. S., & Manning, M. R. (1986). Occupational stress: Its causes and consequences for job performance. *Journal of Applied Psychology, 71,* 618–629.

55. See Note 41.

56. Chandola, T., Brunner, E., & Marmot, M. (2005). Chronic stress at work and the metabolic syndrome: Prospective study. *British Medical Journal.* Online first: bmj.com. From: http://stress.about.com/gi/dynamic/offsite.htm?zi=1/XJ&sdn =stress&zu=http%3A%2F%2Fpress.psprings.co.uk%2Fbmj %2Fjanuary%2Fworkstress.pdf.

57. Frese, M. (1985). Stress at work and psychosomatic complaints: A causal interpretation. *Journal of Applied Psychology, 70,* 314–328. Quick, J. C., & Quick, J. D. (1984). *Organizational stress and preventive management.* New York: McGraw-Hill.

58. Tosevski, D. L., & Milovancevic, M. P. (2006). Stressful life events and physical health. *Current Opinion in Psychiatry, 19,* 184–189. Cooper, C. L. (1996). *Handbook of stress, medicine, and health.* London: CRC Press.

59. Ostry, A., Stefania, M., Tansey, J., Dunn, J., Hershler, R., Chen, L., Louie, A., & Hertzman, C. (2006). Impact of fathers' physical and psychosocial work conditions on attempted and completed suicide among their children. *Public Health, 6,* 77–85. Also available from: http://www.biomedicalcentral.com/1471-2458/6/77.

60. Carey, E. (2006, March 27). Child suicides linked to paternal job stress: 15-year study of 30,000 B.C. sawmill workers. *Toronto Star,* p. 7.

61. Daw, J. (2001, August). Road rage, air rage, and now desk rage. *Monitor on Psychology, 32*(7). 9–10.

62. The list: Desk rage. *Business Week* (2000, November 27), p. 12.

63. Lorenz, I. (2004, December 20). 7 tips for combating desk rage. CNN.com/CareerBuilder.com. From: http://www.cnn.com/2004/US/Careers/08/13/boss.spying/index.html.

64. Bakker, A. B., Schaufeli, W. B., Sixma, H. J., Bosveld, W., & Van Dierendonck, D. (2000). Patient demands, lack of reciprocity, and burnout: A five-year longitudinal study among general practitioners. *Journal of Organizational Behavior, 21,* 425–441.

65. Latack, J. C., & Havlovic, S. J. (1992). Coping with job stress: A conceptual evaluation framework for coping measures. *Journal of Organizational Behavior, 13,* 479–508.

66. Society for Human Resource Management. (2006). *Annual benefits survey.* Alexandria, VA: SHRM.

67. Employee Assistance Professionals Association. (2006). Recent EAP cost/benefit statistics research: 2000–present. From: http://www.eapassn.org/ public/articles/EAPcostbenefitstats.pdf.

68. Flora, C. (2004, January/February). Keeping workers and companies fit. *Psychology Today,* pp. 36–40. Also available from: http://www.psychologytoday.com/articles/pto-3285.html.

69. Trocki, K. F., & Orioli, E. M. (1994). Gender differences in stress symptoms, stress-producing contexts, and coping strategies. In G. P. Keita & J. J. Hurrell, Jr. (Eds.), *Job stress in a changing workforce* (pp. 7–22). Washington, DC: American Psychological Association.

70. Iwanski, Y., MacKay, K., & Mactavysh, J. (2005, First Quarter). Gender-based analyses of coping with stress among professional managers: Leisure coping and non-leisure-coping. *Journal of Leisure Research.* From : http://www.findarticles.com/p/articles/ mi_qa3702/is_200501/ai_n9520740.

71. See Note 68.

72. Stephens, C., & Long, N. (2000). Communication with police supervisors and peers as a buffer of work-related traumatic stress. *Journal of Organizational Behavior, 21,* 407–424.

73. Beehr, T. A., Jex, S. M., Stacy, B. A., & Murray, M. A. (2000). Work stressors and coworker support as predictors of individual strain and job performance. *Journal of Organizational Behavior, 21,* 391–405.

74. See Note 64.

75. Singer, T. (2000, October 17). The balance of power. *Inc. 500,* pp. 105–108, 110.

76. Benson, H. (1993). The relaxation response. In D. Goleman & J. Gurin (Eds.), *Mind/body medicine* (pp. 233–257). New York: Consumer Reports Books. Domar, A. D., & Dreher, H. (1996). *Healing mind, healthy woman.* New York: Henry Holt.

Case in Point Sources

Sharpe, E. K. (2005). "Going above and beyond": The emotional labor of adventure guides. *Journal of Leisure Research, 37.* From: http://www.findarticles.com/p/articles/mi_qa3702/is_200501/ai_n9520743/pg_8. Wanderlust Tours. (2006). About Wanderlust Tours. From: http://www.wanderlusttours.com/aboutus/index.html.

Chapter 6

Preview Case Sources

Ford Motor Company. (2006). Diversity of our people: Ongoing efforts. From: http://www.ford.com. Garsten, E. (2002, January 13). Awareness of Islam aim of diversity effort at Ford. *Chicago Tribune,* p. S8. Work & Family Newsbrief. (2001, December). Ford workers learn about Islam. From: http://www.findarticles.com/p/articles/mi_m0IJN/is_2001_Dec/ai_80745803.

Chapter Notes

1. McGuire, W. J. (1985). Attitudes and attitude change. In G. Lindzey & E. Aronson (Eds.), *Handbook of social psychology* (3rd ed.). (Vol. 2, pp. 233–346). New York: Random House.

2. U.S. Bureau of Labor Statistics (2000). *Labor participation rates.* Washington, DC: Author.

3. Gill, D. (1999, December 6). Diversity 101. *Business Week,* p. F12.

4. Conlin, M., & Zellner, W. (1999, November 22). The CEO still wears wingtips. *Business Week,* pp. 85–86, 88, 90.

5. Tsui, A. S., Egan, T. D., & O'Reilly, C. A., III. (1992). Being different: Relational demography and organizational attachment. *Administrative Science Quarterly, 37,* 549–579.

6. Nicholson, N. (1995). Organizational demography. In N. Nicholson (Ed.), *Blackwell encyclopedic dictionary of organizational behavior* (pp. 833–834). Malden, MA: Blackwell. Pfeffer, J. (1985). Organizational demography: Implications for management. *California Management Review, 38,* 67–81.

7. Wagner, W. G., Pfeffer, J., & O'Reilly, C. A. (1984). Work group demography and turnover in top management groups. *Administrative Science Quarterly, 29,* 74–92. Godthelp, M., Glunk, U. (2003). Turnover at the top: Demographic diversity as a determinant of executive turnover in the Netherlands. *European Management Journal, 21,* 614–626.

8. Watson, W., Stewart, W. H., Jr., & BarNir, A. (2003). The effects of human capital, organizational demography, and interpersonal processes on venture partner perceptions of firm profit and growth. *Journal of Business Venturing, 18,* 145–164.

9. Webber, S. S., & Donahue, L. M. (2001). Impact of highly and less job-related diversity on work group cohesion and performance: A meta-analysis. *Journal of Management, 27,* 141–162.

10. Gregory, R. F. (2001). *Age discrimination in the American workplace: Old at a young age.* New Brunswick, NJ: Rutgers University Press.

11. Raines, C. (1997). *Beyond generation X. A practical guide for managers.* Menlo Park, CA: Crisp.

12. U.S. Census Bureau. (2005, July 19). 15th anniversary of Americans with Disabilities Act: July 26, 2005. *Facts for Features.* CB05-FF.10-2. From: http://images.google.com/imgres?imgurl=http://www.census.gov/pubinfo/www/broadcast/photos/img/100_0118_sm.jpg&imgrefurl=http://www.census.gov/Press-Release/www/releases/archives/facts_for_features_special_editions/004998.html&h=271&w=185&sz=79&hl=en&start=65&tbnid=KhHd426qTarX8M:

&tbnh=108&tbnw=73&prev=/images%3Fq%3Dworking%2
Bwith%2Bdisabilities%2B%26start%3D60%26ndsp%3D20
%26svnum%3D10%26hl%3Den%26lr%3D%26sa%3DN.

13. Magill, B. G. (1999). *Workplace accommodations under the ADA*. Washington, DC: Thompson Publishing Group.

14. Morris, K. (1998, November 23). You've come a short way, baby. *Business Week,* pp. 82–83, 86, 88.

15. Steinberg, R., & Shapiro, S. (1982), Sex differences in personality traits of female and male master of business administration students. *Journal of Applied Psychology, 67,* 306–310.

16. CATALYST (2006). *The glass ceiling.* New York: Author (from the World Wide Web: www.catalystwomen.org/press/ factslabor00.html. Bureau of Labor Statistics, 2006; Catalyst, Census of Women Corporate Officers and Top Earners; 2006 Census of Women Board Directors of the *Fortune* 1000.

17. Ragins, B. R. (2004). Sexual orientation in the workplace: The unique work and career experiences of gay, lesbian and bisexual workers. In J. Martoccio (Ed.), *Research in personnel and human resources management* (Vol. 23, pp. 35–120). San Diego, CA: Elsevier.

18. Hereck, G. M. (1998). *Stigma and sexual orientation: Understanding prejudice against lesbians, gay men, and bisexuals.* Newbury Park, CA: Sage. Also see Ragins, 2004; Note 17.

19. Martinez, M. N. (1993, June). Recognizing sexual orientation is fair and not costly. *HRMagazine,* pp. 66–68, 70–72 (quote, p. 68).

20. Fernandez, J. P., & Barr, M. (1993). *The diversity advantage.* New York: Lexington Books.

21. U.S. Equal Employment Opportunity Commission. (2006). National-Origin Based Charges, VY 1992–2005. From: http://www.eeoc.gov/stats/origin.html.

22. Yang, C. (1993, June 21). In any language, it's unfair: More immigrants are bringing bias charges against employers. *Business Week,* pp. 110–112 (quote, p. 111).

23. Tannenbaum Center for Religious Understanding. (2001). *Survey on religious bias in the workplace.* New York: Author.

24. Pew Research Center for the People and the Press. (2001). *Americans improve their view of Muslims.* Washington, DC: Author. Online, at: http://www.people-press.org/.

25. Carnevale, A. P., & Stone, S. C. (1995). *The American mosaic.* New York: McGraw-Hill.

26. Towers Perrin. (1992). *Workforce 2000 today.* New York: Author.

27. See Note 26 (quote, p. 1.).

28. See Note 26.

29. See Note 26.

30. Kravitz, D. A., & Klineberg, S. L. (2000). Reactions to two versions of affirmative action among whites, blacks, and Hispanics. *Journal of Applied Psychology, 85,* 597–611.

31. Hagenbaugh, B. (2004, August 27). Women's pay suffers setback. *USA Today,* Money section. From: http://www .usatoday.com/money/workplace/2004-08-26-women_x .htm. Polus, S. (1996). Ten myths about affirmative action.

Journal of Social Issues, 52, 25–31. Howard, L. (206). Wage disparity: Still a concern. From the Web at: http://www.mtsu .edu/~berc/tnbiz/women/pdfs/wages.pdf.

32. Thomas, R. R., Jr. (1992). Managing diversity: A conceptual framework. In S. E. Jackson (Ed.), *Diversity in the workplace* (pp. 305–317). New York: Guilford Press.

33. Kahn, J. (2001, July 9). Diversity trumps the downturn. *Fortune,* pp. 66–72 (quote, p. 70).

34. Murray, K. (1993, August 1). The unfortunate side effects of "diversity training." *New York Times,* pp. E1, E3.

35. Gottfredson, L. S. (1992). Dilemmas in developing diversity programs. In S. E. Jackson (Ed.), *Diversity in the workplace* (pp. 279–305). New York: Guilford Press.

36. Carnevale, A. P., & Stone, S. C. (1995). *The American mosaic.* New York: McGraw-Hill.

37. What's it like to work at Allstate? Diversity. (2003). From: http://www.allstate.com/Careers/PageRender.asp?Page= diversity.htm.

38. Gardenswartz, L., & Rowe, A. (1994). *The managing diversity survival guide.* Burr Ridge, IL: Irwin.

39. Battaglia, B. (1992). Skills for managing multicultural teams. *Cultural Diversity at Work, 4,* 4–12.

40. Wright, P., Ferris, S. P., Hiller, J. S., & Kroll, M. (1995). Competitiveness through management of diversity: Effects of stock price valuation. *Academy of Management Journal, 38,* 272–287.

41. Gingold, D. (2000, July 26). Diversity today. *Fortune,* special section, pp. S1–S23.

42. Finnigan, A. (2001, April). Different strokes. *Working Woman,* pp. 42–64.

43. See Note 42.

44. See Note 42.

45. Gardenswartz, L. & Rowe, A. (1994). *The managing diversity survival guide.* Burr Ridge, IL: Irwin.

46. Rynes, S., & Rosen, B. (1995). A field survey of factors affecting the adoption and perceived success of diversity training. *Personnel Psychology, 48,* 247–270.

47. American Psychological Association Division 42 Online. *Letters for media interviews: Job satisfaction.* From: http:// www.division42.org/PublicArea/Media/PrReleases/ job_satisfaction.html. Anderson, P. (2000, October 24). Job satisfaction: Oxymoron. CNN.com career trends. From: http://www.cnn.com/2000/CAREER/trends/10/23/ job.dissatisfaction/#chart.

48. Herzberg, F. (1966). *Work and the nature of man.* Cleveland, OH: World.

49. Judge, T. A. (1992). Dispositional perspective in human resources research. In G. R. Ferris & K. M. Rowland (Eds.), *Research in personality and human resources management* (Vol. 10, pp. 31–72). Greenwich, CT: JAI Press.

50. Judge, T. A., & Ilies, R. (2004). Affect and job satisfaction: A study of their relationships at home and at work. *Journal of Applied Psychology, 89,* 661–673.

51. Arvey, R. D., Bouchard, T. J., Jr., Segal, N. L., & Abraham, L. M. (1989). Job satisfaction: Genetic and environmental components. *Journal of Applied Psychology, 74,* 187–192.

52. Cropanzano, R., & James, K. (1990). Some methodological considerations for the behavioral-genetic analysis of work attitudes. *Journal of Applied Psychology, 71,* 433–439.

53. Watson, D. (2000). *Mood and temperament.* New York: Guilford Press.

54. Illies, R., & Judge, T. A. (2003). On the heritability of job satisfaction: The mediating role of personality. *Journal of Applied Psychology, 88,* 750–759.

55. Salancik, G. R., & Pfeffer, J. R. (1978). A social information processing approach to job attitudes. *Administrative Science Quarterly, 23,* 224–252. Zalesny, M. D., & Ford, J. K. (1990). Extending the social information processing perspective: New links to attitudes, behaviors, and perceptions. *Organizational Behavior and Human Decision Processes, 47,* 205–246.

56. Agho, A. O., Price, J. L., & Mueller, C. W. (1992). Discriminant validity of measures of job satisfaction, positive affectivity and negative affectivity. *Journal of Occupational and Organizational Psychology, 65,* 185–196.

57. Smith, P. C., Kendall, L. M., & Hulin, C. L. (1969). *The measurement of satisfaction in work and retirement.* Chicago: Rand McNally.

58. Stanton, J. M., Sinar, E. F., Balzer, W. K., Julian, A. L., Thorensen, P., Aziz, S., et al. (2002). Development of a compact measure of job satisfaction: The abridged Job Descriptive Index. *Educational and Psychological Measurement, 62,* 173–91.

59. Weiss, D. J., Dawis, R. V., England, G. W., & Loftquist, L. H. (1967). *Manual for the Minnesota Satisfaction Questionnaire* (Minnesota Studies on Vocational Rehabilitation, Vol. 22). Minneapolis, MN: Industrial Relations Center, Work Adjustment Project, University of Minnesota.

60. Heneman, H. G., III., & Schwab, D. P. (1985). Pay satisfaction: Its multidimensional nature and measurement. *International Journal of Psychology, 20,* 129–141.

61. Judge, T. A., & Welbourne, T. M. (1994). A confirmatory investigation of the dimensionality of the Pay Satisfaction Questionnaire. *Journal of Applied Psychology, 79,* 461–466.

62. Sutton, R. I., & Callahan, A. L. (1987). The stigma of bankruptcy: Spoiled organizational image and its management. *Academy of Management Journal, 30,* 405–436.

63. Hardy, G. E., Woods, D., & Wall, T. D. (2003). The impact of psychological distress on absence from work. *Journal of Applied Psychology, 88,* 306–314.

64. Boswell, W. R., Boudreau, J. W., & Tichy, J. (2005). The relationship between employee job change and job satisfaction: The honeymoon-hangover effect. *Journal of Applied Psychology, 90,* 882–892.

65. Mitchell, T. R., & Lee. T. W. (2001). The unfolding model of voluntary turnover and job embeddedness: Foundations for a comprehensive theory of attachment. In B. M. Staw & R. I. Sutton (Eds.), *Research in organizational behavior* (Vol. 23, pp. 189–246). San Diego, CA: Elsevier.

66. Lee, T. W., Mitchell, T. R., Holtom, B. C., McDaniel, L., & Hill, J. W. (1999). Theoretical development and extension of the unfolding model of voluntary turnover. *Academy of Management Journal, 42,* 450–462.

67. Judge, T. A., Heller, D., & Mount, M. K. (2002). Five-factor model of personality and job satisfaction. *Journal of Applied Psychology, 87,* 530–541.

68. Judge, T. A., Bono, J. E., & Patton, G. K. (2001). The job satisfaction–performance relationship: A qualitative and quantitative review. *Psychological Bulletin, 127,* 376–407.

69. Schneider, B., Hanges, P. J., Smith, D. B., & Salvaggio, A. N. (2004). Which comes first: Employee attitudes or organizational financial and market performance? *Journal of Applied Psychology, 88,* 836–851.

70. Goddard, J. (2001). High performance and the transformation of work: The implications of alternative work practices for the experience and outcomes of work. *Industrial and Labor Relations Review, 54,* 776–806.

71. Barling, J., Kelloway, E. K., & Iverson, R. D. (2003). High-quality work, job satisfaction, and occupational injuries. *Journal of Applied Psychology, 88,* 276–283.

72. Weiss, H. M. (2002). Deconstructing job satisfaction: Separating evaluations, beliefs, and affective experiences. *Human Resource Management Review, 12,* 173–194.

73. Judge, T. A., & Illies, R. (2004). Affect and job satisfaction: A study of their relationship at work and at home. *Journal of Applied Psychology, 89,* 661–673.

74. Reingold, J. (1999, March 1). Why your workers might jump ship. *Business Week,* p. 8. Anonymous. (1999, July–August). To attract talent, you've gotta give 'em all. *Management Review,* p. 10. Anonymous. (1999, July–August). Employee loyalty surprisingly strong. *Management Review,* p. 9. The list: Hot seat in the corner office. (2000, February 14). *Business Week,* p. 8.

75. Snape, E., & Redman, T. (2003). An evaluation of a three-component model of occupational commitment: Dimensionality and consequences among United Kingdom human resource management specialists. *Journal of Applied Psychology, 88,* 152–159. Meyer, J. P., Allen, N. J., & Smith, C. A. (1993). Commitment to organizations and occupations: Extension and test of a three-component conceptualization. *Journal of Applied Psychology, 78,* 538–551.

76. O'Reilly, B. (1994, June 13). The new deal: What companies and employees owe each other. *Fortune,* pp. 46–47, 50, 52 (quote, p. 45).

77. Lee, K., Carswell, J. J., & Allen, N. J. (2000). A meta-analytic review of occupational commitment: Relations with person- and work-related variables. *Journal of Applied Psychology, 85,* 799–811.

78. Clugston, M. (2000). The mediating effects of multidimensional commitment on job satisfaction and intent to leave. *Journal of Organizational Behavior, 21,* 477–486.

79. Lee, T. W., Ashford, S. J., Walsh, J. P., & Mowday, R. T. (1992). Commitment propensity, organizational commitment, and voluntary turnover: A longitudinal study of organizational entry processes. *Journal of Management, 18,* 15–32.

80. Johns, G., & Xie, J. L. (1998). Perceptions of absence from work: People's Republic of China versus Canada. *Journal of Applied Psychology, 83,* 515–530.

81. Bond, M. H. (1986). *The psychology of the Chinese people.* New York: Oxford University Press.

82. Hui, C., Lam, S. S. K., & Law, K. K. S. (2000). Instrumental values of organizational citizenship behavior for promotion: A field quasi-experiment. *Journal of Applied Psychology, 85,* 822–828.

83. Rosen, R. H. (1991). *The healthy company.* Los Angeles: Jeremy P. Tarcher (quote, pp. 71–72).

84. Center for Economic and Social Justice. (2004). On (and off) the road to justice-based management: Allied Plywood Corporation. From: http://www.cesj.org/jbm/casestudies-vbm/alliedplywood.html.

Case in Point Sources

Chevron Products Company. (2006). Diversity. From: http://www.chevron.com/social_responsibility/diversity/ Labich, K. (1999, September 6). No more crude at Texaco. *Fortune,* pp. 205–206, 208, 210, 212. Roberts, B., & White, J. E. (1999). *Roberts vs. Texaco: A true story of race and corporate America.* New York: Avon. Statistics appear on the Texaco Web site: www.texaco.com.

Chapter 7

Preview Case Sources

"Defining Google" (2005, January 2). CBSNews.Com, *60 Minutes.* From: www.cbsnews.com/stories/2004/12/30/60minutes/main6640 63.shtml. Kennedy, S. D. (2004, April). A love/hate relationship. *Information Today, 27*(4), pp. 15–16. Rubenking, N. J. (2004, December 28). MSN Search prepares to battle Google. *PC Magazine, 23*(23), p. 41. Stone, B., & Levy, S. (2004, December 27). Google's two revolutions. *Newsweek, 145*(1), p. 70. From: www.google.com.corporate.

Chapter Notes

1. Latham, G. P., & Pinder, C. C. (2005). Work motivation theory and research at the dawn of the twenty-first century. In S. Fiske (Ed.), *Annual review of psychology* (Vol. 56, pp. 485–516). Palo Alto, CA: Annual Reviews.

2. Mitchell, T. R., & Daniels, D. (2003). Motivation. In W. C. Borman, D. R. Ilgen, & R. J. Klimoski (Eds.), *Handbook of psychology, Vol. 12: Industrial and organizational psychology* (pp. 215–254). New York: Wiley.

3. The Gallup Poll. (2006). From: jttp://poll.gallup.com/.

4. Robson, C. (2004). What motivates workers today? London: Hays Office Support. From: http://www.hays.com/uk/index .jsp?Channel=office&Content=/uk/jobseekers/office/ what-motivates-office-workers-today.htm.

5. Benson, S. G., & Dundis, S. P. (2003). Understanding and motivating health care employees: Integrating Maslow's hierarchy of needs, training, and technology. *Journal of Nursing Management, 11*(5), 315–320. Pfeffer, J. (1998). *The human equation.* Boston: Harvard Business School Press.

6. Maslow, A. H. (1987). *Motivation and personality* (3rd ed.). Boston, MA: Addison-Wesley.

7. Where's my Stairmaster (1999, October). *Across the Board,* p. 5.

8. Yen, L., & Edington, M. P. (2001). Changes in health risks among the participants in the United Auto Workers–General Motors LifeSteps Health Promotion Program. *American Journal of Health Promotion, 16*(1), 7–15.

9. Barnes, E. S. (2003, July). No-layoff policy. *Workforce,* pp. 96–99.

10. Klubnik, J. P. (1995). *Rewarding and recognizing employees.* Chicago: Richard D. Irwin. Leverence, J. (1997). *And the winner is. . . .* Santa Monica, CA: Merritt.

11. Shepherd, M. D. (1993, February). Staff motivation. *U.S. Pharmacist,* pp. 82, 85, 89–93. (quote, p. 91).

12. Wahba, M. A., & Bridwell, L. G. (1976). Maslow reconsidered: A review of research on the need hierarchy theory. *Organizational Behavior and Human Performance, 15,* 212–240.

13. Kanfer, R., & Heggestad, E. D. (1997). Motivational traits and skills: A person-centered approach to work motivation. In L. L. Cummings & B. M. Ataw (Eds.), *Research in organizational behavior* (Vol. 19, pp. 1–56). Greenwich, CT: JAI Press.

14. Kanfer. R, Wanberg, C. R., & Kantrowitz, T. M. (2001). Job search and emolyment: A personality-motivational analysis and meta-analytic review. *Journal of Applied Psychology, 86,* 837–855.

15. Cline, M. (2001, September). Cut agent turnover by hiring for motivational fit. *Call Center Management Review,* pp. 2–3.

16. Kanfer, R., & Ackerman, P. L. (2000). Individual differences in work motivation: Further explorations of a trait framework. *Applied Psychology: An International Review, 40,* 479–486.

17. See Note 2.

18. Locke, E. A. (2004). Goal-setting theory and its applications to the world of business. *Academy of Management Executive, 18*(4), 124–125

19. Locke, E. A., & Latham, G. P. (1990). *A theory of goal setting and task performance.* Englewood Cliffs, NJ: Prentice-Hall.

20. Mento, A. J., Locke, E. A., & Klein, H. J. (1992). Relationship of goal level to valence and instrumentality. *Journal of Applied Psychology, 77,* 395–406.

21. Latham, G. P. (2004). The motivational benefits of goal-setting. *Academy of Management Executive, 18*(4), 126–129.

22. Gellatly, I. R., & Meyer, J. P. (1992). The effects of goal difficulty on physiological arousal, cognition, and task performance. *Journal of Applied Psychology, 77,* 696–704.

23. Latham, G. P., & Seijts. G. H. (1999). The effects of proximal and distal goals on performance on a moderately complex task. *Journal of Organizational Behavior, 20,* 421–429.

24. Locke, E. A., & Latham, G. P. (2002). Building a practically useful theory of goal setting and task motivation: A 35-year odyssey. *American Psychologist, 57,* 705–717.

25. Miner, J. B. (2003). The rated importance, scientific validity, and practical usefulness of organizational behavior theories. *Academy of Management Executive, 2,* 250–268.

26. Mitchell, T. R., & Daniels, D. (2003). Observations and commentary on recent research in work motivation. In L. W. Porter, G. A. Bigley, & R. M. Steers (Eds.), *Motivation and work behavior,* 7th ed. (pp. 26–44). Burr Ridge, IL: McGraw-Hill/Irwin (quote, p. 29).

27. Latham, G., & Baldes, J. (1975). The practical significance of Locke's theory of goal setting. *Journal of Applied Psychology, 60,* 122–124.

28. Locke, E. A., & Latham, G. P. (1984). *Goal setting: A motivational technique that works!* Englewood Cliffs, NJ: Prentice-Hall.

29. See Note 21.

30. Wright, P. M., Hollenbeck, J. R., Wolf, S., & McMahan, G. C. (1995). The effects of varying goal difficulty operationalizations on goal setting outcomes and processes. *Organizational Behavior and Human Decision Processes, 61,* 28–43.

31. Bernstein, A. (1991, April 29). How to motivate workers: Don't watch 'em. *Business Week,* p. 56.

32. From: www.va.gov/budget/perfplan/keygoals.htm.

33. From: www.coeur.com/performance-goals.html.

34. Kerr, S., & Landauer, S. (2004). Using stretch goals to promote organizational effectiveness and personal growth: General Electric and Goldman Sachs. *Academy of Management Executive, 18*(4), 134–138.

35. See Note 34.

36. Latham, G. P., Erez, M., & Locke, E. A. (1988). Resolving scientific disputes by the joint design of crucial experiments by the antagonists: Application to the Erez-Latham dispute regarding participation in goal setting. *Journal of Applied Psychology, 73,* 753–772.

37. Ludwig, T. D., & Geller, E. S. (1997). Assigned versus participative goal setting and response generalization: Managing injury control among professional pizza deliverers. *Journal of Applied Psychology, 82,* 253–261.

38. Shaw, K. N. (2004). Changing the goal-setting process at Microsoft. *Academy of Management Executive, 18*(4), 139–142.

39. Langley, M. (2003, June 9). Big companies get low marks for lavish executive pay. *Wall Street Journal,* p. C1.

40. Friedman, T. L. (1999). *The Lexus and the olive tree.* New York: Anchor Books.

41. Colquitt, J. A., & Greenberg, J. (2003). Organizational justice: A fair assessment of the state of the literature. In J. Greenberg (Ed.), *Organizational behavior: The state of the science,* 2nd ed. (pp. 165–210). Mahwah, NJ: Lawrence Erlbaum. Adams, J. S. (1965). Inequity in social exchange. In L. Berkowitz (Ed.), *Advances in experimental social psychology* (Vol. 2, pp. 267–299). New York: Academic Press.

42. Elovainio, M., Kivimäki, M., Vahtera, J., Keltangas-Järvinen, L., & Virtanen, M. (2003). Sleeping problems and health behaviors as mediators between organizational justice and health. *Health Psychology, 22,* 287–293. Elovainio, M., Kivimäki, M., & Vahtera, J. (2002). Organizational justice: Evidence of a new psychosocial predictor of health. *American Journal of Public Health, 92,* 105–108. Taris, T. W., Kalimo, R., & Schaufeli, W. N. (2002). Inequity at work: Its measurement and association with worker health. *Work & Stress, 16,* 287–301.

43. Harder, J. W. (1992). Play for pay: Effects of inequity in a pay-for-performance context. *Administrative Science Quarterly, 37,* 321–335.

44. From: http://sportsillustrated.cnn.com/2005/hockey/nhl/ 01/03/bc.hkn.gretzky.lockout.ap/index.html.

45. Greenberg, J. (1993). Stealing in the name of justice: Informational and interpersonal moderators of theft reactions to underpayment inequity. *Organizational Behavior and Human Decision Processes, 54,* 81–103.

46. Jones, D. A., & Skarlicki, D. P. (2003). The relationship between perceptions of fairness and voluntary turnover among retail employees. *Journal of Applied Social Psychology, 33,* 1226–1243.

47. Mowday, R. T., & Colwell, K. A. (2003). Employee reactions to unfair outcomes in the workplace: The contributions of Adams's equity theory to understanding work motivation. In L. W. Porter, G. A. Bigley, & R. M. Steers (Eds.), *Motivation and work behavior,* 7th ed. (pp. 65–82). Burr Ridge, IL: McGraw-Hill/Irwin.

48. From: http://1912.history.ohio-state.edu/pullman.htm.

49. From: http://members.tripod.com/~mr_sedivy/colorado21 .html.

50. From: http://www.internationalist.org/teamsters.html.

51. From: http://www.cupe.sk.ca/nr-sept23-02.htm.

52. From: http://www.boston.com/business/articles/ 2005/01/05/united_locked_in_standoff_with_unions/.

53. Martin, J. E., & Peterson, M. M. (1987). Two-tier wage structures: Implications for equity theory. *Academy of Management Journal, 30,* 297–316.

54. 2004 Retail Food and Meat Agreement negotiations update for Aug. 30, 2004. From: http://www.ufcw588.org/ 588Aug30Hotline.htm. Ross, I. (1985, April 29). Employers win big on the move to two-tier contracts. *Fortune,* pp. 82–92.

55. Greenstein, T. N. (1995). Gender ideology and perception of the fairness of the division of household labor: Effects on marital quality. *Social Forces, 74,* 1029–1042.

56. Frisco, M. L., & Williams, K. (2003). Perceived housework equity, marital happiness, and divorce in dual-earner households. *Journal of Family Issues, 24,* 51–73.

57. See Note 56.

58. Kehler, H. (2004, June 9). Unions accepting a two-tier pay system are giving a major concession to bosses. *The Labor Educator.* From: www.laboreducator.org/twotierpay.htm.

59. From: http://www.eiro.eurofound.eu.int/1997/05/inbrief/ de9705113n.html.

60. Baron, J., & Kreps, D. M. (1999). *Strategic human resource management.* New York: John Wiley & Sons.

61. Colquitt, J. A., Greenberg, J., & Zapata-Phelan, C. P. (2005). What is organizational justice? A historical overview. In J. Greenberg & J. A. Colquitt (Eds.), *Handbook of organizational justice* (pp. 3–55). Mahwah, NJ: Lawrence Erlbaum.

62. Hodge, W. A., (2003). *The role of performance pay systems in comprehensive school reform.* Lanham, MD: University Press of America. Lawler, E. E., III. (1967). Secrecy about management compensation: Are there hidden costs? *Organizational Behavior and Human Performance, 2,* 182–189.

63. Lewicki, R. J., Wiethoff, C., & Tomlinson, E. C. (2005). What is the role of trust in organizational justice? In J. Greenberg & J. A. Colquitt (Eds.), *Handbook of organizational justice* (pp. 222–257). Mahwah, NJ: Lawrence Erlbaum.

64. Porter, L. W., & Lawler, E. E., III. (1968). *Managerial attitudes and performance.* Homewood, IL: Irwin.

65. Serwer, A. (2005, January 25). Toyota rolls out a new economy-class drug plan. *Fortune,* p. 47.

66. Bilkovski, S. D. (2004). Work force motivation: A novel application of expectancy theory in emergency medicine. *Annals of Emergency Medicine, 44*(4), Supplement 1, S130. Lord, R. G., Hanges, P, J., & Godfrey, E. G. (2003). Integrating neural networks into decision-making and motivational theory: Rethinking VIE theory. *Canadian Psychology, 44,* 217.

67. Zippo, M. (1982). Flexible benefits: Just the beginning. *Personnel Journal, 17*(4), 56–58.

68. Levering, R., & Moskowitz, M. (2005). The 100 best companies to work for. *Fortune,* pp. 72–76, 78, 80, 82, 84, 86, 88, 90. Schafer, S. (1997, August). Battling a labor shortage? It's all in your imagination. *Inc.,* p. 97.

69. Stern, J. M., & Stewart, G. B., III. (1993, June). Pay for performance: Only the theory is easy. *HRMagazine,* pp. 48–49.

70. Heneman, R. L. (2000). *Business-driven compensation policies.* New York: AMACOM. Schuster, J. R., & Zingheim, P. K. (1992). *The new pay: Linking employee and organizational performance.* New York: Lexington Books.

71. Chu, K. (2004, June 15). Firms report lackluster results from pay-for-performance plans. *Wall Street Journal,* p. D1.

72. Curry, S. (1997, August 18). Surprise! Money talks loudest. *Fortune,* p. 227.

73. Markham, S. E., Dow, S. K., & McKee, G. H. (2002). Recognizing good attendance: A longitudinal, quasi-experimental field study. *Personnel Psychology, 55,* 639–660.

74. National Association for Employee Recognition. From: http://www.recognition.org/index.asp?cid=189&tid=694.

75. Harrington, A. (2005, January, 24). Hall of fame. *Fortune,* pp. 94–95.

76. Nelson, B. (2004). Low-cost recognition ideas. Nelson Motivation. From: http://www.nelson-motivation.com/recideas.cfm.

77. Ettore, B. (1998, May). The brave new world of executive compensation. *Management Review,* p. 8.

78. Rodric, S. (2001). *The stock options book.* Oakland, CA: National Center for Employee Ownership.

79. Merck & Co. (2004). *Annual report: 2004.* Whitehouse, NJ: Author.

80. Griffin, R. W., & McMahan, G. C. (1994). Motivation through job design. In J. Greenberg (Ed.), *Organizational behavior: The state of the science* (pp. 23–44). Hillsdale, NJ: Lawrence Erlbaum.

81. Rigdon, J. E. (1992, May 26). Using lateral moves to spur employees. *Wall Street Journal,* pp. B1, B9.

82. Campion, M. A., & McClelland, C. L. (1991). Interdisciplinary examination of the costs and benefits of enlarged jobs: A job design quasi-experiment. *Journal of Applied Psychology, 76,* 186–198.

83. Campion, M. A., & McClelland, C. L. (1993). Follow-up and extension of the interdisciplinary costs and benefits of enlarged jobs. *Journal of Applied Psychology, 78,* 339–351.

84. Lonergan, J. M., & Maher, K. J. (2000). The relationship between job characteristics and workplace procrastination as moderated by locus of control. *Journal of Social Behavior and Personality, 15,* 213–224.

85. Luthans, F., & Reif, W. E. (1974). Job enrichment: Long on theory, short on practice. *Organizational Dynamics, 2*(2), 30–43.

86. Steers, R. M., & Spencer, D. G. (1977). The role of achievement motivation in job design. *Journal of Applied Psychology, U62,* 472–479.

87. Goldman, R. B. (1976). *A work experiment: Six Americans in a Swedish plant.* New York: Ford Foundation.

88. Winpisinger, W. (1973, February). Job satisfaction: A union response. *AFL-CIO American Federationist,* pp. 8–10.

89. Hackman, J. R., & Oldham, G. R. (1980). *Work redesign.* Reading, MA: Addison-Wesley.

90. Levine, R., & Levine, S. (1996). Why they are not smiling: Stress and discontent in the orchestral workplace. *Harmony, 2,* 15–25.

91. Graen, G. B., Scandura, T. A., & Graen, M. R. (1986). A field experimental test of the moderating effects of growth need strength on productivity. *Journal of Applied Psychology, 71,* 486–491.

92. Hackman, J. R., & Oldham, G. R. (1976). Motivation through the design of work: Test of a theory. *Organizational Behavior and Human Performance, 16,* 250–279.

93. Johns, G., Xie, J. L., & Fang, Y. (1992). Mediating and moderating effects in job design. *Journal of Management, 18,* 657–676.

94. Orpen, C. (1979). The effects of job enrichment on employee satisfaction, motivation, involvement, and performance: A field experiment. *Human Relations, 32,* 189–217.

95. Ropp, K. (1987, October). Candid conversations. *Personnel Administrator,* p. 49.

96. Hackman, J. R. (1976). Work design. In J. R. Hackman & J. L. Suttle (Eds.), *Improving life at work* (pp. 96–162). Santa Monica, CA: Goodyear.

97. Callari, J. J. (1988, June). You can be a better motivator. *Traffic Management,* pp. 52–56.

98. Magnet, M. (1993, May 3). Good news for the service economy. *Fortune,* pp. 46–50, 52.

99. Finegan, J. (1993, July). People power. *Inc.,* pp. 62–63.

100. See Note 99.

Case in Point Sources

Amnesty International. (2004). Facts and figures: The work of Amnesty International. From: http://web.amnesty.org/pages/aboutai_facts. Voluntary Matters 3. (2004). *Amnesty International UK.* From: http://www.voluntarymatters3.org/motivation/case_studies/case_study2.html.

Chapter 8

Preview Case 0Sources

Lashinsky, A. (2006, June 12). RAZR's edge. *Fortune,* pp. 124–126, 129–130, 132. Moto Info (2006, June 1). Motorazr V3i Dolce & Gabbana. From: http://www.motorola.com/motoinfo/product/details.jsp?globalObjectId=151. Mobile Tracker. (2006). From: http://www.mobiletracker.net/archives/2006/08/26/mobile-phone-market-share.

Chapter Notes

1. Turner, M. E. (2000). *Groups at work: Theory and research.* Mahwah, NJ: Lawrence Erlbaum. Cartwright, D., & Zander, A. (1968). Origins of group dynamics. In D. Cartwright & A. Zander (Eds.), *Group dynamics: Research and theory* (pp. 3–21). New York: Harper & Row.

2. Toothman, J. (2000). *Conducting the experiential group: An introduction to group dynamics.* New York: John Wiley. Bettenhausen, K. L. (1991). Five years of groups research: What we have learned and what needs to be addressed. *Journal of Management, 17,* 345–381.

3. Forsyth, D. L. (1999). *Group dynamics* (3rd ed.). Belmont, CA: Wadsworth.

4. Long, S. (1984). Early integration in groups: "A group to join and a group to create." *Human Relations, 37,* 311–332.

5. Tuckman, B. W., & Jensen, M. A. (1977). Stages of small group development revisited. *Group and Organization Studies, 2,* 419–427.

6. Gersick, C. J. G. (1988). Time and transition in work teams: Toward a new model of group development. *Academy of Management Journal, 31,* 9–41.

7. Gersick, C. J. G. (1989). Marking time: Predictable transitions in task groups. *Academy of Management Journal, 32,* 274–309.

8. Romanelli, E., & Tushman, M. L. (1994). Organizational transformation as punctuated equilibrium: An empirical test. *Academy of Management Journal, 37,* 1141–1166.

9. Biddle, B. J. (1979). *Role theory: Expectations, identities, and behavior.* New York: Academic Press.

10. Jackson, S. E., & Schuler, R. S. (1985). A meta-analysis and conceptual critique of research on role ambiguity and role conflict in work settings. *Organizational Behavior and Human Decision Processes, 36,* 16–78.

11. O'Keefe, B. (2006, June 15). Hoop dreams. *Fortune,* p. 122.

12. Benne, K. D., & Sheats, P. (1948). Functional roles of group members. *Journal of Social Issues, 4,* 41–49.

13. Hackman, J. R. (1992). Group influences on individuals in organizations. In M. D. Dunnette & L. M. Hough (Eds.), *Handbook of industrial and organizational psychology* (2nd ed.) (Vol. 3, pp. 199–268). Palo Alto, CA: Consulting Psychologists Press.

14. Feldman, D. C. (1984). The development and enforcement of group norms. *Academy of Management Review, 9,* 48–53.

15. Wilson, S. (1978). *Informal groups: An introduction.* Englewood Cliffs, NJ: Prentice-Hall.

16. Greenberg, J. (1988). Equity and workplace status: A field experiment. *Journal of Applied Psychology, 73,* 606–613.

17. Stryker, S., & Macke, A. S. (1978). Status inconsistency and role conflict. In R. H. Turner, J. Coleman, & R. C. Fox (Eds.), *Annual review of sociology* (Vol. 4, pp. 58–90). Palo Alto, CA: Annual Reviews.

18. Jackson, L. A., & Grabski, S. V. (1988). Perceptions of fair pay and the gender wage gap. *Journal of Applied Social Psychology, 18,* 606–625.

19. Torrance, E. P. (1954). Some consequences of power differences on decision making in permanent and temporary three-man groups. *Research Studies: Washington State College, 22,* 130–140.

20. Hare, A. P. (1976). *Handbook of small group research* (2nd ed). New York: Free Press.

21. Aronson, E., & Mills, J. (1959). The effects of severity of initiation on liking for a group. *Journal of Abnormal and Social Psychology, 59,* 178–181.

22. Long, S. (1984). Early integration in groups: "A group to join and a group to create." *Human Relations, 37,* 311–322.

23. Cartwright, D. (1968). The nature of group cohesiveness In D. Cartwright & A. Zander (Eds.), *Group dynamics: Research and theory* (3rd ed.) (pp. 91–109). New York: Harper & Row.

24. George, J. M., & Bettenhausen, K. (1990). Understanding prosocial behavior, sales performance, and turnover: A group-level analysis in a service context. *Journal of Applied Psychology, 75,* 698–709.

25. Douglas, T. (1983). *Groups: Understanding people gathered together.* New York: Tavistock.

26. Aiello, J. R., & Douthitt, E. A. (2001). Social facilitation from Triplett to electronic performance monitoring. *Group Dynamics, 5,* 163–180.

27. Aiello, J. R., & Douthitt, E. A. (2001). Social facilitation from Triplett to electronic performance monitoring. *Group Dynamics: Theory, Research and Practice, 5,* 163–180. Zajonc, R. B. (1965). Social facilitation. *Science, 149,* 269–274.

28. Zajonc, R. B. (1980). Compresence. In P. B. Paulus (Ed.), *Psychology of group influence* (pp. 35–60). Hillsdale, NJ: Lawrence Erlbaum.

29. Geen, R. B., Thomas, S. L., & Gammill, P. (1988). Effects of evaluation and coaction on state anxiety and anagram performance. *Personality and Individual Differences, 6,* 293–298.

30. Aiello, J. R., & Svec, C. M. (1993). Computer monitoring of work performance: Extending the social facilitation framework to electronic presence. *Journal of Applied Social Psychology, 23,* 538–548.

31. Alge, B. J. (2001). Effects of computer surveillance on perceptions of privacy and procedural justice. *Journal of Applied Psychology, 86,* 797–804. Ambrose, M. L. Adler, G. S., & Noel, T. W. (1998). Electronic performance monitoring: A consideration of rights. In M. Schmeinke (Ed.), *Managerial ethics: Moral management of people and processes* (pp. 61–80). Mahwah, NJ: Lawrence Erlbaum Associates.

32. Steiner, I. D. (1972). *Group processes and productivity.* New York: Academic Press.

33. Shepperd, J. A. (1993). Productivity loss in performance groups: A motivation analysis. *Psychological Bulletin, 113,* 68–81.

34. Latané, B., Williams, K., & Harkins, S. (1979). Many hands make light the work: The causes and consequences of social loafing. *Journal of Personality and Social Psychology, 37,* 822–832.

35. Kravitz, D. A., & Martin, B. (1986). Ringelmann rediscovered: The original article. *Journal of Personality and Social Psychology, 50,* 936–941.

36. Karau, S. J., & Williams, K. D. (1993). Social loafing: A meta-analytic review and theoretical integration. *Journal of Personality and Social Psychology, 65,* 681–706.

37. Latané, B., & Nida, S. (1980). Social impact theory and group influence: A social engineering perspective. In P. B. Paulus (Ed.), *Psychology of group influence* (pp. 3–34). Hillsdale, NJ: Lawrence Erlbaum.

38. Earley, P. C. (1993). East meets west meets mideast: Further explorations of collectivistic and individualistic work groups. *Academy of Management Journal, 36,* 19–348.

39. Nordstrom, R., Lorenzi, P., & Hall, R. V. (1990). A review of public posting of performance feedback in work settings. *Journal of Organizational Behavior Management, 11,* 101–123.

40. Bricker, M. A., Harkins, S. G., & Ostrom, T. M. (1986). Effects of personal involvement: Thought-provoking implications for social loafing. *Journal of Personality and Social Psychology, 51,* 763–769.

41. George, J. M. (1992). Extrinsic and intrinsic origins of perceived social loafing in organizations. *Academy of Management Journal, 35,* 191–202.

42. Albanese, R., & Van Fleet, D. D. (1985). Rational behavior in groups: The free-riding tendency. *Academy of Management Review, 10,* 244–255.

43. Miles, J. A., & Greenberg, J. (1993). Using punishment threats to attenuate social loafing effects among swimmers. *Organizational Behavior and Human Decision Processes, 56,* 246–265.

44. Katzenbach, J. R., & Smith, D. K. (1993, March-April). The discipline of teams. *Harvard Business Review, 71*(2), 111–120.

45. Harari, O. (1995, October). The dream team. *Management Review,* pp. 29–31.

46. "Six Teams That Made Business History." (2006, June 12). *Fortune,* special section. Also available from: http://money.cnn.com/2006/05/31/magazines/fortune/sixteams_greatteams_fortune_061206/index.htm.

47. Mohrman, S. A. (1993). Integrating roles and structure in the lateral organization. In J. R. Galbraith & E. E. Lawler, III (Eds.), *Organizing for the future* (pp. 109–141). San Francisco: Jossey-Bass.

48. Tuckman, B. W., & Jensen, M. A. (1977). Stages of small group development revisited. *Group and Organization Studies, 2,* 419–427.

49. See Note 46.

50. Katzenbach, J. R. (1998). *Teams at the top.* Boston: Harvard Business School.

51. Herbelin, S. (2000). *Work team coaching.* Riverbank, CA: Riverbank Books. Chang, R. Y. (1999). *Success through teamwork.* San Francisco: Jossey-Bass. Sundstrom, E. (1998). *Supporting work team effectiveness: Best practices for fostering high performance.* San Francisco: Jossey-Bass.

52. Ray, D., & Bronstein, H. (1995). *Teaming up.* New York: McGraw-Hill.

53. Wellins, R. S., Byham, W. C., & Wilson, J. M. (1991). *Empowered teams.* San Francisco: Jossey-Bass.

54. Fisher, K. (1999). *Leading self-directed work teams.* New York: McGraw-Hill.

55. Moravec, M., Johannessen, O. J., & Hjelmas, T. A. (1997, July/August). Thumbs up for self-managed teams. *Management Review,* pp. 42–47. Manz, C. C., & Sims, H. P., Jr. (1993). *Business without bosses.* New York: Wiley.

56. Osburn, J. D., Moran, L., Musselwhite, E., & Zenger, J. H. (1990). *Self-directed work teams.* Burr Ridge, IL: Irwin.

57. 1996 Industry report: What self-managing teams manage. (1996, October). *Training,* p. 69.

58. Duarte, L. L., & Snyder, N. T. (2000). *Mastering virtual teams.* San Francisco: Jossey-Bass.

59. Coovert, M. D., & Foster, L. L. (2001). *Computer supported cooperative work.* New York: Wiley.

60. Lipnak, J., & Stamps, J. (2000). *Virtual teams* (2nd ed.). New York: Wiley.

61. Hackman, J. R. (2002). *Leading teams: Setting the stage for great performance.* Boston, MA: Harvard Business School Press. Hackman, J. R. (1987). The design of work teams. In J. W. Lorsch (Ed.), *Handbook of organizational behavior* (pp. 315–342). Englewood Cliffs, NJ: Prentice-Hall.

62. See Note 65 (quote, pp. 338).

63. Sheridan, J. H. (1990, October 15). America's best plants. *Industry Week,* pp. 28–64.

64. Beyerlein, M. M., Kennedy, F., & Beyerlein, S. (2006). *Advances in interdisciplinary studies of work teams.* San Diego, CA: Elsevier. Fisher, K. (1993). *Leading self-directed work teams.* New York: McGraw-Hill.

65. Lawler, E. E., III., Mohrman, S. A., & Ledford, G. E., Jr. (1992). *Employee involvement and total quality management.* San Francisco: Jossey-Bass.

66. Hackman, J. R. (Ed.) (1990). *Groups that work (and those that don't).* San Francisco: Jossey-Bass.

67. Pearson, C. A. L. (1992). Autonomous workgroups: An evaluation at an industrial site. *Human Relations, 45,* 905–936.

68. Wall, T. D., Kemp, N. J., Jackson, P. R., & Clegg, C. W. (1986). Outcomes of autonomous workgroups: A long-term field experiment. *Academy of Management Journal, 29,* 280–304.

69. Robbins, H., & Finley, M. (1995). *Why teams don't work.* Princeton, NJ: Peterson's/Pacesetters Books.

70. Demos, T. (2006, June 12). Cirque du balancing act. *Fortune,* p. 114.

71. Stern, A. (1993, July 18). Managing by team is not always as easy as it looks. *The New York Times,* p. B14.

72. See Note 71.

73. See Note 71.

74. See Note 71.

75. See Note 71.

76. Maginn, M. D. (1994). *Effective teamwork.* Burr Ridge, IL: Business One Irwin.

77. Salas, E., Edens, E., & Nowers, C. A. (2000). *Improving teamwork in organizations.* Mahwah, NJ: Lawrence Erlbaum.

78. Dumaine, B. (1994, September 5). The trouble with teams. *Fortune,* pp. 86–88, 90, 92 (quote, p. 86).

79. Barner, R. W. (2001). *Team troubleshooter.* Palo Alto, CA: Davies Black. Maruca, R. F. (2000, November). Unit of one. *Fast Company,* pp. 109–140.

80. Hackman, J. R., & Wageman, R. (2005). When and how team leaders matter. In B. M. Staw & R. M. Kramer (Eds.), *Research in organizational behavior* (Vol. 26, pp. 37–74). San Diego, CA: Elsevier.

81. Redding, J. C. (2000). *The radical team handbook.* New York: Wiley. Caudron, S. (1994, February). Teamwork takes work. *Personnel Journal,* pp. 41–46, 49 (quote, p. 43).

82. Caudron, 1994; see Note 81 (quote, p. 42).

83. Stewart, G. L., & Manz, C. C. (1997). Leadership for self-managing work teams: A typology and integrative model. In R. P. Vecchio (Ed.), *Leadership: Understanding the dynamics of power and influence in organizations* (pp. 396–410). Notre Dame, IN: University of Notre Dame Press.

84. Sundstrom, E., DeMeuse, K. P., & Futrell, D. (1990). Work teams: Applications and effectiveness. *American Psychologist, 45,* 128–137.

85. Levine, R. (2005, June 15). The new right stuff. *Fortune,* pp. 116, 118.

86. Hirschfeld, R. R., Jordan, M. H., Felid, H. S., Giles, W. F., & Armenakis, A. A. (2006). Becoming team players: Team members' mastery of teamwork knowledge as a predictor of team task proficiency and observed teamwork performance. *Journal of Applied Psychology, 91,* 467–474.

87. McDonough, E. F., Kahn, K. B., & Bardczak, G. (2001). An investigation of the use of global, virtual, and collocated new product development teams. *Journal of Product Innovation Management, 18,* 110–120.

88. Lau, D. C., & Murnighan, J. K. (1998). Demographic diversity and faultlines: The compositional dynamics of organizational groups. *Academy of Management Review, 23,* 325–340.

89. Cramton, C. D., & Hinds, P. J. (2005). Subgroup dynamics in internationally distributed teams: Ethnocentricism or cross-national learning. In B. M. Staw & R. Kramer (Eds.), *Research in organizational behavior* (Vol. 26, pp. 231–263). San Diego, CA: Elsevier.

90. See Note 78 (quote, p. 88).

91. See Note 78 (quote, p. 90).

92. See Note 78 (quote, p. 88).

93. Anonymous. (1994, December). The facts of life for team-building. *Human Resources Forum,* p. 3.

94. McDermott, L. C., Brawley, N., & Waite, W. W. (1998). *World class teams.* New York: Wiley.

Case in Point Sources

Shields, D. (2006). *The tour.* Salt Lake City, UT: Three Story Press. Hochman, P. (2006, June 15). Pack mentality. *Fortune,* pp. 145, 147–150, 152. Wheatcroft, G. (2005). *Le Tour: A history of the Tour de France.* London: Simon & Schuster UK. Liggert, P., Raia, J., & Lewis, S. (2005). *Tour de France for dummies.* Hoboken, NJ: Wiley. Tour de France. (2006). From: http://www.letour.fr/indexus.html.

Chapter 9

Preview Case Sources

The Home Depot Web site (2006): www.homedepot.com/HDUS/EN_US/ corporate/about/about.shtml. Brown, J. (2004, June). The Home Depot's communication makeover. Integrated Solutions for Retailers. From: www.ismretail.com/articles/2005_06/040604.htm. Bowne Global Solutions (2005). Home Depot. From: www.bowneglobal.com/english/exp_cs_homedepot.htm. Sharing success. (2005). *Hewitt Magazine Online,* Vol. 7, no. 3. From: was4.Hewitt.com/Hewitt/resource/rptspubs/Hewitt_magazine/vol7_iss3.htm.

Chapter Notes

1. The Home Depot (2005). First quarter financial facts, 2005. From: http://ir.homedepot.com/downloads/1q04factsheet.pdf. News release. (2004, February 6). Home Depot and AARP launch national hiring partnership. From: http://ir.homedepot.com/ReleaseDetail.cfm?ReleaseID=128328.

2. World Communication Awards (2006). Past winners, 2005. From: http://wca.totaltele.com/Custom_7525.stm#2004.

3. International Directory of Business Biographies. (2006). Ben Verwaayen, 1952–. From: http://www.referenceforbusiness.com/biography/S-Z/Verwaayen-Ben-1952.html.

4. Mintzberg, H. (1973). *The nature of managerial work.* New York: Harper & Row.

5. Von Krogy, G., Ichio, K., & Nonaka, I. (2000). *Enabling knowledge creation: How to unlock the mystery of tacit knowledge and release of the power of innovation.* New York: Oxford University Press. Witherspoon, P. D. (1997) *Communicating leadership: An organizational perspective.* Boston: Allyn & Bacon.

6. Jupiter Media Metrix. (2006). From: www.jupitermedia.com. Olsen, S. (2002, March 21). Spam flood forces companies to take desperate measures. CNet news.Com. From: http://news.com.com/Companies+taking+desperate+steps+against+spam/2009-1023_3-864815.html?tag=nl.

7. Ferris Research. (2006). From: http://www.ferris.com/

8. Postini. (2005, March 20). Postini resource center: E-mail stats. From: http://www.postini.com/stats/.

9. See Note 4.

10. Lengel, R. H., & Daft, R. L. (1988). The selection of communication media as an executive skill. *Academy of Management Executive, 2,* 225–232.

11. Yates, J., & Orlikowski, W. J. (1992). Genres of organizational communication: A structurational approach to studying communication and media. *Academy of Management Review, 17,* 299–326.

12. Szwergold, J. (1993, June). Employee newsletters help fill an information gap. *Management Review,* p. 8.

13. Sibson and Company, Inc. (1989). *Compensation planning survey, 1989.* Princeton, NJ: Author.

14. Brady, T. (1993, June). Employee handbooks: Contracts or empty promises? *Management Review,* pp. 33–35.

15. Anonymous. (1993, November). The (handbook) handbook. *Inc.,* pp. 57–64.

16. Level, D. A. (1972). Communication effectiveness: Methods and situation. *Journal of Business Communication, 28,* 19–25.

17. Klauss, R., & Bass, B. M. (1982), *International communication in organizations.* New York: Academic Press.

18. Gantenbein, D. (2002, September). Communicate correctly. *Home Office Computing,* pp. 39–40.

19. Daft, R. L., & Lengel, R. H. (1984). Information richness: A new approach to managerial behavior and organizational design. In L. L. Cummings & B. M. Staw (Eds.), *Research in organizational behavior* (Vol. 6, pp. 191–233). Greenwich, CT: JAI. Daft, R. L., & Lengel, R. H. (1986). Organizational information requirements, media richness and structural design. *Management Science 32,* 554–571. Daft, R. L., Lengel, R. H., & Trevino, L. K. (1987). Message equivocality, media selection, and manager performance: Implications for information systems. *MIS Quarterly, 22,* 355–366.

20. Daft, R. L., Lengel, R. H., & Trevino, L. K. (1987). Message equivocality, media selection, and manager performance: Implications for information systems. *MIS Quarterly, 11,* 355–366.

21. East Side Teachers Association Update. (2003, March 20). San Jose, California. From: www.eastsideta.org/030321.htm.

22. Hickson, M. L., Stacks, D. W., & Moore, N-J. (2003). *Nonverbal communication: Studies and applications,* 4th ed. Los Angeles, CA: Roxbury.

23. Rafaeli, A., Dutton, J., Harquail, C., & Mackie-Lewis, S. (1997). Navigating by attire: The use of dress by female administrative employees. *Academy of Management Journal, 40,* 9–45.

24. Greenberg, J. (1989). The organizational waiting game: Time as a status-asserting or status-neutralizing tactic. *Basic and Applied Social Psychology, 10,* 13–26.

25. Zweigenhaft, R. L. (1976). Personal space in the faculty office: Desk placement and student-faculty interaction. *Journal of Applied Psychology, 61,* 628–632.

26. Barnum, C., & Wolnainsky, N. (1989, April). Taking cues from body language. *Management Review,* pp. 3–8.

27. DuBrin, A. J. (2001). *Leadership* (3rd ed.). Boston: Houghton Mifflin.

28. "An open message with General Motors" (2005, February 22). NevOn: Neville Hobson's Weblog: Comment and Opinion on Business Communication and Technology. From: http://nevon.typepad.com/nevon/2005/02/an_open_convers.html. Hobson, N. (2005, April 8). GM: Poster Child for the Executive Blog. From: http://www.webpronews.com/news/webdevelopmentnews/wpn-42-20050408GMPosterchildfortheexecutiveblog.html.

29. Craiger, P., & Weiss, R. J. (1998, June). Traveling in cyberspace: Video-mediated communication. *The Industrial-Organizational Psychologist,* pp. 83–92. Boeing Company Web site: www.boeing.com.

30. Diamond, L., & Roberts, S. (1996). *Effective videoconferencing.* Menlo Park, CA: Crisp.

31. Jupiter Research. (2005, March). From: www.jupiterresearch.com/bin/item.pl/home.

32. Gartner Group. (2002, March 19). GartnerG2 says e-mail marketing campaigns threaten traditional direct mail promotions. From: http://www3.gartner.com/5_about/press_releases/2002_03/pr20020319b.jsp.

33. Saunders, C. C., Robey, D., & Vavarek, K. A. (1994). The persistence of status differentials in computer conferencing. *Human Communication Research, 20,* 443–472.

34. Postini Resource Center (2005, March). E-mail stats. From: www.postini.com/stats/.

35. Jenkins, S. (2004, September 15). Veritas institutes e-mail free Fridays. *Oracle Headline News.* From: http://dba-oracle.com/oracle_news/2004_9_15_2004.htm. Muktarsing, N. (2001, July 22). Companies rediscover the power of speech. *London Sunday Mail,* p. 8.

36. Goldsborough, R., & Page, L. (2005, February). How to respond to flames (without getting singed). *Information Today, 22*(2), pp. 23–24.

37. Alonzo, M., & Milam, A. (2004). Flaming in electronic communication. *Decision Support Systems, 36,* 205–214. Reinig, B. A., & Mejias, R. J. (2004). The effects of national culture and anonymity on flaming and criticalness in GSS-supported discussions. *Small Group Research, 35,* 698–723.

38. Nancarrow, B. (2005). Multi-platform graphical emoticons quick reference. From the Internet at http://computer-ease.com/emoticon.htm.

39. Shiu, E., & Lenhart, A. (2004, September). How Americans use instant messaging. Pew Internet and American Life Project. From: www.pewinternet.org/pdfs/PIP_Instantmessage_Report.pdf.

40. See Note 39.

41. Walther, J. B., & Addario, K. P. (2001). The impacts of emoticons on message interpretation in computer-mediated communication. *Social Science Computer Review, 19,* 324–347.

42. Wolf, A. (2000). Emotional expression online: Gender differences in emoticon use. *CyberPsychology & Behavior, 3,* 827–833.

43. Employee Monitoring Guide. (2006). From: http://www.computer-monitoring.com/employee-monitoring/stats.htm.

44. Gartner Group. (2006). From: http://www.gartner.com/. Also see Note 39.

45. American Management Association (2005). *Electronic monitoring and surveillance survey.* New York: Author.

46. Yang, C. (2005, August 8). The state of surveillance. *Business Week,* pp. 55–56.

47. Zuboff, S. (1988). *In the age of the smart machine: The future of work and power.* New York: Basic Books.

48. Caplan, S. E. (2005). A social skill account of problematic Internet use. *Journal of Communication, 55,* 721–736.

49. Argyris, C. (1974). *Behind the front page: Organizational self-renewal in a metropolitan newspaper.* San Francisco: Jossey-Bass.

50. Hawkins, B. L., & Preston, P. (1981). *Managerial communication.* Santa Monica, CA: Goodyear.

51. Towers Perrin HR Services. (2005). From: www.towersperrin.com/hrservices/global/default.htm.

52. D'Aprix, R. (1996). *Communicating for change: Connecting the workplace with the marketplace.* San Francisco: Jossey-Bass.

53. Smith, M. (2005). *Performance measurement and management.* Newbury Park, CA: Sage.

54. Tesser, A., & Rosen, S. (1975). The reluctance to transmit bad news. In L. Berkowitz (Ed.), *Advances in experimental social psychology* (Vol. 8, pp. 192–232). New York: Academic Press.

55. Ptacek, J. T., Leonard, K., & McKee, T. L. (2004). "I've got some bad news. . .": Veterinarians' recollections of communicating bad news to clients. *Journal of Applied Social Psychology, 34,* 366–390.

56. Heath, C. (1996). Do people prefer to pass along good news or bad news? Valence and relevance of news as predictors of transmission propensity. *Organizational Behavior and Human Decision Processes, 68,* 79–94.

57. Walker, C. R., & Guest, R. H. (1952). *The man on the assembly line.* Cambridge, MA: Harvard University Press.

58. Luthans, F., & Larsen, J. K. (1986). How managers really communicate. *Human Relations, 39,* 161–178.

59. Kirmeyer, S. L., & Lin, T. (1987). Social support: Its relationship to observed communication with peers and superiors. *Academy of Management Journal, 30,* 137–151.

60. Hackman, J. R. (2002). *Leading teams.* Boston: Harvard Business School Press.

61. Read, W. (1962). Upward communication in industrial hierarchies. *Human Relations, 15,* 3–16.

62. Glauser, M. J. (1984). Upward information flow in organizations: Review and conceptual analysis. *Human Relations, 37,* 613–643.

63. Orrick, Herrington & Sutcliffe, LLP. (2005). Wrongful termination. From: www.orrick.com/practices/employment/ wrongfulTermination.asp.

64. Munter, M. (2002). *Guide to managerial communication,* 6th ed. Upper Saddle River, NJ: Prentice Hall.

65. Lind, E. A., Greenberg, J., Scott, K. S., & Welchans, T. D. (2000). The winding road from employee to complainant: Situational and psychological determinants of wrongful termination claims. *Administrative Science Quarterly, 45,* 557–590.

66. Coulson, R. (1981) *The termination handbook.* New York: The Free Press.

67. Caplan, G., & Teese, M. (1997). *Survivors: How to keep your best people on board after downsizing.* Palo Alto, CA: Davies-Black.

68. Lee, F. (1993). Being polite and keeping MUM: How bad news is communicated in organizational hierarchies. *Journal of Applied Social Psychology, 23,* 1124–1149.

69. Kiechel, W., III. (1990, June 18). How to escape the echo chamber. *Fortune,* pp. 129–130 (quote, p. 130).

70. Gibson, J.W. (1985, March). Satisfaction with upward and downward organizational communications: Another perspective. *Proceedings of the Southwest Academy of Management,* p.150.

71. Frank, A. D. (1984, December). Trends in communication: Who talks to whom? *Personnel,* pp. 41–47.

72. Rogers, E. M., & Rogers, A. (1976). *Communication in organizations.* New York: Free Press.

73. Kitchen, P. J., & Daly, F. (2002). Internal communication during change management. *Corporate Communications, 7*(1), 46–53.

74. Fiol, C. M. (1995). Corporate communications: Comparing executives' private and public statements. *Academy of Management Journal, 38,* 522–536.

75. Cheng, E. W., Li, H., Love, P. E. D., & Irani, Z. (2001). Network communication in the construction industry. *Corporate Communications, 6*(2), 61–70.

76. Harcourt, J., Richerson, V., & Waitterk, M. J. (1991). A national study of middle managers' assessment of organization communication quality. *Journal of Business Communication, 28,* 347–365.

77. Krackhardt, D., & Hanson, J. R. (1993, July–August). Informal networks: The company behind the chart. *Harvard Business Review,* pp. 104–111.

78. Zenger, T. R., & Lawrence, B. S. (1989). Organizational demography: The differential effects of age and tenure distributions on technical communication. *Academy of Management Journal, 32,* 353–376.

79. Ibarra, H. (1992). Homophily and differential returns: Sex differences in network structure and access in an advertising firm. *Administrative Science Quarterly, 37,* 422–447.

80. Lesley, E., & Mallory, M. (1993, November 29). Inside the Black business network. *Business Week,* pp. 70–72, 77, 80–81.

81. Brass, D. J. (1985). Men's and women's networks: A study of interaction patterns and influence in an organization. *Academy of Management Journal, 28,* 327–343.

82. Krackhardt, D., & Porter, L. W. (1986). The snowball effect: Turnover embedded in communication networks. *Journal of Applied Psychology, 71,* 50–55.

83. Duncan, J. W. (1984). Perceived humor and social network patterns in a sample of task-oriented groups: A reexamination of prior research. *Human Relations, 37,* 895–907.

84. Baskin, O. W., & Aronoff, C. E. (1989). *Interpersonal communication in organizations.* Santa Monica, CA: Goodyear.

85. Foxnews.com. (2006, January 4). Mine officials: 'We sincerely regret' mixed messages about miners. From: http://www.foxnews.com/story/0,2933,180507,00.html.

86. Mitchell, G. (2006, January 4). Media report miracle mine rescue—then carry the tragic truth. *Editor and Publisher.* From: http://www.editorandpublisher.com/eandp/news/ article_display.jsp?vnu_content_id=1001804359.

87. McCarthy, E. (2003, May 1). Jousting with rumor mills. *Washington Post,* p. E1.

88. Raine, L. (2005, January). The state of blogging. Pew Internet & American Life Project. From: www.pewinternet.org/pdfs /PIP_blogging_data.pdf.

89. Baker, D. (2003, March 20). Organizations find no comfort from alarming Internet rumors. NSI Partners. From: www.nsipartners.com.

90. Walton, E. (1961). How efficient is the grapevine? *Personnel, 28,* 45–49.

91. Mishra, J. (1990, Summer). Managing the grapevine. *Public Personnel Management,* pp. 213–228.

92. Layoff rumors anger law firm. (2001, November 28). *New York Lawyer.* From: www.nylawyer.com/pay/01/112801a.html.

93. Thibaut, A. M., Calder, B. J., & Sternthal, B. (1981). Using information processing theory to design marketing strategies. *Journal of Marketing Research, 18,* 73–79.

94. Schiller, Z. (1995, September 11). P&G is still having a devil of a time. *Business Week,* p. 46.

95. The Coca-Cola Company. (2005). From: http://www2.coca-cola.com/contactus/myths_rumors/.

96. See Note 87.

97. Tannen, D. (1995). *Talking 9 to 5.* New York: Avon.

98. Tannen, D. (1998, September–October). The power of talk: Who gets heard and why. *Harvard Business Review,* pp. 137–148.

99. See Note 90 (quote, p. 148).

100. Munter, M. (1993, May–June). Cross-cultural communication for managers. *Business Horizons,* pp. 75–76.

101. Mellow, C. (1995, August 17). Russia: Making cash from chaos. *Fortune,* pp. 145–146, 148, 150–151.

102. Hodgson, J. D., Sango, Y., & Graham, J. L. (2000). *Doing business with the new Japan.* Oxford, England: Rowman & Littlefield. Ueda, K. (1974). Sixteen ways to avoid saying no in Japan. In J. C. Condon & M. Saito (Eds.), *International encounters with Japan,* pp. 185–192. Tokyo: Simul Press.

103. Alessandra, T., & Hunksaker, P. (1993). *Communicating at work.* New York: Fireside.

104. Adler, N. (1991). *International dimensions of organizational behavior,* 2nd ed. Boston: PWS/Kent.

105. Chronicle of Higher Education. (2005). From: http://chronicle.com/free/it/jargon.htm.

106. See Note 45.

107. Ivy Sea Online (2005). Think good communication's a "no-brainer"? Real-world results of unmindful communication. From: www.ivysea.com/pages/ca0299_1.html.

108. Rowe, M. P., & Baker, M. (1984, May–June). Are you hearing enough employee concerns? *Harvard Business Review,* pp. 127–135.

109. Burley-Allen, M. (1982). *Listening: The forgotten skill.* New York: John Wiley & Sons.

110. Brownell, J. (1985). A model for listening instructions: Management applications. *ABCA Bulletin, 48*(3), 39–44.

111. Austin, N. K. (1991, March). Why listening's not as easy as it sounds. *Working Woman,* pp. 46–48.

112. See Note 103.

113. Penley, L. E., Alexander, E. R., Jernigan, I. E., & Henwood, C. I. (1991). Communication abilities of managers: The relationship to performance. *Journal of Management, 17,* 57–76. Seyper, B. D., Bostrom, R. N., & Seibert, J. H. (1989). Listening, communication abilities, and success at work. *Journal of Business Communication, 26,* 293–303.

114. Brownell, J. (1990). Perceptions of effective listeners: A management study. *Journal of Business Communication, 27,* 401–415.

115. High Gain. (2005). *The listening organization.* Sebastopol, CA: Author.

116. Nichols, R. G. (1962, Winter). Listening is good business. *Management of Personnel Quarterly,* p. 4.

117. See Note 103.

118. McCathrin, Z. (1990, Spring). The key to employee communication: Small group meetings. *The Professional Communicator,* pp. 6–7, 9.

119. Vernyi, B. (1987, April 26). Institute aims to boost quality of company suggestion boxes. *Toledo Blade,* p. B2.

120. Taft, W. F. (1985). Bulletin boards, exhibits, hotlines. In C. Reuss & D. Silvis (Eds.), *Inside organizational communication,* 2nd ed. (pp. 183–189). New York: Longman.

121. Flag Bank. (2005, December). Merger information. From: http://www.flagbank.com/merger_info.htm.

122. See Note 118.

123. Beck, S. M. (1997, September 7). How'm I really doing? No, really. *Business Week,* pp. ENT 10–ENT 11.

124. Schnake, M. E., Dumler, M. P., Cochran, D. S., & Barnett, T. R. (1990). Effects of differences in superior and subordinate perception of superiors' communication practices. *Journal of Business Communication, 27,* 37–50.

125. Whetten, D. A., & Cameron, K. S. (1995). *Developing management skills,* 3rd ed. New York: HarperCollins.

126. Dubrin, A. J. (2001). *Leadership,* 3rd ed. Boston: Houghton Mifflin.

127. Tannen, D. (1998, February 2). How you speak shows where you rank. *Fortune,* p. 156.

128. Wurman, R. S. (2000). *Understanding.* Newport, RI: TED Conferences.

Case in Point Sources

Cold Stone Creamery has ambitious growth plans. (2005, February). *Dairy Foods, 106*(3), p. 18. The scoop on Cold Stone. (2005, April). *Business 2.0,* p. 64. Opening for business. (2005, March). *Chain Store Age, 81*(3), p. 106. From: www.coldstonecreamery.com/images/secondary/pyramid1.pdf.

Chapter 10

Preview Case Sources

Burrows, P. (2005, August 1). HP minus iPod: Why it makes sense. *Business Week,* pp. 23–24. Fried, I. (2005, July 29). HP to stop selling Apple's iPod. *CNet News.* From: http://news.com.com/HP+to+stop+selling+Apples+iPod/2100-1047_3-5810643.html. Cohen, P. (2004, August 27). HP debuts its own iPod. *PC World.* From: http://www.pcworld.com/news/article/0,aid,117623,00.asp.

Chapter Notes

1. Mintzberg, H. J. (1988). *Mintzberg on management: Inside our strange world of organizations.* New York: Free Press.

2. Drucker, P. F. (2006). *Brainy quote.* From: http://www.brainyquote.com/quotes/authors/p/peter_f_drucker.html.

3. Allison, S. T., Jordan, A M. R., & Yeatts, C. E. (1992). A cluster-analytic approach toward identifying the structure and content of human decision making. *Human Relations, 45,* 410–72.

4. Harrison, E. F. (1987). *The managerial decision-making process* (3rd ed.). Boston: Houghton Mifflin.

5. Wedley, W. C., & Field, R. H. G. (1984). A predecision support system. *Academy of Management Review, 9,* 696–703.

6. Nutt, P. C. (1993). The formulation process and tactics used in organizational decision making. *Organization Science, 4,* 226–251.

7. Nutt, P. (1984). Types of organizational decision processes. *Administrative Science Quarterly, 29,* 414–450.

8. Cowan, D. A. (1986). Developing a process model of problem recognition. *Academy of Management Review, 11,* 763–776.

9. Dennis, T. L., & Dennis, L. B. (1998). *Microcomputer models for management decision making.* St. Paul, MN: West.

10. Fulk, J., & Boyd, B. (1991). Emerging theories of communication in organizations. *Journal of Management, 17,* 407–446.

11. Power, D. J. (2000, September 24). Supporting business decision-making. From: http://www.dssresources.com/dssbook/ch1sbdm.pdf.

12. Sainfort, F. C., Gustafson, D. H., Bosworth, K., & Hawkins, R. P. (1990). Decision support systems effectiveness: Conceptual framework and empirical evaluation. *Organizational Behavior and Human Decision Processes, 45,* 232–252.

13. Stevenson, M. K., Busemeyer, J. R., & Naylor, J. C. (1990). Judgment and decision-making theory. In M. D. Dunnette & L. M. Hough (Eds.), *Handbook of industrial and organizational psychology* (2nd ed.) (Vol. 1, pp. 283–374). Palo Alto, CA: Consulting Psychologists Press.

14. Harris, R. (1998, July 2). Introduction to decision making. *Virtual salt.* From: http://www.virtualsalt.com/crebook5.htm.

15. See Note 14.

16. Dutta, A. (2001). Business planning for network services: A systems thinking approach. *Information Systems Research, 12,* 260–283. Hill, C. W., & Jones, G. R. (1989). *Strategic management.* Boston: Houghton Mifflin.

17. Crainer, S. (1998, November). The 75 greatest management decisions ever made. *Management Review,* pp. 16–23.

18. Amit, R., & Wernerfelt, B. (1990). Why do firms reduce business risk? *Academy of Management Journal, 33,* 520–533.

19. Roepik, D, & Gray, G. (2002). *Risk: A practical guide to deciding what's really safe and what's really dangerous in the world around you.* New York: Houghton Mifflin.

20. The Odds. (2006). Funny2.com. From: http://funny2.com/odds.htm.

21. Provan, K. G. (1982). Interorganizational linkages and influence over decision making. *Academy of Management Journal, 25,* 443–451.

22. Galaskiewicz, J., & Wasserman, S. (1989). Mimetic processes within an interorganizational field: An empirical test. *Administrative Science Quarterly, 34,* 454–479.

23. Parsons, C. K. (1988). Computer technology: Implications for human resources management. In G. R. Ferris & K. M. Rowland (Eds.), *Research in personnel and human resources management* (Vol. 6, pp. 1–36). Greenwich, CT: JAI Press.

24. Simon, H. A. (1987). Making management decisions: The role of intuition and emotion. *Academy of Management Executive, 1,* 57–64.

25. Kirschenbaum, S. S. (1992). Influence of experience on information-gathering strategies. *Journal of Applied Psychology, 77,* 343–352.

26. Simon, H. (1977). *The new science of management decisions* (2nd ed.). Englewood Cliffs, NJ: Prentice-Hall.

27. Lampton, B. (2003, December 1). "My pleasure"—The Ritz-Carlton Hotel Part II. *Expert Magazine.* From: http://www.expertmagazine.com/artman/publish/article_391.shtml.

28. Case, J. (1995). *Open-book management.* New York: HarperBusiness.

29. Tschohl, J. (2006). Empowerment: The key to customer service. *M&T Bank Business Resource Center.* From: http://www.mandtbank.com/smallbusiness/brc_humanresources_empowerment.cfm.

30. Sifonis, J. (2002, November–December). Empowering employees. *IQ Magazine: Cisco Systems.* From: http://www.cisco.com/web/about/ac123/iqmagazine/archives/2001_2002/empowering_employees.html.

31. Rowe, A. J., Boulgaides, J. D., & McGrath, M. R. (1984). *Managerial decision making.* Chicago: Science Research Associates.

32. See Note 31.

33. Murninghan, J. K. (1981). Group decision making: What strategies should you use? *Management Review, 25,* 56–62.

34. Janis, I. L. (1982). Groupthink: *Psychological studies of policy decisions and fiascoes* (2nd ed.). Boston: Houghton Mifflin.

35. Morehead, G., Ference, R., & Neck, C. P. (1991). Group decision fiascoes continue: Space shuttle *Challenger* and a revised groupthink framework. *Human Relations, 44,* 531–550.

36. Eaton, J. (2001). Management communication: The threat of groupthink. *Corporate Communication, 6,* 183–192. Janis, I. L. (1988). *Crucial decisions: Leadership in policy making and crisis management.* New York: Free Press.

37. Morehead, G., & Montanari, J. R. (1986). An empirical investigation of the groupthink phenomenon. *Human Relations, 39,* 391–410.

38. Schweiger, D. M., Sandberg, W. R., & Ragan, J. W. (1986). Group approaches for improving strategic decision making: A comparative analysis of dialectical inquiry, devil's advocacy, and consensus. *Academy of Management Journal, 29,* 51–71.

39. Schweiger, D. M., Sandberg, W. R., & Rechner, P. L. (1989). Experiential effects of dialectical inquiry, devil's advocacy, and consensus approaches to strategic decision making. *Academy of Management Journal, 32,* 745–772.

40. Cosier, R. A., & Schwenk, C. R. (1990). Agreement and thinking alike: Ingredients for poor decisions. *Academy of Management Executive, 4,* 610–74.

41. Sloan, A. P., Jr. (1964). *My years with General Motors.* New York: Doubleday.

42. Johnson, R. J. (1984). Conflict avoidance through acceptable decisions. *Human Relations, 27,* 71–82.

43. Neustadt, R. E., & Fineberg, H. (1978). *The swine flu affair: Decision making on a slippery disease.* Washington, DC: U.S. Department of Health, Education and Welfare.

44. Hurry up and decide (2001, May 14). *Business Week,* p. 16.

45. Breen, B. (2000, September). What's your intuition? *Fast Company,* pp. 290–294, 296, 298. 300. Klein, G. (1999). *Sources of power.* Cambridge, MA: MIT Press.

46. Wild, R. (2000, September). Think fast! *Working Woman,* pp. 89–90.

47. Linstone, H. A. (1984). *Multiple perspectives for decision making.* New York: North-Holland.

48. Simon, H. A. (1979). Rational decision making in organizations. *American Economic Review, 69,* 493–513.

49. Adler, N. J. (1991). *International dimensions of organizational behavior.* Boston: PWS-Kent.

50. Roth, K. (1992). Implementing international strategy at the business unit level: The role of managerial decision-making characteristics. *Journal of Management, 18,* 761–789.

51. March, J. G., & Simon, H. A. (1958). *Organizations.* New York: Wiley.

52. See Note 29.

53. Simon, H. A. (1957). *Models of man.* New York: Wiley.

54. Shull, F. A., Delbecq, A. L., & Cummings, L. L. (1970). *Organizational decision making.* New York: McGraw-Hill.

55. Browning, E. B. (1850/1950). *Sonnets from the Portuguese.* New York: Ratchford and Fulton.

56. Mitchell, T. R., & Beach, L. R. (1990). ". . . Do I love thee? Let me count . . ." Toward an understanding of intuitive and automatic decision making. *Organizational Behavior and Human Decision Processes, 47,* 1–20.

57. Beach, L. R., & Mitchell, T. R. (1990). Image theory: A behavioral theory of image making in organizations. In B. Staw and L. L. Cummings (Eds.), *Research in organizational behavior* (Vol. 12, pp. 1–41). Greenwich, CT: JAI Press.

58. Dunegan, K. J. (1995). Image theory: Testing the role of image compatibility in progress decisions. *Organizational Behavior and Human Decision Processes, 62,* 710–786.

59. Dunegan, K. J. (1993). Framing, cognitive modes, and image theory: Toward an understanding of a glass half full. *Journal of Applied Psychology, 78,* 491–503.

60. Gaeth, G. J., & Shanteau, J. (1984). Reducing the influence of irrelevant information on experienced decision makers. *Organizational Behavior and Human Performance, 33,* 263–282.

61. Ginrich, G., & Soli, S. D. (1984). Subjective evaluation and allocation of resources in routine decision making. *Organizational Behavior and Human Performance, 33,* 187–203.

62. Levin, I. P., Schneider, S. L., & Gaeth, G. J. (1998). All frames are not created equal: A typology and critical analysis of framing effects. *Organizational Behavior and Human Decision Processes, 76,* 141–188.

63. Kahneman, D., & Tversky, A. (1984). Choices, values, and frames. *American Psychologist, 39,* 341–350.

64. Highhouse, S., & Yüce, P. (1996). Perspectives, perceptions, and risk-taking behavior. *Organizational Behavior and Human Decision Processes, 65,* 151–167.

65. Levin, I. P., & Gaeth, G. J. (1988). Framing of attribute information before and after consuming the product. *Journal of Consumer Research, 15,* 374–378.

66. Levin, I. P. (1987). Associative effects of information framing. *Bulletin of the Psychonomic Society, 25,* 85–86.

67. Meyerowitz, B. E., & Chaiken, S. (1987). The effects of message framing on breast self-examination attitudes, intentions, and behavior. *Journal of Personality and Social Psychology, 52,* 500–510.

68. Frisch, D. (1993). Reasons for framing effects. *Organizational Behavior and Human Decision Processes, 54,* 391–429.

69. Nisbett, R. E., & Ross, L. (1980). *Human inference: Strategies and shortcomings of social judgment.* Englewood Cliffs, NJ: Prentice-Hall.

70. Maule, A. J., & Hodgkinson, G. (2002). Heuristics, biases and strategic decision making. *Psychologist, 15,* 68–71.

71. Kahneman, D., & Tversky, A. (1973). On the psychology of prediction. *Psychological Review, 80,* 251–273.

72. Gaeth, G. J., & Shanteau, J. (1984). Reducing the influence of irrelevant information on experienced decision makers. *Organizational Behavior and Human Performance, 33,* 187–203.

73. Power, D. J., & Aldag, R. J. (1985). Soelberg's job search and choice model: A clarification, review, and critique. *Academy of Management Review, 10,* 48–58.

74. Soelberg, P. O. (1967). Unprogrammed decision making. *Industrial Management Review, 8,* 110–129.

75. Langer, E., & Schank, R. C. (1994). *Belief, reasoning, and decision making.* Hillsdale, NJ: Lawrence Erlbaum.

76. Loouie, T. A., Curren, M. T., & Harich, K. R. (2000). "I knew we would win:" Hindsight bias for favorable amd unfavorable team decision outcomes. *Journal of Applied Psychology, 85,* 264–272.

77. Moon, H., & Conlon, D. E. (2002). From acclaim to blame: Evidence of a person sensitivity decision bias. *Journal of Applied Psychology, 87,* 33–42.

78. Conlon, D. E., & Garland, H. (1993). The role of project completion information in resource allocation decisions. *Academy of Management Journal, 36,* 402–413.

79. Crockett, R. L., & Yang, C. (1999, Aug. 30). Why Motorola should hang up on Iridium. *Business Week,* p. 46.

80. Bobocel, D. R., & Meyer, J. P. (1994). Escalating commitment to a failing course of action: Separating the roles of choice and justification. *Journal of Applied Psychology, 79,* 360–363.

81. Staw, B. M. (1981). The escalation of commitment to a course of action. *Academy of Management Review, 6,* 577–587.

82. Whyte, G. (1993). Escalating commitment in individual and group decision making: A prospect theory approach. *Organizational Behavior and Human Decision Processes, 54,* 430–455.

83. Simonson, I., & Staw, B. M. (1992). Deescalation strategies: A comparison of techniques for reducing commitment to losing courses of action. *Journal of Applied Psychology, 77,* 411–426.

84. Garland, H., & Newport, S. (1991). Effects of absolute and relative sunk costs on the decision to persist with a course of

action. *Organizational Behavior and Human Decision Processes, 48,* 55–69.

85. Ross, J., & Staw, B. M. (1993). Organizational escalation and exit: Lessons from the Shoreham nuclear power plant. *Academy of Management Journal, 36,* 701–732.

86. Whyte, G. (1991). Diffusion of responsibility: Effects on the escalation tendency. *Journal of Applied Psychology, 76,* 408–415.

87. Staw, B. M., Barsade, S. G., & Koput, K. W. (1997). Escalation at the credit window: A longitudinal study of bank executives' recognition and write-off of problem loans. *Journal of Applied Psychology, 82,* 130–142.

88. Heath, C. (1995). Escalation and de-escalation of commitment in response to sunk costs: The role of budgeting in mental accounting. *Organizational Behavior and Human Decision Processes, 62,* 38–54.

89. Tan, H., & Yates, J. F. (1995). Sunk cost effects: The influences of instruction and future return estimates. *Organizational Behavior and Human Decision Processes, 63,* 311–319.

90. Davis, J. H. (1992). Introduction to the special issue on group decision making. *Organizational Behavior and Human Decision Processes, 52,* 1–2.

91. Delbecq, A. L., Van de Ven, A. H., & Gustafson, D. H. (1975). *Group techniques for program planning.* Glenview, IL: Scott, Foresman.

92. Hill, G. W. (1982). Group versus individual performance: Are N +1 heads better than one? *Psychological Bulletin, 91,* 517–539.

93. Wanous, J. P., & Youtz, M. A. (1986). Solution diversity and the quality of group decisions. *Academy of Management Journal, 29,* 141–159.

94. Yetton, P., & Bottger, P. (1983). The relationships among group size, member ability, social decision schemes, and performance. *Organizational Behavior and Human Performance, 32,* 145–149.

95. See Note 94.

96. See Note 94.

97. Osborn, A. F. (1957). *Applied imagination.* New York: Scribner's.

98. Bouchard, T. J., Jr., Barsaloux, J., & Drauden, G. (1974). Brainstorming procedure, group size, and sex as determinants of the problem-solving effectiveness of groups and individuals. *Journal of Applied Psychology, 59,* 135–138.

99. Kelley, T. (2001, June–July). Reaping the whirlwind. *Context,* pp. 56–58.

100. Bottger, P. C., & Yetton, P. W. (1987). Improving group performance by training in individual problem solving. *Journal of Applied Psychology, 72,* 651–657.

101. Dalkey, N. (1969). *The Delphi method: An experimental study of group decisions.* Santa Monica, CA: Rand Corporation.

102. Van de Ven, A. H., & Delbecq, A. L. (1971). Nominal versus interacting group processes for committee decision making effectiveness. *Academy of Management Journal, 14,* 203–212.

103. See Note 102.

104. Gustafson, D. H., Shulka, R. K., Delbecq, A., & Walster, W. G. (1973). A comparative study of differences in subjective likelihood estimates made by individuals, interacting groups, Delphi groups, and nominal groups. *Organizational Behavior and Human Performance, 9,* 280–291.

105. Ulshak, F. L., Nathanson, L., & Gillan, P. B. (1981). *Small group problem solving: An aid to organizational effectiveness.* Reading, MA: Addison-Wesley.

106. Willis, R. E. (1979). A simulation of multiple selection using nominal group procedures. *Management Science, 25,* 171–181.

107. Stumpf, S. A., Zand, D. E., & Freedman, R. D. (1979). Designing groups for judgmental decisions. *Academy of Management Review, 4,* 581–600.

108. Rogelberg, S. G., & O'Connor, M. S. (1998). Extending the stepladder technique: An examination of self-paced stepladder groups. *Group Dynamics, 2*(2), 82–91. Rogelberg, S. G., Barnes-Farrell, J. L., & Lowe, C. A. (1992). The stepladder technique: An alternative group structure facilitating effective group decision making. *Journal of Applied Psychology, 77,* 730–737.

109. Harmon, J., Schneer, J. A., & Hoffman, L. R. (1995). Electronic meetings and established decision groups: Audioconferencing effects on performance and structural stability. *Organizational Behavior and Human Decision Processes, 61,* 138–147.

110. Colquitt, J. A., Hollenbeck, J. R., Ilgen, D. R., LePine, J. A., & Sheppard, L. (2002). Computer-assisted communication and team decision-making performance: The moderating effect of openness to experience. *Journal of Applied Psychology, 87,* 402–410.

111. Lam, S. S. K., & Shaubroeck, J. (2000). Improving group decisions by better pooling information: A comparative advantage of group decision support systems. *Journal of Applied Psychology, 85,* 564–573.

Case in Point Sources

Director of College Recruiting, Jim Goodman, answers your draft questions. (2005, April 22). Denver Broncos. From: http://www.denverbroncos.com/page.php?id=334&storyID=4082. Esterson, E. (1998). Game plan. *Inc. Tech.,* pp. 43–44.

Chapter 11

Preview Case Sources

Top Stories. (2006, April). View from the top: Southwest Airlines' Kelleher advises managing in good times for the bad. Stanford Graduate School of Business. From: http://www.gsb.stanford.edu/news/headlines/vftt_kelleher.shtml/. Trottman, M., & McCartney, S. (2004, July 26). Southwest's CEO resigns, citing personal reasons. *Wall Street Journal,* pp. A1, A2.

Chapter Notes

1. Banstetter, T. (2006, June 2). Union leader: American efforts failing. *Dallas Star-Telegram.* From: http://www.dfw.com/mld/dfw/news/14730064.htm.

2. Dabos, G. E., & Rousseau, D. M. (2004). Mutuality and reciprocity in the psychological contracts of employees and employees. *Journal of Applied Psychology, 89,* 52–72.

3. Rousseau, D. M. (1995). *Psychological contracts in organizations: Understanding written and unwritten agreements.* Thousand Oaks, CA: Sage.

4. Rousseau, D. M. 2001. Schema, promise and mutuality: The building blocks of the psychological contract. *Journal of Occupational and Organizational Psychology, 74,* 511–541. Rousseau, D. M., & Schalk, R. (2000). *Psychological contracts in employment: Cross-national perspectives.* Thousand Oaks, CA: Sage.

5. See Note 2.

6. Rousseau, D. M., & Parks, J. M. (1993). The contracts of individuals and organizations.
In L. L. Cummings & B. M. Staw (Eds.), *Research in organizational behavior* (Vol. 15,
pp. 1–43). Greenwich, CT: JAI Press.

7. Hui, C., Lee, C., & Rousseau, D. M. (2004). Psychological contract and organizational citizenship behavior in China: Investigating generalizability and instrumentality. *Journal of Applied Psychology, 89,* 311–321.

8. Power, S., & Walker, M. (2004). Less leisure in Germany. *Wall Street Journal,* July 26, A13.

9. See Note 4.

10. Raja, U., Johns, G., & Ntalianis, F. (2004). The impact of personality on psychological contracts. *Academy of Management Journal, 67,* 350–367.

11. Judge, T. A., Heller, D., & Mount, M. K. (2002). Five-factor model of personality and job satisfaction: A meta-analysis. *Journal of Applied Psychology, 87,* 530–541.

12. Lewicki, R. J., McAllister, D. J., & Bies, R. J. (1998). Trust and distrust: New relationships and realities. *Academy of Management Review, 23,* 438–458.

13. Lewicki, R. J., & Wiethoff, C. (2000). Trust, trust development, and trust repair. In M. Deutsch & P. T. Coleman (Eds.), *The handbook of conflict resolution* (pp. 86–107). San Francisco: Jossey-Bass.

14. Lee, C., Tinsley, C. H., & Chen, Z. X. (2000). Psychological normative contracts of work group members in the U.S. and Hong Kong. In D. M. Rousseau & R. Schalk (Eds.)., *Psychological contrasts in employment: Cross-cultural perspective* (pp. 87–103). Thousand Oaks, CA: Sage.

15. See Note 7.

16. Costa, P. T., & McCrae, R. R. (1992). *The NEO-PI Personality Inventory.* Odessa, FL: Psychological Assessment Resources.

17. Podsakoff, P. M., MacKenzie, S. B., Paine, J. B., & Bachrach, D. G. (2000). Organizational citizenship behaviors: A critical review of the theoretical and empirical literature and suggestions for future research. *Journal of Management, 26,* 513–563.

18. Settoon, R. P., & Mossholder, K. W. (2002). Relationship quality and relationship context as antecedents of person- and task-focused interpersonal citizenship behavior. *Journal of Applied Psychology, 87,* 255–267. McNeely, B. L., & Meglino, B. M. (1994). The role of dispositional and

situational antecedents in prosocial organizational behavior: An examination of the intended beneficiaries of prosocial behavior. *Journal of Applied Psychology, 79,* 836–844.

19. Zellars, K. L., Tepper, B. J., & Duffy, M. K. (2002). Abusive supervision and subordinates' organizational citizenship behavior. *Journal of Applied Psychology, 87,* 1068–1076.

20. Podsakoff, P. M., MascKenzie, S. B., Paine, J. B., & Bachrach, D. G. (2000). Organizational citizenship behaviors: A crucial review of the theoretical and empirical literature and suggestions for future research. *Journal of Management, 26,* 513–563.

21. Tansky, J. W. (1993). Justice and organizational citizenship behavior: What is the relationship? *Employees' Responsibilities and Rights Journal, 6,* 195–207.

22. Ladd, D., & Henry, R. A. (2000). Helping coworkers and helping the organization: The role of support perceptions, exchange ideology, and conscientiousness. *Journal of Applied Social Psychology, 30,* 2028–2049.

23. See Note 1.

24. Fomburn, C. J. (1996). *Reputation.* Boston, MA: Harvard Business School Press.

25. Zeng, M., & Chen, X. P. (2003). Achieving cooperation in multiparty alliances: A social dilemma approach to partnership management. *Academy of Management Review, 38,* 587–605.

26. Komorita, M., & Parks, G. (1994). Interpersonal relations: Mixed-motive interactions. *Annual Review of Psychology, 46,* 183–207.

27. Falk, A., Gachter, S., & Kovacs, J. (1999). Intrinsic motivation and extrinsic incentives in a repeated game with incomplete contracts. *Journal of Economic Psychology, 20,* 251–284.

28. Knight, G. P., Dubro, A. F., & Chao, C. (1985). Information processing and the development of cooperative, competitive, and individualistic social values. *Developmental Psychology, 21,* 37–45.

29. Beersma, B., Hollenbecvk, U. R., Humphrey, S. E., Moon, E., Conlon, D. E., & Ilgen, D. R. (2003). Cooperation, competition, and team performance: Toward a contingency approach. *Academy of Management Journal, 46,* 572–590.

30. Koza, M., & Lewin, A. Y. (1998). The evo-evolution of strategic alliances. *Organizational Science, 9,* 255–264.

31. Zeng, M., & Chen, X. P. (2003). Achieving cooperation in multiparty alliances: A social dilemma approach to partnership management. *Academy of Management Review, 28,* 587–605.

32. Thomas, K. W., & Schmidt, W. H. (1976). A survey of managerial interests with respect to conflict. *Academy of Management Journal, 10,* 315–318.

33. Dirks, K. T., & McLean Parks, J. (2003). Conflicting stories: The state of the science of conflict. In J. Greenberg (Ed.), *Organizational behavior: The state of the science,* 2nd ed. (pp. 283–324). Mahwah, NJ: Lawrence Erlbaum.

34. Jehn, K., & Mannix, E. (2001). The dynamic nature of conflict: A longitudinal study of intragroup conflict and performance. *Academy of Management Journal, 44,* 238–251.

35. East, G. (2004). Graves museum shut; future uncertain. *South Florida Sun-Sentinel,* July 24, p. B6.

36. Bragg, T. (1999, October). Ten ways to deal with conflict. *IIE Solutions,* pp. 36–37.

37. See Note 36.

38. Resume: Howard Schultz. (2002, September 9). *BusinessWeek Online.* From: http://www.businessweek.com/magazine/content/02_36/b3798005.htm.

39. Lee, M. (1998, October 12). "See you in court—er, mediation." *Business Week Enterprise,* pp. ENT22, ENT24.

40. Richey, B., Bernardin, J. J., Tyler, C. L., & McKinney, N. (2001). The effect of arbitration program characteristics on applicants' intentions toward potential employees. *Journal of Applied Psychology, 86,* 1006–1013.

41. Bordwin, M. (1999). Do-it-yourself justice. *Management Review,* pp. 56–58.

42. Lynch, J. F. (2001). Beyond ADR: A systems approach to conflict management. *Negotiation Journal, 17,* 207–216.

43. Bennett, R. J., & Robinson, S. L. (2003). The past, present, and future of workplace deviance research. In J. Greenberg (Ed.), *Organizational behavior: The state of the science* (pp. 52–70). Mahwah, NJ: Lawrence Erlbaum.

44. KnightRidder/Tribune News Service. (2004). Wal-Mart discrimination case huge for women. *Fort Wayne News Sentinel,* July 28, p. 3.

45. Gundlach, M. J., Scott, D. S., & Martinko, M. J. (2003). The decision to blow the whistle: A social information processing framework. *Academy of Management Review, 28,* 107–123. Miceli, M., & Near, J. (1992). *Blowing the whistle.* Lexington, MA: New Lexington Press.

46. Fricker, D. G. (2002, March 27). Enron whistle-blower honored in Dearborn. From: www.freep.com/money/business/htm. Anonymous. (2000, April). Paul van Buitenen: Paying the price of accountability. *Accountancy, 125*(1), 280. Taylor, M. (1999, September 13). Another Columbia suit unsealed. *Modern Healthcare, 29*(37), 10. Ettore, B. (1994, May). Whistleblowers: Who's the real bad guy? *Management Review,* 18–23.

47. Australian Compliance Institute, July 16, 2004. Australians are reluctant whistleblowers. *The Age,* p. 112.

48. Gjersten, L. A. (1999). Five State Farm agents fired after accusing company of consumer abuse. *National Underwriter, 103*(51), 1, 23.

49. Rothstein, K. Class act for hire: Fired whistleblowing teacher looks for work. *Boston Herald,* July 6, 2004.

50. See Note 49.

51. Martucci, W. C., & Smith, E. W. (2000). Recent state legislative development concerning employment discrimination and whistle-blower protections. *Employment Relations Today, 27*(2), 89–99.

52. Jones, M., & Rowell, A. (1999). Safety whistleblowers intimidated. *Safety and Health Practitioner, 17*(8), 3.

53. Bidoli, M., & Eedes, J. (2001, February 16). Big Brother is watching you. *Future Company.* From: www.futurecompany.co.za/2001/02/16/covstory.htm.

54. Mastrangelo, P., Everton, W., & Jolton, J. (2001). *Computer misuse in the workplace.* Unpublished manuscript. University of Baltimore. Lim, V. K. G., Loo, G. L., & Teo, T. S. H. (2001, August). *Perceived injustice, neutralization and cyberloafing at the workplace.* Paper presented at the Academy of Management, Washington, D.C.

55. Douglas, S. C., & Martinko, M. J. (2001). Exploring the role of individual differences in the prediction of workplace aggression. *Journal of Applied Psychology, 86,* 547–559.

56. National Institute for Occupational Safety and Health, Centers for Disease Control and Prevention. (1993). *Homicide in the workplace.* [Document # 705003]. Atlanta, GA: Author.

57. Baron, R.A. (2004). Workplace aggression and violence: Insights from basic research. In R.W. Griffin & V. O'Leary-Kelly (Eds,), *The dark side of organizational behavior,* pp. 23–61. San Francisco: Jossey-Bass.

58. Neuman, J. H. (2004). Injustice, stress, and aggression in organizations. In R.W. Griffin & V. O'Leary-Kelly (Eds,), *The dark side of organizational behavior,* pp. 62–102. San Francisco: Jossey-Bass.

59. Glomb, T. M., & Liao, H. (2003). Interpersonal aggression in work groups: Social influence, reciprocal, and individual effects. *Academy of Management Journal, 46,* 386–396.

60. Dietz, J., Robinson, S. A., Folger, R., Baron, R. A., & Jones., T. (2003). The impact of societal violence and organizational justice climate on workplace aggression. *Academy of Management Journal, 46,* 317–326.

61. See Note 60.

62. Armour, S. (2004). Probe shows traits of violence-prone workers. *SA Today,* July 15, 2004.

63. LeBlanc, M. M., & Kelloway, E. K. (2002). Predictors and outcomes of workplace violence and aggression. *Journal of Applied Psychology, 87,* 444–453.

64. Varita, M., & Jari, R. (2002). Gender differences in workplace bullying among prison officers. *European Journal of Work and Occupational Psychology, 11,* 113–126.

65. Cowie, H., Naylor, P., Rivers, I., Smith, P. K., & Pereira, B. (2002). Measuring workplace bullying. *Aggression and Violent Behavior, 7,* 33–51.

66. Namie, G. (2000). *U.S. hostile workplace survey, 2000.* Benicia, CA: Campaign Against Workplace Bullying.

67. Namie, G., & Namie, R. (2001). *The bully at work.* Naperville, IL: Sourcebooks.

68. Kooker, N. R. (2000, May 22). Taking aim at crime—stealing the profits: Tighter controls, higher morale may safeguard bottom line. *Nation's Restaurant News, 34* (21), 114–118.

69. Jabbkerm, A., (2000, March 29). Agrium seeks $30 million in damages in embezzlement case. *Chemical Week, 162*(13), 22.

70. Greenberg, J. (1998). The cognitive geometry of employee theft: Negotiating "the line" between taking and stealing. In. R. W. Griffin, A. O'Leary-Kelly, & J. M. Collins (Eds.), *Dysfunctional behavior in organizations: Nonviolent dysfunctional behavior* (pp. 147–194). Stamford, CT: JAI Press.

71. Greenberg, J. & Tomlinson, E. (2005). Methodological issues in the study of employee theft. In R. Griffin & A. O'Leary-Kelley (Eds.), *The dark side of organizational behavior.* San Francisco: Jossey-Bass.

Case in Point Sources

King, B. (2005, September 28). How Britain lost Sendo. *The Register.* From: http://www.theregister.co.uk/2005/09/28/how_britain_lost_sendo/. Orlowski, A. (2003, January 26).

Microsoft's master plan to screw phone partner: Full details. *The Register.* From: http://www.theregister.co.uk/2003/01/06/microsofts_masterplan_to_screw_phone/. Charny, B. (2003, January 14). Sendo sues Microsoft over "secret plan." *CNET News.com.* From: http://zdnet.com.com/2100-1106-980463.html. Reinhardt, A., & Greene, J. (2003, February 10). Death of a dream. *BusinessWeek,* pp. 44–45.

Chapter 12

Preview Case Sources

Barancik, S., & Hundley, K. (2005, April 25). A law firm's sexual harassment case: An inside story. *St. Petersburg Times.* From: http://www.sptimes.com/2005/04/24/Business/A_law_firm_s_sexual_h.shtml. Trigaux, R. (2005, March 30). H&K's handling sets a troubling standard. *St. Petersburg Times.* From: http://www.sptimes.com/2005/03/30/Columns/ HK_s_handling_sets_a_.shtml.

Chapter Notes

1. Martin, S. (2005, April 5). Holland & Knight: One of the last sex harass suits for BigLaw. Law.com Blog Network. From: http://legalblogwatch.typepad.com/legal_blog_watch/2005/ 04/ holland_knight_.html.
2. Yukl, G. (2006). *Leadership in organizations* (6th ed.). Upper Saddle River, NJ: Prentice Hall.
3. Yukl, G., & Tracey, J. B. (1992). Consequences of influence tactics used with subordinates, peers, and the boss. *Journal of Applied Psychology, 77,* 525–535. Schriesheim, C. A., & Hinkin, T. R. (1990). Influence tactics used by subordinates: A theoretical and empirical analysis and refinement of the Kipnis, Schmidt, and Wilkinson subscales. *Journal of Applied Psychology, 75,* 246–257.
4. Yukl, G., Falbe, C. M., & Young, J. Y. (1993). Patterns of influence behavior for managers. *Group & Organization Management, 18,* 5–28.
5. Offermann, L. R. (1990). Power and leadership in organizations. *American Psychologist, 45,* 179–189.
6. Falbe, C. M., & Yukl, G. (1992). Consequences for managers of using single influence tactics and combinations of tactics. *Academy of Management Journal, 35,* 638–652.
7. Brinkley, C. (2001, Sept. 7). In Las Vegas, casinos take a big gamble on the highest rollers. *Wall Street Journal,* pp. A1, A8.
8. Seifert, C. F., Yukl, G., & McDonald, R. A. (2003). Effects of multisource feedback and a feedback facilitator on the influence behavior of managers toward subordinates. *Journal of Applied Psychology, 88,* 561–569.
9. Podsakoff, P. M., & Schriesheim, C. A. (1985). Field studies of French and Raven's bases of power: Critique, re-analysis, and suggestions for future research. *Psychological Bulletin, 97,* 387–413.
10. Huber, V. L. (1981). The sources, uses, and conservation of managerial power. *Personnel, 51*(4), 62–67.
11. Kipnis, D., Schmidt, S. M., Swaffin-Smith, C., & Wilkinson, I. (1984, Winter). Patterns of managerial influence: Shotgun managers, tacticians, and bystanders. *Organizational Dynamics,* 58–67.
12. Stewart, T. (1999, November 6). CEOs see clout shifting. *Fortune,* p. 66.
13. Kahn, R. L., Wolfe, D. M., Quinn, R. P., Snoek, J. D., & Rosenthal, R. A. (1964). *Organizational stress: Studies in role conflict and ambiguity.* New York: Wiley.
14. See Note 13.
15. Heathfield, S. (2006). Inspirational quotes for business: Empowerment and delegation. About.com. From: http://humanresources.about.com/od/workrelationships/a/quotes_empower.htm.
16. See Note 15.
17. Thomas, K.W., & Velthouse, B.A. (1990). Cognitive elements of empowerment: An "interpretive" model of intrinsic task motivation. *Academy of Management Review, 15,* 666–681.
18. Arnold, J. A., Arad, S., Rhoades, J. A., & Drasgow, F. (in press). The empowering leadership questionnaire: The construction of a new scale for measuring leader behaviors. *Journal of Organizational Behavior.*
19. Ford, R. C., & Fottler, M. D. (1995). Empowerment: A matter of degree. *Academy of Management Executive, 9,* 21–29.
20. Dumaine, B. (1990, May 7). Who needs a boss? *Fortune,* pp. 52–54, 56, 58, 60.
21. Shipper, F., & Manz, C. C. (1991). Employee self-management without formally designated teams: An alternative road to empowerment. *Organizational Dynamics, 20*(3), 48–61.
22. Sherman, J. (1994). *In the rings of Saturn.* New York: Oxford University Press.
23. National Union of Public and General Employees (2004). Provincial employees suffering most from downsizing. *NUPGE,* August 4, p. 23.
24. DeGus, A. (1997). *The living company.* Boston: Harvard Business School.
25. See Note 24.
26. DuBrin, A. J. (1994). *Contemporary applied management* (4th ed.). Burr Ridge, IL: Irwin.
27. Patalon, W., III. (1992, June 14). Xerox's gateway to the world. *Rochester Democrat and Chronicle,* pp. 1F–2F.
28. Lesser, Y. (1992, May). From the bottom up: A toast to empowerment. *Human Resources Forum,* pp. 1–2.
29. Omni Hotels takes highest honors among upscale hotels in J.D. Power and Associates study. (2005, July 26). Omni Hotels press release. From: http://www.omnihotels.com/AboutOmniHotels/Press/PressReleases/050726PressRelease.aspx.
30. Byham, W. C., & Cox, J. (1991). *ZAPP: The lightening of empowerment.* New York: Harmony.
31. Seibert, S. C., Silver, S. R., & Randolph, W. A. (2004). Taking empowerment to the next level: A multiple-level model of empowerment, performance, and satisfaction. *Academy of Management Journal, 47,* 332–349.
32. Triandis, H.A. (1995). *Individualism and collectivism.* Boulder, CO: Westview Press.
33. Robert, C., Probst, T. M., Martocchio, G., Drasgow, F., & Lawler, J. J. (2000) Empowerment and continuous improvement in the United States, Poland, and India: Predicting fit on the basis of the dimensions of power distance and individualism. *Journal of Applied Psychology, 85,* 643–658.

34. Kirkman, B. L., Rosen, B., Tesluk, P. E., & Gibson, C. B. (2004). The impact of team empowerment on virtual team performance: The moderating role of face-to-face interaction. *Academy of Management Journal, 47,* 175–192.

35. Gresov, C., & Stephens, C. (1993). The context of inter-unit influence attempts. *Administrative Science Quarterly, 38,* 252–276.

36. Pfeffer, J., & Salancik, G. (1978). *The external control of organizations.* New York: Harper & Row.

37. Salancik, G., & Pfeffer, J. (1974). The bases and uses of power in organizational decision-making. *Administrative Science Quarterly, 19,* 453–473.

38. Boeker, W. (1989). The development and institutionalization of subunit power in organizations. *Administrative Science Quarterly, 34,* 388–410.

39. Lawrence, P. R., & Lorsch, J. W. (1967). *Organization and environment.* Cambridge, MA: Harvard University Press.

40. Miles, R. H. (1980). *Macro organizational behavior.* Glenview, IL: Scott, Foresman.

41. Hickson, D. J., Astley, W. G., Butler, R. J., & Wilson, D. C. (1981). Organization as power. In L. L. Cummings & B. M. Staw (Eds.), *Research in organizational behavior* (Vol. 4, pp. 151–196). Greenwich, CT: JAI Press.

42. U.S. Equal Employment Opportunity Commission. (2006). Sexual harassment. From: http://www.eeoc.gov/types/sexual_harassment.html.

43. Roberts, B. S., & Mann, R. A. (2006). Sexual harassment in the workplace: A primer. University of Akron. From: http://www3.uakron.edu/lawrev/robert1.html.

44. See Note 43.

45. Employment Law Learning Technologies and Littler Mendelson (2002, April 11). *Compliance training brings superior ROI to organizations.* From: http://www.dvinitiative.com/ resources/sexual_costs.asp.

46. Stop Violence Against Women (2003, November 1). Effects of sexual harassment. From: http://www.stopvaw.org/Effects_of_Sexual_Harassment.html.

47. Myths about Sexual Harassment. (2002). University of California Women's Center. From: http://www.sa.ucsb.edu/women%27scenter/sexualharassment/mythsaboutsexual.asp.

48. U.S. Equal Employment Opportunity Commission. (2006). Questions & answers for small employers on employer liability for harassment by supervisors. From: http://www.eeoc.gov/policy/docs/harassment-facts.html.

49. Ura, A. (2003, July/August). HR policy trends challenge small companies. Michigan Manufacturers Association. From: http://images.google.com/imgres?imgurl=http://www.mma-net.org/content/images/enterprise/hrtrend03b-big.jpg&imgrefurl=http://www.mma-net.org/publications/publications_ent.asp%3FEntArticleID%3D93&h=490&w=691&sz=32&hl=en&start=75&tbnid=D4oXfRfLSCdEGM:&tbnh=97&tbnw=137&prev=/images%3Fq%3Dsexual%2Bharassment%2Bpolicy%26start%3D60%26ndsp%3D20%26svnum%3D10%26hl%3Den%26lr%3D%26sa%3DN.

50. Drory, A., & Romm, T. (1990). The definition of organizational politics: A review. *Human Relations, 43,* 1333–1354.

51. Ferris, G. R., & Kacmar, K. M. (1992). Perceptions of organizational politics. *Journal of Management, 18,* 93–136.

52. Rosen, R. H. (1991). *The healthy company.* New York: Jeremy P. Tarcher/Perigree (quote, p. 71).

53. Carter, N. M., Gartner, W. B., Shaver, K. G., & Gatewood, E. J. (2003). The career reasons of nascent entrepreneurs. *Journal of Business Venturing, 18,* 13–39.

54. Mulder, M., de Jong, R. D., Koppelaar, L., & Verhage, J. (1986). Power, situation, and leaders' effectiveness: An organizational field study. *Journal of Applied Psychology, 71,* 566–570.

55. Greenberg, J. (1990). Looking fair vs. being fair: Managing impressions of organizational justice. In B. M. Staw & L. L. Cummings (Eds.), *Research in organizational behavior* (Vol. 12, pp. 131–157). Greenwich, CT: JAI Press.

56. Boeker, W. (1992). Power and managerial dismissal: Scapegoating at the top. *Administrative Science Quarterly, 37,* 400–421.

57. Liden, R. C., & Mitchell, T. R. (1988). Ingratiatory behaviors in organizational settings. *Academy of Management Review, 13,* 572–587.

58. Biberman, G. (1985). Personality and characteristic work attitudes of persons with high, moderate, and low political tendencies. *Psychological Reports, 57,* 1303–1310.

59. Kirchmeyer, C. (1990). A profile of managers active in office politics. *Basic and Applied Social Psychology, 22,* 339–350.

60. Allen, R.W., Madison, D. L., Porter, L.W., Renwick, P. A., & Mayer, B. T. (1979). Organizational politics: Tactics and characteristics of its actions. *California Management Review, 22,* 77–83.

61. Ferris, G. R., Frink, D. D., GilGalang, M. C., Zhou, J., Kacmar, K. M., & Howard, J. L. (1996). Perceptions of organizational politics: Prediction, stress-related implications, and outcomes. *Human Relations, 49,* 233–266.

62. See Note 60.

63. Wayne, S. J., & Ferris, G. R. (1990). Influence tactics, affect, and exchange quality in supervisor-subordinate interactions. *Journal of Applied Psychology, 75,* 487–499.

64. See Note 63.

65. Bartol, K. M., & Martin, D. C. (1990). When politics pays: Factors influencing managerial compensation decisions. *Personnel Psychology, 43,* 599–614.

66. Cropanzano, R. S., Howes, J. C., Grandey, A. A., & Toth, P. (1997). The relationships of organizational politics and support to work behaviors, attitudes, and stress. *Journal of Organizational Behavior, 18,* 159–181.

67. Kacmar, K. M., Bozeman, D. P., Carlson, D., & Anthony, W. P. (in press). A partial test of the perceptions of organizational politics model. *Human Relations.*

68. Randall, M. O., Cropanzano, R., Bormann, C. A., & Birjulin, A. (in press). Organizational politics and organizational support as predictors of work attitudes, job performance, and organizational citizenship behavior. *Journal of Organizational Behavior.*

69. Hochwarter, W. A., Witt, L. A., & Kacmar, K. M. (2000). Perceptions of organizational politics as a moderator of the

relationship between conscientiousness and job performance. *Journal of Applied Psychology, 85,* 472–478.

Case in Point Sources

General Motors. (2006, April). Senior leadership: John F. Smith. From: http://www.gm.com/company/ investor_information/corp_gov/bios/smith_john.htm. Blumenstein, R. (1997, October 23). How the Smith boys grew up to be CEOs. *Wall Street Journal,* pp. B1, B12.

Chapter 13

Preview Case Sources

Foust, D. (2006, August 7). Queen of pop. *Business Week,* pp. 44–50, 53. Reuters. (2005, March 24). Coke shakes up global marketing team. *New York Times,* p. C5. Coca-Cola Web Site. (2006). Our Company: Mary E. Minnick. From: http://www2.coca-cola.com/ourcompany/bios/bio_08.html. *Fortune's* Most Powerful Women in Business: 2005 (2006). CNN Money.com. From: http://money.cnn.com/magazines/ fortune/mostpowerfulwomen/snapshots/30.html

Chapter Notes

1. Yukl, G. (2006). *Leadership in organizations* (6th ed.). Upper Saddle River, NJ: Prentice Hall. Lord, R. G. (2001). The nature of organizational leadership: Conclusions and implications. In S. J. Zaccaro & R. J. Klimoski (Eds.), *The nature of organizational leadership: Understanding the performance imperatives confronting today's leaders* (pp. 413–436). San Francisco: Jossey-Bass. Yukl, G. (2002). *Leadership in organizations* (5th ed.). Upper Saddle River, NJ: Prentice Hall.

2. House, R. J., & Podsakoff, P. M. (1995). Leadership effectiveness: Past perspectives and future directions for research. In J. Greenberg (Ed.), *Organizational behavior: The state of the science* (pp. 45–82). Hillsdale, NJ: Lawrence Erlbaum.

3. Bennis, W. G., & Nanus, B. (1985). *Leaders: The strategies for taking charge.* New York: Harper & Row (quote, p. 4).

4. See Note 1.

5. Locke, E. A. (1991). *The essence of leadership.* New York: Lexington Books.

6. Cialdini, R. B. (1988). *Influence* (2nd ed.). Glenview, IL: Scott, Foresman.

7. Famous Quotes and Quotations. (2006). From: http://www.famous-quotes-and-quotations.com/ leadership-quotes.html.

8. Kotter, J. P. (1990). *A force for change: How leadership differs from management.* New York: The Free Press.

9. Geier, J. G. (1969). A trait approach to the study of leadership in small groups. *Journal of Communication, 17,* 316–323.

10. Kirkpatrick, S. A., & Locke, E. A. (1991). Leadership: Do traits matter? *Academy of Management Executive, 5,* 48–60. (quote, p. 58).

11. Barker, R. A. (2001). The nature of leadership. *Human Relations, 54,* 469–494.

12. House, R. J., Shane, S. A., & Herold, D. M. (1996). Rumors of the death of dispositional research are vastly exaggerated. *Academy of Management Review, 21,* 203–224.

13. See Note 9.

14. Chan, K-Y., & Drasgow, F. (2001). Toward a theory of individual differences and leadership: Understanding the motivation to lead. *Journal of Applied Psychology, 86,* 481–498.

15. Zaccaro, S. J., Foti, R. J., & Kenny, D. A. (1991). Self-monitoring and trait-based variance in leadership: An investigation of leader flexibility across multiple group situations. *Journal of Applied Psychology, 76,* 308–315.

16. Avolio, B. J., & Walumbwa, F. O. (2006). Authentic leadership: Moving HR leaders to a higher level. In J. Martoccio (Ed.), *Research in personnel and human resources management* (Vol. 25, pp. 273–304). San Diego, CA: Elsevier.

17. Chemers, M. M. (2001). Efficacy and effectiveness: Integrating models of leadership and intelligence. In R. E. Riggio & S. E. Murphy (Eds.), *Multiple intelligences and leadership* (pp. 139–160). Mahwah, NJ: Lawrence Erlbaum.

18. Lord, R. G., DeVader, C. L., & Alliger, G. M. (1986). A meta-analysis of the relation between personality traits and leadership perceptions: An application of validity generalization procedures. *Journal of Applied Psychology, 61,* 402–410.

19. Rubin, R. S., Bartels, L, L, & Bommer, W. J. (2002). Are leaders smarter or do they just seem that way? Exploring perceived intellectual competence and leadership emergence. *Social Behavior and Personality, 30,* 105–118.

20. Goleman, D., Boyzatis, R., & McKee, A. (2002). *Primal leadership: Realizing the power of emotional intelligence.* Boston: Harvard Business School. George, J. M. (2000). Emotions and leadership: The role of emotional intelligence. *Human Relations, 53,* 1027–1055. Aditya, R., & House, R. J. (2001). Interpersonal acumen and leadership across cultures: Pointers from the GLOBE study. In R. E. Riggio & S. E. Murphy (Eds.), *Multiple intelligences and leadership* (pp. 215–240). Mahwah, NJ: Lawrence Erlbaum. Caurso, D. R., Mayer, J. D., & Salovey, P. (2001). Emotional intelligence and emotional leadership. In R. E. Riggio & S. E. Murphy (Eds.), *Multiple intelligences and leadership* (pp. 55–74). Mahwah, NJ: Lawrence Erlbaum.

21. Offerman, L. R., & Phan, L. U. (2001). Culturally intelligent leadership for a diverse world. In R. E. Riggio & S. E. Murphy (Eds.), *Multiple intelligences and leadership* (pp. 187–214). Mahwah, NJ: Lawrence Erlbaum.

22. Anonymous. (1999, October 11). Molding global leaders. *Fortune,* p. 270.

23. Stein, N. (2000, October 2). Global most admired companies: Measuring people power. *Fortune,* pp. 273–288.

24. See Note 21 (quote, p. 283).

25. See Note 21 (quote p. 285).

26. Sagie, A., Zaidman, N., Amichai-hamburger, Y., Te'Eni, D., & Schwartz, D. G. (2002). An empirical assessment of the loose-tight leadership model: Quantitative and qualitative analyses. *Journal of Organizational Behavior, 23,* 303–320.

27. Muczyk, J. P., & Reimann, B. C. (1987). The case for directive leadership. *Academy of Management Review, 12,* 637–647.

28. Chen, C. C., & Meindl, J. R. (1991). The construction of leadership images in the popular press: The case of Donald

Burr and People Express. *Administrative Science Quarterly, 36,* 521–551.

29. Likert, R. (1961). *New patterns in management.* New York: McGraw-Hill. Stogdill, R. M. (1963). *Manual for the leader behavior description questionnaire, form XII.* Columbus, OH: Ohio State University, Bureau of Business Research.

30. Weissenberg, P., & Kavanagh, M. H. (1972). The independence of initiating structure and consideration: A review of the evidence. *Personnel Psychology, 25,* 119–130.

31. Vroom, V. H. (1976). Leadership. In M. D. Dunnette (Ed.), *Handbook of industrial-organizational psychology* (pp. 1527–1552). Chicago: Rand-McNally.

32. See Note 3.

33. Band, W. A. (1994). *Touchstones.* New York: Wiley (quote, p. 247).

34. Blake, R. R., & Mouton, J. J. (1969). *Building a dynamic corporation through grid organizational development.* Reading, MA: Addison-Wesley.

35. Lee, C. (1991). Followership: The essence of leadership. *Training, 28,* 27–35 (quote, p. 28).

36. Graen, G. B., & Wakabayashi, M. (1994). Cross-cultural leadership-making: Bridging American and Japanese diversity for team advantage. In H. C. Triandis, M. D. Dunnette, & L. M. Hough (Eds.) *Handbook of industrial and organizational psychology* (2nd ed.) (Vol. 4, pp. 415–466). Palo Alto, CA: Consulting Psychologists Press.

37. Phillips, A. S., & Bedian, A. G. (1994). Leader-follower exchange quality: The role of personal and interpersonal attributes. *Academy of Management Journal, 37,* 990–1001.

38. Dunegan, K. J., Duchon, D., & Uhl-Bien, M. (1992). Examining the link between leader-member exchange and subordinate performance: The role of task analyzability and variety as moderators. *Journal of Management, 18,* 59–76.

39. Duarte, N. T., Goodson, J. R., & Klich, N. R. (1993). How do I like thee? Let me appraise the ways. *Journal of Organizational Behavior, 14,* 239–249.

40. Deluga, R. J., & Perry, J. T. (1991). The relationship of subordinate upward influencing behaviour, satisfaction and perceived superior effectiveness with leader-member exchanges. *Journal of Occupational Psychology, 64,* 239–252.

41. Ferris, G. R. (1985). Role of leadership in the employee withdrawal process: A constructive replication. *Journal of Applied Psychology, 70,* 777–781.

42. Scandura, T. A., & Schriesheim, C. A. (1994). Leader-member exchange and supervisor career mentoring as complementary constructs in leadership research. *Academy of Management Journal, 37,* 1588–1602.

43. Sheard, A. G., & Kakabadse, A. P. (2001). Key roles of the leadership landscape. *Journal of Managerial Psychology, 17,* 129–144. Zenger, J. H., Musselwhite, E., Hurson, K., & Perrin, C. (1994). *Leading teams: Mastering the new role.* Homewood, IL: Business One Irwin.

44. Zenger, J. H., Musselwhite, E., Hurson, K., & Perrin, C. (1994). *Leading teams: Mastering the new role.* Homewood, IL: Business One Irwin.

45. LaBarre, P. (1999, April). The agenda—grassroots leadership. *Fast Company,* pp. 115–126.

46. See Note 29 (quote pp. 116, 118).

47. Pascale, R. (1998, April–May). Grassroots leadership: Royal Dutch Shell. *Fast Company,* pp. 110–120.

48. Lord, R. G., & Maher, K. (1989). Perceptions in leadership and their implications in organizations. In J. Carroll (Ed.), *Applied social psychology and organizational settings* (Vol. 4, pp. 129–154). Hillsdale, NJ: Lawrence Erlbaum.

49. Heneman, R. L., Greenberger, D. B., & Anonyuo, C. (1989). Attributions and exchanges: The effects of interpersonal factors on the diagnosis of employee performance. *Academy of Management Journal, 32,* 466–476.

50. Mitchell, T. R., & Wood, R. E. (1980). Supervisors' responses to subordinate poor performance: A test of an attribution model. *Organizational Behavior and Human Performance, 25,* 123–138.

51. Baker, W. D., & O'Neal, J. R. (2001). Patriotism or opinion leadership? The nature and origins of the "rally 'round the flag" effect. *Journal of Conflict Resolution, 45,* 661–687.

52. Bass, B. M. (1985). *Leadership and performance beyond expectations.* New York: Free Press.

53. House, R. J. (1977). A 1976 theory of charismatic leadership. In J. G. Hunt & L. L. Larson (Eds.), *Leadership: The cutting edge* (pp. 189–207). Carbondale, IL: Southern Illinois University Press.

54. See Note 38.

55. Conger, J. A. (1991). Inspiring others: The language of leadership. *Academy of Management Executive, 5,* 31–45.

56. House, R. J., Woycke, J., & Fedor, E. M. (1988). Charismatic and noncharismatic leaders: Differences in behavior and effectiveness. In J. A. Conger & R. N. Kanungo (Eds.), *Charismatic leadership* (pp. 122–144). San Francisco: Jossey-Bass.

57. See Note 1.

58. Zachary, G. P. (1994, June 2). How "Barbarian" style of Philippe Kahn led Borland into jeopardy. *Wall Street Journal,* p. A1.

59. Mumford, M. D., & Van Doorn, J. R. (2001). The leadership of pragmatism: Reconsidering Franklin in the age of charisma. *The Leadership Quarterly, 12,* 279–309.

60. See Note 7 (quote, p. 44).

61. See Note 1.

62. Tichy, N. M. (1993). *Control your destiny or someone else will.* New York: Doubleday Currency.

63. Stewart, T. A. (2002, March 2). America's most admired companies. *Fortune,* pp. 70–82.

64. Morris, B. (1995, December 11). The wealth builders. *Fortune,* pp. 80–84, 88, 90, 94.

65. Hater, J. J., & Bass, B. M. (1988). Superiors' evaluations and subordinates' perceptions of transformational and transactional leadership. *Journal of Applied Psychology, 73,* 695–702.

66. Fiedler, F. E. (1978). Contingency model and the leadership process. In L. Berkowitz (Ed.), *Advances in experimental social psychology* (Vol. 11, pp. 60–112). New York: Academic Press.

67. Hersey, P., & Blanchard, K. H. (1988). *Management of organizational behavior.* Englewood Cliffs, NJ: Prentice-Hall.

68. House, R. J., & Baetz, M. L. (1979). Leadership: Some empirical generalizations and new research directions. In B. M. Staw (Ed.), *Research in organizational behavior* (Vol. 1, pp. 341–424). Greenwich, CT: JAI Press.

69. Whitworth, L., House, H., Sandahl, P., & Kimsey-House, H. (1998). *Co-active coaching: New skills for coaching people toward success in work and life.* Palo Alto, CA: Davies-Black.

70. Halberstam, D. (2005). *The education of a coach.* New York: Hyperion. Wolfe, R. (1998). *The Packer way.* New York: St. Martin's. Holtz, L. (1998). *Winning everyday.* New York: Harper Business.

71. Bradley, Bill. (1998). *Values of the game.* New York: Artisan.

72. Milbank, D. (1990, March 5). Managers are sent to "charm schools" to discover how to polish up their acts. *Wall Street Journal,* pp. A14, B3.

73. Vroom, V. H., & Jago, A. G. (1988). *The new leadership: Managing participation in organizations.* Englewood Cliffs, NJ: Prentice Hall. Vroom, V. H., & Yetton, P. W. (1973). *Leadership and decision making.* Pittsburgh: University of Pittsburgh Press.

74. Kerr, S., & Jermier, J. M. (1978). Substitutes for leadership: Their meaning and measurement. *Organizational Behavior and Human Performance, 22,* 375–403.

75. Sheridan, J. E., Vredenburgh, D. J., & Abelson, M. A. (1984). Contextual model of leadership influence in hospital units. *Academy of Management Journal, 27,* 57–78.

76. Podsakoff, P. M., Niehoff, B. P., MacKenzie, S. B., & Williams, M. L. (1993). Do substitutes for leadership really substitute for leadership? An empirical examination of Kerr and Jermier's situational leadership model. *Organizational Behavior and Human Decision Processes, 54,* 1–44.

77. Meindl, J. R., & Ehrlich, S. B. (1987). The romance of leadership and the evaluation of organizational performance. *Academy of Management Journal, 30,* 91–109.

78. Pernick, R. (2001). Creating a leadership development program: Nine essential tasks. *Public Personnel Management, 30,* 429–444.

79. Day, D. V. (2001). Leadership development: A review in context. *Leadership Quarterly, 11,* 581–613.

80. Atwater, L. E., Ostroff, C., Yammarino, F. J., & Fleenor, J. W. (1998). Self-other agreement: Does it really matter? *Personnel Psychology, 51,* 577–598.

81. London, M., & Smither, J. W. (1995). Can multi-source feedback change perceptions of goal accomplishments, self-evaluations, and performance related outcomes? Theory-based applications and directions for research. *Personnel Psychology, 48,* 803–839.

82. Walker, A. G., & Smither, J. W. (1999). A five-year study of upward feedback: What managers do with their results matters. *Personnel Psychology, 52,* 393–423.

83. Leung, T. K., & Wong, Y. H. (2001). *Guanxi: Relationship marketing in a Chinese context.* Binghamton, NY: Haworth Press. Luo, Y. (2000). *Guanxi and business.* River Edge, NJ.: World Scientific Publishing.

84. Balfour, F., & Einhorn, B. (2002, February 4). The end of guanxi capitalism? *Business Week,* pp. 122–123.

85. Wood, E., Whiteley, A., & Zhang, S. (2002). The cross model of guanxi usage in Chinese leadership. *Journal of Management Development, 21,* 263–271.

86. Olivero, G., Bane, D. K., & Kopellman, R. E. (1997). Executive coaching as a transfer of training tool: Effects of productivity in a public agency. *Public Personnel Management, 26,* 461–469.

87. Giber, D., Carter, L., & Goldsmith, M. (1999). *Linkage: Inc.'s best practices in leadership development handbook.* Lexington, MA: Linkage Press.

88. Marquardt, M. J., & Revans, R. (1999). *Action learning in action.* Palo Alto, CA: Davies-Black.

89. Pedler, M. (1997). Interpreting action learning. In J. Burgoyne & M. Reynolds (Eds.), *Management learning: Integrating perspectives in theory and practice* (pp. 248–264). London: Sage.

90. Dotlich, D. L., & Noel, J. L. (1998). *Action learning: How the world's top companies are recreating their leaders and themselves.* San Francisco: Jossey-Bass.

91. See Note 83.

Case in Point Sources

Farrell, G. (1998, December). "My mouse is my fist." *Business 2.0,* pp. 72–74, 76, 78, 80, 82, 84. From: www.agency.com/ourcompany/.

Chapter 14

Preview Case Sources

Lohr, S. (2006, April 20). Earnings and sale get surge at Apple. *New York Times,* p. B1. From: http://www.iht.com/articles/2006/04/20/business/apple.php. Markhoff, J. (2006, April). Windows or Mac? Apple says both. *New York Times,* p. C7. From: http://www.nytimes.com/2006/04/06/technology/06apple.html?ex=1146024000&en=6e742a151ef99052&ei=5070. *Business Week.* (2004, October 12). Voices of the innovators: The seeds of Apple's innovation. Business Week Online. From: http://www.businessweek.com/bwdaily/dnflash/oct2004/nf20041012_4018_db083.htm.

Chapter Notes

1. Saporito, B. (1992, August 24). A week aboard the Wal-Mart express. *Business Week,* pp. 77–81, 84.

2. Flynn, J., Del Valle, C., & Mitchell, R. (1992, August 3). Did Sears take other customers for a ride? *Business Week,* pp. 24–25.

3. Martin, J. (2005). Organizational culture. In N. Nicholson, P. G. Audia, & M. M. Pillutla, *The Blackwell encyclopedia of management: Organizational behavior* (2nd ed.) (Vol. XI, pp. 271–278). Malden, MA: Blackwell. Schneider, B. (1990). *Organizational climate and culture.* San Francisco: Jossey-Bass.

4. Collier, R. (2006, April 24). A step ahead of the curve: Success of its hybrid cars fuels Toyota's rise in industry. *San Francisco Chronicle,* p. A1. From: http://www.sfgate.com/cgi-bin/article.cgi?f=/c/a/2006/04/24/TOYOTA.TMP. McGregor, J., Arndt, M., Berner, R., Rowley, I., Hall, K., Edmonson, G., Hamm, S., Ihlwan, M., & Reinhardt, A.

(2006, April 24). *Business Week.* From: http://www
.businessweek.com/magazine/content/06_17/b3981401.htm.
Warner, F. (2002, August). In a word, Toyota drives for
innovation. *Fast Company,* pp. 36–38. From: http://www
.fastcompany.com/magazine/61/toyota.html.

5. Schein, E. H. (1992). *Organizational culture and leadership:
A dynamic view* (2nd ed.). San Francisco, CA: Jossey-Bass.

6. Knight, T. (2004, October). Build a strong foundation: High
performance begins with culture. *CPA Leadership Report.*
From: http://www.cpareport.com/Newsletter%20Articles/
2004%20Articles/BuildaStrongFoundation_Oct_2004.htm.

7. Martin, J. (1996). *Cultures in organizations.* New York:
Oxford University Press.

8. Perna, J. (2001, July 15). Reinventing how we do business.
Vital Speeches of the Day, 67(19), 587–591.

9. The Disney Institute & Eisner, M. D. (2001). *Be our guest:
Perfecting the art of customer service.* New York: Hyperion.

10. Barrett, C. (2006, January). Coleen's corner: Managers in
training. *Spirit Magazine,* p. 12. From: http://www
.southwest.com/about_swa/.

11. Nash, G. D. (1992). *A. P. Giannini and the Bank of America.*
Norman, OK: University of Oklahoma Press.

12. Anonymous. (1999, April). Toxic shock? *Fast Company,* p. 38.

13. Rosen, R. H., & Berger, L. (1992). *Healthy company: Eight
strategies to develop people, productivity, and profits.* New
York: J. P. Tarcher.

14. Institute for Business, Technology, and Ethics. (2004). Eight
traits of a healthy organizational culture. From: http://www
.ethix.org/8%20traits.pdf. Barry, L. L. (1999). *Discovering
the soul of service: Nine drivers of sustainable business success.* New York: The Free Press.

15. Vlamis, A., & Smith, B. (2001). *Do you? Business the
Yahoo! way.* New York: Capstone.

16. Garr, D. (2000). *IBM redux: Lou Gerstner and the business
turnaround of the decade.* New York: HarperCollins.

17. Meridden, T. (2001). *Big shots: Business the Nokia way.*
New York: Capstone.

18. Florea, G., & Phinney, G. (2001). *Barbie talks!: An expose
of the first talking Barbie doll.* New York: Hyperion.

19. Tsui, A., S., Zhang, Z.-X., Wang, H., Xin, K. R., & Wu, J.
B. (2006). Unpacking the relationship between CEO leader-
ship behavior and organizational culture. *Leadership
Quarterly, 17,* 113–137.

20. Freiberg, K., Freiberg, J., & Peters, T. (1998). *Nuts!:
Southwest Airlines' crazy recipe for business and personal
success.* New York: Bantam Doubleday Dell.

21. Cameron, K. S., & Quinn, R. E. (1999). *Diagnosing and
changing organizational culture: Based on the competing
values framework.* Reading, MA: Addison-Wesley. Berrio,
A. A. (2003). Organizational culture assessment using the
competing values framework: A profile of Ohio State
University extension. *Journal of Extension, 41*(2). From:
http://www.joe.org/joe/ 2003april/a3.shtml.

22. Kauffman, J. (2005). Lost in space: A critique of NASA's
crisis communications in the Columbia disaster. *Public
Relations Review, 31,* 263–275.

23. Welch, J. (2005). *Winning.* New York: Harper Collins.

24. Welch, J. (1995, February). Interview with Jack Welch.
Business Today. From: http://www.1000ventures.com/
business_guide/ mgmt_new-model_25lessons-welch.html.

25. Berrio, A. A. (2003). An organizational culture assessment
using the competing values framework: A profile of Ohio
State University extension. *Journal of Extension, 41*(2).
From: http://www.joe.org/joe/2003april/a3.shtml.

26. Baker, S., Crockett, R. O., & Gross, N. (1998, August 10).
Can CEO Ollila keep the cellular superstar flying high?
Business Week, pp. 55–57, 59. From: http://www
.businessweek.com/1998/32/b3590001.htm.

27. Hamm, J. (2006, May). The five messages leaders must
manage. *Harvard Business Review,* pp. 115–123.

28. See Note 27 (quote, p. 123).

29. Waterman, R. J., Jr. (1993). *Adhocracy.* New York: W. W.
Norton.

30. Deering, A., Dilts, R., & Russell, J. (2003, Spring).
Leadership cults and cultures. *Leader to Leader, 28,* 36–43.

31. Martin, J., Sitkin, S. B., & Boehm, M. (1985). Founders and
the elusiveness of a cultural legacy. In P. J. Frost, L. F. Moore,
M. R. Louis, C. C. Lundberg, & J. Martin (Eds.),
Organizational culture (pp. 99–124). Beverly Hills, CA: Sage.

32. Dobrzynski, J. H. (1993, April 12). "I'm going to let the
problems come to me." *Business Week,* pp. 32–33.

33. Lemon, M., & Sahota, P. S. (2004). Organizational culture
as a knowledge repository for increased innovative capacity.
Technovation, 24, 484–498. Walsh, J. P., & Ungson, G. R.
(1991). Organizational memory. *Academy of Management
Review, 16,* 873–896.

34. Reitman, J. (1998). *Bad blood: Crisis in the American Red
Cross.* New York: Pinnacle Books.

35. Ornstein, S. L. (1986). Organizational symbols: A study of
their meanings and influences on perceived psychological
climate. *Organizational Behavior and Human Decision
Processes, 38,* 207–229.

36. Martin, J. (1982). Stories and scripts in organizational settings. In A. Hastorf & A. Isen (Eds.), *Cognitive social psychology* (pp. 255–306). New York: Elsevier-North Holland.

37. Ransdell, E. (2000, January–February). The Nike story? Just
tell it. *Fast Company,* pp. 44, 46.

38. Carroll, P. (1993). *Big blues: The unmaking of IBM.* New
York: Crown.

39. Branwyn, G. (1997). *Jargon watch: A pocket dictionary for
the jitterati.* San Francisco, CA: Hardwired.

40. Neuhauser, P. C. (1993). *Corporate legends and lore: The
power of storytelling as a management tool.* New York:
McGraw-Hill (quote, p. 63).

41. Mars, Inc. (2006). The five principles. From:
http://www.mars.com/About_us/The_Five_Principles/.
Brenner, J. G. (1999). *The emperors of chocolate: Inside the
secret world of Hershey and Mars.* New York: Random
House.

42. Manley, W. W., II. (1991). *Executive's handbook of model
business conduct codes.* Englewood Cliffs, NJ: Prentice-Hall
(quote, p. 5).

43. Walter, G. A. (1985). Culture collisions in mergers and acquisitions. In P. J. Frost, L. F. Moore, M. R. Louis, C. C. Lundberg, & J. Martin (Eds.), *Organizational culture* (pp. 301–314). Beverly Hills, CA: Sage.

44. Vlasic, B., & Stertz, B. A. (2001). *Taken for a ride: How Daimler-Benz drove off with Chrysler.* New York: Harper Business. Naughton, K. (2000, December 11). A mess of a merger. *Newsweek,* pp. 54–57. Elkind, P. (1998, November 9). A merger made in hell. *Fortune,* pp. 134–138, 140, 142, 144, 146, 149, 150. Burrough, B., & Helyar, J. (1990). *Barbarians at the gate.* New York: Harper Collins. Muller, J. (1999, November 29). Lessons from a casualty of the culture wars. *Business Week,* p. 198. Muller, J. (1999, November 15). The one-year itch at DaimlerChrysler. *Business Week,* p. 42.

45. Smith, B. W. (2005, May 3). *Corporate culture clashes thwart mergers and acquisitions.* Indianapolis, IN: Smith Weaver Smith. From: http://www.smithweaversmith.com/corporate%20culture%20clash.htm.

46. Charan, R. (2006, April). Home Depot's blueprint for culture change. *Harvard Business Review,* pp. 60–70.

47. See Note 46 (quote, p. 64).

48. Home Depot. (2006). Investor relations: 2005 financial highlights. From: http://ir.homedepot.com/.

49. Fischer, I., & Frontczak, D. (1999, September). Culture club. *Business 2.0,* pp. 196–198.

50. Whitehead, J. (2004, April). Full circuit. *HRO Today.* From: http://www.hrotoday.com/Magazine.asp?artID=736.

51. Collins, J. (2001). *Good to great.* New York: HarperCollins.

52. Amabile, T. M. (1988). A model of creativity and innovation in organizations. In B. M. Staw & L. L. Cummings (Eds.), *Research in organizational behavior* (Vol. 10, pp. 123–167). Greenwich, CT: JAI Press.

53. Runco, M. A. (1991). *Divergent thinking.* Westport, CT: Greenwood.

54. The Drucker Foundation, Hesselbein, F., & Johnston, R. (2002). *On creativity, innovation, and renewal: A leader-to-leader guide.* New York: John Wiley & Sons.

55. Amabile, T. M. (2000). Stimulate creativity by fueling passion. In E. A. Locke (Ed.), *The Blackwell handbook of principles of organizational behavior* (pp. 331–341). Oxford, England: Blackwell.

56. Kabanoff, B., & Rossiter, J. R. (1994). Recent developments in applied creativity. In C. Cooper & I. T. Robertson (Eds.), *International review of industrial and organizational psychology* (Vol. 9, pp. 283–324). London: Wiley.

57. Michalko, M. (1998, May). Thinking like a genius: Eight strategies used by the supercreative, from Aristotle and Einstein and Edison. *The Futurist,* pp. 21–25.

58. Kabanoff, B., & Bottiger, P. (1991). Effectiveness of creativity training and its reaction to selected personality factors. *Journal of Organizational Behavior, 12,* 235–248.

59. Muoio, A. (2000, January–February). Idea summit. *Fast Company,* pp. 151–156, 160, 162, 164 (quote, p. 152).

60. Gogoi, P. (2003). Thinking outside the cereal box. *BusinessWeek,* pp. 74–75.

61. Sittenfeld, C. (1999, July–August). This old house is a home for new ideas. *Fast Company,* pp. 58, 60.

62. Amabile, T. M., Conti, R., Coon, H., Lazenby, J., & Herron, M. (1996). Assessing the work environment for creativity. *Academy of Management Journal, 39,* 1154–1184.

63. Oldham, G. R., & Cummings, A. (1996). Employee creativity: Personal and contextual factors at work. *Academy of Management Journal, 39,* 607–634.

64. Zhou, J. (2003). When the presence of creative coworkers is related to creativity: The role of supervisor close monitoring, developmental feedback, and creative personality. *Journal of Applied Psychology, 88,* 413–422.

65. Amabile, T. M., & Conti, R. (1999). Changes in the work environment for creativity during downsizing. *Academy of Management Journal, 42,* 630–640.

66. Dahle, C. (2000, January–February). Mind games. *Fast Company,* pp. 169–173, 176, 178–179.

67. Shalley, C. E. (1991). Effects of productivity goals, creativity goals, and personal discretion on individual creativity. *Journal of Applied Psychology, 76,* 179–185.

68. Sutton, R. I., & Hargadon, A. (1996). Brainstorming groups in context: Effectiveness in a product design firm. *Administrative Science Quarterly, 41,* 685–718 (quote, p. 702).

69. Buchannan, L. (2000, September). Send in the clowns. *Inc.,* pp. 89–94. Hemsath, D., & Yerkes, L. (1998). *301 ways to have fun at work.* San Francisco, CA: Berrett Koehler. Weinstein, M. (1997). *Managing to have fun at work.* New York: Fireside.

70. Kushner, M. (1990). *The light touch.* New York: Fireside. Vikesland, G. (2006). Rules for having fun at work. From: http://www.employer-employee.com/april2002tips.html.

71. Zachary, P. C. (2000, July). Mighty is the mongrel. *Fast Company,* pp. 270–272, 276, 278, 280, 282, 284.

72. Zachary, G. P. (2000). *The global me: New cosmopolitans and the competitive edge.* New York: Public Affairs Books.

73. Casson, M. (1990). *Enterprise and competitiveness.* New York: Oxford University Press.

74. Busentiz, L. W., Gomez, C., & Spencer, J. W. (2000). Country institutional profiles: Unlocking entrepreneurial phenomena. *Academy of Management Journal, 43,* 994–1003.

75. McGregor, J. (2006, April 24). The world's most innovative companies. *Business Week,* pp. 62–68, 70, 72, 74.

76. David, H. (2006, April 24). Creativity pays. Here's how much. *Business Week,* p. 76.

77. See Note 76 (quote, p. 76).

78. Christensen, C. M., & Raynor, M. E. (2003). *The innovator's solution.* Boston, MA: Harvard Business School.

79. Tucker, R. B. (2002). *Driving growth through innovation.* San Francisco, CA: Berrett-Koehler.

80. Von Hippel, E. (2005). *Democratizing innovation.* Cambridge, MA: MIT Press.

81. Davila, T., Epstein, M. J., & Shelton, R. (2006). *Making innovation work: How to manage it, measure it, and profit from it.* Upper Saddle River, NJ: Prentice Hall. Chakravorti, B. (2003). *The slow pace of fast change: Bringing innovations to market in a connected world.* Boston, MA: Harvard Business School Press. Chesbrough, H.W. (2003). *Open innovation: The new*

imperative for creating and profiting from technology. Boston, MA: Harvard Business School Press.

82. Bernard, S. (2005, April 18). The perfect prescription: How the pill bottle was remade—sensibly and beautifully. *New York.* From: http://newyorkmetro.com/nymetro/health/features/11700/index.html.

83. See Note 52.

84. Davila, T., Epstein, M., & Shelton, R. (2005). *Making innovation work: How to manage it, measure it, and profit from it.* Upper Saddle River, NJ: Pearson. Ricchiuto, J. (1997). *Collaborative creativity.* New York: Oakhill.

85. Hamel, G. (2000, June 21). Re-invent your company. *Fortune,* pp. 99–104, 106, 110, 112, 116, 118 (quote, p. 100).

86. Hamel, G. (2000). *Leading the revolution.* Boston, MA: Harvard Business School Press.

87. DiCarlo, L. (2004, October 30). IBM chief's $200 million bet on U.S. talent. *Forbes.* From: http://www.innovateamerica.org/hot_topics/hot_topics.asp?id=21.

88. First National Bank. (2006). Rewarding innovation a key focus at FNB. From: https://www.fnb.co.za/news/archive/2005/20051118innovation.html.

89. 3M. (2002). *A century of innovation: The 3M story.* Minneapolis, MN: Author. From: http://multimedia.mmm.com/mws/mediawebserver.dyn?000000JHT4507Da0nDa000rvRlWH3e_W-.

Case in Point Sources

Hof, R. D. (2004, August 19). Voices of the innovators: Jeff Bezos: "Blind-Alley" explorer. Business Week Online. From: http://www.businessweek.com/bwdaily/dnflash/aug2004/nf20040819_7348_db_81.htm. Spector, R. (2000). *Amazon.com: Get big fast.* New York: HarperCollins. Schlegelmilch, B., Diamantopoulos, A., & Kreuz, P. (2003) Strategic innovation: The construct, its drivers and its strategic outcomes. *Journal of Strategic Marketing, 11*(2). From: http://search.epnet.com.gateway.library.qut.edu.au/direct.asp?an=10779277&db=bsh.

Chapter 15

Preview Case Sources

CNNMoney. (2006, March 21). Commercial Metals Company reports strongest second quarter in its history. From: http://money.cnn.com/services/tickerheadlines/prn/200603210855PR_NEWS_USPR_DATU026.htm. Commercial Metals Company Web site: http://www.comercialmetals.com. *Commercial Metals Company 2006 Annual Report.* Dallas, Texas: Commercial Metals Company.

Chapter Notes

1. Daft, R. L. (2007). *Essentials of organization theory and design* (9th ed.). Cincinnati, OH: South-Western.

2. Miller, D. (1987). The genesis of configuration. *Academy of Management Review,* 12, 686–701.

3. Galbraith, 1. R. (1987). Organization design. In J. W. Lorsch (Ed.), *Handbook of organizational behavior* (pp. 343–357). Englewood Cliffs, NJ: Prentice-Hall.

4. Hendricks, C. F. (1992). *The rightsizing remedy.* Homewood, IL: Business One Irwin.

5. Swoboda, F. (1990, May 28–June 3). For unions, maybe bitter was better. *Washington Post National Weekly Edition,* p. 20.

6. Blanchard, M. R. (1995). Delayering and span of control: A model to assess appropriate management size during downsizing: A continuing process of organizational renewal. *Clinical Laboratory Management Review,* 9, 430–432, 434–439.

7. Urwick, L. F. (1956). The manager's span of control. *Harvard Business Review, 34*(3), 39–47.

8. Speen, K. (1988, September 12). Caught in the middle. *Business Week,* pp. 80–88.

9. Green, H., & Moscow, A. (1984). *Managing.* New York: Doubleday.

10. Dalton, M. (1950). Conflicts between staff and line managerial officers. *American Sociological Review,* 15, 342–351.

11. Chandler, A. (1962). *Strategy and structure.* Cambridge, MA: MIT Press.

12. Navran, F. J. (2002). *Truth and trust: The first two victims of downsizing.* Athabaska, Alberta, Canada: Athabasca University Press. Mitchell, R. (1987, December 14). When Jack Welch takes over: A guide for the newly acquired. *Business Week,* pp. 93–97.

13. Lawrence, P., & Lorsch, J. (1967). *Organization and environment.* Boston: Harvard University.

14. Pitta, J. (1993, April 26). It had to be done and we did it. *Forbes,* pp. 148–152.

15. Merholz, P. (2002, April 30). The pendulum returns: Unifying the online presence of decentralized organizations. Adaptive Path Essay Archives. From: http://www.adaptivepath.com/publications/essays/archives/000028.php.

16. Schminke, M., Ambrose, M. L., & Cropanzano, R. S. (2000). The effect of organizational structure on perceptions of procedural fairness. *Journal of Applied Psychology,* 85, 294–304.

17. Schminke, M., Cropanzano, R. S., & Rupp, D. E. (2002). Organizational structure and fairness perceptions: The moderating effects of organizational level. *Organizational Behavior and Human Decision Processes,* 89, 881–905.

18. Bahrami, H. (1992). The emerging flexible organization: Perspectives from Silicon Valley. *California Management Review, 34*(4), 33–52.

19. Anders, G. (2003). *Perfect enough: Carly Fiorina and the reinvention of Hewlett-Packard.* Middlesex, England: Portfolio.

20. Hewlett Packard: About us. (2003). From: http://www.hp.com/hpinfo/abouthp/.

21. Mee, J. F. (1964). Matrix organizations. *Business Horizons, 7*(2), 70–72.

22. Bartlett, C. A., & Ghoshal, S. (1990). Matrix management: Not a structure, a frame of mind. *Harvard Business Review, 68*(3), 138–145.

23. Wall, W. C., Jr. (1984). Integrated management in matrix organizations. *IEEE Transactions on Engineering Management, 20*(2), 30–36.

24. Davis, S. M., & Lawrence, P. R. (1977). *Matrix.* Reading, MA: Addison-Wesley.

25. Goggin, W. (1974). How the multidimensional structure works at Dow Corning. *Harvard Business Review, 56*(1), 33–52.

26. See Note 25.

27. Ford, R. C., & Randolph, W. A. (1992). Cross-functional structures: A review and integration of matrix organization and project management. *Journal of Management, 18,* 267–294.

28. See Note 27.

29. McGregor, D. (1960). *The human side of enterprise.* New York: McGraw-Hill.

30. Argyris, C. (1964). *Integrating the individual and the organization.* New York: Wiley.

31. Likert, R. (1961). *New patterns of management.* New York: McGraw-Hill.

32. Duncan, R. (1979, Winter). What is the right organization structure? *Organizational Dynamics,* pp. 59–69.

33. Burns, T., & Stalker, G. M. (1961). *The management of innovation.* London: Tavistock.

34. Deveney, K. (1986, October 13). Bag those fries, squirt that ketchup, fry that fish. *Business Week,* pp. 57–61.

35. Kerr, P. (1985, May 11). Witch hazel still made the old-fashioned way. *New York Times,* pp. 27–28.

36. Morse, J. J., & Lorsch, J. W. (1970). Beyond Theory Y. *Harvard Business Review, 48*(3), 61–68.

37. Mintzberg, H. (1983). *Structure in fives: Designing effective organizations.* Englewood Cliffs, NJ: Prentice Hall.

38. Livesay, H. C. (1979). *American made: Man who shaped the American economy.* Boston: Little, Brown.

39. See Note 1.

40. Harrigan, K. R. (2003). *Vertical integration, outsourcing, and corporate strategy.* Frederick, MD: Beard Group.

41. Mohrman, S. A., Cohen, S. G., & Mohrman, A. M., Jr. (1997). *Designing team-based organizations.* San Francisco: Jossey-Bass.

42. GE: Just your average everyday $60 billion family grocery store. (1994, May 2). *Industry Week,* pp. 13–18.

43. Ashkenas, R., Ulrich, D., Jick, T., & Kerr, S. (1998). *The boundaryless organization: Breaking the chains of organizational structure.* San Francisco: Jossey-Bass.

44. Dees, G. D., Rasheed, A. M. A., McLaughlin, K. J., & Priem, R. L. (1995). The new corporate architecture. *Academy of Management Executive, 9,* 7–18.

45. See Note 44.

46. Tully, S. (1993, February 3). The modular corporation. *Fortune,* pp. 106–108, 110.

47. Werther, W. B., Jr. (1999, March–April). Structure-driven strategy and virtual organizational design. *Business Horizons,* pp. 13–18.

48. Byrne, J. (1993, February 8). The virtual corporation. *Business Week,* pp. 99–103.

49. Sherman, S. (1992, September 21). Are strategic alliances working? *Fortune,* pp. 77–78 (quote, p. 78).

50. Nathan, R. (1998, July–August). NEC organizing for creativity, nimbleness. *Research Technology Management,* pp. 4–6.

51. Moore, J. F. (1998, Winter). The rise of a new corporate form. *Washington Quarterly,* pp. 167–181.

52. Chesborough, H. W., & Teece, D. J. (1996, January–February). When is virtual virtuous? Organizing for innovation. *Harvard Business Review, 96,* 65–73.

53. See Note 52.

54. Nakarmi, L., & Einhorn, B. (1993, June 7). Hyundai's gutsy gambit. *Business Week,* p. 48.

55. Gerlach, M. L. (1993). *Alliance capitalism: The social organization of Japanese business.* Berkeley, CA: University of California Press.

56. Miyashita, K., & Russell, D. (1994). *Keiretsu: Inside the Japanese conglomerates.* New York: McGraw-Hill.

57. Kanter, R. M. (1994, July–August). Collaborative advantage: The art of alliances. *Harvard Business Review,* pp. 96–108.

58. See Note 57.

59. Hansen, M. T., Chesbrough, H. W., Nohria, N., & Sull, D. N. (2000, September–October). Networked incubators: Hothouses of new economy. *Harvard Business Review,* pp. 74–84.

60. Albrinck, J., Irwin, G., Neilson, G., & Sasina, D. (2000, third quarter). From bricks to clicks: The four stages of e-volution. *Strategy and Business,* pp. 63–66, 68–72.

61. Fletcher, N. (1988, December 10). U.S., China form joint venture to manufacture helicopters. *Journal of Commerce,* p. 58.

62. Bransi, B. (1987, January 3). South Korea's carmakers count their blessings. *The Economist,* p. 45.

63. Mason, J. C. (1993, May). Strategic alliances: Partnering for success. *Management Review,* pp. 10–15.

64. Newman, W. H. (1992). Focused joint ventures in transforming economies. *The Executive, 6,* 67–75.

65. Lewis, J. (1990). *Partnerships for profit: Structuring and managing strategic alliances.* New York: Free Press.

66. Weisul, K. (2001, March 6). Minority mergers. *Business Week,* Frontier section, pp. F14–F19.

67. Vanhonacker, W. (1997, March–April). Entering China: An unconventional approach. *Harvard Business Review, 97,* 130–131, 134–136, 138–140.

68. Earley, P. C., & Erez, M. (1997). *The transplanted executive: Why you need to understand how workers in other countries see the world differently.* New York: Oxford University Press.

Case in Point Sources

Lamm, M. D. (2004, June 1). Why alliances fail. *Pharmaceutical Executive.* From: http://www.pharmexec.com/pharmexec/article/articleDetail.jsp?id=98299. Lamm, M. D. (2004, May 1). Dangerous liaisons. *Pharmaceutical Executive.* From: http://www.pharmexec.com/pharmexec/article/articleDetail.jsp?id=95090.

Chapter 16

Preview Case Sources

PBS. (2002, February 27). *NewsHour with Jim Lehrer transcript: A nursing home alternative.* From: http://www.pbs.org/newshour/bb/health/jan-june02/eden_2-27.html. Salter, C. (2002, February). (Not) the same old story. *Fast Company,* pp. 78–80, 82, 84, 86. The Eden Alternative.

(2006). Our ten principles. From: http://www.edenalt.com/10htm. SPORG.com. (2006). The Eden Alternative: Helping the Eden Alternative grow through your donations (SPORG id 3927). From: http://www.sporg.com/servlet/LinkToEventServlet?EventId=3927. Thomas, W. H. (1996). *Life worth living: How someone you love can still enjoy life in a nursing home.* Acton, MA: VanderWyk & Burnam. Thomas, W. H. (1999). *Learning from Hannah: Secrets for a life worth living.* Acton, MA: VanderWyk & Burnam.

Chapter Notes

1. Vaughn, J. (2005, November 21). GM employees face news of layoffs. National Public Radio. From: http://www.npr.org/templates/story/story.php?storyId=5022706.

2. Dawson, P. (2004). *Understanding organizational change: The contemporary experience of people at work.* Thousand Oaks, CA: Sage. Sherman, S. (1993, December 13). How will we live with the tumult? *Fortune,* pp. 123–125.

3. Haveman, H. A. (1992). Between a rock and a hard place: Organizational change and performance under conditions of fundamental environmental transformation. *Administrative Science Quarterly, 37,* 48–75.

4. Smith, D. (1998, May). Invigorating change initiatives. *Management Review,* pp. 45–48.

5. Nystrom, P. C., & Starbuck, W. H. (1984, Spring). To avoid organizational crises, unlearn. *Organizational Dynamics,* 44–60.

6. Reese, J. (1993, July 26). Corporate Methuselahs. *Fortune,* pp. 16, 15.

7. Kanter, R. M. (1991, May–June). Transcending business boundaries: 12,000 world managers view change. *Harvard Business Review,* pp. 151–164.

8. Miller, K. L. (1993, May 17). The factory guru tinkering with Toyota. *Business Week,* pp. 95, 97.

9. Levy, A. (1986). Second-order planned change: Definition and conceptualization. *Organizational Dynamics, 16*(1), 4–20.

10. A master class in radical change. (1993, December 13). *Fortune,* pp. 82–84, 88, 90.

11. Woodyard, C. (2005, February 21). Multilingual staff can drive up auto sales. *USA Today.* From: http://www.usatoday.com/money/autos/2005-02-21-ethnic-cars-usat_x.htm?POE=click-refer.

12. Stewart, T. A. (1993, December 13). Welcome to the revolution. *Fortune,* pp. 66–68, 70, 72, 76, 78.

13. National Performance Review. (1997). *Serving the American public: Best practices in downsizing.* Washington, DC: Author. Also available online at: http://govinfo.library.unt.edu/npr/library/papers/benchmrk/downsize.html.

14. Bureau of Labor Statistics. (2006). From: http://jobsearchtech.about.com/gi/dynamic/offsite.htm?site=http://www.bls.gov/mls/home.htm.

15. Cameron, E., & Green, M. (2004). Making sense of change management. London: Kogan Page. David, F. R. (1993). *Concepts of strategic management.* New York: Macmillan.

16. Mead, R. (1998). *International management* (2nd ed.). Malden, MA: Blackwell.

17. Taylor, B. (1995). The new strategic leadership—driving change, getting results. *Long Range Planning, 28*(5), 71–81.

18. Tripas, M., & Favetti, G. (2000). Capabilities, cognition, and inertia: Evidence from digital imaging. *Strategic Management Journal,* 21, 1147–1161.

19. Spooner, J. G., & Kanellos, M. (2004, December 8). IBM sells PC group to Lenovo. CNET News. From: http://news.com.com/IBM+sells+PC+group+to+Lenovo/2100-1042_3-5482284.html.

20. Bellis, M. (2006). Inventors of the modern computer. From: http://inventors.about.com/library/weekly/aa031599.htm.

21. Travis, L. (2004, December 15). *India offshore outsourcing frees up $30B domestically.* Boston, MA: AMR Research. From: http://www.amrresearch.com/Content/View.asp?pmillid=17845.

22. Guptill, B., & McNee. B. (2005). *Outsourcing transformed: New models and methods.* Westport, CT: Saugatech Technology. From: http://www.saugatech.com/170order.htm.

23. Christensen, H. K. (1994). Corporate strategy: Managing a set of businesses. In L. Fahley & R. M. Randall (Eds.), *The portable MBA in strategy* (pp. 53–83). New York: Wiley.

24. Markides, C. (1997, Spring). Strategic innovation. *Sloan Management Review,* 9–23.

25. Collis, D. J., & Montgomery, C. A. (1995, July–August). Competing on resources: Strategy in the 1990s. *Harvard Business Review,* 73, 118–128.

26. Goldstein, A. P. (2001). *Reducing resistance: Methods for enhancing openness to change.* Champaign, IL: Research Press. Judson, A. S. (1991). *Changing behavior in organizations: Minimizing resistance to change.* Cambridge, MA: Basil Blackwell.

27. Dean, J. W., Jr., & Scharfman, M. (1996). Does decision process matter? A study of strategic decision-making effectiveness. *Academy of Management Journal,* 29, 368–396.

28. Porter, M. (1996, March 14). "It's time to grow up." *Far Eastern Economic Review,* pp. 1–2.

29. Lasserre, P., & Putti, J. (1990). *Business strategy and management: Text and cases for managers in Asia.* Singapore: Institute of Management.

30. Yoshimori, M. (1995). Whose company is it? The concept of the corporation in Japan and the West. *Long Range Planning, 28*(4), 33–34.

31. Nadler, D. A. (1987). The effective management of organizational change. In J. W. Lorsch (Ed.), *Handbook of organizational behavior* (pp. 358–369). Englewood Cliffs, NJ: Prentice-Hall.

32. Katz, D., & Kahn, R. L. (1978). *The social psychology of organizations* (2nd ed.). New York: Wiley.

33. Beer, M. (1980). *Organizational change and development: A systems view.* Glenview, IL: Scott, Foresman.

34. Wanberg, C., & Banas, J. T. (2000). Predictors and outcomes of openness to change in a reorganizing workplace. *Journal of Applied Psychology, 85,* 132–142.

35. Nadler, D. A. (1987). The effective management of organizational change. In J. W. Lorsch (Ed.), *Handbook of organizational behavior* (pp. 358–369). Englewood Cliffs, NJ: Prentice Hall.

36. Reich, R. B. (2000, October). Your job is change. *Fast Company,* pp. 140–148, 150, 152, 154, 156, 158.

37. Dutton, J. E., Ashford, S. J., O'Neill, R. M., & Lawrence, K. A. (2001). Moves that matter: Issue selling and organizational change. *Academy of Management Journal, 44,* 716–736.

38. Huey, J. (1993, April 5). Managing in the midst of chaos. *Fortune,* pp. 38–41, 44, 46, 48.

39. Senge, P. M. (1990). *The fifth discipline.* New York: Doubleday.

40. Kotter, J. P. (1995, March–April). Leading the change: Why transformation efforts fail. *Harvard Business Review,* pp. 59–67. Kotter, J. P., & Schlesinger, L. A. (1979, March–April), Choosing strategies for change. *Harvard Business Review,* pp. 106–114.

41. Collarelli, S. M. (1998). Psychological interventions in organizations. *American Psychologist, 53,* 1044–1056.

42. Pascale, R., Millemann, M., & Gioja, L. (1997, November–December). Changing the way we change. *Harvard Business Review,* pp. 127–139.

43. Watkins, J. M., & Mohr, B. J. (2001). *Appreciative inquiry: Change at the speed of imagination.* New York: John Wiley & Sons.

44. Whitney, D., & Sachau, C. (1998, Spring). Appreciative inquiry: An innovative process for organization change. *Employment Relations Today, 25,* pp. 11–21.

45. Bushe, G. R., & Coetzer, G. (1995). Appreciative inquiry as a team-developed intervention: A controlled experiment. *Journal of Applied Behavioral Science, 31,* 13–30.

46. Sugarman, H. C. (2006). The United States Navy: A case study in leadership development. From: http://appreciativeinquiry.case.edu/uploads/Navy%20-%20mini%20case%20summary.doc.

47. Pascale, R. T., & Miller, A. H. (1999, fourth quarter). The action lab: Creating a greenhouse for organizational change. *Strategy & Business,* pp. 64–72.

48. See Note 47.

49. Porras, J. I., & Robertson, P. J. (1992). Organization development: Theory, practice, and research. In M. D. Dunnette & L. M. Hough (Eds.), *Handbook of industrial and organizational psychology* (2nd ed., Vol. 3, pp. 719–822). Palo Alto, CA: Consulting Psychologists Press.

50. White, L. P., & Wotten, K. C. (1983). Ethical dilemmas in various stages of organizational development. *Academy of Management Review, 8,* 690–697.

51. The International Organization Development Code of Ethics. (2006). Organizational Development Network: Organization and Human Systems Development Credo. From: http://hometown.aol.com/odinst/ethics.htm.

52. Jaeger, A. M. (1986). Organizational development and national culture: Where's the fit? *Academy of Management Review, 11,* 178–190.

53. Kedia, B. L., & Bhagat, R. S. (1998). Cultural constraints on transfer of technology across nations: Implications for research in international and comparative management. *Academy of Management Review, 13,* 559–571.

54. Trepo, G. (1973, Autumn). Management style *a la française. European Business, 39,* 71–79.

55. Blunt, P. (1988). Cultural consequences for organization change in a southeast Asian state: Brunei. *Academy of Management Executive, 2,* 235–240.

Case in Point Sources

Royal Bank of Canda. (2006, February). *RBC Letter: The reality of aging.* From: http://www.rbc.com/community/letter/february2006.html. NCR. (2000). Royal Bank of Canada. From: http://www.teradatalibrary.com/pdf/eb1323.pdf.

Appendix 1

1. Schwab, D. P. (1999). *Research methods for organizational studies.* Mahwah, NJ: Lawrence Erlbaum.

2. Simek, Z., & Veiga, J. F. (2001). A primer on Internet organizational surveys. *Organizational Research Methods, 4,* 218–235.

3. Edwards, J. A. (2003). Measurement of OB constructs. In J. Greenberg (Ed.), *Organizational behavior: The state of the science* (2nd ed.). Mahwah, NJ: Lawrence Erlbaum.

4. Greenberg, J., & Folger, R. (1988). *Controversial issues in social research methods.* New York: Springer-Verlag.

5. Eisenhardt, K. M. (1989). Building theories from case study research. *Academy of Management Review, 14,* 532–550.

Appendix 2

1. Meager, N. (1995). Occupations. In N. Nicholson (Ed.), *The Blackwell encyclopedic dictionary of organizational behavior* (pp. 352–354). Cambridge, MA: Blackwell.

2. Salary.Com. (2006). From the Web at: http://swz.salary.com/salarywizard0.

3. Driver, M. J. (1994). Careers: A review of personal and organizational research. In C. L. Cooper & I. T. Robertson (Eds.), *Key reviews in managerial psychology: Concepts and research for practice* (pp. 237–269). New York: John Wiley & Sons.

4. Pepin, J. (2002, March). Burger meister: Ray Kroc. Time 100 Polls. From the Web at: http://www.time.com/time/time100/builder/profile/kroc.html. Love, J. F. (1995). *Grinding it out.* New York: Bantam.

5. Holland, J. (1973). *Making vocational choices: A theory of careers.* Englewood Cliffs, NJ: Prentice Hall. Gottfredson, G. D., & Holland, J. L. (1990). A longitudinal test of the influence of congruence: Job satisfaction, competency utilization, and counterproductive behavior. *Journal of Consulting Psychology, 37,* 389–398.

6. Cluskey, G. R., & Vaux, A. (1997). Vocational misfit: Source of occupational stress among accountants. *Journal of Applied Business Research, 12,* 43–54.

7. Savickas, M. L., & Spokane, A. R. (1999). *Vocational interests: Meaning, measurement, and counseling* use. Palo Alto, CA: Davies Black.

8. Lawrence, B. (1995). Career anchor. In N. Nicholson (Ed.), *The Blackwell encyclopedic dictionary of organizational behavior* (pp. 44–45). Cambridge, MA: Blackwell.

9. Schein, E. H. (1978). *Career dynamics: Matching individual and organizational needs.* Reading, MA: Addison-Wesley.

10. Hecker, D. E. (2005, November). Occupational employment projections to 2014. *Monthly Labor Review,* pp. 70–101.

11. Nicholson, N. (1995). Career plateauing. In N. Nicholson (Ed.), *The Blackwell encyclopedic dictionary of organizational behavior* (pp. 49–50). Cambridge, MA: Blackwell.

12. Branch, S. (1998, March 16). MBAs: What they really want. *Fortune,* p. 167.

13. Penna Sanders & Sidney Career Consulting, (2001, November). *Taking the plunge.* Research report available at: www.pennasanderssidney.com/research/report-takingtheplunge.html.

14. Bolles, R. N. (2006). *What color is your parachute?* Berkeley, CA: Ten Speed Press.

15. See Note 14.

16. Hanisch, K. A. (1995). Retirement. In N. Nicholson (Ed.), *The Blackwell encyclopedic dictionary of organizational behavior* (pp. 490–491). Cambridge, MA: Blackwell.

17. Hanisch, K. A., & Hulin, C. L. (1990). Job attitudes and organizational withdrawal: An examination of retirement and other voluntary withdrawal behaviors. *Journal of Vocational Behavior, 37,* 60–78.

18. Hanisch, K. A. (91994). Reasons people retire and their relations to attitudinal and behavioral correlates in retirement. *Journal of Vocational Behavior, 45,* 1–16.

19. Forum for Investor Advice (1999, July 26). Work 'til you drop. *Business Week,* p. 8.

20. Decker, J. P. (1999, November 22). Why pro golfers can't wait to hit the big five-oh. *Fortune,* p. 76.

21. Thornton, E. (1999, August 9). No room at the top. *Business Week,* p. 50.

22. Hirsch, W. (1995). Succession planning. In N. Nicholson (Ed.), *The Blackwell encyclopedic dictionary of organizational behavior* (pp. 544–54AII). Cambridge, MA: Blackwell.

23. Rothwell, W. J. (2000). *Effective succession planning: Ensuring leadership continuity and building talent from within.* New York: AMACOM.

24. Bianco, A., & Lavelle, L. (2000, December 11). The CEO trap. *Business Week,* pp. 86–92.

25. Darwin, A. (2000). Critical reflections on mentoring in work settings. *Adult Education Quarterly, 50,* 197–211.

26. Ragubsm, B. R., & Scandura, T. A. (1999). Burden or blessing? Expected costs and benefits of being a mentor. *Journal of Organizational Behavior, 20,* 493–509.

27. Ragins, B. R., Cotton, J. L., & Miller, J. S. (2000). Marginal mentoring: The effects of type of mentor, quality of relationship, and program design on work and career attitudes. *Academy of Management Journal, 43,* 1179–1194.

28. Clutterbuck, D., & Ragins, B. R. (2002). *Mentoring and diversity: An international perspective.* Burlington, MA: Butterworth-Heinemann. Wickman, F., & Sjodin, T. (1997). *Mentoring.* Chicago: Irwin.

Glossary

360-degree feedback. The process of systematically giving and receiving feedback between individuals at various organizational levels.

abilities. Mental and physical capacities to perform various tasks.

abusive supervision. A pattern of supervision in which a boss engages in sustained displays of hostile verbal and nonverbal behaviors.

achievement motivation (or need for achievement). The strength of an individual's desire to excel—to succeed at difficult tasks and to do them better than other persons.

action lab. An OD intervention in which teams of participants work off-site to develop and implement new ways of solving organizational problems by focusing on the ineffectiveness of current methods.

action learning. A leadership development technique involving a continuous process of learning and reflection that is supported by colleagues and that emphasizes getting things done.

action plan. A carefully specified set of guidelines indicating exactly what needs to be done to attain desired results.

ad hoc committee. A temporary committee formed for a special purpose.

additive tasks. Types of group tasks in which the coordinated efforts of several people are added together to form the group's product.

adhocracy. A highly informal, organic organization in which specialists work in teams, coordinating with each other on various projects (e.g., many software development companies).

adhocracy culture. In the competing values framework, organizations that emphasize flexibility while also paying a great deal of attention to the external environment; characterized by recognition that to succeed an organization needs to be highly innovative and constantly assessing what the future requires for it to survive.

administrative model. A model of decision making that recognizes that people have imperfect views of problems, which limits the making of optimally rational-economic decisions.

affective commitment. The strength of a person's desire to work for an organization because he or she agrees with it and wants to do so.

affective conflict. A form of conflict resulting when people experience clashes of personality or interpersonal tension, resulting in frustration and anger.

affective events theory (AET). The theory that identifies various factors that lead to people's emotional reactions on the job and how these reactions affect those individuals.

affiliate networks. Satellite organizations affiliated with core companies that have helped them develop.

affirmative action laws. Legislation designed to give employment opportunities to groups that have been underrepresented in the workforce, such as women and members of minority groups.

agreeableness. A tendency to be compassionate toward others; one of the Big Five personality dimensions.

alternative dispute resolution (ADR). A set of procedures, such as mediation and arbitration, in which disputing parties work together with a neutral party who helps them settle their disagreements out of court.

analytical model of the decision-making process. A conceptualization of the eight steps through which individuals and groups make decisions: identify the problem, define objectives, make a predecision, generate alternatives, evaluate alternatives, make a choice, implement choice.

anger. A heightened state of emotional arousal (e.g., increased heart rate, rapid breathing, flushed face, sweaty palms, etc.) fueled by cognitive interpretations of situations.

anger management. Systematic efforts to reduce people's emotional feelings of anger and the physiological arousal it causes.

appreciative inquiry (AI). An OD intervention that focuses attention away from an organization's shortcoming, and toward its capabilities and its potential; based on the assumption that members of organizations already know the problems they face and that they stand to benefit more by focusing on what is possible.

apprenticeship programs. Formal training programs involving both on-the-job and classroom training usually over a long period, often used for training people in the skilled trades.

arbitration. A process in which a third party (known as an arbitrator) has the power to impose, or at least to recommend, the terms of an agreement between two or more conflicting parties.

asynchronous communication techniques. Forms of communication in which senders and receivers must take turns sending and receiving messages.

attitudes. Relatively stable clusters of feelings, beliefs, and behavioral intentions toward specific objects, people, or institutions.

attribute framing effect. The tendency for people to evaluate a characteristic more positively when it is presented in positive terms than when it is presented in negative terms.

attribution. The process through which individuals attempt to determine the causes behind others' behavior.

attribution approach (to leadership). The approach to leadership that focuses on leaders' attributions of followers' performance—that is, their perceptions of its underlying causes.

authentic leaders. Highly moral individuals who are confident, hopeful, optimistic, and resilient, and who are highly aware of the contexts in which they operate.

autocratic (leadership style). A style of leadership in which the leader makes all decisions unilaterally.

autocratic-delegation continuum model. An approach to leadership describing the ways in which leaders allocate influence to subordinates. This ranges from controlling everything (autocratic) to allowing others to make decisions for themselves (delegating). Between these extremes are more participative forms of leadership— consulting and making joint decisions.

autonomous change. A change in one part of an organization that is made independently of the need for change in another part.

availability heuristic. The tendency for people to base their judgments on information that is readily available to them although it may be potentially inaccurate, thereby adversely affecting decision quality.

avoidance. See *negative reinforcement.*

avoidance goal orientation. The desire to achieve success to avoid appearing incompetent and to avoid receiving negative evaluation from others.

awareness-based diversity training. A type of diversity management program designed to make people more aware of diversity issues in the workplace and to get them to recognize the underlying assumptions they make about people.

baby boom generation. The generation of children born in the economic boom period following World War II.

balanced contracts. Psychological contracts that combine the open-ended, long-term features of relational psychological contracts with the well-specified reward-performance contingencies of transactional contracts.

bargaining (negotiation). The process by which two or more parties in dispute with one another exchange offers, counteroffers, and concessions in an attempt to find a mutually acceptable agreement.

behavioral component (of attitudes). Our predisposition to behave in a way consistent with our beliefs and feelings about an attitude object.

behavioral sciences. Fields such as psychology and sociology that seek knowledge of human behavior and society through the use of the scientific method.

benchmarking. The process of comparing one's own products or services with the best from others.

Big Five dimensions of personality. Five basic dimensions of personality that are assumed to underlie many specific traits.

binding arbitration. A form of arbitration in which the two sides agree in advance to accept the terms set by the arbitrator, whatever he or she may be.

blogs (Web logs). Web pages in which people express their personal experiences and feelings; an Internet-based diary.

bogie rumors. Rumors that are based on people's fears and anxieties.

bottom line mentality. The belief that an organization's financial success is the only thing that matters.

boundaryless organization. An organization in which chains of command are eliminated, spans of control are unlimited, and rigid departments give way to empowered teams.

bounded discretion. The tendency to restrict decision alternatives to those that fall within prevailing ethical standards.

bounded rationality. The major assumption of the administrative model—that organizational, social, and human limitations lead to the making of satisficing rather than optimal decisions.

brainstorming. A technique designed to foster group productivity by encouraging interacting group members to express their ideas in a noncritical fashion.

brown bag meetings. Informal get-togethers over meals in which people discuss what's going on in their company.

bureaucracy. An organizational design developed by Max Weber that attempts to make organizations operate efficiently by having a clear hierarchy of authority in which people are required to perform well-defined jobs.

burnout. A syndrome of emotional, physical, and mental exhaustion coupled with feelings of low self-esteem or low self-efficacy, resulting from prolonged exposure to intense stress, and the strain reactions following from them.

business continuity plans. Systematic sets of plans designed to help organizations get up and running again in the event of a disruption of some sort.

business ethics. The study of people's tendencies to behave in morally appropriate ways in organizations.

cafeteria-style benefit plans. Incentive systems in which employees have an opportunity to select the fringe benefits they want from a menu of available alternatives.

calculus-based trust. A form of trust based on deterrence; whenever people believe that another will behave as promised out of fear of getting punished for doing otherwise.

career. The evolving sequence of work experiences over time.

career anchor. A person's occupational self-concept based on his or her self-perceived talents, abilities, needs, and motives.

career plateau. The point at which one's career has peaked and is unlikely to develop further.

career development interventions. Systematic efforts to help manage people's careers while simultaneously helping the organizations in which they work.

case method. A research technique in which a particular organization is thoroughly described and analyzed for purposes of understanding what went on in that setting.

centrality. The degree to which an organizational unit has a key impact on others because it has to be consulted and because its activities have immediate effects on an organization.

ceremonies. Celebrations of an organization's basic values and assumptions.

channels of communication. The pathways over which messages are transmitted (e.g., telephone lines, mail, etc.).

charisma. An attitude of enthusiasm and optimism that is contagious; an aura of leadership.

charismatic leaders. Leaders who exert especially powerful effects on followers by virtue of the attributions followers make about them. Such individuals have high amounts of self-confidence, present a clearly articulated vision, behave in extraordinary ways, are recognized as change agents, and are sensitive to the environmental constraints they face.

child-care facilities. Sites at or near company locations where parents can leave their children while they are working.

circumplex model of affect. A theory of emotional behavior based on the degree to which emotions are pleasant or unpleasant and the degree to which they make one feel activated (i.e., feeling alert and engaged).

clan culture. In the competing values framework, an organization characterized by a strong internal focus along with a high degree of flexibility and discretion; with goals that are highly shared by members of the organization and high levels of cohesiveness, such organizations feel more like extended families than economic entities.

classical organizational theory. An early approach to the study of management that focused on the most efficient way of structuring organizations.

classical organizational theory. Approaches assuming that there is a single best way to design organizations.

classroom training. The process of teaching people how to do their jobs by explaining various job requirements and how to meet them.

coalition-building. A form of social influence in which an individual seeks the assistance of others in a coalition by telling them about the support he or she already has.

code of ethics. A document describing what an organization stands for and the general rules of conduct expected of employees (e.g., to avoid conflicts of interest, to be honest, and so on).

coercive power. The individual power base derived from the capacity to administer punishment to others.

cognitive appraisal. A judgment about the stressfulness of a situation based on the extent to which someone perceives a stressor as threatening and is capable of coping with its demands.

cognitive component (of attitudes). The things we believe about an attitude object, whether they are true or false.

cognitive intelligence. The ability to understand complex ideas, to adapt effectively to the environment, to learn from experience, to engage in various forms of reasoning, and to overcome obstacles with careful thought.

cognitive moral development. Differences between people in the capacity to engage in the kind of reasoning that enables them to make moral judgments.

cohesiveness. The strength of group members' desires to remain a part of the group.

collaboration. A form of social influence in which an individual makes it easier for a target person to agree to a request.

collectivistic cultures. Cultures in which people placed high value on shared responsibility and the collective good of all.

command group. A group determined by the connections between individuals who are a formal part of the organization (i.e., those who legitimately can give orders to others).

communication. The process by which a person, group, or organization (the sender) transmits some type of information (the message) to another person, group, or organization (the receiver).

competing values framework. A conceptualization of organizational culture that specifies that cultures of organizations differ with respect to two sets of opposite values: (1) valuing flexibility and discretion as opposed to stability, order, and control, and (2) valuing internal affairs as opposed to what's going on in the external environment.

competition. A pattern of behavior in which each person, group, or organization seeks to maximize its own gains, often at the expense of others.

competitive advantage. The benefits enjoyed by an organization to the extent that its customers perceive its products or services as being superior to the products or services of another organization.

competitors. People whose primary motive is doing better than others, besting them in open competition.

compressed workweeks. The practice of working fewer days each week, but longer hours each day (e.g., four 10-hour days).

computer-assisted communication. The sharing of information, such as text messages and data relevant to the decision, over computer networks.

computerized performance monitoring. The process of using computers to monitor job performance.

computer-mediated communication. Forms of communication that are aided by the use of computer technology (e.g., e-mail, instant messaging).

confirmation candidate. A decision alternative considered only for purposes of convincing onself of the wisdom of selecting the implicit favorite.

conflict. A process in which one party perceives that another party has taken or will take actions that are incompatible with one's own interests.

conglomerate. A form of organizational diversification in which an organization (usually a very large, multinational one) adds an entirely unrelated business or product to its organizational design.

conjunctive statements. Statements that keep conversations going by connecting one speaker's remarks to another's.

conscientiousness. A tendency to show self-discipline, to strive for competence and achievement; one of the Big Five personality dimensions.

consensus. In Kelley's theory of causal attribution, information regarding the extent to which other people behave in the same manner as the person we're judging.

consideration. Actions by a leader that demonstrate concern with the welfare of subordinates and establish positive relations with them. Leaders who focus primarily on this task are often described as demonstrating a person-oriented style.

consistency. In Kelley's theory of causal attribution, information regarding the extent to which the person we're judging acts the same way at other times.

constructive organizational deviance. Actions that deviate from organizational norms but are consistent with societal norms.

consultation. A form of social influence in which an individual asks a target person to participate in decision making or planning a change.

contingencies of reinforcement. The various relationships between one's behavior and the consequences of that behavior—positive reinforcement, negative reinforcement, punishment, and extinction.

contingency approach. A perspective suggesting that organizational behavior is affected by a large number of interacting factors. How someone will behave is said to be contingent upon many different variables at once.

contingency approach to organizational design. The contemporary approach that recognizes that no one approach to organizational design is best, but that the best design is the one that best fits with the existing environmental conditions.

contingency theories of leadership. Any of several theories which recognize that certain styles of leadership are more effective in some situations than others.

contingent workforce. People hired by organizations temporarily, to work as needed for finite periods of time.

continuance commitment. The strength of a person's desire to continue working for an organization because he or she needs to do so and cannot afford to do otherwise.

continuous reinforcement. A schedule of reinforcement in which all desired behaviors are reinforced.

conventional arbitration. A form of arbitration in which an arbitrator can offer any package or terms he or she wishes.

conventional level of moral reasoning. In Kohlberg's theory of cognitive moral development, the level attained by most people, in which they judge right and wrong in terms of what is good for others and society as a whole.

convergence hypothesis. A biased approach to the study of management, which assumes that principles of good management are universal, and that ones that work well in the U.S. will apply equally well in other nations.

cooperation. A pattern of behavior in which assistance is mutual and two or more individuals, groups, or organizations work together toward shared goals for their mutual benefit.

cooperators. People who are concerned with maximizing joint outcomes, getting as much as possible for their team.

core competency. An organization's key capability, what it does best.

core self-evaluation. People's fundamental evaluations of themselves, their bottom-line conclusions about themselves.

corporate ethics programs. Formal, systematic efforts designed to promote ethics by making people sensitive to potentially unethical behavior and discouraging them from engaging in unethical acts.

corporate hotlines. Telephone lines staffed by corporate personnel ready to answer employees' questions, listen to their comments, and the like.

corporate image. The impressions that people have of an organization.

corporate social responsibility. Business practices that adhere to ethical values that comply with legal requirements, that demonstrate respect for individuals, and that promote the betterment of the community at large and the environment.

corporate universities. Centers devoted to handling a company's training needs on a full-time basis.

correlation. The extent to which two variables are related to each other.

correlation coefficient. A statistical index indicating the nature and extent to which two variables are related to each other.

correspondent inferences. Judgments about people's dispositions, their traits and characteristics, that correspond to what we have observed of their actions.

counternorms. Practices that are accepted within an organization despite the fact that they are contrary to the prevailing ethical standards of society at large.

counterpower. The capacity to neutralize another's influence attempts.

creativity. The process by which individuals or teams produce novel and useful ideas.

creativity heuristics. Rules that people follow to help them approach tasks in novel ways.

critical incident technique. A procedure for measuring job satisfaction in which employees describe incidents relating to their work that they find especially satisfying or dissatisfying.

cross-cultural training (CCT). A systematic way of preparing employees to live and work in another country.

cross-functional teams. Teams represented by people from different specialty areas within organizations.

cultural due diligence analysis. Before a merger or acquisition is finalized, the process of analyzing the cultures of both organizations to ensure their compatibility.

cultural intelligence. A person's sensitivity to the fact that leaders operate differently in different cultures.

culture. The set of values, customs, and beliefs that people have in common with other members of a social unit (e.g., a nation).

culture clashes. Problems resulting from attempts to merge two or more organizational cultures that are incompatible.

culture shock. The tendency for people to become confused and disoriented as they attempt to adjust to a new culture.

cyberloafing. The practice of using a company's e-mail and/or Internet facilities for personal use.

daily hassles. Unpleasant or undesirable events that put people in bad moods.

daily uplifts. Pleasant or desirable events that put people in good moods.

decentralization. The degree to which the capacity to make decisions resides in several people as opposed to one or just a handful.

decentralization. The extent to which authority and decision making are spread throughout all levels of an organization rather than being reserved for top management (centralization).

decision making. The process of making choices from among several alternatives.

decision stream. An interconnected set of decisions.

decision style. Differences between people with respect to their orientations toward decisions.

decision style model. The conceptualization according to which people use one of four predominant decision styles: directive, analytical, conceptual, or behavioral.

decision support systems (DSS). Computer programs in which information about organizational behavior is presented to decision makers in a manner that helps them structure their responses to decisions.

decoding. The process by which a receiver of messages transforms them back into the sender's ideas.

defensive avoidance. The tendency for decision makers to fail to solve problems because they go out of their way to avoid working on the problem at hand.

Delphi technique. A method of improving group decisions using the opinions of experts, which are solicited by mail and then compiled. The expert consensus of opinions is used to make a decision.

departmentalization. The process of breaking up organizations into coherent units.

dependent variable. A variable that is measured by the researcher, the one influenced by the *independent variable.*

depersonalization. A pattern of behavior occurring in burnout marked by becoming cynical toward others, treating others as objects, and holding negative attitudes toward others.

desk rage. Lashing out at others in response to stressful encounters on the job.

destructive criticism. Negative feedback that angers the recipient instead of helping him or her do a better job.

destructive organizational deviance. A form of behavior that violates both organizational and societal norms.

deviant organizational behavior. Actions on the part of employees that intentionally violate the norms of organizations and/or the formal rules of society, resulting in negative consequences.

direct report Someone in an organization, a subordinate, who must answer directly to a higher-level individual in that organization.

discipline. The process of systematically administering punishments.

discrimination. The behavior consistent with a prejudicial attitude; the act of treating someone negatively because of his or her membership in a specific group.

disjunctive statements. Statements that are disconnected from a previous statement, tending to bring conversations to a close.

display rules. Cultural norms about the appropriate ways to express emotions.

displayed emotions. Emotions that people show others, which may or may not be in line with their felt emotions.

dispositional model of job satisfaction. The conceptualization proposing that job satisfaction is a relatively stable disposition of an individual—that is, a characteristic that stays with people across situations.

disruptive innovation. A form of innovation that is so extreme in nature that it changes the market in which companies operate.

distinctiveness. In Kelley's theory of causal attribution, information regarding the extent to which a person behaves in the same manner in other contexts.

distributive justice. The form of organizational justice that focuses on people's beliefs that they have received fair amounts of valued work-related outcomes (e.g., pay, recognition, etc.).

divergence hypothesis. The approach to the study of management which recognizes that knowing how to manage most effectively requires clear understanding of the culture in which people work.

divergent thinking. The process of reframing familiar problems in unique ways.

diversity management programs. Programs in which employees are taught to celebrate the differences between people and in which organizations create supportive work environments for women and minorities.

division of labor. The process of dividing the many tasks performed within an organization into specialized jobs.

divisional structure. The form used by many large organizations, in which separate autonomous units are created to deal with entire product lines, freeing top management to focus on larger scale, strategic decisions.

dominant culture. The distinctive, overarching "personality" of an organization.

doomsday management. The practice of introducing change by suggesting that an impending crisis is likely.

downsizing. The process of adjusting the number of employees needed to work in newly-designed organizations (also known as rightsizing).

downward communication. Communication from people at higher organizational levels to those at lower organizational levels.

drive theory of social facilitation. The theory according to which the presence of others increases arousal, which increases people's tendencies to perform the dominant response. If that response is well learned, performance will improve. But if it is novel, performance will be impaired.

elder-care facilities. Facilities at which employees at work can leave elderly relatives for whom they are responsible (such as parents and grandparents).

electronic meeting systems. The practice of bringing individuals from different locations together for a meeting via telephone or satellite transmissions, either on television monitors, or via shared space on a computer screen.

e-mail (electronic mail). A system whereby people use personal computer terminals to send and receive messages between one another using the Internet.

emoticons (emotional icons). Symbols typed using characters such as commas, hyphens, and parentheses for purposes of expressing emotions in online communication.

emotional contagion. The tendency to mimic the emotional expressions of others, converging with them emotionally.

emotional dissonance. Inconsistencies between the emotions we feel and the emotions we express.

emotional intelligence (EI). A cluster of skills relating to the emotional side life (e.g., the ability to recognize and regulate our own emotions, to influence those of others, to self-motivate).

emotional labor. The psychological effort involved in holding back one's true emotions.

emotional stability. The tendency to see oneself as confident, secure, and steady (the opposite of neuroticism, one of the Big Five personality variables).

emotions. Overt reactions that express feelings about events.

employee assistance programs (EAPs). Plans offered by employers that provide their employees with assistance for various personal problems (e.g., substance abuse, career planning, financial and legal problems).

employee handbook. A document describing to employees basic information about a company; a general reference regarding a company's background, the nature of its business, and its rules.

employee surveys. Questionnaires designed to assess how employees feel about their organization.

employee theft. The taking of company property for personal use.

employee withdrawal. Actions, such as chronic absenteeism and voluntary turnover (i.e., quitting one's job), that enable employees to escape from adverse organizational situations.

empowered decision making. The practice of vesting power for making decisions in the hands of employees themselves.

empowerment climate. A relatively enduring atmosphere in the workplace that is supportive of empowerment.

empowerment. The passing of responsibility and authority from managers to employees.

encoding. The process by which an idea is transformed so that it can be transmitted to, and recognized by, a receiver (e.g., a written or spoken message).

end-user innovation. The form of innovation in which new ideas are inspired by the individuals who use a company's products.

engagement. A mutual commitment between employers and employees to do things to help one another achieve each other's goals and aspirations.

equalizers. People who are primarily interested in minimizing the differences between themselves and others.

equitable payment. The state in which one person's outcome-input ratios is equivalent to that of another person with whom this individual compares himself or herself.

equity theory. The theory stating that people strive to maintain ratios of their own outcomes (rewards) to their own inputs (contributions) that are equal to the outcome/input ratios of others with whom they compare themselves.

escalation of commitment phenomenon. The tendency for individuals to continue to support previously unsuccessful courses of action.

esteem needs. In Maslow's need hierarchy theory, the need to develop self-respect and to gain the approval of others.

ethical imperialism. The belief that the ethical standards of one's own country should be imposed when doing business in other countries (the opposite of ethical relativism).

ethical relativism. The belief that no culture's ethics are better than any other's and that there are no internationally acceptable standards of right and wrong (the opposite of ethical imperialism).

ethics. Standards of conduct that guide people's decisions and behavior (e.g., not stealing from others).

ethics audit. The practice of assessing an organization's ethical practices by actively investigating and documenting incidents of dubious ethical value, discussing them in an open and honest fashion, and developing a concrete plan to avoid such actions in the future.

ethics committee. A group composed of senior-level managers from various areas of an organization who assist an organization's CEO in making ethical decisions by developing and evaluating company-wide ethics policies.

ethics hotlines (or helplines). Special telephone lines that employees can call to ask questions about ethical behavior and to report any ethical misdeeds they may have observed.

ethics officer. A high-ranking organizational official (e.g., the general counsel or vice president of ethics) who is expected to provide strategies for ensuring ethical conduct throughout an organization.

ethnocentrism. A bias toward one's own subgroup and against other subgroups.

ethnorelativistic thinking. Taking the perspective of another group and understanding how they see the world, including one's own group.

e-training. Training based on disseminating information online, such as through the Internet or a company's internal intranet network.

evaluation apprehension. The fear of being evaluated or judged by another person.

evaluative component (of attitudes). Our liking or disliking of any particular person, item, or event.

evening persons. Individuals who feel most energetic and alert late in the day or at night.

exchange. A form of social influence in which an individual promises some benefits to a target person upon complying with his or her request.

executive coaching. A technique of leadership development that involves custom-tailored, on-on-one learning aimed at improving an individual leader's performance.

executive training programs. Sessions in which companies systematically attempt to develop their top leaders, either in specific skills or general managerial skills.

expatriates. People who are citizens of one country, but who are living and working in another country.

exit strategies. The tactic by which a company withdraws from a market, such as by liquidating its assets.

expectancy. The belief that one's efforts will positively influence one's performance.

expectancy theory. The theory that asserts that motivation is based on people's beliefs about the probability that effort will lead to performance (expectancy), multiplied by the probability that performance will lead to reward (instrumentality), multiplied by the perceived value of the reward (valence).

experimental method. A research technique through which it is possible to determine cause-effect relationships between the variables of interest—that is, the extent to which one variable causes another.

expert power. The individual power base derived from an individual's recognized superior skills and abilities in a certain area.

exploitative mentality. The belief that one's own immediate interests are more important than concern for others.

external causes of behavior. Explanations based on situations over which the individual has no control.

extinction. The process through which responses that are no longer reinforced tend to gradually diminish in strength.

extraversion. A tendency to seek stimulation and to enjoy the company of other people; one of the Big Five personality dimensions.

fair process effect. The tendency for people to better accept outcomes into which they have had some input in determining than when they have no such involvement.

faultline. A condition in which the key attributes of group members are correlated across group membership instead of cutting across group membership.

feedback. Knowledge about the impact of messages on receivers.

feedback. Knowledge of the results of one's behavior.

felt emotions. The emotions people actually feel (which may differ from displayed emotions).

final-offer arbitration. A form of arbitration in which the arbitrator chooses between final offers made by the disputing parties themselves.

first-impression error. The tendency to base our judgments of others on our earlier impressions of them.

first-order change. Change that is continuous in nature and involves no major shifts in the way an organization operates.

five-state mode. The conceptualization claiming that groups develop in five stages—forming, storming, norming, performing, and adjourning.

fixed interval schedules. Schedules of reinforcement in which a fixed period of time must elapse between the administration of reinforcements.

fixed ratio schedules. Schedules of reinforcement in which a fixed number of responses must occur between the administration of reinforcements.

flaming. The practice of overexpressing one's emotions by sending emotionally charged messages to another via e-mail.

flextime programs. Policies that give employees some discretion over when they can arrive and leave work, thereby making it easier to adapt their work schedules to the demands of their personal lives.

formal communication. The sharing of messages regarding the official work of the organization.

formal groups. Groups that are created by the organization, intentionally designed to direct its members toward some organizational goal.

formal status. The prestige one has by virtue of his or her official position in an organization.

framing. The tendency for people to make different decisions based on how the problem is presented to them.

friendship groups. Informal groups that develop because their members are friends, often seeing each other outside of the organization.

functional organization. The type of departmentalization based on the activities or functions performed (e.g., sales, finance).

fundamental attribution error. The tendency to attribute others' actions to internal causes (e.g., their traits) while largely ignoring external factors that also may have influenced behavior.

gatekeepers. People responsible for controlling the flow of information to others to keep them from becoming overloaded.

generalized self-efficacy. A person's beliefs about his or her capacity to perform specific tasks successfully.

globalization. The process of interconnecting the world's people with respect to the cultural, economic, political, technological, and environmental aspects of their lives.

goal commitment. The degree to which people accept and strive to attain goals.

goal framing effect. The tendency for people to be more strongly persuaded by information that is framed in negative terms than information that is framed in positive terms.

goal setting. The process of determining specific levels of performance for workers to attain and then striving to attain them.

goal-setting theory. A popular theory specifying that people are motivated to attain goals because doing so makes them feel successful.

Golem effect. A negative instance of the self-fulfilling prophecy, in which people holding low expectations of another tend to lower that individual's performance.

grapevine. An organization's informal channels of communication, based mainly on friendship or acquaintance.

grassroots leadership. An approach to leadership that turns the traditional management hierarchy upside-down by empowering people to make their own decisions.

great person theory. The view that leaders possess special traits that set them apart from others, and that these traits are responsible for their assuming positions of power and authority.

grid training. A multi-step process designed to cultivate concern for people and concern for production.

group. A collection of two or more interacting individuals who maintain stable patterns of relationships, share common goals, and perceive themselves as being a group.

group decision support systems (GDSS). Interactive computer-based systems that combine communication, computer, and decision technologies to improve the effectiveness of group problem-solving meetings.

group dynamics. The social science field focusing on the nature of groups—the factors governing their formation and development, the elements of their structure, and their interrelationships with individuals, other groups, and organizations.

group structure. The pattern of interrelationships between the individuals constituting a group; the guidelines of group behavior that make group functioning orderly and predictable.

groupthink. The tendency for members of highly cohesive groups to so strongly conform to group pressures regarding a certain decision that they fail to think critically, rejecting the potentially correcting influences of outsiders.

group-value explanation (of organizational justice). The idea that people believe they are an important part of the organization when an organizational official takes the time to explain thoroughly to them the rationale behind a decision.

growth need strength. The personality variable describing the extent to which people have a high need for personal growth and development on the job. The job characteristics model best describes people high in growth need strength.

guanxi. In China, a person's network of personal and business connections.

halo effect. The tendency for our overall impressions of others to affect objective evaluations of their specific traits; perceiving high correlations between characteristics that may be unrelated.

hangover effect The tendency for people's levels of satisfaction to drop over time from when a position is brand new to when one gains more experience with it.

Hawthorne studies. The earliest systematic research in the field of OB, this work was performed to determine how the design of work environments affected performance.

healthy organizational cultures. Organizational cultures in which people feel that they are valued (opposite of toxic organizational cultures).

heuristics. Simple decision rules (rules of thumb) used to make quick decisions about complex problems. (See *availability heuristic* and *representativeness heuristic*.)

hierarchy culture. In the competing values framework, a form of organizational culture in which organizations have an internal focus and emphasize stability and control.

hierarchy of authority. A configuration of the reporting relationships within organizations; that is, who reports to whom.

high performance work systems. Organizations that offer employees opportunities to participate in decision making, provide incentives for them to do so, and emphasize opportunities to develop skills.

hindsight bias. The tendency for people to perceive outcomes as more inevitable after they have occurred (i.e., in hindsight) than they did before they occurred (i.e., in foresight).

Holland's hexagon. A conceptualization specifying the occupations for which people are best suited based on which of six personality types most closely describe them.

Holland's theory of vocational choice. A theory that claims that people will perform best at occupations that match their traits and personalities.

home-stretchers. Rumors designed to reduce the degree of ambiguity in a situation by telling a story about something before it happens.

honeymoon effect The tendency for people to enjoy high levels of satisfaction on new jobs that they have taken in response to dissatisfaction with their old jobs.

honeymoon-hangover effect. The tendency for the honeymoon effect to occur (i.e., for job satisfaction to increase as a dissatisfied person takes a new job) followed by the hangover effect (i.e., for the high levels of satisfaction associated with a new job to decline over time).

horizontal stretch goals. Stretch goals that challenge people to perform tasks that they have never done.

hostile environment sexual harassment. A form of sexual harassment in which individuals are subjected to negative, unwanted, or abusive conditions under which their ability to work effectively and comfortably is compromised.

human relations movement. A perspective on organizational behavior that rejects the primarily economic orientation of scientific management and recognizes, instead, the importance of social processes in work settings.

HURIER model. The conceptualization that describes effective listening as made up of the following six components: hearing, understanding, remembering, interpreting, evaluating, and responding.

hypervigilance. The state in which an individual frantically searches for quick solutions to problems, and goes from one idea to another out of a sense of desperation that one idea isn't working and that another needs to be considered before time runs out.

hypotheses. Logically derived, testable statements about the relationships between variables that follow from a theory.

identification-based trust. A form of trust based on accepting the wants and desires of another person.

idiosyncratic work arrangements (i-deals). Uniquely customized agreements negotiated between individual employees and their employers with respect to employment terms benefiting each party.

image theory. A theory of decision making that recognizes that decisions are made in an automatic, intuitive fashion. According to the theory, people will adopt a course of action that best fits their individual principles, current goals, and plans for the future.

implicit favorite. One's preferred decision alternative, selected even before all options have been considered.

impression management. Efforts by individuals to improve how they appear to others.

improvement teams. Teams whose members are oriented primarily toward the mission of increasing the effectiveness of the processes used by the organization.

incentive stock option (ISO) plans. Corporate programs in which a company grants an employee the opportunity to purchase its stock at some future time at a specified price.

incivility. Demonstrating a lack of regard for others, denying them the respect they are due.

incremental innovation. A slow-and-steady approach to innovation, in which companies exploit existing technology and operate under conditions in which uncertainty about the future is low.

incubator. A company that specializes in starting up new businesses.

independent variable. A variable that is systematically manipulated by the experimenter so as to determine its effects on the behavior of interest (i.e., the *dependent variable*).

individual differences The many ways in which individuals can differ from each other.

individualistic cultures. National groups whose members place a high value on individual accomplishments and personal success.

individualists. People who care almost exclusively about maximizing their own gain and don't care whether others do better or worse than themselves.

informal communication. The sharing of unofficial messages, ones that go beyond the organization's formal activities.

informal communication network. The informal connections between people; the pathways through which they share informal information.

informal groups. Groups that develop naturally among people, without any direction from the organization within which they operate.

informal status. The prestige accorded individuals with certain characteristics that are not formally recognized by the organization.

informate. The process by which workers manipulate objects by "inserting data" between themselves and those objects.

information anxiety. Pressure to store and process a great deal of information in our head and to keep up constantly with gathering it.

information power. The extent to which a supervisor provides a subordinate with the information needed to do the job.

informational justice. People's perceptions of the fairness of the information used as the basis for making a decision.

ingratiation. The process of getting someone to do what you want by putting that person in a good mood or by getting him or her to like you.

initiating structure. Activities by a leader designed to enhance productivity or task performance. Leaders who focus primarily on these goals are described as demonstrating a task-oriented style.

innovation. The process of making changes to something already established by introducing something new; the successful implementation of creative ideas within an organization.

inputs. People's contributions to their jobs, such as their experience, qualifications, or the amount of time worked.

inspirational appeals. A form of social influence in which an individual arouses enthusiasm by appealing to a target person's values and ideals.

instant messaging. The practice of communicating with another online by typing messages into boxes that pop up on the screen as needed.

instrumental conditioning. See *operant conditioning*.

instrumentality. An individual's beliefs regarding the likelihood of being rewarded in accord with his or her own level of performance.

integrative agreement. A type of solution to a conflict situation in which the parties consider joint benefits that go beyond a simple compromise.

interactionist perspective. The view that behavior is a result of a complex interplay between personality and situational factors.

interest groups. A group of employees who come together to satisfy a common interest.

intermittent reinforcement. See *partial reinforcement.*

internal causes of behavior. Explanations based on actions for which the individual is responsible.

interpersonal behavior. A variety of behaviors involving the ways in which people work with and against one another.

interpersonal justice. People's perceptions of the fairness of the manner in which they are treated by others (typically, authority figures).

intrinsic task motivation. The motivation to do work because it is interesting, engaging, or challenging in a positive way.

invalidating language. Language that arouses negative feelings about one's self-worth.

jargon. The specialized language used by a particular group (e.g., people within a profession).

job. A predetermined set of activities one is expected to perform.

job characteristics model. An approach to job enrichment which specifies that five core job dimensions (skill variety, task identity, task significance, autonomy, and job feedback) produce critical psychological states that lead to beneficial outcomes for individuals

Job Descriptive Index (JDI). A rating scale for assessing job satisfaction. Individuals respond to this questionnaire by indicating whether or not various adjectives describe aspects of their work.

job design. An approach to motivation suggesting that jobs can be created so as to enhance people's interest in doing them. See *job enlargement, job enrichment,* and the *job characteristics model.*

job enlargement. The practice of expanding the content of a job to include more variety and a greater number of tasks at the same level.

job enrichment. The practice of giving employees a high degree of control over their work, from planning and organization, through implementing the jobs and evaluating the results.

job satisfaction. Positive or negative attitudes held by individuals toward their jobs.

job sharing. A form of regular part-time work in which pairs of employees assume the duties of a single job, splitting its responsibilities, salary, and benefits in proportion to the time worked.

joint ventures. Strategic alliances in which several companies work together to fulfill opportunities that require one another's capabilities.

Kelley's theory of causal attribution. The approach suggesting that people will believe others' actions to be caused by internal or external factors based on three types of information: consensus, consistency, and distinctiveness.

Kohlberg's theory of cognitive moral development. The theory based on the idea that people develop over the years in their capacity to understand what is right and wrong.

lateral communication. Communication between individuals at the same organizational level.

Law of Effect. The tendency for behaviors leading to desirable consequences to be strengthened and those leading to undesirable consequences to be weakened.

leader. An individual within a group or an organization who wields the most influence over others.

leader match. The practice of matching leaders (based on their LPC scores) to the groups whose situations best match those in which they are expected to be most effective (according to LPC contingency theory).

leader-member exchange (LMX) model. A theory suggesting that leaders form different relations with various subordinates and that the nature of such dyadic exchanges can exert strong effects on subordinates' performance and satisfaction.

leadership. The process whereby one individual influences other group members toward the attainment of defined group or organizational goals.

leadership development. The practice of systematically training people to expand their capacity to function effectively in leadership roles.

leadership motivation. The desire to influence others, especially toward the attainment of shared goals.

learning. A relatively permanent change in behavior occurring as a result of experience.

learning goal orientation. The desire to perform well because it satisfies an interest in meeting a challenge and learning new skills.

learning organization. An organization that is successful at acquiring, cultivating, and applying knowledge that can be used to help it adapt to changes.

legitimate power. The individual power base derived from one's position in an organizational hierarchy; the accepted authority of one's position.

legitimating. A form of social influence in which an individual calls attention to his or her authority to make a request or verifies that the request is consistent with prevailing organizational policies and practices.

line positions. Positions in an organization in which people can make decisions related to doing its basic work.

linear career. The type of career in which someone stays in a certain field and works his or her way up the occupational ladder, from low-level jobs to high-level jobs.

locus of control. The extent to which individuals feel that they are able to control things in a manner that affects them.

LPC. Short for "esteem for least preferred co-worker"—a personality variable distinguishing between individuals with respect to their concern for people (high LPC) and their concern for production (low LPC).

LPC contingency theory. A theory suggesting that leader effectiveness is determined both by characteristics of leaders (their LPC scores) and by the level of situational control they are able to exert over subordinates.

Machiavellianism. A personality trait involving willingness to manipulate others for one's own purposes.

machine bureaucracy. An organizational form in which work is highly specialized, decision making is concentrated at the top, and the work environment is not prone to change (e.g., a government office).

Madison Avenue mentality. A way of viewing the world according to which people are more concerned about how things appear to others than how they really are—that is, the appearance of doing the right thing matters more than the actual behavior.

Malcolm Baldrige Quality Award. An award given annually to American companies that practice effective quality management and make significant improvements in the quality of their goods and services.

management by objectives (MBO). The technique by which managers and their subordinates work together to set, and then meet, organizational goals.

manufacturer innovation. The traditional form of innovation in which an individual or organization develops an innovation for the purpose of selling it.

market concentration strategies. The tactic of withdrawing from markets where a company is less effective, and concentrating resources instead in markets where the company is likely to be more effective.

market culture. In the competing values framework, a form of organizational culture in which organizations are concerned with stability and control, but are external in their orientation; core values emphasize competitiveness and productivity, focusing on bottom-line results.

market-share increasing strategies. A deliberate attempt on the part of a company to develop a broader share of an existing market (such as by widening the range of products, or forming a joint venture with another company that has a presence in the market of interest).

matrix organization. The type of departmentalization in which a product or project form is superimposed on a functional form.

mechanistic organization. An internal organizational structure in which people perform specialized jobs, many rigid rules are imposed, and authority is vested in a few top-ranking officials.

media richness theory. A conceptualization specifying that the effectiveness of any verbal medium depends on the extent to which it is appropriate in view of the ambiguity of the message being sent.

mediation. The process in which a neutral party (known as a mediator) works together with two or more parties sides to reach a settlement to their conflict.

meditation. The process of learning to clear one's mind of external thoughts, often by repeating a single syllable (known as a mantra) over and over again.

member assistance programs (MAPs). Plans offered by trade unions that provide their members with assistance for various personal problems (e.g., substance abuse, career planning, financial and legal problems).

mentor. A more experienced employee who guides a newer employee (see *protégé*) in learning about the job and organization.

mentoring. The process by which a more experienced employee (see *mentor*) advises, counsels, and otherwise enhances the professional development of a new employee (see *protégé*).

metabolic syndrome. A combination of factors (e.g., obesity around the abdomen, high triglyceride levels, glucose intolerance, etc.) that together are linked to such serious maladies as diabetes and hypertension.

middle line. Managers who transfer information between higher and lower levels of the organizational hierarchy. (See *strategic apex* and *operating core*.)

Minnesota Satisfaction Questionnaire (MSQ). A rating scale for assessing job satisfaction in which people indicate the extent to which they are satisfied with various aspects of their jobs.

mission statement. A document describing an organization's overall direction and general goals.

mixed-motive situations. Contexts in which people are interested in both competition and cooperation, to varying degrees.

modular organization. An organization that surrounds itself by a network of other organizations to which it regularly outsources noncore functions.

mood. An unfocused, relatively mild feeling that exists as background to our daily experiences.

mood congruence. The tendency to recall positive things when you are in a good mood and to recall negative things when you are in a bad mood.

moral values (morals). People's fundamental beliefs regarding what is right or wrong, good or bad.

morning persons. Individuals who feel most energetic and alert early in the day.

morphology. An approach to analyzing problems in which basic elements are combined in systematically different ways.

motivating potential score (MPS). A mathematical index describing the degree to which a job is designed so as to motivate people, as suggested by the job characteristics model. It is computed on the basis of a questionnaire known as the Job Diagnostic Survey (JDS). The lower the MPS, the more the job may stand to benefit from redesign.

motivation. The set of processes that arouse, direct, and maintain human behavior toward attaining some goal.

motivational fit approach. The framework stipulating that motivation is enhanced by a good fit between the traits and skills of individuals and the requirements of the jobs they perform in their organizations.

motivator-hygiene theory. See *two-factor theory*.

multinational enterprises (MNEs). Organizations that have significant operations spread throughout various nations but are headquartered in a single nation.

multiple domains of intelligence. Intelligence as measured in several different ways, such as cognitive intelligence (traditional measures of the ability to integrate and interpret information), emotional intelligence (the ability to be sensitive to one's own and others' emotions) and cultural intelligence (awareness of cultural differences between people).

multiple regression. A statistical technique through which it is possible to determine the extent to which each of several different variables contributes to predicting another variable (typically, where the variable being predicted is the behavior in question).

MUM effect. The reluctance to transmit bad news, shown either by not transmitting the message at all, or by delegating the task to someone else.

mutual service consortia. A type of strategic alliance in which two similar companies from the same or similar industries pool their resources to receive a benefit that would be too difficult or expensive for either to obtain alone.

naturalistic observation. A research technique in which people are systematically observed in situations of interest to the researcher.

need hierarchy theory. Maslow's theory specifying that there are five human needs (physiological, safety, social, esteem, and self-actualization) and that these are arranged in such a way that lower, more basic needs must be satisfied before higher-level needs become activated.

negative affectivity. The tendency to experience negative moods in a wide range of settings and under many different conditions.

negative correlation. A relationship between two variables such that more of one variable is associated with less of the other.

negative reinforcement. The process by which people learn to perform acts that lead to the removal of undesired events.

neoclassical organizational theory. An attempt to improve upon the classical organizational theory which argues that economic effectiveness is not the only goal of organizational structure, but also employee satisfaction.

network organization. See *modular organization.*

networked incubator. Partnerships between established companies (often Internet-based firms), which provide valued resources and experience, with start-ups, which are able to develop and market products quickly.

networking. A leadership development tool designed to help people make connections to others to whom they can turn for information and problem solving.

neuroticism. A tendency to experience unpleasant emotions easily; one of the Big Five personality dimensions.

newsletters. Regularly published internal documents, either hard copy or electronic in nature, describing information of interest to employees regarding an array of business and nonbusiness issues affecting them.

noise. Factors capable of distorting the clarity of messages at any point during the communication process.

nominal group technique (NGT). A technique for improving group decisions in which small groups of individuals systematically present and discuss their ideas before privately voting on their preferred solution. The most preferred solution is accepted as the group's decision.

nonprogrammed decisions. Decisions made about a highly novel problem for which there is no prespecified course of action.

nonsubstitutable. The degree to which an organizational unit is the only one that can perform its particular duties.

nonverbal communication. The transmission of messages without the use of words (e.g., by gestures, the use of space).

normative commitment. The strength of a person's desire to continue working for an organization because he or she feels obligations from others to remain there.

normative decision theory. A theory of leader effectiveness focusing primarily on strategies for choosing the most effective approach to making decisions.

norms. Generally agreed on informal rules that guide group members' behavior.

objective tests. Questionnaires and inventories designed to measure various aspects of personality.

observational learning (or modeling). The form of learning in which people acquire new behaviors by systematically observing the rewards and punishments given to others.

obstructionism. Attempts to impede another's job performance.

OCB-I. Acts of organizational citizenship directed at other individuals in the workplace (i.e., helping coworkers in ways that go beyond what is expected) (see *organizational citizenship behavior*).

OCB-O. Acts of organizational citizenship directed at the organization itself (i.e., helping the company in ways that go beyond what is expected) (see *organizational cititzenship behavior*).

occupation. A coherent set of jobs.

offshoring. Short for offshore outsourcing, the practice of using outsourcing services of overseas companies, typically because it allows companies to take advantage of lower labor costs.

old boys' network. A gender-segregated informal communication network composed of men with similar backgrounds.

online surveys. Questionnaires presented to people either via e-mail or using a Web site, which they then complete and return to administrators using the same electronic means.

open systems. Self-sustaining systems that transform input from the external environment into output, which the system then returns to the environment.

openness to experience. A personality variable reflecting the degree to which individuals have intellectual curiosity, value learning, have an active imagination, and are intrigued by artistic endeavors.

openness to experience. A tendency to enjoy new experiences and new ideas; one of the Big Five personality dimensions.

operant conditioning. The form of learning in which people associate the consequences of their actions with the actions themselves. Behaviors with positive consequences are acquired; behaviors with negative consequences tend to be eliminated.

operating core. Employees who perform the basic work related to an organization's product or service.

organic organization. An internal organizational structure in which jobs tend to be very general, there are few rules, and decisions can be made by lower-level employees.

organization. A structured social system consisting of groups and individuals working together to meet some agreed-upon objectives.

organization chart. A diagram representing the connections between the various departments within an organization; a graphic representation of organizational design.

organization chart. A diagram showing the formal structure of an organization, indicating who is to communicate with whom.

organizational behavior. The field that seeks increased knowledge of all aspects of behavior in organizational settings through the use of the scientific method.

organizational behavior management. The practice of altering behavior in organizations by systematically administering rewards.

organizational change. Planned or unplanned transformations in an organization's structure, technology, and/or people.

organizational citizenship behavior (OCB). An informal form of behavior in which people go beyond what is formally expected of them to contribute to the well-being of their organization and those in it (see *OCB-I* and *OCB-O*).

organizational commitment. The extent to which an individual identifies and is involved with his or her organization and/or is unwilling to leave it (see *affective commitment, continuance commitment,* and *normative commitment*).

organizational compassion. Steps taken by organizational officials to alleviate the suffering of its employees or others.

organizational culture. A cognitive framework consisting of attitudes, values, behavioral norms, and expectations shared by organization members; a set of basic assumptions shared by members of an organization.

organizational demography. The nature of the composition of a workforce with respect to various characteristics (e.g., age, gender, ethnic makeup, etc.).

organizational design. The process of coordinating the structural elements of an organization in the most appropriate manner.

organizational development (OD). A set of social science techniques designed to plan change in organizational work settings, for purposes of enhancing the personal development of individuals and improving the effectiveness of organizational functioning.

organizational justice. The study of people's perceptions of fairness in organizations.

organizational memory. Information from an organization's history that is stored through the recollections of events and their shared interpretations by key individuals in the organization who pass it along to others as needed.

organizational politics. Unauthorized uses of power that enhance or protect one's own or one's group's personal interests

organizational structure. The formal configuration between individuals and groups with respect to the allocation of tasks, responsibilities, and authorities within organizations.

organizational structure. The formally prescribed pattern of interrelationships existing between the various units of an organization.

outcomes. The rewards employees receive from their jobs, such as salary and recognition.

outplacement programs. Systematic efforts to find new jobs for employees who are laid off.

outsourcing. The process of eliminating those parts of organizations that focus on noncore sectors of the business (i.e., tasks that are peripheral to the organization), and hiring outside firms to perform these functions instead.

overload. The condition in which a unit of an organization becomes overburdened with too much incoming information.

overpayment inequity. The condition, resulting in feelings of guilt, in which the ratio of one's outcomes-to-inputs is more than the corresponding ratio of another person with whom that person compares himself or herself.

overt aggression. Acts that are outwardly intended to harm other people or organizations.

partial reinforcement. A schedule of reinforcement in which only some desired behaviors are reinforced. Types include: fixed interval, variable interval, fixed ratio, and variable ratio.

participant observation. A qualitative research technique in which people systematically make observations of what goes on in a setting by becoming an insider, part of that setting itself.

participation. Active involvement in the process of learning; more active participation leads to more effective learning.

participative leadership style. A style of leadership in which the leader permits subordinates to take part in decision making and also permits them a considerable degree of autonomy in completing routine work activities.

path-goal theory. A theory of leadership suggesting that subordinates will be motivated by a leader only to the extent they perceive this individual as helping them to attain valued goals.

Pay Satisfaction Questionnaire (PSQ). A questionnaire designed to assess employees' level of satisfaction with various aspects of their pay (e.g., its overall level, raises, benefits).

pay-for-performance. A payment system in which employees are paid differentially, based on the quantity and quality of their performance. Pay-for-performance plans strengthen instrumentality beliefs.

perception. The process through which people select, organize, and interpret information.

perceptual biases. Predispositions that people have to misperceive others in various ways. Types include the *fundamental attribution error,* the *halo effect,* the *similar-to-me-effect, first-impression error,* and *selective perception.*

performance appraisal. The process of evaluating employees on various work-related dimensions.

performance goal orientation. The desire to perform well to demonstrate one's competence to others.

person sensitivity bias. The tendency for people to give too little credit to others when things are going poorly and too much credit when things are going well.

personal appeal. A form of social influence in which an individual attempts to gain a target's compliance by appealing to his or her feelings of loyalty or friendship.

personal identity. The characteristics that define a particular individual.

personal power. The power that one derives because of one's individual qualities or characteristics.

personal support policies. Widely varied practices that help employees meet the demands of their family lives, freeing them to concentrate on their work.

personality. The unique and relatively stable patterns of behavior, thoughts, and emotions shown by individuals.

personalized power motivation. Leaders' desires to influence others (in essence, to lead).

person-centered. See *consideration.*

person-job fit. The extent to which the traits and abilities of individuals match the requirements of the jobs they must perform.

physical abilities. People's capacities to engage in the physical tasks required to perform a job.

physiological needs The lowest-order, most basic needs specified by Maslow's need hierarchy theory, including fundamental biological drives, such as the need for food, air, water, and shelter.

pipe dreams. Types of rumor that express people's wishes.

podcast. A prerecorded message distributed for playback on Apple's iPod MP3 player (i.e., an iPod broadcast).

politics. See *organizational politics.*

position power. Power based on one's formal position in an organization.

positive affectivity. The tendency to experience positive moods and feelings in a wide range of settings and under many different conditions.

positive correlation. A relationship between two variables such that more of one variable is associated with more of the other.

positive reinforcement. The process by which people learn to perform behaviors that lead to the presentation of desired outcomes.

postconventional level of moral reasoning. In Kohlberg's theory of cognitive moral development, the level at which people judge what is right and wrong not solely in terms of their interpersonal and societal obligations, but in terms of complex philosophical principles of duty, justice, and rights.

power. The capacity to change the behavior or attitudes of others in a desired manner.

practical intelligence. Adeptness at solving the practical problems of everyday life.

pragmatic leadership. A type of leadership based on methodically developing solutions to problems and working them through in a thorough manner.

preconventional level of moral reasoning. In Kohlberg's theory of cognitive moral development, the level at which people (e.g., young children and some adults) haven't yet developed the capacity to assume the perspective of others, leading them to interpret what is right solely with respect to themselves.

predecision. A decision about what process to follow in making a decision.

predictive validity. The extent to which the score achieved on a test administered to a person at one time predicts (i.e., is correlated with) some measure of his or her performance at some later time.

prejudice. Negative attitudes toward the members of specific groups, based solely on the fact that they are members of those groups (e.g., age, race, sexual orientation).

prescriptive norms. Expectations within groups regarding what is supposed to be done.

presentism. The practice of showing up for work but being too sick to be able to work effectively.

pressuring. A form of social influence in which an individual seeks a target person's compliance by making demands or threats, or otherwise intimidating him or her.

principles of learning. The set of practices that make training effective: participation, repetition, transfer of training, and feedback. (See *transfer of training*.)

procedural justice. People's perceptions of the fairness of the procedures used to determine the outcomes they receive.

process conflict. A form of conflict resulting from differences of opinion regarding how work groups are going to operate, such as how various duties and resources will be allocated and with whom various responsibilities will reside.

product organization. The type of departmentalization based on the products (or product lines) produced.

production-centered. See *initiating structure*.

productive forgetting. The ability to abandon unproductive ideas and temporarily put aside stubborn problems until new approaches can be considered.

professional bureaucracy. Organizations (e.g., hospitals and universities) in which there are lots of rules to follow, but employees are highly skilled and free to make decisions on their own.

profit strategies. Attempts to derive more profit from existing business, such as by training employees to work more effectively or salespeople to sell more effectively.

profit-sharing plans. Incentive plans in which employees receive bonuses in proportion to the company's profitability.

programmed decisions. Highly routine decisions made according to preestablished organizational routines and procedures.

progressive discipline. The practice of gradually increasing the severity of punishments for employees who exhibit unacceptable job behavior.

proscriptive norms. Expectations within groups regarding behaviors in which members are not supposed to engage.

prosocial behavior. Acts that benefit others.

protégé. An inexperienced employee who receives assistance from a more experienced employee (see *mentor*).

psychological contract. A person's beliefs about what is expected of another in a relationship.

punctuated-equilibrium mode. The conceptualization of group development claiming that groups generally plan their activities during the first half of their time together, and then revise and implement their plans in the second half.

punishment. Decreasing undesirable behavior by following it with undesirable consequences.

Pygmalion effect. A positive instance of the self-fulfilling prophecy, in which people holding high expectations of another tend to improve that individual's performance.

pyramid of corporate social responsibility. The term used to describe an organization's four most basic forms of responsibility, in order from economic responsibility, to legal responsibility, to ethical responsibility, to philanthropic (i.e., charitable) responsibility.

qualitative research. A nonempirical type of research that relies on preserving the natural qualities of the situation being studied.

quality circles (QCs). An approach to improving the quality of work life, in which small groups of volunteers meet regularly to identify and solve problems related to the work they perform and the conditions under which they work.

quality control audits. Careful examinations of how well a company is meeting its standards.

quality of work life (QWL). An OD technique designed to improve organizational functioning by humanizing the workplace, making it more democratic, and involving employees in decision making.

queuing. Lining up incoming information so it can be managed in an orderly fashion.

quid pro quo sexual harassment. A form of sexual harassment in which the harasser requires sexual favors in exchange for some tangible conditions, privileges, or terms of employment from a victim.

radical innovation. A form of innovation in which companies make quantum leaps; involves exploring new technology and operating under highly uncertain conditions.

rally 'round the flag effect. The tendency for followers to make positive attributions about their leaders when they appear to be working to keep things together during a crisis situation.

rational decisions. Decisions that maximize the chance of attaining an individual's, group's, or organization's goals.

rational persuasion. Using logical arguments and factual evidence to persuade others (targets) that an idea is acceptable.

rational-economic model. The model of decision making according to which decision makers consider all possible alternatives to problems before selecting the optimal solution.

rebound effect. The tendency to think about something when you try intentionally not to think about it.

reciprocity. The tendency to treat others as they have treated us, popularly referred to as "the golden rule."

referent power. The individual power base derived from the degree to which one is liked and admired by others.

relational contract. A variety of psychological contract in which the parties have a long-term and widely defined relationship with a vast focus.

reliability. The extent to which a test yields consistent scores on various occasions, and the extent to which all of its items measure the same underlying construct.

religious intolerance. Actions (e.g., personal ridicule, vandalism) taken against a person or group who follows a different faith.

repatriation. The process of readjusting to one's own culture after spending time away from it.

repetition. The process of repeatedly performing a task so that it may be learned.

reporting relationships. Formal connections between people indicating who must answer to whom in an organization.

representativeness heuristic. The tendency to perceive others in stereotypical ways if they appear to be typical representatives of the category to which they belong.

resistance to change. The tendency for employees to be unwilling to go along with organizational changes, either because of individual fears of the unknown or organizational impediments (such as structural inertia).

resource-dependency model. The view that power resides within subunits that are able to control the greatest share of valued organizational resources.

retirement. The phase of people's lives in which they reach the end of their careers and stop working for their primary income.

reward power. The individual power base derived from an individual's capacity to administer valued rewards to others.

rightsizing. See *downsizing*.

risky choice framing effect. The tendency for people to avoid risks when situations are presented in a way that emphasizes positive gains, and to take risks when situations are presented in a way that emphasizes potential losses that may be suffered.

role. The typical behavior that characterizes a person in a specific social context.

role ambiguity. Confusion arising from not knowing what one is expected to do as the holder of a role.

role conflict. Incompatibilities between the various sets of obligations people face.

role differentiation. The tendency for various specialized roles to emerge as groups develop.

role expectations. The behaviors expected of someone in a particular role.

role incumbent. A person holding a particular role.

role juggling. The need to switch back and forth between the demands of work and family.

RSS feed. Information, usually news, delivered to Web sites on a real-time basis, as events occur.

rumors. Information with little basis in fact, often transmitted through informal channels. (See *grapevine*.)

safety needs In Maslow's need hierarchy theory, they are the need for a secure environment, to be free from threats of physical or psychological harm.

satisficing decisions. Decisions made by selecting the first minimally acceptable alternative as it becomes available.

say-do matrix. A way of differentiating systematically with respect to consistencies and inconsistencies in what people say and what they do.

scapegoat. Someone who is made to take the blame for someone else's failure or wrongdoing.

schedules of reinforcement. Rules governing the timing and frequency of the administration of reinforcement.

scientific management. An early approach to management and organizational behavior emphasizing the importance of designing jobs as efficiently as possible.

second-order change. Radical change; major shifts involving many different levels of the organization and many different aspects of business.

selective perception. The tendency to focus on some aspects of the environment while ignoring others.

self-actualization. In Maslow's need hierarchy theory, the need to discover who we are and to develop ourselves to the fullest potential.

self-conscious emotions. Feelings that stem from within, such as shame, guilt, embarrassment, and pride.

self-directed teams. See *self-managed teams*.

self-efficacy. One's belief about having the capacity to perform a task.

self-esteem. The overall value one places on oneself as a person.

self-fulfilling prophecy. The tendency for someone's expectations about another to cause that person to behave in a manner consistent with those expectations. This can be either positive (see the *Pygmalion effect*) or negative (see the *Golem effect*) in nature.

self-managed teams (self-directed teams). Teams whose members are permitted to make key decisions about how their work is done.

self-oriented role. The activities of an individual in a group who focuses on his or her own good, often at the expense of others.

semi-autonomous work groups. Work groups in which employees get to share in the responsibility for decisions with their bosses and are jointly accountable for their work outcomes.

sexual harassment. Unwelcome sexual advances, requests for sexual favors, and other verbal or physical conduct of a sexual nature constitute sexual harassment when this conduct explicitly or implicitly affects an individual's employment, unreasonably interferes with an individual's work performance, or creates an intimidating, hostile, or offensive work environment.

short-term successors. Individuals who are considered suitable candidates, at least temporarily, to fill the position of someone who leaves his or her job unexpectedly.

similar-to-me effect. The tendency for people to perceive in a positive light others who are believed to be similar to themselves in any of several different ways.

simple structure. An organization characterized as being small and informal, with a single powerful individual, often the founding entrepreneur, who is in charge of everything.

situational leadership theory. A theory suggesting that the most effective style of leadership—either delegating, participating, selling, or telling—depends on the extent to which followers require guidance and direction, and emotional support.

skills. Dexterity at performing specific tasks, which has been acquired through training or experience.

skills-based diversity training. An approach to diversity management that goes beyond awareness-based diversity training and is designed to develop people's skills with respect to managing diversity.

skip-level meetings. Gatherings of employees with corporate superiors who are more than one level higher than themselves in the organizational hierarchy.

snowball effect. The tendency for people to share informal information with others with whom they come into contact.

social chameleons. Individuals who figure out what behaviors they believe are considered generally appropriate in their organization, and then go out of their way to make sure that others are aware that they behaved in such a manner.

social dilemmas. Situations in which each person can increase his or her individual gains by acting in a purely selfish manner, but if others also act selfishly, the outcomes experienced by all are reduced.

social emotions. People's feelings based on information external to themselves, such as pity, envy, jealousy, and scorn.

social facilitation. The tendency for the presence of others sometimes to enhance an individual's performance and at other times to impair it.

social identity. Who a person is, as defined in terms of his or her membership in various social groups.

social identity theory. A conceptualization recognizing that the way we perceive others and ourselves is based on both our unique characteristics (see *personal identity*) and our membership in various groups (see *social identity*).

social impact theory. The theory that explains social loafing in terms of the diffused responsibility for doing what is expected of each member of a group (see *social loafing*).

The larger the size of a group, the less each member is influenced by the social forces acting on the group.

social influence. Attempts to affect another in a desired fashion, whether or not these are successful.

social information processing model. A conceptualization specifying that people adopt attitudes and behaviors in keeping with the cues provided by others with whom they come into contact.

social loafing. The tendency for group members to exert less individual effort on an additive task as the size of the group increases.

social needs. In Maslow's need hierarchy theory, the need to be affiliative—that is, to have friends and to be loved and accepted by other people.

social perception. The process of combining, integrating, and interpreting information about others to gain an accurate understanding of them.

social skills. The capacity to interact effectively with others.

social support. The friendship and support of others, which helps minimize reactions to stress.

socialized power motivation. Leaders' interest in cooperating with others, developing networks and coalitions, and generally working with subordinates rather than trying to control them.

socioemotional role. The activities of an individual in a group who is supportive and nurturant of other group members and who helps them feel good.

spam. Unsolicited commercial e-mail messages.

span of control. The number of subordinates in an organization who are supervised by managers.

spinoff. An entirely new company that is separate from the original parent organization, one with its own identity, a new board of directors, and a different management team.

spiral career. The kind of career in which people evolve through a series of occupations, each of which requires new skills and that builds upon existing knowledge and skills.

staff positions. Positions in organizations in which people make recommendations to others, but are not themselves involved in making decisions concerning the organization's day-to-day operations.

stakeholder. Any individual or group in whose interest an organization is run.

standing committees. Committees that are permanent, existing over time.

statements of principle. Explicitly written statements describing the principal beliefs that guide an organization. Such documents can help reinforce an organization's culture.

status. The relative prestige, social position, or rank given to groups or individuals by others.

status symbols. Objects reflecting the position of any individual within an organization's hierarchy of power.

steady-state career. The type of career in which there is a lifetime of employment in a single occupation.

stepladder technique. A technique for improving the quality of group decisions that minimizes the tendency for group members to be unwilling to present their ideas by adding new members to a group one at a time and requiring each to present his or her ideas independently to a group that already has discussed the problem at hand.

stereotype. A belief that all members of specific groups share similar traits and are prone to behave the same way.

stereotype threat. The uncomfortable feeling that people have when they run the risk of fulfilling a negative stereotype associated with a group to which they belong.

stereotypes. Beliefs that individuals possess certain characteristics because of their membership in certain groups.

stonewalling. The practice of willingly hiding relevant information by being secretive and deceitful, which occurs when organizations punish individuals who are open and honest and reward those who go along with unethical behavior.

strain. Deviations from normal states of human functioning resulting from prolonged exposure to stressful events.

strategic alliance. A type of organizational design in which two or more separate companies combine forces to develop and operate a specific business. (See *mutual service consortia, joint ventures,* and *value-chain partnerships.*)

strategic apex. Top-level executives responsible for running an entire organization.

strategic communication. The practice of presenting information about the company to broad, external audiences, such as the press.

strategic contingencies model. A view explaining power in terms of a subunit's capacity to control the activities of other subunits. A subunit's power is enhanced when (1) it can reduce the level of uncertainty experienced by other subunits, (2) it occupies a central position in the organization, and (3) its activities are highly indispensable to the organization.

strategic decisions. Nonprogrammed decisions typically made by high-level executives regarding the direction their organization should take to achieve its mission.

strategic planning. The process of formulating, implementing, and evaluating decisions that enable an organization to achieve its objectives.

stress. The pattern of emotional states and physiological reactions occurring in response to demands from within or outside an organization. See *stressor.*

stress management programs. Systematic efforts to train employees in a variety of techniques that they can use to become less adversely affected by stress.

stressor. Any demands, either physical or psychological in nature, encountered during the course of living.

stretch goals. Goals that are so difficult that they challenge people to rethink the way they work.

strong culture. An organization in which there is widespread agreement with respect to the core elements of culture, making it possible for these factors to exert major influences on the way people behave.

structural inertia. The organizational forces acting on employees, encouraging them to perform their jobs in certain ways, thereby making them resistant to change.

subcultures. Cultures existing within parts of organizations rather than entirely through them.

substantive conflict. A form of conflict that occurs when people have different viewpoints and opinions with respect to a decision they are making with others.

substitutes for leadership. The view that high levels of skill among subordinates or certain features of technology and organizational structure sometimes serve as substitutes for leaders, rendering their guidance or influence superfluous.

succession planning. A person's systematic attempt to identify possible holders of particular positions ahead of time as preparation for his or her departure.

suggestion systems. Formal mechanisms through which employees can present ideas to their company.

support staff. Individuals who provide indirect support services to an organization.

supportive communication. Any communication that is accurate and honest, and that builds and enhances relationships instead of jeopardizing them.

survey feedback. An OD technique in which questionnaires and interviews are used to collect information about issues of concern to an organization. This information is shared with employees and is used as the basis for planning organizational change.

surveys. Questionnaires in which people are asked to report how they feel about various aspects of themselves, their jobs, and organizations.

sustaining innovation. A form of innovation that is incremental in nature; innovation that allows companies to approach their markets in the same manner as they have done in the past.

symbols. Material objects that connote meanings that extend beyond their intrinsic content.

synchronous communication techniques. Forms of communication in which the parties can send and receive messages at the same time.

systemic change. A change in one part of an organization that is related to change in another part of it.

tacit knowledge. Knowledge about how to get things done.

task force. See ad *hoc committee.*

task group. A formal organizational group formed around some specific task.

task-oriented role. The activities of an individual in a group who, more than anyone else, helps the group reach its goal.

team. A group whose members have complementary skills and are committed to a common purpose or set of performance goals for which they hold themselves mutually accountable.

team building. Formal efforts directed toward making teams more effective.

team halo effect. The tendency for people to credit teams for their successes but not to hold them accountable for their failures.

team-based organizations. Organizations in which autonomous work teams are organized in parallel fashion such that each performs many different steps in the work process.

technostructure. Organizational specialists responsible for standardizing various aspects of an organization's activities.

telecommuting (telework). The practice of using communications technology so as to enable work to be performed from remote locations, such as the home.

theory. A set of statements about the interrelationships between concepts that allow us to predict and explain various processes and events.

Theory X. A traditional philosophy of management suggesting that most people are lazy and irresponsible, and will work hard only when forced to do so.

Theory Y. A philosophy of management suggesting that under the right circumstances, people are fully capable of working productively and accepting responsibility for their work.

time management. The practice of taking control over how we spend time.

time-and-motion study. A type of applied research designed to classify and streamline the individual movements needed to perform jobs with the intent of finding "the one best way" to perform them.

time-out. A brief delay in activities designed to reduce mounting tension.

top-down decision making. The practice of vesting decision-making power in the hands of superiors as opposed to lower-level employees.

total quality management (TQM). An organizational strategy of commitment to improving customer satisfaction by developing techniques to carefully manage output quality.

toxic organizational cultures. Organizational cultures in which people feel that they are not valued (opposite of healthy organizational cultures).

training. The process of systematically teaching employees to acquire and improve job-related skills and knowledge.

transactional contract. A variety of psychological contract in which the parties have a brief and narrowly defined relationship that is primarily economic in focus.

transfer of training. The degree to which the skills learned during training sessions may be applied to performance of one's job.

transformational leadership. Leadership in which leaders use their charisma to transform and revitalize their organizations.

triple bottom-line. The contemporary notion that in addition to focusing on an organization's financial performance,

officials also are interested in assuring that their companies are performing well with respect to promoting environmental quality and social justice.

trust. A person's degree of confidence in the words and actions of another.

turnaround strategies. Attempts to reverse a decline in business by moving to a new product line, or by radically restructuring operations.

two-dimensional model of subordinate participation. An approach to leadership that describes the nature of the influence leaders give followers. It distinguishes between leaders who are directive or permissive toward subordinates, and the extent to which they are participative or autocratic in their decision making. Individual leaders may be classified into four types in terms of where they fall when these two dimensions are combined.

two-factor theory of job satisfaction. A theory of job satisfaction suggesting that satisfaction and dissatisfaction stem from different groups of variables (motivators and hygiene factors, respectively).

two-tier wage structures. Payment systems in which newer employees are paid less than employees hired at earlier times to do the same work.

uncertainty. Lack of knowledge about the likelihood of certain events occurring in the future.

unconflicted adherence. The tendency for decision makers to stick to the first idea that comes to their minds without more deeply evaluating the consequences.

unconflicted change. The tendency for people to quickly change their minds and to adopt the first new idea to come along.

underpayment inequity. The condition, resulting in feelings of anger, in which the ratio of one's outcomes-to-inputs is less than the corresponding ratio of another person with whom one compares himself or herself.

unfolding model of voluntary turnover. A conceptualization that explains the cognitive processes through which people make decisions about quitting or staying on their jobs.

unplanned change. Shifts in organizational activities due to forces that are external in nature, those beyond the organization's control.

upward communication. Communication from people at lower organizational levels to those at higher organizational levels.

valence. The value a person places on the rewards he or she expects to receive from an organization.

validating language. Language that makes people feel recognized and accepted for who they are.

validity. The extent to which a test actually measures what it claims to measure.

value-chain partnerships. Strategic alliances between companies in different industries that have complementary capabilities.

value theory of job satisfaction. A theory suggesting that job satisfaction depends primarily on the match between the outcomes individuals value in their jobs and their perceptions about the availability of such outcomes.

variable interval schedules. Schedules of reinforcement in which a variable period of time (based on some average) must elapse between the administration of reinforcements.

variable ratio schedules. Schedules of reinforcement in which a variable number of responses (based on some average) must occur between the administration of reinforcements.

verbal communication. The transmission of messages using words, either written or spoken.

verbal media. Forms of communication involving the use of words (e.g., telephone messages, faxes, books, etc.).

vertical integration. The practice in which companies own their own suppliers and/or their own customers who purchase their products from them.

vertical stretch goals. Stretch goals that challenge people to achieve higher levels of success in current activities.

video-mediated communication (VMC). Conferences in which people can hear and see each other using computers.

virtual organization. A highly flexible, temporary organization formed by a group of companies that join forces to exploit a specific opportunity.

virtual teams. Teams that operate across space, time, and organizational boundaries, communicating with each other only through electronic technology.

virtuous circle. The tendency for companies that are successful financially to invest in social causes because they can afford to do so (i.e., they "do good by doing well") and for socially responsible companies to perform well financially (i.e., they "do well by doing good")

voluntary arbitration. A form of arbitration in which the two sides retain the freedom to reject the agreement recommended by an arbitrator.

voluntary reduced work time (V-time) programs. Programs that allow employees to reduce the amount of time they work by a certain amount (typically 10 or 20 percent), with a proportional reduction in pay.

voluntary turnover. A form of employee turnover in which an individual resigns freely from his or her job.

weak culture. An organization in which there is limited agreement with respect to the core elements of culture, giving these factors little influence on the way people behave.

wedge drivers. Rumors in which people intentionally say malicious things about someone with the intent of damaging that individual's reputation.

wellness programs. Company-wide programs in which employees receive training regarding things they can do to promote healthy lifestyles.

whistle-blowing. The disclosure by employees of illegal, immoral, or illegitimate practices by employers to people or organizations able to take action.

win-win solutions. Resolutions to conflicts in which both parties get what they want.

work group inertia. Forces within a work group that encourage employees to perform their jobs in certain ways, thereby making them resistant to change.

work restructuring. The process of changing the way jobs are done to make them more interesting to workers.

work stress. The harmful physical and emotional responses that people experience on their jobs.

work teams. Teams whose members are concerned primarily with using the organization's resources to effectively create its results.

workplace aggression. Acts of verbal and physical abuse toward others in organizations, ranging from mild to severe.

workplace bullying. The repeated mistreatment of an individual at work in a manner that endangers his or her physical or mental health.

work-related attitudes. Attitudes relating to any aspect of work or work settings.

Photo Credits

Chapter 1   page 4, AP Wide World Photos; page 13, S. C. Williams Library; page 19, © Benjamin Lowy/CORBIS All Rights Reserved; page 25, Elliott Marks/Picture Desk, Inc./Kobal Collection; page 30, AP Wide World Photos; page 33, NewsCom

Chapter 2   page 44, Sergei Karpukhin/AP Wide World Photos; page 54, Steve Schaefer/Agence France Presse/Getty Images; page 57, Bebeto Matthews/AP Wide World Photos; page 61, Chitose Suzuki/AP Wide World Photos; page 65, David Butow/Corbis/SABA Press Photos, Inc.; page 70 (top), Ken Lax/Pearson Education/PH College; page 70 (bottom), Lockheed Martin Ethics Services; page 76, © Martin Rogers/CORBIS All Rights Reserved

Chapter 3   page 91, Corbis Royalty Free; page 105, Jon Feingersh/Masterfile Corporation; page 117, James Marshall/The Image Works; page 118, © Mark Peterson/CORBIS All Rights Reserved; page 119, Darden Restaurants

Chapter 4   page 141 (top), © Michael S. Yamashita/CORBIS All Rights Reserved; page 141 (bottom), Getty Images; page 145, Masterfile Royalty Free Division; page 157, David Frazier/The Image Works

Chapter 5   page 171, © George Shelley/CORBIS All Rights Reserved; page 174, Robert Holmgren/Robert Holmgren Photography; page 179, Inmagine Corporation LLC; page 186, Evan Kafka

Chapter 6   page 211, John Abbott Photography; page 225, Photos.com; page 234, ROMEO GACAD/Agence France Presse/Getty Images; page 239, Menno S. Martin Contractor Limited

Chapter 7   page 252, UAW-GM LifeSteps Program; page 253, Picnic People, Inc.; page 257, 3M; page 267, Tom Hanson/AP Wide World Photos; page 269, AP Wide World Photos

Chapter 8   page 292, Getty Images; page 298, Getty Images; page 302, © Benjamin Lowy/CORBIS All Rights Reserved; page 313, Getty Images; page 317, Fred Prouser/Corbis/Reuters America LLC; page 322, NASA/Johnson Space Center

Chapter 9   page 333, Dan Bosler/Getty Images Inc.–Stone Allstock; page 336, PhotoEdit Inc.; page 344, Boeing Commercial Airplane Group; page 357, Steve Starr/Thomas McClintock; page 360, The Stock Solution; page 367, Ruby Washington/New York Times Agency; page 369, Michael L. Abramson Photography

Chapter 10   page 386, CORBIS–NY; page 391, Ben Margot/AP Wide World Photos; page 403, John Neubauer/PhotoEdit Inc.; page 404, Mark Richards/PhotoEdit Inc.; page 414, Marcio Sanchez/AP Wide World Photos

Chapter 11   page 427, © Bill Varie/CORBIS All Rights Reserved; page 436, © Frank Polich/CORBIS All Rights Reserved; page 441, AGE Fotostock America, Inc.; page 446, J.P. Moczulski/Corbis/Reuters America LLC; page 449, Republished with permission of Globe Newspaper Company, Inc., from the June 18, 2004 issue of The Boston Globe © 2004; page 450, Cindy Manieri

Chapter 12   page 468, SIPA Press; page 473, Corbis/Bettmann; page 477, Ria Fitriana; page 484, CORBIS–NY

Chapter 13   page 511, Getty Images, Inc.; page 514, Corbis Royalty Free; page 523 (left), Walter Bieri/Agence France Presse/Getty Images; page 523 (middle), Anthony Suau/Getty Images, Inc.–Liaison; page 523 (right), Jim Varhegyi/Getty Images Inc.–Hulton Archive Photos

Chapter 14   page 550, Dr. Scott Lieberman/AP Wide World Photos; page 552, Picture Desk, Inc./Kobal Collection; page 555, Julia Malakie/AP Wide World Photos; page 559, John Abbott Photography; page 565, Patrick Collard/AP Wide World Photos

Chapter 15   page 588, Getty Images; page 596, Steve Fecht; page 612, © Jason Reed/CORBIS All Rights Reserved; page 613, © Paul Sakuma/CORBIS All Rights Reserved

Chapter 16   page 624, © Shannon Stapleton/Reuters/CORBIS All Rights Reserved; page 626, Paul Connors/AP Wide World Photos; page 631, Getty Images, Inc.; page 635, Sherwin Crasto/Corbis/Reuters America LLC; page 646, Shepard Sherbell/Corbis/SABA Press Photos, Inc.; page 651, © Ralf-Finn Hestoft/CORBIS All Rights Reserved

Company Index

Name Index

Subject Index